Daniel Raymond

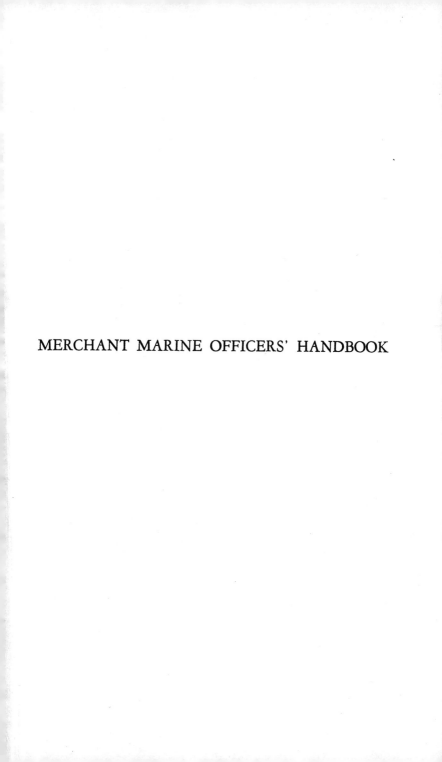

MERCHANT MARINE OFFICERS' HANDBOOK

MERCHANT MARINE OFFICERS' HANDBOOK

By
EDWARD A. TURPIN
and
WILLIAM A. McEWEN
Master Mariners

Fourth Edition

CORNELL MARITIME PRESS, INC.
CENTREVILLE   MARYLAND

Manufactured in the United States of America

First Edition, 1942; Fourth edition, 1965; Reprinted, 1980

PREFACE TO REVISED EDITION

The *Merchant Marine Officers' Handbook* has now been in use for 23 years and, the authors are happy to state, throughout this period it has never ceased to merit and maintain a foremost position of practical usefulness in the Merchant Marine field.

The many changes in rules, regulations, and methods which arise from time to time have been incorporated, as complete as is humanly possible, in the six reprintings of the *Handbook* since its inception. This has proved a strong point in its favor.

It is noteworthy that several maritime academies have been using the book as a text. This encouraging fact alone has further urged both authors and the publisher to provide this New Edition, in order to maintain the *Handbook*'s increasingly popular use for reference purposes on board ship, as well as to meet current requirements for the deck officer's license.

Edward A. Turpin
William A. McEwen

ACKNOWLEDGMENTS

It would be impracticable to recall the many helpful sources, or to correctly list the various books, from which a major part of this *Handbook* has derived, in greater or lesser measure, its store of informative matter. Yet it is with a deeply appreciative spirit that out of the whole range of nautical lore—from Bowditch's masterpiece to Farwell's work on *Rules of the Road*, from Knight's monumental *Seamanship* to the U.S. Coast Guard's massive safety regulations—the authors respectfully have compiled the "digest" here presented.

However, in particular and of more recent date, grateful acknowledgment for valuable assistance is due the following: F. B. Greene, Comdr., U.S.N.R., Recruiting Division, Bureau of Personnel, U.S.N., for up-to-date material for Appendix B; W. B. Durham, Comdr. (retd.), U.S.C.G., for required official C.G. data; also M. V. Foreman, Capt., U.S.C.G.R., of the Military Sea Transportation Service, for obtaining important naval material; William R. Fearn, Lt. Comdr., U.S.C.G., for assembling needed Loran information; and the publisher and authors of *American Merchant Seaman's Manual* and *Modern Marine Engineer's Manual* for permission to use material therefrom.

E. A. T.
W. A. M.

CONTENTS

Chapter 1

THE EVERYDAY LABORS OF A
SHIP'S OFFICER

Textbooks on seamanship are absolutely necessary to pass an examination but they do not give the everyday duties of an officer on a steamer. Many things which are perhaps well known to him he does not take the initiative to do until told. After awhile a captain will come to the conclusion that he is careless or does not know his job. while it may be only that self-confidence is lacking. Seeing these common things in print may give him that confidence, and start him along the right lines.

Let us assume you have just secured your first berth as third mate, on a ship which is to sail the following day. Get your gear together, say your good-byes, and proceed to your ship ready to leave without any further business ashore. Those officers on board have probably had little or no time ashore, and you should be prepared to take over your duties immediately. When you get aboard introduce yourself to the officer on watch, who will show you to the captain. Present your letter of introduction to him, and make it brief; life stories should be avoided.

When your gear is in your cabin, get into a boiler suit and find out all you can about the ship. Leave your unpacking for the evening, but be sure you have your license and are ready to sign on. You should know where all gear is kept. This applies particularly to emergency equipment, breakdown lights, oil lights, fire apparatus, life lines, pilot gear, anchor lights, clusters, where they plug in, etc. Go around with the carpenter and find out the location of the bilge and tank soundings, filling line, wrenches for sideports, etc. Also see that you understand the anchor windlass and sounding machine and find where the sounding tubes, leads and hand lead lines are kept.

In the course of the above mentioned tour you should acquire a fairly good general knowledge of the ship and what is going on. Don't be afraid to ask questions; now is the time, rather than when something is wanted in a hurry and then to have to call the mate out of his bunk to find out where it is.

Your particular care will be, in most ships, the life saving and fire equipment, some or all of the boats, the signaling apparatus and flags. Here is a good time to outline such flag etiquette as will suffice to get you off to a proper start. Flags are not the most important thing for you, but they can cause you a great deal of embarrassment.

In the first place, always check up to see that the sailor or cadet you send to put them up does so properly. If your ship comes into port with an ensign at the gaff and another on the staff aft, upside down, the repercussions will be considerable. This has happened.

Never fly torn flags, especially the ensign; it may be faded and old, but never have it frayed. Always haul down and hoist the ensign slowly, without jerks. Never send it aloft to be broken out. Hoist colors at 8 A.M. and lower them at sunset. If it is not possible to handle all flags together, hoist the ensign first in the morning and haul down the others before it at sunset. Before colors in the morning and after colors at sunset, the ensign and distinguishing flags should be shown when entering port, and should be hauled down immediately on coming to anchor. On entering a foreign port and while there, have the flag of that country at the foremast; some countries impose a fine if this courtesy is omitted. On Decoration Day and on occasions of national mourning the ensign only should be half-masted. Flags should be mast-headed before half-masting them, and should be mast-headed before hauling them down. Saluting with the ensign at half-mast should be done by mast-heading first.*

In dipping to men-of-war, haul the ensign down two-thirds if at the gaff, or take it to the rail if at the flag staff. The ensign should be hauled down in plenty of time so that the intention to dip may be observed by the vessel saluted and a reply made while the vessels are still nearly abreast.

The jack is hoisted only at anchor or alongside, and the jack and the blue peter should be hauled down as soon as the vessel gets away. When sailing from an American port to a foreign country have the flag of that country at the fore, and when returning fly that of the country of departure at the fore. Have your call letters bent together and ready if called for, and don't forget the quarantine flag if you must stop at quarantine.

Keep your mind refreshed on code flags and the meaning of single flag hoists, as well as being proficient in semaphore and blinker. Your proficiency in this respect at the present time will be of more use to the captain than a perfect cartwheel of star position lines out at sea.

Find out where the fire alarm is on the pier, and the shore connection for the fire line. If there is a relief officer for the night, see that he knows these things and the location of the steam smothering line valves and general layout of the ship.

The telegraph, whistle, steering gear and navigation lights are tried an hour or two before sailing, and an appropriate entry made in the log. The second mate looks after the gyro compass, but it will do you no harm to see what he does and that the repeaters and course recorder are checked. Check the latter's time with the ship's time; for with this as with other mechanical aids, if properly installed, maintained and operated, it has been shown that they are so reliable that their mute

---

* The "house flag" is hoisted on the main truck with the Naval Reserve pennant above it on approved vessels of the USNR.

evidence is apt to be given more weight than oral testimony in a court of law. And always bear in mind that every official action of yours will have to undergo the most searching probe if through some accident you land in the hands of the legal inquisition.

If loading is complete, get the draft and at the same time look at the lines and any other connections with the shore to see if the engineers can turn the engines over. Before you notify them look yourself to see that there are no logs or floats which might foul the propeller, and stand by to let them know if they must stop at any time.

See that the engine room clock shows the same time as that on the bridge, so the bell books will correspond. Engine room clocks are often very erratic, but if something occurs where both bell books are called for, don't try to make them jibe afterwards. You will find that the inspectors can dig out such tinkering, which won't help the ship's case, not to mention your own standing.

The rudder, tiller, telltale and midship spoke on the wheel should all be seen in the same straight line, especially if any work has been done on the steering gear or rudder. Naturally, the engineer should be in the steering-engine room at the time the gear is tried, and you should verify this with him. The steering-engine room should always be kept locked in port and the keys kept by an officer, not hanging out for any one to use. Take a look in the steering-engine room yourself, as it is a favorite place for drying clothes, if the crew can get away with it. Of course they wouldn't want their clothes to fall off the line into the grease, but if this happened it would just mean the loss of a shirt to the man, while it might cause the loss of the ship.

There are several other things to see to which the captain should not have to point out to you. Show you are on the job and look to them before being told. See that the binoculars are clear, that the bridge rail has been wiped off, that the megaphone is handy, that the blinker works; know where the breakdown lights are, where the blue lights are and how they ignite, see that you have your whistle and bell book. Have a look at the charts, which the second mate should have put out, and look over the side to make sure the side ports have been secured. Let the mate know if they aren't.

Don't wait until the captain asks you where the quartermaster is. Know beforehand who has the wheel, and make sure he is on the job.

Now some points on working the telegraphs:

The wires from the bridge to the engine-room often go over many leads and have right angled turns. The leverage for working these wires is considerable, so do not go swinging the handle like a madman from full ahead to full astern, to finally telling them down below to *"Stand By."* If you are stopped and told *"Full Ahead"* do not bang the handle back to *Full Astern* and then to *Full Ahead.* Put the handle right on *Full Ahead,* and with all movements try to keep the handle on that side of the dial which the order is on. Otherwise, if the wires carry away—and they sometimes do—it will surely be when you have the handle over at *Full Astern* prior to bringing it to *Full Ahead.* Results, barge sunk.

Another reason why you should not send the pointer all over the dial is that the engineer must wait until you are finished. All this time the last order is being carried out. Get into the habit of working the handles carefully, and at least once in your nautical career you'll be thankful.

When you are docking or undocking, watch the captain or pilot, the quartermaster and the forecastle head. Don't be posturing or adjusting your cap for the benefit of some lady passenger or a señorita on the pier who has caught your eye. With winches making a racket, etc., the pilot may raise his hand to stop the engine or the helmsman put the wheel the wrong way while you are occupied making a public ass of yourself.

At all times when in narrow waters watch the helmsman when altering the course, and see that the wheel house windows are open so that he can hear. Be sure he repeats each order. What with a foreign pilot and foreign sailors, each speaking a different brand of foreign English, anything can happen.

Pilots use magnetic courses, and often give their orders in quarter points. If you will stop to think, this method is very sensible and natural, Southeast having a broader meaning than 135, or Southwest than 225, but many A.B.'s feel that boxing the compass is just an old-fashioned trick of the examiners to catch them.

It is up to the officer of the watch to take an intelligent interest in the navigation, even though a pilot is aboard, and he should report lights or anything unusual to the pilot.

Find out, by day as well as by night, if the master wants a lookout on the forecastle head, and for how long, when leaving or entering a port. If there is any sort of an accident the courts will want to know why he was not there. You don't need to point it out to the Old Man, but remember that a lookout is a lookout and should have no other duties at the time. The courts have held time after time that the chief officer or carpenter, since they have other duties to perform or consider, do not qualify as lookouts.

Of course, you know enough to have the pilot ladder, boat rope and a heaving line ready for the pilot. Also a bucket in case there is something to go ashore which he cannot get in his bag or pocket. Always ask the pilot on which side he wants the ladder, as the side he wishes to use may be the weather side at the moment. Watch when the ladder is being put over to see that some part of it is fast to the ship; it may dip into the sea and be pulled out of the men's hands. Of course they will act very indignant that you should think such a thing could happen, but if it does they'll have an alibi and you'll get the blame. See that it is not made fast to the rail, which is more often than not a painted piece of old pipe, with very little of it landed in the stanchions at each end. An A.B. should look after this job and make the ladder fast, as some ordinaries have very unusual knots of their own. Also, it should be aft of the bow flare and low enough to still reach a rowboat after the bow wave has subsided. Even if the pilot is a young man he should not be expected to be able to put on a monkey act in heavy winter clothes on an icy ladder. And regarding the last remark, try to keep the ladder from getting wet in freezing weather.

Have the boat rope taken well forward and the other end made fast just forward of where the ladder is, with slack enough in the bight to be easily caught and all ready to let go into the boat if necessary. Where to have the after end of the boat rope seems a mystery to many.

Be sure ahead of time that the cluster light will burn and that the cable is long enough to lower the light a few feet over the ship's side. For the same reason, that is, so as not to dazzle the eyes of those who are working the ship, burn the blue flare below the bridge.

There should be a short stepladder for the pilot as he comes over the bulwarks, or have the jacobs ladder next to a rail that unships; and be sure ahead of time that it does unship.

Where a pilot is boarding, an officer should be there to show him the way to the bridge; and at night have a flashlight with you. The men can look after his bag and the boat rope and ladder. When he is leaving, be sure to tell the quartermaster to take his bag down when the ship slows down. Don't expect the quartermaster to think of it without being told.

Another point you will need to watch is wet paint. Don't just say "That's the chief mate's job," and let the men continue painting the rail where the ladder will be, or the gangways, when you know they'll be used before the paint is dry. Show you have a little gumption and stop them; also let the mate know. If he wants to carry on there it's his funeral, but you have done the right thing.

If the other watch have the pilot ladder and gear ready when you come on deck, send a man along to verify it. Then you won't have to sing that old refrain, "The other watch did it," if something is missing.

The log should always be streamed as soon as the pilot is dropped, or at least before taking departure, so that it will be working freely when the readings are taken. As soon as the vessel stops, no matter for how long, haul in the log. When the log is hauled in while the vessel has way upon her, unhook the inboard end of the line and haul this over the opposite quarter while hauling in the rotator. Otherwise the log line is filled with additional turns which make it awkward to coil. When the rotator is on board, haul in the free end and coil down. Always hang up the line to dry before stowing away, clean rotator and wipe off the log.

Don't use the Morse light on a dark night unless it is imperative, as it takes a considerable time to get your eyes accustomed to the darkness after such flashing light, during which time you are useless for keeping a lookout and your bow lookout and the helmsman are watching the blinking also.

If it is a Coast Guard or Navy vessel (double lights) you must answer, and call the captain, especially with traffic about. Naval vessels do not always take into consideration that there is only one man on the bridge of a freighter to do the navigating, watch traffic and the helmsman at the same time he is trying to answer their call.

In other cases in close waters just don't answer. Most of the questions asked are of the "What ship is that?" type, and you can guess what he is going to say after the first word. But the other ship will be quite a time picking your name out and all the time you are blinding yourself. When he has made out your name he's no better off and doesn't really care anyway. So leave the blinker alone until you are in open waters and it is a moonlight night.

When you take your first watch alone on the bridge the Rules of the Road will take on a new meaning, and the conscientious man has a feeling of great responsibility resting upon him. The Rules of the Road cannot be learned from a book, though they should be memorized from the book and visualized at sea carefully, observing while you are quartermaster or cadet how the master or officer of the watch acts in accordance with the rules. The importance of knowing exactly what is required by the rules lies in the fact that the violation of any rule, however slight, is held by the courts to be a presumption of fault, unless it can be proved that the violation could not have caused, or in any way contributed to, the collision. When a collision follows a violation, this is almost impossible to do. First and last remember Rules 27 and 29, that the rules apply to all vessels alike, and that one is entitled to rely on the assumption that they will be obeyed. A disregard of any rule on the basis of convenience, courtesy, good nature, or disbelief in its efficacy places the navigator under a burden of proof that is almost impossible for him to carry.

Again, not only must the rules be obeyed, but the action prescribed by them must be taken in ample time to carry out their purpose. Give plenty of room, and when you give way, do it as soon as possible, don't hang on, keeping the other fellow guessing. Give way so that there is not a shadow of doubt as to what you are doing. Of course, when you do alter course it is the law to blow the necessary signal, and, if the other vessel can be seen, it is never wrong to do so, although many officers forget or do not like to use the whistle.

Another principle of the rules usually overlooked by the mariner in his seagoing practice of the rules is that to avoid liability he must know not only what the rules applicable to a given situation provide, but what the federal courts have interpreted them to mean.

Know when you pass from waters covered by the Inland Rules to those covered by International Rules, or vice versa. There are important differences extending to sound signals as well as running lights. To illustrate, the use of a single blast of the whistle by a privileged vessel holding her course and speed in a crossing situation is proper in certain inland waters, as provided in the pilot rules, but might make the vessel solely liable for a collision which followed the use of the same signal on the high seas, where one short blast indicates a change of course to the right.

Safety lies in keeping awake every moment of the time, with the Rules of the Road, the maneuvering power of your own vessel and of other vessels—sail and steam—constantly in mind. In two minutes a vessel traveling at ten knots will cover 600–700 yards, while two vessels approaching each other on a bow bearing will draw together by half a mile.

A green light a very little on the starboard bow brings a most serious risk of collision, as one vessel may consider that the situation is a case of *meeting* while the other considers it one of *crossing*. The answer is to exchange sound signals while still at a safe distance.

On rivers and in narrow channels ships must pass close to each other; but when in open waters give all craft a wide berth. A small change of course made promptly is safer than a much greater change made after the ships are close aboard. No precaution is too great to prevent accident and loss of life—and, incidentally, to keep your license. You have nothing to gain by going close to another ship, and a jammed steering rod or a feather working out of a feather-way in the steering engine are the ingredients of a nasty accident. And here is an opportune time to remind you again about seeing that there are no clothes lines nor clothes hanging in the steering engine room.

The courts and common-sense say that a vessel must slow down before entering a fog bank and also sound her whistle when that of another vessel is heard within the fog, even if she is running in clear weather outside the bank. Also the rule is imperative that the engines be stopped as soon as the first fog signal is heard apparently forward of the beam. Until the position of the other vessel is definitely ascertained neither vessel is justified in altering course.

There should be no doubt what to do when you see fog setting in. Put the telegraphs on *Stand By*, note the time, call the master, put a man on lookout, blow your whistle and reduce speed before you enter the fog, or directly your visibility is less than two miles.

Instruct the lookout men what bells to strike when they hear or see something in foggy weather, and to point their hand in that direction so you can get its bearing at once.

Many officers let the thought of what others may think outweigh their good judgment, and don't call the master when they should, although they know at the back of their heads that it is time. At night you can only see about half as far as you think if there is the slightest haze around the lights, so start calling the "Old Man" and slowing down in good time and he will have confidence in you.

In fogs that come on suddenly, reduce speed at once. The captain can always go ahead again if he wishes, and you are doing the proper thing. Even if you are going dead slow and you hear a whistle or other sounds before your beam, stop your engine until you know where and what it is. Many cases have been lost because the engines were not actually stopped, which does not mean go astern, for then you destroy steerage way.

Remember that all distances in the light lists and on the chart for visibility of lights are calculated for a height of fifteen feet for the observer's eyes. And when reporting a bearing of a shore light to the captain, give him, besides the bearing, the number of degrees on the bow. He can then tell at once if the ship should be hauled out or in without having to start subtracting course from bearing when perhaps he is half asleep. If you do not see a light when you should, do not hesitate to call him, and so that there is no mistake about it—as many people call the skipper in such a soft voice that it makes him sleep all the sounder. If you send a sailor to call the captain, warn him, especially if it is an emergency, not to turn all the lights on, so that he won't be blind for five or ten minutes after getting on the bridge.

Be sure of the characteristics of the light. It would not do to try to pass inside Barnegat, Fl. W 10 sec., when you intend to pass inside Barnegat Light Vessel, Occ. W 10 sec.

Of course, when you take over the watch you will read and sign the captain's night orders, look over the log, note the barometer, the lights expected, and check the position and the course. You should always verify the course laid off by the captain, though it is not recommended that you make a great show of doing so.

You should arrive on the bridge at least five minutes before eight bells, which will give you a chance to get your eyes accustomed to the darkness. The watch on the bridge is not relieved until the course has been passed, and this should be done in a rapid and business-like manner. The instant the relief repeats the course he is in charge, and if a sudden emergency develops there is no question who it is. If in the midst of a maneuver, the officer of the watch should stay in charge until the maneuver is completed.

Never hesitate when on the bridge with the master to report a light or the loom of one or a noise in a fog, as it is possible that he has not seen or heard it. Don't expect to be congratulated on your alertness when you do, but even the worst grouch prefers to have an officer reporting all he sees to one who sees and hears, but who is too indifferent to say anything until it is perhaps too late.

And here it might be pointed out that it may not be altogether a misfortune to have to start out with the worst old grouch in the company. Going to sea, and particularly your first few trips, will be no bed of roses, and the kind of skipper mentioned will probably seem altogether unreasonable and make a row out of all proportion to your mistake or oversight; but he probably feels it is the way he learned, and you will probably find his bark worse than his bite if you don't always come back with an alibi or act surly or superior. Whatever you do, don't sit down and write the office that you consider life too short to sail with the likes of him. They aren't going to take him off because he doesn't suit you, and if you are transferred it won't do you any good, even if your complaint is justified. As a matter of fact, the office probably knows better than you do how hard he is to get along with, and will think better of you if you can stick it out.

During your night watch stay outside and keep a lookout, and don't spend half the time leaning over the chart in a trance. Of course you know better but many do so anyway; and when the old man steps out of his room there is a clicking of parallel rules or a stepping off of something or other with the dividers—which doesn't fool him at all.

Another way of getting yourself in bad is to spend the watch talking to the man at the wheel. The captain may not say anything, or only drop a hint not to do so, but you can rest assured he does not like it and knows you are not keeping a proper watch and also not helping discipline by a lot of loose talk; which, by the way, applies to passengers also, who feel that an excellent way to start a conversation with the captain is to quote your remarks.

See that the men relieve each other promptly and repeat the course to you, also that they answer properly when spoken to or given an order. Some officers do not know how to speak to the men, and seem half-frightened to start them on a job of work. Don't start with, "I say, George, don't you think you had better," etc. Call the man by his proper name and give a direct order so he will see you know what you want done and can show him, if necessary, how to do it. If a man is too long starting a job, such as first getting a bucket of water and then going almost to the same place for soap, just slowing up until coffee time or eight bells, don't wait until the trip is half over to bring him up with a round turn—do it at once and don't half-apologize for doing so. This doesn't mean to bully or nag, but let him know you are there to see that the work is done. Keeping men up to the mark saves a lot of trouble in the long run. Avoid foul language, as it only shows ignorance or a transparent attempt to be tough on your part. Respect for others creates in them a respect for you, but calling a man out of his name gives him a perfect right to come back at you with the same—which you won't like.

If the vessel is shipping water forward and the lookout has a long way to go to the crow's nest, keep him on the bridge. You not only stop the risk of accident to the man, but you know then that he is keeping a lookout.

Should a high swell come along from ahead and increase rapidly, do not wait until it has smashed in No. 1 hatch before you call the skipper. Let him know and, if necessary, reduce the speed at once. The captain can always put her ahead again if he is willing to risk it a little longer, but you have done the right thing by reducing speed before damage is done. Four hours from a calm to a gale with a very high sea is quite a common thing in a good many seas.

When it starts to rain, slack the signal halyards before they carry away.

Watch that the whistle lanyard doesn't have fathoms of slack to be taken in before it can be blown. Look after worn places too, so it won't be carrying away after one blast when two were intended. Watch the ventilators, and in general take charge of the bridge when you are on it. If you see anything that wants doing, have it done, and don't wait for the officer who relieves you to do it, even if it is only shifting the log over to the lee side.

Unfortunately, many officers lack executive ability for even running a watch—though looking for promotion of course—and have no initiative; in fact, they are quite content to keep a lookout, take the casual observations and write up the scrap log, but show no enthusiasm in using their brains and looking ahead until they become chief officer. These are the gentlemen who have to be told to change a light bulb, keep the compass cover on and the inside of it clean, or take an iron bucket or reel of sounding wire away from the compass, but feel they are imposed upon when they are not allowed to relieve the mate on his vacation.

You should also see that the azimuth mirror is clean and works freely without having to use force and banging the glass on top of the card, which will mean a wait while the card is steadying down again, during which time the object is covered with a cloud and you don't get another chance for twelve hours.

In the morning when you take over the watch try to get a sight and azimuth as soon as possible, in case the sun is obscured later on. If it is still clear, try to get another when the sun is right ahead or astern or on the beam, which line of position will give the speed or tell you definitely whether you are to one side or the other of the course line, even if you are unable to get a noon sight. If the captain says to try to get it abeam and you miss it, don't point out to him that you got it right on the four points though. And stick to tried and true methods with which you are familiar, though you undoubtedly know better than to drop seconds from the chronometer time, as the man who got the sun on the four points did. You have plenty of time for working out your positions, so sacrifice speed for accuracy. And if you wish the old man to have confidence in the accuracy of your work and still wish to use a slide rule for your calculations, you should use it in the privacy of your cabin with all doors locked.

Calculate the time of meridian passage and measure off the distance for the day. If it is cloudy, get an ex-meridian before, in case the sky is overcast at the time of meridian passage. You are expected to get a noon position even if noon is after eight bells, ship's time, so in working it out use Bowditch Table 47 for your longitude, and you will be able to make out your slip and get down to lunch without having to wait until the captain and second mate get away from the chart.

Don't forget to get a time tick and see if the second mate has wound the chronometer as he should. It is his duty, but there's an unfavorable reflection on you if you don't notice a blunder, or ignore it because it is not your job.

This is probably not necessary to point out, but always put down on the chart the true position you get and don't edge it over toward the captain's position. You aren't regarded as an expert navigator but as a beginner, and an honest mistake will be tolerated; but it will be different if the old man makes a mistake and then finds you have also made the same one. Next time he may put down a wrong line on purpose. At any rate, you can't expect him to have confidence in your character thereafter. Just remember that the technical knowledge you acquired to pass the examination is the minimum requirement for your job, and that the intangible known as character is more important. It's a very exceptional third mate who is smart enough to pull the wool over the old man's eyes, as most any trick you can think up has been tried before.

Now a word regarding fire and boat drills: The watchword here is *Take it easy*. Some people are able to create a local panic around their boat at every drill. Just stand back a little, and while the men are taking off the cover see that everyone has something to do, including pursers and engineers. See particularly that no one throws the falls off the cleats—not unusual where some man's enthusiasm exceeds his mentality—that the plug is in, the painter led inside the forward fall, and the davit handles kept under control, so that the weight of the boat does not take charge and break someone's arm.

A very embarrassing necessity for many officers is the talk to the passengers regarding the boat drill. Something along the following line is suggested: "In complying with the rules and regulations for the safety of life at sea, we are having a fire and boat drill, which is for the benefit of all. Please cooperate by wearing your life belts, which are to be found under the lower berth in your cabin. If you are not familiar with the adjusting of life belts, a member of the crew, located at your boat station, will assist you. You will also find a card in your cabin with the number of the boat to which you are assigned. After acquainting yourself with the number of your boat go to B deck. If your boat has an odd number you will find it stenciled overhead on the starboard or right side; if an even number, on the port or left side. The six short and one long blasts of the whistle will be the call to boat stations. The three short blasts will terminate this drill."

In the evening when you relieve the mate for supper, get an amplitude, and if you have an opportunity, take some stars also. Then when you are relieved, take them down to your room and work them out. Don't spread all over the chart table in the way of the mate and the old man if they are also taking star sights. See how your results compare with theirs, and later on, when your star sights are of importance in the navigation of the ship, you will be sure of yourself and will know if you have a personal error, as many persons do with a twilight horizon.

You should get an azimuth at least once each watch, and after the course is changed. But wait long enough for the compass to settle down, and make sure that there is nothing ahead and that the lookout is not watching the porpoises. Try to get your azimuth of an object under 30° altitude, and check your error with the course the captain has laid off. But remember that if there is traffic about or the visibility poor, it is more important to be out there on lookout, since the approximate error is known anyway. And always take a special look at the compass after the wheel is changed, as well as keep an eye on it at all times. The quartermaster may tell you, and believe it himself, that he is right on 220°, when he is actually steering 250°. Always shift from the metal mike to hand in plenty of time before passing another ship, or when you are near land and visibility is not good.

As soon as relieved you should write up the log before going below. The original log book entries (without erasures) are of great value when points of law are being decided with respect to the ship on a voyage.

Care should be taken to enter everything having to do with the state of the weather and the work of the vessel, the posting and relief of the lookout, the correct names of men on lookout, etc. Practice the art of concise writing and stick to facts. The log book entries should always be signed. Remember that if there are any alterations or erasures visible in a log book, even though having no bearing on the immediate matter, the court will presume that since such laxness was apparently customary the log is of little or no value as evidence. If an error is discovered it should not be obliterated, but both it and the corrected entry preserved and initialed by the person responsible. For purposes of record the azimuth book should be regularly written up also.

The following are routine entries required by law, and particular care should be taken to have them correct, both as to form and substance. The test of gear and lights, etc., before sailing, and the radio alarm test on ships with one operator. The time at which watertight doors, sideports and hatches are opened and closed. The draft and freeboard, fire and boat drills, inspection, fumigation, steam smothering line test, Lyle gun fired, boats in water, etc. The search for stowaways before leaving a foreign port and the search for contraband and stowaways the day before arriving at a U. S. port.

If it is the custom of the ship or master to make some certain entry which appears to you to be a useless expenditure of energy, just continue to make it anyway, and you will probably find there is good reason for it. For instance, in a bottleneck harbor like Havana many thousand dollars' worth of damage has been done to vessels a mile or so inside by ships coming past Morro Castle at full speed. If your log and bell book show that the ship was slowed down in time, your vessel will probably be exonerated.

Many officers spend much time in perfecting themselves in deep sea navigation, where the ship is not endangered, but make no effort to acquaint themselves with conditions such as tides, currents, etc., when coming into port, because the captain or pilot will then be taking the responsibility. This is where danger really exists, and if you wait until the burden is upon you to learn these things it may be too late. Always know when the ship has left the high seas and is in inland waters, so as to know what rules apply.

One of the first things you should have done on coming aboard was to familiarize yourself with the sounding machine, fathometer, and find where the hand leads were kept. When you get a sounding don't put the tube and sample of the bottom on the chart for the old man to see. Not that he won't see them, all right.

Very few men in the merchant service have had the necessary practice in swinging a lead. And it isn't likely the owners would appreciate your giving them the practice, with the lead landing on someone's head and a damage suit as a result.

The hand lead and line are in most cases used after the anchor is down, or just before bringing up; anyway the ship is generally stopped. Should there be a little way on the ship, send the lead along about 50 feet, and then throw it overboard. If it is dark, swing the lead a little as you are lowering it, so you will be able to tell when it touches the water, and you can deduct that from the measure in your hand. But the best way of all is to find out what the distance is ahead of time.

If you don't actually have the lead line in your hand, verify what the sailor has sung out as to depth. Soundings should be given in a sharp, clear and decided tone of voice, for while the old-fashioned "song" is being drawled out a steamer may run ashore. If the water is at all shallow, as it will be if the hand lead is being used, sounding is obviously a most important operation. Of course you know all about this, but the thing is to put it into practice.

Perhaps you have never had the opportunity to use a direction finder until you join this, your first ship, as an officer. Try it out so as to get the feel of it before you ever leave the pier, then you will not have the mechanical part to pick up when the captain sends you in to get a bearing if a fog sets in as you are leaving port. If the D. F. does not have a gyro repeater, set it to the true heading and tell the quartermaster to sing out whether he is two degrees to the right or one degree to the left of the course, as the case may be, rather than to say 87° or 84° when he is steering 85°, in which case you will have to consider the steering and standard compass courses as well as the true course. In other words, if the ship isn't steady right on her course at the instant you have the best minimum, your mind will be so confused that you won't know what the bearing is.

Before the ship is in narrow waters, see that the dodger is down, so all hands can see over the top, but make sure it is clear of the telegraph handle.

If you are going to anchor, find out which anchor the pilot wants to use and probable amount of chain, and let the mate know. Of course, you have called out the carpenter and mate in plenty of time. It is a good idea to have a semaphore flag or some prearranged signal to let the mate know when to let go without further orders. Then, when the pilot sings out "Is your anchor ready?"—and all hands have been waiting half an hour to let go—the mate won't drop the hook on the natural assumption that the pilot said "Let go."

Take bearings as soon as anchored, turn out running lights and see anchor lights burning if at night, post your anchor watch and, if there is a stiff breeze or it is night, put over a 14-20 pound drift lead. Have some flares all ready to burn in case a ship comes too close, for he may be able to see your flare before he hears the bell or sees the riding light if it is foggy.

When the ship starts to swing, put the engine on *Stand By* and call the pilot in time if it seems necessary. Of course, have the other anchor ready to let go, with steam on the windlass, and watch bearings.

At the first sign of fog start the bell and post a lookout aft also, and stay on the bridge yourself. There may be a ship just the other side of the fog, although you have not heard his whistle.

Both by day and by night keep a good lookout while at anchor, and if a ship is being carried across your bow you may get clear by slacking cable. Don't just stand by and watch until she hits.

When you are waiting for the doctor to give pratique, see his boat in time so as to have all hands mustered and lined up for inspection directly he boards. There should be an officer at the gangway to meet him and one to see him over the side when he leaves. If you are dopeing off and don't see the yellow flag until just as the doctor is coming alongside, he may see you are not ready and go to the next ship. Then they get the customs first, and your ship gets farther behind all along the line.

If you are to heave up on the pilot's orders, always let the captain know. Foreign pilots in particular are apt to be very officious and quite willing to take a chance with the ship in order to get ashore as soon as possible for their own purposes. Perhaps the skipper would not have allowed the anchor to be started if he had been informed in the first place, but since it is nearly up before he knows about it, he takes the pilot's unsound advice. If the ship is unfortunate enough to get ashore or run into another ship, the pilot may be a bit late getting ashore but that is the end of it more or less, for him. But the ship will have all sorts of trouble and expense, reports to make out, lawyers to see, and you'll all be in the hands of the legal inquisition for a long time if it's a dry docking case. All because the pilot had a date and you didn't notify the captain in time to stop him.

When you get the order to heave up, start a man down the chain locker, while the master, carpenter and bos'n are being called. Put the engine on *Stand By* and call down for water and steam on deck. The hose should have been ready before. Be sure the water valve is open so no pipes will be broken when the engineers start the pumps.

When the officer who is going to heave up arrives, the carpenter should have the friction gear in, and the windlass can be started right away, instead of having to send a man in the chain locker, then having to call for water and steam after he arrives on the forecastle. This might save ten minutes, which in a lifting fog makes the difference between getting on into port and having to wait another 12 hours or more.

Don't let the cadet or quartermaster start to clear up the bridge just as you are making a landing. The extra minute or so gained in getting below is dear to every sailor's heart, but he will be in everyone's way, and the skipper will send him off and give you a few words besides.

When docking you will be handling the telegraph, and can employ your powers of observation in a far more profitable manner than in trying to see if there are any attractive blondes on the pier to meet the ship. See what the chief mate and second mate are up to, and you will be learning to step up the line and can avoid the mistakes they make if you know what it's all about.

The chief officer, or whoever is on the foc'sle head, should always keep an eye on the bridge when entering or leaving port. He can then see at once if those on the bridge want a line shifted or the anchor let go by signs or a wave of a flag, which will stop all shouting. When the anchor is let go, the mate leaning over the side watching the chain run out is not helping anything. He should make sure it's not dropping into a barge and then look towards the bridge to see if they want to hold on or let the other go. On the forecastle head you can estimate the distance from the pier or ship ahead better than those on the bridge, so don't wait until the ship has hit before telling them to go astern. You might have to let go on your own initiative, which you should not hesitate to do if you can thus prevent the stem from hitting the pier or the ship from going ashore. Of course, don't let it go on top of a barge or tug, but something may go wrong in the last movement of the engines, or a line may carry away, and you can prevent damage from resulting. Hold on as soon as the anchor is on the bottom if letting go under these conditions. Otherwise it will be too late to check her way.

When going alongside, the second mate should give the mate a chance to get the bow in first, then he can heave in parallel with the pier, and if she is bound in too tight forward the mate can slack off. If you will stay on the bridge long enough after the engines are rung off and the make-fast order given to see that the ship is actually parallel against the pier, you can save yourself and everyone else a lot of trouble. That is, instead of waiting until everything is all secured, then having to stand by fore and aft again to slack off forward and heave in aft. This is practically a routine on some ships, and if the third mate is awake he can prevent it by telling the mate that the second can't get her in aft. If there is much flare to the bows this situation is more apt to occur, and also by heaving in too much with a flaring bow the mate can do a lot of absolutely needless damage to a crane or warehouse on the pier.

When you are tying up and get an order to slack a line, see that the man at the winch does so 3 or 4 feet at a time, not inches. The usual sailor will slack away a few inches the first order and on being told to slack more will throw the line off altogether.

Another thing is don't let heaving lines be thrown until you are certain they will reach. Usually heaving lines are thrown when there is not a chance of them reaching shore, and then, when you are close enough, everyone is hauling their heaving lines from the water. Remember too that two heaving lines can be bent together as a man walks forward or aft, so that directly he has the line ashore he can let go, and with the other line fast to the mooring line they can start hauling it ashore. If the midships is to land first on the pier, send a man there with the heaving line.

Your next berth will be second mate, so be ready to step into it if there is an unexpected opening. The master may send you aft to make fast instead of calling out the second, or he may have the mate on the bridge to get practice in docking the ship and send you forward, and he'll be watching to see if you can manage.

Your chief concern aft is to see that nothing fouls the propeller, and never signal all clear until you see the lines are aboard and all actually is clear. Never depend on the good sense of the sailors to look over the side to see if the line is all aboard before they stop heaving in. As has been pointed out before, never depend on them for anything but a good alibi if they care enough to give one. They seldom stay on the ship long enough for you to know who can be depended upon, and anyway, if you want to keep out of trouble you must see to things yourself, as the responsibility is yours, and that is why you are given authority to give orders.

When singling up make sure that the engines are not turning over, and leave a short breast as the last rope to let go. This can be taken in most quickly by hand, and make clear to the sailors that it is to be taken in by hand. Rather than do this they will expend twice as much energy and time leading the line along to the winch, then taking in slack and having to throw it off a couple of times because of riding turns. The fact that the engines cannot be turned over and the tide is running out and setting the ship athwart the slip is of no consequence to them.

Remember, too, that when you ring the telegraph to the bridge that it must be read there, then repeated by the engine room telegraph, the order read in the engine room and at last carried out. All very obvious, but it is surprising how often seemingly sensible men do not take such things into consideration.

Very often there is a tug aft while docking; don't think that you must wait for orders from the bridge to tell the tug to keep the stern from coming in too quickly. The tug is there to be used, and you will be to blame if damage is caused. Also remember that the skipper of the tug cannot see how far off the quay the ship is as well as you can. Many officers seem almost frightened to give a tug skipper an order unless it emanates from the bridge, but remember both he and the dock pilot will wriggle out of any blame.

Many young officers have very erroneous ideas regarding fenders. If you are going alongside a barge that has a certain amount of drift before it touches anything that will bring it up, use a fender by all means. But it is far better for a ship's side to take evenly along the quay than to have a fender taking the whole weight between two frames. You have seen that corrugated effect along the sides of some ships.

Last but not least, understand the hand steering gear, see that it is clear, and know how to shift to it in an emergency.

The second mate, as navigating officer, has charge of the chart room. No unauthorized persons should be permitted in this room, or allowed on the bridge either, for as you know, it is required by law, and posted, that the bridge must be kept free from access by persons not directly connected with the navigation of the vessel.

The idea is to look after things without being told. After telling you once and finding that you are too careless or indifferent to remember, the captain will likely look after things himself, having got sick and tired of reminding second mates. And you'll be feeling badly done by when you find the captain doesn't think very highly of you. For instance, be sure and erase the old bearings and positions from a chart at the end of the voyage, and before the chart is put away. Don't plan to do it later on, because you won't.

Before leaving the pier the charts should be ready in the top drawer in the order in which they will be used, and the harbor chart and first coast chart to be used on the table. Look over the Notices to Mariners before leaving port, and post up in a conspicuous place any changes in the lights that will be passed on the voyage. Also post the time of high and low water and information regarding the variable currents along the coast that will be experienced. See that the course record or scrap log for the last time you made this passage is out handy, that pencils have points, pens good nibs, scrap paper handy, dividers not slack or bent and parallel rules not hidden under the charts in the drawer. Check the chronometer and post error, and see that all clocks and the course recorder show the same time. These are all small things and take but a few minutes, but many so-called navigating officers never think of them.

In port there is the usual routine of seeing cargo properly stowed or discharged, which is generally done from the cabin, or by looking down the hatch and asking the hatch foreman when he thinks the hatch will be finished. But there are a few other points that should be looked after in case of damage claims against the ship.

When longshoremen knock off, be sure there are no open hatches without a guard round them, and that hatches are covered if there is a chance of rain. Get hold of the boss stevedore before the last minute, to be sure this is done. And make sure the wooden hatches are on the hatch, not just a tarpaulin pulled over, in which case someone is sure to try to walk across the hatch and fall down into the hold. Bunker hatches in a used alleyway are always a danger too, even with a chain guard around them. The firemen will never think of others in their hurry to get to the forecastle, and the chain won't be put back. It has been found much easier to blame the officer on watch than to blame the whole black gang, so just protect yourself as well as the company.

Take care to check the special cargo, and don't give the keys to someone else. Know where cargo which is likely to be pilfered is stowed, also cargo which is likely to be damaged or to damage other goods. In the case of automobiles, look them over carefully and make a special report on any scratches or torn upholstery, etc.—which will save you a lot of grief in the end, even if the damage seems to be of no consequence. As each deck is finished, see that all cargo for that port is out, as overcarried cargo is a very expensive headache, and a small piece may cause more trouble than a large one. These are just general things to watch, and with every cargo there are special points to be looked after.

Watch the sideports so they do not get damaged on the pier or by lighters, and if you see the longshoremen handling the ship's gear in a manner detrimental to it, stop them, it's what you are there for. But see the boss, and don't go bawling out some winch man who will probably give you a piece of his mind right back, and there's not much you can do about it.

Look after the mooring lines, which should never be left on windlass or winches. Always put them on the bitts. Maybe they will carry away before the shaft is bent, but if you call yourself a seaman see they are made fast in the proper place and attended to. At the same time check up on the rat guards. Fines for their absence is a welcome source of revenue to the officials of many ports. Remember that in the United States an informer who reports a violation regarding rubbish or refuse thrown overboard is entitled to one half of any fine imposed. The amount thrown over is of no consequence and the minimum fine is, in most cases, $250. See also that there is a light on the stern at night, that the whistle is never blown without good reason and that the funnel is not belching smoke. A factory nearby may be making more smoke in an hour than the ship makes in a month, but that won't help you or the ship. You may say it's the engineer's job to watch the fires, but when you see the smoke tell him, for as the Marine Superintendent will point out in no uncertain terms, if there is a fine imposed, your job was to have looked out for the ship's interests.

See that the gangway man is at the gangway at all times, unless properly relieved, and you or someone else is there in his place. If you let him get away with an alibi for being away once, all you can be sure of regarding him is that he will have an alibi the next time also. There should be a lifeline rigged so as to keep those who are a bit unsteady on their feet from falling between the ship and the pier, and he should keep the gangway at a convenient height off the dock. The sailing time should be known and posted on the board for all to see.

Let the gangway man understand that one of the principal things he has to do is to keep possible stowaways off the ship. Some have the idea that it is just the officers' job to find them after they are aboard. It's a sort of game, some think, and very often sailors or firemen will allow a stowaway to hide in their quarters while the routine search for stowaways is on, and he will turn in in one of the men's bunks and pretend to be one of the watch below and also make out if asked a question that he has had too much sherbet. An engineer should be along on the search, to go not only through the bunkers but also the quarters, and if it is a new crowd have a list of their names. Be sure he's a stowaway before you put him ashore. Members of the black gang speaking foreign English have been shoved off in the pilot boat by the mate before now, and it may be some hours before the first assistant discovers he's a man short.

Unfortunately, the man one generally finds at the gangway will challenge any one who looks at all respectable, but any one who looks down and out is allowed on board. Stowaways are the source of endless trouble and inconvenience, and all precautions must be taken to prevent them from coming aboard and in searching for them just before sailing. Men working on board at repairs, etc., should be supplied with some sort of a tag.

Another thing to be guarded against on the gangway is to see that there are not too many people on it. This is especially so at knocking-off time. The same enthusiasm is not shown at turning to, and a rush never occurs then.

Of course, I would not insult any officer's intelligence by asking him if he really thought the quartermaster stopped on the gangway when all the officers have their meals together. If it is really required to have a man on the gangway, and not just a bluff, one officer must be on duty. The idea that an officer may come by is generally enough to keep the man to his post, but the officer should see for himself that he is there.

It is the same at night: Directly the officer lies down on his settee to have forty winks, the watchman will do the same. If the officer wants to do his duty, and perhaps save the ship from fire or other damage or quite a number of people from having their cabins robbed while the occupants are asleep, he had better be around on the job and see that the watchman is also on his.

If you have a shore relief officer, see he understands the layout of the ship, particularly as regards the fire fighting equipment. Also that he knows where the alarm is on the pier, and the shore connections for the fire lines. Where there is any possibility of freezing, the fire-lines should be drained. See that the winches and windlass are out of gear and ready for turning over, and take any other precaution necessary in that particular ship regarding whistle, sanitary lines, fresh water tanks and lines, breakers in the boats and so on. It is a good plan to put a thermometer at the gangway where the quartermaster can keep an eye on it, and let the officer know when it is still two or three degrees above freezing.

Have plenty of light on the gangway and about the decks. The amount of electricity used is of no consequence alongside the possible costs of damage suits or of a mooring line slipped over the side into a junk boat. Don't leave these things for the night mate to attend to.

A fire warp is required by some companies, and it has saved more than one ship from fire. It's a wire lead from the bow along the shed to a post or cleat at the end. In the case of fire in the shed, or on board, the ship can be hauled into the stream even if there is no steam on the main engines.

When you are in port, be sure everything movable is under lock and key, and remember that brass means money for drink most anywhere.

Of course, when the ship is in the shipyard, the only sensible thing you can do is to take your own gear and valuables ashore and get as much of the company's gear as possible into one of the peaks, batten it down, put padlocks on, set a watchman to sit on the hatch, and perhaps with luck and a prayer nothing will be stolen. Just remember that every man and boy has a set of pass keys, and the watchmen are the friends of all.

The following *standing orders* are for your guidance when standing a bridge watch at sea. The captain with whom you serve may have his own in the front of the *Night Order Book.* These you are expected to sign, when read and understood, and then carry out to the letter. They may vary somewhat in wording or emphasis on certain points but will be of the type indicated.

1. Never hesitate to call the captain when in doubt, or to slow down immediately, stop, or start fog signals on your own initiative.

2. Remain on the bridge at all times when under way unless *properly* relieved by a licensed officer.

3. Before taking over the watch, read and sign the night orders, check position and verify the course laid off to see that it is safe and that it is being steered. Note particularly whether compass error has been correctly applied.

4. Fix position by bearings, soundings, etc., as directed; more frequently if in doubt. Use red dark adaptation goggles in the chart room at night.*

5. You are the number one lookout. Keep the seaman on lookout as far forward and low down as weather permits; have running lights reported every half hour; and do not call upon the lookout to perform any other duties.

6. Report all ships to the captain when sighted, and commence taking bearings. If the vessel will pass within one mile notify the captain of this.

7. Obey the Rules of the Road; give all vessels a wide berth and make any course changes ample and definite. Shift from automatic steering to hand while still two miles from the other vessel.

8. See that a good course is steered, check it after the helmsman is relieved, and see that the man relieved repeats the course to you as well as to his relief.

9. Check gyro against standard compass every half hour, or standard against steering compass if you have no gyro.

10. Call the captain when an aid to navigation is sighted, or if it is not sighted at the time expected. Identify all lights by the light list.

11. Make no erasures in the log or bell book; initial all changes.

DECK OFFICERS' DUTIES

One of the best known truisms at sea is the old saying, "different ships, different long splices." With this in mind, the following remarks on the duties of the mates and of night relief officers which have received the endorsement of publication in the *Proceedings of the Merchant Marine Council, USCG,* are submitted for the guidance of young officers.

---

* It must be borne in mind when using these goggles that yellow, red and orange do not show. Hence anything written in red, for emphasis, will be completely lost. New charts use violet or green instead of these colors for this reason.

DUTIES OF THE CHIEF MATE

Next to the Master, the position of Chief Mate is probably the most exacting and responsible position on board a merchant vessel, primarily because he is expected to assume the position and responsibilities of the Master should that officer, for any cause, be unable to perform his duties.

On vessels carrying three licensed mates, the Chief Mate usually stands the morning and evening watches, not only because they are the most desirable watches and are his by prerogative but also that he may have closer supervision of the work going on during the day.

Because of the nature of his position and the broad scope of his duties, it is the practice on larger vessels to assign an additional licensed deck officer to relieve the Chief Mate of his watch standing duty.

It seems to be the impression among certain seafaring personnel and operators of vessels that the fact that the Chief Mate is relieved of watch standing also relieves him of all responsibility toward the vessel other than the maintenance and policing of the deck department, or, in other words, makes the Chief Mate a "glorified Bosun."

In a recent investigation of the grounding of a vessel, it was ascertained that the Chief Mate paid very little if any attention to the navigation of the vessel, being presumably interested in the supervision of maintenance work and discipline of the deck crew.

The Coast Guard believes that the position of Chief Mate is of extreme importance and that it requires considerably more than a mere routine supervision of day work of the crew.

The Chief Mate is second to the master in chain of command and, therefore, is the master's direct representative, and all officers are under his orders in matters pertaining to operation and maintenance of the vessel except insofar as such matters are the direct responsibility of the Chief Engineer, Chief Steward, and heads of other departments. He is in charge of the cleanliness, sanitation, condition, appearance, and safety of his vessel.

The Chief Mate is always on duty and is responsible for the proper execution of the master's orders. He has charge of the maintenance of the vessel's hull and equipment, of lifesaving and fire-fighting apparatus, and of the discipline and efficiency of the crew.

He should arrange and coordinate the ship's work and drills, prepare daily routines, and lay out work for the deck department. He should consult with the heads of other departments relative to coordination of work and drills.

He should correct abuses, prevent infractions of discipline, and suppress disorders.

He shall aid the Master in every way and see that the other officers are vigilant in the performance of their duties and that they conform with orders. He should be able to instruct the watch officers in the performance of duties and take over, if necessary, in the absence of the Master.

He should set an example for the officers and crew under him and should make frequent inspections.

He should be familiar with all parts of his vessel and equipment and make frequent inspections.

As personnel officer of his vessel, he should be familiar with the crew and their abilities and deficiencies.

When not standing a regular watch, the Chief Mate may relieve the watch officer for convenience, and, in any case, should keep close track of the location of the vessel and be ready to assume command if the Master is incapacitated.

In times of emergency or disaster to the vessel, it is expected that the Chief Mate will be in charge of the damage control or emergency squad and direct the crew in combatting the particular peril.

The position of Chief Mate, with its broad administrative and executive authority, requires unusual ability and good old-fashioned common sense and is one toward which all junior officers should aspire.

Captain G. T. Cahling of the SS *Hawaiian Educator*, Matson Navigation Co., has made the following suggestions to assist him and the Chief Mate in running an efficient and safe vessel:

Following is an itemized list of equipment and reports for which condition and proper handling the junior deck officers are held responsible under the direct supervision of the Chief Officer. The work and inspections related to most of these duties shall be made during day work in port when all officers are on watch or when the Chief Officer, in his opinion, can spare a watch officer when watches are not broken in port. It also is expected that junior officers at *all* times do their best in helping the Chief Officer in his work running the ship, by *frequent* inspections of cargo holds and decks, pointing out to him deficiencies found or accident hazards encountered. *Only by teamwork and cooperation can a vessel be efficiently run.*

DUTIES OF THE SECOND OFFICER

1. Cargo stowage plans, including Customs papers, dangerous cargo lineups, etc.

2. Condition of forward lines, windlass and forward telephone.

3. Log properly kept (amount of cargo and oil, gang hours, exceptions, weather conditions, etc.).

4. Commander reports and Operation reports to the Purser.

5. Charts and all navigational books and corrections of same.

6. Notice to the Mariners, Navy and all government instructions.

7. Gyro—upkeep and spare parts.

8. Radar—upkeep and spare parts.

9. Requisitions for the bridge.

10. Request Mate for any assistance needed in performance of above duties.

RELIEF OFFICERS

When discussing the duties and responsibilities of mates and engineers aboard merchant vessels, it is generally taken for granted these officers are thoroughly familiar with their vessels and the owners' operational procedures. Exceptions to this rule, however, are the

Relief Officers, often referred to as "Night Mates" and "Night Engineers."

These officers come aboard a great many ships to relieve the regular officers of the vessel at night or on Saturdays, Sundays and holidays in port. They may be aboard a particular vessel for one watch or several, and then they are off to another ship, which is probably operated by a different steamship company. One night they may stand a watch on a tanker, the next, on a Liberty-type cargo vessel, and possibly the next watch may be on a passenger vessel.

It is evident, therefore, that these officers must familiarize themselves with the vessel and the owner's policies in a minimum of time. There is not time to go over all the ship's gear, nor to go over every detail an officer coming aboard for the next voyage would be expected to check prior to sailing. Still there are many items which must be checked, records to be kept: and, above all, the Relief Officer must be prepared to handle effectively any emergency which may arise.

One of the most practical solutions we have seen to this problem is that employed by the Matson Navigation Company. This company provides each vessel with a looseleaf booklet containing instructions for Relief Officers concerning their duties, company policies and emergency procedures. In addition, this booklet has a diagram of the particular vessel with all the emergency equipment and other facilities clearly marked. Since all vessels have certain characteristics which are different from others, these diagrams are not placed aboard the vessel ready-made. Rather, each diagram has attached to it a series of headings on gummed paper which are cut out when the pamphlet comes aboard and are pasted at the appropriate spot on the diagram to indicate where a particular facility is located, such as the controls for the various fire-fighting equipment, emergency-gear locker, etc. This booklet is printed in large type, with illustrations, and is compact enough that it can be read in a short period of time. There is also a space provided for the Night Orders for the Mate, and also the telephone numbers of all agents and shoreside operation officials to be called in an emergency.

With information such as this at his finger tips, the Relief Officer is better prepared to perform his duties, particularly those of the Relief Mate.

The Relief Engineer, as a rule, knows the type of plant with which a particular vessel is equipped before he comes aboard. With the assistance of the unlicensed personnel, he therefore generally does not require additional instructions.

The booklet referred to above, although brief, is quite comprehensive. Many items are merely touched upon, since they are somewhat routine in nature. Functions, such as log entries, checking drafts, keeping cargo plans, etc., are often overlooked, however, and for this reason a reminder serves a useful purpose.

Relief Mates are also cautioned to give attention to the gangway, especially during the night. Slack hand lines give little protection to someone using the gangway; when they are too tight, there is danger of these lines snapping. The gangway itself may be damaged if the roller is not kept clear of the dock fittings.

Since the cargo operations and tidal conditions will also have an effect on mooring lines, Relief Mates are also cautioned to check them at frequent intervals. These and many other such activities come under the heading of seeing that the vessel is shipshape. They are routine, it is true, but very essential. For example, the value of instructing the Relief Mate to see that adequate lighting is available, especially during cargo operations, or to see that cargo gear is operating safely and properly is easily seen. By locating spare cargo equipment, such as cargo lights, winch runners, tarpaulins, etc., before it is needed, the Relief Mate may easily prevent delay in operations.

Since fire-fighting equipment differs on merchant ships, the Relief Officer should be familiar with the type in use on board the vessel on which he is serving. One vessel may have a carbon dioxide smothering system in the holds, and another may use steam. This is where the book of instructions and the diagram serve their intended purpose best. A short explanation on the operation and location of fire-detecting, fire-alarm, and fire-extinguishing equipment aboard the vessel is invaluable to the Relief Mate.

One point which the Relief Mate must keep constantly in mind is that he may have little assistance from anyone familiar with the vessel's fire-fighting equipment should an emergency arise, since it is quite likely most of the crew will be ashore. For this reason, he must rely to a great extent on shoreside assistance. No time can be wasted in sounding the alarm both on the vessel and ashore. Knowledge of how to go about this before a crisis arises is a valuable asset. Steps then can be taken to locate and isolate the fire and, at the same time, make sure no one is in the affected areas. The shoreside fire department will probably rely on the Relief Mate for information concerning the cargo, location of the fire, fire-fighting equipment available, etc. Here is where advance knowledge regarding these factors will pay off.

There are other casualties that may arise and which the Relief Mate must be prepared to meet. Damage to the ship's structure and gear may occur at any time during cargo operations. Or personnel may be injured about the vessel. It is essential that the Relief Mate know what emergency measures to take, what medical facilities are available, and what reports are required in these instances.

Cargo and ship's stores must also be protected from damage and possible pilferage. Where such conditions do take place, the Relief Mate must know what reports are required. He must also know what company officials are available to assist in correcting such situations. The value of a complete list of emergency telephone numbers supplied to each vessel for use by both the regular and relief officers thus becomes more evident.

Many steamship companies carry specific types of cargoes aboard their vessels. Special means of handling and caring for this cargo in many cases have been developed. This may induce special docking problems, or loading or discharging situations with which a Relief Mate may not be familiar. For this reason, special instructions available to the Relief Mate covering these situations are very helpful.

It is true many of the points covered appear routine to men who make a practice of staying with a particular company or ship trip after trip. The knowledge and experience these men have picked up during this time helps considerably towards efficient operation of their vessel. Some means of imparting this special knowledge quickly to the Relief Officer, aboard for possibly one watch, is essential.

DUTIES OF THE THIRD AND JUNIOR THIRD OFFICERS

1. Navigation.

2. Weather reports and reports to Weather Bureau—pilot charts.

3. Condition of bridge equipment —fathometer—R D F —chronometers—compasses, azimuth circles, binoculars, searchlights, blinkers— navigational lights and spares, CO_2 cabinet, flags and halyards, books, forms and writing equipment.

4. Lifeboats, condition of.

5. General upkeep of the bridge.

6. Sounding machine—Lyle gun and spare parts.

7. Fire-fighting equipment and *report* about same.

8. Condition of afterlines, capstan, and telephone.

9. Bridge *secured* in port—everything locked and covered.

10. Lockers on bridge—gyroroom —box on flying bridge.

11. Station cards in quarters.

12. Draft to Master and Chief Engineer before sailing.

13. Flags properly hoisted in ports.

14. Help Engineer compile overtime according to logbook—All clear to engineroom when last line is in.

15. Request Mate for any assistance needed in performance of above duties.

Finally, all officers are instructed to teach the men on their watch to be on the alert and point out to them *what to look for* when inspecting deck to ascertain that all is well secured at sea—vents trimmed, doors closed, lights on foredeck doused, etc., and last but not least— How to handle a flashlight in order to not blind the men on the bridge. The performance of the watch is judged by the man in charge.

Chapter 2

INSTRUMENTS AND ACCESSORIES
USED IN NAVIGATION

In the following it is presumed that the reader is a licensed officer already familiar with the appearance, construction and use of the various instruments and accessories listed. These notes are intended simply as reminders. For a more elementary or detailed treatment Dutton's, Bowditch or some similar text may be consulted.

Chip Log. Used with a 28-second glass. There are 3600 seconds in an hour and 6080 feet in a nautical mile.

$$X : 6080 = 28 : 3600$$

therefore, $X = 47$ feet 3 inches = distance between knots in log line.

Total log line is 150 fathoms in length, with 15–20 fathoms of stray line from the chip marked by red bunting. Knotted fish line as knots, with a white rag at each .2 K.

Taffrail Log. The faster the vessel the longer the line should be, 150 ft. for a 200-ft. vessel.

Very liable to fouling by gulf weed, etc.

When log is hauled in, unhook the inboard end of the line and trail this over the opposite quarter while hauling in the rotator. Coil down from the rotator.

Forbes' Log. Records speed and miles traveled and consists of a small rotator in a bronze tube projecting through the ship's bottom, which generates an electric current.

Nicholson Log. Similar to the Forbes but depends on the pressure of the water to measure speed.

Engine Revolutions. A curve should be constructed for various conditions of ship's bottom, load and trim.

The Lead. Hand lead—7 to 14 pounds—marked to 25 fathoms.

Deep-sea lead—30 to 100 pounds—marked 100 fathoms or upward. Lines are generally marked as follows:

> 2 fathoms from the lead, with 2 strips of leather
> 3 fathoms from the lead, with 3 strips of leather
> 5 fathoms from the lead, with a white rag
> 7 fathoms from the lead, with a red rag
> 10 fathoms from the lead, with leather having a hole in it
> 13 fathoms from the lead, same as 3 fathoms

15 fathoms from the lead, same as 5 fathoms
17 fathoms from the lead, same as 7 fathoms
20 fathoms from the lead, a line with 2 knots
25 fathoms from the lead, a line with 1 knot
30 fathoms from the lead, a line with 3 knots
35 fathoms from the lead, a line with 1 knot
40 fathoms from the lead, a line with 4 knots

and so on.

Sonic Depth Finder. Based on an average value of 4800 feet per second as the speed of sound in sea water. This being equal to 800 fathoms per second, an elapsed time of one second indicates a depth of 400 fathoms.

Depth indicators vary greatly in details, but all operate on the same principle, and measure the time required for a signal to go to the bottom and echo back. The two general classes are those using a sound in the audible range and those using a sound in the high pitch range above audibility, commonly known as supersonic.

THE SOUNDING MACHINE

Certain precautions are to be observed in the use of the sounding machine. The following quotation is from a report of the U. S. Coast and Geodetic Survey:

Although of undoubted value as a navigational instrument, the sounding tube is subject to certain defects which, operating singly or in combination, may give results so misleading as to seriously endanger the vessel whose safety is entirely dependent upon an accurate knowledge of the depths.

In practical tests, carefully made by surveying parties, where up-and-down casts of the lead were taken with tubes attached to the lead, errors in the tube amounting at times to as much as 25% of the actual depths have been noted. Errors of 10 to 12% were quite common.

It is worthy of note that in the great majority of cases the tubes gave depths greater than the true depths.

The causes of error may be summarized as follows:

1. When ground glass tubes are used, a small deposit of salt on the inside of the tube will cause moisture to creep up in the tube and indicate too great a depth.

2. If the base is not truly cylindrical, readings will be incorrect. This is tested by introducing mercury into the tube.

3. Where the air temperature is higher than that of the water, the air will contract and the depth shown will be about 1% greater for every 3° of change of temperature.

4. The caps that seal the upper end of the tube may not be tight. Some air may then be forced out of the tube, causing the tube to indicate too great a depth.

5. In chemically coated tubes the chemical (chromate of silver) deteriorates with age, and the reading is often guesswork.

6. Errors due to barometric pressure cause an increase as follows: 29.75, 1/40th; 30.00, 1/30th; 30.50, 1/20th; 30.75, 1/15th. . . .

DEVIATION AND COMPASS ADJUSTMENT

Five Methods by which Deviation is Obtained:
1. Bearings of the sun.
2. Comparison with gyro compass.
3. Reciprocal bearings.
4. Bearings of a distant object (6 mi. at least).
5. Ranges.

Order in which Corrections are Made:

1. Place all deck gear in vicinity of compass in normal position; center the compass; check lubber's line.

Note: The static electricity in orlon shirts has been found to affect magnetic compasses.

2. Place quadrantal correctors by estimate.
3. Place heeling magnet with N end up in N latitude, and lower.
4. Remove all but 10° of deviation by Flinders bar, on E or W, if permanent position for that latitude is not known.
5. Head N magnetic and remove all deviation. ⎫
6. Head E magnetic and remove all deviation. ⎬ semicircular
7. Head S magnetic and remove 1/2 deviation. ⎪
8. Head W magnetic and remove 1/2 deviation. ⎭
9. Head NW magnetic and remove all deviation. ⎫ quadrantal
10. Head NE magnetic and remove 1/2 deviation. ⎭
11. Swing ship for residual magnetism and make a deviation table for standard compass heading.
12. On N or S with ship rolling, remove heeling error with heeling magnet, then lower magnet two inches to avoid overcompensation.

Marking of Magnets. The North end is red, and the South end is blue. In other words, red is north-seeking and blue is south-seeking, from which it follows that the North Pole of the earth is blue and the South Pole is red.

CONSTRUCTING A DEVIATION TABLE
(By Bearings of a Fixed Object)

1. Select fixed object—at least 6 miles off if the vessel is to be swung at anchor, and at a greater distance if steamed in a circle. The circle should be as small as possible.
2. Apply variation to true bearing from chart to obtain the magnetic bearing.
3. Observe the bearing of the object by magnetic compass (every 30° at least) as ship swings in a circle.
4. Compare with magnetic bearings, and make deviation table.

To Construct. Draw the *mesial* line about 12 inches down the middle of the paper. Mark top and lower ends of the line *North*; the mid-point *South*; half-way down between N and S. as *East*; and half-way down between S. and N. as *West*.

Graduate the line into points and degrees as on the rim of the compass card, —N, through E, S, and W, to N. At each 5° place a dot alongside the line to facilitate counting.

Through each point of the compass draw a *plain* line at a 60° angle with the mesial line, downward from right to left; and another such line, but *dotted*, downward from left to right. This completes the diagram. Note that now an equilateral triangle is formed by that part of the mesial line between any two points and the plain and dotted lines intersecting such points.

To Plot the Deviation Curve. Lay off on the *dotted* lines the degrees of deviation observed on each *heading by compass*, using the mesial line scale: To the right if E'ly, to the left if W'ly. Draw a fair curve through the plotted values.

To Use the Curve.

"From Compass Course, Magnetic Course to gain:
Depart by dotted, return by plain."
"From Magnetic Course, to Course allotted:
Depart by plain, return by dotted."

SEMICIRCULAR DEVIATION

Semicircular deviation causes: (1) subpermanent, and (2) induced magnetism of vertical iron.

For purposes of compensation this is divided into coefficient *B*—which affects compass on easterly and westerly courses; and coefficient *C*—which affects compass on northerly and southerly courses.

1. Subpermanent Magnetism. The same cycle of deviation is caused by subpermanent magnetism for any ship; i.e., two diametrically opposite headings on which *no deviation* is caused, one of these headings being the *heading on which the ship was built*, with easterly deviation in one semicircle between the two headings, and westerly in the other, with *maximum deviations on the headings* 90° *from the headings of no deviation*. For this reason, the deviation caused by subpermanent magnetism is called semicircular deviation.

2. Induced Magnetism of Vertical Iron. This varies with the latitude, and is taken care of by the Flinder's bar (a soft iron rod placed vertically, generally forward of the compass, and moved up or down). The pole of the induced magnetism in the vertical iron is on the center line of ship abaft the bridge, hence the Flinder's bar is placed forward of the compass.

Flinder's Bar. One-twelfth of its length above compass card, soft iron rods of varying length fit into a brass tube, with wooden filler pieces below to raise iron slightly above card.

Coefficient B. Ship swung magnetic E or W, magnets placed on thwartship line, i.e., pointing *fore and aft.* Coeff. *B* is approximately equal to deviation on E heading (+) or to the deviation on W heading with sign reversed. (More accurately, the mean of these two, with sign of deviation on E heading.)

Coefficient C. Ship swung magnetic N, magnets placed on fore and aft line, i.e., *pointing athwartship.* Coeff. *C* is approximately equal to deviation on N heading, + if easterly. (More accurately as abo mean of N and S with sign of deviation on N.)

QUADRANTAL DEVIATION

Quadrantal deviation is 0° on headings N, E, S, and W magnetic.
It is caused by induced magnetism of horizontal soft iron.
It is corrected by hollow soft iron spheres.
It does not change with latitude.

When a piece of iron is placed in a magnetic field, the lines of force in the field take the path of least magnetic resistance and crowd through the iron, tending to follow the direction of the length of the iron.

When the ship is heading N and S (mag.), these lines of force follow the direction of the length of the ship and no deviation results. When heading E or W (mag.), the lines of force pass through the center line at right angles, and no deviation results.

Coefficient D is caused by the symmetrically placed horizontal iron, the spheres being placed athwartship. Coeff. D is the deviation on the quadrantal points, and is given the sign of the deviation caused when the ship heads NE mag. Normally this deviation is easterly on NE or SW heading, westerly on NW or SE by compass.

Coefficient E causes a quadrantal deviation having a maximum value on the cardinal points. As it arises from horizontal soft iron placed *unsymmetrically*, on a well-placed compass it should not exist. Where present, it is corrected by placing the athwartship spheres at an angle.

Coefficient A is a constant deviation of the compass on all headings. It occurs if the compass is not on the center line of the ship, or if the lubber's line is not accurately placed.

Heeling Error is caused when the ship heels by that subpermanent magnetism which exerted a downward pull before, and now produces deviation; and induced magnetism in the vertical and horizontal iron changing position.

Temporary Magnetism is produced by the earth in the metal of a ship kept for a considerable time on one heading, or where certain iron is subjected to considerable change in temperature, or to shock such as gunfire.

Heeling Adjuster. A small brass box with levels and leveling screws. Contains a dipping needle, its tendency to dip being counteracted by a small sliding weight whose distance from the axis of suspension may be measured by a scale on the glass cover. Needle was exactly balanced before being magnetized, therefore the weight measures the vertical magnetic force.

Deflector. Adjusts compass errors without bearings. Placed on top of the compass needle is the same on four different courses, two of which are opposite to the other two, then the compass should have no error on any heading. It is to assist in bringing about this magnetic condition that the instrument is used.

Finding Variation with No Chart Available. A compass on shore is usually free from deviation. Thus any bearing is magnetic. For a compass on a ship, take the mean of bearings of a shore object on eight equidistant points; this is the magnetic bearing.

Effect of Ship's Position when Building. Given the direction of the ship's head when building as NE, on which points can you expect deviation to be greatest or least?—It is greatest at right angles NW and SE; least in direction built, NE or SW.

Effect of Temperature. Temperature is not felt on a permanent magnet under 130° F.; above this, some magnetism is lost and not regained; at a bright red heat it loses all magnetism. Soft iron at a dull red has maximum induced magnetism.

Permeability. The quality of being susceptible to magnetic flux.

Stowage. Stow magnets with opposite poles adjacent.

Distribution. Many magnets at a distance are better than a few close up.

Isogonic Lines connect points of equal variation.

Agonic Lines connect points where variation is zero.

Isoclinic Lines connect points where dip of magnetic needle is the same.

Isodynamic Lines connect points where intensity of the earth's magnetic force is the same.

Aclinic Line. The magnetic equator.

GYRO COMPASS

The gyro compass improves both the ship's safety and running economy. Its superiority over the magnetic compass lies in the fact that it indicates true North, being unaffected by magnetism, and its directive force is much greater, so that such auxiliaries as the gyro pilot, course recorder and repeaters may be used. Only the Sperry gyro compass is referred to in the following.

The gyro compass indicates true N, as a spinning gyro can be mounted in such a way that it will align its axle with the axis of any angular motion to which it is subjected. This is provided by the earth's rotation. Gravity is always acting at right angles to the direction of the earth's rotation. The earth's horizon is moving in space, thus the gyro, without the ballistic, while maintaining its plane, will appear to move about the earth's horizon one revolution in 24 hours. The gyro is supported in such a manner as to move about (1) its spinning axis, (2) its vertical axis, (3) its horizontal axis.

The gyro compass is based on two properties of the gyroscope:

1. Rigidity, or its tendency to maintain its plane of rotation fixed in space.

2. Precession, or its tendency when subjected to torque (rotational force) to turn about an axis at right angles to the axis of the torque.

The gyroscope by itself does not seek the earth's axis. Gravity, acting on the mercury and causing precession, gives the gyro its directive powers. If the force of gravity was always acting in one direction the compass would precess only in one direction; but since the mercury is equal on both sides (of the ballistic), when the axis is on the meridian, and the force of gravity or torque is exerted from the other side when

SUMMARY OF MAGNETIC COMPASS DATA*

Class of Deviation	Cause	Coefficient	Maximum effect	Magnetism changes with Lat.	Deviation changes with Lat.	How compensated	Magnetic head to correct	Position of correctors	Remarks
Semicircular	(A) Subpermanent magnetism	Part of B and C	90° (app.) from building head's	No	Yes	Permanent magnets	N. or S. and E. or W.	On N. put athwartship magnets red to stbd. for E. dev. On E. put red for'd. for E. dev.	Use least number of magnets at greatest distance for better directive force
	(B) Vertical induction in vertical soft iron	Part of B and C	E. and W.	Yes	Yes	Flinders bar	E. or W.	Usually forward (opp. to ship's vert. soft iron).	Remove all but about 10° dev. by Flinders bar on center line. Make corr. after compensation on magnetic equator or compute
Quadrantal	(A) Induction in symmetrical horizontal soft iron	D	Inter-cardinal points	Yes	No, unless compass needle induce mag. in correctors	Soft iron spheres called quadrantal correctors	Any intercardinal point	Move spheres in if easterly deviation present on NE. or SW.	Place spheres by estimate (mid-position or all way out) before starting to compensate
	(B) Part of induction in unsymmetrical horizontal soft iron	E	Cardinal points	Yes	No	No provision in naval vessels	None	None	Usually negligible
Constant	(A) Part of induction in unsymmetrical horizontal soft iron	Part of A		Yes	No	(A) Not compensated	None	None	Usually negligible
	(B) Instrumental errors of binnacle, lubber's line, etc.	Part of A	Constant	No		(B) If possible, repair defects	None	None	
Heeling	(A) Vertical component of subpermanent magnetism	None	N. and S.	Yes	Yes, except that the deviation due to the induced horizontal mag. in what was previously vert. soft iron does not change	Heeling magnet	Near N. or S.	N. or red end up in N. Latitude, or as determined by heeling adjuster. May find a and λ, and place weight at dist. a Xλ and bring hor. by heeling corrector	If unable to get a or λ, with ship heeled on N. or S., reduce vibration of card to minimum by means of heeling corrector then lower corrector 2"
	(B) Induction in vertical soft iron								
	(C) Induction in transverse soft iron when heeled								

* Reprinted from *Navigation and Nautical Astronomy*, Dutton.

the meridian is passed, the axis is forced to seek the meridian, oscillating back and forth.

To reduce this oscillation, the connecting link between the mercury ballistic and the gyro wheel casing is attached eccentrically (.171 inch), so that each swing of the gyro axle from the meridian is but 1/3 of the preceding swing, the period of oscillation being 85 minutes. (This does not mean that the compass will have settled on the meridian in that time. The length of time depends upon how far it was off in the first place. It means instead that the compass will be passing the meridian in 21 1/4 minutes, 1/4 of an oscillation, as it swings from, say, 30° W to 10° E and back to 3 1/2° W, which is one oscillation.)

It is essential that the period of oscillation of the compass be many times the maximum rolling period of the ship, otherwise the compass might show some deviation before such movements reverse and cancel each other.

Effect of Ship's Speed and Course. The angular movement of the earth's rotation provides the motive force for the North-seeking precessional movement of the compass. But as the ship is travelling over the earth's surface, and therefore the earth's center, the ship's movement is compounded with that of the earth. Thus the meridian is apparently displaced by the angular difference between the true meridian and the virtual meridian, which is dependent upon (1) the ship's speed, (2) the ship's course, since it is only the northerly or southerly components of the course which are to be taken into account, and (3) the latitude, since the higher the latitude the smaller the earth's surface speed and therefore the greater the effect of the ship's speed.

The problem caused by the above factors is automatically solved by a so-called *speed correction* which when set for speed (within 2 k.) and latitude (within 3°), solves the formula and applies the necessary correction to the master and repeater compasses. This also applies the *tangent latitude correction*, which is made necessary by the fact that at all latitudes other than the equator the gyro axle must lag slightly behind the meridian in order to generate a precessional movement to follow the vertical component of the earth's rotation.

The transmitter is attached to the lubber-ring itself so that corrections introduced by the speed and latitude corrector will be included in indications transmitted to the repeaters.

TO START COMPASS AT DOCK

MK VIII

(Indicator-type AC motor, both armature and field winding stationary)

1. Same as MK VI.

2. Close ship's supply switch.

MK VI

(DC, two-pole series wound)

1. Set master compass and repeater to dock heading.

2. Place a small piece of clean paper between the trolley and contactor on each side of the master gyro compass.

3. Close motor-generator switch in downward or "starting" position and allow motor generator to come up to speed.

4. Close compass rotor switch, causing compass rotor to start and AC voltmeter needle to drop, rising slowly as rotor comes up to speed. Rock if necessary.

5. When AC voltmeter reaches 65 volts, lower rotor-case locking screw on master gyro compass and throw motor generator switch upward to "running position."

6. Close DC service switch which starts azimuth motor. Set compass to heading and bubble level.

7. Close repeater switches on control panel.

8. Close battery switch causing storage battery to float on ship's supply.

9. See that the alarm switch on alarm unit in wheelhouse is turned to *Supply* to silence buzzer.

10. Synchronize repeaters exactly with master compass.

11. If compass when started is not exactly on dock heading, allow sufficient time to settle before using. See that bubble of spirit level is in center.

3. Close ship's supply switch on control panel, causing compass rotor to start, and compass ammeter needle to go to extreme right. If necessary, rock compass in plane of rotor until rotor starts to turn.

4. Allow rotor to accelerate for at least 5 minutes, then lower the locking screw on master compass and remove papers. The azimuth motor will now be energized, and the compass should commence to oscillate or "hunt" with a scope of approximately 1°. Set compass on exact heading and set level bubble central.

5. Close repeater switches on control panel.

6. Close battery switch causing storage battery to float on ship's supply.

7. See that the alarm switch on alarm unit in wheelhouse is turned to *Supply* to silence buzzer.

8. Synchronize repeaters exactly with master compass.

9. If compass when started is not exactly on dock heading, allow sufficient time to settle before using. See that bubble of spirit level is in center.

Note: Since 1937 the Mk. XIV compass has replaced the Mk. VIII type on new installations. The principal differences are that the Mk. XIV has substituted a magnetic pick-up for trolleys and contacts, the hunt of the compass has been reduced to 2/10°, and a voltage regulator eliminates the error due to changing voltages. Ball bearings in the Mk. XIV compass make it unnecessary to rock the instrument, as noted in Point 4. In general, however, operation is the same as for the old-type compass.

To Start Compass at Sea. Set master compass and repeater to the approximate meridian.

Follow the same operations as given in the directions for starting at the dock, except that it will be necessary to lower the rotor-case locking screw as soon as the rotor starts, and steady the compass by hand as the ship yaws or rolls in the sea, until it is time to throw the motor-generator switch up to the *Running* position. Level the gyro approximately as before, and synchronize repeaters with master compass.

To Stop Compass at Dock:

1. Open battery switch and ship's supply switch.

2. Open all other switches on the control panel.

3. Lock rotor-case upright by means of locking screw.

4. See that alarm switch on alarm unit is turned to battery to silence buzzer.

5. Inspect, clean and oil.

To Stop Compass at Sea:

1. and **2.** the same as at dock.

3. If ship is not yawing over 10°, proceed as in the directions for stopping compass at dock. If yaw is over 10° and ship is rolling and pitching, leave locking screw down, and steady compass by hand, until rotor comes to rest. Then lock rotor case upright.

When Starting Compass with True Heading Unknown, bring bubble in spirit level to center and note time—one minute later note position of bubble—if 1° to S on level, compass is off 10° to W, if to N, compass is off to E. Precess compass to approximate meridian and allow it to settle.

Constant Error due to:

1. Difference in amount of oil in rotor bearing reservoirs.

2. Wire jammed between phantom and sensitive element.

Variable Error due to:

1. Dirty mercury.

2. Dirty contacts.

Compass Going Around in Circles:

1. Locking latch up.

2. Contactors not properly seated.

Hunt and Transmitter:

1. Hunt, if correct, is about 1°. Small, too rapid hunt due to azimuth motor being too tight.

2. Hunt too slow, then adjusting screw too far out. (In adjusting, vertical screw must be loosened first.)

3. No hunt, then look at commutator brushes on azimuth motor and see if springs have enough tension.

4. Repeaters less than 1/2° out and unable to synchronize with master compass: Move the transmitter on the lubber ring.

5. Hunt transmitted to repeaters: Adjust lost motion device in azimuth motor, which in this case is too much; in the new type transmitter this adjustment can be made on the transmitter, but should be made on the azimuth motor.

Error Due to Voltage:

1. Low voltage causes westerly error.

2. High voltage causes easterly error.

Ten volts either way will give an error of 1°.

One Repeater Goes Out and not the others: Caused by setting the repeaters while repeater switch is in, thus chipping the gears.

Cleaning:
1. Cosine groove each month.
2. Transmitter each month.
3. Collector rings each month.
4. Azimuth motor commutator each month.
5. Trolleys—when blackened, run paper between each day.
6. Contactors—when blackened, run paper between each day.
7. Oil well windows each time oil is changed.

Nothing should be removed but transmitter, the trolley and contacts.

Oiling (Gargoyle Vacuoline, Extra Oil B):
1. Guide—2 drops each month.
2. Stem—2 drops each month.
3. Corrector—felt pad.
4. Azimuth motor bearings—4 places—1 drop per month.
5. Transmitter bearings—4 places—2 drops each month.
6. Wicking in pots of phantom—4 places—each month.
7. Cosine groove roller—2 places—oil each month and grease walls of groove.
8. Ballistic link bearing and lower guide bearing—2 drops each month.
9. Rotor bearing reservoirs—1/16° below dot in glass each week. Renew oil every three months.
10. Gimbal supporting bearings (flip-back cover)—4–5 drops every six months.

Keep oil and grease away from surfaces which conduct electricity. Do *not* oil trolley pinions.

Wicking in mercury pot is to provide ventilation.

Alarm Unit. This contains three dry cell batteries which should be tested individually every three months and renewed every six months.

COURSE RECORDER

All directions necessary for the operation of the course recorder are contained on an engraved instruction plate on the front of the device. The important thing is to keep the record properly. The recorder clock should be checked every watch, and the record itself liberally annotated as regards passing landmarks, alterations of course, and weather conditions. The exact time is of utmost importance if it should be necessary to use the course recorder as evidence in case of accident, collision or stranding.

GYRO PILOT

Condensed instructions for the use of the particular type of gyropilot installed are contained on a framed chart in the wheelhouse.

Care of Control Unit.
1. Bearings of control unit require only a few drops of light oil when general overhaul is made.
2. Keep inner and outer surfaces of follow-up rings clean and bright by means of a clean cloth moistened with alcohol. Occasionally crocus paper may be used, but be sure to wipe off dust afterward.

3. Clean the air gaps between ring sections frequently by passing paper through gaps.

4. See that brushes slide freely in their holders and bear squarely on the ring surface.

5. Apply a little cup grease occasionally to the weather and rudder adjustment lead-screws.

6. Give control lever and adjusting knob shaft a few drops of light machine oil at monthly intervals.

The **Power Unit** is exceptionally rugged, and requires little attention. It is generally under the supervision of the engineers.

CHARTS

Mercator Projection. This is the projection generally used for purposes of navigation proper. Distortion occurs near the poles and where a large extent of surface is covered. It is a development upon a plane surface of a cylinder which is tangent to the earth at the equator.

Constructing a Mercator Chart:

1. Determine limits of the proposed chart.

2. Draw a horizontal line at the bottom if it is to represent North latitude or at the top if South, the middle if both.

3. Divide line into required number of degrees of longitude.

4. Erect perpendiculars at the extremities.

5. Take out meridional parts for desired latitudes, and divide by 60 to reduce to degrees.

6. Lay off these lengths on the perpendicular line for parallels of latitude.

7. Divide spaces between horizontal lines into equal spaces representing 1, 5, or 10 miles.

(**A Loxodromic Curve** is a rhumb line, which is a line on the earth's surface which intersects all meridians at the same angle.)

Gnomonic Projection. In this the earth's surface is projected on a plane, tangent to the earth's surface at a point, by means of rays from the center of the earth. A great circle on this projection is a straight line. Polar charts constructed on this principle have the plane tangent at the pole.

Polyconic Projection. This is a development of the earth's surface on a series of cones, a different one for each parallel of latitude, with each one having the parallel as its base and having its vertex in the point where a tangent to the earth at that latitude intersects the earth's axis. In this projection, the general distortion is less than in any other method, for which reason it is especially adapted to the plotting of surveys.

Chart Symbols, etc., will be found under Piloting.

BAROMETERS

A mercurial barometer, if carried by the ship, should always be employed in meteorological work. The type known as the Kew or marine barometer is especially adapted to ship use, but after reading it must not be left exposed, as it is liable to injury by violent oscillations in heavy weather. The only setting required is to bring the lower edge of the vernier accurately to the level of the top of the mercurial column. It should be hung where the temperature is fairly uniform, in a good light, and away from the jar of machinery. It is essential that the barometer be vertical at the instant of reading. All observations of mercurial barometers are ultimately reduced to a standard temperature (32° F.), to eliminate errors due to expansion. Another final correction is made for latitude, which is for sea level in latitude 45°. Elevation above sea level correction does not apply aboard ship, of course. All instruments may require corrections for their own imperfections.

Aneroid Barometers are liable to many mechanical defects, and the statement that they are "compensated" should not be taken too literally. Tapping on the side or bottom with the fingers will show whether the hand has the necessary freedom of movement. Aneroids suspected of temperature trouble or other failure to register correctly will be tested by the Weather Bureau offices located in most large U. S. seaports. As in mercurial barometers, the instrumental error may be large and undergo irregular changes. Comparisons should be made with the U. S. Weather Bureau at least every 3 or 4 months, In making comparisons, at least three readings should be made at uniform intervals of 12 or 24 hours while the barometer hangs in its accustomed place. In U. S. ports the barometer is read each day at 7:30 A.M. and 7:30 P.M., 75th meridian time. Blank cards for recording comparative readings are supplied by the Weather Bureau.

No attempts should be made to adjust a barometer. Such attempts are likely to increase the irregularities of the instrument.

THERMOMETERS

If two thermometers, one with its bulb moistened, the other with its bulb completely dry, are exposed to a rapidly moving current of air, the thermometer with moistened bulb (the so-called wet-bulb thermometer) will show a lower temperature than the ordinary dry bulb. The difference between the two bears a known relationship to the humidity, the latter being obtained with the aid of appropriate tables. Fine, loosely-woven muslin is used to cover the bulb, and the water for moistening it must be pure and free from salt. In order to protect the thermometers from spray, the direct rays of the sun, and at the same time permit a free circulation of air, a special shelter must be constructed. This shelter should be of wood, with a double roof and louvered sides, painted white and placed so it will not receive warm air issuing from the interior of the vessel.

Temperature Scales:

	Freezing Point	*Boiling Point*
Fahrenheit	32°	212°
Centigrade	0°	100°
Réaumur	0°	80°

Conversion Formulas:

$$F = 9/5C + 32$$
$$C = (F - 32) \times 5/9$$

SEXTANT

Adjustments of the Sextant:

1. Index glass perpendicular to the plane of the limb. Place index bar near the center of the arc. Correct if true and reflected arcs are in a smooth curve.

2. Horizon glass perpendicular to plane of limb. Hold the sextant vertically and bring the direct and reflected images of the horizon line into coincidence; rotate sextant about line of sight; if images still coincide the glasses are parallel.

3. Horizon glass parallel to the index glass. Set index at 0° and clamp; check carefully; direct line of sight at the horizon (or star); the reflected horizon should be an exact continuation of the horizon seen direct.

4. Line of collimation of telescope parallel to plane of limb. Place sextant face up on a table; use star telescope with two parallel cross wires parallel to plane of limb; look along plane of limb to opposite wall (20 ft.) and draw a horizontal line at the height of the limb. Draw another line above equal to the height of the telescope axis above the limb; adjust the telescope so that the second line falls midway between the cross wires when it is correct.

Constant errors of sextant beyond the power of the navigator to correct are practically negligible in a well-made instrument. Possible errors are:

1. Eccentric Error, where the pivot of the index bar is not at the center of curvature of the limb. This would be different for different angles measured. The sextant is examined for this when a certificate is granted, and given *A* if error is 40″ or less, and is tabulated for each 15° of arc. *B* is given if error does not exceed 2′. No certificate granted if error over 3′.

2. Errors of Graduation.

3. Prismatic Error of mirror and shade glass, which is due to lack of parallelism of the two faces.

Sextant covers 1/6 circle and measures an angle of 120°.

Octant covers 1/8 circle and measures an angle of 90°.

Quintant covers 1/5 circle and measures an angle of 144°.

Artificial Horizon. The sextant image is brought tangent to the artificial horizon's reflected image. The observed altitude is double. Apply the index error to this observed altitude and then divide by 2. Now apply corrections for refraction and parallax and for semi-diameter.

After tangency is obtained, the change of altitude of the sun will cause the images to separate or to overlap. In the forenoon if the images separate after tangency, the lower limb is observed; this is reversed in the afternoon.

Molasses, oil or other vicous fluid may, when necessary, be used as a substitute for mercury.

ADJUSTMENTS OF STADIMETER

When the micrometer stands at infinity, both mirrors should be perpendicular to the plane of the instrument, and parallel to each other.

To put the horizon glass perpendicular to the plane of the instrument, look at the horizon glass through the small peep-hole, which is placed near the index glass, before securing the telescope in place. The edge of the silvering of the horizon glass, and the center of the peep-hole are at the same distance above the frame of the instrument. Therefore, if the horizon glass be perpendicular to the plane of the instrument, the observer will see the reflection of one-half of the peep-hole in the silvered part of the horizon glass. If he does not see this, he turns the square head of the screw on the horizon glass, which is perpendicular to the plane of the instrument, until he does see the reflection of one-half of the peep-hole.

To make the index glass perpendicular to the plane of the instrument, hold the instrument with its plane vertical, and look at some small object, like a mast; then, move index glass by means of the regulating screw, which is perpendicular to the plane of the instrument, until the direct and the reflected image of the mast are vertically in line with each other.

To make the mirrors parallel in a vertical plane and perpendicular to the plane of the instrument, hold the instrument with its plane vertical, and move the regulating screws of the horizon glass, which are parallel to the plane of the instrument, until the direct and reflected images of some horizontal line, like the horizon, are in line with each other, the micrometer being at infinity.

During the manufacture of the instrument, the groove in which the micrometer carriage moves and the edge of the index bar are made true, and the micrometer drum is placed on its shaft in such a position that when the infinity mark stands opposite the pointer, the edge of the index bar is parallel to the groove in which the micrometer carriage moves.

The micrometer drum is clamped in position on its shaft by three set screws. After this has been done, it should never thereafter be placed in other positions upon its shaft, unless the point of the micrometer screw should be worn away. If this comes to pass, the direct and reflected images may be in line with each other, when the micrometer carriage is at one part of its movement, and not in line when it is at another part of its movement. For this reason, whenever the micrometer carriage is moved from one "height" to another, it is necessary to vary the alignment of the mirrors.

To readjust when the point of the micrometer screw has been worn away, put the carriage at 200 ft., and turn the micrometer so the infinity mark comes 1/32″ to the right of the reference mark. Align the direct and reflected images; move the carriage to 50 ft.; and see if the direct and reflected images are still in line; if they are, the micrometer screw has been advanced far enough. If the images are not in line, advance the micrometer further, until they remain in line with the carriage at 200 ft. and 50 ft. Then slack up the three set screws; move the micrometer independently of its shaft until the infinity mark opposite the index mark; set up on the set screws.

If the assumed height used is, say 10% too small, the distance given by the micrometer will be 10% too small, and vice versa.

The reading glass over the micrometer should be pushed down close to the micrometer before the stadimeter is put into its box.

In case the edge of the index bar becomes deformed, the instrument should be sent to the repair shop or to the manufacturer for repairs.

CHRONOMETERS

Chronometers should be wound gently, avoiding sudden jerks, and at the same time each day (though constructed to run 56 hours without rewinding). They should be handled as little as possible, and should *always* be kept in the outside cases, screwed down amidships in some secure place, and free from any current of air. The outside case should always be kept closed, except when taking time and winding, as a sudden change of temperature will cause a chronometer to sweat and become rusty. Outside cases are lined and packed for the express purpose of keeping chronometers free from exposure to sea air and sudden changes of temperature. Chronometers should *never* be "set."

When carrying a chronometer to and from the ship, clamp it rigidly in the gimbals; and when transporting for a considerable distance, allow it to run down, dismount it and stay the balance with a cork wedge.

Chronometer Errors. It is more important that a chronometer should have a uniform rate than a small rate. The rate is called positive and marked $(+)$ if the chronometer is gaining, otherwise negative and marked $(-)$. If fast on GCT, the error is positive and marked $(+)$, otherwise negative and marked $(-)$.

Chronometer Correction. To find the GCT, apply the error with the sign just referred to *reversed*.

Time Signals. Radio time signals in the U. S. are sent out from Arlington, Annapolis, and San Francisco at 0000, 0300, 1200, 1600, 1900, and 2200 standard time, 75th meridian.

Comparison of Watch and Chronometer. $C - W$ is the chronometer minus the watch time, and is a quantity which is *always added* to the hack watch reading in order to get the chronometer reading. If, as frequently happens, the watch reads more than the chronometer, so that the watch reading cannot be directly subtracted from the chronometer reading, 12 hours is added to the chronometer to permit the subtraction so that $C - W$ may still be added to W to obtain C.

TABLE SHOWING THE EFFECT PRODUCED BY A CHANGE IN RATE OF A CHRONOMETER

When a chronometer gains on its rate, the computed longitude is to the West of the true longitude. When a chronometer loses on its rate, the computed longitude is to the East of the true longitude. When, on making a well-determined point of land, the longitude by chronometer does not agree with the actual position of the ship, it will be convenient to refer to the following table:

The Land not made so soon as expected	SAILING EAST	SAILING WEST
	THE CHRONOMETER HAS	
	Gained Less or Lost More	Gained More or Lost Less
The Land made unexpectedly	Gained More or Lost Less	Gained Less or Lost More
	THAN ALLOWED FOR	

CHRONOMETER ERROR BY OBSERVATION

1. Take a time sight at a spot ashore of known latitude and longitude. By means of the *artificial horizon* the altitude is observed and the body's *H.A.* computed. The difference between the *G.C.T.* obtained by chronometer and by observation is the chronometer error.

2. At a known spot ashore an altitude of a star is taken E of the meridian, and another when it has exactly the same altitude W of the meridian, noting chronometer time in both cases. The easterly *H.A.* in the first case must equal the westerly *H.A.* in the second, and the middle instant between the two observations is the time of the body's transit. At this instant the body's *R.A.* is equal to the *L.S.T.* By applying the longitude the *G.S.T.* is obtained, and converted to *G.C.T.* The difference between this *G.C.T.* and that obtained by using the middle chronometer time is the chronometer error. (The sun could be used, but it requires an elaborate correction of the middle chronometer instant to obtain the time of transit.)

RADAR

For our purpose the theory behind radar is the same as that behind the fathometer or for obtaining distance off a cliff or iceberg by a whistle's sound.That is, in the latter case, we measure the time elapsed between sending out of the sound and return of the echo, divide by 2 to get the time one way, and multiply by speed of sound, 1120 feet per second. This gives us distance off, in feet. However, speed of radio waves is 186,000 miles per second—nearly a million times that of sound waves. One of the most difficult problems that had to be solved in the development of radar was a technique for measuring time in such infinitesimal amounts. The measure of time used is the *microsecond*, which is one millionth of one second. The radio pulse, which corresponds to the whistle sound and its echo complete their round trip in only a few millionths of a second; then there is a comparatively long wait of a few thousandths of a second before the next pulse is sent out. The echo appears on a cathode-ray tube or oscilloscope (usually called the *scope*), which serves as a visual indicating device for displaying information obtained by the radar system. This cathode-ray tube is a special type of vacuum tube in which electrons emitted from a cathode are accelerated to a very high velocity, then formed into a narrow beam, and finally allowed to strike a chemically prepared screen which fluoresces, or glows, at the point where electrons strike.

BASIC RADAR SYSTEM

Radar systems vary greatly in detail, but principles of operation are essentially the same for all systems. Thus a single basic radar system, Fig. 1, can be visualized in which the functional requirements hold equally well for all specific equipments. There are six essential functional components, as follows:

1. The timer (known also as synchronizer or modulation generator) supplies the synchronizing signals which time the transmitted pulses and the indicator, and which coordinate other associated circuits.

2. The transmitter generates radio-frequency energy in the form of short, powerful pulses.

3. The antenna system takes radio-frequency energy from the transmitter, radiates it in a highly directional beam, receives any returning echoes, and passes these echoes to the receiver.

4. The receiver amplifies the weak radio-frequency pulses returned from target and reproduces them as pulses to be applied to indicator.

5. The indicator produces a visual indication of echo pulses on the scope.

6. The power supply furnishes all a-c and d-c voltages necessary for operation of the system.

There are a number of different kinds of scopes, but one in which we are interested is the PPI, or Plan Position Indicator, Fig. 1. When you view a PPI scope you assume that you are at the center of the screen and everything is reproduced relative to your position.

The picture of the surroundings appears by this simple process: the sweep begins in the center and goes outward toward the edge in direction antenna is pointing, and a bright spot appears at a distance proportional to range of the target. That is all that is needed to draw a true map of everything in the vicinity. The scope shows everything that can reflect radar energy, and shows it in the proper place on PPI chart. You will see islands, ships, planes (if not too high), as well as shore lines and even rain squalls; all objects appearing in their actual positions.

Remember that the sweep moves outward in a direction representing the antenna bearing. Since the antenna can pick up an echo from target only while it is pointing at the target, and since the rotating antenna points in any target's direction for but a short time, you would expect the bright spot to appear for only a moment. As the radar beam swings away from target, you would fail to receive any echo from it, and consequently the beam would no longer make a bright spot. The beam can intensify contacts on only one bearing at a time. This means that in order to continue to see that particular target, the screen must continue to glow after sweep leaves it. In making the cathode-ray tube the screen is painted with a chemical coating that persists in glowing after sweep has left it and has moved to another spot. Image on screen fades slowly, and each time antenna rotates the *picture* is reinforced.

Figure 1 shows the bearing and range markers on PPI scope. By an adjustment of controls, either true or relative bearings of targets may be read directly from calibration scale around the screen, depending on

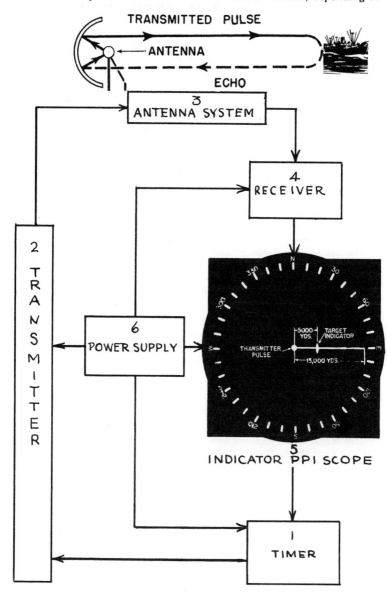

FIG. 1. SINGLE BASIC RADAR SYSTEM.

whether or not a gyrocompass is connected to the system. Any distant object which will reflect a sufficient signal is termed a target.

Range is indicated by radial distance from center of screen at which target appears. Thus range may be estimated from a series of concentric circles that may be put on a transparent overlay or produced electronically on screen. This scale may be changed by means of the controls, giving a choice of, for example, 1-, 5-, 15- or 30-mile scale. Range may also be measured by use of a range marker which appears on the screen as a circle called a *range ring*, whose diameter is controlled by the range knob. By placing this ring over target indication, the range in yards is shown on a scale also controlled by the range knob.

The positions of echo signals on scope indicate range and bearing and do not of themselves reveal any further data. However, with experience the operator is able to interpret what he sees with a surprising degree of detail. Proper manipulation of the gain control is the most important aspect of good radar operation.

INTERPRETATION OF SIGNALS

In general there are four characteristics of the echo signal that may give useful information: its size, its shape, whether it fades or fluctuates or is steady, and movement in range and bearing.

The size of echo signal depends on many factors, and reliance cannot be put on observation of this characteristic alone to estimate the type of target. At ranges greater than 15 to 20 miles, for instance, most ships are hull down so that the echo is returned from the masts and superstructure only.

The shape of an echo may be such that target could not be anything other than a cloud or a storm.

A small vessel or plane may appear and disappear, but if plotting course and speed shows target to be moving at high speed, say 60 knots, it must be a plane, since relative speed of surface vessels rarely if ever exceeds 60 knots. In order to observe these characteristics, the antenna may be stopped. A thorough knowledge of the operating characteristics of a particular piece of radar equipment is necessary before either the capabilities or limitations of the set can be appreciated.

If it is assumed that radio waves travel along perfectly straight paths, curvature of the earth prevents these straight rays from striking objects that are beyond the horizon. If height of antenna is increased, the horizon is extended. However, radio waves, like light waves, must pass through the atmosphere to get from one place to another. Thus, although it is sometimes assumed that both light and radio waves follow perfectly straight paths, properties of the atmosphere are such that waves are made to follow curved paths, and we find that radio waves are subject to refraction, diffraction and reflection from the sea surface. Radio waves in passing through the lower atmosphere are usually bent downward almost twenty times more than light waves, so that the apparent horizon for a radar is approximately 15% greater than the distance to the optical, or sea, horizon.

Radio energy is reflected to some extent at any surface that presents a discontinuity. Reflection takes place best from a plane surface at right angles to the radar beam. A surface of metal presents a very great discontinuity and sends back a strong echo. Although best echoes are obtained from conducting objects, non-conducting targets will also return an echo. Thus, echoes are sometimes received from wooden boats, birds and clouds. Probably a low-lying wooden boat can be detected at a greater distance optically than by radar.

WEATHER EFFECTS

Weather may at times seriously interfere with radar operation. Reasons for this may not be obvious at first. For instance, fine weather with clear skies, little wind, and high barometric pressure may result in very poor performance which will be greatly improved by rainfall. The phenomenon involved in this case is known as *trapping*, that is, the atmosphere has become sufficiently stable to allow stratification so that radio waves become trapped between layers. The most dangerous trapping condition occurs when it accompanies fog and radar detection range is reduced at same time that ordinary visibility is shortened. Other weather conditions that favor trapping are: a moderate breeze that is warmer than the water, blowing from a continental land mass; a cool breeze blowing over the open ocean far from large land masses, especially in the tropical trade wind belt; when smoke, haze, or dust fails to rise, but spreads out horizontally; when air temperature at bridge level on the ship definitely exceeds that of the sea, or when moisture content of the air at bridge level is considerably less than that just above water, and the air is relatively calm.

Roll and pitch of vessel may have a profound effect on radar operation, and in small ships the amount of roll is often enough to prevent reliable use of radar. This is due to the fact that energy transmitted from a radar antenna is confined to a beam, and rolling of the vessel may cause it to miss some targets at times, as shown in Fig. 2A.

Since some energy radiated by radar strikes the sea surface, echoes are returned from the water when surface is disturbed by waves. These echoes are called *sea return*, and they show on PPI scope as an irregular bright area around center of screen. (See Fig. 2C). In very calm water sea return is negligible, but in very rough weather it will be impossible to see targets within several miles of vessel because all echoes are lost in the clutter of sea return. It is frequently possible to estimate direction of the wind from the oval shape of sea return, since stronger echoes are obtained in a direction perpendicular to waves than along their troughs, and fronts of the waves are more nearly vertical and therefore better reflectors than their sloping backs.

The effect of ice formation on radar antenna depends upon whether the antenna is open or covered with a *radome*. In the open type it seems to have little effect other than to put a mechanical load on antenna training mechanism. A coating of ice on the radome may reduce radar performance considerably. Perfectly dry, hard-frozen ice seems to have little effect on performance, but a coating of water on the ice may cause a large reduction in range.

Not all clouds can be seen on a radar scope. Stratus clouds give very little echo or perhaps none at all, and a general overcast sky is often in-

THE ROLL OF A SHIP MAY CAUSE THE BEAM TO MISS THE TARGET

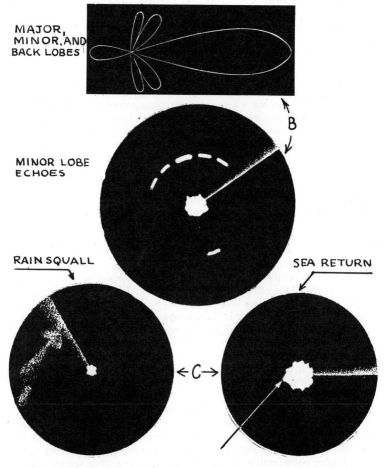

MAJOR, MINOR, AND BACK LOBES

MINOR LOBE ECHOES

RAIN SQUALL

SEA RETURN

FIGURE 2

visible to the radar operator. Thunderstorms and frontal squalls usually produce intense illumination of the scope. Cloud echoes have a nebulous appearance on PPI, and in some cases almost the entire scope may be so covered with cloud echoes as to totally obscure the target.

The foregoing effects of weather have been pointed out so that they may be recognized for what they are, but occasions are rare in which they will seriously affect use of radar.

PHANTOMS

Many peculiar results have been obtained with radar that are variously attributed to phantoms, pixies, gremlins, and the like for want of a reasonable explanation.

Although a directional antenna radiates energy principally in one beam, a small fraction of the energy is radiated in other directions. If echoes are obtained from side lobes as well as main lobe as antenna rotates, an isolated target at close range will produce several spots on PPI scope. (See Fig. 2B). All of these echoes will be at the same range, but they will cover an arc on screen equal to the angle over which minor lobes appear, sometimes over an arc of 50° to 120°. With a high gain, echoes from both main and minor lobes may produce spots of equal intensity. If gain is reduced, side lobe echoes will be less intense and of less angular width than main echoes.

Another cause of phantoms is the fact that energy radiated from a radar antenna may be deflected from its normal straight path by reflection from some part of the ship's structure. This reflected energy can produce echoes from targets at short range, but bearing on which the echo is indicated is false. When the operator becomes thoroughly acquainted with his equipment, he will know the bearings on which to expect doubtful echoes. Plotting contacts of this sort usually reveals their false character.

A radar antenna will have a clear field of view only when there are no obstructions on the ship in the path of radiated energy. Almost all radar equipments have areas of reduced coverage due to this cause, and in some sectors may be completely blind. (See Fig. 3C). The ship may be swung slowly in the smallest possible circle while bearings are taken of a distant object, at 30,000 yards or more to ascertain limits of such impediment, if any. The only cure for a blind zone caused by interference from ship's structure is to relocate the antenna.

RANGE AND BEARING

The minimum range at which radar can detect a target in good weather may be safely assumed to be 400 yards, but in rough water sea return will be strong and may extend 3 miles from vessel, thus preventing detection of targets within this distance. The maximum range obtainable with a radar is a variable quantity.

On long range scales it is impossible for the PPI to paint a sharply defined image, just as it is impossible to paint small letters with too big a brush. Thus, the echoes from two targets which are close together may merge into a single bright spot, though this difficulty may often be overcome by proper adjustment of the gain control, which corresponds to the volume control of a broadcast receiver. To use an extreme case as an example, let us assume that the minimum spot size that can be produced on the scope is .03 inch. Then if a 200-mile range scale is used this spot appears to be a mile in diameter, while if a 20-mile scale is used the spot diameter is only 200 yards.

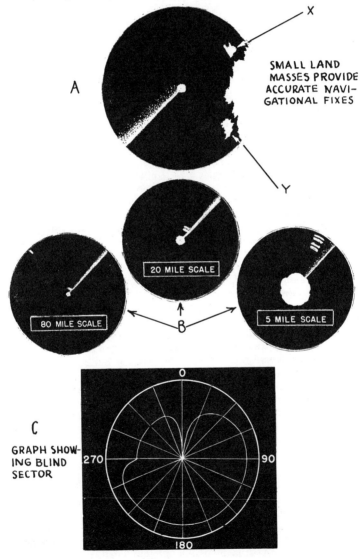

FIGURE 3

Radar bearings are not as accurate as optical bearings under any conditions where target is visible to the eye. In case a radar is installed on a ship without a gyro compass, a rotatable bearing circle is located outside the fixed bearing circle. This bearing circle can be rotated by a knob. The true bearing can be obtained by rotating outer bearing dial to a point where ship's course (or heading) is indicated on outside dial opposite zero of inside dial, which corresponds to the lubber line on a compass. Now the bearing of an object indicated by radar shows relative bearing on inside dial and true bearing on outside dial.

Careful installation of radar is necessary to insure that part of ship's superstructure does not interfere on some bearings. The interference produced by the part of the pulse that is reflected by superstructure may amount to as much as 7°. The accuracy of determination of bearing on PPI scope varies with range, since length of an arc of a given angular length is directly proportional to the radius of the circle on which the arc is drawn. The bearing used should be that obtained by bisecting the target, not by using one tangent of target arc.

MAINTENANCE

Like any complex precision equipment, radar requires careful maintenance. This is simply a systematic application of the old adage, "A stitch in time saves nine." A definite maintenance routine must be carried out. This includes lubrication, cleaning, changing tubes before they fail, and protecting equipment from humidity, dust, and temperature changes.

The data on all parts that require lubrication are given in the manufacturer's instruction book. Both frequency of lubrication and kind of lubricant are specified. Periodic lubrication of the type indicated will eliminate failure of rotating machinery and bearings.

Dust, paint chips, and other foreign matter may accumulate between points where high voltage exists and cause failure through arc-over, since very high voltages are used in some parts of the circuit. To avoid such trouble, equipment should be inspected carefully and often, and dust blown out with an air hose at regular intervals.

The life of components in electronic equipment is in general limited, and experience has shown that nearly 80% of failures that occur are caused by tube failure. Since enough data have been accumulated on the average expected life of tubes used in radar, it is possible to predict approximately when a particular tube is likely to fail. Part of preventive maintenance schedule should include a log of number of operating hours on each tube so that it can be replaced before it fails. Spare tubes are usually mounted in racks within the unit as a means of helping to keep the set in operation. These tubes should be tested before needed for use.

Reliability of radar equipment is affected considerably by humidity and high temperature. In a humid atmosphere collection of moisture on the various elements may cause corrosion of metal parts or deterioration of insulation. If temperature of the radar is allowed to exceed

100° F., life of the vacuum tubes will be shortened and other circuit elements may fail. Adequate ventilation must be provided.

It has also been found that vacuum tubes will operate satisfactorily over longer periods of time if their filaments are continuously heated. Turning on equipment from a cold start causes great stress on tubes. If this stress is repeated by switching equipment on and off frequently, tube life will be seriously shortened. For maximum reliability of the equipment, it is preferable to maintain radar in a stand-by condition rather than fully de-energized while it is not required operationally. This type of operation also has the advantage of keeping humidity low within the unit and of reducing absorption of moisture by the circuit components.

RADAR IN PILOTING

The PPI pattern is a map presentation, but it is not a complete map. Even with receiver gain turned up full, shore line can show only if radar beam reaches it. If it is so low as to be hidden by the earth's curvature, or if it is shadowed by higher headlands in the foreground, no energy can reach it and therefore none can be returned to produce signals on indicator. Signals should not even be expected to appear from all over the land surface that is exposed to radar beam. The configuration of that surface may be such that some parts of it will reflect practically all the pulse off in a direction that will miss the antenna.

A chart of the area can often be easily matched with the PPI shore line but limitations of range and bearing resolution tend to distort the shape of the coast line shown on scope and sometimes this is very difficult.

Most navigational charts do not show contours of the land and even when the contours are shown, it is still not at once apparent just which parts of the shoreline will return echoes and which parts will not. In many cases, for example, high land back from the beach will produce an apparent shore line that will not register with the charted shore. Other factors that may produce a false shore line on the PPI indicator are:

(a) Numerous off-shore rocks or very small islands may produce merging echoes;

(b) Very heavy surf breaking over a reef or sand bar;

(c) A row of pilings off shore;

(d) Many small boats off shore;

(e) A row of sand dunes back of a low shore line.

Another source of difficulty lies in the fact that appearance of a shore line will vary on PPI scope when viewed from different directions. Coral atolls and long chains of islands may produce long lines of echoes when the beam is directed perpendicular to line of islands. However, when the chain of islands is viewed lengthwise, or obliquely, each island may produce a separate spot.

It will be evident then that the maximum range at which land can be detected by radar depends to a great extent on character of the land. Sand spits and smooth clear beaches do not show up at ranges beyond one or two miles because such targets have negligible area than can reflect energy to ship. If waves are breaking over a sand bar on a beach, echoes may be returned from the surf. However, waves may break well out from the actual shore, so that ranging on the surf may be misleading when a radar position is being determined relative to the beach.

Mud flats and marshes generally reflect radar pulses only a little better than a sand spit. The weak echoes that are received at low tide disappear at high tide. Mangroves and other thick growth may produce a strong echo. Therefore, areas that are indicated as swamps on a chart may return either strong or weak echoes, depending on density and size of vegetation growing in the area.

When there are sand dunes covered with vegetation well back from a low smooth beach, an apparent shore line determined by radar will be along the line of dunes rather than the true shore.

Lagoons and inland lakes generally show as blanks on a PPI scope because a smooth water surface returns no energy to radar antenna. In some cases the sand bar or reef surrounding a lagoon may not show because it lies so low in the water.

Submerged objects do not produce radar echoes. If one or two rocks project above the surface, or if waves are breaking over a reef, these may show. When object is entirely submerged and sea is smooth over it, no indication will be seen.

If the land rise is gradual and regular from shore line, no part of the terrain will produce an echo that is stronger than an echo from any other part. Consequently, a general haze of signals will show on the indicator and it will be very difficult to determine distance to any particular part of the land. As a matter of fact, while antenna is held still and ship is not rolling, apparent range to a shore of this sort may vary as much as 1,000 yards. This variation may be caused by slight changes in propagation conditions that cause beam to be moved up and down the slope.

Blotchy signals are returned from hilly ground because the crest of each hill returns a good echo while valley beyond is in shadow. If high gain is used, the pattern may become solid except for very deep shadows.

Low islands may be expected to produce small echoes. However, when thick palm trees or other foliage grow on such island, strong echoes are often produced because surface of the water around the island forms a sort of corner reflector with vertical surfaces of the trees. As a result, wooded islands of all sorts can be detected at much greater range than barren islands.

When the shoreline has a distinctive form that is capable of a precise match, as a steep, vertical cliff that falls down to water's edge, position of ship may be rather quickly determined within the ranging accuracy of the radar. However, when the shore is low and featureless and there is no reliable information available of the topography, an exact match is very difficult to make, and position of ship is correspondingly determined with less certainty.

In piloting a ship tangent bearings are often taken as a means of finding ship's position relative to the land. In cases where it is not possible to identify particular features of the land mass on radar screen, it is not possible to get a fix using radar range and bearing though an approximation may be obtained. However, since width of the radar beam causes echo from any point to appear as an arc, each tangent bearing determined by radar must be corrected by half the beam angle. If this correction is not applied, plotted position of ship will be much closer to the land than is actually the case.

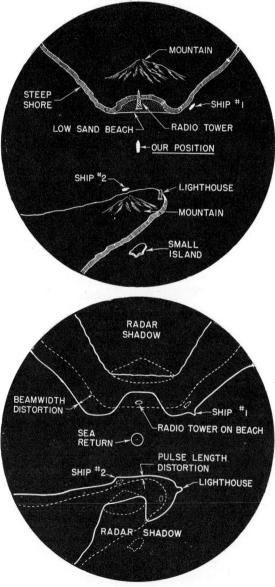

Figure 4

After a landmark has once been identified, however, the navigator is able to determine its bearing to one or two degrees and its range with an accuracy which exceeds that of such optical devices as stadimeters and range finders.

The detection range for tall objects by radar in nautical miles is approximately $\sqrt{2}$ height in feet.

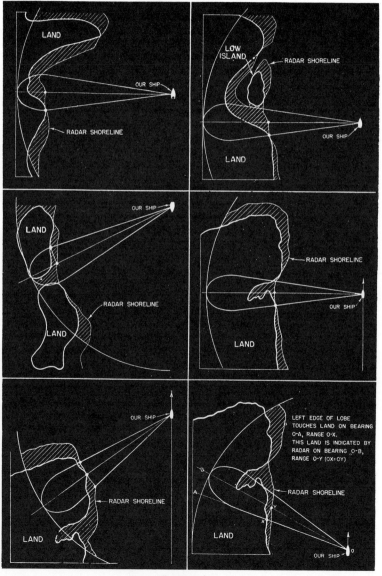

FIGURE 5

Rain, snow, sleet, and clouds generally have the same effect on the picture observed on the scope. If the ship is in the midst of a light rain, Radar operation is usually near normal, but there might be a slight haze on the screen. In the case of heavy concentrations of precipitation, the scope will be blanked out to some degree. However, during this time, the Radar will detect normally in the other areas of the scope if the heavy precipitation is local in nature. Also, targets may be seen on the same azimuth as the storm, but either closer to or beyond it.

The operation of Radar in fog is usually good and usually can be relied upon, although there may be a reduction in the range at which targets are first detected.

Wind, though not a condition of poor visibility, is even a more important factor in the operation of Radar. The effects of wind are most pronounced in open water. The wind by itself gives no trouble, but the attendant sea results in an obscuration of the Radar known as "sea return." This "sea return" can obscure smaller targets. The waves resulting from wind blowing over the water surface present myriads of targets for the Radar signals to detect, with the most pronounced effect being in the direction of the sea. Depending on sea conditions, "sea return" may obscure the scope up to the 10-mile range ring.

Admittedly, merchant marine Radar sets are equipped with devices for minimizing the effect of "sea return" and permitting more or less normal operation of the set. While such devices are quite effective, they do not wholly remove the sea clutter in bad weather. With careful conning of the ship, it is usually possible to pick up large targets, such as ships, before they get close enough to get into the "sea return." It is also possible, in most cases, to properly manipulate the receiver gain control and "sea return" suppressor to detect ships inside the range of the "sea return," because a ship normally gives a larger concentrated echo than do waves. This, of course, depends on the human element. However, the Radar set in this condition is operating at reduced sensitivity and will miss small targets obscured by "sea return" which may still be a source of potential danger to the ship.

Other factors which more or less impose limitations on Radar as tabulated and briefly discussed below:

1. Objects cannot be readily identified unless additional electronics devices (Radar aids) are used in conjunction with the Radar itself, though identification can quite often be accomplished by implication, such as movement, relation to other objects, shape (coastline), and sometimes initial range of detection.

2. Radar chart presentation on the scope requires interpretation due to the line-of-sight characteristics which give shadow effects, that is to say, larger intervening objects may blank out objects behind them.

3. Radar can be used reliably for only slightly over line-of-sight distances.

4. Certain types of objects, because of their characteristics or motion, may go undetected. For example, ice and some other things, due to their physical characteristics and reflecting properties, are relatively poor targets. So is a low-lying point of land. All mariners know the motion of small objects, such as small buoys and boats, caused by bobbing up and down in a seaway, tends to reduce the echo returned to the Radar. These considerations become particularly important when such things as "sea return" and rain are present to reduce the Radar visibility.

While Radar has limitations, its advantages more than compensate for these limitations. The distinct operational advantages are summarized below:

1. It is the best anticollision device perfected to date.

2. It provides greater safety while piloting or making landfalls during periods of low visibility.

3. It indicates continuous instantaneous ranges and bearings of objects.

4. It presents a chartlike picture of the surroundings, the presentation being in the nature of a polar chart with PPI presentation.

5. By observation of the scope movement of objects may be noticed.

To sum up, Radar is definitely not a "cure-all" to replace other devices and methods of navigation, but is rather a supplement to such devices and methods.

LORAN

The principles involved in Loran differ from those of either Radar or Radio Direction Finding. Loran differs from radar in that radio waves are not sent out from the ship to be reflected back, and bearing and distance of a reflecting object is not involved in the record. Nor has it a loop which must be oriented as with the radio direction finder. Loran measures *time* of arrival of signals rather than *direction* of arrival. Reading is made by matching two signals which appear on the scope as shown in Fig. 1.

The principles of transmission and reception which loran utilizes may be stated simply:

(1) Radio signals consisting of short pulses are broadcast from a pair of special shore-based transmitting stations.

(2) These signals are received aboard ship on a specially designed radio receiver.

(3) The difference in time of arrival of signals from two stations is measured on a special indicator. By means of a cathode ray tube, this distance may be measured in microseconds.

(4) This time-difference establishes a single line-of-position by reference to special charts or tables.

(5) Two or more lines-of-position from different pairs of stations are crossed to obtain a fix.

The positional accuracy of the loran system is about that which would be obtained with a direction finder system capable of resolving to 1/50° (one fiftieth of a degree).

Loran has a number of unique features and advantages which no other navigational system enjoys:

(1) It can obtain accurate fixes at ranges of 600 to 700 miles from a transmitting station in daytime and 1,200 to 1,400 miles at night. Accuracy is comparable to that of celestial observations.

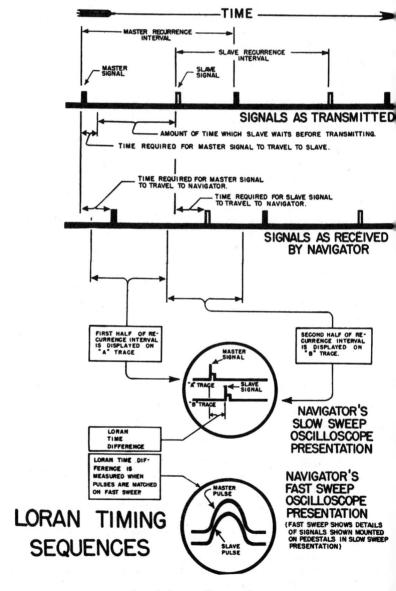

FIG. 6. LORAN TIMING SEQUENCES.

(2) Loran is almost completely independent of weather. It works under all conditions except heavy lightning in immediate vicinity of ship.

(3) Transmission from the ship is not required.

(4) Loran fixes may be obtained by a skilled operator in about two minutes. Calculations are not necessary.

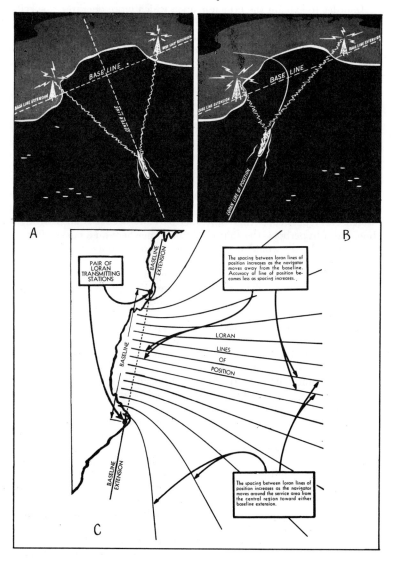

FIGURE 7

(5) Loran fixes are not dependent upon compass, chronometer, or other radio or radar sets; special loran equipment is used.

(6) Because loran measures the difference in time of arrival of radio waves, instead of direction of arrival as in radio direction finding, a simple straight wire antenna without any special requirements may be used.

In order to explain the principle upon which loran operates, a specific illustration will be helpful. A and B, Fig. 7, are two loran transmitting stations, simultaneously sending out pulses of radio energy in all directions. Each pulse lasts about 40 microseconds. These pulses recur at regular intervals but with relatively long periods between pulses (such as 40,000 microseconds). Thus the transmitter is active for 40 microseconds, inactive for 40,000 microseconds, etc.

The line connecting the two stations is called the *base-line;* that bisecting it at right angles, the *center-line.* If stations A and B are transmitting pulses simultaneously a ship located at any point on the center line would receive both pulses at same time. The time difference reading on the loran indicator aboard ship would be zero. Therefore, a ship receiving a time difference of zero would know that it was somewhere on the center line (its line-of-position). See Fig. 7A.

If ship were nearer to station A than station B, (see Fig. 7B), the pulse from station A would arrive first. Because the line of position on which every particular time difference actually occurs is not a straight line, but a hyperbola, the ship would be somewhere on a curved line-of-position, but still would not know the distance from either station or direction of the radio waves.

A series of hyperbolas may be drawn for a pair of stations (Fig. 7C) each representing a constant time difference. The time difference would be zero on center line and a maximum on base line extensions beyond each station.

A system of spacing pulses in a special way provides a method of distinguishing pulses from the two stations, and it is from this identification system that one station of the pair is referred to as the *Master* station and the other the *Slave* station.

After a time-difference reading is obtained, it is necessary only to consult a loran chart or loran tables to find location of line-of-position in regard to the earth's surface.

In order to obtain a fix, ship must obtain lines of position from two pairs of loran stations in the vicinity. Loran stations are always arranged so that two pairs will cover the area. Two operating pairs are usually formed from three stations, by arranging one master station to operate on both pairs, sending out two different sets of pulses to two different slave stations. By establishing two lines of position the navigator can determine where these lines intersect and find his position. If a third pair of stations is present it is wise to check fix by obtaining a third reading and resulting line of position.

Loran charts are marked for latitude and longitude and show positions of important land and water areas. Lines of position with time difference readings are drawn in different colors for each pair of stations in the area. These charts are prepared by the Oceanographic Office.

Loran tables may be used instead of charts and a very complete explanation of use of the tables is incorporated in each set. These should be carefully studied. Loran tables contain in tabular form essentially the same information as loran charts. When loran tables are used, loran lines can be plotted directly on chart or plotting sheet used for regular navigation.

In order to obtain lines of position from a loran chart, it is necessary to identify the pair of stations from which pulses have been received and measured. Pairs of loran stations are identified by three characteristics—radio frequency channel, basic pulse rate, and recurrence rate.

A number of pairs of stations in same vicinity may operate on same radio frequency, but each of these pairs operates on a different pulse recurrence rate. These different rates are identified by numbers 0 to 7 inclusive. All stations on one frequency will appear on the scope but will drift across the screen. The receiver may be adjusted to any desired pulse rate, and then pulses from the pair of stations having that rate will be stationary on the scope, while others continue to drift and are disregarded.

When the navigator wishes to obtain a fix, he obtains from the loran chart for his area information needed for identification of loran stations in the vicinity, sets Channel switch, Basic Recurrence Rate (Base) switch, and Station Selector (Pulse Rate) switch appropriately, obtains a reading for one pair of stations, then sets these switches for another pair of stations in the area, and takes a reading on that pair.

When signals are transmitted from loran stations, some of the waves parallel the surface and are known as ground waves. Fig. 8. Other waves travel upward, encounter electrified layers of the atmosphere known as the ionosphere, and will be reflected to the receiver if conditions are favorable. These reflections are known as *sky waves*.

The navigator may obtain a reading from ground waves or sky waves which appear, but he must be certain that he is matching the corresponding pulses from both stations. Ground waves should always be used if they are present, because they are more stable. Sky waves may be used if the correct ones are matched. At times when pulses are variable and unstable, the navigator must study the scope carefully to make sure that he is using the correct "pips" on the scope.

It may be seen that sky waves travel longer paths than do ground waves, and therefore time necessary for them to reach receiver will be greater than for ground waves. Since Loran charts are computed to show lines of position determined by matching ground waves, a correction must be applied when sky waves are used. These corrections are precomputed, and appear on the charts. They must be added to (if marked *plus*) or subtracted from (if marked *minus*) the time reading given by receiver to determine the line-of-position. This procedure is very similar to that of correction for variation on magnetic compasses and is just as simple.

Many factors enter into reception range of sky and ground waves. Among these are distance from transmitter and time of day, geographical and atmospheric conditions, signal path over water or over land. It is important to understand the effect of these conditions in order to interpret pulses which appear.

Ground waves are strongest near the transmitter. They may be received for a distance of about 700 nautical miles from transmitter by day over sea. At night this may decrease to about 450 nautical miles in heavy static areas. They vary with noise conditions and are not received well over land,

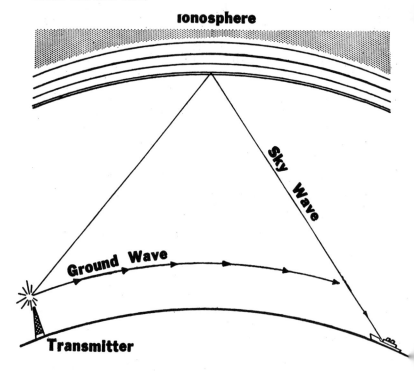

FIGURE 8

Sky waves vary greatly with time of day, seasonal and geographical conditions. They are usually received in sufficient strength to obtain a reading at night only. They are numerous at night, and in medium latitudes may appear in late afternoon and early morning. Sky waves will ordinarily be weak or completely absent in daytime and are too unreliable to be used within 250 miles of a station. Under this distance they need not be used, because the ground waves are available. Best range for sky waves is about 300 to 1200 miles from station.

Reception of both ground and sky waves is better in polar regions than in the tropics. Sky waves may be received in polar regions during most of the day, in winter.

Intervening land greatly reduces range of ground waves, but does not greatly affect sky waves unless land is within 20 or 30 miles of receiver or transmitter. Increased altitude of planes reduces the effect of land.

Because of corrections necessary for sky waves, it is essential to distinguish between ground and sky waves when taking indicator readings. Bearing in mind the type of waves that might be expected, the navigator can determine the type of waves by appearance of signals under observation and spacing of pulses in the train. If frequent observations are taken, changes in location and appearance of pulses will become apparent, and ·the danger of mistaken readings reduced. An operator can easily obtain good readings on strong ground wave signals, but training and experience are necessary to obtain good readings on sky waves.

Accuracy of loran lines of position varies over the service area of each pair of stations. It is very high—a few hundred yards—near base line between stations, very low near base line beyond the stations, and quite high over rest of the area. Except near extensions of base line a rough but usable idea of accuracy may be had from the rule that error will not be more than 1% of distance of stations. For example at 1,000 miles the reading will be within 10 miles of correct value.

Inaccuracies enter from such causes as slightly incorrect maintenance of timing at transmitter stations, uncertainties of sky-wave correction factor, insufficient skill of receiving operator in identifying and matching pulses when taking readings, variable propagation conditions making it difficult to match pulses precisely.

Loran has several features which make it possible to use some new navigational procedures which were not possible by previous navigational methods. One is that accurate knowledge of position is available continuously—from minute-to-minute.

A second feature is that position knowledge is delivered in the form of lines of position which have definite unchanging location on the earth's surface, and receiving equipment, if set for any particular line and left untouched, shows instantly by visual inspection whether the ship is on the line, or to right or left of it. Therefore the ship may be steered along a loran line of position by watching the receiver, as one ordinarily steers by compass.

Some useful practical applications of these features are now in use by ships and aircraft equipped with loran. One is making a landfall and "homing" to harbor. Each spot on the coast, each harbor, each buoy, each airfield, has some loran line of position running through it. The particular line corresponding to any desired destination is determined from loran chart. The ship approaching the coast navigates, well off shore, so as to reach that particular line of position, as read on the receiver. Having reached such line, receiver is allowed to remain on setting for that line, and ship is steered so that receiver continuously corresponds to that setting. This is very simple in practice. The two "pips" are merely kept lined up on the scope. If ship veers right, one pip will move one way, and if she veers left, pip will move the other way. Therefore ship is maintained on a course which is the charted Loran line of position and eventually reaches desired location. The accuracy of maintenance of course by this method, when close to a coast on which stations are located, is within a very few hundred yards.

There are two loran systems in use today: **Loran-A**, the former standard loran, and **Loran-C.**

It is important to remember that **Loran-A** and **Loran-C** are designed to meet two entirely separate sets of requirements. **Loran-A** furnishes long range navigational information of sufficient accuracy to satisfy the general navigator. **Loran-C** was designed to provide very accurate, very long range navigational information to a navigator who has an automatic high precision receiver. The navigator who uses either system in a manner for which it was not designed must not expect to realize the maximum accuracy or utility. Neither navigator when plotting positions will obtain accuracy greater than that dictated by his plotting method and his chart scale.

The following table shows the characteristics of each system.

	Loran-A	**Loran-C**
Frequency	3 channels in the 1850-1950 kc band	100 kc
Range	700 miles, day (ground waves); 1400 miles, night (ground and sky waves)	1200-1500 miles, ground wave.
Time-diff. measurement technique	Manual	Automatic
Transmission	Single pulse	Multipulse
Accuracy	To 1 mile ground, and to 6 miles sky wave	To 1500 feet at 1000 miles
Fix	By plotted position lines	Gives continuous chain

Loran-C was designed to provide a very accurate long-range fix by use of the automatic high precision receiver.

At present (Dec. 1964), the U.S. Naval Oceanographic Office publishes seven loran nautical index charts showing the respective locations of all loran stations, and about 40 "individual rated" loran tables covering the North Atlantic, North, Central, and South Pacific areas, etc.

Loran tables for each pulse rate include, with the main table, a small-scale chartlet which shows the sky-wave correction for the one-hop-E wave.

The charts numbered 1L, 2L, 3L, etc., may be obtained from the U.S. Naval Oceanographic Office, Washington 25, D.C.; also the tables for the various ocean areas listed under H.O. 221 and, as H.O. 15308 and H.O. 15308-1, respectively, the world charts featuring diagrams of **Loran-A** and **Loran-C** coverages, or areas over which the respective systems may be used. (See Figs. 9 & 10.)

Following is an explanation of the symbols shown on the charts.

Figure 9 — Dark shaded areas: Theoretical limits of groundwave (day and night) lines of position; Light shaded areas: Theoretical limits of skywave (night only) lines of position. ●: U.S. operated and funded, 46 stations; ■: Foreign operated — U.S. funded, 1 station; ◉; Foreign operated and funded, 23 stations; ▣: U.S. operated — foreign funded — standby status, 1 station; ▲: Foreign operated and funded — standby status, 9 stations.

Figure 10 — Solid line: Ground wave fix 1500 ft. accuracy contour 95% of the time; standard deviation .1 microsecond. □: U.S. operated and funded; ▣: U.S. funded — host nation operated; —●—: Coverage to be realized when Newfoundland station is completed. Disregard shading and dashed lines.

The accompanying charts have been greatly reduced and are included only as examples to show how **Loran-A** and **Loran-C** function.

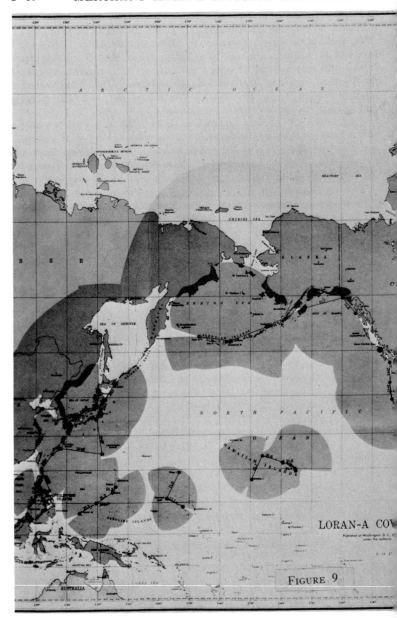

FIGURE 9

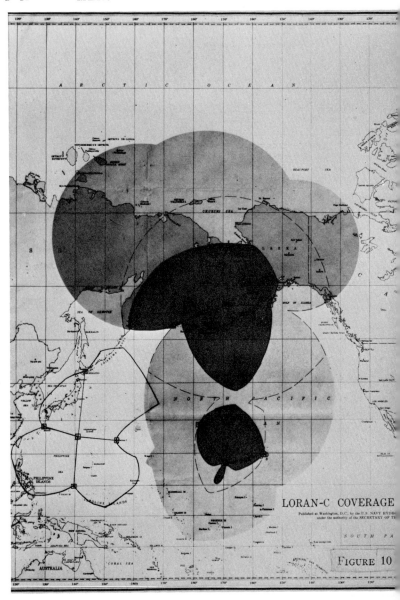

LORAN-C COVERAGE

Published at Washington, D.C., by the U.S. NAVY HYDRO
under the authority of the SECRETARY OF TH

FIGURE 10

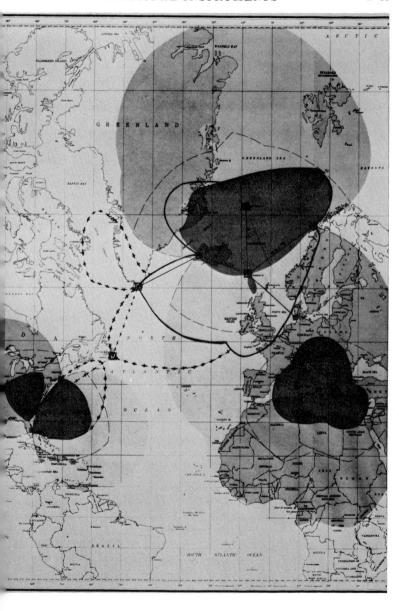

Chapter 3

PILOTING

UNITED STATES BUOYAGE SYSTEM

In approaching the channel, etc., from seaward, *red buoys*, with *even* numbers will be found on the *starboard* side.

In approaching the channel, etc., from seaward, *black buoys*, with *odd* numbers, will be found on the *port* side.

Buoys painted with *horizontal bands* (red and black or black and red) will be found where channel ways lie on either side of them. In general, these buoys have no distinctive shape, but when it is desired to indicate the main or preferred channel, a *can buoy with black band at the top* is used when the important channel is to the *right* for the entering vessel, and a *nun buoy with red band at top* when the important channel is to the *left*.

Buoys painted with *white and black perpendicular stripes* will be found in the *middle* of a fairway and they may be passed close-to.

Offshore buoys along the Atlantic Coast are colored and numbered from north to south, and along the Pacific Coast from south to north, conforming to the order of Light Lists; this does not apply to outside buoys which have a definite approach signification, and which are colored and numbered to conform to the approach. In channels not having a definite approach character, buoys are colored and numbered from north to south or from east to west on the Atlantic Coast and from south to north or from west to east on the Pacific Coast.

All other distinguishing marks on buoys are in addition to the foregoing and may be to mark particular spots. A description of such marks is given in the Light Lists.

Nun buoys, *red* and properly numbered, are usually placed on the *starboard* side and *can buoys*, *black* and properly numbered, on the *port* side of the channels.

Day beacons (except such as are on the sides of channels, which will be colored like buoys) are constructed and distinguished with special reference to each locality, and particularly in regard to the background upon which they are projected.

Buoys maintained by the United States Army Engineers for dredging purposes are painted white with the top, for a distance of 2 feet, painted dark green. (Also see Fig. 1 for characteristics of buoys, etc.)

Special-Purpose Buoys. The meaning of special-purpose buoys:

1. White buoys mark anchorage areas.

2. Yellow buoys mark quarantine anchorage areas.

3. White buoys with green tops are used in connection with dredging and surveying operations.

4. White and black alternate horizontally banded buoys mark fish net areas.

5. White and international orange buoys alternately banded, either horizontally or vertically, are for special purposes to which neither the lateral-system colors nor the other special-purpose colors apply.

6. Yellow and black vertically striped buoys are used for seadrome markings and have no marine significance.

Significance of Light Characteristics. A system of four characteristics of flashes is used on lighted buoys to distinguish their principal purposes, corresponding in part to the color distinctions that are made in buoys for use by day. (*See* Table 1.)

TABLE 1. CHARACTERISTICS OF FLASHES

CHARACTERISTIC OF FLASHING	PURPOSES INDICATED	COLOR OF LIGHT	COLOR OF BUOY
1. *Quick flashing.** Not less than 60 flashes per minute	Isolated dangers, junctions, bifurcations, sharp turns in channels, narrow entrances	White Green Red	Red and black, black and red, black, or red Black and red, or black Red and black or red
2. *Interrupted quick flashing.** Same speed as the preceding but with dark intervals of about 4 seconds	Wrecks	White Green Red	Red and black, black and red, black, or red Black and red, or black Red and black, or red
3. *Short-long flashes.* Groups of a short and a long flash. Groups repeated about 8 times per minute	Midchannels and fairways	White	Black and white vertical stripes
4. *Slow flashing or flashing.* Not more than 30 light periods per minute	Channels sides and coasts	White Green Red	Red or black Black Red

* The first 2 characteristics (quick flashing) are shown on lighted buoys marking features requiring particular attention.

For a complete description of the significance of colors, shapes, and numbers of buoys and the characteristics of lights used on lighted buoys, see the introduction to the Light Lists published by the United States Coast Guard.

AIDS TO NAVIGATION, ETC.

Life-saving station (in general) .... ⚓ L.S.S.

Life-saving station (Coast Guard) .... ⚓ C.G. 161

Lighthouse .... ✹

Lighthouse, on small-scale chart .... •
NOTE.—Light sectors, shown by dotted lines

Light vessels, showing number of mast lights ... ⚓ ⚓

Radio station _____ R.S.○

Radio direction finder station _____ R.C.○
(Radio-compass station)

Radio tower _____ R.T.○

✦ *Radio beacon* _____ R.Bn.○

Water gage _____ ⚓

Beacons — *Lighted* _____ ✶

Not lighted (samples of distinctive top marks) ▲ 𝟙 𝟙 𝟙 𝟙

Buoys —
Buoy of any kind (or red buoy) _____ ⚲
Black _____ ⚲
Striped horizontally (in general) _____ ⚲
Striped horizontally (red and black) ____ ⚲
Striped vertically _____ ⚲
Checkered _____ ⚲
Perch and square _____ ⚲
Perch and ball _____ ⚲   Topmarks used with any buoy symbols
Whistling (or use first six symbols with word "whistling") ⚲
Bell (or use first six symbols with word "bell") ⚲
Lighted _____ ⚲
Mooring _____ ⚓

Anchorage —
Of any kind (or for large vessels) ____ ⚓
For small vessels _____ ⚓

Dry dock _____ ⊃⊐

Floating dry dock _____ ⊂⊃

Patent slip . _____

Leader cable _____ ::::::::::

Range or bearing line _____

Track line _____

Abbreviations for use with hydrographic symbols

Abbreviations relating to lights

F. fixed, Fl. flashing, Occ. occulting, Alt. alternating, Gp. group, R. red, W. white, G. green, B. blue, sec. sector, (U) unwatched, ev. every, m. miles, min. minutes, sec. seconds, vis. visible.

Abbreviations relating to buoys

C. can, N. nun, S. spar, H.S. horizontal stripes, B. black, R. red, W. white, V.S. vertical stripes, G. green, Y. yellow, Ch. checkered.

Abbreviations relating to fog signals

(F.B) fog bell, (F.D) fog diaphone, (F.G) fog gun, (F.H) fog horn, (F.S) fog siren, (F.T) fog trumpet, (F.W) fog whistle, (S.B) submarine fog bell.

Abbreviations relating to bottoms

Cl. clay, Co. coral, G. gravel, M. mud, Oz. ooze, P. pebbles, S. sand, Sh. shells, Sp. specks, St. stones, brk. broken, cal. calcareous, crs. coarse, dec. decayed, dk. dark, fly. flinty, fne. fine, grd. ground, gty. gritty, hrd. hard, lrg. large, lt. light, rky. rocky, rot. rotten, sft. soft, sml. small, spk. speckled, stf. stiff, str. streaky, vol. volcanic, bk. black, br. brown, bu. blue, gn. green, gy. gray, rd. red, wh. white, yl. yellow, srk. stirky.

General abbreviations

Bn. beacon, Rk. rock, Wk. wreck, N.R.S. naval radio station, N.R.C. naval radio direction finder (radio compass) station, P.D. position doubtful, P.A. position approximate, E.D. existence doubtful.

LETTERING

Names of natural land features, vertical lettering.
Names of water features, slanting lettering.

The use of colors is optional

* Hydrographic office and Coast & Geodetic Survey overprint this symbol with a ¼″ (diameter) colored circle.

FIG. 1. STANDARD SYMBOLS ADOPTED BY THE BOARD OF SURVEY AND MAPS.

HYDROGRAPHIC SYMBOLS

Figs. 1 and 2 give standard symbols adopted by the Board of Survey and Maps of the United States. Fig. 1 gives the general symbols and abbreviations for aids to navigation. Fig. 2 shows chart markings for shores, shore lines, obstructions, currents, depths, etc.

HYDROGRAPHY, DANGERS, OBSTRUCTIONS

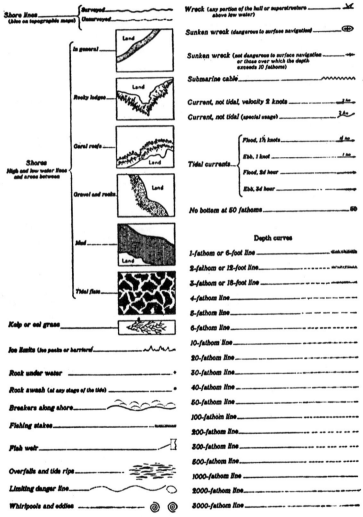

FIG. 2. OTHER STANDARD SYMBOLS. (Figs. 1 & 2 from Dutton, *Navigation and Nautical Astronomy*.)

LIGHTS

Bearings are in degrees true, reading clockwise from 0°, or N; bearings relating to visibility of lights are as observed from a vessel. The azimuth of a range line is given in degrees and minutes when same has been determined with sufficient accuracy for compass error determination, otherwise it is given to the nearest degree.

Heights are referred to mean high water. *Depths* are referred to mean low water. *Distances* are in nautical miles unless otherwise stated.

Unwatched Lights. "U" after the name of a light indicates that the light is unwatched. All lighted buoys are unwatched. Unwatched lights may become irregular or extinguished, although such apparatus has a high degree of reliability.

Reliance must not be placed on floating aids maintaining their exact positions; in cases of uncertainty it is safe to navigate by bearings or angles to fixed objects on shore, and by the use of soundings.

Characteristics. In Table 2 are defined the different classes of lights.

It will be noted that all lights are divided into two general classes; that is, those lights which do not change color and those which do change color. Both classes have the same characteristic phases.

The duration of the light and darkness are computed. In practice they are subject to some degree of fluctuation, owing to slight variations in the working speed of the apparatus. The duration of a flash may also appear to be less than normal when seen from a great distance, and haze has the same apparent effect.

Lights are characterized as *flashing* or *occulting* solely according to the relative durations of light and darkness, without reference to the type of illuminating apparatus employed or relative brilliancy. At short distance, and in clear weather, *flashing* lights may show a faint, continuous light.

The period of a flashing or occulting light is the time occupied by an entire cycle of lights and eclipses; thus, in the case of a flashing light, it is the time from the beginning of one flash to the beginning of the next flash.

In the case of alternating lights, as with all others, the period of the light will be the elapsed time occupied in displaying the entire cycle of changes of which the mechanism is capable.

Caution. The power of a light should always be considered when expecting to make it in thick weather. A weak light is easily obscured by haze, and dependence cannot always be placed on its being seen.

It should be remembered that lights placed at a great elevation are more frequently obscured by clouds, mists, and fogs than those near sea level.

In countries where ice conditions prevail in winter, the windows of unwatched lights may be covered with ice, which will greatly reduce the visibility of the light and may also cause colored lights to appear white.

The apparent characteristic of a complex light may change with the distance of the observer. For example, a light which actually displays in succession a white flash, an interval of fixed white light, a red flash, and another interval of fixed white light, each phase having a different range of visibility, may, when first picked up in clear weather, show as a simple flashing white light. As the vessel draws nearer the red flash will become visible, and the characteristic will be alternating flashing. Later the fixed white light will be seen between the flashes and the official characteristic of the light will be recognized—alternating fixed and flashing (*Alt.F.Fl.*).

All bearings are true and are given in degrees from 0° (north) to 360°. The limits of sectors and arcs of visibility are invariably arranged *clockwise* and are given from seaward *toward* the light.

TABLE 2. CLASSES OF LIGHTS

LIGHTS WHICH DO NOT CHANGE COLOR	CHARACTERISTIC PHASES	LIGHTS WHICH DO CHANGE COLOR
F.—Fixed	A continuous steady light	*Alt.*—Alternating
Fl.—Flashing	(a) Showing a single flash at regular intervals, the duration of light being always less than that of darkness (b) A steady light with, at regular intervals, a total eclipse; the duration of light being always less than that of darkness	*Alt. Fl.*—Alternating flashing
Gp. Fl.—Group flashing	Showing at regular intervals, a group of two or more flashes	*Alt. Gp. Fl.*—Alternating group flashing
Occ.—Occulting	A steady light with, at regular intervals, a sudden and total eclipse; the duration of light being always greater than, or equal to, that of darkness	*Alt. Occ.*—Alternating occulting
Gp. Occ.—Group occulting	A steady light with, at regular intervals, a group of two or more sudden eclipses	*Alt. Gp. Occ.*—Alternating group occulting
F. Fl.—Fixed and flashing	A fixed light varied, at regular intervals, by a single flash of relatively greater brilliancy. The flash may, or may not, be preceded and followed by an eclipse	*Alt. F. Fl.*—Alternating fixed and flashing
F. Gp. Fl.—Fixed and group flashing	A fixed light varied, at regular intervals, by a group of two or more flashes of relatively greater brilliancy. The group may, or may not, be preceded and followed by an eclipse	*Alt. F. Gp. Fl.*—Alternating fixed and group flashing

Light Sectors. In some conditions of the atmosphere white lights may have a reddish hue; the mariner therefore should not trust solely to color where there are sectors, but should verify the position by taking a bearing of the light. On either side of the line of demarcation between white and red there is always a small sector of uncertain color, as the edges of a sector of visibility cannot be cut off sharply.

When a light is cut off by adjoining land, and the arc of visibility is given, the bearing on which the light disappears may vary with the distance of the vessel from which observed. When the light is cut off by a sloping point of land or hill, the light may be seen over a wider arc by a ship far off than by one close-to.

Aeronautical Lights. Aeronautical lights are characterized by great luminous power and altitude. Their effective range is greater than that of most navigational lights, and in some localities they may be the first land falls picked up at night by vessels approaching the coast. Those situated near the coast are accordingly listed in the Light Lists in order that the navigator may be able to obtain more complete information concerning their characteristics, phases, power, height, visibility, description of structures, and hours of exhibition.

These lights are indicated in this List by the designation "Air Light" and are placed in geographic sequence in the body of the text along with lights of strictly navigational character.

It should be borne in mind that these lights are not designed or maintained for marine navigation and that they are subject to changes of which the navigator may not receive prompt notification.

PLOTTING POSITION

In plotting ship's position, remember that you must be certain of the object with which you are working. Positions plotted on objects not properly identified are dangerous. Being certain of the objects, you may use:

a) Two or more bearings or horizontal angles.

b) Bearing and distance.

c) Two bearings of one object with run between bearings.

d) Finally, means of keeping clear of a particular danger without obtaining precise position.

a) Two or More Bearings or Horizontal Angles:

1. Cross bearings of two known objects, whose bearings from the ship differ as nearly as possible by 90°. Taken in rapid succession and corrected for compass error before placing on chart.

2. The 3-arm protractor, consisting of one fixed and two movable arms, with a small hole for pencil marking in the center of the instrument. This requires:

    i. If under way, two observers taking simultaneous sextant angles between three known navigational marks; and

    ii. A large-scale chart for plotting. Advantage is that it gives positions independent of compass error.

b) Bearing and Distance of a Known Object:

1. Bearing as light, or object, breaks over horizon.

The distances at which lights may be seen in clear weather are the geographic ranges computed in nautical miles for a height of the observer's eye of 15 ft. above sea level; the luminous range is given when the light is not of sufficient power to be seen to the limit of its geographic range. These distances may at times be increased by abnormal atmospheric refraction, and, of course, may be greatly lessened by unfavorable weather conditions, due to fog, rain, haze, or smoke. All except the most powerful lights are easily obscured by such conditions.

Under certain atmospheric conditions, especially with the more powerful lights, the glare of the light may be visible beyond the computed geographic range. When approaching a high-power light it evidently may be seen earlier from aloft.

TABLE 3. CONVERSION OF COMPASS POINTS TO THE NEW CARD*

	POINTS	ANGULAR MEASURE		POINTS	ANGULAR MEASURE
NORTH TO EAST			EAST TO SOUTH		
North:		° ′ ″	East	8	90 00 00
N. ¼ E.	¼	2 48 45	E. ¼ S.	8¼	92 48 45
N. ½ E.	½	5 37 30	E. ½ S.	8½	95 37 30
N. ¾ E.	¾	8 26 15	E. ¾ S.	8¾	98 26 15
N. by E.	1	11 15 00	E. by S.	9	101 15 00
N. by E. ¼ E.	1¼	14 03 45	ES. ¾ E.	9¼	104 03 45
N. by E. ½ E.	1½	16 52 30	ESE. ½ E.	9½	106 52 30
N by E. ¾ E.	1¾	19 41 15	ESE. ¼ E.	9¾	109 41 15
NNE.	2	22 30 00	ESE.	10	112 30 00
NNE. ¼ E.	2¼	25 18 45	SE. by E. ¾ E.	10¼	115 18 45
NNE. ½ E.	2½	28 07 30	SE. by E. ½ E.	10½	118 07 30
NNE. ¾ E.	2¾	30 56 15	SE. by E. ¼ E.	10¾	120 56 15
NE. by N.	3	33 45 00	SE. by E.	11	123 45 00
NE. ¾ N.	3¼	36 33 45	SE. ¾ E.	11¼	126 33 45
NE. ½ N.	3½	39 22 30	SE. ½ E.	11½	129 22 30
NE. ¼ N	3¾	42 11 15	SE. ¼ E.	11¾	132 11 15
NE.	4	45 00 00	SE.	12	135 00 00
NE. ¼ E.	4¼	47 48 45	SE. ¼ S.	12¼	137 48 45
NE. ½ E.	4½	50 37 30	SE. ½ S.	12½	140 37 30
NE. ¾ E.	4¾	53 26 15	SE ¾ S.	12¾	143 26 15
NE. by E.	5	56 15 00	SE. by S.	13	146 15 00
NE. by E. ¼ E.	5¼	59 03 45	SSE. ¾ E.	13¼	149 03 45
NE. by E. ½ E.	5½	61 52 30	SSE. ½ E.	13½	151 52 30
NE. by E. ¾ E.	5¾	64 41 15	SSE. ¼ E.	13¾	154 41 15
ENE.	6	67 30 00	SSE.	14	157 30 00
ENE. ¼ E.	6¼	70 18 45	S. by E. ¾ E.	14¼	160 18 45
ENE. ½ E.	6½	73 07 30	S. by E. ½ E.	14½	163 07 30
ENE. ¾ E.	6¾	75 56 15	S. by E. ¼ E.	14¾	165 56 10
E. by N.	7	78 45 00	S. by E.	15	168 45 00
E. ¾ N.	7¼	81 33 45	S. ¾ E.	15¼	171 33 45
E. ½ N.	7½	84 22 30	S. ½ E.	15½	174 22 30
E. ¼ N.	7¾	87 11 15	S. ¼ E.	15¾	177 11 15
SOUTH TO WEST			WEST TO NORTH		
			West	24	270 00 00
South	16	180 00 00	W. ¼ N.	24¼	272 48 45
S. ¼ W.	16¼	182 48 45	W. ½ N.	24½	275 37 30
S. ½ W.	16½	185 37 30	W. ¾ N.	24¾	278 26 15
S. ¾ W.	16¾	188 26 15	W. by N.	25	281 15 00
S. by W.	17	191 15 00	WNW. ¾ W.	25¼	284 03 45
S. by W. ¼ W.	17¼	194 03 45	WNW. ½ W.	25½	286 52 30
S. by W. ½ W.	17½	196 52 30	WNW. ¼ W.	25¾	289 41 15
S. by W. ¾ W.	17¾	199 41 15	WNW.	26	292 30 00
SSW.	18	202 30 00	NW. by W. ¾ W.	26¼	295 18 45
SSW. ¼ W.	18¼	205 18 45	NW. by W. ½ W.	26½	298 07 30
SSW. ½ W.	18½	208 07 30	NW. by W. ¼ W.	26¾	300 56 15
SSW. ¾ W.	18¾	210 56 15	NW. by W.	27	303 45 00
SW. by S.	19	213 45 00	NW. ¾ W.	27¼	306 33 45
SW. ¾ S.	19¼	216 33 45	NW. ½ W.	27½	309 22 30
SW. ½ S.	19½	219 22 30	NW. ¼ W.	27¾	312 11 15
SW. ¼ S.	19¾	222 11 15	NW.	28	315 00 00

(Continued)

TABLE 3—*Continued*

	POINTS	ANGULAR MEASURE		POINTS	ANGULAR MEASURE
SW...............	20	225 00 00	NW. ¼ N..........	28¼	317 48 45
SW. ¼ W.........	20¼	227 48 45	NW. ½ N..........	28½	320 37 30
SW. ½ W.........	20½	230 37 30	NW. ¾ N..........	28¾	323 26 15
SW. ¾ W.........	20¾	233 26 15	NW. by N.........	29	326 15 00
SW. by W........	21	236 15 00	NNW. ¾ W........	29¼	329 03 45
SW. by W. ¼ W....	21¼	239 03 45	NNW. ½ W........	29½	331 52 30
SW. by W. ½ W....	21½	241 52 30	NNW. ¼ W........	29¾	334 41 15
SW. by W. ¾ W....	21¾	244 41 15	NNW.............	30	337 30 00
WSW............	22	247 30 00	N. by W. ¾ W.....	30¼	340 18 45
WSW. ¼ W.......	22¼	250 18 45	N. by W. ½ W.....	30½	343 07 30
WSW. ½ W.......	22½	253 07 30	N. by W. ¼ W.....	30¾	345 56 15
WSW. ¾ W.......	22¾	255 56 15	N. by W.........	31	348 45 00
W. by S.........	23	258 45 00	N. ¾ W..........	31¼	351 33 45
W. ¾ S..........	23¼	261 33 45	N. ½ W..........	31½	354 22 30
W. ½ S..........	23½	264 22 30	N. ¼ W..........	31¾	357 11 15
W. ¼ S..........	23¾	267 11 15	North...........	32	360 00 00

APPLYING COMPASS ERROR—NEW CARD: Add East correct.
Correcting: i.e., compass to magnetic to true: +Easterly
                                               −Westerly
Uncorrecting: i.e., true to magnetic to compass: −Easterly
                                               +Westerly
* Table taken from *Bowditch*, p. 16, 1919 Edition.

Table 4 gives the approximate geographic range of visibility for an object, which may be seen by an observer whose eye is at sea level; in practice, therefore, it is necessary to add to these a distance of visibility corresponding to the height of the observer's eye above sea level.

Distances are found by the formula: Distance in nautical miles = 8/7 $\sqrt{}$ height of object in feet above sea level.

2. Bearing and distance by navigational rangefinder.

To manipulate: On looking into the right eyepiece of the rangefinder, two partial images of the object are seen, one above the other, separated by a fine horizontal line. These images will probably be found displaced relative to one another along the separating line. By suitably rotating the working head, the images may be brought into exact alignment, or as it is generally called, coincidence. The range of the object in yards, metres, cables or other unit can then be read off in the field of the left eyepiece. The operation of determining distance by means of the rangefinder is thus extremely simple and can be performed in a few seconds.

The distances of points of light at night and small objects, such as small rocks, bushes, a line of surf, etc., in the daytime, can be readily measured; for by means of the *astigmatiser* provided in the instrument such small objects can be given the appearance of long vertical streaks, the alignment of which can be easily observed.

The rangefinder gives the distance of a ship from any visible object with great accuracy and in a few seconds, by means of a *single* observation. The 4′ 6″ base instrument measures the distance to about

1/4 sea mile in 10 sea miles
1/16 sea mile in 5 sea miles
6 yards in   1 sea mile.

Compass bearing of a single known object, 78° N.

Range of object given by rangefinder, 5250 yards.

On chart set off bearing line from object and measure along line from object 5250 yards to scale of chart. This gives the ship's position.

TABLE 4. VISIBILITY TABLE

Distances at which objects can be seen at sea according to their respective elevations and the elevation of the eye of the observer

HEIGHT, IN FEET	DISTANCE, IN GEOGRAPHIC OR NAUTICAL MILES	HEIGHT, IN FEET	DISTANCE, IN GEOGRAPHIC OR NAUTICAL MILES	HEIGHT, IN FEET	DISTANCE, IN GEOGRAPHIC OR NAUTICAL MILES	HEIGHT, IN FEET	DISTANCE, IN GEOGRAPHIC OR NAUTICAL MILES
1	1.1	34	6.7	135	13.3	450	24.3
2	1.7	35	6.8	140	13.6	460	24.6
3	2.0	36	6.9	145	13.8	470	24.8
4	2.3	37	6.9	150	14.1	480	25.1
5	2.5	38	7.0	160	14.5	490	25.4
6	2.8	39	7.1	170	14.9	500	25.6
7	2.9	40	7.2	180	15.4	520	26.1
8	3.1	41	7.3	190	15.8	540	26.7
9	3.5	42	7.4	200	16.2	560	27.1
10	3.6	43	7.5	210	16.6	580	27.6
11	3.8	44	7.6	220	17.0	600	28.0
12	4.0	45	7.7	230	17.4	620	28.6
13	4.2	46	7.8	240	17.7	640	29.0
14	4.3	47	7.9	250	18.2	660	29.4
15	4.4	48	7.9	260	18.5	680	29.9
16	4.6	49	8.0	270	18.9	700	30.3
17	4.7	50	8.1	280	19.2	720	30.7
18	4.9	55	8.5	290	19.6	740	31.1
19	5.0	60	8.9	300	19.9	760	31.6
20	5.1	65	9.2	310	20.1	780	32.0
21	5.3	70	9.6	320	20.5	800	32.4
22	5.4	75	9.9	330	20.8	820	32.8
23	5.5	80	10.3	340	21.1	840	33.2
24	5.6	85	10.6	350	21.5	860	33.6
25	5.7	90	10.9	360	21.7	880	34.0
26	5.8	95	11.2	370	22.1	900	34.4
27	6.0	100	11.5	380	22.3	920	34.7
28	6.1	105	11.7	390	22.7	940	35.2
29	6.2	110	12.0	400	22.9	960	35.5
30	6.3	115	12.3	410	23.2	980	35.9
31	6.4	120	12.6	420	23.5	1,000	36.2
32	6.5	125	12.9	430	23.8		
33	6.6	130	13.1	440	24.1		

Nautical miles

55 feet height of observer.......................... visible.... 8.5
200 feet height of light............................ visible.... 16.2

Distance visible.... 24.7

If two known objects are in sight it is not necessary to take a bearing, as the rangefinder can be used to measure the two distances, and by sweeping off these two circles of position on the chart their intersection can be found, which gives the ship's position.

3. Bearing and distance by vertical sextant angle.

Distance off in nautical miles = .56 × height of object in feet ÷ vertical angle in minutes; or else use Bowditch Table entitled *Distance by Vertical Angle.*

4. Bearing and distance by velocity of sound. The speed of sound in air may be utilized to determine the distance by noting the number of seconds elapsed between seeing the flash and hearing the report of a gun fired, and multiplying this elapsed time by .18 or dividing by 5.5 for nautical miles.

c) Two Bearings of One Object with Run Between Bearings.

1. The 4-point or bow and beam bearing, in which the first bearing is taken 45° on the bow and the second when abeam, in which case the distance run between bearings and the distance off when abeam are identical.

2. Doubling the angle on the bow; i.e., when the angular distance on the bow at the second bearing is twice as great as it was at the first bearing, the distance of the object from the ship at the second bearing is equal to the run between bearings.

3. The seven-tenths rule. If bearings of the fixed object be taken at two and four points on the bow (22 1/2° and 45°), seven-tenths (0.7) of the run between bearings will be the distance at which the point *will be passed abeam.*

4. In the following pairs of bearings, the run between bearings is the distance the object *will be passed abeam.*

22°–34°	29°–51°
25°–41°	32°–59°
27°–46°	40°–79°

These rules assume a steady course and make no allowance for current.

TABLE 5. DISTANCE OF AN OBJECT BY TWO BEARINGS

DIFFERENCE BETWEEN COURSE AND SECOND BEARING	DIFFERENCE BETWEEN COURSE AND FIRST BEARING																	
	20°	25°	30°	35°	40°	45°	50°	55°	60°	65°	70°	75°	80°	85°	90°	95°	100°	105°
40°	1.00																	
45	0.81	1.24																
50	0.68	1.00	1.46															
55	0.59	0.84	1.18	1.68														
60	0.53	0.74	1.00	1.36	1.88													
65	0.48	0.66	0.87	1.15	1.52	2.07												
70	0.44	0.60	0.78	1.00	1.28	1.67	2.24											
75	0.42	0.55	0.71	0.89	1.12	1.41	1.81	2.40										
80	0.39	0.51	0.65	0.81	1.00	1.23	1.53	1.94	2.53									
85	0.38	0.49	0.61	0.75	0.91	1.10	1.33	1.64	2.05	2.65								
90	0.36	0.47	0.58	0.70	0.84	1 00	1.19	1.43	1.73	2.14	2.75							
95	0.35	0.45	0.55	0.66	0.78	0.92	1.08	1.27	1.51	1.81	2.22	2.82						
100	0.35	0.44	0.53	0.63	0.74	0.86	1.00	1.16	1.35	1.58	1.88	2.28	2.88					
105	0.34	0.43	0.52	0.61	0.71	0.82	0.93	1.07	1.22	1.41	1.64	1.93	2.33	2.91				
1:0	0.34	0.42	0.51	0.59	0.68	0.78	0.88	1.00	1.13	1.28	1.46	1.68	1.97	2.36	2.92			
115	0.34	0.42	0.50	0.58	0.66	0.75	0.84	0.94	1.06	1.18	1.33	1.50	1.72	1.99	2.37	2.91		
120	0.35	0.42	0.50	0 58	0.65	0.73	0.81	0 90	1.00	1.11	1 23	1.37	1.53	1.74	2.00	2 36	2.8°	
125	0.35	0.43	0.50	0.57	0.64	0.72	0.79	0.87	0.95	1.05	1.15	1.26	1.39	1.55	1.74	1.99	2.33	2.82
130	0.36	0.44	0.51	0.58	0.64	0.71	0.78	0.85	0.92	1.00	1.08	1.18	1.28	1.41	1.56	1.74	1.97	2.28

d) Keeping Clear of a Particular Danger, without obtaining precise position.

1. Following a range.

2. Horizontal danger angle is an application of the principle that the angle subtended by any two points on a circle is the same at every point on its circumference that lies in the same segment. *Requires* two well-marked objects indicated on the chart, lying in the direction of the coast, and sufficiently distant from each other to give a fair-sized horizontal angle. Mark the nearest desired point of approach to the outlying danger. Connect this and the other two marks, forming a triangle. Erect perpendicular bisectors to the sides, and the point

TABLE 6. VERTICAL DANGER ANGLE

DIST., NAU- TICAL MILES	65	70	75	80	85	90	95	100	110	120	130	140	150	160	170	180	190	200
	° ′	° ′	° ′	° ′	° ′	° ′	° ′	° ′	° ′	° ′	° ′	° ′	° ′	° ′	° ′	° ′	° ′	° ′
0.1	6 06	6 34	7 02	7 30	7 58	8 25	8 53	9 20	10 15	11 10	12 04	12 58	13 52	14 45	15 37	16 29	17 21	18 13
.2	3 04	3 18	3 32	3 46	4 00	4 14	4 28	4 42	5 10	5 38	6 06	6 34	7 02	7 30	7 58	8 25	8 53	9 20
.3	2 02	2 12	2 21	2 31	2 40	2 49	2 59	3 08	3 27	3 46	4 05	4 23	4 42	5 01	5 19	5 38	5 57	6 15
.4	1 32	1 39	1 46	1 53	2 00	2 07	2 14	2 21	2 35	2 49	3 04	3 18	3 32	3 46	4 00	4 14	4 28	4 42
0.5	1 14	1 19	1 25	1 30	1 36	1 42	1 47	1 53	2 04	2 16	2 27	2 38	2 49	3 01	3 12	3 23	3 35	3 46
.6	1 01	1 06	1 11	1 15	1 20	1 25	1 30	1 34	1 44	1 53	2 02	2 12	2 21	2 31	2 40	2 49	2 59	3 08
.7	0 53	0 57	1 01	1 05	1 09	1 13	1 17	1 21	1 29	1 37	1 45	1 53	2 01	2 09	2 17	2 25	2 33	2 41
.8	0 46	0 49	0 53	0 57	1 00	1 04	1 07	1 11	1 18	1 25	1 32	1 39	1 46	1 53	2 00	2 07	2 14	2 21
.9	0 41	0 44	0 47	0 50	0 53	0 57	1 00	1 03	1 09	1 15	1 22	1 28	1 34	1 40	1 47	1 53	1 59	2 06
1.0	0 37	0 40	0 42	0 45	0 48	0 51	0 54	0 57	1 02	1 08	1 14	1 19	1 25	1 30	1 36	1 42	1 47	1 53
.1	0 33	0 36	0 39	0 41	0 44	0 46	0 49	0 51	0 57	1 02	1 07	1 12	1 17	1 22	1 27	1 33	1 38	1 43
.2	0 31	0 33	0 35	0 38	0 40	0 42	0 45	0 47	0 52	0 57	1 01	1 06	1 11	1 15	1 20	1 25	1 30	1 34
.3	0 28	0 30	0 33	0 35	0 37	0 39	0 41	0 44	0 48	0 52	0 57	1 01	1 05	1 10	1 14	1 18	1 23	1 27
.4	0 26	0 28	0 30	0 32	0 34	0 36	0 38	0 40	0 44	0 48	0 53	0 57	1 01	1 05	1 09	1 13	1 17	1 21
1.5	0 25	0 26	0 28	0 30	0 32	0 34	0 36	0 38	0 41	0 45	0 49	0 53	0 57	1 00	1 04	1 08	1 12	1 15
.6	0 23	0 25	0 27	0 28	0 30	0 32	0 34	0 35	0 39	0 42	0 46	0 49	0 53	0 57	1 00	1 04	1 07	1 11
.7	0 22	0 23	0 25	0 27	0 28	0 30	0 32	0 33	0 37	0 40	0 43	0 47	0 50	0 53	0 57	1 00	1 03	1 07
.8	0 20	0 22	0 24	0 25	0 27	0 28	0 30	0 31	0 35	0 38	0 41	0 44	0 47	0 50	0 53	0 57	1 00	1 03
.9	0 19	0 21	0 22	0 24	0 25	0 27	0 28	0 30	0 33	0 36	0 39	0 42	0 45	0 48	0 51	0 54	0 57	1 00
2.0	0 18	0 20	0 21	0 23	0 24	0 25	0 27	0 28	0 31	0 34	0 37	0 40	0 42	0 45	0 48	0 51	0 54	0 57
.1	0 18	0 19	0 20	0 22	0 23	0 24	0 26	0 27	0 30	0 32	0 35	0 38	0 40	0 43	0 46	0 48	0 51	0 54
.2	0 17	0 18	0 19	0 21	0 22	0 23	0 24	0 26	0 28	0 31	0 33	0 36	0 39	0 41	0 44	0 46	0 49	0 51
.3	0 16	0 17	0 18	0 20	0 21	0 22	0 23	0 25	0 27	0 30	0 32	0 34	0 37	0 39	0 42	0 44	0 47	0 49
.4	0 15	0 17	0 18	0 19	0 20	0 21	0 22	0 24	0 26	0 28	0 31	0 33	0 35	0 38	0 40	0 42	0 45	0 47
2.5	0 15	0 16	0 17	0 18	0 19	0 20	0 21	0 23	0 25	0 27	0 29	0 32	0 34	0 36	0 38	0 41	0 43	0 45
.6	0 14	0 15	0 16	0 17	0 18	0 20	0 21	0 22	0 24	0 26	0 28	0 30	0 33	0 35	0 37	0 39	0 41	0 44
.7	0 14	0 15	0 16	0 17	0 18	0 19	0 20	0 21	0 23	0 25	0 27	0 29	0 31	0 34	0 36	0 38	0 40	0 42
.8	0 13	0 14	0 15	0 16	0 17	0 18	0 19	0 20	0 22	0 24	0 26	0 28	0 30	0 32	0 34	0 36	0 38	0 40
.9	0 13	0 14	0 15	0 16	0 17	0 18	0 19	0 20	0 21	0 23	0 25	0 27	0 29	0 31	0 33	0 35	0 37	0 39
3.0	0 12	0 13	0 14	0 15	0 16	0 17	0 18	0 19	0 21	0 23	0 25	0 26	0 28	0 30	0 32	0 34	0 36	0 38
.2	0 11	0 12	0 13	0 14	0 15	0 16	0 17	0 18	0 19	0 21	0 23	0 25	0 27	0 28	0 30	0 32	0 34	0 35
.4	0 11	0 12	0 12	0 13	0 14	0 15	0 16	0 17	0 18	0 20	0 22	0 23	0 25	0 27	0 28	0 30	0 32	0 33
.6	0 10	0 11	0 12	0 13	0 13	0 14	0 15	0 16	0 17	0 19	0 20	0 22	0 24	0 25	0 27	0 28	0 30	0 31
.8	0 10	0 10	0 11	0 12	0 13	0 13	0 14	0 15	0 16	0 18	0 19	0 21	0 22	0 24	0 25	0 27	0 28	0 30
4.0		0 10	0 11	0 11	0 12	0 13	0 13	0 14	0 16	0 17	0 18	0 20	0 21	0 23	0 24	0 25	0 27	0 28
.2			0 10	0 11	0 11	0 12	0 13	0 13	0 15	0 16	0 18	0 19	0 20	0 22	0 23	0 24	0 26	0 27
.4			0 10	0 10	0 11	0 12	0 12	0 13	0 14	0 15	0 17	0 18	0 19	0 21	0 22	0 23	0 24	0 26
.6				0 10	0 10	0 11	0 12	0 12	0 14	0 15	0 16	0 17	0 18	0 20	0 21	0 22	0 23	0 25
.8					0 10	0 11	0 11	0 12	0 13	0 14	0 15	0 17	0 18	0 19	0 20	0 21	0 22	0 24
5.0					0 10	0 10	0 11	0 11	0 12	0 14	0 15	0 16	0 17	0 18	0 19	0 20	0 21	0 23

where they meet is the center of a circle through the three points. So long as the sextant angle subtended by the two charted objects is not greater than the angle at the third point on the circle, we will be outside the circle. Similarly, if there is another danger farther off shore we can draw another circle and keep our angle greater than that, thus keeping between the two dangers.

3. The vertical danger angle involves the same general principle. Table 6 may be used, or the following formula:

Required angle in minutes = .56 × height of the object in feet ÷ distance from base of object in miles.

4. The danger bearing. A line is drawn through a navigational mark clear of danger at all points, and its direction noted by compass. As the ship proceeds frequent bearings are taken, and so long as they lie on the safe side of this danger bearing the vessel is on the safe side of the line.

AIDS TO NAVIGATION IN A FOG
Fog Signals

Radiobeacons broadcast simple dot and dash combinations by means of transmitter emitting modulated continuous waves.

Diaphones produce sound by means of a slotted reciprocating piston actuated by compressed air. Blasts may consist of two tones of different pitch in which case the first part of the blast is high and the last of a low pitch. These alternate pitch signals are called "two-tone."

Diaphragm Horns produce sound by means of a disc diaphragm vibrated by compressed air, steam, or electricity. Duplex or triplex horn units of differing pitch produce a chime signal.

Reed Horns produce sound by means of a steel reed vibrated by compressed air.

Sirens produce sound by means of either a disc or a cup-shaped rotor actuated by compressed air, steam, or electricity.

Whistles produce sound by compressed air or steam emitted through a circumferential slot into a cylindrical bell chamber.

Bells are sounded by means of a hammer actuated by hand, by a descending weight, compressed gas, or electricity.

Bells at light stations are operated by clockwork, unless otherwise stated.

Effort is made in all cases to start fog signals as soon as possible after fog has been observed, but there may be some delay depending on the type of equipment in use.

Whistles, Gongs, or Bells on Buoys operated by the action of the sea sound irregularly, and in calm weather are less effective or may not sound.

Air Fog Signals. It has been clearly shown:

1. That fog signals are heard at greatly varying distances.

2. That under certain conditions of atmosphere, when a fog signal is a combination of high and low tones, one of the tones may be inaudible.

3. That there are occasionally areas around a fog signal in which it is wholly inaudible.

4. That a fog may exist at a short distance from a station and not be observed from it, so that the signal may not be sounded.

5. That some fog signals cannot be started immediately, though the endeavor be made to sound them as quickly as possible after signs of fog have been observed.

Submarine Oscillators and Bells are more reliable. Their effective range far exceeds that of air sound signals, and their bearing can be determined with sufficient accuracy for safe navigation in a fog by a vessel equipped with receivers. Even when receivers are not used the submarine bell can be heard from below the water line for distances well outside the range of air fog signals though the bearing cannot then be so well determined.

Soundings should never be neglected. Not to be regarded as fixing a position, they simply afford a check upon the positions obtained by other methods. An exact agreement with depths given on the chart need not be expected, but the soundings should agree in a general way, and a marked departure from the characteristic bottom shown on the chart should lead the navigator to verify his position and proceed with caution; especially is this true if the water is more shoal than expected.

By laying the soundings on tracing paper, along a line which represents the track of the ship according to the scale of the chart, and then moving the paper over the chart, keeping the courses parallel to the corresponding directions on the chart, until the observed soundings agree with those laid down, the ship's position will in general be quite well determined.

TABLE 7. TIME AND DISTANCE

Min.	5	5.5	6	6.5	7	7.5	8	8.5	9	9.5	10	10.5	11	11.5	12	12.5
1	.1	.1	.1	.1	.1	.1	.1	.1	.2	.2	.2	.2	.2	.2	.2	.2
2	.2	.2	.2	.2	.2	.3	.3	.3	.3	.3	.3	.4	.4	.4	.4	.4
3	.3	.3	.3	.3	.4	.4	.4	.4	.5	.5	.5	.5	.6	.6	.6	.6
4	.3	.4	.4	.4	.5	.5	.5	.6	.6	.6	.7	.7	.7	.8	.8	.8
5	.4	.5	.5	.5	.6	.6	.7	.7	.8	.8	.8	.9	.9	1.0	1.0	1.0
6	.5	.6	.6	.7	.7	.8	.8	.9	.9	1.0	1.0	1.1	1.1	1.2	1.2	1.3
7	.6	.6	.7	.8	.8	.9	.9	1.0	1.1	1.1	1.2	1.2	1.3	1.3	1.4	1.5
8	.7	.7	.8	.9	.9	1.0	1.1	1.1	1.2	1.3	1.3	1.4	1.5	1.5	1.6	1.7
9	.8	.8	.9	1.0	1.1	1.1	1.2	1.3	1.4	1.4	1.5	1.6	1.7	1.7	1.8	1.9
10	.8	.9	1.0	1.1	1.2	1.3	1.3	1.4	1.5	1.6	1.7	1.8	1.8	1.9	2.0	2.1
11	.9	1.0	1.1	1.2	1.3	1.4	1.5	1.6	1.7	1.7	1.8	1.9	2.0	2.1	2.2	2.3
12	1.0	1.1	1.2	1.3	1.4	1.5	1.6	1.7	1.8	1.9	2.0	2.1	2.2	2.3	2.4	2.5
13	1.1	1.2	1.3	1.4	1.5	1.6	1.7	1.8	2.0	2.1	2.2	2.3	2.4	2.5	2.6	2.7
14	1.2	1.3	1.4	1.5	1.6	1.8	1.9	2.0	2.1	2.2	2.3	2.5	2.6	2.7	2.8	2.9
15	1.3	1.4	1.5	1.6	1.8	1.9	2.0	2.1	2.3	2.4	2.5	2.6	2.8	2.9	3.0	3.1
16	1.3	1.5	1.6	1.7	1.9	2.0	2.1	2.3	2.4	2.5	2.7	2.8	2.9	3.1	3.2	3.3
17	1.4	1.6	1.7	1.8	2.0	2.1	2.3	2.4	2.6	2.7	2.8	3.0	3.1	3.3	3.4	3.5
18	1.5	1.7	1.8	2.0	2.1	2.3	2.4	2.6	2.7	2.9	3.0	3.2	3.3	3.5	3.6	3.8
19	1.6	1.8	1.9	2.1	2.2	2.4	2.5	2.7	2.9	3.0	3.2	3.3	3.5	3.6	3.8	4.0
20	1.7	1.8	2.0	2.2	2.3	2.5	2.7	2.8	3.0	3.2	3.3	3.5	3.7	3.8	4.0	4.2
21	1.8	1.9	2.1	2.3	2.5	2.6	2.8	3.0	3.2	3.3	3.5	3.7	3.9	4.0	4.2	4.4
22	1.8	2.0	2.2	2.4	2.6	2.8	2.9	3.1	3.3	3.5	3.7	3.9	4.0	4.2	4.4	4.6
23	1.9	2.1	2.3	2.5	2.7	2.9	3.1	3.3	3.5	3.6	3.8	4.0	4.2	4.4	4.6	4.8
24	2.0	2.2	2.4	2.6	2.8	3.0	3.2	3.4	3.6	3.8	4.0	4.2	4.4	4.6	4.8	5.0
25	2.1	2.3	2.5	2.7	2.9	3.1	3.3	3.5	3.8	4.0	4.2	4.4	4.6	4.8	5.0	5.2
26	2.2	2.4	2.6	2.8	3.0	3.3	3.5	3.7	3.9	4.1	4.3	4.6	4.8	5.0	5.2	5.4
27	2.3	2.5	2.7	2.9	3.2	3.4	3.6	3.8	4.0	4.3	4.5	4.7	5.0	5.2	5.4	5.6
28	2.3	2.6	2.8	3.0	3.3	3.5	3.7	4.0	4.2	4.4	4.7	4.9	5.1	5.4	5.6	5.8
29	2.4	2.7	2.9	3.1	3.4	3.6	3.9	4.1	4.4	4.6	4.8	5.1	5.3	5.6	5.8	6.0
30	2.5	2.8	3.0	3.3	3.5	3.8	4.0	4.3	4.5	4.8	5.0	5.3	5.5	5.8	6.0	6.3
31	2.6	2.8	3.1	3.4	3.6	3.9	4.1	4.4	4.7	4.9	5.2	5.4	5.7	5.9	6.2	6.5
32	2.7	2.9	3.2	3.5	3.7	4.0	4.3	4.5	4.8	5.1	5.3	5.6	5.9	6.1	6.4	6.7
33	2.8	3.0	3.3	3.6	3.9	4.1	4.4	4.7	5.0	5.2	5.5	5.8	6.1	6.3	6.6	6.9
34	2.8	3.1	3.4	3.7	4.0	4.3	4.5	4.8	5.1	5.4	5.7	6.0	6.2	6.5	6.8	7.1
35	2.9	3.2	3.5	3.8	4.1	4.4	4.7	5.0	5.3	5.5	5.8	6.1	6.4	6.7	7.0	7.3
36	3.0	3.3	3.6	3.9	4.2	4.5	4.8	5.1	5.4	5.7	6.0	6.3	6.6	6.9	7.2	7.5
37	3.1	3.4	3.7	4.0	4.3	4.6	4.9	5.2	5.6	5.9	6.2	6.5	6.8	7.1	7.4	7.7
38	3.2	3.5	3.8	4.1	4.4	4.8	5.1	5.4	5.7	6.0	6.3	6.7	7.0	7.3	7.6	7.9
39	3.3	3.6	3.9	4.2	4.6	4.9	5.2	5.5	5.9	6.2	6.5	6.8	7.2	7.5	7.8	8.1
40	3.3	3.7	4.0	4.3	4.7	5.0	5.3	5.7	6.0	6.3	6.7	7.0	7.3	7.7	8.0	8.3
41	3.4	3.8	4.1	4.4	4.8	5.1	5.5	5.8	6.2	6.5	6.8	7.2	7.5	7.9	8.2	8.5
42	3.5	3.9	4.2	4.6	4.9	5.3	5.6	6.0	6.3	6.7	7.0	7.4	7.7	8.1	8.4	8.8
43	3.6	3.9	4.3	4.7	5.0	5.4	5.7	6.1	6.5	6.8	7.2	7.5	7.9	8.2	8.6	9.0
44	3.7	4.0	4.4	4.8	5.1	5.5	5.9	6.2	6.6	7.0	7.3	7.7	8.1	8.4	8.8	9.2
45	3.8	4.1	4.5	4.9	5.3	5.6	6.0	6.4	6.8	7.1	7.5	7.9	8.3	8.6	9.0	9.4
46	3.8	4.2	4.6	5.0	5.4	5.8	6.1	6.5	6.9	7.3	7.7	8.1	8.4	8.8	9.2	9.6
47	3.9	4.3	4.7	5.1	5.5	5.9	6.3	6.7	7.1	7.4	7.8	8.2	8.6	9.0	9.4	9.8
48	4.0	4.4	4.8	5.2	5.6	6.0	6.4	6.8	7.2	7.6	8.0	8.4	8.8	9.2	9.6	10.0
49	4.1	4.5	4.9	5.3	5.7	6.1	6.5	6.9	7.4	7.8	8.2	8.6	9.0	9.4	9.8	10.2
50	4.2	4.6	5.0	5.4	5.8	6.3	6.7	7.1	7.5	7.9	8.3	8.8	9.2	9.6	10.0	10.4
51	4.3	4.7	5.1	5.5	6.0	6.4	6.8	7.2	7.7	8.1	8.5	8.9	9.4	9.8	10.2	10.6
52	4.3	4.8	5.2	5.6	6.1	6.5	6.9	7.4	7.8	8.2	8.7	9.1	9.5	10.0	10.4	10.8
53	4.4	4.9	5.3	5.7	6.2	6.6	7.1	7.5	8.0	8.4	8.8	9.3	9.7	10.2	10.6	11.0
54	4.5	5.0	5.4	5.9	6.3	6.8	7.2	7.7	8.1	8.6	9.0	9.5	9.9	10.4	10.8	11.3
55	4.6	5.0	5.5	6.0	6.4	6.9	7.3	7.8	8.3	8.7	9.2	9.6	10.1	10.5	11.0	11.5
56	4.7	5.1	5.6	6.1	6.5	7.0	7.5	7.9	8.4	8.9	9.3	9.8	10.3	10.7	11.2	11.7
57	4.8	5.2	5.7	6.2	6.7	7.1	7.6	8.1	8.6	9.0	9.5	10.0	10.5	10.9	11.4	11.9
58	4.8	5.3	5.8	6.3	6.8	7.3	7.7	8.2	8.7	9.2	9.7	10.2	10.6	11.1	11.6	12.1
59	4.9	5.4	5.9	6.4	6.9	7.4	7.9	8.4	8.9	9.3	9.8	10.3	10.8	11.3	11.8	12.3
60	5.0	5.5	6.0	6.5	7.0	7.5	8.0	8.5	9.0	9.5	10.0	10.5	11.0	11.5	12.0	12.5

TABLE 7. TIME AND DISTANCE (Continued)

13	13.5	14	14.5	15	15.5	16	16.5	17	17.5	18	18.5	19	19.5	20	20.5	Min.
.2	.2	.2	.2	.3	.3	.3	.3	.3	.3	.3	.3	.3	.3	.3	.3	1
.4	.5	.5	.5	.5	.5	.5	.6	.6	.6	.6	.6	.6	.7	.7	.7	2
.7	.7	.7	.7	.8	.8	.8	.8	.9	.9	.9	.9	1.0	1.0	1.0	1.0	3
.9	.9	.9	1.0	1.0	1.0	1.1	1.1	1.1	1.2	1.2	1.2	1.3	1.3	1.3	1.4	4
1.1	1.1	1.2	1.2	1.3	1.3	1.3	1.4	1.4	1.5	1.5	1.5	1.6	1.6	1.7	1.7	5
1.3	1.4	1.4	1.5	1.5	1.6	1.6	1.7	1.7	1.8	1.8	1.9	1.9	2.0	2.0	2.1	6
1.5	1.6	1.6	1.7	1.8	1.8	1.9	1.9	2.0	2.0	2.1	2.2	2.2	2.3	2.3	2.4	7
1.7	1.8	1.9	1.9	2.0	2.1	2.1	2.2	2.3	2.3	2.4	2.5	2.5	2.6	2.7	2.7	8
2.0	2.0	2.1	2.2	2.3	2.3	2.4	2.5	2.6	2.6	2.7	2.8	2.9	2.9	3.0	3.1	9
2.2	2.3	2.3	2.4	2.5	2.6	2.7	2.8	2.8	2.9	3.0	3.1	3.2	3.3	3.3	3.4	10
2.4	2.5	2.6	2.7	2.8	2.8	2.9	3.0	3.1	3.2	3.3	3.4	3.5	3.6	3.7	3.8	11
2.6	2.7	2.8	2.9	3.0	3.1	3.2	3.3	3.4	3.5	3.6	3.7	3.8	3.9	4.0	4.1	12
2.8	2.9	3.0	3.1	3.3	3.4	3.5	3.6	3.7	3.8	3.9	4.0	4.1	4.2	4.3	4.4	13
3.0	3.2	3.3	3.4	3.5	3.6	3.7	3.9	4.0	4.1	4.2	4.3	4.4	4.6	4.7	4.8	14
3.3	3.4	3.5	3.6	3.8	3.9	4.0	4.1	4.3	4.4	4.5	4.6	4.8	4.9	5.0	5.1	15
3.5	3.6	3.7	3.9	4.0	4.1	4.3	4.4	4.5	4.7	4.8	4.9	5.1	5.2	5.3	5.5	16
3.7	3.8	4.0	4.1	4.3	4.4	4.5	4.7	4.8	5.0	5.1	5.2	5.4	5.5	5.7	5.8	17
3.9	4.1	4.2	4.4	4.5	4.7	4.8	5.0	5.1	5.3	5.4	5.6	5.7	5.9	6.0	6.2	18
4.1	4.3	4.4	4.6	4.8	4.9	5.1	5.2	5.4	5.5	5.7	5.9	6.0	6.2	6.3	6.5	19
4.3	4.5	4.7	4.8	5.0	5.2	5.3	5.5	5.7	5.8	6.0	6.2	6.3	6.5	6.7	6.8	20
4.6	4.7	4.9	5.1	5.3	5.4	5.6	5.8	6.0	6.1	6.3	6.5	6.7	6.8	7.0	7.2	21
4.8	5.0	5.1	5.3	5.5	5.7	5.9	6.1	6.2	6.4	6.6	6.8	7.0	7.2	7.3	7.5	22
5.0	5.2	5.4	5.6	5.8	5.9	6.1	6.3	6.5	6.7	6.9	7.1	7.3	7.5	7.7	7.9	23
5.2	5.4	5.6	5.8	6.0	6.2	6.4	6.6	6.8	7.0	7.2	7.4	7.6	7.8	8.0	8.2	24
5.4	5.6	5.8	6.0	6.3	6.5	6.7	6.9	7.1	7.3	7.5	7.7	7.9	8.1	8.3	8.5	25
5.6	5.9	6.1	6.3	6.5	6.7	6.9	7.2	7.4	7.6	7.8	8.0	8.2	8.5	8.7	8.9	26
5.9	6.1	6.3	6.5	6.8	7.0	7.2	7.4	7.7	7.9	8.1	8.3	8.6	8.8	9.0	9.2	27
6.1	6.3	6.5	6.8	7.0	7.2	7.5	7.7	7.9	8.2	8.4	8.6	8.9	9.1	9.3	9.6	28
6.3	6.5	6.8	7.0	7.3	7.5	7.7	8.0	8.2	8.5	8.7	8.9	9.2	9.4	9.7	9.9	29
6.5	6.8	7.0	7.3	7.5	7.8	8.0	8.3	8.5	8.8	9.0	9.3	9.5	9.8	10.0	10.3	30
6.7	7.0	7.2	7.5	7.8	8.0	8.3	8.5	8.8	9.0	9.3	9.6	9.8	10.1	10.3	10.6	31
6.9	7.2	7.5	7.7	8.0	8.3	8.5	8.8	9.1	9.3	9.6	9.9	10.1	10.4	10.7	10.9	32
7.2	7.4	7.7	8.0	8.3	8.5	8.8	9.1	9.4	9.6	9.9	10.2	10.5	10.7	11.0	11.3	33
7.4	7.7	7.9	8.2	8.5	8.8	9.1	9.4	9.6	9.9	10.2	10.5	10.8	11.1	11.3	11.6	34
7.6	7.9	8.2	8.5	8.8	9.0	9.3	9.6	9.9	10.2	10.5	10.8	11.1	11.4	11.7	12.0	35
7.8	8.1	8.4	8.7	9.0	9.3	9.6	9.9	10.2	10.5	10.8	11.1	11.4	11.7	12.0	12.3	36
8.0	8.3	8.6	8.9	9.3	9.6	9.9	10.2	10.5	10.8	11.1	11.4	11.7	12.0	12.3	12.6	37
8.2	8.6	8.9	9.2	9.5	9.8	10.1	10.5	10.8	11.1	11.4	11.7	12.0	12.4	12.7	13.0	38
8.5	8.8	9.1	9.4	9.8	10.1	10.4	10.7	11.1	11.4	11.7	12.0	12.4	12.7	13.0	13.3	39
8.7	9.0	9.3	9.7	10.0	10.3	10.7	11.0	11.3	11.7	12.0	12.3	12.7	13.0	13.3	13.7	40
8.9	9.2	9.6	9.9	10.3	10.6	10.9	11.3	11.6	12.0	12.3	12.6	13.0	13.3	13.7	14.0	41
9.1	9.5	9.8	10.2	10.5	10.9	11.2	11.6	11.9	12.3	12.6	13.0	13.3	13.7	14.0	14.4	42
9.3	9.7	10.0	10.4	10.8	11.1	11.5	11.8	12.2	12.5	12.9	13.3	13.6	14.0	14.3	14.7	43
9.5	9.9	10.3	10.6	11.0	11.4	11.7	12.1	12.5	12.8	13.2	13.6	13.9	14.3	14.7	15.0	44
9.8	10.1	10.5	10.9	11.3	11.6	12.0	12.4	12.8	13.1	13.5	13.9	14.3	14.6	15.0	15.4	45
10.0	10.4	10.7	11.1	11.5	11.9	12.3	12.7	13.0	13.4	13.8	14.2	14.6	15.0	15.3	15.7	46
10.2	10.6	11.0	11.4	11.8	12.1	12.5	12.9	13.3	13.7	14.1	14.5	14.9	15.3	15.7	16.1	47
10.4	10.8	11.2	11.6	12.0	12.4	12.8	13.2	13.6	14.0	14.4	14.8	15.2	15.6	16.0	16.4	48
10.6	11.0	11.4	11.8	12.3	12.7	13.1	13.5	13.9	14.3	14.7	15.1	15.5	15.9	16.3	16.7	49
10.8	11.3	11.7	12.1	12.5	12.9	13.3	13.8	14.2	14.6	15.0	15.4	15.8	16.3	16.7	17.1	50
11.1	11.5	11.9	12.3	12.8	13.2	13.6	14.0	14.5	14.9	15.3	15.7	16.2	16.6	17.0	17.4	51
11.3	11.7	12.1	12.6	13.0	13.4	13.9	14.3	14.7	15.2	15.6	16.0	16.5	16.9	17.3	17.8	52
11.5	11.9	12.4	12.8	13.3	13.7	14.1	14.6	15.0	15.5	15.9	16.3	16.8	17.2	17.7	18.1	53
11.7	12.2	12.6	13.1	13.5	14.0	14.4	14.9	15.3	15.8	16.2	16.7	17.1	17.6	18.0	18.5	54
11.9	12.4	12.8	13.3	13.8	14.2	14.7	15.1	15.6	16.0	16.5	17.0	17.4	17.9	18.3	18.8	55
12.1	12.6	13.1	13.5	14.0	14.5	14.9	15.4	15.9	16.3	16.8	17.3	17.7	18.2	18.7	19.1	56
12.4	12.8	13.3	13.8	14.3	14.7	15.2	15.7	16.2	16.6	17.1	17.6	18.1	18.5	19.0	19.5	57
12.6	13.1	13.5	14.0	14.5	15.0	15.5	16.0	16.4	16.9	17.4	17.9	18.4	18.9	19.3	19.8	58
12.8	13.3	13.8	14.3	14.8	15.2	15.7	16.2	16.7	17.2	17.7	18.2	18.7	19.2	19.7	20.2	59
13.0	13.5	14.0	14.5	15.0	15.5	16.0	16.5	17.0	17.5	18.0	18.5	19.0	19.5	20.0	20.5	60

Echoes. In many inland passages, where the channels are narrow, or along certain coasts which are hilly and mountainous, such as occur in southeastern Alaska, it may prove useful in a fog to sound a whistle or siren and to estimate the distance offshore by the loudness or faintness of the echo and the time it takes to return.

Distance by Velocity of Sound. Speed of sound in air is 1120 feet per second at 60° F., which increases approximately 1 foot per second for each degree rise in temperature. Multiply elapsed time by .18 or divide by 5.5. Remember in using echoes to use 1/2 elapsed time.

Speed of sound in water is 4800 feet per second, in which case multiply seconds by .8 or divide by 1.25 for nautical miles.

RADIO DIRECTION-FINDING DEVICES (Radio compass)

There are several types of radio direction finders; in general, all those in common use afloat find the direction of an incoming radio wave by revolving, centering, or orienting a loop or coil with respect to the direction of the wave. A pointer and a graduated dial are generally used to determine the direction from which the wave comes, or the pointer may be mounted over a gyro repeater in a vessel with a gyro compass.

It is important to note that the bearing of an incoming radio wave is subject to quadrantal deviation not unlike a magnetic compass; therefore, it is necessary to apply to the observed bearing a certain correction which is determined by calibration of the radio direction finder. This deviation, unlike that in a magnetic compass, depends upon the relative bearing of the radio wave from the ship's head rather than principally the ship's structure; and, though subject to some change, may be generally considered constant over a period of several months. In addition, the observed bearing may be affected by variable errors, such as changes in position of wiring, metallic guys, antenna leads, etc. Especially will the open or closed condition of the other radio circuits on board affect the direction of the observed wave. The U. S. Navy requires all antenna circuits, whether sending or receiving, to be open when observing direction by radio direction finder.

Dial Settings of Radio Direction Finders. To avoid interference, it is important to determine and record correct dial settings for each station, and to adhere to them.

Accuracy and Use of Bearings. Long experience with properly installed and correctly calibrated direction finders maintained in good condition indicates an average accuracy of 1° to 2°. Departures from this accuracy will sometimes be experienced when taking bearings from a position close to the shoreline and over land. Night effect, which is sometimes encountered, particularly near sunrise and sunset, and which is usually manifested in very wide or changing minimum, tends to limit the distance at which reliable bearings can be obtained. In observing marine radiobeacons, night effect is not usually encountered at distances less than 30 to 50 miles. The existence of night effect can almost invariably be confirmed by rapidly taking repeated bearings, and when shown to be present, bearings should be used with extreme caution. Serious errors may result in bearings taken if other shipboard antennas are erected close to the direction finder after calibration or if the direction finder, ship's rigging or other equipment affecting direction-finder performance is not maintained in the condition existing at the time of last calibration. Regular and frequent use of the direction finder under all conditions is one of the best means of ensuring ability to obtain accurate bearings and that the direction finder is at all times in proper condition. Clear weather operating periods provide ample opportunity for such use.

Full use should be taken of the opportunity for fixing position by cross bearings on two or more radiobeacons, which is provided through the convenient arrangement of stations as to frequency and sequence of operation, and in most cases their favorable geographic location.

To find whether correct bearing or reciprocal of bearing is being received by direction finder, adjust loop and balance as usual. Turn balance control to extreme left against spring until pointer is on *Sense* position, then turn first to lower readings (counter-clockwise), and if the signal increases the observed bearing is correct. If it increases when turned to higher readings (clockwise), the bearing is 180° in error.

Note: Calibration and accuracy checks of the RDF are made on request to the FCC and consist of comparison of simultaneous visual and RDF bearings on ship's heading 45°, 135°, 225°, and 315°. This should be made before the annual FCC inspection of radio equipment.

Sense Antennas for Radio Direction Finders. The Coast Guard has been informed that on recent inspections of radio direction finding equipment by representatives of the Federal Communications Commission, sense antennas had been improperly maintained in a few instances and that deck officers, on one or more occasions, failed to understand their use.

The sense antenna is used to provide a means for resolving the 180° ambiguity that may exist in a bearing obtained by use of a radio direction finder. In the usual circumstances of navigation at sea, the general direction of a radio beacon is known, so the ambiguity in bearing may not exist. Frequently, any doubt may be resolved by noting the manner in which the bearing changes. However, situations may arise when proper use of the sense antenna can save lives.

One example could well be the location of an emergency transmitter of a lifeboat or airplane in distress. Failure to use the directional capability of the direction finder sense antenna properly could result in your ship heading directly away rather than directly toward the distressed craft.

The necessity for and proper use of the sense antenna may be better understood if the direction finder user understands the basic theory of the direction finder loop. When a loop antenna is rotated, it will produce two nulls (minimum-signal-level points) of the signal from a distant transmitter. These nulls are approximately 180° apart and occur when the plane of the loop is perpendicular to the direction from which the signal is arriving. Since the direction finder pointer cannot identify the actual bearing of the transmitter (true null) from the reciprocal bearing (false null), a sense of direction must be introduced. This is accomplished by combining the loop signal with the signal from a nondirectional sense antenna. Step by step procedure for determining the true null of a radio transmission should be obtained from the operating manual furnished with the specific equipment.

It should be understood that sense antenna installations are usually "hand-tailored" for each type of vessel since its location with respect to the loop antenna, length, and relationship to the ship's superstructure is important. Once the sense antenna has been installed by qualified personnel, its length and location must not be changed. To do so probably will affect the quality of the null, that is, make it too broad or too sharp depending on whether the sense antenna has been shortened or made longer. In some cases, tampering with the antenna may result in complete loss of its ability to provide sense information.

It is recommended that users of the direction finder take practice bearings on signals whose "sense" of direction is already known so that familiarity with the direction finder is acquired.

Special Operation of Radiobeacon Stations. U. S. radiobeacons will broadcast for the purpose of enabling vessels to calibrate their radio direction finders upon request. If it is not practicable to determine the time of calibration sufficiently in advance to contact the District Commander, U. S. Coast Guard, or if the calibration is desired from a remote station where communication is difficult, request may be made directly to the keeper of the station by means of telephone, telegraph, or a whistle signal consisting of three long blasts followed by three short blasts, this whistle signal to be repeated until same is acknowledged by the keeper through the starting of the transmitter. The same group of signals will be sounded at the termination of calibration.

If attention of station or lightship is not attracted by the whistle signals, hoist the international code signal, *J* over *K*, to indicate for radio direction finder calibration.

The work of a station keeper is not confined to standing watch, and there may be times when the whistle request for calibration is not immediately heard, due to the noise from operation station machinery, etc. Usually, a repeated signal not too far from the station will attract the attention of keepers.

Transmission for calibration purposes will be continuous without the 2-minute silent interval unless another station in the same frequency group is in operation at the time. No continuous transmission for calibration will be undertaken during regular schedule periods of operation.

Stations used for calibrating must be within the range of visibility but should not be less than one mile distant.

Radiobeacons

Radiobeacons are the most valuable fog signals, and are also available for navigation in clear weather.

In plotting long-range bearings on a chart of the Mercator projection a correction must be made, as the line of bearing is not a straight line excepting in the meridian. Class A—Range 200 miles; Class B—100 miles; Class C—10 miles.

Distance Finding Stations. At the stations listed in the Light List, the radiobeacon and sound signals are synchronized for distance finding. Whenever the sound signal is operating a group of two radio dashes, a short and long, 1 second and from 3 to 5 seconds respectively, is transmitted every 3 minutes at the end of the radiobeacon minute of operation. A group of two sound signal blasts of corresponding length is sounded at the same time. When within audible range of the sound signal, navigators on vessels with radio receivers capable of receiving the radiobeacon signals may readily determine their distance from the station by observing the time in seconds which elapses between hearing any part of the distinctive group of radio dashes, say the end of the long dash, and the corresponding part of the group of sound blasts, say the end of the long blast, and dividing the result by 5 (or more exactly 5.5) for nautical miles. The error of such observations should not exceed 10%.

Where a submarine oscillator is synchronized with the radiobeacon, the method is the same excepting that the interval in seconds is divided by 1.25 to obtain the distance off in nautical miles.

The 1-second dash preceding the long dash is a stand-by or warning signal as is also the 1-second blast. The latter serves as an identification signal to assure the observer that he is taking time on the correct sound signal blast.

For observations on aerial sound signals a watch with second hand is all that is needed, although a stop watch is more convenient. When observing submarine signals a stop watch or other refined method of time measurement must be used because of the more rapid travel of sound in water.

Observations for distance off at these stations are *not restricted to vessels with direction finders*, but may be made by any vessel having a radio receiver capable of receiving in the band 285 to 315 kilocycles within which radiobeacons are operated. A loud speaker is desirable although not necessary.

An example of the use of these synchronized signals follows: In the case of Chesapeake Lightship if the interval between hearing the end of the long radio dash marking the end of the radiobeacon minute and the end of the long (5-second) blast of the diaphone is 33 seconds, the observer is $33 \div 5.5 = 6$ miles from the lightship.

Caution must be used in approaching radiobeacons on radio bearings, and care must be taken to set courses to pass safely clear. The risk of collision will be avoided by insuring that the radio bearing does not remain constant. This caution is applicable to those lightships and stations which are passed close to.

Warning Beacon on Nantucket Lightship. An auxiliary warning radiobeacon of short range, sounding a warble note, is operated on every third minute immediately following the main radiobeacon and on the same frequency, to warn of proximity to the lightship. This beacon operates 24 hours each day.

Radio Bearings from Other Vessels. Any vessel equipped with a radio-direction finder can give a bearing to a vessel equipped with a radio transmitter. Such service will generally be furnished when requested, particularly by Government vessels. These bearings, however, should be used only as a check, as comparatively large errors may be introduced by local conditions surrounding the radio-direction finder unless known and accounted for. Any radio station, the position of the transmitter of which is definitely known, may serve as a radiobeacon for vessels equipped with a radio-direction finder. However, mariners are cautioned that stations established especially for maritime service are more reliable and safer for use by the mariner, for numerous reasons.

Many navigators are using the ship's radio-direction finder as a help in avoiding collision in fog, detecting with it the presence and observing the direction of approaching vessels.

Accuracy of Bearings. The accuracy with which bearings can be taken depends on various conditions, and while bearings taken by a station can generally be considered accurate to within 2°, the Government cannot accept any responsibility for the consequences of a bearing being inaccurate.

In the case of bearings which cut the coast line at an oblique angle, errors of from 4° to 5° have been reported. Bearings obtained between about one-half hour before sunset and one-half hour after sunrise are occasionally unreliable. It is probable that the accuracy of a bearing is also affected if the ship's transmitting instrument is not adjusted to the correct wave length. Bearings signaled as "approximate" or "second class," should be regarded with suspicion as being subject to considerable error. The maximum distance for which bearings from these stations are accurate is 150 miles.

Conversion of Radio Bearings to Mercator Bearings

The increasing use of radio directional bearings for locations of ships' positions at sea, especially during foggy weather, has made it particularly desirable to be able to apply these radio bearings taken on shipboard or sent out by the shore stations directly to the nautical chart.

These bearings are arcs of the great circles passing through the radio stations and the ship, and unless in the plane of the Equator or of a meridian, would be represented on a Mercator chart as curved lines. Obviously it is impracticable for a navigator to plot such lines on his chart, so it is necessary to apply a correction to a radio bearing to convert it into a Mercator bearing; that is, the bearing of a straight line on a Mercator chart laid off from the sending station and passing through the receiving station.

Table 8 is entered with the difference of longitude in degrees between the ship and station (the nearest tabulated value being used), and opposite the middle latitude between the ship and station, the correction to be applied is read.

The correction is always applied to the observed radio bearing *in the direction of the Equator*, *i.e.*, toward the South in North latitudes and toward the North in South latitudes.

Example: A ship in D.R. Lat. 39° 50′ N., Long. 67° 35′ W., obtains a radio bearing of 299° true on the radiobeacon of Nantucket Shoals Lightship, located in Lat. 40° 37′ N. and Long. 60° 37′ W.

Radiobeacon Lat. 40° 37′ N.   Long. 69° 37′ W.

Ship D.R. Lat.   39° 50′   Long. 67° 35′

Middle Lat.   40° 14′   Long. diff. 2° 02′

Entering *Table* 8 with *Long. difference* 2°, the nearest tabulated value, and opposite *Middle Lat.* 40°, we find the correction is 39′.

The Mercator bearing then will be 299° — 39′ = 298° 21′. It will facilitate plotting if 180° is added or subtracted, and bearing laid off from the position of the radiobeacon; thus, 298° 21′ — 180° = 118° 21′, or true bearing of ship from the lightship in question.

TABLE 8. TABLE OF CORRECTIONS IN MINUTES*

(Difference of longitude in degrees)

Mid. L.	½°	1°	1½°	2°	2½°	3°	3½°	4°	4½°	5°	5½°	6°	6½°	7°	7½°	8°	8½°	9°	9½°	10°
20°	5	10	15	21	26	31	36	41	46	51	56	62	67	72	77	82	87	92	98	103
21°	5	11	16	21	27	32	38	43	48	54	59	64	70	75	81	86	91	97	102	108
22°	6	11	17	22	28	34	39	45	51	56	62	67	73	79	84	90	96	101	107	112
23°	6	12	18	23	29	35	41	47	53	59	64	70	76	82	88	94	100	105	111	117
24°	6	12	18	24	31	37	43	49	55	61	67	73	79	85	92	98	104	110	116	122
25°	6	13	19	25	32	38	44	51	57	63	70	76	82	89	95	101	108	114	120	127
26°	7	13	20	26	33	39	46	53	59	66	72	79	85	92	99	105	112	118	125	131
27°	7	14	20	27	34	41	48	54	61	68	75	82	89	95	102	109	116	123	129	136
28°	7	14	21	28	35	42	49	56	63	70	77	84	92	99	106	113	120	127	134	141
29°	7	15	21	29	36	44	51	58	65	73	80	87	95	102	109	116	124	131	138	145
30°	7	15	22	30	38	45	53	60	68	75	83	90	98	105	113	120	127	135	143	150
31°	8	15	23	31	39	46	54	62	70	77	85	93	100	108	116	124	131	139	147	155
32°	8	16	24	32	40	48	56	64	72	79	87	95	103	111	119	127	135	143	151	159
33°	8	16	25	33	41	49	57	65	74	82	90	98	106	114	123	131	139	147	155	163
34°	8	17	25	34	42	50	59	67	75	84	92	101	109	117	126	134	143	151	159	168
35°	9	17	26	34	43	52	60	69	77	86	95	103	112	120	129	138	146	155	163	172
36°	9	18	26	35	44	53	62	71	79	88	97	106	115	123	132	141	150	159	168	176
37°	9	18	27	36	45	54	63	72	81	90	99	108	117	126	135	144	153	163	172	181
38°	9	18	28	37	46	55	65	74	83	92	102	111	120	129	139	148	157	166	175	185
39°	9	19	28	38	47	57	66	75	85	94	104	113	123	132	142	151	160	170	179	189
40°	10	19	29	39	48	58	68	77	87	96	106	116	125	135	145	154	164	174	183	193
41°	10	20	30	39	49	59	69	79	89	98	108	118	128	138	148	157	167	177	187	197
42°	10	20	30	40	50	60	70	80	90	100	110	120	130	140	151	161	171	181	191	201
43°	10	20	31	41	51	61	72	82	92	102	113	123	133	143	153	164	174	184	194	205
44°	10	21	31	42	52	63	73	83	94	104	115	125	135	146	156	167	177	188	198	208
45°	11	21	32	42	53	64	74	85	95	106	117	127	138	149	159	170	180	191	201	212
46°	11	22	32	43	54	65	76	86	97	108	119	129	140	151	162	173	183	194	205	216
47°	11	22	33	44	55	66	77	88	99	110	121	132	143	154	165	176	186	197	208	219
48°	11	22	33	45	56	67	78	89	100	111	123	134	145	156	167	178	190	201	212	223
49°	11	23	34	45	57	68	79	91	102	113	125	136	147	158	170	181	192	204	215	226

(*continued*)

TABLE 8. TABLE OF CORRECTIONS IN MINUTES* *(continued)*

(Difference of longitude in degrees)

Mid. L.	½°	1°	1½°	2°	2½°	3°	3½°	4°	4½°	5°	5½°	6°	6½°	7°	7½°	8°	8½°	9°	9½°	10°
50°	11	23	34	46	57	69	80	92	103	115	126	138	149	161	172	184	195	207	218	230
51°	12	23	35	47	58	70	82	93	105	117	128	140	152	163	175	186	198	210	221	233
52°	12	24	35	47	59	71	83	95	106	118	130	142	154	165	177	189	201	213	225	236
53°	12	24	36	48	60	72	84	96	108	120	132	144	156	168	180	192	204	216	228	240
54°	12	24	36	49	61	73	85	97	109	121	133	146	158	170	182	194	206	218	231	243
55°	12	25	37	49	61	74	86	98	111	123	135	147	160	172	184	197	209	221	233	246
56°	12	25	37	50	62	75	87	100	112	124	137	149	162	174	187	199	211	224	236	249
57°	13	25	38	50	63	75	88	101	113	126	138	151	164	176	189	201	214	226	239	252
58°	13	25	38	51	64	76	89	102	115	127	140	153	165	178	191	204	216	229	242	254
59°	13	26	39	51	64	77	90	103	116	129	141	154	167	180	193	206	219	231	244	257
60°	13	26	39	52	65	78	91	104	117	130	143	156	169	182	195	208	221	234	247	260

* This table is sufficiently accurate for practical purposes for distances up to 1000 miles.

Chapter 4

TIDES AND CURRENTS

When considering the tides of the world, as apart from those prevailing in any particular locality, it is helpful to remember that all tides fall into one or the other of three broad classes, viz., *Semidiurnal, Diurnal, and Mixed.* Of these, the semidiurnal are the best known and easiest understood, and they prevail in the greatest number of important harbors. As their name denotes, they occur twice a day and they are usually marked by a fairly regular interval between the times of high water and by a reasonably close agreement in the heights of successive tides. In the diurnal group we have those tides that usually have only one appreciable high water in a tidal day. The second tide is so insignificant that it is little more than a variation in the height of low water. The third group is made up of an important type of tide that combines some of the features of the semidiurnal type, with other features of the diurnal type. Two tides occur in a day, but there is often startling difference between the heights of two successive high waters or two successive low waters. These are the "mixed" tides. As illustrating these three types we may take Tyne Piers, Manila and Juneau, Alaska, representing respectively Semidiurnal, Diurnal, and Mixed tides. For the same five days the times of high water at these three places were:

Tyne Piers: 04^h56^m, 17^h11^m, 05^h34^m, 17^h57^m, 06^h16^m, 18^h45^m, 06^h58^m, 19^h38^m, 08^h04^m, 21^h06^m.

Manila: 10^h56^m, 11^h31^m, 12^h13^m, 13^h02^m, 14^h02^m.

Juneau: 01^h56^m, 14^h52^m, 02^h31^m, 15^h41^m, 03^h18^m, 16^h40^m, 04^h14^m, 17^h54^m, 05^h28^m, 19^h20^m.

The high water heights for the same five days were:

Tyne Piers: 13.9 ft., 14.3 ft., 13.9 ft., 14.0 ft., 13.5 ft., 13.2 ft., 12.8 ft., 12.2 ft., 12.1 ft., 11.7 ft.

Manila: 3.7 ft., 3.9 ft., 4.0 ft., 4.0 ft., 3.9 ft.

Juneau: 18.0 ft., 14.7 ft., 17.3 ft., 13.7 ft., 16.3 ft., 12.8 ft., 15.0 ft., 12.1 ft., 13.8 ft., 12.3 ft.

Glancing at these tables we notice that in all groups the time interval between high waters is fairly regular. At Juneau they are alternately over and under 12 hours, but this, although a noticeable feature in many mixed tides, may sometimes be observed in semidiurnal tides. As regards the heights it will be seen that, with the exception of two tides, the heights at Tyne Piers all trend in the one direction: in this case to decrease. The diurnal tides would, if continued, show irregularity in height, while the irregularity of the mixed tide is very obvious. We will briefly investigate the reasons for these different types.

In writing for the information of seamen it is not necessary to discuss the formation of tides in an elementary manner. It is sufficient to say that tides are the result of the centrifugal force of the earth's rotation and the gravitational attractions of the sun and moon. To these three bodies all the variations in tidal phenomena may be directly referred. The centrifugal action of the earth tends to set up a tidal undulation at the points most remote from the sun and moon. The gravitational efforts of these two bodies attract the waters directly under them. We thus get two tides in a lunar day, since the tide set up by the earth's centrifugal force is approximately equal to that set up by the attraction of the moon and sun. The complications that arise in what would otherwise be a comparatively simple system are partly due to the friction between ocean and earth but mainly due to important changes in the relative distances of the three bodies, earth, moon and sun. These distances are three: the angular distance between the sun and moon and the equinoctial and actual distance of the sun and moon from the earth. In all these cases the moon is the predominating factor. In spite of her relative smallness she is so much nearer the earth than is the sun that her gravitational effect is about 2.3 times greater than his. We may say, therefore, that the tides depend mainly on the phases, declination and distance of the moon; these tides being affected by the declination and distance of the sun. The effect of the moon's phase on the tide is really that the moon's tide is increased or decreased by the attraction of the sun. All these factors occur, more or less, in all the tides throughout the world. It is by the preponderating influence of one particular factor that a tide gains its characteristic.

Semidiurnal Type. In British waters, in the Eastern waters of the Atlantic and, with certain exceptions, on the East coast of North America we have the semidiurnal type of tide. Definite and unmistakable effects of changes in the declinations of the sun and moon and in their distances may be observed in these tides, but their main features are a regularity of recurrence, a maximum height about the time of conjunction of sun and moon, and a minimum height about quadrature, when the sun is causing a low water where the moon is raising a high water. The highest tides are called "spring" tides: the lowest tides, "neaps." The mean interval between successive high waters is about 12 hours 25 minutes.

Diurnal Type. With the diurnal type we are introduced to tides in which the predominating factor is the declinational changes in the moon and sun. Because of this connection with the "trope," or turning of the heavenly bodies, they are frequently termed "tropic" tides. As they are prevalent in the tropics, the name is doubly appropriate. An undulation is raised in the latitude of the moon's declination, and another undulation is raised on the opposite side of the earth in the latitude opposite the moon's declination. There is one tide a day in each of these latitudes, except when the declination of the moon is zero. The maximum heights occur with maximum declinations. As a general rule, the range of tropic tides is small, but there are notable exceptions.

At Victoria, B.C., for instance, the range may be more than 9 ft.; at Kua Kam, French Indo-China, it can exceed 12 ft. The time of high water of tropic tides depends on the latitude of the place. If the latitude is the same sign as the declination, high water will follow the superior transit of the moon; if the sign be opposite to the declination, it will follow the inferior transit.

Mixed Type. Between the diurnal and semidiurnal types stand the mixed tides. These are semidiurnal in occurrence, but the effect of the declinational changes is so great that it is only when declination is at zero that the two following tides reach the same height. When declination is great, the difference between alternate tides is great, because one tide has the declinational effect added to it while the other has not. This type of tide prevails on a considerable part of the Australian coast, on the Pacific coast of North America, and on the Eastern shore of Asia and in the adjacent islands. From this it will be seen that they are to be found in many important harbors. As illustrating how closely they approach the tropic tides at certain times, we may consider the tides at Seattle, Wash., for 19–22 October, 1932. The moon's declination was about 28ᶜ N. The heights of high and low water for eight succeeding tides were:

H.W.: 10.7 ft., 09.3 ft., 10.6 ft., 08.9 ft., 10.7 ft., 08.3 ft., 10.9 ft., 7.8 ft.

L.W.: 00.1 ft., 07.8 ft., 00.4 ft., 08.1 ft., 00.7 ft., 08.1 ft., 01.1 ft., 7.6 ft.

On at least two occasions the difference between high and low waters did not exceed 0.2 ft., while the preceding differences exceeded 10 ft.

The moon moves around the earth in an elliptical orbit in about 27 1/2 days. There is, then, a period when she is nearer the earth than at any other time in her orbit. This point of least distance is termed her perigee, or perigean point. Her point of farthest distance is called her apogee. Between her greatest and least distances is a difference of about 31,500 miles, or nearly 1/8 of her mean distance. This causes variations in her gravitational force, which are indicated in the tides. These variations may be detected in all tides, but in certain places— the Bay of Fundy is an outstanding example—the change in height of tide from perigee to apogee is definitely greater than from springs to neaps.

There are other peculiarities of the tides—such as double high waters, as at Southampton—protracted high waters and protracted low waters. These are generally due to local peculiarities and cannot, therefore, be dealt with here. Tidal streams, also, are too extensive a subject for this article, and we will proceed to consider the methods of ascertaining the time and height of high water at ports whose daily tides are not given. The usual method is by the application of time constants. This is known as the non-harmonic method. The daily tide tables of many of the principal ports are given in the publications of the various Governments. With the assistance of a table of constants we may apply a special constant for our port to the time of high water at a tabulated port and so find the time of high water at our secondary port. For instance, by adding 5 hours to the time of H.W. at Gibraltar we obtain the time of H.W. at Sierre Leone; by subtracting 47 minutes from the time of H.W. at Charleston, S.C., we have the time of H.W. at Cape Hatteras. To find the approximate height of tide we take a height between the spring and neap rise according to the moon's age or phase. This method is quick, and generally sufficiently accurate for the ordinary purposes of navigation. Should it be required to obtain a very precise result, recourse should be had to the harmonic constants. The method is involved and lengthy, and too complicated to be discussed here.

Glossary of Tidal Terms. The following abbreviations and terms are usually to be met with in tidal information:

Age of tide. The time that has elapsed since the transit that originated the tide and the occurrence of the tide. Age varies from a negative quantity to $+7$ days, but is generally from $+1$ to $+2$ days. The average for the world is about $+1\frac{1}{2}$ days.

Amphidromic point. A point at which the co-tidal lines meet.

Amplitude. Sometimes used instead of height of tidal undulation.

Anomalistic type of tide varies with moon's distance from earth.

Apogee is the point of moon's orbit farthest away from earth.

Bore is a steep tidal wave found in several rivers.

Change of moon occurs when sun and moon are in conjunction and the moon is invisible. She recommences her phases.

Chart datum is the basis to which chart depths are referred. It is generally below L.W.O.S.T.

Co-tidal lines are lines on a tidal chart that connect all places having the same time of H.W., and also connect those having the same range of tide.

Constituent of a tide is a component part of the undulation due to a particular effect, e.g., moon's declination or sun's distance from earth.

Duration of rise or fall is the time interval between L.W. and H.W., or between H.W. and L.W.

Differences are the differences in time and height between tide at a standard port and tide at a secondary port. Sometimes called *constants.*

Equinoctial tides are extraordinarily high tides occurring about the period of the equinoxes.

Establishment of the port is the time interval between the transit of moon and time of H.W.

H.W. High water.

H.W.F. & C. High water at full and change of moon.

Height of tide. Its height above chart datum.

Lagging. Retardation of the times of H.W. during moon's second and fourth quarters. I.e., the tide is behind the average time of two successive high waters by 12.25 hours. Due to sun's constituent.

Lunitidal interval is the time between moon's transit and next H. or L.W. Varies due to priming or lagging.

M.T.L. Mean tide level.

M.S.L. Mean sea level.

M.S.R. Mean spring rise.

M.N.R. Mean neap rise.

M.H.W.I. Mean high water lunitidal interval.

M.L.W.I. Mean low water lunitidal interval.

M.H.H.W. Mean higher high water—with mixed tides.

M.L.L.W. Mean lower low water—with mixed tides.

Neap tides. Tides with smaller H.W.'s and greater L.W.'s, occurring about quadrature.

Perigee. Point in moon's orbit nearest to earth.

Priming. An acceleration of time of H.W. during moon's first and third quarters. Opposite to lagging.

Phases. Changes in the moon's appearance.

Quadrature. When sun and moon are 90° apart.

Range of tide is distance from L.W. to H.W.; the difference between any low and following high water, or vice versa.

Mean range is the difference in height between mean high water and mean low water.

Spring range is the average difference in height between high and low waters at spring tides or about times of new and full moon.

Diurnal range. Where tide is chiefly diurnal; this is the difference between mean higher high water and mean lower low water.

Rise of tide is distance above chart datum. Same as height of tide.

Retard of tide is age of tide: the interval between transit of the moon at which tide originates and the appearance of the tide itself.

Stand of tide is period at H.W. when level is stationary.

Slack water. When tidal-current has ceased, irrespective of vertical movement.

Standard port. One whose daily tides are tabulated, and to which secondary ports may be applied.

Secondary ports. Those whose differences from a standard port have been calculated and tabulated.

Undulation or tidal wave is the elevation of sea level that causes tides and tidal streams in the vicinity of land.

Spring tide. Caused by moon and sun in conjunction or opposition.

Neap tide. Caused by moon and sun in quadrature.

Mean sea level. Half tide level.

Time of H.W. Time of moon's meridian passage (corrected for longitude) plus establishment of port.

Time of L.W. Can be found approximately by adding or subtracting 6ʰ 13ᵐ (¼ lunar day).

H.W.F. & C. Vulgar establishment—a rough approximation to the establishment of the port—high water lunitidal interval.

Syzygy tide occurs when sun and moon are in opposition or conjunction, as at full or new moon.

Superior and *inferior tides* occur when the moon is above or below the meridian.

TIME OF H.W. BY TABLES*

Table 1. Daily tides at reference stations.

Time is that used at place.

Datum same as for local charts.

Height is added to charted depth.

(Tables give no time of current change or of slack water.)

Table 2. Difference for subordinate stations.

Time: + = later, — = earlier.

Height: + = higher for sub-station, — = lower.

Ratio of Rise (if given) is used to multiply height of both high and low water at reference station.

Ratio of Range as above.

Table 3. Height of tide at any time.

* In the U. S. Government publication on Tides and Currents.

TIME OF HIGH WATER BY CALCULATION

The N. A. GCT of moon's transit will give a very rough approximation of LCT of transit, and adding the H.W. lunitidal interval will give an approximation near enough so we will know whether we want the upper or lower transit tide.

Example		Jan. 19th	
If afternoon (lower transit required) GCT of Gren.		*If forenoon* (upper transit required)	
upper transit for the—	*day hr. min.*		*day hr. min.*
18th Jan.	18—19—59		18—19—59
19th Jan.	19—20—52		
sum including days	38—16—51		
∴ half sum is	÷ by 2 =		
GCT of lower transit	19—08—26		
Bowditch, Table II, corr. for Long. W	+12		+12
LCT of local			
lower transit	19—08—38	*upper*	18—20—11
HW lunitidal interval	—06—32		—06—32
LCT of HW	Jan. 19—15—10		Jan. 19—02—43
Interval to next LW	6—13		6—13
LCT of next LW	Jan. 19—21—23		Jan. 19—08—56

TYPES OF CURRENTS

Tides and currents are intimately related phenomena, or, in fact, may be considered as two different phases of the same phenomenon, since, accompanying the vertical movement of the water caused by the tidal forces of moon and sun, a horizontal movement also takes place, giving rise to currents. In addition, however, to those currents caused by astronomical forces working through the tides, others are brought about by meteorological conditions, and by physical differences in sea water in different parts of the oceans. These astronomical forces, combined with topographical features, as in the case of the tides, and with meteorological and physical conditions, give rise to five types of currents:

1. The rectilinear or reversing type, illustrated by the currents in most inland bodies of water, such as the Hudson River, Chesapeake Bay, Delaware Bay, etc.

2. The so-called hydraulic type, illustrated by the currents in straits connecting two independently tided bodies of water; for example, the East River (New York), Deception Pass (Washington), and Seymour Narrows (British Columbia).

3. The rotary type, illustrated by the currents in the open ocean and along the sea coast.

4. The permanent currents comprising the main oceanic circulation, illustrated by the Gulf Stream of the Atlantic and the Kuroshio or Japanese current of the Pacific.

5. The wind-driven currents of a temporary nature, produced by the friction of local winds on the surface of the water.

The first three types (rectilinear, hydraulic, and rotary) are of tidal origin and are therefore periodic, thus lending themselves to accurate prediction in advance; the last two are non-periodic and are due to meteorological conditions, to dominant winds, to variations in barometric pressures over the oceans, and to differences in temperatures and densities of the sea water in different parts of the oceans. Like the agents which bring them into being, they defy accurate advance predictions.

The first two types (rectilinear and hydraulic) are of interest to the mariner in inland waters only and data for their determination are predicted in advance and furnished in current tables published annually by the important maritime nations.

In a basin like Chesapeake Bay, the wave of high water travels up until it reaches and is reflected back from the head of the bay. There results from this a rather complicated condition of affairs in the bay, with two points of high and two of low water, with points of slack midway between the adjoining high and low.

In a place which lies open at both ends, as the English Channel, or Long Island Sound, the currents flow from both sides toward and away from a certain point; and in the case of the English Channel and Long Island Sound, moreover, the tide turns throughout the whole length of the channel at practically the same moment.

Currents are weaker near shore than in the middle of the channel, and often run in the opposite direction, sometimes with considerable force.

(The most dangerous currents are those encountered beyond the limits where tidal currents are usually looked for. These generally set onto the coast even though the sailing directions give no hint of such danger, and no reason for it is apparent.)

It is only on an open coast line or in a shallow basin that slack water corresponds with high and low. This "slack" water *does not* generally correspond to "high" and "low." Nor is a falling tide necessarily accompanied by a current running out, nor a rising tide by a current running in. In many places high and low water correspond with the maximum strength of the tidal current, the stream of flood commonly running for some time, often hours, after high water, and the ebb runs for some time after low water.

Tidal currents do not always run in and out along the same line, but in many places swing through a complete circle, running at different stages of the tide, from every point of the compass—sometimes directly onshore or offshore.

Duration of Slack. As given in current table (reversing currents), indicate as slack water the instant of zero velocity, which is only momentary. There is a period each side of slack water, however, during which the current is so weak it may be considered negligible for practical purposes. Table 4, sub-tables *A* and *B* of the Current Tables give this.

(Generally, a vessel handles better when running against a current than when running with it. To this there is one exception: Where a sharp turn is to be made, the ship will make it better on a fair tide. In fact it is dangerous to attempt such a turn against a strong head tide, for as the vessel's bow reaches out beyond the point it is caught by the current on the wrong side, giving her a rank sheer across. A moment later, her stern feels the back water sweeping out from the far side of the bend, cutting her stern the wrong way again.)

Rotary Current. The third type of current, while encountered at sea, especially in coastwise traffic, is generally of small velocity, and, since it is rotary in character, its effect becomes nullified through a complete tidal cycle of about twelve and a half hours. This third type, however, being also of tidal origin, lends itself to accurate advance prediction, and in some cases in which the velocity of this type is comparatively high, as for example those currents over the greater part of George's Bank, current roses are provided on the chart. From these data existing local current conditions can be determined by reference to a standard current station for which advance predictions are made.

Permanent Currents. The fourth type (permanent oceanic currents), while of vital interest to the mariner in areas where they are confined, as in the case of the Gulf Stream in the Straits of Florida and along the course of its impingement against the continental shelf, has generally little effect on position determination over the wide expanses of the oceans. In the open ocean these currents are comparatively weak and are at the whim of local winds; they may, therefore, be treated by the mariner in the same manner as the ordinary local wind-driven currents.

The deflective force of the rotation of the earth has a marked effect on both tides and currents, as has been shown by direct observations as well as theoretical considerations. Its action is toward the right (Northern Hemisphere) and a greater range is brought about on the right shore. A comparison, for example, of the mean ranges of the tides at points directly opposite on the eastern and western shores of Delaware and Chesapeake Bays shows an average mean range .3 to .4 ft. greater on the eastern shore, while in the Bay of Fundy the average mean range in the eastern shore is 5.3 ft. greater than directly opposite in the western.

Offshore, and in some of the wider indentations of the coast, this deflective force of the earth's rotation causes the direction of this tidal current to take a rotary motion, its direction changing constantly throughout. A tidal cycle (12^h25^m) is a rotary movement, clockwise in the Northern Hemisphere, at a rate of about 30° per hour.

It is well known that a wind continuing from one general direction for some time will give rise, through friction on the surface of the water, to a current, the velocity of which increases with an increase in the velocity of the wind, and the mariner has accepted that this wind-produced current sets in the same direction as the wind. The deflective force due to the earth's rotation, however, causes a marked deviation of the set of these currents along the coasts and in open ocean areas. In an ocean of infinite depth it can be shown from theoretical considerations that a wind-driven current should be deflected on the surface 45° to the right of the wind direction in the Northern Hemisphere and

45° to the left in the Southern Hemisphere. Near the coast it is to be expected that this deflection should be modified to some extent by the configuration of the bottom and of the shore line. Investigations from comparatively long series of continuous current observations obtained during the past decade at different light vessels along the coast of the United States have verified this theory and brought out the fact, of importance to the mariner, that, contrary to his belief, a local wind creates a current along the coast, setting not in its own direction, but in a direction about 20° to the right of the wind.

While a general law applies to the average current produced by any given wind velocity, it is obvious that along the coast line, the amount of deflection from the wind direction will depend upon the angle of impingement of this current against the coast; in some cases, due to this angle, the deflection is increased and in others decreased. It has been found, however, that the velocity of the current varies nearly in proportion to the wind velocity, and that it is 1.5% to 2% of the wind velocity in miles per hour.

In open ocean areas with plenty of sea room, observations have shown that the actual deflection of wind-driven currents nearly approaches the theoretical value, so we may summarize as follows:

1. The drift of wind-driven currents in the open ocean approximates in knots 2% of the wind velocity in miles per hour.

2. The set of wind-driven currents in open ocean areas is about 40° to the right of the wind direction in the Northern Hemisphere and 40° to the left in the Southern Hemisphere.

The general oceanic circulation gives further evidence of the effect of the deflective force of the earth's rotation on the set of currents. The deep-seated ocean currents of both the Atlantic and the Pacific oceans each comprise two distinct and clearly defined major systems. In each ocean the circulation in the Northern Hemisphere is in a clockwise direction and in the Southern Hemisphere in a counter-clockwise direction. For example, the circulation of the Atlantic Ocean in the Northern Hemisphere comprises on the south the north equatorial current setting westward; on the west and north is the Gulf Stream setting northward and then eastward, and on the east the Canary current setting southward, to complete the circuit. And in the center of this mighty clockwise swirl is the comparatively stagnant Sargasso Sea.

Effects on a Vessel. Accepting these assumptions, which are based both on theory and on direct observations, the effects of wind-driven currents on the determination by the mariner of the dead-reckoning position of a vessel may be discussed in detail. Such a discussion may well be demonstrated by examples, in which the wind directions are assumed to be from both the starboard and port hands, and from various directions relative to the fore-and-aft line of the vessel, since the deflection from a straight path taken by these wind-produced currents causes them to exercise different effects when put in motion by winds from different hands relative to the vessel. In these examples, it is to be understood that the different illustrative cases are assumed to be in the Northern Hemisphere and, therefore, that the deflections are to the right of the wind direction; in the Southern Hemisphere they would, of course, be to the left. Fully to demonstrate these different effects, eight cases have been taken, illustrated by Figs. 1*A* to *H*, inclusive.

Fig. 1*A* illustrates the current effect resulting from a wind 45° on the starboard bow. Assuming the wind velocity to be 35 miles an hour, the resulting current drift would be about 0.7 knot (2% of the wind velocity), setting practically athwartship (40° to the right of the wind direction); and, unless taken into consideration by the mariner and an allowance made, the vessel's position at the end of a 24-hour period would be about 17 miles to port of the course laid down. In order to

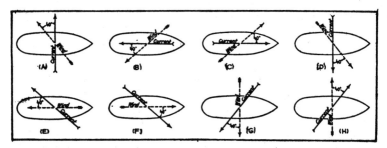

FIG. 1. EXAMPLES OF CURRENT DEFLECTIONS ON SHIP'S COURSE.

demonstrate the fact that a different effect accrues from a similar wind from the other hand, Fig. 1*B* illustrates the effect from a wind 45° on the port bow. Assuming the same wind velocity, the resulting current drift would be 0.7 knot, but setting practically aft and directly against the vessel's progress. In this case, outwardly similar to the last one, the vessel's position at the end of a 24-hour period, however, would be very nearly on the course laid down, but about 17 miles short of her logged distance.

A wind 45° on the starboard quarter produces a current setting practically fair with the vessel's progress through the water (Fig. 1*C*); the logged distance, therefore, will be less than the actual distance made good over the ground. Fig. 1*D* illustrates a wind 45° on the port quarter; the resulting current effect in this case, however, is practically athwartship. But for the deflective force due to the earth's rotation, the resulting current effect in these two cases, apparently quite similar otherwise, would have been identical.

Fig. 1*E*, illustrating a wind from dead ahead, demonstrates that the resulting current sets about 40° across the starboard bow, while in Fig. 1*F*, with the wind dead astern, the resulting current sets about 40° on the port quarter.

With the wind on the port beam (Fig. 1*G*), the resulting current sets 40° on the port bow and, therefore, somewhat against the progress of the vessel over the ground. With the wind on the starboard beam (Fig. 1*H*), the resulting current sets 40° on the starboard quarter and therefore, somewhat fair with the progress of the vessel over the ground.

It must be borne in mind that the effects of current on the dead-reckoning positions, illustrated in Fig. 1, are wholly external to the vessel; that is, the whole mass of water, bearing the vessel, shifts its position in the ocean. This mass movement can, of course, be taken into account in the dead reckoning, either by regarding the current set and drift as a course and distance to be reckoned with, or, in order to follow more closely the track laid down, it can be allowed for by application of the graphic method of the "current rule" with which all mariners are familiar. In the two cases, however, illustrated by Fig. 1*C* and *D*, another problem arises, due to the effects produced by action of the vessel itself. This additional source of error is brought about by the effect on the steering of the vessel, quite probable under the conditions illustrated by these two figures, with the wind on either quarter. This factor should be given consideration by the mariner, irrespective of the effects of the current as illustrated hereinbefore.

If the winds in these two cases are accompanied by a heavy quartering sea, the vessel tends to work to windward, especially to starboard, because of the effect on the steering brought about by the pounding of heavy seas on the quarter. A careful conning of the helmsman under these conditions generally will disclose that when off course, it is usually toward the side against which the following sea is directed. The resulting error is sometimes as much as two- to three-tenths of a mile an hour off the course laid down, depending upon the force of the sea and somewhat upon the vessel.

In making allowance for this correction to the course steered, consideration should be given to the difference in effects of the sea from the starboard quarter and from the port quarter. If the sea is from the starboard quarter, the vessel will work to windward (starboard) the maximum amount, since the current, due to the starboard quartering wind, sets fair with the vessel's course (Fig. 1*C*) and therefore has no compensating effect. On the other hand, the working to windward from a quartering port sea will quite probably be compensated entirely by the effect of the wind-produced current, since the current, due to a port quartering wind, sets practically athwartship (Fig. 1*D*), in a direction opposite to that of the error due to the vessel's working to windward to the port hand. In making steering allowance for the two conditions to make good the course laid down, it is obvious, of course, that the resultant of the two forces must be considered.

At sea, especially in coastwise navigation, constant vigilance on the part of the navigator is the price of safety; for at times wind-driven currents of considerable velocity precede the wind which causes them.

CURRENT DIAGRAMS

(An explanation of those in the U. S. Current Tables)

Current Diagram is a graphic table which shows the velocities of the flood and ebb currents and the times of slack and strength over a considerable stretch of the channel of a tidal waterway. At definite intervals along the channel the velocities of the current are shown with reference to the times of turning of the current at some reference station. This makes it a simple matter to determine the approximate velocity of the current along the channel for any desired time.

In using the diagrams, the desired time should be converted to hours before or after the time of the *nearest* predicted slack water at the reference station.

Besides showing in compact form the velocities of the current and their changes through the flood and ebb cycles, the current diagram serves two other useful purposes. By its use the mariner can determine the most advantageous time to pass through the waterway in order to carry the most favorable current and also the velocity and direction of the current that will be encountered in the channel at any time.

Each diagram represents average durations and average velocities of flood and ebb. The durations and velocities of flood and ebb vary from day to day. Therefore predictions for the reference station at times will differ from average conditions and when precise results are desired the diagrams should be modified to represent conditions at such particular times. This can be done by changing the width of the shaded and unshaded portions of the diagram to agree in hours with the durations of flood and ebb, respectively, as given by the predictions for that time. The velocities in the shaded area should then be multiplied by the ratio of the predicted flood velocity to the average flood velocity (maximum flood velocity given opposite the name of the reference station on the diagram) and the velocities in the unshaded area by the ratio of the predicted ebb velocity to the average ebb velocity.

In a number of cases approximate results can be obtained by using the diagram as drawn and modifying the final result by the ratio of velocities as mentioned above. Thus if the diagram in a particular case gives a favorable flood velocity averaging about 1.0 knot and the ratio of the predicted flood velocity to the average flood velocity is 0.5 the approximate favorable current for the particular time would be 1.0 × 0.5 = 0.5 knot.

THE COMBINATION OF CURRENTS

In determining from the current tables the velocity and direction of the current at any time, it is frequently necessary to combine the tidal current with the wind current. The following methods indicate how the resultant of two or more currents may be easily determined.

Currents in the Same Direction. When two or more currents set in the same direction it is a simple matter to combine them. The resultant current will have a velocity which is equal to the sum of all the currents and it will set in the same direction.

Currents in Opposite Directions. The combination of currents setting in opposite directions is likewise a simple matter. The velocity of the resultant current is the difference between the opposite setting currents, and the direction of the resultant current is the same as that of the greater current.

Currents in Different Directions. The combination of two or more currents setting neither in the same nor in opposite directions, while not as simple as in the previous cases, is nevertheless not difficult, the best way of finding the resulting current being by the graphic method.

Chapter 5

SAILINGS

SYMBOLS AND ABBREVIATIONS

Algebra

a, b, c, d, etc. Known quantities usually represented by letters from the beginning of the alphabet

x, y, z. Unknown quantities represented by letters at the end of the alphabet

(+) Add, or positive

(−) Subtract, or negative

× Multiplication

÷ Division

> Greater than

< Less than

= Equal to

≠ Not equal to

∞ Infinity

~ Difference, meaning algebraic difference. Thus the difference between +4 and −3 is 7

( ) Parentheses

[ ] Brackets

{ } Braces

(All used to group together two or more quantities to be treated as a unit)

$\sqrt{a}$ Is the square root of *a*

$\sqrt[3]{a}$ Is the cube root of *a*

$\sqrt[4]{a}$ Is the fourth root of *a*

Plane Geometry

△ Triangle

⊥ Perpendicular

∥ Parallel

∠ Angle

π Greek letter *pi*, = 3.1416, ratio of the circumference of a circle and its diameter

Trigonometry

sin	Sine
cos	Cosine
tan	Tangent
cot	Cotangent
sec	Secant
cosec	Cosecant

Greek Alphabet

A,	α	Alpha
B,	β	Beta
Γ,	γ	Gamma
Δ,	δ	Delta
E,	ϵ	Epsilon
Z,	ζ	Zeta
H,	η	Eta
Θ,	θ	Theta
I,	ι	Iota
K,	κ	Kappa
Λ,	λ	Lambda
M,	μ	Mu
N,	ν	Nu
Ξ,	ξ	Xi
O,	o	Omicron
Π,	π	Pi
P,	ρ	Rho
Σ,	σ	Sigma
T,	τ	Tau
Υ,	υ	Upsilon
Φ,	ϕ	Phi
Λ,	χ	Chi
Ψ,	ψ	Psi
Ω,	ω	Omega

Aspects

♂ Conjunction, or having the same longitude or right ascension

☊ Opposition, or differing 180° in longitude or right ascension

☐ Quadrature, or having a geocentric angular distance of 90°

Abbreviations

☊ Ascending node
☋ Descending node
N North
S South
E East
W West
° Degrees
′ Minutes of arc
″ Seconds of arc
ʰ Hours
ᵐ Minutes of time
ˢ Seconds of time

Signs of the Planets, etc.

☉ Sun
☾ Moon

☿ Mercury
♀ Venus
⊕ Earth
♂ Mars
♃ Jupiter
♄ Saturn
♅ Uranus
♆ Neptune
♇ Pluto

Signs of the Zodiac

1. ♈ Aries
2. ♉ Taurus
3. ♊ Gemini
4. ♋ Cancer
5. ♌ Leo
6. ♍ Virgo
7. ♎ Libra
8. ♏ Scorpio
9. ♐ Sagittarius
10. ♑ Capricorn
11. ♒ Aquarius
12. ♓ Pisces

STANDARD ABBREVIATIONS IN NAVIGATION

Note: This is the same system of abbreviations as is used in Dutton's *Navigation and Nautical Astronomy.*

Altitude	h	Dead reckoning	*D.R.*
approximate	h_a	Declination	*Dec.* or d
computed	H_c	Departure	p or *Dep.*
intercept	a	Deviation	*Dev.*
observed	H_o	Difference of latitude	l
sextant	h_s	Difference of longitude	D or DLo
Ante-meridian	AM	Distance	*Dist.* or d
Apparent	A	Equation of time	*Eq.T.*
Azimuth	Z	Error	E
Azimuth—from North	Z_n	Greenwich	G
Chronometer		apparent time	GAT
correction	CC	civil time	GCT
minus watch	$C\text{-}W$	sidereal time	GST
time	C	Haversine	*hav*
hack	H	High water	*H.W.*
Colatitude	coL	full and change	HWF and C
Compass		Horizontal Parallax	*H.P.*
error	*C.E.*	Hour Angle	HA or t
per standard	*psc*	Hourly difference	HD
Computed point	*C.P.*	Index correction	IC
Constant for latitude	K	Interval	*Int.*
Correction	*cor.* or c	Knot (s)	*kt.* (s)
Course	C	Latitude	L or *Lat*
from North	C_n	constant for	K
true	*T.C.*	middle	L_m
change of	c/c or *C.C.*	Latitude left	L_1
Day	d	Latitude in or arrived at	L_2

Local		Parallax	*Par.*
apparent time	*LAT*	Parallax and refraction	*p* and *r*
civil time	*LCT*	Patent log	*p.l.*
sidereal time	*LST*	Polar distance	*p*
Logarithm	*log*	Position	
Longitude	λ	dead reckoning	*D.R.*
Longitude left	λ₁	estimated	*E.P.*
Longitude in or arrived at	λ₂	Post meridian	*PM*
Low Water	*L.W.*	Reduction	*Red.*
Lunitidal interval	*Lun. Int.*	Refraction	*Ref.*
Magnetic	*Mag.*	Right ascension	*RA*
Mean time	*MT*	mean sun	*RAMS*
Meridional parts	*M*	Semi-diameter	*S.D.*
Meridional difference	*m*	Sidereal	*S*
Middle latitude	*Lₘ*	Spring	*spg*
Natural	*nat.*	Table	*T*
Nautical	*Naut.*	Time	*T*
Nautical Almanac	*N.A.*	Transit	*tr.*
Neap	*Np.*	Variation	*var.*
Noon		Vertex	*ver.*
local apparent	*LAN*	Versine	*versin.*
local civil	*LCN*	Watch time	*W* or *WT*
Greenwich civil	*GCN*	Zenith distance	*Z*
Observation or observed	*Obs.*		

(Where the same letters have been used as abbreviation of different words, their meanings can always be readily determined from the context.)

PLANE TRIGONOMETRIC FUNCTIONS

In any right triangle, the relation existing between any two of its sides is said to be a *function* of either of the acute angles. The various functions are as follows (*see* Fig. 1):

Function	Description	Of Angle A
sine A	= side opposite ÷ hypotenuse	= $a \div c$
cosine A	= side adjacent ÷ hypotenuse	= $b \div c$
tangent A	= side opposite ÷ side adjacent	= $a \div b$

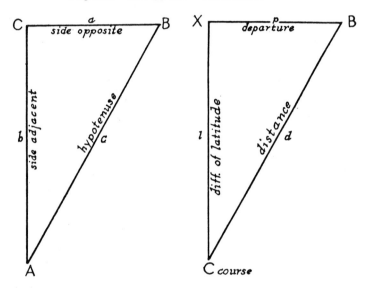

FIG. 1. PLANE RIGHT TRIANGLE.   FIG. 2. PLANE SAILING TRIANGLE.

The above three are the basic functions, and the remaining three are merely reciprocals of these:

cosecant A	= hypotenuse ÷ side opposite	= $c \div a$
secant A	= hypotenuse ÷ side adjacent	= $c \div b$
cotangent A	= side adjacent ÷ side opposite	= $b \div a$

Since the sum of the angles A and B is 90°, each angle is the *complement* of the other, the complement of an angle being equal to 90° − the angle. Any given function of A is the same as the corresponding co-function of B. That is, sine A = cosine B, secant A = cosecant B, etc. In this respect, the "co" is an abbreviation for "complement," or is equivalent to saying "the cosine of A is equal to the sine of the complement of A."

If you are given that the sine of 30° = .5, it follows that the cosecant of 30° = 2, and also that the cosine of 60° = .5.

PLANE SAILING

For a very small area the earth's surface may be assumed to be a plane surface; that is, the spherical form may be neglected without material error. The smaller the area under consideration, the less the error of this assumption.

Let C = course (*see* Fig. 2)
Cos $C = l \div d$, whence $l = d \cos C$
Sin $C = p \div d$, whence $p = d \sin C$
Tan $C = p \div l$

Plane Sailing Used:

1. When the distance is short.
2. When the angle the course makes with the meridian is small.
3. When near the equator.

The problems of plane sailing may be solved in three ways: graphically, by logarithms, and by the traverse tables (Table 2, *Bowditch*).

The Traverse Tables:

1. Find the page where the course is given, either at the top or bottom of the page.

2. Find the given distance in the column marked *Dist.*

3. Opposite the given distance, l is tabulated in the column marked *Lat* and p in the column marked *Dep.*

4. Note that the *Lat* and *Dep* columns, as given at the top and bottom of the page, are interchanged; so when using a course which appears at the bottom of the page, be sure to take the name of these columns from the bottom.

PARALLEL SAILING

If a ship's course is due east or due west she does not change her latitude, and all the distance covered is departure. In this case, the problem is simply to find the difference of longitude corresponding to the departure. The triangle shown in Fig. 3 has no relation to the theory of parallel sailing, but it presents the parts in such relations

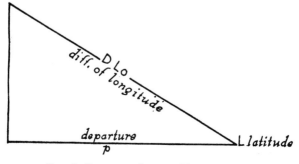

Fig. 3. Parallel Sailing Triangle.

that the formulas of parallel sailing may be deduced therefrom as on a parallel: $DLo = p \sec L$.

In solving a problem in parallel sailing, the computation can be made by logarithms, but the traverse tables are more convenient.

By traverse tables:

Parallel sailing	*Heading in table*
latitude of parallel	course
distance	diff. of lat.
diff. of long.	distance

MIDDLE LATITUDE SAILING

When a ship follows a course obliquely across the meridians remember that the latitude as well as the longitude changes continually. For

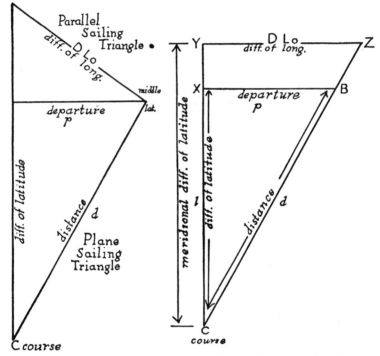

FIG. 4. MIDDLE LATITUDE SAILING.   FIG. 5. MERCATOR SAILING.

practical purposes, involving an ordinary day's run, the departure between two places may be taken as the departure on the middle latitude of the two places, *provided* that the latitude does not exceed 50° and *also provided* that both are on the same side of the equator.

Fig. 4 has no relation to the theory of middle latitude sailing, but presents the parts in such a way that any required formula may be deduced therefrom. It is simply an aid to memory formed by combining the triangles of plane sailing and parallel sailing, substituting middle latitude (L_m) for latitude (L) in the latter.

By traverse tables:

1. Find departure (p) in the latitude column.

2. Find diff. of long. (D Lo) in the distance column.

MERCATOR SAILING

Middle latitude sailing assumes that the departure between two places is equal to the departure between their meridians as measured in their middle latitude. Certain limitations were pointed out, and where greater distances are involved another solution is required.

All the formulas used in Mercator sailing may be deduced from the diagram, Fig. 5, as for a given course the triangles of plane and Mercator sailing are similar triangles. CBX is the triangle of plane sailing, CY is the meridional difference of latitude, i.e. the difference between the meridional parts for any two latitudes. YZ is parallel to XB and CB is extended to Z. YZ is the difference of longitude, and may be found by use of the plane trigonometric functions.

Logarithms are generally used in finding the Mercator course and distance between two points, as the distance is usually beyond the limits of the traverse tables. However, the traverse tables may be used by renaming,

1. the Lat. column the meridional diff. of lat., and,

2. the Dep. column the diff. of long.

Do not use Mercator sailing when the course is near East or West. In this case use middle latitude sailing, as the tangents of angles near 90° vary rapidly in value, and any error in the value of C produces a large error in the computed value of D Lo.

TRAVERSE SAILING AND DEAD RECKONING

When the track of a ship is composed of several rhumb lines it is called a traverse. The net change of latitude made by a ship which sails a traverse is the algebraic sum of the changes of latitude made on each course. Similarly with the departures. The work can be most efficiently performed by adopting a tabular form for the computation and using the traverse tables.

Procedure:

1. Construct traverse form, separate column for each step.

2. Reduce all courses and bearings to *New Card* and points to degrees.

3. Insert variation and deviation.

4. Apply leeway.

5. Determine if set of current is magnetic or true if a known current; enter set as a course and drift as distance.

6. With the true courses and distances, find from the traverse tables the D. Lat. and Dep. corresponding to each course and distance.

7. The total D. Lat. and Dep. made by the ship are found, respectively, by taking the algebraic sum of northerly and southerly differences of latitudes and easterly and westerly departures.

8. The working of the dead reckoning merely involves an application of traverse sailing and middle latitude sailing.

Dead reckoning as defined in Dutton's *Navigation and Nautical Astronomy* has a somewhat different meaning than dead reckoning defined in Bowditch. Dutton refers to the course made by *dead reckoning traces* and, being arrived at mechanically it does not include leeway or drift, but is the sum of courses and distances steered. The dead reckoning position arrived at by use of this Day's Work form is defined by Dutton as *estimated position* or *E. P.*

FORM FOR DAY'S WORK, DEAD RECKONING

TIME	COMPASS COURSE	VAR.	DEV.	LEE-WAY	TOTAL ERROR	TRUE COURSE	PATENT LOG	DIST.	N	S	E	W	DIFF. LONG.

	Latitude	Longitude
	° '	° '
Left at departure (or noon)	...... N or S	...... E or W
Run to......	...... N or S	...... E or W
By D. R. at......	...... N or S	...... E or W
Run to......	...... N or S	...... E or W
By D. R. at......	...... N or S	...... E or W

GREAT CIRCLE SAILING

The shortest distance between two places is that measured along the great circle which passes through them. Under certain circumstances the great circle track is not materially shorter than the rhumb line between two places. These may be summarized as follows:

1. For a small distance, the rhumb line and great circle are nearly coincident.

2. The rhumb line between places that are near the same meridian is very nearly a great circle.

3. The equator is a great circle and parallels near the equator are very nearly great circles. Therefore, *in low latitudes*, parallel sailing is very nearly as short as great circle sailing.

Computation to Determine the Great Circle Track. We have given the latitude and longitude of our point of departure, C, and of destination, B. We must determine the distance, d; the initial course, C, the point at which the great circle track reaches its highest latitude, the vertex, V; and various latitudes of the points m, m' and so on, in order to plot the track on a Mercator chart. (Refer to Fig. 6.)

Form for Initial Course and Distance. Where both latitudes are on the same side of the equator:

$$\text{co } L_1 = 90° - L_1 \text{ and co } L_2 = 90° - L_2.$$

Where departure is on one side of the equator and destination on the other:
$$\text{co } L_1 = 90° - L_1 \text{ and co } L_2 = 90° + L_2.$$

			$\begin{array}{c} co\,L_1 \\ d \\ \hline d \sim \text{co} L_1 \end{array}$
λ_1			
λ_2			
DLo	log hav		
L_1	log cos		log sec
L_2	log cos		
	$\begin{cases} \text{log hav} \\ \text{nat hav} \end{cases}$	════	
$L_1 \sim L_2$	nat hav	────	
d	nat hav	════	log csc
$\text{co}L_2$	nat hav		
$d \sim \text{co}L_1(-)$	nat hav	────	
	nat hav		log hav
C^*			log hav

(Note: $\sim$ means algebraic difference. Thus the difference of latitude between 20° North and 15° South is 35°, whereas the difference between 20° North and 15° North is only 5°.)

Computing the Latitude and Longitude of the Vertex.

$$\sin \text{co } L_v = \sin \text{co } L_1 \sin C$$
$$\tan D Lo_v = \sec \text{co } L_1 \cot C$$

(Note: The vertex may fall beyond the part of the track to be traversed. This does not alter the following explanation of the procedure in determining other points of the track.)

Where the points of departure and of destination are on opposite sides of the equator, the longitude of the equator crossing is the longitude of the vertex, $+$ or $- 90°$.

---

* The quadrant of the initial great circle course is in the same quadrant as the Mercator course when the point of destination is in a higher latitude than the point of departure. In the reverse case the quadrant of the initial course is indeterminate by inspection.

Determining Other Points of the Great Circle Track. Referring to Fig. 6, assume a meridian Am, differing in longitude from the merid-

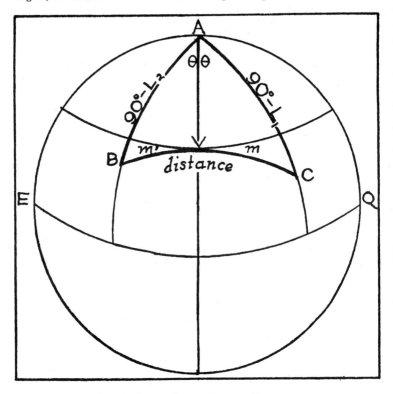

FIG. 6. GREAT CIRCLE SAILING TRIANGLE.

ian of the vertex by a selected angle θ, say 5°. Then, in the right-angled spherical triangle VAm we know the angle VAm (5°) and the side AV, which is the colatitude of the vertex. Then:

$$\text{Cot } L_m = \cot L_v \cdot \sec \theta.$$

This formula gives the latitude of two points on the track whose longitudes differ by the angle θ from the known longitude of the vertex, since latitude of m' is the same as the latitude of m.

By assuming a series of values of θ, say 5°, 10°, 15°, the latitudes and longitudes of a double series of points of the track may be determined, plotted on the chart, and a curve drawn through them which represents the great circle track. This should then be examined to see if it passes clear of dangers to navigation, ice, etc.

Methods of Determining the Great Circle Course:

1. Great circle sailing charts. Of the available methods, that by

means of charts especially constructed for the purpose is considered greatly superior to all others.

A series of great circle sailing charts covering the navigable waters of the globe is published by the U. S. Hydrographic Office. Being on the gnomonic projection, all great circles are represented as straight lines, and it is only necessary to join any two points by such a line to represent the great circle track between them. The courses and distances are readily obtainable by a method explained on the charts. The track may be transferred to a chart on the Mercator projection by plotting a number of its points by their coordinates and joining them with a curved line.

2. By time azimuth method, using regular azimuth tables.

Factors	*Heading in Table*
with lat. of departure (L_1) as the	latitude
with lat. of destination (L_2) as the	declination
with D *Lo* as the	hour angle
enter the tables and	azimuth is the *initial course*

(The latitude of destination will remain constant for all courses. This method applies for finding all other courses, the distance run on each to be such that the distance will keep the azimuth changing approximately 1°.)

COMPOSITE SAILING

This is a combination of great circle and parallel sailing, used when the great circle reaches higher latitudes than is desirable. The shortest track between points where a fixed latitude is not to be exceeded is made up as follows:

1. A great circle through the point of departure tangent to the limiting parallel.

2. A course along the parallel.

3. A great circle through the point of destination tangent to the limiting parallel.

Chapter 6

CELESTIAL NAVIGATION

The purpose of the diagrams and text in the following pages is to explain both graphically and verbally the various terms used in nautical astronomy. In keeping with the intent of this handbook, it is presumed that the reader has been over the ground before, and has an understanding of the subject.

TERMS IN NAUTICAL ASTRONOMY

The Earth's Axis is that diameter about which it rotates.

The Earth's Poles are points at which the axis meets the surface.

The Equator is that great circle of the earth that lies midway between the poles.

A Parallel is a circle on the earth's surface whose plane is parallel to the equator.

A Meridian is a great circle of the earth which passes through the poles.

An Hour Circle is a great circle of the celestial sphere which passes through the poles and a celestial body.

The Vernal Equinox is that equinoctial point which is occupied by the center of the sun on March 21st, at the commencement of spring in the northern hemisphere, also called the first point of Aries (♈).

TIME

Mean Time is measured by the apparent motion of the **mean sun,** an imaginary sun which moves to the East in the equinoctial at a uniform rate equal to the average rate of the true sun in the ecliptic.

Civil Day is the interval between two successive transits of the mean sun across the *lower branch* of the meridian.

Civil Time. Mean time with the origin of the day at lower transit of the mean sun is called civil time. Civil time at any place equals the hour angle of the mean sun +12 hours, dropping 24 hours if the sun exceeds that amount.

When crossing the 180th meridian sailing westward, add one to the date, and if sailing eastward, subtract one from the date, at the same time changing the name of the longitude.

Note: For every 15 degrees one moves east, 1 hr. is added to the time of day, and for every hour one moves west, 1 hr. is deducted from the time of day.

Apparent Time is time measured by the apparent motion of the true sun.

Apparent Noon at any place is the instant of the transit of the true sun over the meridian of the place.

Apparent Solar Day is the interval of time between the successive transits of the true sun across the lower branch of the meridian.

TABLE 1. COORDINATES USED IN NAVIGATION

Subject	Abbreviation	Units of measurement	Measured on	Origin of measurement	Direction of measurement	Measured to	Extreme limits of measurement	REMARKS
Latitude	L	° ′ ″	Terrestrial meridian	Equator	N. or S.	Place	0° and 90°	
Longitude	λ	° ′ ″	Equator	Prime meridian	E. or W.	Meridian of place	0° and 180°	For convenience λ is often expressed in time, i.e., in h-m-s
Declination	Dec or d	° ′ ″	Hour circle through body	Equinoctial	N. or S.	Body	0° and 90°	
Polar distance	p	° ′	Hour circle through body	Elevated pole	From elevated pole	Body	0° and 180°	If L and d are same name, p=90°−d. If L and d are of different name, p=90°+d.
Altitude	H₀	° ′ ″	Vertical circle through body	Celestial horizon	From horizon	Body	0° and 90°	
Zenith distance	z	° ′ ″	Vertical circle through body	Zenith	From zenith	Body	0° and 90°	z=90°−H₀
Azimuth	Zₙ	° ′ ″	Horizon	North point of horizon	Clockwise	Vertical circle through body	0° and 360°	Azimuth is tabulated in Azimuth Tables from either N. or S. point of horizon E. or W. depending whether body is E. or W. of meridian.
Hour angle	H.A.	h-m-s	Equinoctial	Upper branch of celestial meridian	Westward	Hour circle through body	0° and 360°	
Meridian angle	t	h-m-s	Equinoctial	Upper branch of celestial meridian	E. or W.	Hour circle through body	0° and 180°	
Sidereal Hour angle	S.H.A.	° ′	Equinoctial	Vernal equinox	Westward	Hour circle through body	0° and 360°	
Local apparent time	L.A.T.	h-m-s	Equinoctial	Lower branch of local celestial meridian	Westward	Hour circle through true sun	0ʰ and 24ʰ	
Local civil time	L.C.T.	h-m-s	Equinoctial	Lower branch of local celestial meridian	Westward	Hour circle through mean sun	0ʰ and 24ʰ	
Local sidereal time	L.S.T.	h-m-s	Equinoctial	Upper branch of local celestial meridian	Westward	Hour circle through Vernal equinox	0ʰ and 24	
Greenwich mean time	G.M.T.	h-m-s	Equinoctial	Lower branch of Greenwich celestial meridian	Westward	Hour circle through mean sun	0ʰ and 24ʰ	

Equation of Time is the difference between the *true sun's* hour angle and that of the *mean sun*, expressed in time. It is given for each day in the *Nautical Almanac*.

Standard Time. This is the local civil time of meridians known as standard meridians, located 15° of longitude apart, commencing with the meridian of Greenwich as the initial meridian. The time of a standard meridian extends as nearly as practicable 7 1/2° each side of the standard meridian. The system of standard time zones has been extended over the oceanic areas, and the keeping of standard time at sea has been instituted in most navies of the world.

Zone Time is the time of the zone in which the ship happens to be, and is reckoned from 0^h to 24^h. The U. S. Navy uses the 24^h day expressed as a 4-figure group, the first two figures denoting the hour and the second two denoting the minutes. The civil day is used, commencing at midnight, expressed as 0000. Each of the zones is designated by a number representing the number of hours by which the standard time of the zone differs from the Greenwich meridian civil time.

Zone Description is the correction which must be applied to ship's time to obtain the corresponding Greenwich meridian civil time. It is the number of the zone prefixed by the plus sign (+) if in west longitude, or the minus sign (−) if east.

Sidereal and Mean Time. *Civil* time is the hour angle of the mean sun increased by 12. *Sidereal* time is the hour angle of the first point of *Aries*. The *mean* sun is that average place in the equinoctial which the *true* sun is conceived to occupy throughout a given year. *Mean solar* time is that shown on our clocks and is ahead or behind *true solar*, or *apparent*, time by an amount equal to the equation of time. (*See* **Equation of Time.**) Civil time is the mean solar time of the standard meridian adopted for the particular zone or place. (*See* **Standard Time.**)

Daylight Saving Time is advanced time. It is the normal standard time of one zone to the east, i.e., one hour later on the clock than the normal standard time of the zone.

DIAGRAM ON THE PLANE OF THE EQUINOCTIAL

Circle (Fig. 1) represents the equator.

P represents the South Pole.

MPm represents the observer's meridian.

MP = upper branch; Pm = lower branch.

GP is the meridian of Greenwich.

Pg = the 180th meridian.

Arc GM = longitude = angle GPM or 75° W.

* is a star, the hour circle of which is $P*$.

⊙ is the sun; $P⊙$ the sun's hour circle.

♈ is the vernal equinox or the first point of Aries.

S is another star to the eastward.

Longitude (λ) of a place is the arc of the equator intercepted between the prime meridian, Greenwich, and the meridian of the place, measured from the prime meridian east or west through 180° (75° W in Fig. 1).

Hour angle (HA) is the angle at the poles between the meridian of a place and the hour circle of a body measured positively to the westward through 24 hours; or it may be measured as an arc of the equinoctial.

GHA or Greenwich HA of the * is angle $GP* = \lambda + LHA = 75° + 45° = 120°\ GHA$.

LHA or local HA of the * in the figure is angle $MP^* = 45°$.

Meridian Angle (*t*). For a given place the meridian angle, *t*, of a celestial body is the angle at the pole between the meridian of the place and the hour circle of the body measured east or west through 12 hours.

The GHA of the sun (☉'s *GHA*) is the hour angle of the sun measured from the *upper* branch of the Greenwich meridian to the westward through 360°.   In Fig. 1 it is the angle measured by the arc $GSM^* ☉$.

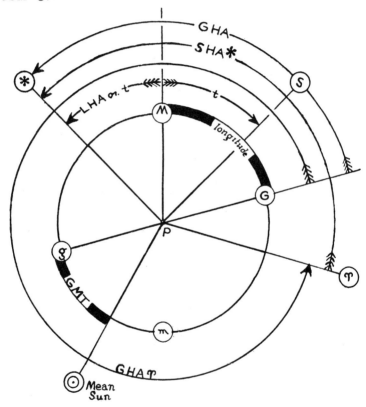

FIG. 1. DIAGRAM ON THE PLANE OF THE EQUINOCTIAL.

Greenwich Mean Time (GMT)   is the angle between the lower branch of the Greenwich meridian (*Pg* = 180th meridian) and the mean sun. In Fig. 1 it is angle $gP ☉ = 3^h$ or 45°. Civil time of any place equals the mean sun $HA + 12$ hours, dropping 24 hours if the sum exceeds that amount. Then $GMT = GHA + 12^h$.

The former *sidereal time* and *right ascension*, which were expressed in hours, minutes, and seconds, have given place to *hour angle of first point of Aries* and *sidereal hour angle*, respectively, expressed in degrees and, minutes of arc.

Our present abridged *Nautical Almanac* gives the *G. H. A.* of Sun, Moon, Aries, Venus, Mars, Jupiter, and Saturn, and the *S. H. A.* of each of 57 selected stars. This information, together with the delineation also given, defines the position occupied by any such bodies or points in the heavenly sphere.

Almost every problem in celestial navigation entails use of the hour angle. Hence, in order to envisage the elements given for a problem's solution, the navigator should thoroughly acquaint himself with the hour angle picture presented in each case.

The H.A., whether sidereal (S.H.A.), Greenwich (G.H.A.), or local (L.H.A.), is measured *Westward* from its point of origin, *i.e.*, from either *Aries*, the Greenwich meridian, or the local meridian. It is perhaps best defined as the arc of the equinoctial intercepted by the respective hour circles passing through the body or point of reference and the meridian in question. It is customarily expressed in degrees and minutes of arc.

TIME DIAGRAM

This is a sketch like Fig. 1, on the plane of the equinoctial. It is invaluable in visualizing a problem, and particularly in determining whether a change of date is involved. Noting the known elements and the elements required to be found, a study of the figure shows very quickly how to combine the known elements to get the unknown elements.

The Zenith of an observer is the point of the celestial sphere vertically over his head.

The Nadir is the point of the celestial sphere 180° from the zenith.

The Equinoctial is that great circle of the celestial sphere which is everywhere 90° from the poles. It is the earth's equator projected on the celestial sphere.

Celestial Meridians are great circles of the celestial sphere passing through the poles. They are the earth's meridians projected on the celestial sphere. The upper branch of an observer's meridian is that half which is terminated by the poles and which passes through the zenith. When we speak of the meridian we usually mean the upper branch of the meridian.

A Vertical Circle is a great circle of the celestial sphere passing through the zenith and the nadir, and which is therefore perpendicular to the celestial horizon. The observer's meridian is the principal vertical circle.

The Prime Vertical is a great circle of the celestial sphere whose plane is at right angles to the observer's meridian, and which passes through the zenith and the nadir.

The North Point of the horizon is the point nearest the North Pole in which the meridian intersects the horizon.

The East Point of the horizon is that intersection of the prime vertical with the horizon which lies to the right of an observer facing North.

DIAGRAM ON THE PLANE OF THE MERIDIAN

The circle (Fig. 2) represents the meridian.

Z represents the zenith.

NS represents the horizon, N being the north point and S the south point. W, the center of the circle is the west point of the horizon.

QQ_1 is the equator. This is drawn so that the angle $ZWQ - 40°$ is equal to the latitude, since by definition *latitude* is the arc of the meridian of a place subtended between the equator and the place, measured N or S from the equator. (Note that NP_n also measures the latitude, since $NWZ = 90° = P_nWQ$, and P_nWZ is common to both right angles.)

Hour Angle has been defined as the arc of the equinoctial intercepted between the meridian and the hour circle. In this case we will

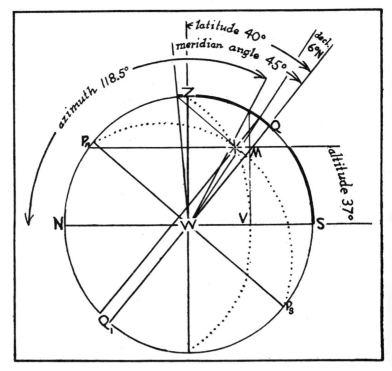

FIG. 2. DIAGRAM ON THE PLANE OF THE MERIDIAN.

show an hour angle of 21 hours or a meridian angle of 3 hours east, which is 45°. $t = 45°$ E. From Q on the upper branch of the meridian in Fig. 2 measure off on the outside circle 45° and drop a perpendicular to QQ_1. The hour circle is then drawn tangent to this perpendicular at M. The foreshortened arc QM then represents 3 hours = 45°. The hour circle is dotted to indicate that it is in the back. An equal westerly meridian angle would be drawn identically the same, except that it would be drawn solid to indicate that it was in front of the figure.

Azimuth, or true bearing of a body, is the angle at the zenith measured by the arc of the celestial horizon between the meridian of the observer and the vertical circle passing through the body.

Suppose that you had to construct the vertical circle for an azimuth of 118.5°. Except that the measurement is made on the horizon, the principal is the same as for the hour or meridian angle. From the north point of the horizon in Fig. 2, measure off 118.5° on the outside circle (meridian) and drop a perpendicular to the horizon. The vertical circle is then drawn tangent to this perpendicular at *V* (dotted to indicate that it is in the back of the figure). The arc *V N* = angle at *Z*, and represents 118.5°.

The Declination of a celestial body is its angular distance from the equinoctial, measured on the hour circle of the body in degrees, minutes and seconds, from 0° to 90°, and named North or South

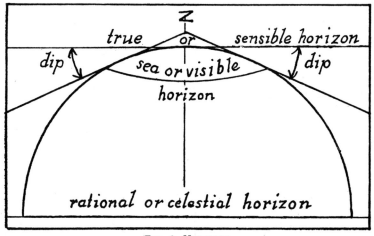

Fig. 3. Horizons.

according as the body is north or south of the equinoctial. Measure off on Fig. 2 the arc, in this case 6° N, on the outside circle (meridian) above the equinoctial, equal to the value of the declination, and draw the diurnal circle of declination parallel to QQ_1.

The point where this diurnal circle cuts the hour, or vertical circle locates the body.

The Altitude of a body is its angular distance above the celestial horizon, measured on the vertical circle of a body from 0° to 90°. From the body draw the altitude circle parallel to the horizon. The amount of arc intercepted above the horizon on the meridian circle is the measure of the altitude, in this case 37°.

See Fig. 3 for illustration of the following definitions.

Rational or Celestial Horizon is the great circle whose plane is perpendicular to the direction of the zenith, and passes through the center of the earth.

Sensible, or True Horizon is the plane passing through the point where the observer stands; it is parallel with the rational horizon, being also perpendicular to the direction of the observer's zenith.

Sea or Visible Horizon is the apparent boundary between the sky and the sea, forming a circle at the center of which the observer stands.

The Polar Distance of a body is its angular distance from the elevated pole, measured on the hour circle of the body in degrees, minutes, and seconds.

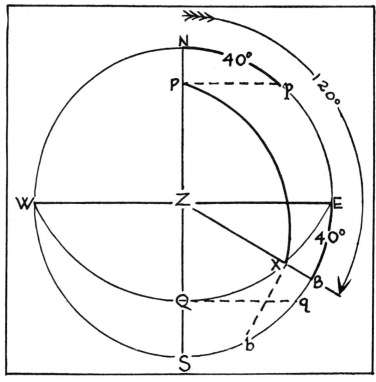

FIG. 4. DIAGRAM ON THE PLANE OF THE HORIZON.
THE ASTRONOMICAL TRIANGLE.

The Zenith Distance of a body is its angular distance from the zenith, measured on the vertical circle passing through the body from 0° to 90°. It is the complement of the altitude.

The Colatitude of a place is 90° minus the latitude.

DIAGRAM ON THE PLANE OF THE HORIZON

1. A circle is drawn (*see* Fig. 4) representing the rational horizon

with the center Z representing the zenith (in this case supposing the observer to be in north latitude).

2. Vertical circles will then appear as radial straight lines. The observer's meridian is shown as a vertical diameter with the upper end N representing the north point of the horizon. Then the east and west points lie 90° from the north and south points.

3. The latitude of the observer may be placed on the meridian by means of the theorem that the latitude of the observer is equal to the altitude of the elevated pole. Thus, with a latitude of 40° N, mark p on the horizon 40° from N and project it back to the meridian at P.

4. The equinoctial passes through the east and west points. A third point of the equinoctial may be obtained by the theorem that the latitude is equal to the declination of the zenith by laying off $Eq = 40°$ and projecting it back to Q as shown. A fair curve may then be drawn through EQW to represent the equinoctial.

5. The azimuth is 120°, and azimuths are measured around to the right (clockwise) through 360° from the north point. Make NEB equal to 120°, and lay off the body's vertical circle radially from Z to B.

6. Now, if the body's altitude is 37°, lay off $Bb = 37°$, and project it on ZB at X.

7. The hour circle of the body may now be drawn as a fair curve, as PX.

PZX is a spherical triangle known as the **astronomical triangle.**
PX = polar distance.
ZX = zenith distance.
PZ = colatitude.

Examples

1. Required the Sun's declination and local hour angle for July 13, 1964, at 9ʰ. 03ᵐ 30ˢ A.M., at a place in Longitude 85°15′ W.

Local civil time, July 13	9ʰ03ᵐ30ˢ
Long. W. from Greenwich	5 41 00
G.M.T., July 13	14 44 30

With this Greenwich Mean Time and Date, enter *Nautical Almanac:*

G.H.A. July 13, 14ʰ	28°34.9′	Declination	21°46.6′N.
corr. for 44ᵐ30ˢ	+11 07.5′	corr.	−.3
G.H.A.	39 42.4′	Declination	21°46.3′N.
add	360 00		
	399 42.4′		
Long. W.	85 15		
Sun's L.H.A.	314°27.4′		

2. Required the local hour angle of star *Rigel* at 10:30 P.M. on Dec. 20, 1964, in Long. 30°15′ E.

G.H.A. *Aries* at 22ʰ00ᵐ Dec. 20	59°30.5′
corr. for 30ᵐ	+7 31.2
G.H.A. *Aries*	67 01.7
S.H.A. *Rigel*	281 47.1
G.H.A. *Rigel*	348 48.8
Long. E.	30 15.0
	379 03.8
Less	360 00.0
L.H.A. *Rigel*	19°03.8′

3. Required the local hour angle and declination of *Venus* on Jan. 22, 1964, at G.M.T. 11ʰ53ᵐ19ˢ in Lat. 35°00′ N. Long. 150°55′ E.

G.H.A. *Venus* at 11ʰ	307°00.6′	Dec.	10°28.7′S.
corr. for 53ᵐ19ˢ	+13 19.8		
v corr.	−0.4	d corr.	−1.1
G.H.A.	320 20	Dec.	10°27.6′S.
Long. E.	150 55		
L.H.A.	471 15		
	360 00		
L.H.A. *Venus*	111°15′		

4. Required the Greenwich hour angle and declination of the Moon on January 2, 1964, at G.M.T. 20ʰ24ᵐ44ˢ.

G.H.A. *Moon* at 20ʰ	251°45.7′	Dec.	16°19.2′N.
corr. for 24ᵐ44ˢ	+5 54.1	d corr.	−3.9
v corr.	+3.9	Dec.	16°15.3′N.
G.H.A. *Moon*	257°43.7′		

5. Required the local mean time of meridian passage of star *Sirius* at a place in Longitude 77°00′ W., on January 4, 1964.

At instant of star's meridian passage, star's S.H.A. = 360° − L.H.A. of *Aries*. Then 360° − S.H.A. = L.H.A. of *Aries*, or,

	360°00′		
S.H.A. *Sirius*	259 06.5	G.M.T. Jan. 5, 4ʰ, G.H.A. *Aries*	163°47.6′
L.H.A. *Aries*	100 53.5		177 53.5
Long. W.	77 00	Increase in 56ᵐ	14°05.9′
G.H.A. *Aries*	177°53.5′	G.M.T. of Mer. Pass. =	4ʰ56ᵐ
		Long. W. −	5 08
		L.M.T. of Mer. Pass. =	23ʰ48ᵐ =11:48P.M.

6. Required the local mean time of meridian passage of the Moon in Long. 80°00′ W. on February 4, 1964.

G.M.T. Mer. Pass. Feb. 3	4^{h}22^m
G.M.T. Mer. Pass. Feb. 4	5 05
Diff. in 1 day	43^m

Long. corr. = $\dfrac{80 \times 43}{360}$ = $-9\frac{1}{2}^m$

G.M.T. Mer Pass. Feb. 4	5^{h}05^m
L.M.T. Mer. Pass. Feb. 4	4^{h}55$\frac{1}{2}^m$

Bear in mind that:

The *solar day* begins with lower transit of Sun, so that elements in our *Nautical Almanac* appear as given for each day *from midnight to midnight,* or from 0^h to 24^h. Civil time 9:15 A.M., accordingly, is expressed 0915, for example, while 3:15 P.M. is 1515; and 15^m past midnight, 0015.

HA is the angle at the pole between the meridian of a place and hour circle of a body. Measured positively to the *westward* through 24 hours.

Finding Greenwich time and date: To the local civil time add the longitude if West; subtract it if East.

Making a general case, *a new date* first comes into effect on the earth at the 180th meridian at the instant of Greenwich Noon.

Crossing 180th meridian, if sailing westward, add one to the date; if sailing eastward, subtract one from the date, at same time changing name of longitude.

CORRECTION OF OBSERVED ALTITUDES

Index Correction depends upon the instrument's error.

Refraction is always subtracted, as is also that correction for combined refraction and parallax of the sun; the correction for combined refraction and parallax of the moon is invariably additive.

Dip is always to be subtracted.

Parallax is always additive; combined parallax and refraction additive in the case of the moon, but subtractive for the sun. As the correction for *parallax of the moon* is so large, it is essential that it be taken from the table with considerable accuracy the corrections for index correction, semi-diameter and dip should therefore be applied first, and the "approximate altitude" thus obtained should be used as an argument in entering the table to find parallax and refraction.

Semi-Diameter is to be added to the observed altitude in case the lower limb of the body is brought into contact with the horizon. and to be subtracted in the case of the upper limb. When the artificial horizon is used, the limb of the reflected image is that which determines the sign of this correction, it being additive for the lower and subtractive for the upper.

LATITUDE

The easiest way to find the manner in which the altitude and declination must be combined to give the latitude is to draw a rough sketch on the *plane of the meridian*, using the knowledge of the approximate latitude to fix the position of the pole and equator. The body may then be placed on the meridian by its declination, and the necessary combination of the altitude and declination may be seen by inspection.

The latitude is the *declination of the observer's zenith*, and the zenith distance is the complement of the true altitude of the body's center. There are the following four possible combinations between the zenith distance of the observer and the body's declination.

Case 1. Declination and latitude of different names, $L = z - d$.

Cases 2, 3, and 4. Declination and latitude of the same name.

Case 2. Declination less than latitude, $L = z + d$.

Case 3. Declination greater than latitude, $L = d - z$.

Case 4. Lower transit. Latitude = the altitude of the elevated pole = polar distance, $90 - d$, plus the altitude; or $L = p + H$.

In observing the meridian altitude of the sun it is usual to wait for it to dip. But it is best to compute the instant of transit, and take the meridian altitude by time rather than dipping. This should always be done with the other heavenly bodies, and especially with the moon, whose rapid motion in declination may introduce greater inaccuracy.

Finding Time of Transit of Sun or Other Bodies. The use of the *GHA* tabulated in the *Nautical Almanac* is recommended as being the same for the sun and for the other celestial bodies. The local time of transit may be found when the longitude is known, as at the time of transit the hour angle of a body is 0 hours or 0° at the local meridian. Similarly, the hour angle of lower transit is 12 hours or 180°.

In west longitude, the *GHA* of the celestial body at local transit is equal to the longitude in arc. In east longitude, the *GHA* at local transit is equal to 360° minus the local longitude. The use of the diagram in the plane of the equinoctial will assist in selecting the correct Greenwich date.

Finding L.A.N. (Todd's Method).

1) Enter traverse tables (Table 3—H.O. 9) with the course that will be made good over the ground (i.e., allowing for current, etc.) and find the departure for one hour's run. Convert this departure into difference of longitude, using Table 4 (Conversion of Departure into Diff. of Long.).

2) The sun moves west at the rate of 900′ of longitude per hour, and if we are moving west we decrease this rate of approach to us by our difference of longitude per hour. If we are moving east we increase its rate of approach to us. Therefore, if moving west, subtract the diff. of long. per hour from 900′; if moving east, add it to 900′.

3) Our hour angle at time of a morning sight, changed to minutes, divided by this rate of change will give us the length of time it will take the sun to go from its position at time of sight to the meridian, i.e., L.A.N. Hence, this interval added to the local time of sight will be our time of meridian passage.

Example:

(1) Course 318° = N 42° W. Speed 15 knots.
Table 3 (Bowditch) gives departure 10 miles.
Table 4   do.   do.   d. long, 13′ (Lat. 39° 30′).
(2) 900′ − 13′ = 887′ = rate of sun's movement per hour.
(3) Hour Angle 58° 14′ at time of A.M. sight (0912).

$$= (58° \times 60) + 14' = 3494'$$

3494 ÷ 887 = 3.94 hrs.   =   3h   56.4m
ship's time of A.M. obs.   =   9h   12.0m

ship's time of L.A. Noon = 13h   08.4m

Constant for Meridian Altitude. (See Appendix D)

Latitude by Polaris. Determine the L.H.A. *Aries* for the proper G.M.T. Then enter Polaris Tables in *Nautical Almanac* for corrections to true altitude to obtain latitude required. A good illustration of the problem is shown with the Tables.

Polaris may be readily picked up in the sextant glass at twilight, before other stars are visible, by computing beforehand the altitude of the star from the approximate *D.R.* position. Set this altitude (with altitude corrections applied in reverse) on the sextant, then look toward the north point of the horizon, and in a few moments the star will be seen in the telescope.

Reduction to the Meridian. Should the meridian altitude be lost, owing to clouds or for other reason, an altitude may be taken near the meridian and the time noted, from which, knowing the longitude, the hour angle may be deduced.

If the observations are within 28ᵐ from the meridian, before or after, the correction to be applied to the observed altitude to reduce it to the meridian altitude may be found by inspection of Tables 29 and 30, Bowditch. Table 29 contains the variation of the altitude for one minute from the meridian, expressed in second and tenths. Table 30 contains the amount in minutes and tenths of arc necessary to reduce the corrected altitude at the time of observation to the corrected altitude at the meridian passage; *it is always additive when the body is near upper transit* and always subtractive when near lower transit.

The resulting latitude from a reduction to the meridian is that of the vessel *at the instant of observation.*

Special Case. When the sun is very near the zenith, Tables 29 and 30 cannot be used; however, with *GHA* as longitude, and declination as latitude, plot a point, and with this as center draw a circle whose radius in miles is equal to the number of minutes in observer's zenith distance. The observer is somewhere on this circle, which may be crossed by the A.M. line of position carried forward to noon.

LONGITUDE—TIME SIGHT

The method for finding longitude at sea is that of the "time sight." The altitude of the body above the sea horizon is measured with a sextant and the chronometer time noted. The problem consists in finding the *LHA* (*t*) from given values of altitude (*h*), latitude (*L*) and polar distance (*p*), and comparing this with the *GHA*, which gives the longitude.

The formula used is:

$$\text{hav } t = \csc p \sec L \cos S \sin (S - h)$$

in which $S = (h+p+L) \div 2$.

Of the three elements used, altitude, declination and latitude, the only uncertain element is the latitude. Results are most accurate when the body is on or near the prime vertical, as then an error of latitude has the least effect.

Where *GHA* is taken directly from the *Almanac* the comparison is similar for all celestial bodies. A time diagram (diagram on the plane of the equinoctial) should be drawn to aid in visualizing the problem. Noting the known elements and the elements required to be found, a study of the figure shows very quickly how to combine the known elements to get the unknown elements.

When using the sun it must be borne in mind that the *Eq. T.* must be applied to *GMT* to obtain *GAT*, which is then compared with the *LAT* obtained from *t* for the longitude.

The "time sight" to give a longitude is generally used only when the latitude has been accurately determined. When latitude is not accurately known, modern navigators prefer to use one of several short methods to obtain a "line of position."

Longitude by Equal Altitudes. When the latitude and the declination differ by less than about 8°, the longitude may be found by altitudes taken within half an hour before and after local apparent noon.

Observe the sun's altitudes and note chronometer time about 15, 10 and 5 minutes before apparent noon. Set sextant and note chronometer times when sun drops to the same altitudes after noon. The mean of the chronometer times is that of local apparent noon. Apply chronometer correction and equation of time. Result is the longitude in time at local apparent noon.

For best results, the azimuth should be 70° to 90° from the meridian.

AZIMUTH

Altitude Azimuth. When the local time is computed from an observed altitude, as in the "time sight," the true azimuth can be computed from the formula:

$$\text{hav } (180 - z) = \sec h \sec L \cos S \cos (S - p)*$$

in which $S = (h+p+L) \div 2$ (as in Time Sight).

The resulting azimuth is to be reckoned from the North in north latitude and from the South in south latitude.

Line of Position. The usual method for finding a line of position

* It may occur that the term $(S - p)$ will have a negative value, but since the cosine of a negative angle less than 90° is positive, the result will not be affected.

where a "time sight" is computed is to assume a latitude, then work a longitude and an azimuth, using the two preceding formulas. This gives one point on the position line. The line of position is then drawn through the determined point at right angles to the direction of the azimuth.

Azimuths in General. The azimuth of a celestial body being so frequently determined for finding compass error, tables are generally employed. The Azimuth Tables (H.O. Pub. No. 71) give azimuths for every 10 minutes between latitudes 71° N and 71° S, and these tables can be used for all bodies where the declination does not exceed 23° N or S. For celestial bodies whose declinations range from 24° to 70°, and latitude extending 70° from the equator, H.O. Pub. No. 120 can be used. Full explanations are in the Tables.

Amplitudes are seldom used in modern practice. The method of obtaining compass error by amplitudes consists in observing the compass bearing of the body when its center is on the true horizon. This requires a small correction found in Bowditch Tables 27 and 28. This correction of the amplitude, as observed in the apparent horizon, is applied *toward the equator*. The formula for amplitude is:

$$\sin \text{Amp.} = \sec L \sin d.$$

It is not recommended that azimuths be taken of objects above 30° in altitude.

Time Azimuths involve considerable calculation, and the Time and Altitude Azimuth ($\sin Z = \sin t \cos d \sec h$) has a defect in that there is nothing to indicate whether the computed azimuth is measured from the north or south point of the horizon. Occasions will be exceedingly rare when there will be any need of these methods, but they may be found in Bowditch if required.

Azimuth Diagrams are accurate enough for the general use of the navigator, and provide a method of finding the azimuth without the tedious interpolation necessary with the azimuth tables. Full explanations for use are printed in the diagram. Captain Weir's azimuth diagram is in popular use. The Hydrographic Office supplies azimuth diagrams to ships of the navy; and that used by the U. S. Coast Guard, "Stereographic Projections for the Identification of Stars and the Approximate Solution of the Astronomical Triangle," is especially recommended for its practicability.

LATEST METHODS IN NAVIGATION

In modern navigation, the navigator solves all observations of celestial bodies, except those for latitude, to determine (1) either the computed altitude of the body or the zenith distance of the body, and (2) its azimuth.

The most widely used formula is the cosine-haversine formula:

$$\text{hav } z = \text{hav } (L \sim d) + \text{hav } \theta$$
$$(\text{hav } \theta = \cos L \cos d \text{ hav } t)$$

It is universally applicable to all the combinations of the values of *t, d* and *L*. There is no ambiguity in the results, and it is unnecessary to keep track of the signs of functions of angles in various quadrants. It is derived from the fundamental formula of spherical trigonometry:

$$\cos a = \cos b \cos c + \sin b \sin c \cos A$$

rearranged for the use of haversines.

The quantity $(L{\sim}d)$ is the difference between the latitude and declination when they are the same name, otherwise it is their sum.

Since $z =$ zenith distance, the calculated altitude $H_c = 90° - z$.

Note that the product of cos L cos d hav t as found by logs must be changed to the natural function in order to be added to the natural haversine $(L{\sim}d)$.

Procedure. The navigator determines the altitude of a celestial body by sextant observation. For the exact instant of observation, determined by the use of a chronometer, he then computes the meridian angle t of the body, using an assumed longitude. He determines the declination of the body at this instant from the *Nautical Almanac*. Thus, knowing the values for meridian angle t and declination d, he assumes a latitude L and solves the astronomical triangle for the body's computed altitude corresponding to his assumed position. The assumed latitude and longitude used in his computations are, in general, near the D.R. or estimated position of the ship at the time of observation (within approximately 40 miles).

The comparison of the computed altitude for his assumed position with the observed altitude obtained by sextant at his actual position enables him to obtain a line of position on which his ship must be. The location of the line of position thus determined is practically independent of any error in his assumptions for all bearings of the observed body.

Short Tabular Methods. Up to the present time, the only element of the astronomical triangle that can be directly measured is the sextant altitude, hence there has been developed but two methods for obtaining line of position. One of these is called the longitude, or "time sight" method, whereby hour angle and azimuth are determined; the other is the intercept method, in which altitude and azimuth are found. This latter method is the one generally adopted.

In the cosine-haversine formula the amount of labor involved from the time the sight is taken until the solution is completed is considerable, with the possibility of some error at each step. In an effort to minimize the amount of calculation required, three prominent methods that have been devised are those of Dreisonstok (H.O. 208), Ageton (H.O. 211) and Tables of Computed Altitude and Azimuth (H.O. 214).

In 1935, Hydrographic Office publications No. 208 (Dreisonstok) and 211 (Ageton) were still the "last word" in navigation. The principal advance since then has been the appearance of various tabulated solutions which have rendered the trigonometric solutions obsolescent.

H.O. 214. These tables consist essentially of tabulated solutions of the astronomical triangle, so arranged as to give the calculated altitude and azimuth by inspection. The scheme of precomputing such values for ready use is a long-established one; in scope, arrangement, and convenience of interpolation these tables are unique. They may be used for all navigational bodies and in both hemispheres. There are no precepts connected with the use of the tables.

For greater convenience in use, H.O. 214 is divided into six volumes, the values of 10° of latitude being included in a single volume. Thus Volume IV covers the latitude belts 30° to 39°, inclusive, north and south. The first volume of H.O. 214 appeared in 1936. The set was not completed until Vol. IX was published ten years later. The printing of H.O. 218 paralleled that of H.O. 214.

The latest addition to this type of celestial table, H.O. 249, was published in June, 1947.

H.O. 249 gives precomputed altitudes and azimuths, correct to the nearest minute and degree, respectively, of 38 stars, plus a simple correction table to obtain latitude by Polaris when that star has an altitude of 15° or more. Arguments for the tables are integral degrees of latitude from 89° N to 89° S and degrees of Local Hour Angles of Aries (LHA γ). From 69° N through 69° S the tabulation is for each whole degree of LHA γ, printed on two facing pages in four columns of 90° each. From 70° N and S to the Poles the tabulation is for 2° of LHA γ, and because of this condensation the data for each degree of latitude is contained on one page consisting of two columns of 180° each of LHA γ.

In the more frequented latitudes for each degree of LHA γ, six stars are listed together horizontally with their computed altitudes and true azimuths. All the stars are of the first or second magnitude and, whenever possible, stars with maximum altitudes of over 45° were used, as, in flying, the chances are better of obtaining sights at the higher altitudes. Computed altitudes are corrected for refraction, based on an assumed flight level of 5000 feet; *no further correction is indicated for shipboard observations of altitudes of 20° or more, although for an altitude of 15° the correction is minus 0.5' and for 10° altitude it is minus 0.7'.* Azimuth is tabulated from N through 360°; hence, no more time need be lost (or errors made!) in figuring westerly azimuths.

The superiority of H.O. 249 over the other tabular methods, such as H.O. 218, for stellar navigation, lies in its simplicity of presentation and its wide selection of stars. No correction to altitudes is required for precession, as in H.O. 218.

Accuracy will not be as great as that obtained from H.O. 214, especially when the latter tables are used with the *Nautical Almanac,* but navigators generally will find that H.O. 249 is entirely satisfactory in this respect, both as to fixes obtained and as an azimuth table.

The *American Air Almanac,* now used universally by American aviators and by many marine navigators, began with the January-April issue of 1941. Since its appearance there has been almost continuous agitation for revision of the *Nautical Almanac.* A new design patterned somewhat after the *Air Almanac* is available for 1950. Under the arrangement in the new almanac the Greenwich hour angle and declination can always be found with two openings of the book. The altitude corrections have also been simplified. Interpolation is not required and parallax and semidiameter of the moon need not be found. The time necessary for working out sights will probably be cut in half. It may have some deflationary effect upon the ego of the navigator, who has always been regarded as somewhat of a savant aboard ship. With the advent of the new type almanac and the use of H.O. 211, H.O. 214, etc., for the solution of the astronomical triangle, the work of the navigator is simplified to such an extent that it can more easily be mastered.

NAVIGATION PRACTICE—DAY'S WORK

1. Departure and continuous dead reckoning plot of position.

2. Star observations during morning twilight, for a fix from two or more lines of position.

3. Sun observation on or near prime vertical for longitude, or at any time for a line of position.

4. Azimuth observation of the sun to find compass error, either in conjunction with the sun sight or as a separate time azimuth observation.

5. Computation of the interval to noon, watch time of local apparent noon, and constants for meridian or ex-meridian sights.

6. Meridian or ex-meridian observation of the sun for noon latitude line. Running fix or cross with Venus line for noon fix. Determine the day's run, the set and drift of current since the previous noon.

7. At least one sun observation during the afternoon for use in case stars are not available at twilight.

8. Azimuth observation of sun for compass error.

9. Star observations during twilight for a fix from two or more lines of position.

IDENTIFICATION OF THE CELESTIAL BODIES

Most navigators have developed their own special method for the identification of the stars and planets in the course of their night watches at sea. The three charts included here show the star groups and their relationship to each other about the two poles and the equinoctial. It is suggested that the navigator trace out his own groups, using as a basis:

1. Ursa Major for stars of high northern declination.

2. Orion for stars in the region of the equinoctial.

3. The Southern Cross for stars of high southern declination.

Others may be traced out by prolonging a line (straight or curved) passing through two known stars, until at a certain distance it passes through a required star, and by the geometrical figures which in many cases three or more bright stars form with each other.

As to the planets, Venus, Jupiter and Mars are brighter than any stars, and do not twinkle like the stars but show a steady light. Venus is never visible more than three hours and eight minutes before sunrise or after sunset. Mars may be distinguished from the other two by its reddish tinge.

The bulky Rude Star Finder which was popular for many years has given way to the handy, compact, round H.O. 2102-D, andRabl's Star Finder now generally used for locating stars.

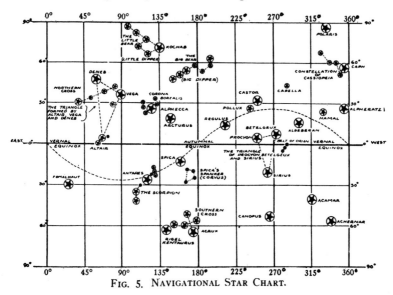

FIG. 5. NAVIGATIONAL STAR CHART.

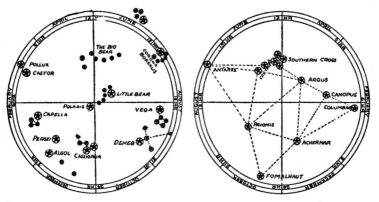

FIG. 6. NAVIGATIONAL STAR CHARTS (for high northern and high southern declinations).

Chapter 7

METEOROLOGY

For introduction we include below three excerpts (on wind circulation, weather forecasting, and air-mass analysis) from "The Weather," an article originally published in the magazine *Fortune*. (Reprinted by permission. Copyright 1940 *Time* Inc. [*Fortune* April 1940]).

Wind Circulation in General. "If the earth were a motionless sphere, the atmosphere would simply follow a perpetual cycle from equator to pole at high altitudes, and back again along the surface. But the earth's topography and rotation cause the disturbances that are weather. . . .

"Equatorial air, rising high out of the **doldrums,** is deflected northeast by the earth's rotation. This strong flow of upper air westerlies is the **antitrade wind.** Cooled, most of it descends at about 30° N. Lat. into a high-pressure belt called the **horse latitudes,** where the stream diverges. Part returns along the surface to the equator as northeast trade winds; the rest continues on course at all altitudes as the **prevailing westerlies** (actually southwesterly) of the middle latitudes. The upper levels of these winds generally travel to the pole, while surface winds blow to about 60° N. Lat. where they encounter a **front of polar air** and bend aloft. Depending on various circumstances, this westerly stream may either double back aloft to the horse latitudes, or climb the polar front and join the upper flow to the pole. Air descended over the pole is deflected by rotation westward—a northeasterly current that meets the prevailing westerlies at the polar front, and there tends to pile up. The only way it can equalize the constant inflow of tropical air from above is to push its frontal barrier south; and this it does when it has built up to a sufficient mass. The break usually occurs at the point of a bulging wave in the front, each wave generating a cyclonic storm. Fully developed, it draws the polar air far to the south, disrupting the normal flow of westerlies, producing cold waves and violent storms in the middle latitudes. Just such a condition was involved in the paralyzing blizzard of February 14 [1940] in the eastern states. . . . "

(**Note:** It is the Master's duty to transmit information regarding tropical storms encountered, ice, derelicts, and other direct dangers to navigation.)

ANALYSIS OF A WEATHER MAP*

Sample Forecast Based on the Chart, (Fig. 1). "A broad current of continental polar air (*cP*) has advanced far southward in the middle section of the country, and is also working rapidly down the North

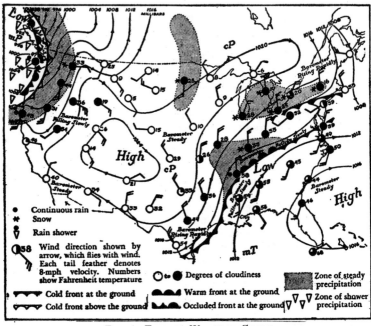

FIG. 1. TYPICAL WEATHER CHART.
(Copyright 1940 *Time* Inc. [*Fortune* April 1940])

Atlantic coast. At the same time, a stream of moist, maritime tropical air (*mT*) from the Gulf of Mexico is spreading northeastward over the Gulf states. The thing to watch is the storm developing over western Tennessee, where the wavelike deformation occurs in the front between the two air masses. Note the zones of precipitation between Arkansas and New York, caused by the moist, warm air flowing up over the cold. The incipient Tennessee storm development must move northeastward and eastward with the direction of movement of the tropical mass. Hence, precipitation is a certainty for the coastal section from Chesapeake Bay northward. But will it be rain or snow, and how much? It's well above 32° at New York City, but the wind directions and rising barometer in New England show that very cold air from Canada is pushing southward. Therefore—snow. How much? That again depends

* This map, Fig. 1, is for the morning of Feb. 13, 1940, the day before the blizzard just mentioned. The map and the accompanying analysis were prepared by Professor Gardner Emmons of New York University.

on what the Tennessee storm does. Either it will not increase much in intensity and will move east rapidly, or it will rapidly intensify and move east slowly. (That is a general rule about storms.) The first alternative means light precipitation of brief duration; the second means a long, heavy snowfall. Now the falling barometers north and south of Tennessee—especially in conjunction with the rising barometer in Texas—indicate that the storm will intensify at a high rate. Another pointer is the steady barometer around the Georgia coast, contrasted with the falling barometer south of Tennessee. This indicates increasing southerly winds from the Gulf, which in turn mean a more intense overrunning of the polar air by tropical air. That is a sure sign of increasingly heavy precipitation—snow in this case—north of the front. So the only logical forecast for New York City and surrounding territory calls for heavy snow and colder during the next 48 hours.''

AIR-MASS ANALYSIS

"Air-mass analysis, which most laymen have heard of as the 'polar-front theory,' is a method of studying the atmosphere as a three-dimensional body, and evaluating surface conditions simply as manifestations of conditions in the upper air. One meteorologist likes to say that air-mass analysis is to old-style forecasting as navy navigation is to a Gloucester fisherman's wind sniffing. The analogy stands up as more than a lecture-platform bromide, for the parallels are striking. The old-line forecaster, like the fisherman, works with limited information and a certain amount of native shrewdness and weather wisdom; and when he misses, blames his luck. The air-mass analyst requires a profusion of data on the atmosphere high above the earth and far afield. When he misses, he blames insufficient data.

"The new concept was first rationalized about 20 years ago by an extraordinary group of Norwegian physicists led by Vilhelm Bjerknes and his son Jakob. This Bjerknes school subordinated the familiar 'highs' and 'lows' of the weather map to the role of secondary symptoms, and identified in the atmosphere specific *air masses* like towering currents. These masses are said to 'originate'—meaning they have had long sojourns—in either tropical or polar regions. and each has its peculiar characteristics of temperature, density, humidity, and dust content, depending on its source. Polar masses are cold, and generally dry in comparison with the warm masses from the tropics. The masses are sometimes pictured as great gaseous tongues, up to 30,000 feet thick, twisting, curling, licking sidewise and up and down over the earth. When a cold, dry tongue from the North meets a moist tongue from the tropics, the surface of contact is called a front, and it is along the fronts that the principal weather disturbances occur.

"There are cold fronts and warm fronts. The cold front, which is the commonest locale of spectacular weather, occurs when an advancing cold mass wedges itself under a warm mass, forcing the warm air to ride up over the top of the cold mass, where it loses its moisture. This front corresponds to the squall line, or trough of the low. When warm air advances to overtake a retreating mass of cold air, the contact surface is called a warm front, but the resulting weather is about the same.

"An air mass may 'originate' over any ocean or continent, and some meteorologists speak punctiliously of 'polar Pacific,' 'tropical Atlantic,' etc. But the Norwegians, holding that the exact source is immaterial, are interested in only two categories—polar and tropical—and two main subdivisions—maritime and continental. The only other significant characteristic is the change the mass may undergo en route, and this the Norwegians classify as 'cold' or 'warm'—which does not mean what it seems to mean. 'Cold' means that the mass, whatever its temperature, is colder than the surface over which it flows. 'Warm' means the opposite. Those attributes are important. A warm mass is cooled from below and becomes stable—i.e., resistant to changes in elevation. It is usually marked by poor visibility, stratus clouds, or fog. A cold mass, heated from below, becomes unstable, ascends in cumulo-nimbus clouds producing showers or thunderstorms.

"In North America, continental polar air can have only one general source—i.e., upper Canada or Alaska. At its source it is markedly stable, since the surface is the coldest and driest to be found anywhere. Moving southward over snow- or ice-covered territory, continental polar changes little; but on crossing open water, the Great Lakes for example, it absorbs moisture, assumes the characteristics of a cold mass, and becomes the source of some of the worst weather in the East.

"Maritime polar masses rarely enter the U. S. from the Atlantic, since the route westerly from Labrador is counter to the normal circulation. When they do—generally in the warm half of the year—they reach the Southeast in a highly unstable condition and give the seaboard some of its worst flying weather. Most of the maritime polar air enters at the Pacific Northwest and spills heavy rains and snows over the Sierra, arrives east of the Rockies dry, stable, and warm. In southeastern U. S. it may become moist again from sojourning over the Gulf, or picking up rainwater from an over-running tropical mass. In winter maritime polar often builds up a high that remains stationary over the Great Basin, then may flow back through the mountains near San Francisco and Los Angeles as a hot, dry easterly. In summer it brings fog to the Pacific Coast, arrives inland dry to steal moisture from vegetation.

ATLANTIC OCEAN

AVERAGE LIMITS OF THE TRADE WINDS					
		Jan. Feb. Mar.	Apr. May June	July Aug. Sept.	Oct. Nov. Dec.
NE Trade	Northern Boundary	Oct. to Apr.—A line drawn from the Canaries to Havana Apr. to Oct.—A line drawn from Madeira to Havana			
	Southern Boundary	2° N	4° N	11° N	6° N
Breadth of variable belt		120 miles	180 miles	500 miles	200 miles

ATLANTIC OCEAN (*Continued*)

		Jan. Feb. Mar.	Apr. May June	July Aug. Sept.	Oct. Nov. Dec.
SE Trade	Northern Boundary	the equator	1° N	3° N	3° N
	Southern Boundary	A line drawn from the Cape of Good Hope to the Isles of Trinidad and Martin Vaz			
Rainy Seasons		Guiana and North Brazil Africa south of the equator	Guiana, Brazil, and Africa (north of the equator) in May and June; Caribbean Sea in June	West Indies and Africa (north of the equator) Brazil in July and Aug.	Guiana in Dec. Africa (south of the equator) in Nov. and Dec.
Cyclones				West Indies	West Indies in Oct. and occasionally Nov.

PACIFIC OCEAN

AVERAGE LIMITS OF THE TRADE WINDS EASTWARD OF THE MERIDIAN OF 160° W.

		Jan. Feb. Mar.	Apr. May June	July Aug. Sept.	Oct. Nov. Dec.
NE Trade	Northern Boundary	28° N	29° N	31° N	28° N
	Southern Boundary	8° N	10° N	12° N	11° N
Breadth of variable belt		300 miles	450 miles	180 miles	300 miles
SE Trade	Northern Boundary	4° N	4° N	9° N	6° N
	Southern Boundary	A line drawn from Juan Fernandez through Easter Is. and the Marquesas	A line drawn from St. Felix Is. toward Tahiti as far as the meridian of 135° W	A line drawn from St. Felix Is. to Tahiti	A line drawn from Valparaiso towards Tahiti as far as the meridian of 135° W
Rainy Seasons		Hawaiian Is. and coast of Ecuador South Pacific Islands	Mexico and Central America in June	Mexico and Central America	Hawaiian Is. and coast of Ecuador in Dec. South Pacific Islands in Nov.–Dec.
Cyclones				Mexico in Aug.–Sept.	Mexico in Oct.

WINDS IN THE INDIAN OCEAN

ARABIAN SEA	BAY OF BENGAL	CHINA SEA
November to March NE Monsoon Moderate and fine	November to March NE Monsoon Moderate and fine	October to April NE Monsoon Blows fresh in Nov., Dec., and Jan.
May to September SW Monsoon Blowing fiercely, with bad weather in June and July; moderating in August	May to September SW Monsoon Blowing fresh, with bad weather in June and July; moderating in August	May to September SW Monsoon Moderate, with rain, strongest in June, July and August
Cyclones in April and May; and from Oct. to Dec.		Typhoons from July to Nov.

EAST COAST OF AFRICA AND THE MOZAMBIQUE CHANNEL

December to March northerly winds	May to November southerly winds

BETWEEN THE EQUATOR AND THE PARALLEL OF 10° S

November to March NW or Middle, Monsoon Light, with squalls, rains and frequent calms. From the Seychelles to the African coast the NE Monsoon prevails	May to September SE Trade Light with frequent calms northward of the parallel of 4° S, and veering to the SW between the meridian of 80° E, and the coast of Sumatra

BETWEEN THE PARALLELS OF 10° AND 27° S

Constant SE Trade—Cyclones from December to April

"Continental tropical occurs only in summer, a hot, parching blast fanning north and east from over Mexico and southwestern U. S. Maritime tropical masses, from whatever ocean, are the wettest of all reaching the U. S., accounting for the heaviest precipitation on both coasts. In summer, if abruptly hiked up over a cold front, they produce heavy line squalls, thunderstorms, even tornadoes. In winter, meeting a cold mass from the North, they give rain or snow. Impeding radiation with their high moisture content, they keep their territories stickily humid."

LOCAL WINDS

NAME	LOCALITY	SEASON	NATURE
Harmattan	C. Verde to C. Lopez	Dec. Jan. Feb.	Very dry from shore
Tornado	W. C. Africa	Mar. to June, Oct. and Nov.	Violent squall from shore, followed by heavy rain
South-Easter	C. of Good Hope	Oct. to April	
North-Easter	C. of Good Hope	May to Sept.	
Westerly	N.C. Africa	Winter	
Easterly	N.C. Africa	Summer	
Sirocco (SE)	Malta and Italy	Summer	Hot and damp
Gregale (NE)	Malta	Winter	
Bora (NE)	Adriatic	Winter	
Etesian (N'ly)	Greek Archipelago	Summer	
Mistral (NW)	Gulf of Lyons		The prevailing wind
Norther	Gulf of Mexico	Sept. to March	
Pampero	Rio de la Plata	July to Sept.	
Easterly	Cape Horn	April to July	
Williwaws	Magellan Straits		Very heavy squalls where high mountains
Norther	Bay of Panama	Dec. to April	
NNW	Red Sea (South)	June to Sept.	
SSE	Red Sea (South)	Oct. to May	
Shamal (NW)	Persian Gulf	General	
Kaus (SE)	Persian Gulf	Dec. to April	Alternate with Shamal
Belot (N to NNW)	Arabia S.C.	Dec. to March	Strong land wind
Elephante	Malabar Coast	Sept. and Oct.	South to SE gale, which closes the SW monsoon
Fort Dauphin (ENE)	Madagascar	General	
Southerly buster	Australian South	Summer	Strong sea breeze which replaces the hot shore wind
Brickfielder (N)	Australian South	Summer	

FOG

Although the substance of fog is the same as cloud, the processes of cloud and fog formation are different. Clouds form chiefly because air rises, expands and cools. Fog results from the cooling of air which remains at the earth's surface. (1) Warm air flowing over cold land or water surfaces; (2) Radiation or ground fog from heat stored by day and radiated at night; (3) Air changing in latitude.

Two other fog processes may exist when the following conditions prevail. (1) Very cold stable air overlies a warm water surface or warm land surface (*vapor*); (2) Rain falls through cool air of high humidity. In this case, the rain both chills and increases the water vapor content of the air through which it is falling. This type of fog is quite common in connection with the storms of the middle latitudes over both water and land surfaces.

British Isles. All seasons, most frequently in the Channel during January and June.

W. C. Africa N of the Equator. November to May.

W. C. Africa S of the Equator. June to August.

N. America, West Coast. Very frequent in summer.

Banks of Newfoundland. All seasons—most frequent in June and July.

Coast of China. January to April.

Japan. April to June.

ICE

North Atlantic. Greatest limit of field ice in March, extending from Newfoundland south to 42° N and east to 44° W, disappearing by August. Icebergs may be met with between April and July North and West of 40° N and 40° W, and sometimes to the east and south of this. Still, some icebergs may remain N and W of 41°N and 38°W in August.

Southern Hemisphere. Greatest number of icebergs in the summer season, November, December and January, and least in June and July. More in March and April than in September and October. During February, in the South Atlantic, the limit of the iceberg region extends as far N as 39° S, while in August they are rarely found northward of the 45th parallel.

Icebergs should be passed to windward to avoid loose ice floating to leeward.

Symbol	Name	Description
 ⌂	Aurora	Popularly called "Northern Lights."
⦶	Corona, Solar	Luminous glow around the sun.
∪	Corona, Lunar	Luminous glow around the moon.
⌓	Dew	Condensed water on grass, stones, etc.
❜	Drizzle	Precipitation of small water droplets.
Ƨ	Dust	Presence of dust in the air.
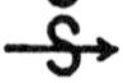 Ƨ→	Duststorm	Dense, blowing dust.
≡	Fog	Moderate, thick, or dense fog. Visibility less than ⅝ mile. Thick fog⁺, dense fog⁺⁺, moderate fog—no sign.
=	Fog, light	Fog with visibility greater than ⅝ mile.
≢	Ice fog	Fog of ice crystals or spicules.
 ⌒•	Fog bow	Arc sometimes seen in fog opposite sun, colorless.
⌊_⌋	Frost	Ice crystals deposited on grass, stones, etc. when temperatures are 32° or lower.
∽	Glaze	Ice layers formed from super-cooled rain or drizzle.
 ⊖⊖	Haze, damp	Like a very thin fog, visibility usually over 1¼ miles.
 ∞	Haze, dry	Very fine dust in air; air seems smoky or opalescent.
▲	Hail	Ice balls, usually fall in thunderstorms.
△	Hail, small	Small ice balls, usually appear glazed.
⊍	Halo, lunar	Luminous ring around the moon.
⊕	Halo, solar	Luminous ring around the sun.
↔	Ice crystals	Fine needles of ice floating in the air.
 <	Lightning, Distant	Lightning in the distance, without audible thunder.
●	Rain	Precipitation of fairly large water drops.
✳	Rain and Snow, Mixed	Precipitation of rain and snow together.
⌒	Rainbow	Colored arc seen opposite the sun in rain.

FIG. 2. SYMBOLS FOR SHOWING THE STATE OF THE WEATHER.

	Rime, Hard	Opaque masses of ice built up on objects.
	Rime, Soft	Ice crystals built up on objects.
	Sandstorm	Dense, blowing sand.
	Showers	Irregular falls of hydrometeors, rain, hail, etc.
	Sleet	Precipitation of ice pellets or frozen rain drops.
	Smoke	Particles of foreign matter in the air from combustion.
	Snow	Precipitation of hexagonal crystals or flakes.
	Snow, blowing	Snow driven up in the air by the wind.
	Snow drifting	Snow driven along the ground by the wind.
	Snow grains	Flattened or oblong grains of snow.
	Snow pellets	Small, round, crisp pellets of snow.
	Thunderstorm	Thunder and lightning in the vicinity.
	Distant Thunderstorm	Thunder and lightning in the distance.
	Visibility, Exceptional	Unusual clearness and transparency of air.

FIG. 2, *continued.*

SYNOPTIC CHARTS

Within the last decade or so, collections of synoptic weather observations have been made readily available to seamen through the medium of scheduled radio broadcasts. These observations, transmitted in code, make it possible for the mariner to prepare his own weather charts. After he has decoded the messages and plotted the data, he is in a position to analyze the chart and to make his own weather prediction. This practice is most advantageous when the ship is in midocean, or at any rate, outside the area covered by official Government weather forecasts.

Outline charts or base maps specially designed for drawing weather maps at sea are furnished by the United States Weather Bureau and some other meteorological services to mariners who cooperate in furnishing weather observations by radio or mail. If suitable base maps are not available they may be improvised; a sheet of transparent paper is placed over an appropriate small scale map and the continental outlines are sketched in; the weather observations are then entered, the paper is removed and the map is completed by drawing the lines of equal pressure—the isobars.

A plan which requires less labor is as follows: A suitable map is covered with tracing paper fastened down with pins or thumb tacks. The observations are entered and the map is completed. The tracing paper is left in place with the meteorological data thereon until time to draw another map. After removal, the tracing paper may be filed away. By this method it is not necessary to sketch in the continental outlines. If any particular map is consulted at a later date it may be placed in position over the base map if the reference points have been marked on the tracing.

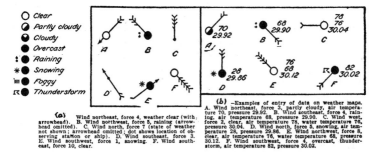

Clear
Partly cloudy
Cloudy
Overcast
Raining
Snowing
Foggy
Thunderstorm

(a) Wind northeast, force 4, weather clear (with arrowhead). B. Wind northwest, force 5, raining (arrowhead omitted). C. Wind north, force 7 (state of weather not shown; arrowhead omitted; dot shows location of observing station or ship). D. Wind southeast, force 3. E. Wind southwest, force 1, snowing. F. Wind southeast, force 10, clear.

(b) —Examples of entry of data on weather maps. A. Wind northeast, force 3, partly cloudy, air temperature 70, pressure 29.92. B. Wind southeast, force 4, raining, air temperature 68, pressure 29.90. C. Wind west, force 2, clear, air temperature 78, water temperature 76, pressure 30.04. D. Wind north, force 5, snowing, air temperature 28, pressure 29.86. E. Wind northwest, force 8, clear, air temperature 76, water temperature 68, pressure 30.12. F. Wind southwest, force 4, overcast, thunderstorm, air temperature 82, pressure 30.02.

Fig. 3. Methods of Entering Data on Weather Maps.

The direction of the wind is shown by an arrow drawn through the station circle. The arrow flies with the wind; that is, the head of the arrow points in the direction *toward* which the wind is blowing.

The force of the wind is shown by barbs (or feathers) on the shaft of the arrow, the number of feathers being equal to the number for wind force on the Beaufort scale.

If preferred, wind force to half scale may be indicated by full barbs and half barbs. The full barb represents two units of force on the Beaufort scale and the half barb one unit; for example, two full barbs and one half barb together indicate force 5. If this practice is adopted, the barbs (or feathers) are all drawn on the same side of the arrow shaft, which is the right side when facing in the direction from which the wind is blowing. The use of full- and half-length barbs (Beaufort half scale) was adopted by the United States Weather Bureau, Effective January 1, 1937.

Examples of different methods of making entries of wind direction and force, with and without station circles and arrowheads, are shown in Fig. 3 (a).

Various methods of entry (arrowheads, state of weather, etc.) are shown in order that the shipmaster may adopt practices suited to his needs. Whatever practice is adopted should preferably be uniformly used on all his maps.

After the entry of wind direction and force has been made, with state of weather when required, figures are placed in a convenient location at the right of the station position to show barometric pressure at time of observation and, if desirable, temperatures of air and water. In the International Code for ships' weather reports, barometric pressure is given in millibars with the first figure (or figures) omitted. Thus, 998 millibars is coded as 98; 1,021 millibars is given as 21.

Temperatures in reports from land stations and from ships cooperating with the Weather Bureau are given in Fahrenheit degrees. The supplemental groups of the code also contain a figure for the difference between air and water temperatures, from which the water temperature may be computed approximately.

If both air temperature and pressure are entered, the figures for temperature are placed above those for pressure. If both air and water temperatures are entered, the first figure is air temperature, the middle figure water temperature, and the last figure barometric pressure. In entering barometric pressure the inches may be omitted and two figures used for hundredths of an inch.

Examples of complete entries, including temperature and pressure, are given in Fig. 3(*b*).

FORMS OF ISOBARS

A number of types of isobars (*see* Fig. 4) are recognized, following the classification made by Abercromby, a noted British meteorologist.

1. The Secondary Low. A small circular depression or a loop in an isobar, accompanied by a cyclonic wind circulation of relatively small extent within, or subsidiary to, the larger, parent cyclone. They usually reach their greatest development if they form on the equatorial side of the principal cyclone center. Some of them attain marked intensity and, in later stages, may exceed the parent cyclone in intensity and extent.

2. The V-Shaped Low. A cyclonic system with isobars taking on the shape of the letter *V* on one side, with the *V* pointing toward the equator. A rapidly veering wind accompanies the passage of the trough of the *V*. In front of the trough there is likely to be much cloud and rain; squalls usually accompany its passage; behind the trough the weather generally clears.

3. Wedge-Shaped Isobars. The poleward protuberance of the isobars of the anticyclone to form an inverted *V*, generally with Lows to the east and west. Wedges are nearly always regions of fine weather, which is of short duration because of the influence of the Low which follows it (Fig. 4).

4. The Saddle or Col. A region between two Highs and two Lows. It is characterized by relatively low pressure with calms or light wind movement in the middle of the region. Conditions in the saddle are favorable for cloudiness and unsettled weather, sometimes with fogs or thunderstorms.

5. Straight or Parallel Isobars. It is frequently the case that the isobars of the outer margin of a Low appear on the weather map as a group of straight or slightly curved lines between the Low and the adjacent High. The character of the weather that prevails over the region of parallel isobars varies with the season and the location of the center of low pressure. The type of weather is dependent to a great extent on the direction in which the isobars run.

The most important single operation in the analysis of ocean weather charts for purposes of weather prediction is the drawing of the isobars for sea level. These lines are commonly thought of as representing nothing more than the distribution of atmospheric pressure at sea level, but in reality they also show something else of more fundamental interest, namely, the character of the horizontal motion of the lowest layers of the atmosphere. This motion, of course, is what we call "wind." The correct drawing of isobars is, therefore, essential to a correct interpretation of the chart and to an accurate forecast of future weather.

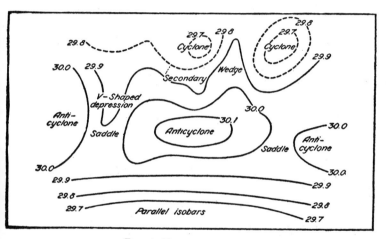

FIG. 4. TYPES OF ISOBARS.

Elementary Rules for Drawing Isobars

It is extremely helpful to remember that isobars are analogous to the depth curves appearing on navigation charts. Just as the 100-fathom curve represents the intersection of the ocean bottom with an imaginary horizontal plane surface 100 fathoms below sea level, so does an isobar on an ocean weather chart represent the intersection of a curved surface of constant atmospheric pressure with the sea-level plane.

The fundamental principle involved in the drawing of isobars may be stated simply as follows: *Every isobar must form a closed curve.* In actual practice it is not possible to make every isobar return to its starting point, because weather charts cover only limited areas, but if isobars are drawn on a globe, it will be seen that they must obey this principle. Therefore, in the analysis of a weather chart it is incorrect to leave "loose ends" of isobars in the *middle* of the chart. It is permissible to terminate an isobar only at the margin or at the edge of the area for which observations are available.

Rule 1. *Proceed with the pencil in such a way as to keep all points where the pressure is higher than the value assigned to the isobar on the same side relative to the direction in which the line is being extended.* It will be extremely helpful in this connection to apply the law of Buys Ballot, which states in effect that the observer, standing with his face to the wind in the Northern Hemisphere, will have lower pressure on his right and higher pressure on his left. From this law it is possible to formulate Rule 2.

Rule 2. *If, on Northern Hemisphere charts, the isobar is traced into the wind* (as shown by the plotted observations of wind direction), *the line must be kept to the right of all points where the pressure is higher than the assigned value and to the left of all points where the pressure is lower. If the isobar is traced down the wind, the line must be kept to the left of all points where the pressure is higher than the assigned value and to the right of all points where the pressure is lower.* Caution should be advised, however, against applying Rule 2 too lavishly over land areas, because the wind directions observed locally at certain stations may not conform to the general pattern of large-scale atmospheric motion, as represented by pressure distribution. This is especially true when the winds are light.

Isobaric Analysis

If barometric observations were infinitely numerous and absolutely accurate, there would be no need for applying analytical methods. One would arrive at the correct picture solely through the use of the elementary technique of drawing isobars. Unfortunately the number of observations is never entirely adequate, nor are the reports completely accurate. The purpose of applying analytical methods is, therefore, to avoid errors and illogical constructions which would result if the isobars were drawn exactly to fit every barometer report.

If one is to render these errors as ineffective as possible, it will be helpful to apply certain principles when drawing isobars on an ocean weather chart.

(1) *Simple isobaric patterns are much more probable than complicated ones, especially when the wind circulation is strong.*

This principle is based primarily on the facts of experience, but it is not unreasonable to expect that small-scale disturbances or eddies in the atmosphere will tend to be absorbed or obscured by large-scale disturbances, if the latter are vigorous. One must, therefore, try to "fair" the isobars and eliminate irregularities which do not show any systematic arrangement. However, if any apparent irregularities do show a systematic arrangement, they should be regarded as real. It is important that they be not overlooked, as they may later develop into major disturbances.

(2) *The isobars should be drawn in such a way as to be in the best possible agreement with the available barometer reports on the one hand and the law of Buys Ballot on the other.*

The relation between wind direction and the direction of the isobars is particularly useful in the analysis of ocean weather charts. From

Buys Ballot's law it follows that the wind blows more or less along the isobars, with relatively low pressure to the left of its course. Because of friction and other forces the true wind at the earth's surface does not blow absolutely parallel to the isobars but is deflected slightly toward the side of lower pressure. Over the ocean the angle between the isobars and the wind direction is usually about 15°.

It will often be helpful to make use of this fact, because **wind direction** reports (at sea) are more reliable than barometer reports. Its practical application takes expression in the following rule: *If it is in no way possible to adjust an isobar to fit both a barometer report and the wind circulation in a reasonable manner, the barometer report should be regarded as incorrect.* An isobar should never be drawn in such a direction with reference to the wind that the wind blows across it from lower to higher pressure.

TABLE 1. WIND FORCE AND DISTANCE BETWEEN ISOBARS OVER OCEAN

OBSERVED WIND FORCE (BEAUFORT)	APPROXIMATE DISTANCE (IN NAUTICAL MILES) BETWEEN ISOBARS FOR EVERY 0.10 INCH			
	30°	40°	50°	60°
4................	230	180	150	135
5................	170	135	110	95
6................	130	100	85	75
7................	105	80	70	60
8................	85	65	55	50
9................	70	55	45	40
10...............	60	45	40	35
11................	55	40	35	30
12................	50 or less	38 or less	32 or less	28 or less

(3) *The isobars should be spaced in such fashion that they shall be in agreement with the observed wind velocities.*

Just as crowded contour lines on a topographic map or chart of soundings represent a steep slope, so do crowded isobars on a weather chart indicate steeply sloping isobaric surfaces. Similarly the speed of the wind is directly proportional to the slope of the isobaric surfaces, just as the speed of the water in a brook is directly proportional to the slope of the hill down which it runs. It follows, then, that the wind velocity is inversely proportional to the distance between isobars.

Table 1 is based on this relation. It shows what the approximate distances are between adjoining isobars for different forces of wind as observed on board ship in different latitudes. The table is computed for isobars drawn for every 0.10 inch. If isobars are drawn for every 5 millibars, the distances should be multiplied by 3/2. It should be stated also that the values apply to isobars which are straight or have only a very small curvature. For isobars near the center of a round *cyclone* the distances corresponding to the stated forces of wind will be considerably *smaller* than those given in Table 1; for isobars near the center of a round *anticyclone* they will be considerably *greater*.

(4) *One should commence drawing isobars where the true pattern is most easily seen. The most difficult parts of the chart should be left until the last.*

From this principle it follows that one should start where the observations are most numerous. If the chart includes coastal areas the isobars should be drawn from the land out over the ocean.

Isobars in regions of high pressure are usually more symmetrical than those in regions of low pressure. Therefore, when observations are no more numerous in one part of the chart as compared with another, it is a good idea to draw the isobars first where the pressure is seen to be relatively high.

(5) *The isobars on the completed chart must be in logical sequence with preceding charts (assuming that the preceding charts have been drawn correctly).*

The successive positions of the Highs and Lows on a series of correctly drawn charts are observed to be free from unsystematic oscillations. This is to be expected because Highs and Lows simply represent large-scale eddies in the general circulation of the atmosphere. Because of their size they possess considerable inertia, and consequently they cannot be quickly set in rapid motion or stopped abruptly. Therefore, a sudden speeding-up during a given 12-hour period followed by an equally sudden slowing-down in the next 12 hours is a highly improbable occurrence. If the isobars on consecutive charts are drawn so as to produce such a result, it is quite certain that the paucity of observations (or a failure to obey principles 2 and 3) has led to an incorrect analysis.

Similarly, abrupt and erratic fluctuations in the direction of movement are illogical. For example, if the distances traveled by a center in successive 12-hour intervals are indicated as being 300 miles toward the southeast on one chart, 600 miles toward the north-northeast on the next chart, and 300 miles toward the east-southeast on the third, it is quite certain that a mistake has been made in the analysis of one or more charts.

Often an apparent irregularity in the progression of a cyclonic center is due to the rapid development of a new cyclone in the southwestern quadrant of the system. This "secondary" may quickly become so much more conspicuous than the original center that it may be regarded mistakenly as the same center which appeared on previous maps. If it is so considered, the chart will not be in logical sequence with the preceding charts. The identity of the original center should be recognized and its position indicated until it is entirely absorbed by the new and more vigorous cyclone.

(6) *When an isobar intersects a line along which there is an abrupt clockwise turning of the wind* (in the Northern Hemisphere), *it must be drawn so as to produce an angle, or corner. The vertex of the angle must point toward higher pressure.*

If one is careful to make the isobars conform strictly to the law of Buys Ballot, one notices that frequently it is necessary to curve them so abruptly that a sharp angle or corner is produced. At first glance this may seem to be an illogical result, but such is not the case. Every sailor knows, for example, how suddenly the wind can *veer* (in the Northern Hemisphere) from SW to NW. The shift is often accomplished in less than a minute. In terms of the law of Buys Ballot this means that there is a 90° change in the direction of the isobars in a distance of less than 1 mile. It is clear, then, that the scale of the ordinary weather chart demands that such a pronounced curvature be represented by an angle in the isobars.

It is important to remember that the characteristic feature of wind-shift lines, or line-squalls, is a *clockwise* shift of the wind in the Northern Hemisphere (*counterclockwise* in the Southern Hemisphere). This means that the corners in the isobars point toward higher pressure. On the other hand, it is not correct under any circumstances to draw angular isobars with the corners pointing *away* from higher pressure. The mathematical and physical proof of this need not be outlined here. It is sufficient to point out that a counterclockwise turning or "backing" of the wind in the Northern Hemisphere is always observed to occur more or less gradually, at least never with the rapidity of the clockwise turning characteristic of a line-squall. These considerations lead to the following generalization: *Although the isobars may be either rounded or V-shaped through the axis of a trough of low pressure, they must always be rounded through the axis of a wedge of high pressure.*

Importance of Correct Isobaric Analysis in Weather Forecasting

When the observations show that a sharp shift of wind occurs along the axis of a trough of low pressure, it is most necessary to represent this fact in the analysis, because of its importance for the weather forecast. Though the phenomenon of the wind-shift line has been recognized for years, its direct and important relation to the structure and development of extra-tropical cyclones has not received full emphasis until comparatively recent times.

In modern meteorological parlance, wind-shift lines are termed **fronts.** Three types of fronts are recognized—**warm** fronts, **cold** fronts, and **occluded** fronts.

It is sufficient to point out here that the meteorological elements of especial interest to the navigator undergo rapid changes with the passage of a front over the ship. Among these elements may be listed the wind direction, wind velocity, character of the sky, and horizontal visibility.

The approach of a well-defined warm front in middle and high latitudes is characteristically indicated by solidly overcast skies with more or less steady rain and diminishing visibility. When the front arrives, the wind *veers* (in the Northern Hemisphere) rather suddenly, the rain stops or diminishes to a fine drizzle, but the sky remains overcast with low clouds, and the visibility becomes very poor.

The conditions following the passage of a warm front are succeeded, sooner or later, by the passage of a cold front. When this occurs heavy rain begins and the wind veers very suddenly (more suddenly than in the case of the warm front passage). The rain does not continue uninterruptedly for any appreciable length of time, however. The visibility improves rapidly, and the sky condition soon changes from a dull overcast to scattered shower clouds separated by clear intervals.

The conditions preceding the arrival of an occluded front are, in general, like those prevailing during the approach of a warm front, while the weather after its passage is typical of the conditions following a cold front.

The reason for the pronounced changes of weather that accompany the passage of a front is that the air currents on opposite sides of the front have their sources in more or less widely separated geographical areas, and hence possess contrasting meteorological properties.

Obviously all these conditions indicate why it is both important and useful to study the wind and pressure fields carefully when drawing isobars. This applies especially to oceanic areas where weather reports from ships are usually widely scattered. If the isobars are drawn in more or less circular fashion around a cyclone, the distribution of the weather elements does not stand out. In this case it would be difficult for the person who attempts to interpret the weather chart to decide when rain would cease or the sky would clear at some stated position, or at what hour a pronounced change of wind might be expected. The proper delineation of the structure of a "low" through recognition of fronts affords a tangible basis for a detailed forecast.

The movement of a cold front depends upon the speed at which the air on the *left hand* side of the cold front (as one faces in the direction of low pressure) is *advancing* in the direction perpendicular to the front. The movement of a warm front depends upon the speed at which the air on the *right hand* side of the warm front (as one faces in the direction of low pressure) is *retreating* in the direction perpendicular to the front. It is a simple matter to compute from wind observations alone the rate at which a front is moving. Often, however, there are no weather reports from vessels in the immediate vicinity of a front. In this case the relationship of distance-between-isobars to wind velocity may be used to advantage; therefore, it is important that the isobars be correctly spaced.

From this discussion it can be seen that, in general, a front remains stationary or moves very slowly when the winds on the cold side of the front are blowing parallel to it, or nearly so. It is useful to remember that the speed of the front is directly proportional to the numbers of isobars which intersect a given portion of its length. This is another reason for the necessity of drawing the isobars correctly. If the isobars are crowded at one portion of a front and widely spaced at another, the latter portion will lag behind and a wave-like deformation of the front will occur. A new cyclone is apt to develop in the region of the deformation.

SUMMARY

The character of the weather and direction of the wind depend entirely on the *shape* of the isobars, while force of wind and intensity of weather depend only on *closeness* of isobars.

1. Simple isobaric patterns are more probable than complicated.

2. Isobars should be in agreement with barometer reports and Buys Ballot's law.

3. Isobars should be in agreement with wind velocities.

4. Commence drawing isobars where pattern is most easily seen.

5. They should be in logical sequence with preceding charts.

6. Where the wind veers suddenly (SW to NW in the Northern Hemisphere) the isobars will produce an angle, the vertex of which must point toward higher pressure.

THE BAROMETER

Weather Indications by the Mercurial Barometer. The barometer rises for northerly winds (winds between NW and NE), for dry or less wet weather, for less wind, or for more than one of these changes, except on a few occasions, when rain, hail or snow, with a strong wind, comes from the North.

The barometer falls for southerly winds (winds between SE and SW), for wet weather, for stronger wind, or for more than one of these changes, except on a few occasions, when moderate wind, with rain or snow, comes from the North.

In the tropics there is little variation of the barometer, except for violent storms or hurricanes, when the mercury falls very low, but quickly returns to its usual state after the storm center has passed.

On some coasts the barometer is differently affected by the wind, according as it blows from the sea or from the land, the mercury rising on the approach of the sea breeze, and falling previous to the setting in of the land breeze.

Weather Indications by the Aneroid Barometer. A rise, with dry air and cold increasing, in summer, indicates wind from the North in northern latitudes, and wind from the south in southern latitudes. If rain has fallen better weather may be expected. A rise, with moist air and a low temperature, indicates both wind and rain from the North in northern latitudes, but from the South in southern latitudes.

A rise, with southerly winds, indicates fine weather in northern latitudes, the conditions being reversed in southern latitudes.

A gradual rise indicates settled weather. A rapid rise indicates unsettled weather.

A steady barometer, with dry and seasonable temperature, indicates a continuance of fine weather.

A fall, with a northerly wind, indicates stormy weather, with rain in summer and snow in winter.

A fall, with increased moisture in the air and the temperature rising, indicates wind and rain from the South.

A fall, with dry air and cold increasing, in winter, indicates snow.

A fall, after very calm and warm weather, indicates rain with squally weather.

A rapid fall indicates stormy weather.

A rapid fall, with westerly winds, indicates stormy weather from the north.

All indications pertaining to the fall of the aneroid apply to northern latitudes; wind directions are reversed in southern latitudes.

Meteorological Information Necessary for Forecasting Weather. Barometer change, humidity change, temperature change, movement of clouds. The distinction between a "high" and a "low" depends not upon the actual height of the barometer, but upon the way in which the wind circulates about the area; or, more accurately upon whether the characteristic pressure is the result of descending or ascending currents, thus:

Low = cyclone = ascending air currents

High = anticyclone = descending air currents

CLOUD FORMS

1. **Cirrus:** detached clouds, delicate and fibrous in appearance, generally white in color. Cirrus appear in the most varied combination of forms, such as tufts, lines drawn across the blue sky, branching feather-like plumes, and are often arranged in bands across the sky. These clouds are very thin, and the sun and the moon can be seen through them. They range in height from 20,000 to 40,000 feet. Cirrus clouds rarely result in rain.

2. **Cirro-cumulus:** patches of white flakes or rounded masses without shadows, arranged in groups or in lines resembling the sand on the seashore. Cirro-cumulus is often called the *mackerel sky*. These clouds range in height from 10,000 to 35,000 feet.

3. **Cirro-stratus:** a thin whitish veil, sometimes covering the sky completely and giving it a milky appearance; at other times presenting a fibrous structure like a tangled web. This cloud is responsible for halos around the sun and moon. This cloud is denser than the cirrus, though its height range is about the same.

4. **Alto-cumulus:** large rounded masses, partially shaded, arranged in groups or lines or waves sometimes so close together that their edges join. They range in height from 2,500 to 28,000 feet. They rarely result in precipitation.

5. **Alto-stratus:** a dense sheet of a gray or bluish color. At times it is very dark and thick, completely hiding the sun or moon. It ranges in height from 8,000 to 32,000 feet.

6. **Strato-cumulus:** large lumpy masses or rolls of dull gray, frequently covering the whole sky. This cloud form is seen more often in the winter, and its usual height is about 2,000 feet, though it may descend to 500 feet and rise to 12,000.

7. **Stratus:** a uniform layer of cloud, not very thick, hovering about 1,000 feet above the ground. Stratus often results in rain or snow.

8. **Nimbo-stratus:** a dense layer of dark, shapeless cloud with ragged edges ranges in thickness from 500 feet to five miles, and hovers usually at a height of 1,000 feet. This is the cloud that brings the steady downpour.

9. **Cumulus:** a thick cloud, dome-shaped with a horizontal base, commonly known as a cauliflower cloud. It is usually very thick, and usually floats at an altitude of 5,000 feet. The cumulus cloud is known as the cloud of fair weather.

10. **Cumulo-nimbus:** the typical thundershower cloud, appears in

great masses in the form of mountains or towers. This is the thickest of all clouds, often reaching a depth of eight miles. This cloud is responsible for what is impolitely called "dirty weather."

Indications by Appearance of Sky. The indications of weather afforded by the colors of the sky, and given herewith, are very useful in predicting approaching weather conditions at sea. A red sky at sunset presages fine weather; a red sky in the morning, bad weather or much wind, if not rain; a gray sky in the morning, fine weather. Soft-looking or delicate clouds foretell fine weather, with moderate or light breezes; hard-edged, oily-looking clouds, wind. A dark, gloomy blue sky is windy, but a light, bright blue sky indicates fine weather. Generally, the softer the clouds look the less wind, although rain may be expected; and the harder, more "greasy," rolled, tufted, or ragged, the stronger the wind will prove. Also, a bright-yellow sky at sunset presages wind; a pale-yellow, wet; and by the preponderance of red, yellow, or gray tints the coming weather may be foretold very nearly—indeed, if aided by instruments, almost accurately.

TABLE 2. BEAUFORT SCALE OF WIND FORCE

Beaufort Number	Wind Character	Appearance of Sea	Nautical M.P.H.
0	Calm	No ripples	0– 1
1	Light airs	Rippled in patches	2–
2	Light breeze	Ripples and wavelets form	– 6
3	Gentle breeze	Occasional whitecaps	7–10
4	Moderate breeze	Spotted with whitecaps	11–16
5	Fresh breeze	Sea covered with whitecaps	17–21
6	Strong breeze	Scud from whitecaps; large waves	22–27
7	High wind (moderate gale)	Waves begin to break; foam blown from crests in lines	28–33
8	Gale (fresh gale)	Foam blown in dense streaks along direction of wind; sea very rough	34–40
9	Strong gale	Dense streaks of foam on all sides	41–47
10	Whole gale	High waves with long overhanging crests and sea white with foam	48–55
11	Storm	Medium size ships lost to sight in troughs and air filled with spray	56–65
12	Hurricane		over 65

TABLE 3. SCALES ON STATE OF SEA, OF SWELL AND VISIBILITY

STATE OF SEA

	Height of wave crest to trough
0 Calm	0
1 Smooth	Less than 1 foot
2 Slight	1 to 3 feet
3 Moderate	3 to 5 feet
4 Rough	5 to 8 feet
5 Very rough	8 to 12 feet
6 High	12 to 20 feet
7 Very high	20 to 40 feet
8 Precipitous	Over 40 feet
9 Confused	

CHARACTER OF SWELL

Scale	Description	Scale	Description
0	No swell.	5	Moderate swell, long.
1	Low swell, short or average length.	6	Heavy swell, short.
2	Low swell, long.	7	Heavy swell, average length.
3	Moderate swell, short.	8	Heavy swell, long.
4	Moderate swell, average length.	9	Confused swell.

VISIBILITY

0 Dense fog. (Objects not visible at 50 yards.)
1 Thick fog. (Objects not visible at 200 yards.)
2 Fog. (Objects not visible at 500 yards.)
3 Moderate fog. (Objects not visible at ½ nautical mile.)
4 Thin fog. (Objects not visible at 1 nautical mile.)
5 Poor visibility. (Objects not visible at 2 nautical miles.)
6 Moderate visibility. (Objects not visible at 5 nautical miles.)
7 Good visibility. (Objects not visible at 10 nautical miles.)
8 Very good visibility. (Objects not visible at 30 nautical miles.)
9 Excellent visibility. (Objects visible at more than 30 nautical miles.)

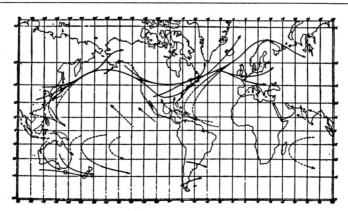

FIG. 5. STORM TRACKS OF THE WORLD.

These storm tracks are indicated on the chart above in Fig. 5.
Solid lines: extra tropical cyclones.
Dotted lines: tropical cyclones.

TROPICAL CYCLONES

HURRICANES	TYPHOONS	CYCLONES
West Indies and East Coast of North America, Mexico and Lower California in North Pacific. Recorded in every month but most in July–October inclusive. South Pacific—90% during December, to March inclusive.	China Sea and in the seas between China and Japan. Have occurred in every month, but principally between May and November, and most frequent in September.	North Indian Ocean. Greatest number in October and November South Pacific Ocean, especially November to May. Unknown in August and September.

PROCEDURE IN TYPICAL CYCLONES
(Refer to Fig. 6 in the following)

1. Frequently a long swell before other signs. May be 1000 miles ahead.

2. Preceded by day of unusual clearness, oppressive temperature and high barometer.

3. Next, oscillating barometer and cirrus haze becoming more dense, the most dense cloud in direction of center.

4. Barometer now falling, more rain, and squalls of increasing force.

5. Find bearing of center.

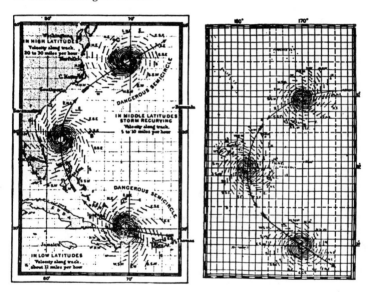

Fig. 6. Course of Cyclones. Northern Hemisphere (left),

Southern Hemisphere (right).

Buys Ballot's Law. When facing the wind, the center is 12–8 points to right in N. Hemisphere (left in S. Hemisphere), wind revolving counterclockwise in N. latitudes (clockwise in S. latitudes); 8 points if barometer has fallen $\frac{1}{2}''$ or more, which indicates near center. Take direction just after a squall. (Movement of lower clouds more accurate than surface wind, if they are visible.)

Face the wind, and the bearing of the center will be somewhere between 90° to 40° to your right. Danger area is 40° to either side of the projected track and 480 miles ahead of the reported center. Recent, closer tracking by Radar and aircraft has shown three other factors to be considered. (1) Buys Ballots law may be in error when the circulation about the typhoon is not circular. Thus, it may be elliptical or very elongated, with two typhoon centers; (2) The angle at which winds blow toward the center varies widely in fast moving typhoons. Directly ahead, the angle is least; to the rear, the angle is greatest; (3) Recent evidence seems to show that typhoons tend to oscillate about a mean path. This oscillation of a few miles may mean the difference between entering and avoiding the eye of the typhoon.

TABLE 4. FOR OBTAINING THE TRUE DIRECTION AND FORCE OF WIND FROM THE DECK OF A MOVING VESSEL

Apparent force of the wind (Beaufort scale)	Speed of the vessel, knots	0		1		2		3		4		5		6		7		8		9		10		11		12		13		14		15		16	
		dir	force	dir	force	dir	force	dir	force	dir	force	dir	force	dir	force	dir	force	dir	force	dir	force	dir	force	dir	force	dir	force	dir	force	dir	force	dir	force	dir	force
0	10	16	3	16	3	16	3	16	3	16	3	16	3	16	3	16	3	16	3	16	3	16	3	16	3	16	3	16	3	16	3	16	3	16	3
	15	16	4	16	4	16	4	16	4	16	4	16	4	16	4	16	4	16	4	16	4	16	4	16	4	16	4	16	4	16	4	16	4	16	4
	20	16	5	16	5	16	5	16	5	16	5	16	5	16	5	16	5	16	5	16	5	16	5	16	5	16	5	16	5	16	5	16	5	16	5
1	10	16	3	16	3	16	3	15	3	15	3	15	3	15	3	15	3	15	4	15	4	16	4	16	4	16	4	16	4	16	4	16	4	16	4
	15	16	4	16	4	16	4	16	4	15	4	15	4	15	4	15	4	15	5	15	5	16	5	16	5	16	5	16	5	16	5	16	5	16	5
	20	16	5	16	5	16	5	16	5	16	5	16	5	16	5	16	5	16	5	16	6	16	6	16	6	16	6	16	6	16	6	16	6	16	6
2	10	15	2	14	2	14	2	13	2	13	3	13	3	13	3	13	3	14	3	14	4	14	4	15	4	15	4	15	4	16	4	16	4	16	4
	15	16	3	15	3	15	3	14	3	14	4	14	4	14	4	14	4	14	4	14	5	15	5	15	5	15	5	15	5	16	5	16	5	16	5
	20	16	4	15	4	15	4	15	4	15	5	15	5	15	5	15	5	15	5	15	5	15	6	15	6	15	6	16	6	16	6	16	6	16	6
3	10	16	1	12	1	11	1	11	2	11	2	11	3	12	3	12	3	13	3	13	4	13	4	14	4	14	4	15	5	15	5	16	5	16	5
	15	16	2	15	3	14	3	13	3	13	3	13	3	13	4	13	4	13	4	14	5	14	5	14	5	15	5	15	5	16	6	16	6	16	6
	20	16	4	15	4	15	4	14	4	14	4	14	4	14	5	14	5	14	5	14	6	15	6	15	6	15	6	15	6	16	7	16	7	16	7
4	10	0	1	3	2	6	2	7	3	8	3	9	4	10	4	11	4	11	5	12	5	12	5	13	6	13	6	14	6	15	6	15	6	15	6
	15	16	1	11	1	10	2	10	2	11	3	11	4	11	4	12	4	12	5	13	5	13	6	14	6	14	6	15	7	16	7	16	7	16	7
	20	16	2	14	2	13	3	13	3	12	4	12	4	12	5	13	5	13	5	13	6	13	6	14	7	14	7	15	7	15	7	16	7	16	7
5	10	0	3	3	4	4	4	5	5	7	5	8	6	9	6	9	6	10	7	10	7	11	7	12	7	13	8	14	8	15	8	16	8	16	8
	15	0	2	4	2	6	3	8	3	9	4	10	5	10	5	11	5	11	6	12	6	13	7	13	7	14	7	14	8	15	8	16	8	16	8
	20	1	1	10	2	10	3	10	3	10	4	11	5	11	5	12	6	12	6	13	7	13	7	13	8	14	8	15	8	15	8	16	8	16	8
6	10	0	4	2	4	3	5	5	6	6	6	7	7	8	7	9	8	10	8	10	8	11	8	12	9	13	9	14	9	15	9	16	9	16	9
	15	0	3	3	3	5	4	6	4	7	5	8	5	9	6	9	6	10	7	11	7	11	7	12	8	13	8	14	9	15	9	15	9	16	9
	20	0	2	4	2	7	3	8	4	9	5	9	5	10	6	11	6	11	7	11	7	12	8	13	8	13	9	14	9	15	9	16	9	16	10
7	10	0	5	1	5	3	5	5	5	6	7	6	8	7	9	7	10	7	11	7	11	8	12	8	13	8	14	8	15	8	16	8	16	9
	15	0	4	2	4	4	5	5	5	6	6	7	6	8	7	9	7	10	7	11	8	11	8	12	9	13	9	14	9	15	9	15	9	16	9
	20	0	3	3	4	5	4	6	5	8	5	9	6	9	7	10	7	11	8	11	8	12	9	13	9	14	9	14	10	15	10	15	10	16	10
8	10	0	6	1	6	3	7	4	7	5	7	6	7	7	8	8	8	8	8	9	10	8	11	9	12	9	13	9	14	9	15	9	16	10
	15	0	6	2	6	3	6	5	6	6	7	7	8	7	8	8	9	8	10	9	10	9	11	9	12	10	13	10	14	10	15	10	16	10
	20	0	5	2	5	4	5	5	6	7	6	7	8	8	8	9	9	9	11	9	11	9	12	10	13	10	14	10	14	11	15	11	15	11	16	11
9	10	0	8	1	8	3	8	4	8	5	8	6	8	7	9	8	9	9	9	9	10	9	11	10	11	10	13	11	14	11	15	11	16	10
	15	0	7	2	7	3	7	4	7	6	7	8	8	8	9	9	9	9	10	10	11	10	11	11	12	11	13	11	14	11	15	11	15	11	16	11
	20	0	6	2	6	3	6	5	7	6	7	8	8	8	9	9	9	10	10	10	11	11	11	11	13	11	14	11	15	11	15	11	16	11
10	10	0	9	1	9	2	9	4	9	5	9	6	9	7	10	8	10	9	10	10	10	11	11	11	12	11	13	11	14	11	15	11	16	11
	15	0	8	1	8	3	8	4	8	5	9	6	9	7	9	8	10	9	10	10	11	11	11	12	11	12	11	13	12	14	12	15	12	16	12
	20	0	7	2	7	3	7	5	8	6	9	6	9	7	9	8	10	9	10	10	11	11	11	12	11	12	12	13	12	14	12	15	12	16	12
11	10	0	10	1	10	2	10	4	10	5	10	6	10	7	11	8	11	9	11	10	11	11	12	12	12	13	13	14	12	15	12	16	12
	15	0	9	1	9	3	9	4	10	5	10	6	10	7	11	8	11	9	11	10	12	11	12	12	12	13	13	12	14	12	14	12	15	12	16	12
	20	0	9	1	8	3	9	4	9	6	10	7	10	8	11	9	11	10	12	11	12	12	12	13	12	13	12	14	12	15	12	16	12
12	10	0	10	1	10	2	10	3	11	5	11	6	11	7	11	8	11	9	12	10	12	11	12	12	12	13	12	14	12	15	12	16	12
	15	0	10	1	10	3	10	4	10	5	10	7	11	8	11	9	11	10	12	11	12	12	12	13	12	14	12	14	12	15	12	16	12
	20	0	9	1	9	3	9	4	10	5	10	7	11	8	11	9	11	10	12	12	12	12	13	12	13	12	14	12	15	12	16	12

First figure column indicates speed of the vessel, knots. Second column gives direction, points off the bow. Third column, true force, Beaufort scale.
Proper allowance should be made for compass variation.

6. Ship's Position in Relation to Storm Track (N. Hemisphere).

a) Wind shifting to right, vessel lies to right of track in dangerous (*navigable* in S. Hemisphere) semicircle.

b) Wind shifting to left, vessel to left of track in navigable (*dangerous* in S. Hemisphere) semicircle.

c) Wind direction steady, force increasing, vessel in track. (Observer in both cases, *a*) and *b*), is assumed to be looking in direction toward which storm is advancing; while in finding bearing of center by Buys Ballot's Law he faces wind.)

7. Center Approaching or Receding.

a) Approaching. Rapidly falling barometer, increase of wind, heavy squalls, intense lightning and rain, heavy, confused sea, continual shifting of winds except on track of center.

b) Receding. Rising barometer, more steady wind, decreasing velocity, clearing, bad sea.

8. Maneuvering to Avoid Center (N. Hemisphere).

a) Dangerous semicircle. Steamers bring wind on starboard bow and make as much way as possible; if must heave-to, do so head to sea. Sail vessels, close hauled on starboard tack, and make as much way as possible; if must heave-to, do so on starboard tack.

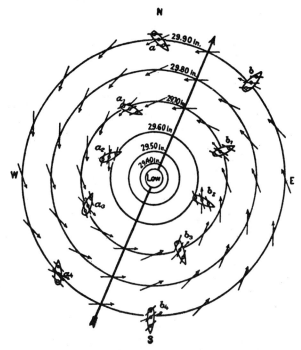

FIG. 7. CYCLONIC STORM IN NORTHERN HEMISPHERE, ILLUSTRATING GRAPHICALLY THE RULES FOR SAILING VESSELS.

b) Navigable semicircle. Bring wind on starboard quarter, note course and hold it. If must heave-to, steamers stern to; sail vessels, port tack.

c) On storm track in front of center. Run for navigable semicircle, with wind on starboard quarter.

d) On track in rear. Have due regard for storm recurving to north and eastward.

(S. Hemisphere)

a) Dangerous semicircle. Steamers bring wind on port bow and have as much way as possible. If must heave-to, put head to sea. Sail vessels, close hauled on port tack, and make as much way as possible. If must heave-to, do so on port tack.

b) Navigable semicircle. Wind on port quarter, note course and hold it. If must heave-to, steamers stern to; sail vessels, starboard tack.

c) On track in front. Run for navigable semicircle, wind on port quarter.

d) On track in rear. Remember storm recurves to south and east.

A general rule for sailing vessels is to always heave-to on whichever tack permits the shifts of wind to draw aft.

ILLUSTRATION OF RULES FOR SAILING VESSELS

For simplicity, on the chart given in Fig. 7 the area of low barometer is made perfectly circular, and the center is assumed to be 10 points to the right of the direction of the wind at all points within the disturbed area. Let us assume that the center is advancing about NNE, in the direction of the long arrow, shown in heavy full line. The ship a has the wind at ENE; she is to the left of the track, or technically in the navigable semicircle. The ship b has the wind at ESE, and is in the dangerous semicircle.

As the storm advances, these ships, if lying-to, a upon the port tack, b upon the starboard tack, as shown, take with regard to the storm center the successive positions $a-a_1$, etc., $b-b_1$, etc. The wind of ship a is shifting to the left, of ship b to the right, or in both cases drawing aft, and thus diminishing the probability of either ship being caught aback, with possible serious damage to spars and rigging. This is a danger to which a vessel lying-to on the opposite tack (i.e., the starboard tack in the left-hand semicircle, or the port tack in the right-hand semicircle) is constantly exposed, the wind in the latter cases tending constantly to draw forward. The ship b is continually beaten by wind and sea toward the storm track. The ship a is drifting away from the track and, should she be able to carry sail, would soon find better weather by running off to the westward.

BAROMETER DIURNAL VARIATION IN THE TROPICS

The Standard Pressure at sea level is 29.9 inches.

The usual pressure in the equatorial low pressure belt is 29.8 inches, increasing north and south to a maximum of 30.1 inches in 35° N and S and thence falling steadily to a minimum of 29.7 inches in 60° N and S. Beyond this it increases slightly toward the poles.

Minimum is at 4 A.M. & 4 P.M.   Maximum is at 10 A.M. & 10 P.M.

The range is greatest at the equator (0.10''), diminishing with increased latitude.

Nonperiodic Variations. Equatorial belt of high pressure (lat. 30° to 35°) is characterized by marked uniformity of barometer, temperature, wind and weather changes.

The following is a rough guide for approximating distance from storm center:

.02–.06	average fall per hour			= 250–150 miles from storm center				
.06–.08	"	"	"	"	= 150–100	"	"	"	"
.08–.12	"	"	"	"	= 100–80	"	"	"	"
.12–.15	"	"	"	"	= 80–50	"	"	"	"

The barometer falls more for high winds than for heavy rains.

A single reading of the barometer is not only useless but is misleading.

Outside the Tropics. A change of .01″ per hour is considered a low rate and .03″ high.

29.5″ is very low in middle latitude, 30.0″ average, and 30.5″ high.

TYPHOON DOCTRINE

Captain Elmer W. Malanot, of the USNS *Marine Fiddler*, has had considerable experience with typhoons and hurricanes and, in 1955, published an article on this subject in the *U.S. Naval Institute Proceedings*, which was widely discussed and subsequently reprinted in the *Proceedings of the Merchant Marine Council USCG*, from which the following extracts are taken.

Generally, cyclones travel in "families" of three to five, following one another across the earth. Upon reaching their greatest violence, they then disappear in the low pressure areas near Iceland or the Aleutian Islands. Danger of heavy weather damage always exists when sailing waters churned by cyclones, for the resultant winds and seas test the master's weather eye and challenge his seamanship.

Now, good seamanship does not necessarily mean sailing through a strong blow bow on into the sea. The practice of meeting dangerous seas bow on dates back to the time when ships were bluff-bowed and sail-propelled. When such vessels were held up to the wind and sea by their sail and helm, they had little or no headway. Whenever they started to fall off, a hard helm usually sufficed to bring them back to meet the sea. For them, heading into the sea was an ideal way of riding out a strong blow.

Modern vessels are different. They carry no sail, and they are usually long and sharp-bowed. Moreover, modern steamers have a deeper design draft aft. The customary deep draft aft and the natural drag of the propeller tend to hold their stern up to the sea. They, consequently, have a tendency to fall off when the sea is on the bow. To head one into the sea requires sufficient steering power for the rudder to hold the vessel's bow on. When this is done, the vessel is forced into the sea to some degree. Sufficient steering power may be developed at a relatively low speed, but even this speed creates a severe strain on the vessel. The rougher the weather, the rougher the seas, the more force it takes to hold the vessel in this position, and the greater the strain to which it is subjected. Consequently, there is a definite danger in pounding into a heavy sea with the modern steam vessel when the weather is too heavy for her to continue on her course.

Ship length, wave period, and speed are important factors to be considered when heading into a rough sea. Small, short ships in a long sea can be perfectly confortable while longer and larger ones make very bad weather. A small craft can climb up and over a wave, riding the slopes, while larger craft will hog and sag, pitch and, in general, be subjected to all the dangers of weather damage. If the speed is such that the wave period corresponds to the period of roll for the vessel, unless speed is decreased, and the relative wave period shortened, the vessel will be subjected to the maximum roll she is capable of. Excess speed will likewise create severe pounding.

A number of modern masters, cognizant of the differences between power-propelled and sail-propelled vessels have experimented with other methods of riding out rough seas. Due to their experiences, opinion is now gaining ground that the present day power-propelled steamers should run slowly before a sea or lie to with the sea astern or on the quarter.

They found that when a steamer is left to herself in a seaway, she will fall off until the sea is abaft the beam. There's a deep roll, but usually an easy roll, with little water taken on board.

They also found that if the roll is dangerous when the vessel is left to herself, the roll can be minimized by turning the engines over just enough to give the vessel steerage way. The vessel may then run safely with the sea aft or quartering, provided she runs very slowly.

I believe that it is high time to break with the old tradition of fighting a typhoon and introduce a new concept of riding it out, with stopped engines, drifting more or less broadside to the wind, which in a typhoon is always from a direction different from that of the biggest and most destructive waves. It will take courage by the Commanding Officer of any vessel to order the engines stopped, when close to the center of a typhoon, and even more courage to order a ship to test this "passive resistance," but I am sure that if this method is adopted, it will save money, lives, and valuable property, especially in time of war.

It is suggested that, in this respect, the following simple instructions should be put in textbooks and typhoon doctrines:

When the center of a tropical storm approaches you, get thirty miles or more sea room around you, assure yourself of the ship's stability and water-tight integrity, and when the wind force rises to 60 knots or more and the sea becomes confused, stop your engines, drift and wait for the storm's dangerous area to pass before you proceed.

STORM WARNINGS

By Visual Display. Flags and lights are displayed at many stations on the Atlantic and Gulf coasts of the United States and at selected places in the West Indies to indicate that high winds in coastal areas are expected. Warnings issued by the Weather Bureau are generally divided into three classes: *Small craft warnings*, *storm warnings*, and *hurricane warnings*.

Small Craft Warning. Strong winds are expected.

A red pennant indicates that strong or fresh to strong winds that will interfere with the safe operation of small craft are expected. Lights are not used to display small craft warnings.

Storm Warnings. Strong winds, gales, or whole gales are expected.

A red flag with a black center indicates that a storm of marked violence is expected. The color and the position of the pennant displayed with the square flag indicates the direction of the expected wind. A red pennant means easterly winds; a white pennant, westerly winds.

By night the approach of storms of marked violence is indicated by: Two red lights, one above the other, for winds beginning from the Northeast; a single red light for winds beginning from the Southeast; a red light above a white light for winds beginning from the Southwest; and a white light above a red light for winds beginning from the North-west.

The pennant above the flag indicates northerly winds; the pennant below the flag, southerly winds.

A red pennant above a red flag indicates winds beginning from the Northeast; a red pennant below a red flag indicates southeast winds; a white pennant above a red flag indicates northwest winds; a white pennant below a red flag indicates southwest winds.

ESTIMATING DISTANCE TO STORM CENTER

A difficult problem encountered in maneuvering a vessel in the vicinity of a tropical revolving storm is estimating the distance from your vessel to the center of the storm. Among the methods employed to make such estimates are those based on the height of the barometer, the rate of change of atmospheric pressure, wind velocity, and direction of greatest cloud density. A description of these methods and their limitations can be found in texts dealing with meteorology, seamanship, and navigation.

The maneuvering board can be used to provide an additional method by using bearings of the storm center based on Buys Ballot's Law. That such bearings have a limited accuracy is obvious.

For this problem, we know that the storm is moving Northeast (045°). Our vessel is on a course of Northwest (315°) at a speed of 10 knots. The following three bearings of the storm center are determined at 3-hour intervals with times as noted:

> Bearing 1   South (180°)   at 0000.
> Bearing 2   160°   at 0300.
> Bearing 3   143.5°   at 0600.

How would you solve this problem to obtain the speed at which the storm was moving, and its distance from the vessel at 0000, 0300, and 0600?

The course and speed of the ship is represented by vector line e . . . m. Northwest (315°) at 10 knots (1 : 1 scale). The direction in which the storm is moving, Northeast (045°) is denoted by the line e . . . m.

If the relative speed between the ship and the storm is constant for the 6-hour period, then the relative distance covered in the two 3-hour periods is equal. The direction of relative motion, which satisfies this condition, can be found by using a straightedge and a pair of dividers for a trial and error solution.

Alternatively, a line may be drawn perpendicular to bearing line **2** at any convenient point, P_2. The distance $P_2 . . . P_3$ intercepted between the bearing lines, 2 and 3 is measured, and an equal distance measured on the line from P_2 to determine the point P_1. A perpendicular to line $P_1 \dots P_2 \dots P_3$ is erected to Point P_1. The intersection of this perpendicular with bearing line 1 determines the point X. A line from X to P_3 will determine the direction of relative motion.

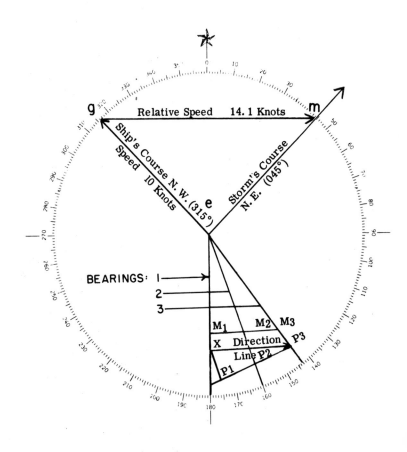

FIG. 8. ESTIMATING DISTANCE TO STORM CENTER.

Hurricane Warnings. Whole gales or winds of hurricane force are expected.

Two square red flags with black centers, one above the other displayed by day, or two red lights with a white light between, displayed by night, indicate the expected approach of a tropical hurricane, or one of the extremely severe and dangerous storms which occasionally occur in more northerly latitudes.

HURRICANE MANEUVERING

Suppose you are at sea when a weather report comes through indicating a hurricane with winds up to 75 miles an hour within 50 miles of its center is making up 100 miles to the south of your position. The report adds that the anticipated direction and speed of movement of the storm is Northwest at 10 knots.

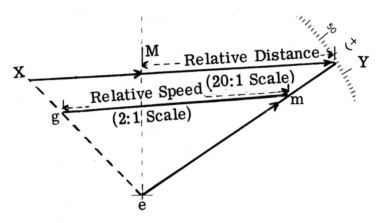

FIG. 9. HURRICANE MANEUVERING.

Your first thought is to put distance between you and the storm. If your vessel has a speed of 15 knots and there is ample sea room in all directions, what course would put at least 200 miles between you and the storm in the minimum length of time?

With the storm center at e, M represents the position of the vessel 100 miles to the north using the scale of 20:1. The dashed line $e—g—X$ represents the direction in which the storm is moving, Northwest (315°).

The length of the line $e—X$ is determined by a ratio:

$\dfrac{\text{Speed of storm}}{\text{Speed of ship}} \times$ desired distance from the center of the storm. In terms of this problem: $\dfrac{10}{15} \times 200 = 133\frac{1}{3}$ miles.

The direction of relative motion is then determined by drawing a line from X through M. This line is extended out to the 200 mile range circle using the 20:1 scale. The course to be steered can be seen as 056.5°. The relative distance $M— Y$ measured on the 20:1 scale is 168 miles.

A line parallel to $X—M—Y$ is drawn from the storm's direction and speed vector at g, using 2:1 scale, until it intersects the 15 knots speed circle of the vessel at m. The length of the line $g—m$, 19.5 miles on the

2:1 scale is the relative speed which results with the vessel on a course of 056.5°.

The time required to complete the maneuver would be:

$$\frac{\text{Relative distance}}{\text{Relative speed}} = \frac{168 \text{ miles}}{19.5 \text{ knots}} = 8 \text{ hours } 37 \text{ minutes.}$$

Analysis of this problem will indicate that it required a determination of a line of relative motion that will combine a maximum relative speed and minimum relative distance compatible for the solution. A similar problem, together with a geometric proof, is contained in

U. S. Small Craft, Gale, Whole Gale and Hurricane Warnings

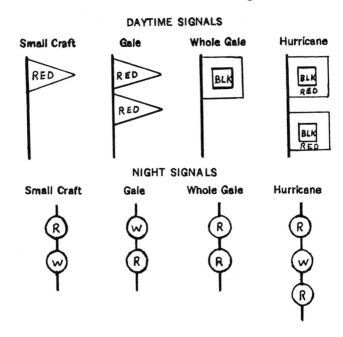

H. O. 217, *Maneuvering Board Manual,* Case XII. Under certain circumstances, this type solution could cause the vessel to go closer to the storm center in the process of reaching a prescribed distance away from it.

In assessing the practical value of problems such as this, the navigator will recognize that storms seldom behave in such exact conformity with the predictions. Several modern textbooks on meteorology and ship handling describe methods for maneuvering which are based on the probable movements of the storm area within a period of time.

Warnings by Radio. Storm warnings, storm advisories, and coastal forecasts issued by the United States Weather Bureau are broadcast promptly and at regular intervals through many United States Naval and Coast Guard radio stations.

These schedules may be obtained from the "Chief, United States Weather Bureau, Washington, D. C." A large number of commercial radio stations also broadcast storm warnings and forecasts although at somewhat irregular intervals.

Radio schedules of storm warnings, forecasts, and weather information broadcast from United States and foreign stations are contained in Hydrographic Office Publication 206 entitled, "Radio Weather Aids to Navigation."

Warnings in Great Britain. A cone displayed with apex down indicates a gale from southward; or if from easterly or westerly direction, is expected to shift to southerly direction.

A cone displayed with apex up indicates a gale from northward; or if from easterly or westerly direction, is expected to shift to northerly direction. Three lights suspended from the corners of a triangle replace the cone at night.

Chapter 8

CARGO

The stowage of cargo should be governed by the following principles:

1. Sound delivery of the cargo by its adequate protection from damage, deterioration, or loss.

2. Consideration of the vessel's earning capacity, in economy of space, in carrying the greatest possible volume and weight of cargo.

3. Protection of ship and crew from danger or injury which might be caused by faulty stowage.

4. Maximum speed and minimum cost in loading and discharging.

DAMAGE

Sound delivery of cargo can be ensured only by the prevention of possible mishap to the goods. The knowledge of what may happen to a cargo during loading, transportation, and discharge, and of the means of averting such losses is perhaps three-fourths the requirements of proper cargo handling and protection.

The various kinds of damage more commonly met with are here noted:

Before Loading. This may be anything from leaky casks to crushed cartons. All packages showing signs of breakage, pilferage, or leakage should be rejected until repaired and put in their original condition by the shipper or the responsible parties receiving the goods for shipment.

By Handling. Careless winch work, as in lowering drafts heavily upon other cargo in holds, or in swinging goods against ship's side or hatch coamings; dragging cargo along dock, or to and from remote places in holds; dropping packages from trucks, cars, tops of tiers, or from the slings; careless sorting and piling; slinging fragile and heavy packages together; tearing by hooks.

By Use of Improper Appliances. Hoisting cargo in slings, trays, or nets not suitable for the packages; lack of landing platforms or chutes when working over cargo already stowed.

Leakage and Drainage. Wet goods should be stowed in compartments set apart for their exclusive use, and drainage and odors from same kept clear of dry cargo.

Dry Cargo Damaged by Wet. Goods such as tea, dried skins, oilcake, paper, and pepper attract and absorb moisture to a ruinous degree. Where dry goods must be stowed in same compartment as wet, extra care should be taken that they do not include such as the above. Dunnage well to keep dry stuff off deck, if stowed with wet goods. If dry cargo is over wet, separate by boards or heavy matting, or by suitable cargo which is not liable to absorb moisture.

Condensation or Sweating. During warm weather wet goods suffer much evaporation; the moisture so released condenses on cool surfaces and causes sweating. When sudden changes of temperature occur, ventilation of holds should be cut down so as to allow the inside and outside air to gradually equalize and so minimize this perhaps the most common of all damage. Where it is proven that reasonable precautions were not taken to prevent sweating, the liability rests with the ship. To avoid this class of damage, goods which will not be affected should be selected for stowage with, or near to, the wet goods; but it is better to place wet goods in compartments thoroughly ventilated and away from local heat, so as to retard evaporation as much as possible.

Results attained by the mechanical air-conditioning and ventilating systems installed in cargo ships of recent years have proven that such treatment of the condensation problem—the cause of much damage in trades in which a considerable range of temperature is experienced— is the final answer. However, with the common, natural ventilating system, there has been in a great many cases some degree of inattention to the cure of this cause of damage on the part of ships' officers in the past, the "not responsible for damage by sweat" clause in the Bill of Lading probably having allowed them to rest comfortably on their oars. But in present-day sweat damage claims, the courts do not lightly treat the responsibility of a vessel for the protection of her cargo, and in order to defeat a claim of this sort, it must be positively shown that "due diligence" was employed to prevent the damage.

A cargo loaded in cold weather will, upon entering rising temperatures, cause considerable sweating if ventilated in the usual way. The increased moisture content of the warmer air meeting the cold cargo and hold surfaces results in the condensation or sweat which we are considering. Therefore, cold cargoes, upon meeting with rising temperatures, should be sealed up, so that the heating of the decks and sides of the ship will act toward drying and warming the cargo and hold atmosphere in much the same way as a heat radiator in a room.

When leaving warmer latitudes, *vigorous* ventilation should be the aim in order to bring the inside and outside temperatures as nearly equal as possible; but, upon a sudden drop in temperature, *check* the ventilation so that condensation caused by the ingress of cold air will be reduced to a minimum.

Generally stated, the ideal condition is reached in combating the "sweat" menace when the hold temperature and the outside air temperature are approximately equal.

Where the nature of the cargo requires it, a record of attention given to ventilation of holds should always appear in the mate's log, special mention being made of uncovering hatches, the necessity for plugging ventilators, and unshipping cowls, etc., in bad weather.

Crushing Damage. Caused by packages subjected to more pressure than they can stand. Cargo in vicinity may suffer damage from contents of crushed packages. Crushing is further aggravated by the ship's motion in a seaway, as when goods stowed near the ends of the vessel are subjected to the effect of pitching in a head sea, or during heavy rolling when cargo in the wings is under extra pressure due to the "scend" of the vessel's roll. The cause of this class of damage is often frail packing; often bad stowage.

Weighty packages should be stowed next to the floor when possible, with lighter cargo over them. Stow light goods in 'tween decks where top weight would be at a minimum. Stow strong packages in the wings; the necessity for compact stowage is here obvious.

Chafing Damage. Caused by the to-and-fro motion arising from the vessel's motion in a seaway, it is mostly found in bale or roll goods, such as cloth, carpets, paper, or linoleum, and coils of cordage, copper piping, etc. Keep such goods away from projecting structural parts of ship's holds, and avoid stowage of same over lively or "springy" cargo. Stow bales on flat; stand them on end in the wings. (If the outer layers of rolled goods are chafed, small damage to the bale results as compared with that due to chafing of the ends.) Compactness of stowage is here of first importance.

Tainting Damage. Cargo giving off fumes or odors should never be stowed in the same compartment with fine goods or food-stuffs; and the best and cleanest dunnage should be exclusively used in stowage of the latter, as contamination by contact with dirty or oil-saturated, or green and stain-producing dunnage wood is sure to bring blame upon the ship for negligence, sooner or later.

A noted source of taint damage is a leaky fuel-oil tank top just below the cargo. Such cargo as creosote, turpentine, most petroleum products, copra, hides, newly-sawn or creosoted lumber, green fruit, onions, certain chemicals, volatile or essential oils, and molasses should never be placed in the same compartment with delicate or edible goods. Keep holds and bilges where fine goods are stowed at all times free from odors. Here it might be noted that the elimination of obnoxious odors left by such commodities as barreled fish, hides, copra, bones, fertilizers, strong liquid chemicals, or oils of many kinds may be effected by freely sprinkling common slaked lime upon the hold ceiling and in the bilges. The lime should stand for a few hours before sweeping up the hold; if necessary, repeat the process; if a clean cargo is to be loaded, use plenty of lime and repeat the sweeping up three or four times, being guided, of course, by the time available for such preparation before loading.

Heating Damage. Many commodities of vegetable or animal origin are susceptible to spontaneous heating, especially where the voyage is lengthy and warm weather prevails. Some cargoes liable to spontaneous heating are the following: bituminous coal, rice, oats, oilseeds, corn, jute, oil-cake, tobacco, pepper, cocoa, copra, hay, wool, nuts.

Not only does deterioration of the goods themselves take place, but the moisture given off by most of those noted is liable to hurt other cargo in the vicinity.

To prevent this class of damage, attention must be given to the following:

1. Stow goods away from boiler-room or engine-room bulkheads and casings, and apart from wet goods.

2. Ventilate thoroughly, and, where cargo is not in bulk, lay deep dunnage to assist in circulation of air.

3. Avoid deep stowage. Better in 'tween decks than lower holds.

4. Keep cargo susceptible to damage by heat or moisture away from goods liable to spontaneous heating.

Beans shipped in a wet or unripe condition have great capacity for heating. Some kinds of nuts require stowage in bins, and must be turned over by shovel from time to time in order to keep down heat and consequent deterioration.

Dust and Stain Damage. Dust-covered packages are never given a hearty welcome by consignees, and claims against the ship have often followed such undesirable delivery, although the goods contained may not have suffered hurt. Avoid such a condition by keeping fine goods safely away from flying dust; if necessary, supply protection by the use of separation cloths.

Oil or acid stains may be the result of using contaminated dunnage or dragging packages over oil-smeared dock floors or dirty decks.

Cargo Mixture. Prevention of this annoyance can only be effected by carefully placing separation marks, by "separation cloths" where, as in the carriage of grain, different lots are shipped, and by arranging the stowage so that no mixture can possibly follow.

Consignments for different ports, or lots of general cargo, may be separated by boards, mats, rope-yarns, between tiers of bags or cases, or wire stretched across metal rails, rods, piping, etc.

Vermin Damage amounts to much less to-day than was the case up to a few years ago, due to the requirements of quarantine laws in fumigation, rat-proofing, placing of rat-guards, etc. Certain woods may carry ants or cockroaches. Maggots breed at an astonishing rate in copra, bones, and some kinds of animal skins. Lice may infest bales of cotton rags; against this, the sanitary condition of such goods is required, in most cases, to be certified by the shipper and endorsed by the consul of the country to which cargo is destined, before shipment is allowed. Grain-carrying ships usually breed rats at a lively rate; a few good traps and a cat or two will at least keep down the increase of the pest until next fumigation time.

Broaching and Pilferage in some general cargo trades amounts to considerable loss each year, according to insurance statistics, and its rate per centum of all cargo damage losses is said to be on the increase. To protect valuable goods from this evil, the "special" cargo locker should be built in the 'tween deck, with its entrance door or doors as near the hatchway as will enable its means of access to be at all times visible from the deck during loading or discharging.

Confine broachable cargo to as few holds as possible, and avoid stowage of same in remote and badly-lighted corners; if possible, have none of these corners. Constant vigilance, and ship and shore co-operation in every means available to prevent this vicious practice, give the only general answer here.

Inherent Vice is the term used to denote a quality of change in some cargoes which damages the commodity itself. This kind of damage allies itself to that of spontaneous heating in that goods in the vicinity of those subject to "inherent vice" may share in the damage from said cause. It is the shipper's lawful duty to inform the carrier of any knowledge he may possess with regard to a particular cargo's inherent vice and the treatment such cargo requires, in order to lessen or prevent any damage arising from this source.

STOWAGE AND EARNING CAPACITY

Consideration of the vessel's earning capacity demands a full cargo to be stowed so that loss of space will be a minimum. This, of course, more especially applies to cargoes which, if so stowed, will fill the ship's entire hold space without sinking her below her load-line marks. As a general rule, where the loading is such that the vessel is immersed exactly to her marks and is filled to capacity, the freight earned is at a maximum; the ship's carrying capacity, both as to weight and volume, is thus wholly in use.

Careful planning of the stowage in advance is therefore most necessary where a full general cargo is offering, for if the weight of the proposed lading will immerse the ship to the allowed load line before her holds are filled, the space has not all been "sold."

If the freight on the weighty cargo figures to advantage when considering the space that may be left unoccupied, all well and good; but it is generally more likely that the earnings would not equal those of the "full and down" cargo. Aside from business policy as to good will of shippers, etc., comparison of weight and volume freight charges is here the key to the situation: a load of cotton will fill a ship to capacity, one of iron ore will leave three-fourths the vessel's space unoccupied; how would the freight on each compare?

Economy of Space naturally calls for the least possible broken stowage, i.e., space not occupied between and around packages, or in way of pillars, brackets, stringers, etc., and space occupied by dunnage. Bulky, heavy weights such as locomotives, boilers, tractors, and other pieces of machinery are noted space-wasters; select such cargo as bales of hay, kegs or bags of bolts, coils of barbed wire, or small sturdy packages, as "filling" or "broken stowage stuff" to fill up the gaps, and "chock off" as with dunnage.

It is good practice to record for future stowage reference the actual **stowage factor** of large consignments of different commodities, noting the particular compartment in which stowed, and the type and capacity of containers. Lumber, barrels, drums, or large cases stow more to advantage in holds nearer amidships than at the ends of the vessel.

The Stowage Factor is customarily stated as the number of cubic feet one ton of 2240 pounds (long ton) of a particular lot of cargo will occupy, when properly stowed and dunnaged, in the ship's hold. Usually the term *measurement cargo* describes goods having a stowage factor of more than 40, while those stowing at or below 40 are termed *dead weight cargo*. Freight rates are generally agreed upon as payable by "dead weight or measurement, ship's option."

PROTECTION OF SHIP AND CREW

Protection of ship and crew from danger might generally be interpreted as the avoidance of any unnecessary risks in stowing a cargo, either due to the actual stowage or to the distribution or disposition of the cargo. Extreme cases under this caption are usually severely dealt with in Admiralty Courts, but the frequency of such is happily on the decrease. The improper vertical distribution of weight, either in the direction of making the vessel "crank" or "top heavy," or of causing excessive rolling, must always be guarded against. Likewise, the fore-and-aft arrangement of weight in the ship should be such that undue local structural stress in a seaway may be prevented. Too much weight in the lower holds will give most ships great stiffness, and heavy, quick rolling in a beam sea is the result. More than is generally realized, a loaded vessel's structure is subjected to severe racking stresses under the stiff condition referred to, the danger of cargo shifting is greatest, and the hazards due to working under such conditions are certainly not in keeping with a healthy *esprit de corps* amongst the crew.

Protection for the crew is required under law by the placing of temporary guard-rails, walks, and suitable means of access to all quarters and spaces used in working the ship, where a deck-load is carried; goods of highly inflammable or corrosive nature are to be carried on deck, where they are always under observation and ready to be thrown overboard, if necessary; and ships are required to avoid the mixture in stowage of certain chemicals with explosives, or other goods giving off odors or gases.

Attention is called to the regulations prescribed by the Secretary of Commerce in the publication *Explosives or other Dangerous Articles on Board Vessels*. It is issued by the U. S. Coast Guard; price $1.00.

SPEED AND COST FACTORS

Maximum speed and minimum cost in loading or discharging are twin brothers in handling cargo. Stowage should be arranged so that as many hatches (and side doors, if any) as possible may be worked at the same time. This, of course, is part of the planning required when loading for two or more ports, and here the value of the **stowage plan** is obvious. The plan shows the disposition of the cargo throughout the vessel, its main objective being to indicate the comparative volume taken up by the various lots of goods; and if cargo is destined for more than one port, the location of consignments for each should always be clearly marked, preferably with distinctive colors.

It has often happened that the *deciding factor in a cargo damage claim has been the evidence offered by the stowage plan*. The plan, therefore, should be drawn up with the greatest care.

The rate of handling drafts of cargo is directly governed by the speed with which the packages can be made up into, and removed from, the slings. Regulate the size of drafts accordingly; faster and better work will be accomplished by keeping a moderate-sized draft moving than by having a heavy one waiting to be dispensed with.

DUNNAGE

The need for heavy dunnage on the floors in present-day steam-vessels is almost nil, unless the presence of liquids requires such protection under other cargo. Perhaps the heaviest dunnage to-day is laid under rice cargoes. We find in rice-loading regulations "6 inches at the bilge, tapering to 3 inches on the floor," and this in addition to the permanent ceiling. As a means of providing *air courses* under the cargo, this is surely good practice for rice, but as a protection from water its value is something akin to keeping one's watch five minutes fast to avoid being too quickly overtaken by the correct time! Provision for draining "sweat drip" from the shell plating, frames, etc., directly into the bilges should prevent this accumulation on the floor or tank top; an efficient cargo hold will have means of such importance as the above, amply supplied. Bilges are made to collect water in the holds; see that these are kept pumped out, and proper drainage takes care of water or other liquid from whatever cause.

The *cargo battens*, or *spar ceiling*, are fitted to prevent cargo from filling the frame spaces, and so interfere with ventilation, or from coming in contact with the frames or shell plating, and thus suffer damage by condensed moisture.

Dunnage serves the following purposes: (1) To protect the cargo from contact with *leakage* from other cargo, from *sweat* which condenses on ship's sides, bulkheads, frames, etc., and which may accumulate on side stringers, brackets, etc.; (2) to prevent *chafing*, and to chock off and secure cargo by filling in broken stowage; (3) to provide *air courses* for the heated moisture-laden air to travel to the sides and bulkheads in its ascent toward the uptake ventilators.

The use of *saw-dust* for absorbing drainage from certain cargoes may be good practice, but its use with barrels of linseed oil or other seed oils is dangerous, due to the liability of spontaneous combustion.

Where certain goods are shipped at a low freight rate, with the understanding that they may be used as dunnage, a clause to that effect should be inserted in the Bill of Lading.

RECEIVING AND DELIVERING CARGO

Receiving Cargo. Packages received in unsound condition cannot be delivered in sound condition. It is therefore necessary that a careful watch be maintained, when loading, for any packages which may have been tampered with, or are broken, or improperly protected; torn or stained bags, leaky, damaged, or repaired casks, etc. Cargo in such unsatisfactory condition should be rejected; but if, after reconditioning and examining contents, it is decided to accept such packages for shipment, the receipt for same should be suitably endorsed. A clean receipt should not be given unless the condition of packages is identical with those unharmed.

When in doubt as to weight, quality, quantity, and condition, *mate's receipts*, and also *bills of lading*, should be marked, "Weight, quality, quantity, and condition unknown."

The Bill of Lading is a negotiable document, is prima facie evidence of shipment of goods on board a particular vessel, and its legal importance consists in the fact that it is a receipt for goods, a contract for carriage, and a title to property.

Foreign Shipments are ordinarily covered by the "order" Bill of Lading, which is one of the parts of the *Documentary Bill*. This consists of the *draft*, or *bill of exchange* (drawn by the seller on the buyer), the *invoice*, the *marine insurance certificate*, and the *Bill of Lading*. Where, in the rarer cases in which the consignee becomes owner of the goods prior to delivery to the carrier, and the cargo is to be shipped directly to the consignee named in the Bill of Lading, the term *straight bill* is used. Shipments of munitions to a foreign power engaged at war are usually negotiated in the latter way.

When required to sign Bills of Lading, shipmasters should be careful to note that the facts concerning the cargo are correctly stated before attesting thereby to the truth of the documents' contents. Notwithstanding any request by shippers, or any clauses in a charter party directing the master to "sign bills of lading as presented," that gentleman is not authorized by any law or established custom to certify the receipt of a quantity of goods which a careful count or tally has shown to have *not* been shipped, to certify the condition of cargo as other than the known fact, or to attest a quality or condition of goods received on board his vessel which quality or condition he is not qualified to determine. The issue of "clean" Bills of Lading is, of course, of much importance to the shipper, and he may "guarantee" the ship immune from all claims for shortage, condition, etc., of his shipment, if the Bills of Lading are signed thus to his advantage. Such a guarantee, however, has no place in the protection of the ship against a consignee's claim, for the reason that the said guaranty has no legal force against a third party. Further, it has always been held by the maritime courts of law that it is the master's duty to protect the consignee or purchaser of the Bill of Lading from being fraudulently dealt with, whenever it is possible for him to do so.

A number of copies of the Bill of Lading are issued, depending upon the number of agents interested. Usually two or three copies are negotiable, any one of which, properly endorsed, gives the holder title, and automatically cancels the others.

Cargo Losses. The term "average," which was formerly used to denote the respective shares that ship, cargo, and freight were required to contribute in settling the total expense incurred in a marine venture, is now the term for a marine loss, and is described as "particular" or "general" according to circumstances.

Particular Average is damage or partial loss to ship, cargo, or freight, and such loss is borne by the individual owners of the property damaged or lost, or by their insurers.

General Average is a loss borne by the ship, cargo, and freight in the proportion of the value of each. Such a loss must be a voluntary sacrifice made by the master or his authority for the purpose of preserving the property of all concerned from a common imminent peril, and such voluntary sacrifice must result in a successful termination of the venture.

Satisfactory evidence is required to show that the voluntary sacrifice was necessary, and proper entries in the ship's log-book should substantiate the same.

The adjustment of general average claims is usually made according to York-Antwerp Rules, 1924, and a clause in the charter party or Bill of Lading is inserted to this effect. The ship may hold the cargo, or require a general average bond, until the claim is satisfied.

Seaworthiness. Although a vessel may be "staunch, tight, and strong," and in every way fitted for safe navigation, she may be still unseaworthy in relation to the safety of certain cargoes, so that the carrier or shipowner would be liable for the loss of, or damage to, cargo resulting from the want of that attribute of seaworthiness necessary to the proper carriage of the particular cargo in question.

The principal factors entering into this condition of seaworthiness are: proper loading; proper stowage; correct relation in stowage of parcels of mixed cargo; ventilation; dunnaging; precautions against the shifting of cargo; deck cargo.

The fitness of a vessel at a particular time for a particular job is, perhaps, the best definition of seaworthiness.

Delivery of Cargo. It is usually the custom to *note a protest* upon arrival at the discharging port, and should there be grounds for anticipating serious damage to cargo, the protest should be extended at once.

All broken receptacles should be attended to by re-coopering, care being taken to preserve the marks and numbers on same. *Broken-up barrels or emptied and torn bags should be landed so as to be tallied, and damage noted.*

Note: Mail must be very carefully checked. Information required, in addition to number and condition of mailbags, is: (1) name of the officer in charge, (2) watchman, (3) postal clerk, (4) number of men working in hold, (5) log time. Receipts required by postal authorities: P.O. Form 2988a—to company, 1 copy; to U.S. mail clerk, 2. Diplomatic 2988c—to company, 1 copy; to U.S. mail clerk, 2. Company forms to be filled out, in addition, will vary as many as 6 to company and to U.S. mail clerk.

NOTES ON IMPORTANT CARGOES

Explosives. Laws to govern the carriage of explosives have been enacted in most countries, and the Navigation Laws of the United States contain such legislation, and empower the Secretary of Commerce to provide the necessary regulations as to the packing and stowing of such cargo.

No explosives should be carried in a hold containing coal, or in a 'tween deck above a hold containing coal, excepting safety cartridges, safety fuses, or percussion caps, unless specially authorized; and no explosives should be carried in a hold containing passengers' baggage.

Ships fitted with wooden masts should have good lightning conductors when carrying any quantity of explosives, and electric light wires must be disconnected in holds where explosives are stowed.

Deck cargo of an inflammable, corrosive, or dangerous nature must not be stowed on the deck of a steamer which carries explosives, unless the engine and boiler space intervenes between the holds in which the explosives are stowed and those over which the deck cargo of a dangerous nature is placed.

No other goods should be stowed in a magazine with explosives.

All explosives must be handled carefully, and where possible, the loading or discharging should be done by hand. Where the use of hoisting gear is made necessary, packages shall be so slung that there will be no danger of any of them dropping from the sling used. Slings of the rope net, basket, or crate type shall be used.

The master or person in charge of the vessel is required to make a careful examination of the gear to be used in the handling of explosives.

In vessels engaged in the foreign or intercoastal trade, a licensed officer shall be assigned to the duty of directing the handling and stowage of explosives or other dangerous articles or substances as cargo.

A fire hose of sufficient length to cover the area of loading or discharging operations shall be laid and connected to an adequate supply of water ready for instant use. *No Smoking* signs shall be posted during the transfer of explosives.

Vapors of inflammable liquids, when mixed with air in proper proportions, will form an explosive concentration. The danger of ignition of same is obvious.

Means of artificial lighting shall be of a vapor-proof type.

Inspection of a dangerous cargo shall be ordered by the master during a voyage to ensure that such cargo is being carried with safety, and that no damage caused by shifting cargo, spontaneous heating, leaking or sifting containers, or from other causes, has been sustained since loading and stowage.

Temperatures of holds containing dangerous goods shall be taken and recorded at proper intervals.

If cargo is found to be in a dangerous condition from leakage, sifting, heat, wetting, or other causes, such condition shall be corrected as the master's judgment shall dictate. Any unusual conditions found during an inspection, and any action taken as a result, shall be entered in the ship's log-book.

Immediately before entering a U. S. port, the master of an ocean-going vessel shall cause an inspection to be made of the holds containing dangerous articles or substances as cargo. Should the presence of fire or any hazardous condition be found, same shall be reported to the U. S. Coast Guard, and advice as to the procedure of entry into port requested.

Magazines. Magazine stowage is required for all high explosives, ammunition, bombs, mines, torpedoes, gunpowder, picric acid, fireworks, blasting-caps (more than 1,000), detonating fuses, and all priming or initiating explosives.

The U. S. Coast Guard regulations require that certain of these shall not be stowed in the same compartment with others as, for example, blasting-caps shall not be stowed with any of the above-named (excepting detonating fuses and primers) or inflammable solids, liquids or compressed gases, acids or corrosive liquids, combustible liquids, or hazardous articles. (*See* following chart.)

Magazines shall be located in the 'tween decks wherever possible, and as far away from living quarters as possible. They must not be built next to a collision, fire-room, engine-room, galley, or coal-bunker bulkhead; but, if it is necessary to place the magazine in proximity to such a bulkhead, a space of at least 4 feet shall intervene between the bulkhead and the magazine side. This space must remain open to free circulation of air, and no cargo shall be stowed so as to obstruct same.

A magazine shall be so located that its door or doors shall be easily accessible from the hatchway. It may be constructed of wood, iron, or steel, but the interior shall be finished with a smooth surface of wood; all nails to be well set in and no projections allowed. Containers must not be allowed to come in contact with any metal surface. Nails to be copper or cement-coated.

Efficient ventilation shall be provided, and any cowl deck ventilators fitted into, or adjacent to, a magazine shall be covered with 30×30 mesh wire screen.

Details of magazine requirements may be found in *Explosives or ther Dangerous Articles on Board Vessels*, issued by the Commerce Department.

Most of the regular steamship lines issue a printed list of dangerous goods which are prohibited as cargo on board their vessels.

Dangerous Goods. The expression "dangerous goods" includes explosives and all substances of an inflammable nature which are liable to spontaneous combustion, either in themselves or when stowed adjacent to other substances, and which, when mixed with air, are liable to generate explosive gases, and so produce suffocation, or poisoning, or tainting of food-stuffs.

Dangerous goods should be stowed as far as possible from bunkers, engine and boiler spaces, etc., and from living quarters, and should be easily accessible from a hatchway. Select the best ventilated compartment in the ship for such goods; this will usually be found in a 'tween deck, and 'tween deck stowage is the most fitting for all-round protection of dangerous cargoes.*

The International Conference for Safety at Sea, 1929, has provided that the carriage on passenger ships, either as cargo or ballast, of goods which, by reason of their nature, quantity, or mode of stowage are, either singly or collectively, liable to endanger the lives of the passengers or the safety of the ship, shall be forbidden; and official notice shall from time to time be issued, showing what goods are to be considered dangerous, and shall indicate the precautions to be taken in the packing and stowing thereof.

Any vessel carrying explosives or other dangerous articles or substances in navigable waters of the United States shall have on board a complete manifest of all dangerous cargo on board, and shall produce

---

* The master should personally sign the dangerous cargo manifest and designate and log the name of the hazardous cargo officer for the voyage.

STOWAGE AND STORAGE CHART OF EXPLOSIVES AND OTHER DANGEROUS ARTICLES

Explosives shall not be stowed together nor with other dangerous articles, except as indicated in this stowage and storage chart.
(Provisions of this chart not applicable to barges)

The following table shows the explosives and other dangerous articles which shall not be loaded or stored together. The letter x at an intersection of horizontal and vertical columns shows that these packages must not be loaded or stored together, for example: blasting caps (4) horizontal column must not be loaded or stored with high explosive (2) vertical column.

Hazardous articles		Dangerous explosives				
		1. Low explosives or black powder	2. High explosives	3. Initiating or priming explosives Wet:—Diazodinitrophenol fulminate of mercury, guanyl nitrosamino guanylidene hydrazine, lead azide, lead styphnate nitro mannite nitrosoguanidine, pentaerythrite tetranitrate, tetrazene	4. Blasting caps with or without safety fuse (including) electric blasting caps A	5. Ammunition for cannon with explosive projectiles, gas projectile, smoke projectiles or incendiary projectiles, ammunition for small arms with explosive bullets
Hazardous articles	22	X	X	X	X	X
Combustible liquids	21	X	X	X	X	X
Poisonous gases or liquids, in cylinders, poison gas label	20	X	X	X	X	X
Compressed noninflammable gases, green label	19	X	X	X	X	X
Acids or corrosive liquids, white label	18	X	X	X	X	X
Inflammable solids or oxidizing materials, yellow label	17	X	X	X	X	X
Inflammable liquids or compressed inflammable gases, red label	16	X	X	X	X	X
Cordeau detonant, safety squibs, fuse lighters, fuse igniters, delay electric igniters, electric squibs or instantaneous fuse	15			X		
Time or combination fuzes	14			X		
Percussion fuzes or tracer fuzes	13			X		
Primers for cannon or small arms, empty cartridge bags — black powder igniters, empty cartridge cases, primed, empty grenades, primed, combination primers or percussion caps, toy caps	12			X		
Small arms ammunition	11			X		
Fireworks	10	X	X	X	X	X
Smokeless powder for cannon or smokeless powder for small arms	9			X		
Ammunition for cannon with empty sand loaded or solid projectiles, or without projectiles	8			X		
Detonating fuzes, boosters (explosive)	7		X	X		X
Explosive projectiles, bombs, torpedoes or mines, rifle or hand grenades (explosive)	6			X	X	
Ammunition for cannon with explosive projectiles, gas projectiles, smoke projectiles or incendiary projectiles, ammunition for small arms with explosive bullets	5			X	X	
Blasting caps, with or without safety fuse (including electric blasting caps) a	4		X	X		X
Initiating or priming explosives Wet: — Diazodinitrophenol, fulminate of mercury, guanyl nitrosamino guanylidene hydrazine, lead azide, lead styphnate, nitro manite, nitrosoguanidine, pentaerythrite tetranitrate, tetrazene.	3	X	X		X	X
High explosives	2			X	X	
Low explosives or black powder	1			X		

Relatively safe explosives / Less danger explosive / Other dangerous articles

No.	Article													
9	Smokeless powder for cannon or smokeless powder for small arms	X			X			X							B X
10	Fireworks	X	X	X	X			X							B X
11	Small arms ammunition	X	X		X										X
12	Primers for cannon or small arms, empty cartridge bags, black powder igniters, empty cartridge cases, primed, empty grenades, primed, combination primers or percussion caps, toy caps	X		X	X		X								
13	Percussion fuzes or tracer fuzes	X	X												
14	Time or combination fuzes	X	X												
15	Cordeau detonant, safety squibs, fuse lighters, fuse igniters, delay electric igniters, electric squibs or instantaneous fuse	X		X	X	X									
16	Inflammable liquids or compressed inflammable gases, red label	X	X	X	X	X	X	X							
17	Inflammable solids or oxidizing materials, yellow label	X	X	X	X	X	X	X							B X
18	Acids or corrosive liquids, white label	X	X	X	X	X	B X	B X							C X
19	Compressed noninflammable gases, green label	X	X	X	X	X	X								
20	Poisonous gases or liquids in cylinders, poison gas label	X	X	X	X	X	X								C X
21	Combustible liquids	X	X	X	X	X									
22	Hazardous articles	X	X	X	X	X	X								

(a) Blasting caps or electric blasting caps in a quantity not exceeding 1000 caps may be stowed or stored with all articles above named except those in columns (1) (2) (3) (5) and (6).

(b) Corrosive liquids (white label) shall not be stowed with inflammable solids and oxidizing materials (yellow label), or with any explosives.

(c) Cyanides or cyanide mixtures shall not be stowed or stored with corrosive liquids.

(d) Charged electric storage batteries shall not be stowed or stored with explosives class A or class B.

(e) Consult detailed regulations of other dangerous articles for provisions regarding "on deck stowage" of such articles on board vessels transporting explosives.

such manifest upon demand of an officer of the Coast Guard, Treasury Department, or any person authorized by the Secretary of Commerce to enforce the provisions of the Department of Commerce regulations for the carriage of dangerous cargoes.

Cargo stowage plans, showing the exact location of any dangerous articles or substances carried on any U. S. vessel, shall be properly prepared, and at least one copy of same retained on shore.

All shipping documents, or copies thereof, pertaining to shipments of dangerous articles or substances shall be preserved for at least one year, and shall be produced upon request of the Secretary of Commerce.

Packages of *dangerous goods carried on deck* should be of a suitable size for easy handling, so that they may be quickly thrown overboard if the safety of ship and crew demands such action.

As an example of a mixture of gases which is very dangerous to life, the fumes emitted by aniline oil, or aniline dyes (by-products of coal tar), combined with the corrosive, pungent fumes of bleaching powder (chloride of lime, calcium hypochlorite, or sodium hypochlorite) have been found to be among the most deadly.

Keep bleaching powder away from corrosive liquids or turpentine.

Cylinders of compressed gas require protection from heat. As the pressure varies directly as the temperature (absolute), a considerable increase of pressure would easily result from a few hours exposure to the sun's rays. An increase of 80° in temperature would increase the pressure from 2000 lbs. per square inch to 2,348 lbs.—not uncommon where cylinders are placed on deck in cool weather and soon afterward exposed to the heat of a tropical sun.

The Coast Guard's "Gray Book" of *Dangerous Cargo Regulations* has been discontinued.

CG–187, *Explosives or Other Dangerous Articles on Board Vessels* is replaced by a new volume of Title 46, *Code of Federal Regulations* In the interest of economy and to avoid duplication of the same information of two Government publications, the Division of the Federal Register has agreed to publish semiannual cumulative pocket supplements of parts 146 and 147, Vol. II of Title 46, *Code of Federal Regulations.*

This publication will contain all Dangerous Cargo Regulation which were in effect on January 1, 1958 and will be divided into parts and subparts exactly the same as CG–187. The supplements will be issued approximately 30 days subsequent to the time the semiannual amendments appear in the Federal Register.

Copies of the new Vol. II of Title 46, *Code of Federal Regulations* containing parts 146 and 147, may be obtained as a sales publication from the Superintendent of Documents, U.S. Government Printing Office, Washington 25, D. C. Price, $5.00.

Dangerous Liquids. Inflammable liquids are those which give off inflammable vapors at a temperature of, or below, 80° F. Combustible liquids are those which give off inflammable vapors only above 80°F.

The term *flash point*, as used in describing dangerous liquids, means that temperature to which the liquid must be heated to give off vapor in sufficient quantity, when mixed with air, to be ignited by a flame.

The term *ignition* or *fire point* refers to that temperature to which the liquid must bè raised before its surface layers will go on fire.

Labels. The regulations require that *dangerous packages are to be labeled* as prescribed for each class of such. Directions as to the necessary caution advised in the handling of the above are printed on the appropriate label. It is the shipper's duty to attach the proper label to each package before it leaves his hands. Labels are required as per the following:

Red label for inflammable liquids, gases, or explosives.

Yellow label for inflammable solids and oxidizing materials.

White label for acids and corrosive liquids.

Green label for non-inflammable gases.

Tear gas label for tear gas producing material.

Bung label for caution notice regarding opening of bung on metal barrels or drums containing inflammable liquids.

Skull and cross-bones label for poisons and poison gases.

"Empty" label for empty containers.

Forbidden on Any Common Carrier. Liquid nitro-glycerine, fulminate in bulk or dry condition, or other like explosive.

Forbidden on Passenger Vessels. Loose hay, cotton, or hemp; camphene, naphtha, benzine, coal oil, etc.; petroleum inflammable under 110° F.; metal polishes inflammable under 300° F.

Permitted on Passenger Vessels under special conditions: Acids, ammonia, baled hay (covered with tarpaulins), on deck only. Gunpowder, by special license, if provided with a metal, or metal-lined container, safe for stowage of same; ammunition for small arms only; alcohol, in cool place; caustic soda, quicklime, in water-tight containers on deck; matches, motion picture films, in fire-proof cases; petroleum, if flash point over 100° F.; gasoline, for, and to be kept in, life-boats using same for motive power.

Petroleum Products. The rules adopted by the Board of Underwriters of New York, which are to be adhered to by their surveyors in the loading of kerosene, gasoline, naphtha, and benzine in cases or drums, contain the following principal points:

All cases are to be stowed on edge (cans right side up). In beam filling only one "flatter" of kerosene is allowed.

Gasoline, naphtha, or benzine must not be stowed with general cargo, and must be kept from touching any iron by boards or proper dunnage.

Gasoline, naphtha, or benzine is not to be stowed in compartments adjoining engine-room or boiler-room bulkheads, unless a temporary bulkhead of wood is constructed not less than 3 ft. from such bulkhead, the intervening space to be filled with sand to a height of 6 ft. Where a permanent bulkhead is fitted, it shall be of wood and shall be 6″ from a fire-room bulkhead, or 3″ from an engine-room bulkhead, the intervening space to be filled with asbestos or silicate of cotton.

No gasoline, or naphtha, or benzine is to be carried in a deck over the engine-room or boiler-room, and none less than 20 ft. from the iron bulkhead of the fiddley, in the 'tween decks.

No coal is to be carried on the same deck with these products unless an iron bulkhead intervenes.

Drums of the above must not be stowed more than 7 high, and must be well dunnaged between each tier.

Heavy oils, such as lubricating, fuel, and gas oils, are not permitted, under any circumstances, to be stowed over cases of refined oil. These must be stowed *under* refined oil, or in blocks by themselves.

This class of cargo *must be thoroughly ventilated* remembering that petroleum gases are heavier than air.

LIQUID CARGOES—GENERAL

Leakage of casks or barrels is often the subject of claims for damage on the ground of improper stowage. Only good casks can be relied upon to withstand the handling from shore to ship and the pressure when stowed in tiers; receipts for casks in any doubtful condition should therefore be suitably qualified for the ship's protection.

Stowage of casks or barrels should be "bilge and cantline," "bung up and bilge free," as in this way less space is occupied and the casks are less liable to damage. This is especially required in the case of combustible liquids; a better stowage for such cargo has not yet been devised, and officers should insist that all barreled liquids be stowed in this manner. Casks standing on their ends under superimposed weight are subjected to a buckling stress which tends to open up their bilge seams. In the "bilge and cantline" style, the strongest part of the cask withstands the top weight; stood on end, the weakest part must uphold it.

Keep the ground tiers *bilge free on all sides*. Use soft wood beds under the quarters. The tiers should be laid straight fore-and-aft, and not follow the curvature of ship's sides; begin laying the barrels at the center line of hold, working toward the wings.

The stowage of strongly made casks of the various types should never exceed the following number in height:

	Capacity	*Height*
Butts or Pipes	130 U. S. gallons	3 tiers
Puncheons	86 " "	4 tiers
Hogsheads	65 " "	6 tiers
Tierces	50 " "	7 tiers
Barrels of Oil	42 " "	7 tiers

Bulk Liquid Cargoes (Petroleum). Today the United States produces and consumes over 60% of the world's supply of petroleum, with the result that the growing demand for facilitating the carriage of crude oil and its products (fuel oil, gasoline, kerosene, etc.) has given the oil tank vessel a place of foremost importance in our Merchant Marine.

The handling of oil cargoes in bulk is highly specialized, and a knowledge of practical tanker work may be acquired only by actual experience in transferring an oil cargo.

In loading, regard must be given the *expansion* of the oil due to increase of temperature, the *coefficient of expansion* being, for instance, .0004 for each degree Fahrenheit in the case of crude petroleum. Allowance for a decrease of *ullage*, or rising of the oil's surface, must be made, therefore, where greater temperatures of both sea and air than those at the place of loading will be met with during voyage.

As when loading full cargoes of ore, coal, grain, etc., the oil should be allowed to flow into as many tanks as possible at the same time, in order to distribute the weight over the greatest possible span of the vessel's length, thus avoiding any undue strain on the structural members of the hull.

Due to the difference in the volume of oil at different temperatures, for commercial reasons the quantity of cargo (usually in barrels) is reduced to that which it would measure at the standard temperature of 60° Fahrenheit.

The *Baumé Gravity* system (slightly modified by the *A.P.I. scale*) is in general use in the handling of bulk oil. For conversion from *Baumé* to *specific gravity*, the following formula is used:

$$\text{Baumé} = (140 \div \text{s.g.}) - 130$$

Fuel oil of specific gravity .933 and Baumé gravity 20 stows at 6.85 barrels, or 38.5 cubic feet to the ton.

(See *Tanker Cargoes*, page 8–26.)

COTTON

Cotton cargoes should be kept separated from coal or coke, any kind of oil, turpentine, resin, gasoline, acids, explosives, tar, or asphalt.

Cotton that has been wet must be kept apart from dry cotton.

Keep fire-damaged cotton on deck and away from the hatches. See that every precaution is taken to prevent outbreak of fire in the cargo and every means available for fighting fire is in good order and ready for instant use.

Attention is called to the Board of Underwriters of New York book of rules for loading cotton with *hazardous* cargo, which may be procured upon request.

GRAIN

The expression "grain-laden ship," in most maritime countries' laws or regulations governing the sea-carriage of grain, means a ship carrying an amount of grain which is more than one-third of the registered tonnage of the vessel; and that third shall be computed, where the grain is reckoned in measures of capacity, at the rate of 100 cubic feet for each ton of registered tonnage; and, where the grain is reckoned in measures of weight, at the rate of two tons weight for each ton of registered tonnage.

The term "grain" means any corn, rice, peas, beans, seeds, nuts, or kernels.

For the carriage of grain, certain rules, which have been made law by some countries, have been laid down with the object of preventing such cargo from shifting, and so minimize the risk of loss of ship and cargo during heavy rolling or listing of the vessel.

Shifting Boards of certain strength are required, as also "feeders" for the feeding, or filling up, of the space in the hold caused by the settling or shifting of the grain.

The shifting boards are usually required to be fitted from deck to deck, and must be at least 2″ in thickness, and of sound lumber.

The rules for loading grain issued by the Board of Underwriters of New York require the unsupported span between *uprights* must not exceed 8 ft. with 2″ boards, 10 ft. with 2 1/2″ boards, or 12 ft. with 3″ boards. Vertical distance between *shores* is to be 7 ft., and the uppermost shore to be within 18″ of the top of the upright. Shores are to be 4″ × 6″ when up to 16 ft. in length; 6″ × 6″ when over 16 and up to 20 ft.; and 8″ × 6″ when over 20 ft. in length.

Wire stays may be used in lieu of shores, but must comply with the rules laid down for such.

Where feeders are not constructed, the rules call for 4 tiers of bagged grain above the bulk cargo, to be stowed up to the deck, upon 2 tiers of boards, the lower boards to be laid not more than 4 ft. apart, and the upper boards not more than 4″ apart. The tiers are to be laid fore-and-aft and athwartships respectively.

When a *full cargo* of bagged grain is carried, shifting boards must be fitted to extend not less than 4 ft. downward from the deck above each hold or 'tween deck.

The foregoing are, in general, the principal requirements in the stowage of grain cargoes. In practice, the rules or laws governing grain loading at a particular port are consulted, and adhered to accordingly.

A point worthy of note is that the "angle of repose" (23° for wheat) is *very much reduced by rolling, pitching*, or shocks on the ship by the sea; movement of cargo is more probable the farther its surface is situated from the center about which the ship rolls. Hence cargo in the upper 'tween decks will shift more easily than cargo in the lower holds.

COAL

Coal of any kind is liable to *spontaneous combustion* when a comparatively long time lying in a hold or bunker. It is said that the coal shipped from Virginia, New South Wales, Calcutta, and the River Clyde is particularly liable to spontaneous ignition.

Coal that has been subjected to much breakage during loading emits an *inflammable gas* (called marsh gas) which, when mixed with the required proportion of air, will explode upon being brought in contact with a spark or flame. Therefore, maintain thorough ventilation of holds during loading, as well as insuring good surface ventilation of the coal on the voyage.

The absorption of oxygen causes the generation of gas by the coal, and the higher the temperature the more rapid is the gas-producing process.

An accumulation of this generated gas very readily lends itself to the spontaneous combustion condition. Thorough surface ventilation is the only effective means for the removal of the gas.

Coal shipped in a wet condition is not thereby necessarily more liable to spontaneous heating than when dry.

Shifting. Precaution against shifting of a coal cargo are necessary in partly filled compartments. Especially is this required on the smaller type of cargo vessels on voyages where bad weather conditions are likely to be met with.

Temperature. Provision should be made for observing the temperature of the body of cargo, and a record of same should be noted in the ship's log.

TIMBER

Timber measurements are the most complicated of all measurements in use for shipping purposes.

The American unit is, in general, the 1,000 board feet, equal in bulk to 83 1/3 cubic feet. In France, Belgium, Italy, etc., the unit is the "stere," which is equivalent to the cubic meter.

The "standard," of which there are several varieties, with no relation to each other whatever, is the unit of measure for wholesale transactions in northern European countries, and, in Great Britain, the "Petrograd standard" is in common use.

To calculate *board measure*, or the number of square feet of planking 1″ in thickness, multiply the thickness by the width (in inches) by the length (in feet) and divide by 12.

Timber Deck Cargoes. As in the case of the carriage of grain, we have no laws enacted for the loading of timber on deck, such procedure being regulated by the Underwriters' surveyors in general.

Timber deck cargo regulations are laid down in the British Merchant Shipping Act, 1932, and the following are the more important points covered therein:

Openings to space below the freeboard deck shall be *closed and battened down*. All fittings, such as hatchway beams, fore-and-afters, and covers shall be in place. Where hold ventilation is needed, the ventilators shall be efficiently protected.

The deck cargo must be *compactly stowed, lashed*, and *secured*; and it must not interfere in any way with the navigation and necessary work of the ship nor with the provision of a safe margin of *stability* at all stages of the voyage, regard being given to addition of weight such as that due to absorption of water, and to losses of weight due to consumption of fuel and stores.

Safe and satisfactory access to crew's quarters, machinery space, and all other parts used in the necessary work of the ship shall be available at all times. Deck cargo in way of openings which give access to such parts shall be stowed so that the openings can be secured against the admission of water.

Efficient protection for the crew in the form of guard-rails or life-lines shall be provided on each side of the deck-load to a height of not less than 4 ft. above the cargo.

Steering-gear arrangements must be effectively protected from damage by the cargo, and, as far as practicable, shall be accessible. Efficient provision shall be made for steering in the event of a breakdown in the main steering arrangements.

Lashings. Over-all lashings of ample strength and in good condition, fitted with releasing arrangements, shall be provided so as to give effective security throughout the length of the timber deck cargo, and releasing arrangements shall be accessible at all times.

Uprights shall be of adequate strength, and may be of wood or metal. The spacing between uprights shall be suitable for the length and character of the timber carried, but shall not exceed 10 ft., and efficient means shall be provided for securing the uprights.

Steamers using *Timber Load Lines* are required to have a forecastle of standard height, and not less in length than 7% of that of the vessel.

In loading deck cargoes, these vessels are required to have the well decks stowed as solidly as possible to a height of at least 6 ft. for ships up to, and including, 250 ft. in length; 7 1/2 ft. for vessels 400 ft. and above in length; and a proportionate intermediate height for vessels above 250 ft., but less than 400 ft. in length.

Lashings are to be not more than 10 ft. apart, and of a *close link chain* not less than 3/4″ or *flexible wire rope* of equivalent strength, fitted with slip-hooks and turnbuckles, to be accessible at all times.

REFRIGERATED CARGOES

Refrigerated cargoes of late years have enormously increased in volume, and today, in addition to the tonnage engaged on regular voyages in the carriage of perishable goods, we have an ever increasing number of tramp steamers equipped with refrigerated space in order to cope with this growing demand.

Refrigerated cargo is divided into three general classes: frozen, chilled, and air-cooled.

Frozen Cargo includes meat, fish, egg products, butter, or such goods as are carried at a temperature of from 10° to 15°F.

Chilled Cargo is usually the term applied to *meats* carried at about 29°. Because of the uniformity and constancy of temperature required, this class of cargo needs the most careful attention for a successful turnout, and to conform to this temperature requirement, the carcasses or quarters of meat are suspended from rails fitted in a fore-and-aft direction on the deckheads.

The refrigeration of frozen and chilled cargoes is effected by *cooled brine* circulated through an arrangement of coils fitted on the bulkheads in the compartments. Special care should be taken to prevent the cargo (more especially meats of any kind) from coming in contact with the piping, and, where dunnage is used to this end, the wood should be cooled to about the same temperature as that of the cargo, in order to avoid the objectionable marking of the goods which would otherwise result.

Some vessels are fitted to carry either frozen or chilled cargo, in which case the insulation provided is heavier than that for chilled cargo only, and the piping heavier than that for frozen goods only.

Air-Cooled Cargo is usually fruits and vegetables, but certain kinds of canned goods, bacon, cheese, eggs, and beer and wines are often included.

The air-cooled system consists of the delivery into, and the extraction from, the holds of cooled air by means of fans, the cooling process being the forcing of the air over coils through which brine at the required temperature is circulated.

Where possible, advantage should be taken of the *stowage of metals under refrigerated cargoes*. Ingots of copper, lead, tin, etc., if spread over the deck of the compartment, will do much toward stabilizing the temperature—a most desirable asset, especially when carrying chilled meats.

Following is a list of refrigerated goods, with the temperatures at which they are commonly carried.

Bananas at about 55°
Beer and Wines at about 42°.
Cheese at 40° to 45°.
Butter at 10° to 15°.
Eggs at 35° to 40°.
Egg Products, or whites and yolks of eggs in dried, powdered, or moist form, at about 10° to 15°.
Fish at 10° to 15°.
Fruits, Fresh: Apples, pears, plums, etc., should not be carried at lower than 33°. Refrigeration is usually considered unnecessary on a North Atlantic crossing, or on a short cool-weather passage, provided the fruit is stowed in well-ventilated compartments; but, where the voyage is lengthy, and especially if passing through the Tropics, a system of refrigeration is indispensable.
Meats: Bacon at 35° to 40°.
            Beef, frozen, at 12° to 15°.
            Beef, chilled, at 29°.
            Pigs, poultry, rabbits, at 12° to 15°.
Milk, in cans or bottles, at 35°.
Vegetables, fresh, 35° to 40°.

LIVE STOCK

Most maritime countries have enacted laws governing the carriage of horses, cattle, sheep, hogs, and goats, which laws should be studied and complied with by the master, so far as they apply to the loading of live stock at the particular port.

The regulations of the U. S. Department of Agriculture, prepared by the Bureau of Animal Industry, should be carefully followed by the master and mates of all vessels engaged in carrying animals from a United States port. These regulations provide for the size of fittings, space, alleys, number of attendants, feed, etc., and cover all points to be considered in the loading and care of animals.

HEAVY WEIGHTS

Where locomotives, boilers, and special heavy lifts are placed in a ship's hold, much broken stowage or unused space is the result. Such freight as baled hay, kegs of bolts, or coils of barbed wire, is often used as a filler, and hence also assist in chocking off or dunnaging.

In addition to the usual precautions taken to safely lift and stow heavy pieces of cargo, care must be taken to spread out the bearing surface, as in the case of placing a locomotive over a double-bottom tank top. Stout timbers laid fore-and-aft, and long enough to distribute the weight over at least two floors, should be prepared to take the bearing points of such weights.

When local stresses due to a heavy weight stowed in a 'tween deck are set up, the deck beams should be shored up from the deck or decks next below.

The hold stanchions, where fitted, are of course important units in the structural strength of the vessel. If it is found necessary to remove any of them when stowing bulky lifts, they should be restored to their original positions before loading cargo on the decks above.

Disposition of Weighty Cargo. Where conditions admit, weighty cargo should not be loaded in the extreme ends of the ship's cargo space. Due to the abnormal moment about the midship point, a vessel heavily loaded at the ends will *steer badly* and will be apt to *ship much water* over the bows in a head sea.

As a rule, stowing heavy cargo toward amidships and in the wings will result in a more comfortable ship in a seaway, and so lessen the probability of damage to cargo through chafing or pressure.

Since the raising or lowering of weights in a ship's hold has a direct effect on the vessel's stability, the distribution of cargo should be consistent with her "stiff" or "tender" qualities, in order to result in an easy-rolling ship in a seaway.

Railway Iron. Differences of opinion exist as to the best stowage for a full cargo of railway iron, which usually includes fish-plates, nuts and bolts, and tie spikes, as well as the rails.

Probably the most favored practice is to lay the ground tier solid (alternate rails base up) and in the fore-and-aft lines; next tier athwartships or obliquely, single rails laid about two feet apart; next tier fore-and-aft, rails close together, and so on; top tier to be laid solid, same as the ground tier, and the whole tommed down from the deckhead. Bundles of fish-plates may be used as dunnage to protect ship's sides from possible movement of the 'thwartship rails. 'Tween deck stowage is solid fore-and-aft, and should take at least one-fourth the cargo. Keep ends of rails away from bulkheads by heavy timber or bundles of fish-plates; also protect masts, pillars, vent shafts, etc., from chafing by placing heavy deals or pieces of dunnage as required.

Structural Steel. Stow fore-and-aft in line with keel. Observe precautions against chafing as for railway iron. If full load, tom down from deck beams, using heavy 'thwartship deals across top of cargo.

STOWAGE PREPARATION NOTES

1. Clean out bilges, limbers, and rose-boxes.
2. See cargo battens and tank covers in place and secured.
3. Have all piping in hold properly protected.
4. See electric wiring is in order.
5. Secure ports and any side openings.
6. Inspect weather deck for leaks, especially around masts.
7. See ladders, hatch strongbacks, and hatch covers in order.

8. Have 3 good tarpaulins for each hatch, good wedges, and battens.

9. Supply clean dunnage for a clean cargo, and *have a clean hold*.

When Discharging: Do not remove damaged cargo until it has been surveyed. Land any empty bags or broken-up containers found in hold after discharge of cargo, so that same may be tallied.

If cargo has been on fire, segregate as follows:

1. Goods that were actually on fire.

2. Goods damaged by water or steam in extinguishing fire.

3. Goods apparently damaged by smoke, fumes, or by being trampled upon, etc., when fighting the fire.

STOWAGE FACTORS AND PERMEABILITIES

Goods	Packing	Stowage Factor	% Permeability (in full hold)
Autos	Cases	about 160	82
Autos	Open	about 250	95
Apples	Barrels	104	61
Apples	Boxes	72	40
Barbed wire	Rolls	55	85
Beans	Bags	60	50
Biscuits	Cases	142	79
Blankets	Bales	153	78
Butter	Boxes	56	20
Canned goods	Cases	50	30
Cardboard	Bundles	210	88
Cartridges	Boxes	30	30
Cement	Bags	35	63
Cement	Barrels	36	72
Cheese	Boxes	45	30
Coffee	Bags	58	42
Cork	Bales	187	24
Corn	Bags	55	42
Dates	Boxes	45	30
Dried fruit	Boxes	45	30
Dry goods	Boxes	100	60
Eggs	Cases	100	45
Flour	Bags	48	29
Flour	Barrels	73	44
Gasoline	Drums	61	40
General cargo	......	70	60
Grapefruit	Boxes	70	46
Hardware	Boxes	50	50
Hay	Bales	120	60
Iron	Pigs	10	17
Lard	Boxes	45	20
Laths	Bundles	107	37
Leather	Bales	80	35
Linseed	Bags	60	50
Machinery	Cases	48	70
Magazines	Bundles	75	70
Meat (cold storage)	......	90–100	66
Newspapers	Bales	120	63
Nitrate	Bags	24	55
Nuts	Bags	70	55

Goods	Packing	Stowage Factor	% Permeability (in full hold)
Oats	Bags	77	48
Oil	Barrels	50	35
Oil	Cases	50	34
Oil	Drums	45	40
Onions	Bags	78	48
Oranges	Boxes	78	46
Paper	Rolls	80	70
Paint	Drums	24	40
Peas	Bags	55	55
Poultry	Boxes	95	60
Potatoes	Bags	60	49
Potatoes	Barrels	75	61
Rags	Bales	149	76
Raisins	Boxes	54	50
Rice	Bags	58	55
Roof-paper	Rolls	80	30
Rope	Coils	72	55
Rubber	Bundles	140	25
Rugs	Bales	146	70
Soap	Boxes	45	20
Soap powder	Boxes	90	70
Sugar	Bags	47	48
Sugar	Barrels	58	60
Starch	Boxes	59	55
Steel rods	. . . . . .	12	28
Tallow	Barrels	66	35
Tea	Boxes	90	80
Thread	Cases	60	45
Tiles	Boxes	50	20
Tin	Sheets	7	15
Tires, auto	Bundles	168	85
Typewriters	Cases	110	80
Waste, cotton	Bales	175	80
Wheat, bulk	. . . . . .	47	45
Wool	Bales	160	30
Zinc	Slabs	7	15

Note: Permeability indicates the percentage of hold space that would be occupied by water were the hold completely filled with the goods noted when totally flooded due to accident, such as stranding or collision. Some idea of the remaining buoyancy, if any, may be gained by a comparison of the figures in the two columns, considering, of course, the weight of the bare product and its packing material.

TANK VESSELS

Tanks. Usually 8 to 12 tanks divided by a continuous longitudinal bulkhead into port and starboard compartments. Surface of oil confined in trunkway. Late construction has two continuous longitudinal bulkheads dividing tanks into 3 compartments with no trunkways.

Pump Room houses all cargo-pumps which are connected to main pipeline of ship. Pump room usually occupies all space between two transverse bulkheads amidships. Some larger tankers have two pump rooms.

Cofferdams separate after end of cargo space from fire-room and bunkers, and for end of cargo space from dry cargo hold. In some ships they separate groups of tanks.

Valves controlling suction and flow in each compartment are worked from the deck. Seat valves at suction ends of lines; gate valves for shut-offs or master valves on main pipe lines.

Air valves on air lines to tanks for controlling gas blow-out system.

Steam valves to control steam heating by coils in tanks.

Master steam valve to fire smothering system, by which all tanks may be supplied with steam at once. Supply of steam may be localized by closing valves at each tank as necessary.

Valve Controls are marked on U. S. tankers as follows:

Color of Paint

Master cargo valves.....................yellow
Starboard cargo line valves.............yellow with green center
Port cargo line valves..................yellow with red center
Bunker fuel oil valves..................black
Live steam valves.......................red
Exhaust steam valves....................blue
Sea water valves........................green
Fresh water valves......................white
Emergency valves........................half red and half black

Summer Tanks. In older construction these were built in wings of first deck from below, between main trunkway and ship's side. No summer tanks in later types, because of the subdivision of tanks into three compartments by two fore-and-aft bulkheads.

Cleaning Tanks. Tanks are cleaned by a whirling spray of hot water in most cases. If the tanks and pipe-line system are to be cleaned for the carriage of a fine grade of oil, a light oil is pumped through the system and re-landed. In any case of cleaning tanks when in port, the "slops" must be transferred to shore or into a barge alongside. The process of steaming tanks for a few hours and hosing down the sides, etc., is in general, falling into disuse.

Expansion of Oil varies slightly with the different products. Crude petroleum has a coefficient of .0004 for each degree Fahrenheit; kerosene, about .0005; gasoline, .0006. One per cent of volume for every 25° temperature change is a useful rule for fuel and heavy oils.

Ullage. Where tanks are to be filled to capacity, the ullage, or distance of the surface of the oil below the tank cover must be governed by the probable expansion on the coming voyage.

A **partly filled tank** of light oil may be filled without hurt to oil by pumping clean water into tank. Oil rests on top of water. Keep water away from fuel oils.

Ballasting Tanker. Fill alternate tanks. Empty tanks may then be inspected, cleaned, valves overhauled, etc.

Gas Free, as referred to tanks, means free from dangerous concentrations of inflammable or toxic gases.

Flame Screen for ullage holes, tank hatches, and vents is a single screen of corrosive-resisting wire of at least 30×30 mesh, or two single screens of at least 20×20 mesh spaced 1/2″ to 1 1/2″ apart.

The danger area is a minimum of 200 ft.

PRECAUTIONS DURING TRANSFER OPERATIONS

1. Display red flag or red light when transferring cargo.

2. Post warning sign at gangway, "No smoking—No open lights—No visitors."

3. Warning sign in radio room not to use equipment when working cargo.

4. Smoking only at designated times and places; safety matches only.

5. Flame screens over tank hatches and ullage holes.

6. Use non-sparking tools.

7. Have sufficient number of crew on duty.

8. Gas mask, fresh air, or oxygen supply apparatus; belt and lifelines.

9. Maintain any electrical connection to shore until cargo hose is removed.

10. Plug scuppers in case of overflow, when water is not used for cooling.

11. Sea valves closed and lashed.

12. Sufficient length of hose to allow for movement of vessel.

13. No repair work in and near cargo spaces unless with senior deck officer's permission.

Duties of Senior Officer during Transfer of Cargo:

1. Supervise operation of cargo valves.

2. Start transfer of cargo slowly.

3. Watch hose and connections for leakage.

4. Watch operating pressure on cargo system.

5. Watch rate of loading to avoid overflow.

Do Not Transfer Cargo:

1. During severe electric storms.

2. If fire breaks out in the vicinity.

3. If a steam vessel comes alongside in way of cargo tanks.

Molasses. Bulk molasses has a specific gravity of about 1.3, and in cold weather thickens and becomes difficult to pump. When transferring this cargo under the conditions noted, it should not be heated above 100° F., in order to avoid sugar deposit.

Molasses tanks should be hosed down with sea water. It has been found that neither fresh water nor steam gives satisfactory results in the operation of cleaning the tanks and pipe-lines used in carrying molasses.

TANKER CARGOES

Kinds of Oils

Liquids having the characteristic of being "greasy" are commonly called oils. In general, oils may be divided into the following 5 classes:

a) **Petroleum Base.** This group includes those oils made by distillation (heating) of crude petroleum, which produces gasoline, kerosene, light fuel oils, heavy oils, lubricating oils, and asphalt.

b) **Coal Base.** This group includes those oils made by distillation (heating) of coal and shale, which produces benzol, toluol, creosote, and coal tar.

c) **Vegetable Oils.** This group includes such products as linseed, tung, cottonseed, olive, palm, and castor oils.

d) **Marine Animal and Fish Oils.** This group includes cod, shark, fish, seal, whale, and porpoise oils.

e) **Animal Oils.** This group includes such products as neat's-foot and lard oil.

While all of these oils are commonly transported in barrels and many of them are transported in bulk, those produced from crude petroleum are by far the most important because of the tremendous quantities which are consumed.

Characteristics of Oils which Relate to Safety

Oils of all kinds may be divided into two classes for purposes of safe handling:

a) **Inflammable,** or those which will give off inflammable vapors at or below 80° F. Thus, if such an oil comes in contact with a flame when the oil temperature is at or below 80° F. it will "flash" (i.e. small flames will pass over its surface). At a temperature not much above its "flash point" such an oil will burn steadily, and this temperature is called its "fire point."

b) **Combustible,** or those which will give off inflammable vapors only above 80° F. Combustible oils are relatively safe to handle and include such petroleum products as kerosene, light and heavy fuels, lubricating oils, etc. Practically all the animal, vegetable, and fish oils are combustible oils and therefore are relatively safe; however, it should be remembered that certain of these oils when mixed with other substances will sometimes ignite of themselves. Thus old rags smeared with linseed oil (or even paint) or sawdust or rags wet with fish oil and kept warm will often ignite from chemical action. Many fires on shipboard have been started in this way and the cause of such fires is referred to as spontaneous ignition, which means the capacity of some substances to ignite from chemical action without being brought in contact with flame.

It will be evident that this characteristic of certain vegetable and fish oils to ignite of themselves when smeared on wood, sawdust, rags, etc., and heated, should be clearly remembered when preparing a cargo hold for barrels of such oils or when wiping paint brushes or the hands on rags in the paint locker. Holds should be thoroughly swept up and oily rags should never be kept in a paint locker or other closed space.

For the purpose of regulating tank vessels the rules of the Bureau of Marine Inspection and Navigation divide all oils into the five following grades:

Inflammable Liquids

Grade A: Any inflammable liquid having a Reid vapor pressure of 14 pounds or more.

Grade B: Any inflammable liquid having a Reid vapor pressure under 14 pounds and over 8 1/2 pounds.

Grade C: Any inflammable liquid having a Reid vapor pressure of 8 1/2 pounds or less and a flash point of 80° F. or below.

Combustible Liquids

Grade D: Any combustible liquid having a flash point below 150° F. and above 80° F.

Grade E: Any combustible liquid having a flash point of 150° F. or above.

Into these five grades all oils may be grouped, and from what has already been said it is apparent that the inflammable oils are those which may be ignited at temperatures below 80° F. whereas the combustible oils (or safer ones) must be heated to above 80° F. before they will flash.

In the three classes of inflammable oils the expression "Reid vapor pressure" is used. This refers to a method of measuring the tendency of these oils to give off inflammable vapors. If such oils are placed in tight containers to which pressure gages are attached it will be found that a moderate pressure exists in the container due to the pressure of the vapors which have escaped from the oil. The pressures given in the definitions of grades, A, B, and C oils are "absolute."

Since the atmospheric pressure is about 14.7 pounds per square inch absolute, it will be seen that only grade A oils will give a vapor pressure greater than atmospheric. The Reid method of measuring vapor pressures consists in placing a small amount of the oil to be tested in a container which is then closed and heated to a temperature of 100° F., at which temperature the pressure within the container is measured by a gage. By this means the tendency of the oil to give off inflammable vapors is measured.

Classification of Oils by Grades

Based on the classification of oils described in the preceding section, the names of the various oils known to commerce may be roughly grouped as follows:

Grade A: "Casing head" (natural) gasoline and very light naphtha.

Grade B: Most commercial gasolines.

Grade C: Most crude oils and some "cut back" asphalts (asphalt thinned with a volatile oil to make it fluid so that it can be used like a paint), creosote, benzol, toluol, alcohol.

Grade D: Kerosene, light fuel oils, and a few very heavy crude oils (Venezuela and Panuco crude).

Grade E: Heavy fuel oils, "Bunker C," Diesel fuel, road oil, lubricating oil, asphalt and coal tar, fish, animal, and vegetable oils.

Having described the various kinds and grades of oils, it is now appropriate to discuss the essential requirements for safely handling them. Since more care must be taken with the inflammable oils (grades A, B, and C) the handling of this group will be described and reference will be made, where appropriate, to the combustible or safer group (grades D and E).

Operations Prior to Transfer of Oil Cargo in Bulk

Upon joining a tank vessel, those whose duties will require them to handle cargo, should familiarize themselves as soon as possible with the arrangement of cargo pumps and the layout of suction and discharge piping and valves. Nearly all tank vessels have individual peculiarities relating to the loading and discharging of cargo and inquiry should be made as to the methods used for loading, "topping off," discharging, and draining.

Prior to starting the transfer of oil cargo in bulk the senior deck officer present should assure himself that the proper signals are displayed (a red flag by day and a red electric lantern by night if the vessel is at a dock). At the gangway or point of approach to the vessel a warning sign should be displayed reading as follows:

WARNING

NO OPEN LIGHTS

NO SMOKING

NO VISITORS

If cargo is being loaded, the sea valves should be tightly closed and lashed and main deck scuppers should be plugged to prevent oil from getting into the harbor. The signal system (telephones, bells, or whistles) used on the dock to regulate the loading should be tested out by the shore personnel.

No repair work should be permitted on the main deck or adjacent to cargo spaces, which might produce a spark. When loading inflammable oils (grades A, B, and C), all fires and open flames under boilers and in ranges should, if possible, be extinguished and in any event no such fires or open flames should be permitted in any compartment which is on and open to that part of the deck on which the cargo hatches and hose are located.

The cargo hose should be properly connected and supported and sufficient men should be available to properly handle the cargo transfer operations.

Inflammable oils (grades A, B, and C) should always be loaded through the tank vessel's pipe lines. Combustible oils (grades D and E), which include such products as kerosene, fuel oils, lubricating oils, etc., are frequently loaded "over all" (by placing the end of the cargo hose in the open tank hatch). This is a safe procedure because such oils do not give off inflammable vapors at usual atmospheric temperatures.

When an inspection by the senior deck officer on duty indicates that the tank vessel is ready and when the terminal representative has indicated his readiness, cargo transfer may be started.

Actual Transfer of Oil Cargo in Bulk

The transfer of bulk oil cargo consists of either loading or discharging. Of these two operations loading requires the greater care. During the loading operation the gases within the cargo tanks are expelled through the tank vents and the ullage (sounding) holes if open. It is usual after loading has started to proceed at a steady loading rate until all tanks are about 90% full and then to reduce the loading rate considerably and "top off," or complete the loading of each tank slowly in order to avoid an "oil spill" or overflow. An oil spill during loading presents one of the principal risks in handling oil cargoes and the topping-off operation should be watched with particular care. Approximately 1 to 3% of the space in each tank should be allowed for the expansion of the oil due to a possible increase in temperature during the voyage. Where the tank vessel is operating on a coastwise or sea voyage, the amount of vapor space in each tank is usually fixed by the gravity of the oil and the draft of the vessel as allowed by the load-line assignment.

The operation and setting of cargo valves during the loading of cargo is an important matter. The senior officer present should supervise the handling of all valves. The dock or terminal man should be given a "standby" order from 5 to 10 minutes before the loading is started, stopped, or reduced in rate. The quick closing of a ship valve may result in bursting the loading hose.

When setting cargo valves in the "open" position it is a good practice first to open the valve all the way, and then to close it about one-fourth turn in order to be certain that the valve is not jammed in the open position. When closing cargo valves it is a good practice to close them tight and then open them one or two turns and then close them tight again. By this means any scale or foreign substance which may have become lodged under the valve gate or disk, preventing it from seating tightly, will be washed clear. As each tank is topped off and its valve is closed, it is a good practice to check the liquid level in it during the time the remaining tanks are being finished to make certain that the valves are not leaking. In the loading of tank vessels the opening and closing of some tank valves change the rate of flow of oil into those tanks where the setting of the valves is not changed.

The discharging of oil cargoes is relatively safe; however, the bursting of the cargo hose as a result of excessive pressure should be carefully guarded against by starting the cargo pumps slowly and observing the pressure gages frequently.

In discharging oil cargoes (except where mixed grades are carried), it is usual to hold until the last one full tank of oil to be used for priming the cargo pumps when suction is lost in draining. During the draining operation the vessel is usually "trimmed by the stern" and frequently listed to port and to starboard to assist the oil to the suctions.

During the transfer of oil cargo, the cargo hose should be frequently inspected to see that it is properly supported. Drip pans or buckets should be placed under the hose connections. When the transfer operation is completed, the cargo hose should be drained back into the vessel's tanks, into buckets or into the shore pipe lines or drainage system.

Maintenance and Care of Equipment

Cargo-handling equipment should be kept in good condition in order to avoid emergency repairs during the period when cargo is being handled. Whenever a tank vessel is gas free, full advantage should be taken of the opportunity to work on cargo pumps, pipe lines, and valves.

The following equipment is required by the tanker rules to be tested or cared for and maintained by the personnel of the tank vessel.

Cargo Hose. Only cargo hose made for oil service and designed for a minimum working pressure of 100 pounds per square inch should be used. Where cargo hose sweats or leaks through the fabric it should be taken out of pressure service.

Particular care should be exercised to see that cargo hose is properly supported and that it is protected against chafing. It should not be bent to too short a radius. Sufficient hose should be used to provide for the movement of the tank vessel, but constant care must be exercised to see that the "bight" of hose is so supported that it cannot become pinched between the dock and vessel's side.

Cargo Pump Relief Valves. These valves should be tested at least once each year to make certain that they function properly at the pressure they are set for.

Cargo Pump Pressure Gages. These gages should be tested at least once each year for accuracy.

Cargo Discharge Piping. Cargo discharge piping should be tested at least once each year at its maximum working pressure.

General Safety Precautions

Matches. Safety matches only should be allowed on tank vessels.

Smoking. Smoking should not be allowed on the weather decks of any tank vessel when loading or discharging cargo, when gas freeing tanks, or when lying at the docks of an oil terminal. The senior officer on each tank vessel should make his own rules for the guidance of the crew as to where and when smoking is permissible.

Static Electricity. When gasoline or similar flammable liquids flow through a hose, when poured from one receptacle to another, and when passed through a filter, dangerous static charges are frequently obtained and fire and explosion may result unless proper precautions are taken. The metal nozzle of the end of the gasoline hose should be bonded to the coupling which is attached to the pump by a copper wire inside the hose and the nozzle should be held in contact with any metal tank or receptacle which is being filled with gasoline. When gasoline is being transferred in large quantities, an insulated copper cable, at least No. 4 US gauge, is connected between the source of supply and the receiving inlet.

Cargo Tank Hatches and Ullage Holes. Tank hatches and ullage (sounding) holes should not remain open without being fitted with flame screens, unless the tank is gas free.

Nonsparking Tools. Tank vessels should be furnished with lead, copper, or other non-sparking hammers or tools for opening and closing cargo tank hatches.

Fresh Air Masks. On manned tank vessels, where the distance from the deck to the bottom of the cargo tank exceeds 15 feet, fresh air breathing apparatus (including belt and life line) is required to be carried.

Fresh Air Breathing Apparatus. This system is the best for use on tank ships (the all-purpose gas mask should not be used in entering compartments on tank ships). The apparatus consists of a large trunk approximately 3 by 2 feet and about 2 feet in depth, which contains the hose, the masks, and a rotary air pump. The mask is adjusted to the wearer in the same manner as the gas mask and the hose is held to the body by a harness similar to an officer's field belt; the hose then being led directly to the pump and attached thereto. This pump may have as many leads from it as desirable, the speed of operation of the pump determining the amount of air thrown out by it and the number of masks which may be attached to it.

In using this apparatus, care must be taken that the hose leads do not foul and that the pump is being operated at sufficient speed to supply all outlets.

Owing to the fact that the hose connections for this apparatus are of rubber, it should not be utilized for fire or where acid has been spilled on the decks.

Ventilation. Ventilation should not be confused with venting. Engine rooms, living quarters, and other spaces where members of crew normally may be employed, are ventilated; cargo tanks, bunker tanks, cofferdams, and water tanks are vented to protect them against excessive internal pressure or vacuum.

The importance of ventilation in working and living spaces where inflammable vapors are likely to accumulate cannot be overemphasized. Even in pump rooms where precautions are taken to eliminate all sources of ignition, ventilation is of primary importance. In working spaces where grinding of tools, electrical sparks, and smoking are normally present, ventilation must often be depended upon to prevent accumulations of inflammable vapors.

As these vapors are heavier than air and tend to settle to the lowest parts of any space, it is desirable to see that ventilators are so set that vapors will be removed from these low places. Particular attention should be given to this fact in the ventilation of spaces containing gasoline engines. Such spaces, as well as pump rooms and hold spaces containing independent cargo tanks, should have at least two ventilators, one extending to the lower part of the space and the other terminating in the upper part, to provide natural change of air. Where necessary, steam or air-actuated ejectors or blowers may be installed to secure adequate ventilation.

Doors and ports which may be closed cannot be depended upon to ventilate enclosed spaces. Other openings provided for natural ventilation should never be shut off or closed. Where mechanical means for ventilation are provided for pump engine, or other engine rooms, it should be remembered to turn them on a sufficient length of time before starting engines to insure the removal of possible inflammable vapors.

Electric Bonding. At some terminals, especially those near cities or large refineries, stray electric currents from trolley tracks or grounded power lines sometimes follow the oil pipe lines down to the dock. Since the hull of the tank vessel (if of steel) offers an excellent ground for these stray currents and since the cargo hose contains metal reinforcing which provides an electrical conductor from flange to flange, it sometimes happens that an electric spark will pass between the hose and ship or shore flanges when the hose is being connected. If oil is around in quantity, it is possible for such a spark to cause a fire.

In order to reduce the chance of fire from these stray currents, some terminals are fitted with electric bonding or grounding cables. These cables should be connected in the following manner: The shore end of the cable is already connected to or grounded on the dock pipe lines. A switch should be provided in the cable. The ship end of the cable should be bolted to a bright metallic part of the ship's hull or cargo lines within a few feet of the hose connection. The following should be the exact sequence of connecting and disconnecting the bonding cable: When connecting cargo hose:

1. See that switch is *open*.
2. Connect bonding cable to ship.
3. *Close* switch.
4. Connect cargo hose.

When disconnecting cargo hose:

1. Disconnect and remove cargo hose from ship.
2. *Open* switch.
3. Remove bonding cable from ship.

In the use of an electric bonding cable the point to be remembered is that the ship should first be grounded before the cargo hose is connected and that this ground connection should be maintained until after the cargo hose is removed.

Handling of General Cargo. No general cargo should be handled during the loading of inflammable oils (grades A, B, and C) without the permission of the senior deck officer present.

Emergencies

Under the tanker rules, the senior officer present on a tank vessel is allowed free exercise of his judgment in pursuing the most effective action in case of emergency. Where an emergency arises during the transfer of cargo, the safest procedure usually is to stop loading or discharging as soon as possible. In an emergency, such as an oil spill or broken cargo valves or pumps, a definite plan should be worked out in advance for correcting the trouble. It is generally best to develop such a plan by discussing the problem with the terminal representative and one or two others on the tank vessel, provided time is available. When the plan has finally been agreed to, every precaution should be taken to insure safety and the work should proceed slowly and carefully.

If the nature of the emergency is such that the vessel, its crew, and surrounding property is hazarded (such, for example, as a serious oil spill) all hands should be called and the terminal executive should be notified. In the presence of known danger, every step should be carefully considered and action should, if possible, be slow and deliberate. Oil spilled on deck should be carefully bailed up with non-sparking bailers or buckets, and the deck should then be mopped up and washed down before loading is resumed.

If it becomes necessary to work on cargo pumps, the cargo pump room should be thoroughly ventilated and freed of gas. When a cargo pump is opened up for repairs it should be first washed out if possible by circulating water through it. After it has been opened up, the repair gang should leave the pump room until dangerous gases have been removed by ventilation. Under such conditions the use of tools or electric portables (extenders) which might produce a spark should be considered as a possible source of ignition.

Cargo tanks which are not known to be gas free should not be entered by anyone not provided with, and experienced in the use of, a fresh air (hose) mask. It should always be remembered that the usual "canister" mask is of no use in entering oil tanks. Only two types of mask can be used—the hose mask where fresh air is pumped to the user through a hose from the deck, and the oxygen breathing apparatus where a supply of oxygen for breathing is carried by the user. The wearer of either type of breathing apparatus should be provided with a safety belt and life line. The life line should be tended by two men from the deck above. Whenever possible, repairs in cargo tanks should not be made until the cargo tank has been gas freed. Under no circumstances should any repairs which require the use of open flames be attempted in cargo tanks until such cargo tanks are gas free.

Cargo transfer operations should be stopped during a severe electrical storm, or if a fire takes place on the tank vessel, or on or in the vicinity of the dock, or if a towboat should come alongside in the way of the cargo tanks while the tank vessel is loading inflammable oils (grades A, B, and C).*

Cleaning and Gas Freeing of Cargo Tanks

See Chapter 14 for full information on this important operation.

The Handling of Oils in Barrels, Drums, and Cases

General. Before stowing oil in barrels or cases, the holds should be thoroughly swept up and all paper, rags, sawdust, and water should

---

* A gasoline hose should never be passed across the deck of one ship or barge to transfer gasoline to another.

be removed. Leaking barrels, drums and cases should be returned to the terminal for repair. Holds in which inflammable oils (grades A, B, and C) in packages are stowed should be well ventilated during transit and especially before unloading. Ventilators to such holds should be screened. Before oil in barrels, drums, or cases is stowed in holds with other inflammable or combustible cargo, the Interstate Commerce Commission regulations and Board of Underwriters rules should be consulted.

Stowage of Combustible Liquids in Barrels. Lubricating oil, turpentine, kerosene, fish oil, and other combustible liquids in barrels should be stowed with the barrel on its side, bung up, and bilge free. Care should be taken that the chimes (ends of staves) are kept free from the sides of the vessel. No barrel should be stowed in a place where there is not sufficient room without bearing its weight on the bilge. All barrels should be stowed in straight tiers fore and aft. In no case should barrels be stowed with the sheer (round off) of the vessel's sides.

The middle of the barrel should be stowed over the four heads of the barrels in the under tier. This will bring the head of each barrel to the bung holes of the under barrels. In places where a barrel cannot be stowed in this manner, wood or suitable dunnage should be fitted in carefully in order to secure the barrels in the tier.

Barrels must not be stowed within 20 ft. of a steam vessel's fiddley or in any compartment liable to excessive heat.

Stowage of Inflammable Liquids in Steel Drums. Steel drums containing gasoline, naphtha, or other inflammable liquid should not be stowed more than seven high on end, and if the full quantity in height is not required, there should not be stowed on top of the drums any cargo the weight of which would exceed that of the drums and contents.

The drums should be well dunnaged between each tier and any broken wing stowage should be filled in with dunnage to equalize the pressure on the lower tiers and make a level. No drums containing inflammable liquids should be used as fillers between the beams under the deck head.

Stowage of Inflammable and Combustible Liquids in Cases. In stowing case oil, all cargo battens should be in place. Missing battens should be replaced with a 1″ board.

Wings should be made up solid with planks or cordwood and boarded over top; also boarded fore and aft on sides to prevent cases being damaged by pressure of the cordwood.

All case cargo should be stowed in straight tiers fore and aft and in no case should such cargo be stowed with the sheer of the vessel.

The first tier in all cases should be cross boarded from wing to wing before the second tier is stowed. The after holds of steam vessels should be cross boarded over the first tier and also cross boarded over the tier that comes level with the top of the shaft tunnel. The tops of shaft tunnels should be made up solid to take the load of the cross boarding, thus making a common level across the vessel. Split wood should be used in chocking cases on tiering height in both the lower hold and between decks.

Cases should be stowed on edge except in beam filling where one "flatter" of combustible oil is allowed. Inflammable oil (gasoline, naphtha, benzene) should be stowed on edge and no "flatters" of this product should be allowed between the beams.

'Tween-deck spaces should be dunnaged 1". 'Tween-deck hatch covers should be in place.

Lubricating oils and kerosene should be stowed under inflammable oils (gasoline, naphtha, and benzene) or in blocks by themselves.

Inflammable liquids (gasoline, naphtha, benzene) should not be stowed in a compartment or hold forward of the boiler room unless the bulkhead separating the hold from the boiler room is made of steel and watertight and with a separate bilge suction to such hold, and then only when approved general cargo such as machinery or oil in cases is stowed 20 ft. forward of the bulkhead.

Inflammable liquids in cases should not be stowed within 10 ft. of the engine-room bulkhead, whether on the deep tank, 'tween decks, or hold.

Compartments in which inflammable liquids in cases are stowed must be properly ventilated. Ventilators must be covered with wire gauze and trimmed during loading. If possible, wind sails should be used while this type of cargo is being loaded and unloaded.

Inflammable liquids such as gasoline, naphtha, or benzene should not be stowed with ordinary general cargo.

CONDENSATION AND HUMIDITY

Considering the necessity of keeping condensation or "sweating" in the cargo holds at a minimum, it may be desirable to ascertain the actual humidity condition existing in the cargo space.

The following table gives the percentage of water vapor present in the atmosphere, given the readings of the wet and dry bulbs of the hygrometer.

HUMIDITY PERCENTAGE TABLE

Air Temp. F.	1°	2°	3°	4°	5°	6°	7°	8°	9°	10°
	Difference between Dry and Wet Bulb readings:									
	Percentage of Water Vapor in Atmosphere.									
24°	87	75	62	50	38	26				
28°	89	78	67	56	45	34	24			
32°	90	80	70	61	51	41	32	23		
36°	91	82	73	64	55	47	38	30	22	
40°	92	84	76	68	59	52	44	37	30	22
44°	92	85	78	70	63	56	49	43	36	29
48°	93	86	79	73	66	60	53	47	41	35
52°	94	87	81	75	69	63	57	51	46	40
56°	94	88	82	77	71	65	60	55	50	44
60°	94	89	84	78	73	68	63	58	53	48
64°	95	90	85	79	74	70	65	60	56	51
68°	95	90	85	81	76	71	67	63	58	54
72°	95	91	86	82	77	73	69	65	61	57
76°	95	91	87	82	78	74	70	66	63	59
80°	96	92	87	83	79	75	72	68	64	61
84°	96	92	88	84	80	77	73	69	66	63
88°	96	92	88	85	81	77	74	71	67	64
92°	96	93	89	86	82	78	75	72	68	65

The **relative humidity,** or percentage of water vapor, having been ascertained by the above table, the "dew point" may be found by means of the next table.

The "dew point" may be defined as the temperature (dry bulb) at which the water content of the atmosphere condenses. Hence the need for regulating ventilation so that the "dew point" may be kept as far away as is possible under the circumstances.

The factor given in the table, when multiplied by the difference between the wet and dry bulb readings, gives the number of degrees to be subtracted from the dry bulb reading in order to obtain the "dew point."

Dry Bulb °F.	Factor	Dry Bulb °F.	Factor
20	8.14	44	2.18
22	7.60	48	2.10
24	6.92	52	2.02
26	6.08	56	1.94
28	5.12	60	1.88
30	4.15	64	1.83
32	3.32	68	1.79
34	2.77	72	1.75
36	2.50	76	1.71
38	2.36	80	1.68
40	2.29	86	1.65
		92	1.62
		98	1.58
		104	1.55

Example. Dry bulb 80°; wet bulb 76°. What is the dew point?

Solution. The difference between the dry and wet bulbs is 4, which, when multiplied by the factor 1.68 (opposite dry bulb 80°) gives 6.7° to be subtracted from 80°. Then $80 - 6.7 = 73.3°$ as the "dew point."

CARGO PROBLEMS

1. A hold is 60′ x 40′ x 10′. We have 16000 cu. ft. of cargo to stow evenly on the floor. To what height will this cargo stow?

(*Ans.* 6′ 8″)

2. 10 triangular piles of piping are on the dock. We wish to stow the piping fore-and-aft in a hold space 42′ x 20′ x 7′. If each pile is 8′ wide at the base, 6′ high, and 20′ long, how high will the piping stow?

(*Ans.* 6′ 00″)

3. A deep tank is 42,280 cu. ft. capacity. It is filled with oil at 37.6 cu. ft. to the ton instead of sea water. Find the difference of weight in tons.

(*Ans.* 83½ tons)

4. A hold of capacity 55000 cu. ft. contains 100 standards of timber at 270 cu. ft. per standard. How many bales of flax can be stowed in the remaining space at 115 cu. ft. per ton, 5 bales to the ton?

(*Ans.* 1217 bales)

5. A cone-shaped pile of coal is to be stowed in a compartment 40 ft. long by 30 ft. wide. The pile is 24 ft. high and 50 ft. wide at the base. How high will the coal stow?

(*Ans.* 13′)

6. Find the amount of rise due to increase of temperature, of oil in a tank, the expansion trunk of which is 30' in length by 10' in width:

4500 barrels are loaded. 6.6 barrels to the ton, and 37 cu. ft. per ton are allowed. Coefficient of expansion is .0004, and expected rise of temperature is 15 degrees (F.) Express result in inches.

(*Ans.* 6 in.)

7. An oil cargo of 75,500 barrels has a temperature of 78 degrees F. If the expansion coefficient is .0004, how many barrels are there in this cargo at the standard temperature of 60 degrees?

(*Ans.* 74960 bbls.)

8. A tank which holds 300 tons of sea water is filled with whale oil to 95% capacity. Find the weight of this oil, its specific gravity being .93.

(*Ans.* 258.6 tons)

9. A 50,000 barrel cargo of oil is found to be 7143 tons weight, the specific gravity of the oil being .933. How many tons of fresh water would there be in the same volume?

(*Ans.* 7656 tons)

10. The above cargo of oil being a full load on a draft of 24' 03", the ship's loaded draft being 25'00" and T.P.I. 57, show that this vessel can just carry the load of fresh water.

11. 100 tons weight of bolts and beans are to be stowed in the same compartment which has a capacity of 4200 cu. ft. The bolts (in kegs) stow at 30, and the beans (in bags) stow at 60.

What is the weight of each that will fill the space?

(*Ans.* 60 tons bolts;
40 tons beans)

12. Loading a steamer, we have a remaining space of 150,000 cu. ft. Present draft is 21' 06" F. and 22' 00" A. Load draft is 27' 00" mean. T.P.I., 50. It is required to fill the cargo space with paper and cement. Paper in rolls stows at 80; cement in barrels at 45.

Find the weight of, and space occupied by each.

(*Ans.* 235.7 tons paper;
2914.3 tons cement)

13. The following is a problem in stowage which requires a practical solution, i.e. kerosene and cotton or hay must not be placed in the same compartment and so on. The cubic capacity of #1 hold is 32,500 cu. ft., #2 40,500, #3 40,000 and #4 30,000; all have an upper 'tween deck, lower 'tween deck and lower hold. The TPI is 30, the ITM is 550 ft. tons, the light displacement is 4000 tons, the light draft is 14' fwd. and 16' aft. The KM (loaded) is 10.02 ft. and the light KG is 8 ft. We have to load the following: 450 t. of kerosene in cases with a stowage factor of 50; 300 t. molasses in hogsheads, stowage factor 60; 325 t. cotton in bales, stow. factor 75; 330 t. flour in bags, stow. factor 45; 295 t. wheat in bags, stow. factor 54; 300 t. hay in bales, stow. factor 150. You are required to load this cargo so as to have a drag of approximately 6" and a safe GM. When you have solved this problem, without too much help, you will have a good understanding of what is involved in properly stowing a ship.

Distances from tipping center	Height of CG above K
#1 hold—110 feet	UTD—21 feet
2 " 70 "	LTD—15 "
3 " 60 "	LH— 6 "
4 " 100 "	

A. One possible solution gives a 6½ inch drag and a GM of 12 inches

Chapter 9

SHIPHANDLING

The actual handling of large vessels is an operation requiring long apprenticeship and much experience. Following is an article on shiphandling by Captain H. A. V. von Pflugk, reprinted by permission from the *U. S. Naval Institute Proceedings*, issue of September, 1941.

Captain von Pflugk's qualifications in this field are demonstrated by his own comment:

"Tips on Practical Shiphandling" is based on the experience gained:

(*a*) While handling a large number of vessels, steam and sail, when captain of tugboats.

(*b*) While handling more than a thousand ships of various sizes and descriptions, from battleships to tramp steamers, from luxury liners to training ships, while Panama Canal Pilot (and later Harbor Master) during the first difficult years before the Canal Channels had been completed.

(*c*) While captain of ocean steamships (including the U.S.S. *Buitenzorg*, 14,500 tons, during the first World War) when I rarely utilized the services of tugboats even under very unfavorable conditions.

Captain von Pflugk's article is followed by a brief summary of the general theory and rules which will help toward an understanding of the action of a particular vessel.

TIPS ON PRACTICAL SHIPHANDLING

By CAPTAIN H. A. V. VON PFLUGK

Can every officer learn to handle a ship expertly?

The answer is very definitely—No!

It isn't his fault. He either hasn't the *knack*, or lacks the opportunity for the practice necessary to gain experience and proficiency in this very fascinating subject.

This article is intended for those who are not satisfied with merely becoming one of the great majority that just "get by," in the hope that even if it isn't in them to become expert, it may at least help improve their work.

Except where stated otherwise, all reference is to a heavy, single-screw ship, under normal conditions, without current or assistance from tugs.

When you step aboard a ship—any ship—do you ever stop to think of the great strides made in ship design during the last few decades, the improved machinery, the modern ordnance, the latest in instruments and new gadgets, the whole the result of the brain and the brawn of thousands of fellow humans? Do you sum it all up as a well-conceived and co-ordinated piece of machinery, the best that we have been able to accomplish so far? Steel and iron and brass and whatnot, inanimate objects transformed by the will and ingenuity of man into a useful but still inanimate whole, a means to an end, be that end making a profit or being offensive to an enemy?

It is of course right and proper that you should give a thought to what went into the creation of the ship, but is that all you think about in that connection? Is that all you feel? If so, your case is pretty hopeless. While you may, in time, attain a certain amount of mechanical proficiency in handling ships, you can never become truly expert at it.

If, on the contrary, with full appreciation of what has been created, you feel, when laying your hand upon the rail, that you are in contact with something alive, responsive to your slightest touch, something that is a part of you, something that you really love, then you are in a good position to become truly expert at shiphandling—if you have the knack and are gifted with good judgment and have an eye for distance and are the calm rather than the excitable type.

Have you ever known anyone who hasn't card sense to become an expert bridge player? No matter how brilliant a man may be in other things, if he hasn't card sense he can never become an expert at cards. Contradistinctively, those who have the knack rarely become very expert at cards unless they have a real liking for them. The knack plus the liking make for perfection. This principle holds true in a great many things—particularly in shiphandling.

This article will not concern itself with theory, or problems in trigonometry, or tactical maneuvering while in formation. It will, on the contrary, confine itself to the practical handling of ships and lines around docks and piers in the harbors. That being established, we must face the sad fact that many shipmasters and naval officers are not proficient in handling ships. (As previously stated, it is not their fault.) Unbelievable as it may seem, there are even a number of tug captains, who certainly have more practice and experience during a given period of time than anyone else, who are far from expert at their job.

A great number of people dearly love the sound of their own voice. When they get on the bridge of a ship they seem to feel that the more noise they make the more important they are, while the tug captains referred to seem to think that the more bells they ring in a given time, the bigger men they are! Then again, some officers, when in command on the bridge, when things don't go the way they expected them to, may try to cover up their own ineptness by shouting, either at the shore gang handling lines, or others, or they may, for the benefit of those with them on the bridge or within sound of their noble voices, make derogatory remarks about the slovenly manner in which the engines are being handled. Everybody is wrong but the captain. He can't be wrong!

What does all the shouting amount to? Merely that the loud one is advertising to all and sundry that he is inefficient in that he either doesn't know how to handle a ship, or in that he has failed to properly train his personnel, has neglected to inform his responsible officers (deck and engine) regarding his standard method and requirements in connection with shiphandling, has neglected to give the Nelsonian touch to his organization.

In contrast, what a great pleasure there is in watching a man who really knows how to handle a ship! There is no excitement, no noise, no confusion. A slight motion of the arm or hand is all that is necessary to convey any and all requirements regarding the handling of any and all lines. With well-trained personnel there is no need for shouting. A calm command in a not too loud voice is all that is necessary for the rudder and the engines. Quiet efficiency!

No man can become expert at everything. This is an age of specialization. That does not necessarily mean that one should confine oneself to a single specialty. Every officer who expects some day to have a command should become as proficient in shiphandling as his make-up will permit. Unfortunately, his opportunities for practical experience in the subject are necessarily limited. There is, as yet, no chair in practical shiphandling at the Naval Academy, nor are there facilities for giving him the opportunity to "try it yourself"—to gain actual experience.

Shiphandling is one of those things that cannot be learned from textbooks, or from watching others. It can only be mastered by doing it yourself—over and over again. Any youngster can learn to do the paper work in navigation. Does that make him a navigator? Would you entrust your ship to him, even after he has watched you do the work for months, or would you wait until he has done it himself over a long period of time under competent supervision? Does a thorough theoretical knowledge of aeronautics enable one to fly?

Popular belief to the contrary notwithstanding, conditions are never exactly the same, even when they appear to be. *One never knows what she may spring on one next!* You may, for instance, be coming into your berth at an open piling pier on a calm day, with no current. You were in the same berth only a few days ago. Conditions are as perfect as they can be, and you are almost close enough to give her a kick back to kill most of the meager headway you have left. Suddenly she takes a rotten sheer, almost as if she were about to turn around and look at you. Why did she do that? The last time you came in here, under conditions not as favorable, she acted perfectly normal. Did the engineer . . . ? (The first reaction of most humans appears to be to look for the cause, for anything going wrong, outside of oneself.) Did, then, the engineer, whose engine had been stopped for a considerable length of time, figuring that your next command will be to reverse, want to "keep her warm," and so gave her "just a few" turns back so as to have her instantly ready for you? That has happened. And the results, in most ships, would very likely be precisely as stated.

Wasn't it high-water slack the last time you came here, and isn't it low-water slack today? Perhaps there is a slight unevenness of the bottom, a hump which, when the deepest end of the ship smelled it, sucked the quarter in toward the pier. Could suction, that greatly underestimated and misunderstood force, be the answer? A few soundings verify and—the mystery is solved.

The foregoing is but one of hundreds of unexpected happenings that may occur at any moment while handling ships. If you were on the alert that time you could have easily broken the suction before she got much of a swing on her (1) if making a port-side landing, by a kick ahead on left rudder, or (2) if making a starboard-side landing, by a small kick back, taking care in this case to give her barely enough to break the suction, and not enough to start her swinging the other way, with her bow toward the pier, for if that happens it will be necessary for you to come ahead on left full rudder (perhaps ahead full) because you must stop that swing, and start her swinging the other way— away from the pier—before you can back again.

One of the most important things to remember in shiphandling is to make very sure that you do not have too much way on the vessel. Speed through the water is very deceiving. When approaching a berth you may feel sure that your ship has hardly any way on her—is, in fact, almost stopped—and you may even feel tempted to give her a kick ahead lest she lose steerageway before reaching her berth, but as soon as you pass the end of the pier you will almost invariably discover that she is moving very much faster than you thought. Too much headway has got more men into trouble than anything else. Remember to leave yourself in a position where you can always come ahead, if need be, for you cannot always come back. It would be well—even for experienced officers—to memorize these words: "You can always come ahead, but you cannot always back," and to think of them whenever they feel tempted.

When handling a ship, avoid the staging of a grandstand play. Even an expert will meet his Waterloo if he undertakes to go in for showmanship. His superior knowledge will "get him by" for a while, perhaps for years, but the law of averages will eventually catch up with him.

There are very good reasons why it is well to have but little headway when entering a slip or approaching a wharf or bulkhead. The most important one is probably the small amount of water under the vessel, which will not only affect her general handling qualities, but will, especially if the bottom is uneven, create a certain amount of suction that may become very dangerous if and when it causes the ship to take a sudden sheer toward the wharf or another vessel. It may be well to note that when the bow of a deep and heavy ship approaches a shoal spot or hump in the slip (with the hump broad on the bow) she will most likely sheer away from it, due to the cushioning effect of the water between the hump and the approaching bow. However, as the vessel passes close by this hump, its passage creates a great deal of suction which, as the stern is neared, will have an ever increasing effect and will draw the quarter in *toward* the hump. This bottom suction is very dangerous, especially when entering or leaving a crowded slip and one must be constantly on the alert to instantly check any tendency to sheer.

The side suction created by close approach to a solid bulkhead or pier is even more dangerous in that its action is much more sudden than that of bottom suction, and its effects, if you have too much way on your ship, may well prove disastrous. The effect of this side suction can, however, be minimized because you can see that the pier is solid below water as you approach it and, being thus forewarned, the prudent man will (*a*) make very sure that his speed is sufficiently low, and (*b*) keep a little farther away and approach his berth at a slightly greater angle than he would were it an open piling pier.

Another type of side suction is that created when one vessel passes near another that is tied up. Even a tug or speedboat passing close aboard can make enough suction to cause a heavy ship to surge in her berth if her lines are at all slack. This, however, is somewhat of a surface suction, in that it does not go down very deep. When a vessel of far greater displacement passes, the amount of suction created is tremendous, and has been known to cause considerable havoc. Lines have been parted, gangplanks pulled overboard, and ships have even been torn away from their berth.

Whenever near anything, especially in a heavy ship, whether maneuvering around docks, or in confined waters, or meeting or passing another vessel in a narrow channel, never forget the effect of suction—between ships as well as between your quarter and shallower water at the edge of the fairway.

A kick ahead full should not be confused with speed. While it is highly desirable, when maneuvering around docks or in confined spaces, to use your engines as gently as practicable—coaxing the ship rather than forcing her—there will be times when you want to give her a quick cant either one way or the other, without materially increasing her headway, as for instance, when she refuses to answer the rudder and takes a sheer towards an obstruction. In such cases it will be found that a short kick ahead full on full rudder will gain much quicker and more satisfactory results than a more prolonged kick under less power, for in the latter case a greater distance will have been covered, both ahead and *toward the obstruction*, before the desired result has been achieved, because in making a short cant or turn, especially when motionless in the water or moving slowly in the same direction in which you propose to use your engine, it is always the strong initial kick that has the greatest turning effect.

Another very good reason for going slow is the many things that may happen suddenly and unexpectedly due to human or mechanical failure. Engineers have been known to make a mistake in answering a signal, engine telegraphs have broken down, helmsmen have inadvertently turned the wheel the wrong way, and the officer in charge forward may misunderstand a command and "hold" the spring instead of "veering" it. If you should be working the ship alongside with an after spring (leading aft) and it *parts*, you are almost certain to get it into your propeller because you now must back, perhaps to keep from ramming the ship in the berth ahead of yours, and the more headway you have the stronger and longer must you back, the stronger suction the action of your propeller creates, drawing the shore portion of the parted spring into it—as sure as fate. If, in any of these events, your headway was what it should be, you will probably have ample time—and space—in which to overcome or counteract whatever happened. If, on the other hand, your way was more than it should have been, it would be well, before blaming others, to remember that it is only human to make a mistake, that you are aware of that fact and should have made allowance for it, and adjusted your speed accordingly, and that, in the final analysis, the blame is solely yours. You are in command, and only you are responsible.

It is well to confine yourself to one line (a forward spring) if it is necessary to make use of any at all in working your ship into her berth. This spring should be the best line in the ship, so that you are not only in a position to check her bow in, but also to work your engine ahead on it if that should seem desirable. Considered the most important line in the ship, it should be treated with the consideration due it, and replaced by an older line as soon as the ship has been secured in her berth. It should then be thoroughly dried and stowed away from exposure to the weather, where it will not be subjected to severe heat or dampness. Whenever a new supply of mooring line comes aboard, the first line to be cut from it should be a forward spring, even though the one in use has seen but very little service. Once you have learned all, or even some of, the many things you can do with just that one line to the pier, you will fully realize its importance and its superiority over every other line in the ship.

Veering any line when there is a heavy strain on it, to reduce or stop the ship's headway, is a deplorable habit possessed by a number of captains. Nothing will ruin a line quicker. You have engines with which to check the vessel's way. Use them! It takes quite a pull for a man to hold a line while veering it when under heavy strain. He may slip and go down, perhaps with his foot caught in a bight, and the line surging out as soon as released from his restraining hold. It will then be too late for you to do anything about it. Don't maim or kill your men! On some foreign-flag ships wire rope is used almost exclusively for mooring lines because it lasts longer and is cheaper. If it is unwise and dangerous to veer a Manila line under heavy strain, it is nothing short of criminal to do so with wire rope which, if and when it takes charge, has been known to cut a man's leg off—to cut more than one man in two. Nevertheless, it is still being done in some ships.

After your vessel is secured in her berth with the usual four essential primary lines (headline, forward spring, after spring, and sternline) by all means use all the wire rope you want to for permanent moorings but remember to give wire rope more scope than you give to Manila especially where there is considerable rise and fall of tide, for, while there is a great deal of stretch in Manila, there is very little in wire.

In making a landing (either side to the pier) the thing to strive for is to have five things happen at the same instant: (1) the ship's headway stopped, (2) light contact with bow to stringpiece, or side to camel, as the case may be (with fenders in between), (3) spring secured (don't veer another inch!), (4) engine begins working ahead very slowly on the spring, and (5) have the ship where she is wanted.

You now have her under absolute control and, with the engine continuing to work ahead dead slow, you can steer the stern alongside. No matter how long it may take to get out the other lines and secure the vessel fore-and-aft, you've got her where you want her and can so hold her indefinitely. If there are no camels between you and the pier, and you think that there may be submerged obstructions, like broken piling, close in, you can keep your stern off any number of feet you like, and hold her there, by a judicious use of your rudder. Then, after the headline and after spring (leading forward) are secured, you can start heaving the stern alongside with a breast at the same time you stop the engine to avoid damage to your propeller. Now you've got her secure and can run out the sternline at your leisure. After you have doubled up fore-and-aft, it would be well to take in your after breast, unless there is definite need for it. Breast lines are undesirable, especially where there is considerable rise and fall of tide, owing to their short scope and consequent need for constant attention and readjustment. Offshore headlines and sternlines to the same pier will answer the purpose in most instances.

Even a new spring has its limitations. You can always increase the number of revolutions, but after your spring has parted it is too late to decrease them. Arrange some special signal between the bridge and the engine-room to indicate when you want the engine worked gradually up to (not down to) "dead slow." Remember that your engineer can't guess what you want; he is not a mind reader. Clear thinking, proper planning, and co-operation from the engine-room are requisite for really good shiphandling. In execution there must be co-ordination of effort similar to that between the seeing-eye dog and its blind master. No matter how good a shiphandler the captain may be, if he hasn't proper co-operation from the engine-room—if the officer at the throttle is not consistent in the execution of signals—the commanding officer is severely handicapped. That is why, in some ships, the same officer is required to handle the engine whenever docking or undocking. When that is not practicable, or not good policy, and there is a decided difference between engineers, it is wise in some instances to know beforehand who is going to be at the throttle, so that you may know in advance whether you can look forward to proper co-ordination of effort or to what you will perhaps consider slovenly work, and act accordingly.

Has it ever occurred to you how sick at heart it probably makes an engineer officer to be in a good ship, with ample power, with well-handled engines, when any of us repeatedly and consistently makes a ness of handling her around docks? They probably do not mind the extra time and labor required for answering innumerable, entirely unnecessary signals half as much as the realization that their captain doesn't "know his stuff." Whenever he makes hard work of handling his vessel, he also makes extra work for nearly the entire ship's company, which, however, is probably not resented nearly so much as the look—or word—of commiseration from the personnel of other, better-handled ships. All hands would much prefer to strut about with a su-

perior smirk on their respective faces and brag about our ship, and ou
"old man," who has got what it takes!

Avoid working your engines too strongly when maneuvering aroun
docks. Whenever your propeller turns over, especially when there i
but little water under you, it creates whirlpools, water currents, eddies
and suction, that throw your ship out of position. If, for instance
you are making a port-side landing at a solid bulkhead, your propeller
in backing, will force a wedge of water between the ship and the berth
and the stronger you have to back, the farther this cushion of wate
will force you away from the wharf, with the result that you wil
probably find yourself in a position whence you have to laboriously
heave the ship alongside. Should you at any time have to heave a ship
into her berth (broadside) it is well to remember to heave one end at
time, alternating, so as to reduce the strain on the lines and heavin
gear, and lessen the chances of parting a line. Do not subject you
gypsy-shaft to too much strain. Stop off and secure to the bitts whil
the other end of the ship is being hove in, so as to avoid bending
shaft while "holding."

What has been said to apply to solid bulkheads, also refers to ope
piers (where the water flows more or less freely under the pier) thoug
to a smaller degree. In nearly all instances there is a slope running u
from the dredged bottom in the slip to the lesser depth of water unde
the open pier, so that, while it does not confine the water near the bot
tom to the same extent as in the case of the vertical wall of a soli
pier, allowance must nevertheless be made for its effect.

It will readily be seen that the answer to a great many things is
Not too much headway!

The officer in charge of the lines aft should be one upon whom yo
can depend to keep his mind on his job. He must be "on his toes,
should have a good fundamental knowledge of shiphandling, an
should be familiar with your method of doing things and your require
ments, so that he will not only be in a position to co-operate intell
gently, but also to anticipate your next move to the extent of being ir
stantly ready for your command whenever it comes. Above all thing
he must keep his lines out of your propeller. Aside from the rednes
of your face, the feeling of embarrassment, of helplessness, or, perhaps
the necessity of being obliged to ask for outside help to get your shi
alongside, there is the delay occasioned by the need of getting a dive
to cut the line from your propeller, or by dry-docking. And it can easi
be avoided by proper planning, proper information, proper trainin
Do not hesitate to go into a huddle with the officers concerned. Ge
them interested in what you are trying to accomplish. It pays!

If, when approaching your slip or wharf, you realize that you hav
too much way on her, by all means back and check your headway be
fore you get too close, and make a new start rather than come in to
fast. Before you start backing to reduce the speed, be sure to give he
a swing on left rudder in order to counteract in advance some of th
contrary action of the propeller's side-pull. The amount of swing
give her depends on the ship, and on her trim. Normally, a singl
screw ship with right-handed propeller will swing her stern to port an

her bow to starboard on reversing the engine, but ships have their own personalities—their individual idiosyncrasies—just like humans. Some will slowly and sedately swing as they should, and instantly recover at the slightest touch of ahead on left rudder, while others wildly start to turn around and look at you, making it necessary to give them a touch of the whip—ahead full—in order to straighten them out. Some ships, especially when deeply laden and with little or no drag, will act almost lifeless in that they will take quite a while to begin swinging, but watch out for them, for, once they have got a good start they are stubbornly persistent, and are difficult to stop. This applies particularly to low-powered ships.

Then there are ships that may, and frequently do, swing their bow to port on backing. That may be due to not having any drag, or being by the head, either with or without a slight starboard list. Should your ship be by the head, with a decided starboard list, her bow will almost certainly swing to port as soon as you start backing.

After you and your ship have become well acquainted, you may feel that you know all about her. You will be wrong! A ship is like a colt that will playfully nip you the minute your back is turned. She can always find a new trick in the bag that she hasn't pulled on you yet, and is only waiting for the psychological moment—when you are not looking—so look!

Suppose you were ordered to bring a strange ship from an anchorage to alongside an inner berth in a crowded slip. A new skeleton crew has preceded you and has her ready to move. You have no information about her handling qualities. To gather the knowledge necessary to handle her to best advantage, as soon as you have started her in, with the ship steadied on a course, give her a kick back, gauge her swing, and note what it takes to get her straightened out. An expert now knows all that is necessary to enable him to do anything with her that may be required. He "has the *feel* of her." But, supposing that you have not as yet become an expert, that you want still more information about her qualities. Give her a good swing to port, then back her until she swings to starboard, then straighten her out. Next, give her right full rudder, then astern full, then see what it takes to straighten her out. Surely, no one can require, or expect to obtain, more information than that regarding the handling qualities of a strange ship.

In maneuvering a ship, the action of the rudder is dependent upon a number of factors and can only become definitely known through trial and error. Some vessels have a clean run, others the reverse. There are proportionately large rudders as well as small ones, ordinary or garden variety rudders, and streamlined and balanced rudders, as well as combinations of two or more. There are only two things that you can fairly well depend upon with a strange ship: (*a*) that it is advisable to turn your rudder in accordance with the direction in which you want the stern to move (twin-screw ships as well as others), and (*b*) when you have a list, the rudder will not have its normal or full effect; the greater the list, the smaller the rudder's effect. This is an important point to remember.

The principal factors that should have careful consideration in connection with the handling of any ship are: (*a*) the weight of the vessel (displacement), (*b*) her speed (power), (*c*) the amount of water under her, (*d*) traffic, (*e*) force and direction of current, (*f*) force and direction of wind, (*g*) space (crowded condition near berth), (*h*) condition of berth, (*i*) whether there are men available ashore for handling your lines, or you must go in close enough to drop some of your crew on the dock from your bow.

In general, the more power a ship has, the easier she is to handle. There is no comparison between the handling of a full-powered (outboard turning), twin-screw ship and that of a heavily laden, low-powered, single-screw freighter, especially if the latter has an old-fashioned engine that wheezes and coughs for a minute or two before it begins to turn over in reverse. (Two minutes and 42 seconds by stop watch have been noted.) Deeply laden, inboard-turning, twin-screw ships of moderate power handled by this writer were very definitely not ladies. The most satisfactory way to turn them in a small space under all weather and current conditions was found to be a judicious alternating between ahead full on all engines and astern full on all engines. Should it suddenly become necessary to stop such a ship's headway in a very narrow channel, stop your engines, then full astern on all engines. She may travel almost a length before she will take a rotten sheer to either one side or the other (you can't tell which side until she does it). Now stop and ahead full on all engines (rudder on side needed) until the sheer is broken, then instantly stop and astern full again on all engines until she takes her next sheer. Repeat as often as necessary, taking care to back as long as possible and to make the kicks ahead brief. This method has been used successfully in Culebra Cut and elsewhere and applied also to triple-screw, 21-knot passenger steamers whose outside propellers were inboard-turning, and whose center engine worked ahead only. Battleships, despite all their weight, handle much easier.

Handling a ship is a one-man job. With few exceptions a pilot is aboard in an advisory capacity only. While the captain retains full jurisdiction and responsibility, it is customary to let the pilot "take her" and, if no tugs are assisting, maneuver the ship into her berth. Should tugs be used, the captain of one of them will mount the ship's bridge and the pilot turns her over to him to berth. This customary procedure does not, however, prevent the ship's captain from handling her himself if he chooses to do so. He of course has that right, but it is not often exercised.

Different ships, different long-splices! One man's method of handling ships may be better—or not so good—as that of another. It is, nevertheless, his method and as he is the one that is handling her, he should not be pestered lest such interference endanger the ship. He has made his plans in accordance with local conditions (knowledge of which is frequently of far greater importance than familiarity with the fine nuances of the ship's individual idiosyncrasies) and should be permitted to carry them out without being subjected to the annoyance of heckling. Such lines as he designates should be handled in the manner directed by him, regardless of the opinion of others. Common sense dictates that there be but one head at any given time.

Most pilots, and the great majority of the tug captains engaged in this work, are proficient in shiphandling—a number are expert at it—but there are some that, while they may have handled ships for years, will make hard work of it because they haven't the knack that would enable them to do it instinctively and smoothly. Should anyone at any time, handle your ship in a manner that, in your considered opinion, endangers her, it is not only your privilege, but your duty to take her away from him and to handle her yourself.

This brings up the fine point of where to draw the obviously rather elastic line. Appearances are frequently misleading to those lacking local knowledge. Dozens of instances could be cited in which it would be dead wrong to take her away from the pilot, and other dozens in which it would be a neglect of duty not to do so. Clear thinking, sound judgment, and an intimate knowledge of shiphandling are requisite here to enable you to do justice to your ship, the other chap, and to yourself.

Never interfere. Either let him do it, or you do it. Handling a ship is very definitely a one-man job!

It is impossible to cover the subject of shiphandling and its various ramifications—its hundreds of possible situations—in one article, one chapter, or, for that matter, in one reasonably sized volume, but it is hoped that this very brief generalization—these few tips—may prove "of service to the Service," and that even experienced officers may find herein a few hints that are helpful.

One more tip: Suppose you have just finished bringing your ship alongside and are pleased with yourself for having made a good job of it. Don't spend too much time patting yourself on the back. Instead, think back over the maneuver step by step and, in being thus critical of your own work, see if you can't find a point or two that could have been done better, and the method. Never be quite satisfied with your own work. Remember the apple: the instant it becomes fully ripe it begins to deteriorate. Even an expert picks up a new wrinkle every so often. No man living knows all there is to know about anything. All of us can always learn more.

STEAMSHIP MANEUVERING

Handling Single-Screw Steam Vessels. Almost all steamers and motor vessels have right-handed propellers; a left-handed screw would, of course, produce the opposite effect to the following general rule:

Engines going ahead, ship's head tends to go to port. Engines going astern, ship's head tends to starboard. The screw exerts its greatest turning effect when engines are going slow ahead or full astern.

Wind effect is greatest on a light vessel, which, for example, will back straight astern due to a breeze on the starboard beam, and in a gale will back almost into the wind's eye.

A ship cants best with hard-over helm and engines full ahead. She will *begin* to cant well when stopped and engines are put full astern;

but, as sternway is gathered, she will tend to straighten out, the rudder being amidships.

Effect of Rudder and Screw. The following table is intended to show the canting effect due to rudder position, ship's way and screw motion, through the cycle from making good headway to making good sternway, the engines going full astern. Bear in mind that the influence of wind pressure or of "smelling the bottom" in shallow water may considerably affect the results noted.

	Way on Ship	*Engines*	*Rudder*	*Ship's Head Cants*
1.	Good headway	Full astern	Amidship	To starboard
2.	Good headway	" "	Right	" "
3.	Now slowing down	" "	"	To port
4.	Now moving astern	" "	"	Either way
5.	Good sternway	" "	"	To port
6.	Good sternway	Full ahead	"	To starboard
7.	Good headway	Full astern	Left	To port
8.	Now slowing down	" "	"	To starboard
9.	Now going astern	" "	"	" "
10.	Good sternway	" "	"	" "
11.	Good sternway	Full ahead	"	To port

Analysis of the table shows that greater rudder effect occurs with faster motion of ship, as in 2, 5, 7, and 10; and greater propeller effect on rudder with her slower motion as in 3 and 8. When these two forces act together the result is very decided as in #6, 9 and 10. In case #4 the two forces are opposed and vessel may swing either way. In #1 and #11 we have the result given as the propeller stream usually has a greater effect on the rudder than does the ship's motion. The limits as to way and engine speed peculiar to the particular vessel should be carefully ascertained by actual experiment, in both loaded and light condition.

Note that between #2 and #3 is a point at which the ship's head will not change. It is often of value to know, especially when docking starboard side to, that with engine going astern and helm hard right the ship will go straight while headway is on her.

Turning Short Around, Single Screw. Put helm hard right, engines full ahead. When a headway is acquired, stop, and go full astern. As the ship gathers sternway, shift helm. When far enough astern, go ahead. Repeat the maneuver if necessary.

If there is not enough room to go ahead and astern, drop anchor and steam round it with helm hard over, paying out just enough cable for the anchor to hold.

If there is not enough room to steam round anchor, place bows against the bank or quay and heave ship around, utilizing wind and current, if possible.

If coming upstream with a flood tide, or down river with the current, sheer toward starboard bank, so bringing bow into slack water and stern into current. Continue as for turning short around with helm and engines.

Turning Circle. The diameter of the ship's turning circle is least at slow speed. At full speed it is about 6 times the vessel's length; and a 12-knot steamer will complete the circle in nearly 8 minutes. The turning center is located at about 1/3 the ship's length from the stem.

The maximum rudder angle should be 35° to 38°.

Stopping. When bringing a ship to rest from full speed ahead and full headway, engines put at full astern power will stop the ship in 4 to 6 lengths.

Head Reach and Advance. The distance that a ship will travel in the direction of the original course from the time that the rudder is put hard over until the course has been altered 90° is called the *advance*. The distance that a ship travels from the time that the order to put engines full astern until the ship is dead in the water is known as *head reach*. The head reach for all types of ships is considerably greater than the advance. However, the advance will be more for a right turn than a left turn, due to the turning bias of a right-handed screw and, of course, Diesel engines are superior to turbines in reversing, since the latter are limited by the power of the astern turbine. Thus, the head reach of a Diesel powered ship is smaller than for the turbine ship. The average advance for most ships is in the neighborhood of 4 ship lengths, while the average head reach is 6 or 7 ship lengths.

CONTROLLABLE PITCH PROPELLER

Some ships are to be equipped with gas turbines. Since the gas turbine cannot be reversed it is planned to equip these vessels with the controllable pitch propeller.

This type of propeller turns at all times in one direction, right handed, we will say. When it is desired to go astern the propeller blades are reversed, the direction of rotation continuing to be right handed.

Vessels so equipped *back to starboard*, even with a hard left rudder. That is, when going ahead the vessel will act the same as any other single screw ship with a right hand screw, but on backing she acts the opposite way.

In turning short these vessels will turn to port in a little over half the time it takes to turn to starboard. That is they will turn best on full ahead with a hard left rudder and full astern and hard right.

In stopping short it is not advisable to use maximum propeller pitch when starting to go astern as this may overload the engine. On first reversing the blades a moderate pitch should be used which is gradually increased to maximum.

Another point to remember is that when you ring up "stop" in docking, the blades will be set at neutral but they will still be revolving. Special care must therefore be taken with the after lines.

When the blades are revolving in neutral the ship may be given very slight headway.

Collision. Approaching nearly head on, observe the cant the reversed screw will produce. Ship approaching fine on port bow, do not go full astern in a single-screw (right-handed) vessel; better stop and hard left, and take a glancing blow.

If your ship makes a hole with her stem in the other vessel's side, try to keep her there and give the people on the injured ship an opportunity of climbing over your bows, or at least keep the water-flow into the vessel in check.

In all cases, stand by and render assistance, if needed. (Note the occurrence in the official log.) See that watertight doors are closed as necessary. The Station Bill should provide for, and drills frequently held in, the manning of hand-operated doors.

* Use of Anchor in Docking. Let us consider some of the ways an anchor can be helpful in docking:

(*a*) In the first hypothetical case we will make a starboard side landing with a single screw right-handed ship, loaded so deep she is "smelling the bottom" and therefore taking a lot of rudder to make her answer with the engine working slow ahead. She will not answer at all with the engine stopped. While still a good distance from the dock, drop the port anchor and little by little give her almost enough chain to stop her with the engine working slow ahead. This will entirely eliminate the likelihood of having too much headway when getting close to the dock and also avoid the danger of hitting the dock when, and if, she is backed for the purpose of stopping.

(*b*) The reader is quite likely to be thinking: The anchor is apt to damage or go through the ship's bottom. Although this could happen, it is a remote probability if the bottom is soft mud and (it might be well to emphasize) if the anchor is dropped in the aforesaid manner, because: (1) the anchor buries itself in the mud; (2) the flukes and crown become balled up with mud; (3) the shank and flukes will not point in the direction which would be necessary to cause them to penetrate. However the anchor can and very often does do serious damage if, when it is dropped, a great deal of chain is paid right out. There are two distinct reasons: (1) By giving too much slack the chain can get foul of the flukes and thereby prevent the anchor from leading properly when it starts to drag. (2) If given too much chain, the anchor—when it strikes—might lie on the bottom with the crown farthest ahead thus making the shank and shackle point aft. In either of these instances, when the strain does come on the chain, the result will be about the same as when a fishhook is backed out of the flesh.

Dropping an anchor is considered so extremely simple that very little if any thought is ever given to doing it properly. Therefore when a mishap occurs it is thought of as being unavoidable, whereas in many cases damage could have been prevented if the anchor had been handled properly.

(*c*) In the next hypothetical case let us go the other extreme and assume we have a ship in ballast or (to use the coined expression) "flying light," with a very strong beam wind blowing on the dock. The dock is parallel to the channel, slack tide. In plenty of time before nearing the dock, drop the lee anchor and little by little "feel" her out until satisfied she has ample chain.

---

* Excerpts from an article titled: *The Use of Anchors in Maneuvering,* by Carlyle J. Plummer in U. S. Naval Institute Proceedings for March 1942 and reprinted in his book, *Ship Handling in Narrow Channels.*

(*d*) It might be well to go into detail as to what is "ample chain." The stronger the wind, the more the chain has to be paid out; and, incidentally, the stronger the engine must be worked. The ultimate purpose is to have the anchor hold the bow up against the wind, and lee rudder hold the stern sufficiently up to windward. Under this kind of control a ship can be barely making headway and still make practically no leeway. The ship is now in such shape that she can be worked right up alongside the dock slow enough to get lines out, both fore and aft, before ever stopping the propeller.

(*e*) Now let us consider the same ship landing at the same dock under the same conditions, except that the wind is blowing heavy off the dock. The same procedure would be carried out. Of course, the opposite anchor would be the lee anchor.

(*f*) Those who are unfamiliar with this maneuver almost invariably contend that, in both of the above cases, the weather anchor would be more effective in holding the bow up to windward, and conversely that the lee anchor would cause its chain to act as a spring line and consequently pull her head down to leeward.

(*g*) Ordinarily these viewpoints are correct, therefore let us try to find out what causes these improbabilities. But first this illustration or comparison: A doctor avoids as much as possible the use of narcotics because he is ever mindful that they can and sometimes do have disastrous consequences. Therefore one of the secrets of their successful use is that they be administered as sparingly as possible. Likewise a "mud pilot" is ever mindful of the serious difficulties that can be caused by dropping an anchor and not being able to hold it, so he avoids its use whenever possible; and one of the secrets of its successful use is that always the minimum scope of the chain, to get the desired results, be paid out.

(*h*) It might be well to repeat that we are considering a light ship with strong beam wind. Now before either anchor would be dropped the ship's headway should be reduced to the minimum. This reduced speed will cause her to go to leeward almost as much as she goes ahead. Under these circumstances if the lee anchor is dropped it will not lead from the hawse pipe but from under the bottom of the ship, and toward the weather side. Therefore, with a very little chain, the anchor will have a great deal of effect, because leading from under the ship will make it more parallel with the bottom and therefore have a decided tendency to help the anchor dig into the mud and hold better.

(*i*) On the other hand, if the weather anchor is dropped, the chain leads directly from the hawse pipe which necessitates considerable chain to keep the effect on the anchor from being just "up and down."

(*j*) The lee anchor will hold with much less pressure on the brake band—under the above conditions—because the bight of the chain pressing so heavily against the side of the ship helps it to be held for the same reason that taking an extra turn on the bitts helps a line to hold.

(*k*) If it were desired simply to hold the bow up then the weather anchor would, in most if not all cases, be preferable. But the anchor is used not only to hold the bow but to help hold the entire ship broadside to the wind. When a ship is in this situation the major concern is to see that the rudder is able to hold her stern up to windward. Of course the most effective way to accomplish this is to go full speed ahead with full lee rudder. In the event the anchor only drags slightly—and, incidentally, that is what we want it to do—there is danger that full ahead on a full lee rudder will not work the stern up, so it is of utmost importance that full use has been made of everything else at our command. In this particular case that thing is the lee anchor. Let us see what it now does. (Keep in mind that the anchor is leading under the bottom and to windward.) When the ship is worked full ahead it causes her to go up to windward until the chain leads aft along the lee side. When this takes place, the chain ceases to serve as a breast line and becomes (according to those who would question its use instead of the weather anchor) a spring line leading from the lee bow and is exceedingly effective in helping the rudder to twist (or swing) the after part of the ship up to windward.

(*1*) Now think—in contrast—what the weather anchor would do. It would act as a spring leading from the weather bow and would cause results exactly opposite to what we desperately need. It would help the wind to throw the stern still more to leeward.

Docking in a Slip. When docking in a slip where uncertain eddy currents prevail, use the *offshore anchor* and a few fathoms of chain to steady the ship's head, if tugs are not at hand. Remember that the anchors are, or should be always ready for letting go when easing the ship in on a dock under any circumstances. Often the inshore anchor, which will "bite" more quickly because of chain leading around and under the ship's bottom, will save the situation where the offshore hook would fail, because of its necessarily longer scope of cable.

Stopping with Spring Line or Anchor Cable. The force required to stop a ship varies as the square of her speed. A vessel of 10,000 tons displacement requires an applied force of 35 tons to stop her within 50 ft., if she is going 2 miles per hour. (Two miles or knots per hour is 3.4 ft. per second.) One-quarter of this force is required if she is moving at 1 mile per hour. Hence the need for gradually taking up the stress on a spring, or on the windlass brake, when moving into berth.—Note what is likely to happen when making a flying or running moor, the term for bringing a ship to a berth between two anchors, one upstream and the other down, if the anchor chain should jam in the hawse pipe!

Engine Bell Signals. The system used on tugs and other coastwise vessels may be conveniently used on the occasion of a sudden mishap to the engine-room telegraph when in close waters. A hand whistle for transmitting the required bridge order through the engine-room skylight will meet the emergency.

Signals are as follows:

When engine is stopped	1 bell means	Slow Ahead
Running full ahead	1 bell means	Slow
Running slow ahead	1 bell means	Stop
Running slow ahead	Jingle means	Full Ahead
When engine is stopped	2 bells mean	Slow Astern
Running astern	Jingle means	Full Astern
Running astern	1 bell means	Stop
Running full ahead	**4 bells mean**	Full Astern
Running slow ahead	**3 bells mean**	Full Astern

The "jingle" on the whistle may be easily recognized by a few successive short, sharp toots.

Signals to Tugs. The following signals are used between U.S. Navy pilots and tug masters. There is no universally accepted system.

In using whistle signals to direct more than one tug, care must be exercised to ensure that the signal is directed to and received by the desired tug. Whistles of a different distinct tone have been used successfully to handle more than one tug.

These signals may be transmitted to the tug by flashing light. However, flashing light signals should be restricted to use only when hand whistle or hand signals cannot be used.

Normally, these whistle signals will be augmented by the hand signals given below.

Hand Signals

HALF SPEED AHEAD OR ASTERN—Arm pointed in direction desired

TUG TO USE RIGHT RUDDER— Hand describing circle as if turning wheel to right (clockwise) facing in the same direction as tug

FULL SPEED (Either)—Fist describing arc (as in "bouncing" an engine telegraph)

TUG TO USE LEFT RUDDER— Hand describing circle as if turning wheel to left ,(counterclockwise) facing in same direction as tug

DEAD SLOW (Either)—Undulating movement of open hand (palm down)

TUG TO RUDDER AMIDSHIP— Arm at side of body with hand extended, swung back and forth

STOP (Either) Open palm held aloft facing tug

CAST OFF, STAND CLEAR— Closed fist with thumb extended, swung up and down

Note: Tug shall acknowledge all of the above signals with one short toot (one second or less) from its whistle, with the exception of the backing signal, which shall be acknowledged with two short toots, and the cast-off signal, which shall be acknowledged by one prolonged and two short toots.

A blast is 2 to 3 seconds' duration; a prolonged blast is 4 to 5 seconds' duration; a short blast is about one second duration.

Steering with Twin Screws. Twin screws are almost always "outturning"; i.e., the starboard screw is right-handed and the port lefthanded. This is the best set-up for maneuvering. When turning the ship short around, one screw going ahead and the other astern, the ship will swing faster if given a little way, ahead or astern, during the maneuver.

When steering by the screws alone, one engine is kept turning at a constant rate (about 3/4 speed), while the other is varied as necessary. The starboard screw working ahead alone will swing the stern to starboard and when going astern will swing the stern to port; naturally the port screw just the opposite.

To turn short around the rudder should be left amidships as in any other position it will oppose the turn.

Backing the screw nearest a solid bulkhead or bank throws a current of water between ship and bulkhead, breasting the ship off.

"Dredging" with the Current. Have just sufficient cable out to check the ship's way. Sheer with the helm. If there is too much way over the ground, pay out more cable.

If you are at anchor in a tideway and a vessel is dragging down upon your ship, then pay out a good length of chain and give the ship a sheer with the helm.

Making a Lee. To make a lee for a lighter, when at anchor in a strong breeze, bend a wire mooring hawser to the anchor cable outside the hawse-pipe, and lead it along to the bitts on the after end of the fore deck. Haul taut and make fast the wire. Slack away on the cable until the hawser straightens out. The vessel will now cant away from the anchor and provide the necessary lee.

Length of Cable at Anchor. The length of cable at single anchor in moderate wind and current should be 5 times the depth of the water in good holding ground. Thus "45 fathoms in the water" is a good order for the mate, upon dropping anchor in 9 fathoms. Give the ship double this amount in a strong current, or if it blows hard; and if a gale is coming on, let go the second anchor before paying out any more chain on the first.

Taking Way Off. In taking way off a steamer the backwash of the screw reaches to about amidships when the vessel's headway is stopped. This is worth bearing in mind when about to anchor on a dark night.

Weighing Anchor. If weighing anchor in a rough sea, leave the anchor under foot until ship may be brought before the sea, to avoid risk of damaging bow plating. It can then be more easily and safely housed.

Making Fast. If making fast stern to, where a swell is likely to make in, as in some Mediterranean ports, use manila or coir hawsers only. Wires will not stand the surging.

Care of Cables When Moored. When moored, and a strong breeze springs up across stream, note that the great spread of the anchors may require slacking away on one of the cables. Two cables leading at a 120° angle are each bearing the same stress as one leading ahead. Therefore pay out on one and lessen the angle.

Going Alongside Another Vessel at Anchor. This may be necessary for the purpose of fueling. Note the other vessels heading when passing astern or request same. Watch out for yawing (carriers may yaw 45° at anchor) and see sponsons or fenders are in place.

Commence approach (assuming to go on other vessel's port side) about 1500 yards off if possible on a course 30°–40° to right of other vessel's heading, headed for bridge. Slow to 4 knots and drop port anchor with 1½–2 times depth in water at 800 yards distance and lock brake. Continue approach altering course to left 5–10 degrees at a time until headed for bow.

Come parallel about 30 feet off and pass after bow spring. Vessel can now be held in any position with engines slow ahead until all lines are secured.

In getting away let go all lines except a short spring from a point well aft. Hold this and allow bow to fall off about 6°, then go ahead. In this position any wind or current tends to separate the two vessels.

Naturally the maneuver can be performed without using the anchor, but by using it the vessel is always under perfect control and can be stopped instantly or swung either way. This may be very important where the other vessel is yawing badly.

Effect of Sea on Steering. Ships have a tendency to fall into the trough when going ahead at an angle with the sea. Backing tends to throw the stern up to the sea.

Effect of Shallow Water on Steering. Steering is usually bad at full speed and propeller slip greatly increased, because of disturbance of natural underbody flow. Engines should never be turned at full speed where the depth markedly affects the steering.

Drifting in Current. A vessel having no way upon her and not affected by wind will lie broadside on the flow or "set" of the current.

Engines Broken Down in Heavy Weather. Hoist "Not Under Command" signal. If the depth of water admits, unshackle cable from anchor and drag enough on the bottom to keep ship out of the trough of sea. In deep water, both anchors lowered out to about 45 fathoms has been found effective toward this end in moderate-sized steamers. A fore-and-aft sail set as far aft as possible will greatly assist the above-mentioned measures, but if cables are not used, set sail as far forward as possible, in order to bring sea abaft the beam.

Here the use of **storm oil** would be of great advantage and, due to ship being stopped and drifting, would have its greatest effect on the heavy sea.

The use of a **drogue** or **sea drag** in this extremity would greatly assist in keeping the vessel more or less end on to the sea. A moderate-sized steamer would fall off sufficiently by the drag of the bight of a heavy manila hawser, with one end made fast on each quarter. The drag of the stopped propeller naturally assists in the situation, and an oil bag in the bight of the hawser would also greatly help. A small line through a block on the hawser's bight may be rigged to haul the oil bag out to its place, or inboard for replenishing.

Provided your ship is not by the head and has no preponderance of superstructure abaft amidships, she will *fall off from the sea easier than you can bring her up to it.* For this reason almost any steamer, when obliged to lie powerless in a heavy sea, should be encouraged to fall off. A sea anchor is not a practical instrument on the modern sea-going steamer.

If it is found necessary to head into the sea, the paying out of cable as referred to, coupled with two or three long bights of your heaviest manila hawsers as a drag, will be found successful, *if your vessel is not more than two or three feet by the stern;* the nearer to even keel the better.

Heaving-To in a Gale. With plenty of sea-room, a vessel generally will lie easiest if engines are stopped and ship is allowed to take her own position relative to sea direction. This is markedly so where ship is not stiffly laden; i.e., if she has a relatively small *GM*. Ships deeply loaded, with large metacentric height, will usually lie best with sea on port quarter, and engines turning slowly astern (right-handed single screw).

Where it is necessary to hold the ship from "sagging down" to leeward, such as when on a lee shore, keep a single-screw steamer with the sea two or three points on port bow, engines slow ahead. If in a light vessel in such circumstances and, due to propeller racing, ship has not power to hold her own, *fill every available double-bottom tank and flood an after hold*, in order to increase the draft and give the screw a better grip in the water.

Some shipmasters prefer to heave-to with the sea on the bow, regardless of ship's load condition. This surely demonstrates want of feeling for the vessel's straining and creaking structure. Avoid, if at all possible, holding a ship up to a heavy sea when obliged to heave-to. It is here worthy of note that, excepting possibly the stranding situation, the structural strength of many vessels has been unnecessarily taxed by their officers forcing them to do what they were never intended to do.

Running Before a Heavy Sea. If running before a heavy sea in a deeply-laden vessel, less water will be shipped if the engines are turning at half speed; and, should it be decided to heave to with ship head to sea, do so with as little way as possible. Use full speed ahead only to give ship a start in swinging.

Fire at Sea. Consider any fire on board, however small, as dangerous and calling for immediate action. If of a serious nature, put ship before the wind or stop her in a calm, in order to reduce the draft or air currents through the vessel to a minimum. Call all hands to stations. If fire is inaccessible and in a hold, apply smothering-line system at once. If it gets out of control, swing out boats and make ready to abandon ship. Head for the nearest port, or beach the vessel if near the coast. Keep owners informed, and send out distress signal by radio.

Stranding. If on a sea-coast, and ship is hard and fast, take immediate steps to prevent her "creeping" farther inshore. Fill up all ballast tanks and, if ship is pounding, flood the lower holds so as to hold ship in position until anchors are laid out in readiness for hauling off. Inform your owners of the situation. If inner bottom is damaged, request assistance from a salvage concern at once. Lay out anchors to heave ship off in the opposite direction to that in which she was heading at time of stranding.

Lighten ship when all ready to heave on anchors, and take advantage of any range of tide by timing your best efforts to be at high water.

Laying Out Anchors. Carry out a kedge a little beyond the spot where your heavy anchor is to be dropped and bend a 2 1/2" or 3" line to it for a "guess-warp." For the heavy anchor use two boats catamaran fashion. Hang the anchor (the spare bower or one of the regular bowers) between the boats from a spar lashed across amidships, and a coil wire hawser attached across after ends of boats. If there is any swell, lash spars across ends of boats also, so that the two will take the swell as one boat, and thus produce no jerky torque on the anchor spar. Buoy each anchor as laid down.

Anchor Raft. With the material at hand, it is perhaps better to construct a raft on which to carry the anchor. Three stout spars lashed together in triangular form, corners strengthened with other spars, empty drums, barrels or tanks secured between spars, and the whole decked over, will make a very satisfactory "ferry" in this work.

A raft of this sort having a 12-ft. side all round, if fully supplied with the buoyant material suggested above, would easily carry 4 tons on a 2-ft. draft.

The use of one boat in carrying out a heavy anchor is not recommended. The method requires the anchor to be slung under the boat, which calls for an extra heavy boat and a much greater depth of water in order to keep the anchor off the bottom, not to mention the danger of capsizing when letting the anchor go.

Jury Rudder. Fasten two steel plates, with wood between, on each side of a cargo boom. Have gooseneck to fit in one of rudder gudgeons. Rig topping-lift over stern to take weight of boom and wires from end of boom to each quarter, thence to winch.

Jury Steering-Gear. Wire pendants attached to tiller. Manila luff tackles secured to pendants and hauling parts led to winch, turns being taken in opposite ways on drumheads. Have tackles fore-and-aft in line with drumheads.

Intercepting Another Vessel for Medical Assistance, etc. The following practical example will probably serve as the best explanation (refer to Fig. 1).

P_1 is your ship, and you wish to intercept P_2 in order to transfer an injured man. You wish to know the course to steer and the time required, with P_2 maintaining course and speed.

eg represents the course of P_2, 40°, and speed 10 K.

gm is the relative movement line, and is taken up to g and laid off; it is the bearing of P_2 from your position P_1 at the moment you start to intercept him.

The length of *em* you have in your speed, 11 K.

Using this as a radius, intercept *gm* as extended from g.

Then the *direction* from e to m (the point of intersection) is the course for you to steer, i.e. 272°.

The *length* of *gm* is the speed at which you are approaching P_2.

Referring back to the positions originally plotted, P_1 and P_2, we find that P_1 to P_2 is 22 miles.

Then the time required to intercept P_2 is 22 divided by 19 K. or 1ʰ 09ᵐ.

Speed and Direction Triangle. (*See* Fig. 1.) The direction of each side of the triangle represents a course (direction of movement), and the length of each side represents a speed (rate of movement); the whole triangle, therefore, represents six elements:

Side eg:
    1. Course of guide
    2. Speed of guide

Side em:
    3. Course of ship
    4. Speed of ship

Side gm:

  5. Direction of relative movement
  6. Rate of relative movement or, briefly, "relative speed"

The direction of movement is always as indicated by arrows, that is, *eg* and *em* are drawn from the center of diagram, *e*, and *gm* is always *from g* toward *m.*

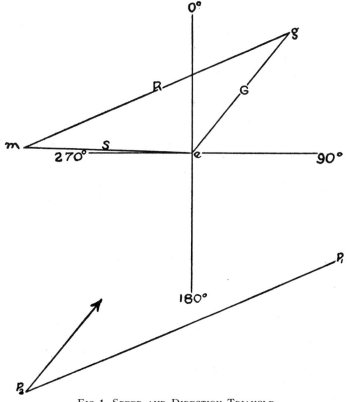

Fig 1. Speed and Direction Triangle.

In the most common problem you know (1) and (2), course and speed of guide, also (5), direction of relative movement (from present to new position).

You decide on your course (3), and want to know what speed to take (4); or,

You decide on your speed (4), and want to know what course to steer (3).

It may be necessary to determine the "time" to reach position. In this case you must determine relative speed (6) from the triangle, and "relative distance," i.e., distance from present to new positions as plotted.

Transfer of Personnel at Sea

Under the exigencies of war the transfer of fuel, stores, provisions, mail and personnel became standard procedure and the feasibility of this operation under almost any conditions was demonstrated. Never-

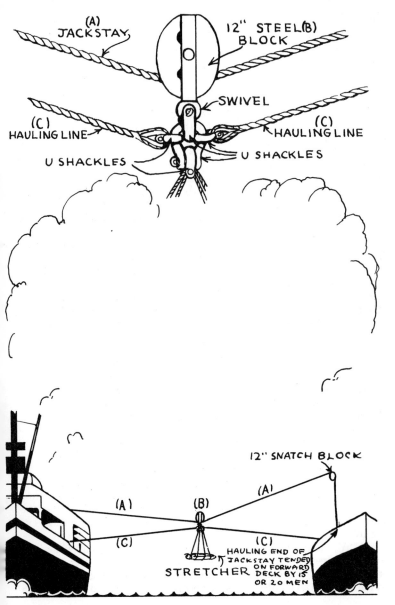

FIGURE 2

theless this remains a dangerous maneuver and is unlikely to be attempted by other than naval vessels in peacetime, except when human life may be at stake. Therefore the transfer of a stretcher case in weather too rough for small boats will be the only one described.

The vessel likely to make least leeway should be to windward and the course chosen should put the wind about two points on the weather bow. The guide ship, A, must maintain a steady course and speed. The smaller or handier ship, B, makes its approach on the other and maintains the proper distance from it.

It should be borne in mind that even if the hulls of two ships travelling on the same course and at the same speed touch, the impact will be less than in any other circumstances and there is less chance of crippling damage. There is generally a tendency for the bows to draw apart and the most danger lies in letting the stern swing in so that the propellers may be damaged.

The gear shown in Fig. 2 should be made ready and the procedure decided upon by both vessels. A should have a marker placed at the position where the jackstay will be made fast. The jackstay should be rigged as nearly level as possible and should be kept taut by hand, using 15–20 men so located as to be free to move fore and aft on deck.

(a) "B" takes station about 300 yards astern and about 60 feet from the wake of "A" on the appropriate quarter.

(b) "B" steadies on the chosen course and speed for a time sufficient to permit an accurate check on that of "A".

(c) After both vessels are ready "B" increases speed *3 knots* by RPM's and *maintains this increased speed for one minute for each 100 yards astern of position*. A stop watch should be used and when one minute has passed for each 100 yards reduce to standard speed of "A" even though still behind position. This holds true for all types of vessels since a ship that is slow to gain way (overcome inertia) is also slow to lose it, and vice versa.

(d) "B" uses the wake of "A" as a primary guide and the stern as a secondary guide. If it is necessary to correct position no sudden changes should be made. Take it easy. 1°–3° alteration in course and 1–5 RPM's in speed is ample, bearing inertia in mind. The helmsman should be given a definite compass course to steer each time a change is made.

(e) A bold approach should be made. It is better to overshoot the mark than to cause delay by too slow an approach as the lines can be passed while "B" drops back into position.

(f) The towline and springline shown in Fig. 3 are not always used but may assist in maintaining position even if no strain is put on them. The eyes of these lines are passed from "A" to "B", "A" tending the lines as necessary. Men with axes should be stationed on "B" to cut the lines in an emergency.

(g) "A" maintains a steady course and speed throughout while "B" adjusts course and speed to maintain position about 60 feet off. This is not difficult if the captain of "B" is on the inboard wing where he can watch the lines and adjust course. Another officer is located where he can watch the lines and adjust course. Another officer is located where he can line up some point on "A" and adjust speed, a turn or two at a time.

(h) "B" should clear the side of "A" by increasing speed and sheering out, using small divergent course changes.

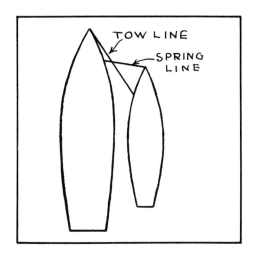

FIGURE 3

RENDERING ASSISTANCE

Vessels in Distress. Whether passengers and crew are to be taken off is to be decided by the master of the disabled vessel. The manner in which they are to be taken off is decided by the commanding officer of a public vessel (U.S.C.G. or U.S.N.) assisting. The matter of rescuing property and personal effects is entirely in the hands of the commanding officer of the assisting vessel.

If a vessel is in tow, it is the right of the towed vessel to let go the tow-line whenever he sees fit. A U.S.C.G. or a U.S.N. vessel must, by law, relinquish a disabled vessel to a privately-owned tug, if such tug can manage the disabled vessel and her charges are reasonable, regardless of distance from port or extent of assistance the public vessel has already given. Similarly with stranding, a public vessel cannot interfere with private enterprise, unless it is manifestly inadequate.

Assisting Vessel Whose Rudder Is Gone. Come up astern of her. Take a good wire from each quarter to your forecastle head. Use anchor cables for catenary spring if bad weather is expected. Let disabled ship go ahead. Steer her by stress on either wire.

Assisting to Haul Off a Stranded Vessel. Where anchorage to seaward is available, and there is a high-water slack in local tidal conditions, both anchors are dropped with about 100 fathoms of cable in the hauling-off direction, with the heaviest hawser or hawsers at hand made fast aft and leading to the stern of the stranded vessel—which is undoubtedly the position in which the maximum power can be exerted to the best advantage. Heave away on your anchors until hawsers are taut; then go ahead on engines as directed by signal from the stranded vessel. This procedure is practicable during slack, or nearly slack water only, for when the current makes across your ship you will do more harm than good by carrying away all your hawsers or pulling obliquely across the line of direction in which the stranded vessel should be moved.

If the tide is such that at highest water the current runs along the coast, proceed as follows: Stem the current and drop the offshore anchor in the direction from the stranded vessel in which it is desirable to haul off, allowing about 100 fathoms cable paid out when as close as practicable to her position. Maneuver ship to sheer inshore toward the stranded vessel, paying out cable as required. When close enough, drop the other anchor to hold your position, and proceed to run a good hawser from your forecastle or fore deck to the stranded vessel's quarter. When all ready, heave up the inshore anchor, heave away on the off-shore cable, hold ship on the "line of haul" with the engines, and give her the necessary cant to seaward as chain cable and hawser are set taut. Complete control of your vessel here enables this combination of windlass and main engine power to fall little short of the first method noted.

Towing Disabled Vessel. For deep sea towing in heavy weather, the chain cable is perhaps the surest tow-line at hand in a merchant vessel. Get up enough chain from the locker as will reach to the stern of your ship. Stretch the chain aft and place a couple of heavy planks between the anchor flukes and the shell plating. Having maneuvered your vessel so the stern will be as close as possible to the bows of the disabled vessel, the latter having unshackled and secured one of her anchors in the meantime, heave the end of her chain on board and shackle it to your cable. The towed vessel will regulate the length of cable by her windlass. Your cable is toggled by the anchor in the hawse-pipe.

Long-distance towing in this fashion has been in several known instances carried out with great success in the heaviest weather. *There are no hawsers or bitts to carry away.*

Wire hawsers suit smooth water conditions, even the heaviest wire hawsers carried on merchant vessels being too light for heavy weather, excepting, of course, where a towing winch is used. *Manila hawsers* have the properties of elasticity and buoyancy in their favor, and for moderate towing work are unequaled, towing machines not considered.

A combination of chain cable and manila hawser has found favor in long-distance towing, but manila of the heavy size required is seldom found on merchant vessels. For any hope of success in deep-sea towing, the towing vessel should have at least a 12″ manila to attach to, say, a 2 1/2″ chain cable leading from the disabled vessel's hawse-pipe. And here the need for rigging a *bridle* from the towing ship's quarters is apparent, since it is practically impossible to properly and securely make fast an unusually large hawser on a merchant vessel's bitts.

A wire and a manila hawser of about 100 fathoms total length and the heaviest obtainable will give satisfactory results, as a rule. The wire should not be less in length than the manila, if leading through a chock, since the accumulation of twisting (greater in the manila than in the wire) due to the vessel's surging in a seaway, must be dissipated throughout the wire's length.

Length of tow-line. The ideal length is such that both vessels are "in step" with the sea or swell conditions at all times. They should always hold the same position with relation to each sea in order to avoid the heavy surges and jerks which would otherwise result.

Storm Oil. The use of storm oil in towing during heavy weather cannot be too strongly recommended. Here the towing vessel is in a position to protect her charge and generally make better time on a passage.

In maneuvering to pick up a tow in bad weather it is well to remember that a *vessel will drift to leeward faster than oil will spread in that direction.* Therefore spread oil well to leeward of the disabled vessel, so that both ships, during the operation of connecting up a tow-line, will be protected by the "oil slick," and a less arduous job will be the result.

The line-throwing gun may be used to advantage in establishing contact under the above conditions.

For storm oil, animal and vegetable oils are the best. Fuel oil thinned out with kerosene has given good results. About 2 gallons per hour is the rate reported by many vessels hove-to in heavy weather. A slow drip from canvas oakum-filled bags, or from rags kept soaked with the oil and placed in waste-pipes will be found effective, but the quantity required will be governed by the effect produced, as observed in any particular case.

In shallow water, where the "run" of the sea is greatest, oil has the least effect. Breakers on a bar during flood tide have been "flattened out" by allowing plenty of oil to spread in ahead of the vessel, but during ebb tide its use is ineffective. In any case, the result of spreading oil in "bar" conditions has been found uncertain.

Rescuing Crew of a Foundering Vessel During Heavy Weather. As in picking up a tow in bad weather, spread oil generously to leeward of the disabled vessel. Make a thorough job of this before attempting to get a boat away, and when ready in position to windward of the wreck your vessel should be well within the oil area. After sending your boat off when to windward and as close as possible to the wreck, the boat having arrived at the lee side of the latter, maneuver ship so as to drift as close astern or ahead of the disabled vessel as possible, spreading oil continuously. You will now be in the best possible position to take the rescued people on board without delay.

The officer in charge of the rescuing boat should have at hand a couple of heaving lines so that, if unable to lie close enough to the wreck, he may have the means with which to drag each person into the boat, while the men at the oars hold her off the vessel's side.

In getting the boat away, the use of frapping lines on the falls, the sea painter, and the necessity for each man in the boat to wear a lifebelt will at once suggest seeing this carried out by a *seaman* under such circumstances. A supply of blankets would not be out of place in the boat, where exposure to cold weather must be endured.

The officer in charge of the boat should consider the probability of encountering, and suffering damage to his boat by, floating wreckage on the lee side of the disabled vessel, especially so during darkness. He should also be advised *to lie alongside to leeward of a drifting vessel in heavy weather in no other position than at right angles to the ship's side,* keeping the boat controlled by the oars at all times. To allow a "broadside on" position in such conditions invites disaster.

In the rare case of the distressed vessel drifting at the same rate as the rescuing ship (which may be noted by the latter during approach across the wind and sea) a boat attached to a good line and managed by her crew may be sent away from a position to windward of the disabled ship. A system of signals should be arranged in order that the line be promptly slacked, hauled in, or held fast, as required by the boat. Each rescued person would be hauled to the boat by line and life-buoy, one end of the life-buoy line on board their vessel, the other in the boat. Oil from the rescuing vessel should be freely used during the operation.

INSTRUCTIONS TO MASTERS OF MERCHANT VESSELS IN CASES OF VESSELS AND AIRCRAFT IN DISTRESS

The increasing volume of transoceanic flights by aircraft means that masters of merchant vessels may be called upon to assist distressed aircraft.

The master of a merchant ship in the vicinity of the vessel or aircraft in distress will materially further the rescue operation if he finds the vessel or aircraft quickly. Radio direction finder and radar help here. If it is a surface vessel in distress, there will be few problems other than those of sound seamanship. The Coast Guard has found the large inflated rubber raft very handy to lay alongside of a vessel in rough sea where a ship's boat might well be smashed. By the use of the rubber raft, people can sometimes be taken from a foundering vessel in a rough sea with less hazard than with the old method of attempting to lie close under power or alongside on a sea painter, with a wood or metal boat.

If the distress call is from a transoceanic passenger plane, the rescuing merchant vessel has a number of new problems:

1. The ditching, i. e., crash landing in the water, will be violent at the very best, with consequent probability of injury and shock to passengers and crew. Suppose a distressed aircraft is coming to you. You picture him landing in the sea like a gull. The gull flies at 20 knots and lands at 5. The airliner lands closer to 100. Try to visualize a ship's boat with cellophane bottom coming into that sea you are looking at at 100 knots. The aircraft may float for hours; it may sink in several minutes.

2. Airborne rubber dinghys do not give the survivors nearly as good protection from the sea as ship's lifeboats.

3. The dinghys are much smaller and have much lower silhouettes than lifeboats and so are harder to find.

4. Extensive floating debris—sometimes even the abandoned hulk itself—usually present when a ship burns, founders, or is stranded, are not present to guide search planes and ships to survivors of aircraft ditchings.

5. The limitations of weight in aircraft baggage allowances, stowage, and the terrific haste with which passengers must expect to abandon a ditched aircraft, point to limited protective clothing for survivors.

6. The round rubber dinghy cannot be rowed or sailed even the hundred miles or so that might make land or put it in a steamer lane.

7. The awkwardness of the round dinghy complicates the problem of rescue if the sea is rough. They do not tow well. They cannot be brought along side on a sea painter under some control like a ship's boat, but will probably be slammed violently into the ship's side, spilling survivors into the sea. (The military type rubber dinghy is shaped like a boat. The air transport type is normally round.)

8. And finally there will not likely be any seamen in the dinghys who can cooperate in their own rescue in simple things like bending lines, rigging bridles to relieve tow pads, heaving lines, fending off with skill, etc.

In all rescue problems it is important to get first things first. Some of these are not obvious to the inexperienced and in the stress and hurry of a rescue others may be overlooked. It is easy to oversimplify a rescue mission in planning; to assume that this or that phase of the rescue does not need your care or assistance. Recently a ship's commander stated: "I won't maneuver to work up a lee for a ditching plane because I don't think he'd hit it anyway, and I might not be in a position to get to him quickly." This was a failure to get first things first. If the pilot kills everybody in the landing, the rescue ship won't save anyone anyway. In ignorance this captain assumed that landing was easy. The records show that many ditching aircraft have killed or injured all or large proportions of the persons aboard on the landing.

The following instructions have been prepared by the Office of the Commander Eastern Area, United States Coast Guard, for the guidance of surface vessels facing the problem of rescue of ditching aircraft. It is believed that a wide dissemination of these instructions to masters will contribute materially to safety of life at sea and to the peace of mind of the conscientious master:

INSTRUCTIONS FOR RESCUE OF DISTRESSED AIRCRAFT PERSONNEL AT SEA

Finding the Aircraft

1. Establish firm communications. You can use *any* frequency in distress cases.

2. Transmit on a frequency between 200 and 1,750 kilocycles for the plane to home to you. If you cannot be sure the plane knows what frequency you will use to home him in, use 500 kilocycles. If you can, use a frequency liable to less interference. Make your call frequently so the plane is sure he is homing on the right ship. Make twenty second dashes. Example: "AUOD .... AUOD.......... AUOD".

3. Track the distressed plane with your own **DF** if possible. If he cannot transmit on a frequency within your **DF** band, ask him to hook his Gibson Girl to his antenna and crank. The Gibson Girl is an emergency transmitter that transmits simultaneously on 500 kilocycles and 8280 kilocycles; power is applied through a hand crank. Many airliners cannot transmit below 2900 kilocycles with regular equipment. If you get bearings send him frequent vectors for comparison with his own. Mark each one either true or magnetic. *A vector is the course that the plane has to follow to reach your ship, disregarding drift, etc.* In other words, a vector is your bearing from the plane. *Example:* **Vector 284 true 1410Z.**

4. Get the distressed plane in your radar screen when and if you can and hold him.

5. Get his **Loran** readings and plot his track as practicable.

6. Long before you estimate he will see you, make black smoke in the daytime, or rotate a powerful searchlight around the sky at night.

7. Always keep in mind that with each engine he loses, he loses a generator too. As his batteries go down he may hear you after he can't transmit. Transmit to him blind if necessary until you are *sure* he can't read you.

8. Head on an intercepting course for him from the first distress signal. He may not be able to reach you **unless** you are proceeding into appreciable worse seas and he states he is sure he can reach you. If you know the seas are much easier an hour or so steaming from your position, ask the distressed pilot if he desires you to proceed to the area of the easier landing condition.

ATLANTIC MERCHANT VESSEL REPORT (AMVER) SYSTEM

Atlantic Merchant VEssel Report (AMVER) System, operated by the United States Coast Guard, is a maritime mutual assistance program which provides important aid to the development and coordination of search and rescue (SAR) efforts in the offshore areas of the North Atlantic Ocean, Caribbean Sea and Gulf of Mexico, north of the Equator and west of Prime Meridian. Merchant vessels of all nations making offshore voyages are encouraged to voluntarily send movement (sailing) reports and periodic position reports to the AMVER Center located at Coast Guard New York, via selected U. S. coastal, extra continental, or Ocean Station Vessel radio stations. Information from these reports is entered into an electronic computer which generates and maintains dead reckoning positions for the vessels while they are within the plotting area. Characteristics of vessels which are valuable for determining SAR capability are also entered into the computer from available sources of information. Appropriate information concerning the predicted location and SAR characteristics of each vessel known to be within the area of interest, is made available upon request to recognized SAR agencies of any nation, or person in distress, for use during any emergency. Predicted locations are only disclosed for reasons related to maritime safety.

GENERAL INSTRUCTIONS

PURPOSE OF AMVER

Several hundred merchant vessels are sailing the North Atlantic area at one time. These vessels have the proven potential for early arrival at the scene of a maritime incident, which is so necessary during a distress. The purpose of AMVER is to make possible maximum efficiency in coordinating assistance offered by merchant vessels to save life and property at sea. AMVER provides information which assists in: determination of most appropriate early assistance; timely resolution of distress cases; and enabling vessels responding to distress calls to continue on their passages with minimum delay.

It is important that information be available to SAR coordinators prior to occurrence of an emergency, so that potential assistance may be utilized effectively and with the least delay to those voluntarily offering aid. Establishing communications is sometimes difficult even when "auto alarms" are used, and determination of SAR capability and intentions of vessels is time-consuming. Communications must be held to a minimum during a distress. Many emergencies require immediate decisions and action. The AMVER Center provides much valuable information concerning those vessels participating in the AMVER program, thereby making possible more timely assistance during emergencies.

AMVER PARTICIPANTS

A vessel is a participant in the AMVER program when she sends a report to the AMVER Center during a passage. An AMVER participant is under no greater obligation to render assistance during an emergency than any vessel who has not made a report during the passage. There is no limitation as to the size of a vessel before she may participate in the AMVER program. This is determined by nature of passage and communication capability.

SAR CHARACTERISTICS OF MERCHANT VESSELS

In addition to the information generated from movement and position reports, the AMVER Center maintains data on the characteristics of active merchant vessels. This data which reflects SAR capability includes the following: Vessel name; international call sign; nation of registry; owner or operator; type or rig; type of propulsion; gross tonnage; length; normal cruising speed; radio schedule; HF and VHF radio frequencies; radio telephone installed; surface search radar installed; doctor normally carried. Vessels can assist the AMVER Center in keeping this data accurate by sending a complete report by message or letter, and then sending corrections as the characteristics change. The corrections may easily be included in regular AMVER reports as remarks.

CONSTRUCTIVE COMPLIANCE—USCFR, TITLE 33

AMVER messages which include the necessary information are considered to be in constructive compliance with provisions of the U.S. Code of Federal Regulations, Title 33, Part 124.10, as revised on 1 January 1962. This regulation requires, with certain exceptions, that the master or agent of each United States registered vessel and every foreign vessel arriving at a United States port (including the Great Lakes) from an offshore passage, give advance notice to the U.S. Coast Guard at least 24 hours prior to arrival. The U.S. Code of Federal Regulations should be consulted to determine the exact current requirements, the exceptions, and the conditions of constructive compliance. The AMVER Center forwards pertinent information to the appropriate Coast Guard officials.

AMVER SYSTEM COMMUNICATION NETWORK

An effective communication network supports the AMVER System. It provides three routes for assistance messages as well as AMVER messages. These routes are: coastal, overseas, and Ocean Station radio stations. Propagation conditions, location of vessel, and message density will normally determine which station may best be contacted to establish communications. To insure that no charge is applied, all AMVER messages should be passed through specified government radio stations. Stations which currently accept AMVER messages and apply no coastal station, ship station, or landline charge are listed on the following page, together with respective call sign, location, frequency bands, and hours of guard. AMVER messages may be sent through commercial stations, but the Coast Guard cannot reimburse the sender for any charges applied.

AMVER MESSAGE ADDRESS

All AMVER messages are addressed to COAST GUARD NEW YORK, regardless of the station to which the message is delivered.

AMVER MESSAGE TYPES AND FORMAT

Any vessel of any nation departing on an offshore passage, a significant part of which is north of the Equator and west of the Prime Meridian (0° Longitude) in the North Atlantic Ocean, Caribbean Sea, or Gulf of Mexico, is encouraged to become a participant in the AMVER System by sending appropriate AMVER messages in four types of formats illustrated on the following page. The messages may be transmitted at any convenient time as long as the information is accurate and the data corresponds to the time specified. The information may be estimated for a short time in the future, for the present, or for a short time past.

The four types of reports are:

Type 1.—The complete Type 1 report consists of nine parts and any pertinent remarks and contains the information necessary to initiate a plot. It is called an initial AMVER message and may be considered a movement report or sailing plan. Type 1 reports may be sent immediately prior to departure, at departure, immediately after departure, or upon entering the Plotting Area, as soon as adequate communications can be established. If the point of departure is not within the Plotting Area, the initial Type 1 report should specify the estimated position, date, and time of entry into the Plotting Area, or a supplemental Type 1 or Type 2 report may be sent upon actual entry into the Plotting Area.

Type D.—The Type D report is a deviation report and need include only information which differs from that previously reported. It is sent when the actual position will vary more than 25 miles from the position which would be predicted based upon data contained in previous reports. It may indicate a change of route, course, speed, or destination, and include any pertinent remarks.

Type 2.—The Type 2 report is considered a position report and includes the date and time of the position. It may contain additional entries and remarks. Experience has shown that occasional position reports are required during long passages to insure that the electronic computer will predict the positions within acceptable accuracy. It is not important that these position reports be sent at any particular time or location, but it is suggested that they be prepared at intervals of approximately 15 degrees of latitude or longitude depending upon direction of advance. The revised diagram of the AMVER Plotting Area contains dashed lines at 0, 15, 30, 45, 60, and 75 degrees of latitude and longitude to serve as a reminder that position reports are desired occasionally. Parts 6, 7, 8, and 9 may be omitted from the message if desired. It is no longer necessary that a Type 2 report be sent exactly at 67° W. longitude, however it may be continued if desired.

Type 3.—A Type 3 report is an arrival report, and is sent upon reaching the harbor entrance at port of destination if within the AMVER Plotting Area, or upon crossing out of the Plotting Area. Parts 6, 7, 8, and 9 may be omitted from the message if desired. Remarks may be included. If communications cannot be established to permit sending the Type 3 report, the electronic computer will automatically terminate the plot at the predicted time of arrival at the destination. However, the report is desired to increase the accuracy of the plot and Type 3 reports are especially desired upon arrival at the harbor entrance of United States ports.

Only these four types of AMVER messages require specific formats. Other operational and administrative messages relating to the AMVER program may use the AMVER System. These may include such things as SAR characteristics of vessels.

ADDITIONAL INFORMATION

Further information concerning the AMVER System may be obtained by writing to Commandant, U.S. Coast Guard, Washington 25, D.C., or by writing or visiting Commander, Eastern Area, U.S. Coast Guard, Custom House, New York 4, N.Y. Officers of the shipping industry and others concerned with maritime safety are welcome to visit the AMVER Center, Room 650A, in the Custom House. Visitors are preferred on weekdays between the hours of 0900 and 1600. The telephone number is currently 212–422–5700, extension 629. The TELEX address is 01–2043. The TWX address is 212–571–0593.

BREAKDOWN OF TEXT OF AMVER MESSAGES

1 NAME	2 CALL SIGN	3 REPORT TYPE	4 POSITION	5 DATE—TIME	6 SAILING ROUTE	7 SPEED	8 DESTINATION	9 ETA
Name of vessel ..	Radio call	1, D, 2, or 3. (See p. 2.)	Latitude and longitude to nearest tenth degree (name of point may be used where convenient. i.e. Ambrose)	Date—Time GMT of position. (Use 6 digits, i.e. 041800 where first 2 is date of month and last 4 are GMT hours and minutes.)	Latitude and longitude to nearest 0.1 degree of each turn point along intended track. Use "RL" for rhumb line, or "GC" for great circle before each point to show method of sailing. When track is to be coastal, state "coastal" for that part of route.	To nearest 0.1 knot.	Next port of call. (Note: for U.S. port located inland, it is recommended that the off-shore point i.e. Cape Henry, etc. be given.)	Estimated time of arrival at destination Use GMT date and time

SAMPLE MESSAGES

Imperial St. Lawrence	HOOX	1	43.5N 70.1W	281100	RL 41.6N 69.7W RL via Windward Passage RL.	15.7	Colon	03090
Parthia..........	GSWQ	1	51.0N 10.3W	092300	GC 42.0N 50.0W RL 40.5N 69.5W RL.	16.5	New York	15110
Argentina........	WMDU	1	Ambrose	061300	GC Equator at 37.0W	23.0	Rio de Janeiro.	16010
Sagami Maru....	JJGF	1	40.5N 73.3W	301300	Coastal RL.........	17.1	Overfalls......	30180
J. L. Luckenbach.	KAEO	D	31.0N 78.0W	261500	....	9.0	In heavy seas...	....
Groote Beer.	PELA	2	39.1N 67.0W	061400	....	15.4	....	....
Godafoss	TFMA	2	42.4N 67.3W	232300	....		....	....
Alcoa Pilgrim...	KKVZ	3	QTP South Pass	092300	....		....	....

WHO ACCEPTS AMVER MESSAGES?—A list of U.S. Coast Guard Radio Stations and Ocean Stations accepting AMVER messag. the frequencies and/or bands guarded by each, and their working frequency in each band is tabulated below:

CG unit's radio call	Unit's location	Frequency and/or HF bands guarded		CG unit working frequency	CG unit's radio call	Unit's location	Frequency and/or HF bands guarded		CG unit wor. ing frequen.
		Day	Night				Day	Night	
NMF	Boston, Mass.....	500 kc 8 mc	500 kc 8 mc	472 kc 8734 kc	NJN	Argentia, Nfld....	500 kc 8 mc 12 mc	500 kc 6 mc 8 mc	427 kc 6477.5 kc 8734 kc 12718.5 kc
NMY	New York, N.Y...	500 kc 8 mc 4 mc	500 kc 8 mc	486 kc 8710 kc 4361 kc	NOC	Bermuda, B.W.I..	500 kc	500 kc	440 kc
NMH	Washington, D.C.	12 mc 16 mc	12 mc	12718.5 kc 17002.4 kc	NMR	San Juan, P.R.....	500 kc 8 mc 12 mc	500 kc 4 mc 8 mc	466 kc 4361 kc 8710 kc 12718.5 kc
NMN	Norfolk, Va......	500 kc 8 mc	500 kc 8 mc	466 kc 8734 kc	NBA*	Balboa, C.Z......	500 kc 8 mc 12 mc 16 mc	500 kc 4 mc 8 mc 12 mc	470 kc 4352 kc 8614 kc 12883 kc 17136.8 kc
NMV	Jacksonville, Fla..	500 kc 8 mc	500 kc 8 mc	457 kc 8734 kc					
NMA	Miami, Fla.......	500 kc 8 mc	500 kc 8 mc	440 kc 8710 kc	4YB	56-30N 51-00W	500 kc	500 kc	466 kc
NOF	St. Petersburg, Fla.	500 kc	500 kc	440 kc	4YC	52-45N 35-20W	500 kc	500 kc	466 kc
NMG	New Orleans, La.	500 kc 8 mc	500 kc 4 mc	428 kc 4361 kc 8710 kc	4YD	44-00N 41-00W	500 kc	500 kc	466 kc
NOY	Galveston, Tex....	500 kc	500 kc	457 kc	4YE	35-00N 48-00W	500 kc	500 kc	466 kc

NOTE: U.S. Interdepartment Radio Advisory Committee (IRAC) Definitions:
DAY—2 hours after sunrise until 2 hours before sunset.
NIGHT—2 hours before sunset until 2 hours after sunrise. (Local time of radio station)
Schedule may be changed due to propagation.

*U.S. Navy Communication Station.

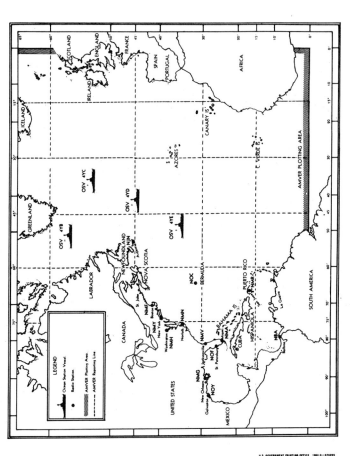

FIG. 4. CHART SHOWING LOCATION OF OCEAN STATION VESSELS, RADIO STATIONS, AMVER PLOTTING AREAS AND AMVER REPORTING LINES.

Assisting the Distressed Aircraft To Land

1. Give him the force and direction of the surface wind. Use degrees and knots and the word "From". *Example:* **Surface wind from 149 true 15 knots.** *Not* "Wind south southeast three-quarters East force four," which doesn't tell a pilot quickly and for sure either the approximate direction of the wind or its velocity.

2. Describe the sea conditions as clearly and accurately as possible. *Example:* **Long swell from 280 true five feet high five hundred feet between crests moving at thirty knots steep wind driven sea from north true four feet high eighty feet between crests moving at twelve knots.** Throw over a life jacket and clock the time between passage of two successive swells under it. Five times the square of this time in seconds equals roughly the distance in feet between crests; three times the time in seconds equals roughly the speed of the swell in knots. Use the same formula for the wind driven sea. Estimate sea or swell height—trough to crest—carefully by eye.

3. To make a lee, circle with hardover rudder at high speed. After completing three or four circles the area inside the ship's turning circle should be considerably smoother than the area outside. Continue the circle until the plane has landed unless the pilot asks you to stop or take some particular heading. Use oil with judgment. Cold bunker or diesel oil should not create a fire hazard but it is sometimes almost useless. It is most worth while for easing a short hard wind-driven sea. Your turning circle creates an area big enough for a good ditching; the plane should travel less than a thousand feet after hitting the water. A smart pilot will elect to land with the most formidable sea on his beam and with some wind ahead if possible.

4. **Night conditions.** After proceeding as above, attempt to mark the circle at four equidistant points with floating lights if possible. The weather marker should be pitched off the fantail and the leeward one from the bow to allow for drift. Try to put these lights down as shortly before the landing as possible to minimize their drifting away or going out. Ask the pilot if he wants the searchlight for landing. If he says "yes," maneuver into position to throw the beam on the water so it hits the plane about one point on the starboard quarter as he lands. The pilot sits on the left hand side of the cockpit and this way he is not blinded. Don't point the searchlight at the plane's cockpit (bow) until the plane is on the water. The result desired is to illuminate the sea for landing without blinding the pilot. The light should come from abaft the plane's beam. If you blind the pilot he may lose control of the plane.

Rescue of Personnel

1. Use lots of lookouts. Try to have a responsible lookout kept over each boat and each raft while it is in the water. Have spare lookouts ready to assist if people in the water get scattered and to relieve difficult stations.

2. Have a boat ready to go over the side *quickly*. Work as fast as you can. The weak or injured are likely to die from exposure. Man the boat with a smart crew. Use a lively pulling boat or a smart handling power boat if possible. In addition to the usual boat box, the following gear will be helpful:

(a) A five- or seven-man dinghy (rubber). Tow astern of boat.

(b) A dozen exposure suits.

(c) About 20 pieces of small line (9 thread is heavy enough) each 8 fathoms long, with a bowline on a bight on one end, and each coiled separately.

(d) Several spare boat hooks.

(e) Several spare kapok life preservers.

(f) A dozen blankets.

(g) Two fire axes.

(h) Two pairs of pliers.

(i) One bolt cutter.

(j) Two pairs horsehide gloves.

(k) Four 5-cell flashlights.

The rubber dinghy can be laid alongside a plane when a boat would sink it quickly. The exposure suits, spare life preservers, and blankets will be useful in rescuing and warming up especially weak or exhausted persons. The boat may well be away from the ship for several hours and rescued people should be kept as warm as possible in the boat. The pieces of 9-thread will be useful to toss to men in the water to drag them into the boat, for men to wear who are going over the side to help especially weak survivors, for bending onto rafts to tow, etc. The fire axes, pliers, bolt cutters, horsehide gloves, and flashlights will be useful if it is necessary to cut or smash an entrance into the fuselage of the plane to get someone out who is caught.

3. The area of the landing should be buoyed to fix a central point for search if some persons are thought to be lost in the vicinity.

4. Rescue or cargo nets should be rigged over the side and if available, volunteers should be ready to go over the side on safety lines to help survivors to and up the nets. Boats may be swamped or smashed against the side in a sea or rattled survivors may try to swim to the ship.

5. Care should be taken not to maneuver the ship into a position where the plane and ship will drift together. Check relative drift carefully and approach the plane from a bearing that will assure no closing on the plane when the ship has no way on. This cannot be emphasized too much. Planes are very fragile and a ship or ship's boat drifting into one in a sea may open compartments that are contributing substantial buoyancy and cause the wreck to sink very quickly. It is important to remember that the plane is drifting faster when plane and ship are on separate wind lines, but when the ship gets the plane close in her lee she blankets the wind from the plane and closes on her very fast. Many planes have been severely damaged this way and rescue efforts blocked or greatly complicated.

6. The number of people in the plane should have been ascertained before she went into the water and all accounted for before search and rescue operations are abandoned. An apparently drowned man floating in his life preserver can sometimes be resuscitated.

Closing the Search

1. When you are satisfied that all hands are accounted for or beyond chance of rescue, send a message to the United States Coast Guard with an unequivocal statement to that effect so that planes and ships that are racing to assist or preparing for searches on the morrow may be released.

ASSISTANCE TO AIRPLANES

Should you be called upon to tow a plane, remember the following:

a) At all times listen to what the aviator has to say. He knows the capabilities of his airplane better than you do.

b) Rig the towline so that the airplane is on the after face of the second wave.

c) Work speed up slowly until the airplane is at least part way up on the step.

d) Place an equal strain on both wing lines and leave sufficient slack for yaw, or the plane will tend to tow by one of the wing lines.

e) Do not attempt to tow to windward at any great speed.

f) Change course slightly to determine the most comfortable towing course.

g) If trying to make port in a heavy sea, tack in if necessary.

h) Use a drogue (bucket) on all headlines at speeds below 10 knots and at higher speeds when the wind is from forward of the beam.

i) Do not worry if the fabric is torn off the lower wings. If the sea is heavy the fabric on the lower wings should be slit to allow any water shipped to drain.

j) Remove all personnel from the airplane.

k) Tow at as fast a speed as possible with safety, for the airplane will ride easier, but do not permit the plane to "bounce" or yaw.

l) Have positive and instant communication between the bridge and poop.

m) Have an axe ready for cutting the towline.

n) Have two good men stationed continually to tend the wing lines, ready to slack one if the other carries away.

TOWING

Towline. Wire rope has proved satisfactory for heavy sea towing. Manila is the most satisfactory line that can be used for light or moderate towing.

A good plan is to combine manila and wire, the towing vessel first paying out the manila hawser, which is hauled across by the tow and secured, after which the towing ship shackles the wire rope to the manila and then starts ahead very slowly, paying out the wire rope as she gathers way.

For towing even a small vessel it must not be overlooked that rough weather may be encountered in almost any towing operation. The full length of a 10-inch manila hawser or a $1\frac{1}{2}''$ diameter wire rope will be none too much.

Where the tow is a vessel whose displacement is large the towline should be made up of two and one-quarter inch diameter wire rope connected to a good length of the tow's anchor cable. The length that is needed will vary with circumstances.

In securing the towline, consideration must be given to the possible necessity for letting go in an emergency. For convenience in letting go, it is desirable to have a break in the line near the stern; that is to say, to have, at or near this point, a shackle connecting two parts of the line, together with some arrangement, like a pelican hook, for slipping quickly.

To have the bitter end of the towline just inside the stern chock on the towing ship means that practically the whole length of the towline must be paid out, and that any variation in length must be taken care of by the tow. If the anchor cable of the tow is in use as a part of the towline, it is very easy to heave in or veer away on the chain, as may be necessary for shortening or lengthening the towline.

If the towing ship is comparatively large and has a chock at the stern, on the centerline, the tow line should be brought in through it. It is a good plan to use a short length of chain for the lead through the stern chock, shackling outside to an eye in the end of the towing hawser and inside to a towing bridle from a firm foundation depending upon the arrangement used for securing. Where the chain is not used for taking the chafe in the stern chock, the towline must be fully protected by chafing gear. Where the strain is not too heavy to be taken by the bitts, the line can be taken around the first bitts, thus leaving the line free to render slightly and so transfer a portion of the strain.

An arrangement with a pelican hook taking the steady strain of towing offers the quickest means for affecting an emergency release.

On board the tow, the hawser is usually secured to the anchor cable or towing bridle; if the anchor cable is not used, it is desirable to use at least a short length of chain to take the chafe in the chock in the same manner as already described for securing on the towing ship.

Where the anchor cable is used, the hawser is secured or shackled to it and the cable veered away to the desired length, after which the windlass brakes are set up and springs or chain stoppers are used to take the real strain of towing. It is well to have a shackle between the windlass and the point to which the springs or chain stoppers are secured and to keep tools at hand for unshackling if it becomes necessary to let go in an emergency. The tow should not let go in this way except in case of extreme emergency, as the line, weighted with a considerable length of heavy anchor cable, would sink immediately, hanging as a dead weight from the stern of the towing vessel, where it would be extremely difficult to handle and would be in danger of fouling the propellers. This applies only to cases where the tow is a vessel of some size, and where she is towing by her anchor cables. It is evident that where a large ship is towing a small one, the natural way of casting off is for the tow to let go, leaving the line to be handled by the large ship. Where the anchor cable of the tow is in use, the natural way to let go is for the tow to heave in her anchor cable and then cast off the towing hawser.

Taking a Disabled Vessel in Tow at Sea. The towing vessel, places herself to windward, if she is drifting faster than the other vessel, and to leeward if she is drifting more slowly, and on the same heading as the disabled vessel; taking care, of course, not to run any risk of drifting into collision, and remembering, as the ships draw together, not to get so close that the rudder cannot be put over for hauling off without danger of throwing the stern into collision with the tow.

The first line to be run will be a light one, by means of which the heavier ones can be hauled across. A 3-inch manila is a convenient size to begin with. If new, so much the better, as it will float freely. If a boat is to be used it should be lowered with the crew and the greater part of the line in it, the line being paid out as the boat pulls away for the other ship.

Maximum Height of Storm Waves. The *fetch* being the distance through which waves are generated by the wind, height of storm waves is indicated in the formal, $H = 1.5\sqrt{F}$, where F is fetch in nautical miles and H is expressed in feet.

TRANSFER PROCEDURE FOR SEAMAN TO USCG AIRCRAFT

Normally, any rendezvous with a merchant ship in response to a MEDICO, more than 50 miles at sea, will be made by an amphibian or seaplane. It should be remembered that even under ideal conditions, an open sea landing is, at best, a hazardous operation. Swells are the greatest hazard to such operation. Since the plane can be damaged by the action of the sea, it is imperative that the transfer of personnel be made as expeditiously as possible so that the aircraft will remain on the water the shortest period of time. Accordingly, the merchant ship captain should do all in his power to expedite the transfer of the patient.

First of all, one of the ship's lifeboats should be manned and ready for immediate launching, with the patient dressed and ready for transfer. The boat used should have good maneuverability, an alert crew and coxswain, and a megaphone for communicating with the aircraft. The crew of the lifeboat should be prepared to pick up survivors should the aircraft break up on landing.

The pilot may decide that the sea conditions are too unfavorable, in which case he will abort the mission. Once the plane is waterborne, the lifeboat can be launched. It should be remembered that the plane will drift to leeward faster than the ship, and care should be taken to see that the ship stays well clear. The lifeboat should not approach the aircraft until the aircraft engines are stopped, or, in the event the pilot does not elect to stop engines, until hailed alongside by the pilot. Without power, the aircraft will drift to leeward rapidly with the bow in the general direction from which the wind is blowing. The coxswain should stand in toward the bow close enough to establish communications with the pilot and to ascertain which hatch the pilot elects to take the patient aboard.

The best procedure is for the boat to pass a line to the bow and discharge the patient through the bow hatch. The pilot may elect to float a rubber life raft aft so that the patient can be put in it clear of the aircraft and then hauled to the side of the aircraft eliminating the necessity of the boat coming alongside. For this operation, the patient should be wearing a life preserver and he should not be strapped to a stretcher or litter unless it is buoyant.

The aircraft hull, wings, and tail surfaces are extremely fragile and should not be bumped by the boat. The slightest damage to wing and tail surfaces may make the aircraft unairworthy, calling for an abortion of the pick-up and possible abandonment and loss of the aircraft.

If the pilot elects to take the patient in the starboard or port hatch, it is wise to stand off a short time and observe the action of the aircraft as it rides succeeding swells, particularly observing the rise and fall of the tail section. *Don't let your boat get trapped under this tail section.* Use no sharp or pointed devices for fending off. The hull is easily punctured.

Helicopter Operations. The helicopter may be used for rescue and MEDICO operations when the merchant ship is not more than 50 miles off the coast.

As soon as communication is established between the ship and the helicopter, it should be ascertained whether the patient is ambulatory or a litter case and whether the ship has a Stokes litter or desires the helicopter to lower one.

Prior to the arrival of the helicopter, the ship's captain should make sure that the hovering area (usually the after hatch) is clear of all rigging and antennas, etc. For example, boom topping lifts should be slackened off if the booms are in their cradles. All loose gear about the hovering area should be removed or secured. The hovering helicopter will produce a downdraft from the rotor blades and any loose articles might be blown into and damage the whirling rotors. For safety reasons, no more than the necessary personnel to accomplish the transfer should be on deck in the hovering area.

The ship should take a course and speed recommended by the pilot. The pilot will endeavor to position the ship in such a manner as to have a resultant wind from the port or starboard bow. He will attempt to avoid a bow wind due to turbulence created by the stacks and superstructure. For nonambulatory cases, a litter will probably·be used. If a litter is to be lowered by the helicopter, the pilot will hover and the litter will be lowered by hydraulic hoist. This litter will have a bridle attached. The deck crew should unhook the litter and cast the hoist free. The helicopter will then fly around in the vicinity of the ship until all is ready for hoisting, and the ship calls him in for pick-up. *Under no circumstances make the hoist hook fast to anything on the deck.*

If the ship is preparing its own litter for hoisting, it should be made buoyant by strapping several life preservers to the sides. It should be bridled so that the patient's feet will hang slightly down. He should have a life preserver on and be securely strapped in the litter.

In the event that obstructions and rigging prevent a safe hover, the helicopter pilot may request that the patient be put in a lifeboat and the pick-up made clear of the ship.

If the patient is ambulatory, the helicopter will lower a special rescue basket or a hoisting sling. Instructions are indicated thereon for their use. No special preparation of the patient is necessary for using these devices other than to have him in a life preserver.

MAN OVERBOARD

The ability of a deck officer to properly maneuver his ship if the cry "man overboard" is heard may well mean the difference between life and death.

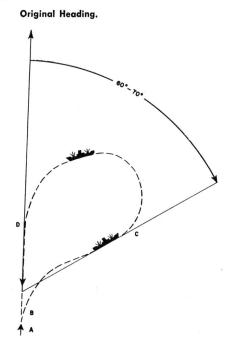

FIG. 5. THE WILLIAMSON TURN.

Standard seamanship texts in the past have skimmed over the subject and summed it up by merely stating the "rule of the thumb" that the vessel's head be put over to the side the man fell from—to throw the screw away from him. While this "rule of the thumb" is excellent, as far as it goes, it does not assist in the recovery of the man.

There is an excellent method which was developed during World War II by Comdr. John A. Williamson, USNR. It is known as the *Williamson Turn* and, while it has received wide publicity and endorsement in navy circles, it is little known among merchant mariners.

The evolution, simple to execute, will give a merchant ship time to turn, stop its engines, and end up in the approximate position as when the alarm was sounded. It is particularly adaptable in rough weather and periods of low visibility, having been developed with night rescue in mind under blackout conditions.

When the alarm is sounded, the conning officer should put the rudder hard over to the side from which the victim fell. With the rudder held hard over, engine speed is maintained until approximately 60° from the original heading. Then, the rudder is eased and put hard over to the opposite direction and held until the ship returns to a reciprocal of the original course. At this point, the engines are stopped, and the vessel will drift down to the victim's position dead ahead.

Experience has indicated that the turn takes approximately *5 minutes longer* than a standard turning circle, and, for that reason, it should not be used if it is possible to keep the victim in sight. It is possible, with calm seas or certain conditions of wind and sea, that a quick turn at full speed or to "back down" would be the best maneuver; however, that is up to the "seaman's eye" of the conning officer.

Figure 5 shows the maneuvers a ship would make in using the *Williamson Turn*.

ICE NAVIGATION PROCEDURE

Increased military activity in polar regions has taken many more merchant ships into these areas in recent years. The following procedure was set up by Capt. D. F. Sargent of the *Mormacisle* and has been passed along by the U.S.C.G. for the benefit of other shipmasters whose vessels may be called upon to navigate in far northern latitudes.

a) Chief Mate to assist Master in conning from flying bridge;

b) One mate and able seaman posted on bow as lookouts to assist in ice conn;

c) One mate on watch on flying bridge;

d) Helmsman steering from flying bridge, 1 hour on, and 1 hour off, because of cold and amount of maneuvering necessary;

e) One mate in wheelhouse plotting continuous position and keeping bells;

f) Carpenter and one dayman sounding all bilges every half hour;

g) Boatswain and one dayman inspecting all holds and deep tanks every half hour at quarter of and quarter past the hour;

h) Chief engineer in engine room pumping bilges in rotation continuously.

NARROW CHANNELS

Turning a bend, going upstream, as the bow clears the bend, the full force of the current strikes it causing a sheer which is increased as the ship nears the opposite bank and the backwater strikes the stern.

Turning a bend, going downstream, here all is favorable, for, as the vessel clears the bend, the current forces the bow around and assists the turn.

Bank cushion is particularly noticeable in narrow reaches with steep banks where draft is nearly equal to depth. A wedge of water forces the bow out while suction of the screw (twin screws in particular) lowers the water level between the quarter and the near bank, drawing the stern in and resulting in a sudden and decided sheer. A single screw ship can break this sheer by backing full with left rudder. A twin screw ship can break the sheer by going full ahead, stop (or back) starboard with full right rudder. If carried across mid-channel, it is advisable to drop the starboard anchor and back both engines.

Where *bank cushion* and *bank suction* may be expected, it is best to proceed at low speed, keeping near the center of the channel with both anchors ready for letting go; and it will be necessary to pass other vessels much closer than would be desirable otherwise. This may be safely done as the wall of water between the bows forces them apart. Then, as they pass abeam, the rudder of each ship is put over toward the other and the sterns swing clear. As the sterns draw opposite, the suction will tend to draw the sterns together so the ships will be straightened out by the time they are clear.

Overtaking and passing in narrow channels is especially dangerous as suction will throw the stern of the passing vessel into the other. If the overtaken vessel stops her engines, the suction will be decreased.

Chapter 10

CARGO GEAR

In recent years speedier loading and discharging have resulted from the enlargement of hatches, the lengthening of cargo booms, the increased power and speed of winches, the removal of obstructions from holds and their enlargement. For instance, great economies have resulted in the handling of structural steel, steel plates and long timber by increasing the length of booms from the former 42–52 foot length to as much as 70 feet, and at the same time cutting back the 'tween deck hatches and making larger main deck hatch openings. Another change has been the placement of masts at each end of large hatches or putting king posts at each of the four corners. In the case of a five-hatch ship so equipped, an increase of 40% results from being able to work seven instead of five gangs. Much faster rigging, stowing and spotting of booms has been effected through the use of electric or hydraulic topping lift winches for individual booms. The use of hatch covers on rollers, removed, replaced and made secure for sea by means of compressed air is proving very efficient.

The four basic loading systems for the typical light lift cargo derrick shown in Fig. 1 are *pick* and *strike*, *Burton*, *married fall* and *house fall*.

In the pick and strike system, the outboard boom lifts the load from the dock high enough to clear the ship's side; it is swung inboard by a lanyard and landed on the ship's deck. The outboard fall is unhooked and swings out for another load. At the same time, the inboard fall is hooked onto the first load and lifts it clear of the deck. Since the inboard boom is spotted over the hatch, the draft swings over and is lowered into the hold. This system is best adapted to loading light materials which are easy to sling or hook on.

The Burton system is a variation of the pick and strike system. While the boom set-up is the same, the draft is not landed on the deck, but when over the deck a wide mouthed Burton hook attached to the inboard fall is inserted into the cargo hook. The result is a temporary married fall arrangement. When the draft is over the hatch with the entire strain on the inboard fall, the deck man (Burton man) snaps the outboard fall loose and returns it to the dock for another load.

The married fall system is the one commonly used, the boom arrangement being as in the foregoing but with the falls joined at the cargo hook. This system has the advantage of being safer and requiring the load to be slung only once. There is the disadvantage that both booms

TYPICAL LIGHT LIFT CARGO DERRICK

SHOWING BLOCK LOCATIONS ON MAST AND BOOM

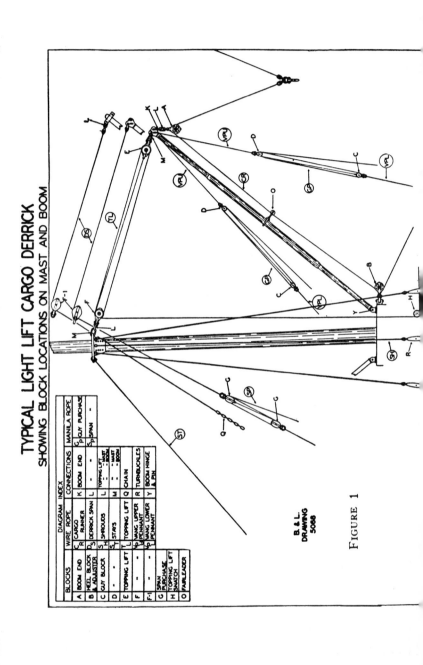

DIAGRAM INDEX

BLOCKS		WIRE ROPE		CONNECTIONS		MANILA ROPE	
A	BOOM END	C	CARGO RUNNER	K	BOOM END	G	GUY PURCHASE
B	HEEL BLOCK & ADAPTER	S₃	DERRICK SPAN	L	TOPPING LIFT - " BOOM	S	SPAN - "
C	GUY BLOCK	S	SHROUDS	L₁	- " - MAST		
D	- "	S₁H	STAYS	M	- " - BOOM		
E	TOPPING LIFT	T	TOPPING LIFT	Q	CHAIN		
F	- "	Vᵤ	VANG UPPER PENNANT	R	TURNBUCKLES		
F-1	- "	Vₗ	VANG LOWER PENNANT	Y	BOOM HINGE & PIN		
G	SPAN PURCHASE						
H	TOPPING LIFT SNATCH						
O	FAIRLEADER						

B. & L.
DRAWING
5068

FIGURE 1

are required for one draft and during most of the operation either one fall or the other is riding along free.

The house fall system is the same as the married fall except that only the boom over the hatch is used aboard ship and in place of the outboard boom a structure on the dock is used on which a block for the dock fall can be secured. This system has the following advantages: (1) A boom is released for loading on the outboard side. (2) The system can be used for working the second deck of a warehouse. (3) Loading can be accomplished from a very narrow deck. There is the disadvantage of greater strain on the ship's gear in this system.

Typical heavy lift or jumbo gear is shown in Fig. 2 . This gear is used for weights of over 5 tons, usually considered the limit for a light lift cargo derrick. A special winch is required for the topping lift as well as for the fall. The guys must be led to winches or capstans.

Electric Winches. Loads cannot be held with lever in *On* position without burning out resistance (*use foot brake*). It is important, when using a heavy derrick, to start the winch at full power; i.e., put control all the way down.

The Harrison Cargo Gear which employs traveling overhead cranes is a recent attempt to save loading time and trials have shown savings of 15% over traditional gear. It replaces both booms and winches. A pivoted joint at the ship's side holds a continuation of the track on which the crane travels in an athwartship direction. This track extension is folded in while at sea. A cargo hook is suspended from a trolley which runs fore and aft on the traveling crane structure. A set of tracks and traveling crane are required for each hatch. With this system a single operator can handle the load all the way, heavier weights can be lifted, there is greater flexibility in placing the load and cargo can be worked either inshore or offshore without stopping for time-consuming changes in the rigging.

CARGO GEAR RECORD BOOK*

"What has a cargo gear record book got to do with safety?" The answer is: "Lots." The ship's cargo gear—and the safety of all who work with it—is only as good as its maintenance." To insure that maintenance is thorough, it is essential that you keep a record of it. Furthermore, you may leave the ship for some reason and, unless your relief knows what has been done to keep the cargo gear in shape, he has two strikes against him before he starts.

Recently, a steamship company operating department wanted to determine the average life of a cargo fall under normal conditions. They wanted the information in order to compare two types of swivels. On ship after ship, they were unable to find out the necessary facts. Records of gear were kept but they were useless when it came to ascertaining specific facts.

Not long ago, a serious accident occurred when an outboard wire guy pennant parted. The obvious question was, did the stevedore put an excessive strain on the gear or was the guy pennant old, neglected,

* Arthur E. Wills (U. S. P & I Agency, Inc.)

or deteriorated for other reasons? The Chief Officer was able to produce a written record of his Cargo Gear Record Book which showed the date the pennant was put into service, date of each slushing, and a record of regular inspections. Naturally, this ship came through the subsequent legal proceedings with a clean bill of health and the Mate received the credit he deserved.

About the same time, on another ship which sustained a bad accident when a cargo fall parted and the load dropped on a longshoreman, the most thorough investigation failed to ascertain when or from where the cargo runner came on board the ship, when it had been put into use, or what maintenance it had received. The Mate had been on board only 6 months and there were no records which could be located that went back before that time.

How are your records? Do you know when each block aloft was checked, the pin pulled, sheaves and shell checked, and a good lubrication applied? When was the last time the goosenecks were lifted, sighted, and lubricated? How long has each manila guyline been in service?

Your cargo gear record book should contain data on the size and make of every piece of cargo gear, equipment, blocks, swivels, hooks, wire and manila line, booms and goosenecks on the ship. It should contain a record of all regular gear inspections and list the times when the gear is greased or slushed. Also, it should contain the date of renewal of every piece of cargo gear and the reason for such replacement.

A well-kept cargo gear record book may not by itself prevent accidents but any Mate who keeps his record book as it should be kept will keep his cargo gear in the way it should be kept up. The two things go hand in hand. Intelligent record keeping makes for intelligent maintenance and safer gear. If an accident does occur which involves the ship's rigging, the well-kept record book will provide conclusive evidence that it was not the fault of the ship's rigging.

Don't forget that the cargo gear record book is not your own personal property but is a part of the ship's records. When you are relieved, turn it over to your relief—and be sure that it is in such shape that you can do so with quiet pride. If you who read this safety letter are not a Chief Mate, keep these facts in mind for use when you become one. A complete and up-to-date cargo gear record book is the trade-mark of a good Mate—*even if you have no port captain who is liable to check it at the end of the voyage*!

ROPE

Manila is the best rope for general service on board ship, and is the fiber generally used, when available, for tackles and mooring lines.

Nylon has been tested and it has been proved that $6\frac{1}{2}''$ nylon rope is equal in strength to $10''$ manila and lasts 15 times as long under trying conditions, as when towing barges alongside in rough weather. Nylon rope stretches 10% and, though costing 5 times as much as manila, it has 10 times more value.

Mexican sisal, in general use during the war, has a tensile strength 20% less than that of the Manila product and is often blended with it in manufacture of the cheaper "manila" grades.

Hemp, though of greater tensile strength than manila, will not stand up to wet conditions of wear and weather in its natural state. When tarred, however, it will outlast either manila or coir under wet conditions, but is heavy and less flexible when so treated, and consequently "unhandy" compared with manila. Today it is confined to such uses aboard ship as for seizing stuff, spun-yarn, ratline stuff, and roping for awnings or heavy weather sails.

Coir Rope has the advantage of greater elasticity or "spring" than the others, though only about 3/4 the strength of manila. It will not absorb water like manila or untarred hemp, and can be depended upon to float where these become waterlogged and sink, a point worth remembering in coral-bottom waters. For lighter-ropes, and as springs used to hold a vessel alongside a pier during a swell, coir is found to give best results.

Breaking Stress. The ultimate strength, or breaking stress, of a rope varies very nearly as the square of its circumference. The breaking stress of good quality manila is, in tons of 2,240 lbs., equal to the rope's circumference squared divided by 2.5, or:

$$B = C^2 \div 2.5$$

where B is the breaking stress in tons,
and C is the circumference in inches.

In allowing for the necessary margin of safety, a definite factor should be decided upon which, when multiplied by the **working load,** will give the ultimate strength of the rope. This figure is called the **safety factor.** For example, a safety factor of 6 means that we shall use a rope which would break under a stress of 6 times the working load.

The safety factor adopted depends upon the degree of use to which the rope is to be subjected; thus, for a new rope used for a single special lift, a safety factor of 3 would seem the adequate figure; while, in the case of boat-falls, a practical safety factor would be 8.

Example. The working stress (or working load) for a boat tackle fall is found to be .6 ton. What size of manila rope, using 8 as a safety factor, is required for the tackle?

$$.6 \times 8 = \text{Breaking stress; or } 4.8 = C^2 \div 2.5$$

then $C^2 = 4.8 \times 2.5 = 12$, and $C = \sqrt{12} = 3.46$, or 3 1/2", circumference of rope.

We might as readily determine the diameter of the rope required by the following method, which is based upon the above formula:

$$\sqrt{B} \div 2 = \sqrt{4.8} \div 2 = 2.2 \div 2 = 1.1'', \text{ diameter of rope.}$$

Rope is put up in coils of 1200 feet and in half coils of 600 feet.

Houseline is a small tarred hemp line of three strands laid left handed.

Roundline is a three stranded, right handed line.

Hambroline is similar to roundline except that the twist is in the opposite direction.

Marline is small line of two strand twisted loosely left-handed.

Spun yarn is two or more yarns loosely twisted.

Rope over 5 inches in circumference may properly be termed a hawser.

To open a coil of Manila rope. Loosen the cover. Lay the coil on the flat side with the inside end at the bottom. Reach through the center of the coil and pull the rope up through the center. Never uncoil the rope from the outside as it will put kinks in it.

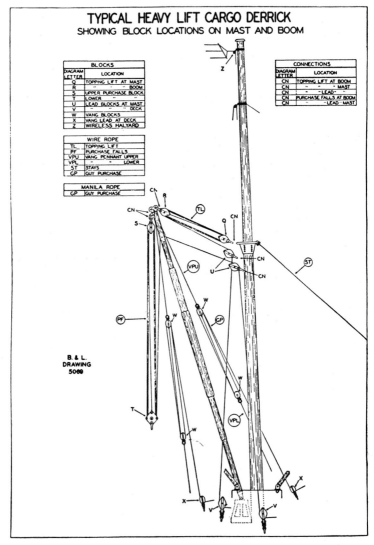

FIGURE 2

How to thoroughfoot a rope. Coil down against the lay. Bring the lower end up through the center of the coil. Coil down with the lay.

CARE AND USE OF ROPE

Make sure the usual right-laid rope unwinds in a counter clockwise direction when removing from the coil.

Store in a dry, unheated location with free air circulation.

Avoid kinks by throwing compensating turns in the rope if its use involves continual twisting in one direction.

Avoid contact or proximity to chemicals, especially acids or alkalis, where fumes may injure the rope. Linseed oil and paint are injurious.

A knot reduces the strength of rope approximately 50%. Splices are stronger. If rope is damaged cut and splice it.

Reverse ropes end for end to give all sections equal wear.

Avoid chafe, sharp bends and the dragging of rope over dirty surfaces.

Do not attempt to add lubrication to a Manila rope. The original lubrication is adequate.

Soft laid rope having relatively less fiber than hard laid is in general weaker. However, the strength of a hard laid rope in a single straight fall may be lower than a softer laid rope because the fibers are bent more as laid. On the other hand the soft laid rope would be weaker as a sling because the loose lay causes the rope to be flattened on sharp angles.

The circumference of Manila rope is most properly measured by taking the mean of five measurements made with a steel or paper strip.

Such a measure may differ as much as 10% from that made with calipers.

The working load should be only 1/8 to 1/5 of the breaking strength of *new* rope.

Avoid the use of blocks too small for the rope. This is especially dangerous as ropes so used may appear perfectly sound on the outside. However, opening up the rope will show many broken fibers owing to the chafing and sliding of the yarns upon one another.

WIRE ROPE

STANDARD HOISTING ROPE
6 STRANDS AND A HEMP CENTER, 19 WIRES TO THE STRAND
PLOW STEEL

Diameter Inches	Circumference Inches	Breaking Strength in Tons	Approximate Weight per 100 Feet in Pounds
1/4	3/4	2.5	10
5/16	1	3.9	16
3/8	1 1/8	5.5	23
7/16	1 3/8	7.3	31
1/2	1 5/8	9.4	40
9/16	1 3/4	11.7	51
5/8	2	14.4	63
3/4	2 3/8	20.6	90
7/8	2 3/4	28.0	123
1	3 1/8	36.5	160
1 1/8	3 1/2	46.0	203
1 1/4	3 7/8	56.5	250
1 3/8	4 3/8	68.0	303
1 1/2	4 3/4	80.5	360

To determine proper working load, divide the breaking strength by five, thus giving a factor of safety of five.

Turning ropes end for end can result in service increases as high as 25%. There is no known means of inspection which will even approximate the strength of corroded rope.

DATA ON MANILA AND WIRE ROPE

MANILA ROPE

THREE STRAND—STANDARD LAY

Threads	NOMINAL SIZE		Net Weight of 100 Feet Pounds	Minimum Length in One Pound Feet	Minimum Breaking Strength Pounds	Approximate Gross Weight Full Coils Pounds
	Circumference Inches	Diameter Inches				
6-Fine	9/16	3/16	1.37	72.9	420	50
6	3/4	1/4	1.71	58.5	550	50
9	1	5/16	2.52	39.6	950	50
12	1 1/8	3/8	3.45	29.0	1,275	50
15	1 1/4	7/16	5.15	19.4	1,750	63
18	1 3/8	15/32	6.14	16.3	2,250	75
21	1 1/2	1/2	7.36	13.6	2,650	90
24	1 3/4	9/16	10.2	9.80	3,450	125
30	2	5/8	13.1	7.65	4,400	160
33	2 1/4	3/4	16.4	6.12	5,400	200
	2 1/2	13/16	19.1	5.23	6,500	234
	2 3/4	7/8	22.0	4.54	7,700	270
	3	1	26.5	3.78	9,000	324
	3 1/4	1 1/16	30.7	3.26	10,500	375
	3 1/2	1 1/8	35.2	2.84	12,000	432
	3 3/4	1 1/4	40.8	2.45	13,500	502
	4	1 5/16	46.9	2.13	15,000	576
	4 1/2	1 1/2	58.8	1.70	18,500	720
	5	1 5/8	73.0	1.37	22,500	893
	5 1/2	1 3/4	87.7	1.14	26,500	1,073
	6	2	105.0	.949	31,000	1,290
	6 1/2	2 1/8	123.0	.816	36,000	1,503
	7	2 1/4	143.0	.699	41,000	1,752
	7 1/2	2 1/2	163.0	.612	46,500	2,004
	8	2 5/8	187.0	.534	52,000	2,290
	8 1/2	2 7/8	211.0	.474	58,000	2,580
	9	3	237.0	.422	64,000	2,900
	9 1/2	3 1/8	264.0	.379	71,000	3,225
	10	3 1/4	292.0	.342	77,000	3,590
	11	3 1/2	360.0	.278	91,000	4,400
	12	4	427.0	.234	105,000	5,225

Standard Coils: 50 pounds and 25 pounds for 6, 9 and 12 thread rope; 200 fathoms and 100 fathoms for all larger sizes.
One Fathom equals Six Feet.

SIZE OF WIRE ROPES TO REPLACE MANILA LINES

Manila rope		Spring lay wire rope		6 x 12 wire rope type "G"		6 x 24 wire rope type "J"		6 x 37 wire rope type "E"	
Circumference	Strength	Diameter	Strength	Diameter	Strength	Diameter	Strength	Diameter	Strength
Inches	Pounds	Inches	Pounds	Inches	Pounds	Inches	Pounds	Inches	Pounds
4	15,000	3/4	17,500	5/8	17,700	--------	--------	1/2	18,600
5	22,500	1	29,300	3/4	25,400	--------	--------	9/16	23,200
6	31,000	1 1/8	37,100	7/8	34,500	3/4	36,900	3/4	40,000
7	41,000	1 3/8	54,600	1	44,800	7/8	49,300	7/8	53,400
8	52,000	1 1/2	70,200	1 1/8	56,700	1	64,000	1	69,400
9	64,000	1 5/8	81,900	1 1/4	69,400	1 1/16	72,200	(1)	(69,400)
10	77,000	1 3/4	95,500	1 3/8	83,800	1 3/16	89,900	1 1/8	87,600
11	91,000	1 7/8	109,200	1 1/2	99,300	1 1/4	99,400	1 1/4	108,000
12	105,000	2	117,000	1 5/8	115,000	1 3/8	120,000	1 3/8	130,000

NOTES:	(1) Most flexible. (2) For mooring: First choice. (3) For towing: First choice where no means for cushioning shock load is available.	(1) Less flexible. (2) For mooring: Second choice. (3) For towing: Second choice where no means for cushioning shock load is available.	Used where other lines not available. Similar to 6 x 12 but less flexible.	(1) Least flexible. (2) For mooring: Not desirable. (3) For towing: First choice where proper provision is made to cushion shock load, and maintain catenary.

ROPE SLINGS

Manila Rope					Wire Rope	
Size		Breaking strength in lbs.	Safe working load in lbs. used straight		Size dia.	Safe working load in lbs. used straight
cir.	dia.					
5/8	3/16	450	90			
3/4	1/4	550	110			
1	5/16	950	190			
1 1/8	3/8	1,300	260		3/8	2,050
1 1/4	7/16	1,750	350			
1 1/2	1/2	2,650	530		1/2	2,700
1 3/4	9/16	3,450	690			
2	5/8	4,400	880		5/8	5,600
2 1/4	3/4	5,400	1,080		3/4	8,050
2 1/2	13/16	6,500	1,300			
2 3/4	7/8	7,700	1,540		7/8	10,800
3	1	9,000	1,800		1	14,000
3 1/4	1 1/16	10,500	2,100			
3 1/2	1 1/8	12,000	2,400		1 1/8	17,600
3 3/4	1 1/4	13,500	2,700		1 1/4	22,000
4	1 5/16	15,000	3,000			
4 1/2	1 1/2	18,500	3,700		1 1/2	32,000
5	1 5/8	22,500	4,500			
5 1/2	1 3/4	26,500	5,300		1 3/4	43,200
6	2	31,000	6,200		2	52,000
6 1/2	2 1/8	36,000	7,200			
7	2 1/4	41,000	8,200			
7 1/2	2 1/2	46,500	9,300		2 1/2	85,600
8	2 5/8	52,000	10,400			
8 1/2	2 7/8	58,000	11,600			
9	3	64,000	12,800			
9 1/2	3 1/8	71,000	14,200			
10	3 1/4	77,000	15,400			

The figures above are for a straight pull on the rope using a safety factor of 5. The loads specified are for each single rope. When used double, or in any other multiple, the load may be increased proportionately. For example, if the sling has 3 legs, the load may be increased three times the load specified above. However, it is most important to consider *the angle between the legs of the sling*. If the angle between the legs is 60°, the safe working load is only ¾ of what it is when the rope is used straight; ⅔ of used straight load if the angle is 90°; ½ if the angle is 120°.

The safe loads with safety factor of 5 to 1 referred to are for slings protected by thimbles and hooks. Any increase in the risk involved by sharp edges, short nips, snaring, or other factors of abuse will decrease the factor of safety.

BLOCKS

Size of Blocks. Where manila rope is used, approximately 3 times the circumference of the rope is the size of block required (length of shell in inches), and the diameter of the sheave should be at least twice the circumference of the rope.

Thus, for a 4″ manila, a suitable block would be one of 12″ shell, with a sheave 8″ in diameter.

For wire rope, the greater the diameter of the sheave the easier it will be on the wire. The diameter of the sheave should always be stipulated when ordering the proper block for a given size of wire.

To find the minimum size of sheave required, multiply the diameter of the wire by 15, or its circumference by 5. Thus, for a wire 3/4″ in diameter, or 2 1/4″ in circumference, a sheave of at least 11 1/4″ (say 12″) in diameter is required.

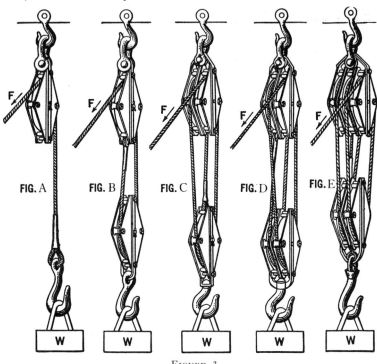

FIG. A FIG. B FIG. C FIG. D FIG. E

FIGURE 3

	Theoretical Power	Actual Power	Mechanical Efficiency
A. Single whip	1F	.90F	90%
B. Gun tackle	2F	1.67F	83%
C. *Luff or "handy billy"	3F	2.33F	78%
D. Twofold purchase	4F	2.86F	72%
E. One double and one triple-sheave	5F	3.35F	67%

* Note—If the double block is movable, theoretical power is 4F.

Purchases such as the single and double Spanish Burton, the bell purchase, etc., which are real oddities on board the ship of today, are not here considered. Any good work on mechanics will illustrate the principle of determining the power-to-weight ratio in any particular setup of blocks, chain hoists, etc.

The allowance of one-tenth the weight for each sheave is greater than the actual friction in well-made modern blocks, but it is on the side of safety—a point of first consideration in the handling of weighty objects by any mechanical means.

The efficiency of wire, properly proportioned, is greater than figures given for manila.

Loads for hook-blocks should be 30–40% less than where shackle-blocks are used.

The proper method of reeving off a triple and triple tackle is as shown below. The stress comes on the center of the blocks and keeps them from toppling. Note that the sheaves in the upper block are at right angles to those in the lower block.

FIG. 4. REEVING TRIPLE BLOCKS.

Many practical men know that when hoisting a weight of p tons with a rope led over one sheave it is necessary to exert a pull of p tons at the other end, but they do not realize that stress in block and its fastening point amounts to 2 p tons. (Easily demonstrated by a spring balance).

The weakest parts of a block are the center pin (which is under sheave stress) and the swivel (which is under tension). Swivel bolt and center pin are generally of same or almost same diameter, and the rup-

Suitable Working Loads for Blocks

Dimensions (inches)		With loose side hooks			With shackles		
Length shell (inches)	For diameter rope	Double and single (pounds)	2 doubles (pounds)	2 triples (pounds)	Double and single (pounds)	2 doubles (pounds)	2 triples (pounds)
3	3/8	200	300	400	400	800	1,200
4	1/2	400	550	700	800	1,400	1,800
5	5/8	500	750	1,000	1,100	1,700	2,100
6	3/4	1,000	1,500	2,000	1,600	2,400	3,000
7	7/8	1,500	2,000	2,500	2,000	3,000	3,700
8	1	1,700	2,450	3,200	2,400	3,600	4,400
10	1 1/8	2,600	3,400	4,200	4,000	5,400	6,400
12	1 1/4	3,000	3,750	4,500	5,000	8,000	10,000
For heavy wide mortise blocks							
6	3/4	1,500	2,000	2,500	1,600	3,000	4,000
7	1	1,700	2,450	3,200	2,000	3,800	4,800
8	1 1/8	2,200	2,900	3,600	2,400	4,700	6,700
10	1 1/4	3,000	3,750	4,500	4,000	7,000	9,000
12	1 1/2	3,600	4,800	6,000	5,000	9,000	12,000
14	1 3/4	4,400	5,700	7,000	6,500	11,000	15,000
16	2	6,000	7,500	9,000	8,000	14,000	18,000

NOTE.—These tables are shown through the courtesy of the Boston & Lockport Block Co. and indicate suitable loads for 1 series of their standard and heavy blocks. These should be used as a guide only in figuring without assuming any responsibility—since the loads will vary between blocks in the manufacturer's line, and between blocks in other manufacturers' lines. Remember, too, that these are suitable working loads for blocks, not rope. Safe working loads for rope are higher than those for blocks.

turing tensile stress may be calculated at half breaking stress when shearing is taken into account. Since swivel is generally forged while center pin is sometimes made of material with a higher breaking strength, the swivel bolt may as a rule be taken as weakest part of a block. If an inspector takes one fifth of tensile strength of swivel he will have a sufficient idea of strength of the block.

TACKLES

1. To find the stress on the hauling part, or the working load on the fall:

Add one-tenth of the weight for each sheave in the purchase to the weight, and divide by the number of parts at the moving block.

Example. Find the stress on the hauling part when lifting 5 tons by a two-fold purchase.

There are here 4 sheaves in the purchase and 4 parts at the moving block (assuming the hauling part leads directly from the upper block), so that:

$(W+.4W) \div 4 = [5+(.4 \times 5)] \div 4 = 7/4 = 1 \ 3/4$ tons stress on hauling part.

2. To find the weight a given purchase will lift:

Multiply the working load of the rope by the number of parts at the moving block, and divide by one plus one-tenth the number of sheaves in the tackle.

Example. How many tons will a three-fold purchase lift if rove with a new 3 1/2″ (circ.) manila rope, using a safety factor of 5?

The working load is here equal to one-fifth of the breaking stress, or:

$1/5 \times (3.5^2 \div 2.5) = 1/5 \times (12.25 \div 2.5) = 1$ ton, working load. There are 6 parts at the moving block (assuming the hauling part leads directly from the upper block), and 6 sheaves in the tackle; so that:

$(1 \times 6) \div (1+.6) = 6 \div 1.6 = 3.75$, or 3 3/4 tons, the load tackle will lift.

3. The mechanical advantage of a purchase is usually stated in the form of a ratio; thus, we say that 1 to 4 is the mechanical advantage of a two-fold purchase (without allowing for friction), 4 being the number of parts at the moving block. Should the tackle be so placed that the hauling part leads through the moving block, the two-fold purchase would have a mechanical advantage of 1 to 5, and the tackle is said to be "rove to advantage."

One-tenth the weight for every sheave in the purchase is the allowance for frictional resistance in the blocks. The mechanical advantage in the case of the example in **1**, allowing for friction, then becomes:

$(1+.4) \div 4 = 14/40$, or, the power is to the weight as 14 is to 40; hence $14/40 \times 5 = 1 \ 3/4$ tons stress on the hauling part.

Allowing for friction, the working load or stress on the hauling part is, where the hauling part leads through the stationary block, equal to:

$12/20 \times$ the weight, for a gun-tackle purchase

$14/40 \times$ the weight, for a two-fold purchase

$16/60 \times$ the weight, for a three-fold purchase

and where the hauling part leads through the moving block:

12/30×the weight, for a gun-tackle purchase
14/50×the weight, for a two-fold purchase
16/70×the weight, for a three-fold purchase

WIRE

The strength of steel wire rope varies with the number of wires in each strand, but for practical purposes a good working formula is:

$$B = C^2 \times 2.5$$

where B is the breaking stress in tons (2,240 lbs.);
and C is the circumference in inches.

This is a safe value for ordinary wire, say of the 6×12 type—i.e., 6 strands of 12 wires each.

Example. For a working load of 2 tons and a safety factor of 4 what size of wire is required?

$$2 \times 4 = C^2 \times 2.5, \text{ or } C^2 = (2 \times 4) \div 2.5 = 3.2$$
$$C = \sqrt{3.2} = 1\frac{3}{4}'', \text{ circumference.}$$

The diameter of the wire might also be found by the following formula derived from the above:

$$D = \sqrt{B} \div 5, \text{ or } \sqrt{2 \times 4} \div 5 = \sqrt{8} \div 5 = 2.8 \div 5 = .56, \text{ or } 9/16'' \text{ diameter.}$$

As a rule, the strength of a wire increases with the number of wires in each strand, so that the above formula will be found to lie on the safe side when the better grade of flexible wire is used. A constant of 3, instead of 2.5 as used in the formula for finding the circumference, would be probably nearer the truth in the case of a 6×37 wire.

The three principal grades of wire rope used aboard ship are mild plow steel, plow steel, and improved plow steel which is the best grade. These are trade names.

Improved plow steel is usually used for cargo handling though plow steel is sometimes used. Improved plow steel generally has better wear resistance and about 15% higher tensile strength.

In describing wire rope, the quality of material (above), type of construction and type of center or core should be included. By type of construction is meant the number and arrangement of the individual wires in the several strands and the direction of helix of the wires in the strand and of the strands in the finished rope.

The type of center, whether fiber or steel, should be specified. Unless a steel center is specified rope with a fiber center will be furnished. Steel centers do not make wire rope appreciably less flexible.

The diameter of a wire rope is half of the circle which will enclose all of its strands. The correct diameter is the greatest diameter of the rope or strand.

Lubrication of wire rope is necessary to have it give maximum service. Flexibility of the rope as a whole is dependent upon the freedom of movement of wire upon wire and strand upon strand. A thorough cleansing before lubrication is important. The lubricant used should be thin enough to penetrate to the center of the rope and it should be sufficiently tenacious not to throw off. There are several compounds on the market that fulfill these requirements and they will give better results than the fish oil, etc. commonly used.

New wire rope can be ruined, before being used, by improper unreeling. It is imperative that the reel or coil rotates as the rope unwinds. Attempts to unwind rope from stationary coils or reels will result in kinking the rope and once a kink is formed, the rope at that point is ruined beyond repair.

While galvanizing considerably lengthens the life of wire it decreases the strength by about 10%. Galvanizing is generally recommended only for standing rigging.

The most commonly encountered forms of abuse of wire ropes are: kinks, untwisting, overloads, jumping off sheaves, improperly attached fittings, improper lubrication and internal wear produced by grit, improperly fitting grooves or broken flanges, sheaves and drums of inadequate size, permitting ropes to overwind or crosswind on drums, dragging ropes over obstacles, exposing rope to moisture, acid fumes or excessive heat, and using rope of incorrect size, construction or grade.

PROPER SIZE OF SHEAVE GROOVES FOR WIRE ROPE

Nominal Diameter of Rope	Groove Diameter Tolerances	
	Minimum	Maximum
1/4″ to 5/16″	+1/64″	+1/32″
3/8″ to 3/4″	+1/32″	+1/16″
7/8″ to 1 1/8″	+3/64″	+3/32″
1 1/4″ to 1 1/2″	+1/16″	+1/8″

Where the angle of embrace is 90° or more the minimum diameter of each sheave should be as follows for the various sizes of rope:

size of wire rope— circumference	diameter of sheave
under 2″	10″
2″ −2 1/2″	12″
2 1/2″–3″	14″
3″ −4″	16″
4″ and over	18″

The minimum diameter of sheaves for any other conditions should be not less than four times the circumference of the rope.

INSPECTION OF RUNNING WIRE AND SHEAVES

Wire runners should be changed when it appears they are becoming flattened out on the drum. Wire should be condemned when outside strands have been worn to 1/2 their diameter but inspection of the inside may show wire should be condemned long before this, particularly with small sheaves.

The sheaves over which wire rope passes should be inspected for wear in respect to diameter of sheave, diameter of the wire bearing groove, sheave's bearings and the edges of the flange.

Do not measure the diameter of a sheave from flange edge to flange edge but from bearing surface to bearing surface. If the diameter is less than that recommended there takes place in the rope a crushing action which increases internal friction and causes nicking of one inside wire by another.

The groove in a sheave should support a wire for nearly 1/2 its circumference i.e. it should lie snugly in the groove. If the groove is too large the rope tends to flatten under tension. If a groove has been worn down by an old rope its diameter will be decreased and a new rope when placed in this groove will be inadequately supported.

Defective bearings in the sheave will cause the sheave to wobble and increase wear on the rope.

A sheave with a broken flange should be replaced as soon as possible as it will nick and cause serious damage to the rope.

WIRE SPLICING

Open Eye Splice. There are a number of ways to make eye splices that are known by different names, depending on their use, when and by whom they are made. For example, the Gun Factory splice is used in handling heavy guns at the factory. The Liverpool splice was so named because it originated on the Liverpool docks and the Logger's splice is used by loggers in snaking out heavy logs.

Directions for Making Liverpool Eye Splice

Fig. 5 shows diagrammatically the method of making this splice. The tucking strands are numbered 1 to 6 in the order that they are tucked. The strands in the standing part are lettered *A* to *F*, as illustrated in the cross section at the right of the figure.

1. Measure off 2′ to 4′ from the end of the rope and seize wire with marline to prevent unlaying while splicing. Unlay the strands back to the seizing, cut out the heart close to the seized end and whip the end of each of the six strands.

2. Bend the wire to form an eye of desired size and seize the two parts together with marline.

3. Stretch the wire about waist high between two permanent objects, or clamp the eye in a vice and secure the standing part to a fixed object.

4. With the strands lying about parallel to the part of the wire through which they are to be tucked and the eye in a vertical position, stand with the eye on your left side and face in the direction in which the tucks are to be made.

5. Divide the tucking strands so that three are on each side of the standing part.

6. Open the standing part through the center with a marline-spike and tuck the top strand over the right side through the opening. This step is shown in Fig. 5 where tucking strand 1 passes under the strands *C*, *B*, and *A* of the standing part.

7. The next strand on the right is tucked through the same opening but comes out under two strands on the right. This step is shown in Fig. 5 where tucking strand 2 passes under the strands *C* and *B* of the standing part and comes out between strands *B* and *A*.

8. The last strand on the right also is tucked through the same opening but comes out under one strand. This step is shown in Fig. 5 where tucking strand 3 passes under strand *C* of the standing part and comes out between strands *C* and *B*.

9. The top tucking strand on the left side is now passed over and around the top strand on the left side of the standing part. This step is shown in Fig. 5, where tucking strand 4 passes over and around strand *D* of the standing part.

10. The next tucking strand on the left is now passed over and around the next strand in the standing part. This is shown in Fig. 5, where tucking strand 5 is passed over and around strand *E* of the standing part.

11. The last tucking strand is passed over and around the last strand of the standing part. This is shown in Fig. 5, where tucking strand 6 passes over and around strand *F* of the standing part.

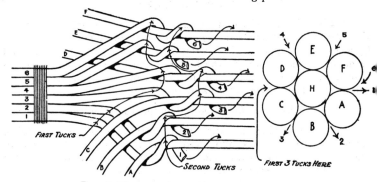

Fig. 5. Making a Liverpool Open-eye Splice.

This completes the first tuck of all six strands. The second tuck for each strand is made by passing the tucking part around and under the strands of the standing part, following the lay of the wire. This second tuck is shown in Fig. 5 by the small arrow marked second tuck.

To finish the splice take one more tuck with each strand in the same manner, pound splice into shape, and cut off ends of tucking strands close to the splice.

Thimble Splice. To fit a thimble in the Liverpool eye, bend the eye around the thimble and secure it in a rigger's vice; if a common vice is used place a kicker against the wire to hold it tight in the thimble groove. Make the tucks as described, but force each tuck close up to the thimble. Seize with marline.

How to Attach a Wire Rope Socket

See Fig. 6 for illustration of the following steps.

1. Measure from end of rope a length equal to basket of socket. Serve at this point with not less than three seizings. Cut out the hemp center but do not cut out wire rope or strand when used as a center. Open strands.

2. Separate wires in strands. Straighten by means of iron pipe. Cleanse all wires carefully with kerosene oil from ends to as near first serving as possible. Wipe dry.

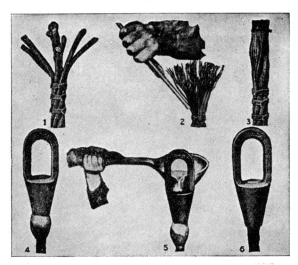

F IG . 6. A TTACHING A W IRE R OPE S OCKET .

3. Dip wire, for three-quarters of the distance to the first seizing, into one-half muriatic acid, one-half water (use no stronger solution and take extreme care that acid does not touch any other part of the rope. Keep wire in long enough to be thoroughly cleaned. Wipe dry. Serve end so that socket can be slipped over all of the wires.

4. Then slip socket over wires. Cut top seizing wire and distribute all wires evenly in basket and flush with top. Be sure socket is in line with axis of rope. Place fire clay around bottom of socket.

5. Pour in molten zinc. Use only high grade zinc heated preferably not above 830° F. Do not use babbit or other antifriction metal

6. Remove all seizings except the one nearest socket. After cooling, preferably slowly, socket is ready for service.

Grommet. A grommet is a ring or strap made of manila or wire rope, and has many uses. It is made of one continuous strand of rope by crossing the strand to form a ring and then following the lay of the rope with each end until three complete turns are formed. (With wire rope make six complete turns.) The ends are then tucked as in a long splice.

Clips. Fig. 7 shows two wrong methods and the right method of attaching wire rope clips. For safety, the U-bolts of clips must all be on the *dead* end of the wire.

SAFETY FACTORS (recommendations of the International Labour Office)

For all metal structural parts in hoisting machinery:
    (a) when safe working load is 10 tons or less   5
    (b) when safe working load is over 10 tons   4
For wooden structural details   8
For chains   4 1/2
For wire ropes as a general rule   5
For fibre ropes   7

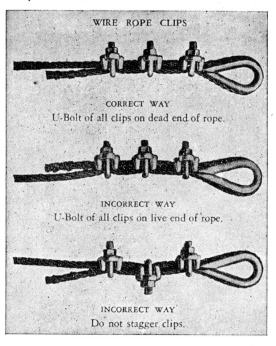

FIG. 7. RIGHT AND WRONG WAYS OF ATTACHING
WIRE ROPE CLIPS.

"Even persons considered to be competent often misjudge the stresses in the gear, if they have to base their judgment on what they observe and have no occasion, or do not know how, to calculate them or find them graphically.

"Calculation of the stresses in gear is a very difficult task which should be performed by naval architects, standardization committees, classification bureaus and the like—as compared with calculation however, the graphical method enables the stresses to be calculated with relative ease."

Friction of the sheaves in the blocks generally estimated at 5% of the load *per sheave*.

CARGO BOOM STRESSES

1. Tension on the Topping-Lift Span. Neglecting the weight of the boom, the stress on the topping lift, when lifting a given weight, is governed by the ratio, "as the length of the span is to the length of the mast"; so that, for the tension on the span, we may write:

Tension on topping-lift span = (length of span ÷ length of mast) × weight.

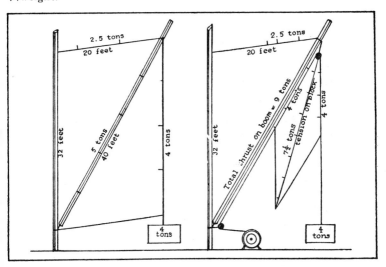

FIG. 8. GRAPHIC ANALYSIS OF A BOOM LOADING PROBLEM.

In the parallelogram laid down to suit a particular case, let the distance between the suspended weight and the end of the boom be equal to the length of the mast, as measured between the heel of the boom and the topping lift. If we divide this distance into as many parts as there are tons in the weight, since the equal and opposite side of the parallelogram is the length of the mast, it follows that the ratio of the length of the mast to the weight will be equal to that of the length of the topping-lift span to the tension on the span.

Hence, (length of mast) ÷ (weight) = (length of span) ÷ (tension on span) from which,

Tension on span = (length of span) ÷ (length of mast) × weight.

Substituting a scale of tons for that of feet as representing the sides and diagonal of the parallelogram of forces, it is readily seen that the stresses sustained by the lift and the boom due to suspending a weight, as in Fig. 8 (left), are directly proportional to the given lengths of mast, boom, and topping-lift span.

Such a figure, however, does not show the whole truth; we do not handle a sling of cargo by merely suspending it at a boom end. A block of some sort must be hung at that point, and the hauling part of the hoisting rig leads from the block down along the boom to a cargo-winch.

What actually takes place is shown in Fig. 9, and a little consideration will show that the tension on the span, unlike the compression or thrust on the boom, remains unaffected by a change in the tackle used in hoisting a given weight.

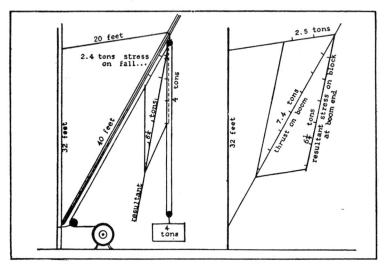

FIG. 9. ANOTHER BOOM LOADING PROBLEM, COMPONENT AND RESULTANT FORCES.

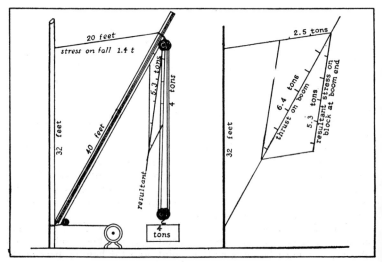

FIG. 10. BOOM LOADING PROBLEM WITH DOUBLE BLOCKS.

Fig. 8 (right) shows the resultant magnitude and direction of the stress on the boom end block where a single fall or runner is in use.

The same weight is shown hoisted by a gun-tackle purchase in Fig. 9 and by a two-fold purchase in Fig. 10. Observe the difference in the thrust on the boom, while the topping-lift tension remains unchanged.

2. Thrust on the Boom. The thrust, or compression on the boom, as we note in the figures shown, is the resultant of the forces (*a*) gravity acting on the suspended weight, (*b*) the tension on the topping-lift span, and (*c*) the tension on the hauling part of the tackle used in hoisting.

However, it is not necessary to lay down a parallelogram of forces in order to determine either the span tension or the boom thrust.

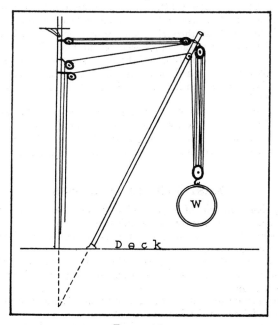

FIGURE 11

Given the lengths of the mast, boom, and span, and the stress on the hauling part of the hoisting rig, all the data for the solution of a simple problem is at hand.

Referring to Fig. 8 , we have:

(length of mast) ÷ (weight) = (length of boom) ÷ (thrust on boom) from which,

Thrust on boom = (length of boom) ÷ (length of mast) × weight which is the thrust due to the suspended weight. To this must be added the tension on the hauling part of the tackle used; whence:

Total thrust on boom = [(length of boom) ÷ (length of mast) × weight] + tension on fall.

Example. With conditions as in Fig. 9 given lengths of mast 32′, boom 40′, span 20′, to find the tension on the span and the thrust on the boom.

Tension on span = 20/32 × 4 = 2.5 tons

Tension on hauling part of tackle = 12/20 × 4 = 2.4 tons

Thrust on boom = (40/32 × 4) + 2.4 = 7.4 tons

The tension on the upper block of the tackle is approximately equal to the weight plus the stress on the hauling part, or: 4 + 2.4 = 6.4 tons.

The greatest stress in this common hoisting rig is always found at the heel of the boom; and, in the usual conditions where the boom is equal to or greater than the mast in length, the thrust on the boom is more than double the weight hoisted, when a single fall or runner is used.

When handling a **heavy lift,** both the topping-lift tension and the boom thrust may be considerably lessened by leading the hauling part or fall of the purchase through a sheave or block at the head of the boom, and thence to a lead block well up the mast. The fall will lead from the lower or moving block of the purchase the tackle being then rove "to advantage." In a similar way the topping-lift tackle should be rigged so that the fall leads from the block at the head of the boom. (*See* Fig. 11.)

Where the boom is stepped at some distance from the mast, as in the case of some heavy weight rigs, in determining the stresses set up the lengths of the mast and boom must be considered as terminating at the point of intersection of the downward extension of each, as in Fig. 11.

MAST AND STAY STRESSES

A graphical solution of any problem in mast and stay stresses is perhaps best arrived at by an application of the parallelogram of forces.* As an illustration, suppose that the tension on the topping lift has been found to be 5 tons, and the thrust on the boom 10 tons. It is required to find the tension on the stay and the thrust on the mast. The boom and the stay are in the same vertical plane, or, the boom is trimmed fore-and-aft.

A plan of the particular rigging conditions is drawn and the procedure is as follows, referring to Fig. 12.

Using any convenient scale, lay off $T\,L = 5$ tons as the tension on the topping-lift span. Then, according to the plan, we have for the tension on the stay $S\,T = 7$ tons, and thrust on the mast $T\,M = 3\,1/2$ tons, due to 5 tons tension on the span.

Note that this thrust on the mast ($T\,M = 3\,1/2$ tons) is the resultant of the two forces $S\,T$ and $T\,L$, or the stress on the stay and the stress on the span respectively. For the total thrust on the mast, we must consider also the vertical component of the thrust on the boom, or $V\,H = 9$ tons.

The *total thrust* on the mast is therefore $T\,M + V\,H = 12\,1/2$ tons.

* Shrouds and stays should be set up to a tension not exceeding 20% of the minimum breaking strength of the wire rope. This will work out to take-up of 1″ for each 60′ of length after sag is eliminated.

The force H Z (= 4 3/4 tons) is the horizontal component of the boom thrust, or what is termed side thrust on the mast.

Cargo-Runner and Guy Stresses. The tension on either leg of a hoisting span may also be graphically determined by the parallelogram of forces method. This is shown in Fig. 13, applying to the rig where two booms are placed to transfer cargo to or from a hatch as indicated.

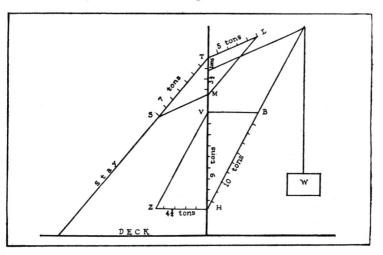

FIG. 12. LOADING PROBLEM ILLUSTRATING PARALLELOGRAM OF FORCES.

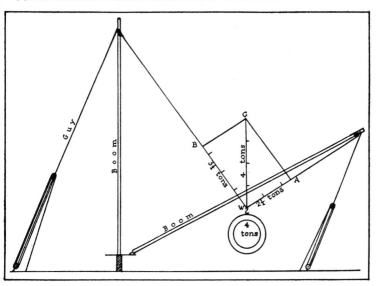

FIG. 13. APPLICATION OF USE OF PARALLELOGRAM
OF FORCES WITH A TWO-BOOM RIG.

The resultant of the two forces $W A$ and $W B$ being equal to the weight, we lay down $G W$ equal to 4 tons in the direction of gravity, and construct the parallelogram to the scale adopted. It is found that the tension on leg $W A$ is 2 1/2 tons, and that on leg $W B$ is 3 1/2 tons.

It is to be noted that, as the boom sustains an equal and opposite force to that of the stress on the runner at any time during the cargo operation, the guy should be placed as nearly as possible in the vertical plane through which the sling travels, or "squarely across the hatch" and the outboard or yard-arm guy should lead as nearly as possible in the fore-and-aft line.

The influence of the angle between the legs of a sling on the actual tension in the legs must be understood. Thus we see:

angle between the legs	safe working load per leg as percentage of the maximum
perpendicular position	100%
45°	90%
90°	70%
120°	50%

With an angle between the legs larger than 120° the highest safe working load allowable is only 25% of that for an angle of 120°, consequently the angle should never exceed 120°.

Hooks are measured by the diameter of the metal at the back of the hook. Shackles are measured by the diameter of the metal at the sides of the shackle. With "D" signifying diameter, the formula for safe working load of hooks is $2/3 \ D^2$ tons; for shackles, $3 \ D^2$ tons.

It is apparent that the strength of the hook is the measure of the strength of the block.

BREAKING LOADS (2000 lbs. (1 ton))

size	hooks	shackles screw pin	round pin
1/2"	1.	8.6	10.2
7/8"	3.6	26.5	31.3
1 1/4"	8.4	47.5	56.
1 3/4"	16.	106.	125.
2"	19.7	128.	151.

These figures are given to show what a great difference there is between the strength of a hook and that of a shackle.

The following formula is commonly used for calculating the breaking load, in pounds, of wrought-iron crane chains—

$$W = 54,000 \ D^2$$

in which W = breaking load in pounds, and D = diameter of bar (in inches) from which the links are made. The working load should never exceed 1/3 the value of W; in many cases, it is 1/4 or 1/5 the breaking load. When a chain is wound around a casting and severe bending stresses are introduced, a greater factor of safety should be used.

TESTING AND INSPECTING CARGO GEAR

The following description of testing and inspection procedures for Liberty and Victory ship cargo handling gear was written by Mr. John M. Roche, Chief Safety Consultant of the U. S. Maritime Commission.

All lines are inspected for size, material and type, while blocks are thoroughly inspected for size, presence of flaws and to make sure that the correct type of block or fall is used in the proper places.

For the type of ship mentioned, all cargo handling gear is designed for a boom angle of 25 degrees from the horizontal for booms up to five tons working load. The long ton of 2,240 pounds is used in figuring all loads and in completing stress strain diagrams. For 15 and 50 ton booms, the minimum boom angle is considered to be 35 degrees with the horizontal.

A factor of safety of 4.3 must be established for all masts, booms, pins, shackles, chains, fittings and other cargo gear. This includes a standing and running rigging except where a lower factor of safety has been approved by the American Bureau of Shipping. Steel of uniform quality and up to requirements and approval of the American Bureau of Shipping is used. Best plough steel is generally acceptable for steel wire.

In making the inspection, either preliminary to installation of gear on the booms, or after installation, it must be made certain that fittings of all types but especially for topping lift blocks and similar attachments have been designed to prevent undue wear by chafing, binding or bonding. Upon subsequent inspection, all chains, shackles, bolts, swivels, chain plates, eye bolts or other forgings must be renewed if the dimensions have diminished more than 15 percent.

It is obvious that frequent inspections would be made on shipboard while the gear is actually in use. On some ships, inspection of all running rigging and gear is a weekly routine.

Reinspections which show steel plates or angle construction having their dimensions diminished by more than 25 percent indicate immediate renewal of the affected parts. Steel wire should be renewed where there is a bad rust formation or more than 10 percent of the composing wires have been broken within a distance of 10 times the circumference of cable. Topping lift steel wires may not be used in any case for a period greater than eight years and, of course, in the case of important alterations or renewals, as well as after an accident, the retesting of all rigging or gear is required before it is put back into use.

The Federal Register of June 5, 1957 states: "An inspection of cargo gear shall be required. A current certificate of the ABS, or other recognized non-profit organization or association, approved by the Commandant, U.S.C.G., relating to tests and surveys of cargo gear may be accepted as *prima facie* evidence of the construction and suitability of such gear. Such certificate shall attest to the fact and so indicate that the standards of the ABS or the International Labor

Organization Convention No. 32, with respect to cargo gear, have been met."

The International Cargo Gear Bureau is a non-profit organization established by the maritime industry to certificate the shipboard safety standards for cargo gear. These standards comply with International Labor Organization Convention No. 32, which has been ratified by most maritime nations.

The certificates, issued by the ICGB, are accepted internationally as *prima facie* evidence of the safety condition of the cargo gear.

The U. S. Coast Guard has given official recognition to the International Cargo Gear Bureau as a qualified organization and announced:

"The valid current certificates and/or registers issued by the International Cargo Gear Bureau, Inc., with home office at 52 Broadway, New York 4, N. Y., attesting to the tests and surveys of shipboard cargo gear on a passenger, cargo, or miscellaneous vessel conducted by or for such Bureau, may be accepted as *prima facie* evidence of the condition and suitability of such gear by the Coast Guard when performing an inspection of a vessel as further description in 46CFR 71,25-25 or 91.25-25."

The procedure for annual and quadrennial inspection, as required by the International Cargo Gear Bureau for certification of cargo gear, follows:

Annual Inspection. A visual examination shall be made and, if it proves satisfactory, then a total of 20% of the gear shall be dismantled to determine the actual internal condition of the goosenecks, heel pins, block pins, sheaves, shackle pins, swivels, etc. This gear shall be stripped on available booms at the various hatches.

If, in the ICGB inspector's opinion, the equipment shows only nominal wear, it shall be greased and reassembled. The booms shall be proof-tested to the required proof load in long tons of 2,240 pounds. All gear inspected will be stenciled with the safe working loads.

Quadrennial Inspection. Details of this fourth year inspection are the same as the annual except that the remaining 40% will be dismantled, thus resulting in 100% of the gear being stripped and inspected over the four-year period.

This method of partial annual inspection of cargo gear by the International Cargo Gear Bureau offers continuous inspection, minimum inconvenience and an improved degree of safety.

Boom Test Procedure. In making boom tests, steam for winch operation during the test must be taken from ship's boilers and through the ship's piping. The initial steam pressure should be 125 pounds at the reducing valve with 10 pounds back pressure. Shore piping or temporary piping is not acceptable for cargo handling gear testing.

General requirements of the test include that all five ton booms and 15 ton booms be tested with an overload of 25 percent with a 50 ton boom being tested with a load of 55 tons. Pig iron, waterfilled tanks or any other load that can be safely attached to the cargo hook may be employed as the test load. Concrete blocks are frequently used and it is urged that where they are employed U-bolts firmly anchored in the block be used in place of eye bolts. Accidents have occurred where the eye has opened and the block dropped.

In the case of five ton booms, all booms must be tested with a boom angle of 25 degrees to the horizontal with a full load, swinging inboard and outboard as far as obstruction permits. At least one five ton boom at each hatch must be lowered with its full test load to the tank top and back to the deck. A hook speed of 120 feet per minute is required and, if all winches are furnished by same manufacturer, the hook speed test may be confined to one winch.

During the test, mechanical brakes must be able to stop and hold the load instantly in any position of the hook.

While the 15 and 50 ton booms are tested in general as already described, a detailed description is as follows:

1) The boom is topped at a 35 degree angle to the horizontal.
2) The load is lifted from either deck, lighter, or pier.
3) With a boom top high enough to clear obstruction, the load is swung over the hatch. The clearance of the hook over the bulwark should be at least 30 feet.
4) The boom is then topped under full load to the last quarter of the hatch nearest the boom.
5) Brakes are tested immediately after the load clears the deck, lighter or pier to make certain they will hold and no slipping will occur. Sudden stops of the load must be avoided.
6) Vang tackles must be winch operated during this test.

For safety it must be demonstrated that all five ton boom topping lifts are long enough to lower the boom into the boom crotch with at least three turns of the wire rope on all drums hooked to or otherwise securely fastened to the gypsy head or winch drum.

All cargo whips must be long enough to lower the hook to the tank top at the last quarter of the hatch nearest the boom with at least three turns of the rope still remaining on the drum and end of the wire rope securely fastened to the drum.

Checking Gear After Testing. Upon completion of these tests described above, a thorough and careful examination must be made of all gear to assure that no permanent deformation, chafing or scoring of pins, pads, cleats or other fittings or gear has taken place or that there is any evidence of over-straining, faulty design or poor workmanship. Any defects found must be remedied immediately and, the extent of the defect will indicate whether additional tests are necessary.

Capacities must be clearly marked on all booms, winches, blocks, chains, etc., either by stamping, center punching or similar indelible and durable marking. These capacities should be underlined with a white paint line one inch wide, framed by a white square. The minimum angle to the horizontal at which a safe working load may be applied must also be marked on all booms.

As a further precaution, all chains, rings, hooks, shackles and swivels in general use should be annealed by a competent plant at least once every twelve months. While this is a recommended practice, inspection will frequently show that shorter intervals are necessary between annealing of such gear.

GENERAL SAFETY RULES*

All gears and friction drives, wherever located, should be completely encased. Where, in the case of gears, this is impracticable, a band guard should be provided with side flanges extending inward beyond the root of the teeth.

Where there is a spoke hazard the spokes should always be covered on exposed side.

All sprocket wheels, wherever located, should be completely encased.

All projecting set screws on moving parts should be removed, or countersunk or headless set screw should be used. No part of the set screw should project above the surface.

Shaft keys, unless enclosed by the housing of the machine, should be flush or protected with cylindrical safety sleeves, or completely enclosed.

Shields or screens should be provided which will prevent contact with crank, connecting rod, valve rod, steam jam cylinder or other moving parts.

Where an edge of cargo or of a landing platform is exposed and there is danger of falls of persons, the edge should be guarded by a life line.

The ship's gear should be so rigged as to protect the winch driver against swinging loads.

All winches operating with a single lever shall be counterbalanced by a weight properly secured.

Extensions on operating levers of winches, of substantial material, where necessary, shall be furnished by the ship, and securely attached to the regular lever.

Winches, conveyors, belts, and all driving gear may be lubricated while in motion only when this can be done by means of suitable contrivances, without danger.

Lubricating and oiling while a machine is in motion may be done only by persons authorized to do so.

Cleaning of machine parts may be done only while the machine is not in motion.

No cargo shall be worked through a section of a hatch unless the strongback of section adjacent to uncovered portion of hatch is bolted to hatch coamings, or otherwise secured or removed.

No cargo shall be hoisted from hatch until hatch covers and strongbacks are off and stowed clear of working gear, except such cargo as must be removed to clear beams.

Strongbacks and hatch covers shall be so stowed as not to interfere with a safe walkway for hatch tenders from rail to hatch coaming, and so that drafts or gear cannot tip same into hatches or over ship's side.

When employees are below, they shall stand in the clear while strongbacks, hatch beams and hatch covers are being taken out or put in place.

* Excerpts from the Pacific Coast Marine Safety Code.

Sling loads or drafts of dunnage shall not be handled over the heads of longshoremen. Where practicable double slings should be used.

Employees shall never ride strongbacks or beams; nor shall they unnecessarily walk or climb upon them while in place. Riding cargo hook prohibited.

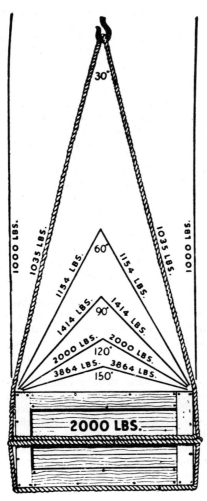

FIG. 14. LOADS ON TWO LEG SLINGS AT VARIOUS ANGLES.

When working cargo over a deck load a safe walkway shall be provided for the hatch tender from rail to coaming. When this is impracticable two hatch tenders shall be used.

Deck loads shall be so stowed as not to interfere with safe operation of winches or to permit loose material falling into hatches or overside.

All decks, floors and other places, shall, as far as possible, be kept clean and free from dust, litter and slipperiness. Grease, oils, etc., shall be immediately covered with sand or other suitable material.

Men should not be hoisted aloft except by hand power; booms should be lowered to deck for changing gear, or making necessary repairs.

The winch fall should be so wound that the lever shall have the same direction of operation as the load being handled. Winches hereafter constructed shall be made so that they can be operated as above recommended.

The boom guys and preventers should be kept as far away from the heel of the boom as possible, but not past the line of the fall. They shall be made fast so as to divide the strain on both. Preventers should be made fast around the head of the boom independent of all other fastenings. Booms shall always be so topped as to avoid undue strain on both boom and topping lift. (Special caution where samson or derrick post is low.) In all "set-ups" the dragging of one fall against the other without plenty of sag is positively dangerous and should be avoided.

When winch controls are located so as to expose winch driver to bight of the fall, an additional preventer shall be placed on the lead block at the heel of the boom. The preventer shall be not less than $5/8$-inch wire cable and preferably $3/4$ or larger.

A sling load or draft shall not be lifted with a chain having a kink in it. A chain shall not be shortened by wiring or tieing. Chains shall not be repaired, even temporarily, by bolting two links together or by the use of wire.

All bridles for removing strongbacks or beams from hatch coamings shall be of sufficient length so that strongbacks can be hooked on without necessitating climbing out on them to do so; shackles or toggles are recommended in place of hooks for handling strongbacks. Hand lines shall be attached of adequate length for use in preventing swinging of hatch beams and strongbacks.

All boom guys and gin blocks shall be secured by shackles.

When deck loads of lumber extend above the bulwarks, there should be a pendant of sufficient length to preclude sending a workman down ship's side to secure or release the boom guy from the deck ring bolt.

The ship shall furnish a sufficient number of approved topping lift stoppers where necessary for safely shifting derrick topping lifts.

Cargo booms should be tested and have approved capacity plainly marked in a conspicuous manner and place, preferably at the heel of the boom.

Cargo falls or ship's hoisting gear shall not be used to move railroad cars on docks.

Hatch rollers shall be so constructed that they can be firmly attached or secured to hatch coamings.

Broken, split, or ill fitting hatch covers shall at once be discarded or repaired. All hatch covers, and fore-and-aft and thwart-ship beams shall, insofar as they are not interchangeable, be kept plainly marked to indicate the deck and hatch to which they belong and their position therein, and a licensed ship's officer should be present and responsible for the proper covering and uncovering of all hatches. Sufficient hatch covers of proper dimensions to insure a tight cover for each deck shall be supplied at all times during Operations.

Adequate hand grips shall be provided on all hatch covers, having regard to their size and weight. Hand grips shall not be secured by means of wood or lag screws; where bolts are used ends of same shall be riveted.

Ship's cargo hoisting falls or whips shall not be used for mooring or shifting ship.

Wire bridles shall have a covering of marline, rubber hose or other suitable protection for men's hands over hook-splice.

Savealls shall be stretched, hung and safely secured to vessel and dock, in line with each hatch when general cargo is being worked.

Inspection of ship's cargo gear should be made by the ship's crew before gear is used for stevedoring Operations. The crew should give all assistance possible to maintain properly ship's cargo gear while in use.

Chapter 11

GROUND TACKLE

The importance of efficient ground tackle—the *anchors, chain cables,* and *windlass*—has been realized for years by the classification societies, and certain standard minima in equipment are prescribed for all vessels according to their *equipment tonnage* (a figure closely approximating the gross tonnage) in order to attain the 100A1 rating, or *class,* under the particular society's rules.

In connection with the requirements of the classification rules, anchors and cables are subjected to certain tests, under the supervision of inspectors, in order to determine that the strength of material and the quality of workmanship attains the standard values set up in the rules.*

All vessels, according to the American Bureau of Shipping Rules, are required to carry two *bower* anchors and cables with each, and an efficient windlass or capstan for weighing anchor. Steam and motor vessels of 380 tons (equipment tonnage) and upwards must carry one *spare bower,* and those of all sizes are required to carry one *stream anchor.* Sailing vessels of any tonnage must carry all four, viz., 2 bowers, 1 spare bower, and 1 stream. Only a seagoing tug is required to carry a kedge anchor.

Anchors. There are several varieties of the "patent", or "stockless" anchor in general use of which the *Admiral, Dunn,* and *Baldt* are perhaps the most commonly met with. A favorite with salvage operators is the *Eels* anchor, characterized by its long flukes which make it an unhandy instrument for stowing, but a first rate "digger-in" for hauling off a stranded vessel.

Weight for weight, however, the old-fashioned anchor takes a better grip of the bottom than the best stockless one yet invented. Its popularity, in spite of its good holding qualities, has lost to the patent type because of its extreme unhandiness for stowing, and the likelihood,

---

* Typical marking (on the stock) of a bower anchor showing besides the number, inspector's initials, date of inspection, classification society and weight (in pounds) appears as follows:

P A 24195
E G P   11   46
123760
AB
8200

when swinging to a change of tide or wind, of the chain fouling the exposed fluke or the stock itself.

INSPECTION OF ANCHOR CHAIN

While it is desirable that chain be ranged and tested (hammer test and visual examination) at regular intervals, the only actual requirement that this be done is found in the ABS instructions for their Special Periodical Survey No. 2. This survey is required 8 years after the vessel is built as a condition for reclassification. The Coast Guard does not require that the chain be ranged and tested at the annual inspection unless there is reason to believe that it is defective. However, if the annual inspection takes place while the vessel is in dry dock, and the chain has been ranged for painting, as is usually the case, the inspector will hammer test the links. (Proceedings of the Merchant Marine Council, USCG, March, 1956.)

The **holding power** of anchors commonly in use depends, of course, upon the character of the bottom, but, under ordinary conditions in good holding ground, the "hook" will withstand a pull of 7 times its weight. This ratio holds good with the outer end of the cable leading up to a 23-degree angle with the shank of the anchor as it rests on the bottom. Thus we find that a bower 8225 lbs. in weight should be good for pull, in the usual mud or clay bottom met with, of about 28 tons, or a value not far off the working load of its 2 5/16-inch wrought iron cable, (or one of 2 inches, cast steel).

Weight of Anchors with Length and
Size of Stud Chain Cable (Wrought
Iron)   required   by   A.B.S.   Rules

Equip't tons	2 Bowers	1 Spare Bower	1 Stream	1 Kedge	Cable Fathoms	Cable Size
100	490	none	140	70	120	11/16"
800	2275	1925	980	420	210	1 3/8"
1400	3465	2940	1435	none	240	1 5/8"
2550	4725	4025	1885	do	240	1 7/8"
5260	7665	6510	2765	do	270	2 1/4"
10300	12005	10220	4305	do	300	2 11/16"
15300	15575	13230	5600	do	330	3"
20400	18900	16065	6825	do	330	3 1/4"
26500	22470	19110	8120	do	330	3 1/2"

The "stockless" anchor's head (the flukes and their connecting arm) must be at least three-fifths that of the anchor in weight.

The stock of the ordinary anchor must be equal in weight to one-fourth that of the anchor exclusive of the stock.

Where approved *cast* or *die-forged steel* chain is adopted, sizes from 3 to 7 sixteenths inch smaller than the wrought iron sizes given in the table are allowed.

MARKINGS

When the tests have been completed satisfactorily, the particulars are stamped on each component as follows:

Stockless Anchor

1. The number of the certificate (furnished by the surveyor), 7147
2. The initials of the surveyor who witnesses the proof test, X.Y.Z.
3. Month and year of test, 6–35
4. Proof test applied, 76,440
5. Signifying that the testing machine is recognized by the committee of the American Bureau of Shipping, AB
6. The weight of anchor, 4,200
7. Signifying that the anchor head has been tested by a surveyor to the American Bureau of Shipping, AB
8. The weight of anchor head, 2,520
9. The initials of the surveyor who witnesses the drop test, X.Y.Z.
10. Month and year of drop test, 6–35

One side of the anchor should be reserved solely for the above marks and the other side used for the maker's name or other trademarks that may be desired. If the design of the anchor does not admit the foregoing marks being placed as indicated, a suitable boss should be cast on each arm, on which the marks can be stamped.

Cable

The shackles and end links of each length and shot, and one link in every 15 fathoms of stud-link chain, when connecting links are used to connect the shots, are stamped as follows:

1. The number of the certificate (furnished by the surveyor), 8442
2. The initials of the surveyor who witnesses the test, X.Y.Z.
3. Month and year of test, 6–35
4. The breaking test, 211,680
5. The proof test applied, 151,200
6. Signifying that the testing machine is recognized by the committee of the American Bureau of Shipping, AB

Cables. The *connecting* shackles are set in the chain cable with their bows toward the anchor. The *joiner* shackle, or that joining anchor and cable, should be attached to a patent anchor with its bow facing inboard. This latter necessity will be realized upon observing how easily the shackle referred to will catch on the lip of a worn hawse-pipe, if set with its bow toward the anchor.

Chain cable is often made today with no other shackles than those required to join it to the anchor. This is the cast steel or die-forged steel chain which is made up into the required length of cable by the use of connecting links. A link of this sort is shown in Fig. 2.

CABLE MARKINGS

It is important that the officers of a ship know at all times the *scope* or amount of cable paid out. To make this knowledge quickly available, a system of cable markings is used. These markings are made with turns of seizing wire at appropriate points in the chain's length and, according to the ideas of the mate, the wire markings may be supplemented by distinctive painted links.

Where the cable is made up of 15-fathom lengths, or 'shots', the time-honored system of markings is as follows:

15 fathoms, one turn of wire on the stud of the first studded link from each side of shackle.

30 fathoms, two turns of wire on second stud from each side of shackle.

45 fathoms, three turns of wire on third stud from each side of shackle.

60 fathoms, four turns of wire on fourth stud from each side of shackle.

75 fathoms, five turns of wire on fifth stud from each side of shackle.

90 fathoms, six turns of wire on sixth stud from each side of shackle.

105 fathoms, seven turns of wire on seventh stud from each side of shackle, and each succeeding 15-fathom mark according to the rule indicated.

Navy Markings

20 fathoms, the first studded link on each side of the shackle has a turn of wire around its stud and is painted white.

20+15 or 35 fathoms, the second studded link on each side of the shackle has two turns of wire around its stud and the two links on either side of the shackle are painted white.

35+15 or 50 fathoms, the third studded link on each side of the shackle has three turns of wire and the three links on either side of the shackle are painted white, etc.

If in addition to the marking described, the shackles and chain are painted, then the following system of colors is used:

20 fathoms	shackle	painted	red
35 "	"	"	white
50 "	"	"	blue
65 "	"	"	red
80 "	"	"	white
95 "	"	"	blue
110 "	"	"	red
125 "	"	"	white
140 "	"	"	blue
155 "	"	"	white

155 to 175, all other links painted red.

All the other links are painted black between shackles 20–140 except as has been noted in previous paragraph.

Between the shackles 140–155, all the other links are painted yellow.

Where a *die-lock*, or any patent detachable link supplants the connecting shackle, it should not be difficult to devise an easily recognized system, such as painting one link for 15 fathoms, two links at the 30-fathom mark, three at the 45-fathom mark, and so on.

Weight of Chain Cable. The weight per fathom of both wrought iron and cast steel or die-forged chain cable is very nearly equal to 57 times the diameter (in inches) of the metal in the link (this is the *size* of the chain) *squared*, expressed in pounds; or W (*in pounds*) $= 57d^2$.

Form of Link. The studded links are made in the following proportions: *Outer length* of link is equal to 6 times the diameter of the metal, and the *outer width* is 3.6 times the diameter of the metal. The *pitch* of the chain is the distance from the center of one link to that of its next neighbor, which also means the *inside length* of the link.

Chain cable stresses. American Bureau of Shipping rules require the breaking test of wrought iron studded link chain cable, expressed in *long tons*, to be approximately 25 times the square of the diameter of the metal (in inches). Cast steel, or die-forged steel stud chain must stand a breaking test, under the same rules, of about 36 times the square of the diameter of the metal.

A *safety factor* of 4 has been considered by many seamen of long experience as an appropriate figure for chain cable, and, although in ordinary use one-fourth of the breaking stress is seldom reached, in view of the violent jerks and surges to which the cable may be subjected under so many different conditions, such as heavy sheering, heaving in a seaway, or bringing up in mooring, this factor seems a fair and reasonable one.

As noted under **anchors,** the holding power of the "hook" is very nearly equal to the working load of the chain cable, and, in this connection, it should be noted that, under any conditions, the tension on the cable is greatest at the lip of the hawse-pipe, and is governed by the weight of the veered chain as well as the actual horizontal pull throughout the cable. The cable takes the form of a parabolic curve known as the *common catenary*, the highest and lowest points of which are coincident with the lip of the pipe and the ring of the anchor.

The following table indicates the tension at the hawse-pipe, in long tons, corresponding to the scope of chain and the angle which the chain makes with the water's surface, or the *angle of lead*, and also gives the horizontal pull on the anchor. The values are given for a 2 1/2-inch wrought-iron chain.

The values for any other size of cable under similar conditions of lead angle and length of chain may be easily computed. The p corresponding to a 2-inch chain, for example, is equal to $(2^2 \div 2\,1/2^2) \times p$, since the p varies directly as the square of the size of chain.

In the chain tension table given, p is the tension in long tons at the hawse-pipe corresponding to the length of chain veered and the *angle of lead* or angle the cable makes with the water's surface. The values below the heavy line indicate the tension has reached the working load of the chain and that the holding power of the anchor, in ordinary circumstances, has attained a maximum. *Provided the forces of wind and current remain undiminished, any further veering of chain at this point will unduly tax both the chain and the holding power of the anchor.*

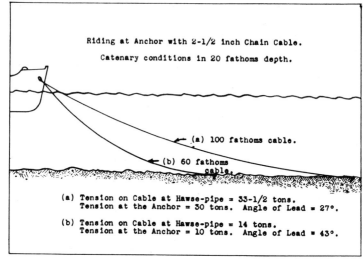

Riding at Anchor with 2-1/2 inch Chain Cable.

Catenary conditions in 20 fathoms depth.

← (a) 100 fathoms cable.

← (b) 60 fathoms cable.

(a) Tension on Cable at Hawse-pipe = 33-1/2 tons.
    Tension at the Anchor = 30 tons. Angle of Lead = 27°.

(b) Tension on Cable at Hawse-pipe = 14 tons.
    Tension at the Anchor = 10 tons. Angle of Lead = 43°.

FIGURE 1

Tension at Hawse-pipe and Anchor on a 2½-inch chain												
Fathoms cable	Angle of lead of cable at surface of water											
	20°		25°		30°		35°		40°		45°	
	p	a	p	a	p	a	p	a	p	a	p	a
30	14	13	11	10	9½	8	8	6½	7½	5½	7	5
45	21	19½	17	15	14	12	12½	10	11	8½	10	7
60	28	26	22½	20½	19	16½	16½	13½	15	11½	13½	9½
75	35	33	28	25½	24	21	21	17	18½	14	17	12
90	**42**	**39½**	34	31	28½	24½	25	20½	22	17	20	14
105	**48½**	**45½**	**39½**	36	33½	29	29	24	26	20	23½	16½
120	**55½**	52	**45**	41	**38**	**33**	33	27	29½	22½	27	19

p = tension on the chain at the hawse-pipe.
a = horizontal tension or pull on the anchor.
Values are given in long tons.
The figures in bold type indicate the working load
of wrought-iron chain cable (37½ tons) is exceeded.

If **towed** by the chain cable, the tension at the hawse-pipe, p, is found by entering the table with the approximate length of cable, measured from the pipe to the *lowest point in the catenary*, and the estimated angle of lead.

The value a indicates the horizontal pull on the anchor, or the horizontal component of the total tension at any point in the catenary.

Maximum Scope of Chain

Depth in fathoms (outboard lip of Hawsepipe to bottom)	5	7½	10	15	20	25	30	35	40	45
Wrought-iron chain (fathoms)	54	66	76	93	107	120	130	140	149	157
Cast-steel chain (fathoms)	64	78	91	110	127	142	155	166	178	188
Die-lock nickel steel chain (fathoms)	78	95	109	133	154	174	188	202	216	228

These figures apply, regardless of the size of the ship, provided the vessel is furnished with a properly balanced outfit of ground tackle.

If longer scopes are used, the chain may be stressed beyond its safe service working load; if shorter scopes are used, the anchor will tend to drag before developing the full safe load on the chain. The scopes shown for the greater depths could be obtained only by bending additional shots to the standard lengths of chain cable. If greater holding power than that given by one anchor with the scope of chain shown in the table is necessary, it is better practice to drop a second anchor, even with moderate scope of its chain, than to rely upon the one anchor with a longer scope. Of course, in the case of extreme necessity, when the greatest holding power is necessary, all anchors should be dropped and the chain veered to the greatest possible scope though if there is ample sea room, it would be better to reduce the scope to the amounts shown in the table and accept the possibility of dragging anchor, rather than risk breaking the chain.

Anchor work. It is an old rule among seamen that you should not drop anchor unless moving over the ground, but this does not mean a speed at which the sparks will fly from hawse-pipe and windlass by a rattling cable doing the showy *flying* or *running* moor stunt. The vessel should be moving just enough to lay the chain clear of the anchor, and if stemming a current, the time to drop the *hook* will be just as the ship begins to gather sternway over the ground.

In *deep anchorages* many an anchor with its entire cable has been lost through attempting to *let go* with the usual brake control as in shallow water. In depths of 10 fathoms or more an anchor should never be *let go by the run*, especially so should there be some way on the vessel over the ground. Always keep the lowering of your anchor in hand, and in depths of 15 fathoms or upwards, lower the anchor with the windlass in gear to within a few fathoms of the bottom, and then let go under brake control. Twenty fathoms of 2 1/2-inch chain cable, plus the anchor's weight—about 7 tons—will easily keep going if paid out *by the run* in comparatively deep water, in spite of an A-1 brake at your command; assuredly so, if the vessel has a couple of knots way on her in the bargain.

Bringing up. In all cases care should be given to braking the wildcat when it is required to hold the cable. Sharp clamping down of the brake produces jerks and unnecessary jolts to your ground tackle which may prove disastrous. The force required to stop a vessel by means of the cable or a mooring line varies directly as the square of the ship's speed, and, by this rule, at 2 knots 4 times the more stress is necessary to bring the ship to rest in a given distance than at 1 knot.

Weighing anchor. When *heaving up* in a swell or seaway, remember to avoid the heavy blows the anchor may deliver to your ship's bow plating. If vessel is rolling enough to swing the anchor about, put her end on to the sea before attempting to heave the *hook* clear of the water.

Stream anchor cable. The American Bureau of Shipping rules prescribe the cable requirements for stream anchor use as well as that of the bower anchors. For example, a steam vessel of 7850 equipment tonnage is required to carry 105 fathoms of a choice of 1 3/8-inch wrought iron stud link chain, 1 7/16-inch short link chain, or 1 1/2-inch steel wire (6 strands of 24 wires each). The break test of the wire is to be 126,000 lbs., or about 56 long tons.

Such a vessel is also required to carry a 130-fathom *tow line* of either a 16-inch (circ.) manila, or a steel wire of the same length 1 13/16-inch in diameter, having a break test of approximately 78 long tons. *The use of this line and the spare bower might easily solve the problem of a lost bower with its cable, and the ship in danger of drifting ashore.*

Short link chain is not prescribed for steam or motor vessels of over 10,300, and *no manila tow line* for those of 11,200 equipment tonnage.

It is noted that our 7850-ton vessel is required to be equipped with at least 4 manila *hawsers* or *warps*, viz., 2 of 8 1/2-inch circumference, and 2 of 7 1/2-inch.

Mooring to a Buoy. In all cases, pass a "hook rope" to hold the bow in position while the moor is being made. This "hook rope" is preferably a 1⅝" spring-laid mooring wire which can be used as a trolley line by which the anchor chain may be lowered to the buoy. A strop to slide down the trolley line is attached to the third link of the chain above the mooring shackle. An easing-out line is also attached at this point and will, as it is eased out, permit the strop to slide down the trolley line carrying the weight of the chain. Thus, there will be sufficient free end of the chain to permit the men on the buoy to shackle onto the buoy.

Testing Cable

As before noted, the American Bureau of Shipping rules specify that chain, shackles, and anchors be given a series of tests to determine their strength and perfection. After passing the tests, each separate connecting unit in the cable must be stamped by the manufacturer in the following manner:

A. The number of certificate (furnished by surveyor).
B. The initials of the surveyor who witnesses the test.
C. Month and year of test.

D. The breaking test (lbs.).

E. The proof test applied (lbs.).

F. Signifying that the testing machine is recognized by the Committee of the American Bureau of Shipping.

NOTES ON THE MAKING OF ANCHOR CABLE

The *stud link* anchor chain cable gets its name from the *stud*, cast or welded across the inside of the link. This stud prevents the link from closing under heavy stress and keeps the link in its proper lengthwise position as the chain is straightened out. It is estimated that the stud adds 15% to the strength of the link.

One method of manufacture is known as drop forging. This means that each link is formed from a straight piece of tested steel bar and welded under a steam hammer, requiring several operations, for each of which the link must be re-heated. The second link is welded into the first and so on until the desired length of chain has been made.

Another method is known as casting. Molds are made of the desired size and the metal is heated to about 3000° Cent. The molten metal is swung over the molds in a pouring ladle, handled by a travelling crane. The pouring is done by an experienced man who must control the flow of the metal in such a way as to prevent air bubbles forming in the casting. After proper cooling time the molds are knocked apart and the chain is ready for cleaning and testing.

A third method is a patented drop forging process called Di-Lok. Di-Lok chain is made of links consisting of a ridged solid section and an open section. The cold ridged section is inserted into the heated open section and the joint is struck in a forming die, locking the extra metal of the open section around the cold lugs of the ridged section. This leaves the link drop forged to shape and size, and the stud is formed a part of the link and not a separate piece. Figure 2 shows the parts of chain links before and after they are united by this mechanically forged lock. The figure also shows one of the patent detachable links now finding favor as a substitute for the shackle.

Cast-steel and di-lock chain have proved their superiority over forged-iron and forged-steel welded chain. Cast-steel chain has a tensile strength about 30 percent greater than wrought-iron chain of the same diameter. Di-Lok chain is approximately 100 percent stronger than wrought-iron chain of corresponding size. In addition, both Di-Lok and cast-steel chain are capable of withstanding great shock. Cast-steel and Di-Lok chain have uniform dimensions and the elastic limit of the links is considerably higher than that of forged iron and forged steel welded chain. Under the usual service conditions, the links of these types of chain do not stretch or become deformed and the chains will operate smoothly over the wildcat during the entire period of their useful life. Cast-steel chain can be distinguished by the fact that the studs are solid and an integral part of the links. The studs of Di-Lok chain are also an integral part of the link.

The mooring swivel is attached five links from the anchor end by means of a detachable link.

This permits the anchor to turn without twisting the anchor chain when the anchor is being lowered or raised. The tapered locking pin Fig. 3*A*. is held in place by a lead plug Fig. 3*B*.

The bitter end should be attached at "A" by means of a pelican hook or lashing so that if it should be necessary to slip the anchor it can be readily released.

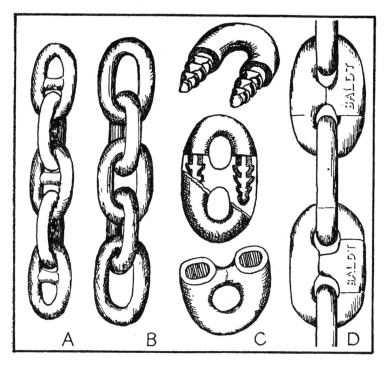

FIG. 2. A) Stud-link Chain. *B*) Close-link Chain. *C*) Di-Lok Link Before and After Joining. *D*) Di-Lok Chain Joined With Detachable Link.

CARE OF ANCHOR CABLES

Ground tackle is very important to the safety of the ship and it is very expensive equipment; therefore it must be given the best of care. Links should be tested when anchor is weighed and at regular intervals the cable should be ranged (laid out) for inspection and overhauling. The shots should be interchanged, the inner ones should be transferred to the outboard and vice versa. This change of position of *shots*, when carried out in a systematic manner, will insure uniform wear of the entire cable.

The Navy method of examining chain links is: Wash the chain with a hose from deck pump while heaving in slowly. Sound each link with a hammer and if one is found with a false ring it must be given a close inspection for defect. The following from Knight's *Modern Seamanship,* tenth edition, will illustrate the importance attached to anchor chain aboard men of war: "If any part of the chain has been reduced by corrosion or wear so that the mean diameter is reduced to 90 per cent of its

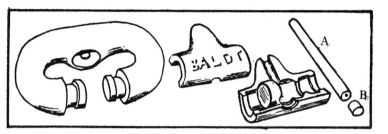

FIG. 3. DETACHABLE LINK.

original diameter, or when the length of 6 links exceeds the original length of these links plus the wire diameter of the chain in inches due to wear or elongation, or a combination of both, that part shall be replaced." In many cases of wrought iron chain, the Navy found that fractures were occurring in links of the outboard shot and inquiry disclosed that they were caused by the end links dropping on the *jew's harp* when the anchor strikes ground. This was eliminated by reeving a length of old manila line through the first few links of the outboard shot.

EXAMINATION OF ANCHORS

Modern stockless anchors are rugged in design and normally require little care. However, flukes should be kept free to move in their proper arc on the shank. The crown socket or pivot bar should be kept free of mud, rocks, etc. The anchor shackle pin in the bower anchors should be examined as they are subject to severe strain, as well as abrasion in the hawse pipes and in use. Should any slackness develop, they must be hardened up (usually by shipyard repair gangs) by heating and peening, or renewed. Spare bower, stream and kedges which are seldom used should have their shackles kept free.

Detecting Flaws in Chain Links, Hooks, Castings, etc. Saturate thoroughly with some light oil long enough to permit the oil to soak into any cracks or pin holes, then wipe off the surface oil. After this has been done, coat the entire surface with whiting. When the whiting has dried, the oil will begin to appear through it wherever there are deep-seated flaws having surface openings. A hammer blow will help bring the oil to the surface.

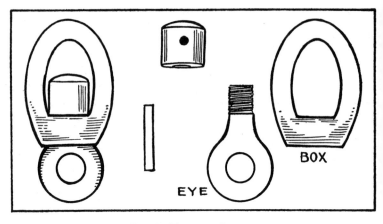

Fig. 4. Mooring Swivel.

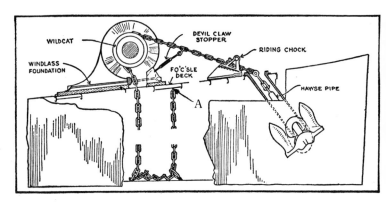

Fig. 5. A Vessel's Ground Tackle.

CHAIN CABLE FORMULAE

Weight of stud cable in lbs.	$= 57d^2 \times$ fathoms
Weight of stud cable in long tons	$= .025d^2 \times$ fathoms
Length of link in inches	$= 6d$ (outside)
Pitch of link (or inside diameter)	$= 4d$
Links per fathom	$= 18 \div d$
Working load, wrought iron cable	$= 6d^2$ (in long tons)
Working load, cast steel cable	$= 9d^2$ (in long tons)

$$d = \text{diameter of metal in link.}$$

The **cable length** is a traditional unit of nautical measure derived from the length of a ship's cable in "the good old days". It bears no relation, however, to the length of a present-day ship's cable.

The majority of recognized authorities appear to favor calling it 120 fathoms, but the following definitions are quoted to give an idea of the difference of thought on the subject.

The *Kedge Anchor* by Brady, published in 1857, says: "Cables take their names from the anchor to which they belong, as the sheet cable, the best bower cable, etc. They are generally 120 fathoms in length."

Admiral Luce, in the 1863 edition of his work on seamanship, gives this definition with an explanation: "Custom has heretofore limited the length of all cables to 120 fathoms for the reason that private rope-walks are seldom long enough to lay up strands of greater length, as a cable will take up one third from the drawing down of the yarns in laying up."

Riesenberg in his *Standard Seamanship for the Merchant Service*, states: "A cable length is 100 fathoms."

Webster's *New International Dictionary*: "The length of a ship's cable, specifically a maritime measure, *sometimes* considered to be about 100 fathoms, that is, 600 feet, an *approximation* to one tenth of a nautical mile. In the U. S. Navy 120 fathoms, or 720 feet; in the British Navy, 608 feet."

Century Dictionary: "An approximate measure of length regarded in maneuvering as 100 fathoms (600 feet or about 1/10 of a nautical mile), and in ordinary use, 120 fathoms (720 feet = the length of a chain or rope cable)".

Chambers' English Dictionary: "A cable is a measure of distance equal to one tenth of a nautical mile."

Chapter 12

SIGNALS

INTERNATIONAL CODE OF SIGNALS

The 1931 International Code of Signals went into effect January 1, 1934. It is published in English, French, German, Italian, Japanese, Spanish, and Norwegian.

The American edition is published by the Hydrographic Office in two volumes. Volume I (H.O. No. 87) is for visual and sound signaling; Volume II (H.O. No. 88) is for radio. Volume I should be on the bridge and immediately available at all times. It will not be wanted frequently, but it may be wanted immediately.

There are four methods of signaling with this code:

1. Flag signaling with the alphabet flags, numeral pennants, substitutes, and answering pennants. (*See* Fig. 1*A*, International Code flags and pennants and 1*B*, International flag signals.)

2. Flashing-light signaling with the International Morse.

3. Sound signaling with International Morse.

4. Semaphore.

The "distant signals" of the former code have been abolished.

NATURE OF SIGNALS

Single-Letter Signals. Urgent or very common use. Also special meanings, between towing and towed vessel, given on page 341 of the Code.

Two-Letter Signals. Generally speaking, these are important signals, many of them indicating various degrees of distress or warning. They should be read, translated, and acted upon with dispatch.

Three-Letter Signals. Used for remaining words, phrases and sentences.

Four-Letter Signals. Those commencing with *A* are used for the geographical section. The remaining four-letter signals are the signal letters of ships, signal stations, etc. The first letter or the first two letters indicate the nationality of a ship.

Five-Letter Signals. These are the call letters of aircraft.

How to Call. If no signal letter is hoisted superior to signal, it is for all ships; in other cases, signal letter of ship is hoisted superior to message. Keep flying until answered.

Note: H.O. 87 is now H.O. 103.

How to Answer. Hoist answering pennant at dip as soon as hoist is seen, and close up as soon as signal is understood. Lower to dip as soon as hoist is hauled down.

How to Complete Signal. Transmitting ship to hoist answering pennant singly after last hoist.

When Signal Is Not Understood. If receiving ship cannot distinguish the signal, she is to keep answering pennant at dip and hoist an appropriate signal to inform transmitting ship of reason.

If she can distinguish the signal but cannot understand its purport she should hoist *V B*.

P refers to position, and is the top letter of the numeral hoist when signaling latitude and longitude.

T refers to time, and is the top letter of the numeral hoist when signaling hours and minutes. (Time as USN: 0000—2359.)

✕ refers to bearings. ✕ at top of numeral hoist: Direction is true. 0°—360°. Each of 32 points of compass allocated a group of three letters.

Answer over E. Means "I am going to spell out words."

Answer over F. End of word or dot.

Answer over G. Word spelling completed.

Radio Signals, Vol. II, are arranged in 5-letter groups representing various words, phrases and sentences. When International Code groups are to be transmitted by radio the message is preceded by *INTCO*.

USCG Identification Procedure for Vessels Entering U. S. Ports

International Code Signals

WD numeral	You should reduce speed to . . . .
K	You should stop your vessel instantly.
OL	Heave to or I will open fire.
C	You have been identified; you may proceed.

SINGLE-LETTER SIGNALS

(Only those marked with an asterisk should be used by flashing.)

 A I am undergoing a speed trial.
 B I am taking in or discharging explosives.
 C Yes (Affirmative).
 D Keep clear of me—I am maneuvering with difficulty.
 E I am directing my course to starboard.
*F I am disabled. Communicate with me.
 G I require a pilot.
 H I have a pilot on board.
 I I am directing my course to port.
 J I am going to send a message by semaphore.
*K You should stop your vessel instantly.
*L You should stop. I have something important to communicate.
 M I have a doctor on board.
 N No (Negative).
*O Man overboard.

*P IN HARBOR (Blue Peter)—All persons are to repair on board as the vessel is about to proceed to sea. (Note.—To be hoisted at the foremast head.)

AT SEA—Your lights are out, or burning bad.

Q My vessel is healthy and I request free pratique.

*R The way is off my ship; you may feel your way past me.

S My engines are going full speed astern.

T Do not pass ahead of me.

*U You are standing into danger.

*V I require assistance.

*W I require medical assistance.

X Stop carrying out your intentions and watch for my signals.

Y I am carrying mails.

*Z To be used to address or call shore stations.

SOME TWO-LETTER SIGNALS

AC to AK	Abandon.
AL to MN	Accident.
AM	Accident has occurred. I require a doctor.
AP	I am aground.
DM to EP	Assistance.
DM	Haste is necessary.
DQ	Am afire and require immediate assistance.
DR	Am proceeding to the assistance of vessel in distress in position indicated.
FD to GD	Boats.
FR	I require a boat. Man overboard.
FX	You should not attempt to land in your own boats.
GU to IT	Caution.
HD	I am engaged in submarine survey work. You should keep clear of me.
JD	You are standing into danger.
JI	I am adjusting compasses.
LS to MG	Distress.
LJ	Am disabled. Will you tow me in?
MH to MK	Doctor
MJ	Have you a doctor?
NC	In distress and require immediate assistance.
NJ to OC	Fire.
PC	Light vessel off station.
PT	I require a pilot.
QL	Infectious disease aboard.
QQ	Suspect infectious disease aboard.
QW	Have mail for you, or vessel indicated.
RK to RQ	Mines.
RO	There is danger from mines in this area.
RV	Where are you bound?
RW	Where are you from?
SC	What is the name of your vessel?

SG	I have orders for you.
ST	I require a police boat.
T X	I am endeavoring to get in touch by radio.
TZ	My radio is not working.
UN to *UT*	Sickness.
UW	Cannot distinguish your flags.
UZ	I wish to signal, come nearer.
VB	Signal not understood but flags distinguished.
VC	Distress signals understood. Assistance coming.
VH	Hoist your signal letters.
YA	I require a tug.
YJ	I require water immediately.
YQ to *ZC*	Weather.

INTERNATIONAL FLAG CODE

(H.O. 87)

Following is an outline to assist in coding:

Page 34: *1-flag signals.*

Pages 35, 45: *2-flag signals.* Mostly distress and maneuvering, and a few in common use.

Pages 46, 47: *3-flag signals.* Compass, bearings, time.

Page 48: *Model verb.*

Page 49: *Punctuation and amplifying phrases.* Amplifying phrases are used to make a message clearer, as: "group follows is a question" and "buoy has broken adrift," is decoded as "has buoy broken adrift?" Correct use essential when communicating with foreign ships.

Pages 51, 199: *3-flag coding.*

Basic language is English.

Basic words and groups arranged alphabetically so far as possible under chief word they contain. Order is 1st, present tense; 2nd, past; 3rd, future.

If large number under one heading, 1st, information or advice; 2nd, orders; 3rd, questions.

When coding look up principal word and see if you can find a complete sentence to fulfill its meaning.

Departures from normal English necessary, as a single word in one language often requires several words in another language. The use of prepositions most difficult, but their use is generally connected with "time" and "place," so Code is arranged accordingly.

The possessive construction ("apostrophe-*s*") is omitted from Code, as there is no equivalent in most foreign languages. Use "of" (belongs to).

A complementary group (i.e., to the object or person indicated) is always signalled *after* the signal to which it refers.

Pages 200, 240: *3-flag decoding.* The signals cannot be used for coding in English, they are inserted solely for the purpose of decoding foreign messages.

Pages 241, 333: *4-flag signals.* All begin with *A* and are geographical.

Names of merchant ships, men-of-war and coast stations will be found in the *Liste Alphabétique d'Indicates d'Appel*, where they are arranged by call letters only, and in the *List of Coast and Ship Stations*, wherein Part *A* is an "Alphabetical Index of Coast Stations," Part *B*, "Particulars of Coast Stations" and Part *C*, "Particulars of Ship Stations," giving names of ships in alphabetical order, call letters and particulars. These books are published by the Bureau of the International Télécommunication Union, Berne, Switzerland. Aboard ship they are kept by the Radio Operator.

DEFINITIONS

Procedure. Denotes the rules drawn up for the conduct of signaling.

Tackline. Is a length of halyard about 6 ft. long, used to separate each group of flags which, if not so separated, would convey a different meaning to that intended.

Bearings. Made by a ship pointing out an object or referring to a position. They are always reckoned from the ship making the signal or from the point of departure, that is, invariably toward the objective.

Bearings and Courses. May be either true or magnetic, but will always be true unless otherwise stated.

Weft. End of a pennant made fast to halliard.

INTERNATIONAL FLAG CODE PROCEDURE

Transmitter	Receiver

To signal Hope Pt., Alaska that you have mail from New London, Conn.

1. *Z* left flying	**1.** Ans. pen. at dip, ans. pen. 2 blocks
2. *A HIJ* (Hope Point, Alaska)	**2.** Same
3. *Q X* (I have mail from · · ·)	**3.** Same
4. *A LGO* (New London, Conn.)	**4.** Same
5. Ans. pen. 2 blocks. (end)	**5.** Same

Passing another ship and wishing to ask "Where are you bound?"

1. *R V* (where are you bound?)	**1.** Ans. pen. at dip, ans. pen. 2 blocks
2. Ans. pen. 2 blocks (end)	**2.** Same
1. Ans. pen. at dip, ans. pen. 2 blocks	**1.** *A BEQ* (Baltimore, Md.)
2. Same	**2.** Ans. pen. 2 blocks (end)

Two ships present besides self. You wish to signal "My lifeboats are damaged and useless."

1. *G HA K*	**1.** Ans. pen. dip, ans. pen 2 blocks
2. *I N K*	**2.** Same
3. Ans. pen. 2 blocks	**3.** Same

REQUIREMENTS REGARDING FLAG SIGNALING

1. Familiarity with the flags and H.O. 87, particularly with that information at the commencement of Vol. I, covering coding and decoding.

   2. Tell nature of a signal by:
- *a)* The number of flags in the hoist
- *b)* The type of flags which compose the group
- *c)* The upper flag

   3. Know where to find and how to look up the names of merchant ships and men-of-war.

   4. Read signal at sight, i.e., know name of flags composing hoist.

   5. Know use of code pennant, numerals and substitutes.

   6. Know the meaning of all single-letter signals.

   7. Know the flags used to indicate quarantine.

   8. Signal some word or words not included in vocabulary of Code.

   9. Have a good knowledge of distress signals.

MORSE SIGNALING

Table 1 gives a list of the Morse symbols* used for visual and sound signaling. A bar over the letters composing a sign denotes that the letters are made as one symbol.

   dot = 1 unit
   dash = 3 units
   interval between flashes = 1 unit
   interval between letters = 3 units
   interval between word or group = 5 units

TABLE 1. INTERNATIONAL MORSE CODE SYMBOLS

ALPHABET

Meaning	Symbol	Meaning	Symbol	Meaning	Symbol
A	·—	H	····	Q	——·—
ä	·—·—	I	··	R	·—·
à	·——·—	J	·———	S	···
B	—···	K	—·—	T	—
C	—·—·	L	·—··	U	··—
CH	————	M	——	ü	··——
D	—··	N	—·	V	···—
E	·	ñ	——·——	W	·——
è	··—··	O	———	X	—··—
F	··—·	ö	———·	Y	—·——
G	——·	P	·——·	Z	——··

NUMERALS		PUNCTUATION		
Meaning	Symbol	Meaning	Sign	Symbol
1	·————	Period (full stop) (.) and decimal point	AAA	·—·—·—
2	··———			
3	···——	Bar indicating fraction (/)	X̄Ē	—··—·
4	····—			
5	·····			
6	—····			
7	——···			
8	———··			
9	————·			
0	—————			

* As given in H.O. 87, page 12.

PROCEDURE SIGNALS AND SIGNS

A A A A etc. Call for unknown ship and general call.

T T T T T etc. Answering sign, continued until transmitting ship ceases to call.

II($\cdots$) Space sign. Used to separate the signs *A A*, *A B*, *W A*, and *W B* from the identifying words or groups which follow them. It is also used to separate whole numbers from fractions.

B T Break sign. Used to precede the text. It is to be repeated back, but its repetition is not acknowledged with *C* by the transmitting ship.

$\overline{EEEEE}$ *etc.* Erase sign. Used to indicate that last group or last word was signaled incorrectly. Answered with the *erase sign*, after which the transmitting ship will repeat the word or group signaled incorrectly and proceed with the message. If it is desired to cancel the whole of a message while in process of transmisssion, the *erase sign* must be made, followed by the *ending sign*, viz.: $\overline{EEEEE}$ $\overline{AR}$.

$\overline{UD}$ Repeat sign. When made singly it signifies "Repeat the last message." To obtain a repetition of a part of a message it is used in conjunction with one of the following signs, thus: "Repeat all after the word *vessel*" is sent, "$\overline{UD}$ *A A II* Vessel."

A A all after

A B all before

W A word or group after

W B word or group before

$\overline{AR}$ Ending sign. Used in all cases to end a message.

De Identity sign, meaning "From $\cdots$." Thus *De G X D E* means "From ship whose signal letters are *G X D E*." This signal is repeated back by the receiving ship, which then makes *De* followed by her own signal letters. This latter is repeated by the other vessel.

C "You are correct." When a word or group in the text of a message, is repeated back, the letter *C* is used by the transmitting ship to indicate that the repetition has been made correctly.

G "Repeat back." It may be inserted at the beginning of the text of a plain language message, and is signaled separately. It signifies "Everything which follows in this message is to be repeated back, word by word, as soon as received."

R signifies "Message received."

T is used to indicate the receipt of each word in the text of a plain language message.

W signifies "I am unable to read your message owing to light not being properly trained (or light burning badly)."

P R B signifies "International Code groups follow."

Component Parts of a Message: 1. Call; **2.** Identity; **3.** Break sign; **4.** Text; **5.** Ending.

PROCEDURE WITH BLINKER

	Transmitter (*WIIT*)		Receiver (*GDBD*)
1.	aa aa aa aa		TTTTT
2.	de WIIT	→	de WIIT
	GDBD	←	GDBD

3. BT	→	BT
4. you		T
should		T
dock		T
at		T
1730		1730 (numerals repeated)
5. C AR		R

(OR USING CODE BOOK)

aa aa aa aa	TTTT
de WIIT	de WIIT
GDBD	GDBD
BT	BT
PRB	PRB
C (your repetition is correct)	
FDU	FDU
C	
T 1730	T 1730
C	
AR	R

MORSE FLASHING EXAMINATION

Must receive three mixed alphabets at speed of 6 words per minute (5 letters to a word), and afterwards a prose message of 10 words to be sent at same speed. After reading, candidate required to send the same at minimum of 6 words. Message equivalent of 20 words or 100 characters. May take 10 words, and have it recorded on files if successful.

Message read by candidate and taken down by another candidate. To be thoroughly tested in various signs and procedure of calling, sending and answering. Spacing and intervals will be particularly noted, and increase of speed at expense of accuracy is discouraged.

SIGNALING BY SOUND*

The misuse of sound signaling being of a nature to create serious confusion in the highways at sea, the captains of ships should use these signals with the utmost discretion. Owing to the nature of the apparatus used (whistle, siren, foghorn, etc.) sound signaling is necessarily slow, and it is for this reason that it is necessary for ships to reduce the length of their signals as much as possible.

(*a*) Sound signaling in fog should be reduced to a minimum. Signals other than the single-letter signals should be used only in extreme emergency and never in frequented navigational waters.

(*b*) For the reasons given in the above articles, the procedure shown below will be carried out in Morse signaling by sound.

HOW TO SIGNAL

The transmitting ship will make the call in the same way that it is made by flashing light. No call or answer will be used when transmitting single-letter signals.

* Articles 117–121, page 22, H.O. 87.

The receiving ship answers with the answering sign.

The transmitting ship then proceeds to signal the remainder of the message right through. The receiving ship does not answer unless she misses a word or group, but waits until the ending ($\overline{AR}$) has been made and then makes *R*.

Should the receiving ship miss a word or group, she is *immediately* to make the repeat sign ($\overline{UD}$), on hearing which the transmitting ship will cease signaling and then go back a few words or groups and continue the message.

Example. S. S. *Beechwood* hearing the sound of another steamer's siren, wishes to transmit the message: "Have just passed floating mines." The other ship is S. S. *Sirius*.

Component	S. S. Beechwood makes—	S. S. Sirius makes—
Call..............	*A A A A A A*, etc.	$\overline{TTTTTTT}$, etc.
Break sign........	$\overline{BT}$	
Text.............	{ Have just passed floating mines	{ No answer unless a word is missed, in which case makes repeat sign $\overline{UD}$. See paragraph above.
Ending...........	*A R*	*R*

Note. It will be observed that the transmitting and receiving ships do not exchange identities despite the use of the general call.

DISTRESS SIGNALS—Surface Vessels

Day	**Night**
1. Gun, etc., every minute	same
2. Code letters *NC*	flames
3. Continuous fog signal	same
4. Square flag and ball	rockets
5. $\overline{SOS}$	$\overline{SOS}$

Submarines—(*Day or Night*)

1. Red smoke bomb—in distress.

2. Yellow smoke bomb—compelled to surface in vicinity of other vessels.

(Submarine in distress on bottom will send up 2 orange buoys with a telephone and telegraph key under a black disc. One is at the bow, the other at stern, each with a cable length of 400 ft. Send position to nearest naval authority immediately.)

Submarine Signal Meanings. Submarine emergency identification colors and meanings are as follows:

(a) *Green.*—Indicates a torpedo has been fired. Will be used to simulate torpedo firing on special exercises, such as convoy exercises.

(b) *Yellow.*—Indicates that submarine is about to come to periscope depth from below periscope depth. Surface craft terminate antisubmarine counterattacks and clear vicinity of submarine. Do not stop propellers!

(c) *Red.*—Indicates an emergency condition within the submarine and she will surface immediately, if possible. Surface vessels clear the area and stand by to give assistance after the submarine has surfaced. In case of repeated red signals, or if the submarine fails to surface within a reasonable time, she may be assumed to be disabled. Buoy the location, look for submarine marker buoy, and attempt to establish sonar communications. Advise naval authorities.

The foregoing, all of which mark the submarine's position, are fired from a submerged signal ejector into the air to a height of about 300 feet, then float downward slowly, suspended from a small parachute, and give colored illumination for about 30 seconds.

Submarines are also equipped with messenger buoys which are about 3 feet in diameter, and are painted international orange. A submarine on the bottom in distress and unable to surface will, if possible, release this buoy. An object of this description which is sighted on the surface of the water should be investigated and naval authorities advised.

Aircraft—(*Day or Night*)

1. Succession of white lights projected into air at short intervals.

2. "Mayday" by radio telephone.

If an aircraft circles about ship and guns motor to attract attention, then heads off, this is a signal to follow, leading you to ship or plane in distress or leading you away from danger.

LIFE SAVING SIGNALS

1. Red light or rocket: "You are seen."

2. Red light or flag: "Haul away."

3. White light of flag: "Slack away."

4. 2 flags, white and red, or white and red lights together, or blue light: "Do not attempt to land in your own boats; it is impossible."

5. Man on shore beckoning, or two torches near together: "This is best place to land."

Any of these signals may be answered from the vessel as follows: In the daytime, waving a flag, a handkerchief, a hat, or even the hand; at night, by firing a rocket, a blue light, or a gun, or by showing a light over the ship's gunwale for a short time and then concealing it.

PILOT SIGNALS

By Day.

1. *G* "I require a pilot."

2. *PT* "I require a pilot."

3. The Pilot Jack hoisted at the fore.

At Night.

1. Blue pyrotechnic light every 15 minutes.

2. A bright white light, flashed or shown at frequent intervals just above the bulwarks for about a minute at a time.

3. *PT* by flashing light.

QUARANTINE SIGNALS

By Day.
Q " My ship is healthy, and I request free pratique."
QQ " My ship is suspect," i.e., " I have had cases of infectious diseases more than 5 days ago, or there has been unusual mortality among the rats on board my ship."
QL "My ship is infected," i.e. " I have had cases of infectious diseases less than 5 days ago."

At Night.
Red light over a white, signifying "I have not received free pratique."
(Only to be exhibited within the precincts of a port. The lights should not be more than 6 ft. apart.)

WARNING SIGNALS

Warning signals for Coast Guard vessels while handling or servicing aids to navigation.
Inland Waters (Inland Rules). *Day*—Two orange and white vertically striped balls in a vertical line not less than 3 feet nor more than 6 feet apart displayed from the yardarm.
Night—Two red lights in a vertical line not less than 3 feet nor more than 6 feet apart.
Vessels, with or without tows, passing Coast Guard vessels displaying this signal, shall reduce their speed sufficiently to insure the safety of both vessels, and when passing within 200 feet of the Coast Guard vessel displaying this signal, their speed shall not exceed 5 miles per hour.
High Seas (International Rules). *Day*—Three shapes not less than 2 feet in width in a vertical line not less than 6 feet apart, the highest and lowest being red globular shapes and the middle being a white diamond shape.
Night—Three lights in a vertical line not less than 6 feet apart, the highest and lowest being red and the middle being white in color.

Distress, Urgency and Safety Procedures for Radiotelegraph and Radio Telephone*
I Distress

a. Frequencies (1) Radiotelegraph   500 KC
                 (2) Radiotelephone 2182 KC
b. Signal (1) Radiotelegraph ...---... *SOS*
           (2) Radio telephone *MA YDA Y*
c. Form of *Distress Call*
     (1) Radiotelegraphy
         Int. Distress Signal, *SOS*, transmitted 3 times
         followed by   *de*
         followed by *call sign of station*, 3 times

* Radio Regulations, International Radio Conference, 1947.

    (2) Radiotelephone

        Int. Distress Signal, *MAYDAY*, spoken 3 times

        followed by words,   *This is*

        followed by identification of mobile station in distress, 3 times

d. Radiotelegraph Alarm Signal

    If possible, transmit 12 dashes in 1 minute, each dash 4 sec. in duration, followed by 1 sec. silence (this signal sent 3 times) followed by sending signal as in C (1).

e. *Distress Message*—The "Distress Call" must be followed as soon as possible by the "Distress Message", as follows:

    (1) Distress call

    (2) Name of station in distress

    (3) Particulars of position

    (4) Nature of distress

    (5) Kind of assistance desired

    (6) Any information which might facilitate rescue

f. Transmission of Radio Location—after transmission of Distress Message, 2 telegraph dashes of approximately 10 seconds each, followed by call sign (to permit the taking of DF bearings).

g. Acknowledgement—vessels receiving the distress message will send:

    (1) Call sign of distressed vessel (3 times)

    (2) *DE*

    (3) Call sign of acknowledging vessel (3 times)

    (4) *RRR*

    (5) Distress Signal

    Then, as soon as possible, the following additional information will be sent by the acknowledging vessel:

    (1) Its name

    (2) Its position

    (3) Course and speed at which proceeding toward the distressed vessel

    (4) *ETA* at scene of distress

h. Other stations must remain silent while distress traffic is in progress. Quiet may be imposed by the signal *QRT SOS*

II Urgency Signal

The safety of ship or person involved. This signal has priority over all communications except *DISTRESS*.

a. Radiotelegraphy: Send *XXX* 3 times, followed by the call and message text.

b. Radiotelephony: Repeat word *PAN* 3 times, followed by call and message text.

III Safety Signal

Safety of navigation or important meteorological warning.

a. Radiotelegraphy: Send *TTT* 3 times, followed by call and message text.

b. Radiotelephony: Repeat word *SECURITE* 3 times, followed by the call and message text.

REQUIREMENTS FOR AUTOALARM RADIO SIGNAL

1. A radio signal is provided for use by vessels in distress for the purpose of actuating the autoalarms of other vessels and thus securing attention to distress calls or messages.

2. The signal consists of a series of 12 dashes, sent in 1 minute, the duration of each dash being 4 seconds, and the duration of the interval between 2 consecutive dashes, 1 second.

3. All radio stations, including government stations and stations on board foreign vessels when within the territorial waters of the U.S., shall give absolute priority to radio communications or signals relating to a ship in distress. They shall cease all sending on frequencies which will interfere with hearing a radio communication or signal of distress, and, except when engaged in aiding or answering the ship in distress, shall refrain from sending any radio communication signals until there is assurance that no interference will be caused with the radio communications or signals relating thereto, and shall assist the vessel in distress so far as possible by complying with its instructions.

4. The autoalarm shall be operated by either 3 or 4 consecutive dashes when the dashes vary in length from 3.5 to as near 6 seconds as possible and the spaces vary in length between 1.5 seconds and the lowest practicable value, preferably not greater than 10 milliseconds.

5. The prescribed frequency is 500 KC.

6. When operated by an alarm signal, or in the event of failure of the apparatus, the autoalarm shall cause a continuous audible warning to be given in the radiotelegraphy operating room, in the radio operator's room and on the bridge.

7. Only one switch for stopping the warning shall be provided and this shall be located on the radiotelegraphy operating room.

8. In ships fitted with an autoalarm, the radio operator shall test the efficiency of the alarm at least once every 24 hours while at sea and report to the master or officer on watch on the bridge whether or not it is in working order.

RADIO EQUIPMENT REQUIREMENTS FOR MOTOR LIFEBOATS

1. It shall be capable of transmitting and receiving in the medium (500 KCS) band; the note frequency shall be between 450 and 1350 cycles per second.

2. The apparatus to be readily portable, watertight and capable of floating in sea water and also capable of being dropped 20 feet into the sea without damage.

3. Designed so as to be used by an unskilled person, the transmitter fitted with an automatic keying device as well as a key for manual transmission. An aerial shall be included, either self-supporting or capable of being supported by the mast of the lifeboat at the maximum practicable height.

4. At sea, a qualified operator shall at weekly intervals bring the battery up to full voltage and shall test the transmitter, using a suitable artificial aerial.

5. The minimum range shall be 25 miles.

NOTICE

Due to periodic changes in RULES OF THE ROAD, readers are advised to procure a copy of the latest U.S. Coast Guard NAVIGATION RULES, International and Inland.

This publication may be obtained upon request from the Coast Guard Marine Inspection Offices or by writing the Commandant (G-WLE/73), U.S. Coast Guard Headquarters, 400 Seventh Street, S.W., Washington, D.C. 20590. It may also be available at U.S. Coast Guard District Offices.

Chapter 13

RULES OF THE ROAD

INTERNATIONAL REGULATIONS FOR PREVENTING COLLISIONS AT SEA

The International Regulations for Preventing Collisions at Sea, 1960, (commonly called the 1960 International Rules of the Road) are contained herein. They will become effective on 1 *September* 1965, replacing the 1948 International Rules of the Road which are now in effect. It should be noted that these new International Rules will *not* be effective on U. S. waters governed by Inland, Great Lakes, or Western Rivers Rules of the Road.

The pending 1960 International Rules of the Road (formally identified as International Regulations for Preventing Collisions at Sea), which are scheduled to replace the 1948 International Rules now in effect, are reprinted in their entirety. There are a number of changes which will be of primary interest to mariners navigating on waters where the International Rules apply.

The most significant change made concerns conduct in restricted visibility. A new Rule 16(c) was adopted to provide for safe navigation by a vessel which detects another vessel outside of visual or audible range. Though not mentioning radar specifically, this rule—when considered together with the preliminary paragraphs to Part C and the Annex entitled "Recommendations on the Use of Radar Information as an Aid to Avoiding Collisions at Sea"—resolves several important questions which presently exist concerning a vessel navigating with the aid of radar.

Other changes of interest are: vessels are defined by their length rather than by tonnage; the use of a white light synchronized with the prescribed whistle signals is permitted; requirements for special lights for ships unable to get out of the way of approaching vessels because of the nature of their work were extended to ships replenishing at sea and ships engaged in the launching or recovery of aircraft; a new provision was added concerning lights and shapes for minesweeping vessels; Rule 9, lights for fishing vessels, was almost completely rewritten; Rule 17, the sailing rule, was modernized. Rule 22 was strengthened to require that a vessel which is directed by these rules to keep out of the way of another vessel shall, so far as possible, take positive early action to comply with this obligation; a new rule was added requiring that in a narrow channel a power-driven vessel of less than sixty-five feet in length shall not hamper the safe passage of a vessel which can navigate only inside such channel; a requirement that a tug and tow carry a prescribed shape in daylight was adopted; specific authorization was provided for the permissive use of navigation lights in daylight in restricted visibility; a definition of "engaged in fishing" was added to include fishing with nets, lines or trawls but not fishing with trolling lines; and the permissive use of colored masthead identity lights by sailing vessels was authorized.

Part A. PRELIMINARY AND DEFINITIONS

Rule 1. (a) These Rules shall be followed by all vessels and seaplanes upon the high seas and in all waters connected therewith navigable by seagoing vessels, except as provided in Rule 30. Where, as a result of their special construction, it is not possible for seaplanes to comply fully with the provisions of Rules specifying the carrying of lights and shapes, these provisions shall be followed as closely as circumstances permit.

(b) The Rules concerning lights shall be complied with in all weathers from sunset to sunrise, and during such times no other lights shall be exhibited, except such lights as cannot be mistaken for the prescribed lights or do not impair their visibility or distinctive character, or interfere with the keeping of a proper look-out. The lights prescribed by these Rules may also be exhibited from sunrise to sunset in restricted visibility and in all other circumstances when it is deemed necessary.

(c) In the following Rules, except where the context otherwise requires:

    (i) the word "vessel" includes every description of water craft, other than a seaplane on the water, used or capable of being used as a means of transportation on water;

    (ii) the word "seaplane" includes a flying boat and any other aircraft designed to manoeuvre on the water;

    (iii) the term "power-driven vessel" means any vessel propelled by machinery;

    (iv) every power-driven vessel which is under sail and not under power is to be considered a sailing vessel, and every vessel under power, whether under sail or not, is to be considered a power-driven vessel;

    (v) a vessel or seaplane on the water is "under way" when she is not at anchor, or made fast to the shore, or aground;

    (vi) the term "height above the hull" means height above the uppermost continuous deck;

    (vii) the length and breadth of a vessel shall be her length overall and largest breadth;

    (viii) the length and span of a seaplane shall be its maximum length and span as shown in its certificate of airworthiness, or as determined by measurement in the absence of such certificate;

    (ix) vessels shall be deemed to be in sight of one another only when one can be observed visually from the other;

    (x) the word "visible", when applied to lights, means visible on a dark night with a clear atmosphere;

    (xi) the term "short blast" means a blast of about one second's duration;

    (xii) the term "prolonged blast" means a blast of from four to six seconds' duration;

    (xiii) the word "whistle" means any appliance capable of producing the prescribed short and prolonged blasts;

    (xiv) the term "engaged in fishing" means fishing with nets, lines or trawls but does not include fishing with trolling lines.

Part B. LIGHTS AND SHAPES

Rule 2. (a) A power-driven vessel when under way shall carry:
- (i) On or in front of the foremast, or if a vessel without a foremast then in the forepart of the vessel, a white light so constructed as to show an unbroken light over an arc of the horizon of 225 degrees (20 points of the compass), so fixed as to show the light 112½ degrees (10 points) on each side of the vessel, that is, from right ahead to 22½ degrees (2 points) abaft the beam on either side, and of such a character as to be visible at a distance of at least 5 miles.
- (ii) Either forward or abaft the white light prescribed in sub-section (i) a second white light similar in construction and character to that light. Vessels of less than 150 feet in length shall not be required to carry this second white light but may do so.
- (iii) These two white lights shall be so placed in a line with and over the keel that one shall be at least 15 feet higher than the other and in such a position that the forward light shall always be shown lower than the after one. The horizontal distance between the two white lights shall be at least three times the vertical distance. The lower of these two white lights or, if only one is carried, then that light shall be placed at a height above the hull of not less than 20 feet, and, if the breadth of the vessel exceeds 20 feet, then at a height above the hull not less than such breadth, so however that the light need not be placed at a greater height above the hull than 40 feet. In all circumstances the light or lights, as the case may be, shall be so placed as to be clear of and above all other lights and obstructing superstructures.
- (iv) On the starboard side a green light so constructed as to show an unbroken light over an arc of the horizon of 112½ degrees (10 points of the compass), so fixed as to show the light from right ahead to 22½ degrees (2 points) abaft the beam on the starboard side, and of such a character as to be visible at a distance of at least 2 miles.
- (v) On the port side a red light so constructed as to show an unbroken light over an arc of the horizon of 112½ degrees (10 points of the compass), so fixed as to show the light from right ahead to 22½ degrees (2 points) abaft the beam on the port side, and of such a character as to be visible at a distance of at least 2 miles.
- (vi) The said green and red sidelights shall be fitted with inboard screens projecting at least 3 feet forward from the light, so as to prevent these lights from being seen across the bows.

(b) A seaplane under way on the water shall carry:
- (i) In the forepart amidships where it can best be seen a white light, so constructed as to show an unbroken light over an arc of the horizon of 220 degrees of the compass, so fixed as to show the light 110 degrees on each side of the seaplane, namely, from right ahead to 20 degrees abaft the beam on either side, and of such a character as to be visible at a distance of at least 3 miles.
- (ii) On the right or starboard wing tip a green light, so constructed as to show an unbroken light over an arc of the horizon of 110 degrees of the compass, so fixed as to show the light from right ahead to 20 degrees abaft the beam on the starboard side, and of such a character as to be visible at a distance of at least 2 miles.

(iii) On the left or port wing tip a red light, so constructed as to show an unbroken light over an arc of the horizon of 110 degrees of the compass, so fixed as to show the light from right ahead to 20 degrees abaft the beam on the port side, and of such a character as to be visible at a distance of at least 2 miles.

Rule 3. (a) A power-driven vessel when towing or pushing another vessel or seaplane shall, in addition to her sidelights, carry two white lights in a vertical line one over the other, not less than 6 feet apart, and when towing and the length of the tow, measuring from the stern of the towing vessel to the stern of the last vessel towed, exceeds 600 feet, shall carry three white lights in a vertical line one over the other, so that the upper and lower lights shall be the same distance from, and not less than 6 feet above or below, the middle light. Each of these lights shall be of the same construction and character and one of them shall be carried in the same position as the white light prescribed in Rule 2(a)(i). None of these lights shall be carried at a height of less than 14 feet above the hull. In a vessel with a single mast, such lights may be carried on the mast.

(b) The towing vessel shall also show either the stern light prescribed in Rule 10 or in lieu of that light a small white light abaft the funnel or after-mast for the tow to steer by, but such light shall not be visiable forward of the beam.

(c) Between sunrise and sunset a power-driven vessel engaged in towing, if the length of tow exceeds 600 feet, shall carry, where it can best be seen, a black diamond shape at least 2 feet in diameter.

(d) A seaplane on the water, when towing one or more seaplanes or vessels, shall carry the lights prescribed in Rule 2(b)(i), (ii) and (iii); and, in addition, she shall carry a second white light of the same construction and character as the white light prescribed in Rule 2(b)(i), and in a vertical line at least 6 feet above or below such light.

Rule 3. Note that the International Rule prescribes two 20-point white lights at least 6 feet apart when towing one vessel regardless of the distance of the latter from the towing vessel. An additional light (making three 20-point white lights) is carried if the tow is over 600 feet long and there are two or more vessels in it.

The Inland Rule requires (1) two white lights not less than 3 feet apart, when towing alongside, and three such lights when towing any number of vessels astern regardless of the tow's length. (2) These lights may be carried forward in the position of the masthead light, or aft on the same mast as the range light. (3) If one of the towing lights is the forward white light required by all steam vessels, each of them shall be 20-point lights; and if one of the towing lights is the range light, each shall be visible all around the horizon.

Rule 4. (a) A vessel which is not under command shall carry, where they can best be seen, and, if a power-driven vessel, in lieu of the lights prescribed in Rule 2(a)(i) and (ii), two red lights in a vertical line one over the other not less than 6 feet apart, and of such a character as to be visible all round the horizon at a distance of at least 2 miles. By day, she shall carry in a vertical line one over the other not less than 6 feet apart, where they can best be seen, two black balls or shapes each not less than 2 feet in diameter.

(b) A seaplane on the water which is not under command may carry, where they can best be seen, and in lieu of the light prescribed in Rule 2(b)(i), two red lights in a vertical line, one over the other, not less than 3 feet apart, and of such a character as to be visible all round the horizon at a distance of at least 2 miles, and may by day carry in a vertical line one over the other not less than 3 feet apart, where they can best be seen, two black balls or shapes, each not less than 2 feet in diameter.

(c) A vessel engaged in laying or in picking up a submarine cable or navigation mark, or a vessel engaged in surveying or underwater operations, or a vessel engaged in replenishment at sea, or in the launching or recovery of aircraft when from the nature of her work she is unable to get out of the way of approaching vessels, shall carry, in lieu of the lights prescribed in Rule 2(a)(i) and (ii), or Rule 7(a)(i), three lights in a vertical line one over the other so that the upper and lower lights shall be the same distance from, and not less than 6 feet above or below, the middle light. The highest and lowest of these lights shall be red, and the middle light shall be white, and they shall be of such a character as to be visible all round the horizon at a distance of at least 2 miles. By day, she shall carry in a vertical line one over the other not less than 6 feet apart, where they can best be seen, three shapes each not less than 2 feet in diameter, of which the highest and lowest shall be globular in shape and red in colour, and the middle one diamond in shape and white.

(d) (i) A vessel engaged in minesweeping operations shall carry at the fore truck a green light, and at the end or ends of the fore yard on the side or sides on which danger exists, another such light or lights. These lights shall be carried in addition to the light prescribed in Rule 2(a)(i) or Rule 7(a)(i), as appropriate, and shall be of such a character as to be visible all round the horizon at a distance of at least 2 miles. By day she shall carry black balls, not less than 2 feet in diameter, in the same position as the green lights.

(ii) The showing of these lights or balls indicates that it is dangerous for other vessels to approach closer than 3,000 feet astern of the minesweeper or 1,500 feet on the side or sides on which danger exists.

(e) The vessels and seaplanes referred to in this Rule, when not making way through the water, shall show neither the coloured sidelights nor the stern light, but when making way they shall show them.

(f) The lights and shapes prescribed in this Rule are to be taken by other vessels and seaplanes as signals that the vessel or seaplane showing them is not under command and cannot therefore get out of the way.

(g) These signals are not signals of vessels in distress and requiring assistance. Such signals are contained in Rule 31.

Rule 4.—This is an International Rule only. A vessel not under command or disabled in inland waters must warn an approaching vessel by the danger signal (see Rule 28 (b)), or if requiring assistance, by distress signal prescribed in Rule 12 to attract attention.

The shapes and lights required by this Rule for a submarine cable-ship at work might be said to be permissible in inland waters, since therein there is no other meaning allotted to this signal; but no such signal is provided in the Inland Rules, and therefore no authority here for the display of such.

Rule 5. (a) A sailing vessel under way and any vessel or seaplane being towed shall carry the same lights as are prescribed in Rule 2 for a power-driven vessel or a seaplane under way, respectively, with the exception of the white lights prescribed therein, which they shall never carry. They shall also carry stern lights as prescribed in Rule 10, provided that vessels towed, except the last vessel of a tow, may carry, in lieu of such stern light, a small white light as prescribed in Rule 3(b).

(b) In addition to the lights prescribed in section (a), a sailing vessel may carry on the top of the foremast two lights in a vertical line one over the other, sufficiently separated so as to be clearly distinguished. The upper light shall be red and the lower light shall be green. Both lights shall be constructed and fixed as prescribed in Rule 2(a)(i) and shall be visible at a distance of at least 2 miles.

(c) A vessel being pushed ahead shall carry, at the forward end, on the starboard side a green light and on the port side a red light, which shall have the same characteristics as the lights prescribed in Rule 2(a)(iv) and (v) and shall be screened as provided in Rule 2(a)(vi), provided that any number of vessels pushed ahead in a group shall be lighted as one vessel.

(d) Between sunrise and sunset a vessel being towed, if the length of the tow exceeds 600 feet, shall carry where it can best be seen a black diamond shape at least 2 feet in diameter.

Rule 5. The International Rule requires the colored side lights only for any vessel being towed, as well as for the sailing vessel, which would include any type of raft, however distinct from a "vessel" in description. The purpose aimed at, in the case of the "vessel towed" is to declare the presence of a possible danger to an approaching vessel.

Rule 6. (a) When it is not possible on account of bad weather or other sufficient cause to fix the green and red sidelights, these lights shall be kept at hand lighted and ready for immediate use, and shall, on the approach of or to other vessels, be exhibited on their respective sides in sufficient time to prevent collision, in such manner as to make them most visible, and so that the green light shall not be seen on the port side nor the red light on the starboard side, nor, if practicable, more than 22½ degrees (2 points) abaft the beam on their respective sides.

(b) To make the use of these portable lights more certain and easy, the lanterns containing them shall each be painted outside with the colour of the lights they respectively contain, and shall be provided with proper screens.

Rule 7. Power-driven vessels of less than 65 feet in length, vessels under oars or sails of less than 40 feet in length, and rowing boats, when under way shall not be required to carry the lights prescribed in Rules 2, 3 and 5, but if they do not carry them they shall be provided with the following lights:

(a) Power-driven vessels of less than 65 feet in length, except as provided in sections (b) and (c), shall carry:

    (i) In the forepart of the vessel, where it can best be seen, and at a height above the gunwale of not less than 9 feet, a white light constructed and fixed as prescribed in Rule 2(a)(i) and of such a character as to be visible at a distance of at least 3 miles.

    (ii) Green and red sidelights constructed and fixed as prescribed in Rule 2(a)(iv) and (v), and of such a character as to be visible at a distance of at least 1 mile, or a combined lantern showing a green light and a red light from right ahead to 22½ degrees (2 points) abaft the beam on their respective sides. Such lantern shall be carried not less than 3 feet below the white light.

(b) Power-driven vessels of less than 65 feet in length when towing or pushing another vessel shall carry:

    (i) In addition to the sidelights or the combined lantern prescribed in section (a)(ii) two white lights in a vertical line, one over the other not less than 4 feet apart. Each of these lights shall be of the same construction and character as the white light prescribed in section (a)(i) and one of them shall be carried in the same position. In a vessel with a single mast such lights may be carried on the mast.

   (ii) Either a stern light as prescribed in Rule 10 or in lieu of that light a small white light abaft the funnel or aftermast for the tow to steer by, but such light shall not be visible forward of the beam.

(c) Power-driven vessels of less than 40 feet in length may carry the white light at a less height than 9 feet above the gunwale but it shall be carried not less than 3 feet above the sidelights or the combined lantern prescribed in section (a)(ii).

(d) Vessels of less than 40 feet in length, under oars or sails, except as provided in section (f), shall, if they do not carry the sidelights, carry, where it can best be seen, a lantern showing a green light on one side and a red light on the other, of such a character as to be visible at a distance of at least 1 mile, and so fixed that the green light shall not be seen on the port side, nor the red light on the starboard side. Where it is not possible to fix this light, it shall be kept ready for immediate use and shall be exhibited in sufficient time to prevent collision and so that the green light shall not be seen on the port side nor the red light on the starboard side.

(e) The vessels referred to in this Rule when being towed shall carry the sidelights or the combined lantern prescribed in sections (a) or (d) of this Rule, as appropriate, and a stern light as prescribed in Rule 10, or, except the last vessel of the tow, a small white light as prescribed in section (b)(ii). When being pushed ahead they shall carry at the forward end the sidelights or combined lantern prescribed in sections (a) or (d) of this ·Rule, as appropriate, provided that any number of vessels referred to in this Rule when pushed ahead in a group shall be lighted as one vessel under this Rule unless the overall length of the group exceeds 65 feet when the provisions of Rule 5(c) shall apply.

(f) Small rowing boats, whether under oars or sail, shall only be required to have ready at hand an electric torch or a lighted lantern, showing a white light, which shall be exhibited in sufficient time to prevent collision.

(g) The vessels and boats referred to in this Rule shall not be required to carry the lights or shapes prescribed in Rules 4(a) and 11(e) and the size of their day signals may be less than is prescribed in Rules 4(c) and 11(c).

Rule 8. (a) A power-driven pilot-vessel when engaged on pilotage duty and under way:

   (i) Shall carry a white light at the masthead at a height of not less than 20 feet above the hull, visible all round the horizon at a distance of at least 3 miles and at a distance of 8 feet below it a red light similar in construction and character. If such a vessel is of less than 65 feet in length she may carry the white light at a height of not less than 9 feet above the gunwale and the red light at a distance of 4 feet below the white light.

   (ii) Shall carry the sidelights or lanterns prescribed in Rule 2(a)(iv) and (v) or Rule 7(a)(ii) or (d), as appropriate, and the stern light prescribed in Rule 10.

   (iii) Shall show one or more flare-up lights at intervals not exceeding 10 minutes. An intermittent white light visible all round the horizon may be used in lieu of flare-up lights.

(b) A sailing pilot-vessel when engaged on pilotage duty and under way:

   (i) Shall carry a white light at the masthead visible all round the horizon at a distance of at least 3 miles.

(ii) Shall be provided with the sidelights or lantern prescribed in Rules 5(a) or 7(d), as appropriate, and shall, on the near approach of or to other vessels, have such lights ready for use, and shall show them at short intervals to indicate the direction in which she is heading, but the green light shall not be shown on the port side nor the red light on the starboard side. She shall also carry the stern light prescribed in Rule 10.

(iii) Shall show one or more flare-up lights at intervals not exceeding 10 minutes.

(c) A pilot-vessel when engaged on pilotage duty and not under way shall carry the lights and show the flares prescribed in sections (a)(i) and (iii) or (b)(i) and (iii), as appropriate, and if at anchor shall also carry the anchor lights prescribed in Rule 11.

(d) A pilot-vessel when not engaged on pilotage duty shall show the lights or shapes for a similar vessel of her length.

Rule 9. (a) Fishing vessels when not engaged in fishing shall show the lights or shapes for similar vessels of their length.

(b) Vessels engaged in fishing, when under way or at anchor, shall show only the lights and shapes prescribed in this Rule, which lights and shapes shall be visible at a distance of at least 2 miles.

(c) (i) Vessels when engaged in trawling, by which is meant the dragging of a dredge net or other apparatus through the water, shall carry two lights in a vertical line, one over the other, not less than 4 feet nor more than 12 feet apart. The upper of these lights shall be green and the lower light white and each shall be visible all round the horizon. The lower of these two lights shall be carried at a height above the sidelights not less than twice the distance between the two vertical lights.

(ii) Such vessels may in addition carry a white light similar in construction to the white light prescribed in Rule 2(a)(i) but such light shall be carried lower than and abaft the all-round green and white lights.

(d) Vessels when engaged in fishing, except vessels engaged in trawling, shall carry the lights prescribed in section (c)(i) except that the upper of the two vertical lights shall be red. Such vessels if of less than 40 feet in length may carry the red light at a height of not less than 9 feet above the gunwale and the white light not less than 3 feet below the red light.

(e) Vessels referred to in sections (c) and (d), when making way through the water, shall carry the sidelights or lanterns prescribed in Rule 2(a)(iv) and (v) or Rule 7(a)(ii) or (d), as appropriate, and the stern light prescribed in Rule 10. When not making way through the water they shall show neither the sidelights nor the stern light.

(f) Vessels referred to in section (d) with outlying gear extending more than 500 feet horizontally into the seaway shall carry an additional all-round white light at a horizontal distance of not less than 6 feet nor more than 20 feet away from the vertical lights in the direction of the outlying gear. This additional white light shall be placed at a height not exceeding that of the white light prescribed in section (c)(i) and not lower than the sidelights.

(g) In addition to the lights which they are required by this Rule to carry, vessels engaged in fishing may, if necessary in order to attract the attention of an approaching vessel, use a flare-up light, or may direct the beam of their searchlight in the direction of a danger threatening the approaching vessel, in such a way as not to embarrass other vessels. They may also use working lights but fishermen shall take into account that specially bright or insufficiently screened working lights may impair the visibility and distinctive character of the lights prescribed in this Rule.

(h) By day vessels when engaged in fishing shall indicate their occupation by displaying where it can best be seen a black shape consisting of two cones each not less than 2 feet in diameter with their points together one above the other. Such vessels if of less than 65 feet in length may substitute a basket for such black shape. If their outlying gear extends more than 500 feet horizontally into the seaway vessels engaged in fishing shall display in addition one black conical shape, point upwards, in the direction of the outlying gear.

NOTE. Vessels fishing with trolling lines are not "engaged in fishing" as defined in Rule 1(c)(xiv).

Rule 9. Under Inland Rules all vessels engaged in fishing carry the same lights, and in no case are required to carry side lights. International Rules prescribe different lights for the various methods of fishing, viz., trawling or dredging, drift-net fishing, and line-fishing. Trawlers at work have very little way upon them. Drifters lie at the lee end of their nets, which may be as long as 1 to 2 miles, and buoyed at various distances. Line-fishing may be carried on by a drifting vessel, or she may tow a set of lines while under way.

Line-fishing work is usually done by day, drift-net fishing by night, and trawling, dredging, or "drag-net" fishing by day or by night.

These International Rules for fishing vessels were principally drawn up for craft on the western coasts of Europe and in the waters of China and Japan.

There are no special fog signals for vessels engaged in fishing under the Inland Rules, all the fog signals prescribed being contained in Article 15.

Rule 10. (a) Except where otherwise provided in these Rules, a vessel when under way shall carry at her stern a white light, so constructed that it shall show an unbroken light over an arc of the horizon of 135 degrees (12 points of the compass), so fixed as to show the light 67½ degrees (6 points) from right aft on each side of the vessel, and of such a character as to be visible at a distance of at least 2 miles.

(b) In a small vessel, if it is not possible on account of bad weather or other sufficient cause for this light to be fixed, an electric torch or a lighted lantern showing a white light shall be kept at hand ready for use and shall, on the approach of an overtaking vessel, be shown in sufficient time to prevent collision.

(c) A seaplane on the water when under way shall carry on her tail a white light, so constructed as to show an unbroken light over an arc of the horizon of 140 degrees of the compass, so fixed as to show the light 70 degrees from right aft on each side of the seaplane, and of such a character as to be visible at a distance of at least 2 miles.

Rule 10. Note that the after range light required for inland steam vessels provides the necessary signal for an overtaken vessel, and that a sea-going steam vessel, or any other type of vessel in inland waters is not required to carry the stern light, if fixed, according to any prescribed rule. The International Rule prescribes the optional stern light to be of a certain construction and character.

Rule 11. (a) A vessel of less than 150 feet in length, when at anchor, shall carry in the forepart of the vessel, where it can best be seen, a white light visible all round the horizon at a distance of at least 2 miles. Such a vessel may also carry a second white light in the position prescribed in section (b) of this Rule but shall not be required to do so. The second white light, if carried, shall be visible at a distance of at least 2 miles and so placed as to be as far as possible visible all round the horizon.

(b) A vessel of 150 feet or more in length, when at anchor, shall carry near the stem of the vessel, at a height of not less than 20 feet above the hull, one such light, and at or near the stern of the vessel and at such a height that it shall be not less than 15 feet lower than the forward light, another such light. Both these lights shall be visible at a distance of at least 3 miles and so placed as to be as far as possible visible all round the horizon.

(c) Between sunrise and sunset every vessel when at anchor shall carry in the forepart of the vessel, where it can best be seen, one black ball not less than 2 feet in diameter.

(d) A vessel engaged in laying or in picking up a submarine cable or navigation mark, or a vessel engaged in surveying or underwater operations, when at anchor, shall carry the lights or shapes prescribed in Rule 4(c) in addition to those prescribed in the appropriate preceding sections of this Rule.

(e) A vessel aground shall carry the light or lights prescribed in sections (a) or (b) and the two red lights prescribed in Rule 4(a). By day she shall carry, where they can best be seen, three black balls, each not less than 2 feet in diameter, placed in a vertical line one over the other, not less than 6 feet apart.

(f) A seaplane on the water under 140 feet in length, when at anchor, shall carry, where it can best be seen, a white light, visible all round the horizon at a distance of at least 2 miles.

(g) A seaplane on the water 150 feet or upwards in length, when at anchor, shall carry, where they can best be seen, a white light forward and a white light aft, both lights visible all round the horizon at a distance of at least 3 miles; and, in addition, if the seaplane is more than 150 feet in span, a white light on each side to indicate the maximum span, and visible, so far as practicable, all round the horizon at a distance of 1 mile.

(h) A seaplane aground shall carry an anchor light or lights as prescribed in sections (f) and (g), and in addition may carry two red lights in a vertical line, at least 3 feet apart, so placed as to be visible all round the horizon.

Rule 12. Every vessel or seaplane on the water may, if necessary in order to attract attention, in addition to the lights which she is by these Rules required to carry, show a flare-up light or use a detonating or other efficient sound signal that cannot be mistaken for any signal authorized elsewhere under these Rules.

Rule 12. The "flare-up" light is now defined as any bright white light conspicuously displayed. In former days it was a flaming torch.

Rule 13. (a) Nothing in these Rules shall interfere with the operation of any special rules made by the Government of any nation with respect to additional station and signal lights for ships of war, for vessels sailing under convoy, for fishing vessels engaged in fishing as a fleet or for seaplanes on the water.

(b) Whenever the Government concerned shall have determined that a naval or other military vessel or waterborne seaplane of special construction or purpose cannot comply fully with the provisions of any of these Rules with respect to the number, position, range or arc of visibility of lights or shapes, without interfering with the military function of the vessel or seaplane, such vessel or seaplane shall comply with such other provisions in regard to the number, position, range or arc of visibility of lights or shapes as her Government shall have determined to be the closest possible compliance with these Rules in respect of that vessel or seaplane.

Rule 14. A vessel proceeding under sail, when also being propelled by machinery, shall carry in the daytime forward, where it can best be seen, one black conical shape, point downwards, not less than 2 feet in diameter at its base.

Part C. SOUND SIGNALS AND CONDUCT IN RESTRICTED VISIBILITY—PRELIMINARY

1. *The possession of information obtained from radar does not relieve any vessel of the obligation of conforming strictly with the Rules and, in particular, the obligations contained in Rules 15 and 16.*
2. *The Annex to the Rules contains recommendations intended to assist in the use of radar as an aid to avoiding collision in restricted visibility.*

Rule 15. (a) A power-driven vessel of 40 feet or more in length shall be provided with an efficient whistle, sounded by steam or by some substitute for steam, so placed that the sound may not be intercepted by any obstruction, and with an efficient fog horn to be sounded by mechanical means, and also with an efficient bell. A sailing vessel of 40 feet or more in length shall be provided with a similar fog horn and bell.

(b) All signals prescribed in this Rule for vessels under way shall be given:
    (i) by power-driven vessels on the whistle;
    (ii) by sailing vessels on the fog horn;
    (iii) by vessels towed on the whistle or fog horn.

(c) In fog, mist, falling snow, heavy rainstorms, or any other condition similarly restricting visibility, whether by day or night, the signals prescribed in this Rule shall be used as follows:
    (i) A power-driven vessel making way through the water shall sound at intervals of not more than 2 minutes a prolonged blast.
    (ii) A power-driven vessel under way, but stopped and making no way through the water, shall sound at intervals of not more than 2 minutes two prolonged blasts, with an interval of about 1 second between them.
    (iii) A sailing vessel under way shall sound, at intervals of not more than 1 minute, when on the starboard tack one blast, when on the port tack two blasts in succession, and when with the wind abaft the beam three blasts in succession.
    (iv) A vessel when at anchor shall at intervals of not more than 1 minute ring the bell rapidly for about 5 seconds. In vessels of more than 350 feet in length the bell shall be sounded in the forepart of the vessel, and in addition there shall be sounded in the after part of the vessel, at intervals of not more than 1 minute for about 5 seconds, a gong or other instrument, the tone and sounding of which cannot be confused with that of the bell. Every vessel at anchor may in addition, in accordance with Rule 12, sound three blasts in succession, namely, one short, one prolonged, and one short blast, to give warning of her position and of the possibility of collision to an approaching vessel.
    (v) A vessel when towing, a vessel engaged in laying or in picking up a submarine cable or navigation mark, and a vessel under way which is unable to get out of the way of an approaching vessel through being not under command or unable to manoeuvre as required by these Rules shall, instead of the signals prescribed in sub-sections (i), (ii) and (iii) sound, at intervals of not more

than 1 minute, three blasts in succession, namely, one prolonged blast followed by two short blasts.

(vi) A vessel towed, or, if more than one vessel is towed, only the last vessel of the tow, if manned, shall, at intervals of not more than 1 minute, sound four blasts in succession, namely, one prolonged blast followed by three short blasts. When practicable, this signal shall be made immediately after the signal made by the towing vessel.

(vii) A vessel aground shall give the bell signal and, if required, the gong signal, prescribed in sub-section (iv) and shall, in addition, give 3 separate and distinct strokes on the bell immediately before and after such rapid ringing of the bell.

(viii) A vessel engaged in fishing when under way or at anchor shall at intervals of not more than 1 minute sound the signal prescribed in sub-section (v). A vessel when fishing with trolling lines and under way shall sound the signals prescribed in sub-sections (i), (ii) or (iii) as may be appropriate.

(ix) A vessel of less than 40 feet in length, a rowing boat, or a seaplane on the water, shall not be obliged to give the above-mentioned signals but if she does not, she shall make some other efficient sound signal at intervals of more not than 1 minute.

(x) A power-driven pilot-vessel when engaged on pilotage duty may, in addition to the signals prescribed in sub-sections (i), (ii) and (iv), sound an identity signal consisting of 4 short blasts.

Rule 15.—Signal blasts here are never given by vessels at anchor. Ringing of ship's bell is never used as an underway signal, excepting that provided in (c)(x) for vessels fishing.

Rule 15 (c)(i).—This is similar to Inland Art. 15 (a), excepting the interval between blasts. Maximum intervals for all fog signals under Inland Rules, and for those given by sailing vessels, all vessels at anchor, and all vessels fishing under International Rules, is one minute.

Note that the fog horn required for sailing vessels and vessels towed must be sounded mechanically; the Inland Rule specifies no particular means for this.

(c)(ii). The two prolonged blasts required by this paragraph, it must be noted, are prescribed for a steam vessel stopped dead in the water on the high seas, and must not be used in inland waters.

(c)(iii). The word "tack" here means the course on which the vessel is sailing relative to the wind direction when closehauled, or nearly so. Thus, "when on the port tack" the wind is on the beam; or forward of the beam, on the port side.

Observing the true direction of the wind, the course on which a sailing vessel may be steering can be estimated to within 2 or 3 points by the one or two blast signal indicating the tack on which she is sailing; she may, however, be heading anywhere on an arc of the compass of 16 points when sounding the 3 blasts "with the wind abaft the beam." The blast here is one of about 2 seconds' duration.

(c)(iv). Where two or more vessels are lying at anchor and made fast together, each vessel in the group must sound the required signal. The courts have stressed this particular duty of vessels anchored in fog, and have on many occasions emphatically declared it necessary that the interval between sound signals be much less than the required maximum of one minute when the signals of an approaching vessel are heard.

(c)(v). Note that the signal for a vessel "not under command" is prescribed by the International Rules only. Also note that a steam vessel when towing is

provided for under Inland Rules, while a vessel when towing is the wording of the International Rule.

From this it follows that a sailing vessel, if towing in inland waters, is required to sound the signals prescribed by subdivision (c)(ii).

Rule 16. (a) Every vessel, or seaplane when taxi-ing on the water, shall, in fog, mist, falling snow, heavy rainstorms or any other condition similarly restricting visibility, go at a moderate speed, having careful regard to the existing circumstances and conditions.

(b) A power-driven vessel hearing, apparently forward of her beam, the fog-signal of a vessel the position of which is not ascertained, shall, so far as the circumstances of the case admit, stop her engines, and then navigate with caution until danger of collision is over.

(c) A power-driven vessel which detects the presence of another vessel forward of her beam before hearing her fog signal or sighting her visually may take early and substantial action to avoid a close quarters situation but, if this cannot be avoided, she shall, so far as the circumstances of the case admit, stop her engines in proper time to avoid collision and then navigate with caution until danger of collision is over.

Rule 16. The necessity for an authoritative definition of moderate speed naturally attaches itself to this article. Consideration of the numerous court decisions and opinions on this point in the past has led to the definition of "moderate speed" by the U. S. Supreme Court as "that speed at which it is possible to stop the vessel's way within half the distance of visibility." Such a speed would, of course, necessitate bare steerage-way in very thick weather, when, if in crowded waters, a vessel should, if practicable, come to an anchor.

It might be noted that, in a few cases of collision, vessels have been found at fault for having left an anchorage in such conditions.

Sound signals in fog may at times be very deceptive as to direction from which they may be heard. Note the words "apparently forward of the beam": if there is the least doubt regarding this direction, it is good practice to assume the signal is forward of the beam, and accordingly stop the engines.

Part D.   STEERING AND SAILING RULES—PRELIMINARY

1. *In obeying and construing these Rules, any action taken should be positive, in ample time, and with due regard to the observance of good seamanship.*

2. *Risk of collision can, when circumstances permit, be ascertained by carefully watching the compass bearing of an approaching vessel. If the bearing does not appreciably change, such risk should be deemed to exist.*

3. *Mariners should bear in mind that seaplanes in the act of landing or taking off, or operating under adverse weather conditions, may be unable to change their intended action at the last moment.*

4. *Rules 17 to 24 apply only to vessels in sight of one another.*

Rule 17. (a) When two sailing vessels are approaching one another, so as to involve risk of collision, one of them shall keep out of the way of the other as follows:

   (i) When each has the wind on a different side, the vessel which has the wind on the port side shall keep out of the way of the other.

   (ii) When both have the wind on the same side, the vessel which is to windward shall keep out of the way of the vessel which is to leeward.

(b) For the purposes of this Rule the windward side shall be deemed to be the side opposite to that on which the mainsail is carried or, in the case of a square-rigged vessel, the side opposite to that on which the largest fore-and-aft sail is carried.

Rule 17.—Rules 21 and 22 should be noted in connection with these sailing rules.

The rule states nothing as to a closehauled vessel's headway. A vessel "hove to" on port tack must, therefore, keep clear of a vessel sailing on starboard tack closehauled, bearing in mind Rules 21, 27 and 29.

Rule 18. (a) When two power-driven vessels are meeting end on, or nearly end on, so as to involve risk of collision, each shall alter her course to starboard, so that each may pass on the port side of the other. This Rule only applies to cases where vessels are meeting end on, or nearly end on, in such a manner as to involve risk of collision, and does not apply to two vessels which must, if both keep on their respective course, pass clear of each other. The only cases to which it does apply are when each of two vessels is end on, or nearly end on, to the other; in other words, to cases in which, by day, each vessel sees the masts of the other in a line, or nearly in a line, with her own; and by night, to cases in which each vessel is in such a position as to see both the sidelights of the other. It does not apply, by day, to cases in which a vessel sees another ahead crossing her own course; or, by night, to cases where the red light of one vessel is opposed to the red light of the other or where the green light of one vessel is opposed to the green light of the other or where a red light without a green light or a green light without a red light is seen ahead, or where both green and red lights are seen anywhere but ahead.

(b) For the purposes of this Rule and Rules 19 to 29 inclusive, except Rule 20(c) and Rule 28, a seaplane on the water shall be deemed to be a vessel, and the expression "power-driven vessel" shall be construed accordingly.

Rule 19. When two power-driven vessels are crossing, so as to involve risk of collision, the vessel which has the other on her own starboard side shall keep out of the way of the other.

Rule 20. (a) When a power-driven vessel and a sailing vessel are proceeding in such directions as to involve risk of collision, except as provided for in Rules 24 and 26, the power-driven vessel shall keep out of the way of the sailing vessel.

(b) This Rule shall not give to a sailing vessel the right to hamper, in a narrow channel, the safe passage of a power-driven vessel which can navigate only inside such channel.

(c) A seaplane on the water shall, in general, keep well clear of all vessels and avoid impeding their navigation. In circumstances, however, where risk of collision exists, she shall comply with these Rules.

Rule 20.—Note that, in the case of a sailing vessel overtaking a powered vessel, Rule 24 makes the former the burdened vessel. This is the only situation in which a sailing vessel must keep clear of a powered vessel.

Rule 21. Where by any of these Rules one of two vessels is to keep out of the way, the other shall keep her course and speed. When, from any cause, the latter vessel finds herself so close that collision cannot be avoided by the action of the giving-way vessel alone, she also shall take such action as will best aid to avert collision (see Rules 27 and 29).

Rule 21. The "privileged" vessel must hold her course and speed until the behavior of the "burdened" vessel shows a collision to be inevitable. Action must be taken by the "privileged" vessel at this critical point, according to Rule 27 "in order to avoid immediate danger." Little or no fault would be found by the court against a "privileged" vessel which, having taken seamanlike action to avoid an impending collision, failed to accomplish her purpose.

The interpretation of "holding course and speed" is held by the courts as not necessarily a steady compass point heading, or a constant rate of speed (as special conditions may occur, particularly in coastal waters), but that course, or track, and speed, variable or otherwise, which the "privileged" vessel might have pursued had there been no other vessel in the vicinity. It is the duty of approaching vessels to observe each other's purposes in navigating in localities where varying compass headings and variations in speed are required.

Perhaps good seamanship and navigational skill, rather than a knowledge of the Rules of the Road are the controlling factors in avoiding collisions under the conditions noted.

Rule 22. Every vessel which is directed by these Rules to keep out of the way of another vessel shall, so far as possible, take positive early action to comply with this obligation, and shall, if the circumstances of the case admit, avoid crossing ahead of the other.

Rule 23. Every power-driven vessel which is directed by these Rules to keep out of the way of another vessel shall, on approaching her, if necessary, slacken her speed or stop or reverse.

Rule 24. (a) Notwithstanding anything contained in these Rules, every vessel overtaking any other shall keep out of the way of the overtaken vessel.

(b) Every vessel coming up with another vessel from any direction more than 22½ degrees (2 points) abaft her beam, i.e., in such a position, with reference to the vessel which she is overtaking, that at night she would be unable to see either of that vessel's sidelights, shall be deemed to be an overtaking vessel; and no subsequent alteration of the bearing between the two vessels shall make the overtaking vessel a crossing vessel within the meaning of these Rules, or relieve her of the duty of keeping clear of the overtaken vessel until she is finally past and clear.

(c) If the overtaking vessel cannot determine with certainty whether she is forward of or abaft this direction from the other vessel, she shall assume that she is an overtaking vessel and keep out of the way.

Rule 24.

The overtaking vessel under International Rules, it must be remembered, should, as in all cases where vessels are required to "take any course authorized by these rules," and are within sight of each other, indicate her change of course by the one or two blast signal. No assent by the overtaken vessel is required. The International signal merely announces the giving-way vessel's action.

Note that the overtaking vessel continues to be the "burdened" vessel until she is "finally past and clear" of the overtaken vessel.

Rule 25. (a) In a narrow channel every power-driven vessel when proceeding along the course of the channel shall, when it is safe and practicable, keep to that side of the fairway or mid-channel which lies on the starboard side of such vessel.

(b) Whenever a power-driven vessel is nearing a bend in a channel where a vessel approaching from the other direction cannot be seen, such power-driven vessel, when she shall have arrived within one-half (½) mile of the bend, shall give a signal by one prolonged blast on her whistle which signal shall be answered by a similar blast given by any approaching power-driven vessel that may be within hearing around the bend. Regardless of whether an approaching vessel on the farther side of the bend is heard, such bend shall be rounded with alertness and caution.

(c) In a narrow channel a power-driven vessel of less than 65 feet in length shall not hamper the safe passage of a vessel which can navigate only inside such channel.

Rule 25. A collision resulting from one of two steam vessels being on the wrong side of the channel leaves such vessel, by this Rule, wholly at fault. Navigation conditions, such as easier steering due to tidal conditions on the left side of the channel, must not induce the careful seaman to depart from this rule.

Rule 26. All vessels not engaged in fishing, except vessels to which the provisions of Rule 4 apply, shall, when under way, keep out of the way of vessels engaged in fishing. This Rule shall not give to any vessel engaged in fishing the right of obstructing a fairway used by vessels other than fishing vessels.

Rule 27. In obeying and construing these Rules due regard shall be had to all dangers of navigation and collision, and to any special circumstances, including the limitations of the craft involved, which may render a departure from the above Rules necessary in order to avoid immediate danger.

Rule 27. This is often called the General Prudential Rule. Its application begins at the time a departure from the steering and sailing rules becomes necessary "in order to avoid immediate danger." In justifying such departure from the rules, it must be clearly shown that the danger of collision or the presence of any other navigational danger was so evident that adherence to the rules was impossible under the circumstances.

Part E. SOUND SIGNALS FOR VESSELS IN SIGHT OF ONE ANOTHER

Rule 28. (a) When vessels are in sight of one another, a power-driven vessel under way, in taking any course authorized or required by these Rules, shall indicate that course by the following signals on her whistle, namely:

One short blast to mean "I am altering my course to starboard".

Two short blasts to mean "I am altering my course to port".

Three short blasts to mean "My engines are going astern".

(b) Whenever a power-driven vessel which, under these Rules, is to keep her course and speed, is in sight of another vessel and is in doubt whether sufficient action is being taken by the other vessel to avert collision, she may indicate such doubt by giving at least five short and rapid blasts on the whistle. The giving of such a signal shall not relieve a vessel of her obligations under Rules 27 and 29 or any other Rule, or of her duty to indicate any action taken under these Rules by giving the appropriate sound signals laid down in this Rule.

(c) Any whistle signal mentioned in this Rule may be further indicated by a visual signal consisting of a white light visible all round the horizon at a distance of at least 5 miles, and so devised that it will operate simultaneously and in conjunction with the whistle-sounding mechanism and remain lighted and visible during the same period as the sound signal.

(d) Nothing in these Rules shall interfere with the operation of any special rules made by the Government of any nation with respect to the use of additional whistle signals between ships of war or vessels sailing under convoy.

Rule 28.—The whistle signals of one or two short blasts, it must be remembered, are purely "helm" or "steering" signals in international waters, and are given only to announce the fact that a change of course as "authorized or required by these rules" is actually being executed by a steam vessel. Since there is no other meaning attached to this international rule, the answering of these signals is wholly at variance with the Rule, and herein lies the great and sometimes awkward difference from the one- and two-blast signals under the Pilot Rules.

Part F. MISCELLANEOUS

Rule 29. Nothing in these Rules shall exonerate any vessel, or the owner, master or crew thereof, from the consequences of any neglect to carry lights or signals, or of any neglect to keep a proper look-out, or of the neglect of any precaution which may be required by the ordinary practice of seaman, or by the special circumstances of the case.

Rule 30. Nothing in these Rules shall interfere with the operation of a special rule duly made by local authority relative to the navigation of any harbour, river, lake, or inland water, including a reserved seaplane area.

Rule 31. *Distress Signals* (a) When a vessel or seaplane on the water is in distress and requires assistance from other vessels or from the shore, the following shall be the signals to be used or displayed by her, either together or separately, namely:

- (i) A gun or other explosive signal fired at intervals of about a minute.
- (ii) A continuous sounding with any fog-signalling apparatus.
- (iii) Rockets or shells, throwing red stars fired one at a time at short intervals.
- (iv) A signal made by radiotelegraphy or by any other signalling method consisting of the group ...---... in the Morse Code.
- (v) A signal sent by radiotelephony consisting of the spoken word "Mayday".
- (iv) The International Code Signal of distress indicated by N.C.
- (vii) A signal consisting of a square flag having above or below it a ball or anything resembling a ball.
- (viii) Flames on the vessel (as from a burning tar barrel, oil barrel, etc.).
- (ix) A rocket parachute flare or a hand flare showing a red light.
- (x) A smoke signal giving off a volume of orange-coloured smoke.
- (xi) Slowly and repeatedly raising and lowering arms outstretched to each side.

NOTE. *Vessels in distress may use the radiotelegraph alarm signal or the radiotelephone alarm signal to secure attention to distress calls and messages. The radiotelegraph alarm signal, which is designed to actuate the radiotelegraph auto alarms of vessels so fitted, consists of a series of twelve dashes, sent in 1 minute, the duration of each dash being 4 seconds, and the duration of the interval between 2 consecutive dashes being 1 second. The radiotelephone alarm signal consists of 2 tones transmitted alternately over periods of from 30 seconds to 1 minute.*

(b) The use of any of the foregoing signals, except for the purpose of indicating that a vessel or seaplane is in distress, and the use of any signals which may be confused with any of the above signals, is prohibited.

ANNEX TO THE RULES

RECOMMENDATIONS ON THE USE OF RADAR INFORMATION AS AN AID TO AVOIDING COLLISIONS AT SEA

(1) Assumptions made on scanty information may be dangerous and should be avoided.

(2) A vessel navigating with the aid of radar in restricted visibility must, in compliance with Rule 16(a), go at a moderate speed. Information obtained from the use of radar is one of the circumstances to be taken into account when determining moderate speed. In this regard it must be recognized that small vessels, small icebergs and similar floating objects may not be detected by radar. Radar indications of one or more vessels in the vicinity may mean that "moderate speed" should be slower than a mariner without radar might consider moderate in the circumstances.

(3) When navigating in restricted visibility the radar range and bearing alone do not constitute ascertainment of the position of the other vessel under Rule 16(b) sufficiently to relieve a vessel of the duty to stop her engines and navigate with caution when a fog signal is heard forward of the beam.

(4) When action has been taken under Rule 16(c) to avoid a close quarters situation, it is essential to make sure that such action is having the desired effect. Alterations of course or speed or both are matters as to which the mariner must be guided by the circumstances of the case.

(5) Alteration of course alone may be the most effective action to avoid close quarters provided that:

    (a) There is sufficient sea room.

    (b) It is made in good time.

    (c) It is substantial. A succession of small alterations of course should be avoided.

    (d) It does not result in a close quarters situation with other vessels.

(6) The direction of an alteration of course is a matter in which the mariner must be guided by the circumstances of the case. An alteration to starboard, particularly when vessels are approaching apparently on opposite or nearly opposite courses, is generally preferable to an alteration to port.

(7) An alteration of speed, either alone or in conjunction with an alteration of course, should be substantial. A number of small alterations of speed should be avoided.

(8) If a close quarters situation is imminent, the most prudent action may be to take all way off the vessel.

In the examination of Rules of the Road, the examiner's duty will be to test the candidate's knowledge of the sense and intention of the Rules of the Collision Regulations. Mere ability to repeat the Rules word for word will not suffice to insure the candidate's passing, nor will the lack of it necessarily entail failure, provided the examiner is satisfied that the candidate grasps the full significance, content, and practical application of the Rules. Examiners will ask for the content of the Rules not by their number, but by the subject with which they deal, and they will discourage the use by candidates of verses as aids to memorizing the Rules. Examiners will not place a candidate for a steam license in the position of handling a sailing ship, but will lay stress on the candidate's ability to recognize a sailing ship's lights and on his knowledge of sailing ship's possible maneuvers according to the direction of the wind. Masters, in addition to knowing Rules of the Road thoroughly, shall be required, under the subject of Admiralty Law, to interpret them as they are required to be interpreted by the law.

The following summary is included as an aid in learning the International Rules.

  I. Enacting Clauses, Scope and Penalty
 II. Lights and So Forth
    1. Lights. Those rules concerning lights, etc.
    2. Power-driven vessels.
      a) masthead, 5′
      b) green starboard, 2′
      c) red port, 2′
      d) inboard screens
      e) range lights
    3. Power-driven vessel towing, 5′.
    4. *a)* vessel not under command, 2′
      b) vessel laying or picking up telegraph cable, 2′
      c) these vessels when making way
      d) these signals not distress signals
    5. Sail vessels and vessels in tow, 2′.
    6. Lights for small vessels, 3′; side lights, 1′.
    7. *a)* power-driven vessels less than 40 tons, 2′
      b) small steamer boats carried by seagoing vessels, 1′
      c) vessels under oars or sails less than 20 tons
      d) rowing boats
    8. Pilot vessels, 3′.
    9. Fishing vessels.
      a) open boats
      b) decked-drift nets 2′
      c) decked-line fishing, 2′
      d) trawling, 2′
        i. power-driven
        ii. sail
      e) oyster dredges, 2′
      f) flare-up light
      g) fishermen at anchor, 2′
      h) stationary because of foul gear
      i) fog signals
      k) day signals
    10. Stern light, 2′.
    11. Anchor lights, 2′. Length 150 ft. or more, 3′.
    12. Special signals.
    13. Naval lights and recognition signals.
    14. Powered vessel under sail by day.
III. **Sound Signals for Fog**
    15. *a)* **Powered vessel under way, 2 minutes**

  b) Powered vessel under way but stopped, 2 minutes
  c) Sail vessel under way, 1 minute
  d) Vessels at anchor or not under way, 1 minute
  e) Small sail vessels and boats, all conditions, 1 minute
  f) Vessel towing or towed, laying or picking up telegraph cable, under way but not under command, 1 minute
16. Speed in fog. Powered vessels stop.
IV. Steering and Sailing Rules*
  17. Sailing vessels.
    a) running free
    b) close hauled
    c) both free—wind on different sides
    d) both free—wind on same side
    e) wind aft
  18. Power-driven vessels meeting end on.
  19. Power-driven vessels crossing.
  20. Power-driven and sail vessels meeting.
  21. Duty to hold course and speed.
  22. Crossing ahead.
  23. Power-driven vessels slacken speed or stop.
  24. Overtaking vessels.
  25. Narrow channels.
  26. Right of way of sail fishing vessels.
  27. General Prudential Rule.
  28. Sound signals for passing steamers. Danger signal.
  29. Precautions, lookout, etc.
  30. Rules not to interfere with local authority.
  31. Distress signals.
  32. Orders to helmsmen.

COLLISION LAW

Jurisdiction in Collision Cases. A vessel may be sued *in rem*, or her owners *in personam* for damages due to fault in collision under Admiralty Law in a U. S. Federal Court. Where a state has enacted laws governing the navigation of public navigable waters within its territory, its courts usually have equal jurisdiction with a Federal Court.

Equal Responsibility for Unequal Fault. Under United States law the liability for collision must be equally divided, regardless of degree of fault, if both vessels are to blame. The courts are concerned with the *fact* of fault only, and damages are equally borne by each vessel.

Limited Liability of a vessel is her value after a collision, plus earnings for the voyage, collected or collectable; thus, if a vessel at fault in and lost due to a collision is of no value, the injured vessel can recover nothing should there be no freight due the lost vessel for the current voyage.

Liability for Death or Personal Injury, however, since 1935 has been extended to a maximum of 60 dollars per gross registered ton, where the

* The applicant for license should know Rules 22, 23, 27 and 29 verbatim.

remaining value of the vessel is less than that amount; but, if the owners of the vessel at fault have guilty knowledge of any circumstances which could have caused such death or personal injury due to a collision, limited liability cannot be invoked.

Government-Owned Vessels cannot be libeled, but for faulty collision damage the government allows itself to be sued *in personam* where a public vessel is involved.

WATERS REFERRED TO IN THE RULES

A *fairway* is interpreted by the courts to include any navigable water on which vessels of commerce habitually move, and therefore embraces the water exterior to a buoyed channel where vessels of light draft frequently navigate, and not merely the channel itself.

A *narrow channel*, by court definition, is a body of water navigated up and down in opposite directions, and does not include harbor waters with piers on both sides, where navigation may be, and frequently is, in any direction.

Limits of Application of International and Inland or Local Rules. The Secretary of Commerce is authorized, empowered, and directed from time to time to designate and define by suitable bearings or ranges with lighthouses, light-vessels, buoys or coast objects, the lines dividing the high seas from rivers, harbors, and inland waters.

The words "inland waters" shall not be held to include the Great Lakes and their connecting and tributary waters as far East as Montreal. (Act for adoption of rules for navigation of harbors, rivers, and inland waters, June 7, 1897.)

DUTY TO STAND BY AFTER COLLISION

In every case of collision between two vessels it shall be the duty of the master or person in charge of each vessel, if and so far as he can do so without serious danger to his own vessel, crew, and passengers (if any), to stay by the other vessel until he has ascertained that she has no need of further assistance, and to render to the other vessel, her master, crew, and passengers (if any), such assistance as may be practical and as may be necessary in order to save them from any danger caused by the collision, and also to give to the master or person in charge of the other vessel the name of his own vessel and her port of registry, or the port or place to which she belongs, and also the name of the ports and places from which and to which she is bound. If he fails to do so, and no reasonable cause for such failure is shown, the collision shall, in the absence of proof to the contrary, be deemed to have been caused by his wrongful act, neglect, or default. (Sept. 4, 1890; 33 U.S.C. 367).

Log Entries. U. S. law provides that, "In every case of collision in which it is practicable to do so, the master shall, immediately after the occurrence cause a statement thereof, and the circumstances under which the same occurred, to be entered in the official log book."

The claim by one of two colliding vessels that one of the other's lights was missing, or that her whistle was not properly acting, would be received with scepticism by the court, if the officers of the other vessel made no entry in their log relative to such a mishap.

PROPER LIGHTS

Side lights must be properly screened and unobstructed. In no case must they be visible from the vessel's own bow. They must show through the specified arcs of the compass. Failure in these requirements will bear strongly against an offending vessel in a collision case.

Lights for vessels at anchor must conform to the regulations, and mere volume of light, such as the illuminated decks of a passenger vessel, does not constitute due notice to approaching vessels.

Flare-up light is nowhere defined in the rules, but by court decisions any efficient white light properly displayed is now accepted as a "flare-up" light, as prescribed in the rules.

A tug is jointly responsible for the lights on her tow if the tow is manned, wholly responsible if the tow is not manned.

A vessel at anchor and made fast to another must show her own proper anchor lights and give her own fog signals.

Moored alongside the end of a wharf in the navigable part of a river or harbor, a vessel must show an anchor light. This is required by the General Prudential Rule, Rule 27: "Due regard shall be had to all dangers of navigation and collision" is the clause which should at once suggest the precaution of carrying a light in this situation, whether expressly required by the rules or not.

PROPER SIGNALS

Meeting under International Rules, the course should never be changed without sounding the whistle signal required, and conversely, a change must be made if the whistle is so sounded.

Leaving a dock or berth, according to Inland and Pilot Rules, immediately after clearing the berth so as to be fully in sight, a vessel shall be governed by the steering and sailing rules; but the courts have decided she is under the special circumstances rule (Rule 27) until she is straightened out on her desired course.

The "half-mile" rule. It is a safe and practical rule to blow the necessary whistle signals when vessels are half a mile from, and approaching each other so as to involve risk of collision. In inland waters the required signals are likely to be heard at this distance; if not, there is still time enough for repetition, and an understanding arrived at, before the vessels get dangerously near each other.

Initial signal by overtaken vessel. In inland waters an overtaken vessel is not obliged to give an initial signal to an overtaking vessel, if it is apparent there is plenty room for a safe passing; but if she sees that danger exists in such a passing, it is her manifest duty to warn the overtaking vessel by sounding the danger signal.

Assent to passing (inland waters). The desire to pass by an overtaking steam vessel having been assented to by the overtaken vessel, the latter does not forfeit her status as the privileged vessel, nor is she responsible for the safety of the overtaking vessel during the act of passing. The overtaken vessel must, however, refrain from crowding out the overtaking one, and she will be held liable for allowing the overtaking vessel to run into a visible danger of which the latter was unaware. The overtaken vessel will never be blamed for holding up an overtaking vessel by the danger signal.

Silence of the overtaken vessel's whistle cannot be regarded as equivalent to assent to passing by the overtaking vessel.

Two blasts in the crossing situation. The courts have been guided in the past by the accepted decision that a two-blast signal in the crossing situation is a direct violation of the rules, and therefore cannot be justified. This is no longer tenable as appears from the following recent decision, which states in effect that the privileged vessel must not "cross" the signal of the other:

"Now, in a crossing situation a privileged vessel faced with a two-blast signal from the burdened vessel, must assume only that it is a special circumstance, an emergency of some sort such as a strong tideway, a tow astern or in the way, or shoal water, which makes it necessary for the burdened vessel to pass ahead of the privileged vessel, and the privileged vessel can only choose between blowing a two-blast assent, or blowing the danger signal. In the latter case both vessels must be stopped or backed till the situation is cleared up."

Two blasts in the crossing situation (Inland) does not have legal sanction, though often used as a practical necessity in such crowded waters as New York harbor. It should never be proposed by the privileged vessel, and should be accepted when proposed by the burdened vessel only when the maneuver indicated can be done with a high degree of safety. The effect of such assent is to take the right of way from the privileged vessel without conferring it on the burdened vessel, and thus to put both vessels under the rule of special circumstances, with the mutual duty of taking any positive action necessary to avoid collision. (Farwell and Prunski)

A proposal contrary to the rules must be taken as a special circumstance, and in every situation (excepting, of course, that of meeting end on) where a steam vessel cannot safely comply with the other's proposal or request, she must sound the danger signal, and stop or reverse her engines, if necessary, until signals are made for passing in safety, and understood.

Headway must be reduced, and both vessels brought to a dead stop, if necessary, whenever it is apparent that one of the approaching vessels ignores or disputes the other's signals, or in any manner acts inconsistently in avoiding collision.

THE MEETING SITUATION

Vessels approaching each other within two points of exactly head on are defined as meeting end on, or nearly end on, and all steam vessels are required by Rule 18 to alter course *to the right*, so as to pass on the port side of each other when in this situation.

The meeting situation is unique in that *both vessels* are "burdened," and therefore each must take definite and positive action to keep out of the other's way; each *must* alter her course, sufficiently and in time, to *starboard*, in order to make the maneuver a safe one, and, both in the International and Inland Rules, each *must* sound the proper whistle signals.

When it is apparent that two meeting vessels would pass clear of each other, if kept on their respective courses, starboard to starboard, the vessel which attempts to make a port-to-port passing is clearly at fault.

Neither vessel being "privileged" in this situation, neither is required to hold course and speed. Both vessels being "burdened" with the duty of avoiding collision, it therefore is manifestly proper, especially in narrow waters, for each to reduce speed and approach with caution until danger of collision is over.

Risk of collision may be said to begin when it is apparent that the respective courses of the approaching vessels, or a small departure therefrom, if continued, would bring about a collision. Such risk is defined as continuing up to the moment when the vessels have so far progressed that any departure from the course by either can *not* bring about a collision.

THE LAW IN FOG

Efficient fog signal. A steam vessel's whistle should be heard at least two miles under favorable conditions, and a fog horn at least one mile.

Excessive speed may perhaps be classed as a breach of good seamanship, and can only be defined as a speed in excess of that which is incompatible with seamanlike prudence under the conditions existing. The distance in which a vessel may be stopped at a given speed should be found by actual experiment, and borne in mind by the officer in charge of a moving vessel.

Collision with a vessel at anchor has been generally looked upon by the courts as positive evidence of excessive speed, the opinion held being that the speed should not be greater than that at which the ship could be stopped within the distance of visibility.

Hearing fog signal of a vessel apparently forward of the beam, the duty of a steam vessel to stop her engines is *absolute*, if the position of the other vessel is not ascertained (Rule 16). The special circumstance rule might be invoked as an excuse for not complying with this article, but positive evidence of an immediate danger, such as a strong current setting down upon rocks or shoals in the vicinity, must satisfy the court.

A vessel must navigate with caution until danger of collision is over. Having collided with a vessel, it would be most difficult to prove in court that the danger of collision was over. Bare steerageway with a proper change of course which could be justified by the reasonable certainty of the bearing of the other vessel's whistle, and timely full-power reversal of the engines if the latter apparently draws more ahead, would be the best seamanlike action in most cases, and would most likely meet with approval by the court.

No vessel is privileged or has the "right of way" when vessels are hidden from each other in fog. The steering and sailing rules are to be obeyed when vessels are within sight of each other.

The danger signal in inland waters is permissible in fog, although both vessels may not be in sight of each other.

A vessel aground in fog, under Inland Rules, is held to be a vessel at anchor so far as the required lights are concerned, but it has been ruled she is not a vessel at anchor as to fog signals. She must sound distress signals, i.e., a continuous sounding with any fog signal apparatus, or by firing a gun (Rule 31).

SPECIAL CIRCUMSTANCES

The situation termed a "special circumstance" (Rules 27 and 29) is one in which *immediate danger* is present. In determining the fact of special circumstance, consideration of convenience or inconvenience in navigating or maneuvering a vessel is totally irrelevant.

A special circumstance "which may render a departure from the rules necessary" applies: (1) in a situation *in extremis*, i.e., where collision is inevitable unless immediate action is taken, whether contrary to the rules or otherwise. (2) Where either vessel is unable to obey the rules with safety due to the presence of a third vessel. Here the worst possible act is to maintain an excessive speed. (3) Where the privileged vessel must act because of the burdened vessel being unable to maneuver properly, such as a tug and her tow in a strong current, or when she is seen by the privileged vessel to be disabled. (4) Where a proposed passing by one vessel, contrary to the rules, is assented to by the other. Neither vessel is then privileged, and both are equally obligated to proceed with caution. The proposal, however, is not binding on the other vessel, but, upon assenting, the situation is at once a "special circumstance." (5) In a situation for which the rules do not specifically provide. The rules do not cover, for example, vessels maneuvering around a wharf, or dredging in a tideway.

Vessels making sternway. It is often a local practice among pilots to consider the stern of the vessel as the bow when going astern, passing signals being given accordingly. However, it has been held in numerous court decisions that the approaching situation given here is one of special circumstances, the practice above mentioned remaining uncensured. A vessel making sternway cannot be regarded as being capable of maneuvering consistently within the requirements of the rules.

Speed in close waters. Excepting the requirement in Rule 16, there is nothing in the rules which limits the speed of vessels, but every vessel is liable for damage caused by her waves to craft lying alongside wharves, to passing tugs and their tows, or small harbor craft in general.

GOOD SEAMANSHIP

In Rule 29 a precaution "may be required by the ordinary practice of seamen, or by the special circumstances of the case." The neglect of one or more of such precautions constitutes ground for presumption of fault in collision cases. The Rule may therefore be referred to as the "good seamanship" or "precautionary" rule.

The carrying of proper lights and signals, the keeping of a proper lookout, the ordinary practice of seamen, and the prompt and prudent action of the mariner under special circumstances *is actually good seamanship.* Its neglect may lead up to the collision situation, may be the direct cause of collision, or may aggravate the damage made in a collision after it has become inevitable. Its continuous and attentive practice not only tends toward avoiding collision generally, but is the mariner's ready tool in avoiding an impending collision with a vessel at fault, or in maneuvering his vessel in order to lessen the damage where collision is unavoidable.

It is said that the first rule of good seamanship is to "keep a proper lookout and obey the rules of the road;" but the mariner must act in accordance with the ordinary practice of seamen and with the special circumstances of the case, as well as with the letter of the law.

Presumption of fault is against (1) a moving vessel colliding with a moored or anchored one; (2) a vessel free to maneuver colliding with a disabled vessel, or one engaged in fishing, or a vessel towing; (3) a vessel steaming against a strong current which collides with one going with the current; (4) a vessel maintaining excessive speed in close waters; (5) a vessel improperly steered or manned.

In the case of a moving vessel *colliding with an anchored one*, a court would probably decide upon equal damage costs only when it is *clearly shown* that (1) the anchored vessel was in an improper position, and that it was not practicable nor safe for the moving vessel to avoid collision; (2) that no lights (or improper lights) were shown on the anchored vessel, and that it was impossible to clear her because of failure to discover her in time, (3) that the anchored vessel failed to maintain an anchor watch, and thus failed to warn an approaching vessel where the circumstances required such vigilance; (4) that the anchored vessel failed to sheer off with the helm, slack away cable, or to take any other proper steps to avoid collision.

A PROPER LOOKOUT

A proper lookout is, by Federal Court definition, a person specially charged with the duty of observing lights, sounds, echoes, or any obstruction to navigation with that thoroughness which the prevailing circumstances permit.

A lookout must have a *reasonable amount of experience* as a seaman; no minimum length of service has been set by the courts as the required qualification for duty as a lookout.

The proper station for a lookout has been defined as "as far forward and as low down as conditions allow."

The degree of vigilance required of the lookout is not specified in the law, but the courts hold that he must be "actually and vigilantly employed in the performance of the duty." The actual degree of vigilance employed in a particular case is likely to be judged by the standard of its effectiveness in preventing collision.

Number of lookouts. According to decisions of the courts, more than one lookout is required under certain conditions, although one with that exclusive duty will ordinarily be sufficient. Good seamanship practice complies with the foregoing obligation in large vessels in stationing as many as four lookout men in thick weather, two of whom usually would be placed aloft.

A lookout astern is required, as held by the courts, when leaving an anchorage or moorings; when actually going astern; at all times when changing course and speed; when under way at night and no fixed stern light is carried.

INEVITABLE ACCIDENT

This term is applied to cases of collision which occur *in spite of the use by both vessels of every means in their power, and a proper display of seamanlike care and nautical skill.* It is usually defined as "something that human skill and foresight could not, in the exercise of ordinary prudence, have provided against."

A case of this sort occurs only when *neither* vessel is at fault, and acting contrary to the law of the road. Less than one per cent of accidents happen in this way. Each vessel in such a case must bear her own damage, and has no claim against the other.

Inevitable collisions in the past have been mostly due to *vis major,* a mechanical failure, or a combination of both.

Vis major or force majeure is defined as the superior force of the elements, such as a violent storm, a whirling current, damage to pilot house by lightning, unexpected sheering of vessel caught in ice.

Mechanical failure as the cause of an inevitable accident means a breakdown of engines or steering-gear in spite of "due diligence" in making frequent periodical inspections of same, and their proper construction when installed in the vessel.

REGULATIONS [1]

TITLE 33—NAVIGATION AND NAVIGABLE WATERS

Chapter I—Coast Guard, Department of the Treasury

Subchapter D—Navigation Requirements for Certain Inland Waters

PART 80—PILOT RULES FOR INLAND WATERS

[1] The regulations in this part are copied from the Code of Federal Regulations of the United States of America, as amended.

AUTHORITY : §§ 80.01 to 80.36 issued under sec. 2, 30 Stat. 102, as amended ; 33 U. S. C. 157. Other statutory provisions interpreted or applied are cited to text.

.

GENERAL

Section 80.01   General Instructions.—The regulations in this part apply to vessels navigating the harbors, rivers, and inland waters of the United States, except the Great Lakes and their connecting and tributary waters as far east as Montreal, the Red River of the North, the Mississippi River and its tributaries above Huey P. Long Bridge, and that part of the Atchafalaya River above its junction with the Plaquemine-Morgan City alternate waterway.

80.02   Definition of steam vessel and vessel under way; risk of collision.—In the rules in this part the words "steam vessel" shall include any vessel propelled by machinery.   A vessel is under way, within the meaning of the rules in this part, when she is not at anchor, or made fast to the shore, or aground.   Risk of collison can, when circumstances permit, be ascertained by carefully watching the compass bearing of an approaching vessel.   If the bearing does not appreciably change, such risk should be deemed to exist.

SIGNALS

80.03   Signals.—The whistle signals provided in the rules in this part shall be sounded on an efficient whistle or siren sounded by steam or by some substitute for steam.

A short blast of the whistle shall mean a blast of about one second's duration.

A prolonged blast of the whistle shall mean a blast of from 4 to 6 seconds' duration.

One short blast of the whistle signifies intention to direct course to own starboard, except when two steam vessels are approaching each other at right angles or obliquely, when it signifies intention of steam vessel which is to starboard of the other to hold course and speed.

Two short blasts of the whistle signify intention to direct course to own port.

Three short blasts of the whistle shall mean, "My engines are going at full speed astern."

When vessels are in sight of one another a steam vessel under way whose engines are going at full speed astern shall indicate that fact by three short blasts on the whistle.

80.1   Danger signal.—If, when steam vessels are approaching each other, either vessel fails to understand the course or intention of the other, from any cause, the vessel so in doubt shall immediately signify the same by giving several short and rapid blasts, not less than four, of the steam whistle, the danger signal.

80.2   Cross signals.—Steam vessels are forbidden to use what has become technically known among pilots as "cross signals," that is, answering one whistle with two, and answering two whistles with one.

80.3   Vessels passing each other.—The signals for passing, by the blowing of the whistle, shall be given and answered by pilots, in compliance with the rules in this part, not only when meeting "head and head," or nearly so, but at all times when the steam vessels are in sight of each other, when passing or meeting at a distance within half a mile of each other, and whether passing to the starboard or port.

The whistle signals provided in the rules in this part for steam vessels meeting, passing, or overtaking are never to be used except when steam vessels are in sight of each other, and the course and position of each can be determined in the daytime by a sight of the vessel itself, or by night by seeing its signal lights. In fog, mist, falling snow, or heavy rainstorms, when vessels cannot so see each other, fog signals only must be given.

80.4   Vessels approaching each other head and head, end on.—When steam vessels are approaching each other head and head, that is, end on, or nearly so, it shall be the duty of each to pass on the port side of the other; and either vessel shall give, as a signal of her intention one short and distinct blast of her whistle, which the other vessel shall answer promptly by a similar blast of her whistle, and thereupon such vessels shall pass on the port side of each other. But if the courses of such vessels are so far on the starboard of each other as not to be considered as meeting head and head, either vessel shall immediately give two short and distinct blasts of her whistle, which the other vessel shall answer promptly by two similar blasts of her whistle, and they shall pass on the starboard side of each other.

The foregoing only applies to cases where vessels are meeting end on or nearly end on, in such a manner as to involve risk of collision; in other words, to cases in which, by day, each vessel sees the masts of the other in a line, or nearly in a line, with her own, and by night to cases in which each vessel is in such a position as to see both the side lights of the other.

It does not apply by day to cases in which a vessel sees another ahead crossing her own course, or by night to cases where the red light of one vessel is opposed to the red light of the other, or where the green light of one vessel is opposed to the green light of the other, or where a red light without a green light or a green light without a red light is seen ahead, or where both green and red lights are seen anywhere but ahead.

80.5   Vessels nearing bend or curve in channel; moving from docks.—Whenever a steam vessel is nearing a short bend or curve in the channel, where, from the height of the banks or other cause, a steam vessel approaching from the opposite direction cannot be seen for a distance of half a mile, such steam vessel, when she shall have arrived within half a mile of such curve or bend, shall give a signal by one long blast of the steam whistle, which signal shall be answered by a similar blast, given by any approaching steam vessel that may be within hearing. Should such signal be so answered by a steam vessel upon the farther side of such bend, then the usual signals for meeting and passing shall immediately be given and answered; but, if the first alarm signal of such vessel be not answered, she is to consider the channel clear and govern herself accordingly.

When steam vessels are moved from their docks or berths, and other boats are liable to pass from any direction toward them, they shall give the same signal as in the case of vessels meeting at a bend, but immediately after clearing the berths so as to be fully in sight they shall be governed by the steering and sailing rules.

80.6   Vessels running in same direction; overtaking vessel.— When steam vessels are running in the same direction, and the vessel which is astern shall desire to pass on the right or starboard hand of the vessel ahead, she shall give one short blast of the steam whistle, as a signal of such desire, and if the vessel ahead answers with one blast, she shall direct her course to starboard; or if she shall desire to pass on the left or port side of the vessel ahead, she shall give two short blasts of the steam whistle as a signal of such desire, and if the vessel ahead answers with two blasts, shall direct her course to port; or if the vessel ahead does not think it safe for the vessel astern to attempt to pass at that point, she shall immediately signify the same by giving several short and rapid blasts of the steam whistle, not less than four, and under no circumstances shall the vessel astern attempt to pass the vessel ahead until such time as they have reached a point where it can be safely done, when said vessel ahead shall signify her willingness by blowing the proper signals. The vessel ahead shall in no case attempt to cross the bow or crowd upon the course of the passing vessel.

Every vessel coming up with another vessel from any direction more than two points abaft her beam, that is, in such a position with reference to the vessel which she is overtaking that at night she would be unable to see either of that vessel's side lights, shall be deemed to be an overtaking vessel; and no subsequent alteration of the bearing between the two vessels shall make the overtaking vessel a crossing vessel within the meaning of the rules in this part, or relieve her of the duty of keeping clear of the overtaken vessel until she is finally past and clear.

As by day the overtaking vessel cannot always know with certainty whether she is forward of or abaft this direction from the other vessel she should, if in doubt, assume that she is an overtaking vessel and keep out of the way.

80.7   Vessels approaching each other at right angles or obliquely.—When two steam vessels are approaching each other at right angles or obliquely so as to involve risk of collision, other than when one steam vessel is overtaking another, the steam vessel which has the other on her own port side shall hold her course and speed; and the steam vessel which has the other on her own starboard side shall keep out of the way of the other by directing her course to starboard so as to cross the stern of the other steam vessel, or, if necessary to do so, slacken her speed or stop or reverse.

If from any cause the conditions covered by this situation are such as to prevent immediate compliance with each other's signals, the misunderstanding or objection shall be at once made apparent by blowing the danger signal, and both steam vessels shall be stopped and backed if necessary, until signals for passing with safety are made and understood.

80.8   Meeting of steam and sailing vessels; right of way.—When a steam vessel and a sailing vessel are proceeding in such directions as to involve risk of collision, the steam vessel shall keep out of the way of the sailing vessel.

80.9   Avoidance of crossing ahead.—Every steam vessel which is directed by the rules in this part to keep out of the way of another vessel shall, if the circumstances of the case admit, avoid crossing ahead of the other.

80.10   Keeping to right in narrow channels.—In narrow channels every steam vessel shall, when it is safe and practicable, keep to that side of the fairway or mid-channel which lies on the starboard side of such vessel.

80.11   Departure from rules.—In obeying and construing the rules in this part due regard shall be had to all dangers of navigation and collision, and to any special circumstances which may render a departure from said rules necessary in order to avoid immediate danger.

80.12   Fog signals.—In fog, mist, falling snow, or heavy rainstorms, whether by day or night, signals shall be given as follows:

A steam vessel under way, except when towing other vessels or being towed, shall sound, at intervals of not more than 1 minute, on the whistle or siren, a prolonged blast.

A steam vessel when towing other vessels shall sound, at intervals of not more than 1 minute, on the whistle or siren, three blasts in succession, namely, one prolonged blast followed by two short blasts.

A vessel towed may give, at intervals of not more than 1 minute, on the fog horn, a signal of three blasts in succession, namely, one prolonged blast followed by two short blasts, and she shall not give any other.

A vessel when at anchor shall, at intervals of not more than 1 minute, ring the bell rapidly for about 5 seconds.

80.13   Speed in fog; pamphlet containing Pilot Rules; diagrams—(a) Moderate speed in fog.—Every steam vessel shall, in a fog, mist, falling snow, or heavy rainstorms, go at a moderate speed, having careful regard to the existing circumstances and conditions.

A steam vessel hearing, apparently forward of her beam, the fog signal of a vessel the position of which is not ascertained shall, so far as the circumstances of the case admit, stop her engines and then navigate with caution until danger of collision is over.

(b) Pamphlets.—All vessels and craft over 65 feet in length upon the waters described in Section 80.01 shall, where practicable, carry on board and maintain for ready reference copies of the current edition of Coast Guard pamphlet CG–169. Nothing in this section shall require copies of this pamphlet to be carried on board any motorboat as defined by section 1 of the Act of April 25, 1940, as amended (54 Stat. 163; 46 U. S. C. 526).

(c) Diagrams.—The following diagrams are intended to illustrate the working of the system of colored lights and pilot rules.

FIRST SITUATION

Here the two colored lights visible to each will indicate their direct approach "head and head" toward each other. In this situation it is a standing rule that both shall direct their courses to starboard and pass on the port side of each other, each having previously given one blast of the whistle.

SECOND SITUATION

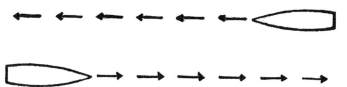

In this situation the red light only will be visible to each, the screens preventing the green lights from being seen. Both vessels are evidently passing to port of each other, which is rulable in this situation, each pilot having previously signified his intention by one blast of the whistle.

THIRD SITUATION

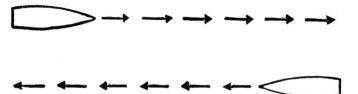

In this situation the green light only will be visible to each, the screens preventing the red light from being seen.   They are therefore passing to starboard of each other, which is rulable in this situation, each pilot having previously signified his intention by two blasts of the whistle.

FOURTH SITUATION

In this situation one steam vessel is overtaking another steam vessel from some point within the angle of two points abaft the beam of the overtaken steam vessel.   The overtaking steam vessel may pass on the starboard or port side of the steam vessel ahead after the necessary signals for passing have been given with assent of the overtaken steam vessel, as prescribed in § 80.6.

FIFTH SITUATION

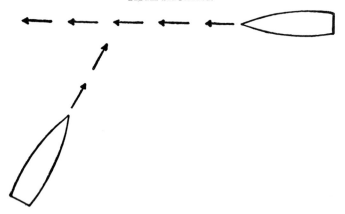

In this situation two steam vessels are approaching each other at right angles or obliquely in such manner as to involve risk of collision, other than where one steam vessel is overtaking another.   The steam vessel which has the other on her own port side shall hold course and speed, and the other shall keep clear by crossing astern of the steam vessel that is holding course and speed, or, if necessary to do so, shall slacken her speed, stop, or reverse.

80.14 Lights; time for.—The following rules in this part concerning lights shall be complied with in all weathers from sunset to sunrise.

80.15 Ferryboats.—(a) Ferryboats propelled by machinery and navigating the harbors, rivers, and other inland waters of the United States, except the Great Lakes and their connecting and tributary waters as far east as Montreal, the Red River of the North, the Mississippi River and its tributaries above Huey P. Long Bridge, and that part of the Atchafalaya River above its junction with the Plaquemine-Morgan City alternate waterway, shall carry the range lights and the colored side lights required by law to be carried on steam vessels navigating those waters, except that double-end ferryboats shall carry a central range of clear, bright, white lights, showing all around the horizon, placed at equal altitudes forward and aft, also on the starboard side a green light, and on the port side a red light, of such a character as to be visible on a dark night with a clear atmosphere at a distance of at least 2 miles, and so constructed as to show a uniform and unbroken light over an arc of the horizon of 10 points of the compass, and so fixed as to throw the light from right ahead to 2 points abaft the beam on their respective sides.

(b) The green and red lights shall be fitted with inboard screens projecting at least 3 feet forward from the lights, so as to prevent them from being seen across the bow.

(c) Officers in Charge, Marine Inspection,[2] in districts having ferryboats shall, whenever the safety of navigation may require, designate for each line of such boats a certain light, white or colored, which will show all around the horizon, to designate and distinguish such lines from each other, which light shall be carried on a flagstaff amidships, 15 feet above the white range lights.

80.16 Lights for barges, canal boats, scows, and other nondescript vessels on certain inland waters on the Atlantic and Pacific Coasts.—(a) On the harbors, rivers, and other inland waters of the United States except the Great Lakes and their connecting and tributary waters as far east as Montreal, the Red River of the North, the Mississippi River and its tributaries above the Huey P. Long Bridge, and that part of the Atchafalaya River above its junction with the Plaquemine-Morgan City alternate waterway, and the waters described in §§ 80.16a and 80.17, barges, canal boats, scows, and other vessels of nondescript type not otherwise provided for, when being towed by steam vessels, shall carry lights as set forth in this section.

(b) Barges and canal boats towing astern of steam vessels, when towing singly, or what is known as tandem towing, shall each carry a green light on the starboard side and a red light on the port side, and a white light on the stern, except that the last vessel of such tow shall carry two lights on her stern, athwartship, horizontal to each other, not less than 5 feet apart, and not less than 4 feet above the deckhouse, and so placed as to show all around the horizon.

---

[2] For a definition of an Officer in Charge, Marine Inspection, see 46 C. F. R. 70.10–33, also same section number in Coast Guard publication entitled "Rules and Regulations for Passenger Vessels," CG–256.

A tow of one such vessel shall be lighted as the last vessel of a tow.

(c) When two or more boats are abreast, the colored lights shall be carried at the outer sides of the bows of the outside boats. Each of the outside boats in last tier of a hawser tow shall carry a white light on her stern.

(d) The white light required to be carried on stern of a barge or canal boat carrying red and green side lights except the last vessel in a tow shall be carried in a lantern so constructed that it shall show an unbroken light over an arc of the horizon of 12 points of the compass, namely, for 6 points from right aft on each side of the vessel, and shall be of such a character as to be visible on a dark night with a clear atmosphere at a distance of at least 2 miles.

(e) Barges, canal boats or scows towing alongside a steam vessel shall, if the deck, deck houses, or cargo of the barge, canal boat or scow be so high above water as to obscure the side lights of the towing steamer when being towed on the starboard side of the steamer, carry a green light upon the starboard side; and when towed on the port side of the steamer, a red light on the port side of the barge, canal boat, or scow; and if there is more than one barge, canal boat or scow abreast, the colored lights shall be displayed from the outer side of the outside barges, canal boats or scows.

(f) Barges, canal boats or scows shall, when being propelled by pushing ahead of a steam vessel, display a red light on the port bow and a green light on the starboard bow of the head barge, canal boat or scow, carried at a height sufficiently above the superstructure of the barge, canal boat or scow as to permit said side lights to be visible; and if there is more than one barge, canal boat or scow abreast, the colored lights shall be displayed from the outer side of the outside barges, canal boats or scows.

(g) The colored side lights referred to in this section shall be fitted with inboard screens so as to prevent them from being seen across the bow, and of such a character as to be visible on a dark night, with a clear atmosphere, at a distance of at least 2 miles, and so constructed as to show a uniform and unbroken light over an arc of the horizon of 10 points of the compass, and so fixed as to throw the light from right ahead to 2 points abaft the beam on either side. The minimum size of glass globes shall not be less than 6 inches in diameter and 5 inches high in the clear.

(h) Scows not otherwise provided for in this section on waters described in paragraph (a) of this section shall carry a white light at each end of each scow, except that when such scows are massed in tiers, two or more abreast, each of the outside scows shall carry a white light on its outer bow, and the outside scows in the last tier shall each carry, in addition, a white light on the outer part of the stern. The white light shall be carried not less than 8 feet above the surface of the water, and shall be so placed as to show an unbroken light all around the horizon, and shall be of such a character as to be visible on a dark night with a clear atmosphere at a distance of at least 5 miles.

(i) Other vessels of nondescript type not otherwise provided for in this section shall exhibit the same lights that are required to be exhibited by scows by this section. (R. S. 4233A, sec. 2, 30 Stat. 102, 38 Stat. 381, as amended, 33 U. S. C. 157, 178.)

Note: The regulations in §§ 80.16 to 80.17, inclusive, are not applicable to rafts. The requirements regarding lights for rafts are in § 80.32.

**80.16a   Lights for barges, canal boats, scows and other nonde-
script vessels on certain inland waters on the Gulf Coast and the
Gulf Intracoastal Waterway.**—(a) On the Gulf Intracoastal Waterway and on other inland waters connected therewith or with the Gulf
of Mexico from the Rio Grande, Texas, to Cape Sable (East Cape),
Florida, barges, canal boats, scows, and other vessels of nondescript
type not otherwise provided for, when being towed by steam vessels
shall carry lights as set forth in this section.

(b) When one or more barges, canal boats, scows, or other vessels
of nondescript type not otherwise provided for, are being towed by
pushing ahead of a steam vessel, such tow shall be lighted by an
amber light at the extreme forward end of the tow, so placed as to be
as nearly as practicable on the centerline of the tow, a green light on
the starboard side of the tow, so placed as to mark the maximum
projection of the tow to starboard, and a red light on the port side
of the tow, so placed as to mark the maximum projection of the tow
to port.

(c) When one or more barges, canal boats, scows, or other vessels of
nondescript type not otherwise provided for, are being towed alongside a steam vessel, there shall be displayed a white light at each
outboard corner of the tow.   If the deck, deckhouse, or cargo of such
barge, etc., obscures the sidelight of the towing vessel, such barge, etc.,
shall also carry a green light upon the starboard side when being towed
on the starboard side of a steam vessel or shall carry a red light on the
port side of the barge, etc., when being towed on the port side of the
steam vessel.   If there is more than one such barge, etc., being towed
abreast, the appropriate colored sidelight shall be displayed from the
outer side of the outside barge.

(d) When one barge, canal boat, scow or other vessel of nondescript
type not otherwise provided for, is being towed singly behind a steam
vessel, such vessel shall carry four white lights, one on each corner or
outermost projection of the bow and one on each corner or outermost
projection of the stern.

(e) When two or more barges, canal boats, scows, or other vessels
of nondescript type not otherwise provided for, are being towed behind
a steam vessel in tandem, with an intermediate hawser, such vessels
shall carry white lights as follows:

(1) The first vessel in the tow shall carry three white lights, one
on each corner or outermost projection of the bow and a white light
at the stern amidships.

(2) Each intermediate vessel shall carry two white lights, one at
each end amidships.

(3) The last vessel in the tow shall carry three white lights, one on

each corner or outermost projection of the stern and a white light at the bow amidships.

(f) When two or more barges, canal boats, scows, or other vessels of nondescript type not otherwise provided for, are being towed behind a steam vessel in tandem, close-up, such vessels shall carry white lights as follows:

(1) The first vessel in the tow shall carry three white lights, one on each corner or outermost projection of the bow and a white light at the stern amidships.

(2) Each intermediate vessel shall carry a white light at the stern amidships.

(3) The last vessel in the tow shall carry two white lights, one on each corner or outermost projection of the stern.

(g) When two or more barges, canal boats, scows, or other vessels of nondescript type not otherwise provided for, are being towed behind a steam vessel two or more abreast, in one or more tiers, each of the outside vessels in each tier shall carry a white light on the outboard corner of the bow, and each of the outside vessels in the last tier shall carry, in addition, a white light on the outboard corner of the stern.

(h) When one or more barges, canal boats, scows, or other vessels of nondescript type not otherwise provided for, are moored to the bank or dock in or near a fairway, such tow shall carry two white lights not less than four feet above the surface of the water, as follows:

(1) On a single moored barge, canal boat, scow, or other vessel of nondescript type not otherwise provided for, a light at each outboard or channelward corner.

(2) On barges, canal boats, scows, or other vessels of nondescript type not otherwise provided for, when moored in a group formation, a light on the upstream outboard or channelward corner of the outer upstream boat and a light on the downstream outboard or channelward corner of the outer downstream boat; and in addition, any boat projecting toward or into the channel from such group formation shall have two white lights similarly placed on its outboard or channelward corners.

(i) The colored side lights shall be so constructed as to show a uniform and unbroken light over an arc of the horizon of 10 points of the compass, so fixed as to show the light from right ahead to 2 points abaft the beam on their respective sides, and of such a character as to be visible at a distance of at least 2 miles, and shall be fitted with inboard screens so as to prevent either light from being seen more than half a point across the centerline of the tow.

(j) The amber light shall be so constructed as to show a uniform and unbroken light over an arc of the horizon of 20 points of the compass, so fixed as to show the light 10 points on each side of the tow, namely, from right ahead to 2 points abaft the beam on either side, and of such a character as to be visible at a distance of at least 2 miles.

(k) The white lights shall be so constructed and so fixed as to show a clear, uniform, and unbroken light all around the horizon, and of such a character as to be visible at a distance of at least 2 miles.

(l) All the lights shall be carried at approximately the same height above the surface of the water and, except as provided in paragraph (h) of this section, shall be so placed with respect thereto as to be clear of and above all obstructions which might tend to interfere with the prescribed arc or distance of visibility.

80.16b Lights for barges, canal boats, scows, and other nondescript vessels temporarily operating on waters requiring different lights.—Nothing in §§ 80.16, 80.16a, or 80.17 shall be construed as compelling barges, canal boats, scows, or other vessels of nondescript type not otherwise provided for, being towed by steam vessels, when passing through any waters coming within the scope of any regulations where lights for such boats are different from those of the waters whereon such boats are usually employed, to change their lights from those required on the waters on which their trip begins or terminates; but should such boats engage in local employment on waters requiring different lights from those where they are customarily employed, they shall comply with the local rules where employed. (R. S. 4233A, sec. 2, 30 Stat. 102, 38 Stat. 381, as amended, 33 U. S. C. 157, 178, Pub. Law 544, 80th Cong.)

80.17 Lights for barges and canal boats in tow of steam vessels on the Hudson River and adjacent waters and Lake Champlain.—All nondescript vessels known as scows, car floats, lighters, and vessels of similar type, navigating the waters referred to in the following rules, shall carry the lights required to be carried by barges and canal boats in tow of steam vessels, as prescribed in such rules.

Barges and canal boats, when being towed by steam vessels on the waters of the Hudson River and its tributaries from Troy to the boundary lines of New York Harbor off Sandy Hook, as defined pursuant to section 2 of the act of Congress of February 19, 1895 (28 Stat. 672; 33 U. S. C. 151), the East River and Long Island Sound (and the waters entering thereon, and to the Atlantic Ocean), to and including Narragansett Bay, R. I., and tributaries, and Lake Champlain, shall carry lights as follows:

(a) Barges and canal boats being towed astern of steam vessels when towing singly shall carry a white light on the bow and a white light on the stern.

SINGLY

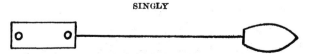

(b) When towing in tandem, "close up," each boat shall carry a white light on its stern and the first or hawser boat shall, in addition, carry a white light on its bow.

TANDEM—CLOSE UP

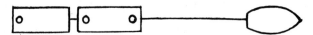

(c) When towing in tandem with intermediate hawser between the various boats in the tow, each boat shall carry a white light on the bow and a white light on the stern, except that the last vessel in the tow shall carry two white lights on her stern, athwartship, horizontal to each other, not less than 5 feet apart and not less than 4 feet above the deck house, and so placed as to show all around the horizon: *Provided*, That seagoing barges shall not be required to make any change in their seagoing lights (red and green) on waters coming within the scope of the rules of this section, except that the last vessel of the tow shall carry two white lights on her stern, athwartship, horizontal to each other, not less than 5 feet apart, and not less than 4 feet above the deck house, and so placed as to show all around the horizon.

TANDEM—WITH INTERMEDIATE HAWSER

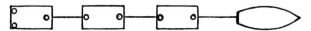

(d) Barges and canal boats when towed at a hawser, two or more abreast, when in one tier, shall each carry a white light on the stern and a white light on the bow of each of the outside boats.

TWO OR MORE ABREAST IN ONE TIER

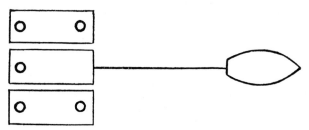

(e) When in more than one tier, each boat shall carry a white light on its stern and the outside boats in the hawser or head tier shall each carry, in addition, a white light on the bow.

TWO OR MORE ABREAST AND IN MORE THAN ONE TIER

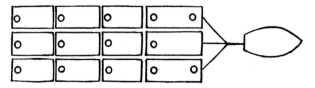

(f) The white bow lights for barges and canal boats referred to in the preceding rules shall be carried at least 10 feet and not more than 30 feet abaft the stem or extreme forward end of the vessel. On barges and canal boats required to carry a white bow light, the white light on bow and the white light on stern shall each be so placed above the hull or deck house as to show an unbroken light all around the horizon, and of such a character as to be visible on a dark night with a clear atmosphere at a distance of at least 2 miles.

(g) When nondescript vessels known as scows, car floats, lighters, barges or canal boats, and vessels of similar type, are towed alongside a steam vessel, there shall be displayed a white light at the outboard corners of the tow.

TOWED ALONGSIDE—VARIOUS POSITIONS

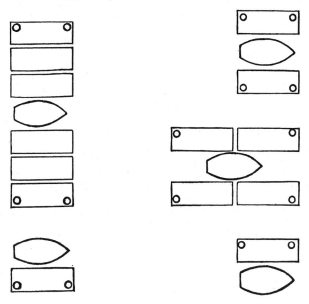

(h) When under way between the hours of sunset and sunrise there shall be displayed a red light on the port bow and a green light on the starboard bow of the head barge or barges, properly screened and so arranged that they may be visible through an arc of the horizon of 10 points of the compass; that is, from right ahead to 2 points abaft the beam on either side and visible on a dark night with a clear atmosphere at a distance of at least 2 miles, and be carried at a height sufficiently above the superstructure of the barge or barges pushed ahead as to permit said side lights to be visible.

PROPULSION OF BARGE OR BARGES BY PUSHING

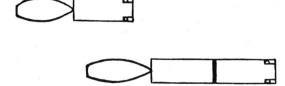

(i) Dump scows utilized for transportation and disposal of garbage, street sweepings, ashes, excavated material, dredging, etc., when navigating on the Hudson River or East River or the Waters tributary thereto between loading points on these waters and the dumping grounds established by competent authority outside the line dividing the high seas from the inland waters of New York Harbor, shall, when towing in tandem, carry, instead of the white lights previously required, red and green side lights on the respective and appropriate sides of the scow in addition to the white light required to be shown by an overtaken vessel.

The red and green lights herein prescribed shall be carried at an elevation of not less than 8 feet above the highest deck house, upon substantial uprights, the lights properly screened and so arranged as to show through an arc of the horizon of 10 points of the compass, that is, from right ahead to 2 points abaft the beam on either side and visible on a dark night with a clear atmosphere a distance of at least 2 miles.

Provided, That nothing in the rules of this section shall be construed as compelling barges or canal boats in tow of steam vessels, passing through any waters coming within the scope of said rules where lights for barges or canal boats are different from those of the waters whereon such vessels are usually employed, to change their lights from those required on the waters from which their trip begins or terminates; but should such vessels engage in local employment on waters requiring different lights from those where they are customarily employed, they shall comply with the local rules where employed.

LIGHTS AND DAY SIGNALS FOR VESSELS, DREDGES OF ALL TYPES, AND VESSELS
WORKING ON WRECKS AND OBSTRUCTIONS, ETC.

NOTE : The regulations in Sections 80.18 to 80.31a are applicable on the harbors, rivers, and inland waters along the Atlantic and Pacific Coasts and the Coast of the Gulf of Mexico as described in Section 80.01.   The same regulations in Sections 95.51 to 95.66 are applicable on the "western rivers."   Similar Department of the Army regulations are applicable on the Great Lakes and their connecting and tributary waters as far east as Montreal and are contained in Sections 201.1 to 201.16 of this title.

80.18   Signals to be displayed by a towing vessel when towing a submerged or partly submerged object upon a hawser when no signals can be displayed upon the object which is towed.—(a) The vessel having the submerged object in tow shall display by day, where they can best be seen, two shapes, one above the other, not less than six feet apart, the lower shape to be carried not less than 10 feet above the deck house.   The shapes shall be in the form of a double frustum of a cone, base to base, not less than two feet in diameter at the center nor less than eight inches at the ends of the cones, and to be not less than four feet lengthwise from end to end, the upper shape to be painted in alternate horizontal stripes of black and white, eight inches in width, and the lower shape to be painted a solid bright red.

(b) By night the towing vessel shall display the regular side lights but in lieu of the regular white towing lights shall display four lights in a vertical position not less than three feet nor more than six feet apart, the upper and lower of such lights to be white, and the two middle lights to be red, all of such lights to be of the same character as the regular towing lights.'

80.19   Steam vessels, derrick boats, lighters, or other types of vessels made fast alongside a wreck, or moored over a wreck which is on the bottom or partly submerged, or which may be drifting.— (a) Steam vessels, derrick boats, lighters, or other types of vessels made fast alongside a wreck, or moored over a wreck which is on the bottom or partly submerged, or which may be drifting, shall display by day two shapes of the same character and dimensions and displayed in the same manner as required by § 80.18 (a), except that both shapes shall be painted a solid bright red, but where more than one vessel is working under the above conditions, the shapes need be displayed only from one vessel on each side of the wreck from which they can best be seen from all directions.

(b) By night this situation shall be indicated by the display of a white light from the bow and stern of each outside vessel or lighter not less than six feet above the deck, and in addition thereto there shall be displayed in a position where they can best be seen from all directions two red lights carried in a vertical line not less than three feet nor more than six feet apart, and not less than 15 feet above the deck.

80.20   Dredges held in stationary position by moorings or spuds.—(a) Dredges which are held in stationary position by moorings or spuds shall display by day two red balls not less than two feet in diameter and carried in a vertical line not less than three feet nor more than six feet apart, and at least 15 feet above the deck house and in such a position where they can best be seen from all directions.

(b) By night they shall display a white light at each corner, not less than six feet above the deck, and in addition thereto there shall be displayed in a position where they can best be seen from all directions two red lights carried in a vertical line not less than three feet nor more than six feet apart, and not less than 15 feet above the deck. When scows are moored alongside a dredge in the foregoing situation they shall display a white light on each outboard corner, not less than six feet above the deck.

80.21   Self-propelling suction dredges under way and engaged in dredging operations.—(a) Self-propelling suction dredges under way and engaged in dredging operations shall display by day two black balls not less than two feet in diameter and carried in a vertical line not less than 15 feet above the deck house, and where they can best be seen from all directions. The term "dredging operations" shall include maneuvering into or out of position at the dredging site but shall not include proceeding to or from the site.

(b) By night they shall carry, in addition to the regular running lights, two red lights of the same character as the white masthead light, and in the same vertical line beneath that light, the red lights to be not less than three feet nor more than six feet apart and the upper red light to be not less than four feet nor more than six feet below the masthead light, and on or near the stern two red lights in a vertical line not less than four feet nor more than six feet apart, to show through four points of the compass; that is, from right astern to two points on each quarter.

80.22   **Vessels moored or anchored and engaged in laying cables or pipe, submarine construction, excavation, mat sinking, bank grading, dike construction, revetment, or other bank protection operations.**—(a) Vessels which are moored or anchored and engaged in laying cables or pipe, submarine construction, excavation, mat sinking, bank grading, dike construction, revetment, or other bank protection operations, shall display by day, not less than 15 feet above the deck, where they can best be seen from all directions, two balls not less than two feet in diameter, in a vertical line not less than three feet nor more than six feet apart, the upper ball to be painted in alternate black and white vertical stripes six inches wide, and the lower ball to be painted a solid bright red.

(b) By night they shall display three red lights, carried in a vertical line not less than three feet nor more than six feet apart, in a position where they can best be seen from all directions, with the lowermost light not less than 15 feet above the deck.

(c) Where a stringout of moored vessels or barges is engaged in the operations, three red lights carried as prescribed in paragraph (b) of this section shall be displayed at the channelward end of the stringout. Where the stringout crosses the navigable channel and is to be opened for the passage of vessels, the three red lights shall be displayed at each side of the opening instead of at the outer end of the stringout. There shall also be displayed upon such stringout one horizontal row of amber lights not less than six feet about the deck, or above the deck house where the craft carries a deck house, in a position where they can best be seen from all directions, spaced not more than 50 feet apart so as to mark distinctly the entire length and course of the stringout.

80.23   **Lights to be displayed on pipe lines.**—Pipe lines attached to dredges, and either floating or supported on trestles, shall display by night one row of amber lights not less than eight feet nor more than 12 feet above the water, about equally spaced and in such number as to mark distinctly the entire length and course of the line, the intervals between lights where the line crosses navigable channels to be not more than 30 feet. There shall also be displayed on the shore or discharge end of the line two red lights, three feet apart, in a vertical line with the lower light at least eight feet above the water, and if the line is to be opened at night for the passage of vessels, a similar arrangement of lights shall be displayed on each side of the opening.

80.24   **Lights generally.**—(a) All the lights required by §§ 80.18 to 80.23, inclusive, except as provided in §§ 80.18 (b) and 80.21 (b), shall be of such character as to be visible on a dark night with a clear atmosphere for a distance of at least two miles.

(b) The lights required by § 80.18 (b) to be of the same character as the regular towing lights and the lights required by § 80.21 (b) to be of the same character as the masthead light shall be of such character as to be visible on a dark night with a clear atmosphere for a distance of at least five miles.

(c) All floodlights or headlights which may interfere with the proper navigation of an approaching vessel shall be so shielded that the lights will not blind the pilot of such vessel.

80.25 **Vessels moored or at anchor.**—Vessels of more than 65 feet in length when moored or anchored in a fairway or channel shall display between sunrise and sunset on the forward part of the vessel where it can best be seen from other vessels one black ball not less than two feet in diameter.

PASSING FLOATING PLANT WORKING IN NAVIGABLE CHANNELS

80.26 **Passing signals.**—(a) Vessels intending to pass dredges or other types of floating plant working in navigable channels, when within a reasonable distance therefrom and not in any case over a mile, shall indicate such intention by one long blast of the whistle, and shall be directed to the proper side for passage by the sounding, by the dredge or other floating plant, of the signal prescribed in the local pilot rules for vessels under way and approaching each other from opposite directions, which shall be answered in the usual manner by the approaching vessel. If the channel is not clear, the floating plant shall sound the alarm or danger signal and the approaching vessel shall slow down or stop and await further signal from the plant.

(b) When the pipe line from a dredge crosses the channel in such a way that an approaching vessel cannot pass safely around the pipe line or dredge, there shall be sounded immediately from the dredge the alarm or danger signal and the approaching vessel shall slow down or stop and await further signal from the dredge. The pipe line shall then be opened and the channel cleared as soon as practicable; when the channel is clear for passage the dredge shall so indicate by sounding the usual passing signal as prescribed in paragraph (a) of this section. The approaching vessel shall answer with a corresponding signal and pass promptly.

(c) When any pipe line or swinging dredge shall have given an approaching vessel or tow the signal that the channel is clear, the dredge shall straighten out within the cut for the passage of the vessel or tow.

NOTE: The term "floating plant" as used in §§ 80.26 to 80.31a, inclusive, includes dredges, derrick boats, snag boats, drill boats, pile drivers, maneuver boats, hydraulic graders, survey boats, working barges, and mat sinking plant.

80.27 **Speed of vessels passing floating plant working in channels.**—Vessels, with or without tows, passing floating plant working in channels, shall reduce their speed sufficiently to insure the safety of both the plant and themselves, and when passing within 200 feet of the plant their speed shall not exceed five miles per hour. While passing over lines of the plant, propelling machinery shall be stopped.

80.28 **Light-draft vessels passing floating plant.**—Vessels whose draft permits shall keep outside of the buoys marking the ends of mooring lines of floating plant working in channels.

80.29 **Aids to navigation marking floating-plant moorings.**—Breast, stern, and bow anchors of floating plant working in navigable channels shall be marked by barrel or other suitable buoys. By night approaching vessels shall be shown the location of adjacent buoys by throwing a suitable beam of light from the plant on the buoys until the approaching vessel has passed, or the buoys may be lighted by red lights, visible in all directions, of the same character as specified in § 80.24 (a): *Provided,* That the foregoing provisions of this section shall not apply to the following waters of New York Harbor and adjacent waters: the East River, the North River (Battery to Spuyten Duyvil), the Harlem River and the New York and New Jersey Channels (from the Upper Bay through Kill Van Kull, Newark Bay, Arthur Kill, and Raritan Bay to the Lower Bay).

80.30   Obstruction of channel by floating plant.—Channels shall not be obstructed unnecessarily by any dredge or other floating plant. While vessels are passing such plant, all lines running thereform across the channel on the passing side, which may interfere with or obstruct navigation, shall be slacked to the bottom of the channel.

80.31   Clearing of channels.—When special or temporary regulations have not been prescribed and action under the regulations contained in §§ 80.26 to 80.30, inclusive, will not afford clear passage, floating plant in narrow channels shall, upon notice, move out of the way of vessels a sufficient distance to allow them a clear pasage. Vessels desiring passage shall, however, give the master of the floating plant ample notice in advance of the time they expect to pass.

NOTE: If it is necessary to prohibit or limit the anchorage or movement of vessels within certain areas in order to facilitate the work of improvement, application should be made through official channels for establishment by the Secretary of the Army of special or temporary regulations for this purpose.

80.31a   Protection of marks placed for the guidance of floating plant.—Vessels shall not run over anchor buoys, or buoys, stakes, or other marks placed for the guidance of floating plant working in channels; and shall not anchor on the ranges of buoys, stakes, or other marks placed for the guidance of such plant.

LIGHTS FOR RAFTS AND OTHER CRAFT NOT PROVIDED FOR

80.32.   Lights for rafts and other craft. (a) Any vessel propelled by hand power, horse power, or by the current of the river, except rafts and rowboats, shall carry one white light forward not less than 8 feet above the surface of the water.

(b) Any raft while being propelled by hand power, by horse power, or by the current of the river, while being towed, or while anchored or moored in or near a channel or fairway, shall carry white lights as follows:

(1) A raft of one crib in width shall carry one white light at each end of the raft.

(2) A raft of more than one crib in width shall carry 4 white lights, one on each outside corner.

(3) An unstable log raft of one bag or boom in width shall carry at least 2 but not more than 4 white lights in a fore and aft line, one of which shall be at each end.   The lights may be closely grouped clusters of not more than 3 white lights rather than single lights.

(4) An unstable log raft of more than one bag or boom in width shall carry 4 white lights, one on each outside corner.   The lights may be closely grouped clusters of not more than 3 white lights rather than single lights.

(c) The white lights required by this section shall be carried from sunset to sunrise, in a lantern so fixed and constructed as to show a clear, uniform, and unbroken light, visible all around the horizon, and of such intensity as to be visible on a dark night with a clear atmosphere at a distance of at least one mile. The lights for rafts shall be suspended from poles of such height that the lights shall not be less than 8 feet above the surface of the water, except that the lights prescribed for unstable log rafts shall not be less than 4 feet above the water.

For lights to be displayed on pipe lines.

Motorboat Act of Apr. 25, 1940. Class A—less than 16 feet in length. Class 1—16 feet or over and less than 26 feet in length. Class 2—26 feet or over and less than 40 feet in length. Class 3—40 feet or over and not more than 65 feet in length.

Rafts and other watercraft navigating by hand power, horsepower, or by the current of the river. *A*. Rafts of 1 crib and not more than 2 in length. *B*. Rafts of 3 or more cribs in length and 1 in width. *C*. Rafts of more than 1 crib abreast.

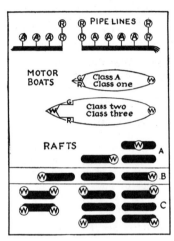

Fig. 1. Other Signals.

SPECIAL DAY OR NIGHT SIGNALS

80.32a Day marks for fishing vessels with gear out.—All vessels or boats fishing with nets or lines or trawls, when under way, shall in daytime indicate their occupation to an approaching vessel by displaying a basket where it can best be seen. If the vessels or boats at anchor have their gear out, they shall, on the approach of other vessels, show the same signal in the direction from the anchor back towards the nets or gear.

80.33 Special signals for vessels employed in hydrographic surveying.—By day a surveying vessel of the Coast and Geodetic Survey, under way and employed in hydrographic surveying, may carry in a vertical line, one over the other not less than 6 feet apart where they can best be seen, three shapes not less than 2 feet in diameter of which the highest and lowest shall be globular in shape and green in color and the middle one diamond in shape and white.

(a) Vessels of the Coast and Geodetic Survey shall carry the above-prescribed marks while actually engaged in hydrographic surveying and under way, including drag work. Launches and other boats shall carry the prescribed marks when necessary.

(b) It must be distinctly understood that these special signals serve only to indicate the nature of the work upon which the vessel is engaged and in no way give the surveying vessel the right-of-way over other vessels or obviate the necessity for a strict observance of the rules for preventing collisions of vessels.

(c) By night a surveying vessel of the Coast and Geodetic Survey, under way and employed in hydrographic surveying, shall carry the regular lights prescribed by the rules of the road.

(d) A vessel of the Coast and Geodetic Survey, when at anchor in a fairway on surveying operations, shall display from the mast during the daytime two black balls in a vertical line and 6 feet apart. At night two red lights shall be displayed in the same manner. In the case of a small vessel the distance between the balls and between the lights may be reduced to 3 feet if necessary.

(e) Such vessels, when at anchor in a fairway on surveying operations, shall have at hand and show, if necessary, in order to attract attention, a flare-up light in addition to the lights which are, by this section, required to be carried.

80.33a Warning signals for Coast Guard vessels while handling or servicing aids to navigation. (a) Coast Guard vessels while engaged in handling or servicing an aid to navigation during the daytime may display from the yard two orange and white vertically striped balls in a vertical line not less than three feet nor more than six feet apart, and during the nighttime may display, in a position where they may best be seen, two red lights in a vertical line not less than three feet nor more than six feet apart.

(b) Vessels, with or without tows, passing Coast Guard vessels displaying this signal, shall reduce their speed sufficiently to insure the safety of both vessels, and when passing within 200 feet of the Coast Guard vessel displaying this signal, their speed shall not exceed 5 miles per hour.

Cross Reference: For rules of the road, see page 1.

UNAUTHORIZED USE OF LIGHTS; UNNECESSARY WHISTLING

80.34 Rule relating to the use of searchlights or other blinding lights.—Flashing the rays of a searchlight or other blinding light onto the bridge or into the pilothouse of any vessel under way is prohibited. Any person who shall flash or cause to be flashed the rays of a blinding light in violation of the above may be proceeded against in accordance with the provisions of R. S. 4450, as amended, looking to the revocation or suspension of his license or certificate.

R. S. 4405, as amended; 46 U. S. C. 375.

80.35 Rule prohibiting unnecessary sounding of the whistle.—Unnecessary sounding of the whistle is prohibited within any harbor limits of the United States. Whenever any licensed officer in charge of any vessel shall authorize or permit such unnecessary whistling, such officer may be proceeded against in accordance with the provisions of R. S. 4450, as amended, looking to a revocation or suspension of his license.

R. S. 4405, as amended; 46 U. S. C. 375.

80.36 Rule prohibiting the carrying of unauthorized lights on vessels.—Any master or pilot of any vessel who shall authorize or permit the carrying of any light, electric or otherwise, not required by law, that in any way will interfere with distinguishing the signal lights, may be proceeded against in accordance with the provisions of R. S. 4450, as amended, looking to a suspension or revocation of his license.

R. S. 4405, as amended; 46 U. S. C. 375.

PART 82—BOUNDARY LINES OF INLAND WATERS

AUTHORITY: §§ 82.1 to 82.275, inclusive, issued under sec. 2, 28 Stat. 672, 33 U. S. C. 151.

GENERAL

Section 82.1 General basis and purpose of boundary lines.—By virtue of the authority vested in the Commandant of the Coast Guard under section 101 of Reorganization Plan No. 3 of 1946 (11 F. R. 7875), and section 2 of the act of February 19, 1895, as amended (28 Stat. 672, 33 U. S. C. 151), the regulations in this part are prescribed to establish the lines dividing the high seas from rivers, harbors, and inland waters in accordance with the intent of the statute and to obtain its correct and uniform administration. The waters inshore of the lines described in this part are "inland waters," and upon them the Inland Rules and Pilot Rules made in pursuance thereof apply. The waters outside of the lines described in this part are the high seas and upon them the International Rules apply. The regulations in this part do not apply to the Great Lakes or their connecting and tributary waters.

82.2   **General rules for inland waters.**—At all buoyed entrances from seaward to bays, sounds, rivers, or other estuaries for which specific lines are not described in this part, the waters inshore of a line approximately parallel with the general trend of the shore, drawn through the outermost buoy or other aid to navigation of any system of aids, are inland waters, and upon them the Inland Rules and Pilot Rules made in pursuance thereof apply, except that Pilot Rules for Western Rivers apply to the Red River of the North, the Mississippi River and its tributaries above Huey P. Long Bridge, and that part of the Atchafalaya River above its junction with the Plaquemine-Morgan City alternate waterway.

ATLANTIC COAST

82.5   **All harbors on the coast of Maine, New Hampshire, and Massachusetts between West Quoddy Head, Maine, and Cape Ann Lighthouse, Mass.**—A line drawn from Sail Rock Lighted Whistle Buoy 1 to the southeasternmost extremity of Long Point, Maine, to the southeasternmost extremity of Western Head; thence to the southeasternmost extremity of Old Man; thence to the southernmost extremity of Double Shot Islands; thence to Libby Islands Lighthouse; thence to Moose Peak Lighthouse; thence to the eastern extremity of Little Pond Head. A line drawn from the southern extremity of Pond Point, Great Wass Island, to the southernmost point of Crumple Island; thence to Petit Manan Lighthouse; thence to Mount Desert Lighthouse; thence to Matinicus Rock Lighthouse; thence to Monhegan Island Lighthouse; thence to Seguin Lighthouse; thence to Portland Lightship; thence to Boon Island Lighthouse; thence to Cape Ann Lighted Whistle Buoy 2.

82.10   **Massachusetts Bay.**—A line drawn from Cape Ann Lighted Whistle Buoy 2 to Boston Lightship; thence to Cape Cod Lighthouse.

82.15   **Nantucket Sound, Vineyard Sound, Buzzard's Bay, Narragansett Bay, Block Island Sound, and easterly entrance to Long Island Sound.**—A line drawn from Chatham Lighthouse to Pollock Rip Lightship; thence to Great Round Shoal Channel Entrance Lighted Whistle Buoy GRS; thence to Sankaty Head Lighthouse. A line drawn from the westernmost extremity of Smith Point, Nantucket Island, to No Mans Land Lighted Whistle Buoy 2; thence to Gay Head Lighthouse; thence to Block Island Southeast Lighthouse; thence to Montauk Point Lighthouse on the easterly end of Long Island, N. Y.

82.20   **New York Harbor.**—A line drawn from Rockaway Point Coast Guard Station to Ambrose Channel Lightship; thence to Navesink (abandoned) Lighthouse (south tower).

82.25   **Delaware Bay and tributaries.**—A line drawn from Cape May East Jetty Light to Cape May Inlet Lighted Bell Buoy 2CM;

thence to Overfalls Lightship; thence to the northernmost extremity of Cape Henlopen.

82.30 Chesapeake Bay and tributaries.—A line drawn from Cape Henry Lighthouse to Cape Henry Junction Lighted Whistle Buoy; thence to Cape Charles Lighthouse.

82.35 Charleston Harbor.—A line drawn from Sullivans Island Coast Guard Station to Charleston Lighted Whistle Buoy 2C; thence to Charleston Lighthouse.

82.40 Savannah Harbor.—A line drawn from the southwestern-most extremity of Braddock Point to Tybee Lighted Whistle Buoy T; thence to the southernmost point of Savannah Beach, bearing approximately 278°.

82.45 St. Simon Sound, St. Andrew Sound, and Cumberland Sound.—Starting from the hotel located approximately ¾ mile, 63½° true, from St. Simon (rear) Lighthouse, a line drawn to St. Simon Lighted Whistle Buoy St. S; thence to St. Andrew Sound Outer Entrance Buoy; thence to St. Marys Entrance Lighted Whistle Buoy 1STM; thence to Amelia Island Lighthouse.

82.50 St. Johns River, Fla.—A line drawn from the east end of the north jetty to the east end of the south jetty.

82.55 Florida Reefs and Keys from Miami to Marquesas Keys.—A line drawn from the east end of the north jetty at the entrance to Miami, to Miami Lighted Whistle Buoy 2; thence to Fowey Rocks Lighthouse; thence to Pacific Reef Lighthouse; thence to Carysfort Reef Lighthouse; thence to Molasses Reef Lighthouse; thence to Alligator Reef Lighthouse; thence to Tennessee Reef Lighthouse; thence to Sombrero Key Lighthouse; thence to American Shoal Lighthouse; thence to Key West Entrance Lighted Whistle Buoy; thence to Sand Key Lighthouse; thence to Cosgrove Shoal Lighthouse; thence to westernmost extremity of Marquesas Keys.

GULF COAST

82.60 Florida Keys from Marquesas to Cape Sable.—A line drawn from the northwesternmost extremity of Marquesas Keys to Northwest Channel Entrance Lighted Bell Buoy 1; thence to the southernmost extremity of East Cape, Cape Sable.

82.65 San Carlos Bay and tributaries.—A line drawn from the northwesternmost point of Estero Island to Caloosa Lighted Bell Buoy 2; thence to Sanibel Island Lighthouse.

82.70 Charlotte Harbor, Fla., and tributaries.—Eastward of Charlotte Harbor Entrance Lighted Bell Buoy off Boca Grande.

82.80 Tampa Bay and tributaries.—A line drawn from the southernmost extremity of Long Key, Fla., to Tampa Bay Lighted Whistle Buoy; thence to Southwest Channel Entrance Lighted Bell Buoy 1; thence to a spire on the northeast side of Anna Maria Key, bearing approximately 109°.

82.89 Apalachee Bay, Fla.—Those waters lying north of a line drawn from Lighthouse Point on St. James Island to Gamble Point on the east side of the entrance to the Aucilla River, Fla.

82.95   Mobile Bay, Ala., to Mississippi Passes, La.—Starting from a point which is located 1 mile, 90° true, from Mobile Point Lighthouse, a line drawn to a point 5.5 miles, 202° true, from Mobile Point Lighthouse; thence to Ship Island Lighthouse; thence to Chandeleur Lighthouse; thence in a curved line following the general trend of the seaward, highwater shore lines of the Chandeleur Islands to the southwesternmost extremity of Errol Shoal (Lat. 29°35.8′ N., Long. 89°00.8′ W.); thence to a point 5.1 miles, 107° true, from Pass a Loutre Abandoned Lighthouse.

82.100   Mississippi River.—The Pilot Rules for Western Rivers are to be followed in the Mississippi River and its tributaries above the Huey P. Long Bridge.

82.103   Mississippi Passes, La., to Sabine Pass, Tex.—A line drawn from a point 5.1 miles, 107° true, from Pass a Loutre Abandoned Lighthouse to a point 1.7 miles, 113° true, from South Pass West Jetty Light; thence to a point 1.8 miles, 189° true, from South West Pass Entrance Light; thence to Ship Shoal Lighthouse; thence to a point 10.2 miles, 172° true, from Calcasieu Pass Entrance Range Front Light; thence to a point 2.5 miles, 163° true, from Sabine Pass East Jetty Light.

82.106   Sabine Pass, Tex., to Galveston, Tex.—A line drawn from Sabine Pass Lighted Whistle Buoy 1 to Galveston Bar Lighted Whistle Buoy 1.

82.111   Galveston, Tex., to Brazos River, Tex.—A line drawn from Galveston Bar Lighted Whistle Buoy 1 to Freeport Entrance Lighted Bell Buoy 1.

82.116   Brazos River, Tex., to the Rio Grande, Tex.—A line drawn from Freeport Entrance Lighted Bell Buoy 1 to a point 4,350 yards, 118° true, from Matagorda Lighthouse; thence to Aransas Pass Lighted Whistle Buoy 1A; thence to a position 10½ miles, 90° true, from the north end of Lopeno Island (Lat. 27°00.1′ N., Long. 97°15.5′ W.); thence to Brazos Santiago Entrance Lighted Whistle Buoy 1.

PACIFIC COAST

82.120   Juan de Fuca Strait, Wash., and Puget Sound.—A line drawn from the northernmost point of Angeles Point to Hein Bank Lighted Bell Buoy; thence to Lime Kiln Light; thence to Kellett Bluff Light; thence to Turn Point Light on Stuart Island; thence to westernmost extremity of Skipjack Island; thence to Patos Island Light; thence to Point Roberts Light.

82.125   Columbia River Entrance.—A line drawn from the west end of the north jetty (above water) to South Jetty Bell Buoy 2SJ.

82.130   San Francisco Harbor.—A straight line from Point Bonita Lighthouse drawn through Mile Rocks Lighthouse to the shore.

82.135   San Pedro Bay.—A line drawn from Los Angeles Harbor Lighthouse through the axis of the Middle Breakwater to the easternmost extremity of the Long Beach Breakwater; thence to Anaheim Bay East Jetty Light 4.

82.140   San Diego Harbor.—A line drawn from the southerly tower of the Coronado Hotel to San Diego Channel Lighted Bell Buoy 5; thence to Point Loma Lighthouse.

82.175 Mamala Bay.—A line drawn from Barbers Point Light-house to Diamond Head Lighthouse.

82.200 Bahia de San Juan.—A line drawn from the northwestern-most extremity of Punta del Morro to Puerto San Juan Lighted Buoy 1; thence to Puerto San Juan Lighted Buoy 2; thence to the northern-most extremity of Isla de Cabras.

82.205 Puerto Arecibo.—A line drawn from the westernmost ex-tremity of the breakwater through Puerto Arecibo Buoy 1; thence through Puerto Arecibo Buoy 2; thence to shore in line with the Church tower in Arecibo.

82.210 Bahia de Mayaguez.—A line drawn from the southernmost extremity of Punta Algarrobo through Manchas Interior Lighted Buoy 3; thence to Manchas Grandes Lighted Buoy 2; thence to the northwesternmost extremity of Punta Guanajibo.

82.215 Bahia de Guanica.—A line drawn from the easternmost extremity of Punta Brea through Bajio La Laja Lighted Buoy 2; thence to the westernmost extremity of Punta Jacinto.

82.220 Bahia de Guayanilla.—A line drawn from the southern-most extremity of Punta Ventana through Bahia de Guayanilla en-trance Lighted Buoy 2; thence to the southeasternmost extremity of Punta Guayanilla.

82.225 Bahia de Ponce.—A line drawn from the southeasternmost extremity of Punta Cuchara through Bahia de Ponce Lighted Buoy 1; thence to Bahia de Ponce Lighted Buoy 2; thence to the southwestern-most extremity of Punta Cabullon.

82.230 Bahia de Jobos.—A line drawn from Punta Arenas through Bahia de Jobos Light; thence to Bahia de Jobos entrance Lighted Buoy 2; thence to the southernmost extremity of Isla Morrillo; thence to the southernmost extremity of Isla Pajaros.

82.235 St. Thomas Harbor, St. Thomas.—A line drawn from the southernmost extremity of Red Point through Lindbergh Bay Buoy 1; thence to Porpoise Rocks Lighted Buoy 2; thence to the southernmost extremity of Flamingo Point; thence to The Triangles Bell Buoy 2; thence to the Green Cay.

82.240 Christiansted Harbor, Island of St. Croix, Virgin Is-lands.—A line drawn from Shoy Point to Scotch Bank Lighted Buoy No. 1; thence to Long Reef Range Rear Daybeacon; thence to shore in range with stack at Little Princess northwestward of leper settle-ment.

82.245 Sonda de Vieques.—A line drawn from the easternmost extremity of Punta Yeguas, Puerto Rico, to a point 1 mile due south of the lighthouse at the entrance to Puerto Ferro; thence eastward in a straight line to a point 1 mile southeast of Punta Este Light, Vieques; thence in a straight line to the easternmost extremity of Punta del Este, Isla Culebrita. A line from the northernmost ex-tremity of Cayo Nordeste to Piedra Stevens Lighted Buoy 1; thence to Las Cucarachas Light; thence to Cabo San Juan Light.

ALASKA

82.275   Bays, sounds, straits and inlets on the coast of south-eastern Alaska between Cape Spencer Light Station and Sitklan Island.—A line drawn from Cape Spencer Light Station due south to a point of intersection which is due west of the southernmost extremity of Cape Cross; thence to Cape Edgecumbe Lighthouse; thence through Cape Bartolome Lighthouse and extended to a point of intersection which is due west of Cape Muzon Lighthouse; thence due east to Cape Muzon Lighthouse; thence to a point which is 1 mile, 180° true, from Cape Chacon Lighthouse; thence to Barren Island Lighthouse; thence to Lord Rock Lighthouse; thence to the southernmost extremity of Garnet Point, Kanagunut Island; thence to the southeasternmost extremity of Island Point, Sitklan Island. A line drawn from the northeasternmost extremity of Point Mansfield, Sitklan Island, 040° true, to where it intersects the mainland.

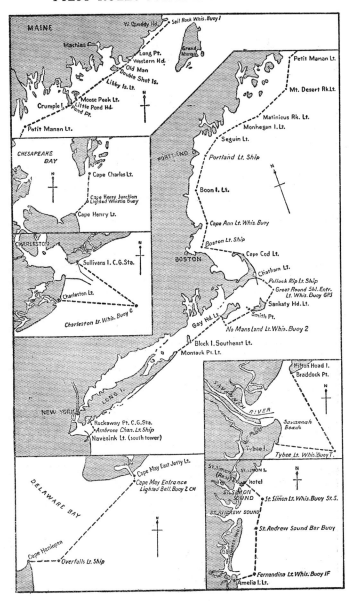

Fig. 2. Atlantic Coast.

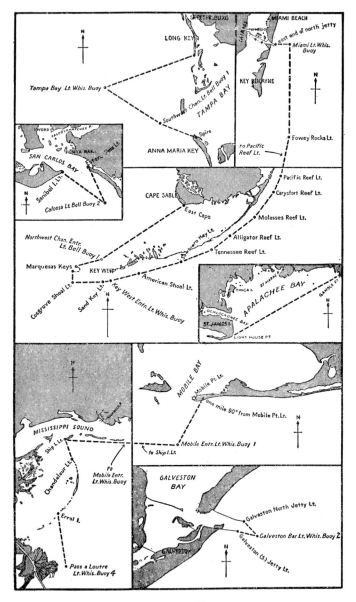

Fig. 3. Gulf Coast.

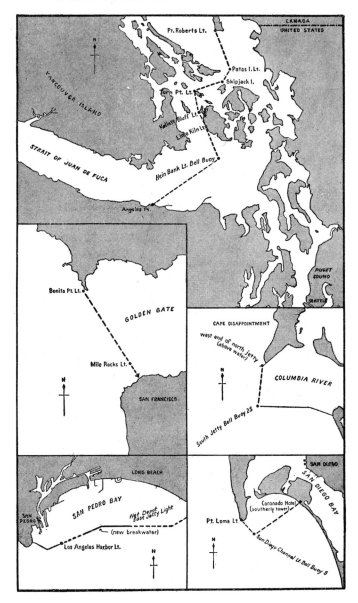

FIG. 4. PACIFIC COAST.

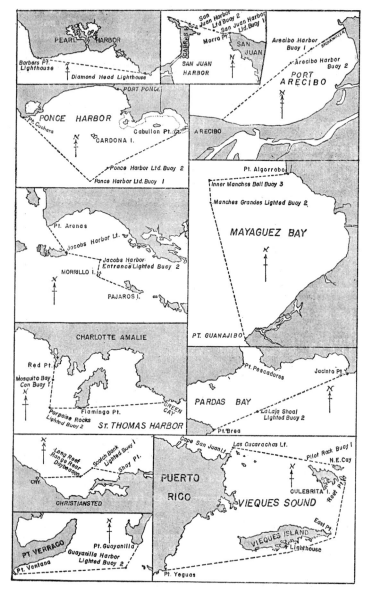

FIG. 5. HAWAII, PUERTO RICO, AND VIRGIN ISLANDS.

POINTS TO BE NOTED IN PILOT RULES

80.03   Short blast is 1 second.
Prolonged blast 4 to 6 seconds. (For vessels under 65 feet in length, 2 seconds deemed sufficient)

80.1   The "danger signal", not less than 4 short blasts.

80.2   *Cross signals forbidden.*

80.3   *Signals for passing to be used whenever steam vessels are passing in any direction within one-half mile of one another, provided they are within sight of each other.*

80.4   Meeting head and head, it is a duty to pass port to port.

80.5   Blast nearing bend, same as Inland Rules. *This is the only signal described as a long blast, and generally in practice is one of about 10 seconds duration. In the light of Rule IX of Article 18, Inland Rules, exchange of signals for meeting and passing immediately after hearing an answer to the bend signal must be understood to mean immediately after sighting each other.*

By International Rules: One short blast means *"I am directing my course to starboard"*; and *has no other meaning.*

By U. S. Pilot Rules: One short blast signifies intention to direct course to own starboard, except when two steam vessels are approaching each other at right angles or obliquely, when it means intention of steam vessel to starboard of the other to hold course and speed.

RADAR AND THE RULES OF THE ROAD

Due to knowledge determined by *radar* of another vessel's presence and movements, during fog or adverse visibility conditions, obviously the onus of taking timely and proper action to avoid risk of collision becomes an obligation of greater moment to a vessel so informed than had she not been thus advantageously equipped. Rules of the Road to be considered:

Until sighting or hearing the other vessel the Rule of Good Seamanship (General Prudential Rule) and the Rule of Special Circumstances apply.

Slowing down to steerageway will seldom cause any trouble, and will often avoid it.

All things being equal, the starboard turn offers the better of choices if a turn is to be made.

The instinctive maneuver of the mariner is to turn to starboard and decrease his speed. There is little wonder that this is the maneuver followed in most cases. Rules of the Road in meeting situations require a starboard turn; the Rules in crossing situations require the burdened vessel to turn to starboard or slow down or both. In most narrow channels, starboard side is the proper side. Situations where port turns are required or desirable are rare in comparison to the standard turn to starboard.

To make the plot referred to: Suppose you are making 15 knots on a course north true and a target is picked up bearing 50° true at a distance of 10 miles. Take the chart and run off a line indicating your

General instructions to serve as a guide

when ships are detected by radar in restricted visibility in open sea.

The International Rules of the Road to be observed.

ANALYSIS ON RADAR AND RULES OF THE ROAD MADE BY SWEDISH GOVERNMENT FOLLOWING ANDREA DORIA STOCKHOLM COLLISION		
Range of radar scale (Use suitable scale)		Watch target carefully, amplify radar picture by plotting if the bearing does not appreciably change at first. Required actions to be made in ample time to enable the ships to pass each other at a safe distance (preferably outside sound range). Compare Steering instructions below. Maneuvers to be positive and clear and easily perceptible by other radar-equipped ships. Check the result of the maneuver by plotting continuously. Watch carefully any simultaneous movements of the approaching ship.
Keep moderate speed. (Int. Rules on Collision, 16A)		Navigate with caution. Proceed at low speed. Avoid alteration of course. Notice any change of scale. Plot more frequently.
	SOUND RANGE	Stop engine, if circumstances permit and if the other ship is forward of the beam (cf. Rule 16B.)
	STOP ENGINES	Keep your course. Navigate with caution. Listen.
	SIGHT RANGE	As soon as ships sight each other, steering and sailing to be governed, solely, by the International Collision regulations of 1948, Part C.
	APP. 3 MI.	Safety first. Stop engines in time. Avoid alteration of course to port. Avoid close-quarter situations while under way. To slacken speed and keep waiting until the other ship has passed, is a way of minimizing the risk of collision and means less loss of time than is ordinarily imagined. Give fog-signals and keep a good lookout. Practice your radar in good visibility.
	APP. 5 MI.	

Where collision risks and movements of approaching ships are ascertained by plotting prior to the distance getting below 5 nautical miles, some of the measures suggested below might generally be taken, before fog-signals are heard or should have been heard.

Situation shown by plotting: change of bearing not appreciable	Suggested measure at the earliest possible moment outside the 5-miles limit and beyond fog-signal range:	Rule 27 to apply, together with the Rules stated below.
1. Ships meet end on, or nearly end on.	Alter course to starboard at least 30°, so as to keep ships clear of each other, even if similar maneuver is taken by the other ship. Maintain course until the other ship is abeam, or danger of collision is over. If necessary, slacken speed still further. Continue plotting.	Rule 18
2. Ships approach one another on crossing courses. Other ship on port side.	Keep course, slacken speed or stop to let the other ship pass ahead, if she is not radar-fitted; if further plotting proves she has got radar and is taking avoiding action astern of your own ship or acts in accordance with alternative 1 below, proceed on your course and navigate with caution. Continue plotting until danger is over.	Rules 19, 22, 23
3. Ships approach on crossing courses: the other ship on starboard.	Alt. 1. Slacken, stop, or reverse; let the other ship pass. Continue plotting. Alt. 2. Alter course to starboard to let the other ship pass clear on port; thus, own ship will pass clear astern of the other, even if she stops and is making no way through the water. Continue plotting. Alt. 3. Combine alt. 1 and 2.	Rules 19, 22, 23
4. Own ship overtaking another straight from the stern.	Alter course at least 30° in the most suitable direction, considering other echoes and circumstances; keep course and continue plotting until danger is over. Where conditions do not permit your ship to pass the other safely, reduce speed and postpone overtaking.	Rule 24
5. Own ship overtaking another on crossing courses.	Slacken speed or alter course--or both--so as to facilitate overtaking at a safe distance astern of the other ship. Continue plotting.	Rule 24, (cf. 22, 23)
6. Own ship overtaken by another.	Continue plotting. No avoiding action on the basis of radar contact. If necessary, sound fog-signals more frequently.	Rule 21

course of north true. Then from a point on this line run off a line 50° true and at a point 10 miles to scale on this line plot the position of the target. Six minutes later the range and bearing is 8 3/4 miles on a bearing of 55°. During this time you have moved ahead 1 1/2 miles. Plot this point and from there run off a line bearing 55° and mark a point 8 3/4 miles from your position. Draw a line joining the two positions of the target and extend it until it crosses your track. With parallel rulers run this line down to the compass rose and you will find that vessel is on a course of 282° true. Then with your dividers determine the distance between points. You will find that during 6 minutes the vessel has moved a half mile, therefore her speed must be 5 knots.

The point at which the two lines cross is 8.1 miles from your position at time of first bearing and is 7.8 miles from first position of target. If both vessels maintain their courses and speeds your vessel will arrive at the point in 32 minutes while it will take the other vessel 1 hour and 34 minutes.

Don't be satisfied with only two bearings. In the instant case target vessel might have increased speed to 15 knots right after the second bearing, thus changing the situation as to involve risk of collision. Unless a continuing plot is made any change in the situation would not be detected.

New Radar Requirement. The U.S. Coast Guard requires that deck officers be qualified as radar observers. This requirement applies to applicants for original licenses and candidates for increase in scope of license or raise in grade.

Candidates must either pass a professional examination in radar or furnish a certificate of completion of an approved radar course.

Maritime Administration Radar Schools are located in New York, San Francisco, and New Orleans. Completion of the 1-week course meets Coast Guard requirements.

This radar course is intended to help the navigator to know the full possibilities of marine navigational radar and to make the best use of it, and also to know its limitations and safeguards to be used.

Radar Plotting. Whether the merchant marine deck officer likes it or not, as long as he is shipmates with radar, he is going to have to become familiar with the maneuvering board and regard it as a radar plotting sheet designed especially to assist him.

The Maneuvering Board. There is no question that maneuvering board problems can be difficult. However, those problems are of no concern to the merchant officer. The Navy has plenty of manpower to look after their involved problems of fleet maneuvering. You, the merchant officer, alone on a dark bridge except for the helmsman, are concerned only with the most elementary problem—how to miss that ship approaching and still keep six inches of water beneath the keel. In short—is the ship ahead on a collision course?

Anyone who has passed his third mate's license examination can solve this simple problem by using the maneuvering board . . . if you can't, it is because you have been led to believe the solution is highly technical.

Unfortunately, textbook discussions of maneuvering boards fail to point out that the standard size form, H.O. 2556a, the 12″ x 12″ sheet, was never meant to be used by a harassed mate alone on a dark bridge. This small scale form was designed for use in a lighted CIC room on a man-o'-war where a petty officer with a wide desk and a drawer of sharp pencils could devote his full time to developing the plot.

Surprising as it will be to most deck officers, for many years the

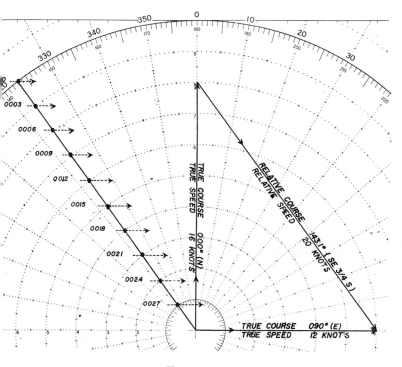

FIGURE 6

TRATED ABOVE is a typical maneuvering board problem for determining true course and of the vessel observed. The pips seen at three-minute intervals show the course and of the observed vessel as seen in the PPI scope. The dashed arrows, which are not ent to the scope observer, show the true course of the observed vessel. To the right is a vector diagram for the solution of the problem of true course and speed. The true of the observing ship is 000° and a speed of 16 knots, employing the 2:1 scale. At ead of the vector arrow of the observing ship is placed the tail of the vectoring arrow senting the relative, or apparent, course and speed. This course is parallel to the course served on the radar scope and the speed is equal to that computed by determining the ce and time between pips. With the known quantities, true course and speed of the ving vessel, and the relative course and speed thus laid down, the true course and speed observed vessel can be obtained by drawing in the third arrow as indicated. Both the e speed and the true speed of the observed vessel must be determined using the 2:1 also.

Hydrographic Office* has published a large scale maneuvering board which has received no publicity. Known as H.O. 2556, it is 24″ x 24″, and is ideal for use on a merchant ship bridge.

The maneuvering board itself is nothing more than a compass rose containing a *nomogram*, or combined speed, distance, and time scale The maneuvering board is used to calculate the *relative motion* of ships moving or maneuvering in formation, and from it the navigator calculates distances, courses, and speeds required for various evolutions. Solution of maneuvering board problems is fairly simple when you understand the fundamentals of relative motion.

Relative Plotting. Motion observed on the PPI scope is relative movement. Actual motion is seen on your PPI scope only when your ship is stationary.

Figure 6 illustrates this point. Your vessel is on course 000° at a speed of 16 knots. Another ship is observed at three-minute intervals and, after plotting, shows a relative course of 143° and a speed of 20 knots. If this data were accepted as indicating the observed vessel's true course and speed, it is obvious how much in error this assumption would be. In the diagram, the small arrows are used to illustrate the true direction of the observed ship, and normally would not appear on a shipboard plot.

The diagram further shows how the relative course and speed obtained from radar observations is plotted to obtain the true course and speed. This differs by a substantial extent from the direction and speed of the pip observed on the PPI scope.

It cannot be overemphasized that radar observations must be translated from relative to true motion before any conclusions can be made on true course and speed.

Relative Motion. Geographical motion is the motion involved in a change of geographical position, as when a ship moves from point A to point B on the chart, or an automobile moves from New York to Kansas City. Relative motion, on the other hand, is the combined result of the geographical motion of moving bodies. For instance suppose two ships sail from the same anchorage, one heading north the other east, and both making 20 knots. Disregarding set and drift each will have a geographical motion of 5 miles in the first 15 minutes but at the end of that time they will be 7 miles apart. Although each has travelled only 5 miles, their relative motion will be 7 miles.

The maneuvering board is used to calculate the relative motion involved in a ship's change of position from one point in a formation to another, and from that the course and speed required to arrive at the given position at a given time.

Navigational Plot. Relative positions of ships in formation may be presented graphically by the navigational plot, and their DR positions run forward to show changing relationships. The navigational plot however, does not usually present a good picture of changing conditions as they appear to an observer on one of the ships, and change of position calculated by this method frequently require a trial-and error solution.

*Now the U.S. Naval Oceanographic Office.

Relative Movement Plot. By the relative movement plot, not only actual motion, but motion relative to a moving point (relative motion) may be determined.

If all the ships in a formation are proceeding at the same speed along the same course, they remain stationary relative to each other; in other words, they have no relative movement. However, if one ship

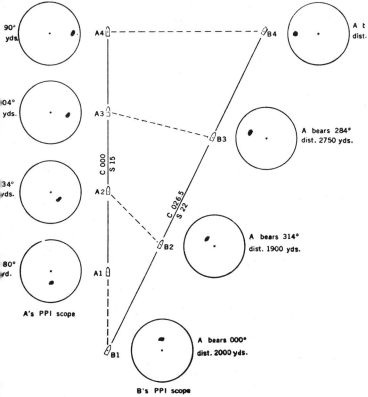

FIG. 7. RELATIVE MOVEMENT ON A NAVIGATIONAL PLOT.

forges ahead or drops behind, then that ship has movement relative to the others, and they have movement relative to it, even though they remain on their former course and continue to run at the same speed.

Relative movement, then, occurs *only when the actual motions of two or more units are not the same.*

Relationship of Relative Movements to Navigational Plot. Figure 7 shows ship A proceeding on course 000° at a speed of 15 knots, while ship B is on course 026.5° at speed 22 knots. When A is at A_1, B is at B_1; When A is at A_2, B is at B_2, etc. The full lines represent the navigational plots of the two ships. The bearing and distance at any time can be determined directly by measurement. Note that in each position illustrated the bearing of B from A is exactly the reciprocal of A's bearing from B.

In Fig. 8 the various positions shown in the PPI scopes of Fig. 7 are plotted on a single scope for each ship. Note that they form a straight line. It can be seen that, although ship B is actually on course 026.5°, its movement *relative* to A is in the direction 062°. Similarly, the direction of relative movement of A with respect to B is the reciprocal of this, or 242°, although A is on the actual course 000°.

The PPI scope permits visualization of relative movement, since the positions of the target ship on the scope are all relative to your

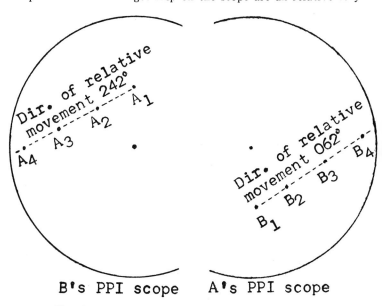

B's PPI scope   A's PPI scope

Fig. 8. Relative Movement on a Radar PPI Scope.

ship. Hence, the motion observed on the PPI scope is *relative movement. Actual motion is seen on your PPI scope only when your ship is stationary.*

Parts of the Relative Movement Plot. The relative movement method consists of two distinct but related parts:

1. Relative Plot.
2. Vector Diagram.

The function of each line and point must be clearly understood, as well as its relationship to every other line and point, if problems are to be solved intelligently.

Relative Plot. It will be noted in Figs. 7 and 8 that the ship on which the radar is mounted remains always at the center of the PPI scope. Therefore, in the relative plot, we have the following rule:

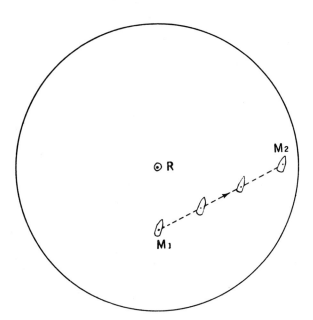

Fig. 9. Elements of a Relative Plot.

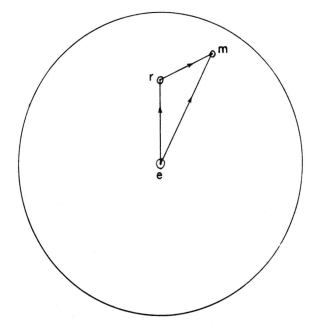

Fig. 10. Vector Diagram.

The ship with respect to which relative movement is to be shown remain fixed on the plot.

This ship, termed the *reference ship*, is placed at the center of the diagram and labeled R (Fig. 9). Since you are usually interested chiefly in the position of other ships with respect to your own, it is preferable to designate your ship as the reference ship. It follows that any ship other than the reference ship will be shown in a different position on the plot, except in the special case of a ship on the same course and speed as the reference ship. Any ship other than the reference ship is called a *maneuvering ship* and is labeled M. Its position at the beginning of a maneuver is labeled M_1 and its position at the end of a maneuver, M_2. When more than two positions of the maneuvering ship are of interest, they are labeled M_1, M_2, M_3, etc., in order.

Figure 9 illustrates the situation in Fig. 7 with A the reference ship and B the maneuvering ship. The line M_1—M_2, called the *relative movement line*, defines:

1. Direction of relative movement of the maneuvering ship with respect to the reference ship.

2. Distance of relative movement (by its length).

(This line gives no clue as to the heading or speed of the maneuvering ship, since the ship heads in the direction of travel through the water and not in the direction of relative movement.)

The relative movement line indicates the actual heading only when the directions of relative and actual motion happen to coincide.

Vector Diagram (Speed Triangle). The vector diagram, sometimes called the speed triangle, is illustrated in Fig. 10. It is used to solve for courses and speeds.

The speed triangle is composed of three vectors, representing the following:

1. The *er* vector.
   a. *Actual course* of the reference ship, indicated by the direction of the line *er*.
   b. *Actual speed* of the reference ship, indicated by the length of the line *er*.
2. The *em* vector.
   a. *Actual course* of the maneuvering ship, indicated by the direction of the line *em*.
   b. *Actual speed* of the maneuvering ship, indicated by the length of the line *em*.
3. The *rm* vector.
   a. *Direction of relative movement* of the maneuvering ship with respect to the reference ship, indicated by the direction of the line *rm*.
   b. *Relative speed, or speed of the maneuvering ship* relative to the reference, indicated by the length of the line *rm*.

Labels Are Important. You can see, then, that each line (or vector) represents both direction (course) and speed. The diagram must be properly labeled for correct interpretation.

Relationship Between Relative Plot and Vector Diagram. Note that direction of relative movement is indicated by both the relative movement line of the relative plot and the vector *rm* of the vector diagram. This is the connecting link between the two diagrams. Since they both represent direction of relative movement, they must in every case be parallel (Fig. 11).

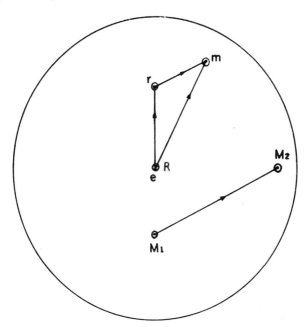

FIG. 11. COMPLETE RELATIVE MOVEMENT PLOT.

The *function* of each diagram must be kept clearly in mind. The *relative plot* indicates bearings and distances. The *vector diagram* indicates courses and speeds.

Use of the Maneuvering Board in Solving Problems. The Hydrographic Office has prepared a plotting sheet to facilitate solution of relative movement problems (Fig. 12).

More recently, BuShips has developed a mechanical maneuvering board to further expedite the solution of relative movement problems. Full instructions are provided with each instrument (Fig. 13).

Maneuvering Board Technique. The following hints on maneuvering board problems are based on the mistakes made in problems by midshipmen at the U.S. Naval Academy.

1. Be sure to read the problem carefully, and be certain you understand it before you proceed with the solution. Check all numbers carefully.

2. Avoid using reciprocals. When a bearing is given, be sure you understand to which ship the bearing applies, and from which ship it is taken.

3. Be particularly careful of the scale of the nomogram at the bottom of the form.

4. Measure carefully. It is easy to pick off the wrong circle, or make an error of 10° in direction. Read the plotted answers carefully.

5. Plot only *true* bearings. If a relative bearing or compass direction is given, convert it to a true direction before plotting.

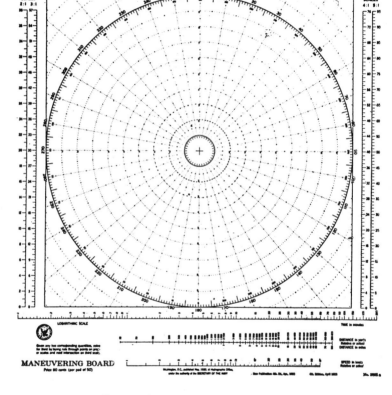

FIG. 12. H.O. MANEUVERING BOARD.

6. Label all points, and put arrowheads on lines as soon as they are drawn.

7. Remember that relative speed is from *r* to *m*. This can be remembered by associating the letters *r* and *m* with relative movement. The arrowhead never points in the opposite direction.

Actual speed vectors always originate at the center of the diagram.

9. Remember that vectors indicate direction of motion as well as speed. Thus, motion along the relative movement line is associated with relative and not *actual* speed. Relative speed is determined when relative distance and time are known. To obtain actual speed, actual distance and time must be known.

10. Remember that the maneuvering board moves with the reference ship; therefore, the reference ship is always at the center of the diagram.

11. Do not attach undue significance to the center of the maneuvering board. This point is used both as the origin of actual speed vectors and the position of the reference ship merely for the sake of convenience.

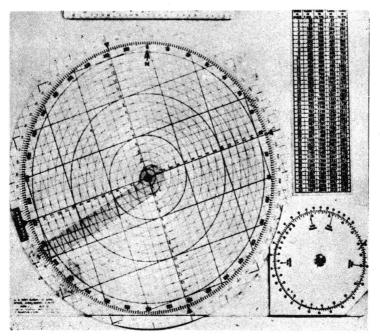

FIG. 13. MECHANICAL MANEUVERING BOARD.

12. Work a problem one step at a time. An entire problem may seem complicated, but each step is simple, and often suggests the next step. Remember that all problems are based on a few simple principles.

It is a good idea to refer back to these suggestions periodically, for practically all mistakes result from the violation of one or more of them, or from poor arithmetic.

Examples of problems the solution of which will be required by the USCG examiners. Each problem involves a determination of course and speed and closest point of approach. The use of a maneuvering board is recommended for solution. The problems represent relative motion interpretation and do not indicate any recommendation for a vessel's action while using radar.

Q. Your vessel is on course 240° True at speed 7 knots. At 1700, a vessel is observed on the PPI scope bearing 000° T at a range of 3

miles. At 1720, the vessel is observed bearing 010° T at a range of
1.5 miles. (1) Assuming that both vessels maintain course and speed,
determine the distance between them at the closest point of approach.
(2) Determine the course and speed of the vessel observed.

A.   (1) 0.5 mile (at 1730). (2) 213.3° and 9.6 knots.

Q.   Your vessel is on course 165° True at speed 17 knots. At 1900,
a vessel is observed on the PPI scope bearing 244° T at a range of
2.2 miles. At 1915, the vessel is observed bearing 225° T at a range
of 1.4 miles. (1) Assuming both vessels maintain course and speed,
determine the distance between them at the closest point of approach.
(2) Determine the course and speed of the vessel observed.

A.   (1) 1 mile (at 1930). (2) 153° and 18.5 knots.

Q.   Your vessel is on course 125° True at speed of 16 knots. At
0100, a vessel is observed on the PPI scope bearing 150° T at a range
of 7 miles. At 0115, the vessel is observed bearing 140° T at a range
of 4.5 miles. (1) Assuming that both vessels maintain course and
speed, determine the distance between them at the closest point of
approach. (2) Determine the course and speed of the vessel observed.

A.   (1) 2 miles (at 0138). (2) 083.1° and 10.75 knots.

Q.   Your vessel is on course 035° True at speed of 19 knots. At
2200, a vessel is observed on the PPI scope bearing 020° T at a range
of 9 miles. At 2206, the vessel is observed bearing 030° T at a range
of 5 miles. (1) Assuming that both vessels maintain course and speed,
determine the distance between them at the closest point of approach.
(2) Determine the course and speed of the vessel observed.

A.   (1) 1.9 miles (at 2213). (2) 168.7° and 26.2 knots.

Q.   Your vessel is on course 205° True at speed of 10 knots. At
0500, a vessel is observed on the PPI scope bearing 230° T at a range
of 9 miles. At 0512, the vessel is observed bearing 220° T at a range
of 6 miles. (1) Assuming that both vessels maintain course and speed,
determine the distance between them at the closest point of approach.
(2) Determine the course and speed of the vessel observed.

A.   (1) 2.9 miles (at 0531). (2) 106.8° and 11.4 knots.

Q.   Your vessel is on course 310° True at speed of 18 knots. At
1100, a vessel is observed on the PPI scope bearing 300° T at a range
of 9 miles. At 1110, the vessel is observed bearing 295° T at a range
of 6 miles. (1) Assuming that both vessels maintain course and speed,
determine the distance between them at the closest point of approach.
(2) Determine the course and speed of the vessel observed.

A.   (1) 1.5 miles (at 1129). (2) The other vessel is practically dead
in the water.

Q.   Your vessel is on course 235° True at a speed of 8 knots. At
1600, a vessel is observed on the PPI scope bearing 165° T at a range
of 7 miles. At 1612, the vessel is observed bearing 155° T at a range
of 5 miles. (1) Assuming that both vessels maintain course and speed,
determine the distance between them at the closest point of approach.
(2) Determine the course and speed of the vessel observed.

A.   (1) 2.7 miles (at 1634). (2) 322.3° and 8.3 knots.

Q. Your vessel is on course 355° True at a speed of 7.5 knots. At 1800, a vessel is observed on the PPI scope bearing 020° T at a range of 6 miles. At 1806, the vessel is observed bearing 020° T at a range of 4 miles. (1) Assuming that both vessels maintain course and speed, determine the distance between them at the closest point of approach. (2) Determine the course and speed of the vessel observed.

A. (1) Vessels are on collision course (at 1812). (2) 213.5° and 13.6 knots.

Q. Your vessel is on course 045° True at a speed 15 knots. At 0900, a vessel is observed on the PPI scope bearing 080° T at a range of 9 miles. At 0912, the vessel is observed bearing 060° T at a range of 7.5 miles. (1) Assuming that both vessels maintain course and speed, determine the distance between them at their closest point of approach. (2) Determine the course and speed of the vessel observed.

A. (1) 7.2 miles (at 0920). (2) 356.9° and 21.6 knots.

Q. Your vessel is on course 110° True at speed 18.5 knots. At 1000, a vessel is observed on the PPI scope bearing 070° True at a range of 9 miles. At 1006, the vessel is observed bearing 073° T at a range of 7 miles. (1) Assuming that both vessels maintain course and speed, determine the distance between them at their closest point of approach. (2) Determine the course and speed of the vessel observed.

A. (1) 1.6 miles (at 1026). (2) 181° and 16.65 knots.

Q. Your vessel is on course 355° True at speed 6 knots. At 0900, a vessel is observed on the PPI scope bearing 020° T at a range of 6 miles. At 0920, the vessel is observed bearing 031° T at a range of 4.3 miles. (1) Assuming that both vessels maintain course and speed, determine the distance between them at their closest point of approach. (2) Determine the course and speed of the vessel observed.

A. (1) 2.5 miles (at 0956). (2) The other vessel is practically dead in the water.

Q. Your vessel is on course 290° True at speed 13 knots. At 1300, a vessel is observed on the PPI scope bearing 250° T at a range of 7 miles. At 1330, the vessel is observed bearing 260° T at a range of 4.9 miles. (1) Assuming that both vessels maintain course and speed, determine the distance between them at their closest point of approach. (2) Determine the course and speed of the vessel observed.

A. (1) 2.5 miles (at 1424). (2) 310.8° and 11.5 knots.

Q. Your vessel is on course 095° True at speed 7 knots. At 1100, a vessel is observed on the PPI scope bearing 110° T at a range of 6 miles. At 1106, the vessel is observed bearing 100° T at a range of 4.7 miles. (1) Assuming that both vessels maintain course and speed, determine the distance between them at their closest point of approach. (2) Determine the course and speed of the vessel observed.

A. (1) 3.1 miles (at 1119). (2) 345° and 12.2 knots.

Chapter 14

SHIP CONSTRUCTION, MAINTENANCE AND REPAIR

HULL CONSTRUCTION

Experience, observation and theoretical analysis make up the basis of ship design, enabling the builder to meet the requirements of strength in ordinary conditions of sea service.

Load, in reference to a ship's structure, denotes the total force that the vessel, or part of the vessel, must withstand when floating in a given condition.

Stress is the amount of load to which a particular member of the structure is subjected. It is usually expressed in pounds per square inch of cross section of the material.

Strain is the amount of actual *yield* of a structural part to the stress applied. Within the *elastic limit*, the deformation or strain produced is proportional to the stress.

Elastic Limit is the point beyond which an added stress will produce deformation of the material.

Longitudinal Framing includes the parts of the structural framework which run in a fore-and-aft direction, and whose chief function is to supply longitudinal strength.

Transverse Framing is made up of the "ribs" of the body, or the parts whose chief function is to give transverse, or athwartship, strength.

Stresses Floating Light are due to unequal distribution of weight. Buoyancy exerts greater upward stress on empty hold compartments than on engine space or on extreme ends of the vessel.

Stresses in the Loaded Condition. Besides the local stresses on frames, beams, etc., the shearing stresses due to differences of weight in adjacent compartments are here usually more marked, and of an opposite name to those in the light condition. The excess buoyancy force under one compartment adjacent to another is the measure of stress on the whole structure, in still water, at the separating bulkhead.

Hydrostatic Pressure. The vertical component of total water pressure on the hull is the measure of buoyancy, and is equal to the vessel's weight or displacement tonnage. Water pressure is exerted in the direction normal to the immersed surface.

Stresses in a Seaway are due to the structure being locally supported in greater measure than usual by a passing wave. A vessel may be lifted at each end while only partly supported amidships in a following, or in a head sea; and may be subjected to racking and twisting stresses in a beam sea, or in a quarterly one.

Resistance to these forces is met by considering the vessel a huge hollow girder made up of an arrangement of small girders. When a bar is bent its upper edge must be stretched or elongated, and its lower edge contracted or compressed. Hence the requisite for a well-formed girder is a concentration of material in its upper and lower parts. The deeper the bar or plate the greater is the resistance to bending or tensile strain on the upper edge and compression on the lower. A bar's resistance to bending varies as the square of its depth and directly as its breadth; added resistance is gained by reinforcing its upper and lower edges with extra material, as the *flange* or the *bulb* ordinarily found on structural steel.

Vessels subject to great stress are those of a large *length-depth* ratio, or a small depth compared with the length. In all vessels longitudinal strength, as in the girder, is mostly required amidships, a reduction being gradually effected toward their ends.

Transverse stresses attain a maximum in a rolling vessel. As in the case of a box, the *racking* and *collapsing* forces set up at the corners must be met at those parts by the required resisting buildup of material.

Local Stresses:

1. Panting. Due to head resistance causing the bows, particularly the bluff type, to work in and out, or "pant," in a seaway.

2. Pounding. Pronounced in full-formed vessels when in a head sea and in the light condition. Fore end of ship descends like a hammer upon the waves.

3. Propulsion by engines. Particularly that due to vibration at stern frame and in engine room.

4. Propulsion by sail. Wind pressure on sails and momentum of masts in rolling is transmitted to hull by masts and shrouds.

5. Deck cargoes cause great twisting and racking stresses in a seaway.

6. Shipping heavy seas causes sudden, severe stresses to decks, bulwarks, bulkheads, etc.

7. Heavy concentrated weights, as engines, boilers, winches, windlass, cranes, anchors, guns, etc.

8. Loading while lying aground, as must be done in certain trades, requires special bottom construction and heavier framing.

STRUCTURE

(For illustration of the parts of a ship and their relative positions, see Figs. 1, 3 and 4.)

Scantlings are the measurements of the various frame-work parts of the structure, as frames, beams, floors, stringers.

A Full Scantling Ship has full strength (per classification society's rules) of structure maintained up to uppermost continuous deck. This type is usually built for heavy deadweight cargoes.

Awning or Shade Deck Ship. Hull below 'tween decks mainly relied upon for strength; affords large proportion of internal space for cargo of light nature or passengers.

Spar Decked Ship. This type has no very clearly defined limits. It is a construction somewhere between the above-noted types.

Shell Plating. Besides providing the watertight covering for the hull, is an important element in longitudinal strength, and binds the whole structure to its work.

Thickness of shell plating varies from 7/20″ in a 162′ vessel to 14/20″ in a 450′ vessel. It is of different thicknesses in different strakes, being thickest in the *sheerstrake, garboard, and bilge.* Plating must be thick-

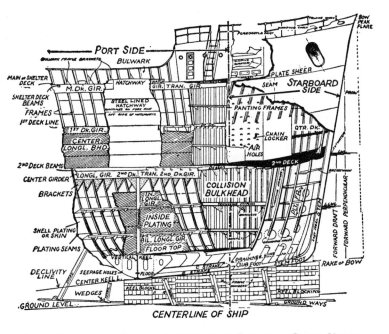

Fig. 1. Sketch of Framing Section of a Bow in a Cargo Vessel.

ened at the bows if ice may be encountered; at the stem and stern where vibration and twisting stresses are to be met; in way of breaks in the continuity of the structure, or where openings must be cut. The principle aimed at is the arranging of the plating so that at all points its strength shall be proportional to the stress to be borne, thus making the strength generally uniform.

For continuity of strength the plates in each strake are staggered, so that as few as possible are joined at the same distance from the vessel's ends. The strakes are usually named *A, B, C,* etc., from the keel upwards, and the plates numbered **1, 2, 3,** etc., from aft forward.

Framing. Framing, both longitudinal and transverse, has two major purposes: to maintain the ship's original form, and to directly provide longitudinal and transverse strength. While providing a means of support and fastening for the shell plating, the framing is dependent upon the latter for keeping it to its work.

Transverse frames are spaced from 20″ to 36″ apart, according to size and type of vessel. Toward the ends this spacing is reduced by a few inches.

In the longitudinal framing system, the heavy transverse frames are of the web, or deep, form, and spaced at intervals of from 12′ to 16′. Between these, the fore-and-aft framing takes care of local stiffness and is the means of support and fastening of the shell plating.

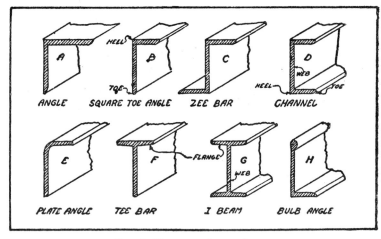

Fig. 2. Types of Angle Irons.

In the transverse framing system, the *frame bar* (or angle bar) extends continuously from keel to weather deck. The long flange points inward at right angles to the fore-and-aft line, and the short flange is shaped to lie flat against the shell plating for a "faying" surface.

The reverse frame bar is similarly shaped, and is riveted to the back of the frame bar for the required strength and rigidity.

A web frame is a specially deep frame built like a girder. Such frames are placed at certain intervals in long holds, or to compensate for the cutting away of frames to provide side openings in the hull, where loss of transverse strength would otherwise occur.

Other structural materials, as the Z bar, the channel bar, and the bulb angle bar, are used for frames, stiffeners, beams, stringers, etc. (*See* Fig. 2.)

Floors are deep plates laid on edge athwartships, against the ship's bottom. Their principal use in the structure is to preserve transverse strength against the inroads of the various vertical stresses common to a vessel's bottom members. They provide the means of fastening the outer and inner bottom plating. In the transverse framing system, they are practically heavy continuations, in way of the ship's bottom, of the ordinary frames.

Beams form the foundation for the decks. They are bracketed to the frames by knee plates at their ends, and so unite the whole transverse section, whose members are the *frame* and *reversed frame*, the *floor*, the *beam*, and the *pillar*, in the ordinary framing system.

Pillars, or hold stanchions, support the beams and so supply the necessary rigidity to the decks.

Longitudinals. These are the keel, keelson, stringer, tank margin plate, and intercostal.

In whatever form constructed, the *keel* is the ship's backbone. Projecting keels are seldom found in modern vessels for the reason that the same, or a greater longitudinal strength may be obtained by building up the required material *inside* the hull. In the latter case the term "keel" denotes the *keel plate* upon which is set the middle-line keelson, the two combined really forming the keel.

The *middle-line keelson*, besides forming the backbone of the hull in combination with the keel plate, forms the fore-and-aft partition of the double-bottom tank system. Also called *center-line girder*.

The *side keelson* is similar to the above, but laid parallel to, and at some distance outward from, the keel.

Bilge keels are usually projecting bulb and angle bars, fitted at the turn of the bilge for the greater part of the vessel's length. Their purpose is to reduce rolling by acting as a brake against the surrounding water.

The *false keel* is a plate or timber bolted to the lower side of the keel for the purpose of protecting it against wear and tear, as in the case of grounding. Also called the *shoe*.

Stringers are girders fitted continuously fore-and-aft to "bridge" the frames and provide longitudinal stiffness generally. In a large vessel the bilge stringer is fitted just above the turn of the bilge, and the hold stringer about half way between the bilge stringer and the deck next above.

Intercostal plates are fitted fore-and-aft between the floors, their chief purpose being to hold the floors from collapsing under vertical stress; they also serve to stiffen the shell and inner bottom plating, and, in the cellular double bottom construction we are here considering, they act as wash plates in restraining the otherwise free movement of water or oil in a "slack" tank.

A *stringer plate* is laid as the outside strake of a deck. It is heavier than the plating of the particular deck and, being strongly attached to the shell plating and the beams, greatly assists the beam knees in their work. It also gives longitudinal tensile strength to the hull.

Stress-Strength Relations. Distribution of material must be consistent with relation to the stresses to be borne by the vessel. Frames and floors usually maintain their maximum size for three-fifths of the vessel's length amidships, being reduced for the remaining one-fifth at each end. *Longitudinal strength* is consistently provided by arrang-

ing the material according to the requisites of the symmetrical girder
we may take the ship to represent. The classification societies have
thoroughly investigated this subject, and have drawn up the requirements for scantlings, plating, etc., at the particular locations in the
structure to suit all classes and types of vessels.

Engine and boiler spaces require specially rugged design and construction, not only to provide for the localized weight of machinery
and probable vibration effect, but because of the necessary break in
the arrangement of transverse strength due to the omission of a considerable number of beams. This latter condition is compensated for

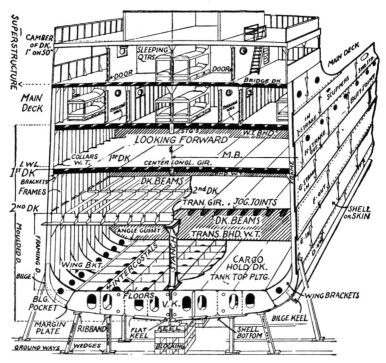

FIG. 3. SKETCH OF MIDSHIP SECTION OF A CARGO VESSEL.

by supplying a few extra heavy beams where possible, and by the use
of *web frames*. The boilers are supported on *stools*, or *cradles*, secured to
the floors, and the engines are fastened down on the *bed-plates*, which
are also secured to the floors.

The **Stern Frame.** The after end of a screw steamer is subjected to
heavy stresses of a shock and vibratory nature, especially during bad
weather at sea, due to the sudden changes of resistances met by both
rudder and propeller. Extra heavy fastening is required at the junction
of the keel with the frame, and the shell plating strakes which terminate at the *stern-post* (or forward part of stern frame) are tap-riveted

to it. The head, or upper part, of the frame, which is usually a continuation of the *rudder-post* (the after member of the frame) is firmly secured to the *transom floor*, which, in the usual run of construction, is the aftermost and deepest floor in the vessel.

Panting Stringers are extra stringers fitted in the bows from abaft the collision bulkhead to the stem, where they are joined by triangular-shaped plates called *breast hooks*. In addition to these stringers, a general strengthening of the bows is effected by an increase of plating thickness and by a closer spacing of the frames, in order to offset panting and pounding stresses. In larger types of vessels extra beams, called *panting beams,* are also provided.

Decks are supported by the beams and by pillars. These supports are designed to withstand any probable temporary load in addition to

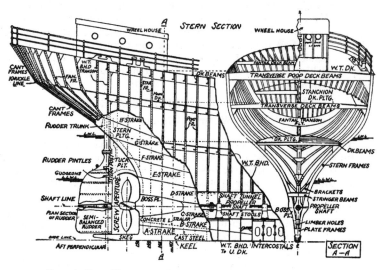

FIG. 4. SIDE VIEW AND SECTION OF STERN, LOOKING AFT.

the fixed weight of houses and deck erections, *winches*, etc. Weather decks must be strong enough to support great weights of water in heavy weather, and the strength of any deck must be consistent with the weight of cargo that may be carried thereon.

The upper deck plating follows a close second to the shell plating as the most important element in the strength of a ship.

Pillars, or small stanchions of round iron, were formerly fitted from keelson to deck under every second beam; but the system now commonly adopted is to fit pillars of large size at greater distances apart, which give increased rigidity and strength while reducing obstructions to a clear hold space.

Masts transmit considerable stresses to the structure when rolling heavily in a seaway, or when heavy cargo is worked by ship's gear.

They are usually stepped on the main deck, and whatever deck or decks they pass through are suitably strengthened in their vicinity.

The masts are stayed in position by *shrouds* and *back-stays* at each side of the ship, and by *stays* leading forward.

Bulkheads are partitions dividing the ship into compartments, some or all of which may be watertight. Keelsons and stringers should be continuous through bulkheads for longitudinal strength. Bulkheads intended to be watertight must be specially strengthened to withstand water pressure, particularly the *collision bulkhead*, which must be situated not less than one-twentieth of the vessel's length from the stem.

Riveting is tested by filling tanks or compartments with water under pressure, or, if this is not practicable, by a powerful jet of water directed on seams and butts.

Water Ballast Tanks must be provided with means for the air to escape freely from all parts of the tanks when being filled with water, in order to eliminate the possibility of the "slack" condition, due to the presence of air pockets in the various upper corners of the tanks.

Each tank must also be fitted with a *sounding-pipe* leading to the ship's working deck, and such sounding-pipes must be kept free from obstruction at all times.

WATERTIGHT DOORS AND ESCAPE PORTS
Watertight Doors

A watertight bulkhead is a bulkhead which has no opening in it. A bulkhead fitted with a watertight door is a watertight bulkhead only to the extent that the vessel's personnel insure, by precept and inspection, that the door is closed and securely dogged. Otherwise, it is a delusion.

When a door must be opened while at sea, the safety valve of the entire bulkhead is lost during such time as the door is open. It might just as well not be in the ship. It is highly desirable, therefore, that the time the door is open and the value of the bulkhead thereby destroyed be kept to a minimum, and that when the door is closed it be properly secured.

Where a door must be repeatedly opened and closed, as, for example, a shaft alley door, it is human nature to become careless. If the door operates stiffly, its whole purpose may be lost sight of in the desire to avoid a little effort. Every man on the ship may be jeopardized by such neglect. The particular individual who temporarily vitiates the integrity of a bulkhead should be concerned with its restoration at the earliest possible moment. The responsible officer authorizing or supervising such opening should satisfy himself of its adequate closing.

Most seamen are familiar with the ordinary watertight door, which is a hinged steel door closing on a rubber gasket and secured by dogs.

The new type watertight door as installed on the newest ships built on Navy plans is more complicated, and every sailor should know how to operate it in an emergency. It is actually a section of the watertight bulkhead cut out and fitted on enclosed slide rail guides and is operated by hydro electric jacks automatically controlled from the bridge. They may also be controlled by local valves which are operated by a lever on either side of the bulkhead. The vertical position of the lever is neutral, movement toward the door will open and away from the door will close it.

Should the hydro electric system fail the doors may be opened manually by means of a ratchet gear located by the door.

Another ratchet gear for controlling the doors manually is located on the next deck above the doors.

Should it be necessary for several persons to pass through this type door it would be good policy for one to hold the lever open until all have passed. These doors are very powerful and should an arm or leg get caught it would mean amputation. In passing through do not release one lever until, with your free hand you have moved the other lever to open position. When the automatic control is on "closed," the door obeys when the hand lever returns to neutral, which it does automatically upon being released.

Hydraulically Operated Watertight Doors—Stone System

The Stone system of watertight door operation is a hydraulic system for operating all of the sliding watertight doors throughout a vessel. A single control on the bridge closes all doors but does not open them, irrespective of whether hydraulic pumps are in operation or not. In addition, each door is provided with local controls and operating gear to enable it to be operated hydraulically from both sides of the bulkhead. (*See* Fig. 5.)

The hydraulic operating gear is so arranged that, when control on bridge is on closed position, any door which opens locally will automatically return to the closed position when local control is released.

The system consists generally of one suction tank, one accumulator tank, two motor-driven hydraulic pumps located in engine room, and the necessary control valves, fittings, mountings, hydraulic rams, etc.

Each door is also provided with manual operation from both sides of the door and remote manual mechanical operation from above the bulkhead deck.

The system has a working pressure of 700 lbs. per sq. in., and a test pressure of 1,400 lbs. The liquid used in the system is oil of anti-freeze quality equal to Socony Vacuum Teleo "A-A."

The power unit consists of two electrically driven pumps, with pressure regulator, together with an air loaded accumulator. Each pump maintains a pressure of 700 lbs. in the system. Pumps are driven through reduction gears by constant speed DC motors and are controlled to automatically start and stop, regulated by the pressure in the accumulator tank. One pump may operate while the other is idle.

The accumulator is charged with air by a motor-driven air compressor.

A master control valve, operated by a small hydraulic ram, is installed in the engine room. This valve directs the flow of fluid under pressure in such a manner that all doors close simultaneously. It is controlled

FIG. 5. HYDRAULICALLY-OPERATED WATERTIGHT DOOR.

from a control valve located in the wheelhouse. A *door control valve* is located at each door for the purpose of local control.

The *door control valve* is operated by suitable levers from both sides of the bulkhead in which the door is located. The levers are so arranged that valves return to their original position when operating lever movement is reversed.

An automatic by-pass valve is fitted on or near door control valve to prevent fluid lock when operating by hand.

Stop Valves. Two stop valves are located at door control valves, one for each main.

Electric alarm bells, controlled from the bridge, are at each door, and commence operating prior to door closing. Mechanical bells are provided at each door to operate while door is closing.

There is provided in the wheelhouse an indicating board which shows

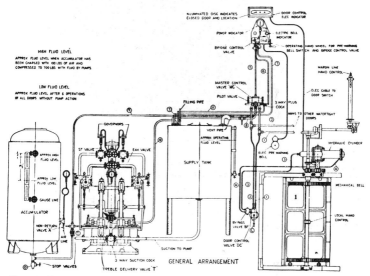

Fig. 6. General Arrangement of Stone Watertight Door System.

by individual electric lights for each door whether door is open or closed.

A valve and switch with power indicator are fitted in the pilot house, and a warning switch for operating electric bell and control valve for closing all doors are interconnected. Warning of 7 to 10 seconds is given before the doors start to close.

Three hand spanners for operating each door by hand are stowed, one at each side of the bulkhead at each door and one above the bulkhead deck. A general arrangement is shown in Fig. 6.

For further details of requirements covering installation and operation of watertight doors, U.S. Coast Guard current regulations for class of vessel concerned should be consulted.

Escape Air Ports

Escape air ports are installed on the *America*. Figure 7 shows this new type of air port in windscoop position.

FIG. 7. ESCAPE AIR PORT.

The operation is through a worm and sector connected to a shaft on which the yoke-carrying light is fixed. By reversing the movement of the handle the light can be locked in windscoop position. By continuous turning of the operating handle in counter clockwise direction the glass is swung outward to full open position, thus allowing for escape through the opening.

SHIPBUILDING TERMS AND ABBREVIATIONS

Following is a glossary of terms used in shipbuilding. It includes names of the many parts of a ship's structure, words related to the building of a ship, terms common to shipyard workers as well as those which will be familiar to any seaman.

Figs.1, 3 and 4, pages 14–3, 14–6, and 14–7,give roughly pictorial views of bow, midship, and stern sections of a ship as she would look on the ways. In some cases these drawings may be helpful in clarifying the terms and definitions in the glossary.

GLOSSARY OF SHIPBUILDING TERMS

Abaft. Toward the stern; aft, relative to.

Abeam. At right angles to the keel.

Aboard. On or in a ship.

Abreast. Side by side.

Abrid. A bushing plate around a hole in which a pintle works.

Accommodation Ladder. Stairs slung at the gangway, down vessel's side to point near water for ship access from small boats.

Aces. Hooks for the chains.

Acorn. A solid piece of metal shaped like an acorn, and used to finish off the top of an upright in a railing constructed of pipe.

Aft, After. Toward the stern. Between the stern and the amidship section of a vessel. **2. After Body.** The section aft of amidships. **3. After Frames.** Radiating cant frames fastened to transom plates. **4. Afterpeak.** A compartment just forward of the stern post. It is generally almost entirely below the load water line. **5. After Perpendicular.** The vertical line through the intersection of the load water line and the after edge of the stern post. On submarines or ships having a similar stern, it is a vertical line passing through the points where the design water line intersects the stern of the ship. **6. After Rake.** That part of the stern which overhangs the keel.

Air Casing. A ring-shaped plate coaming surrounding the stack and fitted at the upper deck, just below the umbrella. It protects the deck structure from heat and helps ventilate the fireroom. **2. Air Port.** An opening in the side of a ship or a deck house, usually round in shape, and fitted with a hinged frame in which a thick glass light is secured. The purpose of the air port is to provide light and ventilation to and vision from the interior.

Air-Tight Door. A door so constructed that, when closed, air cannot pass through. They are fitted in air locks.

Aloft. Above the deck.

Altar. A step in a graving dock.

Amidship(s.) In the longitudinal, or fore-and-aft center of a ship. Halfway between stem and stern. The term is used to convey the idea of general locality but not that of definite extent.

Angle. Same as angle bar. **2. Angle Bar.** A bar of angle-shaped section used as a stiffener and on riveted ships ties floors to the shell. **3. Angle Collar** Angle bent to fit a pipe, column, tank or stack, intersecting or projecting through a bulkhead or deck for the purposes of making a watertight or oiltight joint.

Anneal. To heat a metal and to

cool it in such a fashion as to toughen and soften it. Brass or copper is annealed by heating to a cherry red and dipping suddenly into water while hot. Iron or steel is slowly cooled from the heated condition to anneal.

Aperture. The space provided between propeller and stern post for the propeller.

Appendages. Relatively small portions of a vessel projecting beyond its main outline, as shown by cross-sections and water-sections. The word applies to the following parts of the stern and stern post: the keel below its shell line; the rolling keel or fin; the rudder, rudder post, screw, bilge keel, struts, bossing and skeg.

Apron Plate. A plate fitted in the continuation of the shell plating above the forecastle sheer strake at the stem. These plates are sometimes fitted one in each side of the stem, and serve as foundation for the bow mooring pipes.

Arbor. The principal axis member or spindle of a machine by which a motion of revolution is transmitted.

Arch Piece. The curved portion of the stern frame over the screw aperture, joining the propeller post and stern post.

Astern. Signifying position, in the rear of or abaft the stern; as regards motion, the opposite of going ahead; backwards.

Athwart. Same as abeam.

Auxiliaries. Various winches, pumps motors, engines, etc., required on a ship, as distinguished from main propulsive machinery (boilers and engines on a steam installation).

Auxiliary Foundations. Foundations for condensers, distillers, evaporator pumps or any of the auxiliary machinery in the engine or boiler rooms.

Awash. Even with the surface of the water.

Awning. A canvas canopy spread over a vessel's decks, bridges, etc., for protection against rain and sun.

Back Bar. Used on the opposite side of a bosom bar.

Balanced Frames. The midship frames that arc of equal shape and square flanged. There are thirty or more on a cargo vessel, equally divided between starboard and port sides. **2. Balanced Rudder.** A rudder with its axis halfway between the forward and after edge.

Balk. (In carpentry) a piece of timber from 4″ to 10″ square.

Ballast. Any weight carried solely for the purpose of making the vessel more seaworthy. Ballast may be either portable or fixed, depending upon the condition of the ship. Fixed or permanent ballast in the form of sand, concrete, scrap or pig iron is usually fitted to overcome an inherent defect in stability or trim due to faulty design or changed character of service. Portable ballast, usually in the form of water pumped into or out of the bottom, peak, or wing ballast tanks, is utilized to overcome a temporary defect in stability or trim due to faulty loading, damage, etc.

Ballast Tanks. Tanks carried in various parts of a ship for water ballast, to add weight to produce a change in trim or in stability of the ship.

Barbette. Cylindrical structure built up of armor plates extending from the protected deck of a war vessel to the lower side of the turret shelf plate. They form protective enclosures in which are located the turret stools, shell stowage flats and ammunition hoisting gear for the turrets.

Barge. A craft of full body and heavy construction designed for the carriage of cargo but having no machinery for self-propulsion.

Base Line. A horizontal fore and aft reference line for vertical measurements. This line is perpendicular to the vertical center line. A horizontal transverse reference line for vertical measurements. This line is perpendicular to both the vertical center line and fore-and-aft base line.

Batten. A narrow strip of wood for fairing in lines. Also a strip of wood to fasten objects together. A strip of wood or steel used in securing tarpaulins in place. (*Verb*) To secure by means of battens, as to "batten down a hatch."

Battens, Cargo. A term applied to the planks that are fitted to the inside of the frames in a hold to keep the cargo away from the shell plating; the strips of wood or steel used to prevent shifting of cargo.

Beam. The extreme width of a ship. The athwartship members of the ship's frame which support the decks. **2. Beam Knees.** Angular fittings which connect beams and frames together. **3. Beam Line.** The line showing the top of the frame lines. **4. Beam Plate Angles.** A beam made from a flat plate, with the flange bent at right angles by an angle-bending machine.

Bearding. The line of intersection of the plating and the stem or stern post.

Bearer. A term applied to foundations, particularly those having vertical web plates as their principal members. Also these vertical web plates themselves are called bearers.

Bed Plate. A structure fitted for support of the feet of the engine columns, as well as to provide support for crankshaft bearings. It also helps distribute engine weight and stresses to the ship's structure. The bed plate consists of a series of transverse girders, connecting fore-and-aft members or girders.

Below. Underneath the surface of the water. Underneath a deck or decks.

Bending Rolls. Large machine used to give curvature to plates by passage in contact with three rolls.

Bending Slab. Heavy cast-iron blocks with square or round holes for "dogging down," arranged to form a large solid floor on which frames and structural members are bent and formed.

Berth. A place for a ship.—The distance from frame line to frame line.—A term applied to a bed or a place to sleep. Berths, as a rule, are permanently built into the structure of the staterooms or compartments. They are constructed singly and also in tiers of two or three, one above the other. When single, drawers for stowing clothing are often built in underneath. Tiers of berths constructed of pipe are commonly installed in the crew space.

Between Decks. The space between any two, not necessarily adjacent, decks. Frequently expressed as "Tween Decks."

Bevel. Any angle other than 90° which one surface makes with another. Also to bevel a beam, flange, or plate for vee welding; to tilt a girder to make the sheer bevel. **2. Bevel Square.** A device that can be used to make a close bevel, less than 90°, or an open bevel, more than 90°.

Bilge. The rounded side of a ship where it curves up from the flat bottom plates to the vertical shell plating. (*Verb*) To open a vessel's lower body to the sea. **2. Bilge Keel.** Longitudinal angles welded and riveted back to back on the bilge of a vessel, to check the ship's tendency to roll. **3. Bilge Plates.** The curved shell plates that fit the bilge. **4. Bilge Well.** A bilge well is generally located in the lowest part of the compartment. It is used for drainage and is generally shaped like a box, and fitted to the underside of the inner bottom, with a strainer on top.

Bilges. The lowest portion of a ship inside the hull, considering the inner bottom where fitted as the bottom hull limit.

Bilgeway. Same as bilge.

Binnacle. A stand or case for housing a compass so that it may be conveniently consulted. Binnacles differ in shape and size according to where used and the size of the compass to be accommodated. A binnacle for a ship's navigating compass consists essentially of a pedestal at whose upper end is a bowl-shaped receptacle having a sliding hood-like cover. This receptacle accommodates the gimbals supporting the compass. Compensating binnacles are provided with brackets or arms on either side, starboard and port, for supporting and securing the iron cylinders or spheres used to counteract the quadrantal error due to the earth's magnetization of the vessel. This type of binnacle is usually placed immediately in front of the steering wheel, having its vertical axis in the vertical plane of the fore-and-aft center-line of the vessel.

Birth Marks. A builder's irregularity in construction.

Bitter end. (Nautical) The inboard end of a vessel's anchor chain which is made fast in the chain locker.

Bitts. Cast steel heads serving as posts to which cables are secured on a ship.

Bitumastic. A black, tar-like composition largely of bitumen or asphalt, and containing such other ingredients as rosin, Portland cement, slaked lime, petroleum, etc. It is used as a protective coating in ballast and trimming tanks, chain lockers, shaft alleys, etc.

Bleeders. A term applied to plugs screwed into the bottom of a ship to provide for drainage of the compartments when the vessel is in dry dock

Block. The name given a pulley or sheave, or system of pulleys or sheaves mounted in a frame, and used to multiply power when moving objects by means of ropes run over the sheaves. Single, double or triple when used with the word "block" indicate the number of sheaves it contains. **2. Block and Tackle.** (Block and Falls) —The complete unit of two or more blocks rove up with an adequate amount of rope.

Body Plan. A pair of half transverse end elevations, with a common vertical center line. The right side gives the ship as seen from ahead, the left side from astern. Water lines, buttock and bow lines, diagonal lines, etc., are shown.

Boiler. Any vessel, container or receptacle that is capable of generating steam by the internal or external application of heat. There are two general classes of boilers, i.e., fire-tube and water-tube. **2. Boiler Casing.** A wall protecting the different deck spaces from the heat of the boiler room. **3. Boiler Foundation.** The structure upon which the boiler is secured. It generally consists of girders built up from plates and shapes. In a cylindrical boiler the athwartship girders are often called saddles. **4. Boiler Room.** A compartment in the middle or after section of a vessel where the boilers are placed.

Bollards. Cast steel heads or short columns secured to a wharf or dock, and used for securing the lines from a ship. The bitts on a ship may also be called bollards.

Bolster Plate. A piece of plate adjoining the hawse hole, to prevent the chafing of the hawser against the cheeks of a ship's bow. A plate for support like a pillow or cushion.

Booby Hatch. The cover of a scuttle-way or small hatchway, such as that which leads to the forecastle or forepeak of a vessel.

Boom. A term applied to a spar used in handling cargo, or as the lower piece of a fore-and-aft sail. **2. Boom Table.** An outrigger attached to the mast, or a structure built up around a mast from the deck, to support the heel bearings for booms. Boom tables are necessary to provide working clearances when a number of booms are installed on one mast.

Boot-Topping. Special resistant paint or paints used to coat that portion of a vessel between light and load lines. Also the area to which this paint is applied.

Bosom. The inside of an angle bar. **2. Bosom Bar.** One angle fitted inside another. **3. Bosom Plate.** A plate bar or angle fitted to an angle bar to connect the ends of two angles.

Boss. The part of the propeller to which blades are attached. Also the aperture in the stern frame where propeller shaft enters. **2. Boss Frame.** A frame bent around to fit the boss in way of the stern tube or shaft. **3.**

Boss Plate. The plate fitted around the boss of a propeller post or around the curved frames in way of stern tubes.

Bottom, Outer. A term applied to the bottom shell plating in a double bottom ship.

Bottom Plating. That part of the shell plating which is below the water line.

Bounding Bar. A bar connecting the edges of a bulkhead to tank top, shell, decks, or another bulkhead.

Bow. The fore end of a ship. **Bull-nosed Bow.** Bow with large rounded bow point underneath water line. **Clipper Bow.** A bow with an extreme forward rake, once familiar on sailing vessels. **Flared Bow.** A bow with an extreme flare at the upper and forecastle deck. **Ram Bow.** A bow protruding underneath the water line considerably forward of the forecastle deck. **2. Bow Lines.** Curves representing a vertical section of the bow end of a ship. Similar curves in aft part of hull are buttock lines.

Bracket. A steel plate, commonly with a reinforcing flange, used to stiffen or tie beam angles to bulkheads, frames to longitudinals, etc.

Breadth. The side-to-side measurement of a vessel at any given place. **2. Breadth Extreme.** The maximum breadth measured over plating or planking, including beading or fenders. **3. Breadth, Molded.** See Molded Breadth. **4. Breadth, Registered.** Measured amidships at its greatest breadth to outside of plating.

Break. Of poop or forecastle. The point at which the partial poop or forecastle decks are discontinued.

Breakwater. A term applied to plates fitted on a forward weather deck to form a V-shaped shield against water that is shipped over the bow.

Breaming. Cleaning the barnacles, paint, etc., from a ship's bottom with a blow torch.

Breast Beam. The transverse beam nearest to midship on the poop and forecastle deck. **2. Breast Hook.** A horizontal plate secured across the forepeak of a vessel to tie the fore-peak frames together and unite the bow. **3. Breast Rail.** The upper rail of a balcony on the quarter deck.

Bridge. A high transverse platform, often forming the top of a bridge house, extending from side to side of the ship, and from which a good view of the weather deck may be had. An enclosed space called the pilot house is erected on the bridge in which are installed the navigating instruments, such as the compass and binnacle, the control for the steering apparatus, and the signals to the engine room. While the pilot house is generally extended to include a chart-room and sometimes staterooms, a clear passageway should be left around it. As the operation of the ship is directed from the bridge or flying bridge above it, there should also be clear, open passage from one side of the vessel to the other. **2. Bridge House.** The erection or superstructure fitted about amidship on the upper deck of a ship. The officer's quarters, staterooms and accommodations are usually in the bridge house. **3. Bridge, Navigating or Flying.** The uppermost platform erected at the level of the top of the pilot house. It generally consists of a narrow walkway supported by stanchions, running from one side of the ship to the other and the space over the top of the pilot house. A duplicate set of navigating instruments and controls for the steering gear and engine room signals are installed on the flying bridge so that the ship may be navigated in good weather from this platform. Awnings erected on stanchions and weather cloths fitted to the railings give protection against sun and wind.

Brow. A small curved angle or flanged plate fitted on the outside of the shell of a ship over an air port to prevent water running down the ship's side from entering the open port. Also called a watershed.

Buckle Plate. A plate that has

warped from its original shape; also a plate that is wider at the center than at the ends.

Building Slip. An inclined launching berth where the ship is built.

Bulb Angle. Or bulb angle bar. An angle with one edge having a bulb or swell. **2. Bulb Plate.** A narrow plate generally of mild steel, rolled with a bulb or swell along one of its edges. Used for hatch coamings, built up beams, etc.

Bulge. Same as bilge.

Bulkhead. A partition in a ship which divides the interior space into various compartments. **Afterpeak Bulkhead.** A term applied to the first transverse bulkhead forward of the sternpost. This bulkhead forms the forward boundary of the afterpeak tank and should be made watertight. **Collision Bulkhead.** A watertight bulkhead approximately 25′ aft of the bow, extending from the keel to the shelter deck. This bulkhead prevents the entire ship from being flooded in case of a collision. **Corrugated Bulkhead.** A bulkhead made from plates of corrugated metal or by flat plates alternately attached to the opposite flanges of the bulkhead stiffeners. Corrugated metal bulkheads are used around staterooms and quarters. Corrugated cargo hold bulkheads are generally constructed of flat plates alternately attached to opposite flanges of the stiffeners. **Forepeak Bulkhead.** The bulkhead nearest the stem, which forms the after boundary of the forepeak tank. When this bulkhead is extended from the bottom of the ship to the weather deck, it is also called the collision bulkhead. **Longitudinal Bulkhead.** A partition wall of planking or plating running in a fore-and-aft direction. Oil tankers are required to have at least one fore-and-aft bulkhead in the cargo oil space. Fore-and-aft bulkheads are very common on warships. **Oiltight Bulkhead.** A partition of plating reinforced where necessary with stiffening bars and capable of preventing the flow of oil under pressure from one compart-

ment to another. The riveting must be closer spaced than in watertight work and special care must be taken with the calking. **Partial Bulkhead.** A term applied to a bulkhead that extends only a portion of the way across a compartment. They are generally erected as strength members of the structure. **Screen Bulkhead.** A light bulkhead fitted between engine and boiler rooms, designed to keep dust and heat out of the engine room. Often built around the after ends of boilers. **Swash Bulkhead.** A partial bulkhead used for the same purpose as a swash plate. **Transverse Bulkhead.** A partition wall of planking or plating running in an athwartship direction across a portion or the whole breadth of a ship. The principal function of transverse bulkheads is to divide the ship into a series of watertight compartments so that any rupture of the shell will not cause the loss of the vessel. **Watertight Bulkhead.** A partition of plating reinforced where necessary with stiffening bars and capable of preventing the flow of water under pressure from one compartment to another. **2. Bulkhead Bounding Bar.** A bar used for the purpose of connecting the edges of a bulkhead to the tank top, shell, deck, or to another bulkhead. Angle bars are generally used for this purpose, as both flanges are easily calked. **3. Bulkhead Sluice.** An opening cut in a bulkhead just above the tank top connecting angle, and fitted with a valve which may be operated from the deck above. **4. Bulkhead Stiffeners.** A term applied to the beams or girders attached to a bulkhead for the purpose of supporting it under pressure and holding it in shape. Vertical stiffeners are most commonly used, but horizontal stiffeners or a combination of both may be used.

Bulwark. The upper section of the frames and side plating, which extends above and around the upper deck. **2. Bulwark Stay.** A brace extending from the deck to a point near the top of the bulwark, to keep it rigid.

Bunker. A coal or fuel oil space below decks. **2. Bunker Stays.** Stiffening angles connecting the frames to the bunker bulkheads.

Buoy. A term applied to a floating object that is moored or anchored so that it remains at one place. Buoys are used for marking the places on the water where a ship is sunk, where reefs are below, where the edges of the channel are, or to provide means for mooring a ship at a desired position.

Buoyancy. Ability to float; the supporting effort exerted by a liquid (usually water) upon the surface of a body wholly or partially immersed.

Burr Edge. The rough uneven edge of a punched or burnt hole or plate.

Butt Joint. A joint made by fitting two pieces squarely together on their edges, which is then welded or butt strapped. **2. Butt Strap.** A bar or plate used to fasten two or more objects together with their edges butted.

Buttock. Counter. The rounded-in overhanging part on each side of the stern in front of the rudder, merging underneath into the run. **2. Buttock Lines.** The curves shown by taking a vertical longitudinal section of the after part of a ship's hull, parallel to the keel.

Cabin. The interior of a deck house, usually the space set aside for the use of officers and passengers.

Calk. To tighten a lap or other seam with a chisel tool, either by hand or mechanically.

Cam. A projecting part of a wheel or other simple moving piece in machinery, so shaped as to give predetermined variable motion to another piece against which it acts, in repeating cycles.

Camber. A slope upwards toward the center of a surface, as on a deck amidships for shedding water. This deck camber is usually 1″ on 50″.

Camel. (In engineering) a decked vessel having great stability designed for use in the lifting of sunken vessels or structures. A submersible float used

for the same purpose by submerging, attaching, and pumping out.

Cant. The inclination of an object from the perpendicular. As a verb, to turn anything so that it does not stand square to a given object. **2. Cant Beam.** Any of the beams supporting the deck plating or planking in the overhanging part of the stern of a vessel. They radiate in fan shape from the transom beam to cant frames. **3. Cant Body.** That portion of a vessel's body either forward or aft in which the planes of the frames are not at right angles to the center line of the ship. **4. Cant Frames.** The frames (generally bulb angles) at the end of a ship which are canted; that is, which rise obliquely from the keel.

Capstan, Steam. A vertical drum or barrel operated by a steam engine and used for handling heavy anchor chains, heavy hawsers, etc. The engine is usually non-reversing and transmits its power to the capstan shaft through a worm and worm wheel. The drum is fitted with pawls to prevent overhauling under the strain of the hawser or chain when the power is shut off. The engine may be disconnected and the capstan operated by hand through the medium of capstan bars.

Cargo. Merchandise or goods accepted for transportation by ship. **2. Cargo Hatch.** Large opening in the deck to permit loading of cargo. **3. Cargo Port.** An opening, provided with a watertight cover or door, in the side of a vessel of two or more decks, through which the cargo is received and discharged.

Carlines (Carlings). A short beam running fore and aft between or under transverse deck beams. Also called headers when they support the ends of interrupted deck beams.

Carvel Built. A type of plating made flush by vee butt welding or butt strap riveting.

Casing. The extra case or bulkhead built around the ship's funnel to protect the decks from heat. See *Air Casing*.

Ceiling. The inside skin of a vessel

between decks, or in a small vessel from the deck beams to bilge.

Cellular Double Bottom. A term applied where the double bottom is divided into numerous rectangular compartments by the floors and longitudinals.

Center Line. A horizontal fore-and-aft reference line for athwartship measurements, dividing the ship into two symmetrical halves. A vertical reference line in the center of the body plan, midship section or other sections. **2. Center Line Bulkhead.** A fore-and-aft or longitudinal bulkhead erected on the center line or in the same plane as the keel. Also a reference line scrived on a transverse bulkhead to indicate the center of the ship.

Chain Locker. The compartment for storing the anchor chains, located near the hawse pipes in the bow of the ship. **2. Chain Locker Manger.** See *Manger.* **3. Chain Locker Pipe.** The iron-bound opening or section of pipe leading from the chain locker to the deck, through which the chain cable passes.

Chains. Anchor chains.

Chamfer. A bevel surface formed by cutting away the angle of two faces of a piece of wood or metal.

Chart House. Small room adjacent to the bridge for charts and navigating instruments.

Chase Joint. A kind of plate joint by which an overlap can gradually be made flush. This is done with the aid of liners, and is used on the bow and stern to give the vessel a finer trim.

Check Lines. Used in shaping plates, etc., to make sure that the templates have not changed in size by shrinking or expanding.

Cheeks. The bilgeways, or curve of the bilges.

Chock. (In naval architecture) a small piece of wood used to make good any deficiency in a piece of timber, frame, etc.

Chocks. Deck fittings for mooring line to pass through.

Cleat. A metal fitting having two projecting arms or horns to which a halyard or other rope is belayed. The

deck, side plating, a stanchion, or other convenient structure serves as a support for securing the cleat.

Clip. A 4″ to 6″ angle bar welded temporarily to floors, plates, webs, etc. It is used as a holdfast which, with the aid of a bolt, pulls objects up close in fitting. Also, short lengths of bar, generally angle, used to attach and connect the various members of the ship structure.

Close Butt. A joint fitted close by grinding, pulled tight by clips, and welded.

Club Foot. The flattened, broadened after end of the stem foot.

Coaming. Strictly speaking, coamings are the fore and aft framing in hatchways and scuttles, while the athwartship pieces are called head ledges; but the name coaming is commonly applied to all raised framework about deck openings. Coamings prevent water from running below, as well as strengthen the deck about the hatches.

Cofferdam. A small space left open between two bulkheads as an air space, to protect another bulkhead from heat, fire hazard or collision.

Coffin Plate. The plate used on an enclosed twin bossing, named for its shape. In reality it is an inverted boss plate.

Collar. A ring used around a pipe or mast, or a flat plate made to fit around a girder or beam passing through a bulkhead. They serve to make various spaces watertight.

Collision Mat. A large mat used to close an aperture in a vessel's side resulting from a collision.

Companion. A covering over the top of a companionway.

Companionway. A set of steps or ladder leading up to a deck from below.

Compartment. A subdivision of space or room in a ship.

Compass, Magnetic. The compass is the most important instrument of navigation in use on board ship, the path of a ship through the water depending upon the efficient working and use of this instrument. There are two kinds of compasses, the Dry Card Compass and Liquid Compass. The Dry Compass consists essentially of a number of magnetic needles, suspended parallel to each other and fastened to the rim of a circular disc that has a paper cover upon which are marked the points of the compass and the degrees. This card rests upon a pivot centered in the compass bowl, which in its turn is suspended by gimbals in the binnacle or stand, the latter having means for lighting the card at night and for the adjustment of compass errors due to the magnetism of the ship. In the Liquid Compass, the bowl is filled with alcohol and water, or oil. The needles are sealed in parallel tubes and form a framework which connects the central boss with the outer rim, the whole resting upon a pivot in the compass bowl. Upon the rim are printed the points and degrees. As regards the relative uses of these compasses, it may be said that the dry compass is the standard in the world's Merchant Marine, while the liquid compass is the standard in Navies because of its freedom of vibration from the shock of gunfire, etc.

Composite Vessel. A vessel with a steel frame and wooden hull and decks.

Conning Tower. Protective structure built up of armor plates and having various shapes and sizes.

Counter. That part of a ship's stern which overhangs the stern post.

Countersunk Hole. A hole tapered or beveled around its edge to allow a rivet or bolt head to seat flush with or below the surface of the bolted object. **2. Countersunk Rivet.** A rivet driven flush on one or both sides.

Cradle. A framing built up on the ways and in which the ship rests while being launched.

Crater. A cup-shaped depression in a weld. The arc tends to push the molten metal away from the center of the point being welded, thus forming the crater.

Cribbing. Foundations of heavy blocks and timbers for supporting a vessel during construction.

Cross-Spall. A temporary horizontal timber brace to hold a frame in position. Cross-spalls are replaced later by the deck beams.

Crown. Term sometimes used denoting the round-up or camber of a deck. The crown of an anchor is located where the arms are welded to the shank.

Crow's Nest. A lookout station attached to or near the head of a mast.

Crutches. Same as breast hooks, but fitted at the after end.

Cutwater. The forward edge of the stem or prow of a vessel at the water level.

Dagger. A piece of timber that is fastened to the poppets of the bilge-way and crosses them diagonally to keep them together. Dagger applies to anything that stands in a diagonal position. **2. Dagger Plank.** One of the planks which unite the heads of the poppets or stepping-up pieces of the cradle on which the vessel rests in launching.

Davits. A set of cranes or radial arms on the gunwale of a ship, from which are suspended the lifeboats.

Dead Flat. The flat-surfaced midship section of a vessel on the sides above the bilge, or on the bottom below the bilge. **2. Dead Rise.** The upward slope of a ship's bottom from the keel to the bilge. This rise is to give drainage of oil or water toward the center of the ship.

Deadlight. A shutter placed over a cabin window in stormy weather to protect the glass against the waves.

Deadweight. The total weight of cargo, fuel, water, stores, passengers and crew and their effects that a ship can carry when at her designed full-load draft.

Deck. A platform or horizontal floor which extends from side to side of a vessel. **After Deck.** A term applied to a deck aft to the midship portion of a vessel. **Forecastle Deck.** A deck over the main deck at the bow. **Flush Deck.** A deck running from stem to stern without being broken by forecastle or poop. **Half Deck.** A short deck below the main deck. **Hurricane Deck.** Same as bridge. **Main Deck.** The highest complete deck on a ship: in other words, the highest deck which runs the full length of the ship. **Poop Deck.** The raised deck on the after part of a ship. **Quarter Deck.** A term applied to the after portion of a weather deck. In a warship that portion allotted to the use of the officers. **Shelter Deck.** A term applied to a deck fitted from stem to stern on a relatively light superstructure. The main deck. **2. Deck Beam Dimensions.** The molding of a deck beam is its vertical dimension. Its siding is its horizontal dimension. **3. Deck House.** A small house on the after or midship section of a vessel. **4. Deck Stringer.** The strip of deck plating that runs along the outer edge of a deck.

Deep Frame. A web frame or a frame whose athwartship dimension is over the general amount. **2. Deep Floor.** A term applied to any of the floors in the forward or after end of a vessel. Due to the converging sides of ships in the bow and stern, the floors become much deeper than in the main body. **3. Deep Tanks.** These usually consist of ordinary hold compartments, but strengthened to carry water ballast. They are placed at either or both ends of the engine and boiler space. They usually run from the tank top up to or above the lower deck.

Derelict. A vessel abandoned and drifting aimlessly at sea.

Derrick. A device consisting of a kingpost, boom with variable topping lift, and necessary rigging for hoisting heavy weights, cargo, etc.

Development. The method of drawing the same lines on a flat surface which have already been drawn on a curved surface. The shapes and lines produced by development are the same as though the curved surface from which they are taken were a flexible sheet which could be spread out flat without change of area or distortion.

Diagonal Line. A line cutting the body plan diagonally from the frames to the middle line in the loft layout.

Displacement. The weight in tons of the water displaced by a ship. This weight is the same as the total weight of the ship when afloat. Displacement may be expressed either in cubic feet or tons; a cubic foot of sea water weighs 64 pounds and one of fresh water weighs 62.5 pounds, consequently one ton is equal to 35 cubic feet of sea water or 35.9 feet of fresh water. The designed displacement of a vessel is her displacement when floating at her designed draft.

Dock. A basin for the reception of vessels. "Wet" docks are utilized for the loading and unloading of ships. **2. Dry Docks.** A dock into which a vessel is floated, the water then being removed to allow for the construction or repair of ships.

Dog. A hold fast; a short metal rod or bar fashioned to form a clamp or clip and used for holding watertight doors, manholes, or pieces of work in place. **2. Dog Shores.** The last supports to be knocked away at the launching of a ship.

Dolphin. A term applied to several piles that are bound together situated either at the corner of a pier or out in the stream and used for docking and warping vessels.

Donkey Engine. A small gas, steam or electric auxiliary engine, set on the deck and used for lifting, etc.

Double Bottom. A tank whose bottom is formed by the bottom plates of a ship, used to hold water for ballast, for the storage of oil, etc. Also a term applied to the space between the inner, and outer bottom skins of a vessel. Also applied to indicate that a ship has a complete inner or extra envelope of watertight bottom plating. A double bottom is usually fitted in large ships extending from bilge to bilge and nearly the whole length fore-and-aft.

Doubling Plates. Extra plates (bars or stiffeners) added to strengthen sections where holes have been cut for hawse pipes, machinery, etc. Also laced where strain or wear is expected.

Dowel. A pin of wood inserted in the edge or face of two boards or pieces to secure them together.

Draft (Draught). Of a vessel the depth of a vessel below the waterline measured vertically to the lowest part of the hull, propellers or other reference points. **2. Draft, Aft.** Draft measured at the stern. **3. Draft, Extreme.** Draft measured to the lowest projecting portion of the vessel. **4. Draft, Forward.** Draft measured at the bow. **5. Draft, Load.** Draft at load displacement. **6. Draft, Marks.** The numbers which are placed in a vertical scale at the bow and the stern of a vessel to indicate the draft at each point. **7. Draft, Mean.** The average between draft measured at bow and at stern, or for a vessel with a straight keel, the draft measured at the middle length of waterline.

Drag. The amount that the aft end of the keel is below the forward end when the ship is afloat with the stern end down.

Drain Well. The chamber into which seepage water is collected and pumped by drainage pumps into the sea through pump dales.

Drift Pin. A conical-shaped pin gradually tapered from blunt point to a diameter a little larger than the rivet holes in which it is to be used. The point is inserted in rivet holes that are not fair, and the other end is hammered until the holes are forced to line.

Ductility. That property of a material which permits its being drawn out into a thread or wire.

Duplicating Pipe. A piece of tubing, generally brass, used with paint to transfer rivet hole layout from template to plate. The end of the pipe is dipped in paint, and while still wet is pushed through each template hole, leaving an impression on the plate.

Dutchman. A piece of steel fitted into an opening to cover up poor joints, or the crevices caused by poor workmanship.

Electrode. A pole or terminal in an electrical circuit. See *Polarity.*

Engine Room. Space where the main engines of a ship are located.

Entrance. The forward under-water portion of a vessel at and near the bow.

Erection. The process of hoisting into place and joining the various parts of a ship's hull, machinery, etc.

Even Keel. When a boat rides on an even keel, its plane of flotation is either coincident or parallel to the designed water line.

Expansion Joint. A term applied to a joint which permits linear movement to take up the expansion and contraction due to changes in temperature. **2. Expansion Trunks.** Trunkways extending a short way into oil tanker compartments from the hatches. When the compartment is filled, the trunk is partly filled, and thus cuts down the free surface of the cargo, improving stability. Free space at the top is left for any expansion of the oil.

Eye Bolt. A bolt having either a head looped to form a worked eye, or a solid head with a hole drilled through it forming a shackle eye. Its use is similar to that of a pad eye.

Eyes. The forward end of the space below the upper decks of a ship which lies next abaft the stem, where the sides approach very near to each other. The hawse pipes are usually run down through the eyes of a ship.

Fabricate. To shape, assemble and secure in place the component parts in order to form a complete job.

Fair. To fair a line means to even out curves, sheer lines, deck lines, etc., in drawing and mold loft work.

Fairlead. A term applied to fittings or devices used in preserving the direction of a rope, chain or wire, so that it may be delivered fairly or on a straight lead to the sheave or drum.

Fairwater. Plating fitted, in the shape of a frustrum of a cone, around the ends of shaft tubes and struts to prevent an abrupt change in the stream lines. Also any casting or plate fitted to the hull for the purpose of preserving a smooth flow of water.

Fall. Commonly the entire length of rope used in a tackle, though strictly it means only the end to which the power is applied.

Fantail. The overhanging stern section of a vessel, from the sternpost aft.

Fathom. Six feet. A sea-going measure of length.

Fay. To unite closely two planks or plates, so as to bring the surfaces into intimate contact.

Felloes. Pieces of wood which form the rim of a wheel.

Fender. This term is applied to various devices fastened to or hung over the sides of a vessel for the purpose of preventing rubbing or chafing. On small craft, such as tugboats, it consists of a timber or steel structure running fore and aft along the outside of the vessel above the water line. On the wearing surface, a strip of iron bark or a piece of flat bar iron is attached.

Fidley. Framework built around a deck hatch ladder, leading below. **2. Fidley Deck.** A partially raised deck over the engine and boiler rooms, usually around the smokestack. **3. Fidley Hatch.** Hatch around smokestack and uptake.

Fillet. The rounded edge of a rolled steel angle or bar.

Fin. A projecting keel.

Flagstaff. Flag pole, usually at the stern of a ship; carries the ensign.

Flange. The turned edge of a shape or girder, which acts to resist bending strain. **Blank Flange.** A flange which is not drilled but which is otherwise complete.

Flare. The spreading out from the central vertical plane of the body of a ship with increasing rapidity as the section rises from the waterline to the rail.

Flat. A small partial deck, built level, without curvature.

Floating Drydock. A U-shaped dock with double skins which is filled by opening up the sillcocks, and

allowed to settle so the middle section will be lower than the keel of the ship to be docked. The floating drydock is then placed under the ship and the water pumped out, raising the ship so that repairs can be made on her hull.

Floor Plan. A horizontal section, showing the ship as divided at a water or deck line.

Floors. Vertical flat plates running transverse of the vessel, connecting the vertical keel with the margin plates or the frames to which the tank top and bottom shell is fastened.

Flotsam. The parts of a wrecked ship and goods lost in shipwreck, both found floating.

Fluke. The palm of an anchor. The broad holding portion which penetrates the ground.

Flux. A substance such as borax, used in welding to help in the melting of the metal. Flux also serves to stabilize the electric arc, steady the flow of the filler metal into the weld and protect the weld from oxidation.

Fore and Aft. Parallel to the ship's centerline. **2. Fore, Forward.** Toward the stem. Between the stem and amidships. **3. Fore Peak.** The narrow extremity of a vessel's bow. Also the hold space within it. **4. Fore Rake.** The forward part of the bow which overhangs the keel.

Forecastle. A short structure at the forward end of a vessel formed by carrying up the ship's shell plating a deck height above the level of her uppermost complete deck and fitting a deck over the length of this structure.

Forefoot. The forward end of a vessel's stem which is stepped on the keel.

Forehook. Or breast hook.

Forging. A mass of metal worked to a special shape by hammering, bending, or pressing while hot.

Fork Beam. A half beam to support a deck where hatchways occur.

Foul. A term applied to the underwater portion of the outside of a vessel's shell when it is more or less covered with sea growth or foreign matter. It has been found that even an oily film over the vessel's bottom will retard the speed, while sea growth will reduce a vessel's propulsive efficiency to a large extent. Also, obstructed or impeded by an interference, etc.

Found. To fit and bed firmly. Also, equipped.

Frame Head. The section of a frame that rises above the deck line. **2. Frame Lines.** Lines of a vessel as laid out on the mold loft floor, showing the form and position of the frames. Also the line of intersection of shell with heel of frame. **3. Frame Spacing.** The fore-and-aft distances between frames, heel to heel.

Frames. The ribs of a ship.

Freeboard. The distance from the water line to the top of the weather deck on the side. Sometimes refers to the whole out-of-water section of a vessel's side.

Freeing Ports. Holes in the bulwark or rail, which allow deck wash to drain off into the sea. Some freeing ports have swing gates which allow water to drain off but which automatically close from sea water pressure.

Furrings. Strips of timber or boards fastened to frames, joists, etc., in order to bring their faces to the required shape or level, for attachment of sheathing, ceiling, flooring, etc.

Gadget. A slang term applied to various fittings.

Gage. A standard of measure.

Galley. The space on a vessel in which the food is prepared and cooked.

Galvanizing. The process of coating one metal with another, ordinarily applied to the coating of iron or steel with zinc. The chief purpose of galvanizing is to prevent corrosion.

Gangboard. Same as gangplank. **2. Gangplank.** A board with cleats, forming a bridge reaching from a gangway of a vessel to the wharf.

Gangway. The opening in the bulwarks of a vessel through which persons come on board or disembark. Also a gangplank. **Crew's Gangway.** Used on oil tankers. An elevated runway from poop to midship, and midship to forecastle deck. It affords means of safe passage for crew members when deck is awash in stormy weather.

Gaskets. Packing materials, by which air, water, oil, or steam tightness is secured in such places as on doors, hatches, steam cylinders, manhole covers, or in valves, between the flanges of pipes, etc. Such materials as rubber, canvas, asbestos, paper, sheet lead and copper, soft iron, and commercial products are extensively used. **Gear.** Steering gear, running gear, cleaning gear, etc. A comprehensive term used in speaking of all the implements, apparatus, machinery, etc., which are used in any given operation.

Gib. A metal fitting that holds a member in place, or presses two members together.

Girder. A heavy, main supporting beam.

Girth. The distance measured on any frame line, from the intersection of the upper deck with the side, around the body of the vessel to corresponding point on the opposite side. The half girth is taken from the center line of the keel to the upper deck beam end.

Gooseneck. A return, or 180° bend, having one leg shorter than the other. An iron swivel making up the fastening between a boom and a mast. It consists of a pintle and an eyebolt, or clamp.

Gouge. A tool with a half round cutting edge used to cut grooves.

Grating. An open iron lattice work used for covering hatchways and platforms.

Graving Docks. A dry dock. The vessel is floated in, and gates at the entrance closed when the tide is at ebb. The remaining water is then pumped out, and the vessel's bottom is graved, or cleaned.

Gripe. The sharp forward end of

the dished keel on which the stem is fixed.

Grommet. A ring of fiber usually soaked in red lead or some other packing material, and used under the heads of bolts and nuts to preserve tightness.

Groundways. Large pieces of timber laid across the ways on which the keel blocks are placed. Also the large blocks and planks which support the cradle on which a ship is launched.

Gudgeon. A metallic eye bolted to the sternpost, on which the rudder is hung.

Gunwale. The line where a shelter deck stringer meets the shell. **2. Gunwale Bar.** A term applied to the bar connecting a stringer plate on a weather deck to the sheer strake.

Gusset Plate. A tie plate, used for fastening posts, frames, beams, etc., to other objects.

Gutter Ledge. A bar laid across a hatchway to support the hatches.

Gutterway. The sunken trough on the shelter deck outer edge which disposes of the water from the deck wash.

Guys. Wire or hemp rope or chains to support booms, davits, etc., laterally. Guys are employed in pairs. Where a span is fitted between two booms, for example, one pair only is required for the two.

Half Model. A model of one side of a ship, on which the plate lines are drawn in.

Half-breadth Plan. A plan or top view of half of a ship divided longitudinally. It shows the water lines, bow and buttock lines, and diagonal lines of construction.

Hard Patch. A plate riveted over another plate to cover a hole or break.

Harpings. The fore parts of the wales of a vessel which encompass her bows and are fastened to the stem, thickened to withstand plunging.

Hatch. Hatchway cover. Also used to mean hatchway. **2. Hatch Bars.** The bars by which the hatches are fastened down.

Hatchway. One of the large square openings in the deck of a ship through which freight is hoisted in or out, and access is had to the hold. There are four pieces in the frame of a hatchway. The fore-and-aft pieces are called coamings and those athwart ship are called head ledges. The head ledges rest on the beams and the carlines extending between the beams. There may be forward, main and after hatchways, according to the size and character of the vessel.

Hawse. That part of a ship's bow in which are the hawse holes for the anchor chains. **2. Hawse Hole.** A hole in the bow through which a cable or chain passes. It is a cast steel tube having rounded projecting lips both inside and out. **3. Hawse Pipe.** The tube lining a hawse hole in a ship's bow. **4. Hawse Plug or Block.** A stopper used to prevent water from entering the hawse hole in heavy weather.

Hawser. A cable used in warping and mooring.

Hawsing. (In naval architecture) calking planking with oakum with a large maul or beetle and a wedge-shaped iron.

Head Ledges. See *Hatchway.*

Heel. The convex intersecting point or corner of the web and flange of a bar.

Height. Vertical distance between any two decks, or vertical distance measured from the base line to any water line.

Helm. A term applied to the tiller wheel, or steering gear, and also the rudder.

Helm Port. The hole in the counter of a vessel through which the rudder stock passes.

Hog. A scrub-broom for scraping a ship's bottom under water. **2. Hog Frame.** A fore-and-aft frame, forming a truss for the main frames of a vessel, to prevent bending. **3. Hog Sheer.** The curve of the deck on a vessel constructed so that the middle is higher than the ends.

Hogged. A ship that is damaged or strained so that the bottom curves upward in the middle. Opposite of sagged.

Hold. An interior part of a ship, in

which the cargo is stored. The various main compartments are distinguished as the forward, main, and after holds.

2. Hold Beams. The beams that support the lower deck in a cargo vessel.

3. Hold Fast. A dog or brace to hold objects rigidly in place.

Holiday. Parts of a ship's surface which have been accidentally missed in giving it a coat of paint or other protective preparation.

Hood. A covering for a companion hatch, scuttle or skylight.

Hooding-End. The endmost plate of a complete strake. The hooding-ends fit into the stem or stern post.

Horning. Setting the frames of a vessel square to the keel after the proper inclination to the vertical due to the declivity of the keel has been given.

Horseshoe Plate. A small, light plate fitted on the counter around the rudder stock for the purpose of preventing water from backing up into the rudder trunk. Frequently it is made in two pieces.

Hounding. That portion of a mast between the deck and the hounds.

Hounds. The mast head projections which support the trestle trees and top. Also applied in vessels without trestle trees to that portion at which the hound band for attaching the shrouds is fitted.

Housing. That portion of a mast below the surface of the upper deck.

Hulk. The dismantled hull of an old ship.

Hull. The body of a vessel, not including its masting, rigging, etc.

2. Hull Down. A ship at sea, on the horizon, the hull below the line, and only the masts showing.

Inboard. Looking toward the center from the outside of the ship. **2. Inboard Profile.** A plan representing a longitudinal section through the center of the vessel, showing heights of decks, location of transverse bulkheads, assignment of various spaces and all machinery, etc., located on the center or between the center and the shell on the port side.

Inner Bottom. The tank top.

Intercostals. Plates which fit between floors to stiffen the double bottom of a ship. Intercostal comes from the Latin words *inter*, meaning between, and *costa*, meaning rib.

Isherwood System. A method of framing a vessel which employs closely spaced longitudinals, with extra heavy floors spaced further apart.

Jack Ladder. A ladder with wooden steps and side ropes.

Jackstaff. Flagpole at the bow of a ship.

Jacob's Ladder. A rope ladder with wooden rounds.

Joggle. To lap a joint by keeping one edge straight and bending the other, in order to leave both surfaces even on one side.

Journal. That portion of a shaft or other revolving member which transmits weight directly to and is in immediate contact with the bearing in which it turns.

Jury. A term applied to temporary structures, such as masts, rudders, etc., used in an emergency.

Keel. A longitudinal beam or plate in the extreme bottom of a ship, from which ribs or floors start. **2. Keel Blocks.** Blocks on which the keel of a vessel rests when being built, or when she is in a dry dock. **3. Keel Bracket.** A bracket, usually a triangular plate, connecting the vertical keel and flat keel plates, between the frames or floors of a ship. **4. Keel Docking.** In dry docking, the weight of a ship is carried almost entirely on the keel and bilge blocks. The keel and keelson provide the means of distributing the pressure on the center line and docking keels composed of doubling strips of plate or built-up girders are sometimes fitted on the bottom at a distance from the center line corresponding to the best position for the bilge block. The docking keels are fitted in a fore-and-aft direction, generally parallel or nearly so to the keel. **5. Keel Rider.** A plate running along the top of the floors and connecting to the vertical keel.

Keelson. A large I-beam placed above the vertical keel on the rider plate for reinforcing the keel. The term may also apply to bottom fore-and-aft girders on the sides or at the bilge. See *Side Keelson*.

Kentledge. Pig iron used either as temporary weight for inclining a vessel or as permanent ballast.

Kerf. In joiner work, a slit or cut made by a saw. Kerfs are made where timber joints require adjusting. Also applied to the channel burned out by a cutting torch.

King Posts. The main center pillar posts of the ship. May be used as synonym for samson post.

Knot. A nautical mile. About 6,080'.

Knuckle. An abrupt change in direction of plating, frames, keel, deck or other structure of a vessel. Most frequently used with reference to the line at the apex of the angle dividing the upper and lower part of the stern or counter. **2. Knuckle Line.** A line on the stern of a ship, on the cant frames, which divides the upper and lower parts of the stern.

Landing. The spaced distance from the edge of a bar or plate to the center of the rivet holes. **2. Landing Edge.** Opposite of sight edge, which see.

Lap. A term applied to the distance that one piece is laid over the other in making a lap joint.

Lapstrake. Applies to boats built on the clinker system, in which the strakes overlap each other. The top strake always laps on the outside of the strake underneath.

Launch. To place a vessel in the water after completion, by means of sliding ways.

Laying Out. Placing the necessary instructions on plates, shapes, etc., for planing, shearing, punching, bending, flanging, beveling, rolling, etc., from the templates made in the mold loft or taken from the ship.

Lazy Guy. A light rope or tackle by which a boom is prevented from swinging around.

Length Between Perpendiculars. The length of a ship measured from the forward side of stem to the aft side of the sternpost at the height of the designed water line. **2. Length Over All.** The length of a ship measured from the foremost point of the stem to the aftermost part of the stern.

Lift a Template. Is to construct a template to the same size and shape as the part of the ship involved. To lay out a template is to transfer the size and shape onto the material and work it into the fabricated object.

Lifting. Transferring marks and measurements from a drawing, model, etc., to a plate or other object, by templates or other means.

Light, Fixed. A thick glass, usually circular in shape, fitted in a frame fixed in an opening in a ship's side, deck house, or bulkhead to provide access for light. The fixed light is not hinged. **2. Light Load Line.** The water line when the ship rides empty.

Lightening Hole. A hole cut out of a plate to make it lighter and yet not reduce its strength. Also to make a passage through the plate.

Lighter. A full-bodied, heavily built craft, usually not self-propelled, used in bringing merchandise or cargo alongside or in transferring same from a vessel.

Limber Chains. Chains passing through the limber holes of a vessel, by which they may be cleared of dirt. **2. Limber Holes.** Holes in the bottoms of floors through which bilge water runs through tank sections to a seepage basin, where it is then pumped out. The row of holes constitutes the limber passage.

Liner. A piece of flat steel which may or may not taper to a point. Used to fill out a lap or to form a middle layer between two objects. Also for leveling foundations.

Lines. The plans of a ship that show its form. From the lines drawn full size on the mold loft floor are made templates for the various hull parts.

List. To lean to one side.

Load Water Line. The water line when the ship is loaded.

Locker. A storage compartment in a ship.

Loftsman. A man who lays out the ship's lines in the mold loft and makes the molds or templates therefrom.

Logbook. A continuous operating record of a ship kept by one of its officers. In it are recorded daily all important events occurring on board, also the condition of the weather, the ship's position and other data.

Louver. A small opening to permit the passage of air for the purpose of ventilation, which may be partially or completely closed by the operation of overlapping shutters.

Magazine. Spaces or compartments devoted to the stowing of ammunition.

Main Beam. The main longitudinal beam on a ship, running down the center line and supported as a rule by king posts. Sometimes there are two main beams, on each side of the center line. **2. Main Body.** The hull exclusive of all deck erections, spars, stacks, etc.—the naked hull. **3. Main Breadth Line.** The greatest width of a ship amidships. If a ship's sides tumble home, the main breadth line will be considerably below the bulwarks.

Manger. The perforated, elevated bottom of the chain locker which prevents the chains from touching the main locker bottom, and allows seepage water to flow to the drains.

Manhole. A hole in a tank, boiler or compartment on a ship, designed to allow the entrance of a man for examination, cleaning and repairs.

Manifold. A casting or chest containing several valves. Suction or discharge pipes from or to the various compartments, tanks, and pumps are led to it, making it possible for several pumps to draw from or deliver to a given place through one pipe line.

Margin Plate. A longitudinal plate which closes off the ends of the floors along the midship section.

Marry. To join two ropes' ends so that the joint will run through a block; also to place two ropes alongside each other so that both may be hauled on at the same time.

Mast. A spar or hollow steel pipe tapering smaller at the top, placed on the center line of the ship with a slight afterrake. Masts support the yards and gaffs. On cargo vessels they support cargo booms. **Pair Masts.** A pair of cargo masts stepped on either side of the center line, with their heads connected by spans. **2. Mast Hole.** A hole in the deck to receive a mast. The diameter of the hole is larger than the mast for the purpose of receiving two rows of founded wedges to hold the mast in place. **3. Mast Table.** A structure built up around a mast as a support for the cargo boom pivots.

Messroom. A space or compartment where members of the crew eat their meals; a dining room. A dining room in which officers eat their meals is called a wardroom messroom.

Middle Body. That part of a ship adjacent to the midship section. When it has a uniform cross section throughout its length, with its water lines parallel to the center line, it is called the parallel middle body.

Midship. The middle of the vessel. **2. Midship Beam.** The longest beam transverse or longitudinal of the midship of a vessel. **3. Midship Frame.** The frame at midship, which is the largest on the vessel.

Mold. A pattern or template. Also a shape of metal or wood over or in which an object may be hammered or pressed to fit. **2. Mold Loft.** The large enclosed floor where the lines of a vessel are laid out and the molds or templates made.

Molded Breadth. The greatest breadth of a vessel, measured from the heel of frame on one side to heel of frame on the other side. **2. Molded Depth.** The extreme height of a vessel amidships, from the top of the keel to the top of the upper deck beam. **3. Molded Line.** A datum line from which is determined the exact location of the various parts of a ship. It may be horizontal and straight as the molded base line, or curved as a molded deck line or a molded frame line. These lines are determined in the design of a vessel and adhered to throughout the construction. Molded lines are those laid down in the mold loft.

Molding Edge. The edge of a ship's frame which comes in contact with the skin, and is represented in the drawings.

Monkey Tail. A curved bar fitted to the upper, after end of a rudder, and used as an attachment for the rudder pendants.

Mooring Line. Cable or hawse lines used to tie up a ship. **2. Mooring Pipe.** An opening through which hawse lines pass.

Mortise. A hole cut in any material to receive the end or tenon of another piece.

Mullion. The vertical bar dividing the lights in a window.

Nautical Mile. See *Knot*.

Non-watertight Door. A term applied to a door that is not constructed to prevent water under pressure from passing through.

Oakum. A material made of tarred rope fibers obtained from scrap rope, used for calking seams in a wooden deck. It is also used for calking around pipes.

Offsets are given in feet, inches and eighths of an inch. They are taken from large body plans and give the horizontal distance from the center line to the molded frame line on each of the water lines, which are usually spaced 2'-0" to 4'-0" apart. Offsets also give the height of each buttock above the base line at each frame; the heights of decks from the base line; the location of longitudinals and stringers by half breadths and heights, or heights above the base line intersecting the molded frame lines; and all dimensions such that the entire

molded form of a ship and the location of all members of the structure are definitely fixed.

Ogee. A molding with a concave and convex outline like an *S*.

Oiltight. Having the property of resisting the passage of oil.

Old Man. A piece of heavy bar iron bent to the form of a *Z*. One leg of the *Z* is bolted to the material that is to be drilled, and the drill top placed under the other leg and adjusted so the "old man" holds the drill against the material.

On Board. On or in a ship.

On Deck. On the upper deck, in the open air.

Orlop Deck. The lowest deck in a ship.

Outboard. Away from the keel or center of a vessel on either side. **2. Outboard Profile.** A plan representing the longitudinal exterior of a vessel, showing the starboard side of the shell, all deck erections, masts, yards, rigging, rails, etc.

Overboard. Outside, over the side of a ship into the water.

Overhang. Same as counter.

Oxidation. The combination of a substance or element like wood, iron, gasoline, etc., with oxygen. The process is fundamentally the same whether wood is consumed with fire or iron is turned into rust (iron oxide). In welding the oxygen of the air forms an oxide with the molten metal, thus injuring the quality and strength of the weld.

Oxter Plate. The name of a plate that fits in the curve at the meeting of the shell plating with the top of the sternpost and which is fastened thereto.

Packers. Men who fit lamp wicking, tarred felt or other material between parts of the structure to insure water or oil tightness.

Pad Eye. A fitting having an eye integral with a plate or base in order to distribute the strain over a greater area and to provide ample means of securing. The pad may have either a "worked" or a "shackle" eye, or more than one of either or both. The principal use of such a fitting is that it affords means for attaching rigging, stoppers, blocks, and other movable or portable objects. Pad eyes are also known as lug pads.

Pale. One of the interior shores for steadying the beams of a ship while building.

Panting. The pulsation in and out of the bow and stern plating as the ship alternately rises and plunges deep into the water. **2. Panting Beams.** The transverse beams that tie the panting frames together. **3. Panting Frames.** The frames in the forepeak, usually extra heavy to withstand the panting action of the shell plating.

Paravane. A water plane with a protecting wing placed on bottom forward end of the keel stem. Also a special type of water kite which, when towed with wire rope from a fitting on the forefoot of a vessel, operates to ride out from the ship's side and deflect mines which are moored in the path of the vessel, and to cut them adrift so that they will rise to the surface where they·may be seen and destroyed.

Partners. Similar pieces of steel plate, angles or wood timbers used to strengthen and support the mast where it passes through a deck, or placed between deck beams under machinery bed plates for added support.

Paying. Paying out, slackening away on a rope or chain. Also the operation of filling seams between planks after calking, with melted pitch or marine glue, etc.

Peak. See *Fore Peak* and *After Peak*. **2. Peak Tank.** Tanks in the forward and after ends of a vessel. The principal use of peak tanks is in trimming the ship. Their ballast is varied to meet required changes in trim. Should the after hold be empty, the vessel would ride so high that the propeller would lie half out of water and lose much of its efficiency. Filling the after peak tank forces the propeller deeper into the water.

Peen. To round off or shape an object, smoothing out burrs and rough edges.—(*Noun*) The lesser head of a hammer. It is termed ball when it is spherical, cross when in the form of a rounded edge ridge at right angles to the axis of the handle, and ·straight when like a ridge in the plane of the handle.

Pelican Hook. A fastening used where security and great speed of removal are required.

Pendant. A length of rope, usually having a thimble or block spliced into the lower end for hooking on a tackle.

Perpendicular, After. A line perpendicular to the keel line, drawn tangent to the after contour of the stern. **Forward Perpendicular.** A line perpendicular to the keel line, and intersecting the forward side of the stem at the designed load water line. **Mid or Midship Perpendicular.** A line perpendicular to the keel line taken midway between the forward and after perpendiculars.

Pillars. Vertical columns supporting the decks. Also called stanchions.

Pilothouse. A house designed for navigational purposes. It is usually located forward of the midship section and so constructed as to command an unobstructed view in all directions except directly aft along the center line of the vessel, where the smokestack usually interferes.

Pintle. A metal pin secured to the rudder, which is hooked downward into the gudgeons on the stern post, and affords an axis of oscillation as the rudder is moved from side to side for steering.

Pitch. A term applied to the distance a propeller will advance during one revolution, the distance between the centers of the teeth of a gear wheel, the spacing of rivets, etc.

Pitching. The alternate rising and falling motion of a vessel's bow in a nearly vertical plane as she meets the crests and troughs of the waves.

Plan. A drawing prepared for use in building a ship.

Planking. Wood covering for decks, etc.

Plate, Furnaced. A plate that requires heating in order to shape it as required.

Platform. A partial deck.

Plating. The steel plates which form the shell or skin of a vessel.

Plimsoll Mark. The mark stencilled in and painted on a ship's side, designated by a circle and horizontal lines to mark the highest permissible load water lines under different conditions.

Polarity. The property possessed by electrified bodies by which they exert opposite forces in opposite directions. The current in an electrical circuit passes from the positive to the negative pole. In welding, more heat is generated on the positive pole than on the negative one, so that the welding rod is generally made the negative electrode.

Poop. The structure or raised deck at the after end of a vessel.

Poppets. Those pieces of timber which are fixed perpendicularly between the ship's bottom and the bilgeways at the foremost and aftermost parts of the ship, to support her in launching.

Port. Same as porthole. **2. Port Flange.** A protruding flange above a port to keep drip from entering. **3. Port Gangway.** An opening in the side plating, planking, or bulwark for the purpose of providing access through which people may board or leave the ship or through which cargo may be handled. **4. Porthole.** An opening in the ship's shell plating. **5. Port Lid.** A shutter for closing a porthole in stormy weather. It is hung by top hinges. **6. Port Side.** The left-hand side of the ship looking forward.

Propeller. A propulsive device consisting of a boss or hub carrying radial blades, from two to four in number. The rear or driving faces of the blades form portions of an approximately helical surface, the axis of which is the center line of the propeller shaft.

Propeller Arch. The arched section of the hull above the propeller.

Prow. The part of the bow from the load water line to the top of the bow.

Pump Dale. A pipe to convey water from the pump discharge through the ship's side.

Punch, Center. A small punch used to indent a piece of metal for centering a drill. **Prick Punch.** A small hand punch used to make a very small indentation or prick in a piece of metal.

Quadrant. A fitting on the rudder head to which the steering chains are attached.

Quarter. A side of a ship aft, between the main midship frames and stern. Also a side of a ship forward, between the main frames and the stem.

Quarters. Living spaces for passengers or personnel. It includes staterooms, dining salons, mess rooms, lounging places, passages connected with the foregoing, etc.; individual stations for personnel for fire or boat drill, etc.

Quay. An artificial wall or bank, usually of stone, made toward the sea at the side of a harbor or river for convenience in loading and unloading vessels.

Rabbet. A depression or offset designed to take some other adjoining part; as for example the rabbet in the stem taking the shell plating.

Rail. The upper edge of the bulwarks.

Rake. The forward pitch of the stem. The backward slope of the stern.

Range, Galley. The stove situated in the galley which is used to cook the food. The heat may be generated by coal, fuel oil, or electricity.

Reaming. Enlarging a hole by the means of revolving in it a cylindrical slightly tapered tool with cutting edges running along its sides.

Relief. Any clearance allowed back of the cutting edge to reduce friction —whether on top, bottom or wall of the thread.

Reverse Frame. An angle bar placed with its heel against another angle to give the other angle additional strength. The flanges of deck stiffeners always face outboard.

Ribband. A longitudinal strip of timber following the curvature of a vessel and bolted to its ribs to hold them in position and give stability to the skeleton while building.

Rider Frame. Any frame riveted or welded on another frame for the purpose of stiffening it. **2. Rider Plates.** Bed plates set on top of the center keelson, if fitted, for the pillars to rest on.

Rigging. A term used collectively for all the ropes and chains employed to support the masts, yards, and booms of a vessel, and to operate the movable parts of same.

Rise of Bottom. See *Deadrise*.

Rising Floors. The floor frames which rise fore and aft above the level of the midship floors.

Rivet. A metal pin used for connecting two or more pieces of material by inserting it into holes punched or drilled in the pieces. The end that bears a finished shape is called the head and the end upon which some operation is performed after its insertion is called the point. Small rivets are "driven cold," i.e., without heating, and large ones are heated so that points may be formed by hammering. **2. Rivet Spacing.** A term applied to the distance between the centers in a row of rivets. This distance usually consists of a multiple of the rivet diameter, and depends on whether oil-tightness, watertightness or strength is to be the governing requirement.

Riveting Chain. A term applied to two or more rows of rivets that have their centers opposite each other. A line drawn perpendicular to the edge of the plate through the center of a rivet in one row will also pass through the centers of the corresponding rivets in the other rows.

Roll. Motion of the ship from side to side, alternately raising and lowering each side of the deck.

Rolling Chocks. Same as bilge keel.

Rudder. A swinging flat frame hung to the stern post of a ship, by which the ship is steered. **Bow Rudder.** A rudder placed at the bottom of the forward stem and maneuvered from the forepeak. **Pilot Rudder.** A small rudder fastened to the after part of the regular rudder, which by a mechanical attachment pulls the main rudder to either side. **Streamlined Rudder.** A rudder with a bullnosed round forward edge which tapers regularly to a thin after edge. **2. Rudder Bands.** The bands that extend on each side of a rudder to help brace and tie it into the pintles. **3. Rudder Chains.** The chains whereby the rudder is fastened to the stern quarters. They are shackled to the rudder by bolts just above the water line, and hang slack enough to permit free motion of the rudder. They are used as a precaution against losing a rudder at sea. **4. Rudder Flange.** The flange which ties the main part of the rudder to the rudder stem. It may be horizontal or vertical. **5. Rudder Frame.** A frame within the inner shell, bolted through the latter into the main frame and shell, for the purpose of stiffening the rudder. **6. Rudder Pintle.** See *Pintle*. **7. Rudder Post.** The vertical post in the stern of a vessel on which the rudder hangs. **8. Rudder Stop.** Fitting to limit swing of the rudder. **9. Rudder Trunk or Case.** The well in the stern which holds the rudder stock.

Run. The narrowing sides of a vessel aft where they meet at the hooding-ends.

Sagged. Said of a ship which has been strained so that the bottom drops lower in the middle than it is at stem and stern. Opposite of hogged.

Samson Posts. Short heavy masts used as boom supports, and often used for ventilators as well.

Scantling. A term applied to the dimensions of the frames, girders, plating, etc., that go into a ship's structure. The various classification societies publish rules from which these dimensions may be obtained.

Scarfing. A method of cutting away two pieces so that they fit smoothly into each other to make one piece. They are fastened together by welding, bolting, riveting, etc.

Scrieve Board. A large section of

flooring in the mold loft in which the lines of the body are cut with a knife. Used in making molds of the frames, beams, floor plates, etc.

Scupper. Any opening or tube leading from the waterway through the ship's side, to carry away water from the deck. **2. Scupper Hose.** A temporary canvas hose attached to the outside of a scupper hole, and reaching to the water, to conduct the water clear of the ship's side. **3. Scupper Lip.** A projection on the outside of the vessel to allow the water to drop free of the ship's side. **4. Scupper Opening.** A hole longer than an ordinary scupper with vertical bars, placed on the side of the ship at the deck line to allow deck wash to flow over the side of the vessel. Also called freeing port. **5. Scupper Pipe.** A pipe connected to the scupper on the decks, with an outlet through the side plating just above the water. The water thus diverted from the deck does not discolor the ship's side plating or damage the paint.

Scuttle. A small opening, usually circular in shape, and generally fitted in decks to provide access as a manhole or for stowing fuel, water and stores. A cover or lid is fitted so that the scuttle may be closed when not in use. Also applied to the operation of opening a sea valve or otherwise, allowing the sea to enter a ship for the purpose of sinking her. **2. Scuttle Butt.** The designation for a container of the supply of drinking water for the use of the crew.

Seam. Joint.

Seamstrap. Butt-strap of a seam.

Set Bolt. A bolt used as a drift to force another bolt out of its hole.

Set Iron. Bar of soft iron used on the bending slab to bend frames to the desired shapes.

Set Up. To tighten the nut on a bolt or stud.

Sett Piling. Reinforcing piling in the ground beneath the ways.

Shackle. A link with a bolt fastened through its eyes, used for fastening chains and eye loops together.

Shaft. Long, round, heavy forging connecting engine and propeller. **2. Shaft Alley.** A passageway along the shaft line between the after bulkhead of the engine room and the stern post, affording a means of access to the propeller shaft. **3. Shaft Coupling.** A flange on the end of a shaft section connecting two sections by bolts. **4. Shaft Pipe.** A pipe which passes through a hole in the stern post and through frames with a circular housing. In it are bearings on which the propeller shaft rotates. **5. Shaft Strut.** A bracket supporting the after end of the propeller shaft and the propeller in twin or multiple screwed vessels having propeller shafts fitted off from the center line. **6. Shaft Tunnel.** Same as Shaft Alley.

Shape. Long bar of constant cross section such as channel, T-bar, angle bar, etc.

Shaping. Consists of cutting, bending and forming a structural member.

Shear Legs. Usually two or more timbers or spars erected in the shape of an A-frame with lower ends spread out and upper ends fastened together, from which lifting tackle is suspended. Used for raising and moving heavy weights where a crane or derrick is not available.

Shears. Large machine for cutting plates and shapes.

Sheer. The upward curvature of the lines of a vessel toward the bow and stern. **2. Sheer Plan.** A vertical longitudinal midship section of a vessel, showing plan, elevation and end view, on which are projected various lines as follows: Water line; diagonal line; buttock and bow lines; main-breadth lines; top-breadth lines; top side sheer lines. **3. Sheer Rail.** A rail surrounding a ship on the outside, under the gunwale, on small vessels called guard rail. **4. Sheer Strake.** See *Strake.*

Shell Expansion. A plan showing the shapes and sizes of all plates of the shell plating. **2. Shell Landings.** Points on the frames showing where the edges of the shell plates come. **3. Shell Plating.** See *Plating.*

Shift of Butts. A term applied to

the arrangement of the butt joints in plating. These joints in shell plating should be so shifted that the adjacent strakes of plating have their butts at least two frame spaces apart.

Shifting Beam. A portable beam fitted in a hatchway for the purpose of supporting the hatch covers. The ends of the beams are fitted in slotted carriers attached to the inside of the hatchway coamings.

Shim. A piece of metal or wood placed under the bedplate or base of a machine or fitting for the purpose of truing it up. Also applied to pieces placed in slack spaces behind or under frames, plates or planks to preserve a fair surface.

Ship's Log. See *Logbook*.

Shole. A piece of plank put under a shore where there is no groundway.

Shore. One of the many wooden props by which the ribs or frames of a vessel are externally supported while building, or by which the vessel is held upright on the ways.

Side Keelson. A beam placed on the side of the hull about two-thirds the distance from the center line to the bilgeway. This is used as a stiffener longitudinally for the flat bottom of a vessel.

Sight Edges. The edges of plating that are visible are called sight edges. The sight edge is on the outside of the shell, on the tops of decks and inner bottom plating, and on the opposite side from the stiffeners on bulkheads. The edge that is covered is called the landing edge.

Skeg. The after part of the keel, upon which the stern post rests.

Skin. The plating of a ship. The inside skin is sometimes called the ceiling, the outside skin the case. It consists of steel plates laid in alternate inside and outside strakes.

Skylight. An erection built on a deck, having glass lights in its top and fitted over an opening in the deck for the purpose of admitting light and air to a compartment below.

Sliding Ways. One of the structures on each side of and parallel to the keel, supporting the cradle under the bilgeways on which the vessel rests in launching. The sliding ways form the inclined plane down which the vessel slides, made of planks laid on blocks of wood.

Sluice. An opening in the lower part of a bulkhead fitted with a sliding watertight gate or door having an operating rod extending to the upper deck or decks. These openings are useful in center line bulkheads, as in case of damage to one side of the ship the water may be quickly admitted to the other side before the ship is dangerously listed.

Smokestack. A metal chimney or passage through which the smoke and gases are led from the uptakes to the open air.

Snibs. Handles that can be operated from both sides of a watertight door.

Snipe. To cut a sharp bevel on the end of a stiffener or beam.

Sny. To twist a plate into an uneven warped shape on a mold.

Soft Patch. A plate put on over a break or hole, and secured with tap bolts. It is made watertight with a gasket such as canvas saturated in red lead.

Sole Plate. A plate fitted to the top of a foundation to which the base of a machine is bolted. Also a small plate fitted at the end of a stanchion.

Sounding. Measuring the depth of water or other liquid. **2. Sounding Pipe.** Vertical pipe in oil or water tank, used to guide a sounding device when measuring the depth of liquid in tank.

Span. The distance between any two similar members, as the span of the frames. Also used to describe the length of a member between its supports, as the span of a girder.

Spanner. A form of open-head wrench.

Spar. A pole used for a hoist or in scaffolding.

Specific Gravity. The ratio of the weight of a given volume of any substance to the weight of an equal volume of distilled water, and is found by dividing the first weight by the second. Since the distilled water weighs approximately 62.4 pounds per cubic foot, any substance, a cubic foot of which weighs less than this, has a specific gravity of less than one, and will float on water. Any substance of greater weight per cubic foot has a specific gravity of more than one and will sink.

Spectacle Frame. A single casting containing the bearings for and supporting the ends of the propeller shafts in a twin-screw vessel. It consists of arms of pear-shaped section extending outboard from each side of the center line of the ship to bosses, taking the bearings of the propeller shafts. Used in large merchant vessels in place of shaft struts or brackets.

Spiling. The curve of a plate or strake as it narrows to a point.

Splice. A method of uniting the ends of two ropes by first unlaying the strands, then interweaving them so as to form a continuous rope.

Spot-Faced. Indicates that an annular facing has been made about a bolt hole to allow a nut or head to seat evenly.

Square Frame. A frame having no bevel on its flange. A midship frame.

Stability. Tendency of the ship to remain upright.

Stagger. To zigzag a line, or row of rivet holes, etc.

Staging. Upright supports fastened together with horizontal and diagonal braces forming supports for planks which form a working platform.

Stanchion. An iron post or pillar for supporting the decks.

Stapling. Collars, forged of angle bars, to fit around continuous members passing through bulkheads or decks for watertightness.

Starboard. The right side of a vessel looking forward.

Stateroom. A private room or cabin for the accommodation of passengers or officers.

Stays. The ropes, whether hemp or wire, that support the lower masts, topmasts, topgallant masts, etc., in a fore and aft direction.

Stealer or Steeler. The foremost or aftermost plate in a strake, which is dropped short of the stem or stern post of a vessel.

Steering Gear. A term applied to the steering wheels, leads, steering engine and fittings by which the rudder is turned. **2. Steering Gear Flat.** The deck above the stern overhang, on which the rudder steering mechanism is installed.

Stem. The upright post or bar of the bow. **2. Stem Foot.** The forward end of the keel, into which the stem is fitted.

Stepping-up Pieces. Same as poppets.

Stern. The after part of the vessel. **2. Stern Frame.** Large casting attached to after end of keel to form ship's stern. Includes rudder post, propeller post, and aperture for the propeller. **3. Stern Pipe.** A pipe leading to the opening at the side of poop deck for passing through of cables, chains, etc., for mooring purposes. **4. Stern Post.** The after post to which the rudder is hinged and placed on the skeg, with sufficient clearance for the propeller to revolve. **5. Stern Tube.** The bearing which supports the propeller shaft where it emerges from the ship. A cast iron or steel cylinder, fitted with brass bushings which are lined with lignum vitae or white metal bearing surfaces, upon which the propeller shaft, enclosed in a brass sleeve, rotates.

Stiffener. An angle bar or stringer fastened to a surface to strengthen it and make it rigid.

Stopwater. A wood plug driven through a scarf joint to stop water from leaking into the ship. The term is also applied to pieces of canvas soaked in oil, red lead, etc., placed between the faying surfaces of plates and shapes where water or oil is apt to work its way through.

Strake. A continuous line of plates on a vessel's side, reaching from stem to stern. **Garboard Strake.** The range of plating nearest to the keel on both port and starboard sides. **Gore Strake.**

A strake which ends before reaching the stem or stern post. Such strakes are laid at or near the middle of the ship's sides to lessen the spiling of the plating. **Landing Strake.** The second strake from the gunwale. **Limber Strake.** The strake on the inner skin of a vessel which is nearest to the keel. **Sheer Strake.** The top strake, just under the gunwale.

Stringer. A large beam or angle fitted in various parts of the vessel to give additional strength. Depending on their location, stringers are known as bilge stringers, side stringers, hold stringers, etc. **2. Stringer Plate.** A fore and aft member of deck plating which strengthens the connection between the beams and the frames, and keeps the beams square to the shell.

Strut. A heavy arm or brace.

Superstructure. Any structure built above the uppermost complete deck, such as a pilothouse, bridge, etc.

Swage. To bear or force down. An instrument having a groove on its under side for the purpose of giving shape to any piece subjected to it when receiving a blow from a hammer.

Swash Plates. Plates fixed in tanks to prevent excessive movement of the contained liquid.

Tackle. Any combination of ropes and blocks that multiplies power. A single whip, improperly called tackle, gives no increase in power, but a change in direction of the power applied.

Tail Shaft. The aft section of the shaft, which receives the propeller.

Tank Top. The plating laid on the bottom floors of a ship, which forms the top side of the tank sections or double bottom.

Tanks. Compartments for liquids or gases. They may be formed by the ship's structure as double bottom tanks, peak tanks, deep tanks, etc., or may be independent of ship's structure and installed on special supports.

Tee Bar. A rolled shape, generally of mild steel, having a cross section shaped like the letter *T*. In ship work it is used for bulkhead stiffeners,

bracket and floor clips, etc. The size is denoted by dimensions of its cross section and weight per running foot.

Telegraph. Means of signalling from bridge to engine room, etc.

Template. A pattern made in the mold loft from wood strips or heavy paper.

Tenon. The end of a piece of wood cut into the form of a rectangular prism, designed to be set into a cavity of a like form in another piece which is termed mortise.

Test Head. The head of water corresponding to the pressure prescribed as a test for bulkheads, tanks, compartments, etc. Test heads are prescribed to insure satisfactory water or oil tightness, and also as tests of strength.

Tholes. The pins in the gunwale of a boat which are used for oarlocks.

Thread. The spiral part of a screw.

Thwarts. Boards extending across a rowboat just below the gunwale to stiffen the boat and to provide seats.

Tie Plates. A single fore-and-aft or diagonal course of plating attached to deck beams under wood deck to give extra strength.

Tiller. An arm attached to rudder head for operating the rudder.

Toe. The edge of the flange of an angle.

Toggle Pin. A pin, usually having an eye worked on the head, and having a point so constructed, that a portion of it may turn on a pivot pin, forming a tee shaped locking device to keep the pin in place.

Tongue. The tongue of a sternpost or propeller post is the raised middle section which is fastened to the vertical keel. As a rule the tongue is raised twice as high as the sides of the dished keel.

Tonnage, Gross. The entire internal cubic capacity of a vessel expressed in "tons" taken at 100 cubic feet each. The peculiarities of design and construction of the various types of vessels and their parts necessitate certain explanatory rulings in connection with this term. **2. Tonnage, Net.** The internal cubic capacity of a vessel which remains after the capacities of certain specified spaces have been deducted from the gross tonnage.

3. Tonnage Openings. Openings in shelter deck bulkheads for purpose of economy in tonnage rating.

Top Breadth Lines. The width of a vessel measured across the shelter deck.

Topping Lift. A rope or chain extending from the head of a boom or gaff to a mast, or to the vessel's structure for the purpose of supporting the weight of the boom or gaff and its loads, and permitting them to be rotated at a certain level.

Topside. That portion of the side of the hull which is above the designed water line.

Transom Beam. A strong deck beam in the after end of a vessel directly over the sternpost, and connected at each end to the transom frame. The cant beams supporting the deck plating in the overhang of the stern radiate from it. **2. Transom Frame or Plate.** A horizontal frame under a ship's counter.

Transverse. Placed at right angles to the keel, such as a transverse frame, transverse bulkhead, etc. See also *Abeam* and *Athwart.*

Tread. The length of a vessel's keel.

Treenails. Wooden pins employed instead of nails or spikes to secure the planking of a wooden vessel to the frames.

Trim. The difference in draft at the bow of a vessel from that at the stern.

Tripping Brackets. Flat bars placed at various points on a deck girder or beams as reinforcement.

Trunk Bulkhead. The casing or partition that forms an enclosure running from deck to deck and surrounding the hatch openings.

Try Square. A small and handy instrument for trying the square of surfaces while planing or fairing up with any tool. They come in various sizes and should be handled carefully to avoid knocking them out of true, and thus causing material to be spoiled by inaccurate work.

Tuck. The after part of a ship where the shell plating meets in the run and is tucked together.

Tumble Home. Said of the sides of a vessel when they lean in at the top. When vertical they are called wall-sided; when they lean out, flaring.

Turnbuckles. Used to pull objects together. A link threaded on both ends of a short bar, one left-handed, the other right-handed.

Turrets. Structures designed for the mounting and handling of the guns and accessories (usually main battery guns) of a war vessel. Turrets are constructed so as to revolve about a vertical axis usually by means of electrical or hydraulic machinery.

Tween Decks. The space between any continuous decks.

Umbrella. A metal shield in the form of a frustrum of a cone, fitted to the outer casing of the smokestack over the air casing to keep out the weather.

Unship. To remove anything from its usual place. To take apart.

Upper Deck. A partial deck above the main deck amidships. **2. Upper Works.** Superstructures, or deck erections located on or above the weather deck. Sometimes used with reference to a ship's entire above-water structure.

Uptake. A sheet metal conduit connecting the boiler furnace with the base of the smokestack. It conveys the smoke and hot gases from the boiler to the stack, and should be made double thickness with an air space between to prevent radiation. Swinging dampers for controlling the fires are fitted in the uptake.

Veer. The wind to veer, to change.

Ventilation. The process of providing fresh air to the various spaces, and removing foul or heated air, gases, etc., from them. This may be accomplished by natural draft or by mechanical means.

Ventilators, Bell-Mouthed or Cowl. Terminals on open decks in the form of a 90° elbow with enlarged or bell shaped openings, so formed as to obtain an increase of air supply when facing tne wind and to increase the velocity of air down the ventilation pipe.

Vertical Keel. A plate running in a fore and aft direction connecting to the flat keel and keel rider plates, it is usually connected by two angles at the top and bottom for a riveted job or welded to the keel and keel rider.

Visor. A small inclined awning running around the pilothouse over the windows or air ports to exclude the glare of the sun or to prevent rain or spray from coming in the openings when the glazed frames are dropped or opened. They may be of canvas or metal.

Voice Tube. A tube designed for the carriage of the human voice from one part of the ship to another. In its simplest form the voice tube system includes a speaking connection between the pilot house and engine room only. In large war vessels the system becomes very complicated. Voice tubes are generally made up to about four inches in diameter and fitted with appropriate speaking and listening terminals.

Wake. The disturbed water left behind by a moving ship.

Wales. See *Harpings*.

Wardroom. A room or space on shipboard set aside for use of the officers for social purposes and also used as their mess or dining room.

Water Lines. Lines drawn parallel with the surface of the water at varying heights on a ship's outline. In the sheer plan they are straight and horizontal; in the half-breadth plan they show the form of the ship at each of the successive heights marked.

Waterlogged. A ship full of water but still afloat.

Watertight Compartment. A space or compartment within a ship having its top, bottom, and sides constructed in such a manner as to prevent the leakage of water into or from the space.

Watertight Door. A door so constructed that, when closed, it will pre-

vent water under pressure from passing through.

Waterway. A gutter-like recess on the shelter deck at the midship section of a ship, which delivers excess water to the scupper holes for discharge into the sea. **2. Waterway Bar.** An angle or flat bar attached to a deck stringer plate forming the inboard boundary of a waterway and serving as an abutment for the wood deck plating.

Ways. The timber sills upon which a ship is built.

Web. The vertical portion of a beam, the athwartship portion of a frame. **2. Web Frame.** A frame with a deep web.

Weeping. The very slow issuance of water through the seams of a ship's structure or from a containing vessel in insufficient quantity to produce a stream.

Weigh Anchor. To lift anchor off the sea bottom.

Welding. The method of fastening steel objects together by fusing the metal with a gas flame or an electrical arc. **2. Welding Bead.** A seam made by closing a joint with molten metal applied with a welding stick.

Well. The space between the first bulkhead of a long poop deck or deck house and a forecastle bulkhead. **2. Well Deck.** A sunken deck on a merchant vessel, fitted between the forecastle and a long poop or continuous bridge house or raised quarter deck.

Whaler. Any steel or wooden member used for temporarily bracing a bulkhead, deck section, etc.

Winch. A hoisting or pulling machine fitted with a horizontal single or double drum. A small drum is generally fitted on one or both ends of the shaft supporting the hoisting drum. These small drums are called gypsies, niggerheads, or winch heads. The hoisting drums either are fitted with a friction brake or are directly keyed to the shaft. The driving power is usually steam or electricity but hand power is also used. A winch is used principally for the purpose of handling, hoisting, and lowering cargo from a dock or lighter to the hold of a ship and vice versa.

Windlass. An apparatus in which horizontal or vertical drums or gypsies and wildcats are operated by means of a steam engine or motor for the purpose of handling heavy anchor chains, hawsers, etc.

Wing. The overhanging part of a deck on a ferry boat, or fore and aft of paddle boxes in a side wheeler. Also used to indicate outboard parts of the ship, such as in the wings of the hold. **2. Wing Brackets.** The large brackets which fasten the margin plates to the lower frame ends. (Also known as deep bracket knees and bilge brackets.) **3. Wing Passage.** A passageway below the water line on a man-of-war, used for repairs and inspections. **4. Wing**

Tanks. Tanks located outboard and usually just under the weather deck. They are sometimes formed by fitting a longitudinal bulkhead between the two uppermost decks, and sometimes by working a diagonal, longitudinal flat between the ship's side and the weather deck.

Wire Mesh Bulkhead. A partition built up of wire mesh panel.

Yard. A cross-spar on a mast for spreading a sail or displaying signals, as flags or lights.

Yard-arm. The outer end of a yard.

Zenith. When the sun is in the zenith and observed with a sextant, the arc will be 90° from the horizon.

BLUEPRINT ABBREVIATIONS AND SYMBOLS

To a large degree, learning to read blueprints means learning what blueprint symbols and abbreviations stand for, and also the different kinds of lines used on drawings. Fig. 8 gives these lines and illustrates the use of them. Fig. 9 shows the arc and gas welding symbols approved by the American Welding Society.

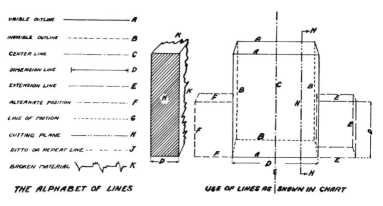

FIG. 8. TYPES OF LINES USED ON DRAWINGS.

In the list which follows, more than one abbreviation is given for many of the words. This is because of the lack of consistency found on drawings. For example, *drawing* will be abbreviated *Drwg., Dwg.* and *Dr. Thk.* and *Tk.* will be found in the same Material List, both standing for *thick*.

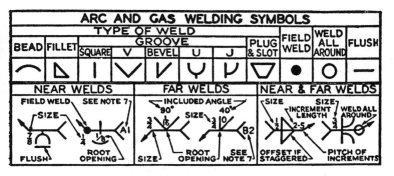

FIG. 9. AMERICAN WELDING SOCIETY SYMBOLS.

A.A.—Anti-Aircraft
A.B.S.—American Bureau of Standards
A.Cant.—After Cant Frames
A.D.—After Draft
A.E.—Air Escape
A.G.—Armor Grating
A.L.—Accommodation Ladder
A.M.C.B.H.—Auxiliary Machine Casing Bulkhead
A.P.—After Perpendicular; Air Port or Porthole
A.S.—Air Scoop; Angle Stiffener
A.S.L.—Abandon Ship Ladder
A.S.R.V.—Angle Stop Radiator Valve
A.S.V.—Angle Stop Valve
A.T.—Airtight
A.T.D.—Airtight Door
Ab., Abv.—Above
Adj.—Adjustable
Aft.B.—Afterbody
Al.—Aluminum
Alt.—Alteration
Amm.—Ammunition
Arrgt.—Arrangement
Assm.—Assembled
Asst.—Assistant
Av. Lub.—Aviation Lubrication

B.—Berth (2-*B.* would mean Two Berths)
B.Bd.—Bulletin Board
B.C.B.H.—Boiler Casing Bulkhead
B.Dk.—Bridge Deck
B.E.—Beveled Edge
B.H.(D.)—Bulkhead (also *Bhd.*)

B.K.—Bar Keel
BL—Base Line (drawn with one letter partly over the other)
B.L.—Base Line; Bow Line
B.R., B.Rm.—Boiler Room
B.S.—Butt Strap
B.W.—Butt Weld
Bal.—Balance
Base L.—Base Line
Bat.—Batten
Bdry.—Boundary
Bel.—Below
Bet.—Between
Bev. Bd.—Bevel Board
Bhd.—Bulkhead
Bil.K.—Bilge Keel, same as Rol. K.
Bkt.—Bracket
Boss. Fr. Aft—Bossed Frames Aft
Boss Plt.—Boss Plate
Br. Dk.—Bridge Deck
Bt.Dk.—Boat Deck
Btk.L.—Buttock Line
Bu., Bur.—Bureau
Bx.K.—Box Keel

C. & R.—Construction and Repair
C.D.—Cofferdam
C.Fr.—Cant Frame
C.L.—Center Line
C.P.—Coaling Port
C.R.—Curtain Rod
C.R.S.—Corrosion-Resisting Steel
C.Sk.—Countersink Holes
C.Sk.O.—Countersink Holes Over
C.T.—Conning Tower
C. to C.—Center to Center

C.V.—Check Valve
C.W.—Cold Water; Continuous Weld
Cab't—Cabinet
Cam'r—Camber
Car.—Carpenter
Ch., Ch.V.—Check Valve
Cir.—Circumference or Circulating
Ck., Csk.—Countersink (see also *C.Sk.*)
Ck.O.S.—Countersink Other Side
Ck.T.S.—Countersink This Side
Cl.—Collar
Clk.—Calk
Col.Bh.—Collision Bulkhead
Comp.—Compartment
Comp. Air—Compressed Air
Cont.—Constant; Continuous
Cont.V.—Control Valve
Csk.O.S.—Countersink Other Side
Csk.T.S.—Countersink This Side

D.—Down (Used around hatches with indicator line —)
D.B.R.—Double Book Rack
D.C.—Deck Covering
D.K.—Duct Keel or Box Keel
D.L.—Dead Light
D.O.—Diesel Oil
D.T.—Dust-Tight
D.W.—Drainwater
Dblr.—Doubler
Det.—Detail
Dia.—Diameter
Dia.L.—Diagonal Line
Disch.—Discharge
Div.—Division
Dk.—Deck
Dn.—Down
Dr.—Door
Drn.—Drain
Dt.C.Sk.—Don't Countersink

E.R.Bh.—Engine Room Bulkhead
E.C.Dn.—Electrical Cables Down
Elev.—Elevation
Emer.—Emergency
Eng.Fdn. (Found.)—Engine Foundation
Eng.Rm.—Engine Room
Exp.M.—Expanded Metal
Exp.T.—Expansion Trunk

F.—Far
F.B.—Flat Bar

F.Cant.—Forward Cant Frames
F.E.—Forward End
F.K.—Flat Keel
F.M.—Fire Main
F.O.—Fuel Oil
F.O.&B.—Fuel Oil and Ballast
F.P.—Fire Plug; Forward Perpendicular
F.Plt.—Face Plate
F.Q.A.W.T.—Flush Quick-Acting Watertight
F.T.—Fume-Tight
F.W.T.—Feed-Water Tank
F.W.T.H.—Flush Watertight Hatch
Fdn.—Foundation
Fe.Bd.—Freeboard
Fl.—Floor
Flg.—Flange
Flg.Plt.—Flange Plate
Flo.B.—Floor Beams
Fo.P.—Forepeak
Focl.Dk.—Forecastle Deck
For., For'd.—Forward
For'd.B.—Forward Body
Fr.—Frame
Ft.—Feet
Fuel P.—Fuel Port
Fwd.—Forward

G.—Gangway
G.P.M.—Gallons per Minute
G.S.H.V.—Glove Stop Hose Valve
G.S.L.C.V.—Globe Stop Lift Check Valve
G.S.R.V.—Globe Stop Radiator Valve
G.S.V.—Globe Stop Valve
G.V.—Gate Valve
Galv.—Galvanize
Gar. Str.—Garboard Strake
Gd.R.—Guard Rail
Gen.—Generator
Gen'l—General
Gir's—Girders

H.—Hatch; Hull
H.D.—Hatch Door
H.L.—Horizontal Line
H.P.—Hawse Pipe; High Pressure
H.Rd.—Half Round
H.S.—Hinged Shelf
H.T.S.—High Tensile Steel; Heat-Treated Steel
H.W.—Hot Water
H.W.T.—Hot Water Tank

Hat.—Hatch
Hd.—Head
Hf.Bh.—Half-Breadth
H'l's—Holes
Hose C.—Hose Connection
HoseR.—Hose Rack
Htg.—Heating

I.—I-Beam
I.B.—Inboard: Inner Bottom
I.D.—Inside Diameter
I K.—Inner Keel
In.—Inch
In.Bd., Inbd.—Inboard (also *I.B.*)
In.Bot.—Inner Bottom
In.Dia.—Inside Diameter
Insul.—Insulation
Int.—Intermittent
Interl'k'd—Interlocked

Jog.—Joggle

K.—Keel
K.P.—King Post
K.R.—Keel Rider
Knu.—Knuckle

L.—Lavatory; Line
L.B.P.—Length between Perpendiculars
L.D.—Load Draft
L.D.B.—Light Distribution Boxes
L.Dk.—Lower Deck
L.H.—Lightening Hole
L.L.—Leave Loose
L.L.L.—Light Load Line
L.L.W.L.—Light Load Water Line
L.O.—Lubricating Oil
L.O.A.—Length Overall
L.P.—Low Pressure; Label Plate
L.S.—Left Side
L.W.L.—Load Water Line
Lb. or #—Pound
Ldg.—Landing
Leg.Bln'k—Legal Blank
Lin.—Liner or Linoleum
Lin. (L)—Light Linoleum
Lin. (M)—Medium Linoleum
Lkr.—Locker
Longl.—Longitudinal
Long's—Longitudinals
Lub.—Lubricating

M.B.—Molded Breadth

M.D.—Molded Depth
M.Dk.—Main Deck
M.E.—Molded Edge
M.H.—Manhole
M.L.—Molded Line
M.P.—Mooring Pipe
M.T.—Mail Tray
Mach.—Machine
Mach'y—Machinery
Mag.—Magazine
Mar.Plt.—Margin Plate
Max.—Maximum
Med.—Medium
Mi.Dk.—Middle Deck
Min.—Minimum
Mk.—Mark
Mld.—Molded
Mn.Drn.—Main Drain
Mo.—Mold
Mrk.—Mark

N.—Near
N. & F.—Near and Far
N.S.—Nickel Steel
N.S.T.—Non-Slip Tread
N.T.D.—Non-Tight Door
N.V.—Needle Valve
N.W.T.—Non-Watertight
No.—Number

O.B.—Outboard
O.D., O.Dia.—Outside Diameter
O.Dk.—Observation Deck
O.G.—Operating Gear
O.G.Dk.P.—Operating Gear Deck Plate
O.K.—Outer Keel
O.S.—Opposite Side
O.S.T.I.—Other Side to Iron
O.T.—Oiltight
Off C.L.—Off Center Line
On C.L.—On Center Line
Op.—Operator
Opp.—Opposite
Opp.H.—Opposite Hand
Outbd.—Outboard
Ov. Bd.—Overboard
Ov. Fl.—Overflow

P.C.—Pitch Circle
P.Dk.—Poop Deck
P.Mk.—Pitch Mark
Pant. Stg's—Painting Stringers
Per., Perp.—Perpendicular

Pl., Plt.—Plate
Plat.—Platform
Plfm.—Platform
Prot.Dk.—Protective Deck
Pt.—Point; Port

Q.A.D.—Quick-Acting Door
Qtrs.—Quarters

R.S.—Right Side
R.B.L.—Raised Base Line
R.F.W.—Reserve Feed Water
R.N.T.H.—Raised Non-Tight Hatch
R.W.T.H.—Raised Watertight Hatch
Ra.K.—Raised Keel
Rad.—Radius
Ref.—Reference
Refrig.—Refrigerator
Rev. S.—Reverse Stiffener
Rivs.—Rivets (also *R'ts*)
Rm.—Room
Rol.K.—Rolling Keel or Fin
R'ts—Rivets

S.A.—Shaft Alley
S.D.H.—Soap Dish Holder
S.F.W.T.H.—Semi-Flush Watertight
    Hatch
S.L.—Safe Locker
S.P.—Sternpost
S.R.—Storage Room
S.S.—Slop Sink
S.T.—Sounding Tube
S.T.A.—Shaft Tunnel Alley
S.T.S.—Special Treated Steel
S.W.—Salt Water or Steel Wire
San.—Sanitary
Scr.Bh.—Screen Bulkhead
Sec.L.—Sectional Line
Sect.—Section
Separ.T.—Separating Tank
Sett.T.—Settling Tank
Sh.—Shore
Shl.Dk.—Shelter Deck
Shr.—Sheer
Spec.—Special or Specification
Specs.—Specifications
Spkg.—Sprinkling
Sq.—Square
St.—Strainer
St.M.—Set Mark

Stanch.—Stanchion
Stg's—Stringers
Stiff.—Stiffener
Str.—Stringer
Suct.—Suction
Swas.Plt.—Swash Plates

T.—Top
T.C.V.—Temperature Control Valve;
    Temperature Check Valve
T.S.—Top Side
T.S.T.I.—This Side to Iron
T.T.—Tank Top
Temp.—Template
Thks.—Thickness
Tk.—Tank; Thick
Tran. Gir.—Transverse Girders
T.P.H.—Toilet Paper Holder
Trans.—Transfer; Transformer;
    Transverse

U.Dk.—Upper Deck
Und.—Underneath

V.—Vent; Void
V.C.—Vertical Cap
V.D.L.—Ventilation Dead Light
V.K.—Vertical Keel
V.G.R.—Vertical Grab Rod
Vert.—Vertical

W.C.—Water Closet
W.L.—Water Level; Water Line
W.P.—Wash Port
W.R.—Wardroom
W.R.H.A.—Winch Resistor House
    Aft
W.R.H.F.—Winch Resistor House
    Forward
W.R.H.M.—Winch Resistor House
    Middle
W.R.S.Rm.—Wardroom Stateroom
W.T.—Watertight
W.T.D.—Watertight Door
W.T.F.—Watertight Flat
W.T.Tr.—Watertight Trunk
Wt.—Weight

X.—Distance Below Deck

Y.—Distance Above Deck

PAINTS AND PAINTING

Paint is made up of two principal parts, the pigment and the vehicle.

Pigment of paint may be defined as the minute particles of insoluble solids that form the body of the paint and remain as the hard opaque surface after the liquid or vehicle has evaporated or deteriorated.

Vehicle of paint is the liquid content which acts as a binding agent between the minute particles of pigment, holding them together as well as to the surface of an object. The vehicle also contains the drying agent. Vehicles are as definitely liquids as pigments are solids.

PIGMENTS

Red Leads come in two basic forms, reddish powder and heavy paste. As red lead and white lead and zinc form the base of most paint it may be well to discuss briefly just what they are and how they are made.

Red lead (Oxide of Lead) is made from metallic lead, by a burning process. Lead melts easily at 620° Fahrenheit, but in this burning process the temperature is boosted to 900° to 1200° Fahrenheit at which point oxygen is induced into the lead producing an oxidizing effect and the resultant compound is the bright reddish powder that we know as red lead.

Litharge. Another form of lead oxide which is made by the same process but at different temperatures. Actually the litharge forms first and as the temperatures are raised and additional oxygen induced red lead is produced.

Fume red lead is a compound of extremely fine particles developed from metallic lead by the heat and oxygen process used in making regular red lead, but it is distilled instead of burned.

Fume red lead is used when a paint pigment of extra fineness is desired, or in other words, a thinner paint film than ordinary red lead, yet having the same dense body with the same covering power. When mixing fume red lead a greater amount of mixing oil per pound is required than for regular red lead.

In mixing red lead powder, it is advisable to mix a little linseed oil with the powder till a pliable paste is reached and let this paste stand at least 24 hours; several days would be better. This allows the oil to completely *wet* all the particles of pigment. Any one who has attempted to make cocoa by adding all the water at the start, then tried to get a good mixture by sheer stirring, will appreciate this point. This is often referred to as breaking up the dry red lead. Add small amounts of oil to the paste, stirring well, until proper consistency is reached.

White Leads (Basic Carbonate). White lead is made by two separate processes; in the first, metallic lead is corroded by acetic acid forming whitish flakes, which are later ground to a fine powder. This is sold either in this form or as paste, the latter being more favored. The second process (basic sulphate) of making white leads is from lead sulphide ore (gelena) by the sublimation process. This process much resembles that of making red lead, in that the ore is roasted, the fumes mixing with oxygen forming the white powder we know as white lead. This process makes finer pigment particles in much the same manner as fume red lead. White lead paste is mixed in the same manner as red lead.

Zinc Oxide is a compound of zinc and oxygen, and is the finest of all white pigments. Due to its extreme hardness zinc oxide is unaffected by either change of temperature or the gases present in the atmosphere. Zinc oxide is used in making white enamels and may be combined with white lead or other pigments.

COLOR PIGMENTS

Color pigments are added to the base pigment to give color to paint. They are made principally from mineral or natural earth colors and from chemical colors. The most common natural earth pigments are, siennas (raw and burnt), umbers (raw and burnt), yellow ochre, and various mineral blacks. The most common chemical colors are chrome yellow, Prussian blue, chrome green, cobalt blue and vermilion.

Carbon Blacks. *Lampblack*, *gas black* and *graphite* are the most common carbon blacks in use aboard ship today. They are pigments of pure ingredients and in themselves will make a very durable paint but their best use is to tint white, red or zinc lead to get a desired shade and because of their extreme opaque quality only a small amount is required with leads to make an excellent black paint.

Drip black, *bone black*, *ivory black* and other blacks of this type are also carbonized products but as they are made from animal and vegetable matter they are naturally of an inferior quality and strength therefore about five times greater amount than carbon black should be used. For tinting purposes these blacks should not be added while in their dry state but mixed with a small amount of linseed oil.

All carbon blacks have a non-drying tendency and when used as pure pigment more driers must be added.

EXTENDERS

Extenders, as the name implies are materials used to extend or increase the pigment base. They are sometimes referred to as auxiliary pigments or inert ingredients, having no chemical action on the compounds of paints.

Some of the more common extenders are: *Silica asbestine, china clay, barytes* and *gypsum.*

VEHICLES

Linseed Oil. The most common vehicle used today in mixing paint is linseed oil. It is obtained from crushed flaxseed and is a natural product. For mixing of paint it is prepared in two forms, the first, *raw oil* which is the product in its original state. The second, *boiled oil,* is produced from the raw oil by dissolving certain drying compounds into it. These compounds may be manganese and lead oxide or cobalt and as they are dissolved by a heat process the term boiled oil has become widely used. Boiled oil is somewhat thicker than raw oil and a shade darker, and since it has been more or less oxidized in its manufacture, has a quicker drying action. Therefore when using boiled oil the amount of driers can be reduced considerably or may be omitted entirely.

China Wood Oil or Tung Oil, as it is sometimes called, is extracted from the nut of a tree which grows along the Tung river in China. It is a stronger drying oil than linseed but has a tendency to skin over in a way that prevents its use in paint. It may be heat-treated in mixtures of resin or linseed oil after which it will dry with a smooth surface. It is more water-resisting than linseed oil but less durable.

Fish Oil being commonly considered a non-drying oil, is seldom used as a binding agent for good paint.

In the preparation of lubricant compounds such as are used for slushing down running rigging and hawsers it is both practical and economical.

THINNERS

Thinners are used in paint to make it thin or to "cut" the oil vehicle and make the paint easier to spread. They also speed the "setting" of the paint. Turpentines are the best and most widely used thinners. They perform a double function in paint because, being oxidizers, they hasten drying by absorbing oxygen from the air.

Gum Turpentine (Gum Turps) is distilled from pine resin.

Wood Turpentine, which is produced by distilling with steam the wood of the pine tree. Wood turpentine is becoming the accepted equal of "gum turps."

Turpentine Substitute is a distillate of crude oil and is of a cheaper grade and should never be used to thin varnishes as it has a tendency to separate the resin from the oils.

Coal Tar Thinners. There are a number of coal tar distillates used as thinners in some grades of paint used for a special purpose. *Naphtha* and *benzol* are the most common.

DRIERS

Certain chemical compounds of a metallic nature have been found to add some drying properties to vehicle oils and by doing so cut down the drying time for paint.

Driers are manufactured chemical products, the most common being "Japan" drier.

VARNISH, SHELLAC, AND LACQUER

Varnish is a compound of resin, boiled oil, thinners and driers. The melted resin is mixed with the boiled oil and the thinners and driers added. Turpentine is commonly used as a thinner for the best varnish. Oxides of lead manganese make good driers.

To prepare the surface for varnish, clean well, fill and rub down.

Dust off all particles and apply varnish with varnish brush by flowing it on in a smooth coating.

At least three days are required for drying.

Shellac in its raw form is a flaky substance taken from a tree that grows in India. The flakes are soluble only in alcohol and as the alcohol evaporates rapidly the shellac soon dries to a hard smooth surface.

There are numerous manufactured substitutes for shellac and most of them have a trade name ending in "lac."

As a filling coat on new wood shellac and its substitutes are widely used.

Lacquer is a compound of shellac, coloring matter and other ingredients dissolved in alcohol. Widely used for decorative work.

Prepared Paints

Paint is supplied to ships in both forms, ready-mixed and unprepared.

The following are the most common ready-mixed paints, their names in most cases define their use:

Hull or freeboard paint (usually black)	Hold paint
Inside flat paint (white & colors)	Deck paint
Gloss paint (inside & outside)	Deck lacquer
Inside enamel (white & colors)	Boottopping
Outside flat (white & colors)	Waterway paint
Outside or cabin enamel (white & colors)	Water line paint
Overhead paint	Spar varnish (outside)
Mast and spar paint	Inside varnish
Stack paint (heat resisting)	Shellacs (clear, white & orange)
Signal color	

The materials for mixing paint usually consist of:

White lead	Linseed oil (boiled or raw)
White zinc	China wood oil
Red lead (powder or paste)	Fish oil
Color pigments (various)	Turpentine (or substitute)
Carbon black (usually lampblack)	Alcohol
Driers	

PREPARATION OF SURFACES

As the priming coat of paint can only be applied once and must touch the metal, it is unreasonable to expect it, no matter how good it is, to stay on a surface that is dirty or rusty. Paint applied over rust does not stop its action, the rusting goes on unhindered and loosens the paint. The best known hand tools for removing rust from metal are the chipping hammer, scraper, and wire brush. There have been many power tools developed in recent years among them the air hammer, rotary scrapers and electric brushers. It is obvious that these power tools can accomplish more, with better results, and are less tiring than the old hand methods.

All surfaces should be dry for the best results, moisture under paint when it is applied will always cause peeling later. Allow the priming coat to dry thoroughly before applying a second coat. Applying a second coat on a surface that is soft will cause alligatoring later on and the ultimate breakdown of the undercoat. Expert opinions have often stressed that paint should not be put on in temperatures lower than 50° F. as moisture from the air very easily condenses and forms on surfaces, and not being apparent, is painted over. This of course, cannot be adhered to in marine painting as vessels seldom remain constantly among ideal conditions, but every effort should be made to have the surface as dry as possible before painting.

Rust. Paint having the dual function of protection and decoration, let us consider the protecting influence of paint and the great marine problem, *rust.*

When iron or steel or any of the crucibles of iron are exposed to the elements, air and water, both containing oxygen in varying degrees which acts upon the surface of metal, oxidizing it, and the resultant chemical action produces a reddish scale *rust*, powdery in its first stages, and of high saturation point, causing the surrounding molecules of iron to be similarly acted upon. Therefore, once this oxidizing starts on metals subject to such reaction, its action is constant unless checked, and by the very fact that rust scale retains moisture easily and can impart some of this oxygen to adjacent iron molecules, the spread of this action, essentially a hydrated form of ferric oxide, will continue.

There are at least four different but plausible theories of the exact chemical action that takes place on iron when attacked by air and moisture, but all agree that oxygen present as well as carbonic acid in all natural water and air are the elements responsible; therefore keep out oxygen in any form and you stop rust; but nature never ends her effort to combine oxygen with iron, in which a separation of these two elements was made when the iron was smelted.

From this it can be seen, that a correctly balanced paint film must be mixed to suit the needs of any particular job with due regard to the exposure to moisture that it must resist.

Galvanized Surfaces. No paint can be guaranteed to stand up satisfactorily on galvanized iron at all times because the coating left by a galvanic process has a tendency to repel paint. Sometimes the paint adheres successfully, other times the paint appears to fall away from the metal. Galvanized iron if left exposed to the elements for at least six months has been known to give paint the necessary surface to take hold successfully. Cleaning galvanized work with ammonia or vinegar before painting has been found to be an aid in making paint adhere to the surface.

It might be mentioned that certain authorities consider that the galvanized surface is ample protection for the metal and should be exposed to the very oxygen and moisture that bare metal is protected from, believing that to deprive this coating of oxygen hastens the breakdown of galvanized surfaces instead of preserving them.

Shellac applied after the surface has been cleaned with vinegar has been found to make a lasting priming coat for galvanized surfaces.

APPLYING PAINT

Priming Coat. Again emphasizing the fact that the priming coat can only be put on once it is very important to brush the paint into the metal if it is to take hold. Do not flow it on, brush it in.

Close inspection of any piece of iron or steel, especially after a good wire brushing, will reveal tiny pores. It is into these pores that the paint must be *worked*. Paint applied in this manner is said to have good *tooth* and will adhere well under the most adverse conditions.

For the primary coat many compounds have been developed, but red lead has always been supreme in this field and is favored by marine and civil engineers all over the world.

A good red lead priming paint should contain turpentine as thinner and a good drier.

Second Coat. It is good policy when applying a second coat of the same color as the priming coat to add a small amount of lampblack or some coloring to give the second coat a different tint. If this is done, missed spots or "holidays" may easily be detected.

Subsequent coats may be the same color as the priming coat or any color desired for decoration.

All paint should be *brushed out thin, not flowed on.*

Types of Brushes. Duster brush, used in cleaning. Sash trim or tool brush, used on small surfaces. Varnish brushes; oval, flat or French bristle. The oval is used in rough work, the flat for medium, and the French bristle for high-grade work. Flat brushes, ranging in size from two to four inches. Wall or surface brushes, from four to six inches. Wire brushes, of various sizes, to brush blisters and rust off iron.

Use of Brush. The following instructions on handling brushes and applying paint are taken from *Sailor's Manual of Paints and Painting* and Riesenberg's *Standard Seamanship:*

1. Hold the brush by the handle and not by the stock, otherwise the hands may become poisoned.

2. Hold the brush at right angles to the surface, with the ends of the bristles alone touching, and lift it clear of the surface when finishing a stroke! Otherwise the surface will be uneven and have laps and spots which give a very poor appearance.

3. Do not cover the brush with the paint; dip the ends of the bristles only. Do not repeat this until the preceding charge has been exhausted.

4. Apply the paint with long strokes parallel to the grain of the wood. If painting along smooth surfaces, draw the brush along the entire surface if not too long so as to show as few breaks as possible.

5. The successive applications should be applied systematically. Be sure on the second application to cross the preceding work at right angles. In each complete application keep all strokes parallel to each other. During the crossing use a medium pressure; in the final application use a light pressure. The final application should be in the length direction of the work.

6. An overhead surface should be systematized thus: Lay off the ceiling panels fore and aft, and the beams athwartship. However, if the panels contain many pipes running parallel with the beams, lay off the ceiling in general, parallel with the beams.

7. Vertical surfaces, bulkheads, etc., should be painted with the lines vertical.

Each succeeding coat of paint should be laid off in the same direction; this is an exception to rule 5.

8. Keep the paint well mixed in the pot during the work.

9. Use two coats of thin or medium paint rather than one of heavy. The reason for this is that a heavy coat will show the brush marks and will give an uneven finish.

10. Wait until the preceding coat is entirely dry before applying the second coat. Paint dries after coming in contact with the air; hence a second coat would retard this process.

Care of Brushes. Good painting calls for good brushes, and a good brush deserves good care. To clean a brush that is not to be used for an indefinite time: rinse well in kerosene, wash in warm soda water or with brown laundry soap, rinse well again in clean water, shake out and hang up to dry. If a brush is to be used again, in a matter of days, it should be kept in a brush keeper, which is usually made from empty kerosene cans or such and partially filled with either kerosene or water. The brush is suspended in the trough by a wire inserted through the handle and hooked on the edge, or by a rod through the handle laid across the opening. In either case the bristles of the brush are kept immersed in the liquid without touching the bottom.

Painting Wrinkles

Handfuls of clean rope yarns make excellent soogee rags and will remove the most stubborn dirt from paint work.

A few turns of rags around a paintbrush just above the bristles will stop the paint working onto the handle. Try this the next time you have to paint the overhead.

Unused portions of a keg of red or white lead or zinc paste may be kept soft and free from skins by pouring water over the surface to the depth of an inch or more and keeping the lid on the keg, first scraping surplus paste down from the sides of the keg. If to be used frequently, a disk of stiff paper cut out to fit the inside of the keg may be placed on the lead.

Manhelpers are used to paint inaccessible places, usually a ship's side, when stagings are not practicable. When vessels are berthed alongside a dock, much of the work is done from the dock or from work boats. Manhelpers are rarely used on deck as no part of deck structures should be considered inaccessible to a seaman. Manhelpers are usually 10′ or over in length, the brush being fastened by yarns to a notch cut about 3″ from one end, the brush secured at an angle of about 45° to the shank.

NOTES ON PAINTING

Too much time is wasted on board ship in scraping paint off screw threads, gaskets, and other places which should never have been painted over in the beginning. A little attention to the following common-sense rules will prevent this waste of time and improve the appearance of the ship:

¶Never, under any circumstances, paint rubber gaskets on water-tight doors, manholes, hatches, etc.

¶Never paint screw threads, compartment name plates, louvres, gauze air screens, zinc protectors on the bottom.

¶Never without orders, paint anything that has not been kept painted.

¶Never paint out lettering without special orders to do so. All the various numbers and letters have definite meanings, and they must not be painted out.

¶As there is a regulation way in which ships must be painted, never paint anything a different color without orders.

¶In painting use only a little paint on the brush, and never paint crosswise; that is, never make the strokes cross; they should always be parallel to each other.

¶Never put the paint on in a thick coat. It will not dry and become hard, but it is easily rubbed off for days afterwards, and catches dirt continually. Put it on in thin coats, and it will dry quickly and form a hard surface.

¶Never paint over a dirty surface, or a rough unprepared surface. Paint is too frequently used to save scrubbing. The surface to be painted must be cleaned and scrubbed down to a smooth surface before any paint is applied.

¶Binding a brush is binding the bristles with twine much the same as the straws of a broom are bound, to keep them from spreading.

¶Generally the brush is held by the handle, but at times the wrist and palm of the hand may get tired and sore, in which case experienced painters have found comfort and ease by changing for a spell and holding the brush by the brindle, or metal band, which allows plenty of play on the brush. Keep the brindle clean.

¶When painting or washing the forward or after ends of deck houses always start at the windward side; in this way no paint or dirty water will be blown onto the finished surface.

¶There is no end of uses for red lead and for structural painting it has no peer. Red lead mixed with a small amount of carbon black makes an excellent hull paint of good body.

¶A new practice is to use an aluminum pigment mixed with zinc oxide and a varnish vehicle for the second coating. This is a good mixture to cover red lead as it dulls the tint and a fine white finish will take well when applied over it.

¶When mixing paint in more than one container, remember to box the contents together to get a uniform paint film. This boxing of paint is very necessary when using colors.

¶Considering the prompt action of driers and turpentine in paint it is advisable not to put these ingredients into the pigment until just before using. While paints should be mixed about 24 hours previous to their use, they should not be allowed to stand for long periods of time unless they are kept in well sealed and airtight containers.

¶When painting the mast or tarring down the rigging a simple way to control the paint or tar when charging the brush is to fit the paint can inside a water bucket and pack old rags around the paint can to keep it centered. In this way the excess paint that drips from the brush as you wipe it over the edge of the can is taken up by the rags and not splattered on the deck below.

¶For a quick set and a good thorough drying, it is suggested that about five ounces of powdered litharge be stirred into the finishing coat. Paints containing litharge should be used within two or three days after preparation. If boiled oil or litharge is used, add only half the specified amount of driers.

¶In cleaning brushes that have been used in shellacs, alcohol will serve better than anything else. After cleaning with alcohol use brown soap and warm water. Shellac brushes should never be allowed to stand long after using, as shellac has a very quick drying point.

¶In revarnishing a surface a light sandpapering before applying varnish will give an ideal finish. In new varnish work, treating the wood to a little tung or raw oil will give the varnish a good hold. Surfaces must be kept free of dust while varnishing, as this will show up in the finished surface. It is not a good idea to varnish in the direct hot sun or damp weather.

¶Linseed oil is very useful to soften brushes that have become stiff.

¶It is necessary to have a hard undercoat for permanence in painting and to attain this do not put too much oil in a priming coat.

¶While the addition of driers to paint is desirable, too much drier will cause too rapid top-drying resulting in a wrinkled effect.

¶One gallon of correctly mixed paint will cover approximately 700 square feet on a smooth metal surface.

¶Running, streaking and sagging may be caused by improper mixing and stirring as well as by applying the paint too thick.

¶To prepare ready mixed paint pour off most of the liquid (vehicle) into another can and stir well the pasty pigment which has settled to the bottom. During the stirring process add small amounts of the liquid and continue stirring until all the liquid is used. Box well the mixed paint before using.

¶Boxing paint means pouring paint, back and forth, from one can to another until the mixture is smooth and free from lumps.

What to Expect of Paint Applied at Varying Temperatures. 100°F.— Setup time of paint may be very rapid, causing brush pull, laps, and very noticeable brush marks, or "orange peel." Thinner often evaporates before paint is applied, making constant thinning necessary. Paint may not bond well.

85°F.—Thinner evaporates too quickly. Paint sets up faster than it should, causing slight brush marks or, if spraying, "orange peel." May be difficult to keep paint from lapping.

70°F.—Paint should not need thinning and should possess the workability and good film properties claimed for it.

55°F.—Paint is too heavy. Thinner needed which injures paint according to amount used.

40°F.—Paint much too heavy to apply unless excessively thinned. Too much thinner cuts the life out of the paint and results in poor film properties and a film too thin to provide adequate protection.

Never paint when the temperature is below 32°F. The thinner evaporates slowly and the oxidation of the vehicle is retarded. As a result, the paint will not dry properly and it will blister in warm weather. The higher the drying temperature, the better, but watch humidity and ventilation.

Spreading Power of Paint. A knowledge of the spreading power of paint is of considerable value in determining the kind to use as well as the amount necessary. Approximate figures given by the Navy Department for the spreading rates of their paints are of value and those of greatest interest follow:

	Sq. Ft.
Hand mixed red lead	450
Anticorrosive-Norfolk No. 17	270
Antifouling-Norfolk No. 19	243
Boottopping, red	405
Boottopping, light grey	684
Outside white	486
Outside black	477
Spar color	495
Inside white	432
Flat white	540
White enamel	540
Spar color for smokestacks	333
Light grey for smokestacks	477
White canvas preservative	70
Under cork	135
Clear shellac	450
Red or yellow shellac	369

Penetrol stops rust action by penetrating through light rust into minute pits and pores in the steel displacing moisture and air from the porous rust by thoroughly wetting the rust particles and separating them from each other and from the steel. (*Scale and loose rust must be removed.*) When in intimate contact with the steel, *Penetrol* insulates anodic from cathodic areas and, when hardened, incorporates the rust as a pigment within its film and bonds to the underlying steel producing a foundation to which paint bonds well. *Penetrol* can be used as a thinner and adds good adhesion, gloss, flexibility and uniformity and it is not affected by temperature as are other thinners. It can be used 50/50 with red lead and can be used as a vehicle for aluminum, though aluminum should not be used as a prime coat on clean steel as, being dissimilar metals, a current is generated, which stimulates corrosion in the presence of moisture and air. A primer should be applied under aluminum.

The authors do not intend to push any proprietary product but it would be a disservice to the reader to omit mention of a product simply because it is unique. This description of the properties and uses of *Penetrol* is based upon its actual use over many years under conditions described. There may be other products that will "fill the bill" as adequately, which is a matter the user must decide for himself.

PAINT FORMULAS

The following red lead formulas were developed by the American Society for Testing Materials and when brushed on a smooth vertical iron surface, will dry with an elastic firmness without running, streaking or sagging.

Dry red lead	20 lbs.	0.274 gal.	
Raw linseed oil	5 pints	0.625 "	
Turpentine	1/2 "	0.125 "	1.024 gal.
Liquid driers	1/2 "		

Red lead paste	20 lbs.	0.446 gal.	
Raw linseed oil	3 pints	0.375 "	
Turpentine	2 gills	0.125 "	0.946 gal.
Liquid driers	2 "		

Pure White Lead Mixture. Paint manufacturers recommended 2 1/2 to 3 gallons linseed oil per hundred pounds of white lead **as a safe ratio between pigment and vehicle.** The following formula is **based on** the foregoing and is recommended where a second coat of pure white lead paint is desired to cover a red lead primary coat.

White lead paste	100 lbs.	Turpentine	1/2 gal.
Raw linseed oil	2 1/2 gals.	Driers	1 pint

Gallons of paint, 6; coverage, 700 sq. ft. per gal.

Outside White. The following formula for finishing coats of white has found much favor aboard ships. The formula calls for raw oil, but boiled oil may be used, in which case the driers may be cut to 1/2 amount specified or omitted entirely.

White lead paste	5 lbs.	Turpentine	3 gills
White zinc paste	9 lbs.	Driers	7 ounces
Raw oil	3 pints		

After this mixture is made add a small amount of Prussian blue, just enough to tint the paint so it is apparent to the naked eye in good light. Paint will dry gloss white.

Hull Black can be made with a red lead base by using the following formula, which will make approximately one gallon of paint:

Red lead paste	4.25 lbs.	Raw linseed oil	.376 gal.
Carbon black in oil	.327 gal.	Turpentine	.058 gal.
Prussian blue in oil	.085 gal.	Driers	.058 gal.

For *light gray* the following formula has been recommended. Gray being a neutral color it is much used in marine painting, many ships using it to paint their hull, house, sun decks, lifeboat interiors, etc. The formula makes approximately six and a half gallons of paint.

White lead paste	100 lbs.	Raw linseed oil	3 1/2 gals.
Lamp black paste (1/4 pint)	.03 gal.	Turpentine	1 pint
French ochre paste (1/4 pint)	.03 gal.	Driers	1 pint

In mixing this formula the French ochre may be omitted and the quantity of lamp black varied to suit the mixer for any particular shade desired.

All of the foregoing formulas call for raw oil, but boiled oil may be used just as well, in which case only half the amount of driers specified need be used or they may be omitted entirely.

Rust Proofing Compounds derived from petroleum and containing certain special rust inhibitors are admirably suited for protection of iron and steel under the very severe moisture conditions under which marine equipment must operate. In many of the locations these petroleum rust preventives give much better protection than hard drying paints chiefly because:—

1. Hard drying paint films crack and allow moisture to get behind them causing rust.

2. Petroleum rustproof coatings remain slightly tacky, and do not harden or crack and they shed moisture like water running off a duck's back. These non-drying coatings are self-sealing and they seal out moisture and air which are necessary for rust formation.

These rustproof compounds are usually marketed in several grades ranging from a heavy one, which must be melted to apply, down to a thin one which can be sprayed. There are some that contain pigments to give color to the coatings.

Although these compounds can be applied with little or no cleaning of the steel surface, it is recommended that very heavy rust and paint scale be hammered loose, scraped or wirebrushed and completely removed from the surfaces to be sprayed or brushed. More effective and economical application can be obtained in this way.

If, however, it is not convenient to remove all the rust before application, the rustproof compound can be applied directly over the rust. The rustproof compound will loosen the rust and make it much easier to remove later by hammering or scraping. The area can then be "spotted up" if the protective layer underneath is not heavy enough.

If necessary these compounds can be applied on surfaces which are slightly damp since they contain inhibitors which give the necessary protection.

The only disadvantage these type products have over hard drying paints is that they cannot be used where personnel will walk on them or otherwise come in contact, or where moving objects might rub against them. The reason is that they do not dry to a hard finish and they are liable to be rubbed off.

INSPECTION OF REPAIRS AND ALTERATIONS

Watertight Boundaries. There are three means of determining the material condition of watertight boundaries and compartments: observation of oil and water leaks from tanks into adjoining spaces; visual examination; air tests. Such leaks are frequently evident at: loose rivet heads; poorly caulked plate laps or stiffeners, and poorly caulked bounding angles.

The visual tests must be depended upon where there are permanent openings to topside as in enginerooms and firerooms, but this does not connote relative lack of importance. This inspection is made by completely closing and darkening compartment on one side of affected boundary, stationing an observer therein, and intensely lighting the other side.

When compartments cannot be filled with oil or water, the only practicable means of establishing degree of watertightness is the air test, wherein compartment is completely closed, and an air pressure applied. The loss in pressure, or "drop" over a specified period, (normally ten minutes), is indicative of degree of tightness.

Air pressure, of course, does not truly simulate the varying hydrostatic pressure placed upon a compartment's bulkheads when it is flooded, and also does not represent the flooded condition as to water pressure, since air test places same pressure on overhead and deck. However, the air test remains our most satisfactory method of detecting leaks in watertight compartments.

Mercury gages are used in place of spring gages because they are more reliable and more sensitive.

Where a compartment air test shows no drop in pressure greater than the initial, or allowable drop, the air test records shall then show the compartment as having passed a "satisfactory" test.

A few precautions must be observed in connection with compartment air testing.

1. In no case should the air test pressure be exceeded. (Serious damage to structure and boundaries of the compartment will result if this warning is disregarded).

2. Be sure cap is replaced on air testfitting when test is completed.

3. *Doctoring* a compartment for the purpose of passing the test is a definite hazard to the ship's safety.

Ship yard air test gangs are wise to all the tricks of air testing, and it requires close attention to detect such questionable methods as may be used.

One method of *doctoring* employed quite often for obtaining watertightness has been the use of a quick drying cement which can be applied to cracks and boundary leaks. When this cement sets up hard and painters coat it over with paint it is very difficult to detect, and only when ship begins working in a seaway will the cement come loose. Other methods, such as wooden plugs, temporary packing, and numerous other tricks, are used.

Another common means of faking an airtest is to file a groove in the valve seat of the valve supplying air to the compartment. This will allow air into compartment although valve is closed tightly and may compensate for a relatively large leak. To guard against this, hose supplying air to compartment must be disconnected when pressure drop is noted.

Still another means for faking a test is for a man inside the compartment being tested to close or plug the opening to mercury gage when pressure is built up. This will indicate a zero drop in pressure on gage, although pressure in compartment may have dropped considerably.

TEMPORARY REPAIRS TO HULL AND EQUIPMENT

In the following suggestions concerning damage control we are concerned only with what you can do yourself. Many casualties may be nullified to a large extent with no special tools whatever, merely using readily available materials and common sense. A high school physics book will be found of value to review the basic laws of mechanics, especially those treating with levers and hydrostatic pressure.

Note: Reports of Ship Structural Failures to USCG. Masters, vessel owners, operators and agents are required to report promptly to the nearest Officer-in-Charge, USCG, any condition which affects the seaworthiness of their vessels. In the case of a Class 1 casualty involving a structural failure, an immediate report is required by dispatch or telephone, and in such cases repairs must not be undertaken until the proposed method of repair has been approved by the USCG. A Class 1 structural failure is any fracture or buckle which has weakened the main hull girder, so that the vessel is lost or is in a dangerous condition. For this purpose any fracture more than 10 ft. long in the strength deck or shell, shall be considered to put the vessel in a dangerous condition.

Pressure on a flooded bulkhead. The pressure on a bulkhead or deck of a flooded compartment depends upon:

(1) The depth of flooding,

(2) The flooded area,

(3) Whether there is any additional pressure caused by the ship's motion, and

(4) Whether or not the compartment is open to the sea.

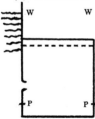 The depth of water in a compartment open to the sea and completely flooded is measured from the ocean surface—not from the overhead. Thus, in the sketch, the pressure on point P is the weight of the column W — P. Even if the lower compartment is not entirely flooded, but contains a layer of entrapped air at the top, the air will be compressed until it assumes the same pressure as the water column.

1. The total pressure on a bulkhead of a flooded compartment is *tremendous*.

2. The pressure is greatest along the deck and least along the overhead.

3. The pressure depends upon the height of water over a given spot.

4. The pressure depends upon how the ship is rolling and pitching.

5. The pressure may depend on how much headway the ship is making.

Since (3), (4) and (5) are variable, it is obvious that the pressure and stress will be variable. When undertaking any shoring operation, you must allow for the maximum stress, with an ample factor of safety.

A bulkhead and its supporting frames make up a sort of spring. It is obvious, therefore, that a bulkhead will bulge and pant as the pressure varies, and it will weave as the ship itself changes shape while working in a seaway. Hence, the pressure on shoring will increase and decrease, and the bulkhead will tend to walk away from the shores. Therefore, *no shoring job can be considered completed until you have taken up all the slack; and when the job is done, you must leave a man to watch it and to tighten up the wedges as they start to work loose.* It should be borne in mind that shoring is intended to support. It is *not* intended to push warped bulkheads back to their original positions or shapes. Excessive shoring pressure may cause a bulkhead to collapse or rupture, especially at boundaries.

Shoring is the process of placing props against the side of a structure, or beneath or above anything, to prevent sinking or sagging.

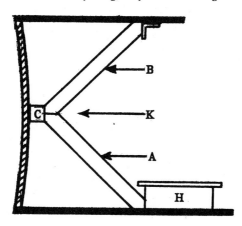

FIGURE 10

The length of a shore in use should NEVER be over thirty times its minimum thickness. Thus, a 4″ x 4″ shore can be ten feet long, a 6″ x 6″ shore can be fifteen feet long, and a 4″ x 6″ shore can be ten feet long. If the proportion of length to thickness is greater than thirty to one, the shore will buckle and may break.

The usual method of installing shores is by a triangulation system, such as that indicated in figure 10. Shores *A* and *B* are in direct compression, and the vector produces a resistance in direction *K*. If shore *A* alone is used, it will be merely leaning against *C*, and will have no value whatever. *B* must be installed.

The pressure on a bulkhead (or deck) must be taken up over a wide area, and not all at one or two points.

Each horizontal strongback must be backed up by a multiplicity of shores exerting a pressure perpendicular to the bulkhead.

If it has been found necessary to shore one bulkhead, and there is any danger of that bulkhead's carrying away, the next bulkhead inboard must be shored as early as possible.

Shores must form a considerable angle with the bulkhead they are supporting.

If a shore in direct compression begins to bow, look out. It may snap in two at any moment.

When using wedges to support a shore, either horizontally or vertically, always use two wedges, driven simultaneously and evenly from both sides. This is to prevent tilting the shore. If there is not room enough to swing a second maul, you can get the same effect by holding a maul against the butt of one wedge and driving on the other.

COFFERDAMS AS LEAK STOPPERS

A method frequently employed in stopping large holes involves the use of cofferdams. A cofferdam, in this case, is a large wall or fence built around the damaged area.

A cofferdam may be built up of steel plates or heavy planks (preferably tongue-and-groove), either directly supported by frames and stanchions, or held securely in place by shores. When constructed, it may be partially or completely flooded. If it were possible to build a cofferdam thoroughly watertight, as by welding plates together and to the ship, no further steps would be necessary.

However, conditions seldom permit you to construct a watertight box. You therefore build a strong retaining wall around the hole, and leave the box open at the top. Then you drop mattresses, pillows, bales of waste, clothing, etcetera into the pen until it is full. As most of these materials will float, you will have to weight them to get them down to the bottom of the cofferdam. When the pen (or box) is full, keep the stuffing materials down by means of iron bars or shores. A cover may be put on the top, if you desire it. It is more reliable than shoring, although the whole structure should be strengthened by shores all around. The fibrous stuffing materials will act as caulking materials to exclude water.

It is possible that the hole will be so large than even mattresses or bales of rags could fall out through the side of the ship. This can be prevented by installing a grating of crossed pipes, timbers or angle irons over the hole before attempting to stuff the box.

The Use of Concrete for Repairs to Hull Damage. With the aid of wood or steel cofferdams, concrete can often be used to great advantage in stopping leaks and to a limited extent to restore strength in damaged machinery supports.

The sand should be coarse, clear and sharp, and should be free of vegetable matter and oil. It should be true sand—not powdered coral.

The materials should be mixed in approximately the following proportions (by volume): 1 High Early Strength Portland Cement, 1 1/2 sand, 2 aggregate.

Fresh water at or above 70° should be used. It should be clean and free of oil and vegetable matter. In an emergency, salt water may be used. The amount of water should be just enough to make a sticky plastic mass of mud that will hang together, but which can still be poured through a large tube. Too much water reduces the strength and watertightness of concrete, and encourages washing away. About 5 1/2 gallons of water for each 100 pounds of cement will make a satisfactory concrete.

Calcium chloride generates heat upon contact with water, and thereby facilitates the setting of concrete under water. Use two pounds of calcium chloride for each 5 1/2 gallons of water, dissolving the calcium chloride in the water before the latter is poured into the dry ingredients.

Concrete should be deposited promptly after it is mixed. For a large job it may be advisable to have two mixing boxes, staggering the batches so as to have a steady flow of fresh concrete.

In depositing concrete above water it is usually necessary to build a form or cofferdam to retain the concrete while it is setting. Frames, bulkheads and other parts of the ship's structure may be used as part of the form. Place the concrete in the form with a shovel or a bucket. Do not drop or throw the material in loosely, as that would tend to entrap air pockets. Press or tamp the concrete tightly into the form. If the concrete settled rapidly, without air pockets, it is a sign that you have used too much water. If time and conditions permit, it is advisable to scrape and to clean metal surfaces against which concrete is to be deposited.

Concrete is usually deposited under water by the use of a chute made of watertight pipe or waterproofed canvas. It may also be made of 1/2″ lumber. The chute, or tube, should be large enough to allow a free flow of the concrete. An inside diameter between four and six inches should suffice. The upper end may be made much larger, to serve as a sort of hopper. The tube is used to avoid dropping the concrete loosely through the water and thereby wasting much of it. The lower end of the tube should be right down in the mass of deposited concrete.

At best, using concrete for under water leak stopping is difficult. The heavier materials will sink to the bottom, but the finer particles tend to wash away—especially the cement. Therefore, every effort must be made to prevent the flow of water through or across the mixture while it is being poured and after it is in place. As a preliminary measure, try to stop or to restrict the flow of water through cracks or holes that are to be patched. Mattresses, pillows, oakum, wedges, plugs and similar materials may be used for this purpose.

After the leaks have been restricted as much as possible, erect a form or cofferdam around the damaged area. Steel plates or lumber (preferably tongue and groove) may be used for this purpose. The form itself should be tight, and it should fit snugly against decks and bulkheads. This is to reduce the washing effect of water. The form is necessarily left open at the top for depositing concrete.

Put the chute well down into the form, with the lower end practically buried in concrete. Fill the chute to a height above the water level, and move the chute along the bottom, gradually depositing concrete as you move along. Continue shoveling concrete into the tube. *Do not* let the concrete pile up at any one point and then try to relocate it with a shovel or a hoe.

In several cases it has been found advisable to install a pipe running from a point near the leaky seam or hole to a point outside the form. The pipe carries away harmful water while the concrete is setting, after which the pipe can be plugged.

Concrete may also be deposited under water by means of bags of about one cubic foot capacity. The bags may be made of a coarse cloth, such as burlap—the common gunny sack. After filling a bag about two thirds full, tie it securely.

DRY-DOCKING

Prior to docking a *docking plan* is furnished the dock superintendent. This is a longitudinal section showing transverse bulkheads, engine and boiler spaces and sea connections. Various cross sections are shown to enable the yard to determine the blocking required. Keel blocks are generally 3 to 4 feet apart. Closer placed blocks may be required for the stem and stern. The bilges and areas under heavy machinery require extra blocking, but the blocks must not obstruct sea connections.

Tail shafts are drawn at times as required by the Local Inspector or Classification Society.

Pitch of propellers with removable blades are checked and hubs examined for cracks.

Plugs in the shell plates on the bottom should be unscrewed so that water can be drained from the inner bottom, or if there are no such plugs a few rivets may be drilled out. See personally that the plugs are replaced.

Dry-docking Requirements Clarified. Dry-docking regulations for passenger, tank, cargo, and miscellaneous vessels—which were considered by the Merchant Marine Council at a public hearing on 7 May, 1957—has resulted in these regulations being clarified and revised.

The major changes in the regulations remove requirements regarding "calendar year" as a period of time in determining when vessels are required to be dry-docked and substitutes instead maximum periods between dry-dockings and aggregate amount of service as the governing factors.

For passenger, tank and cargo vessels, the new regulations include:

Shall be dry-docked or hauled out at intervals not to exceed 18 months if operated in salt water an aggregate of 9 months in the 18-month period since it was last dry-docked or hauled out.

Shall be dry-docked or hauled out at intervals not to exceed 36 months if it operates in salt water an aggregate of 6 months or less in each 12-month period since it was last dry-docked or hauled out. If this aggregate amount of service in salt water is exceeded in any 12-month period since it was last dry-docked or hauled out, the vessel shall be dry-docked or hauled out within 6 months after the end of this period or within the 36-month interval, whichever is earlier.

Shall be dry-docked or hauled out at intervals not to exceed 60 months if it operates exclusively in fresh water.

Regulations for tank barges and wood hull tank vessels follow:

Tank barges used in fresh-water service exclusively need not be dry-docked or hauled out during the first 60-month interval after date of build, but shall be dry-docked or hauled out between that time and the end of the 120th month after date of build, and at least once in each 60-month interval thereafter.

Each wood hull tank vessel shall be placed in dry dock or on a slipway or hauled out for examination not to exceed 48 months.

Precautions During Dry-Docking.

1. No free liquid surfaces in tanks, etc.

2. Vessel trimmed to an even keel.

3. Shift no weights, cargo or water while docked.

4. Make connections between ship and yard fire lines.

5. All closets, drains, etc. shut off.

6. Check bottom plugs, underwater cocks and valves, zinc protectors, and note when removed and when replaced.

7. Bottom cleaned, examined and painted. First, anticorrosive paint, second, antifouling paint which can be applied 2 hours after anticorrosive. Be sure this paint has no contact with the bare metal.

8. Rudder lifted, pintles and gudgeons examined.

9. Repack stuffing boxes and valves of rudder, the propeller gland, etc.

10. Look for corrosion along butts of shell plating and for corroded rivets. Inspect the zincs at stern frames, the propeller struts, shafting, brackets, etc.

11. After undocking, look for leaks where repairs have been made.

The number of times a year a vessel is docked depends on where she runs, if in the tropics it may be every 6 months, elsewhere it may be a year.

Bottom Corrosion. The primary problem concerning bottom corrosion is pitting and the rate of corrosion in these pits. Normal corrosion evenly distributed over the underwater body of a steel hull would amount to a loss of only about 1/8 inch of thickness in 20 years. Pitting can cause more than this in as many weeks.

Pitting is basically an electrochemical effect resulting where an exposed metal surface acts as a positive terminal for an electric current. This current may derive from an electric source ashore or from the galvanic action of dissimilar metals. It is extremely unlikely that electric current generated within the ship when under way can cause any corrosion on the outside of the hull since the current will not be discharged from the plating.

The most likely locations for pitting are those where water turbulence has resulted in the loss of the protecting paint. Typical spots are at the forward edge of the bilge keel, wherever rough welds or patches occur, and in the vicinity of the propeller. Any scratches through the paint are apt to cause particularly severe pitting when an electrical current from ashore, as in electric welding, is led into the ship and escapes through the water instead of through ground return leads. Loss of metal through electrolysis will occur wherever this current leaves the ship, and the smaller this area the more severe the pitting. Direct current will cause more severe pitting than alternating current.

Dissimilar metals coming in contact will set up a galvanic corrosion which is particularly apt to occur at the stern of the ship because of the bronze propeller. This can be detected by the presence of salt deposits and blistered paint in the area. The latter condition is the result of hydrogen gas set free by electrolysis beneath the paint.

The most damaging and widespread galvanic corrosion is due to the presence of mill scale. Mill scale is a sort of slag firmly attached to new steel. The impurities in the mill scale set up electrolytic action with bare steel and can exert this influence through several layers of paint. This corrosion is detected by the presence of white salt deposits where the mill scale has been removed as in the vicinity of welds, by rivet points and at scratches through the paint. At times these salts may be discolored by rust and will have the appearance of conventional anticorrosive or antifouling paint. It should be noted that although it is the steel which is attacked, the fault does not lie in the quality of the steel, as is often presumed, but in the presence of the mill scale. Mill scale is removed in time by natural weathering but sand blasting and pickling are economical in the long run. The latter process consists of soaking the steel plate in a 5% solution of sulphuric acid at 170° F. for 20 minutes, followed by a water rinse.

Some paints contain elements which actually promote electrolysis under certain conditions. Such a paint is the antifouling paint which contains copper, an element toxic to marine life. Unless the steel is protected, this copper will promote electrolysis and pitting of the steel. This is the reason for the 5 coats of paint generally applied to the bare steel of the ship's underwater body. The first coat is more a surface treatment than a protective coat. This primer consists of zinc or lead chromate in a synthetic resin vehicle thinned with a mixture of phosphoric acid and alcohol. When dry, this wash coat forms a phosphate covering over the steel. Several coats of anticorrosive paint follow, the main purpose of which is to protect the steel from the effects of the copper in the two coats of antifouling paint which completes the operation.

Repairs. In repairs as in new construction, faying surfaces of parts to be connected should invariably be well cleaned and unless otherwise specified, given a liberal coating of red lead immediately prior to bolting up. In way of fuel oil compartments, however, red lead should be replaced by a mixture of pine tar and shellac. The only exceptions occur in faying surfaces of fresh water tanks, which are usually left bare, though insides of the tanks are liable to receive some special or patented coating.

Stop Waters. Where flange joints of water and other systems are made to watertight bulkheads, floors, decks, or shell platings, and in any case where watertightness in a steel-to-steel connection is imperative, stop waters are used. These are usually strips of canvas, soaked in raw linseed oil and painted with thick white lead. Similar stop waters should also be placed between all wood-to-steel connections, as in the case of wooden decking. The points in decks, bulkheads, etc., which are pierced by screwed water pipes, steam pipes, conduit, voice and air tubes, etc., are made watertight by use of approved stuffing boxes. Stop waters are also made from flat lampwick or burlap, soaked in a mixture of red and white lead and from tarred hemp felt.

Oil Stops. As the name implies, oil stops are used in way of oil tight work between seams of plates, between angles and plates, beneath staples, collars and laps, and especially where caulking is impractical. They are also made of canvas, but are not treated with oil, being instead saturated with a mixture of 97 parts pine tar and 3 parts shellac, or by some other approved preparation. Rubber is never used in oil tight work.

Stop water and oil stops are frequently required between seams of light plating, due to impracticability of caulking. If an oiltight job is required, stops will be made as above, or by soaking canvas half a day in clear shellac and then coating it with a mixture of one part red lead and three parts shellac.

All bolts used in watertight or oiltight work should have grommets fitted beneath washers. The grommets are made from lamp-wicking soaked either in white lead or in the pine tar shellac combination, depending on nature of the work.

Gaskets are made from a variety of materials and for many purposes, but we are interested only in those used for manholes, and watertight doors and hatches. Rubber is generally used for watertight bolted manholes, but when these covers are to be oiltight gasket is made from canvas treated with tar and shellac, or from a material such as trunk board, treated with wax and varnish. Gaskets of hemp or flax are also used in oiltight work. When large manholes and hatches, secured by dogs, are required to be oiltight, gasket is made from square-braided flax treated with wax and tallow.

Rubber around watertight doors and hatches should never be painted, and bearing surfaces that come in contact with the rubber gasket should be kept bright—a rare sight on anything but naval craft. In fitting a new or repaired door, chalk bearing surface and close door securely by putting down the dogs. When door is opened chalk marks upon rubber will indicate worth of the job.

Doublers. Wherever it is required to strengthen a place by increasing the thickness it is faced with a second plate called a doubler. It is hardly necessary to add that doublers may be applied to almost any part of a ship's structure. Doubling is used in many parts of a vessel during construction, wherever extra strength is considered necessary, but the practice is carried to really great lengths during repairs. Old and rotting ships are literally plastered with doublers inside and out. It is about the cheapest and quickest means of general repair.

Wood Caulking. The technique or, more properly, the art of wood caulking is beyond the scope of this book. Briefly, in large scale deck caulking, as on passenger vessels, seams are first opened up with a reaming iron and, being properly clean and of sufficient depth, are partially filled with cotton spun yarn. Next, a layer of oakum is driven on top of cotton. Further driving may be carried out by two men, one swinging a maul and the other holding the "hawsing" iron. Finally, the caulked seams are filled or "payed" with pitch, poured from a special type ladle. One thread of roven cotton, followed by two threads oakum, suffice for new decks or decks in good condition aboard most commercial vessels, but widely varying quantities are used in special cases. Most small craft use only cotton.

Metal Caulking. A riveted joint is not inherently watertight or oiltight. This is because the surfaces, or edges held together, are not machined or ground. Such connections are made tight by means of caulking. In caulking, a thin fin of metal is sprung from the base plate or structure by use of a chisel, usually pneumatically driven and called a caulking tool.

When fittings, such as pad-eyes, etc., exposed to the weather run rust, this may be stopped sometimes by caulking well all around the fitting; to do this, all paint should be removed from around fitting, and the clean metals caulked together. Where the plate to which fitting is fastened is too thin to admit of caulking, the fitting should be taken off and a stop-water (canvas soaked in red lead) put behind it. Care should be taken in putting on new fittings to always paint well the fitting, and place to which it is to be fastened.

All caulking shall be done in the most thorough manner, metal to metal. Care shall be taken in caulking staples around beveled channels to avoid leakage due to irregularities caused by beveling.

Special care should be taken to secure most thorough caulking of oiltight members; and all edges of plates, angles and clips must be carefully caulked necessary to insure absolute oiltightness. Heads and points of rivets in way of oiltight work must be caulked wherever necessary. All stiffeners, angles, etc., on outside of fuel-oil compartments must be caulked; and laps, seams and butts must be caulked on both sides where deemed necessary.

Wherever there is a possibility that rust streaks would be formed by the drip of water from behind connections, fittings, etc., suitable precautions must be taken for their prevention by caulking, by embedding in red lead, or by both, or by other approved means.

Problems in Welded Assembly. Legitimate mechanics are still necessary for the construction of good riveted bulkheads, but increasing numbers of satisfactory welded bulkheads are being built by helpers and apprentices. Yet, with all its alleged virtues of speed and cheapness, welding is accompanied by a problem which is the despair of all who face it.

Welded metal undergoes unequal contraction and expansion and, in a practical sense, shrinkage. Welded bulkheads shrink, warp, and develop astonishing hills and vales. During welding, a bulkhead may at one moment be a thing of beauty, straight and fair, and the envy of riveters. Seconds later, there is a hollow boom and an ugly bulge bursts into being. Hours later, with the welding nearly completed, the bulkhead is an ugly mass of bumps and buckles, but still in one piece and possibly watertight. It is at this already disheartening stage that an appalling series of staccato reports is liable to occur, as the shrunken bulkhead rips itself free from the shell or deck—and stands there, inches short of its intended boundaries!

The prime cause of these things is known to all concerned, but no one has worked out any sure-fire method for overcoming it. In ship repair work especially, identical conditions are never twice encountered; the combinations of factors involved would have to be estimated in astronomical figures. The problem has been tackled in books filled with charts and graphs and tables, but none of this has any real interest or value to ordinary workers. Every mechanic has his own pet theories and methods, and ship repair welding in general is a haphazard and guesswork proposition at this time. In those yards which have staffs of engineers and sliderule wizards, so-called "welding sequences" are often worked out for particular jobs; and the results are at least no worse than those obtained by the self-styled "practical" men.

In a broad and unscientific way, it is generally agreed that greatest shrinkage occurs transverse to the line of weld, and that it amounts to *approximately* 1/32″ for each welded connection. A shell plate, for example, having three longitudinal connections, is expected to shrink about 1/8″ in width, and is, therefore, laid out a trifle wider than required. Shrinkage also occurs in the length, but it is sometimes possible to take advantage of this; as in edge butts, where an opening of about 1/8″ is desired between plate edges.

Welded bulkhead shrinkage is a more serious problem in repair yards than in well-equipped plants where modern ships are built. Bulkheads for new ships are completely assembled and welded away from ship and, though shrinkage occurs, required dimensions or outline are easily obtained. The welding is completed and bulkhead made ready to enter ship before its final outline is cut. This is rarely practicable in a repair yard. In the latter, bulkhead must be assembled and welded within ship itself. Fitting and erection are not difficult, and when the entire bulkhead has been tackwelded it may present a quite satisfactory appearance. However, when this is done and finishing welds are applied to its seams, butts and stiffeners, bulkhead as a whole shrinks in size, and is liable to break the tack welds about its edges. Or, if edges are welded solid before the central area is, severe strains and tensions will occur which will be greatly increased when seams, etc. are welded. Buckling and warping will be the consequence. One way of overcoming this difficulty is to secure seams and butts in central portion of bulkhead by means of bolts in oversize holes, instead of by unyielding tack welds, and then to work the finishing welds from the outside toward center. This is exact opposite of the system used in welding preassembled new work, where it is usual to commence at the center of a seam and work outwards, ends of the material being left free. The use of automatic welding machine is another advantage in new work, because in their rapid and uniform progress they are not apt to cause nearly as much warping as manual work does.

But under best of conditions, whether in new or repair work, more or less buckling of the bulkhead is bound to occur. The metal in the immediate vicinity of welding shrinks, while remainder of steel is comparatively unaffected. In other words, marked fullness, represented by bulging, occurs in central portion of areas bounded by welding. These bulges are certainly unsightly, especially to persons accustomed to riveted work, but they do not necessarily impair watertightness, strength, or general usefulness of a bulkhead or similar surface. Upon completion of welding, however, an effort is made to bump or fair the bulkhead to reasonable smoothness.

Requirements for Good Riveting. In view of the high stresses to which ship work is subject, and the corresponding necessity of ensuring that riveting shall be efficient, it is important to precede all riveting by proper bolting up. In oiltight work, where parts to be secured are of a good fit, it may be sufficient to use one bolt for every four holes, but the essential requirement is that bolts used shall bring plates, bars, etc., metal-to-metal. In most repair yards, the caliber of work is such as to require a bolt in every other hole and, not infrequently, in every hole. All burrs and chips should, of course, be removed from between the faying surfaces, and buckles and lumps faired out, before any riveting is done. At all events, rivets should not in any case be used to draw the material together.

All riveting should be executed in a careful and workmanlike manner, special care being taken that holes come fair, that rivets fit accurately, and are properly heated for driving, but not burned. Rivets less than 3/8″ in diameter may be driven cold, but when this is done in watertight joints, stop-waters should be fitted to secure tightness. All rivet points should be of adequate strength and properly centered, and—contrary to common practice—snap points should not be reduced from standard sizes by using tools that have been ground down from proper sizes or that are otherwise imperfect. All rivets should be tested and, wherever found, loose rivets, rivets with slack or eccentric points, cracked or eccentric heads or with heads standing off from surface, should be replaced. Plates, angles, etc., should not be marred or show an undue amount of hammer marks around rivet holes.

As a general rule, countersunk heads should be used only where required for mechanical or other special reasons. Where practicable, the panhead rivet should be used, with countersunk points where flush work is required. Special care should be taken that rivets used are of sufficient length to insure a proper point, the aim being to have the rivet a trifle long, if anything. Such cutting as is necessary should be done while rivet is still a dull red.

Although its importance is not realized in some repair yards, rivet holes should be punched small and reamed in work which is subject to test requirements for oiltightness, in work where strength is of special importance, and whenever three or more thicknesses are to be joined. Similar punching and reaming should also be used for rivet holes in plates 1″ or more in thickness. In any case, increase in diameter, due to reaming, should be at least 1/8″.

In plates and shapes of thickness corresponding to a nominal weight of 12 1/2 pounds and less, depth of countersink may be full thickness of material, but in plates and shapes of greater thickness depth of countersink should be approximately 1/16″ less than thickness of material. Where countersinking in accordance with above is not suitable for one of the standard heads of rivets of required diameter, it should be made to suit the nearest standard depth of rivet head. But in no case should depth of countersink be such that head of rivet before driving is less than approximately 1/16″ above surface of the plate or shape.

SHIP PREPARATION OF TANK VESSELS FOR ALTERATION AND REPAIR

C. A. NEUSBAUM*

Toxic Effect of Petroleum Vapors. Vapors given off by crude petroleum, gasoline and other petroleum products cause anesthetic effects when inhaled and, unless precautions are taken, such effects may be encountered by workers during the cleaning operations.

Exposure to petroleum vapors often results in irritation of the eyes and the development of a severe headache. When inhaled in comparatively small quantities these vapors produce merely a mild exhilaration. Upon inhaling the fumes in more concentrated form this condition rapidly develops into complete intoxication accompanied by a tendency on the part of the individual to sing, dance, or otherwise vigorously exert himself. As this stimulated activity wears off the victim's lips lose their natural color and become so stiff that proper enunciation is no longer possible. At this stage, further exposure causes unconsciousness and may result in death.

The toxic effect of gasoline vapors in various degrees of concentration is illustrated by data from the U. S. Bureau of Mines Technical Paper No. 272 as follows:

Air containing .07 to .28% vapors by volume causes slight symptoms of dizziness when inhaled for 14 1/2 minutes.

Air containing 1.13 to 2.22% vapors by volume represents the concentration which causes severe dizziness when inhaled for 3 minutes.

Air containing 2.20 to 2.60% vapors by volume causes intoxication after 10 to 12 breaths.

Flammability of Petroleum Vapor-Air Mixtures. Petroleum vapors are highly flammable and considerable care is required to prevent the occurrence of fires or explosions. When mixed with the proper amounts of air (oxygen) these vapors form explosive mixtures. The explosive mixture range of gasoline in air, for example, is generally accepted to be from 1 to 6% by volume. The lower figure corresponds to the minimum amount and the higher figure to the maximum amount of gasoline vapor capable of producing a flammable mixture. The vapor concentration below which the mixture will not burn is called the "*lower explosive limit*" and the vapor concentration above which the mixture will not burn is called the *upper explosive limit*. For some of the more volatile

* Assistant Director, Standard Inspection Laboratory, Standard Oil Development Company

hydrocarbons, such as commercial propane, the upper explosive limit is 9.5%. The explosive range for natural gas is 4.8 to 13.5%. Although explosive limits have been established definitely for a number of hydrocarbons, it must be remembered that petroleum products seldom are handled as pure hydrocarbons. It is essential, therefore, to consider the lowest and the highest explosive limits of the hydrocarbons of any products or mixtures being handled.

The following table lists several of the more common combustibles with their lower and upper explosive limits:

	Limits of Flammability	
Combustibles	*Lower*	*Upper*
Methane	5.0	15.0
Ethane	3.20	12.50
Propane	2.40	9.50
Butane	1.90	8.50
Pentane	1.45	7.50
Hexane	1.25	6.90
Hydrogen	4.10	74.0
Carbon Monoxide	12.50	74.2
Natural Gas	4.80	13.50
Illuminating Gas	5.30	31.00

Other Gases associated with petroleum products also are toxic if breathed in sufficient quantity. Hydrogen sulphide, most prominent of these gases, is contained in some crude oils and is present also in some unfinished refinery distillates as the result of reaction at high temperature and pressure. Hydrogen sulphide is harmful, even fatal, in relatively small concentrations. It is especially hazardous because of its paralytic effect on the sense of smell, making detection by odor impossible. The U. S. Bureau of Mines has found that a concentration of 0.01% in air will produce irritation of the eyes and other physical disturbances upon exposure for two minutes, with increasingly harmful results upon continuous exposure. Exposure for two minutes in a concentration of 0.07% has resulted in death. Hydrogen sulphide also is explosive in concentrations from 4.3 to 46.0 per cent in air.

Oxygen Deficiency. The atmosphere within clean tanks which have been closed tightly for some time is frequently deficient in oxygen due to rusting of the metals of tanks. Such tanks, therefore, should not be entered until they have been ventilated thoroughly. Normal air contains about 21% oxygen. Air which contains less than 16% will not safely sustain life.

Unless tanks are known to be properly cleaned, there is not assurance that a gas-free atmosphere at time of inspection is a guarantee of safety during repair period which may extend over several days. Numerous cases have been experienced where the atmosphere in tanks showing no signs of gas on one day, showed dangerous amounts twenty-four hours later, presumably because tanks were not cleaned satisfactorily and vaporization of petroleum material took place after analyses were made.

In this connection it seems desirable to point out two fundamental principles. The first is that a certificate of safety is worthless unless the inspector has entered the tank or compartment in question and has examined it carefully for deposits of oil and/or sediment which may generate vapor. Without such an examination, the analysis of the atmosphere means nothing more than that the tank is safe for a man to enter at time of testing. The practice of taking samples by means of a sampling-tube or sampling-bottle lowered from the deck seems entirely inadequate except for preliminary information.

The other fundamental principle is that the maximum permissible content of petroleum vapor is fixed by its effect on men inhaling the atmosphere rather than by the lower limit of the explosive range. The lower explosive limit of different hydro-carbons varies, but 1.0% is perhaps a representative figure. On the other hand, it is stated that petroleum vapors in concentrations of 0.3% or more are intoxicating to some people on exposure for 30 minutes or longer, so that the actual danger limit is far below the explosive limit. It has been experienced that men are able to work in tanks for indefinite periods when a maximum of 0.2% of petroleum vapor calculated as pentane is enforced as a limit.

Cleaning Procedures. It is impossible to specify arbitrarily that a tank of a given size shall be steamed or machine-washed a certain number of hours, since amount of steaming or washing required varies with the nature of oil last carried, atmospheric conditions, and other factors. The intensity and duration of each process rests therefore with the judgment of supervisor and chemist and are governed by conditions and circumstances which necessitate such cleaning.

Butterworth Method. With the Butterworth Method, heated water is directed upon interior surface of tanks by means of high pressure streams from two revolving nozzles. The nozzles are geared to turn simultaneously and slowly in all planes, horizontal to vertical, so that streams from nozzles are directed eventually upon the entire interior surface of tank.

As soon as cargo is pumped out, steam is forced through the heater coils and steam smothering-lines. If condensed steam comes through the heater coils clear, the lines are satisfactory. If steam fails to come through or if the condensate is oily, it is evident the coil is ruptured and that cleaning is necessary before a certificate can be issued for the compartment in which the faulty coil is located. Smothering-lines are steamed for approximately ten minutes. Butterworth machines are next placed in the cargo tanks through special openings or through hatches if vessel is not equipped with such special openings. Generally two machines are operated at the same time, one in each of two main, wing or summer tanks. The hatch and ullage covers are closed but not dogged down. During the period of washing, which normally takes from 1 1/2 to 2 hours per tank, the ship is held at a slight list if necessary to speed the drainage of the tanks to the suction. The cargo pumps are operated slowly to withdraw from the tanks the refuse oil and hot water resulting from the washing operation. For most efficient cleaning operation the water is heated to a temperature of approximately 175°F. The water is supplied at a pressure of approximately 175 pounds per square inch from the vessel's deck fire lines.

After the tanks have been washed sufficiently, the Butterworth machines are removed and the tanks ventilated by means of wind sails, Venturi tubes or air blowers lowered into the tanks through the hatch, or by steam gas suckers installed in the ship's deck discharge lines. When the atmosphere within the tanks has cooled sufficiently for men to enter, a sample of it is obtained by means of a sampling tube or sampling bottle lowered from the deck and analyzed for toxic or combustible gases. If the atmosphere is found to contain not more than 0.2% gas by volume, the supervisor in charge of cleaning enters the tanks to make a preliminary survey before men are sent into the tanks with hand hose to wash toward the suction any sediment or scale left in various parts of the tank. Sediment which is not pumped through the suction line is removed manually.

Manual Method. When Butterworth machines are not available, the approximate time required for steaming is estimated on the basis of previous cargoes. After the heater lines are blown, the hatch covers and ullage holes are closed but not dogged down. Steam at a line pressure of about 75 pounds is allowed to enter the tanks through the smothering lines for the period of time considered necessary to sufficiently soften and loosen oil and sediment on the bulkheads, beams, etc., so as to permit removal with streams of hot water. Upon completion of the steaming, the hatch covers are thrown open and wind sails, air blowers or steam gas suckers are used as described above for purpose of expelling gases and steam. When the tanks have cooled sufficiently, a preliminary test of the atmosphere within is taken. If the gas content is more than 0.2% by volume, further ventilating or steaming and ventilating are required. If the gas content is 0.2% or less, men equipped with hand hose descend the ladders slowly, washing down the top, sides and beams as they go. The water used for washing is at an approximate temperature of 100°F. and at a pressure of about 50 pounds. A convenient means of supplying hot water for washing is provided by a "Y" connection which introduces steam into a nozzle on the fire line and provides a positive regulation of temperature. A careful watch is maintained from deck for the safety of the men below. When the top, sides and beams have been washed thoroughly, work is commenced on the bottom. Starting at the forward outboard corner of the tank the oil and sediment are washed toward the suction from which point they are removed to a barge or a slop tank ashore by means of the ship's pumps which are kept in operation throughout the entire washing period. Any material which is not removed through the suction line is removed manually.

Final Inspection. After all tanks and compartments in question have been washed and cleaned in accordance with either of the above methods, the main pump room bilges are cleaned. Next, water is pumped through all ship's cargo lines and discharged into the slop line. After pumping for a predetermined period, the water is discharged on deck where it is examined by the chemist, the chief officer, and the supervisor in charge of tank cleaning. If the water is clear the cargo lines are considered to be cleaned. Whenever possible, depending on the shifting of ballast, valves are left open to air out the cargo lines.

The tanks then are entered and inspected by a certified chemist; and if found to be cleaned to his satisfaction and if the gas content is 0.2% or less, a Certificate is issued stating the tanks (reported individually) are either *Safe for Men and Fire* or *Safe for Men— Not Safe for Fire*.

Repairs Remote from Cargo Tanks. Whenever a vessel must be dry docked for a survey on account of a seriously damaged bottom or for repairs confined solely to work on the rudder, propeller, tailshaft or other parts remote from the cargo compartments, such tanks may be smothered with steam and sealed prior to the vessel's arrival in the shipyard. In case it is found necessary to do any work in and/or around any of the tanks, the tanks in question are cleaned by either the Butterworth Method or the Manual Method and certified as heretofore described.

Cleaning Cargo Tanks at Sea. Whenever vessels after discharging at one port are ordered to proceed to a shipyard at some other port, it may be necessary to clean the tanks and compartments enroute. The same procedures outlined previously are to be followed except, of course, no certified chemist is present. However, each vessel is provided with a Combustible Gas Indicator by means of which it can be determined if it is safe for members of the crew to enter the cargo tanks to remove sediment and complete the cleaning. Upon arrival at the shipyard, the services of a certified chemist are obtained for a complete inspection. If the chemist is satisfied with the condition of the tanks and the analysis of the atmosphere within the tanks indicates absence of gas, a Certificate is requested. If further cleaning is necessary this is done to the satisfaction of the chemist and a Certificate is obtained before repairs are started.

Whenever it is necessary to carry out emergency repairs (requiring the use of spark producing tools) in a cargo tank while at sea, the tank in question and all adjacent tanks are cleaned, and the atmosphere within tested with a combustible gas indicator in accordance with the approved practice. If the gas content is 0.2% or less, the necessary repairs may be carried out.

Chemist's Certificate. As a convenience for reporting the condition of tanks of a vessel, a ruled form of certificate with blank spaces resembling a conventional diagram of the horizontal cross section of a ship is provided. This certificate, affirming that the atmosphere in the tanks in which repairs are to be made, and adjacent tanks, are safe for the conduct of the work, must be signed by the inspecting chemist and given to the master or officer in charge before the ship is delivered to the contractor or person charged with making repairs.

In order that no possible misunderstanding can occur, the condition of tanks is indicated only by the notations *Safe for Men and Fire, Safe for Men— Not Safe for Fire*, and *Not Safe*.

The notation *Safe for Men and Fire* implies that the tanks so designated as well as the adjacent tanks and compartments have been thoroughly cleaned of residues and deposits on frames and on the bottom which, when disturbed, might produce vapor; and that the gas content of the atmosphere within the tanks is not more than .2% by volume calculated as pentane. Welding, riveting and similar work requiring fire are permitted in tanks so designated.

The notation *Safe for Men— Not Safe for Fire* implies that tanks so designated but not the adjacent tanks have been thoroughly cleaned of residues and deposits on frames and on the bottom which, when disturbed, might produce vapor; and that the gas content of the atmosphere within the tanks is not more than .2% by volume calculated as pentane. Only work not requiring the use of fire or spark producing tools is permitted in such tanks.

The notation *Not safe* is used when oil or dangerous amounts of residues or deposits are present, when leakage from adjacent tanks is possible, or when gas content of atmosphere is greater than .2%. Under such conditions, men are permitted to enter the tanks when an emergency exists but only when equipped with life-lines and fresh air hose masks, and only when a constant watch is maintained on deck for their safety.

The original and one copy of chemist's certificate are retained aboard ship and an entry of their receipt made in ship's log-book. Upon completion of repairs a statement is made by the master or officer in charge on the original certificate to this effect. The certificate then is forwarded to the home office.

Combustible Gas Indicator. Various types of indicators have been used in the past for the detection of petroleum vapors to insure that atmosphere is non-toxic and to guard against fires and explosions. All have employed basic principles, such as diffusion, volume change on combustion, or heat of combustion. Of these, the last-named type seems most suitable for the petroleum industry because of the wide variety of gases which are likely to be encountered.

Chapter 15

SHIP CALCULATIONS AND STABILITY

TONNAGE

Measurement. The "ton" of 100 cubic feet is the unit used in recording the volume of enclosed space in a vessel. *It has no relation to the ton weight.*

Gross Registered Tonnage is the total internal volume of the ship in units of 100 cubic feet.

Under-Deck Tonnage is the space in ton units between the top of the ceiling over the double bottom (if no ceiling, measured from the top of double bottom) and the under surface of the tonnage deck. The tonnage deck is the second deck from below in vessels of more than two decks; otherwise, it is the upper deck.

Net Registered Tonnage is the gross registered tonnage less certain deductions for machinery and passenger spaces, crew's quarters, storerooms, and spaces used in navigating the vessel.

All spaces deducted from the gross tonnage, by U. S. Navigation Laws, must be marked to signify their use, e.g.: "Certified for steering gear," "Certified for master's use."

Weight. The ton weight used is 2240 pounds (the long ton).

Deadweight Capacity is the weight, in tons, of cargo and necessary fuel and stores which a vessel can carry on her load draft.

Displacement Tonnage is the actual weight of the ship and everything on board.

Relative figures in tonnage for a modern freight steamship:

Gross registered tonnage . . . . 6,000 tons of 100 cu. ft.
Net registered tonnage . . . . 4,000 tons of 100 cu. ft.
Deadweight capacity . . . . 10,000 tons of 2240 lbs.
Displacement, loaded . . . . 13,350 tons of 2240 lbs.

Approximate Comparisons Between Some of the Ship Tonnage Relationships (ONI382.6 5-3-51):

To find	Multiply dwt.	by *grt.* by	*nrt.* by
deadweight tons	1.	1.5	2.5
gross register tons	.67	1.	1.67
net register tons	.40	.6	1.
displacement tons	1.5	2.25	3.75

The above is for a standard type cargo vessel, but will vary according to the measurement rules under which determined, as well as for the type of vessel under consideration. In a sailing vessel, the net tonnage may run to nearly 90% of the gross tonnage.

The American Bureau of Shipping and the USCG. The ABS is a nonprofit organization having semigovernmental status. The USCG has a representative on the executive committee of the ABS. The law provides that the USCG may, in certain cases, adopt the plans and specifications of the ABS. In the case of the permanent marking of load line marks, the ABS is authorized to act as inspector so that the marks are correctly placed, but it is not the function of the ABS to inspect vessels loaded and sailing in order to see whether their marks are submerged or visible; this is the function of the USCG.

SHIP DIMENSIONS

Length Between Perpendiculars (or L.B.P.). For vessels with a straight stem, this is taken from the fore part of the stem to the after side of the stern-post. Should the vessel have a clipper or curved stem, the length is measured from the point where the line of the upper deck beams would intersect the fore edge of the stem.

Extreme Breadth. The greatest breadth between the outside surfaces of the shell plating.

Moulded Breadth is the greatest breadth measured between the outside edges of the frames.

Moulded Depth, in 1-, 2-, or 3-deck vessels, is measured at the midlength from top of keel to top of upper deck beams at the side of the vessel. In awning or shelter decked vessels, it is measured from the top of the keel to top of main deck beams at the side of the vessel.

Registered Length is measured from the fore part of the stem under the bowsprit (if any) to the after side of the head of the stern-post.

Registered Breadth. Same as extreme breadth.

Registered Depth of Hold is the distance amidships from top of double bottom, or top of floors, or from a point 2 1/2″ above these points where a wood ceiling is fitted, no matter of what thickness, to the top of the upper deck beams, or second-deck beams in awning or shelter-deck vessels.

Length by American Bureau of Shipping Rules is measured on the estimated summer load line from the fore side of the stem to the after side of the rudder-post, or if no rudder-post, to the center of the rudder stock.

Depth by A.B.S. Rules is measured at the middle of vessel's length (by the same rules) from top of keel to top of deck beams.

Floodable Length is the length of compartment space which can be flooded without causing ship to sink. Such length differs with the location in the fore-and-aft line. What is called the *subdivision factor* multiplied by the floodable length gives the maximum length of each compartment permitted at that location. This is known as the *permissible length,* or the maximum distance between two watertight bulkheads for that locality.

Draft by A.B.S. Rules is the vertical distance in feet from the top of the keel to the center of the load-line disc.

Freeboard is the distance measured vertically downward, at the side of the vessel amidships, from the upper edge of the *deck line* to the upper edge of the load line.

Freeboard Deck. This is the deck from which the freeboard is measured, and is also the uppermost complete deck having means of permanently closing all openings thereon. It is the upper deck in flush-deck ships.

Deck Line is a horizontal line 12″ in length and 1″ in breadth, marked amidships on each side of the vessel, its upper edge passing through the point where the continuation outward of the upper surface of the freeboard deck intersects the outer surface of the shell plating or planking.

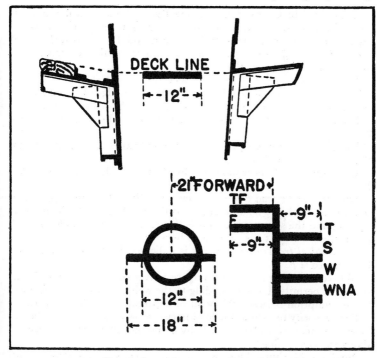

FIG. 1. LOAD LINES FOR STEAMSHIPS.

LOAD LINES FOR OCEAN STEAMERS

The exact location of the **disc** is determined by the rules of the classification society, which take into consideration the details of length, breadth, depth, structural strength and design, extent of superstructure, sheer, and round of beam of the particular ship, as compared with those of a *standard vessel* to which a definite summer freeboard has been allotted. The necessary corrections to the freeboard given the standard ship are made according to the degree of departure in detail that exists in the vessel in question, and this value is the *summer freeboard* assigned the particular vessel.

Load Line Regulations Sect. 43.018: "Notwithstanding the marking of a load line and the issuance of a load line certificate, the certificate will be cancelled if (a) the annual load line inspection required by Sect. 43.012 has not been carried out." Penalty, $500 for each voyage made without a certificate.

Load Line Disc. This is 12″ in diameter, and is intersected by a horizontal line 18″ in length and 1″ in breadth, the upper edge of which passes through the center of the disc. The disc is marked amidships, or at the mid-length between perpendiculars, below the deck line. (*See* Fig. 1.)

Lines Used in Connection with the Disc. The lines which indicate the maximum load line in different circumstances and in different seasons are horizontal lines, 9″ in length and 1″ in breadth, which extend from, and are at right angles to, a vertical line marked 21″ forward of the center of the disc.

The following are the lines used, as shown in Fig. 1:

The *summer load line* is indicated by the upper edge of the line which passes through the center of the disc, and also by a line marked *S*.

The *winter load line* is indicated by the upper edge of a line marked *W*.

The *winter North Atlantic load line* is indicated by the upper edge of a line marked *WNA*.

The *tropical load line* is indicated by the upper edge of a line marked *T*.

The *fresh water load line in summer* is indicated by the upper edge of a line marked *F*. The difference between the fresh water load line in summer and the summer load line is the *allowance* to be made for loading in fresh water at the other load lines.

The *tropical fresh water load line* is indicated by the upper edge of a line marked *TF*.

(Where sea-going steamers navigate a river or inland water, deeper loading is permitted, corresponding to the weight of fuel, etc., required for consumption between the point of departure, and the open sea.)

The *authority* by whom the load lines are assigned may be indicated by letters measuring about 4 1/2″ by 3″ marked alongside the disc and above the center line.

Details of Marking. The disc, lines, and letters are painted in white or yellow on a dark ground, or in black on a light ground. They are also carefully cut in or center-punched on the sides of iron and steel ships, and on wood ships they are cut into the planking for at least 1/8″.

MINIMUM FREEBOARDS FOR OCEAN STEAMERS

Summer Freeboard. The minimum freeboard in summer is the freeboard derived from the freeboard tables of the classification society. This freeboard is not to be less than 2 inches.

Tropical Freeboard. The minimum freeboard in the tropical zone is obtained by deducting from the summer freeboard 1/4″ per foot of summer draft, measured from the top of the keel to the center of the disc. This freeboard is not to be less than 2 inches.

Winter Freeboard. The minimum freeboard in winter is obtained by *adding* to the *summer freeboard* 1/4″ per foot of summer draft.

Winter North Atlantic Freeboard. The minimum freeboard for ships not exceeding 330 ft. in length on voyages across the North Atlantic, north of latitude 36° during the winter months, is the winter freeboard plus 2″. For ships over 330 ft. in length it is the winter freeboard.

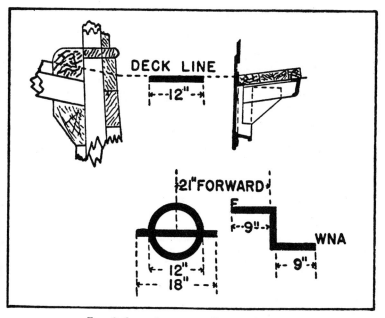

FIG. 2. LOAD LINES FOR SAILING VESSELS.

Fresh Water Freeboard. The minimum freeboard in fresh water is obtained by deducting from the minimum freeboard in sea water the number of inches equal to the displacement in sea water at the summer draft (in tons) divided by 40 times the tons per inch immersion in sea water at the same draft.

Where the displacement at the summer draft cannot be certified, the deduction is to be 1/4″ per foot of summer draft, measured from the top of the keel to the center of the disc.

Sailing Ships. Winter and tropical load lines are not marked on sailing ships. (*See* Fig. 2.) The maximum load line to which sailing ships may be laden in sea water in winter and in the tropical zone is the center of the disc.

Minimum freeboards: No addition to the freeboard is required for *winter* freeboard, nor is a deduction permitted for tropical freeboard.

An increase of freeboard of 3″ is made for voyages across the North Atlantic north of 36° latitude during the winter months.

Steamers Carrying Timber Deck Cargoes. (Fig. 3.) Where the assigning authority is satisfied that the ship is suitable and is equal to the

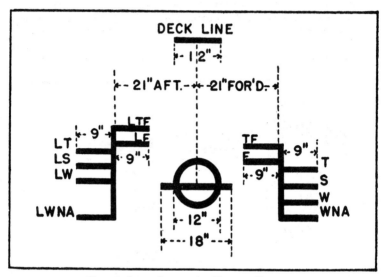

FIG. 3. LOAD LINES FOR TIMBER CARGOES.

requirements for the carriage of timber deck cargoes, a *summer* freeboard is assigned her in accordance with the load line regulations.

The *winter* timber freeboard is obtained by adding to the summer timber freeboard 1/3″ per foot of the moulded summer timber draft.

The *winter North Atlantic* timber freeboard is the same as that prescribed for any ocean steamer.

The *tropical* timber freeboard is obtained by deducting from the summer timber freeboard 1/4″ per foot of the summer timber draft.

Tankers. Load lines for tankers are provided according to the same rules as those for ocean steamers.

Special Lumber Vessels. Load lines for vessels specially constructed for the carriage of complete cargoes of timber (lumber schooner type), and which carry cargoes other than timber, are shown in Fig. 4. This load line is applicable to all seasons and zones. The assignment and certification of the load line is made after consideration of the vessel's experience on voyages carrying complete cargoes of timber, and of the condition of the vessel and her appliances.

The vessels to which this load line applies may be propelled by either sail or steam.

The forward markings shown in Fig. 4 are those required for a *steamer* when carrying cargoes other than complete timber cargoes.

The prescribed load lines for a *sailing vessel* take the place of the above forward markings.

Draft and Freeboard. Draft plus freeboard is constant for any particular vessel. Specifically, it is the sum of the mean draft, when floating at the summer load line, and the corresponding freeboard as given in the Load Line Certificate. By subtracting the mean draft at any time from this constant, we determine the freeboard. This is principally required for entry in the Official Log.

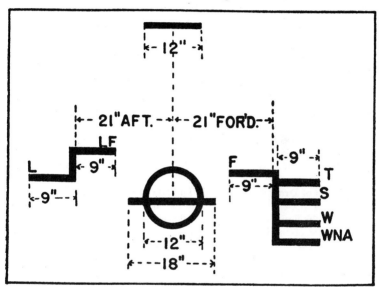

Fig. 4. Timber Load Line in Conjunction With Steamer Load Line for Vessels Constructed for Carrying Full Cargoes of Timber.

Change in Draft Due to a Change in Water Density. Where a vessel proceeds from sea water into water of a given density, the following is true:

Change in draft = (Displacement in tons ÷ $T.P.I.$) × (1025 − Given density) ÷ 1000

which, for fresh water, becomes: (Displacement ÷ $T.P.I$) × (1 ÷ 40).

$T.P.I.$ being the tons per inch immersion at the approximate draft in question.

Example. On a mean draft of 25′ 00″, the displacement is 10,000 tons and the tons per inch immersion 42. Find the increase of draft in water of 1010-oz. density. Also in fresh water.

For 1010 density, Increase = (10,000 ÷ 42) × [(1025 − 1010) ÷ 1000] = 3 1/2″.

For fresh water, Increase = (10,000 ÷ 42) × (1 ÷ 40) = 6″.

When the allowance for fresh water, as given in the Load Line Certificate, is considered when loading to one of the marks in water of known density, then,

Increase allowed in draft = F.W. allowance × (1025 − Density) ÷ 25.

Example. The fresh water allowance being 6″ for the vessel in the above example, what is the increase of draft allowed in water of 1010-oz. density?

$$6 \times [(1025 - 1010) \div 25] = 6 \times (15 \div 25) = 3\ 1/2''.$$

To Find the Draft in water of a given density, the draft in sea water being known: Here the following relation exists, very nearly:

$$\text{(Given density)} \div \text{(Sea water density)} = \text{(Draft in sea water)}$$
$$\div \text{(Draft required)}.$$

Example. Draft in sea water 25′ 00″. Find the draft in water of 1010-oz. density.

$$\text{Draft required} = (1025 \times 25) \div 1010 = 25.37', \text{ or } 25'\ 4\ 1/2''.$$

In most cases the result will be within one inch of the truth, the margin being about 1 1/2″ for vessels of fine form and deep draft. The error always lies on the greater side.

The Allowance for Fresh Water, *in the absence of any other data*, is approximately equal to 1/4″ per foot of summer draft. Thus, if 25′ were the summer draft, 25 divided by 4, or 6 1/4″, is the approximate allowance.

Increase of Draft Due to Heel. The rise of floor being *nil* for a great part of the vessel's length, the amount of draft over and above that shown by the figures on the stem and stern, or the increased immersion of the "turn of the bilge" due to heel, is very nearly equal to half the breadth of the vessel times the sine of the angle of heel.

Example. What is the increase of draft in a ship of 58′ beam when heeled to an angle of 6°?

$$(58 \div 2) \times \sin 6° = 29 \times .104 = 3.02, \text{ or } 3' \text{ increase.}$$

Fresh water (lake or river: Density 1000 ounces per cubic foot or, 62 1/2 pounds per cubic foot.

Volume of 1 ton of 2240 pounds, 35.84 cubic feet or, 1 cubic meter (approx.) or, 269 U. S. gallons or, 1000 liters (approx.).

Sea water: Specific gravity, 1.025, average on all oceans.

Density 1025 ounces per cubic foot, or, 64 pounds per cubic foot.

Volume of 1 ton of 2240 pounds, 35 cubic feet.

Sea water pressure, in pounds per square inch = 4/9 depth (in feet).

SHIP STABILITY

As a first requirement in the practical application of stability principles by a ship's officer, full information concerning his vessel should be at hand. This should include the following:

1. A scale or table showing the displacement and deadweight tonnage, freeboard, tons per inch immersion, and moment to change trim 1″ for any draft.

2. A curve or table of metacenters, showing the height of the metacenter above the keel at any draft.

3. A curve of righting levers, the so-called "stability curve," for two or three different conditions of lading, or *GM* values.

4. Height of the center of gravity above the keel (*KG*) in the light condition, this condition to be particularly defined as to tanks full or empty, and location and weight of fuel and stores on board.

5. Dimensions—length, breadth, depth of hold, etc., and the docking plan, the general arrangement plan, and the capacity plan.

Hydrostatic Curves, also called *Curves of Form* or *Displacement and Other Curves*, can be of very great practical use to the ship's officer. They are drawn up by the ship's designer after long and arduous calculations. The values given by the curves are all based on the underwater form of the ship. Furthermore, the designer assumes the ship to be on an even keel with a straight waterplane. Hence the term static; that is, the values cannot be computed for an infinite number of wave profiles and trimmed waterplanes such as a ship has under dynamic sea conditions. Some of the more important hydrostatic values given by means of the curves include:

1. Displacement in fresh and salt water

2. Moment to change trim 1 inch

3. Height of the transverse and longitudinal metacenters

4. Longitudinal and vertical position of the center of buoyancy

5. Coefficient of fineness

6. Change in displacement for trim

7. Location of the tipping center

8. Wetted surface

Displacement Tonnage is the weight in tons of 2240 pounds of the water a ship displaces when floating, and is equal to the weight of the vessel plus all weights on board. Volume of displacement depends upon the density of the water in which it floats. A ton of sea water = 35 cubic feet; a ton of fresh water, 35.84 cubic feet.

Draft of vessel is approximately one forty-eighth more in *fresh* water than in *sea* water.

Deadweight Tonnage is the carrying capacity of the vessel, or the weight of cargo, fuel, and stores on board when floating at the load draft. The difference between the light displacement and the load displacement is equal to the deadweight tonnage.

Tons per Inch Immersion (T.P.I.) is the figure denoting the number of tons weight required to be taken on board in order to increase ship's mean draft one inch.

Moment to Change Trim One Inch, or inch-trim-moment (*I.T.M.*), is the value in foot-tons of the moment about the transverse axis passing through the center of gravity of the water-plane which will cause a change of one inch in the difference between the forward and after drafts. Such a change is indicated by a half-inch increase in draft at one end of the ship, and a half-inch decrease at the other, where, as is usually the case, the center of gravity of the water-plane is roughly amidships.

Height of the Metacenter above the keel (*KM*) is required in order to find the *GM*, or the measure of the vessel's initial stability. Values of *KM* are shown by a curve, or may be tabulated, for any draft of the vessel. As we are principally concerned with *transverse*, or *sidewise*, stability considerations, unless otherwise noted the transverse metacenter will be hereafter simply termed *metacenter*, as above.

The Righting Arm, or lever, generally referred to as the *GZ* in the transverse stability diagram, is usually found from the curve drawn through a set of these values which have been calculated for each 10° of heel. Since the curve is based upon an assumed value of the *GM*, a correction must be made to the righting levers given thereon where the existing *GM* differs from that used in laying down the curve.

Height of the Center of Gravity above the keel, or the *KG*, is given for a definite light condition of the vessel. Where cargo or fuel are taken on board, this height must be corrected to give the *KG* for the whole system of weights, or the center of gravity above the keel of the entire floating mass.

The Docking Plan shows the particulars as to form of ship's bottom, including rise of floor, fineness toward ends, etc. It is used in preparing a dry dock to receive the vessel.

The General Arrangement Plan shows masts, rigging, booms, boats,

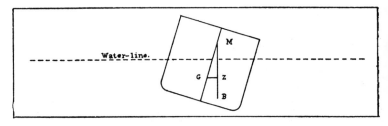

FIG. 5. ILLUSTRATING STABILITY FORMULAE.

hatches, bulkheads, deck erections, hold subdivisions, etc., with useful dimensions, sizes, and volumes of the various units.

The Capacity Plan shows details of capacities of all holds, 'tween deck spaces, tanks, bunkers, and storerooms. Sometimes the general arrangement and the capacity information are combined in one plan.

Stability, or the tendency of a floating body to remain at rest in a certain position, demands that, when the body is inclined by some external force, the vertical through the center of buoyancy (normal to the surface of the liquid in which floating) pass *above* the center of gravity of the body. When it does so, both its weight and the force of buoyancy tend to right the body to its original position.

A ship or other floating body is in vertical equilibrium under the action of gravity (*downward*) and that of buoyancy (*upward*). When the centers of gravity and buoyancy lie in the same vertical line, the body is floating in equilibrium.

Fig. 5 shows that when the vessel is inclined by an external force the center of buoyancy, or center of displaced volume of water, moves toward the low side, and the upward force of buoyancy acts through the extremity of the righting arm, *GZ*. The righting moment, or the length of the righting arm, GZ, multiplied by the vessel's displacement in tons, represents the amount of statical stability the ship possesses at that angle of heel.

Note that the position of G, the center of gravity, determines the value of GZ, so that, in the case of a *low* center of gravity (CG), we have comparatively great stability, or a "stiff" vessel, and conversely, a high CG will produce a "crank," or "tender" vessel.

An infinite number of transverse stability conditions might be indicated by the midship body diagram, but for a given value of GM the following considerations must be noted:

1. At small angles of heel, increase of beam produces greater righting power, or a greater GZ.

2. The limiting angle to which the vessel may heel and still possess righting power is governed by the amount of freeboard. Thus, more important than a broad or narrow beam in governing a vessel's range of stability is whether her freeboard is low or high.

3. The point M, the metacenter, limits the position of G if the ship is to possess stability, and it will be noted that the distance GM, the height of the metacenter *above* the center of gravity, is actually the measure of the vessel's initial stability.

4. A fine-lined vessel has a shorter GZ, or righting arm, than the "full" vessel.

As previously noted, the "stiff" vessel is so named because of her comparatively low center of gravity and great length of GZ. This condition is accompanied by short, sharp rolling in a seaway, and so not a comfortable one for those on board. The probable consequent damage to ship or cargo scarcely needs pointing out.

The "tender" vessel, on the other hand, has a long easy roll, and the opposite condition to that of the "stiff" vessel is observed. Here the center of weight is comparatively high, the GZ short, and, if a good freeboard value is wanting, the danger of capsizing in a heavy sea is always present. However, such a vessel, possessing a high freeboard, might actually have a greater range of stability than had she been in the "stiff" condition with less freeboard.

In looking into the stability question it should be made clear that the object aimed at is something more than a mere knowledge of ship stability. All transverse stability considerations are really focused on the GM which may be regarded as the yardstick used in supplying any vessel with the appropriate measure of righting power. This viewpoint is of prime importance.

The value of GM may be, in most cases of loading and in some cases of ballasting, controlled by the proper vertical distribution of the weight on board ship. An otherwise "stiff" vessel may be changed into an easy one, or a "tender" ship's behavior may be corrected by providing the necessary condition which will result in the degree of stability most suited to the particular vessel.

We shall now examine the properties of the terms used in the conventional transverse stability diagram:

1. *CG*, or the center of gravity.
2. *CB*, or the center of buoyancy.
3. *M*, or the metacenter.
4. *GZ*, or the righting arm.
5. *GM*, or the so-called metacentric height.

1. The *CG*, or center of gravity, is the point at which the total weight of the ship and any other weight on board is taken to be concentrated. If the vessel were suspended at this point she would rest perfectly balanced, due to the fact that equal weight lies at each side of the point indicated.

The vertical position of the *CG* (*VCG*) is usually located with reference to the keel. The value *KG* indicates the height of the *CG* above the keel.

Considered as located in the fore-and-aft line, the *CG* is referred to as the *LCG* (longitudinal center of gravity), and in ship calculations is usually indicated as at a certain distance from a definite midship point.

The position of the center of gravity for a given light condition of the vessel is calculated by the shipbuilder. A simple computation will determine the position of the new *CG* when any subsequent changes in weight distribution, or those due to loading or ballasting, take place.

2. The center of buoyancy, *CB*, may be defined as the geometrical center, or center of gravity of the body of water displaced by a floating vessel. It is the center of the immersed part of the ship.

Since the upward force of buoyancy must equal the downward or gravitational force acting upon the mass of the vessel, the total buoyancy considered as acting through *CB* must uphold the weight of the ship acting downward through its center, *CG*. We then have the *CG* and the *CB* lying in a vertical line, and the vessel floating at rest.

3. The Metacenter. When a vessel is heeled by an external cause, the form of the displaced body of water undergoes a change, and a shift of the center of buoyancy, *CB*, is the result.

The *CB* is now located at some distance from its original position in the direction of the low side of the ship. The line showing the direction of buoyancy force, normal to the water surface, now intersects the vertical line from the center of the keel through the *CG* in the fore-and-aft midship plane. This point of intersection is called the metacenter, and, in most vessels, is fixed up to angles of about 12° of heel.

Usually a *locus of metacenters* is supplied by the shipbuilder, showing the change in the position of the metacenter due to the various angles of heel for at least three different draft conditions. One of these loci should be drawn for the light condition, one for about half-load draft, and another for full-load draft.

4. *GZ*, the righting arm, is drawn from *G* perpendicular to the direction of buoyancy, *BM*. Through its extremity *Z* the force of buoyancy acts, and we see that the *GZ* is the lever length which, when multiplied by the displacement in tons (equal to the buoyancy force) gives the moment about *G*, or the initial work performed in righting the ship. The righting moment, then, is equal to the *GZ* times the displacement, **expressed in foot-tons.**

5. GM, also called the metacentric height, is really the criterion of a vessel's stability. We have seen that the position of G depends upon the distribution of the weight on board the vessel, so that by arranging the weights to give a GM which by experience has been found to be the most satisfactory, we shall have done all that is possible to ensure a vessel's best sea-going behavior.

Note particularly that, while a certain value of GM for one particular vessel may leave nothing to be desired, under similar conditions of loading that of a ship of a different body form may require perhaps as much as a foot of GM more or less than the other as the best value.

THE GM

In the practical application of the information supplied by the shipbuilder we are not interested, as a rule, in the methods used in determining values such as the GZ at various angles of heel for a given condition, the distance of the CB above the keel, or the height of the metacenter, KM.

We are, however, very much concerned with the value of the GM of our particular vessel, and with the information given in the stability curve before us, we should be in a position to provide our vessel with the properties of at least a good "sea-boat."

Later we shall consider the determination of the values referred to; for the present we are concerned with that of the GM.

As already noted, the curve of righting levers, or stability curve, is drawn for a particular value of the GM. The location of M, the metacenter, is readily found from the locus of metacenters, and, being dependent upon the displacement and water-plane area, is capable of being precisely determined. The CG depends upon the distribution of weight in the ship, and in all cases is not so easily arrived at.

The CG for the light condition is a huge calculation, though simple in principle, which takes into account all the weights of the vessel's structural parts, the weights of ballast and fuel on board, and the distance of the center of gravity of each above the keel. The sum of the products of all the weights multiplied by their distances above the keel is divided by the total weight (displacement) and the quotient is then the KG, or distance of the CG above the keel. KM, the height of the metacenter above the keel, having been determined for the particular draft, the GM is then equal to KM minus KG.

The location of G as found by the calculation mentioned may, however, be somewhat in error, for reasons apart from the questionable accuracy of the work, as is apparent to anyone dealing with enormous data detail as are involved in such computations. A check upon the calculated GM is therefore made by carrying out an *inclining experiment*. This is simply listing the vessel by placing a known weight at a certain distance from the fore-and-aft midship line, and noting the angle of heel produced by the resulting moment about the midship line. From this observation a simple calculation derives the GM, and $KG = KM - GM$. The location of G now being established, for any subsequent change in position of, or addition to, the weights on board, a new G, and consequently a new GM, are easily determined.

Note: The International Convention for Safety of Life at Sea of 1948 requires that all mechanically propelled vessels of 500 gross tons or over must be subjected to a stability test if contracted for on or after Nov. 19, 1952. In the U.S., the USCG administers these regulations and conducts the inclining tests. The inclining test of a sister ship may be omitted, and generally is if the CG feels that the results of the first class ship test is sufficiently representative of her sister to warrant it.

A ship is inclined only once unless a major conversion of the ship is undertaken.

After a ship is inclined, the USCG issues a "Stability Letter" setting forth the Master's stability responsibilities. This letter, which is posted under glass in the pilothouse, refers to the information derived from the inclining test.

THE INCLINING EXPERIMENT

Choose a calm day, or a day when the wind is end on to the ship. Have the ship moored only over stem and stern, so heeling will be unaffected. All weights must be stationary, and tanks free from loose water or hardened up.

Place a known weight with its center over the fore-and-aft center line of the vessel, and as nearly amidships as possible. The weight should be accurately known, of a compact nature, and sufficient to incline the ship a few degrees. Note draft and find the displacement from the displacement scale. At center line of vessel suspend two plumb-lines (preferably in hatchways), one forward and one aft, as long as conveniently possible. Both should be freely hung and of equal length. Now fix a transverse batten on which to measure the exact deflection of each plumb-line and carefully measure between the upper edge of each batten and the suspension point of the plumb-line.

Move the weight to starboard as far as possible, and note the distance it has been moved. Note the exact deflections of the plumb-lines.

Shift the weight to the port side the same distance from the fore-and-aft line, and repeat the observation.

Find the mean value of the four deflections noted, and determine the distance ship's center of gravity has moved during the experiment. This is equal to the weight moved multiplied by the distance it has been moved from the fore-and-aft line and divided by the vessel's displacement.

We now have all the required data to solve the problem.

Referring to Fig. $6A$, the center of gravity, G actually moves to G_1, parallel to the movement of the weight, and also parallel to LL_1.

PL_1 is parallel to G_1M, and angle at P is equal to angle at M; therefore triangles LL_1P and GG_1M are similar. The "shift moment" $GG_1 \times W$ is equal to the "shift moment" $d \times w$, or $GG_1 \times W = w \times d$, W being the displacement in tons.

Knowing the length of the plumb-line, PL, the deflection of the plumb-line LL_1, and the shift of the center of gravity, GG_1, we have:
$GG_1 = (w \times d) \div W$.
$PL \div LL_1 = GM \div GG_1$, from which $GM = (PL \times GG_1) \div LL_1$.

Example. A 30-ton weight is moved 25' to one side of the fore-and-aft line in a vessel of 2500 tons displacement. Length of plumb-lines 20', and mean deflection 24". Required, the GM.

Solution: Shift of $CG = GG_1 = (30 \times 25) \div 2500 = .3' = 3.6''$

$$GM = (240 \times 3.6) \div 24 = 36'', \text{ or } 3'.$$

Since the accuracy of GG_1 basically determines the degree of accuracy of the resulting GM, it will be realized that a precise knowledge of the weight and the distance through which it is moved is of first importance, as well as the necessity of taking every precaution to prevent any movement of weight, especially water or fuel oil in slack tanks, in any part of the ship.

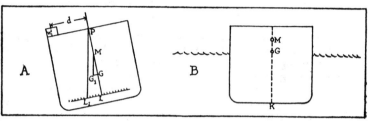

FIG. 6. *A*) MEASURING EFFECT OF SHIFT OF WEIGHT.
B) KM − KG = GM.

There should be little or no difficulty in obtaining the correct values of the plumb-line deflections and lengths.

It must be noted that, should the weight be one placed on board for this special purpose, a correction to the resulting GM must be made when it is removed from the vessel. This correction will be, in the usual case of the weight being above the CG. (Weight removed × Dist. of weight from CG) ÷ (Total displacement − Weight removed), or distance the CG is lowered. This quantity is to be added to the GM found by the test.

If the weight remains on board and is removed to a lower position, as in the case where ballast taken from the hold is used as the weight, then the correction to be added to the GM will be: (Weight × Distance removed) ÷ (Displacement), since, as before, the CG has been lowered by that amount.

In the former case, where the weight is taken on board before the experiment and landed after its completion, the height of the vessel's CG must be known in order to find the vertical distance of the weight from that point. As previously noted, the height of the CG, or $KG = KM - GM$.

FINDING THE GM FOR A LOAD CONDITION

The computation of KG, which is simply an application of the principle of moments about the basic point K in order to find the CG of a vertical system of weights, may best be illustrated by a worked example:

A ship in light condition displaces 2000 tons, the KG being 10', and the *KM* in the load condition 12'. 3500 tons of cargo are loaded 9' above the keel, and 400 tons of fuel 15' above the keel. Find the *GM*.

Solution: (Sum of moments about *K*) ÷ (Total wt. or displacement) = *KG*.

Weight (tons)		Ht. above *K* (feet)	Moment (ft.-tons)
Ship	2000	10	20,000
Cargo	3500	9	31,500
Fuel	400	15	6,000
Total	5900 (tons)		57,500

$$KG = 57,500 \div 5900 = 9.75'$$
$$KM = 12.00'$$
$$GM = 2.25'$$

Assuming the above example is a trial computation for a proposed loading, it is desired to shorten the *GM* by half a foot. How many feet must 500 tons of the cargo be raised to effect this?

Solution: Here it is required to raise the *CG* .5'. By the principle of moments, the weight moved times the distance moved divided by the total weight (displacement) is equal to the shift of the center of gravity (*CG*) of the system:

$$.5' \text{ rise of } G = (500 \times \text{Distance raised}) \div 5900,$$

then,   Distance raised = $(.5 \times 5900) \div 500 = 5.9'$.

So that 500 tons of the 3500 tons cargo must be placed 9+5.9, or 14.9' above the keel.

Note further that 250 tons raised $5.9 \times 2 = 11.8'$ would give the same result; or 1000 tons raised $5.9 \div 2 = 2.95'$ gives a third choice in the matter.

Again, suppose that a *GM* of .75' has been computed for a proposed load condition. It is required to increase the value to 1.5'. Load displacement 8800 tons. How many tons must be moved 8' downward to give the required result?

Solution: $1.5 - .75 = .75'$, shift of $G = (\text{Weight} \times 8) \div 8800$

whence,   Weight = $(.75 \times 8800) \div 8 = 825$ tons.

Stowage must therefore be arranged so that 825 tons of the cargo will be lowered 8'. But 1650 tons lowered 4' would equally accomplish the same purpose, since the *moment* required to produce a lowering of the *G*, or an increase of the *GM*, of .75' is the constant 6600 foot-tons.

Taking another example, assume the vessel to fill a ballast tank whose *CG* is 1 1/2' above the keel. *GM* = 1.5' and *KG* = 18'. Capacity of tank = 100 tons. What will be the effect on the *GM*?

Solution: Distance of *CG* of tank from $G = 18 - 1 1/2 = 16 1/2'$.

Shift of $G = (100 \times 16 1/2) \div (8800 + 100) = 1650 \div 8900 = .19'$.

Therefore $KG = 18 - .19 = 17.81'$

and $GM = 1.5 + .19 = 1.69'$

STABILITY CURVES

The value of the *GM*, as previously noted, must be considered in connection with the curve of righting levers, or what is usually called the stability curve. This curve is often drawn for 3 values of *GM*, each corresponding to a different draft condition: light, half-load, and load. For practical purposes, the necessary corrections to be applied to the righting levers, which are calculated for the nearest condition to that existing, are found by multiplying the difference between the *GM* for which the curve is drawn and the existing *GM* by the sine of the angle of heel—$(GM - G_1M_1) \times$ sine of angle = correction.

While a satisfactory stability condition may be apparent through the information shown on the curve, a later experience may prove the vessel's behavior at sea to be poor. The ship's rolling period is usually the key to this state of affairs. If the sea-wave period and the vessel's period of roll are nearly in agreement when the sea is somewhere near the beam, excessive rolling is the consequence.

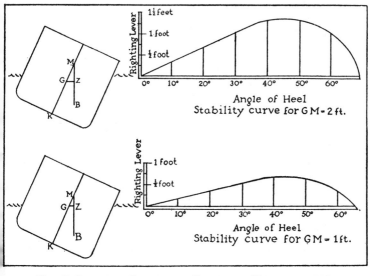

Fig. 7. Stability Curves for Different Values of *GM*.

Experience is undoubtedly the best guide in determining the *GM* which, in a given condition of loading, is most desirable, and will render unnecessary the temporary cures such as altering course or speed, and the probable wasting of time and energy generally, not overlooking the harmful effects on both ship and cargo during heavy rolling in an ordinary seaway.

GM values for vessels of various types and sizes, based upon facts concerning rolling under different conditions, and values of righting levers, have been recommended by naval architects. This information is of much importance in naval and passenger ship construction, but may be classed as simply a rough guide to the cargo vessel's officer. A wide range of conditions of loading is the rule in the average merchant ship, and, while in many instances the best possible GM may be provided, the exception rather than the rule is the order. This is because cargoes seldom accommodate themselves to a model form of stowage which results in the most satisfactory stability condition or general sea behavior of the vessel.

Supposing the stability curve to be that corresponding to a GM of say 2′ at a certain draft, and the present GM has been computed as 1′ at approximately the same draft. It will be noted that the righting levers are shorter and the range of stability is reduced, but actually an easier and more comfortable sea-boat will be the result, provided the vessel's rolling period and the average wave period are not synchronous. (*See* Fig. 7.)

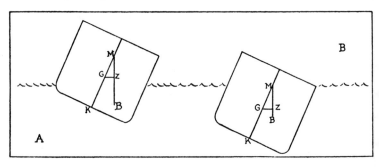

FIG. 8. *A*) LIGHT DRAFT. MAXIMUM RIGHTING MOMENT WILL NOT BE REACHED UNTIL SHIP HAS HEELED ABOUT 20° MORE THAN SHOWN IN SKETCH, *B*) DEEP DRAFT. BECAUSE OF THE DEEP DRAFT CONDITION, MAXIMUM RIGHTING MOMENT IS REACHED AT APPROXIMATELY THE ANGLE OF HEEL SHOWN.

Again, with a given value of GM, it is apparent that the range of stability and the righting levers are directly influenced by the vessel's draft. (*See* Fig. 8.)

A *heavy draft* ship having small righting levers and a good freeboard is usually the best sea-boat. Longer rolling periods and shorter righting levers are co-existent in any case. The greater the displacement, the greater the statical stability, since GZ times the displacement is the measure of the latter; or the righting moment at a given angle of heel, in a given GM condition, increases with the displacement.

Heavily loaded vessels with low freeboard have a comparatively short range of stability, their maximum righting lever being coincident with the immersion of the low side of the freeboard deck, as will be noted by a consideration of the stability diagram. Here a dangerous condition is evident in the case of the "tender" ship (*See* Fig. 8), and one of good initial stability quickly loses her righting lever values when the deck is immersed.

ROLLING

Rolling Period. The rolling *period* is the time taken in seconds from the maximum angle of heel on one side to the maximum angle of heel on the other side. The *interval* of roll, also known as the *full rolling period*, is the total time in seconds for the vessel to roll from starboard to port to starboard (or vice versa). The average of 15 or 20 is usually taken.

Where the vessel's metacentric height GM is known, her full rolling period T can be found by the following empirical formula.

$$T = \frac{.44 \text{ beam (in feet)}}{\sqrt{GM}}$$

where the beam is 40 ft. and the vessel's GM is 1 ft., we have:

$$T = \frac{.44 \times 40}{\sqrt{1}} = 17.6 \text{ seconds}$$

Or, if we find the full rolling period at sea and wish to find the GM, we can do so by the formula above.

The generally accepted metacentric heights considered suitable for different types of vessels are: passenger vessels, 2% of the beam; dry cargo vessels, 5% of the beam; tankers, 8% of the beam.

Among several formulae for finding the period of roll (the single roll, as above defined) the following has been found to give very close results:

$t = .554 \times k \div \sqrt{GM}$, t being the period in seconds, and k the radius of gyration of the mass about the longitudinal axis passing through G.

Also, a close approximation to the truth may be found by the much simpler

$t = .22B \div \sqrt{GM}$, B being the greatest breadth of the ship, and t the period in seconds.

The Wave Period is the elapsed time in seconds between the passing of two successive wave crests over a fixed point.

In the Atlantic, ordinary sea waves have a period of about 8 seconds, and a length of from 200′ to 350′. Storm waves, 10 to 12 seconds period, and length of 500′ to 600′.

In the Pacific, much longer waves prevail, those of ordinary conditions being 600′ to 1,000′ from crest to crest, with a period of from 11 to 14 seconds.

The wave period may be found by the formula:

$t = \sqrt{\text{Length of wave}} \div 5.124$, t being the period in seconds.

Ships of shorter periods than that of the waves are usually subjected in a beam sea to short, quick rolling which naturally results in severe transverse structural stresses. This condition is commonly met with in the smaller type of vessel.

Where the vessel's rolling period happens to be equal to the *half* wave-period, a synchronizing of the passing wave-slope with the *single* roll leaves the ship at the end of her roll when in the trough of the sea; the advancing wave-slope then swings her to the end of her next roll just as the crest of the wave reaches her. A capsizing danger is here obvious. The resistance offered by the underwater body form, air, and skin friction would *probably* break the synchronism and save the situation, but timely action in altering the vessel's compass heading a couple of points would suggest itself to the experienced seaman in order to restore his misbehaving charge "to her four feet."

Equally hazardous is the condition in which the period of roll and the wave period are about the same, which is more likely to occur with a fairly large vessel than with the smaller type.

The most satisfactory rolling period is one which is greater than the half wave-period, and not coincident with the full wave-period. Taking the average Atlantic wave period of 8 seconds, a vessel whose period of roll is 5, 6, 7, or 9 seconds should react favorably to an ordinary beam sea.

It is well to remember that changes in the ship's speed will appreciably affect the period of roll, an increase of speed causing an increased period, and vice versa.

Situated among storm waves of 10 to 11 seconds period, were the period of roll the same value, an uncomfortable experience would be the result; but it is hardly supposed that a shipmaster would proceed beam-on to the sea in an ordinary-sized vessel under such conditions. Large liners, of course, whose periods are usually greater than those of any probable storm waves, and whose great superstructure, acted upon by the heavy wind pressure, considerably obstructs the rolling process, are seldom seriously affected.

The means used to reduce rolling are bilge keels, which are fitted to almost all steam vessels; anti-rolling tanks, which have been installed in a few passenger vessels; and the gyroscope stabilizer.

Of the three mentioned, the last-named has proved to be the most effective. Experiments have shown that on vessels of the destroyer type it is possible to reduce a 30° roll in less than a minute to one of about 2° with the proper gyroscope fly-wheel. It is claimed that the weight of the gyroscopic stabilizer equipment need not be more than 1% of the ship's displacement.

THE BM OR METACENTRIC RADIUS

We have seen that the vector representing the upward force of buoyancy meets the point M, the metacenter, on the midship vertical line. The total buoyancy force concentrated at B, the center of buoyancy, has its origin at that point. We accept the value BM for any given floating position·or draft condition of a vessel as beyond our control. In supplying a ship with the required degree of stability we are limited by the location of M, whether the vessel be upright or not, as to the vertical distribution of weight in the ship. In other words, a desired location of G may be affected by means at our disposal, but M and B, and consequently the distance BM, are laid down by the inexorable laws of nature.

BM (feet) = [Moment of inertia of water-plane] ÷ [Volume of displacement (feet³)] = $I ÷ V$, the numerator I being considered relative to the longitudinal axis.

It will be observed by this formula that the value of BM depends almost wholly upon the volume of displacement, since an ordinary vessel's water-plane area changes comparatively little throughout her range of working drafts. This accounts for the high position of the metacenter at the lighter drafts, so that a given KG results in a greater GM at the light draft than at the load draft.

Also, for a given displacement, the vessel having the greater beam will have the greater BM, since the moment of inertia of the water-plane about the fore-and-aft line varies as the breadth cubed and only directly as the length. We therefore note that the broad-beamed, shallow-draft vessel is characterized by her great metacentric height (GM) because of the comparatively great height of $M(KM)$. This is the "stiff" vessel with the short rolling period.

Considering a narrow-beamed ship, the formula again shows that the BM will be seriously affected by a heavy draft, or increase of displacement. We have here the naturally "tender" vessel in the load condition, and particular care must be taken to keep the G well down.

In ordinary type cargo steamers the BM varies inversely as the draft, nearly. Thus, a vessel of 12,500 tons displacement, 400′ in length, and 55′ beam, at 12′ draft with a BM of about 21′ has at 26′ draft a BM of 10′. In such a steamer the location of the center of buoyancy, or the KB (ship upright), is approximately .55 of the draft above the keel.

The Moment of Inertia of the water-plane, which was given as the numerator in the formula for finding the transverse BM, may be defined as the moment of inertia about the water-plane's longitudinal axis, or the measure of the tendency of the water-plane area to resist motion. In mechanics it is "the sum of the products of the elementary areas into which the area may be conceived to be divided and the squares of their distances from the axis in question."

It can be shown that the moment of inertia of a rectangular-shaped water-plane about the longitudinal axis is equal to the length times the breadth cubed divided by 12, so that for a box-shaped vessel we have:

$$BM = (LB^3 \div 12) \div V = I \div V.$$

From this it may be seen that, as stated in the remarks on the BM, the numerator of the formula varies as the cube of the breadth, without going into the lengthy process of calculating the moment of inertia of an actual ship's water-plane.

The Longitudinal BM, which is required in certain ship calculations, is computed on the same principle. The moment of inertia of the water-plane is considered as about the transverse axis passing through the center of gravity of that area.

Pitching. What has been stated regarding the influence of the BM value on rolling applies similarly in principle to pitching. A vessel of light draft as compared with her load condition will react to a head sea with a much more lively motion, due to the fact that the greater longitudinal BM corresponds to a shorter *pitching period*, just as we have seen that the greater transverse BM (unless counteracted by a raised center of gravity) produces the shorter *rolling period*.

The pitching period has been found to agree closely with the result given by the formula:

$$t = .554k \div \sqrt{LGM},$$

k being the radius of gyration about the transverse axis passing through the center of gravity.

The value of t (in seconds) of course, primarily depends upon the moment of inertia of the mass about the center of gravity, so that greater weight toward the vessel's ends, and a consequent increase in the numerator k, will result in a longer pitching period for a given LGM (longitudinal metacentric height). The same effect on the period of roll is produced by stowing heavy cargo in the wings of the holds, but, due to the comparatively small distance from the midship line to the center of weight, such effect would, in most cases, be negligible.

Unusual weight placed near the ends of the ship produces sluggishness in a head sea, which causes the shipping of heavy water over the bows, a consequent loss of speed, and undue longitudinal stresses on the vessel's structure.

Ballasting. From one-fourth to one-third of the deadweight carrying capacity is, in general, a suitable amount of water ballast to be carried in double bottom and deep tanks of a light ship.

Double bottom tanks alone are seldom adequate for efficient ballasting, considering the difficulties of navigation and wear and tear on the structure in a heavy seaway.

Deep tanks, or wing tanks, as fitted in some better-class cargo types and bulk carriers, are almost a necessity in most trades and absolutely so in stormy waters. The obvious advantages of supplying the needed deadweight as well as a *raised center of gravity* need hardly be commented upon.

Slack water ballast should be particularly guarded against, as having a damaging effect upon tank tops, and causing strained and broken rivets in the tank structure and vicinity.

Filling Ballast Tanks at Sea. Loss of GM due to the consumption of fuel or water may sometimes require filling a ballast tank at sea. It is surely not good seamanship to wait until the vessel is in a tender condition, especially so if rough weather is encountered, before taking such action; and particularly should the tank or tanks be of the undivided type, i.e., a free surface extending from side to side of the entire tank.

It can be shown that the GM is reduced, in the case of a free liquid, by an amount equal to the moment of inertia of the surface of the liquid, divided by the displacement of the vessel, or:

Reduction of $GM = i \div V$, i being the moment of inertia of the free surface, and V the displacement (in ft.³); and it should be noted that i in the formula is independent of the volume of the free liquid, being, for a tank of rectangular form:

$i = (l \times b^3) \div 12$, l and b being respectively the length and breadth of the free surface.

As an example of the effect on the GM of the free liquid surface in a vessel's tanks, consider a double-bottom tank 4' deep, filled to a depth of 3' with sea water; the tank is 50' in width by 52' in length, and the water is free to flow in any direction. Assume the height of the *CG* before running water into tank is 22.8' and ship's displacement 13,000 tons. Weight of water in tank is 220 tons.

Change in *KG* due to water in tank = [(22.8 − 1.5) × 220] ÷ 13,220 = .35'.

Reduction in *GM* due to slack water = $i ÷ V$, or:

$$(50 \times 50 \times 50 \times 52) \div (12 \times 13,220 \times 35) = 1.17'$$

Fall in *CG* due to taking in water	= .35'
Reduction in *GM* due to slack water	= 1.17'
Total reduction in *GM*	= .82'

Instances of such large free surfaces of liquid, of course, would be rare in any vessel. It is worthy of note that, since the value of the moment of inertia of the free surface varies as the cube of the breadth, a watertight center-line division in the tank would result in one-fourth the *GM* reduction due to the free surface in the through tank. The center-line division condition would appear, then, as follows:

Fall in *CG* due to taking in water	= .35'
Reduction in *GM* due to slack water	= .29'
Increase in *GM*	= .06'

The presence of slack water or oil in subdivided tanks, therefore, is not generally a serious condition in ship stability considerations. However, the probably perilous case of a tender vessel having her lower hold half full of water is realized when considering the effect on the *GM* of comparatively large free liquid surfaces as given in the example.

CARGO SHIFTING PREVENTION

The danger attending the carriage of grain cargoes on ocean voyages has long ago been dealt with by the enactment of laws regulating the manner in which such cargoes must be stowed and requiring the provision of means to prevent shifting during heavy rolling or listing.

Where grain is carried in bulk, the holds are to be kept completely filled through the voyage by means of feeders erected in the deck next above, the feeders being required to contain at least 2% of the hold's capacity. Whether the grain is in bags or in bulk, the decks or holds are divided by longitudinal bulkheads or grain-tight *shifting boards*, which must be of suitable strength. The effect of these shifting boards is to reduce the heeling moment of a shifted cargo to about one-fourth of what it would be without them.

In any case where bulk grain, coal, etc., only partially fills the space, special precautions must be taken to prevent the surface from being moved by the rolling or lurching of the ship.

Deck Cargoes. A sufficient margin of stability must be allowed before leaving port, for as fuel is consumed the *CG* is raised and the *GM* reduced. Also the exposed timber or other cargo absorbs spray and rain, thus adding to its weight and raising the *CG* still more.

Care must be taken to properly secure a deck-load of timber against being moved by a boarding sea, and the lashings should be kept tightened up at all times.

LONGITUDINAL STABILITY

The principles applied in *transverse* metacentric stability considerations are identical with those employed in problems relating to trim, as may be seen by Fig. 9.

As in the transverse stability diagram, Fig. 5, *CB*, *CG*, and *M* are in the same vertical line when the ship is floating in equilibrium, or at rest. When the vessel's forward end is depressed by some external

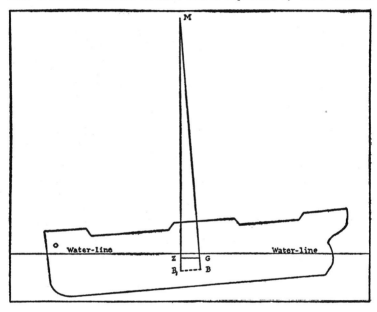

Fig. 9. Illustrating Longitudinal Stability, With Ship Having a Pitching Motion. BB_1 = Movement of Center of Buoyancy; GZ = Righting Lever; M = Metacenter.

cause (as shown in Fig. 9) GZ times the displacement is the measure of the stability, or the righting moment, tending to restore equilibrium. We see, then, that gravity and buoyancy act on exactly the same principles in the longitudinal as in the transverse metacentric system.

Due to the enormous value of the *moment of inertia* of the water-plane about the midship transverse axis in the formula $BM = I \div V$, the longitudinal BM is of much greater length than the transverse BM. Consequently we have great "stiffness" because of the larger GZ values for similar inclinations, as compared with the transverse GZ.

Inch Trim Moment. If, instead of considering the vessel's head temporarily depressed by an external cause, we think of a certain weight on board being moved from amidships well forward as the *internal cause* of the above condition, the vessel will now be floating in equilibrium, with G shifted to G_1, and B shifted to B_1 (Fig. 10).

The distance BB_1 (practically equal to GG_1), multiplied by the displacement is the moment which has caused the draft to increase forward and to decrease aft a certain amount expressed in inches.

The sum of these two changes in the drafts is called the change of trim. The moment which will cause a difference of 1 inch in the forward and after drafts is termed the inch trim moment, or the *I.T.M.*

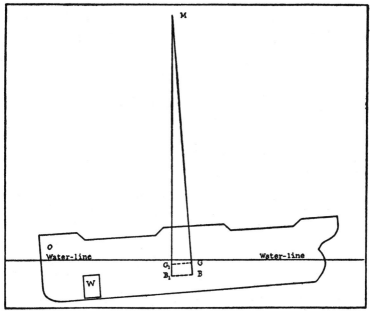

FIG. 10. LONGITUDINAL STABILITY. SHIP IS AT REST, TRIMMED BY THE HEAD. UNDER THE EFFECT OF THE WEIGHT, w, MOVED TO THE FORWARD END. GG_1 = SHIFT OF CENTER OF GRAVITY; BB_1 = SHIFT OF CENTER OF BUOYANCY.

B_1, the center of buoyancy, is the so-called *center of flotation*, or tipping center. (*See* Fig. 10.)

CHANGE OF TRIM

1. When a given weight is placed in a vessel at a given distance forward or abaft the tipping center, or center of flotation, the change of trim due to the moment about that point (expressed by the weight multiplied by the distance) is found by the formula:

$$C = (w \times d) \div I.T.M.$$

where C is the change of trim in inches; w, the weight in tons; d, the distance from tipping center; $I.T.M.$, the inch trim moment.

The $I.T.M.$ may be found by $(k \times t^2) \div b$ where t is the tons per inch immersion; b, the breadth of the vessel; k, a constant depending upon the *block coefficient.*

For coefficient of .65, value of k is 28
"   "   " .70, " " k " 29
"   "   " .75, " " k " 30
"   "   " .80, " " k " 31
"   "   " .85, " " k " 32
"   "   " .90, " " k " 33

Example: 360 tons of cargo are loaded in a vessel 150′ forward of the tipping center; tons per inch are 50; breadth of ship 60′; block coefficient .75. Draft before loading, 20′ 00″ F., and 22′ 06″ A. Find the draft after loading.

For the $I.T.M.$ $(30 \times 50 \times 50) \div 60 = 1250$ foot-tons
For the change of trim $(360 \times 150) \div 1250 = 43″$, or 3′7″
For the increase in mean draft, $360 \div 50 = 7″$

Draft before loading,	20′00″F.	22′06″A.
1/2 trim $+$	1′09 1/2″	$-$ 1′09 1/2″
increase $+$	07″	$+$ 07″
Draft after loading,	22′04 1/2″ F.	21′03 1/2″ A.

Since the change of trim is equal to the sum of the increase of draft at one end of the ship and the decrease at the opposite end, due to the "tipping effect," we apply the *half-trim* in the manner required.

The location of the tipping center is approximately at the mid-distance between perpendiculars. Correctly, it is a point on the vertical line joining the center of gravity, the center of buoyancy, and the longitudinal metacenter of the vessel. In practice, we assume the tipping center to be at the midship point above denoted; and, providing there is not an unusual difference between the forward and after drafts, such assumption in trim calculations will not materially affect the result.

2. When weights are shifted in the fore-and-aft line, the moment found by multiplying the weight by the distance it is moved is that which causes the change of trim. Therefore it is not necessary to know the position of the moved weight relative to the tipping center.

Example: 100 tons of fuel oil are shifted from No. 3 to No. 6 tank, a distance of 110′. The $I.T.M.$ is 550 foot-tons. Draft before shifting fuel is 15′00″ F., and 14′00″ A. Find the new draft.

$(100 \times 110) \div 550 = 20″$ change of trim (by the stern).

Draft before shifting fuel,	15′00″ F.	14′00″ A.
1/2 trim,	$-10″$	$+10″$
New draft,	14′02″ F.	14′10″ A.

Note that in this case we have not added or taken away any weight, so that the tons per inch ($T.P.I.$) value does not enter the calculation.

3. The points forward and abaft the tipping center, at which the loading or discharging of any weight will affect the draft *at one end of the vessel only* are found by the following:

$$2 \ (I.T.M.) \div T.P.I. = \text{distance (in feet) from tipping center.}$$

The number of inches it is required to change the draft at one end of the vessel only will be the effect of loading or discharging a certain weight at the above-noted point, which weight may be found by the formula:

$$1/2 \ (\text{inches change in draft}) \times T.P.I. = \text{weight.}$$

Example: The $I.T.M.$ being 1100 foot-tons and the $T.P.I.$ 45, (*a*) at what distance abaft the tipping center must a weight be loaded so that the forward draft will not change? (*b*) How many tons are required to be loaded at that point to increase the draft 10″ aft?

(*a*) $(2 \times 1100) \div 45 = 48.9$, or 49′ abaft the tipping center.

(*b*) $(10 \div 2) \times 45 = 225$ tons required.

We note in this case that 22.5 tons loaded 49′ *abaft* the tipping center will increase the draft aft by 1″, no change taking place forward.

Tabulated information on the draft and trim effect due to loading, discharging, or shifting cargo or ballast is of much practical value on board ship.

As a suggestion, such information might be calculated for the light and load drafts, the necessary correction for an intermediate draft being estimated and properly applied.

A convenient form of tabulating this data in the case of the ship's *ballast* or *bunker* tanks might be laid down as follows:

EFFECT ON DRAFT DUE TO FILLING TANKS

Fore Peak . . . . sinks 10″ forward; rises 3″ aft.
No. 1 D.B. . . . . "   8″   "   "   2″ "
No. 8 D.B. . . . . rises 3″   "   sinks 6″ "
Etc.

Similarly, the effect due to loading, say, 100 tons of cargo in the center of each hold might be arranged as a table.

CRITERIA OF STABILITY

The following recommendations were drawn up by the American Marine Standards Committee:

a) When subjected to a steady wind abeam of 55 miles an hour for ocean and coastwise vessels (somewhat less for vessels in protected waters) the list should not be such as to immerse more than one-half of the freeboard, or greater than 7°.

b) When all of the passengers who can do so crowd over to one side of the ship, the list must not be such as to immerse more than one-half of the freeboard, or in excess of 7°.

c) When any two adjacent compartments on one side are flooded due to damage, the list must not be such as to immerse more than one-half of the freeboard, or greater than 7°.

d) To reduce probability of shifting of bulk cargoes, the metacentric height (*GM*) should not be so great as to cause the ship to have a complete period roll of less than 10 seconds. The period of roll is defined as the time required for a complete cycle, as from starboard to port and back to starboard again. (*This is the double rolling period. The period mentioned in these pages is the single period, or half of that here quoted.*)

e) In light conditions, vessels with double bottoms must not have a negative metacentric height; other vessels must have a metacentric height of at least one-half foot.

f) A ship should have sufficient stability to prevent an excessive heel in the early stages of flooding of any of the main compartments.

g) A ship should have sufficient stability to prevent an undue angle of leeward roll, if the vessel has been disabled due to loss of rudder or breakdown of propelling machinery, and lies in the trough of the sea during a hurricane.

h) The metacentric height should not be such as to give the ship a natural period of roll which will be liable to synchronize with the period of the waves likely to be met on the route and service for which she is designed.

SYMPTOMS ATTENDING A *TENDER* OR *CRANK* STABILITY CONDITION

(A) Amount of heel caused by a beam wind.

(B) Amount of heel caused by putting the helm over at full speed.

(C) Amount of heel caused (in case of small ships) by slings of cargo hanging overside from derrick heads.

(D) Amount of heel caused by small parcels of cargo stowed on one side of ship.

(E) Ship for no apparent reason takes a list or lists from side to side.

How to Deal with a Tender Ship. The most junior ship's officer should know how to deal with an unstable vessel. This condition can generally be diagnosed before it becomes serious, as the ship herself will give warning that something is amiss by taking a list or listing from side to side for no apparent reason. The following suggestions for dealing with this situation may be useful:

(1) See that all deck openings on ship's sides and lower deck openings near ship's sides are closed and water-tight, so that, in event of increasing list, such openings will not become submerged.

(2) Do no try to correct list of an unstable vessel by shifting weight from low to high side, as this will cause a sudden heel to opposite side with probably increasing list.

(3) Generally, it is not practicable in an emergency, such as a considerable list at sea through instability, to reduce weight above the center of gravity by shifting coal, cargo, or equipment to a lower level, or by jettisoning; but anything which can be done in that respect improves ship's condition. If a deck-load is carried it is usually practicable, because of ship's list (if the situation warrants) to throw overboard part or whole of such load.

(4) If any D.B. tanks containing oil or fresh water are partly full and the situation warrants, such tanks should be filled to capacity with water ballast. This will increase stability in two ways: added weight of water will lower center of gravity and the completely full tank or tanks will obviate the detrimental effect of free liquid surfaces on vessel's *GM*. Of course, if any D.B. ballast tanks are only partly full, these should be completely filled before sacrificing fresh water or oil.

(5) Any D.B. tanks available should be filled with water ballast, commencing with smallest and longitudinally divided tanks. More than one tank should not be filled at same time, unless they are of small dimensions and longitudinally divided; the more tanks with free surfaces, the greater will be the detrimental effect on the *GM*.

(6) A large tank should not be filled whether divided or not, unless it is evident that free liquid surface created will not endanger the vessel.

(7) If a vessel's tanks are undivided, generally those at her extreme ends (because of their limited breadth) are safest to run up first.

(8) Peak tanks, if well below center of gravity of ship and cargo, will be safe to run up; their small breadth minimizes adverse effect on the *GM* due to free water surfaces.

(9) Detrimental effect of free liquid surfaces is greatest when displacement is least and least when displacement is greatest.

(10) Closing water-tight door to shaft tunnel or tunnels and filling with water, if situation warrants, is a safe procedure. Breadth of tunnel being small, effect of free water on *GM* would be negligible.

(11) Running water into empty holds of an unstable or tender vessel will give such water an absolute free surface and consequent effect on *GM* may cause disaster.

(12) Be careful with a vessel in dry-dock. When she takes the blocks or is about to refloat, there will be a period of possible instability. All shores should not be removed until ship is afloat when undocking and some shores should be in position as soon as, or before, she takes blocks when docking. Dry-dock managers usually see to this but there is at least one instance of a large vessel taking a considerable list due to removal of shores before ship was fully afloat. Incidentally, in one such case ship's chief engineer was wrongly blamed for the occurrence on the ground that he emptied one small boiler while vessel was in dock.

USEFUL FORMULAE

1. $GM = KM - KG$ (ship upright). KM = height of metacenter above keel, and KG = height of center of gravity above keel.

2. $\sqrt{GM} = .22b \div t$. b = breadth of vessel, and t = single period of roll in seconds.

3. $KB = .55\,d$ (ship upright). KB = center of buoyancy above keel, and d = mean draft. (A close approximation in cargo steamers.)

4. $BM = I \div V$. I = moment of inertia of water-plane about fore-and-aft axis, and V = volume of displacement.

5. $BM = .08\,b^2 \div d$. b = moulded breadth of vessel, and d = mean draft. (A close approximation in cargo steamers.)

6. $KM = KB + BM.$

7. $LGM = (LBM + KB) - KG.$

8. $LBM = I \div V.$ $I =$ moment of inertia of water-plane about transverse axis, and $V =$ volume of displacement.

9. $I.T.M. = (LGM \times W) \div (12 \times \text{Length}).$ $W =$ displacement in tons, and Length = that between perpendiculars.

10. $T.P.I. = (\text{Area of water-plane}) \div (12 \times 35).$

11. Area of water-plane = Length $\times$ Breadth $\times$ Coefficient of fineness.

12. $GG_1 = (w \times d) \div W.$ $GG_1 =$ shift of center of gravity (in feet); $w =$ weight shifted; $d =$ distance weight is shifted; and $W =$ displacement (in tons).

13. Distance to transversely shift a given weight to bring ship upright: $d = (GM \times \tan \text{heel} \times W) \div w.$

Buoyancy and Stability after Damage. Stability under normal conditions has already been discussed. In general it may be said that modern ships are so designed that lack of stability at sea can only be attributed to negligence, for even the most rudimentary understanding of the subject will suffice to insure safety if put into practice. However, when water is admitted into a vessel as the result of damage an evaluation of the situation and the corrective measures available becomes imperative. A sound decision must be made but there is no time for lengthy mathematical calculations nor can the factors necessary for these calculations be accurately ascertained.

EFFECTS OF ADMISSION OF WATER INTO SHIP

1. Into a central watertight compartment, through being holed below the water-line. Here the vessel's draft increases until the displacement of the undamaged part of the ship is equal to the displacement before the damage. This condition lowers the CG so that the vessel has a greater GM than when she was undamaged.

2. Into a compartment above a watertight flat. The effect of the increased buoyant volume below the watertight flat is to lower the center of buoyancy and to decrease the GM.

3. Flooding an end compartment. Serious consequences are liable to follow if compartment is a large one, such as:

a) A change of trim which may render ship unmanageable;

b) Increased immersion through the water entering other spaces;

c) Pressure on bulkheads and hatches, much increased if ship is damaged forward and making way through the water;

d) Transverse stability may be adversely affected.

4. Flooding a compartment containing cargo. Buoyancy remaining depends upon volume and permeability of the goods.

5. Entrance through a deck opening. The effect upon stability may be serious because the water will accumulate in the lower corner of a compartment and result in an increasing list. If the freeboard is insufficient, capsizing may be the consequence, through the shifting of weight on board, or foundering is accelerated by bringing side or deck openings under water. With ample freeboard, however, a maximum heel will be reached when the righting moment increases more rapidly than the rate at which the inflow increases the heeling moment, provided weights already on board do not shift. If the inflow of water continues from this point, the ship will tend to return to the upright, and, generally, whether the vessel remains afloat or founders will depend upon her amount of reserve buoyancy.

The following *rule of thumb* is used to determine the *danger angle* for permanent list beyond which a vessel may capsize. This *danger angle* may be assumed to occur at one-half the angle of the maximum arm of the intact stability curve for the condition of loading before damage. Fig. 11 depicts the curve of static stability for a vessel in a load condition *M*. The Maximum Righting Arm is developed ordinarily when the angle of heel is 34°; accordingly, the danger angle is 1/2 this figure, or 17°. At a permanent list of 17° danger of capsizing would thus be imminent.

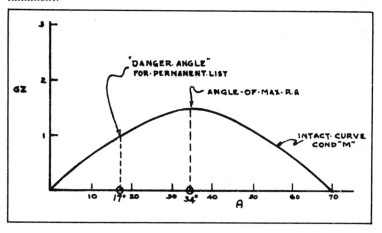

Fig. 11. Static Stability Curve.

The vessel would be in danger of capsizing sooner than this:—
(1) in case of bad weather;
(2) if the deck edge was going under in the roll;
(3) if flooding was progressing;
(4) if list was increasing;
(5) if the ship was *logy*;
(6) if the original *GM* when intact was poor as indicated by *lolling*.

The deck edge going under on the roll is not only evidence of decreasing freeboard and therefore less reserve buoyancy but the righting arm, *GZ*, is very rapidly diminished from the time at which the deck edge is immersed. In other words, the maximum righting moment is attained just before the deck edge is immersed.

If the vessel had a permanent list before being holed the situation is particularly hazardous. This is true as at any angle of heel the upsetting moment due to the off-center weight exceeds the restoring moment, there is no residual dynamic stability. A ship with a permanent list may be *stiff* (in other words have reasonably good *GM* at the position of equilibrium) and yet have poor overall stability. Ships with relatively small initial *GM* are susceptible to this condition.

A ship which has a *logy* roll has a low *GM* and a knowledge of this relation between period of roll and *GM* is useful in giving one the general feel of the ship in relation to her stability as she rolls. However, *timing the roll* is of little practical use in evaluating damaged stability. As pointed out under the discussion of normal conditions the ship's natural period of roll (for small amplitudes) is constant, regardless of amplitude, and varies inversely as the square root of the *GM*. This is so in still water. It is not true if: (1) there is loose water in the ship, (2) the ship is rolling in a seaway, subject to wind and wave action.

Free surface is the most serious and dangerous factor to contend with in a damaged ship. When compartments within the ship are partially full of liquid which is unimpeded in moving as the ship heels, the surface of the liquid tends to remain parallel to the waterline, and is termed free surface. The effect of free surface is to reduce *BM* and *GM*, and can be thus considered to cause a drop in the metacenter. This decrease in *GM* and *BM* is determined only by the extent of the free surface and is independent of depth of liquid and also of the location of the liquid in the ship. Thus a given area of loose water at a given angle of heel will cause the same reduction in *GM* whether it is forward or aft, high or low, on the centerline or off the centerline. This is true as long as the boundaries of the compartment are intact.

If the ship is holed at the waterline, the seas are free to rush in and out of the hole as the ship rolls in a seaway, and the compartments affected, if not completely filled, are said to be *partially flooded, and in free communication with the sea.*

The dynamic effect of the seas rushing in and out of the ship, and the fact that as the ship rolls toward the damaged side, more water is free to come into the ship, tends to increase free surface, list, and bodily sinkage, and aggravates the situation of the damaged vessel. Although these factors are not susceptible of ready calculation, there is always a loss in *GM* and overall stability in this case. Hence, every effort should be made to restrict free communication to the sea after such damage, even though it is impossible to pump out the affected area.

If a considerable quantity of solid matter in a compartment projects through and above the surface of the loose water (for example cargo or turbines in an engine room), and if this solid matter is made fast so that it does not float around and is not permeable itself, then the free surface area and free surface effect will be diminished accordingly.

Lolling may be defined as the listing of a ship with negative initial stability, but with the restoration of positive righting arm at some angle of heel, due to increased breadth of waterplane or of pocketing of free surface. A lolling ship will list with equal facility to either port or starboard, and in a seaway may *flop* from one side to the other. This is a very dangerous condition and may be prevented by proper ballasting and filling fuel oil tanks with water ballast as the tanks are emptied.

Before arriving at a final evaluation and taking corrective measures we must consider the structural damage. Here it is advantageous to think of the ship as a long beam or girder. Its principal strength members are at the top and bottom, where the greatest stresses occur, and these top and bottom flanges are tied together by side-webs. The top flange consists of the main deck plating, especially the deck stringers, plus the sheer strakes of the side plating and any continuous deck girders. The bottom flange consists of the bottom plating, including flat keel, garboard strakes, *B* strakes, bilge strakes, etc., plus the vertical keel and any continuous longitudinal girders in the way of the bottom. If an inner bottom is fitted it also contributes to the lower flange. The transverse frames and continuous transverse bulkheads also contribute greatly to the strength of the hull girder by tieing its various members together, stiffening them, and preventing buckling when under compression.

If the skin of the ship is ruptured and flooding follows, the hydrostatic pressures formerly exerted on the shell plating are now placed on the bulkheads of the flooded compartments. Flooding water will exert a considerable upward pressure against the overhead deck of a flooded compartment if the deck in question is some distance below the waterline. This pressure will be just as great, possibly greater, if there is an air bubble trapped above the flooding water, and will be equal, in tons per square foot, to the depth below the external waterline times 1/35. Therefore give some thought to the problem of shoring weakened decks downward as well as upward, and to the consequences of opening a hatch, scuttle, or manhole over a flooded compartment.

In arriving at a final decision as to the ship's condition and measures to be undertaken, all of the above must be considered in conjunction with the *feel of the ship*—her behavior. In general, a logy ship, lazy to return from deep rolls, is in serious condition. Then too, the weather impending, and course to destination versus course to nearest haven, condition of engineering plant, remaining uncontaminated fuel and reserve feed water all are important factors which must be taken into account.

Hydrostatics. When a solid body is completely immersed in a fluid at rest, the body is buoyed up by a vertical force equal in magnitude to the weight of the fluid displaced.

The pressure on a submerged body is proportional to its depth in the liquid and acts at right angles to the surface of the object. Each square foot of shell surface is subject to a pressure of 1/35 of a ton for every foot of depth of liquid (i.e., 64 lbs. per ft. of depth). The water pressure is applied to the shell and transmitted through the frames, decks and bulkheads. Although the horizontal pressures of the water exerted on each side of the ship cancel each other, the force still acts upon the hull. The decks, transverse framing and bulkheads prevent lateral crushing of the hull by the horizontal pressure of the water.

If the shell of the ship is ruptured and flooding follows, the hydrostatic pressures formerly exerted on the shell plating are now placed upon the bulkheads of the flooded compartments. This is why bulkheads require stiffening to prevent them from bulging, and why bulkheads that are farther below the waterline are thicker, require more stiffening and are given higher test pressures. Flooding water will exert a considerable upward pressure against the overhead deck of a flooded compartment if the deck in question is some distance below the waterline. This pressure will be undiminished if there is an air bubble trapped above the flooding water. Hydrostatic pressures are similarly imposed upon bulkheads and decks by the contents of intact fuel and water tanks—an important factor to be considered when filling these tanks with a line under pressure.

CORRECTIVE MEASURES

In case of widespread flooding following damage the proper steps to take are outlined below.

1. Establish Flooding Boundaries by plugging holes, shoring weakened closures, and shoring the decks and bulkheads subjected to heavy pressures, even if they are apparently intact. At the same time, steps should be going forward to—

2. Suppress Free Surface and at the same time if the situation is serious—

3. Jettison Topside Weights from the centerline or from both sides symmetrically to improve *GM* and overall stability as well as freeboard.

4. After Positive GM Has Been Assured by suppressing free surface and jettisoning, then correct remaining list which is due to inclining moment of off-center flooding by one of the following methods:

a. Jettison from Down Side Only to produce a restoring moment. This also helps *GM* and freeboard.

b. Transfer Liquids from intact wing tanks to any empty double bottom tanks on the centerline, one at a time. Any further creation of free surface effect, such as sluicing tanks from side to side of the ship, leaving double bottoms slack, or pumping down several tanks at one time must be avoided.

c. Pump Liquid Overboard from intact wing tanks on the down side.

5. Correct Excessive Trim by transferring water from one peak tank to another, or by pumping out the down peak tank, and then counterflooding the peak tank at the up end.

The prime effort is on getting water out of the ship. In suppressing free surface, the pumping capacity of the ship's drainage systems must be utilized to maximum effectiveness. This generally means allocating the capacity of the pumps first against those compartments which have suffered the *least* damage, then against the next smallest leakage, and so on up to the limit of the system. In this way pumping capacity is not thrown away on damage that is beyond its ability.

The steps to insure best chances of reaching port may be summarized as:

1. *Slow down: don't drive the ship.*

2. *Adjust course to minimize pitching; do not meet the sea head-on, or run before a following sea; tack if necessary.*

3. *If damage is critical, head for the nearest safe haven: if necessary, beach the ship. Salvage crews can often save a beached ship, seldom a sunken one.*

4. *Shore between decks if stanchions are damaged.*

5. *Shore against panting structure to brace it out.*

Chapter 16

FIRE

The three things necessary for fire are: *Fuel, Oxygen,* and *Ignition temperature.*

When all three are present, fire occurs. Remove one and the fire is out.

Successful fire fighting is the removal of any one of these three factors. Removing the fuel would consist of jettisoning the material or shutting off a fuel line. You can take away the oxygen either by smothering or blanketing the fuel, or by cooling the area down to below the ignition point. If you do either of these things, and therefore eliminate one factor, the fire will go out.

GENERAL MEASURES

1. Consider the fire to be serious. Sound the general alarm and call all hands.

2. Locate and isolate the compartment on fire.

3. Start smothering agencies, steam or carbon dioxide.

4. Batten down all hatches, cover all ventilators, stop ventilating systems, close slop chutes and ash chutes, fire screen doors and port holes.

5. Lay vessel to, deck fire to leeward, hold fire to windward.

6. Detail men to clear and swing out boats.

7. Make dangerous cargo ready to jettison.

Three Classes of Fire

Three different types of fire that may break out aboard ship.

A *Class A* fire is one in *ordinary combustible materials* such as bedding, clothing, wood, canvas, rope, paper, etc. The cooling effect of water will take care of this type of fire. On smaller fires, the standard portable extinguishers may be used.

A *Class B* fire means fire in *inflammable liquids* such as gasoline, oils, grease, paint, turpentine, etc. The thing to do here is to smother the fire so as to exclude oxygen. This can be done by the use of foam, fog-foam, dry chemical (bicarbonate of soda), CO_2 or steam. The cooling of *combustible gases* below ignition temperatures will also solve the problem. Fog is used for this.

To Prevent Fires. Put out cigarettes, cigars and matches; remove all greasy and oily rags; eliminate all breeding places of fire; value the benefits of good housekeeping; educate all hands in fire-prevention methods; never use any but safety matches aboard ship; training in fire fighting pays dividends; fire prevention should be an everyday precaution; inspect equipment frequently; remember your exact duties in fire and boat drills; encourage interest in—*safety always.*

Fire Fighting

The three basic steps in Fire Fighting are: *Locate! Confine! Extinguish!*

Determine quickly the following facts:

1. Where the fire is (not necessarily where the smoke is coming from).

2. What is burning.

3. What is the extent of the fire.

4. What combustibles are in the immediate vicinity—in all surrounding spaces and in the compartments above and below.

5. What vents and other channels there are that would facilitate the spread of the fire.

6. What is the best means to:

    1st—prevent the spread of the fire;

    2nd—put the fire out;

    3rd—avoid affecting stability and buoyancy.

Heat transmission can take place in three ways; radiation, conduction and convection. In radiation heat is radiated in all directions and no medium is required. Heat is transmitted through solids (and liquids and gases as well) by conduction, that is by the molecules of the substance being in contact. In convection portions of liquids and gases that are heated to a higher temperature than the rest of their mass become lighter in weight and move upward into the cooler portions above. These heated gases may be, and often are, carried by drafts to ignite combustibles at some distance away.

Cooling is the commonest method of fire extinguishment. The cooling quality of water is tremendously increased when it has been converted into vapor, a conversion now achieved with fog nozzles. These break up each gallon of water into millions of particles; and as a result, the vastly increased total surface for the absorption of heat makes fog an extremely efficient cooling agent. In addition to its capacity for cooling fire, fog has another virtue in that it dilutes combustible vapors, and when turned to steam by the heat of the fire it forces air away from the fire, thereby removing the oxygen needed to support combustion. Fog is also a more desirable agent than water in situations where water damage must be held to a minimum. Fog is a poor conductor of electricity and can therefore be used on electrical equipment though, if available, carbon dioxide is of course preferable. Not the least of the advantages of the use of fog is the protection afforded the fire fighter by means of the screen it forms between him and the fire. This fog screen protects the fire fighter from the intense heat, and as a result he has greatly increased mobility. Not only does fog dilute vapors, as pointed out above, but to a certain extent it also washes fumes and smoke from the atmosphere.

Two general points on fire fighting. The first concerns the effect of solid streams of water on a shipboard fire as demonstrated in the case of the *Normandie* and numerous others. Bear in mind that a 2 1/2

Fire Fighting Chart			
Combustible	Type fire	Extent	Extinguishing agents
Woodwork, bedding, clothes, combustible stores	A	Small	1. Portable CO_2 extinguishers. 2. Solid water stream. 3. Low-velocity fog. 4. Foam.
		Large	1. High-velocity fog. 2. Solid water stream. 3. Foam. 4. CO_2 (fixed system)
Electrical and radio apparatus	C	Small	1. (De-energize affected circuits). 2. Portable CO_2 extinguishers. 3. High-velocity fog.
		Large	1. (De-energize affected circuits). 2. Portable CO_2 extinguishers or CO_2 hose reel system. 3. High-velocity fog. 4. Foam application.
Paints, spirits, inflammable stores	B	Small	1. Portable CO_2 extinguishers. 2. Low-velocity fog. 3. Foam.
		Large	1. CO_2 (fixed system). 2. High velocity fog. 3. Foam. 4. Installed sprinkling system. 5. Steam smothering.
Explosives	-----	Small	1. Water immersion. 2. Magazine sprinkling. 3. Solid water stream.
		Large	1. Water immersion. 2. Magazine sprinkling and flooding. 3. Solid water stream.
Gasoline and kerosene	B	Small	1. Portable CO_2 extinguishers. 2. Low-velocity fog. 3. Foam. 4. Fog-foam. 5. Installed fog spray (to prevent spread).
		Large	1. Foam. 2. Fog-foam. 3. High-velocity fog. 4. Fog-spray. 5. CO_2 (fixed system). 6. Installed sprinkling system (to prevent spread). 7. Water curtains (to prevent spread).
Fuel oil and Diesel oil	B	Small	1. Portable CO_2 extinguishers. 2. Low-velocity fog. 3. Foam.
		Large	1. Foam. 2. Fog-foam. 3. High-velocity fog. 4. CO_2 (fixed system). 5. Steam smothering.
Incendiary bombs	-----	-----	1. (Throw overboard). 2. Solid water stream. 3. High-velocity fog. 4. Sand. 5. Immersion in water.
Films, celluloid, etc	A	-----	1. Water immersion. 2. Solid water stream. 3. High-velocity fog.

Extinguishing agents are listed in the order of their preferred use.
They act in the follow manner: (1) Water—wetting and cooling, (2) Fog—wetting, cooling, smothering, (3) Foam—smothering, (4) Fog-foam smothering, cooling, (5) CO_2—smothering, (6) Steam—smothering, (7) Sand—smothering.

inch hose under 100 pounds pressure with a one inch outlet delivers one ton of water every minute. The effect on a vessel which is light, improperly ballasted or which has much free surface in its tanks is evident. Of course *an ounce of prevention is worth a pound of cure* for when a fire has started there isn't time for pressing up ballast tanks. But when a municipal fire department has taken over the actual fire fighting the ship's officers should immediately take steps to insure proper stability. The great advantage of fog is particularly noteworthy here for the effectiveness of a given weight of water is increased at least 25 times due to the increase in exposed surface and in addition a considerable portion of this fog is turned into steam which is then carried off in the form of vapor.

The second point concerns protection of men actually engaged at the fire. They should wear sufficient clothing, including gloves, to avoid burns. The asbestos suit is protection against flash burns but if it gets wet the wearer may be scalded inside it. One or two men should assist the nozzle man, on opposite sides, and all these men should be covered by fog to cool the air and absorb fumes and vapors. Fog is particularly effective in absorbing the fumes of anhydrous ammonia. Proper ventilation is a most important consideration for the hot gases and steam must be given some opening ahead of the fire fighters by which these gases may escape to the open. If this is not provided there is danger of envelopment from the rear.

In entering a compartment men should wear oxygen masks and have a steel-wire life line attached.

In a smoke filled or flaming compartment men should keep low, better air being nearer the deck, and there is less danger of flash burns from explosions. Watch out for carbon monoxide.

THE ALL-PURPOSE NOZZLE

The all-purpose nozzle is the basic fitting for fog equipment, the applicators being inserted into it. Note the placement of the holes in the low velocity head shown in Fig. 1 to see how the paired streams come together under pressure and thus break up into fog particles.

The All-Purpose Nozzle is controlled for three operations by a single valve; it can project either a solid stream, a fog or be shut off by this one valve. To put the nozzle in operation the valve handle is pulled back from the *shut* position to the *fog* position, which is half way back to the *open*, or solid stream, position. The fire fighter can remove the high velocity nozzle tip Fig. 2A. and insert the applicator Fig. 2B. if a low velocity is desired.* As already stated the small outlets drilled at converging angles in the head or tip break down the water stream into fog particles by impinging the streams on one another. The fine particles of water in the low velocity fog will remain suspended in the air producing little disturbance over inflammable liquids while absorbing heat and cooling the fire. On the other hand when entering a compartment or passageway the greater force of the high velocity fog will

* These applicators are made in lengths up to 12 feet.

Fig. 1. All-Purpose Fog Nozzle.

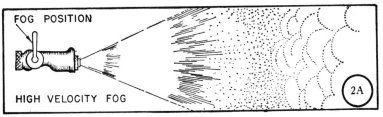

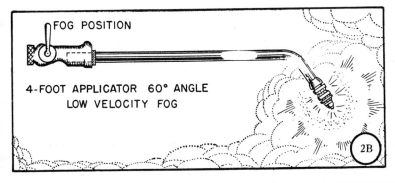

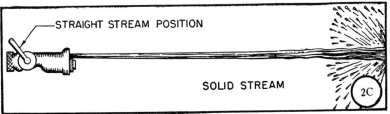

Fig. 2. Fog Nozzle and Tips.

force gases and fumes ahead of the operator, and since it is an integral part of the all-purpose nozzle there is greater freedom of movement in directing it either for fog or a solid stream.

For both the low-velocity head and the high-velocity tip, the water pressure is the same and for best results this should be maintained as close to 100 pounds as possible. Both operate acceptably with a water pressure down to 60 pounds.

Note that there is a separate outlet for the solid stream so that even though the applicator is attached an instant shift may be made to the solid stream by means of the lever.

FOAM

Foam is commonly used as a fire extinguishing agent on tankers carrying gasoline or other petroleum products. It is applied with a hose and nozzle much the same as is water.

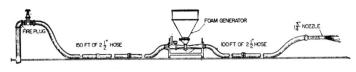

A CHEMICAL FOAM EQUIPMENT (CONTINUOUS-TYPE GENERATOR)

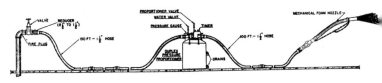

B MECHANICAL FOAM EQUIPMENT (DUPLEX PRESSURE PROPORTIONER)

FIGURE 3

Because oils and grease burn only on the surface, the smothering method is the most satisfactory with such fires. On oil fires in particular foam provides a tight cover and isolates the fire from its source of oxygen. In addition to providing cover, foam retards the formation of vapor on the surface of oil and it has some cooling effect because of its water content. Furthermore, the foam cover remains intact long enough to prevent rekindling, such as would occur if oxygen again reached the surface while sufficient heat was radiated from surrounding surfaces.

The foam is generated by mixing two chemicals, bicarbonate of soda and aluminum sulfate, with water by means of a foam generator. The two chemicals are stored in cans usually of 50 pounds each, the aluminum sulfate cans being marked *A* powder and the bicarbonate of soda cans marked *B* powder. The generator is connected into the fire hose line at a safe distance from the fire. The water is turned on and the buckets of *A* and *B* powder are dumped into the hoppers of the generator. The two powders mix with the water as it passes through the generator and are converted into a thick foam which, when applied to a petroleum fire, spreads a blanket of tough foam bubbles and cuts off the air from the burning liquid, thus starving the fire.

When using foam in machinery spaces it must be borne in mind that it does not run well on solid matter and may pile up in pockets. In this case CO_2 for smothering and fog for cooling and smothering is indicated. If the compartment is cooled to a point at which oil, or other matter, cannot vaporize combustion will stop.

On first thought machinery spaces seem to be all metal but electrical insulation, stores and the oil film over all adds fuel to the fire when the heat becomes high enough for vaporization.

There are two kinds of foam which have proven of great value, they are: Chemical foam and Mechanical foam.

Chemical Foam is produced by adding the dry powder foaming agent to the water stream in a chemical foam generator, Fig. 3. It is discharged through a 1-3/4 inch plain tip nozzle. Chemical foam is tougher and longer lasting than mechanical foam, but does not flow around obstructions as easily. This foam powder is not subject to freezing. Chemical foam cannot be used to produce fog foam.

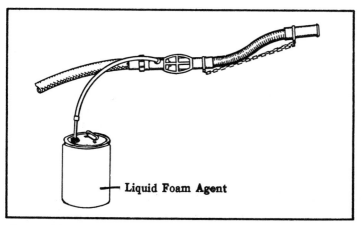

Liquid Foam Agent

FIG. 4. MECHANICAL-FOAM NOZZLE SHOWING USE OF PICK-UP TUBE.

Mechanical Foam is produced by adding the liquid foaming agent to the water stream. The foam does not form until air is introduced to the mixture through a special mechanical foam nozzle (NPU Nozzle). The mixture is then discharged as air-filled bubbles. Mechanical foam makes an effective cover but is not as strong and durable as chemical foam. This means that it is not so effective for highly inflammable substances such as gasoline. However, because it flows freely, mechanical foam will pass readily around obstructions and can be applied more quickly. Because of this, mechanical foam is the better of the two foams to use in engine room and machinery spaces. It is possible to use a mixture of water and mechanical foam liquid through an applicator to form fog-foam. This will give a combined cooling and blanketing effect.

Whether the fire fighter applies chemical or mechanical foam, he employs the same technique, since both kinds of foam should be spread upon a fire in such a way as to avoid undue agitation of the burning oil or gasoline. Therefore, he plays the foam against a bulkhead or other vertical structure if that is practicable and as speedily as possible; he aims the foam stream sufficiently above the deck, in order to break its force before it flows over the fire. Since the rate of application is important he places several such streams in operation as quickly as possible. Applied in this way, foam will flow more gently. The fire fighter continues this operation until the burning area is completely covered with a foam blanket thick enough to smother the fire. Ordinarily, a covering 6 inches thick is sufficient. For gasoline fires it may be necessary to apply a thicker cover. No exact rule for the thickness of the foam blanket can be formulated, except that the fire fighter should use as much foam as is necessary to put out the fire, bearing in mind that the roll and pitch of the ship will effect the foam blanket. Foam is not effective on alcohol fires.

STEAM

Steam as an extinguishing agent is applied through installed flooding systems. Generally speaking, steam is not effective on Class A fires; the combustibles leave embers that cannot be extinguished by a blanket of steam on top of the fire, and the steam does not penetrate sufficiently. In the absence of other extinguishing mediums, however, steam can be used to retard the propagation of flame. For class A fires a penetrating cooling medium, such as water, should be applied with pressure to break down the masses of embers for quicker extinguishment.

On class B fires, steam acts in a manner similar to that of fog, but with very much less cooling effect. Fog cools the fire as it absorbs heat and is converted to steam, and the steam then acts as a smothering agent. This effect is achieved because steam displaces the oxygen of the air which is required for combustion. Steam would not be used if foam or fog were available, because of the quantity required and because it renders a compartment untenable.

Steam is most effective with cased goods, canned goods, barrels or drums where the steam vapor has easy access and can displace the atmosphere. With loosely packed substances such as cereals and baled combustibles steam may have no effect even after weeks of application as the outside saturation protects the material until dried out with conditions existing inside that may cause a new outburst of flame.

Steam is especially dangerous in a coal bunker fire as pockets of gas may be sealed inside which may result in an explosion and a resumption of fire. In this case surface ventilation and the removal of the coal is the method indicated, not steam smothering.

APPLICATION OF THE SOLID STREAM OF WATER

When a fire rages over a large area, as it may on the relatively unobstructed weather deck, the fire fighter may not be able to get close enough to apply fog or foam. He must then resort to a *solid stream of water*, one that will reach across the space between him and the fire with force enough to carry large quantities of water. He relies upon the volume of water and its driving force to beat back the fire, and thus bring down the intensity and permit closer approach. The solid stream would be useful as a means of sweeping burning oil over the side, if a greater hazard would not be created thereby. It would also be useful on occasion to keep burning oil on the surface of the sea away from the vessel. Applied in a low trajectory, the solid stream has a more or less slight emulsifying effect on the surface of viscous oils, such as fuel oil. For deep-seated fire in class A combustibles the solid stream is indicated.

Much of the technique to be adopted in fighting a fire with a solid stream of water is a matter of exercising common sense. The fire fighter realizes that his first consideration is the extinguishment of the fire, but he realizes also that he would not be much of a help in accomplishing this, if he were overcome by heat or fumes. For this reason, if for no other, the nozzle men are advised to bend forward as they approach a fire, and keep their faces as close as practicable to the deck, where the heat is somewhat less intense. The rushing stream has a cooling effect and creates a void into which fresh air is drawn. When they stop moving forward, they should kneel on one knee, in order to breathe on a level closer to the deck. When circumstances warrant it, a fog stream is either played between the nozzle men and the fire, or over them, to serve as a shield as they move forward and approach the fire.

In bringing hose lines into action, the fire fighter considers first the direction in which the greatest exposure or hazard lies. If he can do so, he begins operations between the fire and this hazard. From this point first, and then from others, water is directed on the fire with the all purpose nozzle, which permits the fire fighter to use the fog or the solid stream intermittently; he changes from one to the other as circumstances warrant. In doing so, he remembers that the solid stream is the most efficient for getting water to the seat of a fire in class A materials. The surrounding hazards are protected with fog or, if necessary, with the solid stream. When the fire has been extinguished the fire fighter stands by to watch for rekindling.

Class A fires in compartments most often are attacked from within the compartment. In such situations, if a fire fighter has to enter through a hatch or has to advance more than a few paces beyond a door leading into the compartment, he may have to wear an oxygen breathing apparatus. With this apparatus on he could work safely in the smoke and fumes; and approach the fire closely enough to use the solid stream to the best advantage. His purpose would be to get close enough to the fire in order to direct the stream for a thorough wetting of the combustibles, and also to break down masses that would otherwise burn longer because the water would not penetrate them. For the achievement of this result, fog would not have sufficient drive, and it would remain chiefly over the surface. It would be used, however, to cool the compartment for the comfort and safety of the fire fighter, and to prevent surface propagation of flame.

A large stream carries farther and penetrates better than does a small stream. Therefore, when a quantity of water is to be delivered to one spot, it is better to use one large hose than several smaller ones, even though the quantity of water delivered is the same.

Chemical or mechanical foam in sufficient quantity would form a cover over the class A combustibles, but beneath it they would smolder for some time. If, however, these combustibles are finely divided materials, the foam blanket can be used, but water would be more effective.

With a fireplug pressure of 100 pounds per square inch, two lengths of 2 1/2-inch hose with a nozzle having a 1-inch outlet will discharge 250 gallons per minute, and have an effective reach of 75 feet. With the same fireplug pressure two lengths of 1 1/2-inch hose with a nozzle having a 5/8-inch outlet will discharge 94 gallons of water per minute, and have an effective reach of 65 feet. With a fireplug pressure of 50 pounds per square inch, two lengths of 1 1/2-inch hose with a nozzle having a 5/8-inch outlet will discharge 65 gallons per minute, and have an effective reach of 32 feet. When fog is used the discharge is materially reduced.

Notwithstanding the fact that the fire fighter's job is to get the fire under control and put it out, he must remember that every gallon of water he puts aboard his vessel contributes toward an increase in mean draft, which is nearly always accompanied by a change in trim and the development of a list. A nozzle delivering 250 gallons of water a minute puts over 60 tons of water into the vessel every hour—a ton a minute. Consequently, it is incumbent upon the fire fighter to use the solid stream wisely, and further, to see to it that the water he puts aboard is properly confined, so far as it is possible for him to do so. He must, therefore, close doors, hatches, manholes, and the stops in ventilation ducts and voice tubes. In short, he must take every possible precaution when he uses the solid stream of water, if the stability and the safety of his vessel is not to be jeopardized. He must be alert to the situation and quick to use pumps and drains.

CLASS *A* FIRES

Passenger and Cargo Vessels. Wooden furniture, curtains, drapes etc., are such obviously dangerous combustibles that it is unnecessary to dwell on them. However, there are other combustibles which being built into the ship are seldom thought of as such. Thus the incredibly fast spread of fire on the *Morro Castle* gave rise to many wild and sensational rumors, from that of arson by Cuban Communists to lightning having set the fuel tanks afire. But an oiler, though in broken English, gave the most simple and thoughtful explanation of all, "It was a very de luxe ship, lots of paint and varnish. She burn much quickly."

Paint, varnish, turpentine, linseed oil, etc., will obviously burn in bulk. But paint having in it linseed oil, tung oil and most other mediums is a dangerous anomaly. When old and thoroughly dry it will not burn even when heated with a blowtorch, in fact it will hardly blister. Newer paint will brown and blister when heated with a blowtorch, but it will not burst into flame and burn. BUT paint on bulkheads in a burning compartment will not only burn furiously with a dense and poisonous smoke, it will propagate the fire from one compartment to another. What happens is that the paint on the bulkhead of the next compartment blisters and forms pockets of inflammable vapors arising from the partial decomposition of the organic mediums, such as linseed oil, in the paint. The blisters finally burst emitting jets of hot gases which ignite and burn vigorously.

Red lead and linseed oil primer is especially subject to this action. Zinc chromate and metallic aluminum in *leaf* form have greater fire resistant qualities. These primers can be used in a much thinner film and the thermal conductivity of the aluminum has the effect of dissipating the heat over a larger area, preventing the formation of blisters.

Linoleum consists largely of cork and burlap and if the surface has been waxed repeatedly it becomes an even greater fire hazard. Like paint it does not ignite readily, even under a blowtorch, but in a blazing compartment it burns rapidly, with a heavy and stifling smoke. Linoleum cement, especially when fresh, is highly inflammable.

Cork in slab form and as cork paint is used extensively as an insulating material around iceboxes, as sheathing and to prevent sweating. It burns readily, and makes a dense and suffocating smoke. Lagging on firemains, flushing lines, ventilation and fresh water lines may be covered with hair-felt and canvas to prevent sweating and to preserve temperatures. These are of course highly inflammable and fibre-glass insulation is generally used in new construction.

Sheathing of living spaces and of holds in refrigerated vessels is generally done with slab cork or hair-felt, often covered with sheet metal. This is a tremendous fire hazard.

Cooking fats such as butter, lard, oleomargarine, olive oil and salad oils are not only hazards in themselves but may be spilled onto wooden decks and make them more vulnerable to fire.

Fires in trunks, forced draft ducts and funnel casings are not normally sustained long enough to seriously injure the structure but must be carefully observed for heat conductivity.

When a cabin is burning it may be very dangerous to open the door as a sudden outrush of gas and fumes may result. Knocking a hole in a lower corner of the door and inserting a low pressure applicator would give very effective results.

On entering any smoke filled compartment it is advisable to crawl rather than walk as even when smoke is very dense there is generally a clear space of a few inches near the deck.

When putting a stream of water between crevices in the cargo care must be taken to keep clear of a sudden back rush of hot gases and steam which is likely when the stream hits the heart of the fire. This generation of steam is the best indication that one has hit the fire and the approach to this point is indicated by the rising temperature of any water than can be observed running off. When reaching for the seat of a fire one should bear in mind that high temperature from a ventilator does not necessarily indicate that the fire region is immediately beneath.

Hot gases and fumes rising from a fire in a confined space set up a circulation of air over the region and induce a down draft remote from the fire. It may be possible and to great advantage to get to the level of the fire or underneath it.

Remember that the hose line should lead you back to safety and get out at the first feeling of inertia, it is nature's warning. An unconscious man who must be rescued is not helping matters.

With fire in spaces where acids may be encountered be sure of adequate ventilation.

Nitrates evolve a terrific volume of hydrogen when burning with a consequent danger of rapid flame spread, particularly to leeward.

Procedure using Carbon Dioxide Installation (Mail Room):

1. Make certain there is no one in the compartment.

2. If possible close any openings, but do not delay release of carbon dioxide.

3. Go to cylinder room and open valve marked *Mail Room— Normally Closed.*

4. Pull *local control* handle releasing cylinders intended for Mail Room. Do not release the major control cylinder as this will cause the release of all cylinders.

5. In order to keep the fire under control discharge one cylinder once every four to six hours. The best guide is the fire itself. If smoke increases or bulkheads get warmer discharge gas oftener. The object is to keep the fire under control until arrival at port, and the supply of carbon dioxide is limited.

6. During the foregoing procedure and until arrival at port, keep all openings tightly closed in order to avoid loss of carbon dioxide.

7. Allow no one to enter the space until the atmosphere has been tested with a Flame Safety Lamp.

CLASS *B* FIRES

Procedure in case of small fire in Boiler Room or Engine Room using Carbon Dioxide Installation:

1. Pull control handle in break-glass pull box located next to the hose reel.

2. Lead out hose, which is already connected.

3. Remove as few floor plates as is necessary to gain access to the fire. Direct the gas at the nearest edge of the fire, moving the horn back and forth, chasing the flame as it recedes across the burning area until the fire is extinguished. *Do not direct gas at center of flame.* In case of bulkhead fire start at bottom and chase flame up.

4. Take care not to touch the extinguisher horn to any live electrical equipment.

5. Watch out for rekindling from hot bulkheads, etc.

6. After fire is out ventilate compartment thoroughly before allowing anyone to enter.

Procedure in case of serious bilge fire in boiler room:

1. Sound warning alarm and make certain everyone leaves the boiler room.

2. Close watertight door between boiler room and engine room.

Controls for the carbon dioxide system are located in the engine room adjacent to this door.

3. Open valve in control room marked *Boiler Room Bilge— Normally Closed* and pull the control handle in the break-glass pull box marked *Boiler Room Bilge-Cylinder Control.* (Note:—When the carbon dioxide system is operated as above a pressure-operated valve in the fuel oil line is closed and the blower circuits are automatically shut down.)

4. Test atmosphere with Flame Safety Lamp before again entering boiler room.

Methods found to be successful in fighting fires in machinery spaces may be summed up as follows:

1. Control the supply of air into the compartment.

2. Abandon the idea that volume of water from straight streams is an efficient fire-extinguishing agent for these fires.

3. In the control of ventilation, provide an escape vent from the top side of the compartment to the atmosphere to prevent an explosion from hot gases and provide a ready escape for those gases and steam generated during application of waterfog.

4. Provide foghead equipment, foam proportioners, or foam generators, foam nozzles, high velocity fog nozzles, and portable oxyacetylene burning equipment, and familiarize fire fighters with their use on board vessels.

TANK FIRES—CLASS *B*

Metal that is in contact with a liquid cannot be heated to a red heat and as long as water remains fluid it cannot be heated above 212°F. This indicates that tanks adjoining one on fire should be immediately filled with water to withdraw heat. However, it does not matter how combustible a liquid may be, if in bulk it can easily absorb heat from a bulkhead.

Moreover an oil tank may be burning furiously at the surface and yet, in its early stages, the temperature of the oil will be normal at a level a few inches from the surface. This heated layer may heat downward in the oil at a rate of 15 inches per hour.

When pressing up a burning tank to eliminate air space oil is preferable to water as the oil can do no harm while water introduced into oil which is at a high temperature will generate steam at the surface and cause a froth which has a rapid rate of combustion and a high flash factor by which the flame would be considerably increased.

CLASS *C* FIRE

Fire in electrical generator (turbo-electric drive) using carbon dioxide installation.

The method of combating a generator fire is much different from the usual method of combating fire because of (a) the long deceleration period, (b) leakage of air, (c) speed of the generator, and (d) the nature of the burning material which is slow-burning and incandescent. To overcome these difficulties it is essential to discharge a large volume of carbon dioxide into the ventilating ducts at the first instant of trouble.

After obtaining this fast initial discharge it is necessary to maintain this inert atmosphere during the deceleration. The extinguishing system as installed provides for this situation automatically.

FIRE EXTINGUISHERS

Hand portable fire extinguishers and semiportable fire extinguishing systems, as required by U.S. Coast Guard regulations, are named as to type unit as follows: Soda-acid, foam, carbon dioxide, dry chemical, pump tank (water or antifreeze), cartridge operated (water, antifreeze, or loaded steam), vaporizing liquid (either pump-operated or stored pressure type). Of these, the first four are most commonly installed as hand portable units.

Coast Guard regulations classify extinguishers by a combination letter and number symbol, the letter indicating type of fire the unit could be expected to extinguish, the number denoting the relative size of unit. In this connection, types of fires are designated as follows:

"A" for fires in ordinary combustible materials where quenching and cooling effects of quantities of water, or solutions containing large percentages of water, are of first importance;

"B" for fires in flammable liquids, greases, etc., where a blanketing effect is essential;

"C" for fires in electrical equipment where use of a non-conducting extinguishing agent is of first importance.

The number disignations start with "I" for the smallest to "V" for the largest. Sizes I and II are considered hand portable fire extinguishers; sizes III, IV, and V are considered semiportable fire extinguishing systems which shall be fitted with suitable hose and nozzle or other practicable means so that all portions of the space concerned may be covered. Examples of size graduations for some of the typical hand portable and semiportable systems are set forth in the following table.

Classification		Soda-acid and water, gallons	Foam, gallons	Carbon dioxide, pounds	Dry chemical, pounds
Type	Size				
A	II	2½	2½		
B	I		1¼	4	2
B	II		2½	15	10
B	III		12	35	20
B	IV		20	50	30
B	V		40	100	50
C	I			4	2
C	II			15	10

Effective January 1, 1962, the vaporizing liquid type containing carbon tetrachloride or other toxic vaporizing liquids shall be removed from all vessels.

For details of latest Coast Guard requirements concerning the number, location, size, and type of extinguishers to be carried, the *Rules and Regulations* for class of vessel concerned should be consulted.

Carbon dioxide extinguishers, essentially steel cyclinders made to hold the gas at high pressure, also are extensively installed in batteries of two or more for use against fire in vessel's cargo or store-room spaces, mail rooms, etc. Such are equipped with a 50-foot length of reeled CO_2 hose and horn outlet, or fixed piping with projectors of *horns* around the bulkheads. The size of carbon dioxide cylinders is referred to according to the weight of carbon dioxide they can hold. The cylinders are generally of 15 pounds capacity in the portable extinguishers and of 50 pounds in the installations. The portable cylinders have either a disc-type valve or a squeeze-grip type valve. The installed cylinders have disc-type valves. All carbon dioxide cylinders have safety release discs. The standard pressure in carbon dioxide cylinders in merchant vessels is 600 p.s.i. and 850 p.s.i. in naval vessels at 70°F. Any increase in temperature increases the pressure and three means are resorted to in order to avoid the danger of explosion: the cylinders are never filled to more than 68 percent of their volume capacity, they are strong enough to withstand pressure up to 3,000 p.s.i., and they are equipped with safety valve release discs.

When carbon dioxide is released from an extinguisher cylinder, it expands rapidly to 450 times its stored volume. In consequence of this rapid expansion, it is immediately reduced in temperature to 110° below zero F. and the liquid is vaporized to carbon dioxide gas; some of it, however, forms carbon dioxide *snow* before it returns to the gaseous state.

Once opened (and the sealing disc ruptured), the disc-type valve cannot be closed tightly enough to hold unexpended gas. Any unexpended CO_2 will leak away. The cylinder must be refilled and a new sealing disc inserted in the release valve. The squeeze-grip-type valve, on the contrary, makes a tight seal when the pressure on the *squeeze grip* is released. It can be opened and closed repeatedly without leakage.

If carbon dioxide is put over a fire in time, the fire will go out immediately. It should be applied to the base of the fire first. While operating a disc-type portable cylinder, the fire fighter may shut off the valve for brief intervals without an appreciable loss of carbon dioxide, but the carbon dioxide will leak away in 10 minutes or so once the disc has been ruptured. The squeeze-grip-type likewise may be turned off while in use, but it will hold the carbon dioxide without leakage indefinitely. In continuous operation the 15-pound cylinder, of either type, will expend its contents in about 40 seconds. Carbon dioxide cylinders should be recharged to capacity as soon after use as practicable. *A discharged cylinder must not be returned to its bracket support empty.*

While carbon dioxide extinguishers are designed for hand application, they can be used in a small compartment as a means of providing partial flooding. Two or three portable carbon dioxide extinguishers can be opened and tossed into such a compartment and the doors closed. The carbon dioxide, being heavier than air, will settle and form a blanket over the lower portion of the compartment and, if the compartment is not too large for the amount of CO_2 released, extinguish the fire. Roughly, it may be estimated that one 15-pound cylinder of carbon dioxide will cover the bottom of a compartment 11 feet by 12 feet in dimension to a depth of 1 foot.

To check weight of portable CO_2 cylinders place on platform scale or pick up with the supporting hook on a spring scale.

From the total weight, the following items are deducted for calculating the weight of CO_2 in the cylinder:

(*a*) The known weight of the cylinder when empty (marked on the valve). This is about 30 pounds. Cylinder weights may vary a few pounds.

(*b*) The known weight of the hose and horn. This is about 2 pounds.

(Usually, then, about 32 pounds represents the weight of an empty 15-pound portable cylinder, hose, and horn. The total weight of a fully charged cylinder, therefore, would ordinarily be about 47 pounds.)

Stamped on each cylinder valve are the weight of the cylinder, empty, and without the horn and hose; and the weight of the cylinder, filled to capacity, and without the horn and hose.

NOTE.—The quantity of carbon dioxide in a cylinder cannot be determined by the pressure gage. This is so, because the pressure varies with changes in temperature. The cylinders must be weighed.

CARBON DIOXIDE REQUIREMENTS

When carbon dioxide flooding is resorted to for extinguishing combustible materials subject to quick flash fire (class B) and little or no combustible materials subject to smoldering (class A) are involved, the following quantities would be effective:

Volume of space (cu. ft. net[1]):	*Carbon Dioxide in Lbs.*
100	7.5
140	10
220	15
300	20
375	25
500	35
800	50
1,100	70
1,600	100

For spaces larger than 1,600 cubic feet, the requirements are as follows:[2]

18 cubic feet per pound of gas up to 4,500 cubic feet space.

20 cubic feet per pound of gas up to 50,000 cubic feet space.

22 cubic feet per pound of gas over 50,000 cubic feet space.

[1] Allowance is made for impermeable structures and contents of compartments.

[2] It will be noted that relatively larger quantities of carbon dioxide are required for small spaces than for large ones.

Notwithstanding the low temperature of the expanding carbon dioxide as it leaves the extinguisher cylinder, its cooling effect on fire is slight, and it is employed primarily, therefore, to smother fire. Carbon dioxide is an excellent smothering agent because it will not support combustion and, furthermore, when it has displaced 20 to 30 percent or more of the oxygen in the air, there is not sufficient oxygen left to support combustion. If for instance, the 21 percent oxygen content of the air is reduced to 15 percent or lower, combustion cannot continue. (Some few chemicals, it should be noted, continue to burn until the oxygen of the air is reduced to about 8 percent, and a few others until only about 6 percent of the oxygen remains.)

Inasmuch as carbon dioxide is 1 1/2 times heavier than air, it flows down and over a fire, and, if it is not disturbed by air currents, it will hover long enough to put the fire out—when the concentration is sufficient.

Carbon dioxide is especially effective for extinguishing fires in electrical equipment. When carbon dioxide, a nonconductor of electricity, is used on these (class C) fires, there is no danger of injury to the fire fighter from electrical shock. The electrical circuit should be deenergized to prevent recurrence of the fire.

Applied promptly, carbon dioxide is effective on burning oil. The explanation of this effectiveness lies in the fact that the combustion of oil occurs only at the surface. Except for a layer there, the bulk of the oil is comparatively cool in the early stages of a fire; and there is then less danger of rekindling from glowing bulkheads or overhead structure in case the carbon dioxide should be drawn away from the surface.

The *fire fighter must be warned* that the very qualities which make carbon dioxide a valuable extinguishing agent also *make it dangerous to life*. Certainly, when it replaces oxygen in the air to the extent that combustion cannot be sustained, respiration cannot be sustained either. Prolonged immersion in air thus laden with carbon dioxide causes suffocation, very much as immersion in water does when a person drowns. This gas cannot be seen or smelled and, therefore, it gives no evidence of its presence that can be recognized by the senses. Since it is heavier than air, it does not rise, but remains close to the surface in a deep or shallow pool, according to the area covered and the amount of CO_2 used. With a portable carbon dioxide extinguisher there is practically no danger, inasmuch as its 135 cubic feet of CO_2 in the average compartment lies in a shallow pool, well below the average breathing level.

Anyone who uses a carbon dioxide extinguisher should be warned that the *snow* will blister the skin and cause painful burns if it is allowed to remain on the skin.

When a fire fighter has occasion to enter a compartment that contains carbon dioxide (or any other harmful gas) in a dangerous concentration, he must wear an oxygen breathing apparatus.

Except in an emergency, the fire fighter should not open a CO_2-flooded compartment for at least 10 minutes after it has been flooded. This delay is a precautionary measure to give all burning substances time to cool down below their ignition temperatures, and thereby prevent their reignition upon readmission of air.

Testing of CO_2 Cylinders-Sec. 147-04-1 U.S. Code of Federal Regulations: "If removed from vessel for any purpose (they are) to be tested if previous date shown is lower than 5 years. If not removed, (they) need not be tested until 12 years from previous date has elapsed."

LUX-RICH SYSTEM

Richaudio Fire Detector. The Lux-Rich system for the protection of cargo spaces on passenger and cargo ships is a combination of the Rich detecting system with the Lux extinguishing system. The Rich system, with the Richaudio detector, automatically rings a fire gong at the first trace of smoke in a cargo hold so that the fire can be put out at its in-·ception with the Lux system.

The so-called *electric eye* which is the basis of this system of fire detection is the photoelectric cell which consists of a metal surface, sodium or potassium, placed inside an evacuated glass tube similar in appearance to an electric light bulb. When light waves fall upon this metal surface their energy is absorbed and given to electrons in the metal which emerge with their velocity, i.e. voltage of the current in the circuit, corresponding to the amount of light. A beam of light is set to strike constantly into the eye of the detector. So long as the air is clear it does not interfere with the beam. But as soon as smoke gets into the light beam it changes the amount of energy the tube receives from the light, a relay operates a small electromagnetic switch and sets off the alarm bell.

If line indicator stops (it will not show by a trouble signal), the system is non-operative by audio, but by visual only. Exhaust valve must be set to exhaust into the wheelhouse at all times, at sea or in port.

Three-quarter-inch pipe lines are run from all individual cargo spaces and terminate in the chamber of the Richaudio detector, which is installed on the bridge. Duplicate exhaust fans draw a continuous sample of air through each line into the detector. Any trace of smoke in an air sample is illuminated, giving a visual warning of fire and locating the actual space on fire. The air samples are discharged into the wheelhouse, if desired, thus enabling smell detection also.

The Richaudio detector also rings one or more fire gongs, to attract the attention of the watch to the detector when fire breaks out.

In the Richaudio detector, the air samples from the cargo spaces are passed between a photovoltaic cell and a source of light for *smoke inspection.* If there is any smoke in an air sample, the amount of light reaching the cell is reduced, thus causing the cell to operate the alarm gong and indicate the number of the space in trouble. The detector is equipped with a voltage regulator that compensates for voltage variations in the ship's lines, preventing false alarms due to variations in the intensity of the light source. A light intensity control makes it possible to compensate for aging of the light source and for any dirt that might collect and reduce the amount of light reaching the cell.

The Richaudio detector permits the use of several alarm stations. A fire gong may be installed in the engine room as well as in the wheelhouse so that if there is no watch in the wheelhouse while in port, the alarm will be heard below.

Lux (CO_2) Gas Extinguishing Apparatus. When the Lux system is installed in conjunction with the Rich system, the same pipe lines which are used for smoke detecting are utilized for fire extinguishing. The Lux extinguishing agent is carbon dioxide gas, which is clean, dry. non-corrosive and non-poisonous, and will not support combustion. It puts out fire by smothering it. Sufficient gas is installed, stored under pressure in steel cylinders to extinguish any fire in the cargo spaces. (*See* Fig. 5 .)

FIG. 5. CO_2 CYLINDERS STORED AND HOOKED UP
TO FIRE EXTINGUISHING SYSTEM.

The CO_2 cylinders are stowed in any convenient and accessible place, manifolded together and piped to special three-way valves installed in the smoke detecting lines. When a fire has been detected the proper three-way valve is operated, closing the line to the detecting cabinet and connecting the burning hold with the gas supply. Enough gas is discharged to create an inert atmosphere in the hold. Additional gas is discharged periodically to maintain the inert atmosphere until the hot material has cooled.

Carbon dioxide will not wet, dirty or in any way damage the cargo in the hold. It leaves the unburned cargo in the same condition as it was before the fire.

Engine and Boiler Room Installations. An oil fire in the engine or boiler room spreads rapidly and often drives the crew from the burning space before they can put it out. The Lux bilge flooding system makes it possible to extinguish such fires, even when involving flowing oil, from outside of the fire area.

The system consists of a battery of CO_2 cylinders, manifolded and equipped for simultaneous and instantaneous release, a breakglass pull box control installed outside of the exit from the protected space, a stop valve or valves and distributing pipe with nozzle outlets suitably located in the protected space or spaces.

When released, the CO_2 gas expands 450 times as it leaves the nozzles. It drives over and around boiler foundations, pipe lines and other obstructions. It fills the bilges and the space above the floor plates. All flames are smothered in 10 seconds.

MAINTENANCE

The *Lux* System requires no more than ordinary care to insure its proper operation. As the equipment is only for occasional emergency use, it must be maintained in first class working order at all times.

Monthly Inspection. Make a general inspection to make certain that nothing has been placed to interfere with the operation of cables, levers, and mechanisms used to perform auxiliary operations, or with access to the break-glass pull boxes or valves. Inspect all piping for mechanical breakage. All valves should be operated to make sure that they work freely and do not stick. Check valves to see they are in their normal position.

Yearly Inspection. Weigh all cylinders to detect any possible loss of gas. If any cylinder is found to contain less than 45 pounds of gas, it must be recharged to its full capacity of 50 pounds. Record the net weight of gas in each cylinder on the record card that is framed in the cylinder room. The tare weight of each cylinder is stamped on the neck of the cylinder.

Remove the safety outlets located at the ends of the cylinder manifolds to make sure that the safety disc contained therein is intact. If any disc is found to be damaged, in any way whatsoever, it must be replaced.

Two Year Inspection. Blow out all distributing piping with air or carbon dioxide to make sure that it is not stopped up. *Do not* use water or oxygen for blowing out the pipe lines. The use of oxygen, especially, is dangerous, as the possible presence of even a minute quantity of oil may cause an explosion.

FIRE MAIN

No step should be omitted which will insure that fire fighting equipment will operate efficiently when needed. Therefore, the fire main should receive particular attention. No matter how high the state of mechanical or operational readiness of fire fighting equipment, inadequate water pressure will render it useless.

One of the common causes of fire main trouble is *fouling*, caused by a foreign growth which accumulates inside fire main piping. It is the same type of growth found on the ship's bottom (barnacles). It can build up in a pipe, decreasing its internal cross-sectional area, and resulting in a decreased supply of water to the fire main risers.

There are records of a 6″ fire main being so fouled that the opening was only 2 1/2″ in diameter. This caused a reduction in cross sectional area from approximately 28 square inches to about 5 square inches. This growth will also accumulate on the valve seats, valve discs and stems, thereby preventing the valve from seating properly, or the stem from working freely. Too, when a fire plug or sprinkling valve is open, loose particles of this growth can travel through the system and clog the small orifices in the fog and sprinkler nozzles, as well as the applicators.

Periodic Flushing of all fireplugs under full fire-main pressure is recommended in order that incipient marine growth will be blown out before it has an opportunity to adhere strongly to the fire main. Ships are likewise advised to fill and flush their fire mains with fresh water whenever shore water is available in order to take advantage of the fact that marine growth die upon exposure to fresh water.

This can be accomplished only when a ship is alongside a dock having fresh water connections, and it should be done in the following manner.

1. Secure the fire pumps.

2. Open all cut-out valves.

3. Open pump drains, or engine room and fireroom fire plugs, and drain the system into the bilges.

4. When fresh water has been connected, flush out each riser from the highest fire plug.

This will eliminate or remove all salt water from the system. Keep the fresh water in the system for at least 24 hours; then flush all risers again, using the highest and lowest plugs. Finally, close all valves, disconnect the fresh water, and cut in the salt water.

When alongside a dock, always use dock pressure on the fire main, if possible; otherwise, the ship's pumps will pick up dirt, oil and grease from the surrounding water and further clog the system.

DANGEROUS GASES

Carbon Dioxide. Since carbon dioxide is the gas which the impure blood gets rid of in the lungs, to breathe air which is heavily charged with this gas and correspondingly low in oxygen is bound to starve the blood and produce eventual suffocation. Fires, with their heavy consumption of oxygen and production of carbon dioxide, are the common cause of such a dangerous atmosphere. A concentration of more than 2 or 3% of carbon dioxide will force a man to breathe rapidly and with more or less discomfort.

A person thus has some warning when the proportion of carbon dioxide is gradually increasing, although dependence for safety should not be placed upon this. On the other hand, he has little or no warning when the amount of oxygen is dangerously decreased. The effect of an excessive amount of carbon dioxide is immediately overcome by fresh air, as this gas in itself is not poisonous. Carbon dioxide is heavier than air, and accumulation in unventilated spaces is a common occurrence. In view of this, the oxygen rescue breathing apparatus should be worn when work requiring the entrance into holds, tanks, or similar confined spaces on board ship is to be performed.

Carbon monoxide is a colorless, odorless gas. It is a chemical combination of equal parts of carbon and oxygen. It is formed by smoldering fires or slow rates of oxidation when the amount of oxygen present at the point of combustion is not sufficient to provide two parts of oxygen for each part of carbon burned. Funnel gases, coal gas, gasoline-engine exhaust gases, illuminating gas, and the gaseous products of modern explosives are all rich in carbon monoxide. Many deaths have resulted from the use of portable charcoal stoves in poorly ventilated rooms. The majority of cases of gas poisoning (asphyxiation) is due to carbon monoxide, and unless it is known definitely that some other poisonous gas, such as chlorine or one of the more potent warfare gases, is responsible, it should be assumed that carbon monoxide is the cause of asphyxiation.

Carbon monoxide is rightly classed as a dangerous poison, but in the strictest sense of the word it is not a poison at all because, although it combines with the red coloring matter of the blood and prevents the blood from absorbing a sufficient amount of oxygen, it really does not harm the blood in the least, and after the carbon monoxide has been eliminated the red coloring matter (hemoglobin) is in just as good condition to carry oxygen as before. Hemoglobin absorbs carbon monoxide in the same way as it absorbs oxygen, but the affinity of hemoglobin for carbon monoxide is between 200 and 300 times as strong as its affinity for oxygen. The hemoglobin, therefore, takes up equal quantities of carbon monoxide and oxygen when approximately 0.1 per cent of carbon monoxide is present in the air.

Death or serious after effects from carbon-monoxide poisoning are due to *degeneration of the delicate nerve cells in the brain caused by oxygen starvation* and not to any direct effect on the body caused by carbon-monoxide gas. In air containing 2 to 5 per cent of carbon monoxide, death follows almost as quickly as in drowning. Roughly, it may be stated that a man who has breathed air containing 0.2 per cent of carbon monoxide 4 or 5 hours, or 0.4 per cent for 1 hour will die. The breathing of air containing lower percentages of carbon monoxide causes effects proportionate to the amount present and length of time breathed. Carbon monoxide is one of the most potent poisonous gases and is the most common dangerous gas encountered on board ship. *Its special element of danger is its failure to give any warning symptoms before asphyxiation takes place.*

One exposed to carbon monoxide in dangerous concentrations will be affected as follows: if he has been breathing even small amounts for a long time a tight feeling across the forehead will be the result, and this will be followed by a throbbing headache. In addition he becomes nervous, depressed, and dizzy. The face may become flushed and the eyeballs become bright red. A sickness in the stomach together with vomiting may occur. If exposed for too long a time the victim will pass out.

To render first aid, carry the patient to the fresh air at once. If he has stopped breathing or is gasping give artificial respiration, which practice should be known by every seaman.

Loosen the man's clothes. Rub his hands and feet. Keep his body warm with blankets and hot water bottles (don't let the bottles burn him). Keep him at rest.

Never let a carbon monoxide victim get up and walk about until he is entirely recovered! Many lives have been lost because people thought the victim could walk off the effects right after he came to. Exercise simply speeds up the attack of the monoxide on the heart. When this happens, the patient may collapse and die before help can reach him. Keep the man "turned in"—it may be several days before he gets over being uncomfortable, dizzy and nauseated!

Many other harmful gases, chlorine, ammonia, hydrogen sulphide, sulphur dioxide, etc., are produced by various conditions. A cargo fire may create an atmosphere which is not only dangerous because of smoke produced and oxygen used up, but also because of the harmful gases generated by the combustion of the materials making up the cargo. Burning wood gives off a high percentage of carbon monoxide. Burning rubber produces both sulphur dioxide and carbon monoxide.

In case of fire, smoke presents another hazard in addition to the lack of oxygen and the presence of harmful gases. Smoke is very irritable to the air passages. The choking and coughing which results from breathing smoke-filled air sometimes prevents nearly all the inhaled air from reaching the lungs. Since this air is generally poor to begin with, quick suffocation will result if there is no escape to the open air.

Phosgene is a colorless, very poisonous gas heavier than air and has a distinct odor which resembles new mown hay or ensilage. When carbon tetrachloride strikes a smoldering fire in a place already filled with carbon monoxide, phosgene and chlorine are immediately formed. Since phosgene is decomposed when it comes into contact with water and forms hydrochloric acid this is what takes place in the lungs and bronchial tubes when it is inhaled.

Chlorine is greenish-yellow, heavier than air and very poisonous, though not explosive nor inflammable. It has a very irritating effect on the throat and lungs and a stifling odor so it is easily detected. Even the least amount that can be detected by odor, about 4 parts per million of air, is dangerous. Its effects are somewhat relieved by inhaling ammonia or alcohol vapor.

Sulphur dioxide is a colorless gas, suffocating and irritating, with a strong sulphurous taste. This gas is twice as heavy as air and is not explosive nor flammable. Being very irritating to the eyes and throat it may be detected in mixtures of less than 20 parts per million by the coughing it causes, and exposure to 100 parts per million are seldom fatal even as long as 1/2 hour. It is used as a bleaching agent, in fumigation, and as a refrigerant in mechanical refrigerators.

Ammonia is colorless, transparent, with a sharp burning taste and a very penetrating, overpowering odor. If breathed in large amounts suffocation results. It is heavier than air and will not burn in air nor support combustion. It is principally used in ice plants and petroleum refineries. Ammonia overcomes to a large extent the effects of chlorine, bromine vapor, sulphur dioxide, and hydrochloric acid, when inhaled.

Nitrous oxide is a colorless gas with a faint but pleasant odor and a sweet taste. It is the so-called laughing-gas as when inhaled in small quantities it causes more or less nervous excitement. Nitrous oxide does not burn but it supports the combustion of many substances; it is soluble in water. It is formed by the action of nitric acid on metallic or organic materials and by the burning of articles made of nitrocellulose such as movie film, x-ray film and plastic products. In this group are included brushing lacquers and many toilet articles. It is possible to inhale sufficient fumes from the burning of such articles to cause death without having experienced a great deal of discomfort at the time of inhaling. When cotton or rayon cloth are burned in a deficient oxygen supply nitrous oxide is sometimes formed.

Hydrogen sulphide is a poisonous, colorless, inflammable gas, heavier than air with the characteristic odor of rotten eggs. There is seldom enough of this gas produced at a fire to endanger life but it is produced to some extent by the burning of wool and rubber materials and it is found in tanks that have contained certain types of crude oil.

Hydrogen cyanide, the gas used in death chambers for capital punishment, is colorless, flammable and lighter than air. It is used in fumigation.

Methyl chloride, which is used extensively in mechanical refrigerators, is moderately flammable and very poisonous.

Explosive gases are methane, acetylene, hydrogen, ethylene and the compressed cooking gases such as propane and butane; the refrigerant ethyl chloride and, as mentioned already, carbon monoxide.

Many items of cargo are characterized by their ability to make unventilated spaces dangerous. This comes about in either of two ways—by the generation of gases which will not support life, or by the absorption of the oxygen in the space. Suspect any confined space until it has been inspected or well ventilated.

Linseed oil paints, red lead in particular, absorb oxygen and generate carbon monoxide. Tanks or compartments which have been closed immediately after painting are especially dangerous. However, a rusty unpainted tank may be deficient in oxygen for the moist steel surface consumes oxygen by rusting. Oxygen in such tanks has been found to be reduced to less than 4%; free air normally contains 21% by volume.

Oxygen is removed by the decomposition of most organic substances and some give off toxic gases as well. Molasses residue, coal, whale oil, old bones, linseed oil cake, resin, tobacco, latex, potatoes, oranges, rice bran, castor pumice, hides, coffee have all caused the deaths of stevedores and seamen who were careless or ignorant of this danger.

Dry ice, used to pack fruit, is of course nothing but solidified carbon dioxide which turns back to a gas as it melts.

Of all ordinary cargoes petroleum products present the most hazardous conditions from fire, explosion and asphyxiation. Methods of washing, steaming and gas freeing tanks are familiar to those handling such cargoes and are described under Ship Maintenance, Chapter 14 of this book. It is well to remember that tanks tested gas free in the early morning have been found to be explosive after several hours' exposure to the hot sun. Rust, scale, slop oil and residue in the bottoms or internal framing, cargo lines, steam smothering coils, pipe handrails etc., may release sufficient gas to cause the concentration to rise to a dangerous point.

FRESH AIR BREATHING APPARATUS

Fresh Air Breathing Apparatus. This equipment consists of a trunk about 3 ft. long, 2 ft. wide and 2 ft. deep, which contains the hose, the masks and an air pump. The mask is adjusted to the wearer in the same manner as the all-purpose gas mask, and the hose is held to the body by a harness similar to an officer's field belt; the hose is then led directly to the pump and attached.

The pump may have as many leads going from it as desirable, the speed of operation determining the amount of air produced, and consequently the number of masks that can be attached.

When using the breathing apparatus, care should be taken that the hose leads do not foul and that the pump is being operated at sufficient speed to supply all outlets.

The hose being of rubber, it should not be used around fire or where acid has been spilled.

The only limitations to the fresh-air breathing apparatus are the length of hose which is generally less than 150 feet and the places which may be traversed without the hose becoming entangled led. Since fresh air is provided for respiratory purposes there is no time limit to its use, and the equipment can be worn with safety in any concentration of gas and in any oxygen deficiency.

OXYGEN BREATHING APPARATUS

Oxygen breathing apparatus is independent of outside air and is especially suited for use in air dangerously low in oxygen content, or in a dangerous concentration of poisonous or asphyxiating gases where gas masks cannot be used.

The apparatus consists of a mouthpiece or facepiece with tubes, having inhalation and exhalation valves, leading to a breathing bag containing air, a reducing valve, an oxygen cylinder, and a canister of chemicals for purifying the air exhaled. (*See* Fig. 7 .)

The mouthpiece is secured in place tightly by head bands. The remainder of the apparatus is held in place either on the chest or the back by a harness.

In operation, the main oxygen valve on the cylinder is opened, oxygen passes from the cylinder through the reducing valve and into the breathing bag at a pressure of about 3 pounds per square inch. Air exhaled goes through the exhalation valve to the purifier, and thence into the breathing bag where it is mixed with oxygen. Thence it is drawn through the mouthpiece by inhalation.

Cylinders containing excess moisture should not be used. To ascertain whether excess moisture is present, disconnect the cylinder and then open its main valve. If water is blown from the bottle, it should not be used until cleaned.

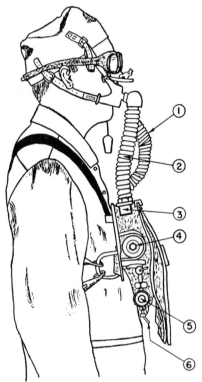

Fig. 6. Oxygen Breathing Apparatus. 1. Exhalation Tube. 2. Inhalation Tube. 3. Gauge. 4. Reducing Valve. 5. Main Bottle Valve. 6. By-Pass Valve.

When assembled, all valves, fittings, etc., should be carefully examined for leaks, which should be immediately stopped.

The nose clip should be so tight that breathing through the nose is impossible. The mouthpiece should also be tested for tightness.

Goggles should be worn with oxygen breathing apparatus if it is used in a gas or smoke which affects the eyes.

INSTRUCTIONS FOR USE OF OXYGEN BREATHING APPARATUS

1. A can of purifying chemicals, called cardoxide, is furnished with each new apparatus. Pour the contents of the can into the regenerator. The half-hour type holds one pound, the one-hour type two pounds.

2. Remove the oxygen cylinder from the apparatus and test it in accordance with the instructions on the tag attached to each cylinder.

3. Replace the oxygen cylinder on the apparatus. Tighten coupling nut to the main valve outlet; also tighten the coupling nuts on both ends of the by-pass tube (the tube connecting the small outlet on the by-pass side of the valve to the cooler).

FIG. 7. OXYGEN BREATHING APPARATUS. THE MAN
IS CARRYING A FLAME SAFETY LAMP.

4. Test the apparatus for tightness before placing in wearing position, as follows:

Place the apparatus in an upright position so the breathing bag is in a vertical position, or in such position that the metal plate mounted at the center of the bag does not press against the admission valve stem (which is inside the bag). This will prevent unnecessary oxygen escaping through the circulation system.

5. The pressure gage valve (on the line extending from the reducing valve to the pressure gage) should be open at all times.

6. Open the main cylinder valve until the gage shows the pressure in the cylinder. A full cylinder should register 125 to 135 atmospheres.

7. Close the main cylinder valve. If there are no leaks, the pressure gage hand will remain constant. If there are any leaks, the hand will slowly move toward zero. If this condition exists, go over all connections to see that they are tight. First look for a leak at the pressure gage valve. There is a packing inside this valve which dries and shrinks slightly. To take up this shrinkage, loosen the lock nut and tighten the packing nut immediately under the hand wheel, just enough to stop the leak.

8. With all connections tight, now place the apparatus in the wearing position, adjust mouthpiece (or facepiece, as the case may be).

9. To adjust mouthpiece, place it in the mouth with the inner rubber flange between the teeth and lips, with the two rubber lugs between the upper and lower teeth. Adjust straps on the mouthpiece in the apparatus cap buckles. Leave nose clip off and breathe through nose until apparatus is cleared of dead air.

Moisture in Oxygen Bottle. To test for moisture in the oxygen bottle hold the bottle, fully charged, in a vertical position with the valve down. Open and close main valve quickly. Water blown from valve shows moisture has gathered. Valve should be removed and bottle drained and cleaned. This is important, as water or sediment forced into the breathing apparatus system may cause trouble. A metal tube projects into the oxygen bottle from the end of the closing valve in order to draw the oxygen free from sediment.

Testing Air Tightness of Bottle. To test oxygen bottle and main closing valve for air tightness, immerse the complete bottle with valve under water. Any air bubbles indicate leaks. Place a metal cap on the outlet end of the closing valve, open main valve and immerse in water. Any leaks around the packing gland or stem will be shown by escaping air bubbles. When the apparatus is completely assembled, test main oxygen valve after opening by using soap suds around packing gland and stem.

Valve Safety Cap. A safety cap is attached to the closing valve as required by the Interstate Commerce Commission, to provide for escape of the oxygen without rupture of the cylinder if it is exposed to fire. The safety cap contains Rose metal, which melts at 94° C. (about 200° F.), and a frangible copper disc that will rupture if the pressure is increased beyond the safety factor of the material. The design of the cap with Rose metal against the copper disc increases the safety factor and prevents the disc from blowing out unless heat is applied. If heat is applied the Rose metal will run out and the copper disc will rupture and permit the escape of the oxygen.

By-Pass Valve. The apparatus is equipped with a by-pass valve so that the wearer can be supplied with oxygen in case some working part fails. It is never kept open, but turned on and off quickly, since the pressure is too great for the strength of material used in construction of the apparatus, and one could not inhale or exhale because of the high pressure. It would also be dangerous to the lungs.

When the by-pass valve is opened the oxygen has free access to the lungs, there being only the inhalation valve between it and the mouth. It should not be used when reducing and admission valves are supplying sufficient oxygen, since pressure is developed against exhalation which may prove very uncomfortable.

Reducing Valve. The reducing valve is made without adjusting screws. Proper adjustment is made by the manufacturer, and when necessary the valve should be sent back to him for repairs. If the safety valve whistles, or excessive pressure is indicated at the reducing valve by a testing gage, or no oxygen is supplied to the wearer the reducing valve is in need of repair. To test its pressure simply attach a low pressure gage to the outlet end. The proper pressure is about 3 lbs.

Admission Valve. The admission valve is the valve for admitting oxygen into the breathing bag, which acts as a reservoir and reduces resistance to breathing. The breathing process deflates and empties this bag. The bumper plate on the bag automatically opens the admission valve, thereby admitting oxygen as needed.

To test admission valve open main oxygen valve, holding breathing bag plate outward so that admission valve seat is closed, then close main oxygen valve. Then open and close admission valve seat, observing the movement of the pressure gage hand, and stopping as the pressure is reduced.

Safety Valve. When reducing valve pressure reaches about 7 lbs. above atmospheric pressure the safety valve opens, sounding a whistle and releasing the excessive reducing valve pressure. Further increased pressure opens additional ports in the safety valve, allowing the oxygen to escape more rapidly.

When safety valve begins to whistle close main oxygen valve and use by-pass valve by opening and closing momentarily. Retreat to fresh air at once.

Operation of Admission and Reducing Valves. As the pressure in the circulatory system builds up, the breathing bag inflates, closing the admission valve by raising the bumper plate from the piston of the admission valve. Then the oxygen pressure below the seat of the admission valve increases so that the bellows of the reducing valve extends, drawing the attached lever arm down over the seat of the reducing valve. This closes the orifice of the reducing valve and shuts off high pressure of the oxygen valve.

Testing Cooler Tube. Close admission valve seat and blow through tube, or attach low pressure testing gage to reducing valve and tube. Turn on oxygen, close stop cock of low pressure gage, read both gages. Then close oxygen valve. Open stop cock of low pressure gage. Any leaks in tube will show on gages.

Mouthpiece Valves. There are four valves in the metal mouthpiece of the apparatus: inhalation, exhalation, saliva and relief valves. The first two are set close together to reduce the dead air space to a minimum.

Testing the Mouthpiece. Place a solid plug in the exhalation side, holding thumb over mouthpiece. Immerse all parts in water and blow through inhalation side. Any air bubbles indicate leaky joints. With solid plug in exhalation coupling, or with the hand held over its end, exhale through the rubber mouthpiece. If unable to exhale the inhalation valve is free from leaks. Place the plug in the inhalation coupling, or hold hand over end, then inhale. If unable to inhale, the exhalation valve is free from leaks. Remove plugs, then inhale and exhale through mouthpiece several times, observing that valves open and close freely. Test valve in saliva trap and release valve by having plugs in inhalation and exhalation couplings, then push up on saliva trap or release valve and inhale. If unable to inhale the valve is free from leaks.

Testing Complete Apparatus. To test complete apparatus for air tightness, hold thumb over mouthpiece opening, then open main oxygen valve. By pressing down on the admission valve inflate the breathing bag fully. Then after closing main valve observe whether the bag deflates or the pressure gage hand moves toward zero. No change will indicate an air tight apparatus, and also that the admission and reducing valves are in good order.

Removing Excessive Nitrogen. To remove excessive nitrogen from the air circulatory system inhale from the apparatus and exhale to the outside air at least four times before adjusting the nose clip.

The release valve should be used about every 15 to 20 minutes to avoid accumulations of nitrogen.

To adjust facepiece, grasp the head straps with both hands, insert chin well into the lower part of facepiece, and pull head straps back over the head. Tighten the head strap as follows:

Tighten the two bottom straps first, just enough to take up the slack. Tighten the two side straps.

Place the palms of the hands at the junction of the straps on top of the head, sliding them toward the back of the head. This feature is important, as it forces the chin into the bottom of the facepiece and pulls the top of the facepiece tightly against the forehead.

Again tighten the bottom straps, then the side straps. The top straps seldom need pulling up, never more than one or two notches.

To determine if the facepiece is tight, grasp the inhalation tube (on the right) between the palms of the hands, closing it completely. Now inhale deeply but slowly. If there are no leaks around the sides of the facepiece, it will collapse against the face.

Clear the circulation system of any possible dead air as follows:

Mouthpiece type: Before placing the nose clip in position inhale through the mouth and exhale through the nose. Repeat this procedure until you have drawn all air possible from the apparatus—that is, until you can no longer inhale. Now open main cylinder valve, inhale twice, discharging exhaled air to the outside atmosphere. Now place the nose clip in position and you are ready to proceed.

Facepiece type: Inhale, then shut off the exhalation tube with the palms of the hands (the tube on the left), and exhale with lifting one edge of the facepiece slightly away from the face. When you have drawn all air possible from the apparatus open the main cylinder valve, inhale twice, discharging the exhaled air to the outside atmosphere. You are now ready to proceed.

Gas masks, as distinguished from the oxygen breathing apparatus, protect the wearer from acid gases (such as carbonic), ammonia, organic vapors, smoke and dust. Some types protect from carbon monoxide gas, while others do not. Only the oxygen breathing apparatus will serve where there is a deficiency of oxygen.

US Navy Type Oxygen Breathing Apparatus. This type of apparatus, found on many merchant vessels, does not have a cylinder with oxygen under pressure as does the other type already described. The canister in this type apparatus contains chemicals which absorb the CO_2 and water vapor from your breath, producing a chemical reaction which provides a fresh supply of oxygen. The instructions listed below must be followed in detail. REMEMBER YOU MUST BREATHE FRESH AIR *INTO* THE APPARATUS AS IT IS THE MOISTURE IN YOUR BREATH WHICH ACTUATES THE CHEMICAL.

1. Adjust the facepiece and test it by inhaling while pinching both breathing tubes. If the facepiece collapses, it is airtight. If there is any leak at all, adjust the facepiece further.

2. Grasp both breathing tubes with one hand and squeeze tightly; depress the starter valve and inhale deeply. Release the starter valve and tubes and then *exhale into* the apparatus.

3. Repeat this procedure until the breathing bags are fully inflated. Do this at least four times, better fifteen.

4. Lift one side of the facepiece with one hand and deflate the breathing bags with the other hand.

5. Repeat the above steps—further adjustment of the facepiece of course may be omitted so long as there are no leaks—until.the canister becomes warm at the *top and bottom*. It is absolutely necessary that the canister, top and bottom, be warm before you risk your life in smoke or gas-filled spaces. Oxygen is not produced until the chemical reaction starts and the chemical reaction makes the canister warm. In cold weather this procedure may take much longer. You must wait until the canister becomes warm; but you may hurry the process by exercising (jumping, squatting, simulating running) with the breathing bags full.

6. Immediately after inflating the bag, turn the pointer on the timer dial to number 30. The pointer will return to zero as the apparatus is used, and at zero a warning bell will ring. If there has been no noticeable resistance to breathing, reset the pointer for an additional 15 minutes work. The approximate life of a canister in use is 45 minutes, but conditions can shorten this time.

7. To remove a spent canister, spread your legs apart, bend slightly forward, turn the handwheel counterclockwise to the extreme down position, depress the canister stop and, with a quick forward motion, swing the bail (bottom frame) outward. The canister will then drop out of the apparatus.

Precautions to Observe in Using Oxygen Breathing Apparatus:

1. Don't go into the danger area until you are sure the apparatus is working correctly. Don't forget to start the timer each time you start a new canister.

2. If the bag takes extra time to fill and yet deflates rapidly, do not use the apparatus unless you first find and stop the leaks.

3. Excessive fogginess of the facepiece lenses and increased resistance to exhalations indicate that the bag is overinflated, or that the canister is exhausted. If the canister is exhausted, get a new one, or go into fresh air.

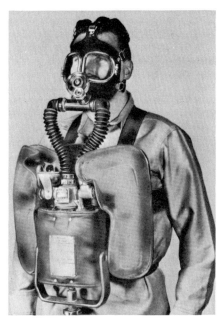

Fig. 8. Chemox Oxygen-Breathing Apparatus. (M-S-A)

4. A canister in use becomes very hot. Do not touch one without suitable protection for your hands.

5. The chemicals used in the canister are caustic and can burn your skin badly; if a canister should be open, handle it with care.

6. Because the chemicals contain so much oxygen, they will cause combustion, perhaps explosion of any flammable materials with which they come in contact. Do not throw or permit a used canister to bounce into the bilges or onto a deck where oil, grease, or gasoline may be present. Do not throw it overboard if there is an oil slick on the water. If possible do not dispose of the used canister until the ship is underway; then throw it overboard. By all means do not allow any liquid, especially oil, grease, etc., to enter the opening of a used canister; and never hold your face or any part of your body over a canister opening.

GAS MASKS

The third type of respiratory protector is the canister-type gas mask. This item consists of a facepiece, an inhalation tube, and a canister. There are various types of canisters and, therefore, it is important to know what gases will be encountered in entering the space and to confirm from the label on the canister that it is designed to give protection from the gases in question.

Fig. 9. Gas Mask With Canister.

A gas mask consists of a facepiece with glass eyepieces which is held in place by head bands, and is connected by corrugated tubing to a canister held against the chest and supported by a harness about the neck and body. (*See* Fig. 9.)

In use, the head bands are so adjusted that the facepiece is held very tightly against the face so as to prevent the entrance of gases under the mask. The facepiece should be tested for tightness by holding the palm of the hand over the bottom of the canister and inhaling strongly. The facepiece should collapse against the face and remain there as long as the breath is held and the hand remains in place.

Air or gases enter the canister through a check valve in its bottom, pass through the purifying chemicals contained in it, and then leave the top of the canister, being inhaled through the corrugated tube. The inhaled dry air enters the facepiece through tubes and is discharged over the eyeglasses to prevent fogging.

Canisters should be kept absolutely dry, as moisture causes deterioration of the contents.

In connection with the canisters, it is important to be familiar with the time limits of their usefulness. Canisters are constructed with a hole in the bottom through which gases pass. At time of manufacture this hole is covered with a seal. With this seal intact, the canister may be used any time within 5 years from the date of manufacture which is noted on the canister. Before the canister is put to use this seal must be removed and the date of breaking the seal must be entered on the canister in ink. Do not enter this date with pencil because it will possibly become illegible after a short period of time. One year from this date of breaking the seal, the canister should be discarded even though it may not have been put to much service. In use the canister life should be based on the timer or when it is noticed that gases are passing through. However, a canister should not be used for more than 2 hours even though the timer may not show complete exhaustion of the canister and even though the passage of gases is not noticed by the wearer's sense of smell or taste. The service life of a canister as set forth above is based on a gas concentration of less than 2 percent. With a higher concentration, the service life will naturally be less and this should be kept in mind. The time limits of usefulness as set forth above are not to be considered as minimum periods of positive usefulness since the chemicals in the canisters deteriorate more rapidly in damp atmospheres, resulting in a shorter life than that indicated. The atmospheric condition surrounding the place of stowage has a considerable bearing on the shelf life of canisters and therefore the time limits as given should be considered as average limits under normal conditions only.

In using this type of mask it is very essential that the wearer know its protective limitations. The most important limitation is that the mask provides no protection in spaces where there is an oxygen deficiency. The air we breathe contains approximately 20 percent oxygen and 80 percent nitrogen. The gas mask will not afford protection when the oxygen content has been reduced to 16 percent. In order to detect the oxygen deficiency the flame safety lamp is used. This lamp will not burn when the deficiency of oxygen reaches the low point of 16 percent. Therefore, before using the canister-type mask, a flame safety lamp should be lowered into the space to be entered to first ascertain whether there is an oxygen deficiency. If the lamp goes out, the fresh-air mask or the oxygen-breathing apparatus must be used because the canister gas mask will afford no protection. Whenever this type of mask is worn the flame safety lamp should be carried along by the wearer of the mask. When the flame safety lamp goes out, he will know that a location has been encountered which is deficient in oxygen and a withdrawal to fresh air should be made at once.

FLAME SAFETY LAMPS

The flame safety lamp has its limitation in that it will not reveal the degree of concentration of gases other than oxygen. It is possible to have sufficient oxygen in a space to support life and still have a concentration of carbon monoxide which will produce death. For this reason care must be exercised in entering spaces with a canister-type gas mask. Where possible, it is desirable to have the atmosphere of the space chemically analyzed so that a true picture of the hazards of the space to be entered can be known by the individual concerned.

The flame safety lamp is so constructed that it can be used with safety in spaces containing combustible gases. The lamp is equipped with a gauze mesh which permits the entry of gases. Should these gases be combustible, the ignition and burning is confined within the lamp so that the atmosphere outside the lamp will not be ignited with possibly an explosion. However, acetylene and hydrogen gases are of such light character that they will penetrate the fine gauze protector in the light and cause an explosion before the presence of the gas is known.

As flame safety lamps are now required equipment aboard passenger vessels it is essential that all licensed officers and engineers become familiar with their use and operation.

Normal air contains 21% oxygen. Candles or flame safety lamps cease to burn when the oxygen content is lowered to 16%. (Unconsciousness occurs in humans when the oxygen content drops to 10%.) Therefore, the user is warned of oxygen deficiency in time to withdraw to a place of safety.

Flame safety lamps should be used to test the oxygen content before men are allowed to enter places where oxygen deficiency is liable to occur, such as holds in which a fire has been smoldering, or where solid CO_2 has been used as a refrigerant, or in deep tanks which have been filled with oil or molasses and which have not been thoroughly aired out; or in fuel or water tanks which may have been sealed for some time, etc.

As a special safety precaution men wearing gas masks in any part of the vessel where a deficiency of oxygen might be encountered should carry a flame safety lamp.

Fuel Specifications. Successful operation of the flame safety lamp depends in large part on use of proper fuel. Gasoline that contains tetra-ethyl lead is not satisfactory nor is the so-called third structure white gasoline even though this latter is lead free. In order to light the cold lamp with the re-lighting device, a fuel having a flash point sufficiently low to insure the presence of an inflammable fuel-vapor mixture at the open end of the wick is required. The U. S. Bureau of Mines recommends the following fuel for permissible safety lamps (Koeler & Wolf):

"Trade Name of Fuel: Atlantic 70 Naphtha; Freedom safety lamp fuel; Gulf safety lamp fuel; Waverly safety lamp fuel.

"Lamps for which these fuels are suitable are often referred to as naphtha-burning lamps' or just 'naphtha lamps.' 'Naphtha' is an indefinite term, in that there is no general agreement as to what constitutes a naphtha. However, to some refiners it means a straight-run distillate, one that has no part produced by cracking. In this respect all of the above fuels may be classed as naphthas.''

Container for Reserve Fuel. Even though the lamp is not used there will be a gradual loss of fuel through evaporation from the wick. It is, therefore, advisable to have available a reserve supply of fuel. One satisfactory method of keeping a small reserve handy is to use a one pint copper-plated engineer's filler with screw cap on the filler spout.

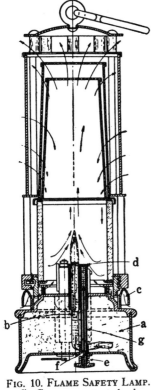

This filler should be kept filled with fuel and stored near the lamp.

Precautions in Using. The following precautions should be observed in using a flame safety lamp:

Be sure that the lamp is locked.

Examine the lamp carefully to see that it is in good condition before using it. Do no carry the key which opens the lamp with you.

Do not attempt to open the lamp in hold or tank. Always take into fresh air.

Be sure that lamp gauze is clean. Do not use one with rust, dirt, or oil on gauze.

Do not let lamp smoke. Soot may fill up the gauze.

Lamps that have not been used for some time may have rusty gauzes and hardened wick or gummy fuel. Do not use such a lamp.

Action of Fuel in Lamp. Fig. 10 shows a sectional view of a typical flame safety lamp. The parts shown are—

a) Cotton in base of lamp which absorbs the fuel.

b) Wick.

c) Bottom inlet ring through which most of the air that supports combustion enters.

FIG. 10. FLAME SAFETY LAMP.

d) Cover cap to tube in which wick adjuster is contained.

e) Control handle for wick adjuster.

f) Rod connecting control handle with wick adjusting mechanism.

g) Tube containing wick adjusting mechanism.

The arrows show the path of air into and out of the lamp.

Assembling Errors. When properly assembled, a flame safety lamp may be introduced into an explosive mixture of gases and air. However, it should not be so used unless absolutely necessary. A flame safety lamp is safe only when in perfect condition and used with care and discretion. The following errors may be made in assembling lamps:

1. Leaving out one or both gaskets or using a broken glass.

2. Placing gaskets in underfeed lamps so the inlet passage under the glass is obstructed.

3. Leaving out one of the gauzes in double gauze lamps.

4. Placing on top of glass an expansion ring designed to be placed under the glass.

5. Placing expansion ring upside down, thus destroying its usefulness.

6. Failure to screw the fuel vessel far enough in to make a tight fit between the glass globe and the gaskets.

7. Leaving off the deflection rings that prevent air from flowing directly into the lamp.

8. Leaving off the shield or bonnet when the lamp is to be used in a strong air current.

9. Placing a defective gauze in a lamp.

Care of Wicks. The wick should be renewed when it is believed that it has become stiff and when there is a characteristic gummy deposit around the wick and wick tube. The cotton in the fuel reservoir should be renewed about once a year. In packing the lamp the base should be filled with cotton uniformly distributed and a wick trailed out through the cotton in intimate contact with the fuel supply. No more fuel should be placed in the base than can be absorbed in the cotton. After filling the fuel reservoir it should be inverted, and any free liquid allowed to drain out. Be certain that filler cap is screwed on tightly.

Flame safety lamps are gas testing devices and dependable only when properly assembled, properly fueled and properly used. They indicate deficiency in oxygen as well as explosive atmospheres. Keep them in good condition and test them frequently.

Life Line. No individual should be permitted to enter any dangerous space without having a life line attached to him and without having a man on deck continually observing his actions so that aid can be called immediately when assistance is needed. By means of the life line, rescue can be easily performed without further endangering the lives of others.

The steel-wire life line is a 50-foot length of 3/16-inch, 7 by 9 aircraft cable, equipped at each end with a stout hook that is closed with a snap catch. The line has a maximum of pliability and it will slide freely around obstructions.

The uses of the life line are manifold; and while most of them are precautionary, rescue is often effected with the life line as a means of hauling an injured person to safety. The line is manned by a fellow fire fighter who stands by ready to haul away on signal or when he believes his charge is in trouble. He must be careful to prevent snagging of the line, by paying it off the coil in his hand as the line is extended. For hauling a stricken person to safety and for lowering a rescue party into a compartment, and for various other uses, the steel wire life line is indispensable.

One important precaution in the use of the life line is obvious, but it is set down here because in the excitement of a fire it may be forgotten. It is this: a stricken person must never be hauled up by a life line that is attached to his waist. He may be dragged along a deck a short distance, but his weight must never be suspended on a line attached to his waist. If he is not wearing any sort of harness, the line must be made fast so that it passes under his arms and meets either at the front or the back. The tender should wear gloves and try to keep the line in contact with grounded metal, and away from electrical equipment.

CO ALARM AND DETECTORS

Carbon Monoxide Alarm. The CO (carbon monoxide) alarm is an automatic device installed in spaces where carbon monoxide is likely to accumulate. As mentioned before, this gas is highly poisonous in small concentrations and to know of its presence is important.

A small fan, direct-connected to a 1/80 HP motor, pulls in a continuous sample of air at the rate of 20 (7/10 cu. ft.) liters per minute through a screened intake funnel which contains a replaceable filter for trapping entrained dust. The air is passed over electric heater coils, and enters a divided, insulated cell containing active and inactive Hopcalite, respectively, in its two compartments. Any CO present is converted into CO_2 (carbon dioxide) with liberation of heat in proportion to the amount of the gas in the air.

The heat liberated is measured by thermo-couples and is indicated on a dial in terms of CO concentration. The dial is graduated from 0 to .02% carbon monoxide. When the needle reaches the .02% mark, a magnet pulls the needle over to the stop-post, which closes the alarm circuit. The magnet holds the alarm circuit closed and continues the insistent ringing of the gong, until the needle is turned back by hand. By this means, it is assured that the alarm will be heard and heeded, and the ventilation arrangements changed.

CO Ventilation Control. The ventilation control is essentially the same as the alarm, except that the bell and bell-ringing transformer are replaced by a secondary relay which is energized when the point of the indicating relay contacts the magnetic stop post at .02% CO concentration. This relay starts the ventilation motors, in some cases through an external power relay. At the same time a reset mechanism is put into operation. This mechanism will stop the ventilating system motors when the CO content of the air has been reduced below the danger point.

CO Detector. This is a small instrument with four main parts: a rubber bulb used for pumping an air sample from a suspected space or vessel through the instrument; a detector tube containing a chemical which changes color in proportion to the amount of CO in the air sample; another chemical in the barrel which removes other gases which would affect the detector; and a color chart against which the color of the detector is checked to determine the percentage of CO present. Two valves, inlet and outlet, keep the air moving through the instrument in one direction. (*See* Fig. 11.)

To operate, squeeze bulb ten or fifteen times before detector tube is inserted to remove any gas remaining from previous test. Break the tips from ends of detector tube, place tube in holder on top of barrel. Squeeze bulb ten times, then compare the color of the material inside the detector tube with the color in the color scale. Six or seven tests in low concentrations can usually be made with each tube, provided they are made within a short period of time.

Combustible Gas Indicators. Combustible gas indicators measure the degree of explosive gases present in any space, tank, compartment, etc. By means of a sampling line, a length of small tubing, an air sample is drawn out of the space and through the measuring instrument. A meter indicates the concentration of the explosive gas in the air under

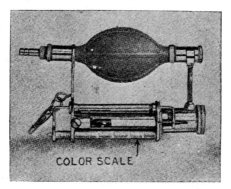

FIG. 11. CO DETECTOR: BULB, DETECTOR TUBE, AND COLOR SCALE.

test. It is graduated to read in percentage of the low explosive limit concentration. (*See* Fig. 12.)

The gas sample may be drawn into the instrument by means of a small piston-type hand pump, an aspirator bulb, or motor-driven pump in the case of the non-portable gas alarm. The sample flows over a hot platinum wire which forms a part of a balanced electrical circuit. Current for the circuit is supplied by two small dry cell batteries. This detector unit is balanced against the filament of a small electric light bulb burning in an inert gas. The combustible gas in the air sample

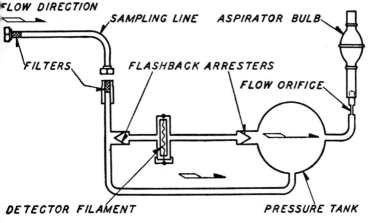

FIG. 12. COMBUSTIBLE GAS INDICATOR, DIAGRAMMATIC LAYOUT.

burns easily in the presence of the platinum detector filament, which heats up during the combustion according to the amount of gas burned. This increases the wire's resistance and causes the electrical circuit to become unbalanced. The unbalancing of the circuit in turn causes a movement of the pointer of the electrical meter which is directly proportional to the concentration of combustible gas in the sample.

Combustible Gas Alarm. The combustible gas alarm operates in the same manner as the portable instrument. When the combustible gas concentration exceeds that for which the instrument is set to operate, the alarm circuit closes and the alarm signal (bell, light, horn or siren) operates until the gas concentration is lowered.

Two small pilot lights indicate normal operation. When the alarm circuit closes, these lights go out and a red warning light inside the instrument case flashes on.

Like the portable indicator, the alarm may be specially calibrated for any particular gas, and adjusted to give alarm at any desired degree of concentration. It may also be hooked up to operate ventilating fans or blowers.

Breathing Cycle. An average man at rest will breathe about every 5 seconds, drawing in about one quart of air at a breath. This air is spread out in the lungs, entering small cells through the walls of which the impure blood moves, given off carbon dioxide and taking up oxygen from the inhaled air. The breath leaving the lungs then carries away the carbon dioxide. The re-oxygenated blood goes from lungs to heart, from which it is pumped through the body again. The oxygen carried in the blood is used in reaction with the body tissues. The result of this reaction, which is actually a form of combustion, is to use up the oxygen and produce carbon dioxide. The blood then carries the carbon dioxide back through the heart to the lungs, thus completing the cycle.

To cut off or replace this vital supply of oxygen with other gases is to bring about starvation of the body tissues, beginning with the brain. As a result unconsciousness comes early in the process of asphyxiation.

The lower processes of the body, or those which go on automatically, such as respiration, circulation of the blood, etc., can and do go on even when the person is unconscious, but usually in asphyxiation, soon after unconsciousness develops, respiration also ceases, so that most asphyxiated persons are not only unconscious but also are not breathing. In this stage of asphyxiation, provided that the heart has not yet been sufficiently affected to prevent its functioning, the patient can be benefited by artificial respiration.

By making a person breathe artificially we get oxygen back into the lungs where it can be absorbed by the blood and taken to the various vital centers of the body. Those parts that were affected last usually recover first, which is the reason, during artificial respiration, that the patient may begin to breathe even before he wakes up or becomes conscious. As respiration improves and more oxygen is brought to the vital centers of the body, the higher centers are finally reoxygenated and the person becomes conscious once more.

INHALATOR

The inhalator is used in connection with the Schaefer respiration method to give the victim a more stimulating mixture of oxygen and carbon dioxide than he can get from the open air, which contains only about 21% oxygen. The mixture used with the inhalator is generally 93% oxygen and 7% carbon dioxide, the latter acting to stimulate the breathing action, while the high concentration of oxygen hastens recovery by saturating the blood with oxygen.

Circulation Through Inhalator. The oxygen-carbon dioxide mixture is contained in cylinders charged to a pressure of 135 atmospheres, from which it passes through a reducing valve into a breathing bag. This bag makes each respiration visible to the operator. The volume of flow to the breathing bag is regulated by a volume control valve after the gas has passed through the reducing valve.

The facepiece or half mask is provided with three check valves, one for inhalation, one for exhalation and a third to provide extra air from the outside if the patient requires more at any inhalation than the breathing bag can supply.

A T-cock connection which by-passes the volume control valve makes possible quick assembly of an auxiliary attachment of supply hose, breathing bag and mask for independent treatment of a second victim at the same time.

Method of Operating. Open volume control valve, open one manifold valve and the cylinder valve next to it. Inflate the rubber cushion which forms the rim of the half mask and place the mask over the patient's mouth and nose. After the breathing bag has been inflated, set the volume control at a point on the dial where the bag will neither collapse nor become too full and distended. Change the setting at intervals, if required, in order to maintain this condition. If one cylinder becomes empty, close the manifold valve adjacent to it, and open the manifold and cylinder valves of the second cylinder, thus continuing the treatment without interruption. The empty cylinder should then be replaced with a fully charged one. Continue to use the inhalator until the patient is conscious and breathing normally.

Each cylinder contains when fully charged 16 cubic feet of gas, and will last about 1 1/2 hours at normal operating conditions. Both cylinders should never be turned on at the same time.

General Precautions Against Fire:

1. Smoking in holds prohibited.
2. Wire mesh guards in ventilator cowls.
3. Investigate the least odor of smoke.
4. Only safety matches permitted aboard.
5. Persons handling explosives to wear rubber boots. Coamings, hatches, gangway and rails to be protected with matting and wood.
6. Paint-lockers well ventilated, and no open lights allowed.
7. Oily rags thrown overboard immediately after use.
8. Electric wiring insulated and armored.

See to it that vents and galley hoods are free of oil and grease, and that containers of inflammable liquids are closed and properly stowed. Boatswain's stores (such as lines, paints, etc.) and ship's stores should be stowed with care (see Spontaneous Combustion). Prevent the accumulation of oil and grease in the bilges. Keep quarters and workshops free of waste and materials.

Of all the causes of fires the most common is *smoking*. Observe the smoking regulations. Carelessly tossed matches and butts cause more fires than all the other hazards together. *

FUEL OIL SAFETY PRECAUTIONS

Deck officers of tankers are of course thoroughly familiar with the dangerous potentialities of the cargo they are handling. However, those who have not sailed on tankers are not always aware of the dangerous nature of fuel oil vapor when mixed with air.

Fuel oil itself is inert, nonexplosive, very difficult to ignite in bulk, and not capable of spontaneous ignition. The vapor from this oil, however, is explosive when mixed with air. This vapor is heavier than air and tends to accumulate in low levels, such as bilges and bottoms of tanks where it may remain undiscovered until ignited by a naked light or spark. It is always present in a partly filled oil tank, or one that has contained fuel oil and from which the vapor has not been removed by artificial means, and it is expelled through the vents from the fuel oil tanks while they are being filled. A leak allowed to continue in any part of the oil-burning system may result in an accumulation of this explosive vapor, unless such leak is located in the path of air to the furnace. Ignition of the vapor may be caused by an open light, electric spark, or spark made by striking metal, the heat of the filament of a broken electric lamp, smoking, sparks from funnel or galley, or fires under boilers.

Tank Vessels. No transfer under following conditions:

1. During severe electrical storms.
2. If fire occurs in the vicinity.
3. If a towboat comes alongside in way of cargo tanks.

Rules and regulations for tank vessels during transfer operations:

1. Display red flag or red light.
2. Warning sign at gangway: "No open lights—No smoking—No visitors."
3. Warning sign in radio room not to use equipment.
4. Smoking only at designated times and places. Safety matches only.
5. Flame screens over tanks and ullage holes.
6. Non-sparking tools provided.
7. Have at hand fresh air or oxygen masks; belt and life lines.

---

* "In the nineteen-twenties there was an inexplicable epidemic of fires in jute cargoes out of Calcutta. The Calcutta Underwriters Association in collaboration with the jute trade, organised a series of experiments consisting of stowing jute in containers reproducing the conditions of a ship's hold. Some jute was stowed wet, some with matches and oily waste mixed with it, some in normal conditions and so forth, but not only did no fire result, but the extent to which the jute engendered heat spontaneously was negligible. The negative result of the experiments led to a search for some causes of the fires other than spontaneous combustion, and this in turn led to the tightening up of the regulations against smoking at jute loading ports. The result was instantaneous and startling. The epidemic of fires in jute cargoes died down and since then outbreaks of fire in jute cargoes have been very infrequent."—Nautical Magazine.

8. Sufficient number of crew on duty.

9. Any electrical connection to shore maintained until cargo hose removed.

10. Scuppers plugged except where water used for deck cooling; sea valves closed and lashed.

11. Sufficient hose for movement of vessel.

12. No repair work in cargo spaces except with deck officer's special permission.

The spilling or pumping of oil into harbors creates one of the gravest fire and explosion hazards to vessels and waterfront installations. The Oil Pollution Act, 33 U.S.C. 431–437, seeks to prevent these dangers by making it unlawful for any person to discharge oil from a vessel into the coastal navigable waters of the United States. Violators of the act are subject to a criminal penalty of imprisonment of not less than 30 days nor more than 1 year and to a fine of not less than $500 nor more than $2,500. The violating vessel may be proceeded against for the collection of the monetary penalties.

The reasons this law should be implicitly obeyed are obvious and practical. Yet this act is frequently violated. For example, during the year 1944, in the 8th Naval District Gulf Coast area, 121 cases of violation were reported.

FLASH POINTS AND IGNITION TEMPERATURES

(Degree, Fahrenheit)

	Flash point	Ignition temperature
Alcohol (grain)...............................	55	700
Ether...	−49	356
Fuel oil (heavy)..............................	150–250	695
Gasoline......................................	−45	495
Kerosene......................................	100	490
Linseed oil (boiled)..........................	403	650
Linseed oil (raw).............................	432	650
Lubricating oil (cylinder)....................	535	783
Lubricating oil (turbine).....................	400	700
Turpentine....................................	95	464

Classification of Flammable Liquids

Class I—Liquids with flashpoint below 25 degrees F.

Ether	Naptha
Carbon bisulphide	Benzol
Gasoline	Collodion

Acetone

Class II—above 25 degrees and below 70 degrees F.

Alcohol   Toluol
Amyl acetate   Ethyl acetate
                    Methyl acetate

Class III—above 70 degrees and below 187 degrees F.

Kerosene   Amyl alcohol
                    Turpentine

SPONTANEOUS COMBUSTION

A common cause of fire aboard ship is spontaneous combustion, which can generally be traced to ignorance or carelessness. The term means a fire which starts without the aid of such outside sources as a spark, open flame, overheated pipe, etc.

Such occurrences seem mysterious unless we realize that combustion is not limited to the production of open flames; it is happening all the time about us. Paint drying is in a state of combustion. So is rusting iron, rotting wood and it is even taking place in the body as the tissues consume oxygen. In every case heat is given off in this chemical process by which oxygen combines with another chemical or compound releasing energy in the form of heat.

If the speed of oxidation is increased so that heat is generated faster than it is dissipated the ignition temperature of the substance will be reached. Breaking the substance into small particles so that more surface area is exposed will increase the rate of oxidation. Particles of coal dust or linseed oil on a piece of waste satisfy this condition and are a common cause of fire. A rag with only 3 to 5 percent saturation with paint or oil may ignite. This applies to all animal and vegetable fats such as lard, tallow, turpentine, peanut oil and other oils that are not petroleum products.

Some substances ignite spontaneously if they are damp, but not wet. An example is *green* hay stored before it is thoroughly dry.

It is often found that a quite low initial heat is sufficient to start the process. Thus the sun's rays or wood heated for a long time by steam pipes have started fires even though this heat was well below the ignition temperature of about 500 degrees F.

Articles Liable to Spontaneous Combustion:

1. Coal temperature over 140° F. is dangerous. Avoid breaking, avoid sticks or rags in coal. Ventilate well. Small coal most dangerous.

2. Practically all animal products, such as leather, wool, fish, guano.

3. Vegetable products, such as malt, bran, hops, cereal grains, seeds, hay, clover, grass, flax, hemp, jute, tow, rope.

4. Chemicals, such as nitric acid, nitro compounds, sulphur compounds, superphosphates, soda, burnt lime, etc. Carbon bisulphide particularly, which can be ignited by heat of sun.

5. Finely divided substances, such as sawdust, cork dust, insulating materials, drill turnings, disinfecting powders, gas purifying materials, lampblack, etc.

6. Varnishes, lacquers, driers.

7. Cloth, oil cloth, oily rags, etc.

8. Cotton, particularly in combination with turpentine, rosin, cottonseed oil, and petroleum, all of which products are forbidden as cargo on cotton-laden ships.

9. Scrap rubber.

Sulphuric acid with its strong affinity for water can easily start a fire and in combination with particles of sugar and potassium chlorate the result is violent. Other substances such as turpentine catch fire when brought into contact with chlorine, bromine or iodine. Even water will start a fire when it comes in contact with ordinary quicklime in the right proportion.

Explosions in tanks and pipe lines are sometimes the result of spontaneous combustion. A heated tank containing a hydro-carbon vapor, air, and a coating of finely divided coal dust may be as dangerous as a bomb. Under such conditions the hydro-carbons oxidize rapidly building up a large amount of heat. The vapor ignites, burning slowly at first, and the contents of the tank expand under the heat thus generated. The pressure resulting from this expansion in turn produces more heat until the whole body of unburned vapor takes fire at once building up the enormous pressure which results in an explosion.

EXPLOSIVES

The regulations of the United States Coast Guard require a permit to be obtained by every vessel loading or unloading explosives and certain piers or areas are designated for this purpose. Vessels having these highly dangerous cargoes on board are not permitted to enter congested areas in our ports. Vessels that have such dangerous cargoes on board are not permitted to become immobile. It is required that the vessel be ready to move, that a sufficient number of the crew to constitute a standby watch be on board and on duty. If for any reason the ship must be immobile, it is required that tugs stand by during that period. Personnel engaged in handling and stowing this dangerous cargo of explosives or ammunition are required to have an explosive handling permit issued by the Captain of the Port. Before securing this permit, the applicant is checked as to his qualifications for this task, and also for subversive tendencies. No unauthorized persons are permitted to be in the hold of a vessel taking on or discharging cargoes of explosives. Certain other prescriptions are laid down to safeguard the actual handling of the explosives. Regardless of the functions performed by the military personnel in supervising the loading or unloading of explosives, these functions do not relieve the masters of the vessels from the responsibility of providing security for their vessels.

It has been the experience of the Coast Guard that one of the most effective functions which it undertakes in providing for the security of vessels and our ports is its fire prevention and firefighting activity. When a vessel applies for a permit to load explosives, it is inspected. All potential fire hazards are eliminated or safeguarded before the vessel may proceed to an explosives loading terminal. During the time the vessel is at the terminal, constant inspections are made to insure, as far as is humanly possible, that no fire hazards exist. The vessel's fire-fighting equipment is checked and so placed as to be instantaneously available in usable condition while dangerous cargo is being handled on board. This includes operation of the fire pumps on the vessel itself. If a vessel is at an explosives loading pier, land lines are run out prepared for instant use. It is customary also to moor one of the Coast Guard fireboats alongside the vessel or the pier while the operation is under-way. In some areas, especially where the pier water supply may be inadequate or of low pressure, the Coast Guard provides mobile pumper units manned by men trained in firefighting on board vessels. To handle oil fires, foam and log nozzles are provided by the Coast Guard and ready for instant use. All of this equipment is modern and up-to-the-minute, and is manned by trained personnel of the Coast Guard.

The existing regulations governing the handling, stowage, and transportation of explosives and ammunition are not restrictive or onerous. They are not the brain child of a theorist. They represent the learning of many men and the experiences of many casualties. Prior to promulgation, they were passed upon and agreed to by a group of qualified and experienced men drawn from the Ordnance Departments of the Army and Navy, the Transportation Corps of the Army and Navy, the 40 years experience of the heads of the Bureau of Explosives, the experiences of the promulgating agency, the U. S. Coast Guard, the vessel underwriters, and vessel operators of this country.

The regulations have the authority of law. To protect your own life and limb, observe them.

STATIC ELECTRICITY HAZARD

The possibilities for more or less serious consequences from the static electricity hazard are many and varied; and this is so for reasons which need no elaboration here. Attention is therefore confined to the nature of the hazard, and to a few of the possibilities and precautions. Although the generation of static electricity cannot be prevented, it is often possible to prevent its accumulation, and thus prevent the occurrence of static sparks when, in particular, an explosive vapor is present or within probable range for contact.

Static electricity is a stationary charge of electricity that is generated by friction between two solid substances or a solid substance and a liquid (such as friction resulting from the passage of a liquid through a hose) or by solid substances coming together and separating, or by various sorts of motion of a person or a material. It accumulates on surface; but if the surface is moist, the static charge is dispersed. For this reason persons whose skin is habitually dry readily accumulate static electricity on the surface of their bodies, and they should exercise extreme precaution in dry air containing explosive vapor, when operating machinery or using sparking tools.

When a sufficient charge of electricity has accumulated on a surface, and the object (or person) so charged comes close to one that is not grounded or one that is not equally charged, the two charges neutralize by jumping the gap. The spark produced across this gap will ignite any explosive vapor in the vicinity.

Accumulation of static electricity can be prevented by grounding machinery. When advisable to do so, each individual machine is grounded. The fire fighter is not called upon to perform this task, but he should understand the principle involved, especially in view of the fact that he may have occasion to use equipment when a static electricity hazard is present.

The fire fighter may be called upon to set up an electric blower in order to vent a compartment of explosive vapors. He should see to it that the blower is grounded, unless it is of non-sparking design. If he has occasion to put water into an empty gasoline tank, he must ground the nozzle. This is necessary because of the high probability that the tank contains gasoline vapor. For the same reason, gasoline pipes and their outlets must be grounded; the friction of the moving gasoline is a possible source of static electricity. Filtering materials of chamois or leather would contribute to the static electricity hazard, and consequently they are not used for filtering gasoline, unless this hazard is guarded against. Chamois, for instance, may be used for filtering gasoline if it is used with a 40-mesh wire gauze, and with the hose nozzle grounded. Wire gauze alone may be used with safety for filtering gasoline, and if it is so used the hose nozzle would also be grounded.

Another method of preventing the accumulation of static electricity is to maintain a relative humidity of 40 to 50 percent in enclosures containing flammable liquids. This amount of moisture provides a means for the static charge to leak away. A third method is to use so-called static neutralizers. These produce ionization in the air, and thus make it a conductor of electricity, to carry off the static charge.

REGULATIONS CONCERNING FIRE PROTECTION*

Following the *Morro Castle* fire disaster of September 8, 1934, in which 124 persons perished, all passenger vessels 100 gross tons or over, built or converted after May 27, 1936 were required to submit plans for approval to the Bureau of Marine Inspection, now under the Coast Guard, embodying the following features, which are outlined with later amendments included.

Certain elements of design and construction practices, especially in passenger quarters, were found to be faulty; having the practical effect of forming flues tending to provide excellent methods of increasing combustion and communicating fire from compartment to compartment through the over-all length of the structure. These faults were pointed out and design requirement altered to provide fire stops in an effort to isolate a fire within a compartment in which it initially occurs. These provisions apply primarily to passenger-carrying vessels and do not have specific applicability to cargo vessels.

Hull, bulkheads, decks and deck houses to be of steel with the in-

* See CG 227, *Laws Governing Marine Inspection*, Chapter IV, Art. 46, page 110, for requirements concerning Safety Certificates which are good for 1 yr. and which must be posted under glass.

terior boundaries of various type of fire retardent materials depending
on their location. These are broadly grouped into materials which are
absolutely fireproof and those which are slow burning such as wood
treated with fireproofing solutions. However, the futility of treating
wood in an attempt to render it fireproof was demonstrated in the fire
aboard the *USS Wakefield* in September 1942. During the construction of this vessel, as the *S/S Manhattan*, the builders went beyond the
requirements then in effect, 1932, in an attempt to comply with the
spirit of the 1929 Safety of Life-at-Sea Convention. Joiner work was
wood chemically *fireproofed*, and a considerable amount of this wood
was removed upon her conversion to a Navy transport. Nevertheless
the vessel was gutted in a fire at sea which fortunately has not gone
down as a major disaster because of the splendid rescue work of the
USS Brooklyn, no lives being lost.

Absolutely fireproof are sheet products of asbestos such as Marinite,
used for staterooms and passageways, and marine sheathing which is
stronger but heavier and is used for hull lining and such locations requiring greater strength. Metal bulkheads with insulation between
have also been developed and by careful design the increase in weight
has not been as great as was originally expected, though topside weight
has increased.

Deck coverings within accommodations are required to be of incombustible material such as magnesite, a cement. Windows in these locations must be fitted with wire inserted glass and must have metal
frames. Rugs and carpets, though permitted, are required to have fire
resisting qualities.

Steel escape stairways to weather decks must be fitted in each main
vertical zone and, except in machinery spaces, they must be enclosed.
The Regulations define *main vertical zones* for fire resisting bulkheads
as being continuous, side to side, with a distance between them not to
exceed 131 feet. Open stairways are permitted only if they lie wholly
within a public space and in this case they are not to be considered as
a means of escape.

Doors in main vertical bulkheads must be of incombustible materials
and be capable of being opened from either side by one person. In addition they must be of the self closing type and capable of release from
the open position either at the door or from the wheelhouse. This is
done by holding the door in the open position by a magnet arrangement
so that when current is cut off the magnet, the doors swing shut by
means of the self closing spring feature. Holdback hooks are explicitly
forbidden.

All insulation must be incombustible for which fiber glass or asbestos
materials are used.

Nitro-cellulose paints or those producing noxious fumes are not permitted and warning is given that an excessive number of coats of paint
renders a surface highly flammable. War experience showed that paint
which appeared highly fire resistant under test became one of the principal means by which fire was spread when high temperatures were
reached over large areas. In general the thicker the paint film the more
readily it will burn. This subject is dealt with more fully later on.

Automatic fire dampers of 1/8 inch steel plate are required in all ventilation ducts unless these ducts are to be closed by hand by a crew member regularly assigned to this duty. These dampers must be inspected annually. The fusible link melts at a temperature of 165 degrees F.

It is also required that means be provided for shutting off the ventilating system's fans, one switch to be in the wheelhouse and another switch in the passageway just outside the main entrance to the machinery space.

Furniture or drapes in corridors and stairway enclosures must be incombustible, and while this is not required of drapes and upholstery in staterooms the furniture itself must be incombustible.

Since 1916 the Rules have called for a fire detecting system on passenger ships which would report *the presence or indication of fire in various compartments of the vessel which are not accessible to observation.* Amendments to this rule now require that passenger and crew quarters on passenger vessels be protected with an automatic sprinkler system or an automatic fire detecting system and that a manual fire-alarm system be also installed. On some large vessels the fire detecting system (usually on the thermostatic principal) reports the exact compartment, but generally the zone type system is used. This latter system is less desirable as invaluable time may be lost in locating the fire within the zone.

When the requirement regarding fire detecting systems for staterooms was put into effect it was realized that the electric thermostat system might actually increase the fire hazard in cargo spaces and that a basic change in the method of fire detecting for holds was necessary. This resulted in a system which draws samples of air from each individual cargo space to a cabinet located in the wheelhouse where it passes a photoelectric eye and is then discharged, within the wheelhouse. The presence of smoke causes an alarm to ring when passing the electric eye and its presence can also be detected by odor due to the discharge within the wheelhouse. The foregoing requirement applies to all passenger vessels over 5000 gross tons.

Despite all precautions there is nothing that can be done to render a ship's cargo non-inflammable and as far back as 1870 the U.S. Government passed a law requiring the fitting of pipes which would bring steam from the boilers into any of the cargo spaces for the purpose of smothering fire. Carbon dioxide is now generally used in preference to steam as it will extinguish the fire as effectively without doing damage to cargo, and it can be combined with the smoke detecting system, making use of the same pipes.

Since 1921 a foam or carbon dioxide system for smothering fire has been required for oil-fired boiler rooms on passenger vessels. The use of carbon dioxide permits a combination system whereby the same installation can be used for both cargo spaces and boiler room.

Such spaces as paint and oil lockers, motion picture booths, etc., must be protected by a steam or carbon dioxide system.

The *Morro Castle* disaster also brought about the regulation that a fire patrol be employed to visit all parts of a passenger vessel accessible to passengers and crew, except machinery spaces and occupied quarters, every 20 minutes between the hours of 10 P.M. and 6 A.M. A loudspeaker system with a talk-back arrangement was also required at this time.

The electrical installations aboard ship are governed by a standard known as *Recommended Practice for Electrical Installations on Shipboard* prepared under the auspices of the American Institute of Electrical Engineers. Vibration, dampness and corrosion are the principal problems which must be guarded against.

A thorough knowledge of the layout of the ship is essential for the ship's officer. Relationship of tanks, bunkers and holds to the other sections of the ship, the recognition of the vertical zone boundaries, watertight bulkheads, the location of insulated spaces, storerooms, electric motors and resistor houses and a knowledge of the water, steam and carbon dioxide outlets of the ship's fire control system are all very important factors for those charged with the responsibility of fighting fire aboard a vessel.

The simple and obvious fact, that the divisions of a ship are formed by metal bulkheads that easily conduct heat from one compartment to another, must be continually borne in mind. Asbestos materials used in the passenger spaces will resist flame spread but cannot resist heat. A sheet of asbestos over wood will not positively protect the wood, the heat will pass through to char and ultimately ignite the wood.

Summary of Regulations Pertaining to Fire Protection:

Fire bulkheads. Required on all passenger vessels, and to be constructed of fire-resisting material effective for one hour against fire temperatures of 1500° F. Mean distance between two adjacent fire-resisting bulkheads in a superstructure not to exceed 131 ft.

Requirements for lamp and paint locker. In all vessels to be wholly and tightly lined with metal and fitted with steam pipes of not less than 3/8″ diameter. All such pipes to be supplied with valves on deck where they are accessible at all times.

Fire patrolman. On all passenger vessels with berths or staterooms. To cover completely all parts of the vessel accessible to passengers and crew every 20 minutes, and report to bridge every hour between 10 P.M. and 6 A.M., except machinery spaces and occupied quarters. Failure to follow a prescribed route to be recorded, and reason given. To have no other tasks, wear uniform and badge, carry flashlight.

Alarm bells in all sleeping quarters, unless watchman always on duty, on vessels over 100 t. gross, 7 inches in dia. and operated by open switch from bridge.

Woodwork around stoves, stove pipes, in lamp lockers, etc., to be protected by metal and a 1-inch air space.

Electric wiring to be covered with iron conduit or armored casing in all places where it is liable to mechanical injury, as in bunkers, cargo spaces, storerooms. Splices to be secure without solder, but soldered afterward.

Fire detecting or sprinkler system required on all vessels of over 150 ft. in length with sleeping quarters for passengers. In exceptional conditions a watchman is permitted instead, who must visit such parts as directed every 10 minutes and keep a time-clock record.

Steam smothering lines to be tested with at least 50 lbs. air pressure.

Smoke-pipe systems (Richaudio). To wheelhouse, or where a 24-hour watch is kept. To have an audible alarm there and in engine room.

Gasoline tanks. Where allowed, as for emergency lighting, to have 2 approved fire extinguishers within 5 ft.

Fire line hydrants. To be so arranged that any part of the vessel can be reached with water with full capacity of the pumps by means of a single 50 ft. length of hose.

Fire line. To be no less in diameter than hose and so that it is at least 1 1/2" dia. Tested to 100 lbs. pressure per sq. in.

Hand pump or rotary pump. Driven by an engine independent of main engine to deliver full pressure.

Steam fire pumps on vessels over 3000 t. to have double acting fire pump of 1000 cu. in. capacity. All steam fire pumps to be supplied with pipes and valves for pumping and discharging water from holds overboard.

Fire hose. All lengths to be tested at each inspection to 100 lbs. pressure. Couplings securely fastened to hose. One length at all times attached to outlet of fire main and provided with nozzle. May be uncoupled on freight vessels where it would interfere with loading or discharging.*

Approved Types of Fire-Detecting Systems:

a) Electrical as Henschel transmitting temperature changes by electricity.

b) Pneumatic tube systems using thermostats composed of copper tubing containing air the expansion of which produces visual and audible signals. Aero automatic system.

c) Smoke pipe systems as the Richaudio which besides giving notice by sight and smell is made audible by means of the photo-electric cell.

Fire-Fighting Systems and Apparatus:

Overhead water sprinkling system. Required on all steamers carrying passengers which also carry freight upon a main deck which is accessible to passengers or crew while being navigated. Also in passenger steamers with a galley below the main deck.

Portable fire extinguishers. Vessels over 1000 t. gross must carry not less than 8 on deck, 2 in fireroom and 1 for each additional machinery space.

Oxygen breathing apparatus. Class *A* vessels, 50 to 100 passenger staterooms, require 2 masks, 1 in pilot house and 1 in engine room. Class *B* vessels, more than 100 passenger staterooms, require 4 oxygen apparatuses or masks, 2 in pilot house, 1 in engine room and 1 in radio room. Apparatus is good for one-half hour's use.

Flame safety lamp. Required on Class *B* passenger vessels, more than 100 passenger staterooms.

Axes. All steamers over 1000 tons must carry not less than 8 axes, located so as to be readily found, and not to be used for general purposes.

* Suitable spanners must be secured to each hydrant or nearby.

Pipes for steam smothering system must have main and branches not less than 1 1/2 inches in dia. and pipes of not less than 3/4 inches dia. to all lamp lockers, oil rooms, etc. Valves to be in not more than two places, enclosed in boxes or casings, and marked "Steam Fire Apparatus."

Carbonic acid gas, or other kind if approved, may be substituted for steam.

Passenger vessels using oil fuel must have CO_2 or foam system in engine room. Also two or more CO_2 extinguishers and a sand box with 10 cu. ft. of sand.

EXTRACTS FROM COAST GUARD REGULATIONS

Steam Smothering Lines

The main pipes and their branches, on steamers carrying passengers or freight, to convey steam from the boilers to the hold and separate compartments of the same shall be not less than $1\frac{1}{2}$ inches in diameter. Steam pipes of not less than three-fourths of an inch in diameter shall be led to all lamp lockers, oil rooms, and like compartments, which lamp lockers, oil rooms, and compartments, in all classes of vessels, shall be wholly and tightly lined with metal. All branch pipes leading into the several compartments of the hold of the vessel shall be supplied with valves, the handles distinctly marked to indicate the compartment or parts of the vessel to which they lead.

These valves or their handles shall be placed in not more than two places on the most suitable and accessible deck of the vessel and so arranged that all can be inclosed in cabinets, boxes, or casings, the doors of which shall be plainly marked with the words "Steam fire apparatus."

Steam smothering lines shall be tested with at least 50 pounds air pressure with ends of the smothering lines capped, or by blowing steam through the lines, and a survey made for detecting corrosion and defects, using the hammer test or such other means as may be necessary.

On all oil-tank steamers the valves, instead of being located near the hatches on the upper deck, shall be all in an accessible house in which the operator is well protected from heat and smoke: *Provided*, That on oil-tank steamers a main line of steam smothering pipe of sufficient area to supply all branch pipes leading from the same to the tanks may be run the entire length of the deck, and only the main stop valve of the main line shall be required to be housed. All branch pipes shall be provided with valves which shall be left open at all times, so that the steam may enter all compartments simultaneously. Such branches as may not be required after the fire is definitely located may be shut off, in order that the entire system may be concentrated on one tank.

Carbonic Acid (CO_2) Smothering System

Provided, That carbonic-acid gas or other extinguishing gases or vapors may be substituted in place of steam as aforesaid and for the above-described purposes, and may be used on cargo vessels, using oil for fuel, in the fire hold, fireroom bilges, and pump rooms, when such gas or vapor and the apparatus for storing, producing, and distributing same shall have been approved by the Board of Supervising Inspectors.

At annual inspections, all carbon dioxide (CO_2) cylinders, whether fixed or portable, shall be examined externally and replaced if any corrosion is found; and also shall be checked by weighing to determine contents, and if found to be more than 10 per cent under required contents of carbon dioxide, the same shall be recharged.

On all vessels where a carbon dioxide system is installed, there shall be sufficient carbon dioxide to give a 30% concentration in largest cargo hold.

The largest cargo hold is to be considered the space from the shelter deck to top of cargo tank top and between the bulkheads.

Provided further, That pipes for conveying steam from the boilers, or pipes for conveying carbonic-acid gas or other extinguishing vapors for the purpose of extinguishing fire, shall not be led into the cabins or into other passengers' or crew's quarters.

Foam Type Smothering System

Provided further, That in the compartments or oil tanks of oil-tank vessels the foam-type fire-extinguishing system may be substituted for steam, or other extinguishing gases or vapors, and may also be used in the fire hold, fire-room bilges, and pump rooms on vessels using oil for fuel when such foam-type fire-extinguishing system is completely installed in accordance with drawings or blue prints and specifications approved by the supervising inspector of the district where it is installed. The foregoing system may be of type employing either two-solution tanks or one or more generators using an approved dry chemical mixture.

Any special type of appliance, fire-extinguishing medium, or arrangement approved by the Board of Supervising Inspectors may be used.

Motor vessels of 50 gross tons and over, carrying passengers or freight for hire, shall be equipped with efficient means for extinguishing fire in the hold and the different compartments thereof in which cargo is carried; also in lamp lockers, oil rooms, and like compartments.

Fire Equipment for Vessels Using Oil for Fuel

Steam-propelled vessels burning oil for fuel, and sea-going vessels in excess of 300 gross tons propelled by internal combustion engines, except such vessels engaged in fishing, oystering, clamming, crabbing, or any other branch of the fishery or kelp or sponge industry, shall be fitted with the fire-fighting equipment of the type and character specified below.

(1) In each fire room a metal receptacle containing not less than 10 cubic feet of sand, sawdust impregnated with soda, or other approved dry materials, and scoop or shaker for distributing same: *Provided, however,* That vessels of 1,000 gross tons and under using oil as fuel, shall be fitted with a metal receptacle containing not less than 5 cubic feet of sand, sawdust impregnated with soda, or other approved dry material, and scoop or shaker for distributing same.

(4) (*a*) On all steam propelled vessels having one boiler room, there shall be provided one fire extinguisher of the foam type of at least 40 gallons rated capacity or one carbon dioxide (CO_2) extinguisher of at least 100 pounds. If the vessel has more than one boiler room, an extinguisher of the above type shall be provided in each boiler room.

(*b*) On all steam propelled vessels of 1,000 gross tons and under, foam type fire extinguishers of at least 20 gallons rated capacity or carbon dioxide (CO_2) extinguishers of at least 50 pounds may be used in lieu of the capacities required in (*a*) above.

(*c*) Extinguishers fitted in compliance with (*a*) and (*b*) above, shall be equipped with suitable hose and nozzles on reels, or other practicable means, easy of access and of sufficient length to reach any part of the boiler room and spaces containing oil-fuel pumping units.

(5) (*a*) Steam-propelled passenger vessels burning oil for fuel shall be fitted with an approved fixed carbon dioxide or foam type system for extinguishing fire in the bilges of each fire room. If engine and boiler rooms are not entirely

separate, or if fuel oil can drain from the boiler room bilge into the engine room, the combined engine and boiler rooms shall be considered one compartment. The system shall be capable of being operated from a convenient and accessible point outside of space protected.

(b) Passenger vessels propelled by internal-combustion engines shall be fitted with an approved fixed carbon dioxide system for extinguishing fire in the machinery space. The system shall be capable of being operated from a convenient and accessible point outside of space protected.

(6) All vessels propelled by internal-combustion engines shall be equipped with the following foam type or carbon dioxide fire extinguishers in the machinery spaces:

(a) One approved 12-gallon foam type extinguisher or one approved 35-pound carbon dioxide extinguisher.

(b) One approved 2½-gallon foam type, or 15-pound carbon dioxide extinguisher for each 1,000 B.H.P. of the main engines, or fraction thereof.

(c) The total number of 2½-gallon foam type or 15-pound carbon dioxide extinguishers carried in compliance with (b) above, shall not be less than two, and need not exceed six.

(d) When a donkey boiler fitted to burn oil as fuel is located in the machinery space, there shall be substituted for the 12-gallon foam or 35-pound carbon dioxide unit required by (a) above, one approved 40-gallon foam or one approved 100-pound carbon dioxide unit.

(7) (a) On all passenger vessels there shall be provided in the machinery spaces, which contain electric propelling motors and generators of the open type, at least one 15-pound carbon dioxide extinguisher for each such electric propelling motor and generator unit.

(b) On all passenger vessels, small compartments containing auxiliary internal-combustion engines, such as emergency generators, etc., shall, in addition to any other extinguishers required, be provided with one approved 15-pound carbon dioxide or 2½-gallon foam extinguisher for each such compartment. This extinguisher shall be located outside of and adjacent to the entrance of the compartment.

(8) *Carbon dioxide system requirements.* (a) When a carbon dioxide (CO_2) smothering system is fitted in the boiler room, the quantity of carbon dioxide carried shall be sufficient to give a gas saturation of 25 per cent of the gross volume of the largest boiler room from tank top to top of the boilers. Top of the boilers is to be considered as the top of the shell of a Scotch or leg type of boiler, and the top of the casing or drum, whichever is the higher, on water-tube boilers.

(c) The whole charge of gas shall be capable of being released simultaneously by operating one valve and control. All cylinders shall be completely discharged in not more than two minutes. The arrangement of the piping shall be such as to give a general and fairly uniform distribution over the entire area protected. An alarm which shall operate automatically with the operation of the system shall be provided to give a warning in the space when the carbon dioxide is about to be released. Provision shall be made to prevent the admission of air into the lower parts of the boiler or engine room while the system is in operation.

(9) *Foam smothering system requirements.* (a) When a foam type system is fitted, its capacity shall be such as to rapidly discharge over the entire area of the bilge (tank top) of the largest boiler room a volume of foam six inches deep. The arrangement of piping shall be such as to give a uniform distribution over the entire area protected. The system shall be completely discharged in not more than three minutes.

(*b*) The foregoing system may be of a type employing either two-solution tanks or one or more generators using an approved dry chemical mixture. All containers and valves by which they are operated shall be easily accessible and so placed that they will not readily be cut off from use by an outbreak of fire.

Fire Hazards. Following forbidden on passenger vessels:

1. Loose hay, cotton or hemp.
2. Camphene, naphtha, benzene, coal oil, etc.
3. Petroleum inflammable under 110° F.
4. Metal polishes inflammable under 300° F.

Articles Permitted on Passenger Vessels Only Under Special Conditions:

1. Acids have various special regulations for different kinds, but in general must be carried on deck, packed in an absorbent and, if a mixed shipment, not more than five 1-lb. or 1-pint bottles in a single case.
2. Alcohol if stowed in a cool place and packed to prevent leakage.
3. Ammonia in cylinders on deck.
4. Ammunition plainly marked, under special restrictions.
5. Asphalt, disinfectants, petroleum, require a special license if their flash point is under 110° F.
6. Empty gasoline cylinders may be accepted if carefully drained and steamed out.
7. Gunpowder only under special license.
8. Caustic soda and quicklime in watertight containers on deck.
9. Matches in strong and tight metal-lined chests, marked with name and stowed away from heat. Fiber containers not acceptable.
10. Moving-picture films may be transported only under special conditions.
11. Gasoline only in tanks of lifeboats, or for wireless or lighting auxiliary.
12. Baled hay, cotton or hemp, where allowed on deck, must be covered with a tarpaulin.

(*Note*: By definition, a combustible liquid is one with a flash point above 80°F.) See page 8-28.

STANDARD STATION BILLS

A standard form of station bill has been prepared which includes, as far as practicable, the suggestions submitted by and representing the consensus of opinion of the U. S. Coast Guard Merchant Vessel Inspectors, and others concerned. This proposed form will meet with the requirements of all inspected vessels. The minimum emergency signals and instructions have been incorporated in this proposed form and the continuous ringing of the General Alarm Bells has but one meaning, Fire and Emergency. The crew, trained to recognize this signal, shall proceed to their emergency stations immediately and carry out their allotted duties quickly and effectively. In the event of an actual collision, or stranding, those men assigned to fire hose, hydrants, axes, extinguishers, etc., must assist in closing all airports, side scuttles, side ports, watertight doors, and ventilator ducts in the vicinity of their stations.

Section 18, Rule V, provides that the master of any vessel may establish additional emergency signals as will provide that all the officers, crew, and passengers of the vessel will have positive and certain notice of the existing emergency. Therefore, where collision drills are conducted on a particular type vessel, it is recommended that the emergency signal for collision stations, "Eight bells sounded on the general alarm bells," like striking time on the ship's bell, be adopted to eliminate the confusion of additional whistle signals. As the alarm bells can be heard by the entire crew at all times, upon hearing the first two bells of the group, the crew would instantly be alert and ready to respond to the emergency.

The Ten Standard Instructions provide for all anticipated emergencies which may occur on board the various types of vessels. Where one or more of these instructions does not apply to a particular type of vessel, they need not be considered. The crew, however, will be familiar with all Standard Instructions in the event they are transferred to a vessel to which they are applicable.

The advantages of this form are numerous. For instance, if a member of the crew wishes to find his emergency stations, he can look under the respective department in the left-hand column and follow down until he arrives at his rating and number and then read to the right in each column for his station and duties at each emergency drill. With this form in use throughout the merchant service, the crew will become thoroughly familiar with it and need not study and interpret a different form each time they change ships.

The preparation of station bills would be facilitated by indicating the berth or article number (instead of names) of the individual members of the crew, with the emergency duties assigned to them. A number and card would be fixed to each berth or issued to each member of the crew at the time of signing articles. This supplementary station bill card should show the emergency duties in detail, location of the station, and all signals connected with these duties, should be included. In order to provide for a permanent assignment to lifeboats, the station bills should be made up on the basis of maximum passenger and crew capacity.

Electric lifeboat winches must be equipped with limit switches and an emergency disconnect switch and the station bill must provide for a person stationed at each such switch with no additional duties during the hoisting of lifeboats. See *Electrical Engineering Regulations*: CG-259.

On board these vessels employing large crews, it is recommended that the station bill be made up in sections and posted in the mess room, quarters or passageway adjacent to the quarters of each department.

Whatever lifeboats, life rafts, or buoyant appliances are provided against the contingency of the vessel having to be abandoned, the use to which they will be put when the emergency arises must depend on the efficiency of the crew. It is not enough that individual members of the crew should be experts in the management of a boat. Well organized teamwork is necessary and the organization must cover not only the lowering and handling of the boats or rafts, but also the mustering of all on board at their stations. No amount of material improvement in equipment and arrangement can take the place of a well-instructed, disciplined and properly organized crew. The establishment of uniformity is essential.

The duties connected with the assisting and controlling of the passengers should normally be assigned to certain members of the steward's department. In emergencies they shall warn all passengers, assist them to obtain and put on life preservers and direct them to their emergency stations. They are to keep order in the stairways, passages, and doorways, impressing on passengers the serious danger of injury from leaping overboard. In this connection, the importance of using the side ladders for the purposes of entering the boats should it prove necessary to embark in them after they had been lowered into the water, should be pointed out. At drills they should explain to the passengers the process of abandonment and emphasize that the general alarm signal is not in itself a signal to abandon ship, but is intended to secure the orderly assembly of passengers at the appointed stations.

On all vessels, the allocation of members of the crew to the duties of distributing the life preservers to the passengers in various parts of the vessel, and preparing and launching the life rafts and buoyant apparatus, should receive special attention.

Instruction cards for passengers posted in the staterooms must clearly state the various emergency signals and the location of the allotted emergency station of the occupants.

In assigning the crew to stations and duties comparable to their regular work, consideration should be given to the quarters and working station of personnel. For example, a room steward's lifeboat and the passengers in his care should be located on the same side of the vessel as their room section, and in the case of Firemen No. 1, No. 2, and No. 3, on vessels employing only three firemen, all should be assigned to one station such as watertight door No. 5, located near the fire room. As the standard instructions state that all persons on watch must remain on watch during emergency drills, this station will be protected at all times by the two firemen not on watch. It is recommended that all personnel standing watch be detailed in this manner as far as possible.

UNITED STATES COAST GUARD

SPECIMEN OF A STANDARD STATION BILL PREPARED FOR FREIGHT AND TANK SHIPS CARRYING PERSONS IN ADDITION TO CREW

STATION BILL
SIGNALS

_____   _____
(Name of ship)   (Name of company)

FIRE AND EMERGENCY—Rapid ringing of the ship's bell and continuous ringing of general alarm bells for a period of at least 10 seconds.
ABANDON SHIP—7 short blasts and 1 long blast on the whistle and the same signal on the general alarm bells.
MAN OVERBOARD—Hail, and pass the word "MAN OVERBOARD" to the bridge.
DISMISSAL—From FIRE AND EMERGENCY stations, 3 short blasts on the whistle and 3 short rings on the general alarm bells.

WHERE WHISTLE SIGNALS ARE USED FOR HANDLING BOATS

Lower boats—1 short blast on whistle
Stop lowering boats—2 short blasts on whistle
Dismissal from boat stations—3 short blasts on whistle

INSTRUCTIONS

1. Entire crew shall familiarize themselves with the location and duties of their emergency stations immediately upon reporting on board.
2. Each crew member shall be provided with an individual supplementary station bill card which must show in detail the special duties to perform.
3. Entire crew shall be instructed in the performance of their special duties and crew on watch will remain on watch on signal for emergency drill.
4. Every person participating in the abandon-ship drill will be required to wear a life preserver and entire boat crew shall assist in removing covers and swinging out boats.
5. Emergency Squad will assemble with equipment at scene of action immediately upon the emergency signal.
6. Stewards' department will assemble and direct passengers, properly dressed and wearing life preservers, to embarkation stations.
7. Person discovering FIRE shall immediately notify the bridge and fight the fire with available equipment.
8. Immediately upon the FIRE AND EMERGENCY signal, fire pumps to be started, all watertight doors, ports, and air shafts to be closed, and all fans and blowers stopped. Fire hose to be led out in the affected area as directed.
9. Upon hearing the signal, "MAN OVERBOARD," throw life ring buoys overboard, stop engines and send lookout aloft. Emergency boat crew consisting of all seamen shall immediately clear lee boat for launching.
10. During periods of low visibility, all watertight doors and ports below the bulkhead deck shall be closed, subject to the Master's orders.

No.	RATING	FIRE AND EMERGENCY STATIONS	No.	ABANDON SHIP—BOAT STATIONS
		DECK DEPARTMENT		
A.	Master	On the bridge. In command, all operations.	A.	Lifeboat No. 1	In command. On bridge in charge all operations.
1.	Chief Mate	At scene of emergency. In charge.	1.	Lifeboat No. 2	In command. In charge launching lifeboats amidship.
2.	2d Mate	On the bridge. Relieve the watch.	2.	Lifeboat No. 3	In command. On the bridge. Relieve the watch.
3.	3d Mate	Prepare all lifeboats for launching. In charge.	3.	Lifeboat No. 4	In command. In charge launching lifeboats aft.
4.	Radio Operator	Radio room. At instruments.	4.	Lifeboat No. 1	Attend Master's orders and instructions.
5.	Boatswain	Emergency squad. Provide life lines.	5.	Lifeboat No. 1	2d in command. Attend forward gripes and falls.
6.	Able Seaman	Emergency squad. Relieve the wheel.	6.	Lifeboat No. 2	2d in command. Attend forward gripes and falls.
7.	Able Seaman	Emergency squad. Provide extra length of hose and spanner.	7.	Lifeboat No. 3	2d in command. Attend forward gripes and falls.
8.	Able Seaman	Emergency squad. Provide fire extinguisher.	8.	Lifeboat No. 4	2d in command. Attend forward gripes and falls.
9.	Able Seaman	Emergency squad. Provide fire ax.	9.	Lifeboat No. 1	Release boat chocks and secure drain cap.
10.	Able Seaman	Emergency squad. Provide fresh air mask.	10.	Lifeboat No. 2	Release boat chocks and secure drain cap.
11.	Able Seaman	Assist 3d Mate prepare lifeboats for launching.	11.	Lifeboat No. 3	Release boat chocks and secure drain cap.
12.	Able Seaman	Assist 3d Mate prepare lifeboats for launching.	12.	Lifeboat No. 1	Lead out and attend boat painter.
13.	Able Seaman	Assist with fresh air mask.	13.	Lifeboat No. 2	Lead out and attend boat painter.
14.	Able Seaman	Assist 3d Mate prepare lifeboats for launching.	14.	Lifeboat No. 3	Lead out and attend boat painter.
15.	Ordinary Seaman	Bridge. Act as messenger.	15.	Lifeboat No. 4	Release boat chocks and secure drain cap.
16.	Ordinary Seaman	Emergency squad. Act as messenger.	16.	Lifeboat No. 1	Lead out and attend boat painter.
17.	Ordinary Seaman	Assist 3d Mate prepare lifeboats for launching.	17.	Lifeboat No. 2	Lead out and attend boat painter.
		ENGINE DEPARTMENT		
18.	Chief Engineer	In charge of Engine Department.	18.	Lifeboat No. 1	Assist in general operations.
19.	1st Assistant	Engine room. In charge.	19.	Lifeboat No. 2	Assist in general operations.
20.	2d Assistant	In charge of fire room and steam smothering apparatus.	20.	Lifeboat No. 3	Assist in general operations.
21.	3d Assistant	Attend main steam smothering line.	21.	Lifeboat No. 4	Assist in general operations.
22.	Jr. Engineer	Attend CO² or foam smothering system.	22.	Lifeboat No. 1	Turn out forward davit and assist at forward falls.
23.	Jr. Engineer	Attend CO² or foam smothering system.	23.	Lifeboat No. 2	Turn out forward davit and assist at forward falls.
24.	Jr. Engineer	Engine room. At fire pumps.	24.	Lifeboat No. 3	Turn out forward davit and assist at forward falls.
25.	Pumpman	Assist 2d Assistant Engineer in fire room.	25.	Lifeboat No. 4	Release after gripes and attend after falls.
26.	2d Pumpman	Emergency squad. Assist with fresh air mask.	26.	Lifeboat No. 4	Lead out and attend boat painter.
27.	Electrician	Engine room. At main panel.	27.	Lifeboat No. 4	Assist in general operations.
28.	Machinist	Engine room. Assist at fire pumps.	28.	Lifeboat No. 1	Turn out forward davit and assist at forward falls.
29.	Oiler	Engine room. Assist at fire pumps.	29.	Lifeboat No. 2	Release after gripes and attend after falls.
30.	Oiler	Engine room. Trim ventilators as directed.	30.	Lifeboat No. 3	Release after gripes and attend after falls.
31.	Oiler	Engine room. Trim ventilators as directed.	31.	Lifeboat No. 4	Release after gripes and attend after falls.
32.	Oiler	Assist at steam smothering manifold.	32.	Lifeboat No. 1	Turn out after davit and assist at after falls.
33.	Oiler	Assist at CO² or foam smothering system.	33.	Lifeboat No. 2	Turn out after davit and assist at after falls.
34.	Oiler	Engine room. At portable fire extinguisher.	34.	Lifeboat No. 3	Turn out after davit and assist at after falls.
35.	Watertender	Fire room. Assist 2d Assistant Engineer.	35.	Lifeboat No. 4	Turn out after davit and assist at after falls.
36.	Watertender	Emergency squad. Provide wrenches and pliers.	36.	Lifeboat No. 1	Assist release gripes and turn out davits.
37.	Watertender	Engine room. Assist at fire pumps.	37.	Lifeboat No. 2	Assist release gripes and turn out davits.
38.	Fireman	Fire room. Assist 2d Assistant Engineer.	38.	Lifeboat No. 1	Turn out forward davit.
39.	Fireman	Fire room. Assist 2d Assistant Engineer.	39.	Lifeboat No. 2	Turn out forward davit.
40.	Fireman	Fire room. Assist 2d Assistant Engineer.	40.	Lifeboat No. 3	Turn out forward davit.
41.	Fireman	Fire room. Assist 2d Assistant Engineer.	41.	Lifeboat No. 3	Assist release gripes and turn out davits.
42.	Fireman	Fire room. Assist 2d Assistant Engineer.	42.	Lifeboat No. 4	Assist release gripes and turn out davits.
43.	Fireman	Fire room. Assist 2d Assistant Engineer.	43.	Lifeboat No. 3	Turn out davits and assist at falls.
44.	Storekeeper	Emergency squad. Provide inhalator.	44.	Lifeboat No. 2	Turn out davits and assist at falls.
45.	Wiper	Engine room. Act as messenger.	45.	Lifeboat No. 1	Turn out after davit.
46.	Wiper	Assist 3d Officer prepare lifeboats for launching.	46.	Lifeboat No. 1	Stand by life ring buoy, ready for use.
47.	Wiper	Emergency squad. Assist with fresh air mask.	47.	Lifeboat No. 4	Stand by life ring buoy, ready for use.
48.	Wiper	Emergency squad. Assist with inhalator.	48.	Lifeboat No. 1	Turn out davits and assist at falls.
		STEWARDS' DEPARTMENT		
49.	Chief Steward	Arouse, warn, and direct passengers. In charge.	49.	Lifeboat No. 1	Arouse, warn, and direct passengers. In charge.
50.	Chief Cook	Secure galley.	50.	Lifeboat No. 3	Lead out and attend boat painter.
51.	2d Cook	Assist Chief Cook secure galley.	51.	Lifeboat No. 4	Lead out and attend boat painter.
52.	Messman	Close all ports and doors amidship.	52.	Lifeboat No. 1	Turn out forward davit.
53.	Messman	Close all ports and doors starboard side aft.	53.	Lifeboat No. 2	Turn out after davit.
54.	Messman	Close all ports and doors port side aft.	54.	Lifeboat No. 3	Turn out after davit.
55.	Messman	Arouse, warn, and direct passengers.	55.	Lifeboat No. 2	Arouse, warn, and direct passengers.
56.	Utilityman	Secure mess rooms aft.	56.	Lifeboat No. 4	Turn out after davit.
57.	Utilityman	Assist 3d Mate prepare lifeboats for launching.	57.	Lifeboat No. 3	Stand by life ring buoy, ready for use.
58.	Galleyman	Assist 3d Mate prepare lifeboats for launching.	58.	Lifeboat No. 4	Stand by life ring buoy, ready for use.

NOTE.—For additional information see notice entitled STATION BILLS, DRILLS AND REPORTS OF MASTERS, Form 809 A.

_____
Master.

This specimen station bill has been prepared for freight and tank ships that carry a crew of 35 to 58 persons and are equipped with 4 lifeboats. In view of the various types of fire fighting and lifesaving equipment on board vessels of this class, this specimen is to be used only as a guide in making up suitable station bills in compliance with the regulations. Copies of this specimen may be obtained from the office of the Merchant Marine Inspector in Charge, U. S. Coast Guard.

Chapter 17

EMERGENCIES IN GENERAL

EMERGENCY SIGNALS

Fire Signals in Port. The question of a standard, audible fire signal to be used by vessels in port and not under way is certainly a problem worthy of careful consideration.

It is time to discontinue the establishment of conflicting and confusing local signals. The fates cannot be tempted indefinitely. The situation is dangerous, and its successful resolution rests upon the cooperation of the various communities throughout the land. This is the time for the local adoption of the best signal available, the distress signal.

The distress signal is well known. It is simple, dramatic and effective. It is used by mariners for all types of distress when under way, whether in port or at sea. What would be more logical than to have its use extended by local adoption to vessels not under way? Let there be a continuous blast of the whistle on the waterfront and there will be no question of fire. Heads will turn, traffic will stop. What might have become a conflagration will be of no more consequence than a routine blaze.

The objection that the continuous sounding of a fog signal apparatus is the international distress signal and, therefore, disqualified for use by vessels sounding a cry of fire in port is exceedingly naive. If a fire on board, or a fire in the immediate vicinity of the vessel, does not place a vessel in distress, what does? Moreover, since provisions for the continuous sounding of the fog signal apparatus found in Rule 31 of the International Rules have been extended by the Pilot Rules to cover all United States ports, it most certainly is not merely an international distress signal, but also our nationally accepted distress signal.

It is not intended to question the right to establish a local audible fire signal for use by vessels in port and not under way. Admittedly, the statutory and regulatory requirements concerning the use of the distress signal apply to vessels under way. What is desired is clarity and unanimity, effectiveness, in dealing with this important problem. The same people man the same ships, whether or not they be under way. They should not be required to flip pages in a desperate search for the local fire signal at a time of stress, nor should they be required to painstakingly give the required combination of exactly timed blasts in the futile hope someone will recognize their need for assistance. How can any community risk its welfare on such a slim margin of human frailty?

1. *Fire-alarm signals. a*) The general fire alarm signal shall be a continuous rapid ringing of the ship's bell for a period not less than ten seconds supplemented by the continuous ringing of the general alarm bells for not less than ten seconds.

b) For dismissal from fire-alarm stations, the general alarm bells shall be sounded three times, supplemented by three short blasts of the whistle.*

2. *Boat station or boat drill signals. a*) The signal for boat drill or boat stations shall be more than six short blasts and one long blast of the whistle, supplemented by the same signal on the general alarm bells.

b) Where whistle signals are used for handling boats, they shall be as follows: To lower boats, one short blast of the whistle; to stop lowering the boats, two short blasts of the whistle; for dismissal from boat stations, three short blasts of the whistle.

3. *Other emergency signals.* The master of any vessel may establish such other emergency signal, in addition to the above, as will provide that all the officers and all the crew and passengers of the vessel will have positive and certain notice of the existing emergency.

The signals used for assembly of the emergency squad should not conflict with the navigational signals or those used for a general alarm.

EMERGENCY SQUAD

During the past few years, the masters of Ocean, Coastwise, and Great Lakes passenger ships have organized and trained a squad of men for the special duty of handling almost any emergency that might occur on board ship. This so-called emergency squad, consisting of from 6 to 24 men depending on the size of the crew, are selected for their skill in their special calling, such as able seamen, quartermasters, boatswains, carpenters, electricians, and deck engineers, or oilers. They are placed under the charge of the Chief Officer and trained to respond promptly to such emergencies, as fire aboard ship, man overboard, steering gear casualties, and collision; and to handle them effectively.

The master of the ship designates a signal for calling the emergency squad. On ships that are fitted with a loudspeaker system, the squad may be called by means of loudspeakers placed advantageously in the crew quarters. In case a fire-alarm is turned in over the manual alarm call box system, fire-alarm bells ring in the pilot house, engine room, and crew quarters. Immediately upon the sounding of the manual fire-alarm bell, the fire pumps are started, so that by the time the emergency squad arrives at the scene of the alarm, water under pressure is available for fighting. In addition to the manual alarm system,

---

* Port Authorities of the United States and Canada, and possessions of the U. S., have adopted as the signal for ships afire in port *and not underway*—five prolonged blasts (each of 4 to 6 seconds duration) on the whistle or siren. This signal is not a substitution for, but may be used in addition to, other means of indicating fire aboard a vessel and may be repeated at intervals.

the fire-alarm may be given by the melting of a sprinkler head or the sounding of an automatic fire-detection system. The alarm or fire in a cargo space may be indicated in the pilot house by either the audible alarm or the detection of smoke through the smoke-detection system.

The importance of organizing and training an emergency squad cannot be over-emphasized. This squad should be carefully selected from the crew for their experience, intelligence, and endurance. On the signal, the squad should assemble near the emergency lifeboats or bridge with fire axes, crowbar, fire extinguishers, extra lengths of hose, gas masks, lifelines, first-aid kit, safety-lamp, flashlight, etc., and then proceed to the scene of action under proper direction and take over the real work of clearing away wreckage, fighting fires, etc. In the event of a man overboard, the emergency squad shall assist the emergency boat crew to clear away and swing out the lee boat and tend the boat falls or winch; assist the boat crew into life preservers and, if necessary, fill in the vacant thwarts to man the boat in the shortest possible time. This squad and all officers should be instructed in the operation of the emergency steering gear, auxiliary lighting system, oxygen-breathing apparatus, steam smothering and CO_2 control valves and cut-off valves to fuel oil system. On vessels where the size of the crew permits, the carpenter, plumber, machinist, and electrician should be included in this squad.

Men must be assigned to closing all ports and overboard discharge valves (except those in the engine room) below the bulkhead or main deck under proper direction. Watertight doors should in all cases be closed immediately upon receipt of the emergency signal. After a collision, the machinery for closing these doors may be damaged.

Men from each lifeboat should be assigned to the embarkation deck to assist passengers entering the boat and capable men must be assigned to lead out and tend painters.

The practice of assigning a small group of men in charge of a deck officer to prepare all lifeboats and swing them out ready for lowering on the emergency signal is to be encouraged. In the event the emergency gets beyond control, the boats are ready to abandon ship and the crew is assigned to abandon ship stations accordingly.

Only competent men should be entrusted with the command or second in command of lifeboats. A comprehensive knowledge of the boat problem is necessary so that under various circumstances a lifeboat may be launched successfully. Hesitation and insufficient leadership are direct incentives to accident. This consideration demonstrates that the boat commander and the man attending the releasing gear have responsible tasks and that skilled cooperation is absolutely necessary. The lifeboat commander has charge of the entire operation and should be in the boat during the operation of lowering because it is he who must decide the opportune moment for releasing the boat falls.

Competition among the ships of a company and among the boat crews aboard the individual vessel is to be encouraged. Competition with or without prizes has a tendency to increase the interest of the crew, resulting in a higher degree of efficiency and cooperation at emergency drills.

The practice of conducting a combined fire and boat drill has apparently been adopted by all ship masters because of its convenience. Emergency drills conducted on specific days at the same hour do not demonstrate crew efficiency. This practice finds the crew waiting for the fire signal with the life-belts already on, the engineers warned well in advance of the imminent use of the fire pumps. That portion of the crew on watch during these prearranged drills are not mustered at their emergency stations during the entire voyage.

It is also the custom at emergency drills to ring the engine room telegraph as a signal to start the fire pumps. These pumps should be started immediately upon the emergency signal as adequate relief valves will dispose of excess pressure.

Although the size of the crew is limited on freight and tank vessels, each member of the crew must be assigned to definite duties in emergencies, such as, leading out fire hose, steam-smothering system, putting plug in No. 2 boat or forward fall of No. 1 boat, etc.

As many cargo vessels and tank ships are certificated to carry persons in addition to crew under the Merchant Marine Act of 1920, the steward's department should assist these passengers with life preservers and direct them to the allotted lifeboats.

Cargo vessels equipped with watertight doors should have men assigned to close these doors. The crew, divided as equally as possible and assigned to all lifeboats, should be mustered at these drills. While it is true that these vessels carry sufficient lifeboats on each side for all persons on board, conditions may exist on the vessel whereby the crew cannot reach their respective boats. Therefore, all boats should be manned, and as many as possible launched in case of emergency.

An emergency station list or booklet supplied to each officer, containing each emergency station, its location and person assigned to that station, along with his duties, would be valuable at all drills and should be provided.

If the location of the alarm is known, the emergency squad may be dispatched by means of the loudspeaker or other signals directly to the scene, without the necessity of their reporting to the pilot house. The first of the squad on the scene lead out adjacent hoses and start to extinguish the fire. Sometimes the fire may readily be put out by the use of fire-extinguishers, which the squad gathers on its way to the fire. A well-trained squad should arrive at the designated location on the largest ship within a minute or two. The Chief Officer, or officer who first arrives on the scene, immediately estimates the situation and directs a messenger from the squad to inform the officer of the deck watch, either by means of talk-back loudspeakers, telephone, voice tube, or by proceeding to the bridge, of the location of the fire, probable seriousness of the situation, and whether or not it is necessary to change course or stop the vessel to make a lee. Upon receipt of word on the bridge, it may readily be determined if it is necessary to sound the general fire-alarm signal.

The members of the emergency squad take such immediate steps as the occasion requires to fight the fire with water, close adjacent fire-screen doors and airports to stop the draft, arrange for the stopping of the ventilation system in that part of the ship, and warn the passengers in adjacent accommodations.

If the general fire-alarm has sounded, the squad directs all members of the crew assigned to adjacent hoses to lead in all hoses possible to bear, without delay, in order to apply as large a volume of water as possible on the fire. Hoses may be coupled together, some may be passed from deck to deck, and streams from as many hoses as reach played on the fire. The officer in charge keeps the Master informed of the progress attained, and if he believes it necessary he may advise stopping the ship and clearing away the boats, if quick control of the fire is not possible.

The emergency squad provides fire axes, crowbars, fire extinguishers, spare lengths of fire hose, nozzle and spanners, flashlights, gas masks and oxygen-breathing apparatus, and a safety flame lamp.

All members of the squad should be thoroughly trained in the use of gas masks for rescue purposes, and instructed in the limitations of possible use of the all service gas masks, and use of the safety flame lamp. The oxygen-breathing apparatus should be reserved for service when it is necessary to furnish oxygen to the would-be rescuer, in cases of oxygen depletion within a compartment. The gas masks of oxygen-breathing apparatus should be kept in the containers until actually necessary to use them. This is to prevent damage to the equipment. Instructions for the use of this equipment are printed inside the cover of the container, and should be carefully observed. Men entering smoke-filled compartments should wear a safety belt fitted with a line, to enable them to be dragged to safety.

The emergency squad responds to all man-overboard calls and prepares to swing out the emergency boat on the designated or lee side, assists the emergency boat crew into life preservers, tends the falls or mechanical lowering gear, and frapping lines, and, if necessary, men from the squad fill in vacant thwarts to expedite launching of the boat. If necessary to use storm oil, a man from the squad is detailed for the purpose, and at least one man keeps watch on the person overboard until relieved by regular lookouts. At nighttime the searchlights are manned. The squad hangs an ordinary rope net cargo sling over the side, aft of the emergency boat, for picking up the boat crew in case the boat is overturned when launching. This sling may be used to pick up tired or exhausted persons, in view of the fact that a person may easily entangle his arms and legs in the net and be hoisted aboard in safety. As soon as one boat is cleared away and lowered, the remainder of the squad prepares the other boat for lowering, and then provides heaving lines to pass the sea painter to the boats and arranges for hoisting the boat or boats upon their return. A pilot's ladder is also hung over the side to take the crew aboard.

In case of collision, the squad reports to the scene and immediately starts closing hand-operated watertight doors adjacent to the damage, closes airports and ventilation ducts passing through the boundary watertight bulkheads, and makes every effort to localize the damage and to enhance the watertight integrity of the ship in the vicinity of damage. The Chief Officer instructs his messenger to report the extent of the damage to the Master or Officer of the deck watch, with such recommendations as are necessary. All overboard discharges in the vicinity are closed and preparations are made to effect temporary repairs, if feasible. Soundings are taken of adjacent compartments to determine if leakage has occurred. The squad provides topping mauls, crowbars, and wrenches to assist in closing watertight doors that may be sprung and need persuasion to close effectually. Flashlights should be provided at nighttime, and cargo lights rigged at the scene as soon as possible, to provide illumination.

Emergency Steering Gear Drill. Fire drills and lifeboat drills are a regular part of shipboard routine, but there are other emergency evolutions that can well be practiced at a drill. An emergency steering gear drill is an example.

Too often, the emergency steering gear is never activated until an actual emergency arises. Then, when time is of the essence, there is much confusion and delay while unfamiliar personnel trace out lines and valves.

In addition to the drill, the instructions for changing over to emergency steering should be stenciled on the bulkhead in large letters. Should the occasion arise when the engineers and other key personnel are not around, someone not familiar with the gear can activate it by following the instructions.

The emergency squad is thoroughly trained in the methods of changing over from the regular steering gear to all auxiliary steering gears, and instructed in the manning and steering of the ship by all possible steering gears. This instruction is given by the officers with special instructions regarding the handling of mechanical parts given by the Chief Engineer. All deck and engine officers should be thoroughly instructed in changing steering gears. All clutches, pins, and couplings are marked, numbered, or lettered, and a sign at each station is posted, showing all instructions for changing from one method of steering to another. Members of the squad take their stations at each steering wheel, and man voice tubes and telephones promptly so that the vessel may be steered from any steering station without delay. All members of the squad are instructed to center the steering wheels and gears amidship before shifting gears or clutches.

The emergency squad quickly proves itself invaluable aboard ship, and in many cases emergencies have been met successfully by the squad without calling the entire crew to emergency stations. However, the alert officer of the watch or ship master never hesitates to sound the general alarm without delay if the emergency warrants such action.

BOATS *

Lowering a boat in heavy weather demands calm and quick judgment, resourcefulness and courage from a ship's officer. The following can only broadly outline the proper procedure in such an emergency, where so many different perils must be dealt with.

---

* Be guided by instructions in CG-175, *Manual for Lifeboatmen.*

The vessel should first be hove to in a position which will reduce motion to a minimum, and which will offer the best possible lee for the boat to be launched. Some vessels are better in the trough, some with the sea on the bow, and some with a quartering sea. However, it is best when possible to lie a few points off the wind, and see that the boat is lowered on the side opposite the bow which is taking the sea. When lying broadside to the wind, getting the boat away is almost impossible, for the leeway of the ship causes her to set down on top of the boat. In any case, the condition, size, etc., of the ship determine the maneuvering to be done in each particular situation.

The boat's gear, in general, should be stripped of everything that is unnecessary. But never discard the spare oars, bailers, bucket, axes, storm oil, sea anchor, and lamps and flares if it is night. Gear not in use should be stowed clear and immediately accessible in the bottom of the boat.

In ships fitted with the old type of davits, lowering the boat calls for especially careful preparation. The danger is very great that the boat will swing heavily against the ship's side when being lowered, and receive heavy damage before reaching the water.

Figure 1 shows the use of frapping lines and traveling lizard with an old fashioned davit. Some adaptation of these should be used in heavy weather plus heavy steadying lines received to bow and stern. A fender made of the boat cover rolled up fairly tight may be used as well.

The boat's painter should not be passed inboard. A boat rope should be passed from as low down and as far forward as possible, into the boat, and the end given a dry turn around the foremost thwart on the inboard side. Station a good man at the other end to veer or take up slack on this line as the boat is lowered.

Generally speaking, launching a boat requires speed and close timing, especially if not fitted with releasing gear. Take full advantage of a long, high sea, or a downward roll, to lift the boat and give good slack on the falls. Also, the downward roll acts to put the boat well away from the ship's side. Of course, the rope lengths attached to the shackles, as mentioned above, must be cast off just before the boat is waterborne. Cast off and overhaul falls when letting go, and drop the boat on an even keel. To immediately trice up falls clear of the boat when they are let go, heaving lines can be attached to the lower ends of their standing parts. When shipped, the rudder should be angled slightly to steer the boat off the ship. The engine, if a motor boat, should be running before the boat hits the water.

Rigidly superintend the position of rescued persons in the boat. As far as possible they should be kept below the thwarts. If they are allowed to sit on the thwarts the stability of the boat may be endangered, and an extra surface is offered to the wind. Also, in case the boat broaches to, those on the thwarts will probably be thrown to leeward. This risk is considerably reduced if they are kept on the bottom boards.

If fenders have been used when lowering, remove them as soon as the boat is waterborne. Also, in cases of "fending off," keep the implement used for fending well clear of the boat.

Hoisting in Heavy Weather. What appears to be but a slight sea, from the bridge, is sufficient to make hooking on and hoisting a very difficult operation. Rules cannot be established, skill and common sense are essential.

Hooking on and the first moments thereafter are the critical ones. On the ship preparations consist of providing a bow line, stern line, steadying line, and fenders; overhauling the falls, and preparing them so that once hooked on, the boat can be hoisted quickly so it will not

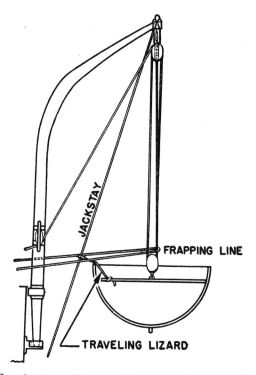

JACKSTAY

FRAPPING LINE

TRAVELING LIZARD

FIG. 1. USE OF FRAPPING LINES AND TRAVELING LIZARD.

crash into the water again as the ship rolls, resulting in a violent and possibly destructive jerk.

In the boat it is essential that bow and stern be hooked at the same time which in a seaway requires nerve and skill on the part of men concerned.

Automatic Releasing Hook. When an automatic releasing hook is used on the boat falls of a small boat, the hook is hauled into the hoisting ring and hooked on with the aid of a lanyard.

In most boats, it is both convenient and safe for the man hooking on the falls to stand toward the center of the boat from the falls and haul the lanyard and point of the hook toward him. The use of the lanyard eliminates any danger of the block falling on the man's hand because the lanyard can be rove through the ring in the boat while the block is at a safe distance from him.

Therefore, when an automatic Releasing Hook is used the point of the hook can be pointed *toward the center* of the boat.

When the simple hook is used, conditions involved must determine the method to be used.

If there is a limited space between the ring and the sides of the boat, it would be extremely dangerous to attempt hooking on with the point of the hook toward the center of the boat. The man handling the hook would have to place his hand in a confined space and his chances of getting it out of there unmangled would not be good.

Therefore, the point of the hook would face *away from* the center of the boat.

The tricing line used to get the lower block and hook clear of the boat when it was released can be of great assistance for hooking on if it is attached, above the hook, at about its mid length so one end can be retained on board and one passed to the boat.

To avoid having the boat crash into the water again careful timing is necessary. When the ship begins to roll towards the boat, or when the ship is on a high wave, lower the hook and hook in quickly. Once hooked start hoisting as rapidly as possible.

Swinging against the ship's side may be minimized by the use of steadying lines forward and aft and the proper placement of fenders. The lines should be tended so that the slack is taken in or held as the boat starts to swing.

If making way through the water or pitching badly, long bow and stern lines should be used to reduce surging.

BOARDING A WRECK

It is best in most cases to approach and board a vessel whether stranded or afloat from the lee side. Greatest danger lies in the sea crashing the boat against the vessel or in being swamped as the sea breaks away from it. The sea is always more violent on the weather side of vessel. A vessel stranded broadside to the sea presents such hazards as wreckage alongside which may damage your boat and the possibility of a falling mast, stove-in lifeboat or other gear that may have become awash. The presence of these dangers may make it advisable to carry out your rescue from bow or stern. To board a wreck that is stranded on a smooth beach it is well to anchor lifeboat to windward and veer down with caution until close enough to reach the vessel with a heaving line.

To carry out rescue from drifting wreck come in from leeward keeping sharp lookout for floating wreckage. In a strong wind lay off and heave a line aboard. Instruct a seaman aboard the wreck (if there be one) to fasten the line to one person's body with a French bowline and have the person jump overboard. Haul him aboard and repeat the operation. Remember that there is plenty of danger of swamping if you take your boat alongside a wreck that is rapidly drifting to leeward. If you must go alongside, do so with bow or stern to sea ladder or gangway and hold your boat at right angles to the wreck. From this position it will be much safer when pulling away.

A wrecked craft with very low freeboard is best boarded from the weather quarter. This action cuts down the danger from her main booms, chains, etc.

USE OF OIL FOR MODIFYING THE EFFECT OF BREAKING WAVES

Many experiences of late years have shown that the utility of oil for this purpose is undoubted and the application simple. The following may serve for the guidance of seamen whose attention is called to the fact that a very small quantity of oil skillfully applied may prevent much damage, both to ships (especially of the smaller classes) and to the boats, by modifying the action of breaking seas. The principal facts as to the use of oil are as follows:

1. On free waves—that is, waves in deep water—the effect is greatest.

2. In a surf or waves breaking on a bar, where a mass of liquid is in actual motion in shallow water, the effect of the oil is uncertain, as nothing can prevent the larger waves from breaking under such circumstances, but even here it is of some service.

3. The heaviest and thickest oils are most effectual. Refined kerosene is of little use; crude petroleum is serviceable when nothing else is obtainable; but all animal and vegetable oils, and generally waste oil from the engines have great effect.

4. A small quantity of oil suffices, if applied in such a manner as to spread to windward.

5. It is useful in a ship or boat, either when running or lying to or in wearing.

6. No experiences are related of its use when hoisting a boat at sea or in a seaway, but it is highly probable that much time would be saved and injury to the boat avoided by its use on such occasions.

7. In cold water the oil, being thickened by the lower temperature and not being able to spread freely, will have its effect much reduced. This will vary with the type of oil used.

8. For a ship at sea the best method of application appears to be to hang over the side, in such a manner as to be in the water, small canvas bags capable of holding from 1 to 2 gallons of oil, the bags being pricked with a sail needle to facilitate leakage of the oil. The oil is also frequently distributed from canvas bags or oakum inserted in the closet bowls. The positions of these bags should vary with the circumstances. Running before the wind they should be hung on either bow —for example, from the carhead—and allowed to tow in the water. With the wind on the quarter the effect seems to be less than in any other position, as the oil goes astern while the waves come up on the quarter. Lying-to, the weather bow, and another position farther aft seem the best places from which to hang the bags, using sufficient line to permit them to draw to windward while the ship drifts.

9. Crossing a bar with a flood tide, to pour oil overboard and allow it to float in ahead of the boat, which would follow with a bag towing astern, would appear to be the best plan. As before remarked, under these circumstances, the effect cannot be so much trusted. On a bar with the ebb tide running it would seem to be useless to try oil for the purpose of entering.

10. For boarding a wreck it is recommended to pour oil overboard to windward of her before going alongside. The effect of this must greatly depend upon the set of the current and the circumstances of the depth of water.

11. For a boat riding in bad weather from a sea anchor it is recommended to fasten the bag to an endless line rove through a block on the sea anchor, by which means the oil can be diffused well ahead of the boat and the bag readily hauled on board for refilling if necessary.

LANDING THROUGH SURF

Lifeboats are designed for deep water operation and landing one through a surf requires certain variations from the landing craft procedures with which many became familiar during the war. The greatest danger is from broaching and capsizing.

The cause of a boat's broaching to, when running before a broken sea or surf, is that her own motion being in the same direction as that of the sea, whether it be given by motor, oars or sails or by the force of the sea itself, she opposes no resistance to it, but is carried before it. Thus, if a boat be running toward shore, and her stern to the sea, the effect of a surf is to throw up the stern, and as a consequence depress the bow. Not having sufficient inertia to allow it to pass, the stern is raised high and the wave carries the boat before it on its front side, the bow all the time being deeply immersed in the hollow of the sea, where the water offers a resistance, while the crest of the sea forces the stern onward.

It will often happen that the bow will be driven under water and then the buoyancy being lost forward, the sea pressing on the stern will throw the boat end over end. Or it may be that even though the bow does not become submerged the resistance forward will slightly turn to boat's head, and the force of the surf being transferred to the opposite quarter, she will in a moment be turned round broadside to the sea and be capsized.

Experienced surfmen have long used the trick of beaching their boats stern first. The boat is turned around outside the line of breakers and proceeds toward the beach in reverse. As a heavy breaker bears down on the boat the engine is shifted to forward speed and the boat is propelled seaward to meet the wave and begins backing shoreward again after the sea has passed. It is easier to prevent the boat from broaching in this manner.

When the boat approaches the beach bow first, the same maneuver is used but in reverse. In this case, the boat engine is reversed upon the approach of a large breaker. When the wave has picked up the boat, the engine is shifted to forward speed again and revved up for the drive to the beach.

A Drogue is almost always used when taking a motor whaleboat or a motor boat through the surf. The standard drogue is a conical-shaped bag somewhat the shape of a wind sock at an airfield and is about 2 feet wide at the mouth and about 3 feet long. It serves to control the speed of the boat and to keep it from broaching.

The drogue is towed by a *towing line* and a *tripping line* is attached to its mouth. When the tripping line is slackened, the bag fills with water and offers considerable resistance to the forward motion of the boat. When the tripping line is tautened, the bag empties and tows flat, offering little if any resistance.

In operation, allow the drogue to fill on the approach of a large sea and to empty as the boat starts to ride the back of the wave toward the beach.

Another method of getting a boat to the beach without broaching and swamping is that in which an anchor is dropped outside the surf line. The anchor line is then payed out as the seas carry the boat toward the beach. The taut anchor line prevents the boat from doing anything but riding the seas head-on.

This maneuver has the advantage of making it much easier to retract the boat from the beach. The anchor method cannot be used, however, when there is a strong current running parallel to the beach, because the current would swing the boat broadside to the seas.

The following general rules may therefore be depended on when running before, or attempting to land, through a heavy surf or broken water:

1. As far as possible avoid each sea by placing the boat where the sea will break ahead or astern of her.

2. If the sea be very heavy, or if the boat be very small, and especially if she have a square stern, bring her bow round to seaward and back her in, rowing ahead against each heavy surf that cannot be avoided sufficiently to allow it to pass the boat.

3. If it be considered safe to proceed to the shore bow foremost, back the oars against each sea on its approach, so as to stop the boat's way through the water as far as possible, and if there is a drogue, or any other instrument in the boat that may be used as one, tow it astern to aid in keeping the boat end-on to the sea, which is the chief object in view.

4. Bring the principal weights in the boat towards the end that is to seaward, but not to the extreme end.

5. If a boat, worked by both sails and oars, be running under sail for the land through a heavy sea, her crew should, under all circumstances, unless the beach be quite steep, take down her masts and sails before entering the broken water, and take her to land under oars alone, as above described.

BOAT DRILL COMMANDS

All hands remain seated, except two bow men who stand-by to fend off.

1. Stand-by your oars:
   a) Oarlocks in place.
   b) Oars on gunwale placed behind oarlock of seat behind you, blade flat.
2. Out oars:
   Oars are put in oar locks horizontal and blade flat, do not let oar touch water.
3. Stand-by to give way:
   The blade is brought forward and vertical ready for stroke.

4. Give way together:

All hands start stroke and keep in time with stroke oar.

Port stroke oar keeps in time with starboard stroke.

The hands grip handle of oar only.

5. Oars:

Finish stroke and hold your oar horizontal and blade flat.

6. In bows:

Two bow men boat their oars and stand-by, rest continue rowing.

7. Way enough:

All hands swing their oars in a 45° angle and boat them.

These are the main commands in leaving and arriving.

There are other commands: Boat the oars, Toss oars, Let fall, Trail oars, Stern all, Point the oars, Back water port, Back water starboard, Hold water port, Give way starboard, or vice versa, and Hold water.

Having headway, give Hold water command first and then Stern all, when required to stop quickly or to make sternway.

Note: The stroke oar in the lifeboat is the oar nearest the stern in a single-banked boat; in a double-banked boat, the port and starboard oars nearest the stern are both stroke oars, the port stroke taking his timing from the starboard stroke.

RESCUING A DROWNING PERSON

1. Before jumping into the water to save a drowning person, undress as quickly as possible. If there is any object lying about that may be thrown to the person in the water, such as a life buoy, or other buoyant object that may help to keep a person afloat, throw it to him before jumping overboard.

2. On swimming up to a person in the water, assure him with a loud and firm voice that he is safe. If he is struggling, do not seize him at once, but keep off for a few seconds until he becomes quiet; it is sheer madness to take hold of a man when he is struggling in the water; if you do so, you run a great risk. Always endeavor to make your approach from behind. It is important to retain your presence of mind and a clear, cool head, and to keep at a safe distance until the person is nearly exhausted.

3. When he has ceased to struggle, get close to him, and grasping him firmly by the hair of his head, turn him as quickly as possible upon his back, give him a sudden pull, which will cause him to float, then throw yourself on your back also and swim for the shore—one or both your hands having hold of his hair, you on your back and he on his, and, of course, his back to your stomach. In this way you will get more quickly and safely to shore than by any other plan. One great advantage of this method is that it enables the swimmer to keep his head up and also to hold up the head of the person whom he is trying to save.

4. There is probably no such thing as a "death grasp." When a drowning man begins to grow weak and to lose consciousness, he gradually slackens his hold until he quits it altogether. No apprehension need therefore be felt in regard to a "death grasp" when attempting to rescue a drowning person.

5. After a person has sunk to the bottom, if the water is smooth, the exact place where the body lies may be known by the air bubbles which will occasionally rise to the surface, allowance being made, of course, for the motion of the water, which, in a tideway or stream will have carried the bubbles out of a perpendicular course as they rise to the surface. Often a body may be regained from the bottom, before it is too late for recovery, by diving for it in the direction indicated by these bubbles.

6. In rescuing a person by diving to the bottom after him, the hair of his head should be seized with one hand only, and the other should be used with the feet in raising yourself and the drowning person to the surface.

7. If the accident occurs some distance out at sea, it is sometimes a great mistake to try to get to land. If there is a strong outsetting tide, and you are swimming either alone or while holding a person who cannot swim, get on your back, and float till help comes. Many a man exhausts himself by trying to stem the billows for the shore on a backgoing tide, and sinks in the effort, whereas, if he had floated, a boat or other aid might have reached him.

8. These instructions apply alike in all circumstances, whether they involve rough sea or smooth water.

INSTRUCTIONS TO MARINERS IN CASE OF SHIPWRECK

Coast Guard (lifesaving) stations and houses of refuge are located upon the Atlantic and Pacific seaboards of the United States, the Gulf of Mexico and Lake coasts.

The stations are manned throughout the year by crews of experienced surfmen.

All lifesaving stations are fully supplied with boats, wreck guns, beach apparatus, restoratives, and clothing provided by the Blue Anchor Society, women's national association for the shipwrecked requiring it, etc.

Houses of refuge are supplied with boats and restoratives but not manned by full crews; an officer in charge, and at places, one or two additional men reside in each, who are required to make extended excursions along the coast after every storm, with a view to ascertaining if any shipwreck has occurred and finding and succoring any persons that may have been cast ashore.

Houses of refuge are located exclusively upon the east coast of Florida, where the requirements of relief are different from those of other portions of the seaboard.

The lifesaving stations are provided with International Code of Signals, and other means of visual signaling, and vessels can, by opening communication, be reported; or obtain the latitude or longitude of the station, where determined; or information as to the weather probabilities in most cases; or, where facilities for the transmission of messages by telephone or telegraph are available, request for a tug or Coast Guard cutter will be received and promptly forwarded.

All services are performed by the lifesaving crews without other compensation than their pay from the Government.

Destitute seafarers are provided with food and lodging at the nearest station by the Government as long as necessarily detained by the circumstances of shipwreck, and, if needed, with clothing provided by the Blue Anchor Society.

The station crews patrol the beach from 2 to 4 miles each side of their stations between sunset and sunrise, and if the weather is foggy the patrol is continued through the day. A continuous lookout is always maintained at every station night and day.

Each patrolman carries warning signals. Upon discovering a vessel standing into danger he ignites one of these, which emits a brilliant red flame of about 2 minutes duration, to warn her off, or should the vessel be ashore, to let her crew know that they are discovered and assistance is at hand.

If the vessel is not discovered by the patrol immediately after striking, rockets, flare-up lights, or other recognized signals of distress should be used. If the weather be foggy, some recognized sound signal should be made to attract attention, as the patrolman may be some distance away at the other end of his beat.

Masters are particularly cautioned, if they should be driven ashore anywhere in the neighborhood of the stations, to remain on board until assistance arrives, and under no circumstances should they attempt to land through the surf in their own boats until the last hope of assistance from the shore has vanished. Often when comparatively smooth at sea a dangerous surf is running which is not perceptible 400 yards offshore, and the surf when viewed from a vessel never appears as dangerous as it is. Many lives have been lost unnecessarily by the crews of stranded vessels being thus deceived and attempting to land in the ship's boats.

The difficulties of rescue by operations from the shore are greatly increased in cases where the anchors are let go after entering the breakers, as is frequently done, and the chances of saving life correspondingly lessened.

Rescue with the Lifeboat or Surfboat

The patrolman after discovering your vessel ashore and burning a warning signal, hastens to his station or the telephone for assistance. If the use of a boat is practicable, either the large lifeboat is launched from its ways in the station and proceeds to the wreck by water, or the lighter surfboat is hauled overland to a point opposite the wreck and launched, as circumstances may require.

Upon the boat reaching your vessel the directions and orders of the officer in charge (who always commands and steers the boat) should be implicitly obeyed. Any headlong rushing and crowding should be prevented, and the captain of the vessel should remain on board, to preserve order, until every other person has left.

Women, children, helpless persons, and passengers should be passed into the boat first.

Goods or baggage will positively not be taken into the boat until all are landed. If any person be passed in against the remonstrance of the officer in charge, he is fully authorized to throw the man overboard.

Rescue with Breeches Buoy or Life Car

Should it be inexpedient to use either the lifeboat or surfboat, recourse will be had to the wreck gun and beach apparatus for the rescue by the breeches buoy or the life car.

A shot with a small line attached will be fired across your vessel. Get hold of the line as soon as possible and haul on board until you get a tailblock with a whip or endless line rove through it. The tailblock should be hauled on board as quickly as possible to prevent the whip drifting off with the set or fouling with wreckage, etc. Therefore if you have been driven into the rigging, where but one or two men can work to advantage, cut the shot line, and run it through some available block, such as the throat or peak halyards block, or any block which will afford a clear lead, or even between the ratlines, that as many as possible may assist in hauling.

Attached to the tailblock will be a tally board with the following directions in English on one side and French on the other:

"Make the tail of the block fast to the lower mast, well up. If the masts are gone, then to the best place you can find. Cast off shot line, see that the rope in the block runs free, and show signal to the shore."

The above instructions being complied with, the results will be as shown in Fig. 2–A .

As soon as your signal is seen a 3-inch hawser will be bent onto the whip and hauled off to your ship by the lifesaving crew.

If circumstances permit, you can assist the lifesaving crew by manning that part of the whip to which the hawser is bent and hauling with them.

When the end of the hawser is got on board, a tally board will be found attached, bearing the following directions in English on one side and French on the other:

"Make this hawser fast about 2 feet above the tailblock, see all clear and that the rope in the block runs free, and show signal to the shore."

These instructions being obeyed, the result will be as shown in Fig. 2–B. Take particular care that there are no turns of the whip line around the hawser. To prevent this, take the end of the hawser up between the parts of the whip before making it fast.

When the hawser is made fast, the whip cast off from the hawser, and your signal seen by the lifesaving crew, they will haul the hawser taut and by means of the whip will haul off to your vessel a breeches buoy suspended from a traveler block, or a life car, from rings running on the hawser.

Figure 2–C represents the apparatus rigged, with the breeches buoy hauled off to the ship.

If the breeches buoy be sent, let one man immediately get into it, thrusting his legs through the breeches. If the life car, remove the hatch, place as many persons therein as it will hold (four to six) and secure the hatch on the outside by the hatch bar and hook, signal as before, and the buoy or car will be hauled ashore. This will be repeated until all are landed. On the last trip of the life car the hatch must be secured by the inside hatch bar. In many instances two men can be landed in the breeches buoy at the same time by each putting a leg through a leg of the breeches and holding onto the lifts of the buoy.

Children when brought ashore by the buoy, should be in the arms of older persons or securely lashed to the buoy. Women and children should be landed first.

In signaling as directed in the foregoing instructions, if in the daytime, let one man separate himself from the rest and swing his hat, a handkerchief, or his hand; if at night, the showing of a light and con-

FIG. A
TAIL-BLOCK HAULED
OFF BY FIRST LINE
FROM SHORE

FIG. B
HAWSER HAWLED OFF
BY WHIP

FIG. C
BREECHES
BUOY

BREECHES BUOY IN USE

Fig. 2. Rigging and Handling a Breeches Buoy.

cealing it once or twice will be understood; and like signals will be made from the shore.

Circumstances may arise, owing to the strength of the current or set or the danger of the wreck breaking up immediately when it would be impossible to send off the hawser. In such a case a breeches buoy or life car will be hauled off instead by the whip or sent off to you by the shot line, and you will be hauled ashore through the surf.

If your vessel is stranded during the night and discovered by the patrolman—which you will know by his burning a brilliant red light— keep a sharp lookout for signs of the arrival of the lifesaving crew abreast of your vessel.

Some time may intervene between the burning of the light and their arrival, as the patrolman may have to return to his station, perhaps 3 or 4 miles distant, and the lifesaving crew draw the apparatus or surfboat through the sand or over bad roads to where your vessel is stranded.

Lights on the beach will indicate their arrival, and the sound of cannon firing from the shore may be taken as evidence that a line has been fired across your vessel. Therefore upon hearing the cannon, make strict search aloft, fore, and aft, for the shot line, for it is almost certain to be there. Though the movement of the lifesaving crew may not be perceptible to you, owing to the darkness, your vessel will be a good mark for the men experienced in the use of the wreck gun, and the first shot seldom fails.

Important. Remain by the wreck until assistance arrives from the shore, or as long as possible. If driven aloft, the inshore mast is the safest.

If not discovered immediately by the patrol, burn rockets, flare-ups, or other lights, or if the weather be foggy, fire guns or make other sound signals.

Make the shot line fast on deck or to the rigging to prevent its being washed into the sea and possibly fouling the gear.

Take particular care that there are no turns of the whip line around the hawser before making the hawser fast.

Send the women, children, helpless persons, and passengers ashore first.

Make yourself thoroughly familiar with these instructions, and remember that on your coolness and strict attention to them will greatly depend the chances of success in bringing you and your people safely to land.

Life-Saving Signals

The following signals shall be used by life-saving stations and maritime rescue units when communicating with ships or persons in distress and by ships or persons in distress when communicating with life-saving stations and maritime rescue units. The signals used by aircraft engaged in search and rescue operations to direct ships are indicated in sub-paragraph (*d*) below. An illustrated table describing the signals listed below shall be readily available to the officer of the watch of every ship to which this Chapter applies.

(*a*) *Replies from life-saving stations or maritime rescue units to distress signals made by a ship or person* :—

Signal	Signification
By day—Orange smoke signal or combined light and sound signal (thunderlight) consisting of three single signals which are fired at intervals of approximately one minute.	"You are seen—assistance will be given as soon as possible."
By night—White star rocket consisting of three single signals which are fired at intervals of approximately one minute.	(Repetition of such signals shall have the same meaning.)

If necessary the day signals may be given at night or the night signals by day.

(b) *Landing signals for the guidance of small boats with crews or persons in distress :—*

Signal	Signification

By day—Vertical motion of a white flag or the arms or firing of a green star-signal or signalling the code letter " K " (— · —) given by light or sound-signal apparatus.

By night—Vertical motion of a white light or flare, or firing of a green star-signal or signalling the code letter " K " (— · —) given by light or sound-signal apparatus. A range (indication of direction) may be given by placing a steady white light or flare at a lower level and in line with the observer.

" This is the best place to land."

By day—Horizontal motion of a white flag or arms extended horizontally or firing of a red star-signal or signalling the code letter " S " (· · ·) given by light or sound-signal apparatus.

By night—Horizontal motion of a white light or flare or firing of a red star-signal or signalling the code letter " S " (· · ·) given by light or sound-signal apparatus.

" Landing here highly dangerous."

By day—Horizontal motion of a white flag, followed by the placing of the white flag in the ground and the carrying of another white flag in the direction to be indicated or firing of a red star-signal vertically and a white star-signal in the direction towards the better landing place or signalling the code letter " S " (· · ·) followed by the code letter " R " (· — ·) if a better landing place for the craft in distress is located more to the right in the

" Landing here highly dangerous. A more favourable location for landing is in the direction indicated."

Signal	Signification
direction of approach or signalling the code letter " L " (· — · ·) if a better landing place for the craft in distress is located more to the left in the direction of approach.	
By night—Horizontal motion of a white light or flare, followed by the placing of the white light or flare on the ground and the carrying of another white light or flare in the direction to be indicated or firing of a red star-signal vertically and a white star-signal in the direction towards the better landing place or signalling the code letter " S " (· · ·) followed by code letter " R " (· — ·) if a better landing place for the craft in distress is located more to the right in the direction of approach or signalling the code letter " L " (· — · ·) if a better landing place for the craft in distress is located more to the left in the direction of approach.	" Landing here highly dangerous. A more favourable location for landing is in the direction indicated."

(*c*) *Signals to be employed in connection with the use of shore life-saving apparatus :—*

Signal	Signification
By day—Vertical motion of a white flag or the arms or firing of a green star-signal. *By night*—Vertical motion of a white light or flare or firing of a green star-signal.	In general—" Affirmative." Specifically:— " Rocket line is held." " Tail block is made fast." " Hawser is made fast." " Man is in the breeches buoy." " Haul away."
By day—Horizontal motion of a white flag or arms extended horizontally or firing of a red star-signal. *By night*—Horizontal motion of a white light or flare or firing of a red star-signal.	In general—" Negative." Specifically:— " Slack away." " Avast hauling."

(*d*) *Signals used by aircraft engaged on search and rescue operations to direct ships towards an aircraft, ship or person in distress* (see explanatory NOTE below):—

(i) The following procedures performed in sequence by an aircraft mean that the aircraft is directing a surface craft towards an aircraft or a surface craft in distress:—

(1) circling the surface craft at least once;

(2) crossing the projected course of the surface craft close ahead at a low altitude, opening and closing the throttle or changing the propeller pitch;

(3) heading in the direction in which the surface craft is to be directed.

Repetition of such procedures has the same meaning.

(ii) The following procedure performed by an aircraft means that the assistance of the surface craft to which the signal is directed is no longer required: —

—crossing the wake of the surface craft close astern at a low altitude, opening and closing the throttle or changing the propeller pitch.

NOTE: Advance notification of changes in these signals will be given by the Organization as necessary.

Chapter 18

UNITED STATES NAVIGATION LAWS*
AND SHIP'S BUSINESS

The purpose of this chapter is to give significant excerpts from the laws and regulations which have been established on the many phases of ship operation. Selection has been made according to the importance and usefulness of the information for the ship's officer.

These excerpts deal with: Registry, Arrival and Departure, Seamen, Master, Pilot, Towage, etc.; Cargo, Passengers, Charters, Salvage, Admiralty Law, Ship's Papers, Inspections, the Ship in General, Fire, Life-Saving Apparatus. They are in no sense complete, but simply provide a shortcut through the thousands of pages of maritime law.

Registry is required for vessels engaged in foreign trade and with our insular possessions (except Hawaii and Puerto Rico). Permitted to vessels engaged in domestic trade under certain requirements.

Enrollment and License. Required for vessels 20 t. (gross) or over in the coasting trade or fisheries. Liable to forfeiture if they proceed on a foreign voyage without becoming registered.

License alone is required for vessels 5–20 t. in the coasting trade or fishing, and for pleasure yachts which latter are permitted to travel to foreign or domestic ports but not to carry passengers or cargo for hire.

Vessels less than 5 t. may not be licensed, nor may pleasure vessels less than 16 t. be documented except under special instructions.

Registry and Nationality. By U. S. law, if a ship is actually owned by U. S. citizens, her nationality is U. S. and she is entitled to protection accorded U. S. property throughout the world, regardless of the fact that for any reason she may not be entitled to, or may not desire to take, U. S. registry.

In the case of a corporation organized under the laws of the U. S., or of any state, the president and managing directors must be U. S. citizens. The vessel itself must have been (1) built in the U. S.; (2) captured by citizens and condemned as a prize of war; (3) forfeited for a breach of U. S. laws; or (4) if built abroad, certified by the Coast Guard as safe to carry dry and perishable cargo.

Original Registry—Procedure for Documenting Vessels:

1. Presentation of "Builder's Certificate" giving date and place of building, general description, time of building and of completion, and place where hull was constructed.

* More appropriately MARINE LAWS.

2. Surveyors Certificate of Measurement by Surveyor of Customs.

3. Securing and marking of official number (assigned by Bureau of Marine Inspection and Navigation). Deeply carved or otherwise permanently marked on her main beam.

4. Marking of official tonnage (as above).

5. Marking of name and of home port. Name on each bow and on stern and home port on stern, light on dark or dark on light ground in letters not less than 4″ high, and on each outer side of pilot house in letters not less than 6″ high. The *home port* may be either the port where documented, or place in same district where built, or where one or more of the owners reside.

6. Evidence that number, tonnage, name and home port are properly marked.

7. Owner's oath. Documentation void without this and, if false, vessel is forfeit.

8. Master's oath (penalty if false citizenship, etc.: $1000). Every change of master must be reported at first port and indorsed on register.

9. Special oath by a corporation that the controlling interest is free from any alien trust or obligation.

10. Evidence of outstanding Certificate of Inspection (i.e., Local Inspector's Certificate).

Draft of every registered vessel is to be marked on stem and stern posts in English feet or decimeters, in either Arabic or Roman numerals, the bottom of each numeral indicating the draft.

Marking of Load Lines and Certificate. Done by classification society concerned in accordance with International Load Line Convention, 1930, and Coastwise Load Line Act, 1935, as amended June 20, 1936, Commandant of Coast Guard being responsible U. S. authority in administration.

With every change in status of a vessel a new registry must be secured and vessel documented anew where vessel is sold, altered or renamed. The steps are the same as for a new vessel except for the first steps which are in the preceding document.

Bill of Sale. Must comply with registry in every detail or vessel is deprived of U. S. character.

Recording of Bill of Sale at Collector of Customs:

1. Name of vessel.

2. Time and date receiving bill of sale.

3. Name of parties to sale.

4. Interest in vessel to be sold.

Change of Name. Can be made by Commissioner of Customs only. If otherwise made, vessel is subject to forfeiture. Change is executed by Collector of Customs.

Coastwise Trade. Not permitted to foreign-built U. S. owners' vessels unless registered and owned by U. S. citizens on Feb. 1, 1920, and at all times thereafter. A foreign wreck purchased and repaired by U. S. citizens at a cost equal to three times the value of the vessel wrecked may be enrolled and engage in coastwise trade. Trade between the U. S., Puerto Rico, Hawaii and Alaska is deemed coastwise; that with

the Philippines, Guam, Tutuila, Wake, Midway and Kingman Reef
is not.

Foreign-Owned Vessels are prohibited from transporting passengers
or cargo between domestic ports either directly or by way of a foreign
port.

Inspection of Vessels is by the U. S. Coast Guard, who must approve
all plans for the construction or alteration of passenger vessels before
such work is begun. Annual inspection of all vessels is required and no
vessel will be granted clearance from a U. S. port without having on
board an unexpired certificate.

Foreign Vessels, when in U. S. ports, are subject to inspection, but
her equipment may be different from that of a U. S. vessel if it is in
accordance with the rules of her flag as regulated according to treaty.

ENTRY AND CLEARANCE

All vessels under registry (as distinguished from vessels enrolled or
licensed) are required to enter and clear at every port, except where
bound from a point in one state to one in an adjoining state. Except as
provided in the following:

All vessels engaged in the coasting trade must enter and clear on
their arrival at or departure from each port. If under 20 t. (and properly licensed) and laden wholly with U. S. goods, or with foreign goods
in packages as imported not exceeding $400 in value, or of aggregate
value not over $800, they may trade from a customs district in one
state to a customs district in the same or an adjoining state, without
entering or clearing. If over 20 t., such vessels are permitted to trade
without entering or clearing, from one customs district in the same
Great District to another in the same Great District, or from a state in
one Great District to an adjoining state in another Great District. The
5 Great Districts referred to are not the same as the Customs Collection Districts. They are (1) Atlantic Coast from Canada to Mexico
(2) Puerto Rico (3) Pacific Coast (4) Alaska (5) Hawaii.

In the case of vessels in the foreign trade or coming from one Great
District to another, and which are required to be registered, the law requires the surrender and filing of manifests, bill of health and crew
lists. When the formalities have been complied with, the vessel is
posted in the custom house as entered.

Vessels Not Required to Enter:

1. Vessels of war and public vessels.

2. Passenger vessels making 3 or more trips per week to foreign
ports. But they must report baggage and merchandise to collector
within 24 hours.

3. Licensed yachts or undocumented U.S. pleasure vessels not engaged
in trade and not having visited any hovering vessel.

4. Vessels entering in distress to bunker or for stores and leaving
within 24 hours and not landing or taking aboard passengers or
merchandise. Master. or owner or agent to report and take oath to the
above.

5. Tugs to Canada, when towing vessels which are required to enter
and clear.

UNITED STATES COAST GUARD
OFFICE OF MERCHANT MARINE SAFETY

The Commandant, U.S. Coast Guard, is now vested with plenary powers in administration and execution of all Merchant Marine matters as formerly carried on by the *Bureau of Marine Inspection and Navigation* under the Secretary of Commerce.

Generally, the functions of the former *Board of Supervising Inspectors* are now under the *Chief, Office of Merchant Marine Safety,* which office includes, in the main, the joint activities of the *Merchant Marine Technical, Merchant Vessel Personnel,* and *Merchant Vessel Inspection Divisions.* However, the *Merchant Marine Council,* which consists of the responsible officers (now numbering about 12) of all divisions, etc., engaged in Merchant Marine interests, forms the governing body, as directly under the Commandant, in all matters of legislation, policy, and general safeguarding of the nation's maritime interests as entailed chiefly in requirements for safe navigation, proper construction, and competent manning of our merchant vessels.

At the office of each Coast Guard District Commander is stationed the *Marine Inspection Officer* who, in turn, is over the *Officer in Charge, Marine Inspection* at each principal port within the several districts, as indicated below.

*Marine Inspection Offices.**

1st C.G. Dist. . . . . *Boston,* Providence, Portland.
2nd C.G. Dist. . . . . *St. Louis,* Pittsburgh, Cincinnati, Louisville, Nashville, Memphis, Cairo, Dubuque, Huntington.
3rd C.G. Dist. . . . . *New York,* New London, New Haven, Albany, Philadelphia.
5th C.G. Dist. . . . . *Norfolk,* Baltimore, Portsmouth, Wilmington.
7th C.G. Dist. . . . . *Miami,* Charleston, Savannah, Jacksonville, San Juan, P. R., Tampa.
8th C.G. Dist. . . . . *New Orleans,* Mobile, Port Arthur, Houston, Galveston, Corpus Christi.
9th C.G. Dist. . . . . *Cleveland,* Oswego, Buffalo, Toledo, Detroit, St. Ignace, Duluth, Chicago, Milwaukee, Ludington.
11th C.G. Dist. . . . *Long Beach* (California), San Diego, Wilmington.
12th C.G. Dist. . . . . *San Francisco.*
13th C.G. Dist. . . . . *Seattle, Portland, O.*
14th C.G. Dist. . . . . *Honolulu.*
17th C.G. Dist. . . . . *Juneau,* Ketchikan, Anchorage.

These offices handle the following matters:

1. Assigns the official number to a vessel.

---

* Head office in italics.

2. Must approve any change of vessel's name.

3. Must approve all plans for construction or alteration of passenger vessels before work is done.

4. Must inspect all vessels annually.

5. Inspects foreign vessels in cases where such is done in U. S. ports.

6. Licenses all deck and engineer officers.

7. Grants certificates of competency to crew members.

8. Investigates marine casualties.

The Secretary of Commerce. May investigate any phase of ship operation, including maritime labor relations, construction and operating costs here and abroad, charge of discrimination between shippers, contracts between carriers, and charges of unfair competition by one carrier with another. It is also empowered to study and develop new trade routes and new ideas in the field of ship construction, and to cooperate with the navy in national defense policies.

One of its most important functions is the administration of construction differential subsidies and operating differential subsidies both of which are restricted to ships in foreign trade.

LAWS GOVERNING PROCEDURE OF ARRIVING AND DEPARTING

Radio Pratique. Covers the permission granted (request made 12 to 24 hours before expected arrival) to selected passenger vessels, whereby they may enter certain U. S. ports without stopping at quarantine. Requirements in brief: (1) acceptable ship's doctor employed aboard; (2) no calls at ports having or suspected of having quarantinable diseases; (3) no bird of parrot family; (4) maintained relatively rat free; (5) maintained in sanitary condition; (6) no known or suspected quarantinable or unusual incidence of other communicable disease aboard.

Boarding. Not stopping for boarding vessel—penalty $1000 to $5000.

Unauthorized persons boarding arriving vessel before inspection— $100 or 6 mo. or both, and master to hold such person.

Hindering boarding officer—fine of $500 to $1000.

Quarantine Regulations. Entry of vessel in violation of quarantine laws—a fine up to $500, which is a lien on the vessel.

Unauthorized entry within or departure from quarantine grounds or anchorages—fine of $300 or 1 year or both.

False statement relative to vessel or passenger—$500 or 1 year or both.

Quarantine hours of inspection are fixed by the Surgeon General.

Bill of Health. Two copies to be obtained from U. S. consul or from Medical Officer, where one is detailed by President: $5000 fine if none obtained. Original goes to Collector of Customs and duplicate to quarantine officer at time of inspection. *See* ship's papers, pages 18 44 and 45.

Free pratique is on white paper, and indicates the vessel has met requirements and no further quarantine formalities required.

Provisional pratique is on yellow paper, and it requires the observance of additional quarantine procedures, which are specified thereon.

Cargo can be removed from a quarantined vessel only under permission and supervision of Collector.

Immigration. Responsibility for bringing in diseased aliens rests with the company.

Penalty for illegal transportation of immigrants—$1000 fine per person, plus such sum as immigrant has paid as fare.

Immigration Examination. In the absence of suitable facilities as to space, lighting and assistance, or of proper cooperation, examination will not be made. The determination of the citizenship of a passenger or member of the crew rests solely with the immigration officer before whom the person appears, and not with medical or other officers. Disabled or sick persons unable to appear for inspection with comfort and safety may be examined in their quarters.

The *Alien Crew List* must not be confused with the working crew Crew List. Although Quarantine Doctor or Customs Boarding Officer may be satisfied with either, Immigration Officer must be supplied the Alien List made out in the proper form. The form is made out after ship sails and any crew member failing to join need not be shown. Failure to show any new members who join subsequently makes vessel liable for a $400 fine in each instance. Although called *Alien* Crew List, every crew member must be listed, master included. When Immigration Officer boards, original of the list is submitted to him, he interviews each person and retains list for his files. At least 10 copies of the Alien Crew List should be made, or more depending on number of ports of call. Upon arrival at first foreign port the document is visaed by U.S. Consul and certified as to the number of names appearing on it.

Alien crew members may be subjected to intensive physical examination on each arrival in a U. S. port, particularly for venereal disease.

Entry. Report of arrival must be made by master to nearest Custom House within 24 hours after arrival from a foreign port, or if a foreign vessel from a domestic port, or if a U. S. vessel carrying bonded merchandise or foreign merchandise not already entered.

The *time of arrival* shall be that time when the vessel first comes to rest, whether at anchor or at a dock, in any harbor within the customs territory of the U.S. (19 C.F.R. 4.2(b)). The *report of arrival* may be filed by the master, or owner or agent (19 C.F.R. 4.2(c)).

Preliminary entry may be made and permission obtained to discharge baggage.

Formal entry must be made by master to Custom House within 48 hours after arrival from a foreign port.

Master must produce and deposit with Collector:
1. Crew list.
2. Register.
3. Clearance and Bills of Health from foreign port.
4. Original and copy of official manifest. Master takes oath as to

register and also that manifest is made out as required. It must contain names of ports at which cargo was loaded and ports of destination (bulk cargoes may state "for orders"); description of vessel; marks and description of merchandise; names of consignees; passengers and baggage; ship's stores and sea stores aboard, which are to be kept aboard, including fuel. All must be separately specified, and if landed without permit are subject to forfeiture and a penalty to the master equal to value of articles.

Drugs not manifested subject master and owners to various heavy fines, unless it is proved that the highest degree of diligence and care was taken to find same, and such search was entered in the log.

Duty on repairs is to be 50% on cost thereof in such foreign country. Vessel may be seized and forfeited if they are unreported. Remission is made for necessary repairs, (1) if due to stress of weather or other casualty, (2) if U. S. equipment or labor was used.

Arrival at Another Port. Master to present permit issued at first port of arrival and a certified copy of the manifest within 24 hours.

Licensed deck officer or purser may make entry and clearance whenever statutes make this the duty of master, but this does not relieve the master of liability.

Clearance may be refused to any vessel declining to receive cargo in good condition and properly presented, if there is space for same, provided it is merchandise for which vessel is adapted.

Official Crew List is to be produced to first boarding officer at first port of call in U.S., and also all persons named therein, unless person was discharged before a U.S. consul or proof is submitted that he has died, absconded or been impressed. Penalty for failure to produce person, $400.

A crew list containing the name of even one alien seaman must be visaed by a U.S. consular agent for the U.S. Immigration Service. If all on the crew list are U.S. citizens, no letter or other certification attesting the fact will be issued.

1. Duplicate list required to be delivered to Collector of Customs; to be in one uniform handwriting without erasure or interlineation.

2. Owners to obtain from Collector of Customs a true and certified copy of articles containing names of crew.

3. To contain all conditions of contract and to be submitted to U. S. consul if called for.

4. All interlineations, erasures or writing in a different hand from original to be deemed fraudulent.

5. Penalty to master for sailing without same or failing to produce them, $100.

6. It is the duty of the boarding officer to report all violations. This Crew List is issued by the collector of the last port of clearance from the U. S., the collector having retained the original sworn to by the master and having furnished the master with a certified copy.

The ship's register is deposited in the Custom House and obtained before clearance.

A coasting manifest is required in the case of the clearance of a vessel in the coastwise trade which is under registry, or which for any other reason desires a clearance.

Shipping Articles are required in both the foreign and domestic trade. Foreign articles are to be signed before the Shipping Commissioner. This includes Intercoastal. Foreign doesn't include trade between U. S. and British North American possessions, West Indies and Mexico. Must contain the following:

1. Nature of voyage, duration, and port or country at which voyage is to terminate.

2. Number, description, and nature of employment of crew.

3. Time at which seamen are to be aboard to begin work.

4. Capacity in which each is to serve.

5. Wages.

6. Scale of provisions.

7. Regulations as to conduct, fines, or other lawful punishment.

8. Any stipulations regarding allotment of wages.

LAWS RELATING TO SEAMEN

A seaman may be defined as any person who signs a ship's articles. But the correct definition must be found under the law covering the case, as the U. S. Public Health service includes the master as one of the crew; but where discipline or a lien for wages is concerned, he is not a member of the crew.

Duties of master and owner to the seamen are to pay wages when due; to see that the voyage is legal, ship seaworthy and fully manned, equipped and supplied, that reasonable steps will be taken to care for seamen sick or injured, that voyage is performed without undue delay or deviation, and that men are fairly treated.

A *stowaway* is not a seaman in the eyes of the law. Signing him on the articles changes his status, however.

Seaman's Wages are secured by a maritime lien which comes ahead of all others, with the exception of salvage liens in certain cases.

The master is not ordinarily considered as justified in discharging a seaman for a single fault unless it is of a highly aggravated character, showing him to be an unsafe or unfit man to have on board.

If discharged before commencement of voyage, without fault and without his consent, or before he has earned one month's wages, he is entitled to wages earned plus wages for an additional month.

If vessel is wrecked, voyage and wages end but seaman is entitled to transportation home.

Wages Payable. If coastwise, within 2 days of termination of agreement; if foreign, within 24 hours after cargo unloaded or 4 days after discharge. Delayed payment entitles seaman to 2 days' extra pay for each day delay. If the voyage is foreign or intercoastal, discharge and payment of wages to be made in presence of Shipping Commissioner (if not, penalty is $50).

Master must furnish wage account to seaman 48 hours before paying him off*or, if discharged before Commissioner, then to such Commissioner, with full and true account of wages and deductions.

* Penalty $50. (46 U.S.C., par. 642).

Receiving remuneration from a seaman for securing employment for him, either directly or indirectly, is an offense punishable with a fine of $200 and 6 months.

Discharge in foreign ports may be made before U. S. consul, if agreements and law are complied with. Consul is to see that wages are received.*

Continuous Discharge Books and Certificates of Identification:

1. Every seaman to have one or the other.

2. Must furnish proof of citizenship.

3. No seaman to be employed until he has exhibited above except in a foreign port.

4. Discharge to be entered in book by a commissioner.

5. Certificate in lieu of book if desired. No reference to character or ability in book.

6. Record to be kept in Washington.

7. No person or company to require book if seaman prefers certificate. (Penalty, $1000 or 1 year.)

8. Penalty for false statements in application: $1000 or 1 year.

Illegal Shipment. If man is signed on through force, misrepresentation or while intoxicated or under influence of drugs, any person knowingly aiding or abetting such shall be fined not more than $1000 or imprisoned 1 year or both, and such unlawful shipment is void.

Penalty for accepting seamen engaged in violation of law is $200 to master, mate or other officer responsible.

Undermanning. In cases of desertion or casualty, master must, if obtainable, replace deserters by men of the same or higher rating, and report same to U. S. consul at first port of arrival.

Shipment in foreign port must be before U. S. consul, and if seaman was engaged in a foreign port, master shall not be required to reship such seaman in a U. S. port. Replacement may be other than U. S. citizen, who may fill vacancy until arrival at first U. S. port.

Owners or masters may ship seamen in certain cases where no Shipping Commissioner shall have been appointed.

Shipment without agreement makes vessel subject to $200 fine.

Minimum age is 15 years, unless it is a vessel on which owner's family only is employed. Fourteen years permitted if employed for education.

Forecastle Card. A legible copy of the Articles must be posted (omitting signatures) where accessible to crew (Penalty $100).

Wages and clothing of seamen *exempt from attachment*, except by court order for support of wife or minor children. Person attaching such clothing liable to 6 months imprisonment, $500 fine or both.

Allotments are valid only if made in writing and signed and approved by shipping commissioner. They can be made only to seaman's grandparents, parents, wife, sister or children or to certain savings banks or to U. S. postal savings.

---

* In this case the consul gives the master a certificate stating amount of wages received, when and where seaman signed off, etc. One copy is attached to the Articles and one to Official Crew List, thus accounting for the seaman.

If the shipping agreement has been completed the master must provide a job on a vessel agreed to by the seaman, or give him one month's extra wages.

Wages are settled by *mutual release* signed by master or owner and seaman before Shipping Commissioner, which is then signed and attested by him. This is a mutual discharge in settlement of all claims. Wages cannot be dependent on freight earned, and the seaman cannot forfeit his lien upon the ship by any agreement.

A seaman has no right to wages when he neglects or refuses to work, or when lawfully imprisoned for own fault.

Other circumstances affecting the seaman's right to wages are venereal disease, negligence, insolence, disobedience.

Wages when vessel sold in foreign port. To pay off before consul with certified crew list. Besides wages, master to provide employment on a vessel agreed upon, or provide passage home, or deposit with consul amount sufficient to defray such expenses.

On foreign discharge, when seaman makes *justifiable complaint*, master must pay wages, plus one extra month's wages, and provide transportation home as above.

Advances. It is unlawful to pay any seaman wages in advance of the time when he has actually earned them, or to pay them to anyone else. Fine of $25 to $100 and 6 months to person doing so.

Seamen are entitled to 1/2 of balance due at each port where cargo is loaded or delivered, provided this does not occur oftener than once in 5 days or more than once in same harbor on same entry. As penalty to ship, seaman is released from his contract if the advance is refused. This applies to foreign vessels in U. S. waters.

Overdue Wage Claims, if overdue 10 days or more, can be settled by a simplified and speedy procedure on application to a district judge, justice of the peace or U. S. commissioner who can attach the vessel. This does not prevent further suit.

Wages and Effects of Deceased Seaman. Entry in log as follows:

1. Amount of money left by deceased.

2. In case of sale, description of each article sold and sum received for each.

3. Statement of sum due as wages, and deductions if any.

Proceedings in regard to effects:

1. If vessel proceeds direct to U. S. port, deliver effects to Shipping Commissioner within 48 hours. Receipt given.

2. If in a foreign port, report to U. S. Consul and, if deemed best, deliver effects and money and receive receipt which shall be presented to Shipping Commission on return to U. S.

3. Penalty for neglect of master to comply with foregoing is 3 times the values of the wages and effects or, if not ascertained, $200.

Protection, Liabilities, etc.

Destitute seamen—Foreign port. Master must transport, upon request of U. S. consul, any destitute seaman (not more than one man for every 100 tons burden, and provided seaman has no contagious disease) from a foreign to a U. S. port to which vessel is bound. Seaman required to do duty, if able, according to his abilities. Consul required to furnish destitute seaman with subsistence and return passage, with penalty to master of $100 for each seaman refused.

Soliciting of seamen as lodgers within 24 hours after arrival of vessel is punishable by a fine of $50 or 3 months' imprisonment.

Complaints regarding provisions and water may be made by any 3 or more seamen of a U. S. vessel bound foreign or intercoastal to any commander of U. S. Navy vessel, consular officer, Shipping Commissioner of chief officer of customs, who shall examine such water and provisions. If master does not comply with their judgment, he is liable to $100 fine. If no reasonable grounds for complaint, parties complaining to pay costs of survey. Master must permit seamen shore leave to make above complaints, if not, penalty of $100.

Allowance for reduction of provisions, except where a seaman is lawfully undergoing confinement. If reduced 1/3 of quantity specified by law, allowed $.50 per day. If reduced more than 1/3, or if bad quality, $1 per day. Reduced or not allowed under special circumstances.

Weights and measures for measuring provisions must be kept aboard, penalty $50 if not.

An unseaworthy vessel knowingly sent to sea subjects person responsible to a fine of $1000 or 5 years.

Inspection for seaworthiness shall be made by surveyors on complaint filed through master by 1st and 2nd officers or a majority of the crew. If master refuses to file such complaint, he is liable to $500 fine. Master submits complaint to a local judge or justice who appoints the 3 best qualified persons who can be secured. A doctor is appointed if matter regards provisions. Master and crew shall in all respects conform to judgment of surveyors. If complaint is justified, master is to pay costs of survey; if unjustified, cost of survey and reasonable damages for detention to be deducted from the wages of the complaining seamen.

Refusal to proceed when vessel found seaworthy, after such inspection by surveyors on complaint, subjects such persons to loss of wages.

If in a foreign port, procedure is the same except that the U. S. consul or officer in command of any naval or government vessel takes the place of the judge in securing surveyors, etc.

Discharge of crew on account of unseaworthiness. If defects or deficiences cannot be removed in a reasonable time, or if due to neglect or design, crew is entitled to 1 month's wages above that due, or sufficient money for return to U. S., or employment on a ship agreed to by them.

Ship Owner's Liability covers sickness, injury or death while under articles after reporting for duty, except for injury or sickness incurred other than in service of ship, by own willful act, default or misbehavior, or if such was intentionally concealed when engaged.

His liability comprises also medicine, medical treatment and board and lodging until cured or declared incurable, unless limited by law to no less than 16 weeks, or if covered by other compensation laws. Also if unable to work, shipowner to pay full wages while on board and, if there are dependents, to pay wages after landed until cured or declared incurable, unless limited to not less than 16 weeks. If landed during voyage, seaman to be returned to home port or one mutually agreed upon. Shipowner is to defray burial expenses and safeguard deceased or injured man's property. Equal treatment must be given, irrespective of nationality, domicile or race.

Compensatory damages for pain and suffering are not included under maintenance and cure.

Indemnity damages allowed where vessel was unseaworthy (covers a wide range) in respect to accident or where necessary equipment not supplied or kept in order.

Jones Act (1920) gives an injured seaman a right to recover damages for pain and suffering, even if his injury was due to the negligence of a "fellow-servant," i.e., the master or another seaman, and even though vessel is seaworthy. Act also gives a deceased seaman's personal representative the right to sue the shipowner. Does not apply to seamen injured on shore in service of the vessel, and suits under the act are barred after two years have elapsed from time of injury.

Accepting wages, care and cure to end of voyage or during period incapacitated by injury does not cancel the right to sue for compensation under the Jones Act.

Medicine Chests are required on vessels of 75 t. and over, bound from U. S. to foreign port or between Atlantic or Pacific Coasts.

Lime or lemon juice, sugar and vinegar (or other antiscorbutics) required on vessels bound around Cape Horn or Good Hope, which are to be served within ten days after salt provisions are started and to continue as long as salt provisions mainly are served. To serve 1/2 oz. of lemon or lime juice and sugar per day and 1/2 pint vinegar per week for each member of crew. Penalty of $500 to master or owner if not on board and $100 per offense if not served out.

Slop Chest required on above vessels, to contain a complement of clothes, including caps, boots, shoes, under and outer clothing and everything necessary to wear for each man. Also a full supply of tobacco and blankets, to be sold to seaman for his own use at not more than 10% above wholesale cost at port of commencement of voyage. Does not apply to vessels in trade with Canada, Newfoundland, Bermuda, Bahamas, West Indies, Mexico or Central America. Penalty, $500.

Warmth and Clothing. Vessels on foreign voyage exceeding 14 days to be provided with at least one suit of woolen clothing for each seaman, and in foreign and domestic trade a safe and warm room for all seamen in cold weather. Penalty, $100.

Crew Accommodations. To be washed out every 3–4 months and painted at least every 2 years. Not to be located forward of collision bulkhead. To have 120 cu. ft. and at least 16 sq. ft. floor space per man. Quarters to be securely constructed, properly lighted, drained and ventilated. To be protected from weather, sea and odors given off by cargo or bilge water. To have two exits, to be kept free of goods, stores or cargo.

Wash room. At least one outfit for each two men of the watch. A separate place for firemen, etc., and if there are over 10 to accommodate 1/6 of them at one time. To have hot and cold running water.

Hospital. Required on vessels making voyages of 3 or more days at sea with a crew of 12 or more seamen. One bunk for each 12, but no more than 6 bunks required.

Watches, Hours of Labor, Legal Holidays:

1. Three watches for all.

2. To work 8 hours only in one day, except in case of extraordinary emergency affecting safety of vessel, life, or property.

3. Seamen not to be shipped to work in fireroom, nor firemen on deck.

4. In a safe harbor no seamen to do any unnecessary work on Sundays, New Years, 4th of July, Labor Day, Thanksgiving or Christmas. This not to prevent dispatch of vessel.

5. If foregoing not complied with, owner is liable to a penalty of $500 and seaman entitled to discharge and wages earned.

Duties of Seaman. To obey all lawful commands, to have training and experience necessary for berth, to report on board at agreed time, to perform duties in a seamanlike manner, and to submit to normal discipline.

SOCIAL SECURITY ACT

Old-age and survivors insurance was extended to seamen by the 1939 amendments to the Social Security Act. All work done by seamen on or in connection with an American vessel is now covered by the act (a) if the contract for service is entered into within the United States or (b) if during the performance of the contract for service the vessel touches at a port in the United States.

For the security trust fund your employer takes 1% of your wages and adds an equal amount to it. The account number on your social security card and your name will identify you when you file a claim for benefits. For your own record the employer is required to give you a statement of security taxes deducted from your wages.

Benefits. Benefits are paid monthly to qualified wage earners 65 or older. Also to members of wage earners' families, as follows: wives 65 or over, unmarried children under 16, or under 18 if in school. Also to surviving dependents, as follows: widows 65 or older, widows of any age with children of the deceased in their care who meet the above conditions, and parents 65 or older if no widow or children have been left.

Fully Insured. A calendar quarter is 3 months. A quarter of coverage is a calendar quarter in which you have earned $50 or more in a job covered by the Act. To be fully insured, a seaman must have had half as many quarters of coverage as there were calendar quarters after January 1940, or after he reached 21, whichever is later, and before he reached 65 or died. Minimum requirement is 6 quarters. But 40 quarters of coverage will bring full insurance, regardless of the rule just given. Fully insured means you are eligible for benefits listed above.

Currently Insured. A worker is currently insured if he has been earning at least $50 in covered jobs for each of not less than 6 of the 12 quarters before he died. Then, if he leaves a widow with one or more children she will get three-quarters of his primary benefit until the youngest child is no longer eligible. Each child also gets an amount equal to half the primary benefit.

Single workers with no dependents get only this primary benefit. Wives over 65 and children get amounts monthly equal to half of this. Widows over 65 get three-fourths the primary benefit. Minimum and maximum benefits are $10 and $85.

For a more complete explanation and further details, inquire at the postoffice for address of nearest Social Security Board field office.

VARIOUS OFFENSES AND PENALTIES

1. Desertion: Forfeiture of effects and wages left aboard. (It must be shown that seaman left without intention to return. Not desertion if he leaves because of cruel treatment or threats, or if he leaves because of a deviation or change of voyage not provided for in the articles.)

2. Neglect or refusal to join or absence without leave within 24 hours of sailing (when not amounting to desertion): forfeiture of 2 days' pay.

3. Quitting vessel without leave before vessel is placed in security: loss of one month's pay.

4. Willful disobedience of any lawful command at sea: is placed in irons until disobedience ceases, with loss of up to four days' pay, or imprisonment for one month.

5. Continued willful disobedience to lawful command, or continued willful neglect at sea: is placed in irons, on bread and water (with full rations every 5th day), until disobedience shall cease, with loss of up to 12 days' pay for every day's continuance, or up to 3 months' imprisonment.

6. Assaulting master or other officer: imprisonment up to 2 years.

7. Willful damage to vessel, stores or cargo, or embezzling from same: loss of wages equal to amount of loss, and up to 12 months' imprisonment.

8. Malingering: to feign illness or inability in order to avoid doing one's duty; to shirk.

9. Smuggling, for which convicted: liable to pay master or owner sum sufficient to reimburse them for loss or damage thus entailed, and liable to 12 months' imprisonment.

Entry of offenses in log. Upon commission of any of the foregoing offenses, entry is to be made on the day on which committed and signed by master and mate and one of crew; before next arrival in port, or if in port then before departure, offender to be furnished with a copy of entry and have same read over to him distinctly. A statement to this effect and his reply, if any, to be entered in log book also in the same manner. If there are any subsequent legal proceedings, log book is to be produced.

Power to punish rests with the master, and cannot be delegated to any other officer except in an emergency.

Duty of consular officer is to discountenance insubordination by every means in his power and to call on local authorities if necessary.

Disposal of forfeitures. First applied toward any expenses occasioned by the desertion, etc., and remainder paid over to Shipping Commissioner. Double the amount involved is the penalty for noncompliance.

Drunkenness or neglect of duty. Where vessel or persons damaged or endangered through such neglect or refusal, twelve months' imprisonment.

Wearing of sheath knives is prohibited. Master liable to $50, if permitted, one-half of which goes to informer.

Corporal punishment prohibited, and any master or other officer found guilty may be fined up to $1000, imprisoned up to 5 years, or both. Master is liable if he fails to surrender offender.

CRIMES COMMITTED AT SEA

A crime consists in the violation of a public law either forbidding or commanding an act to be done. Classified as treason, felonies, and misdemeanors. Felonies are crimes punishable by death or imprisonment, misdemeanors are less important.

Criminal Jurisdiction. Merchant vessels are regarded for many purposes as floating portions of the country to which they belong and the particular state where their home port is located. No crime can escape punishment because committed on shipboard or the high seas.

The jurisdiction of every independent nation over the merchant vessels of other nations within its boundaries is absolute and exclusive, and arrests may be made thereon and offenders removed for trial according to the laws of the locality. The right of local authorities to search a vessel in their ports for a person charged with crime is established unless modified by treaty.

The master is bound to submit to the jurisdiction within which his vessel lies.

Right of the government to prosecute is not barred by lapse of time unless provided by law. In Federal courts indictment is usually required within 3 years, but term does not run while the offender is a fugitive from justice.

Barratry includes any act done by master or crew, with criminal intent, in violation of their duty to the shipowner and without his connivance, such as casting away of the vessel for insurance, bottomry or respondentia. Penalty $10,000 or 10 years, or both.

Mutiny, where by a general combination the crew refuses obedience to the master's lawful orders, is punishable by up to $2000 fine, up to 10 years, or both. Mere refusal of duty or disobedience by seaman, while liable to punishment by the master, is not mutiny, and the conduct may be very aggravating without amounting to mutiny. Mutiny is particularly an attempt to usurp command from the master.

Inciting to mutiny on shipboard by one of crew, that is, one who incites another to disobey or resist the lawful orders of the master or other officer, or incites him to refuse or neglect his proper duty, or makes a riot, or unlawfully confines the master is liable to $1000 fine, or 5 years imprisonment, or both.

Laying violent hands on commander to hinder his fighting in defense of vessel or goods. Imprisonment for life.

Murder. First degree, if premeditated; punishment of death. Second degree, if unpremeditated; punishment up to 10 years.

Manslaughter. First degree, voluntary in a sudden quarrel or heat of passion: 10 years. Second degree, involuntary but in commission of an unlawful act, or of a lawful act without due caution: 3 years or $1000, or both.

Mayhem. Intent to maim or disfigure: $1000 fine, 7 years, or both.

Attempted Murder or Manslaughter. Not more than 20 years.

Arson. Maliciously setting fire: Up to $5000, 20 years, or both.

Robbery. Using force or fear to take anything of value: 15 years.

Assault. Intent to murder or rape: 20 years. With intent to commit other felony: $3000 or 10 years or both. Intent to harm without just cause with a dangerous weapon: $1000 or 5 years or both.

Unlawfully strike, beat, or wound another: $500 or 6 months, or both.

Unlawfully assaulting another: $300 or 3 months, or both.

Rape. Punishment is death, imprisonment for any number of years, or for life.

Carnal knowledge with a female under 16 years: first offense, 15 years; second offense, 30 years.

Seduction by any one employed on a U.S. vessel: $1000 or 1 year.

Death from Negligence, misconduct, etc. Caused by anyone employed on a vessel, or owner or officer of a corporation: $10,000 or 10 years, or both.

Larceny of personal property, if value over $100, up to $5000 fine or 5 years, or both; if under $100, up to $1000 fine or 1 year, or both.

Receiving Stolen Property. With knowledge of felony, $1000, or 3 years, or both.

Obtaining money falsely. Up to $5000 fine, or 5 years, or both.

Perjury. Up to $2000 fine, or 5 years, or both.

Forgery. Up to $1000 fine, or 3 years, or both.

Breaking and Entering Vessel to commit a felony, cutting cable, cordage, etc.: Up to $1000 fine, or 5 years, or both.

Plundering Vessel by surpise or force: Up to $5000, or 10 years, or both.

Piracy. Life imprisonment.

Wrecking or plundering a wreck: $5000 or 10 years. For obstructing the escape of a person from a wreck, or showing a false light, or extinguishing a true light, imprisonment for from 10 years to life.

Conspiracy against United States. $10,000 fine, or 2 years or both.

Ill-treatment of Crew. A master or officer who wounds or imprisons without justifiable cause or withholds suitable food or inflicts any cruel or unusual punishment is liable to a $1000 fine or 5 years or both.

Abandonment of seaman by a master while abroad, maliciously and without justifiable cause, of forcing any officer or mariner of vessel ashore in order to leave him behind, or refusing to bring him home again if he is in a condition to come home and willing: Master is subject to a fine of $500, or 6 months, or both.

Running Away With or Yielding up Vessel, or cargo to the value of $50. $10,000 fine or 10 years or both.

Destruction of Vessel at sea by owner, life imprisonment. By person other than owner, 10 years.

Smuggling. Employment or permitting employment of vessel in smuggling; $5000 fine or 2 years or both. If vessel fitted out for smuggling, registry, etc. is revoked, and if Secretary of Treasury deems it desirable vessel is destroyed.

Packages of Fermented Liquor knowingly shipped in interstate commerce and not plainly marked subjects person to fine of $1000 or 1 year or both.

Stowaways who arrive in the U.S. or stowaways in the U.S. are liable to a fine of $1000 or imprisonment for 1 year (June 1940).

Stowaways are trespassers and the ship owes them no duty save to set them off the vessel without wilful or wanton disregard of their safety.

Penalty for aiding stowaways. Fine of $1000 or imprisonment for 1 year or both.

MERINT

Since the timely receipt of intelligence sightings is vital to the defense of the United States so that United States Military Forces can take prompt defensive action, it is urgent that all United States merchant ships and fishing vessels properly relay such information.

To promulgate the correct procedure for making such reports, the United States Navy has printed the pamphlet *MERINT* which is available for use on merchant vessels and fishing vessels. It will be distributed to vessels by the United States Naval Sea Frontier Commanders. Any inquiries concerning the issue of this publication should be directed to the United States Naval District Commandant, Operations Officer.

Abstracts of certain pertinent portions of this pamphlet are as follows:

How to Report:

1. Merchant ships will employ normal international commercial communication procedure.

2. *MERINT* reports should be transmitted in plain language to the nearest United States military or commercial radio station, as appropriate. When passed to commercial stations, a report should contain instructions to pass to the nearest Military Command and to either Commander Western Sea Frontier or Commander Eastern Sea Frontier for sightings in the Pacific or Atlantic areas respectively.

When to Report:

1. Immediately (except when within territorial waters of other nations, as prescribed by International Law).

2. When the situation changes sufficiently to warrant an amplifying report.

Delayed Reports. In the event a *MERINT* report cannot be made by radio, the master is requested to report the details of the *MERINT* sighting to the appropriate United States military or consular authorities. This report should be submitted immediately upon arrival in port by any available means.

What to Report. Report immediately by radio all airborne and waterborne objects which appear to be hostile, suspicious, or unidentified. As a result of these reports, United States Forces are enabled to take prompt defensive or investigative action.

What to Report Immediately:
1. Guided missiles.
2. Unidentified flying objects.
3. Submarines.
4. Group or groups of military vessels.
5. Formations of aircraft which appear to be directed against the United States, its Territories, or possessions.

What Not to Report:
1. Surface craft or aircraft in normal passage.
2. Known United States military vessels, including submarines.
3. Known United States Government vessels.
4. Known United States or allied military aircraft.

Contents of Reports. *MERINT* reports shall contain the following as applicable in the order listed.
1. *MERINT* will always be the first word of the text.
2. Ship's position at time of sighting.
3. Nature of object(s) sighted.
4. Direction of sighted object's (s') travel.
5. Observations of aerial sightings the altitude expressed as low, medium, or high.
6. Date-time group, expressed in Greenwich mean time (G.M.T.).
7. Signature.
Every effort shall be made to obtain a reply from receiving station to insure that message has been received.

Types of Reports:
1. *MERINT* reports—Initial sighting report.
2. Amplifying report—Additional information that becomes available to any *MERINT* observer and is of importance.
3. Cancellation report—When a *MERINT* report is nullified by a subsequent observation, a cancellation report should be made.

THE MASTER

1. In charge of the navigation, care and management of his vessel.
2. Appointed by the owner, or in some cases by charterers, no formalities are required (except that the Register must be endorsed at Custom House on taking over), and his contract need not be in writing.
3. His wages are a matter of contract, and he has no lien on the ship.
4. As agent of the owner he has the power to bind the owner by acts done within the scope of his authority, such as for supplies, pilotage, labor, stevedoring, towage and the like.

5. His authority is according to the law of the ship's flag. On shipboard his authority is supreme except, possibly, in the presence of the owner.

Duty in Collision. Duty of master of vessel in collision to give aid, his name and name of his vessel, port of registry, ports from and to which bound, and stay by until he has ascertained that the other vessel has no further need of assistance, as long as this can be done without serious danger to his own vessel, crew, or passengers. If not done, he shall be presumed to be at fault, and burden of proof to contrary is placed on him. Liable to fine of $1000 and 2 years.

Danger Messages. The master of every ship which meets with dangerous ice, a dangerous derelict, a dangerous tropical storm or any other direct danger to navigation is bound to communicate the information, by all means of communication at his disposal, to ships in the vincinity, and also to the competent authorities at the first point of the coast with which he can communicate. (*Int. Convention for the Safety of Life at Sea.*)

Speed Near Ice. When ice is reported on or near his course, the master of every ship at night is bound to proceed at a moderate speed or to alter his course so as to go well clear of the danger zone. (*Int. Convention for the Safety of Life at Sea.*)

Duty to Crew:

1. Sufficient provisions.

2. Proper medical care.

3. Protection from unlawful violence.

4. Criminally liable for abandoning sailors in a foreign port.

Owner's Agent. The master acts as such in all matters fairly within the scope of his authority, but has no more authority to bind the owner than any other special agent.

1. Bottomry bonds,[1] respondentia[2] bonds and the right to sell vessel or cargo, under certain circumstances, are now pretty well out of date, due to modern communications.

2. Master can sue in behalf of the owner in the case of collision or damage in foreign ports.

3. Where general average has been declared he must obtain a bond for the payment of the general average contributions before delivery of cargo at port of discharge.

Personal Liability is practically unlimited, as suit may be brought against him for almost anything, and there is no limitation, such as the value of the ship in the case of an owner.

1. Fines for violations of customs, immigration, postal, navigation and shipping laws are his personal liability.

---

[1] *Bottomry bond.* A contract in the nature of a mortgage, by which the ship is pledged in security for money borrowed for a specified use, such as repairs. It is payable on the arrival of the ship at her port of destination, and if the vessel is lost, owner loses his money and interest. Bottomry should be advertised, and the lowest rate of interest accepted. If more than one bond is raised, the last is paid first, as it enables vessel to complete her voyage.

[2] *Respondentia* is a loan on the cargo, to be repaid if the goods arrive, but lost if the borrower is exonerated.

2. Civilly responsible for seaman's wages, damages to cargo and all injuries resulting from negligence.

3. Performance of assigned duties by officers and crew is his responsibility.

4. Pilot does not relieve him from responsibility for navigation.

Rights of Master:

1. Wages according to contract, of course, but no lien on the ship. Has a lien on "freight" (money), however.

2. Entitled to extra wages for services outside line of duty.

3. Right to money advanced by him to ship.

4. Right to care and cure for injuries sustained in service of the ship. He is a seaman within the meaning of the Jones Act.

Relations to Cargo:

1. Must see that bill of lading is correct. (*See* below.)

2. Proper stowage and carriage of cargo is his personal responsibility, even though the stevedoring is done by an independent company.

3. Must see vessel is not overladen.

4. Must pursue voyage without deviation or delay except for purpose of saving life.

5. May jettison cargo to lighten vessel, but cannot give it away.

Duties in Disaster:

1. Last man to leave the vessel.

2. Bound to use all reasonable efforts to save everything possible.

  a) must be diligent to obtain aid of salvage

  b) cargo, so far as possible, to be saved, stored, and transshipped to destination

  c) wreck itself to be preserved so far as possible

3. Makes provision for return of crew.

4. Communicates promptly with owners and underwriters.

5. Remains in charge until lawfully suspended.

BILL OF LADING

Forms differ greatly in contents and legal effect but have the common feature of (1) an acknowledgment of receipt of goods, (2) a description by which they can be identified, (3) an agreement to carry to destination and deliver, (4) rate of freight and exception to certain perils. Signed by master and, as it is *negotiable*, the same as a check. Master may be held for fraud or negligence if goods are not as stated. When quantity, quality and contents are unknown, master should write on the Bill of Lading "not responsible for quantity, qualities, or contents." *Deck cargo* should be annotated, "Goods stowed on deck at shipper's risk."

Two Main Groups:

1. Straight bill, ordinarily rarely used, except in wartime, unless consignee becomes owner of the goods prior to delivery to the carrier.

2. Order form, in which the holder of the Bill of Lading is entitled to possession of the goods. Title to the goods may be transferred by endorsement of bill. Generally three copies, one being stamped. The master keeps one, the merchant keeps one and sends one to his agent or consignee.

Protest. Should be noted in case of damage or suspicion thereof due to heavy weather. It is made within 24 hours after the vessel's arrival by going before a notary and stating that it is expected the cargo is damaged owing to heavy weather. Next have hatches surveyed, and obtain certificate that they are all in good order.

Extending the Protest. Having the cargo surveyed and bringing such of crew as have knowledge of the facts involved as witnesses before the notary, who will then write up the facts from the log entries, clearly and precisely, and have the witnesses' signatures attached.

Survey is made by two competent persons, such as two shipmasters, two engineers, or a shipmaster and merchant, according to the nature of the damage. They give a written report on the case, and when repairs are finished they should give another certificate to that effect.

THE PILOT

Pilot's Authority. The local pilot employed for the occasion is in charge of the navigation while on the bridge, but the master does not relinquish all authority simply because a pilot is aboard. It has been held that the master should interfere "in cases of the pilot's incapacity, in cases of danger which he does not foresee, and in all cases of great necessity. The master has the same power to displace the pilot that he has to remove any subordinate officer of the vessel. He may exercise it, or not, according to his discretion."

It has been held, too, that the responsibility for the safety of the ship rests upon the master. The pilot has charge of the navigation, but the master may advise him, and even displace him "in case of manifest incompetency." Where danger is obvious or apparent, the court has expressed an opinion that it is proper for the master to assert his authority.

Similarly, when an officer has been placed in charge of the watch by the master, the officer has a duty to interfere when the vessel is standing into danger. At the very least, he should call the pilot's attention to the hazard and, if the pilot takes no action, notify the master. For greatest safety, officers should keep a constant check on the ship's position, and see that the pilot's orders for changes in course and speed are promptly carried out. In some waters, the Panama Canal in particular, by law, pilot assigned to a vessel shall have control of movements and navigation of such vessel.

Registered vessels are subject to compulsory pilotage in U. S. waters where such is required. The state may make it a criminal offense for a pilot not duly qualified to take a vessel through their waters. Ships are not absolutely bound to accept the services of such pilots but must pay their fees, in whole or part, if services are tendered and declined.

Enrolled and licensed vessels are exempted by Federal Statute from compulsory pilotage.

Liability of Shipowner for Pilot's Negligence. When a vessel of a class which is not required to take a pilot does take one voluntarily, the pilot becomes the agent of the owner, and the latter is responsible in the same respect as in the case of the master. When the pilot is compulsory, the owner is exempt from liability for the pilot's negligence, as he is not selected by the owner. However, if the master "takes over," the owner is responsible. Under "in rem" proceedings, though, the liability of the vessel may be quite different from that of her owner, as the ship is here personified and is held responsible for wrongful acts directed by those in charge of her.

Liability of Pilots and Pilots' Associations. The pilot himself is liable for his own negligence, both to the owner of the vessel which he is piloting and to third persons injured by this negligence. Pilotage associations are generally exempted from liability.

Pilot's duty when he has taken charge of a vessel at sea is to stay by her, unless discharged, until she reaches her destination, or some place of safety.

Pilot's Rights. He has a lien upon the vessel for services rendered, and he may recover damages for personal injuries sustained by him as a result of the negligence of those in charge of the vessel.

TOWAGE

Duty of Tug. Disaster does not necessarily absolve the contract of towage. On the contrary, the tug is not relieved from its obligations because unexpected difficulties occur, and must do all in its power short of sacrificing its own safety. The tug engages to make the trip or voyage without delay or deviation or undue peril; to be sufficiently equipped and manned and in all respects seaworthy; to exercise reasonable diligence and the ordinary skill of the profession, in case of storm or danger, to protect the tow by seeking a port of refuge, or slowing, stopping, sounding, and otherwise exercising due care until the storm subsides. She is, however, only bound to do what is consistent with her own safety, and may therefore abandon the tow under circumstances of great peril. The tug is bound to see that the tow is properly made up for the proposed voyage, to know the sailing qualities of the vessels in charge and the character of the waters before them.

Duty of Tow. To be properly manned and equipped, and to carefully follow the tug, to be vigilant to observe all orders and signals, and must be ready in case of emergencies to cast loose from the tug and from other tows. Where negligence of the tug causes tow to inflict damage, a maritime lien for tort arises against the tug.

COLLISIONS (*See* Rules of the Road, Chapter 13)

Collision. In maritime law collision is the impact of ship against ship, although usage is increasing the scope of the word so as to include contact with other floating bodies.

Liability depends on negligence or fault causing or contributing to the disaster.

Test of negligence. The primary question is whether there has been a violation of any regulations or rules of navigation.

Damages in Collision Cases:

1. Where both vessels are at fault the damages are divided between them, and the one whose damage is the larger receives from the other one-half the difference between their respective losses. This rule is harsh on the ship which suffers only slight damage in the collision. The divided damage rule applies only where the litigation is before a court of admiralty. If the suit is brought in a common law court and it is shown that both sides were at fault, neither will be given an award, since contributory negligence is a ban to recovery of damage in a common law action.

2. Where a vessel has been damaged solely through the fault of another vessel, her owner is entitled to recover monetary damages sufficient in amount to put him in the same financial position as though the collision had not occurred.

3. Where there has been a total loss, the owner is entitled to recover from the vessel at fault the value of his vessel at the time of the collision, plus the net freight lost for that particular voyage. Where the vessel has been sunk, and it is shown that the cost of raising her plus the cost of repairs will exceed the value at the time of the collision, he is entitled to claim for a total loss.

4. If a collision occurs without negligence or fault on the part of either vessel, each party bears its own loss.

Reports of accidents must be made within 5 days to nearest Officer in Charge, Marine Inspection, or at vessel's home Coast Guard District. (*See also* page 18-19.)

Evidence in Collision Cases. The party alleging negligence must bear the burden of proof in establishing it. He must show fault on the part of the other vessel as well as due care on his own. By an act of Congress, the so-called "Stand-By" Act, failure of a vessel to stay by another which she has collided with, until there is no further need of assistance, raises the presumption that she is at fault in the collision. This presumption, however, is not conclusive, and may be rebutted by testimony.

The facts at issue are shown by the testimony of those who saw or participated. These facts generally come from the officers and crews of the vessels involved and every man ought to be accounted for. Extreme contradictions are to be expected in the evidence, as there is a natural tendency on the part of crew and passengers to be loyal to their own ship and to impute every fault to the one which runs into her. The courts seldom attempt to reconcile conflicting testimony, but frequently decide on the conceded facts and probabilities. The evidence of disinterested parties is of much weight.

WHARVES AND WHARFAGE

Liability for Unauthorized Structures. The harbor waters of the U. S. are under the joint control of the War Dept. and the particular state having jurisdiction over the waters. The erection of a wharf, pier, or breakwater without the authority of the War Dept., or without its approval of the plans, subjects the owner to criminal prosecution, and conviction carries heavy penalties. The government may also enforce the removal of such structure.

The Lien for Wharfage can be enforced in admiralty against a foreign vessel by the wharf owner, as this is a maritime contract. Generally the local state law provides for a lien for wharfage against domestic vessels, but the law is not uniform.

Public and Private Wharves. The owner of a public wharf must allow others to use it on payment of reasonable wharfage, whereas the owner of a private wharf has the right to use it as he wishes, the same as any other piece of real property.

Liability for Damage to Wharves. A vessel is not liable "in rem" for damage to a wharf, as an admiralty court has no jurisdiction to decide cases involving injuries to land structures. Nor is the owner liable "in personam" where the vessel is in charge of a compulsory pilot at the time of damage. If in charge of the master or a voluntary pilot, the owner is liable in common law.

Liability of Wharf Owners for Damage. Injuries received by a ship at a wharf are admiralty cases, and the libel is placed against the wharf owner. A wharf owner does not become an insurer of the safety of vessels using his premises, but is held to a very high degree of care in ascertaining that the premises are reasonably safe and that there is sufficient depth of water to accommodate the particular vessel. He must warn users of his wharf of any hidden dangers, even those beyond the immediate confines of the pier.

CARGO

Cargo Damage Claims. These constitute the great bulk of maritime litigation. Cargo is generally insured "from warehouse to warehouse." Suit is generally brought by the underwriter against the ocean carrier in the name of the cargo owner to recover the amount of loss or damages.

A common carrier or "general ship" must serve all who apply, in the order of application and without discrimination.

A private carrier is usually engaged in the bulk trade where all space must be reserved for one shipper.

An implied *warranty of seaworthiness* on the part of the vessel's owner lies in the contract of carriage, i.e., the Bill of Lading.

Liability of Common Carriers. Before the passage of the Harter Act and the Carriage of Goods by Sea Act of 1936, the only excuses for damages were (1) "an act of God," which means a casualty arising independently of human action or fault that could not have been guarded against by reasonably expected means; (2) "acts of public enemies," i.e., the armed forces of the country's enemies, and includes losses due to delay when eluding the enemy; (3) "inherent vice," by which is meant the natural deterioration of goods without fault on the part of the vessel.

Harter Act on Bills of Lading (1893):

1. All clauses purporting to relieve the carrier from liability for negligence in care and custody of cargo are void.

2. No clause is given effect which lessens the obligation of the carrier to properly stow and care for cargo.

3. The cargo owners must prove negligence; if they fail to prove it, the ship is excused. This is the real benefit to the carrier of the exceptions in the Bill of Lading.

The Harter Act also provides that if the owner of a vessel exercises due diligence to make her in all respects seaworthy and properly manned, equipped, and supplied at the beginning of the voyage, the vessel and her owner shall not be liable for errors in navigation and management of the vessel. The catch is that "in all respects seaworthy" is almost impossible to provide, and was changed by the *Carriage of Goods by Sea Act* of 1936, by which the shipper must show the damage was due to the unseaworthiness.

The Harter Act is a compromise between American shipping and carrying interest, which exempts the carrier from liability for many acts of negligence for which they were formerly responsible, and against which they could not stipulate.

Carriage of Goods by Sea Act of 1936. Through this the benefit of the general exceptions are to some extent lost, as they are limited to those set forth in the act as uncontrollable causes. However, the act benefits the shipowner in that if he can show due diligence on his own part he may not be held liable for certain errors of navigation or management. In practice, the court gathers all facts and decides whether or not the vessel was seaworthy. Act does not apply coastwise unless specified in Bill of Lading.

Due Diligence Means:

1. More than obtaining certificates of seaworthiness from Lloyds or some other classification society. What counts is what the surveyor did by way of inspection, as may be shown under a cross examination.

2. It requires that the holds be clean and that the scuppers and rose boxes be clean and free of obstructions before loading.

3. With respect to rivets, seams and metal parts of the vessel in general, it does not require that all rivets and seams be hammer-tested prior to the beginning of the voyage, but an experienced man should at least visually examine the riveted surfaces and hammer-test any rivets he suspects may be loose.

4. With respect to oil cargo tanks, it requires that the tank be placed under the pressure of a head of water, preferably to the level of the weather deck, and that the seams be inspected within a few days prior to the loading of the oil cargo.

5. With respect to fuel supply, it is shown by an excess of 20 to 25% over that required for the particular passage.

Overloading is a serious offense where that condition has contributed to lo s or damage.

Unexplained sea water damage to underdeck cargo in a seaworthy vessel renders her liable.

Perils of the Sea:

a) Sweat. Weather sufficiently heavy to require a well-found ship to cover or unship her ventilator cowls is a peril of the sea. The same severity of weather would not exonerate the vessel in the event of salt-water damage due to failure of some part of the hull, nor would it excuse the vessel for the shifting and breakage of cargo.

b) Sea water damage occasioned by heavy weather.

c) Breakage and shifting occasioned by heavy weather.

It must be shown that the weather was of such severity as to amount to a peril of the sea under the circumstances. Weather amounting to a sea peril in one trade might not in another, and, in the same trade, heavy weather experienced in the summer, when such weather was unusual, might be considered a peril while it would not be so considered in winter. The courts have placed great weight on structural damage as a corroboration of the testimony of the officers and log entries. Propeller slip, and the gyro compass record are also of value.

Latent Defects. (A customary exception in Bills of Lading.) An example is the breaking of a propeller shaft, the latent defect in which no amount of inspection would have revealed at the beginning of the voyage. The Bill of Lading must contain this exception, however, to make it effective, and should contain the additional phrase "even though existing at the beginning of the voyage."

Error of Navigation or Management. There is no hard and fast rule to differentiate between this and negligence in care and custody of cargo, which is not excusable. Negligent stranding or collision are within this exemption, and the carrier is exonerated from claims by the cargo owner if due diligence has been exercised with regard to providing navigating equipment and in the selection of the navigating personnel. Equipment includes up to date charts, sailing directions, light lists, "Notice to Mariners," etc. It is the duty of the owners, and not of the officers of the ship, to supply this material.

Ventilation. In a general cargo vessel, where the nature of the cargo is such that no obnoxious fumes are given off and the main purpose of ventilation is to eliminate sweat and stains, a vessel proceeding from a cold to a warm climate can avoid sweat to a great extent by shutting off ventilation entirely, as the warm, moist air coming in contact with the relatively cold cargo will condense on the exposed surfaces of the cargo. Yet the courts place entirely too much reliance upon the questionable benefit of opening hatches, and might hold the ship responsible for failure to ventilate. *See* page 8–2.

"Apparent good order and condition" in the Bill of Lading applies merely to the external appearance of the merchandise. The carrier may be held liable for fraud if a clean Bill of Lading is given a shipper in exchange for a letter by which the shipper agrees that the carrier will not be held liable for some existing damage, and the Bill of Lading is subsequently turned over to a third party.

Liability for Negligent Stowage. Where the ship is seaworthy at the time of loading, the carrier is liable for damage to cargo if the stowage itself was negligent and the faulty stowage contributed to the damage, even though the weather encountered amounts to a *peril of the sea.*

Deck Stowage. Where goods are shipped under a clean Bill of Lading, it is understood that they are to be stowed under deck unless there is an agreement with the shipper for deck stowage, or unless a custom prevails whereby goods of that particular class are regularly stowed on deck. Even though the Bill of Lading contains the clause "on deck at owner's risk," the carrier is liable for any damage due to improper stowage or failure to secure the cargo properly.

Stowage of Dangerous Cargoes. Note that, where sulphuric acid is stowed on deck, leakage from it may eat around the rivet heads of the deck and cause sea water was well as acid to leak below. If a dangerous cargo has been shipped without its true nature being disclosed, the carrier may, after ascertaining its true nature, take whatever steps are necessary to protect the other cargo and vessel, even to the extent of destroying it.

Damage from Fire. Liability for damage by fire differs radically from liability for other types of cargo damage, in that it is necessary to show some fault on the part of the owner of the vessel in order to recover for fire damage. When the vessel is owned by a corporation there must be neglect on the part of some officer or agent possessing the power of management, such as a marine superintendent.

Deviation is an unwarranted departure from the usual or advertised route of the vessel. The effect of a deviation is to deprive the carrier of the benefit of all the exceptions contained in the Bill of Lading with the exception of the benefits of the fire statute, unless the fire is the result of such deviation. However, by the Harter Act and the Carriage of Goods by Sea Act the carrier is relieved of liability for deviation occasioned by attempts to save life or property.

The stowage of cargo on deck without the authority of the shipper and contrary to the existence of such a custom in the trade is considered a deviation.

It is not deviation to put into a port of refuge for the purpose of repairs, even though the unseaworthiness which rendered the repairs necessary existed at the beginning of the voyage.

Technical Defenses in Cargo Damage Claims:

a) Notice of claim clause. Under the Harter Act, the carrier was permitted to insert in the Bill of Lading a clause relieving it from liability if claim for cargo damage was not made within a specified time, provided reasonable opportunity for inspection was given the consignee.

b) Clauses limiting the time to sue. The general maritime law does not contain a statute of limitations, whereby suits are barred if not commenced within a certain length of time after the right to sue arises. However, by the doctrine of "laches" unreasonable delay on the part of the person bringing action bars recovery.

Under the Carriage of Goods by Sea Act, all suit for cargo damage must be brought within one year from the date of delivery.

c) Invoice value and agreed value clauses. Under the Harter Act, carriers were permitted to insert in their Bills of Lading clauses whereby the damages were to be based upon invoice value at the port of shipment, providing the freight rate was fixed on that basis. In the absence of agreement to the contrary, damages are based upon market value at the port of destination on the arrival date.

PASSENGERS

Carriage of Passengers. A cargo vessel may not carry more than 12 persons in addition to crew in either the foreign or domestic trade. The relationship between the passenger and carrier is a contractual one, and begins as soon as the individual is accepted as a passenger. The carrier is obliged to exercise a very high degree of care to protect the safety of the passenger while on its property. This duty begins at the time the passenger first enters the premises of the carrier for the purpose of boarding the vessel and terminates when the passenger leaves the premises of the carrier at destination.

Liability of Carriers for Acts of the Crew. The law affords a passenger absolute protection against negligent or malicious acts of members of the crew occurring on board the vessel, and the carrier cannot plead as a defense that the crew member acted outside the scope of his employment.

Passengers are obliged to submit to lawful regulations, and the carrier's employees are entitled to use such force as is necessary to compel them to obey lawful commands. But if the force used is unreasonable under the circumstances, the carrier is liable in damages.

The Safety Convention of 1948 permits the carriage of a larger number of persons than otherwise permissible in order to avoid a lack of life-saving capability.

Liability of Carriers for Acts of Fellow Passengers. The carrier owes a duty to passengers to protect them from a fellow passenger's negligent acts, where the carrier's employees know of the acts and where the exercise of proper precautions would prevent injury. This is not the case where carrier has no knowledge of the conduct of the passengers, or where the injury is one which would not normally be expected to follow from the conduct of fellow passengers.

Duty to warn passengers of dangers which they as persons unfamiliar with vessels and the sea in general, do not recognize as such is well established, but there is no duty to warn where the danger is perfectly obvious even to a person unfamiliar with ocean travel.

Contracts between Carriers and Passengers. The contract is usually set forth in the passage ticket, and clauses inserted purporting to relieve the carrier of liability for negligence are unenforceable and void as contrary to public policy. This also refers to clauses limiting claims for injury or death.

Baggage includes such articles as are normally carried by a passenger for his own use, not only while on board the vessel, but for his trip in general. Unless a Bill of Lading is issued, the carrier is liable for all damage except that caused by perils of the sea. Some cases distinguish between baggage carried in the hold and that kept in the stateroom, and indicate that, as to the latter, the carrier is liable only for negligence. Value of baggage may be limited by the ticket unless a higher rate is paid.

A balement is the delivery of a thing of a personal nature by one person to another, to be carried and delivered to a third. The article must be put in actual charge of the carrier.

Rights of Passenger Injured in a Collision. When due to the sole fault of the vessel on which he is traveling, he may recover against his vessel, just as he may recover against it for any other act of negligence. If the other vessel is solely at fault, he may recover against that vessel. Where both are blameless, he has a right against neither. If both are to blame, he may sue one or both, and each vessel pays half. If a passenger is killed in a collision, his personal representative may bring suit against the offending vessel on behalf of relatives.

Passengers may be called upon to work for the safety of the vessel by the master. This is not a voluntary act but a legal duty for which no salvage is paid. This extends only to assisting the crew under the direction of the ship's officers. Beyond that, if a passenger plans or directs work himself (as a civil engineer might), this warrants payment of salvage.

Deck passenger space must not be infringed upon by cargo.

Parts of vessel assigned to passengers are not to be visited or frequented by officers, seamen, or others employed aboard, except with master's permission. Subjects person to fine of $100 or 20 days' imprisonment.

Foreign private steam vessels carrying passengers from U. S. ports are subject to the same provisions and inspection as U. S. vessels, unless exempted because that country has similar regulations.

A passenger vessel is one carrying more than 12 persons in addition to the crew.

A "new" passenger ship is one whose keel is laid on or after date of coming into force of International Convention for Safety at Sea, 1960. (1965) An "existing" ship is one other than a "new" ship.

Laws governing marine inspection—Title LII. At least two copies of this publication must be kept aboard to be exhibited to passengers on request. (Penalty $20.)

CHARTERS

Voyage or time charter merely gives the charterer the exclusive right to carrying capacity of the vessel.

Bare boat or demise charter provides that the vessel is to be operated by the charterer, who is to hire the crew, pay all expenses of operation, and in general exercise command over the vessel as owner.

Seaworthiness. Under a demise charter the maintenance of seaworthiness is up to the charterer, whereas under the time charter the owner must keep the ship in a seaworthy condition, and hire may cease when the vessel becomes unfit to perform her voyages.

Re-delivery at Termination of Charter. Under a demise charter the charterer must return the vessel in the same condition as received, reasonable wear and tear excepted. If the vessel is lost during the charter, he is liable to the owner.

Under a time charter the charterer may be liable for any damage caused by his own acts, but if the vessel becomes damaged or lost through the fault of the master or officers of the vessel, the loss must be borne by the owner.

Time Charter—Duration of Carrier's Liability. Begins when he receives goods for immediate transportation and ends when he gives notice of the arrival of the goods and has afforded the consignee a reasonable opportunity to remove them; or it may be stipulated to end when goods are put ashore.

Master states that the ship is tight, seaworthy, and in every respect fit for the intended voyage.

Merchant states that he will load the vessel with a full cargo, also load and unload within lay days, or pay demurrage as per charter.

A penalty for non-performance makes the charter party binding.

Charter is made legal by the stamp and signatures of witnesses.

Considerations in accepting charter for a foreign port are the depth of water, the general despatch, the expenses at the port, how the cargo is loaded, etc.

Freight is earned and payable when cargo has been transported and is ready for delivery, unless otherwise specified.

Dead freight is freight claimed for balance of cargo required to complete loading, i.e., when charterer does not fill space.

Demurrage is the amount of penalty to be paid by the charterer for delaying the vessel after her lay days are expired. Claimed day by day and on Saturday for Sunday. *Despatch money* is the reverse of demurrage, a bonus for quick despatch. *Warranty* is a clause stating that a vessel must not deviate from the voyage, and warrants to sail on or before a certain date.

Lay days or hours. The number of days or in some cases hours in which cargo is to be loaded and discharged.

Liabilities of Owner and Charterer as to Third Persons. In a demise charter the charterer is responsible just as if he were the owner. Under either form of charter the vessel may be liable "in rem" for her torts, regardless of the personal liability of her owner or charterer. It is therefore frequently provided in bare boat charters that the charterer shall indemnify and hold the owner blameless for all damage resulting from "in rem" liability of the vessel, arising during the life of the charter party through the fault of the charterer or his agents.

Charter party clauses (1) frequently provide that the charterer shall not have the right to incur any liens on the vessel; (2) state that the vessel is to be employed between safe ports; (3) cover insurance of vessel; (4) state time and terms of redelivery; (5) include charterer's right of cancellation or damages if vessel is late, right of withdrawal of vessel if charter hire not paid in advance or as agreed; (6) include breakdown clause (if vessel broken down more than 24 hours, hire ceases during that time, or as agreed).

SALVAGE

Salvage is a reward granted by a court of admiralty for services rendered in saving a vessel or its cargo, in whole or in part, from a marine peril. The reward is usually generous in order to encourage others to perform salvage services when the occasion arises. Three elements are necessary in a valid salvage claim: (1) a marine peril; (2) service must be voluntarily rendered when not required as an existing duty or from a special contract; (3) success in whole or in part, or evidence that the service rendered contributed to success. The service need not be the sole means of bringing the vessel to safety, nor is it essential that the vessel salved be on the high seas at the time the service is rendered. The placing of a navigator on board a vessel whose own officers had died or become incapacitated by illness has been held to give rise to a valid claim for salvage.

Life Salvage. If human lives alone are saved no enforceable right to salvage arises, no matter how meritorious the service may be. The saving of life at sea is looked upon as a duty owed by all seafarers to persons whose lives are in peril. But if property is also saved, a statute known as the Salvage Act now allows life salvors to share in the award, even in cases where the life salvors had no part in salving the property.

Salvage Contracts. There is no obligation upon the masters of the distressed and rescuing vessels to enter into any contract. If they do make such an agreement, they have authority to bind their owners, subject to the judgment of the courts, which will review an oppressive salvage contract.

Salvor's Lien. Ordinarily it is the salvor's duty to promptly place the property in possession of the court by libelling it for salvage at the first opportunity.

Amount of Reward. Usually regulated by the value of the property saved and the value of that engaged in the operation; the degree of risk or peril and the time and expense of the salvors. Expenses of volunteer salvors cannot be recovered as such. Success is essential; there can be no salvage award for the most meritorious service if unsuccessful. Salvage is generally not allowed in an amount exceeding 50% of the value of the things saved.

The proportion to owners and crew varies according to the amount of risk or loss borne by each. Where the charterer by the terms of the charter party bears the risk of loss, then it is the charterer and not the owner who benefits from the award.

Services rendered by the crew do not ordinarily entitle them to salvage, no matter how extraordinary their service. However, if a vessel has been justifiably abandoned, then those who before were members of the crew, are entitled to salvage if their efforts contributed to salving the vessel. Capture of a vessel by an enemy and her subsequent recapture and salvage by the crew entitle them to salvage, but in the case of a mutiny it does not.

Government Vessels. Suits may be brought "in personam" against the U. S. for salvage services rendered to public vessels. It is not customary for a public vessel to press a claim for salvage.

Salvor's negligence or misconduct reduces the amount awarded sufficiently to make repairs or replacements. Where one vessel negligently causes damage to another and then renders aid, it is not entitled to salvage. If the salvors are guilty of plundering the salved vessel, they forfeit their right to a salvage award.

Taking possession of a derelict does not confer ownership on the possessor, in fact, salvor is strictly accountable for all property aboard. If the crew left with the distinct intention to return, the vessel is not a derelict. Prima facie, however, a deserted vessel at sea is a derelict. Salvage of derelicts is always liberally rewarded and, if destroyed in good faith, as a menace, there is no liability to the owner.

Finders. The person who finds property lost at sea, or cast upon the shore, is protected against the interference of third parties.

Salvage applies only to a vessel or her cargo or freight (objects in tow are cargo). It does not apply to buoys, government mails, the personal belongings of crew or passengers.

Statutory Regulations. Remuneration is not affected by the fact that the same person owns both vessels. Master must render assistance to every person found at sea who is in danger of being lost, as far as he can do so without serious danger to his own vessel ($1000 fine or 2 years or both); salvage suits must be brought within 2 years.

WRECKS

Wreck includes ships and cargoes or any part thereof which have been cast on shore by the sea.

Flotsam. Goods or wreckage which float from a lost vessel.

Jetsam. Goods jettisoned or thrown overboard for safety of ship and cargo.

Lagan. Also *ligan*; jettisoned goods sunk at sea and marked by a buoy for intended recovery.

Liabilities of Owner of Wreck. It is a general doctrine of the law that the owner of a vessel wrecked without his personal fault may relieve himself from all further personal liability on its account by abandoning it. In such case he is under no obligation to remove it, and this abandonment is not required in any formal way but is shown by evidence of acts and intention. A notice to the U. S. Engineer of the district is sufficient. A vessel sunk voluntarily by the owner cannot thus be abandoned. Where the owner does not abandon he remains liable in many respects for damage from it as an obstruction, etc., and must mark it day and night.

Rights of Landowner. He is under no obligation to save a wreck or goods, but he cannot prevent others from doing so, as this is not regarded as trespass. If he does save anything he has the rights of salvage.

Owner's Rights. Title to his wrecked ship or cargo remains in the owner until divested by his own act or by law. He has the right to enter upon the lands of another, upon which it may be cast, for the purpose of removing it; if prevented from doing so he can bring action in common law. In case of abandonment to the underwriters, they become full owners.

Constructive total loss is the condition of a wreck when the cost of salvage exceeds the value of the vessel.

MARITIME LIENS

Maritime liens are perhaps the most distinguishing feature of Admiralty Law. A maritime lien is one against a vessel ("in rem"), and may arise not only where a debt is owing but also where a tort has been committed by the vessel. The first are "contract liens," such as those for wages, towage, supplies, stevedoring, wharfage, etc. Tort liens generally arise against a vessel at fault in a collision.

Liens follow a vessel wherever she may go, and may be enforced by legal proceedings in any admiralty court throughout the world which obtains jurisdiction over the vessel by having her taken into custody by the proper officer.

Enforcement of liens is by "libeling" the ship, and a U. S. Marshal takes possession, in which case the vessel is unable to sail until the owners put up a surety bond.

Characteristics of the Maritime Lien. As soon as the services are rendered, the materials supplied, or the tort committed, as the case may be, the lien arises. The lien not only follows wherever the vessel may go, but continues despite change of ownership. Thus one may buy a ship in absolute ignorance of any liens and later find she is so covered with liens as to be virtually worthless.

In the U. S. the ship herself is liable for her own torts in all cases except where the persons operating her have absolutely no right to do so. In England the ship is not liable for torts except in cases where the owners are liable.

The Maritime Lien Act. Permits liens on a ship to one supplying necessaries upon order of the owner or a person authorized by the owner. Frequently charter parties provide that the charterer shall not have the right to incur liens on the vessel.

Liens of Master and Seamen. Seamen have a lien for wages on their ship and on the freight. The master has a lien against the freight, or the cargo if freight has not been paid, but not against the ship.

Liens on Cargo. The shipowner has a lien against cargo for general average, demurrage, and freight. A lien on cargo can only arise after it has been delivered to the ship, and depends on possession. Thus, if the freight has not been paid but the shipowner delivers the cargo, he cannot thereafter enforce any lien against it. This is because the cargo may be sold over and over again, while the sum involved in the case of a ship is too large to permit this.

Priority of Liens. (1) Seaman's wages; (2) Salvage (in some cases comes first); (3) Collision and other tort liens; (4) Liens for necessaries such as repairs, supplies, towage, etc.; (5) Bottomry bonds; (6) Non-maritime claims. Within their class recent liens outrank earlier ones.

Cancellation of Liens. Once a ship sale takes place under the direction of the court, all liens are extinguished, and anyone filing a claim after that time will receive nothing.

The Ship Mortgage Act permits a preferred mortgage on the ship for a sum advanced the owner. This mortgage takes precedence over all claims against the vessel except "preferred maritime liens" and court expenses.

Preferred maritime liens are those for damages arising out of tort, for wages, general average and salvage. An ordinary ship mortgage, not made as prescribed by statute, does not have preference over any maritime lien.

Limitation of Liability. Subject to certain exceptions, the extent of the responsibility of a shipowner for contracts made in relation to the ship and for torts in which the ship is involved is limited to an amount equal to the value of his interest in the vessel and the pending freight.

The ordinary run of marine accidents falls under the limitation statute, since the owner usually has no personal connection with the accident whatever. If one should knowingly send an unseaworthy vessel on a voyage, he would not be allowed to limit his liability due to such unseaworthiness, and would be liable to claims even exceeding the value of the vessel. Similarly, if there is so called "priority of knowledge" on the part of an officer or supervising agent of a corporation; priority of knowledge of a master is now considered that of a corporate owner.

In the case of fire, exemption from liability is absolute, and cargo-owners may not recover even the value of shipowner's interest in the vessel or her pending freight.

Liability may be limited as regards death or personal injury claims, as well as regards those for damage to property. This is true where either passenger or seamen are killed or injured, but the law was amended in 1935 and 1936 so that damages may total a sum equivalent to the vessel's gross tonnage multiplied by $60. Also in personal injury cases under the new amendments, "priority of knowledge" of the master of the vessel is considered "priority of knowledge of the owner."

GENERAL AVERAGE

General average— "Act of Man" is an adjustment of a loss between all interested parties, the loss being a willful act of the master in order to save the vessel and cargo.

Particular average—"Act of God" is a loss due to ungovernable circumstances, and for which one party only is liable.

Average adjuster. A person who draws up the average bond.

Average bond. An agreement that all interested parties must sign, before delivery of cargo, admitting their liability to a proportionate share of the loss under general average.

Three Essentials of a General Average Act:

1. Must be successful, that is, something must be saved as a result of the sacrifice.

2. Must be a common danger in which ship, cargo, and freight all participate; a danger imminent and apparently inevitable except by voluntarily incurring the loss of a portion of the whole to save the remainder. A mistaken belief as to the existence of a peril, followed by a sacrifice, does not give rise to a claim of general average.

3. The sacrifice must be voluntary and result from the exercise of discretion of the master or officer in charge. If the sacrifice is made by strangers to the venture, such as port officials or municipal authorities, without the concurrence of the master, it does not give rise to a right of general average. Where the master concurs in the action of the local authorities, or where he summons them and they assist in carrying out his orders, the sacrifices are subject to general average.

General Average Expenses. May include ordinary port expenses, pilotage, unloading and reloading, storage, etc., where they were incurred by a vessel which was disabled at sea through no fault of her own and which puts into a port of refuge. Salvage services voluntarily incurred at the discretion of the master are properly included in general average.

Effect of Unseaworthiness and Negligent Navigation:

a) If cargo owners can show the vessel was unseaworthy at beginning of the voyage and that this was part cause for the loss or sacrifice, the owner is not entitled to contribution in general average.

b) The Harter Act (1893) relieves the owner from liability for errors in navigation and management if the owner has exercised due diligence to make her in all respects seaworthy and properly manned, equipped and supplied at the beginning of the voyage. The so-called "Jason Clause" inserted on bills of lading provides for general average if the foregoing situation exists.

c) The fact that the shipowner may under some circumstances be deprived of the right to contribution from cargo does not prevent cargo owners among themselves from claiming general average contributions.

General average adjustments are made by specialists who are known as adjusters. The values upon which contributions are based are values at the end of the voyage, and, in the case of damage to a vessel, the value at the end of the voyage before repairs are made.

The York-Antwerp Rules generally govern the adjustments. It is the duty of the master to cause a general average adjustment to be made and to retain cargo at the port of destination until its contributions are paid, or security for payment is given in the form of a bond for an amount sufficient to cover the estimated amount of the contribution.

LAW IN GENERAL

Law is a system of principles and rules of human conduct, either laid down or recognized by the governing powers.

Civil law may be defined, in one sense, as a written body of law. This form of law had its origin in the Roman Empire, and was codified in the Justinian Code. The laws of Continental Europe, Latin America, Scotland, Louisiana and Japan are based on this system. It is an attempt to draft definite rules to govern human conduct.

Common law is unwritten in that a great part of the law is never set down in the form of definite rules; instead, the judges decide cases according to custom and precedent. This is the law of England and the U. S.

Criminal proceedings are those instituted by the government authority to discourage conduct which is harmful to the public in general.

Civil proceedings are usually instituted by private attorneys on behalf of private persons (called plaintiffs), their object being to obtain damages from the "defendant" or to restrain him. There are two classes:

1. Contract actions for some breach of contract.

2. Tort actions which are not based on any agreement, but have as their object the recovery of damages for some breach of duty independent of contract, such as assault and battery, libel and slander, fraud and deceit, stealing. The same wrong may subject the defendant to a criminal prosecution as well as a civil tort action, such as reckless driving in which someone is injured.

Common law and statutory law. Lawyers refer to that part of the law which is codified as "statutory law," and that which is based on custom or precedent as "common law."

Chancery (or equity) cases were those referred to the King's Chancellor because of the inadequacy of existing laws. The principles on which he acted were known as principles of equity or good conscience. The Chancellor had power to compel a defendant by an injunction, and if he disobeyed he could be imprisoned for contempt of court.

A case *in common law* is decided upon the way it is presented to the jury, the jury deciding questions of fact and the judge deciding questions of law. If a contract is broken damages are given.

A case *in chancery or equity* is heard before a judge only, who decides questions both of law and fact, and if a contract is broken, compels an action.

Prima facie case is one which is apparently established by evidence adduced by libellant in support of his case which, if uncontradicted or unexplained would support a recovery for libellant.

Quit claim title. The title is not guaranteed in any way by the giver of the title. He merely says he gives up whatever title he has, and perhaps he has none.

Procedure in Civil Court Action:

1. Plaintiff files a brief with Clerk of the Court, giving the facts as he sees them and what he intends to prove, a copy going to defendant.

2. Defendant reads brief and files a counter brief, which goes back to the plaintiff. This may go on for a long time without a court case, and can be compromised at any point of the proceedings if the parties will agree to it.

3. When the parties reach an impasse, the court steps in and the trial is the final show.

4. The trial resembles a stage play put on after much rehearsal for the benefit of the jury. Witnesses are heard, examined and cross-examined, the mode of presentation being of first importance in a jury trial.

5. Before the case goes to the jury for the verdict each lawyer draws up the instructions he wants the judge to give the jury. This is argued in privacy before the judge, who then decides himself on what his instructions will be.

6. The judge instructs the jury, which then retires. An "instructed verdict" is one where the judge points out to the jury that only one verdict can be arrived at. Should this be the case, if the jury insists on giving another verdict a mistrial will be declared, and the verdict will be thrown out as contrary to law.

ADMIRALTY LAW

Admiralty court practice in general is governed by the Admiralty Rules of the Supreme Court and is free from many of the technical rules of procedure used in the common law courts.

Admiralty trials are heard by a U. S. District Court sitting as a Court of Admiralty, in which case there is no jury, both questions of fact and questions of law being decided by the district judge.

Testimony by deposition is taken where the witnesses will be at sea at the time of trial, in which case the witness is placed under oath and is examined by his own and by the opposing lawyer. This testimony is reduced to writing and later read to the judge at the trial.

Interlocutory Decree. As a general rule the court merely determines whether the libellant is entitled to damage.

Final Decree. Later a commission determines the amount and reports same to the court.

Appeals. Admiralty differs from common law procedure in that, in case of an appeal, a new trial is held (*de novo*). Further testimony is generally restricted to new matters unknown previously. Appeals are heard by three judges. There is no right of further appeal from the circuit court of appeals to the U. S. Supreme Court except in most exceptional cases.

Proceedings "in rem." This procedure does not exist in common law. The vessel is itself treated as a person responsible for its wrong.

Proceedings "in personam." Here the proceedings are against the owners.

Proceedings "in personam" with warrant of foreign attachment. In this case, if the vessel of a foreign owner escapes, proceedings may be taken against other vessels or property of the same owners.

The Libel is the statement of the party's claim and the relief or remedy which he desires.

The Writ or Process. Upon the libel being properly filed, a writ of attachment is prepared and delivered to the marshal, which commands him to arrest and take the ship, goods or other things into his possession for safe custody, after which a public notice is published in a newspaper.

Owner's Rights. The owner whose vessel is seized in Admiralty is entitled to release her immediately by giving a bond to secure payment of the libellant's claim.

Damages in Admiralty. Where both parties are at fault, the damages are divided between them. In common law, one guilty of contributory negligence cannot obtain judgment against a wrongdoer.

Jurisdiction in admiralty in the U. S. is restricted to maritime matters generally, and includes maritime contracts, maritime torts, and services of a maritime nature. If the court lacks jurisdiction, its decision will be set aside. Admiralty jurisdiction extends to all waters which are in fact navigable. It is unnecessary that the transportation involved be interstate or foreign, as maritime jurisdiction is entirely independent of the commerce clause. Vessels included in admiralty jurisdiction must actually be an instrument of commerce and navigation; so a vessel, until she is launched and completed, is not within admiralty jurisdiction; but, like any other piece of construction, is subject to the local laws of the state where the work is carried on.

A corporation is a legal person having an individuality distinct from its stockholders. Thus a corporation, although owned and directed by aliens, if registered in the U. S., is an American corporation, except where otherwise expressly defined by law, as is the case with vessels in the coasting trade, in which 75% of the interest in the corporation must be American owned.

Public vessels of the U. S. cannot be proceeded against "in rem" but may be "in personam."

Public vessels of a foreign nation are given immunity as the property of a sovereign, when actually used for public purposes.

Admiralty Jurisdiction. Admiralty has jurisdiction in contract cases where the subject matter of the contract is maritime, i.e., where it relates to commerce and navigation. A contract to build a ship is not maritime but, once she has become engaged in commerce and navigation, most contracts made in reference to her are considered maritime, such as hiring of master and crew, purchase of supplies, loading, stowage and discharge of cargo, towage, salvage, pilotage, wharfage, lockage and canal tolls. Marine insurance is a maritime contract, but a contract to sell an existing vessel is not, nor is an ordinary mortgage, though one under the Ship Mortgage Act of 1920 is. Bills of Lading, charter parties, etc., are maritime contracts, but the use of a vessel as a place for storage is not.

Admiralty jurisdiction over equitable matters. Admiralty courts cannot reform a contract, grant an injunction, grant specific performance of a maritime contract or compel an accounting, except the most simple. It has jurisdiction of a proceeding to obtain possession of a vessel or to determine title or ownership.

In tort cases. Jurisdiction is clear where the wrong occurs on navigable waters, but there is doubt in border-line cases such as fire or other damage to a wharf arising from the ship.

The case of a person injured on or by falling from a gangway comes under admiralty.

Longshoremen are protected by a special act, the U. S. Longshoremen's and Harbor Worker's Act of 1927. Seamen on navigable waters are protected by the Jones Act (1920) in cases of injury.

Admiralty jurisdiction *in cases of wrongful death* is covered by the "Wrongful Death on the High Seas Act" of 1920, which gives dependents the right to sue.

Admiralty has jurisdiction over *crimes committed below the low water mark* of the shore.

Longshoremen's and Harbor Worker's Compensation Act provides for the payment of compensation to maritime workers injured on navigable waters, including any drydock, but specifically excludes the master or members of the crew of any vessel. It does not apply to injuries occurring on land or piers, in which case injuries are covered by state laws. The amount recoverable is determined by a compensation commissioner within certain maximum limits for particular injuries fixed by the act.

Fatal injuries to longshoremen must be reported to the USCG on Form 2692, as such a fatal injury is classified as a "Marine Casualty." This is in addition to the required report to the U.S. Bureau of Employees' Compensation under the above act.

Report of Probable Loss of Vessel. Must be made by managing owner or agent to the collector of customs of the port to which vessel belonged, whenever he has reason, owing to non-appearance of vessel or other circumstances, to expect the vessel is lost. Penalty, $100.

First Duties on Being Appointed Master:

1. Get letter of appointment from owners or agents, and at the custom house have name put on ship's register.
2. Inspect vessel and equipment, and see that all necessary repairs are made.
3. See if certificate of inspection and articles are in order.
4. See if station bills, licenses, etc., are in place.
5. Check over stores and crew list. See that vessel is fully found.
6. Obtain all vouchers and accounts from former master and, if in a foreign port, make an entry in official log, with both signing it.
7. Interview chief engineer, and ascertain fuel on board, consumption, average r.p.m., etc.
8. Information regarding cargo, insurance, mails, charter.
9. Become familiar with plans of vessel.
10. Check medicine chest, slop chest.

Required Monthly Reports to Officer in Charge, Marine Inspection:

1. Fire and boat drills.
2. Passengers carried.
3. General condition of vessel and equipment.

Report of Accidents. Any U. S. vessel which has sustained or caused any accident involving the loss of life, the material loss of property, or any serious injury to any person, or has received damage affecting her seaworthiness or efficiency, must file a report with the collector of customs within 5 days. Managing owner, agent or master may file report giving all details; penalty for non-compliance, $100.

THE SHIP'S LOG

Official Log Book (supplied by Shipping Commissioner).

1. Legal convictions of crew members and punishment.
2. Offenses by crew members which it is intended to prosecute.
3. Punishments inflicted on board.
4. Conduct, character, and qualifications of each of crew.
5. Illness or injury of crew member.
6. Deaths.
7. Births.
8. Marriages.
9. Desertions.
10. Wages of crew member who dies, his effects and their disposition.
11. Sale of effects of one who dies.
12. Collisions—strandings.
13. Freeboard, port and starboard, at time of leaving port, with vessel's draft, indicating allowance, if any, for density of water; and all entries required by U.S. Coast Guard Rules and Regulations for class of vessel concerned, such as fire and boat drills, W/T door exercises, opening of hatches, ports, etc.
14. Search for contraband and stowaways.

All entries to be signed by master or mate (to be entered as soon as possible after occurrence) no entries to be made more than 24 hours after arrival. $25 fine to master for violation. $150 fine to anyone making an entry 24 hours after arrival.

Drills to be reported monthly by master, and also number of passengers carried and general condition of vessel and equipment.

The official logbook contains information about a ship and its crew that is not found in any other single document. The entries are required by law and pages 1 and 2 of each logbook spell out the statutory requirements.

In the course of maintaining discipline aboard vessels and attempting to improve the standard of conduct of merchant seamen, there have been some comments by persons connected with the marine industry. These comments have generally followed either of two lines of thought. One, that crew members too often escape proper disciplinary action, and the other that crew members are unduly disciplined. Whatever the merits of the respective comments, a more rigid compliance with the statutes pertaining to the official logbook would alleviate some of the reasons for such comments.

Upon receiving notice of an alleged act in violation of one of the statutes covered by Revised Statute 4450, as amended, or upon receipt of a signed complaint, an investigation is conducted by the local Merchant Marine investigating unit. If at the conclusion of the investigation, it is the opinion of the investigating officer that there has been a violation of the law, the crew member in question is presented with a formal charge supported by fact statement specifications, and action instituted under Revised Statute 4450, as amended. In deciding whether a charge is in order, consideration is also given to the statutory penalties that may be invoked by the master at the time of the violation. A hearing is subsequently scheduled, at which time the U.S. Coast Guard, as complainant must offer sufficient competent evidence to establish a prima facie case. The person charged may then offer evidence in defense or mitigation, the conclusion being an order handed down by the hearing examiner.

The U.S. Admiralty Courts and the U. S. Coast Guard hearing as provided by revised Statute 4450, that portion of the United States Judiciary System concerned with marine cases, have recognized the peculiar nature of seafaring and the transient nature of seafaring personnel. To facilitate the expeditious handling of marine cases, wide latitude is allowed in obtaining depositions of seafaring witnesses. However, many times it is difficult to obtain the necessary witnesses as they usually scatter when the ship's articles are terminated. The official logbook serves the court as a silent witness and under some circumstances, is treated as competent evidence sufficient in itself to establish a prima facie case. The official logbook of a vessel has a historical background that has vested in it inherent powers and authority found in few other documents. The United States has long recognized the status of this document and as far back as 1878 certain laws were enacted setting forth statutory requirements that must be met. (Title 46 U.S.C. 201, 202, 203, and 703.)

The effect of these laws and later amendments has been that the legal integrity of the logbook and the entries therein is maintained so long as the statutory requirements are adhered to. Should there be an omission of any of the requirements however, the logbook entries then cease to have any legality or authority other than that accorded any memoranda made in the regular course of business.

There are many occasions when the crew member to be charged is not located until a long period of time has elapsed since the alleged offense. Witnesses by then have scattered and the U. S. Coast Guard in presenting the evidence necessary to establish a prima facie case, must rely soley on the pertinent logbook entries. The statute 46 U. S. C. 702 places it in the discretion of the court, in this case, the hearing examiner, to order a dismissal for failure of the log entry to meet the requirements as provided by law. Consequently, it is possible that a serious breach of conduct could be and frequently is dismissed due to the insufficiency of the evidence. By the same token, an injustice could be done the crew member in the equally possible situation where the entry is allowed to stand, establishing a prima facie case; where the crew member was not accorded his right to reply to the log. This lack of reply to the log entry possibly gives rise to an inference of guilt, or admission by silence.

The usual omissions in making log entries are those requiring the entry to be read to the crew member, his reply noted, and a copy presented to him; and failure to make the entry within the prescribed period of time.

Thus it is seen that much of the responsibility for the outcome of disciplinary proceedings rests with the master of the vessel. It is his statutory obligation to see that the seaman has a chance to reply to the alleged offense. Failure to do so not only is in violation of the law but eventually may have an adverse effect in the meting out of justice. Aside from the master's responsibility to see that the law is not violated, he should also bear in mind the penalty provided by law for making an improper log entry. This penalty is prescribed in 46 U. S. C. 203 as $25 for each offense.

In addition to complying with the basic essentials to make the log entries conform with the law, the master should appreciate the fact that the context of the entry will reflect his attitude and the extent of his investigation or lack of investigation. This entry assumes a great deal of importance, when, as often is the case, there are no other witnesses and the logbook entry must stand alone as the only evidence in support of the allegation. The defendant's testimony often can offset the weight of a valid log entry because of its brevity. In view of the weight attached to the pertinent entry it should, as a minimum contain these points: (An outline of the incident, names of witnesses, and a brief comment on the persons involved. While the last point might be considered hearsay in nature, it would still be admissible as the expressed opinion of the master of the vessel.

Recommendations for making an official log entry:

1. Meticulous care in stating the offense of the crew member.

2. Confronting the crew member with the accusation and accurately recording his reply.

3. Disclose source of information; i.e., whether the master himself witnessed part or all of the incident, and if not, name the persons who did witness it.

4. Witnesses to logging: The statute requires a witness to the entry. Masters frequently confuse this with a witness to the incident or subject matter of the logging. Where several officers or seamen merely sign the log entry under the caption "witnesses" they must be treated only as witnesses to the logging. A simple notation "witnesses to the incident" will distinguish the signatories, strengthen the log entry, and aid the investigating officer in any subsequent investigation.

Consider the following entries:

Port Elizabeth
August 13, 1953
6:00 p.m. Joseph Blank (Z-0210), A.B., was drunk and unfit for duty 8-12 A.M. today and did not assist in securing for sea and unmooring afternoon and evening. The vessel sailed at 6:00 P.M. For these offenses he is logged and fined two days' wages amounting to $20.96.
s/ ch. mate   s/ master
s/ Crew Member witness to incident
August 14, 1953
L. 34-30 S, Lo. 21-46 E
9:35 A.M. The above entry having been read to Blank and copy of it given to him, his reply; "I'm sorry, hope it won't happen again."
s/ ch. mate witness   s/ master

Referring to the statutes as heretofore mentioned, it may be seen that the above entries are proper in every respect and meet the requirements at law.

Now let us examine several similar but improper entries:

6/20/52
London
2200 H. Coffee absent without leave from watch disobeyed order to remain aboard. Fined two days' pay on each charge. $33.05.
At sea
7/30/51
41-42 N, 12-11 W
Jonas Jones, A.B., charged with being absent without leave and drinking intoxicants while on duty. This is the second offense. Logged two days' pay. $16.33.
s/ ch. mate   s/ master

It is to be noted one entry is unsigned; neither of the above entries were read to the seamen; no copy of the entry was furnished to the seamen; no reply of the seamen was recorded. Because of the defects of these entries, the seamen would have every right to contest them:

(1) Before a Shipping Commissioner in connection with deducting the amount of the logging from his wages;

(2) Before a Hearing Examiner.

The following entries were presumably made in accordance with the provisions of item 9 of section 201:

9/22
Dakar, Senegal
Paid off Buck Dollar 1st Asst.
11/10/52
Gibraltar
Paid off Sam Hose in connection with legal proceedings.
11/14/51
Paid off Hirman Ham misconduct.

Referring to item 9, it may be seen that these entries are unsigned and completely void of the specific manner and cause of discharge in a foreign port.

Defective entries of this nature certainly enhance a claim for wages for wrongful discharge—and are the measure of carelessness.

To be complete, an entry of this type should be somewhat as follows:

Alexandria, Egypt
14 July 1953
10:30 A.M. Local police authorities aboard to advise that Robert Jones (Z-41690), Messman, was being held in custody for assault upon a civilian at 4:00 A.M. this morning. Wage voucher and personal effects left with American Consul.
s/ ch. mate   s/ master
April 20, 1953
Yokohama, Japan
4:30 P.M. Graham Masters, Z-00131-D2, Oiler, failed to join vessel before departing Yokohama today, April 20, 1953, at 4:00 P.M. His pay with net earnings of $671.21, plus overtime and all personal gear to be detained by master until final port of discharge in the U.S.A.
s/ chief engineer   s/ master

Item 5 of section 201, herein quoted, is a very important matter, and when recording the facts in the logbook, it should be stated specifically what action was taken by the Master with respect to the nature of an illness or injury and the medical treatment afforded.

Thus, the following entry is clearly inadequate:

9/24/52
At Sea
1100. Joe Brigg (Z-0120), O. S., injured left leg and foot, first aid given.
s/ ch. mate   s/ master

A proper entry, on the other hand, is as follows:

Wednesday
25 March 1953
At Sea
0930. Robert Blank (Z-2345) DK/Maint., sustained bruised and lacerated 1st and 2nd fingers of left hand and a bruised 3rd finger of same hand as a result of hand being caught in a jamming door. TREATMENT: Fingers cleaned with soap and water and coated with Tincture of Merthiolate, gauze bandages applied. Blank relieved from duty.
s/ ch. mate   s/ master
s/ witness to accident

These sample entries should be sufficient for the instant purpose.

It is to be hoped the foregoing has crystallized the requirements of 46 U. S. C. 201, 202, 701, and 702, for there are additional statutory and regulatory requirements relative to entries in the official logbook to be considered and pointed out.

46 *U. S. C. 85* (*e*) states:

It shall be the duty of the master of every vessel subject to this act and to the regulations established thereunder and of every foreign vessel exempted pursuant to section 5 before departing from her loading port or place for a voyage by sea, to enter in the official logbook of such vessel a statement of the position of the load-line mark applicable to the voyage in question and the actual drafts forward and aft at the time of departing from port as nearly as the same can be ascertained.

In the official logbook, provisions are made for entering the "governing load-line mark," in addition to spaces for entering the port of sailing; date of sailing; the draft forward and aft; and the load-line mark, port and starboard. Nevertheless, it has feen found that some masters are not making the proper entries, particularly with respect to the applicable "governing load-line mark" such as "Winter —Tropical—Summer or Winter North Atlantic," or as applicable "30′ All Seasons."

Regulations 21-22, Chap. II, and *26, Chap. III* of International Convention for Safety at Sea, 1960, also require official logbook entries of all fire and boat drills, testing of watertight doors, etc. For example:

9-3-53
At Sea
L. 36°-13′ N, Lo. 8°-22′ W
3:20 P.M. Held fire and boat drill. Passengers and crew mustered and instructed. Six lengths of hose stretched with full pressure on same. Tested watertight doors. All equipment found in good condition.
s/   ch. mate   s/   master
8/29/53
Cannes
6:45 A.M. Opened side ports and W. T. doors "DI."
4:45 P.M. Secured all side ports and W. T. doors "DI."

THE SHIP'S PAPERS

1. The register. Her evidence of nationality. Gives name of master, and all necessary data as to home port, size, owner, etc. Must be endorsed on back for each change of master.

2. Classification certificate. Issued by American Bureau of Shipping (ABS) or British Corp. (BC) after annual inspection. Not a government paper. Calls for surveys every 4 years, and special survey when required, also whenever drydocked, calked or repaired.

3. International load line certificate. Issued by ABS or BC, and the U. S. Coast Guard.

4. Certificate of inspection is issued by the U. S. Coast Guard. It must be taken to the Custom House first time ship is cleared after inspection, and must be framed.

5. Receipts for tonnage tax levied by U. S. government on net tonnage at first port of entry. Not more than 5 payments in one year.

6. Tonnage certificate for Panama and Suez Canals.

7. Articles of agreement. Describe voyage and duration, names, ratings, and pay of crew, and when service starts. Crew list is a separate paper. Articles in duplicate.

8. Clearance. Official permission to sail.

9. Official crew list. This must be exact, and is presented in duplicate when applying for clearance. One copy is left at the Custom House and one is taken to sea.

10. Bill of health. (Port sanitary statement where issued by U. S. P.H.S.) One copy is issued to ship by U. S. Public Health Service when requested. Two copies must be secured by all vessels clearing for U. S. from foreign and insular ports. It is issued by U. S. consul at port of departure (first foreign port at which cargo or passengers are taken for a U. S. port) and all subsequent ports, provided there are U. S. consuls in these ports. Issued in duplicate, the duplicate copy being given to the boarding quarantine officer and the original presented with the quarantine pratique to the collector of customs at time of entry. (Not required by vessels plying regularly between certain nearby ports unless a quarantinable disease is present there.)

A Consular Bill of Health is issued by the consular representative of the country to be visited by the ship. For a U. S. vessel in a foreign port having no U. S. Consul a local Bill of Health is obtained from the port doctor and this will suffice in a U. S. port after being sworn to by the master.

11. Charter party. Contract between owner and shipper where vessel is under charter.

12. Manifest. A detailed account of cargo on board for the custom officials.

13. Passenger list. Part of manifest.

14. Bill of Lading. A receipt for cargo and contract to deliver same. Signed by master when all cargo aboard.

15. Stores list. A complete list showing all unbroken and broken stores.

16. Consular invoice. Details of cargo—value, marks, insurance—the name of the vessel, destination and name of consignee.

17. Fumigation certificate or Deratization or Deratization exemption certificate. Valid for 6 months.

18. Log-books (a) Official. Supplied to ship by Shipping Commissioner and taken up by him. (*See* p.18–39.)—(b) Rough.—(c) Smooth. Written up by chief officer from rough log and signed by master.

19. *a*) Quarantine declaration. Embodies essential data upon which granting of pratique is premised.

b) Certificate of discharge from quarantine or pratique. The permission granted by quarantine officials to hold communication with the shore. White is free pratique. Yellow is provisional or conditional.

Tonnage Taxes. The rule adopted by almost all maritime nations is that tonnage taxes shall be collected not on gross but on net tonnage. Tonnage tax is levied on every vessel engaged in trade upon her arrival by sea from a foreign port, unless she is in distress. Not levied on more than five entries at the same rate during one year. Top varies from 2 to 6 cents per ton. North and Central America, West Indies (Cuba and Bermuda), Caribbean Coast of South America and Newfoundland, also Norway and Sweden, 2 cents. Six-cent rate applies to all other trade.

Navigation Fees. Vessels engaged in foreign trade with other than Canadian ports are subject to navigation fees upon entry. Thus, if less than 100 t. burden the fee is $1.50. Over, it is $2.50. Her clearance fee is at the same rate.

SHIP'S BUSINESS—CHECK-OFF LIST

Papers Required when leaving U. S. for Foreign Port

1. Register—obtained at Custom House. Certificate of Payment of Tonnage Tax is attached to Register.

2. Articles (2 copies)—obtained at U. S. Coast Guard Shipping Commissioners.

3. Copy of Official Crew List (no changes or erasures), (2 copies to Custom's Collector—one returned)—Waivers, if any, as issued by U.S.C.G. are exhibited on clearing.

Check names on Crew List against Articles.

4. Official Log Book—obtain from Shipping Comm.

5. Fumigation Certificate.

6. Bill of Lading (from agents).

7. Copy of Charter.

8. Manifest (from agents).

9. Bill of Health—signed by consul of country of destination. In some cases copies of manifest and crew list, all stamped and signed by Consul are required.

10. Clearance from Custom House. U.S. Port Sanitary Statement, U.S. Public Health Form, is attached to back of clearance.

11. Changes in Crew (Report)—Before being cleared for a foreign port the master is required to report to the Immigration Office changes which have taken place in the crew including (1) deserting seamen (2) seamen left in hospital (3) seamen discharged (4) seamen signed on at the port.

12. The following may be required as noted: Load Line Certificate when renewed; Radio Telegraphy Certificate when renewed; Inspection Certificate, if not on file or when renewed; Chief Mate's License and Master's License if new to ship.

Papers on Arrival at an American Port

I. Quarantine Doctor requires the following papers

1. 1 set all Consular Bills of Health from foreign ports of call.

2. 1 quarantine information slip. This should be prepared before vessel's arrival.

3. 1 Crew List
4. 1 Passenger List.
5. 1 Copy of Cargo Manifest.
6. 1 *Meat Certificate.*

II. Immigration Inspector
1. 1 Form *Report of Diseases, Births & Deaths.*
2. 1 Form 660 *Report of Boarding Office.*
3. 1 *Alien Crew List.*

III. Customs Boarding Office
1. 3 copies of complete ship's manifest including (a) List of all cargo on board; (b) Stores list; (c) List of crew purchases.
2. 3 copies of Passenger List (if any carried).
3. 1 copy of Crew List

IV. On entering a Custom House (within 48 hours)
1. The Register
2. Official Crew List
3. Bill of Health & last clearance
4. 2 copies Official Manifest

REPORTS IN CASE OF MAJOR MARITIME CASUALTIES

Salvage Required. Report to owners by radio giving position, weather, condition of vessel particularly with respect to machinery, steering gear and propeller; amount and rate of leakage, if any, in each compartment; nature of assistance available in vicinity; opinion on whether this available assistance is adequate and recommendations.

If possible make any necessary agreements on a *no cure-no pay* basis.

Report promptly to owners on arrangements made and on the progress of operations.

Upon conclusion of the salvage service report all details to owners including:—voyage; signed extracts of deck and engine room log books insofar as they pertain to salvage services; latitude and longitude when assistance was requested and when assisting vessel arrived; conditions which made it necessary to engage assistance; condition of weather at time of asking assistance and thereafter in detail until completion; full description of salvage operation, omitting no details and showing equipment of the salvage vessel and the equipment of own vessel, used, lost or destroyed; details of damage if sustained by salving vessel, time and place of completion of salvage operation; terms of agreement entered into with the salvors.

Report of Stranding. Latitude and longitude; description of place; time of stranding; position of vessel on strand and nature of bottom; state of tide at time of stranding; rise and fall of tide; condition of wind and sea; draft of vessel before stranding; draft of vessel on strand, forward and aft, stating at what stage of the tide draft was taken; soundings all around vessel and stage of tide; rate of leakage in various compartments and state whether pumps are controlling leakage; apparent condition of rudder, steering gear, engines and propeller; tonnage of cargo on board and brief description of stowage recommendations; cargo lightered or jettisoned to refloat vessel.

Salvage Services Rendered to Other Vessels. Report to owners name and nationality of the vessel assisted and the nature of the service rendered. Obtain from the Master of the salvaged vessel a written acknowledgement of the nature of the service rendered and an acknowledgement that you have left the salved vessel in good safety in the custody of her Master.

If it is evident that the salved vessel will remain in port an ample length of time, await instructions from owners regarding security from the salved vessel. If the salved vessel may leave port before instructions are received, ask your agents to engage reputable counsel to take whatever legal action may be necessary to obtain security.

Prepare immediately a detailed report of the services rendered, signed by you and your officers and despatch two signed copies to owners, one by air mail and one by steamer mail, giving the same information as under **Salvage Required.**

Full information on U.S. Coast Guard procedure in casualties or accidents may be found in publication CG-200, *Marine Investigation Regulations and Suspension and Revocation Proceedings.*

NOTICES REQUIRED BY LAW TO BE POSTED

1. Certificate of Inspection.
2. Loadline certificate.
3. Stability test certificate.
4. Licenses of master, mates, and engineers to be placed under glass in conspicuous place within 48 hours of going on duty. If not done, subject to fine of $100 or revocation of license.
5. Inland or River Steamers Carrying Passengers—(3 copies)
6. Forecastle card. (Shows substance of Articles of Agreement)
7. Station Bill (a copy posted for each department).
8. Emergency alarm signals.
9. How to adjust life preservers—in every cabin and stateroom and in conspicuous places about decks.
10. Gun and rocket apparatus. Pilot house, engine room, seamen, firemen, stewards (5 copies).
11. Pilot rules.
12. Ferryboats, etc. Lights.
13. SAFETY FIRST.
14. "Only certain persons allowed in pilot house and on navigator's bridge." (3 copies, one in wheelhouse)
15. "Station bills, drills, and reports of master." Form 809A (3 copies posted). A station bill is reproduced on page 16-58.
16. Atomic attack instructions.

Duties of mates to:
1. Assign space to deck or steerage passengers, and see such space not encumbered by cargo.

2. Examine all marks on packages, to see no combustible or dangerous articles aboard.

INSPECTIONS

Annual inspection*by the Coast Guard is made upon the written application of the owner, master or agent. This must be done once a year, and defective life preservers, fire hoses, etc., are to be destroyed in the presence of the owner or master. The Inspector of Hulls inspects every accessible part of the hull steel with a hammer, and the scuppers, sanitary and other discharges, except in the engine room. Licensed officers must assist inspectors and point out any defects known to them, under penalty of suspension or revocation of license. No inspector is to impart the name of such licensed officer or source of his information to anyone other than his superiors. To do so subjects him to dismissal.

Reinspections are made as often as may be thought necessary to detect any neglect to comply with requirements. If inspectors' orders are not carried out, vessel's certificate of inspection will be revoked.

Certificate of inspection or licenses signed by one local inspector only are not valid.

Outboard shaft must be drawn for examination once every 3 years.

When docked for repairs inspectors must be notified, and no repairs or alterations affecting safety shall be made without the knowledge of the local inspectors.

Crew quarters on U. S. vessels shall be inspected by local inspector at least once each month, or at such times as the vessel shall enter a U. S. port. If quarters are not in proper condition certificate of inspection shall be withdrawn, and master is subject to a penalty of $500.

RULES AND REGULATIONS (Not Given Elsewhere)

Steering-gear test is to be made by a licensed officer of the vessel 12 hours before leaving port, if the voyage is to be more than 24 hours in duration.

Unnecessary whistling is prohibited within any harbor limits of the U. S. License may be suspended or revoked.

Passing dredges. The usual signals for passing when within a distance of not over 1 mile, which are to be answered by the plant. Plant to give the danger signal if vessel cannot pass.

Speed passing dredges is to be reduced sufficiently for safety, and within 200 ft. it is not to be over 5 M.P.H. When passing over lines, engine must be stopped.

Light draft vessels are to pass outside the buoys when possible.

Anchors of plant are to be marked by buoys, and at night by a beam of light or red lights.

Dredges not to obstruct the channel unnecessarily.

Vessels not to run over buoys, stakes, etc., or to anchor on ranges.

* In 1956, the requirements concerning annual inspection were amended to provide that vessels not carrying passengers shall be inspected once every 2 yrs. instead of annually, but the annual inspection of passenger vessels is still required.

Dredges to move out of the way on sufficient notice being given, unless otherwise prescribed by special regulations.

Tows of seagoing barges are limited to 5 vessels, including the towing vessel. Hawsers limited to 75 fathoms from the stern of one to the bow of the next.

Searchlights must not be flashed into the pilot house of an approaching vessel. License may be suspended or revoked.

Unauthorized lights which might interfere with the signal lights are prohibited. License may be suspended or revoked.

Cabin watchman to be on duty during night in passenger quarters, reporting to bridge at least every hour. He is to carry a dry cell flashlight, to be in uniform and carry a badge marked *Watchman.*

Lookout is to be at or near bow at all times during the night. No boy to be on lookout except for learning. (Amendment to Seaman's Act.)

Wheel. In narrow or crowded waters or when visibility is low, none below rating of A.B. to take the wheel. No boy to take wheel except for learning. (Amendment to Seaman's Act, Mar. 4, 1915.)

Deck boy is not qualified to fill the place of an O.S. until he has had 6 months' service as deck boy. (Amendment to Seaman's Act.)

Stand-by man on passenger steamers is to be in or near the pilot house at night.

Notice to mariners and charts must be kept at hand and available at all times, and licensed officers and pilots must keep themselves acquainted with the lastest aids.

All officers of U. S. vessels must be full citizens.

No officer to take charge of a watch unless he has had at least 6 hours off duty within 12 hours preceding sailing. No more than 8 hours on in 24 hours in port, nor more than 8 in 24 at sea, except in an emergency.

Oil Pollution Act:

Q. What is the *Oil Pollution Act* and to whom does it apply?

A. Except in case of emergency imperiling life or property, or unavoidable accident, collision, or stranding, it shall be unlawful for any person to discharge, or permit the discharge of, oil by any method into or upon the coastal navigable waters of the United States from any vessel using oil as fuel or any vessel carrying or having oil in excess of that necessary for its lubricating requirements.

Q. What precautions must be taken to avoid harbor pollution when taking fuel oil or petroleum cargoes?

A. When taking on fuel oil or petroleum cargoes, the following precautions should be taken against harbor pollution:

1. Scuppers should be plugged to prevent any overflow going overboard.

2. Drip pans should be provided under hose connections, vent pipes, etc.

3. Mooring lines should be carefully tended and hose should be of proper length to allow for any motion of the vessel alongside dock.

4. Hose should be in good condition, connections properly made,

with efficient gaskets, and properly suspended to avoid kinking or crushing between ship and dock.

5. Proper signals should be arranged between ship and dock to stop the flow of oil when necessary.

6. Hoses should be carefully drained before being disconnected, and blanked off, if necessary, to prevent dripping of any oil remaining in the hose.

7. Ballast discharge valves should be tightly closed and lashed or sealed if necessary.

8. Topping off tanks should proceed at a reduced rate with care to prevent spill.

9. Sawdust, rags, and on tankers, nonsparking tools should be available for cleaning decks in event of any spillage.

Q. When oil is discovered in a vessel's bilge wells at the time soundings are taken, what steps should be taken to prevent oil pollution of coastal waters?

A. When oil is discovered in a vessel's bilge wells at the time of taking bilge soundings, the engineers must be notified not to pump bilges overboard if the vessel is in coastal waters or where the contaminated bilge water may drift into coastal waters. The bilges may, if necessary, be pumped into a tank for future discharge either ashore or at sea when no danger of polluting coastal waters exists.

Q. What precautions should be taken by vessels pumping bilges, ballast, or oil overboard at sea to avoid pollution of coastal waters?

A. When pumping bilges, ballast, or oil overboard, every effort must be made to avoid pollution of coastal waters. If possible, pumping should be confined to such time as the vessel is at a maximum distance from coastal waters. Should it be necessary to pump bilges or ballast which may contain oil where the oil may pollute coastal waters, the pump discharge should be kept under constant visual observation, preferably on deck. If the discharge shows signs of oil, the bilge or ballast water should be pumped into one of the vessel's tanks, and then disposed of in port where such facilities as slop tanks, oil separation plants, and sludge barges are available to handle it; or the vessel may carry the oil or slops until she is far enough from shore to dispose of it without danger of pollution of coastal waters.

Consideration in all cases must be given to tide and currents which may cause oil to drift into coastal waters even though discharge takes place at a distance from the coast.

Q. What precautions must be observed when taking on water ballast to avoid danger of oil pollution, cargo damage, and structural damage to the vessels?

A. When taking on water ballast, it is necessary to avoid overflowing the tanks as such overflow would cause any oil floating on top of the water in the tanks to run on decks and overboard with consequent pollution of the water. When cargo is stowed in holds adjacent to the tanks being filled, a wise precaution is to sound the bilges frequently in order to detect any leakage into the cargo space as soon as possible. The tanks being filled should be sounded frequently not only to prevent spillage, but also to avoid putting an unnecessary head of water pressure on the tank top. Unless tanks being filled from deck sounding pipes or filling lines are sounded frequently and watched carefully with the above possibilities in mind, it is often wiser to fill through an open manhole with a man detailed to watch the operation. This method would prevent a head on the tank being filled and would preclude overflow on deck or overboard.

Vessels fitted with overflow below the main deck to avoid excessive head on tanks must see that such valves are in good condition to perform their function; however, such overflow must be avoided in coastal waters where oil pollution ruins beaches, destroys wildlife, etc.

Deposit of refuse in New York Harbor and adjacent waters prohibited (similar laws in other ports). Refers to placing, discharging, etc., any kind of refuse, dirt, cinders, ashes, etc., into the tidal waters noted. Punishable by a fine of $250 to $2500 and imprisonment for 30 days to 1 year. One-half of fine to go to informer reporting such act. (Throwing overboard a scuttle of ashes at a prohibited place makes the employee so doing liable to above punishment, but does not affect the vessel.) *The Auger Head* (D.C.N.J. 1890).

Anchorage grounds and harbor regulations generally are established by the Secretary of the Army. Enforcement of such regulations is by the Coast Guard.

Obstructing navigable channels subjects party responsible to a fine of $500 to $2500 and 30 days to a year imprisonment, or both.

REGULATIONS REGARDING SHIP IN GENERAL

Fire bulkheads, etc. See provisions regarding fire in Chapter 16.

Watertight bulkheads. a) All passenger vessels must have a forepeak or collision bulkhead watertight up to the bulkhead deck. Not less than 5% of the length of the vessel nor more than 10 ft. plus 5% from the forward perpendicular. *b*) An afterpeak bulkhead and bulkheads dividing the machinery space from cargo and passenger space forward and aft. *c*) In all cases, stern tubes shall be enclosed in watertight spaces.

Two means of escape must be provided from all spaces where passengers or crew may be quartered or employed.

Storm oil must be carried on all steamers over 200 t. (30 gal.) to 5000 gross t. and over (100 gal.). To be accessible and available at all times.

Steamer's name must be on all equipment, such as hose, axes, boats, oars, life rafts, floats, barrels and tanks.

Hatches. The duty of the master is to see that all hatches are secured in a watertight manner by gaskets and screws, or tarpaulins, battens and wedges.

Auxiliary lighting system is required on passenger vessels, and is to be located above the deep load line and operated from the pilot house.

Sanitary condition of the vessel is the duty of the master and chief engineer.

Steamers using bell signals between pilot house and engine room to have tube to return sound of signals to pilot house. Where telegraphs are used, the signal is to be repeated back.

Airports in hull of passenger vessels must be provided which are 16 inches or more in diameter. Those that open into passageways to have a life line fastened overhead in the passage of at least 2 inches circumference; to be knotted every 3 ft., and of sufficient length to reach the water at the lightest sea draft.

Extra steering apparatus is required on all steamers, and there must be efficient communication between the pilot house and the emergency steering station and the steering-engine room. Emergency wheel to be on after weather deck.

Where the distance between steamer deck houses is more than 150 ft., a wire cable must be stretched between them, not less than 6 ft. above the deck and equipped with a traveller and endless whips and loose rings and lanyards. Failure to have such cable stretched and traveller attached at all times when vessel is loaded and being navigated is cause for suspension of license of master.

A whistle must be used for signals on a motor vessel.

The fog bell must be of bronze or brass and not less than 8″ outside diameter.

Steam whistles are required to be placed not less than 6 ft. above the top of the pilot house.

Mechanical deep-sea sounding apparatus, in addition to ordinary deep-sea hand lead, is required on all steamers of over 500 t. gross.

Radio installation is required on all ships of U. S. registry engaged in international trade, except those in trade between the U. S. and Canada, and vessels under 1600 t. gross. Apparatus to have a minimum range of 200 miles.

Direction finder and a signal lamp are required on all ocean passenger vessels of 5000 t. gross and over. The apparatus shall be inspected and approved by the Federal Communications Commission and at all times be kept in efficient condition. Signal lamp on all ships over 150 t. gross on international voyages.

An emergency transmitter and receiver must be provided on all passenger vessels, independent of the propelling machinery.

Prior to departure from port, and each day at sea, the emergency power and radio must be tested.

Auto alarm is required on all ships which do not have a continuous radio watch. It must give an audible alarm, if out of order, to the operator's room, his cabin, and to the bridge. The only switch for stopping it must be in the operator's room.

A special clock and emergency light must be provided for the operator's room.

All passenger ships must have at least two operators; and there must be two on all ships 5000 t. gross or over if they have no auto alarm.

Lifeboat portable radio apparatus. Coast Guard regulations not only require the carriage of this equipment on all vessels on an international voyage carrying less than 20 lifeboats which do not have at least one lifeboat on each side of the vessel fitted with a fixed radio installation, but say: "It shall be the duty of the master to require that all batteries for all fixed and portable radio apparatus for lifeboats are brought up to full charge weekly if the batteries are of a type which require recharging;" and "In any case, the transmitter shall be tested weekly using a suitable artificial aerial."

The equipment is to be stowed in the radio room, chartroom, or other suitable location ready to be moved to one or other of the lifeboats in the event of an emergency.

Designed so that it may be used in an emergency by any member of the crew, it is recommended that fundamentals of the portable radio be passed on to every man aboard ship in the event the radio officer is incapacitated in time of emergency.

Pilot Ladders

Ships engaged on voyages in the course of which pilots are likely to be employed shall comply with the following requirements respecting pilot ladders:

(a) The ladder shall be kept in good order and for use only by officials and other persons while a ship is arriving at or leaving a port, and for embarkation and disembarkation of pilots.

(b) The ladder shall be secured in a position so that each step rests firmly against the ship's side and so that the pilot can gain safe and convenient access to the ship after climbing not less than 5 feet (or 1·5 metres) and not more than 30 feet (or 9 metres). A single length of ladder shall be used capable of reaching sea level in all normal conditions of trim of the ship. Whenever the distance from sea level to the point of access to the ship is more than 30 feet (or 9 metres), access from the pilot ladder to the ship shall be by means of an accommodation ladder or other equally safe and convenient means.

(c) The treads of the ladder shall be not less than 19 inches (or 48 centimetres) long, 4½ inches (or 11·4 centimetres) wide and 1 inch (or 2·5 centimetres) in depth. Steps shall be joined in such a manner as will provide a ladder of adequate strength whose treads are maintained in a horizontal position and not less than 12 inches (or 30·5 centimetres) or more than 15 inches (or 38 centimetres) apart.

(d) A man-rope, properly secured, and a safety line shall be available and ready for use if required.

(e) Arrangements shall be such that:
  (i) The rigging of the ladder and the embarkation and disembarkation of a pilot is supervised by a responsible officer of the ship.
  (ii) Handholds are provided to assist the pilot to pass safely and conveniently from the head of the ladder into the ship or on to the ship's deck.

(f) If necessary spreaders shall be provided at such intervals as will prevent the ladder from twisting

(g) At night a light shining overside shall be available and used and the deck at the position where the pilot boards the ship shall be adequately lit.

(h) Ships with rubbing bands or other ships whose construction makes it impossible to comply fully with the provision that the ladder shall be secured at a place where each step will rest firmly against the ship's side shall comply with this provision as closely as possible.

MARKING EQUIPMENT & SIGNS

The following instructions have been taken from the *Proceedings of the Merchant Marine Council.*

Requests have been received from shipbuilders and others for information concerning the proper marking of fire and emergency equipment, fire doors, watertight doors, lifeboat embarkation stations and direction signs, and the wording of stateroom notices on vessels when not otherwise specifically stated in the General Rules and Regulations. The following recommendations are made for the purpose of effecting uniformity in such markings:

GENERAL ALARM BELL SWITCH

The general alarm bell switch in the pilothouse or fire-control stations to be clearly marked with lettering on a brass plate or with a sign in red letters on suitable background: "GENERAL ALARM."

GENERAL ALARM BELLS

Mark in red paint at least one-half-inch letters, "GENERAL ALARM"—"WHEN BELL RINGS GO TO YOUR STATION".

MANUAL ALARM BOXES

If not clearly marked "FIRE ALARM—BREAK GLASS" or "IN CASE OF FIRE BREAK GLASS", to be marked "IN CASE OF FIRE BREAK GLASS" in one-half-inch letters. Each box to be numbered using 1-inch figures and red paint.

MANUAL ALARM BELLS

The manual alarm bells on bridge, in engine room and in fire-control station and crew quarters to be marked "MANUAL FIRE ALARM" in 1-inch letters, red paint.

SPRINKLER ALARM BELLS

On bridge, in engine room and fire-control station, mark "SPRINKLER ALARM ZONE" in at least 1-inch red letters.

STEAM FIRE-SMOTHERING APPARATUS

Indicate by a sign the location of the "STEAM FIRE APPARATUS". CO₂ fire-extinguishing system to be similarly and appropriately marked "CO₂ FIRE APPARATUS". Use 3-inch red letters. The valves of all branch pipes leading to the several compartments to be distinctly marked to indicate the compartments or parts of the vessel to which they lead.

FIRE HOSE STATION

"FIRE STATION NUMBER——" at each fire hose valve to be marked in 2-inch red letters.

SUPERVISED PATROL STATIONS

Each key station shall be numbered.

EMERGENCY SQUAD EQUIPMENT

Lockers containing equipment for use of emergency squad to be marked "EMERGENCY SQUAD EQUIPMENT", Lockers where self-contained breathing apparatus is stowed to be marked "SELF-CONTAINED BREATHING APPARATUS" or "GAS MASK."

FIRE EXTINGUISHERS

Number or tag each fire extinguisher and mark location where stowed in corresponding numbers in 1-inch letters.

EXIT LIGHTS

To be red glass marked "EXIT" and to be so arranged in corridors that they can be seen from a distance.

EMERGENCY LIGHTS

Stencil a letter "E" at each light in 1-inch letter with red paint.

FIRE SCREEN DOORS

Number each fire screen door in 2-inch letters. Color most legible in contrast to background.
Viz: "F. S. D. 1", etc.

ILLUMINATED EXIT SIGNS

The word "EXIT" in red letters to be installed as required to direct passengers or crew to nearest means of escape to the open deck, when all fire doors and watertight doors are closed.
Small rooms or spaces having a secondary means of escape shall have the sign in red letters "EMERGENCY EXIT" directing attention to such escape.

WATERTIGHT DOORS

Number each watertight door in at least 2″ figures and letters, "W. T. D. 1", 2, 3, etc. Color to be in contrast to color of doors.
Mark location of all watertight door remote operating stations in at least 2-inch figures and letters and indicate the number of the door. Mark direction of operation of lever or wheel provided to close or open the door at all watertight door operating stations. Color of sign to contrast with background.

LIFEBOAT STATIONS

Suspend from overhead at each boat station on embarkation deck a sign marked in 4-inch letters "LIFEBOAT STATION NO. 1", 2, etc. If there is no overhead structure at a boat station, place a similar sign in a position where it will readily be seen.

EMBARKATION DIRECTION SIGNS—TO LIFE-BOATS

Locate signs in alleyways, corridors, and stair wells. These signs to be of at least 1-inch letters with arrows indicating the shortest route to follow to reach lifeboats. The arrow to be of appropriate dimensions, viz.,

TO BOATS
→

TO BOATS
←

The signs near the exits to the embarkation deck should be marked with the numbers of the boat stations nearest to such exits, viz.,

TO BOAT STATIONS
NOS. 1, 2, 3
(or 2, 4, 6, etc.)
→

Any conbination of arrows and at least 1-inch lettering which will clearly indicate the direction to be followed will be acceptable. It is recommended that the signs directing the way to the odd-numbered boats be green and those directing the way to the even-numbered boats be red in color.

STATEROOM NOTICES

Framed notices to be conspicuously posted in the stateroom indicating the following:
"EMERGENCY SIGNALS.
"FIRE AND EMERGENCY—CONTINUOUS RAPID RINGING OF THE SHIP'S BELL AND OF THE GENERAL ALARM BELLS FOR A PERIOD OF NOT LESS THAN TEN SECONDS.
"ABANDON SHIP (OR BOAT STATIONS)—MORE THAN SIX SHORT BLASTS AND ONE LONG BLAST OF THE WHISTLE SUPPLEMENTED BY THE SAME SIGNAL ON THE GENERAL ALARM BELLS."
State location of life preservers.
Include instructions and picture showing how to wear life preservers.
"THE OCCUPANTS OF THIS ROOM ARE ASSIGNED TO LIFEBOAT NO. ——. ALL PASSENGERS ARE REQUIRED TO PUT ON A LIFE PRESERVER AND GO TO THEIR LIFEBOAT STATIONS WHENEVER GENERAL ALARM BELL RINGS.
"THE ROOM STEWARD WILL PROVIDE LIFE PRESERVERS FOR CHILDREN."

CHILDREN'S LIFE PRESERVERS

Mark the lockers or boxes in which the children's life preservers are stowed and also the number contained therein. 2-inch figures and letters.
Viz: 20
CHILDREN'S LIFE PRESERVERS

INSTRUCTIONS FOR CHANGING STEERING GEAR

Instructions in at least ½-inch letters and figures to be posted at each emergency steering station and in the steering engine room, relating in order the different steps to be taken in changing to the emergency steering gear. Each clutch, gear, wheel, lever, or valve which is used during the change-over to be numbered or lettered on a brass plate or painted so that the markings can be recognized at a reasonable distance. Indicate each clutch or pin to be "in" or "out" and each valve which is to be "opened" or "closed" in shifting to any means of steering for which the vessel is equipped. Include instructions to line up all steering wheels and rudder amidship before changing gears.

RUDDER ORDERS

At all steering stations, there shall be installed a suitable notice on the wheel or device or in such other position as to be directly in the helmsman's line of vision, to indicate the direction in which the wheel or device must be turned for "right rudder" and for "left rudder."

MARKING OF EQUIPMENT

All lifeboats, rafts, floats, buoyant apparatus including equipment, also life preservers, ring buoys, fire hose, axes, etc. to be painted or branded with the name of the vessel and numbered as required in accordance with the General Rules and Regulations.

Existing signs, markings and posters that are in general conformity with the above may be accepted if they adequately serve their purpose.

LIFESAVING APPARATUS

Boats—Requirements

General Qualifications of a Lifeboat:

1. Properly constructed of materials approved by steamboat inspectors.

2. Form and proportion to have ample stability in a seaway.

3. Sufficient freeboard when fully loaded.

4. Structural strength sufficient to permit safe loading with a full complement and equipment.

5. Internal buoyancy apparatus of non-corrosive material.

6. Equipment of good quality, efficient for purpose, and kept in good condition.

7. All equipment to be in place before vessel leaves port, and to remain so.

8. Loose equipment securely attached.

9. Cubic capacity not less than 125 cu. ft. coastwise or 180 cu. ft. for ocean steamers.

Apparatus and Equipment:

Embarkation aids—ladders. Required from boat deck to water, one for each set of davits. To be free and convenient with no entanglements.

Weight of a person is taken as 140 lbs. in testing boats in davits at annual inspection, or 165 lbs. in determining freeboard.

Reels, boxes, or covered tubs required for boat falls on steamers of over 1000 t. gross.

Illumination for boat launching operations required where deck is 30 ft. or more above water. To be in emergency lighting system.

Unlawful to stow in lifeboat any article other than those required by regulations.

Care of Lifeboats. To be stripped, cleaned, thoroughly overhauled, and painted once a year at least.

Numbering and Marking of Boats. To be numbered in 3-inch letters on each bow, starting with the forward boat on the starboard side as #1. Cubic capacity and number of persons allowed to be on each bow in 1 1/2-inch letters. Number of persons allowed to be marked on at least 2 thwarts in 3-inch letters. Lettering to be dark on a light ground, or light on a dark ground.

Davits. To be of such strength that boat can be lowered with full complement when vessel has 15° list. The gear to be of sufficient power so that boat can be turned out against the maximum list.

Lifeboats and Rafts on Ocean Vessels. All persons on board to be accommodated in lifeboats. Total of 25% of persons in life rafts, life floats, and buoyant apparatus.

Emergency boat. One lifeboat on each side of Class *A* and *B* vessels must be so designated. It must have at least 4 life lines on span between davit heads; a releasing gear capable of release under tension; a sea painter passed along forward and attached to boat when vessel is at sea, by a long eye, stop and toggle.

Mechanical Means for Lowering. On passenger vessels where boat deck is 20 ft. or more above water, wire falls and mechanical means for lowering each boat is required. Brakes must fall to "ON" position, and the two falls must be separate.

Air Tanks of Lifeboats. Must be entirely independent of hull, and of a capacity not less than 1.5 cu. ft. for each person in a metallic boat or 1 cu. ft. in a wooden boat. To be firmly fastened to the hull and protected by gratings. No more than 50% of air-tank capacity to be in ends of boats.

Loudspeaker System. Required on all passenger vessels where lifeboats are stowed more than 100 ft. from navigating bridge.

1. At lifeboat stations, port and starboard.

2. Embarkation deck, port and starboard.

3. Main quarters for crew.

4. Public spaces as required.

Tests made every week and entered in log.

Crew to be Exercised at Oars at least every 3 months, that is, all members but females.

Manning of Boats. ("Laws Governing Marine Insurance," Jan. 1941, page 128.) A deck officer or certificated lifeboat man to be placed in charge of each boat or life raft, and a second in command to be nominated. To have list of crew and see that they are acquainted with duties. See that there is—

A man capable of working motor in each motorboat.

A man capable of working wireless and searchlight in boats with this equipment.

Life Rafts

1 Boat hook
2 Drinking cups
1 Jackknife (with can opener)
Life line, as boats
Matches, as boats
2 Signaling mirrors
4 Oars
Storm oil, as boats
Painter
Provisions, as boats

5 Rowlocks
Sea anchor, as boats
Distress signals, as boats
Water, as boats
Water light

Buoyant Apparatus

Life line
Painter, as boats
Self-igniting water light (if capacity less than 25 persons, no light required)

Tests for Lowering Boats:

1. Vessel upright in smooth water.
2. Time starts from beginning of removal of boat covers.
3. Only the regular number of hands employed.
4. Two men and full equipment aboard during lowering.
5. Maximum time allowed is ten minutes.

Motorboats. Required on all vessels of over 2500 t. gross, carrying passengers, and going 200 miles offshore. If more than 6 lifeboats are required, the vessel is to carry 2 motorboats. The motor to propel boat, when fully loaded, at 6 k., and to have fuel for 24 hours at this speed. Motor to be in watertight enclosure and operated ahead and astern for at least 5 minutes each week, which is to be entered in the log.

RAFTS AND BUOYANT APPARATUS

Rafts:

1. To be of a size and strength to be handled without apparatus and, if necessary, to be thrown from deck where stowed.
2. Tanks to have 3 cu. ft. for each person, and to be tested by air pressure of 1 lb. per sq. in.
3. To have 4 sq. ft. of deck area for each person, and deck to be at least 6 inches above water when loaded.
4. Tanks to be as near as possible to sides.
5. To be reversible and fitted with 4-inch bulkheads of wood on each side.
6. At least one-half of all rafts to have a capacity of more than 1 persons.

Letter Identification	ITEM	Ocean & Coastwise	Great Lakes	Lakes, Bays, Sounds & Rivers	Ocean & Coastwise		Great Lakes		Lakes, Bays, Sounds & Rivers	Ocean & Coastwise	Great Lakes	Lakes, Bays, Sounds & Rivers	Tank Barge All Waters
					Other than Seagoing Barges	Seagoing Barges	Vessels Carrying Cargo	Other					
a	Bailer	1	1	None	1	None	None	None	None	1	1	None	None
b	Bilge Pump	¹1	None	None	¹1	None	None	None	None	1	None	None	None
c	Boathooks	2	1	1	²2	2	1	1	1	2	None	None	⁸2
d	Bucket	2	1	1	2	1	1	1	1	2	1	1	1
e	Compass and Mounting	1	None	None	1	None	None	None	None	1	None	None	None
f	Ditty Bag	1	None	None	1	None	None	None	None	1	None	None	None
g	Drinking Cups	1	None	None	1	None	None	None	None	1	None	None	None
h	Fire Ext. Motor Prop. Only	2	2	2	2	1	2	2	2	2	2	None	⁹1
i	First Aid Kit	1	²1	None	1	2	²1	None	None	1	None	None	1
j	Flashlight	²1	None	2	1	None	2 1	None	2 1	1	1	None	None
k	Hatchets	2	2	1	2	2	2	1	2	1	2	None	None
l	Heaving Line	2	None	None	1	None	1	1	1	1	2	1	None
m	Jack Knife	1	None	None	2	None	None	None	None	1	None	None	None
n	Ladder Life Boat Gunwale	³1	None	None	³1	1	None	None	None	1	None	None	⁹1
o	Lantern	1	1	None	1	1	None	None	None	³1	None	None	None
p	Lifeline with Seine Floats	1	1	1	1	1	1	1	1	1	1	1	None
q	Life Preservers	2	2	2	2	2	2	2	2	2	2	1	2
r	Lockers	1	1	2	2	None	None	2	2	1	1	1	None
s	Mast & Sail Oar Prop. Only	1	None	None	1	None	None	None	None	1	None	None	None
t	Matches (Boxes)	2	1	1	2	2	1	1	1	1	1	1	⁸2
u	Milk Cond. (Lbs./Person)	1	None	None	2	None	None	None	None	1	None	None	None
v	Mirrors Signaling	2	None	None	2	None	None	None	None	³1	None	None	⁸2
w	Oars	⁴1 Unit	⁴1 Unit	1 Unit	⁴1 Unit	⁴1 Unit	⁴1 Unit	⁴1 Unit	⁴1 Unit	⁴1 Unit	⁴1 Unit	None	None
x	Oil Illum. Qts.	1	1	None	1	None	None	None	None	1	1	None	⁴1 Unit
y	Oil Storm Gals.	1	1	None	1	None	None	None	None	1	1	None	None
z	Painter	2	1	1	2	None	2	None	None	2	1	None	None
aa	Plugs	1	1	1	1	1	1	1	1	1	2	1	1
bb	Provisions (Lbs./Person)	2	None	None	2	None	None	None	None	1	None	None	None
cc	Radio Installation	⁵1	None	1 Unit	None	None	None	None	None	2	None	None	None
dd	Rowlocks	⁵1 Unit	1 Unit	None	None	1 Unit	1 Unit	1 Unit	1 Unit	None	None	1 Unit	¹⁰1 Unit
ee	Rudder & Tiller	1	1	None	1	1	1	1	1	1	1	1	⁹1
ff	Sea Anchor	1	1	None	1	1	None	1	None	1	1	None	None
gg	Searchlight	⁵1	⁵None	⁵None	⁵None	⁵None	None	None	None	2	None	None	None
hh	Signals Floating Orange Smoke	2	2 None	None	2	2 None	2 None	2 None	2 None	2 None	2 None	None	None
ii	Signals Red Hand Flare	1 Unit	⁶1 Unit	None	1 Unit	None	1/2 Unit	None	None	2	None	None	None
jj	Signals Red Parachute Flare	1 Unit	1 Unit	None	⁷1 Unit	1/2 Unit	1/2 Unit	None	None	1 Unit	1/2 Unit	None	None
kk	Tool Kit Motor Prop. Only	1 Unit	1 Unit	1 Unit	1 Unit	1 Unit	1 Unit	1 Unit	1 Unit	1 Unit	1/2 Unit	1 Unit	None
ll	Water Qts./Person	3	None	None	3	1	1 Unit	1 Unit	1 Unit	3	None	1 Unit	⁹1

1. Motor propelled lifeboats, certified for 100 or more persons, shall be fitted with an additional hand bilge pump of an approved type or a power bilge pump.
2. Optional - See footnote 6.
3. Not required on lifeboats of less than 60 person capacity.
4. For description of items see Tables.
5. Required only on motor-propelled lifeboats fitted with radio cabin.
6. An approved flashlight, item (j) or 12 approved parachute red flare distress signals, item (jj) may be substituted for 6 of the required 12 hand red flare distress signals.
7. Vessels in coastwise service need only carry 1 unit for each 5 life-boats or fraction thereof.
8. Only 1 required on other than seagoing barges.
9. Seagoing barges only.
10. Lifeboats on barges need only carry 4 rowlocks.

7. To be stripped, cleaned, and painted at least once a year.

Buoyant Apparatus (Buoyant deck seats, chairs, etc.):

1. Must require no adjustments.

2. To be effective and stable, floating either side.

3. To have line becketed around, or pendants.

4. To be of a size, strength, and weight to be handled without apparatus, and thrown from a deck where stowed, at least 60 ft.

5. Weight not to exceed 200 lbs.

6. Air cases or equivalent buoyant objects placed as near as possible to side.

Lifeboats, life rafts, life buoys and life preservers are not buoyant apparatus.

Stowage of Buoyant Apparatus:

1. Shall not impede launching of boats nor marshalling of persons.

2. So as to be readily launched.

3. Secured only by readily slipped lashings; may be stowed in tiers, but must be kept from sticking together.

4. A means provided to prevent shifting.

Life Preservers. To be of reversible type, with an unbleached cotton covering of not more than two pieces, 52 inches in length when laid flat. To sustain a direct downward pull of 20 lbs. for 24 hours, straps of 1 1/4-inch tape to sustain a strain of 175 lbs. One for every person on board, plus an extra 10% for children on passenger vessels. Located in cabins and so as to be readily accessible. If 7 ft. above deck, to be provided with some means for immediate release and distribution.

Ring Life Buoys. Before being covered, buoys to support a weight of 200 lbs. Glue to be insoluble in water and to stand 2 lbs. steam pressure for 30 min. One-half the buoys to have lights attached, and one buoy on each side to have 15 fathoms of line attached. To sustain a downward pull of 32 lbs. for 24 hours. Not less than 30 inches outside diameter or 17 inches inside.

Self-Igniting Water Lights. To be nonexplosive, remain upright in the water, to be of at least 150 candlepower and burn 45 minutes, to have no obnoxious fumes, to reignite automatically if extinguished.

Line–Throwing Gun. Bronze, 200 lbs. weight limit, 2 1/2-inch bore, range 1400 ft., elevation 35°. Equipment: (*a*) 6 (17–18 lbs.) service projectiles; (*b*) 4 service lines 7/32 to 9/32 inch in dia., 1700 ft. in length, with tag in each end and faked in box; (*c*) auxiliary line of 3-inch manila, 1500 ft.; (*d*) 5–6-oz. service charges, limit 8 oz.; (*e*) 25 primers.

Drill to be held and gun fired at least every 3 months with half a powder charge and any ordinary line of proper length.

In firing, (1) service charge is 5 oz.; (2) wet at least one fathom of line from shank; (3) put 3 slack half-hitches around shank; (4) hang bight over side; (5) place faking box in direction of line of fire but not too close; (6) see that all is clear of rigging, etc.

Line-carrying gun instructions posted. Five copies, one each in pilot house, engine room, seamen's, firemen's and stewards' mess. Instructions as follows: (1) Secure small line shot over vessel, and haul out tail block with endless line rove through. (2) When secure, signal ashore. (3) Shore crew hauls out hawser by endless line. (4) Secure the hawser 2 ft. above tail block. (5) When sure of no turns, signal for breeches buoy.

Equipment Requirements. Depending on type of vessel concerned, one of the Coast Guard current publications "Rules and Regulations" should always be available on board. These are: CG–256 for *Passenger Vessels*; CG–257 for *Cargo and Miscellaneous Vessels*; CG–237 for *Tank Vessels*.

Lifesaving Signals. See page 17-18.

Chapter 19

ENGINEERING FOR DECK OFFICERS

PROPULSION

Marine propulsion equipment is primarily designed to overcome resistance of the vessel to the water. This resistance consists of two parts: frictional resistance created by rubbing water against the surface of the ship, and residual, which is produced by waves thrown by the ship itself.

The needed power is the main consideration in the selection of suitable equipment. The weight of the complete plant, space occupied by it, initial cost, reliability, length of life, flexibility, quietness of operation, cost of upkeep, type and cost of fuel, availability of fuel among national resources, labor conditions existing in industry, speed of the vessel, revolutions per minute of propeller, and the number of propellers—all these factors have to be taken into consideration in the final selection of the proper machinery. Generally speaking, equipment on naval vessels will be different from that on the tramp or liner. The amount of power required depends on dimensions of the hull, which in turn is affected by the type of propulsive equipment.

In the beginning of the design, a rough approximation is usually made of suitable machinery in order to get the weight and space requirement to proceed with the design of the hull. Then the final adjustments and alterations are made in the engine design to suit the ship. The determination of the resistance of each form of vessel is a complicated problem, and it is the general practice to determine resistance and needed power to overcome that resistance by utilizing past experience for similar forms of hulls.

Propeller Revolutions. The effective limits for revolution of propeller varies from 65 to 450 r.p.m. The low limit is set for merchant vessels, and the high used on Navy vessels. It is customary to rely on previous experience of others in preliminary estimates of r.p.m. of the propeller. The diameter of the wheel has an influence on the propeller efficiency.

Propeller efficiency decreases with smaller diameters of propeller and with increase of r.p.m. of the shaft. The numbers of screws varies from one to four, and influences the number of prime movers and affects the whole plant. Propulsive efficiency is highest for the single screw, when it is equal to 75 per cent, drops down to 68 per cent for twin screw, and decreases to 60 per cent for a quadruple drive. Judging from efficiency alone, it is desirable to have single-screw ships; however, other points have to be taken into consideration. Maneuverability possible with two or more propellers is much better than with one. The extra propeller will give extra speed. Certain types of prime movers cannot be built in large sizes, and this fact also is in the favor of the multiple screw. The loss of one screw would not be fatal to a ship having two or more wheels. All these questions have to be considered when selecting the most desirable number of propellers for the ship in question.

The following types of machinery are used as propulsive drives and will be compared: (1) reciprocating steam engine; (2) direct connected turbine; (3) geared tubine; (4) combination steam engine and turbine; (5) diesel; (6) gas turbine; (7) electric drive, both turbine and diesel-driven.

The types of propulsion in use on vessels of U. S. Registry in 1947 was as follows:

reciprocating	65%
Diesel	19%
geared turbine	15%
turbo-electric	1/2 of 1%
Diesel electric	less than 1/2 of 1%

The whole question of selection of type of propulsive machinery is involved and to some extent contradictory. Each problem has to be considered individually. The selection depends on estimated power dimensions and purpose of the ship and calculated speed. The Naval vessels, freighters, and luxury liners, all present different requirements. The waters where the ship is to operate and the number of ports of call have to be considered, as well as the fuel to be used, depending on availability and cost. The highest thermal efficiency is not always the major issue if it leads to very complicated plants with high initial cost.

Modern power plants require the service of highly trained operating personnel and might lead to interruption in service due to lack of repair crews. It is of interest to note that before the outbreak of World War II, out of 30,000 ships with about 70,000,000 gross registered tons, only 4 per cent of the total number and 14 per cent of the total tonnage were steam turbine-driven. Approximately 66 per cent of the total number were equipped with reciprocating steam engine, which equals 60 per cent of the total tonnage. Nineteen per cent of the total number and 24 per cent of the tonnage operated on Diesel and about 10 per cent of the number with 2 per cent in tonnage were sailing vessels equipped with auxiliary drives.

The steam engine, which was the prime mover in the major part of the prewar world's fleet, is still useful on small and medium-sized vessels where fuel of inferior grades is available. The reciprocating engine has attractive features of ruggedness and simplicity. It can be operated in the remote corners of the world with lack of highly trained mechanics. The initial low cost is a great advantage in favor of reciprocating engine. On small ships it can operate in competition with Diesel when finer grades of oil are not available. On larger ships the competition is between steam turbine and Diesel, with possibility for combustion turbine in the future.

Table 1 gives the relative comparison of various types for ships of 10,000 tons. Chart includes weights of boilers and reduction gears for gas and steam turbine; Diesel is direct connected with 105 r.p.m. on shaft.

Selection of number of machines depends on the number of wheels required by design and the fact that some types of equipment like Diesels are not built yet in very high capacity units. Steam plants can use any kind of fuel. This offers a possibility of patronizing the local fuels for ships of coastwise service or between ports of the same nation. The turbines are very efficient on high speed and high horsepower rating and can be built in one high capacity unit.

Beyond about 6,000 horsepower the present Diesel becomes too bulky and thus takes too much space. Greater radius of operation permissible on the same amount of fuel with Diesel-equipped ships makes Diesel very attractive for vessels designed to operate with few ports of call. Diesels are very suitable for use on underwater crafts. High pres-

TABLE 1. COMPARISON OF DIFFERENT DRIVES FOR SHIPS OF 10,000 TONS
WITH 6,200 S. HP. AND SPEED OF 16 KNOTS

Type of Drive	Specific Weight— Lbs. per S. HP.	Fuel Consumption Lbs./S. HP.	Steam Pressure Lbs./sq. in.	Total Weight of Machinery In Tons
Scotch boiler, turbine............	208	.88	235	590
Modern boilers, turbines.........	84.0	.68	530	237
Diesel, double-acting, two-stroke compressorless.............	188.0	.389	.....	530
Gas turbine (estimated).........	32.0	.636	.....	90

(From "Some Reflections on the Propulsion of Ships by Means of Combustion Turbines," by R. Schmid, The Brown Boveri Review, October, 1942.)

sure and temperature, so beneficial to operation of steam turbine, constitute danger of deadly leaks and consequent injuries to operating crews.

The reduction of starting time to a very few minutes, against hours needed on steam-operated plants, is one more factor in favor of Diesel-driven ships, and explains why small Diesels are enormously popular on fishing boats, pleasure yachts, small Navy craft, etc.

The gas turbine is probably the ship's power plant of tomorrow. After the problems of high temperature and overall efficiency of compressor and turbine are solved, the combustion turbine will offer a great opportunity due to its simplicity of operation and considerable reduction in weight. But it can be expected that introduction of the gas turbine will be rather slow, as has been past experience with any new type of propulsive machinery.

The electric drive, with its flexibility, reliability, and quietness of operation, has to compete with a geared turbine and Diesel. The limitation in manufacturing of reduction gears was one reason why electric drive was adopted on many ships where geared turbine was originally on the plans. In the future it can be expected that electric drive will be used on special vessels where its advantage of extra available auxiliary power and remote control is paramount.

THE STEAM ENGINE

The glorious saga of the sailing vessels started to decline in the beginning of the Nineteenth Century with the invention and application of the steam engine as a propulsive drive. First steam engines were used only as auxiliaries and gave a great deal of trouble, but improvement in design gradually overcame the obstacles. The first steam-operated ships had paddle wheels and operated on very low pressure. Reliability of the engine was bad and history records a few cases where sailing ships were victorious in maintaining schedules against steam-operated engines. Gradually, however, the steam engine spelled doom for the sails.

The main advantages of reciprocating steam engines are simplicity and ruggedness of operation due to which it is much easier to train operating engineers and to do repair work at sea. Most sea-going engineers are familiar with repairs and maintenance of the steam engine. Due to this familiarity with the equipment, it is much easier for the owner to find experienced personnel to operate the steam engine. The reciprocating engine can also be built much faster than other types. Most effective speed range for the steam engine corresponds to the speed of a screw propeller so that no reduction gears are necessary. Cost of installation is low. The weight of the complete plant is heavier than any other, and this disadvantage increases rapidly with increase in size of plant, which makes steam engine installation prohibitive on ships requiring huge amounts of power. Common to all types of reciprocating engines, the wear is high due to unbalance of reciprocating motion. This disadvantage is balanced to some extent by the ease of repair and the ruggedness of the engine. The steam engine can take certain overloads, but its thermal efficiency is low and equal to about 15 per cent.

The steam engine can operate on saturated and super-heated steam. It can be used on both low and high pressure and with any kind of boiler and fuel. Due to their simplicity, the construction of steam engines can be undertaken much faster than any other drive, and this is one of the reasons why Liberty ships are equipped with reciprocating steam engines.

Triple, quadruple expansion and uniflow engines are types of steam engines used on ships today. The four-cylinder triple-expansion engine with two low-pressure cylinders decreasing the size of each cylinder and making the turning moment more uniform, has met with much success. The use of multi-cylinder engines reduces the initial condensation and reduces losses. The uniflow engine is utilizing the principle of steam flowing in one direction. In the uniflow engine the steam enters the cylinder at the end after being passed through steam-jacketed heads. And, after cut-off and expansion have taken place, the steam is exhausted through ports arranged around the center of the cylinder which are uncovered by the piston at the end of the power stroke as shown in Fig. 1. Consequently, the steam has a uni-directional flow. Hence, the derivation of the name *uniflow*. This results in better thermal efficiency and the steam combustion pounds per indicating hp. per hour, as claimed by some manufacturers of uniflow engines, varies between 11.67 and 12.30.

The steam engine has a long life, and fuel consumption varies, depending on the plant and type of engine, between 1.4 (for installation with old-type engine and Scotch-Marine boiler steam plant) and .80 or better for the modern plant.

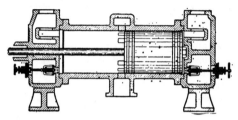

Courtesy Skinner Engine Co., Erie, Pa.

Fig. 1. Arrangement of Cylinder in Typical Uniflow Engine.

THE STEAM TURBINE

With larger and faster ships the steam turbine came into existence as a propulsive drive. The first application was made by the end of the last century. The steam turbine has a thermal efficiency of about 24 per cent and has a uniform turning moment. The fuel consumed varies with size and is better for larger plants—between .60 and .50 pounds of oil per shaft horsepower. Most economical speed of the steam turbine is close to the velocity of steam and is much higher than any permissible r.p.m. of screw propeller. This was a great disadvantage of the turbine in the beginning and designers spent a great deal of time in trying to reduce the turbine speed by compounding it and using a few stages, but even then the speed of the direct drive was much higher than speed of the propeller. Direct drive turbine application on ships had few stages with pressure drops in each stage and consequently results in reduction in speed. Turbine is very economical for large blocks of power and can be used at different pressures and temperature. The modern high-pressure installations are considerably lighter than those of twenty years ago, due to the reduction in size made possible by application of high temperature and high pressure, as well as the use of steel and fabricated structures instead of cast iron. One of the advantages of the turbine is the possibility of using oil-free condensate for feeding boilers. The turbine installation requires extra turbine for astern operation, since the turbine is not a reversible machine. The *SS Lusitania* and the *SS Mauretania* were examples of the direct-connected turbine. These installations were heavy and large. The disagreement between speeds of propeller and direct-connected turbine necessitated the use of reduction between the prime mover and the propeller shaft. Mechanical gears, hydraulic and electric drive, are means of reducing the turbine speed.

The first successful installation of geared turbine was made in 1912 on the *USS Neptune*. Geared turbine makes it possible to operate both turbine and propeller at the most efficient speed, but gears are introducing extra loss and reducing the efficiency of the whole plant by from 2 to 4 per cent. In spite of that, geared turbine weighs less than the reciprocating engine, direct Diesel or geared Diesel, and compares favorably with electric drive. The weight of plant varies from about 350 pounds per horsepower at low capacity to 280 pounds per shaft horsepower at high capacity of the plant.

The cost of installation of geared turbine is higher than for reciprocating engine and Diesel—in the range of low horsepower capacity of the plant—but lower than turbo-electric in plants of over 6,000 horsepower range. The weight of the whole steam plant is affected by the water in which the vessel must navigate. A ship designed for tropical waters will have increased weight due to large condensers and might differ from one designed to operate in cool waters as much as 6 per cent.

Three basic principles and their combinations are used in marine practice:

(a) Reaction—Parsons.

(b) Single velocity extraction impulse elements.

(c) Multi-velocity extraction impulse elements (Curtis).

The turbine installation offers certain possibilities of flexibility by the use of hydraulic coupling between the main turbine and auxiliary. By drainage of this coupling the speeds below 60 per cent, as well as during maneuvers, the generator for ship's service power can be disconnected from the main turbine and connected to the auxiliary turbine. The astern turbine usually provides between 70 to 80 per cent of ahead rating and rotating of reverse turbine on main shaft might lead to undue heating.

Many difficulties were experienced in production of gears, but gradual development in methods and speed of production made it possible for gears to follow very closely the manufacture of turbines. Thus, one of the important bottlenecks in gear production was eliminated.

The degree of precision in manufacture of gears closely resembles that in the watchmaker's skill. Quite a few problems present themselves during manufacture. The need for precision in making of gears has resulted in the fact that gears are now manufactured in special air-conditioned rooms and during the last few days the work is uninterrupted. The delay in delivery of gears led to adoption of some other types of propulsive equipment as emergency substitutes for otherwise desirable geared turbines.

The exhaust turbine used in connection with the steam engine offers some possibilities in increasing thermal efficiency of the steam engine. The *SS Amon* and *SS Amasis*, of the Hamburg-American Line, were two of a few ships equipped with combination of steam turbine drive. The main advantages in such a combination are the use of high vacuum and absorption of periodical torque peaks of the reciprocating engine during each revolution by the turbine. However, due to the dual and rather complicated nature of this drive, it was never adopted for general use.

ELECTRIC DRIVE

Two types of electric drive are in use—turbo-electric and Diesel electric. Both D.C. and A.C. equipment is used. Turbine is used in large power plants to take advantage of the steam turbine at high speeds, for generation of alternating current, and change from high speed alternator to the normal speed of the propeller; is usually done by reduction in speed of motor by increase in number of poles. With turbo-electric drive no extra turbine is needed for reversal of speed, which is accomplished electrically. The expected decrease in weight due to elimination of reversing turbine is compensated by installation of motors and control switchboards. The weight of the turbo-electric plant is less than directly connected or geared Diesel when the size of the power plant is large, but is slightly greater than the geared turbine installation of the same capacity.

The fuel consumption depends on the type of boiler and efficiency of turbine, and is larger at low capacities of the plant, averaging about .70 pounds per shaft horsepower, and goes down to .60 pounds per shaft horsepower at 8,000 horsepower on the shaft. Generally speaking, it is slightly more than the fuel consumption of the geared turbine on corresponding sizes.

The first application of turbo-electric drive was made in 1912, when installation was made on board the *USS Jupiter*, a collier converted into an aircraft carrier—the *USS Langley*, which was sunk in the beginning of this war after a number of years of successful operation.

The electric drive permits a great flexibility in design so far as location of equipment is concerned, mainly in the possibility to separate motor room from the engine room and locating them some distance apart. This makes it possible to reduce the shaft alley and to utilize the space for cargo holds.

In the electric drive, full power is available in reverse operation and offers an extra maneuverability not available on geared turbine when only 70 to 80 of capacity is available on reverse turbine.

The installation of electric drive requires the services of qualified electricians to do the work on complicated electrical circuits, but operation of the ship can be done by regular licensed engineers, inasmuch as it is simple to operate and easy to learn and does not require the knowledge of involved control circuits.

The availability of extra auxiliary power is one of the main advantages of electrical propulsion, in both the cases of Diesel and turbine drive. On some types of ships the ship's service generators can be reduced, provided that the ship's service requires extra power during standstill, like pumps on tankers, tugboats, self-loading freighters, and fishing vessels. The extra ship's service load can be obtained from main propulsion units connected to the ship's service switchboard and used on winches, pumps, etc.

The quietness of operation, very important as an attractive feature on passenger vessels, on turbo-electric drive stands in advance of any other drive thus far developed. The progress in elimination of *singing* of geared turbine promises quite satisfactory operation so far as noise elimination is concerned, but reduction of noise can be accomplished easier with electric equipment. However, completely noiseless operation can hardly be expected. With any drive the turbine installation is highly desirable on alternating current due to the possibility for reduction in size of generating units. On Diesel electric drive, due to limitation in size of individual Diesel, a power plant with a few independent units is necessary. The electric drive offers a possibility of using a multiplicity of prime movers to repair one of the units without greatly jeopardizing the availability of power on all shafts, and in the case of casualty to one of the propulsion motors, by electrical switching full power is still available on the remaining motors.

One of the best examples of long life of a ship with electrical equipment is the *SS Oriente*, which had a million miles to her record during nine years of service without any replacement in the machinery. The possibility of separating the engine room from the motor room, the elimination of long shaft alley, raises the objection that it is desirable to have communication between the two sections of the ship without the necessity of going on deck, and some reports indicate that short shafts transfer the vibration of the propeller directly to the motor and is thus undesirable.

Diesel engines are used to the best advantage in the 1200 r.p.m. region, where high-speed Diesels are economical, and, generally speaking, selection between Diesel and turbine will be governed by the relative advantages of turbine and Diesel engine as a prime mover for the ship.

The direct current installation on high-powered ships is undesirable, since the inherent limit on voltage of D.C. machinery, the increase in weight of cables and machinery itself, and the fact that A.C. machinery is about 4 per cent more efficient than D.C. equipment.

On smaller types of vessels, or when a great variation of speed of the auxiliary machinery is needed, the direct current has preference over alternating current, but where auxiliaries are running at constant speed, for example pumps on tankers, the more rugged A.C. drive is preferable due to simplicity of induction motors used for the auxiliary. In the conventional type of D.C. drive, the speed of the motor can be altered by varying the field current or changing the voltage through the armature circuit. The motors can be reversed by changing the direction of the current in the field, or through the armature. The demand for maneuverability of naval vessels leads to adoption of wound rotor induction motor drive, while on merchant ships the synchronous type of motor can be used. The A.C. motors are reversed by changing the position of two of the three main power leads. The speed of the synchronous motors can only be changed by altering the speed of the generators. The first installation of induction type A.C. motor drive on battleships was made in 1918 on the *USS New Mexico*. Since that time, with certain variations and improvements, it has been installed on a number of ships. The synchronous motor drive has one extra advantage due to constant speed characteristics—it does not race with conditions of heavy sea.

The possibility of remote control from the pilot house is one of the advantages of electrical propulsion of great importance on rescue ships, ice breakers, etc. The initial cost of electrical installation is slightly higher than geared turbine.

DIESEL DRIVE

The acceptance of Diesel in marine practice was for years jeopardized by lack of experience in maintenance and repair and lack of properly trained personnel to operate the Diesel-propelled ships. The thermal efficiency of Diesel is about 30 per cent or slightly higher.

Fuel consumption averages about .40 pounds per shaft horsepower. The initial cost is higher than any other type except electric drive, and it increases with increase in the size of the plant. For a single unit the cost becomes prohibitive with the high capacity plant. The weight of the Diesel compares unfavorably with turbo-electric and geared turbine. The most economical Diesels are built in sizes from two to three thousand horsepower. The larger plant should be a combination of small units used on separately propelled shafts or as a Diesel electric drive.

Diesel is reversible and, therefore, does not require the extra unit as does the geared turbine. The reduction in standby losses through elimination of boilers and the necessity of keeping steam is advantageous. The starting time is a few minutes against hours for the steam plant. The upkeep is high and maintenance work is complicated in comparison with steam engine and requires specialized mechanics.

In spite of the very low fuel consumption, the economy is handicapped by higher cost of Diesel oil. The needed carrying capacity for fuel oil is much lower with the Diesel plant, thus giving Diesel-operated ships increased radius of operation.

The direct Diesels are large and bulky. Thus, the adoption of geared Diesel is becoming more and more popular. Gears have a loss of from 4 to 5 per cent, and naturally increase the cost of the Diesel operation; but the additional weight of gears is compensated by a corresponding decrease in weight of high-speed engines. The gears are also necessary due to the slight difference between efficient speed of the propeller and natural speed of the Diesel engine. Due to limited capacity needed for fuel oil, Diesel is most advantageous on long cruises with few ports of call.

The four-cycle Diesel is better known to operating personnel. Certain improvements in the two-cycle Diesel balances the advantages of the four-cycle engine. Generally speaking, the two-cycle machine is more attractive due to smaller weight, from about 60 to 65 per cent; the four-cycle machine space requirement is less, by an average of 40 per cent, and the turning moment is more uniform. The two-cycle machine can operate on cheaper fuel. The disadvantages, together with higher fuel consumption, are high lubrication cost and requirements for special cooling. More breakdowns were experienced with two-cycle than with four-cycle machines. The exhaust turbo-charger has been used with four-cycle machines on the *M. S. Reine Del Pacifico* of the Pacific Steamship Navigation Company of Liverpool. The ship was built in 1930 with additional weight increase from 2 to 3 per cent, with compensating increase in power of 50 per cent. A turbo-charger can be installed separately with a great degree of flexibility, and the quantity and pressure of charged air is proportional to all loads.

Fuel consumption experienced on this type of plant was lower than regular Diesel. However, like any other new installation, the design met with criticism which slowed its adoption.

THE GAS TURBINE

The principles of gas turbine are used in turbo-charger with the Diesel engine and a few installations with gas turbine as a prime mover were put into use in Switzerland. The application and development of gas turbine has been the dream of engineers for years and was handicapped by poor efficiency of both compressor and the turbine.

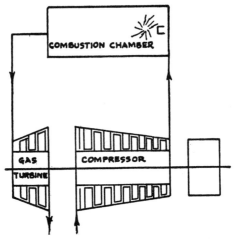

FIG. 2. SCHEMATIC ARRANGEMENT OF COMBUSTION TURBINE.

The principle upon which this prime mover operates consists of burning fuel in air and using the air as a heat carrier and transforming the heat into mechanical energy in the turbine. The simplest form of combustion turbine consists of a turbo-compressor, compression chamber, and a gas turbine, as shown in Fig. 2. A small fraction of the compressed air serves for a combustion of the fuel, which is injected in the form of a fine spray. The rest of the air is mixed with the gas to lower the temperature to insure absolute reliability of the turbine and the most sensitive part of the blades. High temperature experienced in turbines was one of the handicaps in the development of this type of prime mover. The most attractive feature in the combustion turbine is the decrease in weight.

The thermal efficiency of simple cycle combustion turbine is about 22 per cent, and the weight is about one-half of the turbo installation of the same capacity. Like the steam turbine, the gas turbine is not reversible and possible variation in speed is about 30 to 40 per cent. The application of variable pitch propeller with the gas turbine installation is one of the possible solutions for a change in speed. An extra turbine for astern operation can be installed, but will lead to additional weight. The combination of independent Diesel and combustion turbine plant was considered for use on naval vessels where cruising requirements are different from speed required for extensive maneuvering of the ship. This combination offers a high economy over gas turbine at rated capacity and high speed and operation of the Diesel for cruising. The simplicity of the gas plant is one of the attractive features of this design. The maximum limit set up at present for gas turbine is about 7,500 horsepower. It is possible to use turbine as part of the electric drive.

PREPARATIONS FOR GETTING UNDER WAY

Reciprocating Engines. Preparations for getting under way consist of warming up the main engines and starting the necessary auxiliaries. Variations in detail are introduced depending on the size of the engines, method of lubrication, arrangement of steam piping, and whether or not the auxiliaries are independently driven.

The larger the engine the longer the time required for warming up. Should the warming-up process be unduly hastened, there is danger of unequal expansion causing cracked cylinder castings. Very large engines require from *1 1/2 to 2 hours*; other engines a length of time in proportion to their size. It must be remembered that unless an actual emergency exists, it is much better to allow too much rather than too little time for warming up.

Turbines. Preparations for getting under way consist of starting the necessary auxiliaries and warming up the main turbines. During this warming-up process, the temperature of the various parts of the installation is raised from the temperature of the surrounding atmosphere to approximately that reached during the early stages of operation. While this change in temperature is taking place, the metals in the various parts of the installation expand, and, in order to prevent inefficient operation and damage, due to distortion, the procedure must be such that all parts of the main turbines are evenly and gradually heated.

In warming up turbines, every effort must be made to get the rotors turning over as soon as possible after steam has been admitted to the turbine. To accomplish this end, two methods are approved, namely, that used on geared and small direct-drive turbines called spinning, and the continuous jacking and heat-soaking process used with large direct-drive turbines. Both of these methods insure a uniform heating around the circumference and along the axis of the rotor, and diminish chances of distortion due to locally heating one part of the turbine.

If the rotor and the casing are not evenly heated, unequal expansion, resulting in the distortion of the rotor or the casing or both, will take place.

Six hours from lighting up to ready are required for the Parsons turbines and four hours for Brown-Curtis turbine.

HORSEPOWER

IHP. Indicated HP is the power produced in the cylinders.

SHP. Shaft HP is about 90% of the IHP.

BHP. Brake HP may for all practical purposes be taken as identical with shaft HP.

Effective HP in driving the ship is taken roughly as 50% of the indicated HP.

Formula for HP: $HP = 2\ plan \div 33,000$.

p = mean effective pressure in lb. per sq. in. on piston.

a = area of piston in sq. in.

l = length of stroke in ft.

n = number of revolutions per min.

$2\ ln$ = distance travelled by piston in ft. per min.

$2\ plan$ = ft.-lbs. of work per min.

Turbine Engines. Calculation of SHP is determined by means of a *Torsion Meter*, which records the angular twist of the revolving shaft. The torque movement is made to a graduated scale. From the rigidity of the material and the r.p.m. the HP is:

$SHP = (\text{Scale reading} \times \text{r.p.m.}) \div (\text{Constant of torsion meter})$.

SAMPLE PROBLEMS ON FUEL CONSERVATION

Determine how much the speed of a ship should be reduced in order to make port on the amount of fuel at hand.

Determine r.p.m. to consume a certain amount of fuel; the amount of fuel consumption being known on certain r.p.m.

Determine distance on fuel consumption at reduced or increased speeds.

Determine amount speed must be reduced to conserve fuel and reach port with a safe margin.

1. Within 3 knots on either side of the normal speed, in vessels capable of 15 knots, the consumption of fuel varies approximately as the cube of the speed.

Example. At 12 knots, fuel consumption per day = 140 barrels. Find consumption at 10 knots.

$$140/C = 12^3/10^3. \quad C = (140 \times 1000) \div 1728 = 81 \text{ barrels}.$$

Example. Given a speed of 11 knots and a consumption of 120 barrels. Find speed on 100 barrels fuel.

$$120/100 = 11^3/S^3. \quad S = \sqrt[3]{(100 \times 1331) \div 120} = 10.35 \text{ knots}.$$

2. Based upon the above, it is found that the consumption varies as the speed squared times the distance covered, or:

$$c \div C = (s^2 \times d) \div (S^2 \times D)$$

or (Old consumption) ÷ (New consumption) = (Old speed² × Old dist.) ÷ (New speed² × New dist.).

Example. 1000 barrels of fuel are consumed at a speed of 11 knots over a distance of 2200 miles. What speed is necessary to cover the remaining distance of 2000 miles on 700 barrels fuel remaining?

$$1000 \div 700 = (11^2 \times 2200) \div (S^2 \times 2000)$$

$$S = \sqrt{(700 \times 121 \times 2200) \div (1000 \times 2000)} = \sqrt{93.17} = 9.65 \text{ knots.}$$

3. Within the same range of speed as noted in **1,** the consumption varies as the displacement to the two-thirds power, or:

$$c \div C = w^{2/3} \div W^{2/3}$$

or (Old consumption) ÷ (New consumption) = (Old displacement$^{2/3}$) ÷ (New displacement$^{2/3}$).

Example. A vessel of 10,000 tons displacement burns 210 bbls. of fuel when fully loaded. Find her daily consumption at the same speed after discharging 4500 tons of cargo, allowing a constant of 28 bbls. per day for auxiliary purposes.

$$c = 210 - 28 = 182 \text{ bbls. per day for steaming.}$$

$$
\begin{aligned}
w = \text{old displacement} = &\quad 10{,}000 \text{ tons} \\
\text{less cargo discharged} &\quad \underline{4{,}500 \text{ tons}} \\
W = \text{new displacement} = &\quad 5{,}500 \text{ tons}
\end{aligned}
$$

$$182 \div C = 10{,}000^{2/3} \div 5500^{2/3} \text{ from which } C = (182 \times 5500^{2/3}) \div 10{,}000^{2/3}$$

$$\log C = \log 182 + 2/3 \log 5500 - 2/3 \log 10{,}000$$

$$= 2.2601 + 2/3 (3.7404) - 2/3 (4.0000)$$

$$= 2.2601 + 2.4936 - 2.6667 = 2.0870 = \log 122.$$

$$\text{Steaming consumption therefore} = 122 \text{ bbls.}$$

$$\text{adding for auxiliary purposes} \quad 28 \text{ bbls.}$$

$$\text{total new daily consumption} = 150 \text{ bbls.}$$

4. Under similar conditions of weather and sea, the speed varies directly as the revolutions.

Example. Given a speed of 15 knots on r.p.m. 90. What should the r.p.m. be for 12 1/2 knots?

$$90 \div \text{Revs.} = 15 \div 12\ 1/2, \text{ whence r.p.m. required} = (90 \times 12\ 1/2) \div 15 = 75, \text{ ans.}$$

Speed by Engine Revolutions.

$$[60 \times \text{r.p.m.} \times \text{Pitch} \times (1 - \text{Slip})] \div 6080 = \text{Speed in nautical miles.}$$

Example. Given r.p.m. 70; pitch, 20′; slip, 12%. Find the speed per hour.

$$[60 \times 70 \times 20 \times (1 - .12)] \div 6080 = 12.16 \text{ knots per hour.}$$

Slip. Slip is expressed as a percentage of engine speed or distance.

Example. Speed of ship by measured mile observation is 12.16 knots; engine speed, 13.82. Required: the % slip.

$$(13.82 - 12.16) \div 13.82 = 1.66 \div 13.82 = \text{Slip} \div 100.$$

whence, Slip $= (1.66 \times 100) \div 13.82 = 12.01\%.$

Example. Distance by observation 450 miles; by engine 425.5. What is the % slip?

$$(450 - 425.5) \div 425.5 = 24.5 \div 425.5 = \text{Slip} \div 100.$$

whence, Slip $= (24.5 \times 100) \div 425.5 = -5.76\%.$

Note that the slip is negative, which is the term used in such cases. The "slip" being that of the engine's work, it is here a minus quantity because the vessel has out-run the screw distance by 24.5 miles.

FUEL OIL

Fuel oil is measured by the gallon and the 42 gallon barrel to find the weight of a gallon of oil, knowing its specific gravity, multiply the weight of a gallon water at 60° F. (8.328 lb.) by the specific gravity of the oil.*

Specific Gravity of an oil is the ratio at 60° F. of the weights of a given volume of oil and water. The specific gravity is important since fuel oils are purchased by volume (barrels and gallons) at a given temperature. Average weight of oil for boilers 8.0 to 8.3 lb. per gallon; 42 gallon = 1 barrel 6.67 banels = 1 ton (2,240 lb.); 1 ton = 37.5 cubic foot; 1 barrel (42 gallon) = 5.61 cubic foot.

Flash Point of an oil is the lowest temperature at which the vapors arising ignite momentarily or flash when a flame is passed over the surface, without setting fire to the oil. 150° F. is the usual minimum.

Fire Point is the lowest temperature at which an oil continues to burn from its own vapors. The fire point is usually 25 to 50° F. above the flash point.

Fuel Oil for Boilers. Bunker C or No. 6 Fuel Oil is for oil burners equipped with preheaters that will permit heating the oil to reduce viscosity to 150° Saybolt Universal. The characteristics of the oil include flash-point minimum 150° F; water and sediment maximum 2 percent.

Fuel Consumption (oil) per brake horsepower per hour including power plant and auxiliaries: steam engines to 1.3 lb., geared turbines 0.54 to 0.90, Diesel engine 0.40 to 0.60.

FUEL-OIL TANKS

Fuel-oil tanks may be classed as follows: 1. Storage tanks: 2. Service tanks: 3. Gravity tanks.

Storage tanks are located in double bottoms and coffer-dams adjacent to engine rooms and firerooms. Fuel oil in the storage tanks is heated so as to reduce viscosity to the point where the pumps will take suction. It is usually heated by steam coils located near the suction pipe in the tanks. All steam joints inside the tanks are welded to prevent leakage of water into the oil.

Service tanks are double bottoms under the engine room from which oil is taken by a booster pump and discharged to a gravity tank or fuel-oil service pump. Service pumps may take suction direct from the service tanks. Service tanks are intended to give a ready supply of oil near the pumps. Only the newest installations have service tanks.

Gravity tanks are fitted with steam-heating coils, automatic heat control, and electric water detectors. They are used to supply oil by gravity flow to service pumps. No gravity tanks are fitted in some older installations.

* Characteristics of fuel oil are discussed under Cargo: Tank Vessels.

All fuel-oil tanks are fitted with vent pipes, sounding tubes, and steam fire-extinguisher connections. Storage tanks on some ships are fitted with the pneumercator system which registers the amount of oil in each tank at a gage located in some central place such as the log room. Each tank may be entered by means of one or more manholes. Some tanks are fitted with salt-water connections to expel gases and wash out the tanks. Where no such connections are fitted a salt-water hose can be used.

FEED TANKS

Feed tanks are grouped as feed-and-filter tanks and reserve feed tanks.

The feed-and-filter tank, commonly known as the *hot well*, receives the fresh water which is drawn from the condenser and discharged by the air pump or condensate pump into the filter compartment of this tank. In large vessels there is a feed-and-filter tank in each engineroom, in small vessels only one feed-and-filter tank is fitted and all air pumps discharge into it. The filter compartment is located in the upper part of the tank, is separated from the feed tank proper by a horizontal plate, and is divided into several filtering chambers by vertical plates alternately secured to the top and bottom of the filter compartment. The filtering material most generally used is a fibrous marine growth called *loofa*. The vertical plates force the water to flow back and forth through the filtering material until it flows from the last filter chamber through an opening in the bottom of the filter tank into the feed tank below.

A large pipe connects the bottom of the feed tank to the main feed pump suction main, to the auxiliary feed pump suction main, and to the port use feed pump suction pipe. The suction pipes from the feed-and-filter tanks are cross-connected, but cut-out valves are fitted so that the tanks can be isolated.

FEED AND BOILER WATER TESTS

The exact condition of the boiler water must be known at all times in order to guard against sudden condense leakage or of contamination. The test for this is known as the *salinity test* but many ships have direct-reading salinity indicators, some of which are equipped with alarms, which is of course the best method of control.

The Alkalinity Test determines whether the alkalinity of the water is high enough to help control corrosion without being so high as to form deposits and cause damage itself.

The Soap Hardness Test is a measure of the most commonly found scale-forming salts which may be present.

The Chloride Test is used as a general test of the fitness of the evaporated water for use as boiler feed since it indicates the total concentration of soluble salts in the water.

PROPELLERS

Whenever a ship is docked, the propellers are cleaned, polished, and examined for defects such as cracks, nicks, bent blades, etc.

Where a small crack exists, **V** out and weld, or a 1/8-inch hole may be drilled at its end to prevent the crack from extending. Fill the drilled hole with solder.

Where slight nicks appear, file and dress smooth.

Where moderate bends or curled edges exist, they may be straightened by peening the bend on the concave side with a large air-hammer and round-edged calking tool. By this means, the metal on the inside of the bend is stretched.

Where bends of great degree exist, the use of heavy sledges will be necessary; or the propeller may have to be removed and taken to the shop if the damage is so extensive as to affect the pitch of the propeller.

The pitch can be defined as the longitudinal distance which the ship would be driven for one revolution were the propeller to work in a smooth, unyielding surface, as for example, the corresponding surface of a fixed nut. To preserve the pitch of a propeller, the shape and setting of the blades must at all times correspond to the specifications for the propeller.

A change in the designed pitch caused by a bent blade, or improperly set blade will not only decrease the efficiency of the propeller, but will cause considerable vibration. Increase in vibration is especially noticeable with a damaged high-speed propeller.

PROPELLER TERMS

Angle. The angle formed between the blade at any point and a plane perpendicular to its axis.

Cavitation. Formation of a space or cavity at back of blades, caused by atmospheric pressure being unable to press water to back of blades at high speed and increasing slip.

Expanded Blade Area. Widths of blade set on plane surface.

Leading Edge. Edge which strikes water first.

Negative Slip. Ship's speed greater than screw speed.

Pitch. Distance that a screw would advance in a solid in one revolution.

Positive Slip. Difference between speed of ship and speed of screw, when speed of the screw is the greater.

Projected Blade Area. Actual area of blade as seen from aft looking forward.

A propeller is right-handed if it turns clockwise when the observer stands off and looks forward, the ship going ahead. A left-handed propeller is the opposite. The driving face of a blade is at the rear, the back of a blade is its forward side. The face is what acts on the water and gives the forward thrust.

PIPE AND FITTINGS

Pipe installation must provide for the conveyance of steam, hot and cold water, oil, air, refrigerating gases, chemicals used in fire fighting, and other materials, all at varying degrees of pressure and temperature.

Each complete installation is divided into separate sections, in accordance with what is to flow through the pipes.

Tracing. The first thing to be known about any pipe line is what is in it, and how to trace it.

Most pipe lines can be identified and traced by their color markings. Of these there are two distinct standard systems in use, with some ships or company fleets having their own systems. The new man should learn what system is in use, and should memorize it.

STANDARD PIPE LINE MARKINGS

Distinctive Markings for Piping, AMSC 16, Developed By American Marine Standards Committee

The markings consist of painting the edges of flanges adjacent to valves and of such other flanges on a pipe line as deemed necessary for convenient identification of the function of the pipe, also bands of distinctive colors on the pipe on each side of the flange.

Steam
    Supply, black on flange, 4″ white adjacent on each side.
    Exhaust, red on flange, 4″ white adjacent on each side.
Fuel Oil
    Suction, black on flange, 6″ red white red on each side.
    Delivery, red on flange, 6″ red white red on each side.
Common Suction and Delivery
    Red and black on flange, 6″ red white red on each side.

Ventilation
    Supply, black on flange, 4″ yellow on each side.
    Exhaust, red on flange, 4″ yellow on each side.
Pneumatic
    Black on flange, 4″ black on each side.
Fresh water
    Suction, black on flange, 4″ lead color on each side.
    Delivery, red on flange, 4″ lead color on each side.
Salt water
    Suction, black on flange, 4″ green on each side.
    Delivery, red on flange, 4″ green on each side.
Hot water
    Red on flange, 6″ lead green lead on each side.

NAVAL REQUIREMENTS FOR MARKING PIPING

Air
    Compressed: 1 yellow 2″ band.
    Ventilation: 2 yellow 1″ bands.
Fire extinguishers, other than water: 1 brown 2″.
Gas
    Refrigerant: 3 yellow 1″.
Hydraulic
    Power: 1 blue 2″.
    Control: 2 blue 1″.

Oil
    Fuel: 1 red 2″.
    Diesel (white D on red band): 1 red 2″.
    Gasoline: 2 red 1″.
    Lubricating: 3 red 1″.

Steam
    Supply: 1 black 2″.
    Exhaust: 2 black 1″.

Water drainage and Drains: 1 green 2″.

Fire: 2 green 1″.

Flushing, flooding, etc.: 3 green 1″.

Fresh water: 4 green 1″.

Brine: 5 green 1″.

Identification striping is painted on the piping as a circumferential band or bands, and of the color, width and number indicated above.

The bands are painted in conspicuous locations and at suitable intervals so that the lead of the piping may be easily followed.

Each line must have at least one striping designation in each compartment through which it passes.

Identification bands must not be placed on flanges, fittings, or valves.

The body of piping is painted the same color as that of the adjacent bulkheads and decks.

Galvanized metal pipe lagging is not painted or striped.

Vessels carrying both Diesel and boiler fuel oil have a white "D" stenciled on the band on Diesel fuel oil piping.

PIPING SAFETY PRECAUTIONS

To prevent water hammer, drain steam piping of water before admitting steam.

Before opening large steam valves, open bypasses to warm lines and equalize pressures; if bypasses are not fitted, crack valves.

Open trap bypasses when admitting steam to piping.

After remaking steam joint, tighten nuts after steam is turned on.

See that line is clear when breaking flange joints.

Do not use piping for hand or foot holds, or as hangers for chain hoists.

Secure copper and brass piping free from contact with bilges.

Keep inlet valve to reducing valves fully open.

Drain exposed auxiliary machinery and break drains to prevent freezing.

PIPING
General

Main Steam Pipes. Boilers to main engines. In use only when under way.

Auxiliary Steam Pipes. To these pipes connections are made for auxiliaries. No connections to main steam pipes.

Expansion Glands. Fitted in runs of piping to take up any expansion due to temperature changes.

Main Exhaust Pipe. Main engines to the main condenser.

Auxiliary Exhaust Pipe. Runs whole length of ship, with numerous connections. Carries return steam to condenser.

Main Feed Pipe. From main feed pump to feedwater heater and boilers.

Main Drain. Located under floor plates, on top of double bottoms, and used for draining hull of water in cases of emergency. Usually along starboard side of ship, with a branch to each circulating engine. Extends through machinery spaces, and can be operated from deck above if compartment is flooded.

Auxiliary Drain. Runs full length of ship on opposite side from main drain. All fire and bilge pumps connected to it, and the pipe itself has connections to any compartment in the ship.

Galvanic Action. Great care must be taken to avoid this reaction, which may be caused by proximity of copper or metal bilge pipes to the steel structure of the ship. It will be set up not only if copper, brass or lead are in contact with steel, but also if both are immersed in the same bilge or sea water.

VENTILATION SYSTEMS

It is considered that an average person requires 1800 cu. ft. of air per hour and for comfort the temperature and humidity must be considered. Air in living quarters should be changed every 5–10 minutes.

Ventilation may be by the supply system in which fresh air is drawn down ventilators by fans and discharged to compartments. The pressure is thus raised and foul air forced out.

In the exhaust system the pressure in the compartment is reduced and fresh air enters through the ventilators. The exhaust system is used where it is necessary to remove odors, smoke or gases.

Sometimes a combination of supply and exhaust is used in which case the two openings are placed as far away from each other as practical. As warm air rises exhaust openings are located near the deckhead while supply openings are near the deck.

An understanding of the ventilation system is important to a deck officer in case of fire.

BILGE, BALLAST, FIRE AND SANITARY SYSTEMS

The bilge drainage system removes water that may collect from sweating or other causes in the bilges, on tank tops, water tight flats, etc. This system may consist of a main suction line between engine and boiler rooms with an auxiliary line running fore and aft with branches to different compartments. These suction pipes have perforated nozzles at their ends to act as strainers.

Sluice valves are fitted in the boiler room and engine-room bulkheads. These may be opened to permit water from a flooded boiler room to run into the main suction to be pumped out.

An auxiliary suction line extends fore and aft along the tank top. It has connections to the fire and bilge pumps and also to the hand pumps with branches to the double bottoms and other compartments. Compartments not directly connected to this line are drained by sluice valves being operated from above the water-line.

In some ships pipes are run to every compartment and connected to a common manifold which is connected to the bilge or main condenser pump. By this means any compartment can be drained independently.

The main condenser circulating pump is fitted with an emergency bilge suction in the engine room so that it may be used as an emergency bilge pump in the event of rupture.

The ballast system comprises pipe lines to fore and aft peaks, double bottoms and deep tanks so fitted that these tanks may be filled with sea water when necessary for stability.

Pumps on the fire system may be used for other purposes provided one of the required pumps is kept available for immediate use on the fire system. However, no pump having a connection to an oil line can be used as a fire pump. Where two or more pumps are required they are not located in the same space. All fire line pipes on exposed decks are required to be protected against freezing or fitted with cutout valves so that the entire exposed piping system can be shut off and drained in cold weather. A deck officer should know where this drain is located.

It is not permissable to pipe salt and fresh water to the same fixture, if the fresh water system also conveys drinking water.

The fire main piping may be installed as either a single-line system or a loop system. *Risers* are pipes which extend from the main to upper levels. Pipes from the risers lead to fire-plugs.

The single line system consists of one line of piping running fore-and-aft. The loop system consists of two fore-and-aft runs of pipe separated by the width of the ship throughout their length, and joined together at their ends to form a loop.

In the event of damage, likely to be accompanied by fire, the location of cut-out valves (usually at water tight bulkheads) is important so that pressure on the fire line may not be lost through a ruptured main.

Heating systems are steam, electric or air conditioning.

Steam Heating may be either a one or two pipe system. The one pipe system has only one pipe to the radiators, the condensed steam draining back by gravity to a point of removal. The two pipe system has a supply line to the radiators and a return line from them to a tank from which it is pumped to the hot well or a feed tank. The two pipe system has a by-pass from the return to the condenser so that the radiators and pipe lines may be sucked dry in case the ship is laid up in freezing weather.

Electric Heaters have been installed in staterooms and living quarters of Diesel-electric and turbine-electric vessels.

Air Heaters may have steam or electricity as the source of heat connected to a fan that forces the heated air through ducts to the quarters to be heated.

Chapter 20

STEERING GEAR, WINDLASSES, CAPSTANS
AND GYPSIES

STEERING GEAR

When steam power for ship propulsion was introduced, it brought about many problems aboard vessels, the first and probably most important of which was to emphasize the inadequacy of hand-powered steering gear apparatus. The rapid increase in the size and speed of steamships resulted in a correspondingly greater turning effort required at rudder stocks. Therefore, it was only a natural sequence of events that led to the introduction of steam-powered steering gear.

Today all large commercial and naval vessels are equipped with power-driven steerers of either steam or electro-hydraulic design. Most large vessels are also arranged with an auxiliary hand-operated steering apparatus, either built into the power-driven steering gear or furnished as an entirely separate unit.

Inasmuch as the simple hand-operated steering apparatus is still used on small boats and as an auxiliary on larger vessels, a review of its operation is in order. Such a review should benefit students having no previous knowledge of this subject. Similarly, it will refresh the memory of those who at some time during their lives were employed aboard ship. Fig. 1 illustrates a typical hand-steering arrangement.

It will be noted that the principal parts include a steering wheel A with drum B, upon which the tiller lines C (or cables) wind and unwind as the wheel is turned by the helmsman. This causes a corresponding movement of the tiller quadrant D, which is rigidly fastened to the rudder stock.

The tiller lines are arranged on the drum B in such a manner that by turning the wheel A in one direction, say toward starboard, the corresponding shortening of the starboard cable will act on the rudder to bring the bow of the vessel to starboard. Turning the wheel A in the opposite direction will, of course, produce the opposite result, or swing the bow of the vessel to port. The tiller lines are supported on the required number of sheaves, which also serve to reduce cable friction as much as possible. To maintain adequate tension in the lines, turnbuckles are sometimes used to take up any slack likely to occur. This is necessary to insure the same movement of the quadrant as at the steering wheel.

The size of cables, steering wheel and drum depend upon the size of the ship and the type of service to be performed. When used as an auxiliary only, the type of service is, of course, a factor of lesser importance.

Fig. 2 shows a modification of the simple wheel and drum, and, while often employed as the only means of steering on barges and small tow-boats, its application as an auxiliary gear for poop-deck steering on larger river and bay boats is rather frequent.

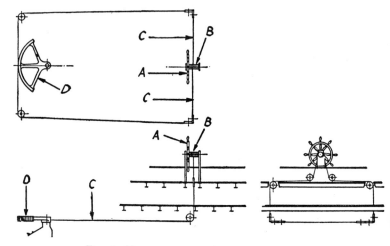

FIG. 1. HAND-STEERING ARRANGEMENT.

The principal advantage of this unit is the spur gear reduction which together with the large diameter steering wheel, permits a heavy pull with much less effort required, than on the simple wheel and drum previously described. The drum is grooved for wire rope, although it is replaced with a sprocket when tiller lines of chain are employed.

Referring to Fig. 2, pinion A, keyed to shaft B, meshes with and drives gear C, which is rigidly bolted to the grooved winding drum D. A fair-lead or sheave E is mounted on each shaft F and serves to properly guide the tiller line in the grooves of the drum. The fair-leads are free to revolve as well as move axially on their respective shafts.

A screw compressor brake (partially concealed) is also included in the unit, and permits holding the rudder in any desired position when maneuvering. The brake consists of a forged steel circular band G with a friction type lining, and which is brought to bear on the periphery of a flanged extension of the winding drum D. The band is operated through a toggle and screw arrangement by the handwheel H. Turning the wheel in one direction applies the brake and turning it in the opposite direction releases

The application of this gear may be more readily grasped by imagining it in place of the simple wheel and drum shown in Fig. 1.

Another type of hand-steering device which has been in use for many years and which has retained its popularity to this day on small vessels and barges, is Napier's Differential Screw Gear. This type gear is always linked directly to the tiller, there being no tiller lines required. Fig. 3

shows a typical design comprising a right- and left-hand threaded screw shaft A, mounted on the self-aligning bearing B and the bearing C, the screw shaft carrying the travelling nuts D and E. The bearing C is pivoted between the tiller casting F and the crosshead G so as to permit the tiller casting which is mounted on and rigidly fixed to the rudder stock H, to turn. The travelling nuts connect to the tiller casting by means of pairs of links K and L. As the screw shaft is revolved by the helmsman, the travelling nuts move toward or away from each other, according to the direction of rotation given the wheel M. Since the tiller casting F is con-

Fig. 2. Hand Steering Gear.

nected to the travelling nuts by the links K and L, it follows that the former turns accordingly, thereby causing the rudder to turn.

Usually, the unit is placed aboard the vessel with the bearing B aft of the rudder stock, in which case the helmsman stands at the side of the screw shaft A between the wheel M and tiller casting F. Under such conditions, the screw threads and the links are so arranged that when the helmsman turns the wheel M clockwise or to starboard, it causes the tiller casting F to turn counterclockwise, swinging the bow of the vessel to starboard. As the wheel M is turned counterclockwise, the tiller casting turns clockwise, thereby causing the bow of the vessel to swing to port. This type steering apparatus is also arranged with the steering-wheel end positioned aft of the rudder stock, thereby allowing the helmsman to stand directly behind the wheel.

FIG. 3. DIFFERENTIAL SCREW GEAR.

In view of the pitch angle of the threads on the screw shaft, the gear is non-overhauling. Consequently, it is not necessary for the helmsman to hold the wheel in position.

The screw gear is also used in some cases as an auxiliary hand gear with power-driven gears.

POWER-DRIVEN STEERING GEAR

The importance of the power-driven steering gear, as probably one of the most vital elements of mechanism aboard ships, cannot be overemphasized. It must be thoroughly dependable under all conditions of service and, therefore, must be both ruggedly built and as foolproof as possible. It must be of sufficient capacity and extremely responsive to the wishes of the helmsman so that maximum maneuverability is obtained. This is particularly necessary in docking and often in congested harbors and ship lanes where rapid changes in the direction of the ship must at times be made to avoid collision. Obviously these requirements cannot be met in the case of large vessels unless efficient and powerful power-driven steering gear is used.

It is not possible to classify steering gear of the steam or the electro-hydraulic type with respect to certain sizes or types of vessels. They are installed on ships of a wide range in tonnage including the largest afloat. Direct electric-driven steering gear, however, is generally confined to the medium- and smaller-sized vessels.

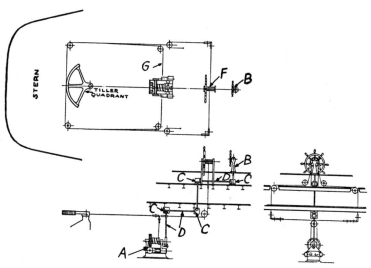

FIG. 4. TILLER LINE ARRANGEMENT WITH POWER STEERING GEAR.

Power steering gear in the medium and smaller type vessels is generally located where convenient and is, therefore, in many cases a considerable distance from the rudder stock. This is possible because the forces required to turn the rudder are of moderate magnitude and can, therefore, be readily transmitted by means of cable or chain. However, in the large commercial and naval vessels, this is not practical. The enormous turning effort required at the tiller would necessitate very heavy chain or cable, thereby resulting in cumbersome and impractical arrangements. In view of this, steering gear in large ships is in all cases located in the immediate region of the rudder, obviating the necessity for cable or chain between gear and tiller. Therefore, it might be said that power steering gear for medium- and smaller-sized vessels is of the indirect type, requiring the use of tiller lines; and for large vessels it is of the direct-connected type, connecting directly to the tiller.

Fig. 4 shows a typical tiller line arrangement for medium and smaller vessels using power steering gear. It will be noted that it resembles very closely the hand-steering arrangement shown in Fig. 1 except that the power-driven steering unit A and steering station B is added. The steering unit shown is operated through sets of mitre gears C and shafting D which extend to the steering column B located just forward of the emergency handwheel and drum F. Often two or three steering stations are used to permit operation from various parts of the vessel. As an example, the vertical shaft leading to the steering column B in Fig. 4 might be extended vertically through the column to the deck above and connected to a second steering station at that point. A third steering station may also be found on the poop deck, in which case either horizontal length of shaft D would be extended aft and then vertically by means of additional mitre gears and shafting finally connecting to the steering station on the poop.

With the tiller-line arrangement, shown in Fig. 4, the steering engine is connected to the quadrant by a single purchase. When steering by power, the hand steering wheel and drum F may be unshackled or permitted to run, but when steering by hand, the power gear cables G must be unshackled, since the winding drum of the power gear is non-overhauling.

There are, of course, many other tiller-line arrangements in use. This is brought about by either the requirements of the particular design of steering gear apparatus used or the individual choice of the shipowner or builder. For example, a double-purchase arrangement may be employed. Such an arrangement allows the handwheel and drum or the engine to be made the standing part and, therefore, eliminates entirely the necessity for unshackling. In other words, when steering by power, the handwheel and drum is locked in the helm position, and when steering by hand the power drum is held. This type of arrangement is shown in Fig. 5.

On more modern boats, of medium size particularly, the auxiliary handwheel and drum is eliminated, the steering gear being designed so that the same steering column may be used for both hand- and power-steering. This is accomplished by means of a clutch built into the steering gear. Fig. 6 illustrates a drum type, steam steering gear in which this arrangement is incorporated, the jaw clutch located at G and a second clutch mounted on the drum shaft (not shown) serving to engage the engine for steam-steering or to disengage it for hand-steering. The clutch is operated by the separate handwheel B at the engine or by a chain or rope drive from the pilothouse. When operated from the pilothouse, the chain engages a sprocket (not shown) mounted immediately behind the wheel B. Shaft C leads to the steering column in the pilothouse or to other steering points on the ship.

Before proceeding further on the subject of power-type steering gear it will be well to bear in mind that any steering apparatus as a whole is generally constructed in three distinct parts; namely, the control gearing, the prime mover, and the rudder mechanism. The two latter items are self-explanatory but will be described later in connection with each type of steering gear covered.

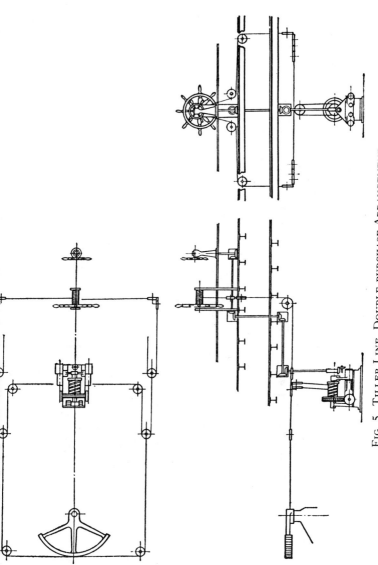

Fig. 5. Tiller Line, Double-purchase Arrangement.

The control gearing consists primarily of the steering station, the transmission lines and the follow-up mechanism. In Fig. 4, for example, the steering station is represented by B and the transmission lines by the sets of mitre gears C and shafting D. The follow-up mechanism consists of gearing and linkage, or a combination of both, and connects the transmission lines to the actuating valve or switch of the prime mover. It serves to maintain the movement of the rudder proportional with that of the steering wheel.

The steering station and transmission lines may be either of the strictly mechanical type, as referred to in Fig. 4, or of hydraulic or electric design. They are all applicable with practically any design of power-steering gear. When of hydraulic design, the hydraulic telemotor system, consisting of a transmitter and receiver unit connected by piping, is employed. This type is described at length in connection with the electro-hydraulic steering gear although, as mentioned, it is equally applicable to any other type

Fig. 6. Drum Type, Steam Steering Gear.

of power-driven steering gear. Steering stations and transmission lines of electric design are either of the contactor or synchronous type. The contactor type, known as the Sperry System consists of a transmitter and receiver unit connected to a contactor panel by electric wiring, the contactors being arranged to give step-by-step control of the receiver unit from the movement of the steering wheel at the transmitter unit. The synchronous type, known by the trade names *Selsyn, Synchro-Tie* and *Synchro-Lock,* consists essentially of two motors, one operated at the sending point as a generator and called the "transmitter," and one operated at the receiving point as a motor and known as a "receiver." Both units are connected by electric wiring, the transmitter and receiver operating in synchronism as the operator turns wheel (or knob) transmitter.

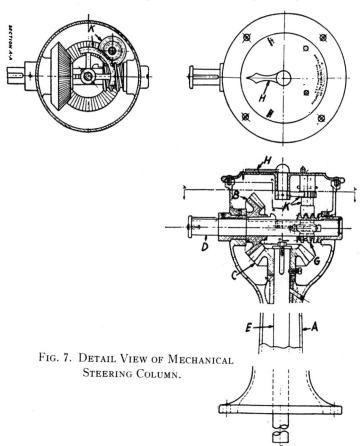

Fig. 7. Detail View of Mechanical Steering Column.

MECHANICAL-TYPE STEERING COLUMNS

Figs. 7 and 8 show the mechanical type of steering station, found on vessels of all sizes and types. It consists essentially of the column A within which the set of mitre gears B and C are mounted and keyed to their respective shafts D and E. Shaft D also carries the handwheel N as well as the small worm G. Movement of the handwheel N is transmitted to the actuating valve of the prime mover through the gears B and C and shaft E, the latter connecting to transmission lines of mitre gears and shafting as referred to in Fig. 4. On top of the column A, a dial and pointer H is provided to give the helmsman an indication of the rudder's position. The pointer is driven from the shaft D through the worm G and quadrant arrangement K. Obviously, any movement of the handwheel correspondingly changes the position of the pointer on the dial. The handwheel N is usually constructed of a built-up mahogany rim, with ash or locust spokes. The column A is made of non-magnetic material, generally bronze or brass, so as not to affect the accuracy of the compass. Of course, when the column is located at a point on the ship other than the pilothouse, the steering wheel may be of brass construction, when exposed to the elements.

Frequently, two steering stations are located one above the other; for instance, in the pilothouse and on the deck above (sometimes referred to as the flying bridge). In an arrangement of this nature, a steering column, as shown in Fig. 8 is employed in the pilothouse, and the type shown in Fig. 7 is placed on the flying bridge, the shaft E in Fig. 7 being extended down and fitted with the jaw clutch L in Fig. 8. The jaw clutch permits engaging or disengaging the two steering stations. When steering from the pilothouse, the jaw clutch L (Fig. 8) is disengaged so that the wheel on the upper steering station does not turn. When steering with the steering column on the flying bridge, the clutch L is engaged and the movement of the wheel is transmitted through the lower steering station to the steering gear. The steering wheel N in Fig. 8 which would be employed in the pilothouse column is provided with the pin M held in place by a spring to permit disengaging the wheel so that it will not turn when steering from the upper steering station.

INDIRECT-CONNECTED STEERING GEAR

The heavier type of steering gear, Fig. 9, illustrates a typical gear driven by a reversing-type, duplex steam engine. As with all drum-type steering gear, this unit connects to the tiller quadrant by means of wire cable or chain and is usually located either on the deck below the pilothouse or in the engine room of the vessel. Being arranged for power-drive only, it is employed in conjunction with a tiller line arrangement of the type illustrated in Fig. 4, which requires a separate gear for emergency hand operation.

The double-cylinder engine K drives the crankshaft L, having the cranks M opposite each cylinder set ninety degrees apart to avoid stalling when one crank is on dead center. Each cylinder is supplied with steam by a piston-type valve O which is actuated by the eccentric P. Worm R is also mounted on the crankshaft, and meshes with and drives worm wheel S, which is rigidly bolted to the flange Y of the winding drum T by the bolts U. Drum T is grooved to receive the tiller cables, the ends of which are fastened to the drum by the stud bolts V.

As with practically all modern steering gear installed on vessels today, this unit is equipped with a follow-up control mechanism. The function of the follow-up mechanism is to maintain the rudder movement proportional to the control-setting at the steering wheel; for example, similar to that obtained with the simple wheel and drum described in Fig. 1. To accomplish this on the steam steering gear, shown in Fig. 9, it is necessary to have the steam to the engine valves O controlled automatically so that the rudder movement produced by the engine is kept proportional to the movement given the steering wheel by the helmsman. Such control is

FIG. 8. STEERING COLUMN ARRANGED FOR CONNECTION TO COLUMN ON FLYING BRIDGE.

obtained through the use of a piston-type control valve X actuated by the steering wheel through a system of linkage and gearing, the valve X simultaneously responding to the movement of the winding. drum T, through gear E. The control valve supplies steam to both cylinders K through the valves O, and the ports are arranged in such a manner that when the piston of the control valve is in its mid-position, no steam flows to either cylinder; in other words, the engine is at rest. When the piston of the control valve is not in mid-position, steam flows to the cylinders and the engine operates. The follow-up mechanism is, therefore, arranged so that the control valve is not in mid-position so long as the steering wheel is moving (in either direction) but is brought to mid-position as soon as the wheel is brought to a halt.

FIG. 9. DRUM TYPE, STEAM STEERING GEAR.

Fig. 10 shows a diagrammatic view of the follow-up mechanism and may be used as a guide in the description of its operating principle which follows: The reference letters in Figs. 9 and 10 refer to the same parts.

Rotary motion is given to the shaft A from the rotation of the steering wheel in the pilothouse. The threaded shaft B, which is prevented from rotating by the follow-up gears E and F when the engine is at rest, is pulled endwise by the rotation of mitre gears C and D upon rotation of shaft A. Gear D, which is threaded to fit shaft B, is held longitudinally by the bearing G. This makes it a block through which the shaft B is drawn. The endwise motion of shaft B controls the opening of the control valve X which admits steam to the main valves of the engine cylinders. This endwise motion is transmitted to the piston rod of the control valve through the lever J and link H, the latter connecting to the piston rod of the control valve X.

Steam having been admitted to the cylinders during the turning of the shaft A, the revolving of the drum T rotating the follow-up gears E and F, returns the control valve to a neutral position when shaft A ceases to turn, thereby stopping the steam flow to main valves O and causing the steering engine to come to a stop. It is thus seen that the movement of the steering wheel in the pilothouse admits steam to the engine and the motion of the engine itself, through the gears E and F, cuts off the steam when the steering wheel is brought to a halt.

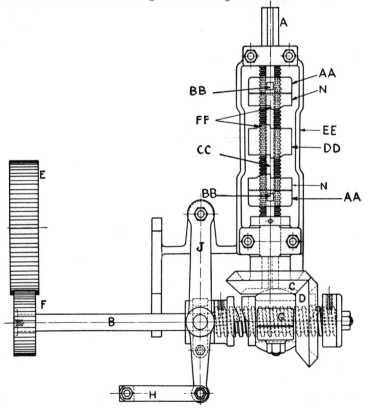

Fig. 10. Follow-up Mechanism of Steering Gear in Fig. 9.

Stops N are mounted on the vertical shaft A and are provided to regulate the number of turns of the steering wheel from hardover to hardover. These stops are screwed on the threaded portion of the shaft A and are, therefore, adjustable to agree with the distance the rudder should travel to prevent swinging the rudder beyond the hardover position, thus undue strains on the cable and connections between the rudder quadrant and the engine are avoided. The stops are held in their proper location by the collars AA which are fixed in position by the set screw BB seated in a slot CC provided on the shaft A. The collars AA are not screwed on the shaft A but are bored to slide over the threads. It will be noted that matched teeth are provided on the adjacent faces of the collars AA and the stops N, and serve to prevent the stops N from turning. The travelling nut DD, screwed on shaft A, is permitted to ride vertically between the stops N, but is prevented from turning on the shaft by means of an extension piece moving in a vertical slot at the rear of the housing EE. Obviously, the stops N are positioned on the shaft so that they are equidistant from the nut DD when the rudder is in the center or helm position.

When the shaft A is rotated by the steering wheel the nut DD moves up or down according to the direction in which the wheel is turned. By continuing to turn the wheel in one direction, the travelling nut will finally bear up against and clutch one of the stops N. In other words, further rotation of shaft A is prevented since the travelling nut itself cannot rotate. When this occurs, it indicates to the helmsman that the hardover position has been reached. It might be mentioned that the shoulders FF on the travelling nut DD and on the stops N make contact before the adjacent sides of each pair meet. This prevents whatever possibility of jamming might exist when turning the wheel in the opposite direction.

The number of turns of the steering wheel from hardover to hardover varies from 6 to 10 according to the size of the vessel and, in general, this applies regardless to the type of power-steering gear employed, assuming the steering-wheel form of control is used.

While the drum-type steering unit shown in Fig. 9 is designed for power operation only, it is also built with provision for hand-steering from the same steering column. Fig. 6 shows a gear of this type and of similar construction to the unit just described, except that clutches are incorporated to permit the two forms of operation. By turning the handwheel B in one direction, a clutch (not shown) mounted on the drum shaft disconnects the worm wheel from the winding drum E and through a system of linkage F a second clutch G engages the pinion A with the shaft H. When this has taken place, the unit is ready for hand operation, steering being effected from the pilothouse through the transmission shaft C which in turn drives the winding drum E through the set of bevel gears K, pinion A and spur gear L. When the handwheel B is turned in the opposite direction, the clutch mounted on the drum shaft engages the worm gear with the winding drum E and clutch G disengages pinion A, permitting it to run free on shaft H. The unit is then ready for power-drive, the engine operating a worm (not shown) which drives the winding drum E through worm gear P.

Fig. 11 shows another form of drum-type steering gear similar in construction and operation to the gear illustrated in Fig. 9 except that it is arranged for motor-drive. Clutches A and B engage or disengage the power-drive through the operation of the handwheel C at the unit or from the pilothouse by the use of chain transmission engaging the sprocket D.

The motor E drives the spur-gear reduction F which in turn drives the

FIG. 11. DRUM TYPE ELECTRIC STEERING GEAR.

worm wheel G through a worm (not shown). It will be observed that the unit in other respects is the same as that shown and described in Fig. 6, in so far as arrangement of gearing and clutches are concerned.

The motor is equipped with an electric brake H which stops the motor immediately upon the interruption of current. This is necessary to eliminate drift of the motor which would carry the rudder past the angle desired by the helmsman.

Fig. 12 illustrates a modern, electric-driven steering gear for small vessels. It is also of the indirect-connected type, requiring the use of tiller lines, and consists essentially of a grooved drum, a reduction gear and an electric motor. The motor frame A, either of open or totally enclosed construction, is attached through the adaptor piece B to the gear housing C The motor shaft drives a train of spur gears enclosed within the housing C, the slow-speed shaft end E extends through the housing and drives the winding drum F through the spur gears G and H.

Tiller lines of wire rope are employed on this type of gear and are fastened to the drum by the cleats J. Steering is accomplished from the pilothouse by the use of a master switch connecting to a contactor panel at the gear unit by electric wiring.

FIG. 12. ELECTRIC-DRIVEN STEERING GEAR FOR SMALL VESSELS.

DIRECT-CONNECTED TYPE STEERING GEAR

Napier's screw steering gear. This is probably the oldest form of gear used aboard ship and while it is gradually becoming obsolete in power-operated form, there are many applications still in use. Many naval vessels were at one time equipped with the screw steering gear. As mentioned previously, it is still widely employed in hand-operated form on small vessels and is also found as an auxiliary hand gear on some larger ships. For power operation, steam engines or electric motors are used.

Fig. 13 illustrates a typical gear arranged with steam-engine drive. Fig. 14 shows a diagrammatic plan view of the same gear. The letter designations in both figures refer to the same parts.

The unit consists essentially of a double-cylinder, reversing-type steam engine driving a right- and left-hand threaded screw shaft through a spur gear reduction. Provision for auxiliary hand steering is also incorporated through the use of a manually-operated jaw clutch which permits disengaging the power drive. On the particular gear illustrated in Fig. 13, a hydraulic-telemotor type of transmission is employed when steering by power, the receiver unit of which is shown located in the foreground. A follow-up mechanism is also incorporated in the steering gear and serves to maintain the rudder movement proportional to the movement given the steering wheel by the pilot.

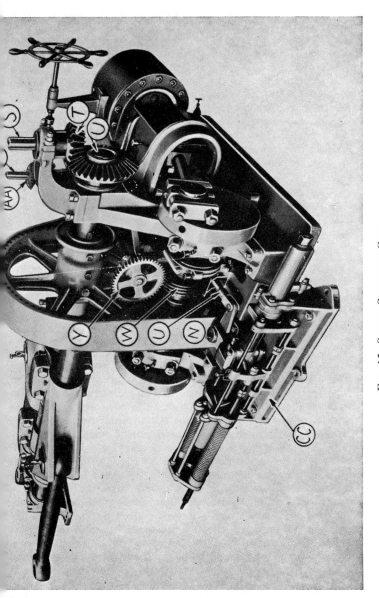

Fig. 13. Screw Steering Gear.

Referring to Fig. 13, the right- and left-hand screw shaft A is supported by the bearings B and C upon which the two travelling nuts D and E move with respect to each other. The nuts are mounted on the guide rods F which also prevent them from turning with the screw shaft. Attached to each travelling nut is the link G, the opposite end of which connects to one side of the double-pronged tiller H sometimes referred to as a crosshead, the latter being rigidly connected to the rudder stock K. Revolving the screw shaft A in one direction causes the travelling nuts to move toward each other and revolving the shaft in the opposite direction results in the movement of the travelling nuts away from each other. Since the crosshead H is connected to the nuts D and E through links G, it is obvious that any movement of the nuts will in turn cause the rudder stock K and, therefore, the rudder itself, to revolve.

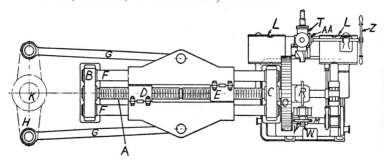

FIG. 14. PLAN VIEW OF GEAR IN FIG. 13.

The engine L drives the crankshaft M upon which a spur pinion (concealed in casing N, Fig. 13) is mounted. This pinion meshes with and drives the spur gear O which is free to turn on the screw shaft A, when the jaw clutch R is in the disengaged position. In other words, the engine may be disconnected from the screw shaft A to permit steering by hand, through the transmission shaft S and bevel gears T and U. To steer by power, the clutch R is engaged with the spur gear O as shown in Fig. 14. The power is, therefore, transmitted from the engine to the screw shaft A through the spur-gear reduction O and the jaw clutch R.

When steering by power the engine is operated from the pilothouse by a hydraulic telemotor, the receiver unit CC of which connects to a piston-type control valve T at the engine through the rod U (Fig. 13). As the steering wheel is turned, its motion is transmitted through the receiver and the rod U which opens the control valve, thereby starting the engine. As the engine starts, the worm W on the crankshaft M engages the worm wheel Y transmitting its motion to the control valve in such manner as to return the valve to its neutral position, hence causing the engine to stop when the steering wheel comes to a halt. In other words, so long as the steering wheel is moving, the engine continues to operate, but as soon as the wheel is stopped, the engine, by virtue of the follow-up mechanism (W and Y), is also stopped. It is, therefore, seen that this mechanism automatically maintains the movement of the rudder proportional to the movement given the steering wheel by the helmsman.

The handwheel Z, sometimes referred to as the trick-wheel, is provided to permit operation in the steering-engine compartment during emergencies or for convenience when adjustments in the unit are necessary. The handwheel connects to the control valve through the bevel gears AA and other gears (not shown) and is, of course, used in connection with the power-drive only. In addition to the hydraulic-telemotor system, a mechanical-transmission system of shafting and sets of mitre gears are sometimes used with the power-drive in which case connection is made with the shaft at BB leading to the control valve of the engine.

With this type of steering gear there is usually no provision in the mechanism for absorbing excessive rudder shock, consequently, it is necessary that the construction of the screw-gear portion of the machine must be as rugged as possible.

ELECTRIC SCREW STEERING GEAR

Fig. 15 illustrates a screw steering gear arranged for electric-motor drive. The principle of operation of this gear is, of course, similar to that just described, except that an electric motor replaces the steam engine. The motor A drives through the double-spur reduction gear B and C to

FIG. 15. SCREW STEERING GEAR WITH ELECTRIC DRIVE.

operate the screw shaft D. The clutch E is provided to permit operation of the screw by either the power-drive or by hand, similar to that described for the steam-operated gear.

The gear shown is of the non-follow-up type and is controlled through a master switch in the pilothouse.* It is also found in the follow-up type,

---

* An electric brake is incorporated to eliminate drift of the motor as the electric current is cut off during steering operations.

in which case a controller designed on the differential principle, rotates against the direction of the screw shaft, so that when the steering wheel is halted, the screw shaft itself, by actuating the controller differential gearing, shuts off the current.

QUADRANT-TYPE STEERING GEAR

Of the mechanical-type, direct-connected, power-driven steering gears used on large vessels, the Wilson Pirrie Quadrant Steerer appears to be the most common.

Fig. 16 shows a typical gear of this design. It will be noted that dual-

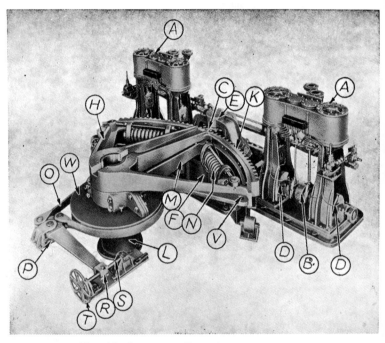

FIG. 16. QUADRANT TYPE STEERING GEAR.

engine drive is used; either engine being held in reserve as a spare drive. The power unit may be arranged either athwartship, as shown, or fore and aft; also dual-drive combinations of one steam and one electric motor, or two electric motors can be used. Steam engines of either horizontal or vertical type may be employed.

Referring to Fig. 16, the double-cylinder, reversing-type steam engines A drive the crankshaft B, the cranks D being set 90 degrees apart to insure rotation. The crankshaft B carries a worm which drives the vertical shaft E through a worm wheel. The worm and worm wheel are enclosed in the oil-tight case F, and are, therefore, not visible. Upon shaft **E** is mounted the pinion **C** which meshes with and drives the quadrant **H** through the rack **K**. The quadrant is freely mounted on the rudder stock **L** and is connected to the tiller **M** through the buffer springs **N**. The tiller **M** is, of course, rigidly connected to the rudder stock. In other words, the quadrant, being freely mounted on the rudder stock, operates the tiller through the buffer springs which serve to relieve any excess rudder shock, thereby preventing damage to the gear mechanism. This flexible arrangement permits the use of a positive drive and is the principal feature of the quadrant type of gear.

FIG. 17. QUADRANT TYPE STEERING GEAR COMMON ON LIBERTY SHIPS.
(Sumner Iron Works)

Hand-operated rudder brakes are also incorporated, and are a requirement of the American Bureau of Shipping for all ocean-going vessels. The brake shown in Fig. 16 is of the screw-compressor type and consists of a forged-steel band O operated through the toggle and lever arrangement P by the threaded nut R, travelling on the screw shaft S. Turning the handwheel T in one direction tightens the brake band O around the large disc W. which is rigidly connected to the rudder stock. The purpose of the rudder brake is, of course, to provide a means for locking the rudder in position when the vessel's steering apparatus has become disabled and is primarily used in emergencies of this kind.

The control gearing usually includes a follow-up type of mechanism. With the particular gear shown in Fig. 16, a positive automatic follow-up mechanism, similar to that described in Fig. 10, is employed, including adjustable-limit stops to regulate the number of turns of the steering wheel from hardover to hardover.

Any type of steering station may be employed with the quadrant steerer. Many units are equipped with the mechanical-steering station illustrated in Fig. 7 with transmission lines of mitre gears and shafting. Also, the Hydraulic Telemotor System and electrical-control systems of contactor or synchronous design, are employed on gears of this type.

With the quadrant-type steerer, an independent gear is required for emergency hand-steering, or sometimes relieving-tackle is employed. In the latter case, the tackle is attached to the lugs V at each side of the quadrant, provisions existing whereby the entire gear unit, including the pinion C, may be moved clear of the quadrant rack. The quadrant is then free to swing through the use of relieving-tackle.

Fig. 17 shows a quadrant-type steering gear employed on many "Liberty" ships. It will be noted that it is similar to that shown in Fig. 16, except that only one vertical-type engine is used. The rudder brake shown consists of the lever arm A carrying a friction block which bears against the grooved segment B by turning the handwheel C. The rudder is thus locked in position or released through operation of the wheel.

ELECTRO-HYDRAULIC STEERING GEAR

In view of its many advantages over all other types, the electro-hydraulic steering gear has become increasingly popular in recent years and is employed on vessels covering a wide range in tonnage, including the largest afloat. Many gears of the electro-hydraulic type are installed on U. S. Maritime Cargo Ships, and may also be found on most modern naval vessels, of the destroyer size and above.

The electro-hydraulic steering gear, using a radial piston pump, was first introduced in the U. S. about 20 years ago. Its development was largely due to the Hele-Shaw pump, an English invention brought to this country about the year 1917 and manufactured by the American Engineering Company.

It is unquestionably the most efficient method of steering, and requires not only a minimum of power to perform its work, but is extremely responsive and reliable in operation. In addition to the fact that it comprises fewer working parts, is much lighter in weight and requires less headroom than other types of equal capacity, its inherent design characteristics permit many arrangements of the cylinders, pumps and control equipment to suit the space requirements of the particular vessel.

The electro-hydraulic steering gear is built in both direct- and indirect-connected form. Since the principles governing the operation of most types are practically the same, only those connecting direct to the tiller and as usually found on larger vessels will be described.

Fig. 18 shows a steering gear with Hele-Shaw hydraulic system used on many commercial vessels. The unit comprises a double-ended ram A operating between two opposed hydraulic cylinders B and C and driven by either of two prime movers, each consisting of a constant-speed motor D driving a variable-delivery reversible hydraulic pump E. The ram moves axially into and out of the opposed cylinders B and C through the medium of fluid power (oil under pressure), the fluid being forced into one cylinder causing the ram to move toward and into the opposite cylinder. Since the entire system is filled at all times, the fluid in the opposite cylinder is returned to the pump for delivery to the first cylinder. By reversing the stroke of the pump the operation is reversed, hence the ram moves in the opposite direction.

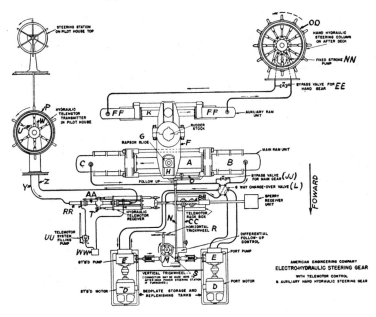

FIG. 18. ELECTRO-HYDRAULIC STEERING GEAR, DIAGRAMMATIC VIEW.

The movement of the ram is transmitted to the rudder stock through the tiller F having a sliding insert G—an arrangement known as a Rapson Slide. The insert (or shoe) is connected to the ram A and operates in the slot H provided in the tiller, thereby providing a progressive increase in leverage as the maximum rudder angle is approached. It will be noted that the tiller is of double-pronged design to permit connection in the same manner to the auxiliary hand-steering ram K.

Two pumping units are usually incorporated, as shown; either one can be used for regular steering, while the second unit serves as a spare. Each pumping unit is of equal capacity, and capable of supplying the required amount of power to operate the rudder under maximum conditions. The pump in use and its electric motor run continuously in one direction while the vessel is under way.

Quick change over from one pumping unit to the other can be made by operation of the 6-way valve L. All piping from both pumps is connected to the valve, and from this point one line leads to each main cylinder as shown. The valve may be operated manually from the steering-gear compartment or by electrical means from the pilothouse.

Practically all electro-hydraulic steering gear used in medium and larger-size vessels is equipped with follow-up control mechanisms. As mentioned previously in connection with the drum-type steerer in Fig. 9, the purpose of the follow-up control is to maintain the movement of the rudder closely in step with the steering wheel. In the case of the steering unit shown in Fig. 18, this mechanism consists essentially of a differential gear and cam arrangement (enclosed in the housing M) which serves to control the discharge of oil from either of the pumps E, to the cylinders B and C. This mechanism is actuated by the steering wheel to place the pump on stroke, and simultaneously responds to the movement of the steering ram A through the follow-up shaft N to return the pump to a neutral or no-discharge position after steering wheel is brought to a halt. In other words, while the steering wheel P is in motion the pump is on stroke and fluid is forced into one steering cylinder and out of the opposite one, thereby resulting in movement of the ram A. After wheel is brought to a halt, the pump is returned to a no-discharge position the moment the ram reaches the position established by the steering wheel. It should be noted that movement of the ram is continuously transmitted to the control box M through a pinioned shaft N (or follow-up), engaging a rack O attached to and moving with the steering ram A. This rack O may be more clearly seen in the shop view of the gear in Fig. 28.

The control mechanism M has storage motion characteristics in that the steering wheel may be turned faster than the ram is moving, and also in that only a slight movement of the wheel places the pump on stroke. Large steering gear is designed so that the rudder can be moved from hardover to hardover (through an angle of approximately 70°) in 30 seconds and requiring approximately 10 revolutions of the steering wheel. With this type of control, the wheel can be turned within this range in less time than it takes the rudder to move through the same distance. This is a very desirable feature, as it allows the helmsman reasonable freedom, insofar as the speed at which he can turn the wheel is concerned. For instance, assuming the telemotor wheel P and rudder is at hard-aport and it is desired to move it over to hard-astarboard in the shortest interval of time, the helmsman may turn the wheel as fast as he can until the telemotor dial indicator shows hard-astarboard. While the rudder started to move with the steering wheel it did not reach the hard-astarboard position until after the steering wheel had reached it. In other words, the rudder movement lagged behind the steering wheel, and it was not necessary for the pilot to limit the speed of the wheel to the corresponding speed at which the rudder was turning.

The steering gear shown in Fig. 18 can also be operated from the steering-gear compartment or from the after deck as indicated by the horizontal and vertical trick wheels R and S respectively. These connect to the follow-up control mechanism, and are provided with clutches to permit disengagement of either or both when not in use.

FIG. 19. ELECTRO-HYDRAULIC GEAR TRANSMITTER UNIT.

Relief valves (not shown) are fitted in the hydraulic system, and act to prevent damage to any part of the gear, should excessive rudder shock occur. Assuming sudden shock does occur, the relief valve opens, thereby permitting the discharge of oil from the cylinder under excessive pressure, and therefore permitting the rudder and ram to change their position. The moment this change occurs, it is transmitted through the follow-up shaft N and mechanism M to the pump, and pumping action starts as soon as the stress is relieved, thereby returning the rudder to its position as established by the steering wheel before the shock occurred. Obviously, the valve is a very vital part of the apparatus, as it provides positive relief and complete recovery from shock, by virtue of the follow-up mechanism incorporated in the gear.

The steering gear is controlled from the pilothouse by a hydraulic telemotor system. As mentioned previously, this system is applicable to most other types of power steering gears, and is widely employed on medium and large-size vessels. It consists essentially of a transmitter unit Fig. 19, located in the pilothouse, and a receiver unit Fig. 20, placed at the steering gear, the transmitter merely serving to transmit the instructions of the helmsman to the steering gear via the receiver. The transmitter and receiver are connected together by copper tubing, as shown in Fig. 18, there being no hydraulic connection whatsoever with the main hydraulic pumping system.

The transmitter unit, Fig. 19, comprises two plungers, each operating in the vertical cylinders U and W, and driven through rack and pinion gearing (not shown), and an internal gear PP from the steering wheel P. The receiver unit, Fig. 20, consists of a double-ended ram AA

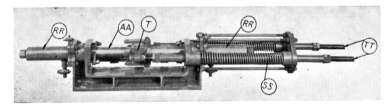

FIG. 20. HYDRAULIC TELEMOTOR RECEIVER UNIT.

operating in two opposed horizontal cylinders RR. Heavy coil springs SS are incorporated in the receiver unit to assist in bringing the ram AA promptly to the center position when the steering wheel is returned to midship.

The receiver ram AA is arranged with a crosshead T, which serves to transmit the movement of the steering wheel P to the control mechanism at the steering gear through the rods TT, the rack BB and the pinioned shaft CC.

Referring to Fig. 18, the operation of the telemotor system is as follows:

Turning the steering wheel P in the direction of the arrow, plunger

U in the transmitter unit is depressed and the plunger W rises. Since the entire system is filled with fluid, it follows that the fluid displaced by plunger U is forced through the copper tubing Y into cylinder RR of the receiving unit, thereby causing a corresponding movement of the receiver ram AA. The receiver ram in turn transmits its movement to the steering-gear control mechanism M, through the rack BB and pinioned shaft CC. Obviously, as the steering wheel P is turned in the opposite direction, the cylinder W is depressed, causing ram AA of the receiver unit to reverse its direction of movement, and in turn causing the pinioned shaft CC to revolve in the opposite direction.

The telemotor system also includes an automatic equalizing and replenishing valve DD, Fig. 19, which equalizes the system every time the steering wheel passes the helm position, and at the same time supplies sufficient fluid to maintain the system in a solid condition. This valve is served by a supply tank referred to in the manufacturer's instructions accompanying Fig. 21.

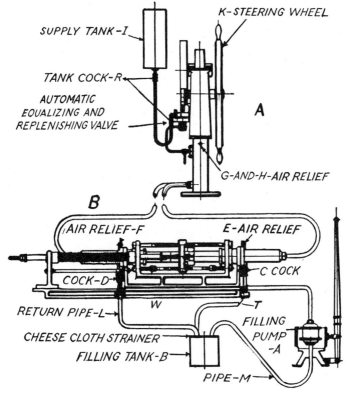

FIG. 21. INSTALLATION DIAGRAM OF RE-CENTERING TELEMOTOR.
A. FORWARD TELEMOTOR.   B. AFTER TELEMOTOR.
SEE OPERATING INSTRUCTIONS ON NEXT PAGE.

The telemotor system also incorporates a hand-operated filling pump UU diagrammatically indicated in Fig. 18. This pump is used when nlling the system and is located at the steering gear together with a suitable filling tank WW.

The manufacturer's instructions for installing, filling and placing the telemotor in operation accompany Fig. 21. It might be mentioned that the telemotor described in this section is of the outside-packed type, obviating the necessity of disassembling the unit when repacking. Telemotors of the inside-packed type are also found on shipboard.

In addition to the hydraulic telemotor system of control, many vessels are also equipped with the Sperry unit, which is of electrical design and is usually provided with the extremely valuable "Iron Mike," by which a set course can be automatically maintained. The Sperry unit is of the contactor type, and consists of a transmitter and receiver unit connected to a contactor panel by electric wiring. The contactors are arranged to give step-by-step control of the receiver unit from the movement of the steering wheel at the transmitter. The receiver is shown in Fig. 18 connected to the opposite end of the telemotor rack BB. Provisions for engagement or disengagement of either the telemotor or the Sperry unit are in the steering gear compartment.

A smaller double-ended ram arrangement is provided aft of the rudder stock, as shown, and is operated through the use of a small Hele-Shaw fixed stroke pump NN, receiving its power from the helmsman as he turns the steering wheel OO. This arrangement is provided for auxiliary

---

INSTRUCTIONS FOR INSTALLING, FILLING, AND OPERATING THE RE-CENTERING TELEMOTOR FOR OPERATING STEERING GEAR
(Refer to Fig. 21)

General:

1) In the installation of piping, avoid locations where temperature varies greatly during 24 hours—avoid proximity to hot pipes and the engine room where possible. Pipes should not run over the top of boilers or superheaters or close to smokestacks.

2) Run the pipe line as straight as possible, avoiding sharp bends and pockets which form air traps and increased friction of moving liquid. Care should be taken to avoid reduction of area of pipes at bends. The bottom of supply tank should be not less than 36" above the highest point of pipe line. The return pipe L should end 2" above the top of filling tank. The pipe line should not be brazed, as this practice tends to cause reduction of pipe area and fragments of solder in pipe line. Brazing also prevents disconnection of pipe to remove obstructions.

3) On ships which are to work in tropical climates where extreme heat may be expected the system should be filled with clean, fresh water, whereas in colder climates glycerine should be added as per following schedule:

Freezing Point	Glycerine	Freezing Point	Glycerine
+15°F.	30%	— 5°F.	50%
+ 5°F.	40%	—20°F.	55%
		—30°F.	60%

Any mixture over 60% glycerine is too thick to operate properly. Telemotor liquid starts to congeal at about 15°F. In temperate climate use of at least 30% glycerine is advisable. It adds body and lubricating qualities to liquid.

Filling:

4) Regardless of composition of liquid, it is essential that it be free from dirt or foreign matter, and must be strained through several layers of cheesecloth before entering the filling tank. Water should be passed freely through the system from the top down until it is thoroughly cleansed of dirt and small particles before filling with liquid to be used in system. The filling tank is to be kept at least two-thirds full so that no air will be drawn through the pump.

5) Always fill the system from the lowest point which should be the after end. Fill the filling tank **B** with the liquid to be used in the system and have at hand an extra bucket of strained liquid to replenish the supply in the filling tank.

Next, open cocks **C** and **D** on after telemotor, place a man at hand pump and proceed to pilothouse. Close cock **R** under supply tank, set steering wheel **K** on center, which will open automatic equalizing valve. Returning to after telemotor, have pump operated. The liquid will pass through one side of system, through by-pass valve and then through opposite side of system to filling tank through return pipe **L**. By closing cock **D** the system would be quickly filled, but it is well to consider elimination of air at this time. Open cock **D** wide to observe that a full volume of liquid passes through system. Next, gradually close cock **D** and have pumping operation continue until there are no air bubbles visible in liquid flowing into filling tank. Finally, close cocks **C** and **D** and system will be filled.

6) The supply tank **I** can be filled by hand or by means of hand pump by the following operation, after the system has been filled by method as described above. Open cock **C** and equalizing valve, by putting steering wheel in central position, and tank cock **R**. By operation of hand pump the liquid will be pumped up into supply tank. Take care not to overflow the tank. Next close cock **C**, having tank cock **R** open. If the system is free from air, the telemotor is in condition for operation. Tank cock **R** should be open at all times except during filling operation.

Elimination of air from system:

7) All the air must be eliminated from the system to permit telemotor to operate and function properly. A thorough test under pressure should be made for air leaks at all the cocks, valves, pipe union couplings, and at forward and after telemotor packing. This packing should be set up just tight enough to prevent leaks. If too tight at forward telemotor, it makes movement of wheel difficult; or if too tight at after telemotor, it will prevent centering springs from bringing telemotor to absolute center.

8) If air is present in system after the filling operation, it can be detected by movement of steering wheel to port and starboard. Air can then be located in one side of system or the other, or in both sides, by failure of after telemotor to respond to movement of wheel. Air is generally expelled through the forward end, as this is the high point.

9) With the system filled, tank cock **R** open, and by-pass valve opened by placing steering wheel in central position, alternately open and close air relief cocks **G** and **H** on forward telemotor, to allow the collected air to escape through the cocks. Repeat this operation as long as there is evidence of air in the system, the liquid passing through cocks to be returned to supply tank. If, by movement of steering wheel, the liquid is found "solid," telemotor is ready for operation.

10) If air still exists in the system, open automatic equalizing valve by placing steering wheel in central position; and with tank cock **R** open, alternately open air relief cocks **E** and **F** on after telemotor, closing cocks as air ceases to flow.

11) If above methods fail to remove all the air from system it will be necessary to install pipes as shown in dot-and-dash lines **W** and **T** so that the pump can be connected to both cylinders. Liquid can then be pumped up through either side of system.

To expel air by this method, open the air cocks **G** or **H** on forward telemotor, on the side on which there is the greater quantity of air, then pump slowly until several buckets of liquid have passed through the cock. Repeat this operation on other side of system.

Leaks:

12) Leaks in the piping system should be eliminated both on account of loss of liquid and to allow accurate functioning between forward and after telemotor. It is essential that, when filling the system, all small particles are eliminated from the telemotor piping.

---

hand-steering purposes. The steering wheel and pump are connected through an inverse spur-gear reduction HH illustrated in Fig. 22, the entire unit being mounted on a hollow bed plate which serves as an oil reservoir.

The operating principle is simple. As the helmsman turns the wheel in one direction the pump forces oil into one of the cylinders FF (Fig. 18) resulting in the movement of the ram K and the simultaneous discharge of oil from the opposite cylinder. This action is reversed as the helmsman turns the wheel in the opposite direction, since the Hele-Shaw pump is of the reversible type. It is, of course, important that the main or power-driven steering apparatus is disconnected before the hand-operated ram is brought into use. This is accomplished by opening the by-pass valve JJ incorporated in the piping to the large rams and closing the valve EE in the lines of piping to the small cylinders. The power drive should also be shut down before the valves are operated. To steer under power drive the valve EE should, of course, be opened and the valve JJ closed.

Fig. 22. Auxiliary Hand Gear Steering Column.

There are also two relief valves BBB and two check valves CCC (Fig. 22), the former serving to prevent damage to the mechanism, due to excessive rudder shock, and the latter to permit the introduction of the necessary oil to the system to replace any loss through leakage. Since the reversible-type pump discharges through either of the flanges AAA, one relief and one check valve are required in each pipe line.

The Hele-Shaw pumping unit is, of course, an important element in the electro-hydraulic type of steering gear and, as mentioned previously, has been largely responsible for the development of the gear. The design and principle of operation of the pump should therefore be included in this discussion.

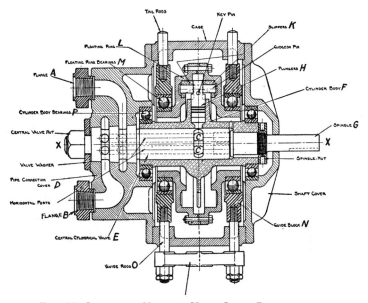

FIG. 23. SECTIONAL VIEW OF HELE-SHAW PUMP.

Fig. 23 shows a sectional view of the pump's construction and also gives the names of the various parts, referred to in the following.

Oil is drawn into and discharged from the pump, through the flanges A and B mounted on the pipe connection cover D, in which is located a stationary central cylindrical valve E. The central valve is equipped with ports C which serve to transmit the fluid to and from the rotating cylinder body F. The cylinder body, mounted and free to turn on the cylindrical valve E, is supported by ball bearings P, and is rotated through the spindle G by the electric motor D (Fig. 18). In the periphery of the cylinder body, steel plungers H, usually 7 in number, are mounted. The end of each plunger carries a pair of slippers K, the outer faces of which are shaped to ride in the floating ring L.

This floating ring is in turn mounted on two large ball bearings M situated on each side of the cylinder body, the outer races of these bearings being fitted in the guide blocks N. Guide rods O connect to the guide blocks and extend out through the case of the pump, and serve as the means to change the position of the floating ring with respect to the axis X-X of the pump. Therefore, by moving the guide rods in either direction, the stroke of the plungers H is altered, which changes the rate of discharge of the pump.

Fig. 24 shows a descriptive view of the Hele-Shaw pump with all parts in approximate relation to each other. Fig. 25 also shows a cutaway section of the assembled pump.

To illustrate the principle of the Hele-Shaw pump, a series of line drawings appear in Fig. 26. It will be noted that only one plunger is shown in these diagrams, for the purpose of simplicity, although there are usually 7 equally spaced about the periphery of the floating ring. Diagram A shows the floating ring in the neutral position, that is, the axis of the floating ring coincides with the axis of the pump. In this position, as the cylinder body rotates, no pumping action occurs, since the

FIG. 24. "EXPLODED" VIEW OF HELE-SHAW PUMP.
(Pump case not shown.)

PARTS LIST

1. Central cylindrical valve
2. Valve washer
3. Cylinder body
4. Spindle
5. Spindle nut
6. Floating ring bearing
7. Plunger
8. Slippers
9. Floating ring
10. Cylinder body bearing
11. Guide block
14. Pipe connection cover
15. Shaft cover

plunger remains at a constant distance from the stationary central valve during the rotation.

In diagram B the floating ring has been moved to the right, causing the plunger, as it rotates toward the right side, to move toward the center or axis of the pump; and as it rotates to the right side, it is moving away from the axis of the pump. Accordingly, during the upper half of the rotation from X to Y, the piston is moving away from the central valve and produces the suction stroke, sucking oil into the cylinder body. During the other half of the revolution, or from Y to X, as shown in diagram C, the plunger is being forced in toward the central valve, thereby discharging the oil it sucked in. It is therefore seen that pump suction occurs in the upper port of the central valve and discharge occurs through the lower port of the central valve.

Diagram D shows the action that would take place when the pump is stroked in the opposite direction, or to the left. Of course, when this occurs the suction and discharge ports are reversed and suction from the bottom port and discharge from the upper port of the valve is obtained.

It will therefore be seen that moving the crosshead indicated in Fig. 23 toward or away from the axis of the pump effects a change in the relationship of the floating ring with respect to the pump's axis X-X, causing a corresponding change in the discharge as well as the direction

FIG. 25. CUT-AWAY VIEW OF HELE-SHAW PUMP.

of flow of the fluid. The crosshead in Fig. 23 is also clearly shown in Fig. 18, and it will be noted that it connects to, and is actuated by, the differential follow-up control mechanism.

Since the essential elements in the electro-hydraulic steering gear have now been described, it will be well to review its operation. Arrows indicated on Fig. 18 show the movement of the steering wheel, flow of oil and movement of rams to give left rudder, or in other words, to swing the bow of the vessel to port. Also, the 6-way change-over valve L is arranged to permit use of the starboard pumping unit. It will be noted

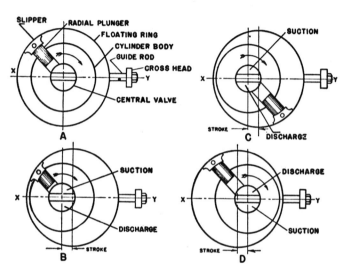

FIG. 26. DIAGRAMS ILLUSTRATING THE OPERATION OF THE HELE-SHAW PUMP.

that a steering column of the mechanical type shown in Figs. 6 & 7 is located on top of the pilothouse with shaft extended and connecting to the wheel P of the telemotor transmitter, thereby permitting telemotor operation from either the pilothouse or the pilothouse top.

Therefore, standing at either steering station, counterclockwise rotation of the wheel causes plunger U in the telemotor transmitter to be depressed and plunger W to rise, thereby moving the fluid to and from the telemotor receiver, in the direction of the arrows on the pipe lines Y and "Z". As a result, the receiver ram AA moves to the port side, causing the rack BB to actuate the control mechanism M (through the rotation of the pinioned shaft CC), in such a manner that the operating pump is placed on stroke, discharging oil to the steering cylinder B. The ram A then moves to starboard, the oil from cylinder A returning to the pump for delivery to cylinder A. Both cylinders have the same area; therefore the same quantity of oil returns to the pump from one cylinder that is pumped to the opposite cylinder, neglecting any slight amount of leakage. To maintain the system full of oil at all times, check valves are incorporated similar to the arrangement on the hand gear in Fig. 22. It should be borne in mind that the steering wheel P during this action is still being turned and the ram A is still moving, also that the movement of the ram is continuously followed by the control mechanism M through the shaft N.

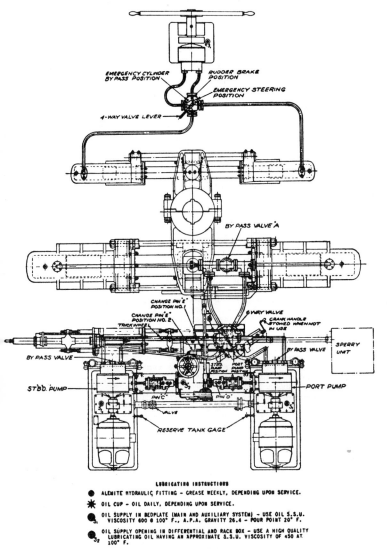

FIG. 27. OPERATION AND LUBRICATION DIAGRAM OF THE ELECTRO-
HYDRAULIC STEERING GEAR SYSTEM.
SEE OPERATING INSTRUCTIONS ON NEXT PAGE.

Assuming that the steering wheel is now brought to a halt, the ram A and therefore the follow-up shaft N continue to operate until the pump is returned to neutral through the differential control mechanism M acted upon by the shaft N.

It is therefore seen that the motion of the steering wheel places the pump on stroke and moves the ram, while the motion of the ram through the operation of the follow-up shaft N returns the pump to the no-discharge position when the steering wheel is brought to a halt.

Turning the telemotor steering wheel in the opposite direction obviously reverses the foregoing operation; all arrows shown in Fig. 18 also change their direction, except those indicating the rotation of the pump E and motor D. It should be noted that, even though the rudder is at rest and the pump is in the neutral or no-discharge position, the pump and motor nevertheless run continuously and in one direction at all times during steering operations.

OPERATING INSTRUCTIONS

(Refer to Fig. 27.)

Steering gear can be operated by either pump unit.

Make certain that motors run in direction as indicated by arrows on the pumps.

The small by-pass valve on the make-up piping on the pump should be kept closed, and opened only to by-pass oil.

Expel air from system by opening air cocks alternately on piping under pressure, opening cock when ram moves.

Move 6-way valve to port position, then to starboard position, to permit oil to flow into hydraulic pumps by turning crank handle to either pump.

Make certain that the stops on the differential control box and after hydraulic telemotor are set to correspond to the rudder working angle.

Keep pins C and D in at all times.

Keep pin E in at all times except when operating by trickwheel.

Keep clutch on forward telemotor disengaged except when operating from pilothouse top.

Operating either power unit, close by-pass valve A in main piping; turn 4-way valve lever to emergency cylinder by-pass position.

1) To operate steering gear through telemotor system, using port power unit: Close by-pass valve at forward telemotor. (This opens electric circuit in Sperry unit.) Push port pump starting button in pilothouse until light shows on port station. (This moves 6-way valve to port pump, starts port pump motor and stops starboard pump motor.)

2) To operate steering gear through telemotor system using starboard power unit: Proceed as in operation (1), using starboard push button in pilothouse.

3) To operate steering gear through Sperry unit, using port power unit: Open by-pass valve at forward telemotor. (This closes electric circuit to Sperry unit and allows liquid to by-pass in telemotor system.) Start Sperry unit. Push port button in pilothouse.

4) To operate steering gear through Sperry unit, using starboard unit: Proceed as in operation (3), and press starboard unit button in pilothouse.

5) To operate steering gear from after steering station: Open by-pass valve at forward telemotor. (This closes electric circuit to Sperry unit and allows liquid to by-pass in telemotor system.) Change to pump unit required from pilothouse.

6) To operate steering gear from trick station at steering gear: Bring rams to midship. Remove change pin E from position (1) and place in position (2). Change to pump unit required from pilothouse. Operate through trick wheel for unit operating.

7) When operating with emergency hand gear: Turn 4-way valve to emergency steering position. Open by-pass valve A in main piping.

8) For rudder breaking: Turn 4-way valve to rudder break position.

9) For emergency operation of 6-way valve, turn crank handle to port or starboard as desired.

Lubrication: Keep reserve tanks, which are part of bedplate, two-thirds full.

Keep oil clean.

Keep valve closed in line connecting both reserve tanks.

Operating instructions for the electro-hydraulic steering gear just described accompany Fig. 27. Fig. 28 represents the actual gear but with the smaller ram for hand steering omitted.

FIG. 28 (top). ELECTRO-HYDRAULIC STEERING GEAR ASSEMBLY.
FIG. 29 (bottom). STEERING GEAR ASSEMBLY TEST BLOCK.

Fig. 29 shows a shop assembly view of the entire apparatus mounted on the test-block. The steering stations are, of course, not in the proper location, as found aboard ship. This particular gear includes the auxiliary hand-steering rams, the construction and application of which are more clearly observed in the side view in Fig. 30. It will be noted that separate valves "A" are incorporated in the pipe lines to each pumping unit, in lieu of the 6-way valve shown in Fig. 28.

FIG. 30. SIDE VIEW OF STEERING GEAR TEST BLOCK ASSEMBLY.

This arrangement is often preferred, since it permits steering with both pumps simultaneously, thereby resulting in more rapid changes in rudder movement—an advantage when moving in congested ship lanes. Normally, however, one pumping unit is employed, the second being reserve as a spare. It might also be mentioned that the differential control mechanism is designed so as to control one or more pumping units at one time. It is possible to disconnect either pump from the differential control unit M by removing the pin B from the control rod C. The control rod is fitted with a spring which serves to protect the control mechanism in the event of a hydraulic lock in the idle pump.

Fig. 31 shows another gear arrangement employed on large naval and commercial vessels, and consists of two sets of double opposed rams A and B, which connect directly to the rudder stock C through a double pronged tiller D of the Rapson Slide type. Two pumping units E are incorporated, the piping being arranged with a 6-way valve, which permits the use of either pump. It will be noted that the gear is provided with two differential control boxes, each serving its respective pumping

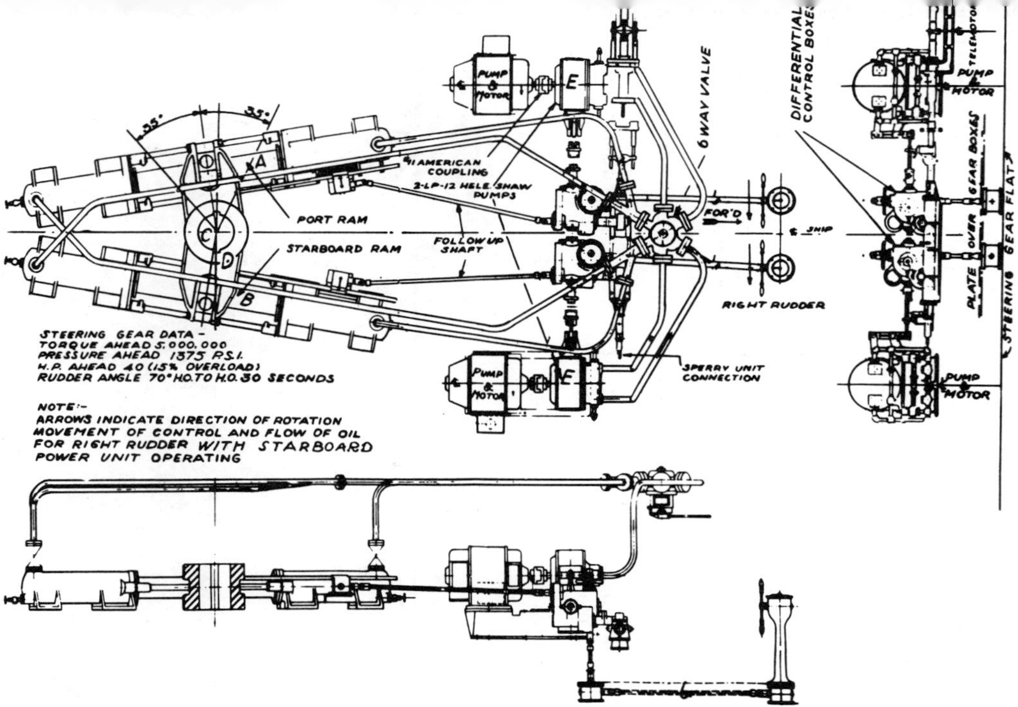

35°
35°
A
B
C
D
E
E
PUMP & MOTOR
PUMP & MOTOR
4/1 AMERICAN COUPLING
2-LP-12 HELE SHAW PUMPS
PORT RAM
STARBOARD RAM
FOLLOW UP SHAFT
6 WAY VALVE
FOR'D
℄ SHIP
RIGHT RUDDER
SPERRY UNIT CONNECTION
DIFFERENTIAL CONTROL BOXES
TELEMOTOR
PUMP & MOTOR
PUMP & MOTOR
PLATE OVER GEAR BOXES
STEERING GEAR FLAT
STEERING GEAR DATA -
TORQUE AHEAD 5,000,000
PRESSURE AHEAD 1375 P.S.I.
H.P. AHEAD 40 (15% OVERLOAD)
RUDDER ANGLE 70° H.O. TO H.O. 30 SECONDS
NOTE:-
ARROWS INDICATE DIRECTION OF ROTATION
MOVEMENT OF CONTROL AND FLOW OF OIL
FOR RIGHT RUDDER WITH STARBOARD
POWER UNIT OPERATING

FIGURE 31

unit. In fact, the arrangement as a whole actually consists of two separate steering gears, either one of which can steer the vessel. The principal advantage of the double ram-type gear shown is, of course, the fact that very large torques can be developed. Also, the arrangement of rams with respect to the center line of the ship permits its application in cases where the available space at the stern of the vessel is limited.

Fig. 32 shows a shop view of another form of electro-hydraulic steering gear, which is referred to as the link-type gear. This type is also used on many large naval and commercial vessels, and employs two double opposed rams A, each connecting to one side of a double-pronged tiller or cross-head B through the 4 large links C. In other respects, this gear is similar to the arrangement shown in Fig. 31, except that a small overhead tank P, driven by a motor-operated pumping unit E, is incorporated. This tank is used to replenish the system. While it is not necessary with the Hele-Shaw system, it is sometimes furnished as the requirement of the shipbuilder. The overhead replenishing tank is necessary, however, with other types of pumping units, such as the axial piston pump, which is also employed on electro-hydraulic steering gear.

The link-type gear shown in Fig. 32 is also employed on many U. S. Maritime Commission C-3 cargo vessels.

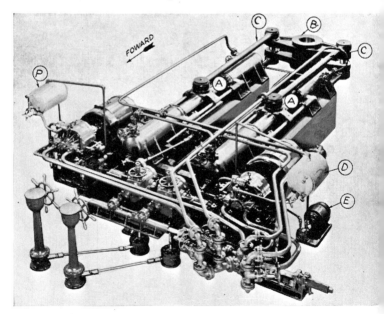

FIG. 32. ELECTRO-HYDRAULIC DOUBLE-RAM STEERING GEAR, LINK TYPE

TELEMOTOR

The most efficient connecting device is the *telemotor*, which transmits the wheel motion to the steering engine through pipes, by hydraulic pressure

Types. Telemotors are of two basic types, namely, the *inside packed* (or piston type) and *outside packed* (or hydraulic ram).

The Brown telemotor is an example of the first type, employing a single cylinder forward and a corresponding cylinder at the steering engine. The piston in each cylinder is rendered pressure-tight by means of leather piston-rings. The after cylinder is fitted with centralizing springs which serve to return the rudder automatically to midship position when hydraulic pressure is removed. The forward cylinder is arranged to by-pass both sides of the piston when the steering wheel is amidships, thus permitting the centralizing springs to synchronize the rudder with the steering wheel.

The hydraulic ram principle is utilized in three telemotors in common use, namely, the American Engineering Company telemotor, the Mactaggart-Scott telemotor, and the Bethlehem telemotor. Each of these types employs double cylinders forward and aft. The rams are packed externally by means of glands and special sea-ring packing. All are fitted with after centralizing springs similar to those used in the Brown telemotor.

The American Engineering Company and the Mactaggart-Scott telemotors are not regularly provided with automatic equalizing valves, although special valves can be obtained for the purpose. The Bethlehem telemotor employs a mechanically operated by-pass valve for equalizing when the wheel is amidships.

Figure 33 is a sketch of a telemotor. The wheels are geared to a plunger in a double-ended cylinder (J), and as the wheel is turned the liquid, a mixture of water and glycerin, in the cylinder is forced through the pipe to a similar cylinder (B) at the steering engine, and moves the piston by the same amount as the plunger at the wheel and it actuates the controlling valve on the steering engine through the connecting rod (N). The liquid is forced back through the other pipe by the other side of the piston in cylinder (B). When the steering wheel is turned the other way the direction of flow in the telemotor system is reversed and the steering engine is reversed. In all steering engines there is a followup motion which closes off the control valve very quickly after the motion of the steering wheel has stopped. Otherwise the engine would continue to operate the rudder to the maximum or to its limiting stops.

Telemotor Maintenance. In order to obtain the best steering results, it is absolutely necessary to maintain the telemotor in good condition. The maximum advantage of fine rudder control can only be obtained when faults such as lost motion and air leaks are eliminated. A regular routine of steering-gear tests should be included in the preparations for getting under way. In this routine, attention should be given to the points which follow.

Tests for Air. Have steam turned on the steering engine and put helm hard over by hand several times in each direction to determine the condition of the rudder follow-up. If air is present in the system the rudder will follow the wheel very sluggishly and will not run to the hard-over position unless wheel is turned past the usual angle.

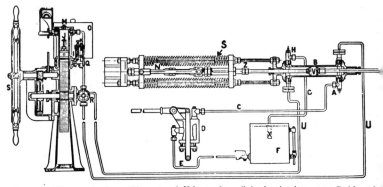

FIGURE 33. Telemotor, showing working parts: *A*. Valve to after cylinder for charging system; *B*. After telemotor cylinder; *C*. Charging line from pump; *D*. Hand-charging pump; *E*. Pump suction; *F*. Filling tank; *G*. Overflow line used in charging; *H*. Valve on overflow line; *I*. Valve casing cover on cylinder (*J*); *J*. Forward telemotor cylinder; *K*. Removable plug to inlet valve (*L*); *L*. Inlet valve from expansion tank (*O*); *M*. Removable plug for air escape in charging; *N*. Connecting rod from telemotor piston rod to engine control valve; *O*. Expansion tank kept half filled with liquid; *P*. Outlet valve allows for expansion of liquid; *Q*. Clean out pocket; *R*. Bypass valve allows wheel movement without operating telemotor; *S*. Springs to return wheel amidships if system leaks; *T*. Forward piston; *U*. Pressure transmitting pipes from forward to after cylinder; *V*. After piston; *X*. Filter for liquid; *Z*. Nuts for connecting and adjusting piston rod.

To remove air, pump up the telemotor with hand by-pass valve open, circulating the liquid briskly until it is observed to flow for each stroke of the pump, and not in a steady stream. Close the after telemotor discharge valve and maintain pressure on the pump, at the same time bleeding the air from the highest part of the forward telemotor by slacking back the relief-nuts or opening air-cocks. Try the after telemotor air-cocks as well. Hold the air-cocks or relief-nuts open until a rush of liquid displaces the air. Then close all valves, closing pump discharge valve last. It may be necessary to circulate liquid more than once before all air is expelled from the system.

Testing for Leaks. Hold steering wheel hard over on each side and examine telemotor glands forward and aft for leakage. Set up on gland nuts just tight enough to hold pressure. Do not jam the nuts tighter than necessary, as to do so causes unnecessary stiffness of operation.

Block the steering wheel hard over on each side and note if rudder creeps back slowly toward center. A tight system should hold rudder without creepage for one half hour. If the rudder creeps when the wheel is blocked as above, the system has a leak at one or more of the following points:

(a) Telemotor piston leathers.
(b) Telemotor glands.
(c) Telemotor automatic by-pass valve (if fitted).
(d) Leaky flange connections or joints.

GYRO-PILOT

The gyro-pilot or "Iron Mike" is a mechanical-electrical arrangement which, by means of the gyro-compass, will steer a ship automatically on a set course. There are three types: the single unit which has direct electrical control between the wheel and the rudder; the two-unit which has an electrical transmission system for controlling the steering engine; and the triple steerer which has direct electrical control between the wheel and the rudder, plus provision for returning control to the wheel by means of the hydraulic telemotor.

Figure 34 shows the mechanism of a single-unit gyro-pilot in simplified diagrammatic form. Departures of the ship from the set course are immediately detected by the master compass and transmitted to the repeater motor indicated on to the left of the diagram. The repeater motor, acting through a differential gear and an adjustable lost motion device turns the contactor roller shown in the center of the diagram. Movement of the contactor roller completes an electrical circuit through one or the other of the contactor rings surrounding the roller. This circuit, acting through electro-magnetic relays, starts an electric motor which moves the rudder in the proper direction to correct the deviation from the course. Movement of the rudder is transmitted back to the gyro-pilot where, acting through another lost motion device, it turns the contactor rings so as to bring the insulated segment over the contactor roller, thus opening the electrical circuits and stopping the motor, leaving a certain amount of rudder applied to return the vessel to the course. As the ship responds, the repeater motor causes the contactor roller to engage with the opposite segment of the contactor ring, thus returning the rudder to the midship position. The elementary action of the gyro-pilot mechanism will be more clearly understood by referring to Fig. 35 in which:

(A) shows the ship on a straight course with rudder amidships.
(B) shows that the ship has departed from a straight course, thus causing the roller to make contact with one segment of the contact ring, thereby energizing the steering engine.
(C) shows that the steering engine has moved, corrective rudder has been applied to the ship and the contact ring has followed the roller, thus stopping the steering engine.
(D) shows that the ship has returned to the set course, thus moving the roller and energizing the steering engine in the reverse direction.
(E) shows that the rudder has moved to the midship position, thus bringing the roller to the neutral position again and stopping the steering engine.

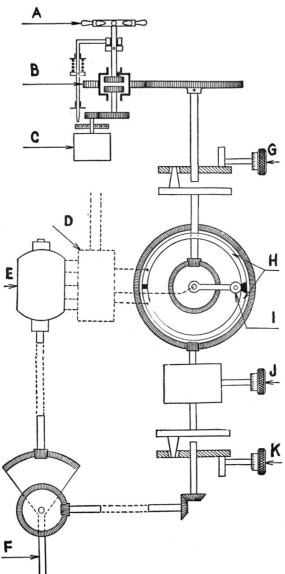

A. Single-unit gyro-pilot. With gyro-pilot steering wheel in this position (pulled out), wheel sets course and vessel is steered automatically through master gyro-compass. When pushed in, repeater motor is locked and wheel controls rudder.

B. Differential gear.

C. Repeater motor connected to master compass.

D. Electro-magnetic relay panels.

E. Steering motor.

F. Rudder.

G. Adjustable lost motion device for permitting weather yaw.

H. Contact rings. These, together with contact roller, control the steering motor through the electro-magnetic relay panel.

I. Contact roller.

J. Lever or gear system for the ratio of movement between the rudder and contact rings.

K. Adjustable lost motion for setting "Initial" and "Meeting" rudder

FIG. 34. MECHANISM OF GYRO-PILOT IN SIMPLIFIED DIAGRAMMATIC FORM.

Referring to Fig. 34, rudder drive indicated by the dotted lines below the electric motor (E) is accomplished as follows:

(1) In a single-unit gyro-pilot by a chain and sprocket drive to the ship's steering wheel.

(2) In a two-unit gyro-pilot by a direct control of the steering engine.

Repeat back of the rudder position, as indicated by the horizontal dotted lines at the bottom of Fig. 34, is accomplished as follows:

(1) In a single unit gyro-pilot by mechanical connections from the ship's steering wheel.

(2) In a two-unit gyro-pilot by electrical transmission from the rudder head.

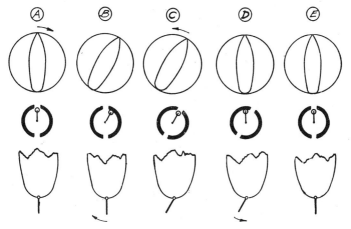

FIG. 35. SHOWING CONTACT AND FOLLOW-UP ACTION AS SHIP LEAVES COURSE AND IS RETURNED BY PROPER RUDDER ACTION.

In the two-unit gyro-pilot shown in Fig. 36, the selector lever on the side of the gyro-pilot has three positions: *Gyro, Hand* and *Off*. When the lever is set to the *Hand* position, it locks the repeater motor and automatically sets both lost motion adjustments to zero.

Weather and Rudder Adjustments. In order that the gyro-pilot may be useful under all conditions, facilities are provided in the equipment to take care of the variable factors which influence the steering of the vessel, such as weather conditions and the characteristics of the ship itself. In rough weather, for instance, it is desirable to let the ship have a small amount of "weather yaw". This is accomplished by means of the weather adjustment. The rudder adjustment varies the amount of rudder applied for a given amount of departure from the set course.

The weather adjustment is simply a means of introducing any desired amount of lost motion between the repeater motor and the signal trolley. For example, when set for 1 degree, the ship can yaw that amount each side of the set course without moving the trolley. When the yaw exceeds the amount for which the weather adjustment is set, the trolley is moved and rudder is applied to correct the deviation from the course.

The weather adjustment is set to zero except in rough weather when it is desirable to allow the ship to respond somewhat to the temporary action of heavy seas. Under such conditions the weather adjustment is opened out as required to prevent racing of the steering engine back and forth.

The rudder adjustment provides a means of controlling the amount of rudder applied for a given departure from the course. The usual position of the rudder adjustment knob is between 0 and 2 for a light ship and between 2 and 4 for a loaded ship. The effect of this adjustment is to delay the follow-up movement of the outer rings until a certain amount of initial rudder movement has taken place. For example, suppose the rudder adjustment is set for 3 degrees. The ship yaws from her course sufficiently to cause the trolley to energize the servo motor. The drive-motor is energized, and the rudder is moved 3 degrees before it is stopped. Thereafter, any further deviation from the course causes the rudder to move in proportion to the degree of deviation. The amount of the initial rudder movement required in either direction depends upon whether the ship is light or loaded. By means of the rudder adjustment this first rudder movement can be made longer than those that follow, the purpose being to apply sufficient rudder on first making contact to check the ship's angular momentum. If the first movement of the rudder is not sufficient, additional rudder movements are given until the momentum is checked. These succeeding movements, however, are made smaller purposely in order to avoid returning the ship with too much rudder.

Under fairly uniform conditions of sea the initial rudder adjustment can be set so that the first rudder application is sufficient to bring the ship back to her course.

The rudder adjustment also provides the means for "meeting" the ship as she returns to the course. For example, suppose the movement of the ship is checked and she starts returning to the set course. The trolley in the signal ring assembly then makes contact with the opposite segment, thus reversing the servo motor. The drive-motor is started in the opposite direction and continues to run until the servo motor has taken out all of the "plus and minus" set in the rudder adjustment and the follow-up ring has caught up with the trolley. This does not occur until the rudder has moved over to the opposite side, thus "meeting" the ship as she returns to the course.

When the rudder adjustment is properly made, the movement of the ship's head is small and is under the control of several influences such as propellers, slight lateral and longitudinal motions, seaway, wind, and even warping and bending of the ship. Thus, the ship's head often crosses the movement of the rudder and the rudder is

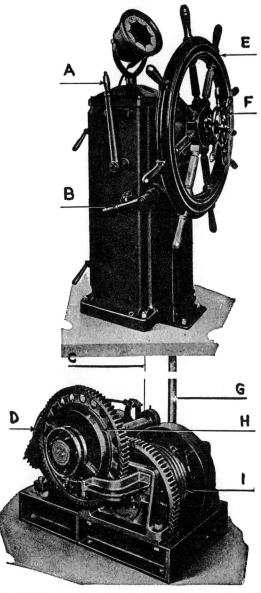

A. Selector lever permits instantaneous shift to direct control of rudder. Thus all methods of steering control are instantly available in the wheelhouse.

B. Lever for engaging and disengaging the large hand steering wheel.

C. Electrical connections for controlling the steering engine.

D. Electric steering motor.

E. Large wheel used for direct control of rudder in case of emergency.

F. Use of adjustments, wheel and selector lever same as on, two-unit gyro-pilot.

G. Mechanical connections for hand steering and for repeating movements of the rudder back to the control unit on the bridge.

H. Magnetic clutch for automatically disconnecting the steering motor from the rudder drive when resorting to hand steering.

I. Rudder is operated by steel cables which pass around this drum.

FIG. 36. TRIPLE-STEER GYRO-PILOT CONNECTED TO DRUM TYPE STEERING ENGINE. A GYRO-REPEATER COMPASS IS MOUNTED ON TOP OF STAND.

restored to a central position with the ship steadied on the course. This condition occurs in automatic steering with about the same frequency as it does with hand steering. The automatic method is more accurate, because it is more sensitive in its response than is a human helmsman, and because it permits precise control of initial rudder.

Course Changes. The gearing between the signal and control systems is such that course changes can be made while steering "gyro" simply by turning the pilot wheel in the desired direction. The rate of the course change can be controlled by turning the gyro-pilot steering wheel at a sufficient rate to hold the wheel pointer at the desired angle from its central position. Pilot wheel control is then superimposed upon the signal from the servo motor. The operation of the servo motor is unaffected; and after the ship has attained the new course the gyro-pilot will continue to control the rudder automatically. One wheel turn gives a course change of approximately 3 degrees. If the pilot wheel is turned, for example, one full turn, while the control lever is set for *Gyro* steering, the rudder will be applied, and as the ship responds, the signal system actuated through the repeater motor will operate to restore the rudder to the midship position, leaving the ship steadied on a new course which is approximately 3 degrees at variance with the previous course.

Also for course changes the control lever can be moved to the *Hand* position and the rudder applied by turning the pilot wheel as necessary. The repeater motor now is locked and the signal circuit inoperative, so that the rudder, instead of being returned to the midship position, will remain at an angle which is proportional to the angle through which the pilot wheel is turned. Therefore, the ship will continue to turn until the rudder has been restored to the midship position by opposite movement of the pilot wheel.

The rudder order indicator on the top of the control unit binnacle shows the "order" to the rudder. In automatic steering, the order originates in the servo motor. In hand electric steering the order originates in the pilot wheel. The angle through which the rudder has actually been moved is indicated on the ship's rudder angle indicator.

Hand Steering. Moving the control lever from the *Gyro* to the *Hand* position locks the repeater motor mechanically. The entire signal circuit including the weather and rudder adjustments is now inoperative because with the repeater motor locked there can be no movement of the signal trolleys, and therefore no movement of the servo motor and the outer rings of the signal ring assembly. The rudder is now controlled by means of the pilot wheel which operates through a differential and train of gears to drive the contact rings of the control ring assembly. When the pilot wheel is turned, the control circuit, through the relays on the motor control panel, actuates the drive-motor in the same manner as it does for automatic steering, the follow-up transmitter and receiver causing the trolleys to follow the contact rings and open the circuit so that rudder application is always proportional to the angle through which the pilot wheel is turned.

Steering with Ship's Wheel. When the control lever on the gyropilot is moved to the *Off* position, the control switch in the binnacle is opened and the magnetic clutch on the power-unit disengaged. The rudder is controlled through the ship's hydraulic telemotor system by means of the ship's wheel.

GYRO-STABILIZER

The rolling motion of a ship is the result of fluid pressure acting upon the hull and the shifting of that pressure from one side to the other. Waves do not beat against the side of a ship as they do against a breakwater. Since the ship is free to rise and fall, the bulk of each wave passes underneath the hull of the vessel, imparting to the vessel a comparatively slight roll.

It is easily understood, therefore, that a comparatively small counteracting force applied at the instant each roll starts would be sufficient to quench the effect of the wave upon the ship. The gyro-stabilizer acts in such a manner as to do this, precessing back and forth in a fore-and-aft direction while resisting the action of the waves from side to side.

In actual practice a gyro-stabilizer is controlled by a motor which regulates its precessional rate and angular movement to make them conform to the existing wave characteristics. Controlled precession, or the counteraction of the stabilizer against the tendency of the vessel to roll, is obtained through the use of a sensitive control gyro which precesses instantly at the very beginning of the rolling movement. In so doing it closes a pair of contacts which, acting through a relay panel, start the precession motor to precess the large stabilizing gyro instantly to apply the necessary stabilizing force to the ship.

A gyro-stabilizer is essentially a gyroscope, the motions of which are controlled and operated electrically. Primarily, a gyroscope consists of a flywheel so mounted that only one point, its center of gravity, is in a fixed position, the flywheel being free to turn in any direction about this fixed point.

The flywheel revolves in a concentric inner ring. This ring in turn revolves in an outer ring about an axis always at right angles to the axis of rotation of the flywheel. The outer ring also revolves in a supporting frame about an axis always at right angles to the axis of rotation of the inner ring.

The principle involved is the same as that employed in tops used as toys by children.

WINDLASSES, CAPSTANS AND GYPSIES

Considerable confusion has always existed as to the correct meaning of the words "windlass," "capstan," and "gypsy." While the word "gypsy" is of relatively recent usage, the words "capstan" and "windlass" have been used interchangeably in the long past and it has only been within the last half century that the meaning of each term has been more definitely established, particularly in the case of the windlass. The gypsy, for instance, is still often referred to as a capstan, and vice versa.

Present-day usage of the word "windlass" generally implies a chain sprocket or sprockets, known as wildcats, mounted on a vertical or horizontal shaft, hand- or power-operated, or both, and used primarily for handling an anchor by means of chain.

The word "capstan" describes a vertical-barrelled, rotative device arranged for either hand operation or hand and power operation with pawls at its base to prevent it from reversing, and generally used for warping or pulling objects in a horizontal direction. It is sometimes used for handling ground tackle or the like.

The "gypsy" is a vertical-barrelled device, direct-connected to a reduction gear and always power-operated. It is used largely for the rapid handling of tow lines and for warping purposes. The name "gypsy" is not universally accepted and many machines meeting this description are found designated as capstans, although no provision is made for hand operation.

WINDLASS

A ship's windlass is designed primarily for handling the anchor, but it is frequently used for handling lines and warps, as well. Its evolution stretches back several centuries, beginning when anchors, because of the increasing size of vessels, became too heavy to be hoisted hand over hand. From the vertical log, forerunner of the capstan, through the horizontal log, predecessor of the winch, the ship's windlass of today has emerged —a highly mechanized piece of equipment. Although it is used intermittently, and then only for brief periods, it must be of sturdy construction and capable of handling all loads required of it under the most severe conditions. Windlasses of many designs are used on shipboard. Hand-operated windlasses are found on very small vessels, but on the larger ships they are always power-operated, in view of the heavy anchors which must be raised. In addition to the wildcats, which handle the anchor chains, windlasses are usually equipped with warping heads (sometimes referred to as gypsy heads) for warping purposes and for the handling of cargo.

Hand-operated windlass. Very small vessels are usually equipped with hand-operated windlasses of the pump-brake type, similar to that shown in Fig. 37. It will be noted that this type consists of a horizontal shaft A upon which two wildcats B and two warping heads C are mounted.

FIG. 37. HAND-OPERATED WINDLASS.

The warping heads are usually equipped with raised projections or whelps D to increase the hold on the lines. The wildcats are, of course, used for hoisting the anchor and are designed to fit the size and type of anchor chain employed on the particular vessel. They are connected to the shaft A by locking mechanisms E which permit each wildcat to be operated independently, or both simultaneously. Engaging or disengaging the wildcat from shaft A is accomplished by inserting the bar F in the locking mechanism as shown, and turning the latter in one direction or the other, to obtain the result desired. When independent use of the warping heads is desired, the wildcats are disconnected from the shaft A through the locking mechanism E and then held by friction-band brakes.

Friction-band brakes are generally incorporated on hand-power windlasses of the type illustrated. These brakes, mounted on one flange of each wildcat, are brought into action when dropping the anchor. They consist of a forged steel band G connected to a cam and rod arrangement H and operated by the hand lever K. Pulling the lever K in one direction causes the band G to grip the wildcat flange, resulting in the braking operation. Pushing lever K forward to a vertical position releases brake.

Hoisting of the anchor is accomplished through the use of the pump-brake levers L and L. one man stationed at each lever and each man pressing down alternately with the other, in pumping fashion. The levers connect to and actuate toggle-operated shoes S, Fig. 38 (which ride on

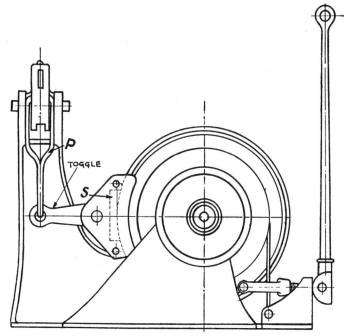

FIG. 38. SIDE VIEW OF WINDLASS IN FIG. 37.

the flange of each locking head), through the links P. Each shoe grips and turns the flange on its upstroke and releases itself from the flange on its downstroke. Since one link P is attached to each side of the fulcrum arm O it follows that the locking heads turn with the operation of the levers L and L. Several combinations of power and speed are obtained by shifting the links P into the several notches R provided in the fulcrum arm O.

Usually, only one anchor is raised at a time although it is possible to raise both anchors during the same operation. It should also be mentioned that a device known as a chain stopper (see Fig. 48) prevents the chain load from overhauling the wildcat when the toggle shoe S is released on its downstroke.

Power-type windlass. Power-type windlasses with hand-pump brakes, incorporated for stand-by use, are also found on many smaller vessels as well as on towboats. Fig. 39 illustrates one of this type arranged for gasoline-engine drive. This design is similar in principle to the pump-brake windlass described in Fig. 37, except that a spur gear A and a worm gear reduction B is incorporated due to the use of a power-type prime power C. This type of windlass is also found frequently arranged for motor drive on boats having sufficient power available to enable the windlass to perform its work. The pump-brake mechanism is disconnected when the power-drive is employed.

FIG. 39. POWER-DRIVEN WINDLASS WITH AUXILIARY PUMP
BRAKES INCLUDED.

Steam spur-gear windlass. On large steam vessels, steam-driven, spur-geared windlasses are generally employed, of the type illustrated in Fig. 40. Assemblies and sectional views of the windlass are shown in Figs. 40–45, the letter designations in all illustrations, including Fig. 40, referring to the same parts.

It will be noted that the machine is a self-contained unit driven by a horizontal piston-valve engine A mounted on the same bedplate. The unit is usually located on board ship so that the cylinders are set forward, thereby allowing the power unit to be placed well up in the bow. Operator's control levers B and C are grouped conveniently together at the after-end of the machine, as shown. The unit must, of course, be bolted very securely to the ship's structure to avoid the possibility of its tearing loose during operation.

The windlass is controlled through a piston-type reverse valve D, the engine driving the wildcats and warping heads through a double reduction or cut-tooth spur gearing. The gearing is protected by shrouded gear guards, which also serve as a safety precaution to those working close to the unit.

FIG. 40. STEAM-DRIVEN, SPUR-GEARED WINDLASS.

Referring to Fig. 41 (see Figs. 43 – 45), the steam cylinders A drive the crankshaft E upon which the sleeve pinion F is freely mounted and which, in turn, carries the keyed gear G. In addition to the eccentrics H of the engine, the crankshaft E also carries the freely mounted pinion K and a jaw clutch L, the latter being provided to engage or disengage the engine from the windlass. When the clutch L has engaged the pinion K, the latter operates the gear M mounted and keyed on intermediate shaft N. Up to this point it is seen that the engine is driving only the warping heads O which are keyed to the intermediate shaft N. Shaft N, however, carries the sliding jaw clutch P and the freely mounted gear R. It, therefore, follows that when the clutch P engages gear R, the latter drives the gear G which in turn operates the main gear S through the sleeve pinion F. Gear S is keyed to the wildcat shaft U. In other words, when it is desired to operate the wildcats under power, gear R must be connected to the intermediate shaft N by the engagement of clutch P. When only the warping heads are to be operated by power, the clutch P must be in the disengaged position, and in this case the chain load must be held by applying the band brakes at the wildcat. The wildcats T are free to turn on the main shaft U but may be connected to it by a locking mechanism consisting of the locking head W, keyed to the shaft U, the locking ring X mounted on the locking head W, and two sliding block keys Y. As the locking ring X is turned (through the use of a bar inserted in holes AA) the annular lugs BB on its periphery, draw the block keys Y into pockets in the side of the wildcat, thereby locking the wildcat to the locking head W. Turning the locking ring X in the opposite direction, withdraws

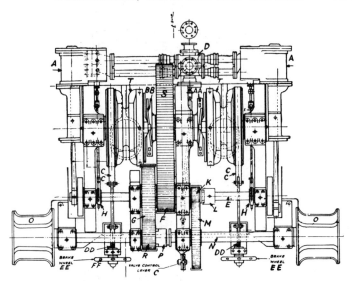

FIG. 41. PLAN VIEW OF WINDLASS.

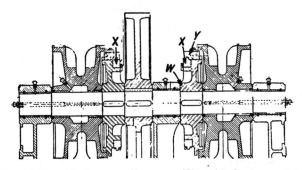

FIG. 42 (detail). SECTION THROUGH WILDCAT SHAFT OF FIG. 41.

the block keys Y from the pocket and the wildcat is again free to turn on shaft U.

Each wildcat is also equipped with a band brake of the screw compressor type. The brake consists of a forged steel band CC which encircles one flange of the wildcat, and connects to a screw shaft DD through a system of links and levers. (See Fig. 45.)

Turning handwheel EE in one direction tightens the band CC around the flange of the wildcat and turning the wheel in the opposite direction releases the band. Holes FF are provided in the rim of the handwheel into which a bar NN may be inserted to gain leverage in the braking

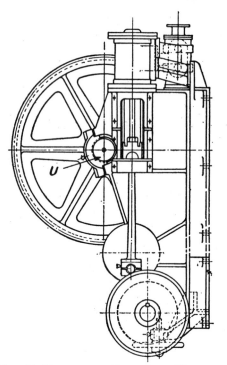

FIG. 43. TRANSVERSE SECTION OF WINDLASS.

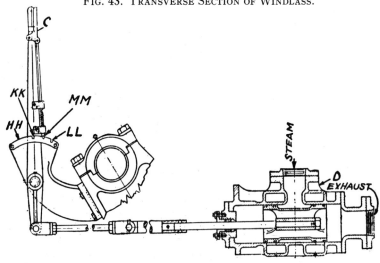

FIG. 44. SECTION THROUGH REVERSING VALVE.

operation. A chain stripper GG is provided at each wildcat to prevent the anchor chain from binding on the wildcat lugs as anchor is hove in.

As mentioned previously, the engine is controlled by the piston-type reverse valve D, an internal view of which is shown in the drawing, Fig. 44 . The valve is operated by the hand lever C, engaging notches in the segment HH. When the lever latch engages the notch KK the windlass operates in one direction and when the lever engages notch LL, rotation in the opposite direction results. When the center notch MM is engaged, no steam is passing to the engine.

The fact that well-designed windlasses are generally of rugged construction enables them to give good service with little attention aside from regular lubrication. Adequate provision for proper lubrication of all working parts is usually found on all modern units.

The manufacturer's operating instructions for the steam spur-geared windlass just described, are given below:

OPERATING INSTRUCTIONS

The windlass is driven by the steam engine and is capable of heaving in both anchors and chains simultaneously, or each anchor and chain independently. The anchors can be paid out simultaneously or independently, either by the use of the mechanical brakes with the block keys disengaged from the pockets of the wildcat, or the use of the steam engine with the block keys engaged in the pockets of the wildcat.

General operation: Before starting windlass:

Oil or grease all bearings as required.

Drain water from steam cylinders and valves.

To line up block keys with slots in wildcats, crack valve and turn engine over slowly until block keys are in line with pockets of wildcat.

Operating of winch heads:

Make certain that the clutch P on the intermediate shaft is disengaged.

Open the throttle valve between the main-steam supply and the steam-engine reverse valve D.

Operate lever C of steam-reverse valve for speed and direction of rotation of winch heads desired.

To drop both anchors simultaneously or independently by using the mechanical brakes:

Pull up on anchor chain sufficiently to remove chain-stopper pawl.

Tighten brakes CC on wildcats and disengage block keys from wildcats using bar in locking rings X (*Warning:* Remove bar from locking ring before further operation.)

Release brakes CC (control the speed of the chains paying out by the use of the brake handwheels).

When the anchors are dropped to the desired depth, apply the brakes on the wildcats and place the chain-stopper pawls in the chain-holding position.

To drop both anchors simultaneously by steam power:

Make certain the clutch P on the intermediate shaft is engaged.

Engage block keys in both wildcats, using bar in locking rings X, and tighten brakes on both wildcats.

Remove chain-stopper pawls from chain-holding positions.

Open throttle valve between main steam-supply and steam-engine reverse valve D.

Release brakes CC on wildcats and drop anchors by operating reverse-valve control lever. (Steam power opposing pull of anchor.)

After anchors are dropped as desired, apply brakes on wildcats, shut down engine and place chain-stopper pawls in the chain-holding position.

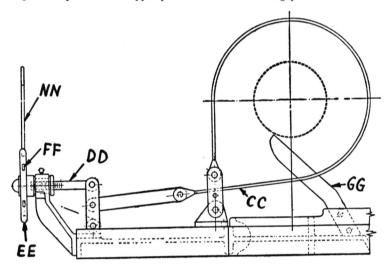

Fig. 45. Side View of Band Brake.

To drop either anchor by steam power:

Make certain the clutch P on the intermediate shaft is engaged.

Apply brakes CC on both wildcats.

Engage block keys in the wildcat to be used.

Disengage block keys from the idle wildcat.

Remove chain-stopper pawl from chain-holding position on chain of anchor to be dropped.

Release brake CC on wildcat to be used and drop anchor by operating reverse valve control lever.

After anchor has been dropped as desired, apply brake CC on wildcat and place chain-stopper pawl in chain-holding position.

To heave in both anchors simultaneously:

Make certain the clutch P on the intermediate shaft is engaged.

Tighten brakes CC on the wildcats.

Engage block keys in wildcats, using bar in locking rings X.

Open throttle valve between main steam supply and steam-engine reverse valve D.

Release brakes CC on the wildcats and heave in anchors by operating reverse-valve control lever.

When anchors are raised, apply brakes on wildcats, shut down engine and place chain-stopper pawls in chain-holding position.

To heave in either anchor:

Make certain the clutch P on the intermediate shaft is engaged.

Apply brakes CC on both wildcats.

Engage block keys in the wildcat to be used.

Disengage block keys from the idle wildcat.

Open throttle valve, release brake on wildcat to be used and heave in anchor by operating lever of steam-reverse valve D.

When the anchor is raised, tighten brake on wildcat. Place chain-stopper pawl in chain-holding position.

FIG. 46. ELECTRIC-DRIVEN, SPUR-GEAR WINDLASS.

Electric spur-gear windlasses of the type shown (Fig. 46) are widely used and may be found on many U. S. Maritime Commission cargo vessels. This type is similar in general construction and design to the steam windlass illustrated in Fig. 40, except that it is electric motor-driven. The motor used with this machine is of watertight construction and has variable speed characteristics. It is also equipped with an electric brake A, which acts to hold the load when the current has been shut off.

Anchor windlasses of the vertical type, driven from below deck by steam engines, motors or hydraulic transmissions are found in a few cases on commercial ships. Fig. 47 illustrates a unit of this design. In the case of naval vessels, however, the vertical windlass is almost always employed. This design is sometimes referred to as a capstan windlass.

The equipment above deck usually consists of a wildcat A and a warp-

ing head B mounted, one above the other, on a vertical shaft, the wildcat being located immediately above the base plate C of the unit, since
it must take the heaviest load and must be in a more direct line with
respect to the hawse pipes. The warping head is keyed to the vertical
shaft, while the wildcat usually is equipped with an individual locking-
head mechanism similar to that described under Fig. 40 although in the
design shown in Fig. 47, the wildcat is driven from the warping head by
means of a block key (not shown). Band brakes are also incorporated,

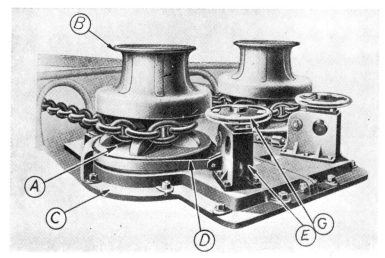

FIG. 47. VERTICAL TYPE ANCHOR WINDLASS.

and, as shown in Fig. 40, are of the screw-compressor type similar in
principle to that used on many of the horizontal-type windlasses, and
consist of a forged steel band D encircling the lower flange of the wildcat.
Both ends of the band connect to a screw-and-toggle arrangement within
the housing E. Turning the handwheel G in one direction, causes the band
D to grip the wildcat flange, and turning it in the opposite direction releases the band.

Vertical-type windlasses are usually found in pairs as shown in the
illustration, in which case each windlass is arranged for operation independently of the other, or simultaneously. There are cases, however, where
only one unit is used, but only on smaller ships.

The principal advantage of the vertical windlass is the small area of
deck space required, as well as the fact that it is adaptable where low
headroom exists. Where the height above deck is extremely limited, the
warping heads B may be omitted, but in such cases they are located at
the side of the windlass although driven from the same power unit from
below deck.

CHAIN STOPPERS

Used in conjunction with practically every windlass is a device known as a chain stopper. There have been many designs used during the past, but the most common found aboard most vessels today are illustrated in Fig. 48.

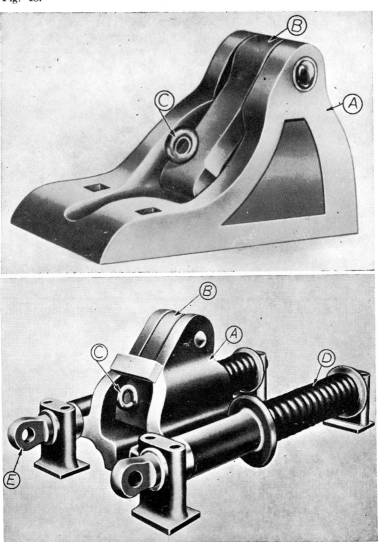

Fig. 48. Chain Stoppers.

The principal purpose of this device is to hold the anchor chain while riding at anchor; thereby absorbing the chain pull which would otherwise continually act on the windlass. It is always located in line with the hawse pipes and the wildcat of the windlass. In both types shown in Fig. 48 the chain is rove through the housing A; the pawl B dropping in place over the chain and bearing against the end of an upright link of the chain. A rope is usually attached to the ring C for releasing the pawl when about to drop anchor, in which case it is necessary to pull up on the anchor slightly before the pawl can be disengaged from the chain. Each anchor chain, of course, has its own chain stopper.

FIG. 49. CHAIN STOPPERS AS INSTALLED.

The common stopper shown at the top of Fig. 48 is used on large commercial vessels. The type illustrated at the bottom is employed on yachts and other types of smaller vessels and is equipped with the coiled steel springs D which are designed to absorb sudden shocks while riding anchor. The eyes E are used to secure the device to the vessel's deck.

The important work of the chain stopper is indicated in the operating instructions given on pages 57 to 59 in connection with the steam spur-gear windlass.

Fig. 49 shows an actual application of the "common" chain stopper in conjunction with a similar form of the electric driven spur-gear windlass described in Fig. 46 .

CAPSTANS

The capstan is used principally for warping purposes. The word warping as used in seamanship means the act of changing a vessel's position with respect to a wharf, dock, or another vessel tied to a wharf, by the manipulation of a common line attached to both objects. The capstan provides the actuating pull to change the position of the ship. Assuming the capstan is located on the vessel, this change is accomplished in general as follows:

One end of the line is attached to a fixed point ashore and is then extended to the capstan; wound around its barrel, and the loose end held by the operator. The barrel is then rotated either by hand or power, and as the loose end is pulled, the rope grips the barrel's surface; in effect, winding in the line between the capstan and the fixed point ashore, thereby bringing the vessel closer to dock. Obviously, if the operator then slacks his line, the vessel will again be free to move away from the dock, since the rope has lost its grip on the barrel of the capstan. This is, of course, only a simple illustration. There are many more complex situations which the experienced seaman and stevedore can handle through the use of the capstan.

Capstans are found in hand- and power-operated form of many sizes and designs. Well-constructed units are designed for maximum strength and durability, and above all, reliability, under the most severe operating conditions. The power-operated types are driven either by steam engines or electric motors. Power-operated capstans are always arranged in such a manner that they can be operated by hand through the use of capstan bars inserted in holes provided in the head of the unit.

In the hand-operated types, the barrels are always arranged to turn in a clockwise direction, while in the power-operated units, they are usually arranged to operate in either direction.

Raised projections or "whelps" are generally provided on the barrel of the capstan to give increased bite to the line. Capstans usually handle Manila line and sometimes wire rope and are not suitable for chain, unless a wildcat is incorporated on the capstan shaft in addition to the capstan barrel. In such cases, the wildcat handles the anchor chain. This arrangement is referred to as either a "capstan windlass" or a "vertical windlass," and was described in connection with Fig. 47.

Hand-powered capstans. Hand-powered capstans are used mostly for barges and docks, although they are also found on many small vessels where power-driven units are not essential. Fig. 50 shows a typical hand-powered capstan, using the conventional capstan bars. All capstans used today are designed with two mechanical speeds. The speeds are obtained through the use of pawls and gears within the capstan, and so arranged that by turning the capstan head A (Fig. 50) in one direction, results in one speed of the barrel B, and by turning it in the opposite direction, a second or lower speed results. With the same force exerted at the end of the capstan bar, a greater pull on the line is obtained when using the lower speed than when the higher speed is employed. The barrel always rotates in a clockwise direction, regardless of which speed is used. Holes C into which the capstan bars are inserted are provided in the capstan head.

Pawls D are also provided on the outside of the lower rim of the barrel and engage pockets cast in the base E of the capstan. The pawls prevent the load from overhauling the rope on the capstan.

Fig. 51 shows another form of hand-powered capstan, having certain advantages over the capstan illustrated in Fig. 50. While the unit shown in Fig. 50 has the pawls D on the exterior of the machine, the form illustrated in Fig. 51 is provided with a pawl enclosed within it, thereby

Fig. 50. Hand-powered Capstan.   Fig. 51. Hand-powered Capstan.

eliminating the possibility of the rope fouling the pawls during operation. Another advantage of the unit shown in Fig. 51 is the fact that the gearing is located in the capstan head, making it more powerful and stronger than the unit illustrated in Fig. 50, which carries the gearing in the base of the machine. Fig. 52 is an internal view of the improved type and it will be noted that the shaft A is supported by and is keyed to the capstan base B. Mounted and free to turn on the shaft A are the capstan head C, the gear D and the capstan barrel E. On the top surface of the barrel E, ratchet teeth F are arranged in such a manner that the pawl G engages them when the capstan head is turned in a clockwise direction. In other words, the barrel E revolves at the same speed as the head C. The second or slower speed is obtained by revolving the capstan head C in the opposite direction, in which case another pawl H engages ratchet teeth S on the flanged surface of the gear D which in turn drives the capstan barrel E through the pinions K meshing with internal gear L. It should be noted that the ratchet teeth S on the flange surface of the gear D are arranged in the opposite direction to the ratchet teeth F located on the capstan barrel. The gears K are mounted on the stationary gear plate N which is keyed to the shaft A. They are two in number, and arranged 180° apart, being free to turn on their respective shafts M.

A pawl O is carried in the base B and prevents the capstan barrel from turning counterclockwise by engaging ratchet teeth P located around the

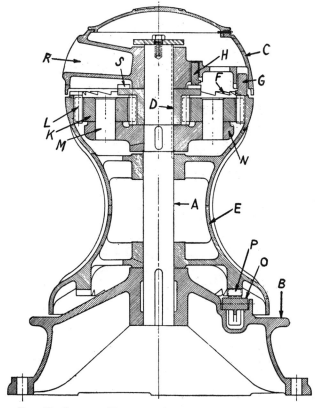

FIG. 52. SECTION THROUGH CAPSTAN SHOWN IN FIG. 51.

inside of the barrel. A small opening (not shown) in the capstan base, into which a bar may be inserted, permits the pawl to be readily lifted to allow the barrel to overhaul in case of a rope jam.

The capstan bars are inserted in the openings R in the capstan head.

Another type of hand-powered unit is the crank capstan shown in Fig. 53 which is designed where space prohibits the use of capstan bars. In this case the capstan head A does not revolve, power being applied by the cranks B operating through bevel gears, located in the capstan head. The internal gearing and pawl arrangement is otherwise the same as that found in the hand-powered capstan using capstan bars, just described. This type also has two mechanical speeds, the change in speed being accomplished by reversing the direction of cranking. The cranks can be unshipped for stowing when not in use.

Power-driven capstans. Power-driven capstans consist primarily of the capstan itself, the reduction unit and the prime mover. Both electric and steam designs are usually either of the deck or laydown type. With

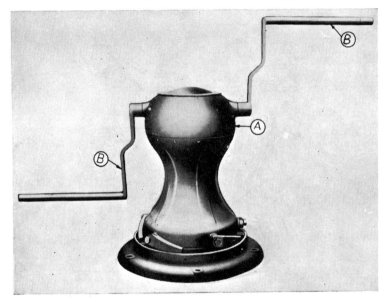

FIG. 53. CRANK CAPSTAN.

the deck type, the entire machine including the reduction gear and prime mover are mounted above deck as illustrated in Fig. 54. The laydown type differs only in that the gear unit and prime mover are situated below deck, being connected to the extended capstan shaft at that point. (See Fig. 55.)

In some cases where reversing features are incorporated, the pawls at the capstan base are eliminated. However, when found on reversing types, the pawls are equipped with thumb screws to hold them in a raised position to permit reverse rotation of the barrel.

Powered capstans generally have two mechanical speeds and are also always arranged to permit operation by hand, using the conventional capstan bars. When hand operation is desired, the reduction gear and prime mover are disconnected from the barrel by removing a block key in the reduction gear, thereby allowing the capstan itself to run free.

The slow mechanical speed on the power-driven capstan is not necessary

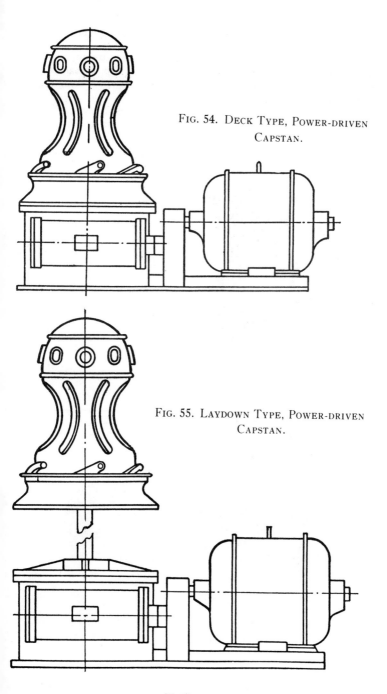

FIG. 54. DECK TYPE, POWER-DRIVEN
CAPSTAN.

FIG. 55. LAYDOWN TYPE, POWER-DRIVEN
CAPSTAN.

when operating under power, since the prime movers are always of sufficient capacity to do the work required through the high mechanical speed. The slow speed is therefore only used, when the capstan is being operated by hand and a heavy pull is necessary.

Electric-powered capstan. Fig. 56 illustrates a typical electric-powered capstan, while Fig. 57 shows the internal arrangement of same.

FIG. 56. SINGLE-BARREL ELECTRIC CAPSTAN, LAYDOWN TYPE.

It will be noted that the motor A drives the capstan shaft B through a set of spur gears C and a worm-wheel reduction D. It should also be observed that the capstan shaft B is connected to the power drive by means of a block key E. This key is removed when it is desired to operate the capstan by hand, and engages the worm wheel with a locking head, the latter being keyed to the capstan shaft B.

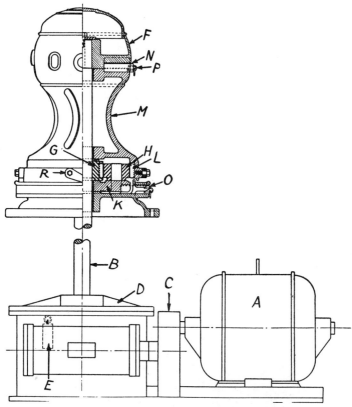

FIG. 57. SECTION THROUGH CAPSTAN SHOWN IN FIG. 56.

The capstan head F and the center gear G are both keyed to the shaft B and, therefore, always revolve with the shaft. Pinion gear H mounted on gear plate K meshes with center gear G and with internal gear L, machined in the barrel M of the capstan. Openings are provided at N in the capstan head and at O in the capstan base, into which a block key P is inserted to permit the use of either the fast or slow mechanical speed.

When the fast mechanical speed is desired, the block key P is inserted in opening N as shown in the illustration. This connects the capstan barrel M to the capstan head F. Since the head F is keyed to the shaft B, it follows that the barrel will always revolve at the same speed as the shaft.

When the slow mechanical speed of the capstan barrel is desired, the key P is removed from opening N and inserted in opening O. Inserting the

Fig. 58. Double Barrel Steam Capstan, Laydown Type.

key in opening O holds gear plate K stationary. Therefore, rotation of shaft B carrying the keyed center gear G revolves the capstan barrel M through the pinion gear H and internal gear L. Although not shown in the illustration, there are three pinion gears H mounted on gear plate K for the purpose of distributing the load more equally on the mechanism and to reduce gear-tooth pressures.

Electric capstans are furnished with motors of open or enclosed construction according to the requirements of the particular installation, but

FIG. 59. STEAM CAPSTAN, DECK TYPE.

in cases where they are exposed to the elements, the motors are usually of watertight design. The motor shown in Fig. 56 is arranged for reversing operation, in which case the capstan barrel may be revolved counterclockwise. Under such conditions, the pawls R are held in a raised position by the thumbscrews S.

The construction and operating principles of the capstan shown in Fig. 57 are also applicable for the steam capstan, except that a double-cylinder steam engine of the reversible or non-reversible type replaces the electric motor A. Also, the spur-gear reduction C (Fig. 57) is eliminated in view of the slower-speed characteristics of the steam engine as compared with the electric motor employed. Fig. 59 shows a typical steam capstan of the non-reversible type, driven by a duplex steam engine through a worm-gear reduction. The engine and gearing are the same as that described and shown in the double-steam capstan in Fig. 58, except that it is of the deck type and of enclosed construction.

There are also capstans of the double-barrel type such as illustrated in Fig. 58. The advantage of this arrangement can be appreciated in cases

FIG. 60. ELECTRIC GYPSY, LAYDOWN TYPE.

where it is desirable to handle two lines at the same time. Although many times, two lines are handled on one head by the practice of marrying the lines, the double-barrel type is more convenient and useful when the work frequently calls for the use of more than one line per capstan.

The unit shown in Fig. 58 is of the laydown type, and of open construction, arranged for steam-engine drive. The engine A drives the crankshaft B carrying the worm C, which in turn meshes with the worm wheel D.

The worm wheel becomes fixed to the shaft E through the use of the block key F inserted in one of the openings G. The locking head H being keyed to shaft E, therefore transmits the power from the worm wheel D to the capstan shaft E. When hand operation is desired, the block key F is removed, thereby disconnecting the power drive from the capstan.

The internal construction of the capstan itself is the same as that described in Fig. 57, the barrel K being driven from the head L by the use of a block key inserted in opening M, or driven from the gears in the base N by inserting the key in an opening at that point (not shown).

If counterclockwise operation of the barrel is desired with the power drive, the engine is reversed and the pawls O are fixed in the raised position by the thumbscrews P, as shown.

GYPSIES

Fig. 60 represents a typical electric gypsy of the laydown type, and of totally enclosed construction. It will be noted that the electric motor A drives the head B through the spur-gear reduction "E" and the worm-gear reduction D. A flexible-type coupling connects the motor shaft with the shaft of the spur gear reduction. Also, the gypsy shaft F is connected to the driving shaft of the worm-gear reduction D by the rigid coupling H, thereby permitting the distance between the head B and the gear mechanism to be varied to suit the requirements of the particular application.

The motor is equipped with an electric brake K enclosed, which acts to hold the load as soon as the current is shut off.

Gypsies are always power-operated and while similar in some respects to the power-driven capstan, they generally have only one mechanical speed and are never arranged for hand operation. Gypsies are driven through spur, herringbone or worm-gear reductions, by steam engines, electric motors or hydraulic transmissions, the gypsy heads being always permanently connected to the gear mechanism. While the earlier designs were arranged for operation in a clockwise direction only, many gypsies today are of the reversing order. In the reversing types, care should be taken, when backing off the load under power due to the tendency for the rope, to "pinch or walk" off the upper flange of the gypsy head. They are also usually designed with variable and high-speed characteristics to meet situations requiring the rapid handling of lines, such as, for example, in tugboat towing operations, where the lines must be brought in rapidly to avoid fouling the propellers of the vessel. Gypsies are also used for warping and mooring purposes.

General. While the large majority of powered capstans and gypsies are non-overhauling by virtue of the usual type worm- and wheel-reduction gear incorporated, there has been a tendency toward the over-hauling type of unit in view of the increased efficiency attainable through the use of high helix-angle, worm-gear reductions. On arrangements of this kind, it is very important that the brakes (which are generally incorporated) should be applied, to avoid the possibility of the load backing off out of control.

In general, capstans and gypsies require very little attention; however, periodic inspection is highly recommended, particularly from the standpoint of insuring adequate lubrication of vital parts.

It is also good practice to start up the unit periodically during long periods of idleness, thereby insuring that the machine is in running condition at all times.

TOWING MACHINES

Before the advent of steam machinery, heavy towing operations were carried out under the most trying conditions, and it was only under the direction of the most skilled that this type of work was performed. In heavy seas and under adverse weather conditions a rigid connection between towing vessel and the vessel in tow was a constant source of danger since the Manila hawser employed had to be possessed of sufficient elasticity to withstand the excessive strains imposed upon it. The hawsers were of large circumference and were, therefore, heavy and extremely difficult to handle, particularly when frozen. It was also impossible to stow them on a drum, due to their bulk. Furthermore, they wore rapidly through chafing and were quickly destroyed in icy waters.

While the Manila hawser is still utilized by tugs in still-water towing, its many disadvantages have gradually led to the use of steel cable, particularly in deep-sea towing operations. Possessed of considerably greater strength than the Manila hawser of equal weight, the steel cable can obviously be smaller in circumference, and, therefore, more readily handled. It also has greater wearing qualities and can be conveniently stowed by winding it on a drum. The wire hawser, however, has relatively little elastic properties, and will, therefore, break under excessive or sudden loads. To compensate for this deficiency, power-operated towing machines having automatic tension, were designed, and are widely used today.

Many large modern vessels whose functions include towing operations are now equipped with towing machines. While many variations of design are found aboard vessels of this nature, the most efficient machines are those of the automatic-tension type driven by either steam or electric power. Fig. 61 shows a modern, steam-operated towing machine which consists of a winding drum A mounted on a shaft supported by the side housings B and driven by the double-cylinder reversing-type steam engine C through the spur-geared reduction D. The engine is controlled by the rocker-type control valve E through operating the hand levers F and G, and also by the automatic control mechanism H, which consists of a travelling yoke on a spiral-screw shaft engaged and held by means of pawls. The automatic-control mechanism operates the rocker-type control valve so that paying out and recovering the line is accomplished automatically.

Operation of the towing machine under working conditions is as follows: The machine is first started manually by means of reverse levers F and control levers G, paying out the line until the tow is at a sufficient distance from the towing vessel. The pawls on the automatic gear H are then thrown in and the reverse lever F put in the "Ahead" position, after which the machine will automatically pay out and recover the hawser. Normally, there is steam cushion in the cylinders of the engine just sufficient to balance the stress on the tow line. In case of a severe strain or a heavy surge on the hawser, the drum overhauls, paying out the line until the strain is relieved or until the pressure in the steam cylinders builds up sufficiently to counteract the pull of the hawser.

It is at this point that the automatic action of the machine manifests itself. As the line pays out, overhauling the drum, the throttle valve of the engine is gradually opened, admitting steam into the cylinders. This action continues until the steam pressure is sufficient to equal the strain and prevents further paying out of the hawser. When the strain is relieved, the engine operates, recovering the line and reversing the action of the automatic control, thus gradually closing the throttle valve until the steam pressure is reduced to where it will just balance the pull on the line.

The drum is provided with a powerful hand brake operated by the handwheel K at the side of the machine near the reverse lever. When towing in still water or light seas, this brake may be set to hold the tow at the desired distance without using steam.

The towing machine is found both with and without the winding device, but the former arrangement is of considerable advantage. The tow is almost never dead astern of the towing vessel, action of the sea causing it to swing to one side or the other. Without the winding device the hawser would pile up, first in one place on the drum, then another, with consequent slipping and cutting unless laid on by hand, which, especially in rough weather, is exceedingly hazardous. The winding device consists of the vertical rolls L mounted on a carriage M which is carried back and forth on guide bars N by means of the diamond-threaded screw O, automatically winding the hawser evenly on the drum. The rolls through which the hawser is guided are of soft iron and prevent chafing of the hawser. Obviously, when the machine is equipped with a winding device, manual labor is practically eliminated on the towing vessel.

The machine is sometimes equipped with an auxiliary shaft carrying either drums or winch heads, which may be used for the rapid handling of loose lines or for warping into dock, etc. The auxiliary shaft is driven directly from the crankshaft and is operated independently of the towing drum. When not in use, it may be disengaged by means of a jaw clutch, in the same manner in which the towing drum is disengaged when the warping heads are used.

The advantages of the automatic towing machine are appreciated by those familiar with the difficulties encountered in handling heavy tows. It permits the use of a steel hawser, which can be much smaller in diameter than a Manila hawser of the same strength, and considerably smaller than the steel line required when towing with fixed bitts. The automatic paying out and recovering of the hawser enables the towing vessel to maintain a uniform distance without danger of parting the tow line. In approaching shallow waters, or narrow or crowded channels, the hawser is shortened by manually operating the throttle valve without slackening the speed of tow. Likewise, when making off into deeper water, the hawser may be lengthened at will by the operator, always enabling him to keep the line off the bottom.

Many towing machines are designed along the same lines as that pictured in Fig. 61 but are not equipped with the automatic tension device or winding device. These are, of course, considerably inferior to the one described in the foregoing and are certainly not as efficient.

FIG. 61. STEAM TOWING MACHINE (AUTOMATIC TENSION TYPE).

WINCHES

POWER-DRIVEN WINCHES

The principal purpose of winches, in general, is cargo-handling. (See general views in Figs. 62 and 63.) However, they are also used for a multiplicity of purposes involving the handling of lines including warping operations. Winches usually consist of a large cable-winding drum mounted on a horizontal shaft and upon one or both ends of which a winch head (sometimes called a gypsy head) is carried. The winding drum and winch head are generally keyed to the shaft and driven through a train of gears by either electric motors, steam engines or electro-hydraulic transmissions. Gasoline and Diesel engines are also employed in a few cases.

In operating the winding drums, one end of a rope (either hemp or wire) is fastened securely to the drum and wound upon it, the other end being carried through blocks to a boom or mast and finally attaching to either the cargo or to the top of the boom for the purpose of lifting, lowering or positioning the load. Normally on single drum cargo winches, the winch heads are often used to top and train the boom; although in the usual practice of burtoning, the booms are fixed in position during the handling of the cargo, in which case two winches and two booms are used in combination to position the load.

In warping ship with the use of the winch, one end of a line is attached to a fixed object on shore (or to another vessel) and is then extended to the winch head, wound around it several times, and the loose end held by the operator. As the operator pulls on the loose end and the winch head

FIG. 62. WINCH IN OPERATION ON MODERN CARGO SHIP.
(Lidgerwood Mfg. Co.)

is turned in the proper direction by the prime mover, the frictional resistance occurring between the rope and the heads' surface causes the latter to wind in the line, hence, pulling the vessel toward the fixed object on shore. During this procedure, it should be noted that the loose end of the line is continually taken off the head by the operator, and it is necessary that he maintain the required pull on the line, otherwise it may loosen its grip on the surface of the head. Obviously, the speed at which the vessel is pulled is determined by the speed of the winch head and the slippage of the rope around the latter. The slippage of the rope may be reduced or eliminated by increasing the frictional resistance of the rope against the heads' surface and may be accomplished by the operator exerting a heavier pull on the loose end or by increasing the number of times the rope is passed around the barrel. Whelps or raised projections on the surface of winch heads are often employed for the purpose of increasing the bite on the rope or, in other words, for reducing slippage.

The fact that winches are often subject to rough weather, rough handling, and abuse, as well as for continuous heavy duty, requires that they should be ruggedly built to withstand the most severe service required of

FIG. 63. VIEW FROM AMIDSHIPS, SHOWING CARGO WINCH INSTALLATION.
(American Hoist & Derrick Co.)

them. They must always be in working order so as to be ready for immediate service. All working parts should be protected by suitable guards and in such a manner as to provide a maximum of safety for those working in their immediate location. All well-designed winches are, as a rule, easily accessible for inspection, lubrication and repairs.

Winches are built with or without drums, although for cargo handling, a drum is always incorporated. Those with winding drums are generally referred to as cargo winches. Winches having only winch heads are generally known as "warping winches," their principal purpose being warping, but they are sometimes employed as a means for topping and training booms, handling hatch covers and loads including cargo. Often they are employed to handle relieving tackle in connection with emergency steering operations.

On older vessels, multiple-drum winches may still be found. These are usually located athwartships and permit a corresponding number of lines to be handled with only one prime mover to be maintained. However, all modern ships are equipped with single- or double-drum units of compact design thereby occupying a minimum amount of deck space and which permits them to be located more advantageously. Two-, three- and four-drum winches are also built but these may be considered for special applications only.

Except for special conditions, all modern power-driven winches are designed to permit hoisting and lowering by power. They are driven by their prime mover through spur, herringbone, helical or worm gearing, or combinations of these, and are arranged to provide one or two mechanical speeds, all speeds being much slower than that of their prime mover.

All winches must be equipped with mechanical brakes in addition to the electric, dynamic or centrifugal braking arrangements usually found on modern electric units, since they are required by some shipping rules at foreign ports.

STEAM CARGO WINCH—SINGLE GEARED

Fig. 64 shows a single-geared, steam cargo winch used for general cargo handling and consisting of a rope-winding drum A, the main gear B, and a winch head C mounted upon a horizontal shaft D supported by the bearings E. A double-cylinder steam engine F equipped with a piston-type reverse valve G forms an integral part of the unit and drives the crankshaft H which carries a spur-gear pinion (not shown). This pinion meshes with and drives gear B. The winding drum A is rigidly bolted to the main gear B which is in turn keyed to the shaft D, the winch head C also being keyed to this shaft. The speed of the drum and winch head and the direction of rotation of same is obtained by operating the reverse-valve lever K which is equipped with a hand latch and notched segment to hold the lever in any desired position.

A foot-lever, operated band brake is incorporated in the unit and consists of a conventional forged-steel band M (asbestos lined) operated by the foot lever L through a toggle and shafting arrangement (not shown). The band encircles and is applied against one flange of the winding drum. The foot lever L is arranged with a counterweight N in such a manner that the band M is released from the drum except when lever is depressed by the operator. Hoisting and lowering are accomplished under power, the band brake being incorporated as a precautionary requirement.

STEAM CARGO WINCH—COMPOUND-GEARED

Fig. 65 illustrates a single-drum cargo winch similar to that shown in Fig. 64 but with compound gearing to provide two mechanical speeds

FIG. 64. STEAM CARGO WINCH, SINGLE-GEARED.

FIG. 65. STEAM CARGO WINCH, COMPOUND-GEARED.

and pulls. While the speed of a winch could be easily controlled by steam-throttling, it is often desired to handle heavy and light loads at the same horsepower, thereby permitting the use of smaller prime movers. This is accomplished by arranging the gear train in such a manner as to provide two speeds, high speed for normal loads, low speed for heavy loads.

In Fig. 65, the double-cylinder steam engine A drives the crankshaft B upon which the two pinions C and D (both concealed) are mounted. Pinion C meshes with gear E while pinions D and F mesh with gear H. Pinions D and F ride free on their respective shafts but may be engaged to their shafts by the jaw clutches K and L. By turning the double-yoked lever M, one gear is engaged and the other gear is disengaged. Rotating the lever in the opposite direction reverses the operation. In other words, it is impossible to engage both gears with their respective shafts simultaneously.

Assuming that the slow speed of the drum is desired, the lever M is rotated clockwise, thereby engaging the gear F with shaft G, and disengaging gear D from shaft Q. The engine then drives the drum P through gears C, E, F and H.

Should the high speed of the drum be desired, the lever M is rotated counterclockwise, thereby disengaging gear F from shaft G and engaging gear D with shaft O. The engine then drives the drum P through gears D and H.

The winch shown is equipped with a piston-type reverse valve, to permit raising and lowering under power and a foot-lever operated band brake S connected through a toggle-shaft arrangement to the lever R. As mentioned previously, this brake is furnished as a precautionary requirement and is seldom used in normal operation, the lowering of the load always being accomplished under power.

While not shown, the winding drum is usually equipped with rope guards similar to those indicated on the winch in Fig. 67. These guards serve to maintain the rope between the confines of the drum flanges.

ELECTRIC CARGO WINCH

Fig. 66 illustrates a modern electric-driven cargo winch having one mechanical speed, although those having two speeds are also widely employed. The unit is of totally-enclosed cast-construction, the gear housing being of horizontal-split design. Electric brakes as well as the conventional band brakes are incorporated.

With this type, the electric motor A drives the winding drum B and winch head C through a train of spur, herringbone or helical gears enclosed in casing D. The motor being arranged for reversing permits hoisting and lowering the load under power, the full-torque electric brake E automatically acting to hold the load as soon as the current to the machine is shut off. The electrical-control equipment consists of a watertight master switch with magnetic panel and resistors. The master switch is usually located on deck close to the hatch, in order that the operator can properly observe the load. The panel and resistors are located either

Fig. 66. Electric Cargo Winch.

Fig. 67. Electric Cargo Winch Aboard Ship.

below deck or in a house on deck. On direct-current applications, dynamic-lowering control is provided which automatically governs the lowering speed of the load.

The mechanical brake consists of the usual forged-steel brake band F, asbestos-lined, and operated through a system of levers and links by a counterweighted foot pedal. The counterweight serves to hold the brake off the drum flange when the foot lever is not depressed by the operator. It should be mentioned that the mechanical brake is a precautionary device, used only in the event of a casualty of the electric brake.

On electric-driven cargo winches of the type shown, but of two-speed

FIG. 68. ELECTRIC CARGO WINCH, WELDED CONSTRUCTION.
(American Hoist & Derrick Co.)

design, a positive jaw-clutch arrangement is incorporated, similar to that illustrated in Fig. 65, to permit the use of either speed, the high speed for normal loads and the low speed for heavy loads.

Fig. 67 shows an actual application aboard ship of the single-speed winch. This form of winch is used on many U. S. Maritime Commission vessels of the cargo type.

Fig. 68 represents another form of motor-driven cargo winch of compact design. With this type, the supporting frames A, winding drum B, and winch head C are of welded-steel construction, while the oil-tight gear casings D are of welded sheet-steel design. The unit is equipped with electric brakes E, emergency band brakes F, herringbone gears, and adjustable rope guards G. Pressure-type lubricating fittings are also incorporated at all bearings.

Fig. 69 illustrates a modern, electrically-driven, single-drum cargo winch of unique design, also found in multi-drum arrangements. It should be noted that the entire unit, including control equipment, is enclosed in a watertight casing with means provided for easy access to each part of the machine. The unit incorporates all of the features of the most modern winch, including electric brakes, emergency foot brakes, herringbone

FIG. 69. SINGLE-DRUM CARGO WINCH.
(Lake Shore Engineering Co.)

cut gears, and is designed for one or two mechanical speeds. The winch incorporates a modern type of dynamic-lowering hoist control. A blower inside the housing provides ventilation for the motor, brake, control panel, and resistor, the air outlet being clearly visible at the lower right of the unit. This type of winch may be found on U. S. Maritime Commission vessels of the cargo type, and is also used on special-purpose vessels where clear decks are essential.

WARPING WINCH

Generally, a warping winch is simply a cargo winch without a winding drum. It is used primarily for warping ship, hoisting boats, and handling booms. It is also often used in conjunction with relieving tackle in emergency-steering operations. Fig. 70 illustrates a winch of this type.

The unit consists of two winch heads A mounted on the shafts B with

FIG. 70. STEAM WARPING WINCH.

FIG. 71. ANOTHER TYPE OF WARPING WINCH.
(American Hoist & Derrick Co.)

extended ends, and driven through a gear mechanism by a steam engine equipped with a piston-type reverse valve D. Hoisting and lowering is accomplished through the operation of the control-valve lever E having a latching device engaging a notched segment with forward, reverse and neutral positions. Grooved drums F are, also, mounted and rigidly fixed to the shaft B for use with relieving tackle in emergency-steering operations.

This type of winch is usually positioned athwartship and often near the stern of the boat. The grooved drums are only furnished in the latter case and when the steering apparatus is of such design to permit their use with relieving tackle. The fact that the winch heads are nearer the sides of the vessel provides very convenient leads for the warp.

Fig. 71 shows a form of warping winch similar to that shown in Fig. 70, but without the grooved drums and arranged for motor drive. In view of the higher-speed characteristics of the motor as compared with engine-drive, the gear reduction consists of a combination, worm and herringbone gear train enclosed in the casings A and B, respectively.

A reversing-type motor is employed and includes fully-housed electric brakes.

BOAT-HANDLING WINCH

Passenger vessels must all be equipped with winches for lifeboat handling. A form of this type is illustrated in Fig. 72 with electric-motor drive and having one mechanical speed, the load being hoisted by power and lowered by gravity.

The unit is equipped with two rope winding drums driven by an electric motor through spur-gear reductions. The gear mechanism is enclosed in oiltight housings and the motor is of watertight construction. This type of winch is equipped with hand-operated as well as centrifugal brakes, both of which are shipping-rule requirements. The centrifugal brake is provided to automatically limit the speed of lowering by gravity, whereas the hand brake is used to control the lowering operation or to hold the load in a suspended position.

Referring to Fig. 72, the electric motor A with a geared head B drives the speed shaft C through the gear reduction D (enclosed). The speed shaft C in turn, operates the shaft E through the gear reduction enclosed within the housing F. Shaft E operates the drums G and H through the (enclosed) gear reduction K. The centrifugal brake L (enclosed) and the hand brake M are both mounted on the speed shaft C.

A jaw clutch N is provided to engage the prime mover when hoisting and is operated by the knob O. Pushing the knob inward engages the motor with the gear mechanism and pulling the knob out disengages it.

The hand brake M (enclosed) is operated by the counterweighted lever S. The brake is of the free-wheeling type, running free when hoisting by power (making it unnecessary to manually release when hoisting) and automatically holding the load when the power is shut off. When lowering by gravity, the brake is manually released by raising the lever S, thereby allowing the brake-wheel and free-wheeling device to rotate as a unit.

Means are provided for hand operation by the use of removable hand cranks. They are not shown but are mounted on the extended shafts R provided for that purpose.

Operation of the machine is as follows: To hoist under power:

1) Push knob O inward to engage motor with gear.
2) Start motor.

FIG. 72. BOAT-HANDLING WINCH. WHILE NOT SHOWN, THE
WINDING DRUMS ARE ALWAYS FURNISHED GROOVED.

When load has been hoisted to the required height and lowering is
desired:

1) Shut off motor.
2) Pull knob O out, thereby disconnecting motor from gear.
3) Allow load to be lowered by gravity by raising the weighted
brake lever S. The load will not drop faster than the centrifugal
brake will allow—which is approximately 30 ft. per minute.

To hoist by hand-cranking, the knob O should be in the "Out" position.

Lifeboat winches should be as foolproof as possible and, therefore, should be constructed and designed in such a manner that accidents will not occur through their use. It is important that the lines leading from each drum should be of such length that the lifeboat will be horizontal during raising and lowering operations. It is equally important to have the lines wind on the drum evenly.

Winches for this purpose should always be ready for instant service and, for this reason, should be inspected periodically and turned over during long periods of idleness to insure that they are in operating condition at all times.

Chapter 21

FIRST AID AND SHIP SANITATION

GENERAL RULES FOR ACCIDENTS

1. Bleeding must receive first attention and be controlled.

2. Do not move patient unnecessarily, particularly in cases of falls, crushing, traffic accidents, etc., as this may cause serious internal injuries. If victim has a broken back, severing of the spinal column may result from any movement; roll him very gently onto a stretcher if he must be removed.

3. In case of skull fracture, bleeding through eyes and ears is most dangerous. Give no sedatives as they would probably kill him.

4. In cases of drowning do not: *a*) Roll patient over barrels, etc.; *b*) Hold body up by feet; *c*) Dash water in patient's face; *d*) Waste time moving patient unless freezing.

5. Give plenty of pure air and keep inquisitive onlookers away.

6. Dry, warm clothing or blankets should be procured as soon as possible, as warmth is essential, especially when severe shock accompanies an accident. Shock may cause death where the injury itself would not.

7. If necessary to remove clothes, slit those on injured parts, particularly in the case of shoes.

8. In case of poisoning and no emetics are handy, put finger down patient's throat and produce vomiting.

FIRST AID AT SEA

Alcoholism (Drunkenness). Induce vomiting with several spoonfuls of mustard dissolved in a pint of warm water, and put patient to bed.

Amputations (Accidental). The first thing is to stop the bleeding and then get the patient into bed; treat for shock and dress the wound.

ARTIFICIAL RESPIRATION

General Instructions. When a person is made unconscious by fumigation gas, by electric shock, drowning or any other cause, and breathing ceases or becomes very shallow, begin artificial respiration. When a person is not breathing, time is of prime importance. Do not wait and look for help to move the victim to a more convenient place, to give stimulants, to loosen tight clothing or for anything else.

The important thing is to get the resuscitation started at once, so get to it.

1) Put the person in the prone (face down) position, with the head turned to one side and the cheek resting on the hands, or one hand.

2) Open the mouth and sweep your finger through to pull the tongue forward and remove any obstruction.

3) Begin artificial respiration and continue without interruption until the patient is breathing spontaneously or is certainly dead.

4) If the subject begins to breathe on his own but still requires

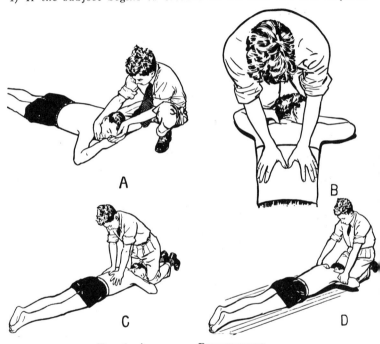

Fig. 1. Artificial Respiration.

help, adjust your rate to his breathing rate; do not attempt to force your rhythm upon him.

5) When help is available or when the victim is breathing without help get the clothing loosened and supply warmth and other measures as needed. Do not interrupt the artificial respiration for any of these purposes.

Arm-Lift Back-Pressure Method: 1) Carry out the first three steps under the general instructions. Note: In carrying out the Schaefer method it was quite necessary to raise the arms in order to have the chest at maximum expansion. In this method this is not necessary and the only reason for having the hand or hands under the face is to keep dirt out of the mouth. In soft ground this is very important. (see A in Fig. 1).

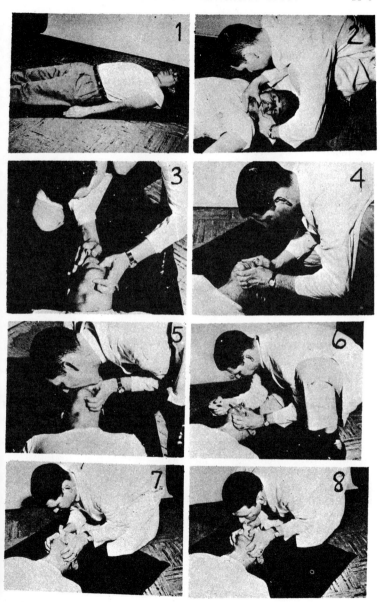

Fig. 2. Mouth-to-Mouth Resuscitation.

2) Kneel at the head of the victim on one or both knees.

3) Place your hands on the victim's back just below the shoulder blades and rock forward to exert a steady gentle pressure on the back to force air out of the lungs. Keep your elbows straight and let the weight of the upper part of your body do the work (see B in Fig. 1).

4) Release the pressure quickly but without giving any extra push at the release (see C in Fig. 1).

5) Rock backward running your hands along the victim's back and arms till you pick up his arms at a point just above the elbows. Continue rocking back, taking the arms upward and towards you. Use just enough effort to feel resistance and tension in the victim's arms. This lifts and expands the chest to permit air to enter (see D in Fig. 1).

6) Rock forward again, placing the victim's arms on the ground and sliding your hands down the arms and back until they come to rest again at the proper pressure point.

7) Repeat the cycle rhythmically at a rate of 10 to 12 complete cycles per minute. Each phase of the cycle should take about 1½ seconds. The rocking motion helps to keep the steady rhythm. The position may be changed from one knee to the other or to both during the operation but it should be done without breaking the rhythm.

8) During resuscitation it may be necessary to change operators. This must be done without losing rhythm of respiration. Thus there is no confusion during change of operator, and a regular rhythm is kept up.

The above quoted instructions plus Fig. 1 should enable the reader to learn the method quickly. If you needed this help, you would certainly hope that someone with you could administer it. Therefore, learn it yourself in case you are called upon for assistance.

Resuscitation is about 90% effective if begun within 2 minutes after breathing stops. About 50% 4 minutes after and about 10% 6 minutes after.

Mouth-to-Mouth Resuscitation (refer to Fig. 2): View 1) Lay victim on back so you can see face. Move injured man carefully.

View 2) Turn head to side, open and clean mouth and throat with cloth or your fingers.

View 3) Pull head back, extending neck. Hold lower jaw up.

View 4) With left thumb between teeth, grasp lower jaw at midline, and lift lower teeth higher than uppers. Close nose with right hand.

View 5) Take deep breath. Put victim's mouth inside your lips and blow into it 12 to 20 times per minute. Watch his chest. When it rises, remove your mouth and let victim exhale passively. If his chest does not rise, improve support of air passageway and blow harder.

View 6) Use an airway tube if it is available.

View 7) To use airway, open mouth and insert along tongue until flange is at his lips. Don't push tongue back in throat.

View 8) Grasp jaw firmly with both hands and pull upward extending neck so chin juts out and front of neck is stretched. Close nostrils by pushing together with the thumbs and blow into airway

Circulation Through Inhalator. The oxygen-carbon dioxide mixture is contained in cylinders charged to a pressure of 135 atmospheres, from which it passes through a reducing valve into a breathing bag. This bag makes each respiration visible to the operator. The volume of flow to the breathing bag is regulated by a volume control valve after the gas has passed through the reducing valve.

The facepiece or half mask is provided with three check valves, one for inhalation, one for exhalation and a third to provide extra air from the outside if the patient requires more at any inhalation than the breathing bag can supply.

A T-cock connection which by-passes the volume control valve makes possible quick assembly of an auxiliary attachment of supply hose, breathing bag and mask for independent treatment of a second victim at the same time.

Method of Operating. Open volume control valve, open one manifold valve and the cylinder valve next to it. Inflate the rubber cushion which forms the rim of the half mask and place the mask over the patient's mouth and nose. After the breathing bag has been inflated, set the volume control at a point on the dial where the bag will neither collapse nor become too full and distended. Change the setting at intervals, if required, in order to maintain this condition. If one cylinder becomes empty, close the manifold valve adjacent to it, and open the manifold and cylinder valves of the second cylinder, thus continuing the treatment without interruption. The empty cylinder should then be replaced with a fully charged one. Continue to use the inhalator until the patient is conscious and breathing normally.

Each cylinder contains when fully charged 16 cubic feet of gas, and will last about 1 1/2 hours at normal operating conditions. Both cylinders should never be turned on at the same time.

Later manifestations: After reaction is fully established, there is great danger of congestion of the lungs, and if perfect rest is not maintained for at least 48 hours, it sometimes happens that the patient is seized with a great difficulty in breathing, and death is liable to follow unless immediate relief is afforded. If the patient gasps for breath, assist the breathing by carefully repeating the artificial respiration. Give oxygen if possible.

Athlete's Foot and Jockey Itch. Use Whitfield's ointment or soak twice daily for 20 min. in a solution of bichloride of mercury or permanganate of potash (1 tablet to 2–3 quarts of water).

Bleeding. Types: Spurting, flowing, oozing.

Spurting bleeding is from a cut artery (**Fig. 3 B**); the blood is bright red, and if the bleeding is not soon checked, the patient may quickly bleed to death. (*See* **Fig. 4 A, B & C.**) The best method of stopping it is to clamp with a forceps and tie both of the cut ends of the artery together with sterile catgut. Usually a tourniquet should be applied first to control the bleeding. Most bleeding can be controlled by simple pressure with a piece of sterile gauze. If this is maintained for 20 or 30 minutes, even fairly large arteries will cease to spurt. This is especially true of the head and neck. If not stopped in this manner, use a clamp and ligature.

Tourniquet. A contrivance used to compress a blood vessel. (*See* Fig. 4*D*.) There are many kinds, but the principle of all is the same. Use rope, string (if heavy enough), or a bandage, handkerchief, necktie, etc. To apply, wrap it around the limb above the bleeding, draw fairly tight, then insert a stick under the wrapping and twist it until the bleeding stops. Care must be taken not to injure the skin, as may happen when the tourniquet is narrow. Under no circumstances should a tourniquet be left on for a period longer than 20 minutes. If it is still necessary after this time it should be loosened, the blood allowed to circulate for a few minutes, then tightened again as necessary.

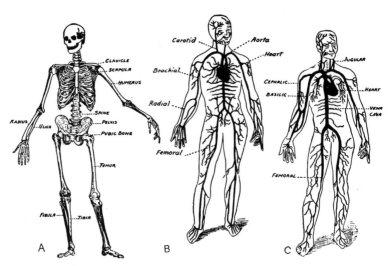

FIG. 3. A) THE HUMAN SKELETON. B) THE ARTERIAL SYSTEM.
C) THE VENOUS SYSTEM.

Bleeding from a vein (**Fig. 3***C*) does not spurt, but wells up and flows from the wound. If the ends of the cut vein can be found, they can be clamped and tied as above, but a tight bandage beyond the wound toward the extremity will control the bleeding so that it will clot when a snug bandage is applied. *Oozing bleeding* needs no special treatment.

Bites. *a*) *Insect.* Apply 1% carbolic acid solution to stop itching, then poultice with a paste of wet soda or soap. *b*) *Rat bites* should be thoroughly washed, first with soap and water, then alcohol. Irrigate the wound with mercurochrome and apply Epsom salts soaks.

Boils or Other Inflammation. Prepare Epsom salts soaks, 1 tablespoon to 1 pint of water, and apply warm.

Broken Bones (Fracture). The first thing is to cut away the clothing from the broken part. Splint the patient where he lies to avoid further damage in moving him. If the broken end is sticking through the skin (compound fracture), pull gently and steadily, tie well-padded boards to the part, apply sterile sulfathiazole powder to the wound and bone fragments and put a clean, sterile dressing over wound before attempting to move the patient. If the skin is not broken (simple fracture), merely pull the parts into approximately normal position and apply splint. The patient can now be moved to a hard bed and, after detailed study of the kind and location of the fracture, proper reduction and splinting may be attempted. (*See* Figs. 3*A* and 4*G* & H.)

Bruises (Contusions). Apply to the skin ice or clothes wrung out in cold water. No treatment is necessary for the "black and blue" discoloration; it will fade away slowly.

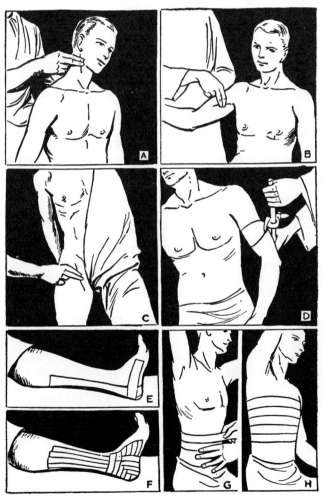

Fig. 4. *A*) Point of Compression for Carotid Artery. *B*) For Brachial Artery. *C*) Femoral Artery. *D*) Windlass Tourniquet. *E*) Strapping an Ankle With Adhesive, First Step. *F*) Strapping Completed. *G*) Strapping Broken Ribs, First Step. *H*) Strapping Completed.

Burns. Cut away the clothes from the burned skin. If the skin is only reddened, apply a clean ointment or linseed oil to the surface. If there are large blisters, they should be drained, best through a hollow needle, going under the good skin a short distance from the blister and then coming up into it. Do not break or remove the skin over a blister but bandage it with a clean, snug dressing. Deep burns with black charred edges should have the dead charred flesh cut away and then be dressed as wounds.

Cramps or Colic. Do not mistake a case of appendicitis for colic. To give cathartics in the situation may cause the patient's death. Put the patient to bed with several hot-water bottles to the flanks and abdomen, then find out whether the cramps are due to appendicitis, abdominal colic, gallstone colic or kidney colic by consulting some medical book such as *The Ship's Medicine Chest*, which should be available on all U. S. vessels. If ice packs are more comfortable than heat, use them. Wrap all ice bags or hot water bottles in a heavy towel to prevent ice or heat burns.

Crushing. Examine for fractures, stop bleeding, and dress as instructed under *Wounds*. If the part is so badly crushed that it is certain not to recover, amputation may be necessary. However, never perform an amputation at sea if it is possible to reach port within several days. Use sulfathiazole powder on all open wounds that cannot be closed.

Dislocation. First, move the patient to a warm comfortable bed and give him a hot drink (whiskey or tea). Then determine the type of dislocation and read up on it before attempting to get it back in place.

Drowning

Rule I. Arouse the patient. Do not move him unless in danger of freezing; instantly expose the face to the air, toward the wind if there be any; wipe dry the mouth and nostrils; rip the clothing so as to expose the chest and waist; give two or three quick, smarting slaps on the chest with the open hand. If the patient does not revive, proceed immediately as follows:

Rule II. To expel water from the stomach and chest: Separate the jaws and keep them apart by placing between the teeth a cork or small bit of wood; turn the patient on his face, a large bundle of tightly rolled clothing being placed beneath the stomach; press heavily on the back over this roll for half a minute, or as long as fluid flows freely from the mouth.

Rule III. To produce breathing: Clear the mouth and throat of mucus by introducing into the throat the corner of a handkerchief wrapped closely around the forefinger; turn the patient on his back, the roll of clothing being so placed as to raise the pit of the stomach above the level of the rest of the body. Let an assistant with a handkerchief or piece of dry cloth draw the tip of the tongue out of one corner of the mouth (which prevents the tongue from falling back and choking the entrance to the windpipe), and keep it projecting a little beyond the lips. Let another assistant grasp the arms just below the elbows and draw them steadily upward by the sides of the patient's head to the ground, the hands nearly meeting (which enlarges the capacity of the chest and induces inspiration). While this is being done let a third assistant take position astride the patient's hips with his elbows resting upon his own knees, his hands extended ready for action. Next, let the assistant standing at the head turn down the patient's arms to the sides of the body the other assistant not releasing the tongue, but changing hands if necessary to let the arms pass. Changing hands will be found unnecessary after some practice. Just before the patient's hands reach the ground the man astride the body will grasp the body with his hands, the balls of the thumbs resting on either side of the pit of the stomach, the fingers falling into the grooves between the short ribs. Now, using his knees as a pivot, he will at the moment the patient's hands touch the ground throw (not too suddenly) all his weight forward on his hands, and at the same time squeeze the waist between them as if he wished to force anything in the chest upward out of the mouth; he will deepen the pressure while he slowly counts 1, 2, 3, 4 (a period of 2 to 2 1/2 seconds) then suddenly let go with a final push, which will spring him back to his first position. This completes expiration.

At the instant of his letting go, the man at the patient's head will again draw the arms steadily upward to the sides of the patient's head as before, holding them there while he slowly counts 1, 2, 3, 4. This completes inspiration.

Repeat these movements deliberately and perseveringly twelve to fifteen times in every minute, thus imitating the natural motions of breathing.

If natural breathing be not restored after a trial of the bellows movement for the space of about four minutes, then turn the patient a second time on the stomach, as directed in Rule II, rolling the body in the opposite direction from that in which it was first turned, for the purpose of freeing the air passage from any remaining water. Continue the artificial respiration from one to four hours, or until the patient breathes according to Rule III, and for a while after the appearance of returning life, carefully aid the first short gasps until deepened into full breaths by carefully timing the movements with the patient's labored breathing. Continue the drying and rubbing, which should have been unceasingly practiced from the beginning by assistants, taking care not to interfere with the means employed to produce breathing. Thus the limbs of the patient should be rubbed, always in an upward direction toward the body. Apply heated objects, etc.

Rule IV. After-treatment: *Externally*, as soon as breathing is established, let the patient be stripped of all wet clothing, wrapped in blankets only, put to bed comfortably warm, but with a free circulation of fresh air, and left to perfect rest. *Internally*, give aromatic spirits of ammonia in doses of a teaspoonful to a tablespoonful, according to the weight of the patient, or hot tea or coffee, every 10 or 15 minutes for the first hour, and as often thereafter as may seem expedient.

Later manifestations: After reaction is fully established, there is great danger of congestion of the lungs, and if perfect rest is not maintained for at least 48 hours, it sometimes happens that the patient is seized with a great difficulty in breathing, and death is liable to follow unless immediate relief is afforded. If the patient gasps for breath, assist the breathing by carefully repeating the artificial respiration. Give oxygen if possible.

Electric Shock. If the patient is still in contact with the live wire, do not touch him, but shut off the current first, or else push him away from the wire with a dry board. Start artificial respiration at once (see *Drowning*). Later, when he is breathing normally, dress the burns.

Eye Splinter. Sit patient down, stand behind him and turn back upper lid. Look for splinter with flashlight. Try to brush it off with a wet gauze over splint; if deeply imbedded, leave it alone, as removal may cause eye to collapse.

Fainting. Get the patient into the open air, loosen his clothing, lay him flat, so that his head is as low as possible, and dash cold water in his face. Try to determine the cause of the faint; especially look up heat exhaustion and apoplexy.

Fits (Spasms). During the fit, the patient should be prevented from injuring himself by striking against surrounding objects. He can be held by several men, or a blanket tied around him. The handle of a spoon, corner of a billfold, or a handkerchief may be stuffed into his mouth to prevent him from biting his tongue. Use a stick to push the handkerchief into his mouth, to avoid bitten fingers.

Gassing. (See *Asphyxia*.)

Gunshot Wounds. Look especially for fractures and for evidences of bleeding internally. If bits of clothing can be seen in the wound they should be fished out. Do not probe around and try to get out the bullet if it is deep. Apply dressing as described under wounds.

Intoxication. (See *Alcoholism*.)

Knife Wounds. Usually the wound is clean. Stop the bleeding as outlined under that heading, and sew the cut edges together. The wound is first cleaned and swabbed out, the first stitch being put midway of the wound, just bringing the edges together. Catgut, silk thread or even horsehair may be used. These materials, especially prepared and sterilized, are usually at hand aboard ship. After putting in the stitches paint the knots and skin with tincture of iodine, wipe excess iodine away with alcohol to prevent burning the skin and dress as any clean wound.

Mortification (Gangrene). Death of a part of the flesh is due to something cutting off its blood supply, and is usually preceded by swelling and a reddish-blue discoloration. These advance signs indicate that something is wrong, and tourniquets, splints, or bandages above the damaged part should be loosened at once. After the tissues are dead, nothing can be done to restore them.

Pain. Pain is an indication that something is wrong, and is nature's way of insisting on rest, since any movement of the sensitive part causes additional pain. In the treatment of pain the underlying cause must be sought and treated. In the meantime, the pain can usually be lessened by rest, hot applications locally to the seat of the pain, and quieting drugs like aspirin, or morphine if necessary.

TABLE 1

Poison	Symptoms	Treatment	Antidote
Alcohol (in any form)	Flushed face, eyes congested, pupils dilated, stupor	Rouse patient, use hot coffee, aromatic spirits of ammonia	Carbonate of ammonia
Arsenic (found in rat poisons, Paris green, Fowler's solution)	Headache, severe pain in stomach, vomiting, collapse	Much lukewarm water, milk, give whites of eggs	Peroxide of iron
Carbon monoxide (gasoline engines exhaust)	Unconsciousness, skin is cherry pink	Administer oxygen, keep quiet and warm	Oxygen
Lead (sugar of lead, lead paint, white lead)	Metallic taste, much thirst, colic, cramps in legs, cold sweat	$\frac{1}{2}$ oz. Epsom salts in tumbler of water, stimulant, soothing liquids	Iodide of potassium or sodium
Opium, morphine, paregoric (in some soothing syrup and cough mixtures)	Skin cold, face pale, respiration and pulse slow, drowsiness	Rouse patient, hot coffee, artificial respiration and oxygen	Slap patient, pinch ears and make him walk around for 24 hrs., if necessary
Chloral hydrate or **barbiturate**	Skin cold, face pale, respiration and pulse slow, drowsiness	Rouse patient, hot coffee, artificial respiration and oxygen	Strychnine
Phosphorus (matches, rat and vermin killers)	Severe abdominal pain, vomiting, skin is dark, nose bleeding	Avoid fats and oils, Epsom salts, stimulants, soothing liquids	Magnesia in water
Ptomaine (decayed meat, fish, etc.—similar to poisoning from infected ripe olives, toadstools, etc.)	Nausea, vomiting, skin cold and clammy, pulse weak, colic, headache, great distress, diarrhea	Powdered charcoal, stimulants	Bismuth and fluids of all sorts freely
Strychnine, nux vomica (in some vermin killers)	Feeling of suffocation, spasms, face blue, exhaustion, jaws locked	Powdered charcoal in large quantity, another emetic, artificial respiration	Bromides, chloral hydrate

TABLE 1 (*Continued*)

II. POISONS FOR WHICH AN EMETIC SHOULD NOT BE GIVEN FIRST.

Poison	Symptoms	Treatment	Antidote
Iodine	Intense scalding pain in throat and stomach, vomiting	Give as much cornstarch paste as stomach will hold	
Mercury, corrosive sublimate (antiseptic tablets)	Very irritating, turning mouth, lips and tongue white, mouth swollen, tongue shrivelled; pain in abdomen; nausea and vomiting, cold, clammy skin prostration, convulsions	Give white of egg or whole egg beaten up; flour and water, but not so good; then emetics, soothing liquids and stimulants	White of egg and milk; induce vomiting with large quantities of soda water or finger down throat
Nitrate of silver, lunar caustic	Black stains about mouth (white at first) acute pain, collapse	Salt in water, or milk; then emetic, afterwards soothing liquids and stimulants	Common salt (sodium chloride)

III. POISONS FOR WHICH AN EMETIC SHOULD NEVER BE GIVEN.

Poison	Symptoms	Treatment	Antidote
Strong corrosive acids: *a*) Acetic *b*) Hydrochloric *c*) Nitric (*aqua fortis*) *d*) Sulphuric (vitriol)	Red stain on clothes, burns or stains about mouth, vomiting, purging, great shock and prostration	An alkali, best is magnesia, lime, baking soda, etc.; afterwards soothing liquids and stimulants; if acid in air passage, inhale ammonia fumes	Alkalies
Oxalic acid (salts of lemon or sorrel)	Much like above, but not so much burning	Magnesia, chalk and water, or lime water, then 1 oz. castor oil and stimulants	Magnesia

TABLE 1 (*Continued*)

III. POISONS FOR WHICH AN EMETIC SHOULD NEVER BE GIVEN.

Poison	*Symptoms*	*Treatment*	*Antidote*
Carbolic acid (phenol), very commonly used in attempts at suicide	A powerful corrosive causing great pain and vomiting; in severe case unconsciousness and early death; odor of acid, burns; pure acid burns white, impure, black	Rinse mouth with pure alcohol, swallow 3–4 spoonfuls alcohol and equal amount water; if above not at hand, use limewater; then 3–4 raw eggs, sweet oil; stimulant, keep warm	Induce vomiting first
Strong caustic alkalies: *a*) Ammonia, (camphor liniment) *b*) Lime, quicklime *c*) Potash *d*) Caustic soda *e*) Lye	Much like corrosive acids; destroys tissues of mouth, vomiting and purging; severe shock and suffocation from swelling	An acid like vinegar, lemon or orange juice, tartaric or citric acids in plenty of water; soothing liquids, stimulants; if cannot swallow, may inhale acetic acid or vinegar from a handkerchief	Acids

Paralysis. Paralysis is usually the result of some injury to the nervous system. If a nerve is cut, the muscles supplied by it are paralyzed until the nerve grows back. If a part of the brain is destroyed, as by a bursting blood vessel in apoplexy, the muscles supplied are paralyzed. Little or nothing can be done for paralysis as an emergency measure. Massage and splinting of the part involved prevents muscular wasting and contracture while new nerve fibers are growing.

Poisoning. In treating poisoning correctly, it is very desirable to know what poison was used. If this is known, look up the specific treatment in Table 1 and give the proper antidote.

If the poison has been taken by mouth, although its nature is unknown, it is always safe to give large amounts of white of egg and then try to induce vomiting by tickling the throat. A stomach tube can usually be passed safely and the stomach washed out, if necessary. Later, a large dose of Epsom salts is helpful in removing the poison which has passed into the intestines.

Respiration, Artificial. (See *Artificial Respiration.*)

Retention of Urine. Retention of urine is usually due to a stricture or enlarged prostate, and comes on slowly. It may be due to rupture of the urethra or disease or injury of the nerves of the bladder. Look up strictures and methods of passing catheters in a medical book.

Rupture (Hernia). The only emergency treatment of rupture is to get the protruding mass back and to keep it back with large pads and snug bandages. To reduce a rupture, the patient should be lying on his back with the knees bent; and while he relaxes as much as possible, by breathing with the mouth wide open, gentle, steady pressure is made with the palms against the mass. It will usually slip back with little trouble, but the difficulty is to keep it back. If nothing else helps, give morphine (1/4 gr.), relax patient and again try reduction. A person with hernia can be cured only by an operation; and a sailor should enter a hospital for repair of the hernia as soon as possible.

Scalds. Scalds are treated like any burn, except that the clothing must always be cut away very carefully so as not to tear open the large blisters. These are then drained and the burns dressed in the usual manner. It is advisable to give morphine at once to patients with severe scalds to relieve the pain.

Shock. Shock is a frequent cause of death and in bombings, torpedo, mine or depth charge explosions, there may be no external injuries. The victim's nervous system is so stunned that it relaxes control over the blood vessels. Blood flows away from the head, arms and legs and collects in the abdomen while some blood fluid seeps into the body's tissues, and the victim actually bleeds to death in his own body.

The shock victim often has a fear of impending disaster; he grows pale and breaks out in a cold sweat; his eyes become glazed and his pulse is rapid and feeble. The most important thing to do right away is to keep him as warm as possible, lay him down so that his head is lower than his feet so the blood will flow to the heart and brain. Wrap him in blankets and apply hot water bottles. A whiff of ammonia or a teaspoonful of aromatic spirits of ammonia in a half glass of water given every thirty minutes, or strong black coffee will all prove helpful. Keep him warm and quiet. This treatment will take care of the vast majority of cases. If further treatment is required, a small dose of morphine (one-sixth grain) or half a cubic centimeter of adrenalin by hypodermic may be life saving.

Spasms. (See *Fits* and look up *Epilepsy.*)

Sprains. Sprains are due to stretching or tearing of the ligaments around a joint. These ligaments are very important structures, as they hold the bones together, and, since they heal slowly, a bad sprain requires splints and careful treatment.

Strangling. Strangling is due to something shutting off the windpipe. It may be around the neck, as in hanging, or may be something caught in the throat. If the patient is strangling, always look and feel down the throat. The throat may be straightened out by putting a pillow under the shoulders, letting the head fall back, and pulling up on the tongue. By doing this, and using a flashlight, it is often possible to see directly down into the larynx ("voice box") and lift out a foreign body, such as a piece of meat, with a pair of forceps, or even with the fingers. Then loosen the clothing around his neck and, if he does not start to breathe, give artificial respiration.

Suffocation. Get the suffocated person into the fresh air and give artificial respiration.

Unconsciousness. Unconsciousness may be temporary and of little importance, as in fainting, but if it lasts for several hours it usually

TABLE 2. COMMUNICABLE DISEASES

Disease	Cause	Source of Infection	Mode of Transmission	Incubation Period	Period of Communicability
*Anthrax	Bacteria	Animals, their hair, hides, bristles	Not transmitted person-to-person, caused by handling hides, etc., while skin abrasions are present		None person-to-person
Chicken pox	Unknown	Discharge from eruption, chiefly from early eruption in nose and mouth	Direct: sick to well; Indirect: articles soiled with discharges	2–3 weeks	Until skin is free from eruption
*Cholera	Cholera vibrio	Bowel discharges and vomited material	Contact cases or carriers, soiled articles, food, water, flies	1–5 days	7–14 days
Dengue	Unknown	Blood of infected person	Bite of mosquito	3–10 days	To 5th day of disease
Diphtheria	Bacillus	Discharges from nose and throat of patients and carriers	Contact cases or carriers, and soiled articles, milk	2–5 days	2–4 weeks
Dysentery 1. Amebic	Ameba	Bowel discharges	Water, food, soiled objects, flies	Unknown	Throughout disease
2. Bacillary	Bacillus	Bowel discharges	Water, food, soiled objects, flies	2–7 days	Until complete recovery
Gonorrhea	Bacteria	Discharges	Contact, and freshly soiled articles	1–8 days	Throughout disease, acute or chronic
Influenza	Unknown	Discharges from mouth and nose	Contact and freshly soiled articles, flies and other insects	24–72 hours	7 days
*Leprosy	Bacillus	Discharges	Close prolonged contact	Prolonged	Throughout disease
Malaria	Animal parasite	Blood of infected person	Bite of mosquito	8 days–3 weeks	Throughout infection
Measles	Unknown	Discharges from mouth and nose	Contact and freshly soiled articles	10 days	9 days
Mumps	Unknown	Discharges from mouth and nose	Contact and freshly soiled articles	12–26 days	Until disappearance of swelling
*Plague, bubonic	Bacillus	Blood of infected man and rats, sputum	Contact and bite of rat flea	3–14 days	Until recovery
*Psittacosis	Unknown	Birds of parrot family and sick canaries	Contact	15 days	Until recovery
Pneumonia	Bacteria	Discharges from mouth and nose	Contact and freshly soiled articles	2–3 days	Until recovery
Scarlet fever	Bacteria	Discharges from mouth and nose	Contact and freshly soiled articles, milk	2–7 days	3 weeks
*Smallpox	Unknown	Discharges from eruption, especially from early eruption in nose and mouth	Contact and soiled articles, flies	8–16 days	Until skin is free from eruption
Syphilis	Spirochaete	Blood, discharges from skin and mucous membrane	Contact, and soiled articles	3–5 weeks	Until skin and mucous membrane are normal
Tetanus (lockjaw)	Bacillus	"Dirt"	Wound infection	8–10 days	Rarely communicable
Trachoma	Unknown	Discharges, chiefly from eye	Contact and freshly soiled articles	Unknown	Until cured
Tuberculosis	Bacillus	Discharges, chiefly from sputum	Contact, soiled articles, food and flies	Unknown	Until recovery
Typhoid	Bacillus	Bowel discharges; urine; carriers	Contact, and food, flies, fingers; carriers; milk and water	7–23 days	Until recovery, and sometimes prolonged thereafter
*Typhus (Spotted fever)	Not definite	Blood of infected person	Lice	5–20 days	Until 36 hours after disappearance of fever
Whooping cough	Bacillus	Discharges from mouth and nose; pets	Contact and freshly soiled articles	Within 10 days	Until recovery
*Yellow fever	Animal parasite	Blood of infected person	Bite of mosquito	3–6 days	During first days of fever

* Quarantinable diseases

indicates a serious condition. Drunken stupor should be recognized as differing from true unconsciousness. Serious injuries, especially head injuries, may give long-continued unconsciousness. Apoplexy, diabetic coma, uremia, poisoning, especially by morphine, are to be considered.

VACCINATION AGAINST SMALLPOX

1. Virus of known potency and unexpired date must be used. The vaccine should be kept in a refrigerator at all times, at a temperature of approximately 40 degrees F.

2. After gently cleansing the skin, one drop of vaccine should be placed on it. The skin should then be drawn tense, and 20 to 30 punctures made through the vaccine into the skin in an area of about 1/8 inch with the point of a sterile needle held parallel to the arm. The excess vaccine should be removed immediately.

3. The results shall be recorded as: (A) Vaccinia, (B) Vaccinoid, or (C) Immune reaction (by Doctor or Master).

4. Vaccinia (A): (Typical Jennerian Vaccinia) No reaction shown for 3–4 days. Vesiculation about the fifth or sixth day with areola present; purulence, with well marked areola about the eighth day.

5. Vaccinoid (B): The papule occurs after two but frequently before five days have elapsed. The reaction is less severe and takes less time to run its course than a *Successful Vaccination*. Vesicles are frequent. Pustules are not always present.

6. Immune Reaction (C): A prompt, sharp reaction, with redness and swelling in the vaccinated area, which reaches its maximum in about 48 to 60 hours and then gradually disappears without formation of vesicles. Reactions which do not appear within the period mentioned should not be classed as immune reactions.

Vomiting. Vomiting is a symptom usually due to an overloaded or poisoned stomach. It should be encouraged rather than suppressed, as it is nature's method of getting rid of what is harmful. Vomiting of greenish material is not in itself serious, but merely indicates that nature is emptying the first part of the small intestine also. However, if the vomiting is long continued or contains foul-smelling black material, it is a sign of serious trouble, usually some obstruction in the intestinal tract, and the patient should have medical attention as soon as possible. Vomiting without sensation of sickness in the stomach occasionally occurs with head injuries or brain disease.

After the action of vomiting is over, a drink of cold lemonade or some whiskey in hot water may help "quiet the stomach."

Wheezing. Wheezing is a noisy rasping sort of breathing heard in asthma, or may be caused by a foreign body in the windpipe, when it is really partial strangulation.

Wounds. Stop the bleeding. (See *Bleeding.*) Foreign bodies, such as bits of cloth, should be lifted out and the wound cleansed by washing with some antiseptic like peroxide or boric acid if it contains dirt. If it looks clean, leave it alone, bring the edges together with adhesive or sutures, apply a clean dressing, and change the dressings daily. The best antiseptic is mercurochrome.

THE MEDICINE CHEST

In the ship's medicine chest are found drugs and chemicals of which the following is a representative list. It also contains surgical instruments and appliances suitable to care for the average emergency case.

Drugs and Chemicals

Caution. Preparations containing opium, such as paregoric, laudanum, camphor and opium pills, etc., should be given only when absolutely necessary, as they are habit-forming.

Antiseptics and Disinfectants

Bichloride of mercury
 (7 1/2-grain tablets and bulk)
Carbolic acid (pure)
Chloride of lime

Solution of cresol (compound)
Formalin
Sulphur
Sulfathiazole powder (50 gr.)

Ointments

Vaseline
Mercury ointment

Ichthyol ointment (20%)
Sulphur ointment
Whitfield's ointment (mild)

External use only:
Permanganate of potash
 (1-grain tablets or crystal form)
Soap liniment
Tincture of iodine
Turpentine

Argyrol solution (20%)
Mercurochrome solution (1%) or merthiolate
Cocaine solution (1%)
Camphorated oil
Picric acid (1/2% solution)

Powders

Calomel
Boric acid

Bismuth subnitrate

Cathartics

Compound cathartic pills
Castor oil

Calomel (1/2 grain)
Epsom salts

Internal Medicines

Aromatic spirits of ammonia
Bicarbonate of soda (baking soda)
Bromide of potash
Capaiba and Santal oil (5-grain tablets)
Sun cholera mixture (5-grain tablets)
Brown's mixture (cough syrup)
Sweet spirits of niter

Ipecac (alcresta) (5-grain tablets)
Aspirin (5-grain tablets)
Quinine sulphate (5-grain capsules)
 Caution: Always give 5 gr. and wait 1/2 hr. If no headache, vomiting or ringing in the ears appears, may give up to 15 gr. twice daily.
Paregoric
Alcohol

Hypodermics

Morphine sulphate (1/4-gr. tablets)
Novocain and adrenalin (1 grain)

Strychnin sulphate (1/30-grain tablets)

Antiseptics and Disinfectants

External Use Only

Bichloride of mercury (poison). One tablet (7 1/2 grains) dissolved in a quart of water makes an antiseptic wash for wounds. When used to make wet dressings the strength should be one tablet to six pints of water. For scrubbing infected decks, quarters, and soaking infected clothing use 1 teaspoonful of the bulk or powdered form to 1 gallon of water.

Carbolic acid—liquid (poison). A useful antiseptic and disinfectant is made by using 1 part of acid to 100 parts of hot water.

Chloride of lime. This is used to disinfect drinking water from an unreliable source. Put 1/2 teaspoonful of this powder to each barrel of water to be treated and mix well.

Solution of cresol, compound (poison). An effective disinfectant is made by adding one tablespoonful of cresol to each quart of water. This is mainly used for disinfecting quarters, clothing and the stools and urine of typhoid and yellow fever patients.

Formalin (poison). This substance is generally used as a disinfectant with permanganate of potash as follows: For every 1000 cubic feet of room space to be disinfected use 1/2 pound of permanganate of potash and from 1 to 1 1/4 pints of formalin. This should be done in a deep pail, when effervescence begins at once. The room should be kept tightly closed for 12 hours. It is very irritable to the mucous membranes of the nose and throat and should be used with great caution.

Sulphur. Sulphur is used to destroy vermin and rats. When it is burned it produces sulphur-dioxide. To effectively fumigate a room, paste paper over all cracks, keyholes, etc. All ports and ventilators should be closed. It is best to burn the sulphur in heavy metal pans to insure complete combustion.

Permanganate of potash. Useful, as an antiseptic, in the treatment of gonorrhea (clap): use 1/4 of a teaspoonful of the crystals of powder in 2 quarts of water or use a one-grain tablet dissolved in a quart of warm water. To make a general antiseptic, use one tablespoonful in a quart of water.

Soap liniment. For use in the treatment of rheumatism, sprains, and bruises.

Tincture of iodine (poison). To disinfect wounds iodine should be diluted with an equal amount of water. Before opening a boil the surface should be painted with tincture of iodine and the edges of all wounds that are to be served should be painted. It is also useful on inflamed surfaces. Do not use a strong solution if the surface painted is to be covered closely as it may blister. Wash off the alcohol.

Turpentine. Used as a liniment in the treatment of bruises and sprains. Do not use too freely or it will cause tender skin to blister.

Argyrol solution (20%). This solution is a valuable preventive of venereal diseases. (*See* Table given on **page** 21–15 .) This strength argyrol solution is also used for the treatment of inflamed eyes by dropping one or two drops inside the lower lid. If this burns the eyes dilute it with an equal amount of sterile water.

Mercurochrome. This antiseptic is used as iodine. It will not blister. It is also valuable as a preventive of gonorrhea by injecting a 1% solution.

Cocaine solution. To be used for one purpose only, the removal of foreign bodies from the eye. Drop one drop of 1 per cent solution on the eye until three drops have been used. The removal of the object will be painless.

Camphorated oil. To be used in case of sprains, bruises, neuralgia, rheumatism or pains and swelling. Rub it on gently. It can also be applied on flannel to the chest and neck for colds.

Picric acid solution (1/2%). Useful in wet dressing to be applied to burns.

Ointments

Vaseline. Especially useful in treating burns as it is non-irritating and its application excludes air.

Ichthyol ointment (20%). Used for reducing swelling of the testicles and pain and swelling of joints.

Mercury ointment (commonly called blue ointment). Used in killing crab lice. Apply to the hairy parts well and let it remain for a day or two. Then bathe well.

Sulphur ointment. Used mainly to kill the parasite causing scabies or itch. Apply for three successive nights, without bathing, then bathe well and change all clothing.

Powders

Calomel. Calomel powder is useful in the treatment of ulcers and sores in venereal disease. It is a good antiseptic powder for any use.

Boric acid. Useful in making a mild antiseptic for wet dressings for wounds and burns. It is also used in an eyewash. The correct strength, for both uses, is four level tablespoonfuls of boric acid dissolved in one pint of boiling water.

Bismuth subnitrate. This is useful in dysentery and diarrhea. Take 1/4 level teaspoonful either mixed with water or dry and follow with water. If taken in 5-grain tablets, take 2 to 4 tablets every 3 hours. Crush before taking.

Cathartics

Compound cathartic pills (C. C. pills). Useful in constipation. One to three should be taken at bedtime.

Castor oil. A safe and effective cathartic. One to three tablespoonfuls should be taken. If lemon juice and a pinch of baking soda are added it will eliminate most of the unpleasant taste.

Calomel (1/2-grain tablets). For a thorough cleaning out one 1/2-grain tablet should be taken every 20 to 30 minutes until six have been taken. When 4 to 6 hours have elapsed it should be followed by a dose of Epsom salts or castor oil. Calomel should not be used frequently as it contains mercury and may cause mercury poisoning.

Epsom salts. Useful in constipation and dysentery. One to two tablespoonfuls should be taken in a glass of hot water to produce prompt results. An enema via catheter is a safe way to make the bowels move (1 quart water with soapsuds).

Internal Medicines

Aromatic spirits of ammonia. Useful in cases of faintness, headache and colic, as a stimulant in shock and heat exhaustion, one-half to one teaspoonful in water every half hour until three doses are taken.

Bicarbonate of soda (baking soda). Will be found useful for relief of sour stomach and heartburn. One-half to one teaspoonful in half a glass of water. This can be repeated if necessary. For painful urination during the acute stage of gonorrhea four 5-grain sodium bicarbonate tablets in water (20 grains) should be taken every two hours.

Bromide of potash (5-grain tablets). To be used in convulsions and delirium tremens. Give three to five tablets dissolved in water, three times a day.

Sun cholera mixture (5-grain tablets). Used to reduce the number of stools in diarrhea, dysentery, and cholera morbus; one tablet should be taken every two hours until relieved.

Sweet spirits of niter. Useful in fevers and colic. Give one-half teaspoonful in sweetened water every 4 hours.

Ipecac (Alcresta) (5-grain tablets). Used in the treatment of amoebic dysentery. Unlike syrup of ipecac they do not cause nausea. They should be given in doses of one to three tablets three times a day as long as the dysentery continues.

Aspirin (5-grain tablets). Aspirin is given to reduce fever, for headaches, colds, and pain. No more than two five-grain tablets every four hours should be given.

Quinine sulphate (5-grain capsules). Quinine is only given in the treatment and prevention of malaria. As a preventive not more than ten grains should be given. In treatment of malaria it is given in doses of 5 to 10 grains every four hours, until 200 grains have been given, then discontinued for 48 hours and then repeated.

Paregoric. This opium compound is given to relieve pain and abdominal cramps. It is given in doses of one to three teaspoonfuls.

Alcohol. Useful as an antiseptic wash for open wounds or washing the surface of the skin that is to be opened. Internally it is given, in an equal amount of water, for shock or collapse from exposure.

Penicillin in tablet form has been found to be very effective in the case of gonorrhea infection. One tablet of 100,000 units should be administered every hour until a total of six (6) tablets have been given. It is advisable to limit the use of penicillin to the above purpose, though it may be used in other infections, where the sulfa drugs have been found ineffective, after a suitable trial. These are tonsillitis, boils, infected wounds, etc.; the method of administration is the same as for gonorrhea.

Penicillin may also be used in severe conditions such as pneumonia, appendicitis, scarlet fever, syphilis and other bacteria infections but in these cases radio advice of a physician should be sought.

It is known that in tetanus, some forms of dysentery, typhoid fever, whooping cough, tuberculosis, typhus and spotted fevers, measles, influenza, poliomyelitis and the common cold penicillin is not effective and should not be used.

Sulfathiazole is now supplied to most vessels for the treatment of gonorrhea. The following is recommended: Four 7 1/2 grain tablets of sulphathiazole are taken every 4 hours for 3 doses, accompanied by a glass of water to which has been added 1/2 teaspoonful of bicarbonate of soda. Following this, two tablets are taken every 4 hours for 3 days, and then 1 tablet morning and night for a period of 1 week. If a temperature of 101 degrees or above is noted, or if there is a bluish color on lips, fingers and toes, the medication should be stopped immediately, a purge given, and then the medication started again in 24 hours and in half the original dosage.

Surgical Supplies for the Medicine Chest

1 reel adhesive plaster (10 yds. by 1″ wide)
1 doz. bandages (1/2 doz. gauze, 1/2 doz. muslin) 5 yds by 2″ wide
1 pair bandage scissors
4 assorted rubber catheters
1 fountain syringe, 2 qt.
3 camel's-hair brushes
2 ice-bags
6 medicine glasses
1 urinal
2 doz. safety pins
1 pr. 6″ shears
3 wooden splints
5 yds. picric acid gauze
6 triangular muslin bandages
12 assorted surgical needles
3 tubes of linen
1 incisor tooth forceps
2 clinical thermometers
50 3″ compressed bandages
1 pr. dressing forceps

1 doz. bandages (1/2 doz. gauze, 1/2 doz. muslin) 3 yds. by 2″ wide
1 doz. bandages (5 yds. muslin by 4″ wide)
3 artery forceps
1 metal catheter
12 urethral syringes
2 hot-water bags
6 medicine droppers
1 bedpan
1 tourniquet
1 pr. blunt end shears
2 sheets of Yucca board
2 pcs. heavy mesh malleable wire gauze
50 yds. sterile gauze, plain
2 nail brushes
6 tubes of catgut
1 spool of silk ligature
1 molar tooth forceps
4 lbs. absorbent cotton
25 1 1/2″ compressed bandages

GLOSSARY

Abdomen. Belly.

Abscess. A local collection of pus.

Acid. Sour, opposite of alkali.

Acute. Sharp, sudden, usually severe.

Adhesive. Sticking plaster of large size used to hold dressings in place and also wound edges together until healing occurs.

Alkali. Opposite of acid, neutralizes acid. Vinegar is an acid; lye is an alkali.

Anaesthesia. Loss of feeling.
  General anaesthesia. Sleep under ether or chloroform.
  Local anaesthesia. Production of loss of feeling in a part.

Antidote. A remedy for counteracting a poison and stopping its action.

Antiscorbutic. A substance, usually a food, used to prevent scurvy.

Antiseptic. A substance which will prevent the growth of germs.

Artificial respiration. Breathing caused by artificial methods.

Bacteria. Germs; very small forms of vegetable life which can be seen only with the microscope.

Bladder. The organ which holds urine, located in the lower abdomen.

Blood clot. Blood which exposed to air has become solid.

Bowel. Intestine; gut.

Bubo. Swollen gland.

Capillary. A very fine blood vessel, too small to see with the naked eye.

Capsule. A small case made of gelatin for giving bad-tasting drugs.

Cathartic. A substance which, when taken by mouth, causes a movement of the bowels.

Caustic. A drug which burns or destroys tissues.

Centigrade thermometer. One in which freezing temperature reads 0° and boiling water 100°.

Charring. To turn black.

Clinical record. A record of occurrences during illness.

Clinical thermometer. A thermometer used to take the body temperature of a person.

Colic. Cramp-like pains, especially in the abdomen.

Collapse. Extreme prostration and depression, with failure of the circulation.

Comminute. Splintered, broken into small pieces.

Compress. A wad of cotton or gauze, applied over wounds or over a painful area.

Constitutio..al. Throughout the whole body or system.

Contamination. To become dirty by touching.

Contused. Bruised.

Counterirritant. Some substance applied to the skin to produce redness.

Cramps. Sharp pains due to spasms of muscles, usually come and go.

Crepitus. A grating sensation which can be felt when broken ends of bones are rubbed together.

Delirium. Condition in which patient is said to be "out of his head."

Diagnosis. The act of distinguishing one disease from another.

Digestion. The process of preparing food taken into the body for use by the body.

Dilute. Not strong.

Disinfection. The destruction of germs.

Disinfestation. Destruction of vermin.

Distended. Filled, enlarged.

Epidemic. Condition in which there are many cases of a disease.

Eruption. A "breaking out," as on the skin.

Excretion. A process by which the body disposes of waste, as in urine or sweat.

Extension. To straighten out; to pull.

Fahrenheit thermometer. One in which freezing temperature is 32° and boiling is 212°.

Fever. Higher body temperature than normal.

Forceps. An instrument with two blades for clamping, grasping, or crushing.

Fumigation. The exposure to poisonous gases or fumes (usually with the idea of killing vermin or germs).

Gangrene. Local death of a part.

Gauze. A very thin cloth used for dressing wounds.

Hemorrhage. Bleeding.

Hypodermic. Under the skin.

Incise. To cut.

Incubation period. The time required for a disease to develop after exposure to it.

Infection. The growth of germs, frequently with the formation of pus.

Inoculation. The intentional introduction of a virus to produce a mild form of disease which will protect against the severe form of that disease.

Inunction. Rubbing medicines or salves into the skin.

Isolate. To separate; to place alone.

Jaundice. Yellowness of the eyes and skin.

Laceration. A torn wound.

Ligate. To tie off, as a blood vessel.

Ligature. A thread for tying a vessel.

Malinger. To pretend; to fake.

Manipulate. To work with the hands; to move and place.

Mucous membrane. The reddish lining of all body cavities which communicate with the air, as the mouth.

Nausea. "Sick at the stomach"; desire to vomit.

Organism. An individual form of life constituted to carry on the activities of life. An animal or plant.

Papular. Composed of papules which are small, round elevations on the skin.

Pox. A term used to designate small-pox or syphilis (great pox).

Pratique. Permission given to a ship that has satisfied the health regulations to enter a port.

Prevalence. To be present and extend widely.

Prophylaxis. The prevention of disease.

Purgative. A medicine which causes the bowels to move freely.

Pus. The creamy discharge from an infected wound.

Relax. To make loose; to slaken.

Retching. Attempts at vomiting without results.

Rupture. To break through.

Saliva. Spit.

Septicemia. Blood poisoning.

Serum. The fluid part of the blood in which the corpuscles float.

Sloughing. The separation and fluffing out of dead tissue from a wound.

Sterile. Free of all germ life.

Sterilization. The process of killing all germs.

Stimulate. To produce activity or quicken and strengthen action, as of the heart.

Stool. Material passed from bowels.

Strangulated. A condition in which a part is pinched or constricted.

Suture. A material used for sewing.

Symptoms. The complaints and discomforts of a patient indicating disease.

Tincture. A medicine dissolved in dilute alcohol.

Ulcer. A local open sore.

Ventilation. The process of continually supplying fresh air.

Vesicle. A blister on the skin or mucous membrane and filled with clear fluid.

Vitality. Life.

SHIP HYGIENE AND SANITATION

Quarantine Inspection. Bills of health must be secured by all vessels clearing for U. S. ports from foreign and insular ports. Issued at port of departure (first foreign port at which cargo or passengers are taken on for a U. S. port), and all subsequent ports, provided there are U. S. consuls in these ports. Issued in duplicate, the duplicate copy being given to the boarding quarantine officer and the original presented, with the quarantine pratique, to the collector of customs at time of entry. Not required on vessels plying exclusively between U. S. and Canada, or certain Mexican ports or ports in the Bahamas, Cuba, and adjacent ports, unless there is a quarantinable disease present in a foreign port of departure.

Free pratique (on white paper) indicates the vessel has met the requirements and no further quarantine formalities are required.

Provisional pratique (on yellow paper) is conditioned upon the observance of additional quarantine procedures which are specified thereon.

Radio pratique covers the permission granted (request made 12 to 24 hours before expected arrival) to selected passenger vessels, whereby they may enter certain U. S. ports without stopping at quarantine. Requirements briefly are:

1. Acceptable ship's doctor employed aboard.

2. No calls at ports having or suspected of having quarantinable diseases.

3. No birds of parrot family aboard.

4. Maintained relatively rat-free.

5. Maintained in a sanitary condition.

6. No known or suspected quarantinable or unusual incidence of other communicable disease aboard.

IMMIGRATION EXAMINATIONS

The primary responsibility for bringing to the U. S. aliens suffering from certifiable diseases or defects rests with the steamship company.

The determination of the citizenship of a passenger or member of the crew resides solely with the immigration officer before whom the person appears, and not with medical or other officers.

In the absence of suitable facilities as to space, lighting and assistance, or of proper cooperation, examination will not be made.

Classes of Diseases and Defects. Class *A* are mandatorily excludable from the U. S. In general, they are mental diseases or deficiencies, tuberculosis, trachoma, epilepsy and certain diseases classed as loathsome or dangerously contagious, among them being included the venereal diseases. Such aliens, passengers or crew, are sent to immigration station or hospital.

Class *B* includes defects or diseases which may affect ability to earn a living. Alien members of the crew with class *B* conditions are not detained unless they seek admission into the U. S.

Class *C* are minor diseases or defects which are not of great consequence, but which are reported to the immigration officer for his information and guidance.

Alien crew members may be subject to intensive physical examinations on each arrival in a U. S. port, particularly for venereal disease.

Disabled or sick persons unable to appear for inspection with comfort or safety may be examined in their quarters.

Hospitalization. Alien passengers requiring treatment for diseases communicable or noncommunicable are sent to the immigration hospital. Only those alien crew members suffering from or suspected of Class *A* conditions are sent to immigration hospital. Citizen crew members of U. S. vessels, regardless of the conditions from which they suffer, are sent to the Marine Hospital, as are alien seamen serving continuously on U. S. vessels.

DOCUMENTS

1. Port sanitary statement issued in U. S. ports for information of foreign quarantine officials.

2. Bill of health—already described.

3. Deratization and deratization exemption certificate, valid for 6 months.

4. Quarantine declaration. Embodies essential data upon which granting of pratique is premised.

5. Certificate of discharge from quarantine or pratique is the permission granted by quarantine officials to the master to hold communication with the shore. *White* is free pratique. *Yellow* is provisional or conditioned.

Shipment of Dead Bodies. A dead body accepted for shipment should be accompanied by a death certificate signed by an accredited physician or health office at the place where death occurred. This certificate should identify the remains and give, in addition to other vital data, the cause, date, and place of death. It should also bear the visa of the U. S. Consul or U. S. Public Health Service officer at the port of embarkation.

Deaths at Sea. When a person dies aboard a vessel, a complete clinical record should be prepared for presentation to the quarantine officer. If not buried at sea, the body should be embalmed and placed in a metal-lined casket which should be hermetically sealed and placed in a specially provided cold storage chamber. The quarantine regulations require that a body dead from cholera, plague or smallpox be wrapped in a sheet saturated with bichloride of mercury, carbolic acid or formalin solution, prior to being placed in the casket.

Certain municipalities, such as New York, require that a transcript of the entry made in the ship's log of a death occurring at sea be submitted to the department of health within three days after the vessel's arrival in port.

Some Guides in Case of Death. Death aboard ship, irrespective of cause, necessitates the preparation of certain documents and fulfilling other arrangements required by law and custom.

Our laws are specific relative to wages, effects, and money; the reporting of any death; and the entries to be made in the official logbook. However, they are silent on other details which prompted a request from a shipmaster that information be published as a guide in the event of a death aboard ship.

In the case of any vessel that does not carry a physican, the master assumes certain responsibilities concerned with death that ordinarily falls into other professions. Statements of a fatally injured or dying person are one of these, and should be recorded for delivery to next of kin and to appropriate officials on shore.

The United States Public Health Service has outlined, in some detail, in *The Ship's Medicine Chest* what can be done when death occurs at sea in the absence of a physician and should be consulted.

An important function for a ship at sea is the notification of the owner or agent so that the next of kin can be contacted relative to the disposition of the body. On cargo and tank vessels where facilities for the proper care of the deceased are limited, the question of burial at sea or not usually is one of an urgent nature.

In a case heard before the District Court for the Southern District of New York in 1940 (*Bambir* v. *Cunard White Star Limited*, 37 F. Supp. 906, affd. 2 C. C. A., 119 Fed. 419), some interesting editorial head notes on the subject of burial at sea were made relative to the judge's decision:

Under common law, the obligation of providing a decent burial for body of deceased person was imposed upon the person under whose roof the death took place.

A death at sea eliminates the usual method of burial, and in such case the master of the ship has an absolute discretion concerning proper disposition of the corpse, the custom of burial at sea having long been sanctioned by usage.

A person who books passage on an ocean-going steamer impliedly acquiesces to be bound by custom of the sea and consents to burial therein in the event of death during the voyage.

The judge said:

It would seem that there is no affirmative duty on the ship's master to embalm the body of a passenger dying aboard ship, in the absence of a special contract. In fact, he is under a duty not to embalm such a body under pain of possible suit for mutilation or unauthorized interference with the body of deceased. *Darey* v. *Presbyterian Hospital*, 202 N. Y. 259, 95 N. E. 695, Ann. Cas. 1912D, 1238.

Who to Notify:

In a domestic port, the master should notify the local police, the agent or owner, Coast Guard, and the coroner.

In a foreign port, notify local police, agent or owner, and United States Consul or merchant marine detail officer.

In all cases, the agent or representative of the ship should be contacted promptly. He will be able to appraise the master of specific details and any unusual port regulations.

The master is required to—

Make suitable entries in the official logbook, which shall include—

Every case of death happening on board, with the cause thereof.

The wages due to any seaman or apprentice who dies during the voyage, and the gross amount of all deductions to be made therefrom.

The sale of effects of any seaman or apprentice who dies during the voyage, including a statement of each article sold, and the sum received for it.

Submit Form CG 2692, Report of Marine Casualty or Accident, to the Officer in Charge, Marine Inspection, in whose district the death occurred, or in whose district the vessel first arrived after such death.

Submit Form CG 1517, Account of Wages and Effects of Deceased or Deserting Seamen, for distribution to the district court, shipping commissioner, and Coast Guard Headquarters.

The master is held directly accountable under Revised Statutes 4540, 46 U.S.C. 623, for the money, wages, and effects of any deceased seaman to the district court in whose jurisdiction such port or destination is situate. This statute spells out the penalties and liabilities the master may incur for failure to account for the seaman's possessions and wages.

The use of Coast Guard Form 1517, as described, will assist the master in providing a detailed inventory for the district court and others concerned.

The master is empowered under Revised Statutes 4538, 46 U. S. C. 621, if he thinks fit to cause all or any of such clothes and effects left on board from a deceased seaman to be sold by auction. If this is done, the master shall sign an entry in the official logbook and cause it to be attested by the mate and one of the crew containing the following particulars: First, a statement of the amount of money so left by the deceased. Second, in case of a sale, a description of each article sold and the sum received for each. Third, statement of the sum due to deceased as wages, and the total amount of deductions, if any, to be made therefrom.

46 U. S. C. 622 explains how the effects and money due a seaman shall be disposed of both in the continental United States and in foreign ports. A consular officer has the option of taking the effects and money due a seaman, giving the master a receipt, or he can require the master to deliver these effects and money at a United States port.

SHIP SANITATION

1. Forepeak—keep neat and orderly, gear on racks, no accumulation of old gear, dust and dirt.

2. Provision Storeroom—provisions on racks and in metal containers, spoiled food burned or thrown overboard.

3. Galley and Pantry—grease, filth and dirt removed frequently with hot water and lye; food in metal containers; particles of food and refuse removed immediately.

4. Refrigeration Room—spoiled stores removed daily; scrubbed frequently.

5. Mess Rooms—swept after each meal and decks scrubbed daily; clean corners and crevices which harbor roaches and flies; no open food or garbage containers.

6. Toilets—should not be used for storage purposes; scrubbed daily.

7. Crew's Quarters—storing of food prohibited; clothing hung up.

8. Bathrooms—cleaned daily; not used for storage of mops, etc.

9. Washrooms—facilities for washing after leaving toilet and before eating; ample supply of hot and cold water, soap and towels. Maintenance of personal cleanliness, especially of food handlers, insisted upon.

10. Shelter Decks—kept clean and excess stores stowed, preferably on racks, so as to prevent harboring rats.

11. Holds—swept or preferably washed down after discharge; bilges inspected and cleaned.

Methods of Controlling Rats:

1. Ratproof construction of new ships.

2. Eliminating harborages and nesting places.

3. Starving rats by removal of grain, etc., from holds, protection of stores, prompt disposal of garbage and water.

4. Trapping, look for runways and nests.

5. Poisoning, doubtful value due to danger to other animals and humans, and hard to be sure it is effective.

6. Fumigation with a deadly gas, such as hydrocyanic acid gas.

SHIP FUMIGATION

Hydrocyanic Acid Gas is one of the most rapidly fatal poisons known to man. Normal breathing in a concentration of 8 ounces or more per 1,000 cubic feet will render a man unconscious in 30 seconds and cause death in from 3 to 5 minutes. In the concentration used to kill rats, 2 ounces per 1,000 cubic feet, a man will lose consciousness within 1 minute and be dead within 10 minutes. Lower concentrations will require correspondingly longer periods of exposure to produce fatal results.

First-aid Treatment. Prompt action in applying proper first-aid treatment will save life. Know what to do and do it promptly.

First: Remove the man to fresh air and induce continued breathing. Call a doctor, but do not send the man to a doctor. Continue first-aid treatment until the doctor arrives.

Second: If the man is breathing, apply smelling salts (weak ammonia fumes or aromatic spirits of ammonia) to his nose. Keep him in fresh air and watch to see that his breathing does not stop. Continue the use of smelling salts at frequent intervals until he has completely recovered. Do not leave him alone until he is normal.

If the man is not breathing, artificial respiration by the Schaefer method must be begun at once. Brief applications of smelling salts should be made during this treatment.

Third: Don't give the patient hypodermic injections at any time. Don't give him alcoholic stimulants of any sort. Don't give any liquid by mouth until the patient is fully conscious. Don't allow anyone affected or overcome to return to work until fully recovered and normal in all respects. Don't rush an unconscious patient to the hospital unless artificial respiration can be continued without interruption and/or the doctor arrives to take charge.

Characteristics of Hydrocyanic Acid. Hydrocyanic acid—HCN—also called hydrogen cyanide, prussic acid, or formonitrile, is a colorless gas, or liquid which evaporates very rapidly and boils at 78° F. It has the odor of bitter almonds.

The gas is lighter than air and, when liberated in the open, dissipates very rapidly. In confined spaces it is very penetrating. Given sufficient time it will actually penetrate a brick wall, and of course goes through cracks in bulkheads or around doors and ports very easily.

The gas also passes out of materials equally quickly. An hour's airing renders a mattress safe to sleep on unless an excessively heavy concentration of gas has been used. Water, however, absorbs hydrocyanic acid and holds it, particularly in cold weather, so that after fumigation moist articles require longer airing than dry ones. Ordinarily, gas absorbed by collections of water (as in the bilges) is given off so slowly that it is not dangerous, but occasionally a relatively large amount is taken up on a cold day, and when a warm day follows, the gas is given off more rapidly.

Methods of Use

Hydrocyanic acid as a fumigant is used in one of three ways:

1. It is generated on the premises by adding sodium cyanide to 50 per cent sulfuric acid.

2. It is supplied already prepared as a liquid in steel cylinders from which it is forced by air pressure and introduced (through pipes or hoses) as a fine spray, which at once evaporates.

3. It is supplied as a solid which is spread on the floor. This may be HCN absorbed in discs of Fuller's earth or absorbent paper, or may be calcium cyanide powder, which absorbs moisture from the air and generates HCN.

The first method seems to be the most prevalent with commercial fumgiators. The preferred method is to use a portable generating apparatus on the dock and to deliver the gas through rubber hose to the desired place.

Warning Gases

1. Warning gases are substances added to the fumigant to warn of the presence of the gas. Hydrocyanic acid has a distinctive odor and may be detected by *experienced* fumigators in quite low concentrations. To the uninitiated, however, its odor does not indicate danger, nor in lethal concentration does it cause discomfort.

2. It is not improbable that much of the controversy that has arisen over the use of a warning gas has been due to method of application. It is recommended that the warning gas chemical be added to the mixture in generating apparatus so that it may have a chance to be diffused all over the space under fumigation.

3. Thoroughly competent fumigators do not rely on warning gases alone. They do, however, use them as a help, both as a warning to others and to assist in detecting the gas themselves.

4. A warning gas is of no avail if the warning that is given is not heeded. Persons who have to enter places that have recently been fumigated should be told what warning gases are and that they should leave a gassy area immediately.

5. Chloropicrin is the best known and most satisfactory of the warning gases. It is commonly called tear-gas for it causes smarting of the eyes and tears to flow. The tendency of this gas to hang as long as or longer than the hydrocyanic acid gas also makes it a desirable warning agent.

6. From 3 to 5 percent of tear-gas is the usual amount used by fumigators; the amount rarely should exceed 10 percent.

7. Masters should insist that a warning gas in quantities of not less than 3 percent always be used when hydrocyanic acid gas is used as the fumigant.

Precautions

The danger present when hydrocyanic acid gas is used as a fumigant should not be minimized and every possible precaution should be taken. The precautions are not numerous; but each one is vital to safe procedure and none should be overlooked.

1. *Preparation*—Fumigating should be done when all cargo has been discharged and rubbish cleaned out of holds. There is less chance under these conditions that pockets of gas will remain. In abnormally low temperatures cyanide loses its effectiveness as a fumigant for certain types of weevils, etc.

An accurate check should be made to see that all members of the ship's crew and other persons are ashore before fumigation is commenced.

A written statement signed by the captain or chief officer should be given the fumigation officer stating that the ship is ready for fumigating.

A guard should be placed at the gangway to prevent *anyone*, except the fumigators, from boarding the ship after the check out has been made without written permission of the fumigation officer.

2. *While fumigating*—Conspicuous signs should be posted at the gangway warning that the ship is being fumigated with cyanide gas. One or more of these signs should be placed on the offshore side of the vessel to warn tugs, barges, or other vessels coming alongside that no one is to board.

In places where the deck of the ship is flush with the dock, the ship should be moored off from the dock to prevent access to the ship except at the gangway.

3. *Ventilation*—The practice of waiting for natural ventilation to air out hatches that have been fumigated should be discouraged, and the use of *mechanically driven pressure fans* should be insisted upon. In this manner a hatch can be thoroughly aired out and enough agitation of the air set up to minimize the danger of gas pockets, especially in empty ships.

In conjunction with the fan a fabric tubing such as canvas can be used to conduct the air; and by a little ingenuity and the use of a couple of lines the air flow can be directed to nearly all parts of a hatch from the main deck. Tubing of various sizes and material can be purchased.

If there is any possibility that the gas may have penetrated the officers' or crews' quarters, all bedding, mattresses, etc., should be hung out in the air for at least 2 hours.

4. *Completion*—When the fumigator has pronounced the ship safe, a signed statement should be demanded of him to this effect before the watchman is taken from the gangway or the crew or others are allowed on board.

DISINFECTING WATER AND CHLORINATING TANKS

A teaspoonful of Chlorinated Lime should be measured out for each 200 gallons of water in the domestic tanks that are to be treated. It should be thoroughly dissolved in a bucket of water and then poured into the ship's tank. The settling of this solution through the water, and the withdrawal of water from the tank is sufficient to cause a thorough mixture. Contaminated water already in the supply pipes should be drawn off at each scuttlebutt and faucet until the treated water flows through the pipes.

Chloride of Lime is a poison and it must be kept dry and used soon after opening.

Approximate and Comparative Measures

60 drops	= 1 teaspoonful
4 teaspoonfuls	= 1 tablespoonful
2 tablespoonfuls	= 1 ounce
2 ounces	= 1 wineglass
2 wineglassfuls	= 1 teacupful
2 teacupfuls	= 1 tumblerful
2 tumblerfuls	= 1 pint

Q. (a) What is the average maximum consumption of fresh water per day per person required in the interests of adequate personal hygiene?
(b) What chemical is used to treat water in order to insure its safety for drinking? (c) How should taps be marked when washwater of doubtful purity is used?

A. (a) 30 gallons per day. (b) Chlorine. (c) Taps should be plainly marked "UNFIT FOR DRINKING."

RULES AND REGULATIONS FOR DECK OFFICER'S LICENSES

10.02–1 Issuance of licenses.

10.02–1(a) Applicants for licenses are charged with the duty of establishing to the satisfaction of the Coast Guard that they possess all of the qualifications necessary, such as age, experience, character and citizenship, before they shall be entitled to be issued licenses. Until an applicant meets this mandatory requirement, he is not entitled to be licensed to serve as an officer on a vessel of the United States. No person who has been convicted by court-martial of desertion or treason in time of war, or has lost his nationality for any of the other reasons listed in 8 U.S.C. 801, is eligible for a license. Neither is a person eligible for a license, who has been convicted by a court of record of a violation of the narcotic drug laws of the United States, the District of Columbia, or any State or Territory of the United States, within ten years prior to the date of filing the application; or who, unless he furnishes satisfactory evidence that he is cured, has ever been the user of or addicted to the use of a narcotic drug.

10.02–1(b) After application to an Officer in Charge, Marine Inspection, any person who is found qualified under the requirements set forth in this subchapter shall be issued an appropriate license valid for a term of five (5) years. In appropriate cases a limitation commensurate with the experience of the applicant shall be placed upon the license.

10.02–1(c) Every person to whom a license is issued shall place his signature and left thumb print thereon, and upon any sheets attached for additional endorsements.

10.02–1(d) Every person who receives a license shall make oath before an Officer in Charge, Marine Inspection, or commissioned officer of the Coast Guard authorized to administer oaths under 50 U.S.C. 732, to be recorded upon his official file, that he will faithfully and honestly, according to his best skill and judgment, without concealment or reservation, perform all the duties required of him by law and obey all lawful orders of his superior officers.

(Sec. 2, 68 Stat. 484; 46 U.S.C. 239b. Treasury Department Order 167–9, August 3, 1954, 19 F.R. 5195)

10.02–3 Original license defined.

The first license issued to any person by the Coast Guard shall be considered an original license, when the United States records show no previous issue to such person.

10.02–5 Requirements for original licenses.

10.02–5(a) *General.* Before an original license is issued to any person to act in a licensed capacity on inspected vessels of the United States, he shall personally appear before an Officer in Charge, Marine Inspection, and present satisfactory documentary evidence of his eligibility in respect to the requirements of this section.

10.02–5(b) *Minimum age.* Any person who has attained the age of 21 years and is qualified in all other respects shall be eligible for a license except that a license as third mate, third assistant engineer or second class pilot may be granted an applicant who has reached the age of 19 years and who is qualified in all other respects, but no such license may be raised in grade before the holder thereof shall have reached the age of 21 years.

10.02–5(c) *Citizenship.* No license shall be issued to any person who is not a citizen of the United States, either native-born or fully naturalized. The Officer in Charge, Marine Inspection, must be satisfied as to the bona fides of all evidence of citizenship presented, and may reject any evidence that he has reason to believe is not authentic. Acceptable evidence of citizenship is described below in the order of its desirability, except that the first six (6) acceptable methods will be assigned equal weight:

10.02–5(c)(1) Birth certificate or certified copy.

10.02–5(c)(2) Certificate of Naturalization.

10.02–5(c)(3) Baptismal certificate or parish record recorded within one year after birth.

10.02–5(c)(4) Statement of a practicing physician certifying that he attended the birth and that he has a record in his possession showing the date on which it occurred.

10.02–5(c)(5) State Department passport.

10.02–5(c)(6) A commission in the United States Navy, Marine Corps, Coast Guard, either regular or reserve; or satisfactory documentary evidence of having been commissioned in one of these services subsequent to January 1, 1936, provided such commission or evidence shows the holder to be a citizen.

10.02–5(c)(7) A continuous discharge book, certificate of identification, or merchant mariner's document issued by the Coast Guard or by the former Bureau of Marine Inspection and Navigation which shows the holder as an American citizen, provided the records indicate that the holder of such continuous discharge book, certificate of identification, or merchant mariner's document produced satisfactory evidence of his citizenship at the time of the issuance of the same.

10.02–5(c)(8) Delayed certificate of birth. If an applicant claiming to be a citizen of the United States submits a delayed certificate of birth issued under a State's seal, it may be accepted as prima facie evidence of citizenship in the absence of any collateral facts indicating fraud in its procurement.

10.02–5(c)(9) For persons deriving citizenship through naturalization of their parents, or for persons born outside the United States who claim to be United States citizens by virtue of their parents having been United States citizens at the time of such birth, a Certificate of Citizenship issued by the United States Immigration and Naturalization Service is acceptable as documentary evidence of citizenship.

10.02–5(c)(10) If none of the requirements set forth in subparagraphs (1) to (9) of this paragraph can be met by the applicant, he should make a statement to that effect, and in an attempt to establish citizenship, he may submit for consideration data of the following character:

10.02–5(c)(10)(i) Report of the Census Bureau showing the earliest record of age or birth available. Request for such information should be addressed to the Director of the Census, Washington 25, D.C. In making such request, definite information must be furnished the Census Bureau as to the place when the first census was taken after birth of the applicant, giving the name of the street and number of the house, or the names of the cross streets between which the house was located if residing in a city; or the name of the town, township, precinct, magisterial district, militia district, beat or election district if residing in the country; also the names of parents, or the names of other persons with whom residing on the date specified.

NOTE: A census was taken in the following years: June 1, 1860, 1870, 1880, and 1900; April 15, 1910; January 1, 1920; April 1, 1930; April, 1940, and April, 1950. (Records for 1890 are not available.)

10.02–5(c)(10)(ii) Affidavits of parents or relatives; or affidavits by two or more responsible citizens of the United States, stating citizenship; school records; immigration records; or insurance policies.

(Sec. 5, 49 Stat. 1935, as amended, sec. 302, 49 Stat. 1992, as amended; 46 U.S.C. 672a, 1132. Treasury Department Order 120, 15 F.R. 6521)

10.02–5(d) *Written application.* The Officer in Charge, Marine Inspection, shall require all applicants for original license to make written application upon Coast Guard Form CG 866.

10.02–5(e) *Physical examination.*

10.02–5(e)(1) All applicants for an original license shall be required to pass a physical examination given by a medical officer of the United States Public Health Service and present a certificate executed by this Public Health Service Officer to the Officer in Charge, Marine Inspection. This certificate shall attest to the applicant's acuity of vision, color sense, and general physical condition. In exceptional cases where an applicant would be put to great inconvenience or expense to appear before a medical officer of the United States Public Health Service, the physical examination and certification may be made by another reputable physician.

10.02–5(e)(2) Epilepsy, insanity, senility, acute venereal disease or neurosyphilis, badly impaired hearing, or other defect that would render the applicant incompetent to perform the ordinary duties of an officer at sea are causes for certification as incompetent.

10.02–5(e)(3) For an original license as master, mate or pilot, the applicant must have either with or without glasses, at least 20/20 vision in one eye and at least 20/40 in the other. The applicant who wears glasses, however, must also be able to pass a test without glasses of at least 20/40 in one eye and at least 20/70 in the other. The color sense will be tested by means of a pseudo-isochromatic plate test, but any applicant who fails this test will be eligible if he can pass the "Williams" lantern test or equivalent.

10.02–5(e)(4) Applicants for original engineers' licenses shall be examined only as to their ability to distinguish the colors red, blue, green, and yellow. No applicant for original license as engineer shall be disqualified for failure to distinguish colors if any of his required experience is served prior to the effective date of the regulations in this part.

10.02–5(e)(5) For original license as engineer the applicant must have, either with or without glasses, at least 20/30 vision in one eye and at least 20/50 in the other. The applicant who wears glasses, however, must also be able to pass a test without glasses of at least 20/50 in one eye and at least 20/70 in the other.

10.02–5(e)(6) Persons serving or intending to serve in the Merchant Marine Service are recommended to take the earliest opportunity of ascertaining, through examination by an ophthalmic surgeon, whether their vision, and color vision where required, is such as to qualify them for service in that profession.

10.02–5(e)(7) Where an applicant is not possessed of the vision, hearing, and general physical condition considered necessary, the Officer in Charge, Marine Inspection, after consultation with the Public Health Service physician, may make recommendations to the Commandant for an exception to these requirements if, in their opinion, extenuating circumstances warrant special consideration. Any requests for a decision by the Commandant must be accompanied by all pertinent correspondence, records and reports. In this connection recommendations from agencies of the Federal Government operating Government vessels as well as owners and operators of private vessels, made in behalf of their employees, will be given full consideration as a determining factor in arriving at a decision.

*   *   *   *   *

§ 10.02–9 Requirements for renewal of license.

(e) * * *

(2) * * * In the event a candidate fails the examination, the provisions of § 10.02–19 shall apply, except in the event of subsequent failures the applicant may be re-examined after a lapse of one month from the date of the last failure.

*   *   *   *   *

10.02–5(f) *First Aid Certificate.* No candidate for original license shall be examined until he presents a certificate from the United States Public Health Service that he has passed a satisfactory examination based on the contents of "The Ship's Medicine Chest and First Aid at Sea," or other manual arranged for the purpose and having the approval of the United States Public Health Service.

10.02–5(g) *Experience or training.*

10.02–5(g)(1) All applicants for original licenses shall present to the Officer in Charge, Marine Inspection, letters, discharges, or other official documents certifying the amount and character of their experience and the names of the vessels on which acquired. The Officer in Charge, Marine Inspection, must be satisfied as to the bona fides of all evidence of experience or training presented and may reject any evidence that he has reason to believe is not authentic or which does not sufficiently outline the amount, type and character of service. Coast Guard issued "certificates of seaman's service" and "certificates of discharge" shall be returned to the applicant. The Officer in Charge, Marine Inspection, shall make entry on the application that service mentioned by these documents has been verified. All other documentary evidence of service or authentic copies thereof shall be filed with the application. No license shall be considered as satisfactory evidence of any qualifying experience required by this paragraph.

10.02–5(g)(2) No original license shall be issued to any person unless 25 percent of the required experience has been obtained within the 3 years immediately preceding the date of application. Service in the armed forces of the United States shall not be counted in computing the 3 years.

10.02–5(g)(3) No original license shall be issued to any naturalized citizen on less experience in any grade or capacity than would have been required of a citizen of the United States by birth.

10.02–5(g)(4) Experience and service acquired on foreign vessels is creditable for establishing eligibility for an original license, subject to evaluation by the Commandant to determine that it is a fair and reasonable equivalent to service acquired on merchant vessels of the United States, with respect to grade, tonnage, horsepower, waters and operating conditions. An applicant who has obtained his qualifying experience on foreign vessels is required to submit satisfactory documentary evidence of such service in the forms prescribed by Subparagraph (1) of this paragraph, which certify the amount, character and scope of his service in these respects.

10.02–5(g)(5) No applicant for a license, who is a naturalized citizen, and who has obtained his experience on foreign vessels, shall be given a grade of license higher than that upon which he has actually served while acting under the authority of a foreign license.

10.02–5(g)(6) Experience in towed barges fitted with sails and rigging is not considered as sail vessel time.

10.02–5(h) *Professional examination.*

10.02–5(h)(1) When the amount and character of an applicant's experience is found to be satisfactory and he is eligible in all other respects, the applicant shall be examined in writing by the Officer in Charge, Marine Inspection: *Provided, however,* That upon navigable waters of the United States newly opened to navigation, and where the only pilots obtainable are illiterate Indians or other natives, the fact that such persons can neither read nor write shall not be considered a bar to such Indians or other natives receiving licenses as pilots if they are otherwise qualified therefor.

10.02–5(h)(2) When the license application of any person has been approved, the Officer in Charge, Marine Inspection, shall give the applicant the required examination as soon as practicable. If applicants for license cannot be examined without material delay by the Officer in Charge, Marine Inspection, of the district in which the application is made, said Officer in Charge, Marine Inspection, shall endeavor, through the Coast Guard District Commander, to arrange for such examination by some other Officer in Charge, Marine Inspection.

10.02–5(i) *Character check and references.*

10.02–5(i)(1) The Officer in Charge, Marine Inspection, shall require each applicant for an original license to have the written endorsement of the master and that of two other licensed officers of a vessel on which he has served. For a license as engineer or as pilot at least one of the other endorsers shall be the chief engineer or licensed pilot, respectively, of a vessel on which the applicant has served. Where no sea service is required for a license, the applicant may have the endorsement of three reputable persons to whom he is known.

10.02–5(i)(2) Fingerprint records on FBI Form "Applicant" shall be submitted to the Commandant on each applicant at the same time application for license is made. The application of any person may be rejected by the District Commander or his authorized representative when derogatory information has been brought to his attention which indicates that the applicant's habits of life and character are such as to warrant the belief that he cannot be entrusted with the duties and responsibilities of the station for which he made application. In the event that an applicant is rejected he shall be advised that he may submit a request to the Commandant for a review of his case. No examination shall be given or temporary permit issued in this type case pending the Commandant's authorization.

10.02–5(i)(3) The fact that an applicant for an original license is on probation as a result of action under R. S. 4450, as amended, does not itself make such an applicant ineligible, provided he meets all the requirements for such original license. However, an original license issued under those circumstances will be subject to the same probationary conditions as were imposed against the seaman's certificates or licenses in proceedings under R. S. 4450, as amended. Any such applicant must file an application for license in the usual manner, and the offense for which he was placed on probation will be considered on the merits of the case in determining his fitness to hold the license applied for. Nothing in the regulations in this subchapter, however, shall be construed to permit an applicant to be examined for an original license during any period when a suspension without probation or a revocation imposed pursuant to R. S. 4450, as amended, is effective against his license or certificate.

10.02–7 Requirements for raise of grade of license.

10.02–7(a) *General.* Before any person is issued a license for raise of grade to act on inspected vessels of the United States, he shall personally appear before an Officer in Charge, Marine Inspection, and present satisfactory documentary evidence of his eligibility in respect to the requirements contained herein.

10.02–7(b) *Surrendering old license.* Upon the issuance of a new license or raise in grade, the applicant shall surrender the old license to the Officer in Charge, Marine Inspection.

10.02–7(c) *Age requirement.* No license may be raised in grade before the holder thereof shall have reached the age of 21 years.

10.02–7(d) *Written application.* The Officer in Charge, Marine Inspection, shall, before granting raise of grade of license, require the applicant to make written application upon the Coast Guard Form 866.

10.02–7(e) *Physical requirements.*

10.02–7(e)(1) No license as master, mate, or pilot shall be raised in grade except upon the official certificate of a medical officer of the United States Public Health Service that the color sense of the applicant is normal. Applicants for raise in grade of engineer's licenses shall not be subjected to such examination. In exceptional cases where an applicant would be put to great inconvenience or expense to appear before a medical officer of the United States Public Health Service, the physical examination and certification may be made by another reputable physician. The test for color vision shall be by means of the "Stillings" test, or failing that, by means of the "Williams" lantern test. A person failing the "Stillings" test and wishing to qualify by the lantern test shall, if the Public Health Station at which he is undergoing test is not equipped with a lantern, pay his own expenses to journey to such station as is equipped with same.

10.02–7(e)(2) In the event it is found that an applicant for raise of grade of license obviously suffers from some physical or mental infirmity to a degree that, in the opinion of the Officer in Charge, Marine Inspection, would render him incompetent to perform the ordinary duties of an officer at sea, he shall be required to undergo an examination by a medical officer of the Public Health Service to determine his competency in such respects. Nothing herein contained shall debar an applicant who has lost the sight of one eye from securing a raise of grade of his license: *Provided*, He is qualified in all other respects; *And provided*, That his vision in his one eye passes the test required for the better eye of an applicant possessed of both eyes. If the applicant subsequently produces a certificate from the Public Health Service to the effect that his condition has improved to a satisfactory degree, or is normal, he shall be qualified in this respect.

10.02–7(f)   *Experience or training.*

10.02–7(f)(1)   Applicants for raise of grade of licenses are charged with establishing to the satisfaction of the Coast Guard that they possess all of the qualifications necessary, such as age, experience, character, and citizenship before they are entitled to a raise of grade of license.

10.02–7(f)(2)   Applicants for raise of grade of license shall present to the Officer in Charge, Marine Inspection, letters, discharges, or other official documents certifying to the amount and character of their experience and the names of the vessels on which acquired. Coast Guard issued "certificates of seaman's service" and "certificates of discharge" shall be returned to the applicant. The Officer in Charge, Marine Inspection, shall make entry on the application that service represented by these documents has been verified. All other documentary evidence of service or authentic copies thereof shall be filed with the application.

10.02–7(f)(3)   No raise of grade of license shall be granted to any applicant unless 25 percent of the required sea service shall have been served within 3 years immediately preceding the date of application. Service in the armed forces of the United States shall not be counted in computing the 3 years.

10.02–7(f)(4)   No sea service acquired prior to the issuance of the license held shall be accepted as any part of the service required for raise in grade.

10.02–7(f)(5)   No license for raise of grade shall be issued to any naturalized citizen on less experience in any grade than would have been required of a citizen of the United States by birth.

10.02–7(f)(6)   Experience and service acquired on foreign vessels while holding a valid U.S. Merchant Marine Officer's license is creditable for establishing eligibility for a raise in grade, subject to evaluation by the Commandant to determine that it is a fair and reasonable equivalent to service acquired on merchant vessels of the United States, with respect to grade, tonnage, horsepower, waters and operating conditions. An applicant who has obtained his qualifying experience on foreign vessels is required to submit satisfactory documentary evidence of such service in the forms prescribed by Subparagraph (2) of this paragraph which certify the amount, character and scope of his service in these respects.

10.02–7(f)(7)   The fact that an applicant for a raise in grade of license is on probation as a result of action under R.S. 4450, as amended (46 U.S.C. 239), does not itself make such an applicant ineligible, provided he meets all the requirements for such raise in grade. However, a raise in grade of license issued under these circumstances will be subject to the same probationary conditions as were imposed against the seaman's certificates or licenses in proceedings under R.S. 4450, as amended. Any such applicant must file an application for license in the usual manner, and the offense for which he was placed on probation will be considered on the merits of the case in determining his fitness to hold the license applied for. Nothing

in the regulations in this part, however, shall be construed to permit an applicant to be examined for a raise in grade of license during any period when a suspension without probation or a revocation imposed pursuant to R.S. 4450, as amended, is effective against his license or certificate.

10.02–7(g)   *Professional examination.*

10.02–7(g)(1)   When the amount and character of an applicant's experience for raise of grade is found to be satisfactory and he is eligible in all other respects, he shall be examined in writing by an Officer in Charge, Marine Inspection: *Provided, however,* That upon waters of the United States newly opened to navigation, and where the only pilots obtainable are illiterate Indians or other natives, the fact that such persons can neither read nor write shall not be considered a bar to such Indians or other natives receiving a raise in grade of license as pilot if they are otherwise qualified therefor.

10.02–9   Requirements for renewal of license.

10.02–9(a)   *Duty of applicants.* Applicants for renewals of licenses are charged with the duty of establishing to the satisfaction of the Coast Guard that they possess all of the qualifications necessary before they shall be issued a renewal of license.

10.02–9(a)(1)   *Written application.* The Officer in Charge, Marine Inspection, shall, before granting renewal of a license, require the applicant to make written application on Coast Guard Form CG–3479.

10.02–9(b)   *Application for renewal.* The applicant for renewal shall appear in person, before an Officer in Charge, Marine Inspection, except as provided in paragraph (g) of this section.

10.02–9(c)   *Fitness.* No license shall be renewed if title has been forfeited or facts which would render a renewal improper have come to the attention of the Coast Guard.

10.02–9(d)   *Period of grace.*

10.02–9(d)(1)   A license shall be renewed within 12 months after the date of expiration as shown on the license held, except when applicant's license has expired beyond the 12 month period of grace during the time of the holder's service with the Armed Forces or the Merchant Marine and there was no reasonable opportunity for renewal. The period of such service following the date of expiration as shown on the license shall be added to the 12 month period of grace.

10.02–9(d)(2)   No license shall be renewed more than 90 days in advance of the date of expiration thereof, unless there are extraordinary circumstances that justify a renewal beforehand, in which case the reasons therefor must appear in detail upon the records of the Officer in Charge, Marine Inspection, renewing the license.

10.02–9(e)   *Masters', mates', or pilots', licenses.*

10.02–9(e)(1)   Every Officer in Charge, Marine Inspection, shall, before renewing an existing license to a master, mate, or pilot who has served under the authority of his license within the three years next preceding the date of application for renewal, or who has been employed in a position closely related to the operation of vessels during the same three year period, require that such licensed officer present an affidavit that he has read within the three months next preceding the date of application the Rules of the Road applicable to the waters for which he is licensed and demonstrate his knowledge of the application of the Rules of the Road.

10.02–9(e)(2) Every Officer in Charge, Marine Inspection, shall, before renewing an existing license to a master, mate, or pilot who has not served under the authority of his license within the three years next preceding the date of application for renewal, or who has not been employed in a position closely related to the operation of vessels during the same three year period, satisfy himself that such licensed officer is thoroughly familiar with the Rules of the Road applicable to the waters for which he is licensed. A written examination may be required for this purpose, or the applicant may be examined orally and a summary of the oral examination placed in the officer's license file.

10.02–9(f) *Physical requirements.*

10.02–9(f)(1) No license as master, mate, or pilot shall be renewed except upon the official certificate of a medical officer of the United States Public Health Service that the color sense of the applicant is normal. Applicants for renewal of license as engineer shall not be subject to examination as to ability to distinguish colors.

10.02–9(f)(2) The color sense will be tested by means of a pseudo-isochromatic plate test, but any applicant who fails this test will be eligible if he can pass the "Williams" lantern test or equivalent. A person failing the pseudo-isochromatic plate test shall, if the Public Health Service Station at which he is undergoing test is not equipped with a lantern, pay his own expenses to travel to such station as is equipped with same.

10.02–9(f)(3) In the event an applicant for renewal of license as master, mate, or pilot is pronounced color blind, the Officer in Charge, Marine Inspection, may grant him a license limited to service during daylight only.

10.02–9(f)(4) In the event it is found that an applicant for renewal of license obviously suffers from some physical or mental infirmity to a degree that, in the opinion of the Officer in Charge, Marine Inspection, would render him incompetent to perform the ordinary duties of an officer at sea, the applicant shall be required to undergo an examination by a medical officer of the Public Health Service to determine his competency. If the applicant subsequently produces a certificate from the Public Health Service to the effect that his condition has improved to a satisfactory degree, or is normal, he shall be qualified in this respect.

10.02–9(f)(5) Nothing contained in this section shall debar an applicant who has lost the sight of one eye from securing a renewal of his license, provided he is qualified in all other respects, and the vision in his one eye passes the test required for the better eye of an applicant possessed of both eyes.

10.02–9(f)(6) In exceptional cases where an applicant would be put to great inconvenience or expense to appear before a medical officer of the United States Public Health Service, the physical examination or certification may be made by another reputable physician.

10.02–9(g) *Renewal by mail.* Where an applicant for renewal would be put to great inconvenience or expense to appear in person before an Officer in Charge, Marine Inspection, or is engaged in a service that necessitates his continuous absence from the United States, his existing license may be renewed by forwarding the following documents to the Officer in Charge, Marine Inspection, of the office which issued the license to be renewed:

10.02–9(g)(1) A letter of transmittal indicating reasons for not appearing in person and stating to the best of his knowledge no physical incapacity exists, together with a properly executed application on Coast Guard Form CG–3479;

10.02–9(g)(2) The oath of office on the form prescribed by the Coast Guard which has been duly executed before a person authorized to administer oaths;

10.02–9(g)(3) The license to be renewed; and,

10.02–9(g)(4) In the case of the renewal of a master's, mate's or pilot's license:

10.02–9(g)(4)(i) Certification by a United States Public Health Service Medical Officer or other reputable physician that color sense is normal; and,

10.02–9(g)(4)(ii) Documentary evidence of service under authority of license within the three years next preceding the date of application or evidence of employment in a position closely related to the operation of vessels within the same three-year period, together with an affidavit that the applicant has read within the three months next preceding the date of application the Rules of the Road applicable to the waters for which he is licensed and demonstration of his knowledge of the application of the Rules of the Road.

(R.S. 4447, as amended, 46 U.S.C. 233. Treasury Department Order 120, July 31, 1950, 15 F.R. 6521)

10.02–9(h) *Reissue of expired license.*

10.02–9(h)(1) Whenever an applicant shall apply for renewal of his license for the same grade, after 12 months after date of its expiration, he shall be required to pass an examination for the same grade of license, of such length and scope as will, in the judgment of the Officer in Charge, Marine Inspection, be sufficient to demonstrate adequately the continued professional knowledge of the examinee, except no professional examination will be required provided the license expired during the time of the holder's service with the armed forces or the merchant marine, and there was no reasonable opportunity for renewal. The Officer in Charge, Marine Inspection, may require a written examination for this purpose.

10.02–9(h)(2) The renewed license shall receive the next higher number of issue of present grade and for the number of issue of all grades.

10.02–13 Sea service as a member of the Armed Forces of the United States and on vessels owned by the United States as qualifying experience.

10.02–13(a) Sea service as a member of the Armed Forces of the United States will be accepted as qualifying experience for an original, raise of grade, or extension of route of license. Such service will be subject to evaluation by the Commandant to determine its equivalence to sea service required on merchant vessels and to determine the appropriate grade, class, and limit of license for which the applicant is eligible. The regulations governing the licensing of merchant marine personnel which are in effect on the date an applicant presents himself for examination shall be applicable in all cases.

10.02–13(b) When any person who has served in a civilian capacity as commanding officer, master, mate, engineer, or pilot, etc., of any vessel owned and operated by the United States, in any service, in which a license as master, mate, engineer, or pilot was not required at the time of such service applies for an examination for license, the

Officer in Charge, Marine Inspection, shall forward the application, together with his comments, to the Commandant for evaluation.

10.02–15 Lifting of limitations.

10.02–15(a) If any Officer in Charge, Marine Inspection, is satisfied by the documentary evidence submitted that an applicant is entitled by experience and knowledge to an increase in the scope of his license, he may change any limitations which he may have previously placed upon the license.

10.02–15(b) No Officer in Charge, Marine Inspection, may change on any license a limitation which he did not place thereon before full information regarding the reason for the limitation is obtained from the Officer in Charge, Marine Inspection, responsible for the same and the applicant has made up any deficiency in the experience required.

10.02–15(c) No limitation on any license may be changed before the applicant has made up any deficiency in the experience prescribed for the license desired and passed the necessary examination.

10.02–19 Reexaminations and refusal of licenses.

10.02–19(a) Any applicant for license or endorsement who has been duly examined and refused may come before the same Officer in Charge, Marine Inspection, for reexamination at any time thereafter that may be fixed by such Officer in Charge, Marine Inspection, but such time shall not be less than 1 month from the date of his last failure. In the case of another failure, he will not be reexamined until after a lapse of at least 6 months from date of last failure.

10.02–19(b) A candidate who has been duly examined and refused a license by an Officer in Charge, Marine Inspection, shall not be examined by any other Officer in Charge, Marine Inspection, until 1 year has elapsed from the date of the last refusal without the sanction of the Officer in Charge, Marine Inspection, that refused the applicant.

10.02–19(c) If the Officers in Charge, Marine Inspection, refuse to grant an applicant the license applied for, they shall furnish him a statement setting forth the cause of their refusal.

10.02–21 Laws, general rules and regulations, and Rules of the Road to be furnished licensed officers.

10.02–21(a) Every master, mate, pilot, and engineer of vessels, when receiving an original license, a renewed license, or a raise of grade of license, shall be furnished at his request with a copy of the "Laws Governing Marine Inspection" and a copy of each of the "Rules and Regulations for Vessel Inspection" distributed by the Coast Guard pertinent to the license issued.

10.02–21(b) Every master, mate, and pilot of vessels and motorboat operator, when receiving an original license, a renewed license, or a raise of grade of license, shall be furnished at his request with a copy of the "Rules of the Road" applicable to the waters for which his license has been issued.

10.02–23 Issuance of duplicate license.

10.02–23(a) Whenever a person to whom a license has been issued loses his license, he shall report such loss to an Officer in Charge, Marine Inspection, who shall issue a duplicate license after receiving from such person a properly executed affidavit giving satisfactory evidence of such loss, and a record of the license from the Marine Inspection Office where it was issued. Such license shall be issued as a duplicate by the addition of the following typewritten endorsement, "This license replaces License Number _____ issued at _____ on the above date," as well as the port and date of the duplicate issue. The duplicate license, issued for the unexpired term, shall have the same force and effect as the lost license.

10.02–23(b) When a person reports the loss of his license, or when it is discovered that any license or license form has been stolen from a Marine Inspection Office or when such lost or stolen licenses are recovered, the Officer in Charge, Marine Inspection, shall immediately report the loss, theft, or recovery to the Commandant giving a description of the license and all facts incident to its loss, theft, or recovery.

10.02–25 Parting with license. If the holder of any license granted to a master, mate, engineer, or pilot, voluntarily parts with it or places it beyond his personal control by pledging or depositing it with any other person for any purpose, he may be proceeded against in accordance with the provisions of R.S. 4450, as amended, looking to a suspension or revocation of his license.

10.02–29 Suspension and revocation of licenses.

10.02–29(a) When the license of any master, mate, engineer, or pilot is revoked such license expires with such revocation and any license of the same type subsequently granted to such person shall be considered in the light of an original license except as to number of issue.

10.02–29(b) No person whose license has been suspended or revoked shall be issued another license except upon approval of the Commandant.

10.02–29(c) When a license which is about to expire is suspended, the renewal of such license may be withheld until the expiration of the period of suspension.

(R.S. 4450, as amended, sec. 2, 68 Stat. 484; 46 U.S.C. 239, 239b. Treasury Department Orders 120, July 31, 1950, 15 F.R. 6521 ; 167–9, August 3, 1954, 19 F.R. 5195)

10.02–33 Right of appeal. Whenever any person directly interested in or affected by any decision or action of any Officer in Charge, Marine Inspection, shall feel aggrieved by such decision or action with respect to the issuance of a license or a certificate, he may appeal therefrom to the District Coast Guard Commander having jurisdiction. A like appeal shall be allowed from any decision or action of the District Coast Guard Commander to the Commandant, whose action shall be final. Such appeals shall be made in writing within 30 days after the date of decision or action appealed from. Pending the determination of the appeal the decision of the Officer in Charge, Marine Inspection, shall remain in effect.

10.05—PROFESSIONAL REQUIREMENTS FOR DECK OFFICERS' LICENSES (INSPECTED VESSELS)

AUTHORITY: Sections 10.05–1 to 10.05–61 interpret or apply R.S. 4417a, as amended, 4426, as amended, 4427, as amended, 4438, as amended, 4438a, as amended, 4439, as amended, 4440, as amended, 4442, as amended, 4443, as amended, 4445, as amended, 4447, as amended, sec. 2, 29 Stat. 188, as amended, sec. 1, 34 Stat. 1411, as amended, secs. 1, 2, 49 Stat. 1544, 1545, as amended, sec. 3, 70 Stat. 152, and sec. 3, 68 Stat. 675 ; 46 U.S.C. 391a, 404, 405, 224, 224a, 226, 228, 234, 230, 231, 233, 237, 367, 390b, 50 U.S.C. 198. Treasury Department Orders 120, July 31, 1950, 15 F.R. 6521 ; 167–14, November 26, 1954, 19 F.R. 8026 ; 167–20, June 18, 1956, 21 F.R. 4894.

10.05–1 Ocean licenses qualifying for all waters. Any license issued for service as master or mate on ocean vessels shall qualify the licensee to serve in the same grade on any waters subject to the limitations of the license and without additional endorsement other than for pilot routes as may be required on the particular waters.

10.05–3 Master of ocean steam or motor vessels.

10.05–3(a) The minimum service required to qualify an applicant for license as master of ocean steam or motor vessels is:

10.05–3(a)(1) 1 year's service as chief mate of ocean steam or motor vessels of 1,000 gross tons or over; or,

10.05–3(a)(2) 1 year's service as chief mate of coastwise steam or motor vessels of 2,000 gross tons or over; or,

10.05–3(a)(3) 2 years' service as second mate of ocean steam or motor vessels of 1,000 gross tons or over while holding a license as chief mate of such vessels; or,

10.05–3(a)(4) 2 years' service as second mate of coastwise steam or motor vessels of 2,000 gross tons or over while holding a license as chief mate of such vessels; or,

10.05–3(a)(5) 1 year's service as master of coastwise steam or motor vessels of 2,000 gross tons or over; or,

10.05–3(a)(6) 2 years' service as master of ocean or coastwise sail vessels of 700 gross tons or over, for license as master of freight or towing steam or motor vessels of not more than 3,000 gross tons; or,

10.05–3(a)(7) 3 years' service as master of steam or motor vessels of 4,000 gross tons or over, except ferry vessels, on the Great Lakes, together with 1 year's service as second mate of ocean steam or motor vessels of 1,000 gross tons or over.

10.05–3(a)(8) 2 years' service as licensed master of ocean or coastwise steam or motor vessels, or as licensed ocean operator of inspected, mechanically propelled passenger-carrying vessels operating on limited ocean or coastwise routes, for a license as master of ocean steam or motor passenger vessels not to exceed 300 gross tons.

10.05–5 Master of coastwise steam or motor vessels.

10.05–5(a) The minimum service required to qualify an applicant for license as master of coastwise steam or motor vessels is:

10.05–5(a)(1) 1 year's service as chief mate of ocean or coastwise steam or motor vessels; or,

10.05–5(a)(2) 2 years' service as second mate of ocean or coastwise steam or motor vessels while holding a license as chief mate of ocean or coastwise steam or motor vessels; or

10.05–5(a)(3) 2 years' service as master of Great Lakes or lake, bay or sound steam or motor vessels of 500 gross tons or over, except ferry vessels, together with 6 months' service as chief mate or 12 months' service as second mate of ocean or coastwise steam or motor vessels, while holding license as master of such Great Lakes or lake, bay or sound vessels; or,

10.05–5(a)(4) 5 years' service on ocean or coastwise sail vessels of 200 gross tons or over, 2 years of which service shall have been as master of such vessels, for license as master of coastwise freight and towing vessels of not over 750 gross tons; or,

10.05–5(a)(5) 1 year's service as a licensed master of ocean or coastwise sail vessels of 700 gross tons or over for a license as master of coastwise freight or towing vessels of not more than 3,000 gross tons; or,

10.05–5(a)(6) 2 years' service as master or first-class pilot of Great Lakes or lake, bay or sound towing steam or motor vessels of 150 gross tons or over, for license as master of coastwise towing vessels of 750 gross tons or under; or,

10.05–5(a)(7) 2 years' service as master of steam vessels of 1,000 gross tons or over, except ferry vessels, on the Great Lakes and other lakes, bays, or sounds, for license as master of coastwise vessels on routes not exceeding 300 miles; or,

10.05–5(a)(8) 2 years' service as a licensed master of steam or motor vessels of 250 gross tons or over, engaged in the ocean or coastwise fisheries, for license as master of coastwise freight or towing vessels of not more than 750 gross tons; or,

10.05–5(a)(9) 1 year's service as licensed master of ocean or coastwise steam or motor vessels, or as licensed ocean operator of inspected, mechanically propelled passenger-carrying vessels operating on limited ocean or coastwise routes, for a license as master of coastwise steam or motor passenger vessels, not to exceed 300 gross tons and limited to the Atlantic, Gulf of Mexico or Pacific Coast of the United States, according to the documented qualifying experience of the applicant.

10.05–5(b) The minimum service required to qualify an applicant for a license as master of motor vessels of not more than 300 gross tons, operated in connection with the offshore mineral and oil industries, limited to a stated distance offshore on the continental shelf of the Atlantic, Gulf or Pacific Coast of the United States, as determined by the Commander of the District in which the license is issued, is:

10.05–5(b)(1) 1 year as a licensed mate of mineral or oil industry vessels; or,

10.05–5(b)(2) 1 year as a licensed master or first-class pilot of inland steam or motor vessels, plus 1 year in the deck department of coastwise vessels or mineral or oil industry vessels; or,

10.05–5(b)(3) 2 years' service as a licensed master of ocean or coastwise uninspected vessels; or,

10.05–5(b)(4) 3 years' service in the deck department of ocean or coastwise vessels of which at least 1 year shall have been as master or person in charge of vessels of at least 50 gross tons. If the required service as master or person in charge has been on vessels of more than 15 and less than 50 gross tons, the service may be accepted as qualifying experience for a license as master of coastwise vessels of not more than 100 gross tons.

10.05–7 Master of ocean or coastwise sail vessels.

10.05–7(a) The minimum service required for a license as master of ocean or coastwise sail vessels of 100 gross tons and over is listed in this paragraph. In order to be eligible for an unlimited license, an applicant must have acquired all of his qualifying service on vessels of 500 gross tons or over.

10.05–7(a)(1) 1 year's service as a licensed master of ocean or coastwise uninspected sail vessels; or,

10.05–7(a)(2) 2 years' service as master of ocean or coastwise sail vessels of 100 gross tons or over; or,

10.05–7(a)(3) 1 year's service as a licensed master of ocean or coastwise auxiliary sail vessels; or,

10.05–7(a)(4) 2 years' service as a licensed mate of ocean or coastwise uninspected sail vessels; or,

10.05–7(a)(5) 2 years' service as a licensed ocean operator of ocean or coastwise sail vessels carrying passengers; or,

10.05–7(a)(6) 5 years' service in the deck department of ocean or coastwise sail vessels, of which at least 1 year shall have been as mate.

10.05–7(b) An applicant who submits satisfactory documentary evidence that he has served as master of ocean or coastwise sail vessels of 100 gross tons or over for a period of at least 1 year, prior to June 1, 1958, shall be eligible without professional examination for a license as master of ocean or coastwise sail vessels of 100 to 700 gross tons, commensurate with his experience: *Provided* That such applicant for a license under the provisions of this paragraph shall fulfill all requirements, other than professional examination, for an original license, including citizenship, physical examination, character and U.S. Public Health Service First Aid Certificate: *And provided further,* That 6 months of the required 1 year of experience shall have been within the 3 years immediately preceding the date of application. Application for the issuance of licenses under the provisions of this paragraph must be filed within a period of 1 year after June 1, 1958. However, if the applicant can show that because of active military service, he was unable to obtain 6 months' service within the past 3 years or to file application within the 1 year period provided, the actual time spent in military service shall not be counted in computing either the 3-year period or the 1-year period specified in this paragraph.

10.05–9 Master of ocean or coastwise steam or motor yachts. The minimum service required to qualify an applicant for license as master of ocean or coastwise steam or motor yachts requiring licensed officers is 3 years' service in the deck department on ocean or coastwise steam, motor, or sailing yachts, of over 100 gross tons.

10.05–11 Master, mate, or pilot of steam or motor vessels operating under special conditions.

10.05–11(a) This section shall apply to every applicant for a license as master, mate, or pilot of steam pilot boats or seagoing motor pilot boats of 300 gross tons or over; or of steam vessels navigating the waters of the whaling grounds in the Alaskan seas; or of steam vessels engaged exclusively in the business of whale fishing; or of steam vessels engaged in the Atlantic, Pacific, or Gulf Coast fisheries; or of steam or sail vessels navigating exclusively between ports in the Hawaiian Islands; or of steam or sail vessels or seagoing motor vessels of 300 gross tons or over navigating exclusively between ports of the Island of Puerto Rico.

10.05–11(b) For original license as master, at least 3 years' experience in the deck department of such vessels is required.

10.05–11(c) For original license as mate, at least 2 years' experience in the deck department of such vessels is required.

10.05–11(d) Any person who has had at least 5 years' experience on sail vessels licensed in the fisheries of the United States, 2 years of which have been as master or mate of such sailing vessels, shall be eligible for a license as master or mate of steam fishing vessels to be employed exclusively in the Atlantic, Pacific and Gulf coast fisheries.

10.05–11(e) Any applicant for original license who has had 3 years' experience in the deck department on steam or motor pilot boats or who has had 2 years' experience in the deck department on steam or motor pilot boats and 1 year's experience on sail pilot boats, shall be eligible for license as mate of steam or motor pilot boats of 300 gross tons or over.

10.05–11(f) Any master's or mate's license issued under this section may be endorsed as pilot on such inland waters on the coasts stated in his license as the appropriate Officer in Charge, Marine Inspection, may find the holder qualified to act on as pilot.

10.05–11(g) An applicant for a master's license of seagoing vessels propelled by internal combustion engines, navigating exclusively between ports in the Hawaiian Islands, shall submit with his application statements duly executed and certified by reputable citizens qualified to judge the character, trustworthiness, and ability of the applicant.

10.05–11(h) The Officer in Charge, Marine Inspection, shall make a diligent inquiry as to the applicant's character and merits, and if satisfied by the oral examination or practical demonstration and the proof of requisite knowledge and skill offered, the Officer in Charge, Marine Inspection, shall issue the license. No certificate from the United States Public Health Service based upon the subject of ship sanitation and first aid shall be required of such an applicant.

10.05–13 Master of Great Lakes steam and motor vessels.

10.05–13(a) The minimum service required to qualify an applicant for a license as master is listed in this paragraph. In order to be eligible for an unlimited license, an applicant must have acquired his service on vessels of 4,000 gross tons or over, except as specified herein.

10.05–13(a)(1) 1 year's service as first class pilot while acting in the capacity of first mate on Great Lakes steam or motor vessels. (No change in existing regulation.)

10.05–13(a)(2) 2 years' service as first class pilot while acting in the capacity of second mate on Great Lakes steam or motor vessels.

10.05–13(a)(3) 4 years' service as first class pilot on Great Lakes steam or motor vessels, one year of which shall have been while acting in the capacity of second mate.

10.05–13(a)(4) 1 year's service as master of Great Lakes steam or motor vessels of 150 gross tons or under while acting under the authority of a first class pilot's license, for a license as master of Great Lakes steam and motor vessels of not over 1,000 gross tons.

10.05–13(a)(5) 1 year's service as master and/or first class pilot on lakes, bays and sounds steam or motor towing vessels, together with 1 year of service as first class pilot on Great Lakes vessels of over 100 gross tons, for a license as master of Great Lakes towing vessels of not over 750 gross tons.

10.05–15 Master of bays, sounds, and lakes other than the Great Lakes, steam and motor vessels.

10.05–15(a) The minimum service required to qualify an applicant for license as master of steam and motor vessels on bays, sounds and lakes other than the Great Lakes is:

10.05–15(a)(1) 1 year's service as first class pilot of steam and motor vessels on bays, sounds and lakes other than the Great Lakes; or

10.05–15(a)(2) 1 year's service as mate of steam and motor vessels on bays, sounds and lakes other than the Great Lakes; or,

10.05–15(a)(3) 1 year's service as master of steam or motor vessels of 150 gross tons or under on bays, sounds and lakes other than the Great Lakes, while acting under the authority of a first-class pilot's license, for a license as master of bays, sounds and lakes other than the Great Lakes, steam or motor vessels of a tonnage commensurate with the experience of the applicant, but of not more than 500 gross tons; or,

10.05-15(a)(4) 2 years' service in the deck department of steam or motor vessels on bays, sounds and lakes other than the Great Lakes, while holding a license as first-class pilot for bays, sounds and lakes other than the Great Lakes, as quartermaster or wheelsman for a license as master of steam and motor freight and towing vessels on bays, sounds and lakes other than the Great Lakes, limited to a gross tonnage commensurate with the experience of the applicant, but not more than 500 gross tons.

10.05–17 Master of river steam or motor vessels. The minimum service required to qualify an applicant for a license as master of steam or motor vessels navigating rivers exclusively is at least 3 years' service in the deck department of steam or motor vessels: *Provided,* That, 1 year of such service shall have been as licensed mate or pilot of steam or motor vessels, and, 1 year shall have been on river steam or motor vessels.

10.05–19 Master of ferry steam or motor vessels.

10.05–19(a) The minimum service required to qualify an applicant for license as master of ferry steam or motor vessels on either the Great Lakes, other lakes, bays and sounds, or rivers is:

10.05–19(a)(1) 1 year's service as first-class pilot; or,

10.05–19(a)(2) 2 years' service as wheelsman or quartermaster while holding a first-class pilot's license; or,

10.05–19(a)(3) 2 years' service in charge of a steam or motor vessel of 150 gross tons or under while acting under the authority of a pilot's license.

10.05–21 Master or pilot of steam yachts. The minimum service required to qualify an applicant for license as master or pilot of steam yachts on either the Great Lakes, other lakes, bays, and sounds, or rivers is 3 years' service in the deck department on board Great Lakes, other lakes, bays, and sounds, or river steam, motor, or sailing yachts.

10.05–23 Master of passenger barges. The minimum service required to qualify an applicant for license as master of barges carrying passengers on either the Great Lakes, other lakes, bays, and sounds, or rivers is 3 years' service in the deck department of such vessels.

10.05–25 Chief mate of ocean steam or motor vessels.

10.05–25(a) The minimum service required to qualify an applicant for license as chief mate of ocean steam or motor vessels is:

10.05–25(a)(1) 1 year's service as second mate of ocean steam or motor vessels of 1,000 gross tons or over; or,

10.05–25(a)(2) 1 year's service as second mate of coastwise steam or motor vessels of 2,000 gross tons or over; or,

10.05–25(a)(3) 2 years' service as officer in charge of a deck watch on ocean steam or motor vessels of 1,000 gross tons or over while holding a license as second mate of such vessels; or,

10.05–25(a)(4) 2 years' service as officer in charge of a deck watch on coastwise steam or motor vessels of 2,000 gross tons or over while holding a license as second mate of such vessels; or,

10.05–25(a)(5) 2 years' service as master of Great Lakes or other lakes, bay, or sound steam or motor vessels of 1,000 gross tons or over except ferry vessels, together with 1 year's service as officer in charge of a deck watch on ocean steam or motor vessels of 1,000 gross tons or over, or together with 1 year of such service on coastwise steam or motor vessels of 2,000 gross tons or over; or,

10.05–25(a)(6) 5 years' service in the deck department of ocean or coastwise sail vessels of 200 gross tons or over, 2 years of such service shall have been as master of such vessels, for license as chief mate of ocean freight or towing vessels of not more than 3,000 gross tons; or,

10.05–25(a)(7) 1 year's service as master of any class of ocean steam or motor vessels of more than 250 gross tons for license as chief mate of ocean freight or towing vessels of not more than 1,500 gross tons.

10.05–25(a)(8) 1 year's service as mate of inspected ocean or coastwise vessels while holding an unlimited license as 3rd mate of ocean steam or motor vessels for a license as chief mate of ocean vessels of less than 1,600 gross tons.

10.05–27 Chief mate of coastwise steam or motor vessels.

10.05–27(a) The minimum service required to qualify an applicant for license as chief mate of coastwise steam or motor vessels is:

10.05–27(a)(1) 1 year's service as second mate of ocean or coastwise steam or motor vessels of 1,000 gross tons or over; or,

10.05–27(a)(2) 2 years' service as officer in charge of a deck watch on ocean or coastwise steam or motor vessels of 1,000 gross tons or over while holding license as second mate of ocean or coastwise steam or motor vessels; or,

10.05–27(a)(3) 1 year's service as master or first-class pilot of Great Lakes or other lakes, bay, or sound steam or motor vessels of 500 gross tons or over, except ferry vessels, together with 1 year's service as officer in charge of a deck watch on ocean or coastwise steam or motor vessels of 1,000 gross tons or over, while holding license as such master or first-class pilot; or,

10.05–27(a)(4) 2 years' service as master or first-class pilot of Great Lakes or other lakes, bay, or sound towing vessels for license as chief mate of coastwise towing vessels of 750 gross tons or under; or,

10.05–27(a)(5) 1 year's service as a licensed master or 2 years' service as a licensed mate on ocean or coastwise steam or motor vessels of 250 gross tons or over engaged in the ocean or coastwise fisheries, for license as chief mate of coastwise freight or towing vessels of 1,000 gross tons or under; or,

10.05–27(a)(6) 5 years' service in the deck department of any ocean or coastwise sail vessel of 100 gross tons or over, 2 years of such service shall have been as master of such vessels, for license as chief mate of freight or towing vessels of 1,000 gross tons or under; or,

10.05–27(a)(7) 2 years' service as first-class pilot, or 2 years' combined service as master and first-class pilot of steam or motor vessels of 1,000 gross tons or over, except ferry vessels, on the Great Lakes and other lakes, bays, and sounds, for license as chief mate of coastwise vessels on routes not exceeding 300 miles; or,

10.05–27(a)(8) 3 years' service in the deck department of ocean or coastwise steam or motor vessels for license as chief mate of coastwise steam or motor vessels of not more than 500 gross tons.

10.05–28   Mate of motor vessels engaged in offshore mineral and oil industries.

10.05–28(a)   The minimum service required to qualify an applicant for a license as mate of motor vessels of not more than 300 gross tons, operated in connection with the offshore mineral and oil industries, limited to a stated distance offshore on the continental shelf of the Atlantic, Gulf or Pacific Coast of the United States, as determined by the Commander of the District in which the license is issued, is:

10.05–28(a)(1)   2 years' service as a licensed officer in charge of a deck watch on mineral or oil industry vessels, or

10.05–28(a)(2)   1 year's service as master or first class pilot of inland steam or motor vessels plus 6 months in the deck department of coastwise vessels or mineral or oil industry vessels, or

10.05–28(a)(3)   1 year's service as a licensed master or 2 years' service as a licensed mate of ocean or coastwise uninspected vessels, or

10.05–28(a)(4)   3 years' service in the deck department of ocean or coastwise steam or motor vessels, including mineral and oil industry vessels.

10.05–29   Second mate of ocean steam or motor vessels.

10.05–29(a)   The minimum service required to qualify an applicant for license as second mate of ocean steam or motor vessels is listed in this paragraph. In order to be eligible for an unlimited ocean license, an applicant must have obtained his service on ocean or coastwise vessels of 1,000 gross tons or over.

10.05–29(a)(1)   1 year's service as officer in charge of a deck watch on ocean or coastwise steam or motor vessels while holding a license as third mate; or,

10.05–29(a)(2)   6 months' service as second mate of coastwise steam or motor vessels; or,

10.05–29(a)(3)   5 years' service in the deck department of ocean or coastwise steam or motor vessels of 1,000 gross tons or over, 2 years of which shall have been as boatswain or quartermaster while holding a certificate as able seaman; or,

10.05–29(a)(4)   1 year's service as first-class pilot of steam or motor vessels of 4,000 gross tons or over, except ferry vessels, on the Great Lakes, or other lakes, bays, or sounds, together with 6 months' service in the deck department of ocean or motor vessels of 1,000 gross tons or over, while holding a license as such first-class pilot; or,

10.05–29(a)(5)   2 years' service as assistant (junior officer of the watch) to the officer in charge of the watch on ocean steam or motor vessels, while holding a license as third mate of such vessels; or,

10.05–29(a)(6)   4 years' service in the deck department of ocean or coastwise sail vessels of 200 gross tons or over, 1 year of such service shall have been as second mate of such sail vessels.

10.05–31   Second mate of coastwise steam or motor vessels.

10.05–31(a)   The minimum service required to qualify an applicant for license as second mate of coastwise steam or motor vessels is:

10.05–31(a)(1)   1 year's service as officer in charge of a deck watch on ocean or coastwise steam or motor vessels while holding a license as third mate; or,

10.05–31(a)(2)   5 years' service in the deck department of ocean or coastwise steam or motor vessels, 2 years of which shall have been as boatswain or quartermaster; or,

10.05–31(a)(3)   1 year's service as first-class pilot of steam or motor vessels of 2,500 tons or over, except ferry vessels, on the Great Lakes or other lakes, bays, or sounds, together with 6 months' service in the deck department of ocean or coastwise steam or motor vessels of 1,000 gross tons or over, while holding a license as such first-class pilot; or,

10.05–31(a)(4)   2 years' service as assistant (junior officer of the watch) to the officer in charge of the watch on ocean steam or motor vessels, while holding a license as third mate of such vessels; or,

10.05–31(a)(5)   1 year's service as a licensed mate on ocean or coastwise steam or motor vessels of 150 gross tons or over engaged in the fisheries, for license as second mate of towing vessels.

10.05–33   Third mate of ocean steam or motor vessels.

10.05–33(a)   The minimum service or training required to qualify an applicant for license as third mate of ocean steam or motor vessels is listed in this paragraph. In order to be eligible for an unlimited ocean license, an applicant must have obtained his service on ocean or coastwise vessels of 1,000 gross tons or over.

10.05–33(a)(1)   3 years' service in the deck department of ocean or coastwise steam or motor vessels, 6 months of which shall have been as able seaman, boatswain, or quartermaster while holding a certificate as able seaman; or

10.05–33(a)(2)   6 months' service as third mate of coastwise steam or motor vessels; or

10.05–33(a)(3)   Graduation from:

10.05–33(a)(3)(i)   The U.S. Merchant Marine Academy (deck);

10.05–33(a)(3)(ii)   The deck class of a state nautical schoolship established under the authority of an Act of Congress approved 4 March, 1911;

10.05–33(a)(3)(iii)   The U.S. Naval Academy; or

10.05–33(a)(3)(iv)   The U.S. Coast Guard Academy; or

10.05–33(a)(4)   Satisfactory completion of the prescribed course (deck) at a U.S. Maritime Service or other Government operated training school, approved by the Commandant, may be accepted as the equivalent of sea service up to a maximum of 4 months, provided the applicant has obtained the additional qualifying experience prior to enrollment; or

10.05–33(a)(5)   1 years' service as second-class pilot of steam or motor vessels of 4,000 gross tons or over, except ferry vessels, on the Great Lakes or other lakes, bays, or sounds, together with 6 months' service in the deck department of ocean steam or motor vessels of 1,000 gross tons or over, while holding a license as such second-class pilot; or

10.05–33(a)(6)   3 years' service in the deck department of steam or motor vessels on the Great Lakes, other lakes, bays, or sounds, or rivers, together with 1 year's service in the deck department of ocean steam or motor vessels, 6 months of which shall have been as able seaman, boatswain, or quartermaster while holding a certificate as able seaman; or

10.05–33(a)(7)   3 years' service in the deck department of steam or motor vessels of 100 gross tons or over engaged in the ocean or coastwise fisheries, together with 6 months' service as able seaman, boatswain, or quartermaster on ocean steam or motor vessels, while holding a certificate as able seaman.

10.05–35 Third mate of coastwise steam or motor vessels.

10.05–35(a) The minimum service or training required to qualify an applicant for license as third mate of coastwise steam or motor vessel is:

10.05–35(a)(1) 3 years' service in the deck department of ocean or coastwise steam or motor vessels, 6 months of which shall have been as able seaman; or,

10.05–35(a)(2) 1 year's service as second-class pilot of steam or motor vessels of 2,500 gross tons or over, except ferry vessels, on the Great Lakes or other lakes, bays, or sounds, together with 6 months' service in the deck department of ocean or coastwise steam or motor vessels of 1,000 gross tons or over, while holding a license as such second-class pilot; or,

10.05–35(a)(3) 2 years' service in the deck department of steam or motor vessels on the Great Lakes or other lakes, bays, or sounds, together with 2 years' service in the deck department of ocean or coastwise steam or motor vessels, 6 months of which shall have been as able seaman; or

10.05–35(a)(4) 2 years' service in the deck department of steam or motor vessels of 100 gross tons or over engaged in the ocean or coastwise fisheries, or any sail vessel of 100 gross tons or over, together with 1 year's service in the deck department of ocean or coastwise steam or motor vessels, 6 months of which shall have been as able seaman; or

10.05–35(a)(5) 3 years' service in the deck department of ocean or coastwise steam, motor, or sail vessels of less than 100 gross tons, together with 1 year's service in the deck department of ocean or coastwise steam or motor vessels, 6 months of which shall have been as able seaman.

10.05–37 Mate of inland or river steam or motor vessels. The minimum service required to qualify an applicant for license as mate of Great Lakes, other lakes, bays, or sounds, or river steam or motor vessels is at least 2 years' service in the deck department of steam, motor, or sail vessels, or barge consorts, 6 months of which service shall have been on steam or motor vessels.

10.05–39 Pilot.

10.05–39(a) *General.* An applicant for an original license as pilot may be given credit for experience on motor vessels of a class not subject to inspection by the Coast Guard and not required to carry a licensed master or a licensed pilot.

10.05–39(a)(1) An applicant for an original pilot's license, endorsement as pilot or an extension of pilot's route shall furnish discharges, letters or other satisfactory documentary evidence, certifying to the names of the vessels, the periods of service, the dates and number of round trips made and the capacity in which the applicant served. Photostatic copies of such letters and documents may be accepted for filing with the application.

10.05–39(b) *Professional requirements.* The minimum service required to qualify an applicant for license as pilot is:

10.05–39(b)(1) 3 years' service in the deck department of ocean, coastwise, Great Lakes or bays, sounds and lakes, other than the Great Lakes, steam or motor vessels, of which 18 months shall have been as able seaman, or service in a capacity at least the equivalent of able seaman. Of the 18 months as able seaman, or equivalent capacity, at least 1 year shall have been on vessels operating on the waters of the class for which pilotage is desired in the capacity of quartermaster, wheelsman, able seaman or equivalent capacity, who stands regular watches at the wheel or in the pilothouse as part of his routine duties; and,

10.05–39(b)(1)(i) 25 percent of such service shall have been obtained within the three years immediately preceding the date of application; and,

10.05–39(b)(1)(ii) The required service shall include a minimum number of round trips over the route for which the applicant seeks license as pilot, as may be fixed by the Officer in Charge, Marine Inspection, having jurisdiction (experience on motorboats as defined by statutes may be accepted by the Officer in Charge, Marine Inspection, for license or endorsement as pilot, but such licenses or endorsements shall be limited to a gross tonnage commensurate with such experience, irrespective of any other license or endorsement held by the applicant) ; and,

10.05–39(b)(1)(iii) One of the required number of round trips shall have been made over the route within the 6 months immediately preceding the date of application; or,

10.05–39(b)(2) 3 years' service in the deck department of any vessel of which at least 1 year shall have been on vessels operating on the waters of rivers while serving in the capacity of quartermaster, wheelsman or deckhand who stands watches at the wheel as part of his routine duties, for license as pilot of river routes. The provisions in Subdivisions 10.05–39(b)(1)(i) through 10.05–39(b)(1)(iii) are applicable to this subparagraph.

10.05–39(b)(3) 2 years' service in the deck department of steam or motor vessels navigating canals and small lakes, such as the New York State Barge Canal and Seneca and Cayuga Lakes in the State of New York, 1 year of which shall have been within the 2 years immediately preceding the date of application, for license as pilot of steam and motor vessels of limited tonnage for the waters and/or routes on which the qualifying service was acquired.

10.05–39(c) *Limitations.* The Officer in Charge, Marine Inspection, issuing a license or endorsement as pilot, shall impose suitable limitations commensurate with the past experience of the applicant, with respect to class of vessels for which valid, tonnage, route and waters.

10.05–41 Pilot of tank vessels of not more than 150 gross tons. All propelled tank vessels regardless of length or tonnage, shall be under the command of a person duly licensed and since propelled vessels of less than 150 gross tons may be in command of a licensed pilot, the license of a candidate who successfully passes an examination for this purpose shall be endorsed as follows: "Pilot for tank vessels not more than _____ gross tons on the waters of _____" (the maximum to be inserted is not to exceed 150 gross tons and the waters covered as may be designated by the Officer in Charge, Marine Inspection).

10.05–42 Endorsement of master's or mate's license as pilot or extension of pilot's route.

10.05–42(a) A master or mate applying for endorsement of his license to act as pilot or a licensed pilot applying for an extension of route, shall make written application on Coast Guard Form CG 866, with documentary evidence of experience acquired by a minimum number of round trips over the particular route or waters for which endorsement or extension of route is desired, as may be required by the Officer in Charge, Marine Inspection, having jurisdiction. One of the required number of round trips shall have been made within the 6 months immediately preceding the date of application. If the applicant is found qualified by experience and written examination as hereafter provided, the endorsement as pilot or extension of route shall be endorsed on his license: *Provided however,* That upon waters of the United States newly opened to navigation, and where the only pilots obtainable are illiterate Indians or other natives, the fact that such persons can neither read nor write shall not be considered a bar to such Indians or other natives receiving extensions of route of licenses as pilots if they are otherwise qualified.

10.05–42(b)   The holder of a license as master or mate of ocean or coastwise vessels who has had recent satisfactory service under the authority of his license is eligible for examination for endorsement as pilot on any waters upon completing the number of round trips over the route required for his grade of license by the Officer in Charge, Marine Inspection, having jurisdiction, while serving in the capacity of quartermaster, wheelsman or able seaman who stands regular watches at the wheel as part of his routine duties. Experience as an observer, properly certified by the master and/or pilot of the vessel is also acceptable in such cases. An endorsement as pilot granted under these provisions shall be limited to the tonnage and class of vessels for which the holder's license as master or mate is valid except as provided in Subdivision 10.05–39(b)(1)(ii).

10.05–42(c)   When an application is made to any Officer in Charge, Marine Inspection, for an extension of route which is outside his jurisdiction he shall request the Officer in Charge, Marine Inspection, having jurisdiction to forward the necessary examination material for examining the applicant. The complete examination file of the applicant shall be returned to the Officer in Charge, Marine Inspection, having jurisdiction, who, if satisfied that the applicant is qualified and capable, shall grant the authority and advise the other Officer in Charge, Marine Inspection, to endorse the license accordingly.

10.05–43   Examination for license as pilot.

10.05–43(a)   An applicant for an original license as pilot or initial endorsement of master's or mate's license as pilot shall be required to pass a satisfactory examination as to his knowledge of the subjects listed in this paragraph:

(1) Rules of the Road.
(2) Inland rules, applicable to route.
(3) Local knowledge of winds, weather, tides, current, etc.
(4) Chart navigation.
(5) Aids to navigation.
(6) Ship handling.
(7) Chart sketch of the route and waters applied for, showing courses, distances, shoals, aids to navigation, depths of water, and other important features of the route.
(8) General: Such further examination as the Officer in Charge, Marine Inspection, may consider necessary to establish the applicant's proficiency.

10.05–43(b)   An applicant for extension of pilot's route shall be examined on the subjects in subparagraphs (1), (2), (7), and (8) in paragraph (a) of this section only.

10.05–45   Examination for license as deck officer of ocean or coastwise steam, motor, or sail vessels.

10.05–45(a)   An applicant for license as deck officer of either ocean or coastwise steam and motor vessels, or sail vessels of 100 gross tons or over, or master of steam and motor yachts, shall pass a satisfactory written examination as to his knowledge of the subjects listed in paragraph (b) of this section. However, if the license to be issued is limited on its face in a manner that would make any of the specific subjects unnecessary or superfluous, the examination should be amended accordingly. Examinations for licenses not incorporated in Table 10.05–45(b) shall be of suitable scope and character to determine the applicant's proficiency.

10.05–45(b)   List of subjects required.

10.05–45(c)(1)   Each applicant for an ocean or coastwise deck license, whether original or raise of grade, shall be required to pass practical tests in signalling. The examination in signalling will consist of an examination in the international flag code and Morse flashing. Candidates will be examined in Morse flashing in groups where practicable.

10.05–45(c)(2)   Candidates shall be able to read a signal at sight, so far as to name the flags composing the hoist; know the use of the code pennant, numeral and substitute pennants, the meaning of all the single letter signals and the flags used to indicate the quarantine signals; be required to signal some word or words not included in the vocabulary of the code; and have a good knowledge of the distress signals. Candidates will be required to attain a speed of six words a minute in Morse flashing. The average length of a word is to be five letters. Candidates who wish to prove their higher proficiency may request to be tested at a minimum speed of ten words a minute in Morse flashing. Such candidates, if successful, will have the results of their examination reported on their official files.

10.05–45(c)(3)   A candidate for license who fails in signalling, but passes in every other subject, will be considered to have failed the examination and shall be so reported; but he may at any time within the six months following his first attempt be reexamined in signalling only, and if he then passes he will be granted a license.

10.05–46   Radar observer.

10.05–46(a)   Every applicant for an original license, raise of grade, or increase in scope of license for service on ocean, coastwise, or Great Lakes vessels of 300 gross tons and over shall be required to demonstrate, by professional examination, his qualifications as a "radar observer."

10.05–46(b)   Applicants for licenses specified in paragraph (a) of this section shall be examined on the following aspects of the proper operation and utilization of marine radar equipment:

10.05–46(b)(1)   Fundamentals of radar:
10.05–46(b)(1)(i)   How radar works.
10.05–46(b)(1)(ii)   Factors affecting the performance and accuracy of marine radar.
10.05–46(b)(1)(iii)   Description of the purpose and functions of the main components that comprise a typical marine radar installation.
10.05–46(b)(2)   Operation and use of radar:
10.05–46(b)(2)(i)   The purpose and adjustment of controls.
10.05–46(b)(2)(ii)   The detection of malfunctioning, false and indirect echoes and other radar phenomena.
10.05–46(b)(2)(iii)   The effect of sea return and weather.

Table 10.05–45(b)—Subjects for Deck Officers of Ocean or Coastwise Steam or Motor Vessels

Subjects	Master				Chief mate		Second mate		Third mate		Mate—Limited mineral and oil industry
	Ocean	Coast-wise	Yachts	Limited mineral and oil industry	Ocean	Coast-wise	Ocean	Coast-wise	Ocean	Coast-wise	
1. Latitude by Polaris	X	X			X		X				
2. Latitude by meridian altitude method							Sun or star.	Sun	Sun	Sun	
3. Fix or running fix	Any body.	Sun or star.	Any body.		Any body.	Sun or star.	do.	do.	do.		
4. Star identification (any method)	X	X	X		X		X				
5. Chart navigation	X	X	X	X	X		X		X	X	X
6. Compass deviation	Any body.	Sun or star.	Sun.		Sun or star.	Sun or star.	Sun or star.	Sun.	Sun.	Sun.	
7. Canceled.											
8. Middle latitude sailing			X						X	X	
9. Mercator sailing	X	X	X								
10. Great Circle sailing	X										
11. Piloting	X	X	X		X	X	X	X	X	X	
12. Aids to navigation	X	X	X	X	X	X	X	X	X	X	X
13. Speed by revolutions	X	X			X	X	X	X	X	X	
14. Fuel conservation	X										
15. Instruments and accessories	X	X	X		X	X	X	X	X	X	
16. Magnetism, deviation and compass compensation	X	X	X	¹ X	X		X		X	X	X
17. Chart construction	X	X									
18. Tides and currents	X	X			X		X		X	X	X
19. Ocean winds, weather and currents	X	X		X		X		X		X	X
20. Nautical astronomy and navigation definitions						X	X		X		³ X
21. International and inland rules of the road	X	X	X	X	X	X	X	X	X	X	X
22. Signaling by international code flags, flashing light; life-saving, storm and special signals	X	X		² X	X	X	X	X	X	X	² X
23. Stability and ship construction	X	X			X	X	X				
24. Seamanship	X	X			X	X	X	X	X	X	X
25. Cargo stowage and handling		X			X	X	X	X	X	X	X
26. Change in draft due to density		X			X	X	X				
27. Determination of area and volume		X									
28. Lifesaving apparatus and fire fighting equipment	X	X	X	X	X	X	X	X	X	X	X
29. Ship sanitation	X	X			X						
30. Rules and regulations for inspection of merchant vessels	X	X	X	X	X	X	X	X	X	X	X
31. Laws governing marine inspection	X	X		X	X	X					
32. Ship's business	X	X		X							
33. Such further examination of a non-mathematical character at the Officer in Charge, Marine Inspection, may consider necessary to establish the applicant's proficiency.	X	X	X	X	X	X	X	X	X	X	X

¹ Practical use of the magnetic compass.   ² Lifesaving, storm, and special signals.   ³ Navigation definitions only.

10.05–46(b)(2)(iv) The limitations of radar resulting from design factors.

10.05–46(b)(2)(v) Precautions to be observed in performing simple maintenance of radar equipment.

10.05–46(b)(2)(vi) Range and bearing measurement.

10.05–46(b)(2)(vii) Effect of size, shape, and composition of ship targets on echo.

10.05–46(b)(3) Interpretation and analysis of radar information:

10.05–46(b)(3)(i) Determining the course and speed of another vessel.

10.05–46(b)(3)(ii) Determining the time and distance of closest point of approach of a crossing, meeting, overtaking or overtaken vessel.

10.05–46(b)(3)(iii) Detecting changes of course and/or speed of another vessel after its initial course and speed have been established.

10.05–46(b)(3)(iv) Factors to consider when determining change in course and/or speed of own vessel to prevent collision on the basis of radar observation of another vessel or vessels.

10.05–46(b)(4) Plotting (any method that is graphically correct may be used):

10.05–46(b)(4)(i) The principles and methods of plotting relative and true motion.

10.05–46(b)(4)(ii) Practical plotting problems.

10.05–46(c) An applicant for a license who fails the "radar observer" examination but passes in every other subject will be considered as having failed the license examination, but he may at any time within 6 months of his failure be reexamined in the "radar observer" subject only; and, if he then passes, he may be granted a license.

10.05–46(d) A certificate of successful completion of a course of instruction of a Maritime Administration or other Government operated school, approved by the Commandant, is acceptable evidence of the holder's qualification as "radar observer" without the examination specified in paragraph (b) of this section.

10.05–46(d)(1) The "Radar Observer Schools" listed in this subparagraph are approved. The approval for a particular school shall be effective for all certificates issued on or after the date of the first class held, as set forth in this subparagraph, and will continue in effect until this approval is suspended, canceled, or modified by proper authority.

10.05–46(d)(1)(i) Maritime Administration Radar Observer School, c/o Atlantic Coast Director, 45 Broadway, New York, New York. Physical location: 45 Broadway, New York, New York. First class held: November 18, 1957.

10.05–46(d)(1)(ii) Maritime Administration Radar Observer School, c/o Pacific Coast Director, 180 New Montgomery Street, San Francisco, California. Physical location: Fort Mason, San Francisco Army Terminal. First class held: March 3, 1958.

10.05–46(d)(1)(iii) Maritime Administration Radar Observer School, c/o Gulf Coast Director, Masonic Temple Building, 333 St. Charles Street, New Orleans, Louisiana. Physical location: New Orleans Army Terminal. First class held: July 14, 1958.

10.05–46(d)(2) The course of instruction in the proper operation and utilization of marine radar equipment is approved as given at the U.S. Merchant Marine Academy, Kings Point, New York. This approval shall be effective for all certificates issued to the deck cadets of the U.S. Merchant Marine Academy and attesting to the successful completion of the course in the proper operation and utilization of marine radar equipment on or after July 17, 1959, and will continue in effect until this approval is suspended, canceled or modified by proper authority.

10.05–46(d)(3)   The course of instruction in the proper operation and utilization of marine radar equipment is approved as given at the U.S. Army Transportation School, Fort Eustis, Virginia. This approval shall be effective for all certificates issued to men attesting to the successful completion of the course in the proper operation and utilization of marine radar equipment on or after June 6, 1960, and will continue in effect until this approval is suspended, canceled, or modified by proper authority.

10.05–46(d)(4)   The course of instruction in the proper operation and utilization of marine radar equipment is approved as given at the State University of New York, Maritime College, Fort Schuyler, New York 65, N.Y. This approval shall be effective for all certificates issued to the deck cadets of the New York Maritime College which attest to the successful completion of the course in the proper operation and utilization of marine radar equipment on or after November 17, 1960, and will continue in effect until this approval is suspended, canceled or modified by proper authority.

* * * *

§ 10.05–46   Radar observer.

(d) * * *
(5) The course of instruction in the proper operation and utilization of marine radar equipment is approved as given at the Maine Maritime Academy, Castine, Maine. This approval shall be effective for all certificates issued to the deck cadets of the Maine Maritime Academy which attest to the successful completion of the course of instruction in the proper operation and utilization of marine radar equipment on or after July 2, 1963, and will continue in effect until this approval is suspended, canceled, or modified by the proper authority.

* * * * *

10.05–47   Examination for license as master of Great Lakes steam and motor vessels.

10.05–47(a)   An applicant for license as master of Great Lakes steam or motor vessels shall be required to pass a satisfactory examination as to his knowledge of the subjects listed in this paragraph:

10.05–47(a)(1)   Rules of the Road.
10.05–47(a)(2)   Deviation by azimuth of the sun.
10.05–47(a)(3)   Deviation by azimuth of Polaris.
10.05–47(a)(4)   Construction of a deviation table by any method:
10.05–47(a)(4)(i)   Azimuth of sun or Polaris.
10.05–47(a)(4)(ii)   Equidistant bearings of a fixed object.
10.05–47(a)(4)(iii)   Ranges.
10.05–47(a)(4)(iv)   Comparison with a gyro or magnetic compass whose deviation is known.
10.05–47(a)(5)   Distance off by bearings and run.
10.05–47(a)(6)   Distance off by distance-finding stations.
10.05–47(a)(7)   Distance off by visibility of lights.
10.05–47(a)(8)   Speed by revolutions and by observation.

10.05–47(a)(9)   Instruments and accessories used in navigation.
10.05–47(a)(10)   Magnetism, deviation, and compass compensation.
10.05–47(a)(11)   Chart navigation and piloting.
10.05–47(a)(12)   Aids to navigation.
10.05–47(a)(13)   Winds and weather.
10.05–47(a)(14)   Signals; storm, wreck, distress and special.
10.05–47(a)(15)   Stability and ship construction.
10.05–47(a)(16)   Cargo stowage and handling.
10.05–47(a)(17)   Seamanship.
10.05–47(a)(18)   Temporary repairs to hull and equipment.
10.05–47(a)(19)   Drills and lifesaving apparatus.
10.05–47(a)(20)   Ship sanitation; Rules and Regulations for Vessel Inspection, and Navigation Laws of the U.S.
10.05–47(a)(21)   Ship's business.
10.05–47(a)(22)   General.
10.05–47(a)(23)   Practical chart work.
10.05–47(a)(24)   Such further examination of a non-mathematical character as the Officer in Charge, Marine Inspection, may consider necessary to establish the applicant's proficiency.

10.05–49   Examination for license as master of bays, sounds, and lakes other than the Great Lakes steam and motor vessels.

10.05–49(a)   An applicant for license as master of bays, sounds, and lakes other than the Great Lakes steam or motor vessels shall be required to pass a satisfactory examination as to his knowledge of the subjects listed in this paragraph:

10.05–49(a)(1)   Rules of the Road applicable to the waters desired.
10.05–49(a)(2)   Distance off by bearings and run.
10.05–49(a)(3)   Speed by revolutions and by observation of landmarks.
10.05–49(a)(4)   Chart navigation and piloting.
10.05–49(a)(5)   Aids to navigation.
10.05–49(a)(6)   Winds, weather, and current.
10.05–49(a)(7)   Signals; storm, wreck, distress, and special.
10.05–49(a)(8)   Stability and ship construction.
10.05–49(a)(9)   Cargo stowage and handling.
10.05–49(a)(10)   Seamanship.
10.05–49(a)(11)   Temporary repairs to hull and equipment.
10.05–49(a)(12)   Drills and lifesaving apparatus.
10.05–49(a)(13)   Ship sanitation; Rules and Regulations for Vessel Inspection, and Navigation Laws of the U.S.
10.05–49(a)(14)   Ship's business.
10.05–49(a)(15)   General.
10.05–49(a)(16)   Practical chart work.
10.05–49(a)(17)   Such further examination of a non-mathematical character as the Officer in Charge, Marine Inspection, may consider necessary to establish the applicant's proficiency.

10.05–51   Examination for license as master of river steam or motor vessels.

10.05–51(a)   An applicant for license as master of river steam or motor vessels shall be required to pass a satisfactory examination as to his knowledge of the subjects listed in this paragraph:

10.05–51(a)(1)   Rules of the Road.
10.05–51(a)(2)   Shiphandling and navigation of river vessels.
10.05–51(a)(3)   Instruments and accessories.
10.05–51(a)(4)   Aids to navigation.
10.05–51(a)(5)   Seamanship.
10.05–51(a)(6)   Ship construction.
10.05–51(a)(7)   Cargo stowage and handling.
10.05–51(a)(8)   Temporary repairs to hull and equipment.
10.05–51(a)(9)   Drills; lifesaving and firefighting equipment and procedures.
10.05–51(a)(10)   Rules and regulations for vessel inspection and navigation laws of the United States; ship sanitation.
10.05–51(a)(11)   Mathematics.
10.05–51(a)(12)   General.
10.05–51(a)(13)   Such further examination of a non-mathematical character as the Officer in Charge, Marine Inspection, may consider necessary to establish the applicant's proficiency.

10.05–53 Examination for license as master of ferry steam or motor vessels. An applicant for license as master of ferry steam or motor vessels on either the Great Lakes, other lakes, bays, and sounds, or rivers shall be required to pass satisfactorily an examination of such length and scope as will satisfy the Officer in Charge, Marine Inspection, that the applicant is capable of handling and navigating such vessels.

10.05–55 Examination for license as master or pilot of yachts on the Great Lakes, other lakes, bays, and sounds, or rivers. An applicant for license as master or pilot of yachts on either the Great Lakes, other lakes, bays, and sounds, or rivers, shall be required to pass a satisfactory examination as to his knowledge in handling such vessels, and his familiarity with the lights, lighthouses, channels, buoys, obstructions, courses, and distances between certain points in the waters for which he makes application for license. He shall

also be examined regarding his knowledge of the Rules of the Road for such waters, the running and anchor lights, fog signals, the use of the lead, signal bells between engineroom and pilothouse, the General Rules and Regulations for Vessel Inspection, and such further examination of a non-mathematical character as the Officer in Charge, Marine Inspection, may consider necessary to establish the applicant's proficiency.

10.05–57 Examination for license as master of passenger barges on the Great Lakes, other lakes, bays, and sounds, or rivers. An applicant for license as master of passenger barges on the Great Lakes, other lakes, bays, and sounds, or rivers shall be required to pass satisfactorily an examination of such length and scope as will satisfy the Officer in Charge, Marine Inspection, that the applicant is capable of handling the class of vessel for which he desires a license.

10.05–59 Examination for license as mate of inland or river steam or motor vessels. An applicant for license as mate of inland or river steam or motor vessels shall be required to pass a satisfactory examination as to his knowledge, experience, and skill in stowage and cargo handling, the operation and handling of fire apparatus, the launching and handling of lifeboats, his knowledge of life preservers and the method of adjusting them, his ability to manage the crew and direct and advise the passengers in case of emergency, his general familiarity with his duties in maintaining discipline and protecting the passengers, and such further examination of a non-mathematical character as the Officer in Charge, Marine Inspection, may consider necessary to establish the applicant's proficiency.

10.05–61 Evaluation of experience not listed. When an applicant presents evidence of service or experience which does not meet the specific requirements of the regulations in this part, but which in the opinion of the Officer in Charge, Marine Inspection, is a reasonable equivalent thereto, the application for license with supporting data shall be submitted to the Commandant for evaluation, together with the recommendation of the Officer in Charge, Marine Inspection.

Appendix B

COMMISSIONS IN THE RESERVE OF THE U. S. NAVY

The purpose of commissioning Merchant Marine officers in the Reserve of the U. S. Navy is to provide a trained force of seagoing personnel for mobilization in the event of a national emergency, for service aboard naval vessels and merchant vessels requisitioned by the Navy; and to provide qualified specialists of the Merchant Marine for mobilization billets in the Naval Establishment connected with the administration and operation of vessels.

SOURCE

Applications for appointment to commissioned grade in the Line (1105) or Supply Corps (3105) are considered from the following sources:

(1) Licensed deck and engineer officers serving in merchant vessels.
(2) Staff officers qualified for Supply Corps duties.
(3) Licensed personnel employed in positions of trust, authority and responsibility ashore in connection with the seafaring profession.
(4) Graduates of the Federal and State Maritime Academies who have successfully completed and prescribed standards.

At the present time, there is no enlisted component of merchant marine personnel. If future needs of the service indicate such a component is desirable, action will be taken accordingly.

PROCEDURE IN MAKING APPLICATION FOR APPOINT-MENT AS OFFICER IN THE NAVAL RESERVE

Applicants for commission should contact the nearest U. S. Navy Recruiting Station and arrange for the processing of their applications.

REQUIREMENTS FOR APPOINTMENT AS AN OFFICER

In addition to the general requirements for commission, the following specific requirements are prescribed for licensed personnel of the merchant marine:

(1) Age—Must be at least 19 years and under 48½ years of age at time of submission of application.

(2) Physical—Must meet the physical standards prescribed in the Manual of the Medical Department for officer personnel.

(3) Educational.

(a) Radiotelegraph Operators—Must have successfully completed two years of work toward a degree in an accredited college or university or must present evidence of eligibility for acceptance without qualification in the junior academic year at an accredited college or university.

(b) Others—No minimum educational requirements.

(4) Professional.

(a) A candidate for commission in the line must be a licensed deck, engineer or radio officer of the American Merchant Marine and be serving in a vessel of not less than 1000 gross tons documented under laws of the United States or on other public vessels thereof. Applicants serving on vessels of less than 1000 gross tons may be appointed by special authority of the Chief of Naval Personnel.

(b) A candidate for appointment in the Supply Corps must be employed on a vessel documented under the laws of the United States. Only chief pursers, pursers, senior assistant and junior assistant pursers (including those assigned to stores duties) who have successfully completed two years of college studies or who have served not less than two years under certificate of registry in one of the purser classifications, will be considered eligible for appointment as commissioned officers in the Supply Corps.

(c) A licensed radio officer applying for appointment in the Naval Reserve must, in addition, hold a valid first-class radiotelegraph operator's license issued by the Federal Communications Commission and be licensed as a radio officer by the Coast Guard. In addition, such officers must have had two years' experience as a radio officer at sea in vessels of the maritime service, one year of which must have included collateral duties as a shipboard administrative officer.

(d) Applications may be accepted from licensed personnel employed in the Merchant Marine Service in a capacity connected with the management, operation, or maintenance of the ships of the Merchant Marine.

(5) Citizenship—All applicants must be citizens of the United States by either birth or naturalization.

(6) Appointment.

(a) The grade in which appointment is made depends on the applicant's age and the total number of years of accumulated seagoing licensed service. Unless otherwise authorized by the Chief of Naval Personnel the maximum age and minimum seagoing licensed experience for appointment in the Naval Reserve of Merchant Marine Officers are:

Maximum Age	Grade	Minimum Seagoing Licensed Experience
48½	LCDR	11 years
39½	LT	7 years
33½	LTJG	3 years
27½	ENS	3 months

(b) In order to establish permanency of duties, applicants serving on board ship must have been employed in their present capacity for at least three months immediately preceding appointment.

With regard to graduates of the merchant marine academies, the following specific requirements are prescribed in addition to the general requirements for commission:

(1) Age—Must be at least 19 years and no more than 27½ years of age at time of appointment as Ensign.

(2) Educational—Must be a graduate of one of the following state or federal maritime academies and must have successfully completed the prescribed course of naval science:

(a) State—California Maritime Academy, Maine Maritime Academy, Massachusetts Maritime Academy, Texas Maritime Academy, and the State University of New York Maritime College.

(b) Federal—U. S. Merchant Marine Academy, Kings Point, New York.

(3) Professional—Must hold unlimited ocean license as deck or engineering officer.

ACTIVE AND INACTIVE APPOINTMENTS

All active appointments will be granted for a minimum active obligated service period of three years.

Inactive Naval Reserve officers appointed under the Merchant Marine Program will be required to sail on their licenses at sea for not less than three years and to participate in Naval Reserve training in accordance with their signed agreements. Those Naval Reserve officers who do not fully meet these requirements will be separated.

GENERAL INFORMATION FOR OFFICERS OF THE NAVAL RESERVE
Pay and Allowances

The 1964 military pay raise was signed into law by the President on 12 August and became effective 1 September 1964. The new pay scales apply both to Regular Navymen and to Reservists on active duty or active/inactive duty for training. In the past, most pay bills covered retired men as well as those on active duty, but this one does not. Only those Navymen who retire or enter the Fleet Reserve after 1 September 1964 will receive any benefit from the new pay rates. On first entry into active service, the pay and allowances of various ranks are:

		With Dependents		No Dependents	
	Base Pay	Quarters	Subsist.	Quarters	Subsist.
CAPT	643.20	170.10	47.88	140.10	47.88
CDR	514.50	157.50	47.88	130.20	47.88
LCDR	434.10	145.05	47.88	120.00	47.88
LT	353.70	130.05	47.88	105.00	47.88
LTJG	281.40	120.00	47.88	95.00	47.88
ENS	241.20	110.10	47.88	85.20	47.88

Naval Correspondence Courses

To provide opportunity for self-study in professional naval subjects, the Navy offers a wide variety of correspondence courses, which are available to all officers, Regular or Reserve, active or inactive. Most of these courses are administered by the Naval Correspondence Course Center, Scotia, New York, with courses in specialized areas offered by the Defense Intelligence School, Naval Submarine School and Naval Security Stations. The Naval War College and the Industrial College of the Armed Forces offer senior courses paralleling some of their resident courses of instruction.

Promotion of Naval Reserve Officers

Normally officers reach the promotion zone to the next higher grade about the time they attain the total years of commissioned service shown in the following table. Provisions in law, however, do permit the accelerated promotion of outstanding officers whose performance indicates them to be definitely among the best fitted of all the officers in the grade concerned. The maximum accelerated promotion flow rate possible must be within the minimum periods of service in grade which is controlled by law. No officer may be considered for promotion to higher grades prior to completing this minimum service. Minimum periods present actual total periods and currently planned stabilized total periods of promotion flow points as indicated in the table.

	(1) Minimum Required Service in Grade	(2) Present Actual Total Service	(3) Planned Stabilized Total Service
Grade			
ENS	$1\frac{1}{2}$	$1\frac{1}{2}$	$1\frac{1}{2}$
LTJG	2	4	4
LT	4	10	10
LCDR	4	16	16
CDR	5	20	22
CAPT	3	29	29

(1) Years of service in grade necessary for eligibility for consideration for promotion.

(2) Total years of commissioned service to reach promotion zone to the next higher grade during recent years.

(3) Total years of commissioned service to reach promotion zone when promotion flow rate becomes stabilized.

The promotion zones are established after a very comprehensive projected study of the grade structure in the U. S. Naval Service has been completed. The purpose of the study is to assure equitable promotion opportunities among succeeding groups of Reserve officers within the authorized grade limitations as established by law.

Official announcement of the promotion zones and the convening dates of the selection boards is made by yearly Bureau of Naval Personnel notices and also by publications, such as: The Naval Reservist, All Hands, and Navy Times.

Selection for promotion to the next higher grade is a competitive process whereby all eligible personnel are competing and being evaluated on the basis of their past demonstrated performance as reported by their reporting seniors, and are further evaluated as to their relative qualifications to serve in the next higher grade upon mobilization of the Naval Reserve. The process of evaluation and classification is performed by a group of experienced senior officers who are ordered to serve as members of the selection board by the Secretary of the Navy. The deliberations of the selection board are in strict confidence, and only the final report listing the recommended selectees is published.

Naval Reserve officers, not on active duty, are required to establish their professional qualification for promotion in addition to being recommended for promotion by a selection board. Individuals who have been recommended for promotion will be advised by the Chief of Naval Personnel of the additional requirements to complete professional qualifications. Qualifications are completed by earning, in grade, a prescribed number of promotion points based on the number of years each officer has been in grade.

Annual Qualification Questionnaires

Inasmuch as promotion, retirement and future assignment may depend on the information obtained from the Annual Qualification Questionnaire, it is in the interest as well as the duty of each officer to prepare, sign and return the form promptly once a year. Appropriate form may be obtained from COMDTS.

Official Letters

The following is for the information of the large number of Naval Reserve officers who have not had active duty, and, consequently, are unfamiliar with procedure for official letters:

From: LCDR Colin Glencannon, 65403, 1105, USNR
      S.S. INCHCLIFFE CASTLE VICTORY
      c/o Loch Steamship Lines
      24 State Street
      New York, New York

To: The Chief of Naval Personnel
Via: Commandant, Third Naval District
Subj: Official letters; preparation of
Ref: (a) NavPers 16138, Chap. 18

1. It is suggested that the following excerpts from reference (a) be published in the Naval Reservist:

(a) The first step in the preparation of an official letter consists of assembling and recording all data pertinent to the subject. Present all facts in a logical sequence.

(b) The next step is to discuss all facts in a clear, decisive manner. Failing to give an exact presentation of facts, omitting supporting details, or neglecting to arrange material so as to lead to definite conclusions, could lead to misinterpretation. On the other hand, properly written letters, leading logically to definite conclusions by the use of a minimum of words and orderly presentation of facts, compel favorable attention.

(c) Letters should be closed with specific requests or recommendations, and in certain cases accomplishments. There is no single form of official letter which fits perfectly all classes of correspondence. However, there are principles of form which, if followed, will reduce the length of letters and lead to the desired sequence of expression. No correspondence form can be used as a substitute for thought and knowledge of subject matter on the part of the writer.

(d) It must be remembered that the official letter is wholly impersonal. The personality of the writer is not to be reflected in the official communication as in personal and familiar correspondence. Navy correspondence is generally confined to the third person.

2. Officers should also be informed of the importance of maintaining a personal file of all official correspondence. It should be started with the first correspondence relating to the officer's naval career. Not infrequently he will find this file of inestimable value in establishing important facts and figures at a later date.

_____

Signature

In addition to the above, officers should remember that all official correspondence must be forwarded through official channels; must be courteous in tone; should always be addressed by title and not by name to officers holding recognized titles; and should not combine unrelated subjects in the same letter, since this causes inconvenience when several departments are involved in answering the letter. If possible, letters should be typewritten.

The file number on correspondence regarding a particular officer shall be the file number assigned him by the Chief of Naval Personnel. This file number should be shown in the upper right-hand corner of correspondence originated by a Naval Reserve officer about himself and shall be used by the Commandant or Chief of Naval Air Reserve Training and by organization commanders having occasion to write about any particular officer.

Appendix C

MATHEMATICS

The following elementary principles of mathematics are discussed briefly, on the assumption that the reader possesses some knowledge of the subject. The explanations and examples given here are intended simply for the purpose of review.

SIGNS AND ABBREVIATIONS

The following signs and abbreviations are employed in this section and in general engineering work.

=	equals	R, r	radius
×	multiplied by	B, b	breadth
÷	divided by: $m \div n$	F	force
/	divided by, in fractions: $3/4 = \frac{3}{4}$	W	weight
+	plus	P	pressure
−	minus	F.	Fahrenheit
°	degrees, temperature, viscosity, etc., and arc	C.	Centigrade
		Hg.	mercury
′	minutes or feet	C.F.M.	cubic feet per minute
″	seconds or inches	r.p.m.	revolutions per minute
y^2, y^3	y squared, y cubed	p.s.i.	pounds per square inch
sin y	the sine of y	kw.	kilowatts
cos	cosine	AC	alternating current
tan	tangent	DC	direct current
sec	secant	B.t.u.	British thermal units
cot	cotangent	GPM	gallons per minute
cosec	cosecant	HP	horsepower
log	logarithm	IHP	indicated horsepower
%	per cent	BHP	brake horsepower
#	pound(s) or number	cc	cubic centimeters
( ) [ ]	parentheses and brackets: in mathematics all operations inside these are to be done first— $5 \times (4+2) = 5 \times 6$	cm.	centimeters
		temp.	temperature
		v.	volts
		H. P.	high pressure
	General Abbreviations	I. P.	intermediate pressure
L, l	length	L. P.	low pressure
W, w	width	B.W.G.	Birmingham Wire Gage
T, t	thickness	π	pi, 3.1416
D, d	diameter or depth	g	acceleration due to gravity

FRACTIONS

Definitions. Such expressions as 2/3, 3/4, and 5/8 are called either proper, simple or common fractions. If a unit of anything, such as a circle, or a unit of length such as a foot, were to be divided into three equal parts, each of the parts would be one-third of the unit (written 1/3); two of the parts would be two-thirds (written 2/3). The expression 5/8 means that a unit has been divided into 8 equal parts, of which 5 have been taken. In each case the number written "below" (at the right of) the slant line indicates into how many parts the unit has been divided while the number written "above" (at the left of) the line indicates how many of the parts have been taken.

Numerator. In the examples 2/3, 3/4 and 5/8 the numbers 2, 3, and 5 respectively, written at the left of the slant line, are called the numerators of the fractions.

Denominator. The numbers 3, 4, and 8 respectively, written at the right of the slant line are called the denominators of the fractions.

Indication of division. In the simple fraction 2/3, the line between the numerator 2 and the denominator 3 is simply a division sign, indicating that the 2 is to be divided by the 3. Thus, any fraction such as 2/3 may also be written $2 \div 3$. This is more fully explained under the discussion of the division of fractions and their conversion into decimals.

The method of writing fractions with a slant line is not considered good practice in engineering drawing. Such a dimension on a drawing as 1 3/16 inches, if carelessly written with a slanting division line instead of the conventional horizontal line, might easily be read incorrectly as 13/16, and 1 7/32 as 17/32. It is therefore suggested that all fractional dimensions on drawings and sketches be written with a horizontal instead of a slanting division symbol: $1\frac{7}{32}$.

Proper fractions. Any fraction whose value is less than unity is called a proper fraction, such as 1/2, 2/3 and 3/4. In a proper fraction the numerator is always less than the denominator.

Improper fractions. A fraction such as 7/7, whose value is unity, is called an improper fraction, as is the fraction 9/7, whose value is greater than unity. In an improper fraction the numerator is always equal to or greater than its denominator.

Mixed numbers. An expression such as 3 5/8 is called a mixed number, because it is made up of a whole number and a fraction.

Compound fraction. The expression 1/2 of 7/8 is called a compound fraction. It means that the fraction 7/8 is to be divided by 2 and could have been written $7/8 \div 2$. Another way in which the same fraction could be expressed is $1/2 \times 7/8$, indicating that the two fractions are to be multiplied by each other.

Complex fractions. Such expressions as $3/4 \div 7/8$ and $1\ 3/4 \div 2\ 7/8$ are called complex fractions. They are fractions in which both the numerator and the denominator may be simple fractions or mixed numbers, or a combination of the two.

To reduce a proper or improper fraction to its lowest terms. Divide both the numerator and denominator of the fraction by their greatest common divisor as, $69/72 = 69 \div 3/72 \div 3 = 23/24$, in which 3 is the largest number which will divide into both the numerator 69 and the denominator 72. As another example reduce the improper fraction 80/64 to its lowest terms. In this case the greatest common divisor of the numerator 80 and the denominator 64 is 16. The example would therefore resolve itself into the expression, $80 \div 16/64 \div 16 = 5/4$. Since 5/4 is still an improper fraction, whose value is greater than unity, the next step is to reduce it to a mixed number, in this case 1 1/4, as will be explained.

To change an improper fraction into a mixed number. Divide the numerator of the fraction by its denominator, as $133/16 = 133 \div 16 = 8 \ 5/16$. Similarly, to change the improper fraction 11/8 into a mixed number, divide numerator by denominator: $11 \div 8 = 1 \ 3/8$.

To change a mixed number into an improper fraction. Multiply the whole number by the denominator of the fraction, and to the product add the numerator of the fraction: $4 \ 3/4 = (4 \times 4 + 3) \div 4 = 19/4$. Likewise $16 \ 1/8 = (16 \times 8 + 1) \div 8 = 129/8$.

To express a whole number or a mixed number in terms of a fraction having a given denominator. Multiply the whole number by that number which is to be the denominator of the fraction, and write the product as the numerator of the desired fraction. For example, 23 in terms of fourths $= 23 \times 4 \div 4 = 92/4$. Likewise 7 in terms of eighths $= 7 \times 8 \div 8 = 56/8$.

To change a fraction with a given denominator into one having a higher denominator. Multiply both terms of the fraction by a number whose product with the denominator of the original fraction will equal the desired higher denominator of the new fraction. For example, change such a fraction as 5/8 into a fraction having 16 as its denominator. Since the required denominator 16 of the required fraction is twice that of the original fraction, multiply both the numerator and the denominator of the original fraction by 2: $5 \times 2 \div 8 \times 2 = 10/16$. To change 3 3/4 into a fraction having 64 as its denominator it is first necessary to change the mixed number to an improper fraction, 15/4. The desired denominator, 64, is 16 times the given denominator 4. Therefore, multiply both terms of the fraction 15/4 by 16: $15 \times 16 \div 4 \times 16 = 240/64$.

To reduce two or more fractions to equivalent fractions having a common denominator. The first step is to find the lowest common denominator of the fractions. With such simple fractions as 1/8, 3/4, 1/2, 5/16, 17/32, it is evident by inspection that the lowest common denominator of all of them is 32, since 8, 4, 2, 16, and 32 are all contained equally in 32.

Having found the lowest common denominator of all the fractions, write beside each of them a horizontal line with the denominator 32 below the line. Then, to obtain the new numerators in each case, divide the denominators of the original fractions into the lowest common denominator and multiply the quotient by the numerator of the original fraction. In the first of the original fractions, 1/8, the denominator 8 divided into 32 is contained 4 times. This quotient 4 is multiplied by the numerator 1 of the fraction. Written mathematically $32 \div 8 = 4 \times 1 = 4$, the numerator of the first new fraction whose denominator is 32.

In changing 3/4, $32 \div 4 = 8 \times 3 = 24$, the numerator of the second fraction. Changing each fraction the same way: $1/8 = 4/32$, $3/4 = 24/32$, $1/2 = 16/32$, $5/16 = 10/32$, $17/32 = 17/32$.

To find the lowest common denominator of two or more proper fractions. To find the lowest common denominator of a group of such fractions as 5/6, 3/4, 15/18, 17/24, write the denominators of the four fractions thus, 6, 4, 18, 24, and divide each denominator by the smallest number that will be equally contained in one or more of the numbers.

2/	6	4	18	24
2/	3	2	9	12
2/	3	1	9	6
3/	3	1	9	3
3/	1	1	3	1
	1	1	1	1

It will be found by inspection that 2 is contained in 6 three times; 2 into 4 twice; 2 into 18 nine times, and 2 into 24 twelve times. This gives the second line of numbers 3, 2, 9, 12. Once more divide by the smallest number that will be contained equally in one or more of the numbers; in this case 2 again. In the event that any of the numbers do not contain the divisor an equal number of times, bring down the number itself in the next row of numbers.

Thus, since the divisor 2 is not contained equally in the first figure 3 of the second row, bring down the number 3 as the first figure in the third row of numbers. As 2 is contained in the second figure 2 once, bring down the figure 1 as the second number in the third row. Since 2 is not contained equally in 9, bring down the number 9 as the third figure in the row. Two is contained in 12 6 times, hence 6 is the last term of the third row.

Proceed in the same manner to divide the third row of numbers, 3, 1, 9, 6, by the smallest number that will be equally contained in one or more of them. Once again using 2 as the divisor, the fourth row of numbers becomes 3, 1, 9, 3. Since 2 is not contained equally in any of the numbers in the fourth row it is evident that the next lowest common divisor is 3. Then, dividing by 3 and bringing down those numbers in which 3 is not contained equally, the fifth row of numbers becomes 1, 1, 3, 1. The lowest common divisor of the fifth row is again 3. Divide as before. This gives the sixth row 1, 1, 1, 1.

Thus the lowest common denominator of the original figures 6, 4, 18 and 24 is the continued product of the divisors 2, 2, 2, 3 and 3, or 72.

With 72 as the lowest common denominator of all of the fractions, the original fractions become: $5/6 = 60/72$, $3/4 = 54/72$, $15/18 = 60/72$ and $17/24 = 51/72$.

Addition of fractions. In the addition of fractions having the same or like denominators it is merely a matter of adding the numerators of the several fractions. Thus, $1/16 + 5/16 + 11/16 + 15/16$ merely indicates that the numerators 1, 5, 11 and 15 are to be added and their sum placed over the common denominator 16 of the fractions: $(1 + 5 + 11 + 15)/16 = 32/16 = 2$.

However, with such fractions as $5/6+7/8$ $+9/12+7/18$ it is evident that sixths, eighths, twelfths and eighteenths cannot be added without first reducing them to equivalent fractions having a common denominator. Use here the method just explained in finding the lowest common denominator. The lowest common denominator of the numbers 6, 8, 12, and 18 is again the continued product of the divisors 2, 2, 2, 3, and 3, or 72. Hence the sum of $5/6+7/8+9/12$

2/	6	8	12	18
2/	3	4	6	9
2/	1	2	3	9
3/	1	1	3	9
3/	1	1	1	3
	1	1	1	1

$+7/18 = 60/72+63/72+54/72+28/72 = 205/72 = 2\ 61/72.$

To simplify the work of adding fractions after having found their lowest common denominator, omit the denominator from the calculations and write down only the numerators of the several fractions. In the above example it is simpler to write down the numerators $60+63$ $+54+28 = 205$, and then $205/72$ or $2\ 61/72$.

Addition of mixed numbers. In adding such mixed numbers as $4\ 1/8$ $+3\ 3/8+5\ 7/8+9\ 5/8$ it is evident that the whole numbers 4, 3, 5, and 9 may be added and likewise the numerators 1, 3, 7 and 5 of the several fractions.

4	1
3	3
5	7
9	5
21	16 = 16/8

A convenient method of arranging such calculations is shown at the left. Since the sum of the numerators of the several fractions is 16/8 or 2, this amount is added to the sum (21) of the whole numbers, making the sum of all the mixed numbers 23. In the event that the fractions in the mixed numbers must be reduced to equivalent fractions with a common denominator, the latter is found as previously explained. In the addition of such mixed numbers as $4\ 2/3+3\ 7/12+2\ 3/16+5\ 10/24$ the lowest common denominator of all the fractions is 48. Hence the problem may be arranged as follows:

4	2/3 = 4	32
3	7/12 = 3	28
2	3/16 = 2	9
5	10/24 = 5	20
	14	89 = 89/48

The improper fraction 89/48, when reduced to a mixed number, is equal to 1 41/48. This amount is added to the sum (14) of the whole numbers making the sum of all the mixed numbers 15 41/48. Another method frequently employed in adding mixed numbers is that of reducing each mixed number to an improper fraction and then to equivalent improper fractions with a common denominator. Using the same mixed numbers as in the previous example, the following is a convenient method for arranging the calculations:

4	2/3 = 14/3	224
3	7/12 = 43/12	172
2	3/16 = 35/16	105
5	10/24 = 130/24	260
		761 = 761/48 = 15 41/48

Subtraction of fractions. When two fractions have the same denominator, subtract the numerator of the smaller fraction from that of the larger: $7/8 - 3/8 = (7-3) \div 8 = 4/8 = 1/2$.

In the case of fractions having unlike denominators, it is again necessary to reduce the fractions to equivalent fractions having the lowest common denominator: $15/16 - 7/8 = 15/16 - 14/16 = 1/16$.

In the subtraction of mixed numbers in which the fractions have the same denominator, subtract the whole numbers from each other and subtract the numerator of one fraction from that of the other: $4\ 5/8 - 2\ 3/8 = 4 - 2$ and $(5-3) \div 8 = 2\ 2/8 = 2\ 1/4$.

In the subtraction of mixed numbers whose fractions have different denominators, as $3\ 7/9 - 2\ 3/5$, it is again necessary to reduce the simple fractions $7/9$ and $3/5$ to equivalent fractions having the lowest common denominator. In this case the lowest common denominator of 9 and 5 is 45, and the fractions then become $35/45$ and $27/45$ respectively. The problem then becomes: $3\ 35/45 - 2\ 27/45 = 1\ 8/45$.

Multiplication of fractions. To multiply two proper fractions by each other multiply their numerators and denominators respectively: $3/4 \times 2/3 = (3 \times 2) \div (4 \times 3) = 6/12 = 1/2$.

To multiply a fraction by a whole number: The whole number is treated as an improper fraction: $6 \times 3/5 = (6 \times 3) \div (1 \times 5) = 18/5 = 3\ 3/5$.

Multiplication of mixed numbers. In the multiplication of mixed numbers such as $4\ 2/3 \times 3\ 5/8$, the first step is to reduce the mixed numbers to improper fractions as $4\ 2/3 = 14/3$ and $3\ 5/8 = 29/8$, after which the problem becomes $14/3 \times 29/8 = (14 \times 29) \div (3 \times 8) = 406/24 = 16\ 22/24$ or $16\ 11/12$.

Cancellation in multiplication. In the multiplication of many fractions the work can be simplified by a method called cancellation.

$$2/3 \times 3/4 = (\overset{1}{\cancel{2}} \times \overset{1}{\cancel{3}}) \div (\underset{1}{\cancel{3}} \times \underset{2}{\cancel{4}}) = (1 \times 1) \div (1 \times 2) = 1/2.$$

In this case the numerator 2 of the fraction $2/3$ and the denominator 4 of the fraction $3/4$ were divided by 2, and the results 1 and 2 respectively were placed as shown. In a similar manner the denominator 3 of the fraction $2/3$ and the numerator 3 of the fraction $3/4$ were both divided by 3. The quotients 1 and 1 were placed as shown, and the two fractions multiplied as previously explained.

In the example $14/3 \times 29/8$ used above, the work could likewise be simplified:

$$\overset{7}{\cancel{14}}/3 \times 29/\underset{4}{\cancel{8}} = 7/3 \times 29/4 = 203/12 = 16\ 11/12.$$

Here the numerator 14 of one fraction and the denominator 8 of the other were both divided by 2, and the quotients 7 and 4 respectively were placed as shown.

Division of fractions. In the division of one fraction by another, that fraction which is the divisor is inverted, and the two fractions are multiplied together. For example, to divide 2/3 by 3/4, invert the divisor 3/4 to 4/3 and then multiply. $2/3 \div 3/4 = 2/3 \times 4/3 = (2 \times 4) \div (3 \times 3) = 8/9$.

Cancellation in division. In division do not try cancellation until the divisor has been inverted, and the problem has the form of multiplication. Then cancel as explained.

$$\overset{2}{4}/5 \div 2/3 = \underset{1}{4}/5 \times 3/2 = 6/5 = 1\ 1/5.$$

Division of mixed numbers. In the division of mixed numbers, the work may be simplified by first reducing the mixed numbers to improper fractions. $4\ 2/3 \div 2\ 1/2 = 14/3 \div 5/2 = 14/3 \times 2/5 = 28/15 = 1\ 13/15$.

Division of a whole number by a fraction. In the division of a whole number by a fraction the whole number is treated as an improper fraction and the two terms of the problem are multiplied together. $5 \div 3/4 = 5/1 \div 3/4 = 5/1 \times 4/3 = 20/3 = 6\ 2/3$.

Division of a fraction by a whole number. As in the previous example, the whole number is again treated as an improper fraction. $3/4 \div 6 = 3/4 \div 6/1 = 3/4 \times 1/6 = 1/8$.

Combined multiplication and division. As has been shown, a problem of division becomes one of multiplication. In combined problems, first invert the divisor so that all factors are multiplied by each other. $1/2 \times 3/4 \div 2/3 = 1/2 \times 3/4 \times 3/2 = (1 \times 3 \times 3) \div (2 \times 4 \times 2) = 9/16$.

To reduce a compound fraction to a proper fraction. As has been explained previously, the mathematical expression 1/2 of 7/8 actually means that 7/8 is to be multiplied by 1/2. So $1/2$ of $7/8 = 1/2 \times 7/8 = 7/16$. And $2/3$ of $3/4 = 2/3 \times 3/4 = 6/12 = 1/2$.

To reduce a complex fraction to a proper fraction. Reduce both the numerator and the denominator of the fraction to improper fractions. Then multiply the numerator of the upper fraction by the denominator of the lower fraction, and the numerator of the lower fraction by the denominator of the upper fraction to form the numerator and denominator respectively of the simple fraction.

$$1\ 3/4 \div 2\ 7/8 = [(4 \times 1 + 3) \div 4] \div [(8 \times 2 + 7) \div 8] = 7/4 \div 23/8 = 7/4 \times 8/23 = 14/23.$$

The example above may also be written as:

$$1\ 3/4 \div 2\ 7/8 = 7/4 \div 23/8 = 7/4 \times 8/23 = 14/23.$$

Another example:

$$1\ 1/2 \div 15 = 3/2 \div 15/1 = 3/2 \times 1/15 = 1/10$$

In complex fractions involving such calculations as addition, subtraction, multiplication or division, these calculations should be performed before the complex fraction is reduced to a simple fraction, as:

$$(3\ 1/2 + 2\ 1/4) \div (2\ 1/2 \times 1\ 3/4) = (7/2 + 9/4) \div (5/2 \times 7/4) = (14/4 + 9/4) \div (5/2 \times 7/4) = 23/4 \div 35/8 = 23/4 \times 8/35 = 1\ 11/35.$$

DECIMAL FRACTIONS

Definitions. A decimal fraction is a fraction whose denominator is ten or some power of ten, such as 9/10, 35/100, or 125/1000. In the notation or writing of decimal fractions the denominator is almost always omitted. Thus, 9/10 is written .9, 35/100 as .35 and 125/1000 as .125. As a means for distinguishing decimal fractions from whole numbers a period (.) is placed before the numerator, as in the case of the 9, 35 and 125 above. This period is called the decimal point.

Consequently, any number with a decimal point before it is a decimal fraction (called a decimal) whose numerator is the number itself, and whose denominator is 1, with as many ciphers after it as there are figures to the right of the decimal point. All numbers to the left of the decimal point are whole numbers.

Decimals are named in accordance with their relation to 1, or unity:

$$
\begin{aligned}
1000.0 &= 10 \times 10 \times 10 = \text{one thousand} \\
100.0 &= 10 \times 10 = \text{one hundred} \\
10.0 &= 10 \times 1 = \text{ten} \\
1.0 &= 1/10 \times 10 = \text{one (unity)} \\
0.1 &= 1/10 \times 1 = \text{one-tenth} \\
0.01 &= 1/100 \times 1 = \text{one-hundredth} \\
0.001 &= 1/1000 \times 1 = \text{one-thousandth} \\
0.0001 &= 1/10,000 \times 1 = \text{one-ten-thousandth} \quad \text{etc.}
\end{aligned}
$$

Since the decimal point is a very important factor in all mathematical work, special care should be taken that it is placed correctly in the results of every calculation.

Converting decimal fractions. To convert a decimal into a common fraction: Write the decimal as the numerator of the fraction. Under it as the denominator write 1, and add as many ciphers as there are places in the decimal. It should be understood that the number of ciphers added make up the equivalent of·tenths, hundredths, thousandths, etc., represented in the numerator.

Examples.

$$
0.75 = 75/100 = 3/4, \quad 0.375 = 375/1000 = 3/8,
$$
$$
0.9375 = 9375/10000 = 15/16
$$

Addition of decimals. Set down the numbers so that all of the decimal points are directly in line, one below the other, then proceed to add the figures as in simple addition.

Examples.

.07 = .070	732.625	.125
.569 = .569	815.9375	.5
.3 = .300	419.21875	.5625
.939 ans.	1967.78125 ans.	1.1875 ans.

Subtraction of decimals. Set down the numbers as in addition, with one decimal point directly under the other, and then proceed as in simple subtraction.

Examples.

```
.9375 = .9375        815.9375
.625  = .6250        732.625
        .3125 ans.   83.3125 ans.
```

Multiplication of decimals. Proceed as in simple multiplication, without regard for the position of the decimal point. Then point off from the right of the product a number of places equal to the sum of the decimal places in both the multiplier and multiplicand.

Examples.

```
        12.25              .375
         .375              .25
        6125              1875
        8575               750
        3675             .09375 ans.
      4.59375 ans.
```

Division of decimals. Proceed as in the division of whole numbers. Move the decimal point in the divisor to the right enough places to change the decimal into a whole number. Then move the dividend's point an equal number of places to the right, adding ciphers to the figure as necessary.

Examples.

```
.75 ÷ .25 =        1.5 ÷ .375 =        3.5 ÷ .3146 =


.25/ .75 =         .375/ 1.5 =         .3146/ 3.5 =

        3. ans.            4. ans.               11.125+ans.
25./ 75.           375./1500.          3146/35000.000
    75                 1500            3146
                                       3540
                                       3146
                                       3940
                                       3146
                                       7940
                                       6292
                                      16480
                                      15730
```

Formulas. Mathematical formulas are rules employed in calculation, whose terms or factors are expressed by letters, characters and symbols. In this manner long, awkward rules may be condensed into short, symbolic expressions. These expressions are also called equations. An equation expresses the equality of two factors $(A = A)$, or operations $(A + B = C \times D)$, and its 2 sides are always connected by the equals $(=)$ sign.

Example.

$$HP = P \times L \times A \times N \div 33,000$$

in which HP = horsepower

P = steam pressure

L = length of stroke

A = area of piston

N = number of strokes per minute

33,000 = unit of power measurement

Let $P = 200$ lb. steam pressure; $L = 4$ ft.; $A = 1017.9$ sq. in. area of piston; $N = 180$ piston strokes per minute.

Then $HP = 200 \times 4 \times 1017.9 \times 180 \div 33,000 = 146,577,600 \div 33,000 = 4441.745 +$ ans.

Transposition of formulas. Any formula or equation having the form $A = B \times C$ can be transposed as follows:

$B = A \div C$ and $C = A \div B$.

$A = B \times C \div D$ can be transposed: $A \times D = B \times C$ and $D = B \times C \div A$ and $B = A \times D \div C$ and $C = A \times D \div B$.

If the equation also involves addition or subtraction of some of its terms, the whole sum or difference must be transposed. Otherwise its value changes. $A = B \div (C + D)$ is transposed to $A \times (C + D) = B$ and $C + D = B \div A$.

However, any term not multiplied or divided by another term, and which is preceded by a plus or minus sign, can be directly shifted to the other side of the equation (other side of the equals sign) by changing its sign. If plus on one side the term will be minus on the other side of the equation, and vice versa. In the example $C + D = B \div A$ just given, $C = B \div A - D$ and $D = B \div A - C$.

Example.

$A + B = C - D$ or $(+)$ $A + B = (+)C - D$

$A = C - D - B$

$B = C - D - A$

$C = A + B + D$ (same as $-C = -D - A - B$)

$D = C - A - B$ (same as $A + B - C = -D$)

From the examples given two general rules should be emphasized. One is that factors multiplied or divided by each other always change their position in regard to the division line when transposed. If above the line on one side of the equation they must be below it on the other side, and vice versa. It is a good idea to keep the division line in your mind's eye, even if the particular problem does not show it. That is to say, $A = A$ is also $A/1 = A/1$.

Actually, when a factor is transposed, both sides of the equation are multiplied or divided by the factor. This is necessary to keep the formula true. If you say that quantity A equals twice quantity B, or 4 equals twice 2, then $A \times C$ would not equal twice quantity B any more than 4×5 would equal twice 2. But $A \times C = 2B \times C$, and $4 \times 5 = 2 \times 2 \times 5$.

Thus $A = B \times C$ becomes $A \div B = B \times C \div B$ and cancelling out the two B's, $A \div B = 1 \times C \div 1$ or C. Using numbers, $10 = 5 \times 2$ becomes $10 \div 5 = 5 \times 2 \div 5 = 2$. Again, $A \times B \div C = D$ becomes $A \times B \times C \div C = D \times C$ and $A \times B = D \times C$. Using numbers again, $6 \times 3 \div 2 = 9$ becomes $6 \times 3 \times 2 \div 2 = 9 \times 2$ and $6 \times 3 = 9 \times 2$.

The second rule to note is the change of sign in factors that are added and subtracted. Similar to the process in equations concerning multiplication and division, the factor to be shifted is added to or subtracted from both sides of the equation. Thus $A + B = C$ becomes $A + B - B = C - B$, which becomes $A + 0 = C - B$, or $A = C - B$. Substituting numbers for letters, $5 + 2 = 7$ becomes $5 + 2 - 2 = 7 - 2$, or $5 = 7 - 2$.

In complex equations, where multiplication, division, addition, subtraction are all included, multiplication and division are done before addition and subtraction.

Examples.

$$12 + 32 \times 9 - 6 = ?$$
$$32 \times 9 = 288$$
$$12 + 288 - 6 = 294, \text{ ans.}$$

$$24 \div 4 + 16 \times 4 = ?$$
$$24 \div 4 = 6$$
$$16 \times 4 = 64$$
$$6 + 64 = 70, \text{ ans.}$$

Special signs. Parentheses ( ) and brackets [ ] are used to specify that additions and subtractions are to be done first instead of following the general rule. Any operations enclosed within them are performed before any others. With the form [( )], the inner operation between the parentheses must be done before the outer one between the brackets.

Examples.

$$(12 - 4) \times 3 + (9 \times 5) = 8 \times 3 + 45 = 24 + 45 = 69$$
$$9 \times (13 - 7) \div 2 + 10 \times 4 = 9 \times 6 \div 2 + 40 = 54 \div 2 + 40 = 27 + 40 = 67$$
$$4 + [16 \times 2(10 - 2) + 6] \div 2 = 4 + (16 \times 2 \times 8 + 6) \div 2 = 4 + (256 + 6)$$
$$\div 2 = 4 + 262 \div 2 = 4 + 131 = 135$$

Parentheses are used in formulas to indicate multiplication, as in the example just above, $2(10 - 2) = 2 \times (10 - 2)$ or 2×8.

Example.

$$3(2 + 4) = 3 \times (2 + 4) = 3 \times 6 = 18$$
$$(6 + 3 - 5) \div 2 = 4 \div 2 = 2$$

The sign $\times$, indicating multiplication, is frequently omitted from formulas, as:

$$ABC = A \times B \times C, \text{ and } ABC \div D = (A \times B \times C) \div D$$

In other cases multiplication is indicated by a dot between the symbols and numbers: $A \times B = A \cdot B$; $5 \times 3 = 5 \cdot 3$.

RATIO AND PROPORTION

The ratio between two quantities, or the ratio of one quantity to another, is the relation between them obtained by dividing the first by the second. The word ratio in this respect is synonymous with quotient.

The colon (:) is used in mathematical expressions to indicate ratio. In the following example 2:4 is read 2 is to 4, or the ratio of 2 to 4. This means $2 \div 4$; so the ratio of 2 to 4 is 1/2. A reciprocal or inverse ratio is the original ratio reversed, or turned upside down. Thus the inverse or reciprocal ratio of 3:6 is 6:3.

Compound ratios involve the products of corresponding terms in two or more simple ratios.

Thus, when $6:3 = 2$, $20:5 = 4$, $63:9 = 7$ the compound ratio is $6 \times 20 \times 63 : 3 \times 5 \times 9 = 2 \times 4 \times 7$.

$$7560:135 = 56:1$$

Proportion is the equality of ratios, as: 8:4 = 12:6.

The foregoing is read, the ratio of 8 to 4 is equal to the ratio of 12 to 6. The expression 16:4::8:2 is read, 16 is to 4 as 8 is to 2. The double colon (::) is a symbol used to express equals, is equal to, or the word as.

The first and fourth terms of a proportion are called the extremes, while the second and third terms are called the means.

The product of the means equals the product of the extremes: If 5:10::3:6, then $10 \times 3 = 5 \times 6 = 30$.

In any proportion involving 4 factors, if 3 of them are known the fourth may be found by one of the following rules:

The first term is equal to the product of the second and third terms, divided by the fourth term.

Thus, $X:7::12:4$ and $X = 7 \times 12 \div 4 = 84 \div 4 = 21$.

The second term is equal to the product of the first and fourth terms, divided by the third term.

Thus, $21:X::12:4$ and $X = 21 \times 4 \div 12 = 84 \div 12 = 7$.

The third term is equal to the product of the first and fourth terms, divided by the second term.

Thus, $21:7::X:4$ and $X = 21 \times 4 \div 7 = 84 \div 7 = 12$.

The fourth term is equal to the product of the second and third terms, divided by the first term.

Thus, $21:7::12:X$ and $X = 7 \times 12 \div 21 = 84 \div 21 = 4$.

The difficulty in all problems in proportion is to state the terms of the proportion in their proper order. If an inspection of the problem indicates that the answer should be greater than the third term, then the greater of the two given terms should be made the second—otherwise the first. Usually the term which is of the same kind as the required, or fourth term, is made the second, while the first and third must be like each other in kind and denomination. To determine which is to be the first and which the second requires a little reasoning.

Consider the following example: If a man shovels 2 tons of coal in 6 hours how long will it take him to shovel 9 tons? Let the number of hours be represented by X. Then write the proportion: 2 (tons): 6 (hrs.) :: 9 (tons):X (hrs.). To find the fourth term apply the given rules: $X = 6 \times 9 \div 2 = 54 \div 2 = 27$ hrs.

PERCENTAGE

Per cent means, literally, "by the hundred." It is a means of expressing the proportion of increase or decrease per 100 parts. As an example: If an article is purchased for $5.00 and sold for $10.00, the profit is 100%; but if it is bought for $5.00 and sold for $2.50, the loss is not 100% but only 50%. The answers to percentage problems are found by setting up proportions. In the first case $5:10::100:X. X = 10 \times 100 \div 5 = 200$, or 100 more than the original 100, or 100%, ans. In the second case, $5:2.50::100:X. X = 50$, and $100 - 50 = 50\%$, ans.

A simpler rule for finding per cent increase or decrease is to divide the increase or decrease by the original amount or value, and then multiply the result by 100.

In engineering practice per cent is a measure of performance efficiency or output as against input. That is, it is the quotient of output divided by input. Any difference between the input and output is loss or waste. Efficiency is almost always less than one (1) when written as a decimal or fraction. Percent efficiency is obtained from multiplying the fraction by 100.

Example. If in heat balance calculations a pound of dry coal produces 14,000 heat units, and the boiler in question absorbs 10,568 heat units per pound of dry coal burned, the efficiency of the boiler = output ÷ input = $10,568 \div 14,000 = .7546$. Then, $.7546 \times 100 = 75.46\%$.

POWERS AND ROOTS

Involution and evolution. Involution is the process of finding the powers of numbers. A power is the product obtained by using a base a given number of times as a factor. Thus, if the base is used twice as a factor, it is raised to the second power; if the base is used three times as a factor, it is raised to the third power. The expression 4^2 means 4 raised to the 2nd power, or 4 "squared," as it is commonly called; 4^3 means 4 raised to the 3rd power, or "cubed." $9^4 = 9 \times 9 \times 9 \times 9$, and is called "the 4th power of 9;" $10^5 = 100,000$, and is called "the 5th power of 10."

In the expression 4^2, 5^3 and 6^9, 4, 5 and 6 are called the *roots* and 2, 3 and 9 the *exponents* or powers of the roots.

Evolution is the opposite of involution in that it has to do with finding the root (or extracting the root) of any number, the power of which is given. The symbol $\sqrt{}$ indicates square root, $\sqrt[3]{}$ indicates cube root, and $\sqrt[4]{}$ indicates the fourth root of the number is to be found.

The square root of numbers may be found by the following rules, but for other roots logarithms are usually employed.

If it is desired to extract the root of a fraction, extract the indicated root of both numerator and denominator separately, as: $\sqrt{16/25} = \sqrt{16} \div \sqrt{25} = 4/5$. But whenever the root of the fraction is not found easily, as above, it is generally preferable to reduce the fraction to a decimal and then find the root of the decimal.

SQUARE ROOT

To find the square root of numbers more difficult than 9, 16, 25, 100, 225 (15^2) or 625 (25^2), a method of long division is used. Take for example, the number 326,041.0

$$32, 60, 41.00/\overline{571.0}$$

$$5^2 = 25$$

$$\underline{107\ /\ 760}$$

$$749$$

$$\underline{1141/\ \ 1141}$$

$$1141$$

Set up as shown above. First of all, mark off steps or groups of 2 figures each, beginning at the decimal point and working both ways. In case of an uneven number of figures to the left of the decimal, the last step will only have one figure. Add ciphers to the decimal side if necessary to make equal steps, or to make extra steps if desired to carry the answer out to several places: 167.00 00 00.

Then proceed as shown in the example. The first step on the left is 32. Take the number (5) whose square is closest to without being greater than 32. Put the 5 at the right as the first figure in the answer, and subtract its square from 32. The result is 7.

To the 7 add the next step complete (60) for the new dividend. For divisor multiply the answer (5) by 2. Now the problem has the shape: 10/760.

Estimate how many times the divisor multiplied by 10 will be contained in the dividend. That is, how many times 100 would be contained in 760. The answer is 7. This 7 must be added to the divisor (10) as well as to the answer. Then multiply the 107 by 7, to give 749. Subtracting gives a remainder of 11, to which is added the next step of 2 figures, 41. Again multiply the whole answer (57) by 2, giving 114 for the next divisor. This brings us to 114/1141. Again find how many times 114×10 is contained in 1141. The answer is 1. Add the one to the divisor, making 1141, and also to the answer, and multiply: $1141 \times 1 = 1141$. Since there is no remainder, the answer is complete at 571, the square root of 326,041.

To prove the answer, square it by multiplying: $571 \times 571 = 326,041$.

Example 2. Find the square root of 17,825.67.

$$1\ \ 78\ \ 25.\ \ 67\ \ 00\ \ 00\ \ 00/\overline{133.5128}$$

$$1^2 = 1$$

$$\underline{23/\ \ \ \ \ 78}$$

$$69$$

$$\underline{263/\ \ \ 925}$$

$$789$$

$$\underline{2665/13667}$$

$$13325$$

$$\underline{26701/\ \ \ 34200}$$

$$26701$$

$$\underline{267022\ /\ \ 749900}$$

$$534044$$

$$\underline{2670248\ /21585600}$$

$$21361984$$

Notice that in the case of Example 2 the square root of the number is imperfect—does not come out even. It was carried out to 4 places for greater accuracy.

Be sure that the whole answer is multiplied by 2 for the divisor of each step: $26 = 13 \times 2$, $266 = 133 \times 2$, $2670 = 1335 \times 2$, etc. Also that before multiplying, the multiplier is first added to the dividend and answer, both: 26 becomes 263×3, 266 becomes 2665×5, 2670 becomes 26701×1, etc. Finally, that in each step not a single figure but a group of 2 is brought down and added to the remainder: 9–25, 136–67, 342–00, etc.

The position of the decimal point is determined by the number of groups. The original number above has 3 groups to the left of the decimal point. Therefore the answer has the same number of digits (3) to the left of its decimal point.

CAPACITIES OF CYLINDRICAL TANKS,
VERTICAL OR HORIZONTAL,
WITH PLANE ENDS

Capacity in gallons per inch of inside length = (inside diam. in inches)$^2 \times .0034$.

Capacity in cu. ft. per in. of inside length = (inside diam. in inches)$^2 \times .0004545$.

In the case of convex dished heads add to the length of the straight side 2/3 of the dish to get an approximate equivalent length of a plane end tank.

Example.

Overall length of tank	240″
Length on straight side	218″
Depth of 2 dished heads	22″
If heads are $\frac{1}{2}$″ thick, deduct	1″
Inside depth of heads	21″

$2/3 \times 21 = 14$, and $14 + 218 = 232″$ equivalent length

If tank has a 60″ outside diameter and a 1/4″ thick plate, then the capacity of the tank will be $(59.5)^2 \times .0034 \times 232 = 2792$ gal., or $(59.5)^2 \times .0004545 \times 232 = 373.2$ cu. ft.

After figuring the total capacity of any diameter horizontal tank with dished heads, a gaging table or gage rod can be made easily from the figures in the following Table 1.

Taking the case of the tank in the example above, and supposing it to be filled to a depth of 27″:

The part of diameter at liquid level is $27 \div 59.5 = 0.454$.

From the table, $0.45 = 0.4364$ capacity. Interpolating, $0.454 = 0.4414$ capacity. Total capacity was 2792 gal. $0.4414 \times 2792 = 1229$ gal. at 27″ level.

If 59 1/2″ is marked off from the end of a gage rod and divided into 100 equal divisions, the fractional capacity can be figured directly from the table and marked on the rod.

Horizontal tanks should always be gaged at the center, as they may not be level.

In the case of very large cylindrical vertical tanks with flat bottoms, a useful and quick method of figuring capacity is to square the diameter in feet, divide by 2, and then deduct 2%. The result is the capacity in gallons per inch of depth.

Examples. If diameter is 20', then $20 \times 20 \div 2 = 200$
Capacity per in., 200 less 2% = 196 gal.

TABLE 1. ESTIMATING CAPACITY OF HORIZONTAL
CYLINDRICAL TANKS

Part of Diam. at Liquid Level	Part of Capacity	Part of Diam. at Liquid Level	Part of Capacity	Part of Diam. at Liquid Level	Part of Capacity	Part of Diam. at Liquid Level	Part of Capacity
.01	.00171	.26	.2066	.51	.5128	.76	.8155
.02	.00476	.27	.2179	.52	.5255	.77	.8263
.03	.00874	.28	.2292	.53	.5383	.78	.8369
.04	.0134	.29	.2407	.54	.5510	.79	.8474
.05	.0187	.30	.2523	.55	.5636	.80	.8576
.06	.0245	.31	.2640	.56	.5763	.81	.8677
.07	.0308	.32	.2759	.57	.5889	.82	.8776
.08	.0375	.33	.2878	.58	.6014	.83	.8873
.09	.0446	.34	.2998	.59	.6140	.84	.8967
.10	.0520	.35	.3119	.60	.6264	.85	.9059
.11	.0599	.36	.3241	.61	.6389	.86	.9149
.12	.0680	.37	.3364	.62	.6513	.87	.9236
.13	.0764	.38	.3487	.63	.6636	.88	.9320
.14	.0851	.39	.3611	.64	.6759	.89	.9401
.15	.0941	.40	.3736	.65	.6881	.90	.9480
.16	.1033	.41	.3860	.66	.7002	.91	.9554
.17	.1127	.42	.3986	.67	.7122	.92	.9625
.18	.1224	.43	.4111	.68	.7241	.93	.9692
.19	.1323	.44	.4237	.69	.7360	.94	.9755
.20	.1424	.45	.4364	.70	.7477	.95	.9813
.21	.1526	.46	.4490	.71	.7593	.96	.9866
.22	.1631	.47	.4617	.72	.7708	.97	.9913
.23	.1737	.48	.4745	.73	.7821	.98	.9952
.24	.1845	.49	.4872	.74	.7934	.99	.9983
.25	.1955	.50	.5000	.75	.8045	1.00	1.000

FINDING AREA OF IRREGULAR PLANE SURFACES

To find the approximate area of a surface like the one shown in the drawing, or of an indicator card, draw a base line, AB, approximately parallel to the central major axis of the figure. Divide the line AB into any number of equal parts, the greater their number the greater the accuracy of the calculation. Place the divisions 1, 2, 3, etc., so that the 2 end divisions are half a space from the ends of the figure. Draw the ordinates 1, 2, 3, etc., perpendicular to the line AB.

Then measure the lengths of the ordinates as included between the sides of the figure, and add their lengths together. Divide this sum by the number of ordinates drawn, and multiply the quotient by the length of the base line (*l*). The result is a close approximation to the area. Rapid and accurate results may be obtained by the use of a planimeter.

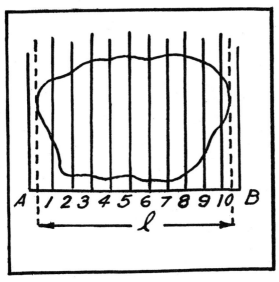

MENSURATION

Square. A plane figure having all 4 of its sides equal to and parallel with each other, and all 4 of its angles right angles.

A = area s = side d = diagonal

then $A = s^2 = 1/2\ d^2$; $s = 0.7071\ d = \sqrt{A}$; $d = 1.414s$ $= 1.414\sqrt{A}$

Example. $s = 12$ in. Then $A = s \times s = 144$ sq. in. $d = 1.414s = 1.414 \times 12 = 16.968$ in.

Rectangle. A plane figure having opposite sides equal to each other and parallel, and all 4 angles right angles.

A = area d = diagonal a & b = sides

then $A = ab = a\sqrt{d^2-a^2} = b\sqrt{d^2-b^2}$

$d = \sqrt{a^2+b^2}$; $a = A \div b = \sqrt{d^2-b^2}$; $b = A \div a$ $= \sqrt{d^2-a^2}$

Parallelogram. Any quadrangle (4-sided figure) whose opposite sides are parallel with each other. It includes the square and rectangle, though generally is taken to mean an oblong with opposite angles equal to each other but none of them right angles.

If A = area, then $A = ab$, $a = A \div b$, $b = A \div a$

Note: The altitude, or height, of all parallelograms is always measured at right angles (perpendicular) to the base. It is not equal to the length of the side.

Trapezium. A quadrilateral (4-sided plane figure) none of whose side are equal or parallel, and none of whose angles are equal.

If A = area, then $A = [b(H+h)+ch+aH] \div 2$

Note: Any quadrilateral may be divided into 2 triangles by drawing a diagonal, as shown, and the sum of the areas of the 2 triangles is equal to the area of the quadrilateral. The methods employed in finding the areas of triangles are explained in subsequent examples.

Trapezoid. A quadrilateral having only 2 of its opposite sides parallel, but not of the same length. None of its angles are right angles or equal to each other.

If A = area, then $A = (c+b)a \div 2$

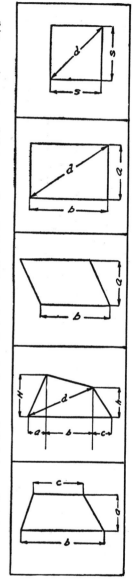

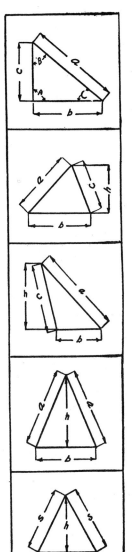

Triangle, right-angled. A plane figure having 3 sides and 3 angles, one angle of which is a right angle. A right angle is an angle of 90°, formed by the intersection of 2 sides perpendicular to each other. In the figure the angle A is a right angle; a is the hypotenuse, which is always the side opposite the right angle; c is the height of the triangle, often called the altitude; and b is the base.

If $A =$ area, then $A = bc \div 2$; $a = \sqrt{b^2 + c^2}$; $b = \sqrt{a^2 - c^2}$; $c = \sqrt{a^2 - b^2}$

Triangle, acute-angled. A plane figure of 3 sides in which each angle is less than 90°. The angles may or may not be equal to each other.

If $A =$ area, then $A = bh \div 2$. If $S = 1/2(a+b+c)$, then $A = \sqrt{S(S-a)\ (S-b)\ (S-c)}$

Triangle, obtuse-angled. A plane figure of 3 sides in which one of the angles is greater than a right angle (90°).

If $A =$ area, then $A = bh \div 2$. If $S = 1/2\ (a+b+c)$, then $A = \sqrt{S(S-a)\ (S-b)\ (S-c)}$, and is found by the same operations as used for the acute-angled triangle. To find the altitude of both kinds of triangle, use of trigonometry is necessary. See below.

Triangle, isosceles. A plane figure of 3 sides, two of which are equal to each other. In every isosceles triangle the angles opposite the equal sides are also equal to each other; and the line h, dropped perpendicularly upon the base as shown, will besect the base and divide the isosceles triangle into 2 equal right-angled triangles.

So the solution of right-angled triangles may be used to find the value of h. In the formula $c = \sqrt{a^2 - b^2}$, let $c = h$ and $b = 1/2$ the base of the isosceles triangle.

Triangle, equilateral. A plane figure of 3 sides in which all 3 sides and angles are respectively equal to each other. Each of the angles in an equilateral triangle equals 60°.

Note: The same rules and formulas apply to equilateral triangles as used with isosceles triangles.

Circle. A closed plane figure generated by a point revolving around a fixed center, and at all times equally distant from this center.

The circumference of a circle is equal to its diameter multiplied by a constant, π, called pi. This constant $=3.1416^+$, or, for purposes of rough calculation, 22/7.

The area of a circle is equal to π multiplied by the square of the radius. $A = \pi r^2$.

The diameter is any straight line passing through the center and ending on the circumference of the circle. $2r = d$.

Arc. The circumference of a circle contains 360°. Any part of the circumference is an arc (l).

Circular sector. A sector of a circle is defined as a part of its area bounded by 2 of its radii and the included arc.

$A =$ area, $l =$ length of arc, $a =$ center angle, deg. Then $A = rl \div 2 = 0.008727ar^2$; $l = \pi ra \div 180$; $a = 57.296l \div r$; $r = 2A \div l = 57.296l \div a$

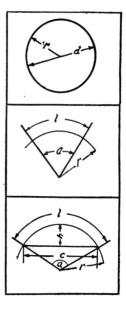

Chord. A chord is any straight line drawn between any 2 points on the circumference of a circle, except a straight line through the center of the circle, which is the diameter.

Circular segment. That part of the area of a circle bounded by a chord and the enclosed arc.

$A =$ area; $l =$ length of arc; $c =$ chord; $h =$ perpendicular distance from center of chord to arc of circle; $a =$ center angle in deg.

Then $c = 2\sqrt{h(2r-h)}$; $l = 0.01745ra$; $h = r - 1/2 \sqrt{4r^2 - c^2}$; $r = (c^2 + 4h^2) \div 8h$; $a = 57.296l \div r$; $A = rl \div 2 - c(r-h) \div 2$

Circular ring. A circular, or annular, ring is the plane surface between 2 concentric circles; that is, between 2 circles having the same center but different diameters.

$A =$ area $= \pi(R^2 - r^2)$

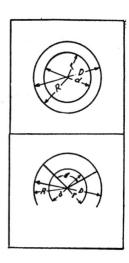

Ring sector. A ring sector corresponds to the segment of a circle. It is that part of a circular ring between 2 radii of the concentric circles and the arc of the circumference of the outer circle.

$A =$ area; $a =$ center angle, deg.; $A = a\pi \div 360 (R^2 - r^2)$

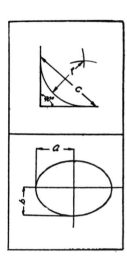

Spandrel. A spandrel, or fillet, is that section of material usually placed in the angles and corners of patterns, etc.

At times, in estimating accurately the weight of castings, it is necessary to calculate the area of fillets having various radii (r).

$A = $ area $= r^2 - (\pi r^2 \div 4) = 0.215 r^2$. If $c = $ length of chord, $A = 0.1075 c^2$.

Ellipse. An ellipse, sometimes called an oval, is a plane figure formed by the arcs of circles which have radii proportional to and concentric with each other, with relation to the central axes of the ellipse.

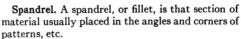

$A = $ area $= \pi ab$. $P = \pi \sqrt{2(a^2 + b^2)}$, approximately.

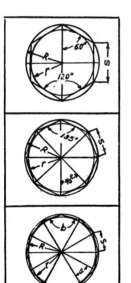

Hexagon. A plane figure having 6 sides and 6 angles. Hexagons may be regular or irregular. In a regular hexagon the 6 sides and angles are respectively equal to each other.

$R = $ radius of circumscribed circle; $r = $ radius of inscribed circle; $s = $ length of side; $A = $ area $= 2.598 s^2 = 2.598 R^2 = 3.464 r^2$; $R = s = 1.155 r$; $r = 0.866 s = 0.866 R$

Octagon. A plane figure having 8 sides and angles. Octagons may be regular or irregular. In a regular octagon the sides and angles are all respectively equal to each other.

$A = $ area; $R = $ radius of circumscribed circle; $r = $ radius of inscribed circle.

$A = 4.828 s^2 = 2.828 R^2 = 3.314 r^2$; $R = 1.307 s = 1.082 r$; $r = 1.207 s = 0.924 R$; $s = 0.765 R = 0.828 r$

Polygon. A plane figure having 3 or more sides. It may be classed as regular or irregular, depending on whether sides and angles are all equal or not. Polygons are named for the number of their sides: pentagon, 5 sides; hexagon, 6 sides; octagon, 8 sides; etc.

$A = $ area; $n = $ number of sides; $a = 360° \div n$; $b = 180° - a$

$A = nsr \div 2 = ns\ 2\sqrt{R^2 - (s^2 \div 4)}$; $R = \sqrt{r^2 + (s^2 \div 4)}$; $r = \sqrt{R^2 - (s^2 \div 4)}$; $s = 2\sqrt{R^2 - r^2}$

VOLUMES OF SOLIDS

Prism. A prism is a solid body in which the upper and lower surfaces are similar equivalent polygons in parallel planes, and whose sides are parallelograms.

Cube. A cube is a prism having 6 faces, all of which are perfect squares of equal areas.

A = area of surface; V = volume; then $A = 6s^2$ and $V = s^3$, while $s = \sqrt{A \div 6} = \sqrt[3]{V}$

Example. Let $s = 9$ in. Then $A = 6 \times 9^2 = 486$ sq. in.

$V = 9^3 = 9 \times 9 \times 9 = 729$ cu. in.

Rectangular prism. A rectangular prism is a solid body bounded by 6 sides, all of which are rectangles, with the ends and opposite sides respectively equal to each other.

V = volume = abh; A = area = $2ab + 2ah + 2bh$

Prismoid. A prismoid, sometimes called a prism, is a solid body having end areas (A) of any shape, but equal to and parallel with each other, while the remaining 4 sides may be rectangles of any size.

A = area of end surfaces; V = volume = lA; s = area of entire outer surface = $2A$ + surface areas of the 4 sides. End areas, volume and surface areas are entirely dependent upon the size and shape of the prismoid.

Pyramid. A pyramid is a solid body having a plane surface as a base, with any number of triangularly shaped faces or sides converging at a point or apex.

a = area of total surface except the base = area of one side multiplied by the number of sides, if the base is a regular polygon and all of its sides are equal. If the base is irregular, then the area (a) is equal to the sum of the respective areas of all the sides. To find the areas of the sides, see the rules for finding areas of triangles. The slant height is also the height of the triangle formed by the sides (given a regular pyramid).

For area (A) of base, see rules for finding areas of polygons. Volume (V) = $1/3hA$

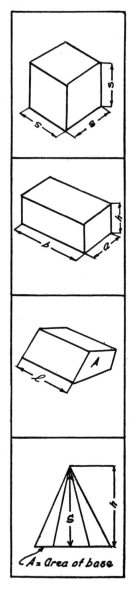

MATHEMATICS

C–23

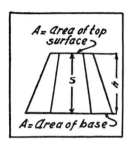

Pyramid, truncated. Also called the frustrum of a pyramid, is that section of a pyramid remaining after any part of the apex or top section has been removed, leaving a solid body whose top and bottom surfaces are similar in shape and parallel with each other. The sides are the remaining sections of the sides of the original pyramid. Like pyramids, truncated pyramids may be regular or irregular.

A = area of base and a = area of top (see areas of polygons)

s = slant height; h = altitude, or height; S = total surface, the sum of the areas of sides, top and base;

V = volume = $1/3h(A + a + \sqrt{Aa})$

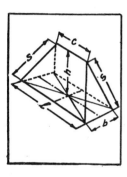

Wedge. A solid body having 5 plane sides, the base being a rectangle, the ends triangles, while the 2 sides may be rectangles or trapezoids.

h = altitude; l = length of base; b = width of base; s = length of sides, or slant height; c = length of top edge.

S = surface area = the sum of areas of all surfaces

V = volume = $(c + 2l)bh \div 6$

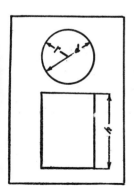

Cylinder. A solid body having a base and a top of equal circular areas, parallel with each other, while its surface, or side, is likewise circular, in conformity with the circles forming the base and top.

A = area of outer cylindrical surface = $2\pi rh$

S = total area of ends and cylindrical surface = $A + 2\pi r^2$

V = volume = $2r^2h = 0.7854d^2h$

Cylinder, portion of. Assume a portion of a cylinder as shown (it may be part of an elbow in a ventilating duct). Let its diameter be 16 in., length H, 20 in., and length h, 10 in. Find the area of its cylindrical surface and its volume.

$A = \pi r(H+h) = 3.1416 \times 8(20+10) = 3.1416 \times 240$
$= 753.98$ sq. in.
$V = 1.5708 r^2(H+h) = 1.5708 \times 8^2(20+10)$
$= 3014.936$ cu. in.

Cylinder, portion of. Required, to find the volume and cylindrical surface area of a part of a cylinder, as shown.

$S =$ cylindrical surface area $(c/2 \pm a \times$ length of arc $efg) \times h \div (r \pm a)$. $A =$ area of end surface = area of circle with diameter d, minus area of the segment bounded by the chord eg.

$V =$ volume $= (2/3 \times C^3 \div 8 \pm a \times A) \times h \div (r \pm a)$

Note: In solving the formulas above, use $(+)$ when the end area (A) is larger and $(-)$ when it is smaller than that of $1/2$ the base circle.

Cylinder, hollow. A tube similar in form to a cylinder, but having a concentric cylindrical section removed from its center.

$A =$ surface area (see Cylinder)
$V = \pi h(R^2 - r^2) = \pi ht(2R-t) = \pi ht(2r+t) = \pi ht$
$(R+r)$

Cone. A cone is a form of cylindrical pyramid with a circular base and an outer surface conforming in shape with the base, but tapering and converging to a point or apex.

$A =$ area of conical surface $= \pi r\sqrt{r^2+h^2} = \pi rs$
$= 1.5708 ds$
$V =$ volume $= \pi r^2 h \div 3 = 1.0472 r^2 h = 0.2618 d^2 h$

Truncated cone. Or the frustrum of a cone, is that section of a cone remaining after any part of the apex or top of the cone has been removed, leaving a solid body in which the top and bottom surfaces are similar in shape and parallel with each other.

$A =$ area of conical surface $= s(R+r) = 1.5708$
$s(D+d)$
$V =$ volume $= 1.0472\ h(R^2 + Rr + r^2)$
$a = R-r;\ s = \sqrt{a^2+h^2} = \sqrt{(R-r)^2 - h^2}$

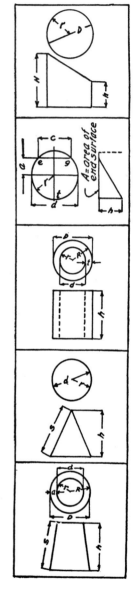

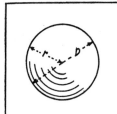

Sphere. A sphere or ball, is a solid body all points on whose surface are equally distant from its center.

$A = 4\pi r^2 = 12.5664 r^2$

$V = 4\pi r^3 \div 3 = 4.1888 r^3$

If $D = 6$ in., then $r = 3$ in., and $A = 12.5664 \times 3^2 = 113.1$ sq. in.

$V = 4.1888 \times 3^3 = 113.1$ cu. in.

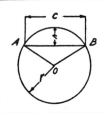

Spherical sector. Also called a spherical conic section, is a section of a sphere such as that shown, in which AOB is conical in form, while the remaining portion is a segment of the sphere.

$A =$ total area of spherical and conic surface $= \pi r(2h + c/2)$

$c = 2\sqrt{h(2r - h)}$

$V = 2\pi r^2 h \div 2$

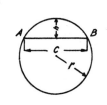

Spherical segment. Any portion of a sphere having as its base a flat, circular plane, such as AB, and as its surface a portion of the surface of the sphere.

$A =$ area of spherical surface $= 2\pi rh = \pi(c^2 \div 4 + h^2)$

$V = \pi h^2(r - h \div 3) = \pi h(c^2 \div 8 + h^2 \div 6)$

$c = 2\sqrt{h(2r - h)}$

$r = (c^2 + 4h^2) \div 8h$

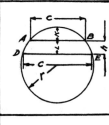

Spherical zone. That portion or section of a sphere having parallel circular areas as its base and top.

$A =$ area of spherical surface $= 2\pi rh$

$V = 1.5708h(C^2 \div 4 + c^2 \div 4 + h^2 \div 3)$

As in the spherical segment, $c = 2\sqrt{K + (2r - K)}$

$C = 2\sqrt{(K + L)\ (2r - K - L)}$

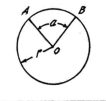

Spherical wedge. That part of a sphere shown by the section AOB.

$A =$ area of spherical surface $= a \div 360 \times 4\pi r^2$

$V = a \div 360 \times 4\pi r^3 \div 3 = 0.0116 a r^3$

Ellipsoid. A solid body, the section of which through one axis is an ellipse, and through the other axis either an ellipse or a circle. If it is the latter, it is called a spheroid.

If a, b, and c are the semi-axes, then

$V = 4\pi \div 3 \times abc = 4.1888\ abc$

If the solid is a spheroid in which $b = c$, then

$V = 4.1888ab^2$; and $A = 4\pi \div \sqrt{2} \times b\sqrt{a^2 + b^2}$

Hollow sphere. As the name implies, it is a solid body with its central part or core removed.

A = surface area (same as for sphere)

$V = 4\pi \div 3(R^3 - r^3) = \pi \div 6(D^3 - d^3)$

Annular ring or torus (circular section). An annular ring is a complete circle formed by a cylindrical-shaped body such as a round bar or tube.

A = area of surface = $4\pi^2 Rr = 39.478\,Rr$

$V = 2\pi^2 Rr^2 = 19.739\,Rr^2$

Annular ring, square section. A = area = $(2\pi r \times 2) + (2\pi R \times 2) + [2 \times 2\pi(R - r)]$

$M = (R - r) \div 2 + r = R - (R - r) \div 2$

$V = 2\pi M(tw)$

Barrel. V = approximate volume. When the sides are bent to the arc of circle, $V = \pi h \div 12(2D^2 + d^2)$

$= 0.262h(2D^2 + d^2)$

When the sides are bent to the arc of a parabola, $V = 0.209h(2D^2 + Dd + 3 \div 4d^2)$

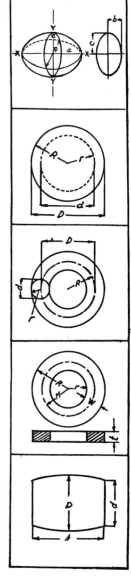

LOGARITHMS

The **logarithm (log)** of a given number is the power of a fixed number called the **base** which equals that given number. Thus, given 3 as the base, 3 to the 4th power, or 3^4, equals 81, and the log of 81 is 4. Given $10^2 = 100$; here the small 2 or the exponent is the logarithm of 100, or the base 10 is raised to the 2nd power to equal 100. The numbers 81 and 100 corresponding to the logs 4 and 2 are called the **antilogs.**

In navigational work the **common,** or **Briggs,** logarithmic system is used. The **Napierian,** or **hyperbolic,** log tables use the base **e** = 2.71828+.

1. The logarithm consists of the **index,** or **characteristic,** and the **mantissa.** The mantissa is given in the log table and is a decimal fraction. The index and the mantissa together constitute the logarithm. It is easily seen that, while the log of 100, using the base 10, is exactly 2, a little stretch of imagination is required to accept the conclusion that the log of, say, 101 is equal to 2.00432. Here again the base 10 has been raised to the 2.00432 power in order to equal 101. Again $10^{2.00432} = 101$; $10^{2.00000} = 100$. We see, then, that the log is simply an *exponent* of 10 in the *common log* system, or the number of times *10* is used as a multiplying factor in order to equal the number in question.

2. It is to be noted that the mantissa is always a positive value, while the index may be either positive or negative, depending upon whether the number whose log is required is greater or less than 1. The rule for expressing the index is readily seen from the following:

Numbers	Logarithms
78540.5	4.89509
7854.05	3.89509
785.405	2.89509
78.5405	1.89509
7.85405	0.89509

The index is written as 1 less than the number of digits to the left of the decimal point. The whole number 78540 contains 5 digits, therefore the log index will be 4, index and mantissa together showing us the power to which 10 has been raised to equal 78540.5, or 4.89509 is the log of 78540.5.

3. Since the index becomes negative for the logs of numbers less than 1, we meet the awkward condition of a *positive mantissa* and a *negative index* in such logs as those indicated below:

Numbers	Logarithms
.785405	$-1 + .89509$
.0785405	$-2 + .89509$
.00785405	$-3 + .89509$
.000785405	$-4 + .89509$
.0000785405	$-5 + .89509$

4. In order to obviate this mixture of the plus and minus, $+10$ is added to the negative index with the result that $+10 - 1 = .89509$ becomes 9.89509. This gives us the rule that *the index of any decimal number less than 1 is expressed as the number of zeros to the right of the decimal point subtracted from 9*. We have then for the foregoing:

Numbers	Logarithms
.785405	9.89509
.0785405	8.89509
.00785405	7.89509
.000785405	6.89509
.0000785405	5.89509

5. How to use log tables. Logs can be found for numbers from 1 to 999 in the following *Table of Logarithms to Base* 10. These are 4-figure logs and are correct to 4 places. Navigational log tables usually give 5-place logs. 6-place logs are the most convenient, perhaps, in that the necessity for interpolation is generally obviated.

The left hand column runs from 10 to 99. Across the top of the page is another subdivision from 0 to 9. To find the log of 783, first run down the column to 78. Then move over from 78 to the log (or, properly, the *mantissa* of the log) which lies directly under the 3 of the top horizontal column and on the 78 line. The value given is 8938. Now add the index, which is 2, or 1 less than the number of digits to the left of the decimal point in the example. Thus the log of 783 is 2.8938.

To find the log of a decimal such as 0.0563 or 0.000254, treat the decimals as if they were whole numbers, 563 and 254. The log of 0.000254 is thus $-4 + .4048$, or 6.4048, found by running down to 25 and across to 4, and then prefixing the index as shown in paragraphs 3 and 4.

Use of proportional parts. With a number like 6.357 the tables give the log for only the first three numbers. Again, run down to 63 and over to 5. The log of $6.35 = 0.8028$.

The figure 7 in 6.357 may be written 6.35–7/10. In other words, the number is 7/10 of the way between 6.35 and 6.36. The log of 6.36 is 0.8035. Subtracting log 6.35 from log 6.36, or 0.8028 from 0.8035 gives 0.0007. Then 7/10 of this difference between the two logs $= 0.0007 \times .7 = 0.0005$ (app.). Add this to 0.8028, which gives 0.8033, the log of 6.357.

As a simplification, the log tables include a list of **proportional parts.** At top right the figures running horizontally from 1–9 indicate the parts (tenths) which are to be taken of the difference between logs of any two consecutive numbers. In the vertical columns are given the corresponding values. For example, running across horizontally from 70, the proportional parts are listed in order as 112 234 456. The average difference between logs for numbers between 700 and 709 runs between 6 and 7. Thus .2 of this difference is roughly, 1, .6 is 4, .9 is 6.

In the example worked out above, 6.357, after finding the log for 635 start at the top of the table at 7 under proportional parts, and run down to the horizontal 63 column. The two meet at 5. Thus .0005 checks with the calculation worked out as being .7 of 7/10 of the difference between the logs of 635 and 636.

Example. Find the log of 0.001032.

$$\text{Mantissa of } 103 = \ .0128$$
$$\text{From prop. parts} \text{---} 2 = \ +8$$

$$.0136$$

Index or Characteristic of log = 7.

$$\log = 7.0136 \text{ ans.}$$

To find the antilog. The antilog is the number corresponding to a given log. Look up the log in the log tables which is closest to (but smaller than) the decimal part of the log given. Remember to use only the mantissa in these steps. This will give the first 3 places in the required number. For the fourth place subtract from the given log (mantissa) the log (mantissa) in the table, multiplying the remainder by 100 and divide by the difference between the found log in the table and the one next higher to it. Put the quotient on the end of the first three figures. Point off according to rule, with one more figure to the left of the decimal point than the number in the index. For minus indices add one less zero to the right of the decimal point than the number in the index.

Example. Find the antilog of 1.3216. The log next lower than .3216 in the table is .3201. The number corresponding to this log is 209. The next higher log (for 210) is .3222.

$$\text{Then} \quad 3222 - 3201 = \quad 21$$
$$3216 - 3201 = \quad 15$$
$$15 \times 100 \div 21 = \quad 7$$
$$\text{and} \quad 209 + 0007 = 2097$$

The index is 1, so that the antilog becomes 20.97.

6. Calculations with logs. When dealing with logarithms the following statements are always true.

$$\log \text{ of base } (10) = 1 \qquad \log (x \div y) = \log x - \log y$$
$$\log 1 = 0 \qquad \log x^n = n \log x$$
$$\log (xy) = \log x + \log y \qquad \log \sqrt[n]{x} = 1/n \log x$$
$$\log 1/x = -\log x$$

7. Multiplication. Find the product of .0055 $\times$ 3.14 $\times$ 670 and of 65.2 $\times$ 95.07.

Log .0055 = 7.7404	Log 65.2 = 1.8142
log 3.14 = 0.4969	log 95.07 = 1.9780
log 670. = 2.8261	
	log 6197. = 3.7922
11.0634 − 10	
11.57 ans.	6197 ans.

Since we have used the *positive* index in the log of .0055, by adding

10 to the *negative* index, we subtract 10 from the sum of the logs. The resulting sum of the logs in such a problem might give an index of 21, 35, etc. We reject the tens and call the index 1, 5, etc.

8. Division. Find the quotient of 17.62 ÷ 20.5, and of .173 ÷ .004.

Log 17.62 = 1.2460	Log .173 = 9.2380
log 20.5 = 1.3118	log .004 = 7.6021
log .8595 = 9.9342	log 43.24 = 1.6359
.8595 ans.	43.24 ans.

Note that 10 is added mentally to the index of log of 17.62. This is one of the advantages of the positive index where the log of the divisor is greater than that of the dividend.

An expression such as $652 \times .017 \div 3.14$ is simplified by first performing the multiplication as indicated. Computed by logs we have $(\log 652 + \log .017) - \log 3.14 =$

$$= (2.8142 + 8.2304) - 0.4969$$
$$= 1.0446 - 0.4969 = \log 3.53. \qquad 3.53 \text{ ans.}$$

9. To raise a number to any power. The general rule is $log\ x^n = n\ log\ x$. Find the value of 18.3^4.

$$\text{Log } 18.3 \times 4 = 1.2625 \times 4 = 5.0500 = \log 112{,}000 \text{ ans.}$$

(The last two digits in the answer are approximate, since a 4-figure log table is accurate to 4 places only).

In the case of the number being less than 1, multiply the negative index and the mantissa separately, and find their algebraic sum, as follows:

Find the value of $.0134^{0.85}$.   Log .0134 = −2. + .1271.

$.85 \times -2 = -1.70.$ $.85 \times .1271 = .1080.$
$-1.70 + .1080 = -1 + .5920 = 9.5920 = \log .3908 \text{ ans.}$

10. To find the root of any number. The rule is indicated in the formula, $log\ \sqrt[n]{x} = 1/n\ log\ x$. Divide the log of the number by the root index; the quotient is the log of the root required. If the number is a decimal fraction, increase the index of its log by a number of tens which shall be less by one than the root index, before dividing by the latter.

Required the cube root of 789, and of .789:

789 log = 2.8971	.789 log = 9.8971
dividing by 3,	increase by 20.
9.24 ans. log = 0.9657	dividing by 3)29.8971
	.924 ans. log = 9.9657

TABLE 2. LOGARITHMS TO BASE 10

Num-ber	0	1	2	3	4	5	6	7	8	9	Proportional Parts								
											1	2	3	4	5	6	7	8	9
10	0000	0043	0086	0128	0170	0212	0253	0294	0334	0374	4	8	12	17	21	25	29	33	37
11	0414	0453	0492	0531	0569	0607	0645	0682	0719	0755	4	8	11	15	19	23	26	30	34
12	0792	0828	0864	0899	0934	0969	1004	1038	1072	1106	3	7	10	14	17	21	24	28	31
13	1139	1173	1206	1239	1271	1303	1335	1367	1399	1430	3	6	10	13	16	19	23	26	29
14	1461	1492	1523	1553	1584	1614	1644	1673	1703	1732	3	6	9	12	15	18	21	24	27
15	1761	1790	1818	1847	1875	1903	1931	1959	1987	2014	3	6	8	11	14	17	20	22	25
16	2041	2068	2095	2122	2148	2175	2201	2227	2253	2279	3	5	8	11	13	16	18	21	24
17	2304	2330	2355	2380	2405	2430	2455	2480	2504	2529	2	5	7	10	12	15	17	20	22
18	2553	2577	2601	2625	2648	2672	2695	2718	2742	2765	2	5	7	9	12	14	16	19	21
19	2788	2810	2833	2856	2878	2900	2923	2945	2967	2989	2	4	7	9	11	13	16	18	20
20	3010	3032	3054	3075	3096	3118	3139	3160	3181	3201	2	4	6	8	11	13	15	17	19
21	3222	3243	3263	3284	3304	3324	3345	3365	3385	3404	2	4	6	8	10	12	14	16	18
22	3424	3444	3464	3483	3502	3522	3541	3560	3579	3598	2	4	6	8	10	12	14	15	17
23	3617	3636	3655	3674	3692	3711	3729	3747	3766	3784	2	4	6	7	9	11	13	15	17
24	3802	3820	3838	3856	3874	3892	3909	3927	3945	3962	2	4	5	7	9	11	12	14	16
25	3979	3997	4014	4031	4048	4065	4082	4099	4116	4133	2	3	5	7	9	10	12	14	15
26	4150	4166	4183	4200	4216	4232	4249	4265	4281	4298	2	3	5	7	8	10	11	13	15
27	4314	4330	4346	4362	4378	4393	4409	4425	4440	4456	2	3	5	6	8	9	11	13	14
28	4472	4487	4502	4518	4533	4548	4564	4579	4594	4609	2	3	5	6	8	9	11	12	14
29	4624	4639	4654	4669	4683	4698	4713	4728	4742	4757	1	3	4	6	7	9	10	12	13
30	4771	4786	4800	4814	4829	4843	4857	4871	4886	4900	1	3	4	6	7	9	10	11	13
31	4914	4928	4942	4955	4969	4983	4997	5011	5024	5038	1	3	4	6	7	8	10	11	12
32	5051	5065	5079	5092	5105	5119	5132	5145	5159	5172	1	3	4	5	7	8	9	11	12
33	5185	5198	5211	5224	5237	5250	5263	5276	5289	5302	1	3	4	5	6	8	9	10	12
34	5315	5328	5340	5353	5366	5378	5391	5403	5416	5428	1	3	4	5	6	8	9	10	11
35	5441	5453	5465	5478	5490	5502	5514	5527	5539	5551	1	2	4	5	6	7	9	10	11
36	5563	5575	5587	5599	5611	5623	5635	5647	5658	5670	1	2	4	5	6	7	8	10	11
37	5682	5694	5705	5717	5729	5740	5752	5763	5775	5786	1	2	3	5	6	7	8	9	10
38	5798	5809	5821	5832	5843	5855	5866	5877	5888	5899	1	2	3	5	6	7	8	9	10
39	5911	5922	5933	5944	5955	5966	5977	5988	5999	6010	1	2	3	4	5	7	8	9	10
40	6021	6031	6042	6053	6064	6075	6085	6096	6107	6117	1	2	3	4	5	6	8	9	10
41	6128	6138	6149	6160	6170	6180	6191	6201	6212	6222	1	2	3	4	5	6	7	8	9
42	6232	6243	6253	6263	6274	6284	6294	6304	6314	6325	1	2	3	4	5	6	7	8	9
43	6335	6345	6355	6365	6375	6385	6395	6405	6415	6425	1	2	3	4	5	6	7	8	9
44	6435	6444	6454	6464	6474	6484	6493	6503	6513	6522	1	2	3	4	5	6	7	8	9
45	6532	6542	6551	6561	6571	6580	6590	6599	6609	6618	1	2	3	4	5	6	7	8	9
46	6628	6637	6646	6656	6665	6675	6684	6693	6702	6712	1	2	3	4	5	6	7	7	8
47	6721	6730	6739	6749	6758	6767	6776	6785	6794	6803	1	2	3	4	5	5	6	7	8
48	6812	6821	6830	6839	6848	6857	6866	6875	6884	6893	1	2	3	4	4	5	6	7	8
49	6902	6911	6920	6928	6937	6946	6955	6964	6972	6981	1	2	3	4	4	5	6	7	8
50	6990	6998	7007	7016	7024	7033	7042	7050	7059	7067	1	2	3	3	4	5	6	7	8
51	7076	7084	7093	7101	7110	7118	7126	7135	7143	7152	1	2	3	3	4	5	6	7	8
52	7160	7168	7177	7185	7193	7202	7210	7218	7226	7235	1	2	2	3	4	5	6	7	7
53	7243	7251	7259	7267	7275	7284	7292	7300	7308	7316	1	2	2	3	4	5	6	6	7
54	7324	7332	7340	7348	7356	7364	7372	7380	7388	7396	1	2	2	3	4	5	6	6	7

Log π = 0.49715. Log_e = 2.3025851 × Log_{10}

TABLE 2. LOGARITHMS TO BASE 10 (*continued*)

Num-ber	0	1	2	3	4	5	6	7	8	9	Proportional Parts								
											1	2	3	4	5	6	7	8	9
55	7404	7412	7419	7427	7435	7443	7451	7459	7466	7474	1	2	2	3	4	5	5	6	7
56	7482	7490	7497	7505	7513	7520	7528	7536	7543	7551	1	2	2	3	4	5	5	6	7
57	7559	7566	7574	7582	7589	7597	7604	7612	7619	7627	1	2	2	3	4	5	5	6	7
58	7634	7642	7649	7657	7664	7672	7679	7686	7694	7701	1	1	2	3	4	4	5	6	7
59	7709	7716	7723	7731	7738	7745	7752	7760	7767	7774	1	1	2	3	4	4	5	6	7
60	7782	7789	7796	7803	7810	7818	7825	7832	7839	7846	1	1	2	3	4	4	5	6	6
61	7853	7860	7868	7875	7882	7889	7896	7903	7910	7917	1	1	2	3	4	4	5	6	6
62	7924	7931	7938	7945	7952	7959	7966	7973	7980	7987	1	1	2	3	3	4	5	6	6
63	7993	8000	8007	8014	8021	8028	8035	8041	8048	8055	1	1	2	3	3	4	5	5	6
64	8062	8069	8075	8082	8089	8096	8102	8109	8116	8122	1	1	2	3	3	4	5	5	6
65	8129	8136	8142	8149	8156	8162	8169	8176	8182	8189	1	1	2	3	3	4	5	5	6
66	8195	8202	8209	8215	8222	8228	8235	8241	8248	8254	1	1	2	3	3	4	5	5	6
67	8261	8267	8274	8280	8287	8293	8299	8306	8312	8319	1	1	2	3	3	4	5	5	6
68	8325	8331	8338	8344	8351	8357	8363	8370	8376	8382	1	1	2	3	3	4	4	5	6
69	8388	8395	8401	8407	8414	8420	8426	8432	8439	8445	1	1	2	2	3	4	4	5	6
70	8451	8457	8463	8470	8476	8482	8488	8494	8500	8506	1	1	2	2	3	4	4	5	6
71	8513	8519	8525	8531	8537	8543	8549	8555	8561	8567	1	1	2	2	3	4	4	5	5
72	8573	8579	8585	8591	8597	8603	8609	8615	8621	8627	1	1	2	2	3	4	4	5	5
73	8633	8639	8645	8651	8657	8663	8669	8675	8681	8686	1	1	2	2	3	4	4	5	5
74	8692	8698	8704	8710	8716	8722	8727	8733	8739	8745	1	1	2	2	3	4	4	5	5
75	8751	8756	8762	8768	8774	8779	8785	8791	8797	8802	1	1	2	2	3	3	4	5	5
76	8808	8814	8820	8825	8831	8837	8842	8848	8854	8859	1	1	2	2	3	3	4	5	5
77	8865	8871	8876	8882	8887	8893	8899	8904	8910	8915	1	1	2	2	3	3	4	4	5
78	8921	8927	8932	8938	8943	8949	8954	8960	8965	8971	1	1	2	2	3	3	4	4	5
79	8976	8982	8987	8993	8998	9004	9009	9015	9020	9025	1	1	2	2	3	3	4	4	5
80	9031	9036	9042	9047	9053	9058	9063	9069	9074	9079	1	1	2	2	3	3	4	4	5
81	9085	9090	9096	9101	9106	9112	9117	9122	9128	9133	1	1	2	2	3	3	4	4	5
82	9138	9143	9149	9154	9159	9165	9170	9175	9180	9186	1	1	2	2	3	3	4	4	5
83	9191	9196	9201	9206	9212	9217	9222	9227	9232	9238	1	1	2	2	3	3	4	4	5
84	9243	9248	9253	9258	9263	9269	9274	9279	9284	9289	1	1	2	2	3	3	4	4	5
85	9294	9299	9304	9309	9315	9320	9325	9330	9335	9340	1	1	2	2	3	3	4	4	5
86	9345	9350	9355	9360	9365	9370	9375	9380	9385	9390	1	1	2	2	3	3	4	4	5
87	9395	9400	9405	9410	9415	9420	9425	9430	9435	9440	0	1	1	2	2	3	3	4	4
88	9445	9450	9455	9460	9465	9469	9474	9479	9484	9489	0	1	1	2	2	3	3	4	4
89	9494	9499	9504	9509	9513	9518	9523	9528	9533	9538	0	1	1	2	2	3	3	4	4
90	9542	9547	9552	9557	9562	9566	9571	9576	9581	9586	0	1	1	2	2	3	3	4	4
91	9590	9595	9600	9605	9609	9614	9619	9624	9628	9633	0	1	1	2	2	3	3	4	4
92	9638	9643	9647	9652	9657	9661	9666	9671	9675	9680	0	1	1	2	2	3	3	4	4
93	9685	9689	9694	9699	9703	9708	9713	9717	9722	9727	0	1	1	2	2	3	3	4	4
94	9731	9736	9741	9745	9750	9754	9759	9763	9768	9773	0	1	1	2	2	3	3	4	4
95	9777	9782	9786	9791	9795	9800	9805	9809	9814	9818	0	1	1	2	2	3	3	4	4
96	9823	9827	9832	9836	9841	9845	9850	9854	9859	9863	0	1	1	2	2	3	3	4	4
97	9868	9872	9877	9881	9886	9890	9894	9899	9903	9908	0	1	1	2	2	3	3	4	4
98	9912	9917	9921	9926	9930	9934	9939	9943	9948	9952	0	1	1	2	2	3	3	4	4
99	9956	9961	9965	9969	9974	9978	9983	9987	9991	9996	0	1	1	2	2	3	3	3	4

Natural Trigonometric Functions

Degrees	SINES							Cosines
	0′	10′	20′	30′	40′	50′	60′	
0	0.00000	0.00291	0.00582	0.00873	0.01164	0.01454	0.01745	89
1	0.01745	0.02036	0.02327	0.02618	0.02908	0.03199	0.03490	88
2	0.03490	0.03781	0.04071	0.04362	0.04653	0.04943	0.05234	87
3	0.05234	0.05524	0.05814	0.06105	0.06395	0.06685	0.06976	86
4	0.06976	0.07266	0.07556	0.07846	0.08136	0.08426	0.08716	85
5	0.08716	0.09005	0.09295	0.09585	0.09874	0.10164	0.10453	84
6	0.10453	0.10742	0.11031	0.11320	0.11609	0.11898	0.12187	83
7	0.12187	0.12476	0.12764	0.13053	0.13341	0.13629	0.13917	82
8	0.13917	0.14205	0.14493	0.14781	0.15069	0.15356	0.15643	81
9	0.15643	0.15931	0.16218	0.16505	0,16792	0.17078	0.17365	80
10	0.17365	0.17651	0.17937	0.18224	0.18509	0.18795	0.19081	79
11	0.19081	0.19366	0.19652	0.19937	0.20222	0.20507	0.20791	78
12	0.20791	0.21076	0.21360	0.21644	0.21928	0.22212	0.22495	77
13	0.22495	0.22778	0.23062	0.23345	0.23627	0.23910	0.24192	76
14	0.24192	0.24474	0.24756	0.25038	0.25320	0.25601	0.25882	75
15	0.25882	0.26163	0.26443	0.26724	0.27004	0.27284	0.27564	74
16	0.27564	0.27843	0.28123	0.28402	0.28680	0.28959	0.29237	73
17	0.29237	0.29515	0.29793	0.30071	0.30348	0.30625	0.30902	72
18	0.30902	0.31178	0.31454	0.31730	0.32006	0.32282	0.32557	71
19	0.32557	0.32832	0.33106	0.33381	0.33655	0.33929	0.34202	70
20	0.34202	0.34475	0.34748	0.35021	0.35293	0.35565	0.35837	69
21	0.35837	0.36108	0.36379	0.36650	0.36921	0.37191	0.37461	68
22	0.37461	0.37730	0.37999	0.38268	0.38537	0.38805	0.39073	67
23	0.39073	0.39341	0.39608	0.39875	0.40142	0.40408	0.40674	66
24	0.40674	0.40939	0.41204	0.41469	0.41734	0.41998	0.42262	65
25	0.42262	0.42525	0.42788	0.43051	0.43313	0.43575	0.43837	64
26	0.43837	0.44098	0.44359	0.44620	0.44880	0.45140	0.45399	63
27	0.45399	0.45658	0.45917	0.46175	0.46433	0.46690	0.46947	62
28	0.46947	0.47204	0.47460	0.47716	0.47971	0.48226	0.48481	61
29	0.48481	0.48735	0.48989	0.49242	0.49495	0.49748	0.50000	60
30	0.50000	0.50252	0.50503	0.50754	0.51004	0.51254	0.51504	59
31	0.51504	0.51753	0.52002	0.52250	0.52498	0.52745	0.52992	58
32	0.52992	0.53238	0.53484	0.53730	0.53975	0.54220	0.54464	57
33	0.54464	0.54708	0.54951	0.55194	0.55436	0.55678	0.55919	56
34	0.55919	0.56160	0.56401	0.56641	0.56880	0.57119	0.57358	55
35	0.57358	0.57596	0.57833	0.58070	0.58307	0.58543	0.58779	54
36	0.58779	0.59014	0.59248	0.59482	0.59716	0.59949	0.60182	53
37	0.60182	0.60414	0.60645	0.60876	0.61107	0.61337	0.61566	52
38	0.61566	0.61795	0.62024	0.62251	0.62479	0.62706	0.62932	51
39	0.62932	0.63158	0.63383	0.63608	0.63832	0.64056	0.64279	50
40	0.64279	0.64501	0.64723	0.64945	0.65166	0.65386	0.65606	49
41	0.65606	0.65825	0.66044	0.66262	0.66480	0.66697	0.66913	48
42	0.66913	0.67129	0.67344	0.67559	0.67773	0.67987	0.68200	47
43	0.68200	0.68412	0.68624	0.68835	0.69046	0.69256	0.69466	46
44	0.69466	0.69675	0.69883	0.70091	0.70298	0.70505	0.70711	45
Sines	60′	50′	40′	30′	20′	10′	0′	Degrees
	COSINES							

NATURAL TRIGONOMETRIC FUNCTIONS

Degrees	COSINES							Sines
	0′	10′	20′	30′	40′	50′	60′	
0	1.00000	1.00000	0.99998	0.99996	0.99993	0.99989	0.99985	89
1	0.99985	0.99979	0.99973	0.99966	0.99958	0.99949	0.99939	88
2	0.99939	0.99929	0.99917	0.99905	0.99892	0.99878	0.99863	87
3	0.99863	0.99847	0.99831	0.99813	0.99795	0.99776	0.99756	86
4	0.99756	0.99736	0.99714	0.99692	0.99668	0.99644	0.99619	85
5	0.99619	0.99594	0.99567	0.99540	0.99511	0.99482	0.99452	84
6	0.99452	0.99421	0.99390	0.99357	0.99324	0.99290	0.99255	83
7	0.99255	0.99219	0.99182	0.99144	0.99106	0.99067	0.99027	82
8	0.99027	0.98986	0.98944	0.98902	0.98858	0.98814	0.98769	81
9	0.98769	0.98723	0.98676	0.98629	0.98580	0.98531	0.98481	80
10	0.98481	0.98430	0.98378	0.98325	0.98272	0.98218	0.98163	79
11	0.98163	0.98107	0.98050	0.97992	0.97934	0.97875	0.97815	78
12	0.97815	0.97754	0.97692	0.97630	0.97566	0.97502	0.97437	77
13	0.97437	0.97371	0.97304	0.97237	0.97169	0.97100	0.97030	76
14	0.97030	0.96959	0.96887	0.96815	0.96742	0.96667	0.96593	75
15	0.96593	0.96517	0.96440	0.96363	0.96285	0.96206	0.96126	74
16	0.96126	0.96046	0.95964	0.95882	0.95799	0.95715	0.95630	73
17	0.95630	0.95545	0.95459	0.95372	0.95284	0.95195	0.95106	72
18	0.95106	0.95015	0.94924	0.94832	0.94740	0.94646	0.94552	71
19	0.94552	0.94457	0.94361	0.94264	0.94167	0.94068	0.93969	70
20	0.93969	0.93869	0.93769	0.93667	0.93565	0.93462	0.93358	69
21	0.93358	0.93253	0.93148	0.93042	0.92935	0.92827	0.92718	68
22	0.92718	0.92609	0.92499	0.92388	0.92276	0.92164	0.92050	67
23	0.92050	0.91936	0.91822	0.91706	0.91590	0.91472	0.91355	66
24	0.91355	0.91236	0.91116	0.90996	0.90875	0.90753	0.90631	65
25	0.90631	0.90507	0.90383	0.90259	0.90133	0.90007	0.89879	64
26	0.89879	0.89752	0.89623	0.89493	0.89363	0.89232	0.89101	63
27	0.89101	0.88968	0.88835	0.88701	0.88566	0.88431	0.88295	62
28	0.88295	0.88158	0.88020	0.87882	0.87743	0.87603	0.87462	61
29	0.87462	0.87321	0.87178	0.87036	0.86892	0.86748	0.86603	60
30	0.86603	0.86457	0.86310	0.86163	0.86015	0.85866	0.85717	59
31	0.85717	0.85567	0.85416	0.85264	0.85112	0.84959	0.84805	58
32	0.84805	0.84650	0.84495	0.84339	0.84182	0.84025	0.83867	57
33	0.83867	0.83708	0.83549	0.83389	0.83228	0.83066	0.82904	56
34	0.82904	0.82741	0.82577	0.82413	0.82248	0.82082	0.81915	55
35	0.81915	0.81748	0.81580	0.81412	0.81242	0.81072	0.80902	54
36	0.80902	0.80730	0.80558	0.80386	0.80212	0.80038	0.79864	53
37	0.79864	0.79688	0.79512	0.79335	0.79158	0.78980	0.78801	52
38	0.78801	0.78622	0.78442	0.78261	0.78079	0.77897	0.77715	51
39	0.77715	0.77531	0.77347	0.77162	0.76977	0.76791	0.76604	50
40	0.76604	0.76417	0.76229	0.76041	0.75851	0.75661	0.75471	49
41	0.75471	0.75280	0.75088	0.74896	0.74703	0.74509	0.74314	48
42	0.74314	0.74120	0.73924	0.73728	0.73531	0.73333	0.73135	47
43	0.73135	0.72937	0.72737	0.72537	0.72337	0.72136	0.71934	46
44	0.71934	0.71732	0.71529	0.71325	0.71121	0.70916	0.70711	45
Cosines	60′	50′	40′	30′	20′	10′	0′	Degrees
	SINES							

NATURAL TRIGONOMETRIC FUNCTIONS

Degrees	TANGENTS							Cotangents
	0'	10'	20'	30'	40'	50'	60'	
0	0.00000	0.00291	0.00582	0.00873	0.01164	0.01455	0.01746	89
1	0.01746	0.02036	0.02328	0.02619	0.02910	0.03201	0.03492	88
2	0.03492	0.03783	0.C4075	0.04366	0.04658	0.04949	0.05241	87
3	0.05241	0.05533	0.05824	0.06116	0.06408	0.06700	0.06993	86
4	0.06993	0.07285	0.07578	0.07870	0.08163	0.08456	0.08749	85
5	0.08749	0.09042	0.09335	0.09629	0.09923	0.10216	0.10510	84
6	0.10510	0.10805	0.11099	0.11394	0.11688	0.11983	0.12278	83
7	0.12278	0.12574	0.12869	0.13165	0.13461	0.13758	0.14054	82
8	0.14054	0.14351	0.14648	0.14945	0.15243	0.15540	0.15838	81
9	0.15838	0.16137	0.16435	0.16734	0.17033	0.17333	0.17633	80
10	0.17633	0.17933	0.18233	0.18534	0.18835	0.19136	0.19438	79
11	0.19438	0.19740	0.20042	0.20345	0.20648	0.20952	0.21256	78
12	0.21256	0.21560	0.21864	0.22169	0.22475	0.22781	0.23087	77
13	0.23087	0.23393	0.23700	0.24008	0.24316	0.24624	0.24933	76
14	0.24933	0.25242	0.25552	0.25862	0.26172	0.26483	0.26795	75
15	0.26795	0.27107	0.27419	0.27732	0.28046	0.28360	0.28675	74
16	0.28675	0.28990	0.29305	0.29621	0.29938	0.30255	0.30573	73
17	0.30573	0.30891	0.31210	0.31530	0.31850	0.32171	0.32492	72
18	0.32492	0.32814	0.33136	0.33460	0.33783	0.34108	0.34433	71
19	0.34433	0.34758	0.35085	0.35412	0.35740	0.36068	0.36397	70
20	0.36397	0.36727	0.37057	0.37388	0.37720	0.38053	0.38386	69
21	0.38386	0.38721	0.39055	0.39391	0.39727	0.40065	0.40403	68
22	0.40403	0.40741	0.41081	0.41421	0.41763	0.42105	0.42447	67
23	0.42447	0.42791	0.43136	0.43481	0.43828	0.44175	0.44523	66
24	0.44523	0.44872	0.45222	0.45573	0.45924	0.46277	0.46631	65
25	0.46631	0.46985	0.47341	0.47698	0.48055	0.48414	0.48773	64
26	0.48773	0.49134	0.49495	0.49858	0.50222	0.50587	0.50953	63
27	0.50953	0.51320	0.51688	0.52057	0.52427	0.52798	0.53171	62
28	0.53171	0.53545	0.53920	0.54296	0.54674	0.55051	0.55431	61
29	0.55431	0.55812	0.56194	0.56577	0.56962	0.57348	0.57735	60
30	0.57735	0.58124	0.58513	0.58905	0.59297	0.59691	0.60086	59
31	0.60086	0.60483	0.60881	0.61280	0.61681	0.62083	0.62487	58
32	0.62487	0.62892	0.63299	0.63707	0.64117	0.64528	0.64941	57
33	0.64941	0.65355	0.65771	0.66189	0.66608	0.67028	0.67451	56
34	0.67451	0.67875	0.68301	0.68728	0.69157	0.69588	0.70021	55
35	0.70021	0.70455	0.70891	0.71329	0.71769	0.72211	0.72654	54
36	0.72654	0.73100	0.73547	0.73996	0.74447	0.74900	0.75355	53
37	0.75355	0.75812	0.76272	0.76733	0.77196	0.77661	0.78129	52
38	0.78129	0.78598	0.79070	0.79544	0.80020	0.80498	0.80978	51
39	0.80978	0.81461	0.81946	0.82434	0.82923	0.83415	0.83910	50
40	0.83910	0.84407	0.84906	0.85408	0.85912	0.86419	0.86929	49
41	0.86929	0.87441	0.87955	0.88473	0.88992	0.89515	0.90040	48
42	0.90040	0.90569	0.91099	0.91633	0.92170	0.92709	0.93252	47
43	0.93252	0.93797	0.94345	0.94896	0.95451	0.96008	0.96569	46
44	0.96569	0.97133	0.97700	0.98270	0.98843	0.99420	1.00000	45
Tangents	60'	50'	40'	30'	20'	10'	0'	Degrees
	COTANGENTS							

NATURAL TRIGONOMETRIC FUNCTIONS

Degrees	COTANGENTS							Tangents
	0'	10'	20'	30'	40'	50'	60'	
0	∞	343.77371	171.88540	114.58865	85.93979	68.75009	57.28996	89
1	57.28996	49.10388	42.96408	38.18846	34.36777	31.24158	28.63625	88
2	28.63625	26.43160	24.54176	22.90377	21.47040	20.20555	19.08114	87
3	19.08114	18.07498	17.16934	16.34986	15.60478	14.92442	14.30067	86
4	14.30067	13.72674	13.19688	12.70621	12.25051	11.82617	11.43005	85
5	11.43005	11.05943	10.71191	10.38540	10,07803	9.78817	9.51436	84
6	9.51436	9.25530	9.00983	8:77689	8.55555	8.34496	8.14435	83
7	8.14435	7.95302	7.77035	7.59575	7.42871	7.26873	7.11537	82
8	7.11537	6.96823	6.82694	6.69116	6.56055	6.43484	6.31375	81
9	6.31375	6.19703	6.08444	5.97576	5.87080	5.76937	5.67128	80
10	5.67128	5.57638	5.48451	5.39552	5.30928	5.22566	5.14455	79
11	5.14455	5.06584	4.98940	4.91516	4.84300	4.77286	4.70463	78
12	4.70463	4.63825	4.57363	4.51071	4.44942	4.38969	4.33148	77
13	4.33148	4.27471	4.21933	4.16530	4.11256	4.06107	4.01078	76
14	4.01078	3.96165	3.91364	3.86671	3.82083	3.77595	3.73205	75
15	3.73205	3.68909	3.64705	3.60588	3.56557	3.52609	3.48741	74
16	3.48741	3.44951	3.41236	3.37594	3.34023	3.30521	3.27085	73
17	3.27085	3.23714	3.20406	3.17159	3.13972	3.10842	3.07768	72
18	3.07768	3.04749	3.01783	2.98869	2.96004	2.93189	2.90421	71
19	2.90421	2,87700	2.85023	2.82391	2.79802	2.77254	2.74748	70
20	2.74748	2.72281	2.69853	2.67462	2.65109	2.62791	2.60509	69
21	2.60509	2.58261	2.56046	2.53865	2.51715	2.49597	2.47509	68
22	2.47509	2.45451	2.43422	2.41421	2.39449	2.37504	2.35585	67
23	2.35585	2.33693	2.31826	2.29984	2.28167	2.26374	2.24604	66
24	2.24604	2.22857	2 21132	2.19430	2.17749	2.16090	2.14451	65
25	2.14451	2.12832	2.11233	2.09654	2.08094	2.06553	2.05030	64
26	2.05030	2.03526	2.02039	2.00569	1.99116	1.97680	1.96261	63
27	1.96261	1.94858	1.93470	1.92098	1.90741	1.89400	1.88073	62
28	1.88073	1.86760	1.85462	1.84177	1.82907	1.81649	1.80405	61
29	1.80405	1.79174	1.77955	1.76749	1.75556	1.74375	1.73205	60
30	1.73205	1.72047	1.70901	1.69766	1.68643	1.67530	1.66428	59
31	1.66428	1 65337	1.64256	1.63185	1.62125	1.61074	1.60033	58
32	1.60033	1.59002	1.57981	1.56969	1.55966	1.54972	1.53987	57
33	1.53987	1.53010	1.52043	1.51084	1.50133	1.49190	1.48256	56
34	1.48256	1.47330	1.46411	1.45501	1.44598	1.43703	1.42815	55
35	1.42815	1.41934	1.41061	1.40195	1.39336	1.38484	1.37638	54
36	1.37638	1.36800	1.35968	1.35142	1.34323	1.33511	1.32704	53
37	1.32704	1.31904	1.31110	1.30323	1.29541	1.28764	1.27994	52
38	1.27994	1.27230	1.26471	1.25717	1.24969	1.24227	1.23490	51
39	1.23490	1.22758	4.22031	1.21310	1.20593	1.19882	1.19175	50
40	1.19175	1.18474	1.17777	1.17085	1.16398	1.15715	1.15037	49
41	1.15037	1.14363	1.13694	1.13029	1.12369	1.11713	1.11061	48
42	1.11061	1.10414	1.09770	1.09131	1.08496	1.07864	1.07237	47
43	1.07237	1.06613	1.05994	1.05378	1.04766	1.04158	1.03553	46
44	1.03553	1.02952	1.02355	1.01761	1.01170	1.00583	1.00000	45
Cotangents	60'	50'	40'	30'	20'	10'	0'	Degrees

TANGENTS

Natural Trigonometric Functions

Degrees	SECANTS							Cosecants
	0′	10′	20′	30′	40′	50′	60′	
0	1.00000	1.00000	1.00002	1.00004	1.00007	1.00011	1.00015	89
1	1.00015	1.00021	1.00027	1.00034	1.00042	1.00051	1.00061	88
2	1.00061	1.00072	1.00083	1.00095	1.00108	1.00122	1.00137	87
3	1.00137	1.00153	1.00169	1.00187	1.00205	1.00224	1.00244	86
4	1.00244	1.00265	1.00287	1.00309	1.00333	1.00357	1.00382	85
5	1.00382	1.00408	1.00435	1.00463	1.00491	1.00521	1.00551	84
6	1.00551	1.00582	1.00614	1.00647	1.00681	1.00715	1.00751	83
7	1.00751	1.00787	1.00825	1.00863	1.00902	1.00942	1.00983	82
8	1.00983	1.01024	1.01067	1.01111	1.01155	1.01200	1.01247	81
9	1.01247	1.01294	1.01342	1.01391	1.01440	1.01491	1.01543	80
10	1.01543	1.01595	1.01649	1.01703	1.01758	1.01815	1.01872	79
11	1.01872	1.01930	1.01989	1.02049	1.02110	1.02171	1.02234	78
12	1.02234	1.02298	1.02362	1.02428	1.02494	1.02562	1.02630	77
13	1.02630	1.02700	1.02770	1.02842	1.02914	1.02987	1.03061	76
14	1.03061	1.03137	1.03213	1.03290	1.03368	1.03447	1.03528	75
15	1.03528	1.03609	1.03691	1.03774	1.03858	1.03944	1.04030	74
16	1.04030	1.04117	1.04206	1.04295	1.04385	1.04477	1.04569	73
17	1.04569	1.04663	1.04757	1.04853	1.04950	1.05047	1.05146	72
18	1.05146	1.05246	1.05347	1.05449	1.05552	1.05657	1.05762	71
19	1.05762	1.05869	1.05976	1.06085	1.06195	1.06306	1.06418	70
20	1.06418	1.06531	1.06645	1.06761	1.06878	1.06995	1.07115	69
21	1.07115	1.07235	1.07356	1.07479	1.07602	1.07727	1.07853	68
22	1.07853	1.07981	1.08109	1.08239	1.08370	1.08503	1.08636	67
23	1.08636	1.08771	1.08907	1.09044	1.09183	1.09323	1.09464	66
24	1.09464	1.09606	1.09750	1.09895	1.10041	1.10189	1.10338	65
25	1.10338	1.10488	1.10640	1.10793	1.10947	1.11103	1.11260	64
26	1.11260	1.11419	1.11579	1.11740	1.11903	1.12067	1.12233	63
27	1.12233	1.12400	1.12568	1.12738	1.12910	1.13083	1.13257	62
28	1.13257	1.13433	1.13610	1.13789	1.13970	1.14152	1.14335	61
29	1.14335	1.14521	1.14707	1.14896	1.15085	1.15277	1.15470	60
30	1.15470	1.15665	1.15861	1.16059	1.16259	1.16460	1.16663	59
31	1.16663	1.16868	1.17075	1.17283	1.17493	1.17704	1.17918	58
32	1.17918	1.18133	1.18350	1.18569	1.18790	1.19012	1.19236	57
33	1.19236	1.19463	1.19691	1.19920	1.20152	1.20386	1.20622	56
34	1.20622	1.20859	1.21099	1.21341	1.21584	1.21830	1.22077	55
35	1.22077	1.22327	1.22579	1.22833	1.23089	1.23347	1.23607	54
36	1.23607	1.23869	1.24134	1.24400	1.24669	1.24940	1.25214	53
37	1.25214	1.25489	1.25767	1.26047	1.26330	1.26615	1.26902	52
38	1.26902	1.27191	1.27483	1.27778	1.28075	1.28374	1.28676	51
39	1.28676	1.28980	1.29287	1.29597	1.29909	1.30223	1.30541	50
40	1.30541	1.30861	1.31183	1.31509	1.31837	1.32168	1.32501	49
41	1.32501	1.32838	1.33177	1.33519	1.33864	1.34212	1.34563	48
42	1.34563	1.34917	1.35274	1.35634	1.35997	1.36363	1.36733	47
43	1.36733	1.37105	1.37481	1.37860	1.38242	1.38628	1.39016	46
44	1.39016	1.39409	1.39804	1.40203	1.40606	1.41012	1.41421	45
Secants	60′	50′	40′	30′	20′	10′	0′	Degrees
	COSECANTS							

NATURAL TRIGONOMETRIC FUNCTIONS

Degrees	COSECANTS							Secants
	0′	10′	20′	30′	40′	50′	60′	
0	∞	343.77516	171.88831	114.59301	85.94561	68.75736	57.29869	89
1	57.29869	49.11406	42.97571	38.20155	34.38232	31.25758	28.65371	88
2	28.65371	26.45051	24.56212	22.92559	21.49368	20.23028	19.10732	87
3	19.10732	18.10262	17.19843	16.38041	15.63679	14.95788	14.33559	86
4	14.33559	13.76312	13.23472	12.74550	12.29125	11.86837	11.47371	85
5	11.47371	11.10455	10.75849	10.43343	10.12752	9.83912	9.56677	84
6	9.56677	9.30917	9.06515	8.83367	8.61379	8.40466	8.20551	83
7	8.20551	8.01565	7.83443	7.66130	7.49571	7.33719	7.18530	82
8	7.18530	7.03962	6.89979	6.76547	6.63633	6.51208	6.39245	81
9	6.39245	6.27719	6.16607	6.05886	5.95536	5.85539	5.75877	80
10	5.75877	5.66533	5.57493	5.48740	5.40263	5.32049	5.24084	79
11	5.24084	5.16359	5.08863	5.01585	4.94517	4.87649	4.80973	78
12	4.80973	4.74482	4.68167	4.62023	4.56041	4.50216	4.44541	77
13	4.44541	4.39012	4.33622	4.28366	4.23239	4.18238	4.13357	76
14	4.13357	4.08591	4.03938	3.99393	3.94952	3.90613	3.86370	75
15	3.86370	3.82223	3.78166	3.74198	3.70315	3.66515	3.62796	74
16	3.62796	3.59154	3.55587	3.52094	3.48671	3.45317	3.42030	73
17	3.42030	3.38808	3.35649	3.32551	3.29512	3.26531	3.23607	72
18	3.23607	3.20737	3.17920	3.15155	3.12440	3.09774	3.07155	71
19	3.07155	3.04584	3.02057	2.99574	2.97135	2.94737	2.92380	70
20	2.92380	2.90063	2.87785	2.85545	2.83342	2.81175	2.79043	69
21	2.79043	2.76945	2.74881	2.72850	2.70851	2.68884	2.66947	68
22	2.66947	2.65040	2.63162	2.61313	2.59491	2.57698	2.55930	67
23	2.55930	2.54190	2.52474	2.50784	2.49119	2.47477	2.45859	66
24	2.45859	2.44264	2.42692	2.41142	2.39614	2.38107	2.36620	65
25	2.36620	2.35154	2.33708	2.32282	2.30875	2.29487	2.28117	64
26	2.28117	2.26766	2.25432	2.24116	2.22817	2.21535	2.20269	63
27	2.20269	2.19019	2.17786	2.16568	2.15366	2.14178	2.13005	62
28	2.13005	2.11847	2.10704	2.09574	2.08458	2.07356	2.06267	61
29	2.06267	2.05191	2.04128	2.03077	2.02039	2.01014	2.00000	60
30	2.00000	1.98998	1.98008	1.97029	1.96062	1.95106	1.94160	59
31	1.94160	1.93226	1.92302	1.91388	1.90485	1.89591	1.88709	58
32	1.88708	1.87834	1.86970	1.86116	1.85271	1.84435	1.83608	57
33	1.83608	1.82790	1.81981	1.81180	1.80388	1.79604	1.78829	56
34	1.78829	1.78062	1.77303	1.76552	1.75808	1.75073	1.74345	55
35	1.74345	1.73624	1.72911	1.72205	1.71506	1.70815	1.70130	54
36	1.70130	1.69452	1.68782	1.68117	1.67460	1.66809	1.66164	53
37	1.66164	1.65526	1.64894	1.64268	1.63648	1.63035	1.62427	52
38	1.62427	1.61825	1.61229	1.60639	1.60054	1.59475	1.58902	51
39	1.58902	1.58333	1.57771	1.57213	1.56661	1.56114	1.55572	50
40	1.55572	1.55036	1.54504	1.53977	1.53455	1.52938	1.52425	49
41	1.52425	1.51918	1.51415	1.50916	1.50422	1.49933	1.49448	48
42	1.49448	1.48967	1.48491	1.48019	1.47551	1.47087	1.46628	47
43	1.46628	1.46173	1.45721	1.45274	1.44831	1.44391	1.43956	46
44	1.43956	1.43524	1.43096	1.42672	1.42251	1.41835	1.41421	45

	60′	50′	40′	30′	20′	10′	0′	
Cosecants				SECANTS				Degrees

Appendix D

TABLES AND USEFUL INFORMATION

COMMON CONVERSION FACTORS

Multiply	*By*	*To Obtain*
Barrels (fuel oil)	42.	gallons (fuel oil)
British gallon	1.2	U. S. gallons
B.t.u.	778.	foot-pounds
Centimeters	0.3937	inches
Centimeters of mercury	0.1934	pounds per square inch
Cubic feet	1728.	cubic inches
Cubic feet	7.48	gallons
Cubic feet (fresh water)	62.5	pounds of fresh water
Cubic feet (sea water)	64.	pounds of sea water
Cwts.	50.8	kilograms
Fathoms	6.0	feet
Feet	30.48	centimeters
Feet	0.3048	meters
Feet of water	0.434	pounds per square inch
Force de cheval	0.98633	horsepower
Gallons	231.	cubic inches
Gallons of water	8.33	pounds of water
Gallons per min.	0.1337	cubic feet per min.
Grams	15.432	grains
Grams	0.035274	ounces
Hectares	0.00386	square miles
Hectoliters	2.75	bushels
Hectoliters	26.42	gallons
Horsepower	33000.	foot-pounds per minute
Horsepower	550.	foot-pounds per second
Horsepower	0.746	kilowatts
Horsepower (boiler)	33472.	B.t.u. per hour
Horsepower-hours	2245.	B.t.u.
Inches	2.54	centimeters
Inches of mercury	0.491	pounds per square inch
Inches of mercury	2.540	centimeters
Kilograms	35.274	ounces
Kilograms	2.2046	pounds
Kilometers	3281.	feet
Kilometers	1093.633	yards
Kilometers per hour	.621	miles per hour
Kilowatts	1.34	horsepower
Kilowatt-hours	1.34	horsepower-hours
Knots per hour	1.152	miles per hour
Liters	35.2	fluid ounces (imp.)
Liters	0.2642	gallons

Multiply	*By*	*To Obtain*
Liters	1.760	pints
Meters	3.281	feet
Meters	1.0936	yards
Miles	1.609	kilometers
Miles (land)	5280.	feet
Miles (nautical)	6080.	feet
Miles per hour (land)	88.	feet per minute
Miles per hour (land)	0.8684	knots per hour
Ounces (avoir.)	28.35	grams
Ounces (troy)	31.1035	grams
Pints	0.56793	liters
Pounds	453.6	grams
Pounds	0.4536	kilograms
Pounds per square inch	2.307	feet of water
Pounds per square inch	2.036	inches of mercury
Pounds per square inch	144.	pounds per square foot
Quarts (dry)	67.20	cubic inches
Quarts (liquid)	57.75	cubic inches
Rods	16.5	feet
Square miles	640.	acres
Square miles	259.02	hectares
Tons (long)	2240.	pounds
Tons (short)	2000.	pounds
Tons (long) fresh water	35.84	cubic feet of fresh water
Tons (long) sea water	35.	cubic feet of sea water
Yards	0.9144	meters

TEMPERATURE SCALE CONVERSIONS

F = Fahrenheit $F = 9/5C + 32°$

C = Centigrade $C = (F - 32°) \times 5/9$

ENGLISH STANDARDS OF WEIGHTS AND MEASURES
WEIGHT
Avoirdupois

16 drachms or 437.5 grains	= 1 ounce (oz.)
16 ounces or 7000 grains	= 1 pound (lb.)
100 pounds	= 1 hundredweight (cwt.)
20 cwt. or 2000 lbs.	= 1 ton (T.)

Long-Ton Table

16 ounces	= 1 pound
112 pounds	= 1 hundredweight
20 cwt. or 2240 lbs.	= 1 ton

Troy

24 grains	= 1 pennyweight
20 pennyweights	= 1 ounce
12 ounces	= 1 pound
1 carat	= 3.168 grains (.205 gram)

Apothecaries' Measure

20 grains	= 1 scruple	8 drachms	= 1 ounce
3 scruples	= 1 drachm	12 ounces	= 1 pound

MEASURES OF LENGTH

Inch	= 72 points or 12 lines
Nail, 1/16	= 2 1/4 inches
Palm	= 3 inches
Hand	= 4 inches
Link	= 7.92 inches
Quarter (or a Span)	= 9 inches
Foot	= 12 inches
Cubit	= 18 inches
Yard	= 36 inches
Pace, military	= 2 feet, 6 inches
Pace, geometrical	= 5 feet
Fathom	= 6 feet
Rod, pole, or perch	= 5 1/2 yards
Chain (100 links)	= 22 yards (4 poles)
Cable's length	= 100 fms., 600 ft.
Furlong	= 40 rods, 220 yards
Mile	= 8 furlongs, 80 chains, 320 rods, 1,760 yards, 5,280 feet, 63,360 inches

Mile geographical, Admiralty measured mile, or Nautical mile, 6,080 feet = 1.151 Statute mile

League	= 3 miles
Degree	= 60 geographical, or 69.12 statute miles

SURFACE

144 square inches	= 1 square foot
9 square feet	= 1 square yard
30 1/4 square yards	= 1 square rod
160 square rods	= 1 acre
640 acres	= 1 square mile

CUBIC OR SOLID MEASURE

Cubic foot	= 1,728 cu. in.
Cubic yard	= 27 cu. ft.
Cord of wood	= 128 cu. ft. (8×4×4)
Shipping ton	= 40 cu. ft., merchandise
Shipping ton	= 42 cu. ft. of timber
Perch of masonry	= 24 3/4 cu. ft. (16 1/2 ft. × 1 1/2 ft. ×1 ft.)

LIQUID MEASURE

The Gill contains 8.665 cu. in.
The Pint contains 4 gills or 34.660 cu. in.
Quart = 2 pints = 8 gills
Gallon = 4 quarts = 32 gills

	Gals.	Qts.	Pts.
Firkin or Quarter Barrel	9	36	72
Anker (10 gallons)	10	40	80
Kilderkin, Rundlet, or 1/2 Barrel	18	72	144
Barrel	36	144	288
Tierce (42 gallons)	42	168	336
Hogshead of Ale (1 1/2 barrel)	54	216	432
Puncheon	72	288	576
Butt of Ale (3 barrels)	108	432	864

Wines are usually measured as follows:

	Gals.
Pipe of Port	=115
Pipe of Teneriffe	=100
Pipe of Marsala	= 93
Pipe of Madeira and Cape	= 92
Pipe of Sherry and Tent	=108
Butt of Lisbon & Bucellas	=117
Aum of Hock & Rhenish	= 30
Hogshead of Claret	= 46
Hogshead of Port	= 57
Hogshead of Sherry	= 54
Hogshead of Madeira	= 46

```
1 gallon U. S.              = 231 cubic inches
1 gallon British imperial = 277.274 cubic inches
To reduce British to U. S. gallons multiply by 1.2
To convert U. S. to British gallons divide by 1.2
```

Water

```
1 U. S. gallon            = 231 cubic inches
1 imperial gallon         = 277.274 cubic inches
1 imperial gallon         = 0.16045 cubic foot
1 imperial gallon         = 10 lb.
1 cubic foot of sea water  = 64.00 lb.
1 cubic inch of sea water  = 0.037037 lb.
1 cubic foot of water      = 6.23 imperial gallons
1 cubic foot of water      = 28.375 litres
1 cubic foot of water      = 62.35 lb.        ⎫
1 cubic inch of water      = 0.03616 lb.      ⎬ Distilled
1 cylindrical foot of water = 48.96 lb.       ⎪ fresh water.
1 cylindrical inch of water = 0.0284 lb.      ⎭
The capacity of a 12″ cube = 6.232 gallons
```
1 cubic foot of ice   =57 lb.
Volume of 1 ton of 2240 lb. of fresh water =35.84 cu. ft., or 1 cubic meter
(specific gravity, 1.000; density 1000 oz.   (approx.), or 269 U. S. gallons, or
per cu. ft., or 62 1/2 lb. per cu. ft.)   1000 liters (approx.)
Volume of 1 ton of 2240 lb. of sea water =35 cu. ft.
(specific gravity, 1.025; density 1025 oz. per cu. ft., or 64 lb. per cu. ft.)

APOTHECARIES' FLUID MEASURE

```
60 minims               = 1 fluid drachm
8 drachms               = 1 fluid ounce
1 fluid ounce U. S.   = 1.805 cubic inches
1 fluid ounce British = 1.732 cubic inches
```

DRY OR CORN MEASURE

Quart	=	2 pints
Pottle	=	2 quarts
Gallon	=	4 quarts
Peck	=	2 gallons
Bushel	=	4 pecks
Strike	=	2 bushels

```
Coomb         =   4 bushels
Quarter       =   8 bushels
Load          =   5 quarters
Last          =  10 quarters
Boll of Meal = 140 lbs.
2 Bolls       =   1 sack
```

The British bushel contains 1.2837 cu. ft. = 1.032 U. S. bushels

BOARD MEASURE

Number of feet = length in feet × width in feet × thickness in inches

THE METRIC SYSTEM

There are three principal units—the **meter,** the **liter** (pronounced lee-ter), and the **gram,** the units of length, capacity, and weight, respectively. Multiples of these units are obtained by prefixing to the names of the principal units the Greek words *deca* (10), *hecto* (100), and *kilo* (1,000); the submultiples, or divisions are obtained by prefixing the Latin words *deci* (1/10), *centi* (1/100), and *milli* (1/1000). These prefixes form the key to the entire system.

MEASURES OF LENGTH

```
10 millimeters........... =1 centimeter........... =      .394 in.
10 centimeters........... =1 decimeter........... =      3.937 in.
10 decimeters........... =1 meter.............. =       3.281 ft.
10 meters.............. =1 decameter........... =      32.809 ft.
10 decameters........... =1 hectometer......... =    109.363 yd.
10 hectometers........... =1 kilometer........... =1,093.63  yd.
```

MEASURES OF SURFACE (NOT LAND)

```
100 sq. millimeters...... =1 sq. centimeter........ =   .155 sq. in.
100 sq. centimeters...... =1 sq. decimeter....... =15.5    sq. in.
100 sq. decimeters....... =1 sq. meter........... =10.764 sq. ft.
```

MEASURES OF VOLUME AND CAPACITY

```
10 milliliters............ =1 centiliter........... =   .61  cu. in.
10 centiliters............ =1 deciliter........... =  6.10  cu. in.
10 deciliters............ =1 liter................ =61.02  cu. in.
10 liters................ =1 decaliter........... =  .353 cu. ft.
10 decaliters............ =1 hectoliter........... = 3.53  cu. ft.
10 hectoliters............ =1 kiloliter............. =35.31  cu. ft.
```
The liter is equal to the volume occupied by 1 cu. decimeter.

MEASURES OF WEIGHT

```
10 milligrams........... =1 centigram........... =      .154 gr.
10 centigrams........... =1 decigram........... =     1.54  gr.
10 decigrams........... =1 gram.............. =    15.43  gr.
10 grams................ =1 decagram........... =   154.32  gr.
10 decagrams........... =1 hectogram........... =    .220 lb., avoir.
10 hectograms........... =1 kilogram........... =   2.204 lb., avoir.
1,000 kilograms......... =1 ton................ =2,204    lb., avoir.
```

The gram is the weight of 1 cu. cm. of pure distilled water at a temperature of 39.2° F.; the kilogram is the weight of 1 liter of water; the ton is the weight of 1 cu. m. of water.

METRIC EQUIVALENTS OF POUNDS, FEET, ETC.

The following table will be found valuable for reference by masters, officers, and stewards in their dealings with ship chandleries and other supply stores in countries where the metric system is used:

Pounds	Kilos.	Pounds	Kilos.
1	= .454	60	= 27.270
2	= .909	70	= 31.815
3	= 1.363	80	= 36.360
4	= 1.818	90	= 40.905
5	= 2.272	100	= 45.450
6	= 2.727	200	= 90.900
7	= 3.161	300	= 136.350
8	= 3.636	400	= 181.800
9	= 4.090	500	= 227.250
10	= 4.545	600	= 272.700
20	= 9.060	700	= 318.150
30	= 13.635	800	= 363.600
40	= 18.180	900	= 409.050
50	= 22.725	1,000	= 454.500

1,000 kilos. = 1 metric ton (Tonelada metrico)

	Centimeters		Centimeters
1 inch	= 2.54	7 feet	= 213.00
1 foot	= 30.48	8 feet	= 243.84
1 yard	= 91.44	9 feet	= 274.32
2 feet	= 61.00	10 feet	= 304.80
3 feet	= 91.44	11 feet	= 335.28
4 feet	= 122.00	12 feet	= 365.76
5 feet	= 152.00	13 feet	= 396.24
6 feet	= 182.88	14 feet	= 426.72

LIQUID MEASURES

1 gill	=	.142 liter
1 pint	=	.568 liter
1 quart	=	1.136 liters
1 gallon	=	4.543 liters
1 peck	=	9.087 liters
1 bushel	=	36.347 liters
1 quarter	=	290.781 liters
1 ounce, avoir.	=	2.83 decigrams
1 pound, avoir.	=	.45 kilogram
1 hundredweight, avoir.	=	50.80 kilograms
1 ton, avoir.	=	1,016.05 kilograms
1 pennyweight, troy	=	1.55 grams
1 ounce, troy	=	31.10 grams
1 pound, troy	=	373.24 grams

NAUTICAL MILES TO KILOMETERS

Nautical Miles	Kilometers	Nautical Miles	Kilometers
1	1.8532	20	37.064
2	3.7064	30	55.596
3	5.5596	40	74.128
4	7.4128	50	92.660
5	9.2660	60	111.190
6	11.1190	70	129.720
7	12.9720	80	148.250
8	14.8250	90	167.880
9	16.7880	100	185.320
10	18.5320	110	203.850

KILOMETERS TO NAUTICAL MILES

Kilometers	Nautical Miles	Kilometers	Nautical Miles
1	.5396	20	10.792
2	1.0792	30	16.188
3	1.6188	40	21.584
4	2.1584	50	26.980
5	2.6980	60	32.375
6	3.2375	70	37.771
7	3.7771	80	43.167
8	4.3167	90	48.563
9	4.8563	100	53.959
10	5.3959	110	59.355

VALUE OF MISCELLANEOUS FOREIGN MEASURES

The following list contains the value of various foreign measures. Many of the equivalents are probably only approximately correct, while several of these countries have now adopted the metric system.

Argentine Republic. 1 frasco = 2.5 qt., 1 baril = 20.1 gal., 1 libra = 1 lb., 1 vara = 34.1 in., 1 arroba (dry) = 25.3 lb., 1 quintal = 101.4 lb.

Belgium. 1 last = 85.1 bu.

Brazil. 1 arroba = 32.4 lb., 1 quintal = 130 lb.

Chile. 1 fanega (dry) = 2.5 bu., 1 vara = 33.3 in.

China. 1 catty = 1.3 lb., 1 picul = 133.3 lb., 1 chik = 14 in., 1 tsun = 1.4 in., 1 li = 2,115 ft.

Costa Rica. 1 manzana = 1.8 A.

Cuba. 1 vara = 33.4 in., 1 arroba (liquid) = 4.3 gal., 1 fanega (dry) = 1.6 bu., 1 libra = 1 lb.

Denmark. 1 tonde (cereals) = 3.9 bu., 1 centner = 110.1 lb.

Greece. 1 livre = 1.1 lb., 1 oke = 2.8 lb., 1 quintal = 123.2 lb.

Japan. 1 sun = 1.2 in., 1 shaku = 11.9 in., 1 ken = 6 ft., 1 sho = 1.6 qt., 1 to = 2 pk., 1 koku = 4.9 bu., 1 catty = 1.3 lb., 1 picul = 133.3 lb.

Mexico. 1 carga = 300 lb.; other measures same as Cuba and Argentine Republic.

Peru. 1 vara = 33.4 in., 1 libra = 1 lb., 1 quintal = 101.4 lb.

Portugal. 1 almuda = 4.4 gal., 1 arratel = 1 lb., 1 arroba = 32.4 lb.

Russia. 1 vedro = 2.7 gal., 1 korree = 3.5 bu., 1 chetvert = 5.7 bu., 1 funt = .9 lb., 1 pood = 36.1 lb., 1 berkovets = 361.1 lb., 1 verst = 0.66 mi.

Siam. 1 catty = 1.3 lb., 1 coyan = 2,667 lb.

Spain. 1 pie = .9 ft., 1 vara = .9 yd., 1 arroba (liquid) = 4.3 gal., 1 fanega (liquid) = 16 gal., 1 butt (wine) = 140 gal., 1 last (salt) = 4,760 lb.

Sweden. 1 tunna = 4.5 bu., 1 skålpun = 1.1 lb., 1 centner = 93.7 lb.

Turkey. 1 pik = 27.9 in., 1 oke = 2.8 lb., 1 cantar = 124.7 lb.

Uruguay. 1 cuadra = 2 A., 1 suerte = 2,700 cuadras, 1 fanega (single) = 3.8 bu., 1 fanega (double) = 7.7 bu.

Zanzibar. 1 frasila = 35 lb.

NAUTICAL MEASURES

6 feet	= 1 fathom
600 feet (approx.)	= 1 cable
6,080 feet	= 1 sea or nautical mile
3 nautical miles	= 1 league

A *Sea or Nautical Mile* is the average length of one minute of arc of a great circle of the earth, namely 6,080 feet. The Admiralty Measured Mile for speed trials is the same distance.

A *Knot* is a speed of one nautical mile per hour. The term is often erroneously used as meaning a nautical mile.

LENGTH OF EUROPEAN MEASURES OF DISTANCES COMPARED WITH THE NAUTICAL MILE OF 6,080 FEET

	Length in Nautical Miles		Length in Nautical Miles
Nautical Mile	1.000	German Ruthen	4.064
British Statute Land Mile	0.868	Italian Mile	1.000
Austrian Mile	4.094	Norwegian Mile	6.097
Danish Mile	4.064	Russian Verst	0.576
French Kilometer	0.539	Swedish Mile	5.769
German Geographical Mile	4.000		

SOUNDINGS UPON FOREIGN CHARTS ARE EXPRESSED THUS:

		Eng. ft.		Eng. fm.
Austrian	meter	= 3.281	or	0.547
Austrian	faden	= 6.223	or	1.037
Belgian	metre	= 3.281	or	0.547
Chilian	metro	= 3.281	or	0.547
Danish	favn	= 6.176	or	1.029
Dutch (European)	meter	= 3.281	or	0.547
Dutch (European)	vadem	= 5.905	or	0.984
Dutch (Batavian)	vadem	= 5.905	or	0.984
French	metre	= 3.281	or	0.547
German	meter	= 3.281	or	0.547
Italian	metro	= 3.281	or	0.547
Japanese	fathom	= 6.000	or	1.000
Norwegian	meter	= 3.281	or	0.547

Norwegian........................favn   = 6.176 or 1.029
Portuguese.......................metro = 3.281 or 0.547
Russian.........................Sazhene = 6.000 or 1.000
Spanish..........................metro = 3.281 or 0.547
Spanish..........................braza = 5.492 or 0.915
Swedish..........................meter = 3.281 or 0.547
Swedish..........................famn   = 5.844 or 0.974
United States...................fathom = 6.000 or 1.000

It will be observed that several nations use both meters and fathoms; generally in such cases the meter is employed in modern charts.

SPECIFIC GRAVITY OF DIFFERENT SUBSTANCES
(Compared with Water as 1.00)

Liquids, etc.		Timber		Metals	
Alcohol	.80	Apple	.79	Bar Iron	7.79
Beer	1.02	Ash	.84	Brass	8.40
Cider	1.02	Beech	.85	Cast Iron	7.21
Granite	2.72	Cedar	.61	Copper	8.69
Gravel, Sand	2.65	Cherry	.72	Gold	19.26
Olive Oil	.92	Cork	.24	Lead	11.35
Petroleum	.78–.94	Ebony	1.33	Mercury	13.57
Porter	1.04	Fir	.55	Platinum	19.50
Sea Water	1.03	Mahogany	1.00	Silver	10.51
Turpentine	.99	Maple	.75	Steel	7.83
Wine	1.00	Oak	1.17	Tin	7.29
		Pear	.66	Zinc	7.19
		Poplar	.38		
		Walnut	.70		

WEIGHT AND SPECIFIC GRAVITY OF LIQUIDS

Liquid	Specific gravity	Weight of 1 Cubic Inch in Lb.
Acid, Acetic	1.10	.040
Acid, Hydrochloric	1.22	.044
Acid, Nitric	1.42	.051
Acid, Sulphuric	1.86	.067
Oil, Light Lubricating	.900	.0326
Oil, Medium Lubricating	.908	.0328
Oil, Heavy Lubricating	.912	.0331
Oil, Linseed	.95–.97	.0344–.0351
Oil, Whale	.94	.034
Water, Fresh	1.00	.03616
Water, Sea	1.026	.0370
Petrol	.75–.78	.0271–.028
Paraffin	.87	.032

DECIMAL EQUIVALENTS OF FRACTIONS

Fractions	Decimals	Fractions	Decimals	Fractions	Decimals	Fractions	Decimals
1–64	.015625	17–64	.265625	33–64	.515625	49–64	.765625
1–32	.03125	9–32	.28125	17–32	.53125	25–32	.78125
3–64	.046875	19–64	.296875	35–64	.546875	51–64	.796875
1–16	.0625	5–16	.3125	9–16	.5625	13–16	.8125
5–64	.078125	21–64	.328125	37–64	.578125	53–64	.828125
3–32	.09375	11–32	.34375	19–32	.59375	27–32	.84375
7–64	.109375	23–64	.359375	39–64	.609375	55–64	.859375
1–8	.125	3–8	.375	5–8	.625	7–8	.875
9–64	.140625	25–64	.390625	41–64	.640625	57–64	.890625
5–32	.15625	13–32	.40625	21–32	.65625	29–32	.90625
11–64	.171875	27–64	.421875	43–64	.671875	59–64	.921875
3–16	.1875	7–16	.4375	11–16	.6875	15–16	.9375
13–64	.203125	29–64	.453125	45–64	.703125	61–64	.953125
7–32	.21875	15–32	.46875	23–32	.71875	31–32	.96875
15–64	.234375	31–64	.484375	47–64	.734375	63–64	.984375
1–4	.25	1–2	.5	3–4	.75		

DECIMAL EQUIVALENTS OF A FOOT

Inch	0	1/16	1/8	3/16	1/4	5/16	3/8	7/16	Inch
0	.0000	.0052	.0104	.0156	.0208	.0260	.0313	.0365	0
1	.0833	.0885	.0937	.0990	.1042	.1094	.1146	.1198	1
2	.1667	.1719	.1771	.1823	.1875	.1927	.1979	.2031	2
3	.2500	.2552	.2604	.2656	.2708	.2760	.2813	.2865	3
4	.3333	.3385	.3437	.3490	.3542	.3594	.3646	.3698	4
5	.4167	.4219	.4271	.4323	.4375	.4427	.4479	.4531	5
6	.5000	.5052	.5104	.5156	.5208	.5260	.5313	.5365	6
7	.5833	.5885	.5937	.5990	.6042	.6094	.6146	.6198	7
8	.6667	.6719	.6771	.6823	.6875	.6927	.6979	.7031	8
9	.7500	.7552	.7604	.7656	.7708	.7760	.7813	.7865	9
10	.8333	.8385	.8437	.8490	.8542	.8594	.8646	.8698	10
11	.9167	.9219	.9271	.9323	.9375	.9427	.9479	.9521	11

Inch	1/2	9/16	5/8	11/16	3/4	13/16	7/8	15/16	Inch
0	.0417	.0469	.0521	.0573	.0625	.0677	.0729	.0781	0
1	.1250	.1302	.1354	.1406	.1458	.1510	.1563	.1615	1
2	.2083	.2135	.2188	.2240	.2292	.2344	.2396	.2448	2
3	.2917	.2969	.3021	.3073	.3125	.3177	.3229	.3281	3
4	.3750	.3802	.3854	.3906	.3958	.4010	.4063	.4115	4
5	.4583	.4635	.4688	.4740	.4792	.4844	.4896	.4948	5
6	.5417	.5469	.5521	.5573	.5625	.5677	.5729	.5781	6
7	.6250	.6302	.6354	.6406	.6458	.6510	.6563	.6615	7
8	.7083	.7135	.7188	.7240	.7292	.7344	.7396	.7448	8
9	.7917	.7969	.8021	.8073	.8125	.8177	.8229	.8281	9
10	.8750	.8802	.8854	.8906	.8958	.9010	.9063	.9115	10
11	.9583	.9635	.9688	.9740	.9792	.9844	.9896	.9948	11

ELECTRICAL MEASURES

The Ohm. Measure of resistance offered by materials to the flow of electricity. Approximately 70 to 80 ft. of good iron wire of 1/16 inch diameter has a resistance of one ohm. A megohm is a resistance of one million ohms.

The Volt = the electromotive force which applied to a conductor with a resistance of one ohm will maintain in it a current of one ampere.

The Farad = the capacity of a condenser such as to be charged to a potential of one volt by one coulomb. The microfarad is a millionth part of a farad.

The Ampere = the current driven through one ohm by one volt. A milliampere is the thousandth part of an ampere.

The Coulomb = the quantity of electricity given by one ampere in one second.

The Joule = the energy expended in one second by one ampere flowing through one ohm.

The Watt = the power of a current of one ampere under a pressure of one volt = 44.23 approximate foot lbs. per minute. 746 watts = one horsepower. A kilowatt is a thousand watts.

The Henry = the induction in a circuit when the pressure is one volt while the current varies one ampere per second.

SHIP MENSURATION

Simpson's First Rule and the Trapezoidal Rule. These are used for computing ship's waterplane areas and hull volumes.

Computing area. (Note: If the figure comes to a point, the first (or last) ordinate is zero.)

h = the space between ordinates (h = 12 in example below). The ordinate is the vertical height of line, as shown in Fig. 1.

The number of spaces must be *even* in Simpson's rule but may be odd or even in the Trapezoidal Rule.

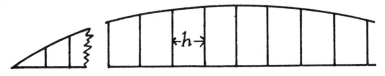

FIG. 1. ILLUSTRATING SIMPSON'S RULE.

Simpson's First Rule

ordinate	multiplier	function of area
6	1	6
13	4	52
15	2	30
16	4	64
17	2	34
16	4	64
14	1	14
		264, sum

Trapezoidal Rule

ordinate	multiplier	function of area
6	1/2	3
13	1	13
15	1	15
16	1	16
17	1	17
16	1	16
14	1/2	7
		87, sum

area $= h/3$ (sum of functions)
or $12/3 \times (264) = 1056$ sq. ft.

area $= h$ (sum of functions)
or $12\ (87) = 1044$ sq. ft.

These are both inexact, of course, but the closer approximation is in favor of Simpson's first rule.

Computing Volume. Here the principle is the same as that used in computing the areas above. The functions of areas become the ordinates in the above form. The product of this area used as an ordinate, and the multiplier gives the function of volume. The sum of these functions of volume is then taken and treated as above to obtain the volume of the entire shape. Always use the work form and Simpson's Rule.

GALVANIZED IRON RIGGING AND GUY ROPE

Composed of 6 Strands and a Hemp Center, 7 Wires to the Strand

Diameter in inches	Approx. circumference in inches	Approx. weight per foot	Breaking strength in tons of 2000 lbs.	Circum. of manila rope of nearest strength
1¾	5½	4.60	37.00	10
1⅝	5⅛	3.96	32.40	9
1½	4¾	3.38	27.70	8½
1⅜	4⅜	2.84	23.70	7½
1¼	3⅞	2.34	19.90	7
1⅛	3½	1.90	16.50	6
1¹/₁₆	3⅜	1.70	14.80	5½
1	3⅛	1.50	13.20	5¼
⅞	2¾	1.15	10.20	4¾
¾	2⅜	.84	7.10	3¾
⅝	2	.59	5.30	3¼
9/16	1¾	.48	4.32	3
½	1⅝	.38	3.43	2½
7/16	1⅜	.29	2.64	2¼
⅜	1⅛	.21	1.95	2
5/16	1	.15	1.36	1½
9/32	⅞	.125	1.20	1⅜
¼	¾	.090	.99	1¼
7/32	11/16	.063	.79	1⅛
3/16	⅝	.040	.61	1

EXTRA PLIABLE HOISTING ROPE

Composed of 6 Strands and a Hemp Center 37 Wires to the Strand

Diameter in inches	Approx. circumference in inches	Approx. weight per foot	Breaking strength in tons of 2000 lbs.
3½	11	19.00	451.0
3¼	10¼	16.37	392.0
3	9⅜	13.95	337.0
2¾	8⅝	11.72	285.0
2½	7⅞	9.69	237.0
2¼	7⅛	7.85	194.0
2	6¼	6.20	155.0
1¾	5½	4.75	119.5
1⅝	5⅛	4.09	103.3
1½	4¾	3.49	88.2
1⅜	4⅜	2.93	74.3
1¼	3⅞	2.42	61.5
1⅛	3½	1.96	49.9
1	3⅛	1.55	39.5
⅞	2¾	1.19	30.5
¾	2⅜	.87	22.8
⅝	2	.61	16.1
½	1⅝	.39	10.6
⅜	1⅛	.22	6.1
¼	¾	.10	2.8

SAFE WORKING LOADS (new gear)

C = circumference in inches
Manila rope: $C^2 \div 7 =$ tons
Running wire: $C^2 \times .4 =$ tons
Standing wire: $C^2 \times .8 =$ tons

d = diameter in inches
Chain: $8d^2 =$ tons
Hook: $2/3d^2 =$ tons (d = diameter at lower quarter)
Shackle: $3d^2 =$ tons
Ring-bolt: $2d^2 =$ tons

USEFUL INFORMATION

Rope. Weight of manila (in pounds) $= .2 \times \text{circ.}^2 \times \text{fathoms}$
$= 2/11 \times$ weight of same size wire
Weight of wire (in pounds) $= \text{fathoms} \times \text{circ.}^2$

Chain. Weight of chain cable (in pounds) $= 57 \times d^2$
Links per fathom, chain cable $= 18 \div d$
(d = diameter of iron in link)

MANILA ROPE TABLE

Approximate Size, Weight and Strength of Manila Rope

Circumference Inches	Diameter (Nominal) Inches	Length of Coil (Approx.) Feet	Gross Wgt. of Coil (Approx.) Pounds	Length per Pound (Min.) Feet	Breaking Strength (Min.) Pounds
$\frac{5}{8}$	$\frac{3}{16}$ (6 thd.)	2,650	35	76.0	450
$\frac{3}{4}$	$\frac{1}{4}$ (6 thd.)	1,920	35	55.0	600
1	$\frac{5}{16}$ (9 thd.)	1,935	55	35.0	1,000
$1\frac{1}{8}$	$\frac{3}{8}$ (12 thd.)	1,690	65	26.0	1,350
$1\frac{1}{4}$	$\frac{7}{16}$ (15 thd.)	1,200	63	19.0	1,750
$1\frac{3}{8}$	$\frac{15}{32}$ (18 thd.)	1,200	75	16.0	2,250
$1\frac{1}{2}$	$\frac{1}{2}$ (21 thd.)	1,200	90	13.3	2,650
$1\frac{3}{4}$	$\frac{9}{16}$	1,200	125	9.61	3,450
2	$\frac{5}{8}$	1,200	160	7.52	4,400
$2\frac{1}{4}$	$\frac{3}{4}$	1,200	200	6.00	5,400
$2\frac{1}{2}$	$\frac{13}{16}$	1,200	234	5.13	6,500
$2\frac{3}{4}$	$\frac{7}{8}$	1,200	270	4.45	7,700
3	1	1,200	324	3.71	9,000
$3\frac{1}{4}$	$1\frac{1}{16}$	1,200	375	3.20	10,500
$3\frac{1}{2}$	$1\frac{1}{8}$	1,200	432	2.78	12,000
$3\frac{3}{4}$	$1\frac{1}{4}$	1,200	502	2.40	13,500
4	$1\frac{5}{16}$	1,200	576	2.09	15,000
$4\frac{1}{2}$	$1\frac{1}{2}$	1,200	720	1.67	18,500
5	$1\frac{5}{8}$	1,200	893	1.34	22,500
$5\frac{1}{2}$	$1\frac{3}{4}$	1,200	1,073	1.12	26,500
6	2	1,200	1,290	0.927	31,000
$6\frac{1}{2}$	$2\frac{1}{8}$	1,200	1,503	.800	36,000
7	$2\frac{1}{4}$	1,200	1,752	.685	41,000
$7\frac{1}{2}$	$2\frac{1}{2}$	1,200	2,004	.600	46,500
8	$2\frac{5}{8}$	1,200	2,290	.524	52,000
$8\frac{1}{2}$	$2\frac{7}{8}$	1,200	2,580	.465	58,000
9	3	1,200	2,900	.414	64,000
$9\frac{1}{2}$	$3\frac{1}{8}$	1,200	3,225	.372	71,000
10	$3\frac{1}{4}$	1,200	3,590	.335	77,000
11	$3\frac{1}{2}$	1,200	4,400	.273	91,000
12	$3\frac{3}{4}$	1,200	5,225	.230	105,000

Carrying capacity of lifeboat. 1/10 (length × breadth × depth × .6) = number of persons

Sea water pressure. Lbs. per square inch = 4/9 depth (in feet)

Area of wetted surface (approx.). Length × (breadth + depth) = square feet

Anti-corrosive paint covers about 270 sq. ft. per gallon

Anti-fouling paint covers about 240 sq. ft. per gallon

STABILITY FORMULAE

GG_1 the shift G

1. $GG_1 = \dfrac{d \times w}{W}$

d the distance through which
w the weight has been moved

2. $GM = GG_1 \cot \theta$

3. $GM = \dfrac{d \times w}{W} \cot \theta$ (p. 337)

W the ship's displacement

GM the metacentric height

4. $GZ = GM \sin \theta$

θ the angle of keel

5. $ITM = \dfrac{LGM \times W}{12L}$

GZ the righting arm

6. ITM (approx.) $= \dfrac{30 \, (TPI)^2}{B}$ (p. 351)

ITM inch-trim-moment

LGM longitudinal GM

7. $LGM = \dfrac{L^2}{12D}$(box-shape)

BM the metacentric radius, i.e., the height of the transverse meta-center above the center of buoyancy

8. Total trim $= \dfrac{\text{trim moment}}{ITM}$

9. $TPI = \dfrac{L \times B \times \text{coefficient}}{12 \times 35}$

CG the center of gravity

CB the center of buoyancy

10. $BM = \dfrac{B^2}{12D}$ (box-shaped vessel)

L length between perpendiculars

B breadth

11. $BM = \dfrac{B^2}{6D}$ (triangular body, apex down)

D draft

12. CB above keel $= .537 \, D$ (approx.)

13. Increase in draft due to flooded compartment (ft.) $\left.\right\} = \dfrac{\text{volume of flooded compartment (cu. ft.)}}{\text{intact waterplane area (sq. ft.)}}$

14. Increase in draft due to list (approx.) $= B/2 \sin \theta$

15. To increase draft at one end without changing it at the other:—

$\dfrac{2 \, ITM}{TPI}$ = distance in feet forward or abaft the tipping center where cargo should be placed to increase draft at one end only.

16. Reduction in GM due to a free surface of water $= \left(\dfrac{35\delta}{36}\right)\dfrac{i}{V}$

$i = LB^3 \div 12$
$V =$ volume of displacement of ship, i.e., displacement in tons $\times 35$.
$\delta =$ density of the liquid having the free surface.

NAVIGATION FORMULAE

(See abbreviations in chapter on Sailings, Chapter 5.)

Plane sailing:	*Parallel sailing:*
$l \quad = d \cos C$	$D \, \text{Lo} = p \sec L$
$p \quad = d \sin C$	$p \quad = D \, \text{Lo} \cos L$
$\tan \, C = p \div l$	

Middle latitude sailing:

When C and d are given	When l and D Lo are given
$l \quad = d \cos C$	$p \quad = D \text{ Lo } \cos L_m$
$p \quad = d \sin C$	$\tan C = p \div l$
$D \text{ Lo} = p \sec L_m$	$d \quad = l \sec C$

Mercator sailing:

Coordinates of places given; to find course and distance.

$l \quad = L_1 - L_2$, or $L_2 - L_1$

$D \text{ Lo} = \lambda_1 - \lambda_2$, or $\lambda_2 - \lambda_1$

or $\lambda_1 + \lambda_2$, or $360° - (\lambda_1 + \lambda_2)$

$m \quad = M_1 - M_2$ or $M_2 - M_1$

$\tan C = D \text{ Lo} \div m$

$d \quad = l \sec C$

Coordinates of the point of departure and course and distance run given; to find coordinates of point of arrival.

$l \quad = d \cos C$

$L_2 \quad = L_1 \pm l$

$m \quad = M_1 - M_2$ or $M_2 - M_1$

$D \text{ Lo} = m \tan C$

$\lambda_2 \quad = \lambda_1 \pm D \text{ Lo}$

Great circle sailing, course and distance (in form for working):

$$\begin{array}{r} \text{co } L_1 \\ d \\ \hline d \sim \text{co } L_1 \end{array}$$

λ_1		
λ_2		
D Lo	l hav	
L_1	l cos	l sec
L_2	l cos	
	l hav	
	n hav	
$L_1 \sim L_2$	n hav	
d	n hav	l csc
co L_2	n hav	
$d \sim \text{co } L_1$	−n hav	
	n hav	l hav
C		l hav

Latitude and longitude of vertex:

$$\sin \text{ co } L_v = \sin \text{ co } L_1 \sin C$$
$$\tan D \text{ } Lo_v = \sec \text{ co } L_1 \cot C$$

Point m, *whose longitude differs* $\theta°$ *from longitude of vertex:*

$$\cot L_m = \tan \text{ co } L_v \sec \theta$$

Time sight:

$$S = (h + p + L) \div 2$$

$$\text{hav } t = \csc p \sec L \cos S \sin (S - h)$$

Altitude azimuth:

$$\text{hav } (180 - z) = \sec h \sec l \cos S \cos (S - p)$$

Amplitude:

$$\sin \text{ Amp} = \sin d \sec l$$

Time and altitude azimuth:

$$\sin z = \sin t \cos d \sec h$$

Time azimuth:

$$S = (p + \text{co } L) \div 2 \qquad\qquad D = (p \sim \text{co } L) \div 2$$

$$\tan x = \sin D \csc S \cot 1/2t \qquad \tan y = \cos D \sec S \cot 1/2t$$

$$z = x + y \text{ or } x - y$$

1st case—if S is less than 90°, take the sum of angles $x + y$, provided the polar distance is greater than the co-lat.; take difference if polar distance is less than co-lat.

2nd case—if S is greater than 90°, always take the difference of x and y and subtract it from 180°; the result will be the true azimuth.

Cosine-haversine formula:

$$\text{hav } ZD = \text{hav } t \cos d \cos l + \text{hav } (d \sim l)$$

Constant for Meridian Altitude. The declination and altitude correction being known, it is found convenient to find the constant which, when applied to the meridian altitude, gives the latitude. The four possible cases are here given with the signs to be used, the value of the constant being that in the parentheses.

I. Lat. and dec. same name; lat. greater—Lat. $= (90 + \text{dec.} - \text{corr.}) - \text{alt.}$

II. Lat. and dec. same name; dec. greater—Lat. $= (-90 + \text{dec.} + \text{corr.}) + \text{alt.}$

III. Lat. and dec. opposite names—Lat. $= (90° - \text{dec.} - \text{corr.}) - \text{alt.}$

IV. Lower transit.—Lat. $= (90° - \text{dec.} + \text{corr.}) + \text{alt.}$

The correction is assumed to be positive in the above. If otherwise, reverse the sign of *corr.*

INDEX

INDEX